Geography in Focus

Ian Cook

Bob Hordern

Helen McGahan

Penny Ritson

CPL

Causeway Press

Contents Summary

Contents

Chapter 3 Settlement — 138

Chapter 4 Primary production — 194

Contents

Chapter 8   Weathering and slopes   344

Chapter 9   Drainage basins   386

Chapter 10   Glaciation   424

Contents

CHAPTER 1 Population

Introduction

The study of population is called demography. Demography examines birth and death rates, population policies and the impact of migration. The study of population also involves looking at where people live and why they live in certain locations. In addition, it raises issues about economic growth and standards of living. The world's population is growing rapidly. During 1999, the total reached 6 billion and, according to United Nations estimates, will reach 9.5 billion in 2050. It is forecast that falling birth rates will cause the world's population to stabilise at approximately 10.5 billion some time after 2100.

Chapter summary

Unit 1.1 investigates the main trends in population growth.
Unit 1.2 considers where people live.
Unit 1.3 looks at migration and its impact on population.
Unit 1.4 examines the relationship between population and resources.
Unit 1.5 investigates the impact of ageing populations.
Unit 1.6 looks at political and social change in nation states and within the European Union.

Unit 1.1 Population trends

key questions

1 Why and how is demographic data collected?
2 What factors affect population growth?
3 What factors affect birth rates?
4 What factors affect death rates?
5 How do changes in birth and death rates relate to development?
6 What is population structure?
7 What are the main trends in world population growth?
8 What are the main population trends in the UK?

1. Why and how is demographic data collected?

All governments collect population data. The statistics are used by governments for a variety of reasons. In some cases it might be to assess the number of people who should pay taxes. In other cases it might be to predict the demand for services such as health care, education and housing. For example, a government needs to know how many teachers to train and how many hospitals to build.

During 1998, an official report in the UK suggested that 5 million new homes would be needed by 2015. This estimate was based on demographic data which included the rate of population growth, the number of people in each age group and trends in marriage and home ownership.

Governments use a number of different methods to gather population data.

- **Census** The main source of population data is a census. In the UK there is a census every 10 years and the first was in 1801. The aims of a census are to provide information on the number of people resident in a country and where they live. The characteristics of the population are recorded by asking questions on people's ages, gender and family size. In the UK, at the time of

Figure 1.1 A new housing development

Governments need accurate demographic data to plan housing needs.

the census, each household is given a form to complete. It is the legal responsibility of the head of household to complete it accurately.

- **Sample surveys** A sample survey is a method of gathering information in which a sample of people are asked questions. Surveys might be used to update census information or to fill in gaps where data is incomplete. In the UK, for example, the Labour Force Survey gathers data on the size of the working population.
- **Registration** This involves people reporting information to the government. The system has the advantage that events are recorded as they happen rather than just at the time of a census. In the UK, people are legally required to register births, deaths and marriages at the local Registry Office. In France and Germany, people must register their place of residence.

Population statistics are never completely accurate. There are a number of difficulties in using a census or sample survey to gather information.

- If districts are not mapped carefully when planning a census, some households may be omitted.
- Counting and surveying homeless people is difficult because they have no fixed address.
- Some people cannot read or write. Failure to understand the census questions can lead to inaccurate answers. People in some low income countries might not know their precise date of birth because it has never been written down.
- A census costs money to prepare and administer. Low income countries may not be able to afford a full census on a regular basis.
- Remote parts of countries with poor transport links pose a problem in surveying people who live there. Collecting information from nomadic peoples (eg, herders who move from place to place with their animals) is difficult.
- Countries with different ethnic groupings may have particular difficulties in obtaining accurate information. If the census is only written in the majority language, there may be problems. Also, if there is a history of conflict between rival ethnic groups, minorities might be reluctant to provide accurate population data.
- Civil wars or conflict, such as in southern Sudan, make it impossible to collect accurate data.

One of the main problems with using registration as a source of demographic data is that some people might not register.

- Illegal immigrants in France or Germany, for instance, are unlikely to register their address for fear of being deported.
- In China, couples are allowed to have only one child if they wish to keep all the benefits provided by the state. Due to the desire of many couples to have a son, the birth of baby girls may therefore go unreported. (A detailed case study on Chinese population policy is provided later in this unit.)

2. What factors affect population growth?

Whether the world's population grows or not depends on two factors: fertility and mortality. Fertility refers to the number of children that are born, mortality refers to the number of people who die. The most widely used measure of fertility is the birth rate. The most widely used measure of mortality is the death rate. Migration can also affect the population size of a particular country or region. (This topic is covered in unit 1.3.)

Figure 1.2 China

The total fertility rate in China fell from 6.4 in 1965 to 1.7 in 1996.

Birth rate

The **birth rate** is the number of live births in a year, measured per 1,000 people. It relates the number of births to the total population. The **fertility rate** is a more specific measure. It is the number of births in a year per 1,000 women who are in the normal reproductive age group (15-44 years). **The total fertility rate** (TFR) is the average number of children a woman will have throughout her childbearing years.

The total fertility rates in 1996 in China and the UK were almost identical at 1.7 children per woman. However, in China, the birth rate was 18 per 1,000 while in the UK it was 13 per 1,000. Although in both countries each woman had, on average, the same number of children, in China there was a larger proportion of women of childbearing age - so the birth rate was higher.

Death rate

The **death rate** is the number of deaths in a year, measured per 1,000 people. It relates the number of deaths to the total population. The **infant mortality rate** is an 'age specific' death rate and is the number of children who die each year before they are 1 year old, measured per 1,000 live births.

Most high income countries have a low death rate and a high average **life expectancy** (this is the number of years a person can expect to live). Because their populations have a high life expectancy, these countries have a relatively large number of people in the older age groups.

Rate of natural increase

The difference between the birth rate and the death rate is called the rate of natural increase if it is a positive number, or natural decrease if the number is negative. It is usually expressed as a percentage.

Natural increase/decrease = birth rate - death rate.

For example, in 1996, in China the birth rate was 18 per 1,000 and the death rate was 7 per 1,000. So,

Rate of natural increase = 18 - 7 per 1,000
= 11 per 1,000 (or 1.1 percent) per annum

Figure 1.3 Population change in England and Wales

Date	Birth rate (per 1,000)	Death rate (per 1,000)	Rate of natural increase (%)	Population (millions)
1750	36	32	0.4	6.5
1801	36	25	1.1	8.9
1851	35	23	1.2	7.9
1901	28	16	1.2	32.5
1951	15	12	0.3	43.8

During the nineteenth century, death rates fell while birth rates remained relatively high. This caused a high rate of natural increase. During the twentieth century, birth rates fell at a faster rate than death rates and this caused a lower rate of natural increase.

A 1.1 percent rate of increase means that a population doubles in 65 years (assuming the rate remains constant). This is a 'medium' rate of rise in world terms. Between 1985 and 1995, the population of Malawi rose at a rate of 3.1 percent per year. At this rate the population doubles within 24 years. In Saudi Arabia the rate of increase was 4.3 percent per year, resulting in a doubling in 18 years. At the other end of the scale, in Denmark for example, over the same period population was rising by 0.2 percent per year. At this rate, it takes 347 years to double.

Throughout the twentieth century, the world's population had a high rate of natural increase. As a result, between 1900 and 1999, world population rose from 1.5 billion to 6 billion. This 'explosion' was largely due to a fall in death rates while birth rates remained high. A similar pattern had occurred earlier in England and Wales (see figure 1.3). Between 1801 and 1901, the population of England and Wales rose by over 250 percent. This was due to a high rate of natural increase that was caused primarily by a fall in the death rate.

Replacement rate

Assuming there is no migration, a population is stable (ie, it does not grow or decline) if the number of live births in one year is equal to the number of deaths. This occurs when the total fertility rate is approximately 2.1. In other words, if each woman has, on average, 2.1 children, the number of new babies will 'replace' the number of people who die.

Activity) Population change

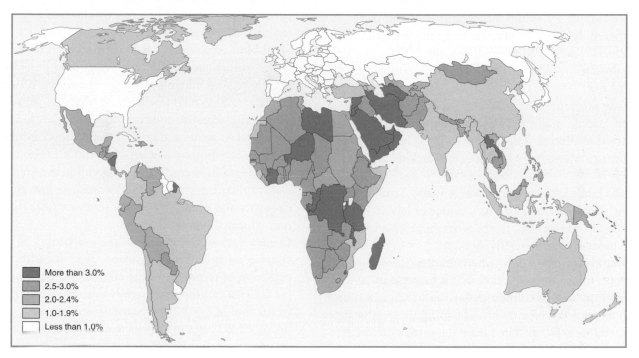

▲ **Figure 1.4 World population growth (average annual percentage change) 1985-95**

 Questions

1 With reference to the data in figure 1.5, briefly explain what is meant by birth rate and death rate.

2 With reference to figure 1.4, describe the main trends in world population growth between 1985 and 1995.

3 Using data from figure 1.5, explain how birth rates and death rates affect population growth.

	Birth rate	Death rate
	per 1,000 population 1992	per 1,000 population 1992
Low and middle income countries		
Sub-Sahara Africa	44	15
East Asia and Pacific	21	8
South Asia	31	10
Eastern Europe and Central Asia	6	10
Middle East and North Africa	34	8
Latin America and Caribbean	26	7
High income countries	13	9

Note: *high income countries include the USA, Canada, Western Europe, Japan, Australia and New Zealand.*

▲ **Figure 1.5 Birth rates and death rates**

3. What factors affect birth rates?

Birth rates are influenced by a range of social and economic factors.

- **Age structure** (ie, the proportion of people in each age group): in rapidly increasing populations where there is a high proportion of people in the reproductive age group, birth rates will tend to be high simply because there are large numbers of potential parents. In populations where there is a large proportion of elderly people, the birth rate will tend to be low.
- **Infant mortality**: in areas where infant mortality is high, people might have many children just to ensure that some survive. This is true in those less developed countries where basic health care is lacking and diet is poor.
- **Child labour**: in countries where many families are poor, children are valued as a source of labour in the home, on the farm or in the workshop. This causes the birth rate to be relatively high.
- **Compulsory education**: when children have to go to school, rather than work, children become an economic burden to their parents rather than a source of income. The introduction of compulsory education is therefore a factor that causes the birth rate to fall.
- **Social services**: the lack of pensions and state support in most poor countries means that children are relied upon to look after parents when they are older. So, the more children a couple have, the more secure they will be in their old age. In countries which provide social services, parents need fewer children to support them when they are old.

Figure 1.6 Birth rates in different continents

Continent	Birth rate per 1,000 (1997)
Africa	40
North America	14
South America	25
Asia	24
Europe	10
Oceania	19

Africa has by far the highest birth rate. Reasons include the high rates of child mortality, the need of many families to have children as a form of 'cheap' labour, the lack of state funded social care and, in some cases, social attitudes favouring large families.

- **Religion and culture**: culture and tradition might encourage people to have large families and discourage the use of family planning and contraceptives. For example, in parts of South America where Catholic teaching is strong, many people accept the Church's view that contraception is morally wrong. In some cultures - for example in parts of East Africa - having many children is regarded as a status symbol.
- **Status and educational level of women**: in regions where women are literate, birth rates tend to be lower than in regions where women do not receive a basic education. This might be because educated women have better access to contraceptive advice, or it may be related to status and employment opportunities. For instance, literate women may find it easier to take up paid employment, and having children would disrupt their careers. Educated women in low income countries also tend, on average, to marry later than non-educated women.
- **Contraception and abortion**: the availability of contraception and legal abortion, together with the provision of family planning clinics, make it easier for couples to limit their family size. However, this factor should not be overstated. There are well documented cases of aid agencies giving contraceptive pills to women in countries such as Bangladesh, and the pills being thrown away. Only when people see that it is in their personal and economic interest to limit their family size do they use contraceptives.
- **Government policies**: government policies can have an impact on the birth rate. This factor is outlined in more detail below.

Government policies

In many low income countries, a reduction in the birth rate is seen as a vital element in reducing poverty. Countries where populations are rising at 3 or 4 percent per year have to increase food output by that amount just to stand still. So, strategies to reduce birth rates are widely used by governments. Where a policy of population control is successful, living standards can rise because there are less mouths to feed and the amount of food and income available per person increases.

When living standards rise, this in itself can cause the birth rate to fall. This is because increased prosperity can bring about the conditions in which

Figure 1.7 Child labour and education

When compulsory education is introduced, children are no longer a source of income or labour for their parents. There is therefore less incentive to have children.

The precise reasons for this are unclear but it seems likely that the introduction of a state funded compulsory education system was a factor. So was the downward trend in infant mortality rates, partly caused by better nutrition but also by improved public sewerage and drinking water systems.

Official population policies can have a dramatic effect on birth rates. Sometimes such policies work (see the case study on China overleaf) but there are also examples of less successful policies. India is an example. It was the first country to introduce a birth control policy. Its early campaigns were to encourage male sterilisation. These started in the 1950s and continued into the 1970s when they reached a peak of 8 million men being sterilised in 1977. However, the policy was unpopular - particularly with men - and not very effective in reducing the birth rate. The main reason was that many families did not see it in their interests to limit their number of children. As a result, the Indian population is rising at a significantly faster rate than the Chinese. In 1997, the population of India was 961 million, rising by 17 million each year. In China, the much larger population of 1.2 billion was rising at the lower rate of 13 million each year.

As part of its birth control policy, India made abortion legal in 1972. Also, the minimum age of marriage was raised to 18 for females and 21 for males - but this age limit is difficult to enforce, particularly in rural areas. Many Indian people remain fearful and suspicious of birth control policies following the sterilisation programme. Another factor at work in India is that tradition and religion play an important role in many people's lives. Islam and Hinduism are the two main religions, and neither officially accepts contraception or family planning.

Although the birth rate in India is relatively high (29 per 1,000 in 1996, compared with 18 per 1,000 in China), it is falling. One factor that seems to be having an impact is the improving status of women and the rising rate of female literacy. In areas where literacy is high, couples tend to have a maximum of two children. In areas where few women are educated and literate, families of five or more children are common.

people want fewer children. For instance, if people have higher incomes, they can afford to buy better quality food. Improved nutrition for mothers (and young babies) causes the infant mortality rate to fall - so people need fewer children to make sure that some survive.

Another important reason why increased prosperity leads to lower birth rates is that rising incomes generally provide governments with higher tax revenues. These can be used to fund programmes of social improvement - which, in turn, lead to people wanting fewer children. For instance, from about 1870 onwards, there was a marked fall in Britain's birth rate.

Activity Population policy in China

China operates the most severe, and controversial, family planning programme in the world. It started in the 1970s with campaigns to encourage later marriage and the use of contraception. Fertility rates fell but the very high proportion of young people in the population meant that the decline in the birth rate was slow. So, in 1979 the 'One Child' policy was imposed. The impact was dramatic. The 1970 birth rate of 33 per 1,000 fell to 18 per 1,000 in 1996. China's population was 800 million in 1970, 1.2 billion in 1996 but is now forecast to stabilise at 1.6 billion in 2045. Without the strict policy, the Chinese government estimates, by 1998, there would have been 300 million extra people.

When the government first announced the policy, in 1979, it said there was no alternative. In order to prevent catastrophic famines in the future, the policy had to be enforced. The result was a system of social control that many view as unacceptable. However, there has not been a famine since the policy started and the country is now self sufficient in food.

Chinese policy in action

A typical example of how the policy works in practice is the experience of Chi An, a nurse in the Manchurian city of Shenyang. In 1981 she was recruited to manage the birth control programme in a large factory with many women workers. The factory was given an annual birth quota. If Chi An kept the number of births under target, she and the factory would get a bonus. If she allowed even one more baby to be born over the quota, there would be a fine.

Each January, the factory family planning committee announced the names of the women whose applications to bear a child had been approved. Chi An spent most of her time pressing women with 'unauthorised' pregnancies to have an abortion. Those who refused were locked in a warehouse and threatened. Chi An always met her target but, in 1984, the factory quota was cut from 322 to 65 births per year. Chi An was told, 'to reduce the population, use whatever means you must, but do it'. Birth control workers resorted to coercion. Forced abortions, and sterilisations of women who had one child, became commonplace.

In rural areas, the policy was more difficult to enforce than in urban areas. Social control over the scattered rural population was more difficult so, in some cases, local officials took drastic and punitive action to enforce the policy. In Hunan province, for example, there are well documented cases of houses being demolished as punishment for disobeying the rules. In the village of Xiaoxi, a man named Huang Ziming, his wife and three children were ordered out of their house. It was then dynamited into rubble. Nearby, a notice was placed saying, 'Those who do not obey the family planning authorities will lose everything'.

In 1993, the Chinese government passed laws forbidding demolition of houses and the physical abuse of people who broke the One Child rule. However, similar cases are still sometimes reported - particularly in rural areas. In order to provide a 'carrot' as well as a 'stick' in its policy, the government has introduced a system of benefits and preferential loans for people who obey the rule.

Results of the Chinese policy

The result of the policy has been, in urban areas, that most families have only one child. In rural districts, family sizes have been cut dramatically, but do not yet match the urban pattern. There is now some evidence that the policy is being relaxed in rural areas. Couples are allowed to have two children without penalties if the births are at least five years apart and are planned under the quota system. This is to increase the chance of having a male heir who can carry on the family farm.

The sex ratio of registered births in China is currently 118 boys to 100 girls (the natural rate is 106 boys to 100 girls). One explanation is that the births of many girls, especially in rural areas, are simply not registered. Another reason is that prenatal screening during pregnancy allows the sex of the unborn child to be determined and many more unborn females are aborted than males.

The China News Service has reported that, in some rural areas, the ratio of newborn boys is 144 to 100 girls. This imbalance is not confined to China but exists in many less developed countries with family planning programmes. Parents want male heirs to carry on the family tradition and to support them in old age. Girls are seen as a burden because they will marry into another family.

The Chinese government has started campaigns to persuade parents that a daughter is as much a blessing as a son. 'Mothers, value your daughters,' is one slogan used. But, it remains a difficult issue. There have been many reports of husbands abandoning and divorcing their wives if a daughter is born, so they can remarry and try for a son. Local government officials have been warned that if they allow scanning to detect and abort female babies, they will be sacked. Nevertheless, the practice remains widespread.

The sex imbalance may, in the future, create new social problems because there will be a shortage of wives. Already, in rural districts, some reports suggest that women have been kidnapped and sold as brides. The next generation of children will be raised without aunts, uncles or cousins. The traditional extended family will virtually disappear in urban areas. It remains to be seen what the long-term consequences will be.

Questions

1 Explain why, despite the birth rate almost halving between 1970 and 1996, China's population continued to rise rapidly.
2 Discuss alternative policies for reducing the birth rate which the Chinese government might have adopted.
3 Draw up a table that summarises the positive and negative effects arising from the One Child policy.

Falling birth rates

Some population policies can work too well. Fewer people in the economically active age groups can lead to declining industrial productivity and decreasing revenue from taxes. A decline in the working population can weaken a country politically and can cause a labour shortage.

This is true of Singapore which adopted an anti-birth policy in 1966. Measures included a sliding scale of child benefit that was more generous to families with one child than to families with several children. Another method was the introduction of a welfare and pension system that reduced the need for children as security for old age. As a result, the total fertility rate fell to 1.6 by the mid-1980s. This was below the replacement rate. Singapore now has a large number of foreign workers who make up almost one quarter of the total working population.

The Singapore government's policy on fertility was reversed in 1987 and the slogan used previously 'Stop at two' was replaced by 'Have three or more if you can afford it'. The policies were selective, however. In an attempt at social engineering, the Premier of Singapore Lee Kuan Yew wanted well-educated families to have more children. The best-educated women, who were often in top careers, were encouraged to get married and have children. Female graduates were targeted in government campaigns, and financial incentives were offered for a third and fourth child.

At the other end of the social scale, poorer families and less educated parents were offered cash incentives to have sterilisations. Fees in hospitals were increased as

Figure 1.8 Singapore

Singapore has developed into a high income economy. Population control has been so successful in Singapore that there has been a labour shortage.

a deterrent to less well-off women from having more children. The population policies in Singapore provide one of the clearest examples of how economic measures can be used to influence birth rates.

If a country's population starts to decline, or growth is slow, there can be a political impact. For two hundred years, successive French governments have been concerned that the relatively low birth rate in France has meant a loss of influence and power. In 1800, at the time of the Napoleonic Wars, France had a population of 20 million - the same as Russia. It could enlist bigger armies than any other Western European country. But, first Russia, then Germany, overtook France in population. In order to try and encourage a higher birth rate, the French government has used a policy of generous child benefits to persuade families to have more children.

Activity) **Will Europe's population decline?**

In many European countries, the total fertility rate has fallen below the replacement rate. This is the case in those Eastern European countries which have suffered economically since the collapse of communism. For example, in 1996, the total fertility rate in Romania was 1.3 and the annual rate of population change was -0.4 percent. However, low fertility rates are not confined to Eastern Europe. For example, in both Italy and Spain, the 1996 fertility rate was just 1.2. In Western Europe as a whole, people are choosing to have fewer children.

Because fertility rates are much higher in Africa and south Asia, the proportion of the world's population living in these low income regions is rising. In 1900, Europe had approximately 25 percent of the world's population, and three times the population of Africa. By 2050, Europe is expected to have only 7 percent of the world's population and just one third of Africa's population.

Figure 1.9 Projected populations in 5 European countries ▶

Country	1998 total (millions)	2050 projection (millions)	Decline in population (millions)
Russia	147.4	121.2	26.2
Italy	57.4	41.2	16.2
Ukraine	50.9	39.3	11.6
Spain	39.6	30.2	9.4
Germany	82.1	73.3	8.8

'I just don't want children'

This attitude is typical of a growing number of women in Europe. Many say: 'I have a career and I enjoy my work. Why should I give up these advantages? If I stop work, I shall lose pay and also lose touch with my work colleagues. There is also the danger that I shall not get back my former position and status in the company.'
The freedom, lifestyle and income that couples can enjoy if they do not have children are important reasons why more women are childless. In Britain, 11 percent of women born in 1940 had no children but this rose to 21 percent of women born in 1960.
If fertility rates continue to decline, what can governments do to halt this trend? Relaxing immigration controls is one answer, though this might be politically unpopular.

Another solution is to give tax incentives or bigger social security benefits to families with children. An alternative policy might be to pass laws that force employers to give lengthy periods of parental leave to mothers and fathers of small children.

Adapted from the Observer, 11th August 1999

Questions

1 What factors will affect the size of the European population in 2050?
2 Outline the possible impact of low fertility rates in European countries.

4. What factors affect death rates?

A variety of factors affect the death rate.
- **Public health care**: ie, the provision of clean drinking water and the safe disposal of sewage. The contamination of drinking water by sewage, causing diseases such as cholera and typhoid, is a major cause of high death rates in low income countries. The World Health Organisation estimates that one sixth of all diseases in the world are caused by contaminated water.
- **Nutrition, diet and lifestyle**: in low income countries, a key factor is the intake of sufficient nutritious food to withstand illness and disease. The highest death rates are in sub-Sahara Africa where the United Nations estimates that 40 percent of the population are undernourished. In high income countries, overeating, smoking and lack of exercise are important factors (this issue is covered more fully in unit 2.3, Health and Welfare).
- **Medical care**: this factor includes both the treatment and prevention of disease. The way in which preventative medicine can reduce the death rate is illustrated by the worldwide campaign against smallpox. As recently as the 1960s, two million people died of this disease each year. After a mass vaccination campaign, smallpox has now been completely eradicated. The standard of health provision in terms of vaccinations, medicine, hospitals and clinics is much higher in Western countries than in low income countries. In the UK, in 1995, there was one doctor per 667 of the population. In Sierra Leone, there was one doctor per 10,820 people. This is a factor in explaining the difference in death rates between countries.
- **Wars**: in very exceptional cases, such as in Cambodia during the 1970s or Rwanda during the 1990s, deaths from wars or civil disturbance have outnumbered deaths from other causes.
- **Age structure**: in 'young' populations, the death rate tends to be lower than in in 'old' or ageing populations. This is simply because, on average, young people are less likely to die than older people.

The factors that affect death rates tend to be different in high income and low income countries. Africa stands out as the continent with the highest death rate (see figure 1.10). It is the least developed economically and many African countries have very low average incomes. Public health care and sanitation are often at a low standard and, in many locations, there is no clean drinking water. Food supply is largely dependent on subsistence farming and, when the harvest fails, people go hungry. During the 1990s, parts of southern Africa have experienced a rising death rate due to AIDS. The impact and spread of AIDS is described later in this unit.

Figure 1.10 Death rates in different continents

Continent	Death rate per 1,000 (1997)
Europe	12
Asia	8
Africa	14
North America	9
South America	7
Oceania	9

Figure 1.11 Water in sub-Sahara Africa

The provision of clean water is one of the most important factors in cutting death rates.

Since the 1970s, there have been civil wars or unrest in many African countries including Ethiopia, Sudan, Chad, Liberia, Sierra Leone, Nigeria, Zaire (Democratic Republic of Congo), Rwanda, Burundi, Angola, Zimbabwe and Mozambique. Vaccination programmes, public health and agricultural investment have all been disrupted in these countries.

Figure 1.10 shows that Europe, perhaps surprisingly, also has a relatively high death rate. This is mainly due to the high number of elderly people in the population. Because death rates are calculated per 1,000 of the whole population, a large proportion of people in older age groups, relative to the number of younger people, will result in a high death rate. In Britain, for example, the number of people aged 65 and over is expected to outnumber those aged under 16 by 2008 - for the first time ever. Because the death rate for over-65s is naturally higher than for under-16s, the overall death rate will tend to rise, even though the population is becoming healthier and the life expectancy is increasing.

The political upheaval that eastern Europe has undergone since the collapse of communism in the early 1990s has reduced living standards for many people. Poverty, poorer diets and the breakdown of health systems have caused lower life expectancy in Russia and other countries. If sub-regions of Europe are examined, the marked difference in death rates can be seen (see figure 1.12).

Figure 1.12 Death rates in Europe

Sub region	Death rate per 1,000 (1997)
Northern Europe	11
Western Europe	10
Eastern Europe	14
Southern Europe	9

Improvements in public health care, diet and medical provision have a dramatic and rapid effect on death rates. According to the World Health Organisation, the single most

Figure 1.13 Life expectancy and access to clean drinking water

Country	Life expectancy (years) 1996	% Population with access to clean drinking water
Ethiopia	49	18
Mozambique	46	22
Nigeria	52	40
Haiti	57	42
Ecuador	69	58
Bangladesh	57	78
Mexico	71	78
Philippines	65	81
UK	76	100
Japan	79	100

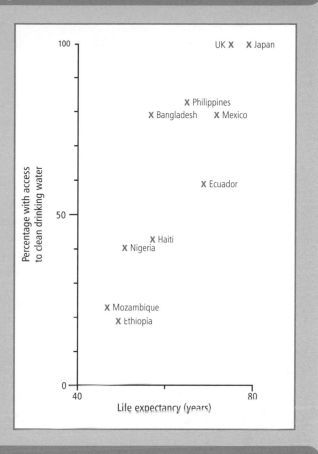

effective measure is the provision of clean drinking water, ie uncontaminated with sewage. This requires piped water from clean sources and a separate sewerage system. Figure 1.13 shows how life expectancy and access to safe drinking water are linked.

Figure 1.14 shows how, in some countries, such as Indonesia and Egypt, death rates have fallen rapidly. In Sri Lanka, the decline came before 1965. On the other hand, Mozambique, disrupted for many years by civil war, has not managed to achieve a comparable breakthrough. For the UK and Denmark, with their similarly ageing populations, death rates are stable or even rising.

When death rates fall, people on average live longer. However, life expectancy in high income countries is only increasing very slowly.

Advances in medical science are helping to raise life expectancy. On the other hand, the 'diseases of affluence' such as cancer and heart disease are working in the opposite direction. These 'life style' diseases are due in part to unhealthy diet, smoking and lack of exercise (see unit 2.3).

Figure 1.14 Death rates in selected countries

Country	Death rate per 1,000		
	1965	1988	1997
Sri Lanka	8	6	5
Indonesia	20	9	8
Egypt	19	9	9
Mozambique	27	24	21
Denmark	10	12	12
UK	12	11	11

Activity **AIDS**

Throughout history, there have been outbreaks of disease that have had a major impact on death rates. For example, the Black Death in the Middle Ages killed up to one third of the population, and Spanish flu, between 1918 and 1920, killed more people than died in World War One. AIDS is a modern epidemic. Its impact has, so far, been very different in the West compared with the low income countries of southern Africa.

Since 1980, when AIDS (Acquired Immune Deficiency Syndrome) was first identified, the disease has claimed an estimated 12 million lives world wide. By 1998, nearly 31 million people were infected with the AIDS virus, HIV. Of these 1.1. million were children and 4.6 million of the total had full blown AIDS. AIDS is the name given to the various medical symptoms experienced by people who have contracted the HIV (human immunodeficiency virus). The time scale between becoming HIV positive and showing AIDS symptoms is extremely variable.

The United Nations estimate that 2.5 million people died of AIDS in 1998. In sub-Sahara Africa, it is a major cause of death. For example, in Zimbabwe infection rates are as high as 17,500 per 100,000 people and are rising. In some hospitals, seven out of every ten pregnant women have tested HIV positive. In Botswana, it is believed that 25 percent of the adult population is infected. The spread of the disease is rapid. Health officials in South Africa estimated in 1998 that 1,500 people were infected every day with HIV.

There are a number of reasons why Africa is the continent most affected by AIDS. It is believed that HIV first developed there, possibly by cross-species contamination from monkeys. Many countries have low literacy rates so public education campaigns about AIDS are difficult to organise. Also, the disease is quickly spread because there are so many migrants - either refugees from war or economic migrants looking for work.

As there is no cure at present, AIDS has the potential to cause a rapid rise in death rates around the world. This has tremendous implications for economic output. A country's productive potential relies upon a healthy workforce. If a large proportion become ill, famine and starvation might follow. The burden of looking after orphans and sick people places a massive strain on the resources of low income countries.

Figure 1.15 shows that the spatial impact has been very uneven. It is some of the world's lowest income countries that have been most affected. Already life expectancy is falling across southern and East Africa - reversing trends and putting the clock back 30 years.

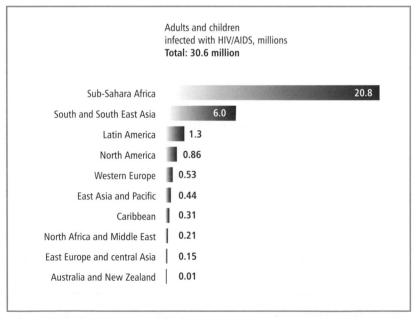

▲ Figure 1.15 The regional impact of AIDS, 1998

AIDS is contracted when the HIV causes a body's natural defences to weaken against previously non-life threatening illnesses. It tends to affect limited groups of people due to the ways in which it is transmitted. HIV is contracted in three main ways:

- through sexual intercourse with an infected person
- by transmission of the virus from mother to unborn child
- through infected blood, eg sharing needles or infected blood transfusions.

AIDS has a long incubation period. This means that HIV can be carried in a person's body for a very long time before any symptoms appear. Therefore it can be transmitted unknowingly. As a result, its spread is not only local but over large distances as someone can travel to another part of the country or the world and unwittingly infect someone there.

AIDS in the UK

The UK was one of the first countries to take the threat of the disease seriously. Although the government's use of emotive advertising in the early 1990s was criticised as alarmist, the effect on numbers of infections was claimed to be successful. For the first time, the number of AIDS cases fell in 1997. (In September of that year the number of cases had fallen by 30 percent compared to the previous 12 months). Those dying from infection have roughly kept in line with the numbers who have become infected. Since records have been kept, it is estimated that there have been 15,000 cases of AIDS in Britain, 72 percent of whom are known or believed to have died.

Most cases have been in large urban centres such as London and Edinburgh. Unprotected sex with an infected person, and needle sharing between heroin addicts, have been the main routes of infection. In the UK and the USA, AIDS is often associated with the gay community. However, on a world wide scale, this is a misleading perception. In Africa, for instance, the overwhelming majority of cases are contracted through heterosexual sex.

The UK experience suggests that by using public awareness campaigns, by promoting the use of condoms, by screening blood products for HIV and by organising needle exchanges, the spread of disease can be controlled. In the late 1990s, by screening pregnant women and then using new medical techniques, it became possible to reduce the risk of passing HIV to unborn children. It seems that, in the UK at least, AIDS will not have the massive impact on death rates that was once feared. New, expensive drug therapies are allowing some HIV patients to live near normal lives. Unfortunately, these 'cocktails' of drugs cost $15,000 per year per patient to administer. At this price, the entire health budget of Kenya would be spent in just six hours if all HIV patients in that country were to be treated.

Questions

1 Outline the possible impact of AIDS on sub-Sahara Africa compared with the UK.
2 Why might countries in sub-Sahara Africa find it more difficult to reduce the rate of HIV infection than a country such as Britain?
3 With reference to the world pattern of AIDS infection, suggest reasons why its spread has been so rapid.

5. How do changes in birth and death rates relate to development?

Changes in a country's birth and death rates, and total population, can be shown on a **Demographic Transition Model** (DTM). The DTM in figure 1.16 is based on the experience of the UK and other high income countries. It highlights the fact that populations rise rapidly when death rates fall. There is a close correlation between the level of social and economic development and the stages of the model. Less developed (ie, low and middle income) countries are in Stages 1, 2 and 3 of the model. More developed (ie, high income) countries are in Stage 4.

Death rates decline when there is improved public health, food supply and medical care. Birth rates start to decline later. This is partly because it takes time for families to adjust when, for example, infant mortality rates fall. Once the birth rate falls to a level that matches the death rate, the population stabilises.
The Demographic Transition Model is useful for comparing different countries but it does have certain weaknesses:

• It is based on the experience of industrialised countries. Less developed countries in other parts of the world, with different cultures, religions and levels of industrialisation, are unlikely to go through exactly the same pattern of change. Some countries have industrialised much faster than the UK. Malaysia and South Korea, for example, have witnessed rapid changes in population growth over a much shorter time scale than the model suggests.

• Death rates in the UK fell steadily, partly due to the social and economic effects of the Industrial Revolution. Some less developed countries have not had this experience. The slower decline of their death rates is caused by an inability to provide an adequate food supply, sanitation or medical care.

• In many European countries birth rates have fallen below death rates. It will take time, however, to see whether this is a long term trend and becomes a general pattern. If so, a Stage 5, with a declining population, will have to be added to the DTM.

6. What is population structure?

Population structure is the proportion of a population in each age group. It can be illustrated by using a population pyramid. This graph is a visual representation of how many people there are in each age group and provides an indication of life expectancy because it shows the number of elderly people. In addition, it shows the ratio of males to females. A population pyramid can also show where migration has had an impact on the population.

Each stage of the Demographic Transition Model has a corresponding population pyramid. Generally, the more pyramidal the shape, the less developed is the country. A wide base indicates a high birth rate and a narrow peak shows that there are low numbers in the older age groups - meaning a high death rate. This is typical of Stages 1 and 2 in the DTM. The Congo provides an example (see figure 1.18). On the other hand, a more narrow based, column shape illustrates a low birth rate, low death rate and high life expectancy; Japan is an example. This is typical of Stage 4 in the DTM. Where a country is moving from Stage 3 into Stage 4, eg Jamaica, the population pyramid is a column shape for lower age groups and then tapers for higher age groups.

Information on the percentage of people in different age groups can be used to calculate the dependency ratio of a population. This is the size of the 'dependent' population as a proportion of those who are 'economically active' (ie, those in the work force or who are of working age). In the UK, the dependent population is defined as those aged under 16 and over 65 (for men) and over 60 (for women).

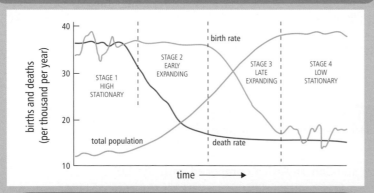

Figure 1.16 The Demographic Transition Model

In Stage 1, birth rates and death rates are high, so population is relatively stable. Population increases rapidly in Stage 2 when the death rate falls and the birth rate stays high. In Stage 3, the birth rate starts to fall but, because it is still higher than the death rate, the population continues to grow. In Stage 4, the birth rate has fallen to match the death rate and the population is once again stable.

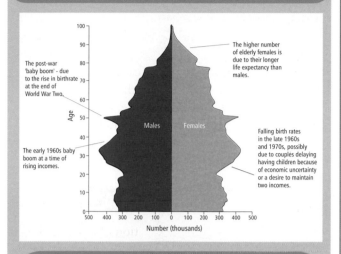

Figure 1.17 Population pyramid, England and Wales, 1997

The post-war 'baby boom' - due to the rise in birthrate at the end of World War Two.

The early 1960s baby boom at a time of rising incomes.

The higher number of elderly females is due to their longer life expectancy than males.

Falling birth rates in the late 1960s and 1970s, possibly due to couples delaying having children because of economic uncertainty or a desire to maintain two incomes.

Males Females

Age

Number (thousands)

The population pyramid shows the number of people (on the horizontal axis) who are in each age group (shown on the vertical axis). Reasons for fluctuations in the birth rate of England and Wales are shown on the graph.

Therefore the people in the economically active population are those aged between 16 and 60/65 years.

$$\text{The dependency ratio} = \frac{\text{numbers in non-economically active population}}{\text{numbers in economically active population}} \times 100$$

In the UK, in 1980, the dependency ratio was 55. This meant that for every 100 people of working age in 1980 there were 55 dependent upon them. By 1997, the ratio was 61. The bigger the dependent population, the more has to be paid in pensions, health care and education. The issues raised by an ageing population and the rising dependency ratio are covered in more detail in unit 1.5.

Note that unemployment is not taken into account in the dependency ratio. The whole of the 16-60/65 population is defined as economically active.

Therefore the tax burden on the working population is actually much higher in countries where levels of unemployment are high, or where few females are in paid employment or when many people have taken early retirement.

7. What are the main trends in world population growth?

The world population is rising at a rapid rate. The total population is projected to rise from just over 6 billion in 2000 to over 10 billion in 2100, and then to stabilise at around 10.5 billion. This is the 'mid estimate' of the United Nations Population Fund published in 1999. The rapid rise is because death rates have fallen, or are falling, and this had not been matched by an equivalent fall in birth rates. The downward trend in death rates is expected to continue. The population will stabilise when, and if, birth rates fall as low as death rates.

Small changes in birth rates and fertility can make a huge difference to population projections. For instance, if total fertility rates stabilise at 2.2 children per woman, the world's population will reach 18.3 billion by 2150. But, if the total fertility rate stabilises at 1.8, the population in 2150 will be just 6.4 billion.

On a global scale, the rate of population growth slowed from the highest level of increase, 2.1 percent per year in 1965-70, to 1.5 percent per year in the late 1990s. United Nation estimates for future growth have been scaled down because of rapidly falling fertility rates in some countries. This has been particularly true in South and East Asia. For

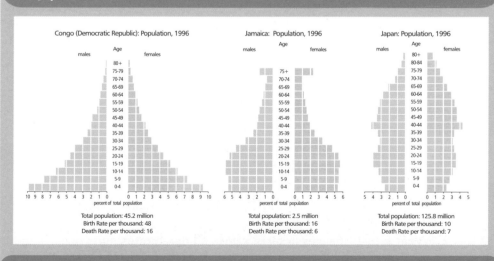

Figure 1.18 Population pyramids for Congo (Democratic Republic), Jamaica and Japan, 1996

Congo (Democratic Republic): Population, 1996

males   Age   females

percent of total population

Total population: 45.2 million
Birth Rate per thousand: 48
Death Rate per thousand: 16

Jamaica: Population, 1996

males   Age   females

percent of total population

Total population: 2.5 million
Birth Rate per thousand: 16
Death Rate per thousand: 6

Japan: Population, 1996

males   Age   females

percent of total population

Total population: 125.8 million
Birth Rate per thousand: 10
Death Rate per thousand: 7

Average annual population growth rate: Congo 3.2, Jamaica 1.0, Japan 0.3.

example, in Bangladesh, the total fertility rate fell from 6.2 children to 3.4 in just ten years between 1986 and 1996. The world's population will stabilise in a hundred years if current trends continue and if Africa and the Middle East follow the same pattern as in other regions.

As with all projections, there is a wide margin for error. Nobody knows, for example, how long the enforced population policies in China, the AIDS epidemic in Africa, and falling European birth rates will continue. Also, of course, there might be completely unforeseen events - perhaps wars, natural disasters or new strains of disease.

There are differences in population growth between low income and high income countries (see figure 1.19). In general, less developed countries have a higher rate of population growth than more developed countries. There are, however, significant differences between less developed countries. Birth rates have fallen markedly in Latin America and in China. But Africa and the Middle East (ie, western Asia) still have high birth rates.

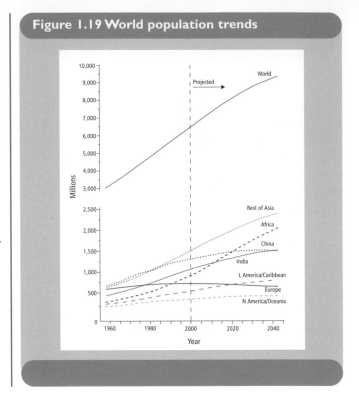

Figure 1.19 World population trends

Activity — Demographic transition on a world scale

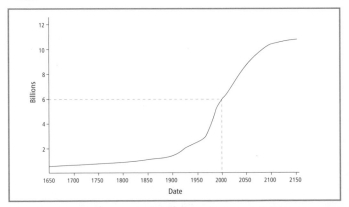

Figure 1.20 shows actual and projected changes in world population - based on the United Nations Population Fund (UNFPA) 'medium variant' projection published in 1999.

◄ **Figure 1.20 World population growth.**

Questions

1 Briefly describe and explain the world demographic transition that occurred up to the year 2000.
2 What future changes in birth rates and death rates must occur if the UNFPA projection is to be accurate?

8. What are the main population trends in the UK?

The population of the UK is growing slowly. In 1997, the population was 59 million, the death rate was 10.7 per 1,000 and the birth rate was 12.3 per 1,000. So there was a rate of natural increase of 1.6 per 1,000 (0.16 percent). The total had grown by 3 million over the previous 20 years and is projected to increase by another 2 million. A peak of just over 61 million is expected in 2020. From then on, the population is projected to decline.

Declining fertility rates are one reason for the population trend. Women are not having as many children as previously, and fewer women are having children. However, there are a relatively large number of women in the reproductive age group and this explains why the population will grow slightly. The total fertility rate in the UK was 1.7 in 1997, having fallen from 2.9 in 1964. Reasons for the falling fertility rate include the increased participation of women in paid employment and the higher proportion of women entering higher education. These factors have caused some women to marry later and delay having children. The better the pay and prospects for working women, the greater the sacrifice is involved in having a career break for children. At the same time, the contraceptive pill has made it easier for couples to choose when and if they will have children. In addition, the availability of legal abortion has provided the opportunity to end unwanted pregnancies.

Another factor affecting the population total is increasing life expectancy. Life expectancy in the UK rose from 73.8 to 79.5 for women and from 67.9 to 74.3 for men between 1961 and 1996. This was due to a number of reasons. Advances in medical care - for example the flu vaccination for elderly people - have contributed. So has the improvement in housing, with fewer people living in cold and damp homes. Better working conditions, and the decline of heavy industries such as coal and steel, have cut the number of work related diseases. The consequence has been an increase in the number of people over the state retirement age (60/65) from 9.1 million in 1971 to 10.7 million in 1997.

Activity ▶ Population structure

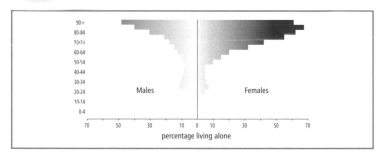

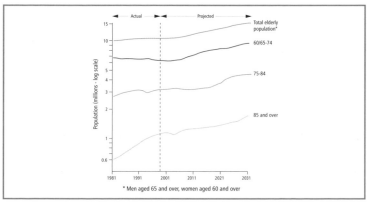

◀ **Figure 1.21 Living alone**
The population 'pyramid' shows the proportion of the population in Great Britain who were living alone at the time of the 1991 Census.

Questions

1 Describe what the data in the graphs show.
2 Suggest reasons for the patterns shown.

◀ **Figure 1.22 The number of elderly people, Great Britain, 1981-2031**
The graph shows the number of elderly people in broad age groups between 1981 and 2000, and projections until 2031.

unit summary

1 Governments gather demographic information for a variety of purposes. One is to plan social needs (such as housing, health care and schools). The main methods of collecting data are by census, registration and sample surveys.

2 World population change depends upon the birth rate and the death rate. In any particular country or region, migration will also affect population size.

3 Changes in birth rate, death rate and population size can be shown on a Demographic Transition Model. The rapid rise in world population has been caused mainly by a fall in the death rate. The rate of population growth is now slowing mainly because of a fall in the birth rate.

4 The proportion of a population in each age group is known as the population structure. It can be illustrated diagrammatically by a population pyramid.

5 The world's population is rising rapidly, but at a slightly slower rate than at its peak. If current trends continue, the world's population will stabilise at about 10.5 billion in 100 years time.

6 The UK's population is increasing very slowly and is expected to peak at 61 million. Life expectancy is rising and the total fertility rate is falling.

key terms

Census - a national demographic data collection process in which everybody is required to take part.

Birth rate - the total number of births in a year measured per 1,000 people.

Death rate - the total number of deaths in a year measured per 1,000 people; the term 'mortality rate' is also used.

Demographic Transition Model - a model that describes and projects population change over time.

Fertility rate - the number of live births in a year per 1,000 women who are in the normal reproductive age group (15-44 years).

Infant mortality rate - the number of children who die each year before they are one year old, measured per 1,000 live births.

Life expectancy - the average number of years that a person can expect to live.

Population pyramid - a graph showing the proportion of males and females in each age group of the population. It provides a visual display of a country's population structure.

Rate of natural increase / decrease - the difference between the birth rate and the death rate.

Registration - notifying the government of information such as births, deaths, marriages and place of residence.

Replacement rate - the total fertility rate required to stabilise a population.

Total fertility rate - the average number of children borne by women during the whole of their child bearing years; the term 'total period fertility rate' is also sometimes used.

Unit 1.2 Population distribution and density

1 What is population distribution and density?
2 What factors influence population distribution and density?

1. What is population distribution and density?

Population distribution is a way of describing where people live. It also describes how 'spread out' a population is. An even distribution means that, within a region, each area has the same number of people living in it. An uneven distribution means that the population is unevenly spread out - for example, people might be concentrated in particular towns or cities.

Population density is a numerical measure of how many people live in a given area. The method of calculation is:

$$\text{Population density} = \frac{\text{population total}}{\text{area}}$$

For example, the population of Hong Kong in 1996 was 6,310,000. Its land area is approximately 1,000 square kilometres.

Therefore its population density is:

$$\frac{6,310,000}{1,000} = 6,310 \text{ people per square kilometre.}$$

A **densely populated** area has many people living in it and a **sparsely populated** area has few people in it. Greater London with its population density of 4,400 people per square kilometre (1995) can be described as densely populated. At the other end of the scale, the Scottish Highlands with a population density of 8 people per square kilometre can be described as being sparsely populated.

Population densities are average figures for a given area and do not necessarily indicate the population distribution. For instance, within the Scottish Highlands, the population distribution is uneven. People tend to be concentrated in towns and villages between which there are areas of almost empty countryside.

Figure 1.23 The world population distribution

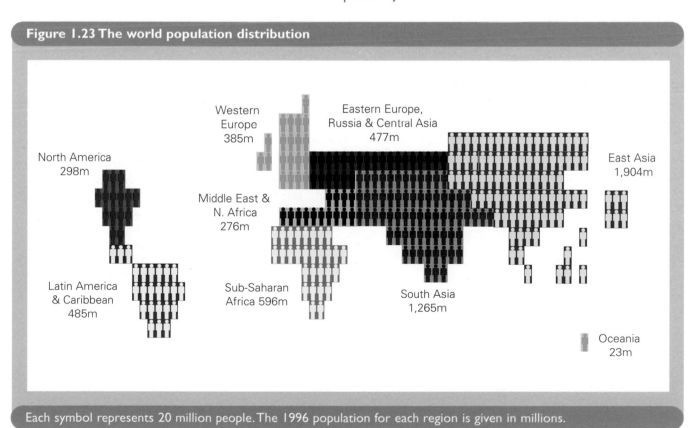

Western Europe 385m

Eastern Europe, Russia & Central Asia 477m

North America 298m

East Asia 1,904m

Middle East & N. Africa 276m

Latin America & Caribbean 485m

Sub-Saharan Africa 596m

South Asia 1,265m

Oceania 23m

Each symbol represents 20 million people. The 1996 population for each region is given in millions.

Figure 1.24 World population density

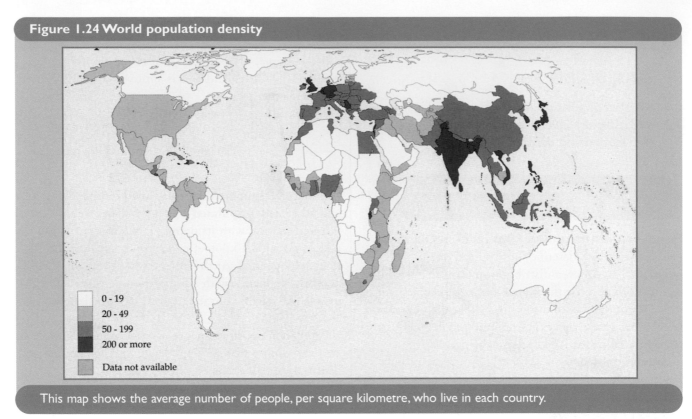

0 - 19
20 - 49
50 - 199
200 or more

Data not available

This map shows the average number of people, per square kilometre, who live in each country.

Figure 1.23 shows that Asia contains more than half the world's population. The diagram distorts the geographical areas but provides a good visual representation of population distribution - ie, where people live. So, for example, Oceania (Australia, New Zealand and the Pacific islands) appears small compared with its size on conventional maps. This is because it has a relatively small population.

Figure 1.24 shows that countries with the highest population densities are in Europe and South and East Asia. The lowest population densities are found in Australia, Russia, Canada and Brazil. Africa and South America are, in general, much less densely populated than South and East Asia.

Figure 1.25 shows the population totals and densities for a selected range of countries. City states like Singapore have the highest population densities. Canada is a thousand times less crowded than Singapore. However, as noted previously, population

densities are averages and there are variations within the borders of each country. So, for example, in Canada, within Toronto and Montreal there are districts with population densities that are as high as Singapore's.

In terms of world rankings, the UK has a relatively high population density. For the world as a whole, excluding Antarctica and Greenland, the population density is approximately 43 people per square kilometre. If all the world's population lived at the same density as people in Singapore, everyone would fit into a country the size of Mexico.

Figure 1.25 Selected population densities, 1996

Country	Area (thousands of sq. km)	Population in millions (rounded to nearest million)	Population (per square km)
Algeria	2,382	28	12
Bangladesh	144	120	833
Canada	9,976	30	3
Mexico	1,908	93	49
Singapore	1	3	3000
United Kingdom	242	58	240

Activity | **UK population distribution and density (1997)**

Figure 1.26 UK population data ▶

Country	Area (square kilometers)	Population total (millions)	Population density (people per square km)
United Kingdom	241,752	59.0	244
England	130,423	49.3	378
Northern Ireland	13,483	1.7	126
Scotland	77,080	5.1	66
Wales	20,766	2.9	140

Questions

1 Describe the population distribution within the UK in 1997.
2 With reference to the data, explain the difference between population density and population distribution.

2. What factors influence population distribution and density?

Put simply, population distribution refers to where people live and population density refers to how closely packed together they are. The factors which influence population distribution and density are generally the same. They can be classified as either physical or human. Climate, relief (ie, landscape features), natural vegetation and water supply are all physical factors. The location of industry, communications and political decisions are all human factors. Sometimes these factors are divided into positive (which attract people to an area) and negative (which discourage people from living there).

Before industrialisation, the physical factors which affected food production were the most important influences on distribution and density. This is because most people were farmers or relied on the food output from nearby farms. As technology has advanced, so the human factors have tended to become more dominant. Bulk transport systems allow food to be transported relatively cheaply to most places in the world. People are now able to live comfortably in harsh physical conditions such as the Libyan desert or the north Alaskan tundra. In both locations, oil wealth pays for the support systems that enable people to survive.

However, it is most unlikely that populations will ever be high in those regions where physical conditions are most severe.

Climate

The main impact of climate on population distribution and density is through its effect on farming. Extremes of climate discourage people from living in an area. Northern Alaska and the Sahara Desert are examples of hostile environments that are 'too cold' or 'too dry'. Although, clearly, it is possible for people to live in these areas, the extreme climate makes agriculture difficult and expensive. So, for example, in the Arctic the growing season is too short for crops to ripen. In the Sahara Desert, crops will not grow without irrigation. It is generally only in those climatic regions favourable to agriculture that large rural populations can be sustained.

Amazonia is sometimes described as being 'too wet' to support a high population density. While it is the case that heavy rainfall can quickly wash away topsoil, and hot, humid conditions favour the spread of disease, these factors can be overstated. The example of Java in South East Asia, with its hot and wet climate and high population density, casts some doubt on the importance of this factor. This point is developed in the section on natural vegetation that follows.

A climate with reliable rainfall and a growing season

long enough for crops to ripen is favourable to farming. North West Europe is a region where climate acts as a positive factor. Countries which have relatively large populations and high population densities, such as England and France, are largely self sufficient in food. This is due to their efficient agriculture which is made possible, in part, by their climate. Regions with growing seasons that allow two crops to be grown each year, for example the Ganges Delta, can support even larger populations and higher population densities.

Natural vegetation

Dense forest was, at one time, a barrier to large scale human settlement because it was difficult to clear. Grassland and regions with light vegetation were more attractive to farmers. In Britain, for example, most of the early agricultural settlements were on higher ground where forest cover was thin. These areas could be turned into pasture or cropland more easily than the dense oak forests in lowland areas. But, over time, population

Figure 1.27 Farming in Western Europe

In Western Europe the growing season is long enough and there is sufficient rainfall to allow efficient agriculture.

pressure led to most of the lower woodland being cleared. This same process is occurring in those remaining forest areas of the world where the climate is favourable to agriculture.

In South East Asia, the natural vegetation is mainly tropical rain forest but, where it has been cleared, the land supports large populations. The river deltas and flood plains of these regions are traditionally associated with rice growing. This is a very nutritious and productive crop. Land planted with rice can support far more people than any indigenous (native) crop of either South America or Africa. The practice of growing rice in paddy fields has the additional advantage of protecting the soil from erosion by the heavy rainfall. The consequence of this farming system is that high rural population densities can be supported in places such as Java and Vietnam, despite the negative physical factors that have restricted population growth in the Amazon or Congo basins.

Relief

This factor refers to altitude, angle of slope and aspect (ie, the direction that a slope faces). It is easier and cheaper to build houses, roads and towns on flat land. It is also easier to farm on flat land because agricultural machinery cannot be used safely on slopes that are much steeper than 10 degrees. It is possible to terrace steep slopes but this is very costly and time consuming. For these reasons, population densities tend to be higher on plains, and lower in mountainous areas.

Large rural populations, living at a relatively high density have arisen on some areas of low lying, flat or gently rolling land. Parts of north Germany, the Netherlands and Belgium are examples of such regions within Europe. In the same continent, the Alps have a relatively low population density because of the mountainous terrain and extreme weather conditions. There are, of course, variations even within the Alps. Flat, lower valleys have higher population densities than the upper slopes. The higher the altitude, the colder the weather and shorter the growing season. The physical factors of relief and climate combine to produce unfavourable conditions for farming or settlement.

In the Alps, north facing slopes tend to be wooded and sparsely populated. South facing slopes tend to be used for pasture and settlements (see unit 12.4). The aspect creates micro-climatic variations because south facing slopes receive more sunshine hours and more overhead sunshine than north facing slopes. The resulting higher temperatures also cause more evaporation and less waterlogging. In the southern hemisphere, it is the north facing slopes that are warmer and more productive for farmers.

Soils

For those regions that rely on agriculture, soil fertility is a key factor in determining population size and density. Flood plains often support large populations because the soil is made fertile by river deposits of silt and mud. For example, the Ganges Delta, the Nile Valley and the flood plains of Eastern China sustain some of the highest rural population densities in the world.

Rich volcanic soils, such as those found in parts of Java, allow very productive farming and also support large rural populations.

Rivers and water supply

Rivers provided the main long distance transport method between many early settlements. The valleys of the Rhine, Loire, Seine and Thames in Western Europe have all become densely populated, at least in part because of their importance as routeways.

Figure 1.28 Farming on terraces

Aspect, altitude and angle of slope are important influences on settlement and population distribution. Only where large amounts of labour or machinery are used to build terraces is it possible to farm on steep slopes.

The presence of water in a desert enables irrigation and provides drinking water. The Nile in Egypt and the Tigris in Iraq are the only source of drinking water for many people and both rivers enable very productive farming along their banks.

Natural resources

Coal and other minerals have attracted large populations in many parts of the world. In particular, during the early nineteenth century, the coalfields of Western Europe and North East USA saw a rapid increase in their urban populations. Factories with coal burning boilers and furnaces were built on the coalfields because it was expensive and impractical to transport large amounts of coal.

Now, although most industries are 'footloose', ie they are not tied to a particular power source, many remain close to the coalfields. For example, the Ruhr coalfield in Germany attracted steel, engineering, textile and chemical industries in the nineteenth century. Today, the region is still a major industrial centre even though steam power is no longer used. The industries and population will remain in place until some new economic reason causes them to relocate. This factor, causing industries to stay in their original locations, is called 'inertia'.

Industry

In countries that are industrialised, human factors tend to be more important than physical factors in affecting population distribution and density. People are attracted to areas of industry in order to gain jobs and improve their standard of living. The movement to these areas began in the mid-eighteenth century in the United Kingdom. The 'Agricultural Revolution' led to the introduction of machinery into farming and released large numbers of workers from the land. During the Industrial Revolution, cities of northern England such as Manchester and Leeds attracted large numbers of people. The same process of industrialisation and urbanisation has occurred throughout the developed world and has started in many low income countries.

When industrialisation occurs, lines of transport and communication tend to develop between markets and sources of raw materials. Along these routes, towns and cities grow - particularly at points where goods are handled and trans-shipped. For this reason, large populations have grown near ports such as Rotterdam, Liverpool and New York.

Political

Governments might directly or indirectly influence where people live. For example, in Indonesia there are government policies to encourage people to move from Java, the most densely populated island, to other less populated islands. Another example comes from Brazil. The creation of Brasilia as the capital was a political move by that country's government to divert development away from the cities of Rio de Janeiro and Sao Paulo, and attract people further inland.

Two of the most densely populated places on Earth, Hong Kong and Singapore, developed largely as a result of political decisions made by Britain to set up colonial trading posts. These Asian city states are built on islands with very limited space for their growing populations.

In most countries of the world, capital cities tend to attract large populations because they are the centre of communication, commerce and administration. For example, London is by far the largest city in the UK and it has a high population density. Not only is it the seat of national government, it is the headquarters of many national and transnational companies.

Figure 1.29 London

Capital cities attract population because they are the centres of government and commerce. Many company headquarters are located in London because it is a focus of communications for the whole country.

Activity — UK population distribution and density (1997)

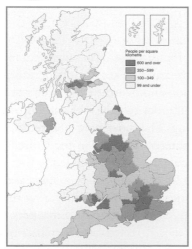

▲ Figure 1.30 UK population distribution

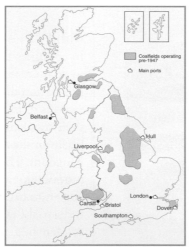

▲ Figure 1.31 UK coalfields and ports

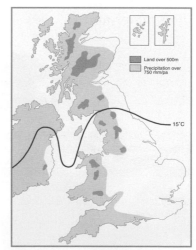

▲ Figure 1.32 UK precipitation, 15°C July isotherm and relief

Questions

1 Briefly describe the distribution and density of population within the UK.
2 Suggest reasons for the population distribution and density within the UK.

unit summary

1 People are not evenly spread over the Earth's surface. Asia contains over half the world's population.
2 Physical and human factors combine to influence population distribution. These factors can be classified as being either positive or negative.
3 People are attracted to regions where farming is productive or where industry can provide an income.
4 On a world scale, population densities are highest in Europe and South and East Asia. They are lowest in northern Russia, Canada, Australia, Brazil and the Saharan countries of North Africa. In general, people avoid hostile environments that are too cold or too dry for agriculture.

key terms

Densely populated - a relatively large number of people living in a given area.

Population density - the number of people living in a given area, usually measured as number of people per square kilometre.

Population distribution - where people live, and how 'spread out' a population is over a particular country or region.

Sparsely populated - a relatively small number of people living in a given area.

Unit 1.3 Migration

key questions

1 What are the main trends in migration?
2 Why do people migrate?
3 What is the impact of migration?
4 What is the pattern of UK migration?

1. What are the main trends in migration?

Migration is normally defined as a permanent or semi-permanent change of residence by an individual or group of people. Other forms of 'geographical mobility' include people commuting to work, people going on holiday and the seasonal movement of farm workers. These are not migrations because they involve people who intend to return to their place of origin. They are known as **circulation**.

Migrations can be classified by cause:

• **Forced migration** - typically caused by war, political persecution or natural disaster.

• **Voluntary migration** - typically caused by a desire to improve standards of living or to change job or place of residence (for example on retirement).

In practice, distinguishing between forced and voluntary migration is not always straightforward. This is because some **economic migrants** (ie, voluntary migrants wishing to improve their standard of living) claim that they are refugees (ie, they are being forced to flee from persecution). They claim **asylum** (ie, shelter from persecution) to get round immigration controls which most countries have imposed. It is therefore difficult to assess accurately how many people are genuinely in each category.

Between 1985 and 1995, there were 5 million asylum seekers to Western Europe, North America, Japan and Australasia. Since then, there has been a further rise in numbers. Countries use different criteria for deciding on refugee status. For example, in the UK, refugees are granted asylum if they can prove that they are genuinely in danger of persecution. This persecution might be by their own government or by any other group within the country, for example by armed rebels. In France, people are only granted asylum if they are in danger of persecution by their own government. So, even within the European Union, there is inconsistency in the way that migrants are classified and treated.

Countries also use different definitions of what is an

economic migrant. The UK, for example, classifies people who work or study abroad for a year or more as migrants - even though many of these people intend to return 'home' eventually. Other countries only count people who intend to make a permanent move as migrants. The outcome is that all statistics on migration have to be treated with great caution.

Migrations can also be classified by distance travelled:

- **Intra-regional** - this is movement within a region; for example rural to urban migration during urbanisation, and urban to rural migration during counterurbanisation (see units 3.3 and 3.4).
- **Inter-regional** - this is movement between one region and another, for example from the West Midlands to East Anglia. Both intra-regional and inter-regional movements are sometimes called 'internal migration'.
- **International** - this is movement across a national boundary. It is sometimes called 'external migration'. When people leave a country they are called **emigrants**. When they enter a new country they are called **immigrants**.

When people flee across a national boundary, they are called refugees. When they flee to another part of the same country they are classed as **Internal Displaced Persons (IDPs)**. National and international statistics on migration, refugees and IDPs are collected by two agencies - the International Organisation for Migration

(IOM) and the United Nations High Commission for Refugees (UNHCR).

Recent trends in voluntary migration

The direction of movement for economic migrations has changed during the last century. From the beginning of the twentieth century, until the late 1950s, the biggest movements were from Europe to the 'New World', mainly the United States of America, Australia and Canada. Since the 1950s, movement has been dominated by economic migrants from low income countries to North America and Western Europe.

There are two main sources of European immigrants. One group of immigrants comes from former Asian, African and Caribbean colonies (eg, Algeria and West Africa to France; India, Pakistan and the West Indies to the UK). The other main source has been the Mediterranean region with most of these migrants moving northwards (eg, Italians to Switzerland and Turkish people to Germany).

In the United States and Canada, the main source of economic migrants since the 1960s has been Mexico, other Latin American countries and Asia.

A major post-war migration caused by non-economic factors has been of Jewish people to Israel. The desire to build a Jewish homeland has been the main driving force. Many Jewish people fled Germany and mainland

Figure 1.33 Large scale migrations since the mid-1980s

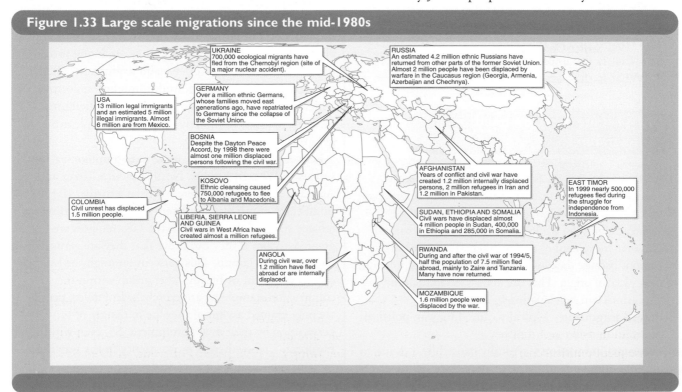

Europe in the 1930s as refugees from persecution. Only later did they move to Israel in large numbers, often from Britain or the USA which had given them temporary refuge. Since the 1980s, a new wave of migrants has moved to Israel from the former Soviet Union. Greater freedom of movement in Russia and the other former communist states has given many Jewish people the chance to move to their new homeland.

The break-up of the Soviet Union has resulted in large population movements. Most of the migrants are ethnic Russians. They do not wish to remain in the new states where they feel they are not welcome. These states include the Baltic countries, such as Latvia, the central Asian countries such as Tajikistan, and the Caucasus countries such as Georgia and Armenia. An estimated 4.2 million ethnic Russians moved to Russia between 1992 and 1998, and a further 3 million are expected to migrate by 2005.

Activity) **US immigration**

(The statistics in figures 1.34 and 1.35 are for legal immigrants; ie, people who have been accepted by the US Immigration Service. They do not include people who have entered the United States illegally.)

Figure 1.34 Immigration 1820 - 1996 (in millions) ▼

Top ten countries of last residence	
All countries	63.1
Germany	7.1
Mexico	5.5
Italy	5.4
UK	5.2
Ireland	4.8
Canada	4.4
Soviet Union (former)	3.7
Austria	1.8
Hungary	1.7
Philippines	1.4

Figure 1.35 Immigration 1981 - 1996 (in millions) ▼

Top ten countries of last residence	
All countries	13.5
Mexico	3.3
Philippines	0.8
Vietnam	0.7
China (and Taiwan)	0.5
Dominican Republic	0.5
India	0.5
Korea	0.4
El Salvador	0.3
Jamaica	0.3
Cuba	0.2

Question

I Compare the recent (ie, 1981-1996) migration to the USA with the longer term pattern (ie, 1820-1996).

Recent trends in forced migrations

According to the UNHCR, the total number of refugees and Internal Displaced Persons was 5.7 million in 1980, 14.9 million in 1990 and 22.7 million in 1997. Wars and consequent political change are the main causes of forced migration.

In the 1990s, the biggest number of refugees has been in Africa - as a result of civil wars. The biggest single movement was the 1.7 million people who fled from Rwanda in 1994/95. In Angola there were 1.2 million people displaced by civil war in 1994 and, in Mozambique, 1.6 million refugees have returned home following the 1992 peace settlement. In 1998/99, there were 800,000 refugees from Liberia and 250,000 from Sierra Leone.

In other regions of civil war and conflict, 3.2 million people have fled Afghanistan and 670,000 have left Bosnia. Another 950,000 remain displaced within the former Yugoslavia. War and civil disturbances in Kosovo in the late 1990s added almost 1 million to the number of temporary refugees in the Balkans.

The biggest number of long standing refugees are 2.8 million Palestinians. Many fled from their homes during fighting at the time Israel was formed in 1948. Four generations have lived in camps in Gaza, the West Bank, Syria, Lebanon and Jordan. Most of the camps now have the appearance of semi-permanent settlements with concrete and brick buildings and utilities.

Who migrates?

There is an important difference between voluntary and forced migrations in terms of who moves. In forced migrations, generally everyone moves, young and old, single and married, rich and poor. The reason is that

everyone is fleeing from danger. Economic migrants, however, are different. They tend to be young adults, often male, who find it easier to move than older people who have possibly started careers, set up homes and had families. Social customs and tradition sometimes make it difficult for single females in some less developed countries to migrate. This is partly due to cultural and religious beliefs about the role of women. For instance, in most Muslim countries it would not be acceptable for a young woman to leave home and seek a job in another country. In other cases it is because the daily tasks traditionally done by women tie them to the home more than men. For example, in many rural areas of Africa, women are expected to do the cooking, child rearing, fetching water, collecting firewood and farming.

The pattern of migration into Western Europe has mainly been of young men moving to find work. Once these men became established, wives and other relatives followed. In some cases, the intention was to earn enough money and then return 'home' to retire. However, once families were raised in the new countries, and children perhaps no longer knew the old language, going home became much more difficult. Throughout Western Europe, millions of people of Asian, African-Caribbean and African ethnic backgrounds have been born since the 1950s and know no other home.

There are some exceptions to the general pattern of young male economic migrants. For example, tens of thousands of young adult females have left the Philippines to find domestic work as cleaners, maids and childminders. They have moved to Japan, Hong Kong, Singapore and the Gulf Arab states such as Kuwait and Bahrain. It is socially acceptable in the Philippines for women to take up paid employment, and working abroad can make a big contribution to family income.

Figure 1.36 Refugees from Kosovo

Refugees are one type of migrants. These people are fleeing from fighting in Kosovo in 1999.

Activity | The age structure of ethnic minorities in the UK

In official UK statistics, the ethnic minority population is defined as non-white migrants and their descendants.

Figure 1.37 Population by ethnic group and age, UK 1996 (percentages) ▼

Ethnic group	Age							All
	0-9	10-19	20-29	30-44	45-59	60-74	75+	
Ethnic minorities	21	18	18	25	12	5	0.7	100
White	12	12	15	22	18	14	6	100

Questions

1 Compare the age structure of the ethnic minority population with that of the white population.
2 Suggest reasons for the different age structures.
3 How might the different age structures affect the demand for schooling, pensions and other social services?

2. Why do people migrate?

A number of theories have been developed to explain and predict migration patterns. In the late nineteenth century, Ravenstein suggested some general 'laws' based on his studies of migration within Britain. His ideas related to voluntary, economic migrants, at a time of rapid urbanisation.

Ravenstein's suggested that:

- most migrants travel relatively short distances, and far fewer travel long distances; this is an example of 'distance decay' which also applies to other types of geographical mobility. (Distance decay can be defined as an inverse relationship between the number of people who move and the distance they travel; ie, most people do not move far.)
- migrations are often counter-balanced by movements in the reverse direction
- migration occurs in waves; ie, large groups of people tend to move together
- migration often takes place in 'steps'; ie, people travel to one place, then later they move on to another - and so on
- most migrants are adults.

The idea that migration occurs in steps is based on widespread evidence. Examples include the East European Jews who travelled to Britain in the late nineteenth century on their way to the United States. Many broke their journeys in places like Hull and the East End of London. Some of these migrants decided to move no further.

Similarly, there is strong evidence that many Irish people came to Britain in the 1950s and 60s to earn enough money to emigrate to the USA. Again, many found jobs, married and decided to stay. These examples support the idea of another writer on migration, Stouffer. He suggested that 'intervening opportunities' might be an important factor in determining a migrant's eventual destination. The example of Jewish people moving from Eastern Europe to the USA, but stopping in London and finding a job - and staying, illustrates the point.

In the 1940s, Zipf suggested that migration between two places depended upon the size of their populations and the distance between them. The idea is based on Newton's gravity equation which is used in physics. The 'pull' between two objects (eg, the Earth and the Moon) is related to their mass and the distance between them. So, in the context of migration, the larger the populations of two places, and the nearer they are to each other, the bigger the expected flow of people - and vice versa. Modified forms of this 'gravity model' are still used as the basis of some population movement predictions.

At its simplest, the gravity model can be expressed as:

$$Fab = \frac{(Pa \times Pb)}{Dab^2}$$

Where a and b are two places, Fab is the population flow between them, Pa and Pb are their respective populations and Dab is the distance between them.

The gravity model has been criticised on a number of grounds. It is a law of physics and there is no theoretical reason why the movement of people should be caused by a force similar to gravitational pull. Nor does the model take into account 'intervening opportunities' between the two places. In reality, there are many other factors such as political boundaries, immigration controls and transport costs that make it difficult to predict population movement. For instance, the movement between two cities in North America will be very different if, in one case, they are both within the USA, and in the other case, one is in the USA and the other is in Mexico. The border controls make movement far more difficult between the two countries than within the USA. Even if the border crossing was opened, the flow might be expected to be mainly from Mexico to the USA, no matter how big the cities are - because of the difference in standard of living. The gravity model takes no account of such factors.

Factors that cause people to migrate

Reasons why people may wish to leave an area are sometimes called push factors. Reasons why they are attracted to another area are called pull factors. Push factors tend to be negative reasons whereas pull factors tend to be positive. They usually work together. For example, in a war zone, people are 'pushed' from danger and they are 'pulled' towards safe areas. Likewise, for economic migrants, people are 'pushed' because of unemployment or low wages and they are 'pulled' by the prospect of a job or higher wages.

War There are many instances of forced migrations caused by war or civil disturbance. For example, in Rwanda, decades of ethnic conflict climaxed in 1994 when the Hutu ruling group organised the massacre of rival Tutsis. Approximately 500,000 Tutsis were killed and 700,000 fled to refugee camps. Then the Rwandese Patriotic Front (RPF), composed largely of Tutsis, retaliated and overcame the Hutu government. An estimated 1.7 million Hutus fled, fearing reprisals for the genocide that had occurred. These Hutus moved to Zaire (now the Democratic Republic of Congo), Tanzania and Burundi.

In Zaire, ethnic Tutsis, feeling threatened by the Hutu influx, established their own rebel army. They gained control of Zaire and drove 500,000 Hutus back into Rwanda. Another 400,000 Hutus fled into dense rain forest. By 1998, almost 250,000 Hutus were still unaccounted for, either living in hiding or killed in revenge for what had happened in Rwanda.

Government decisions Sometimes governments promote migration within countries to relieve population pressure or to help develop regions with low population densities. Indonesia provides an example - people from the densely populated island of Java have been given financial incentives to settle in islands such as Borneo (Kalimantan) and New Guinea (Irian Jaya). This has resulted in ethnic tensions because the newcomers are different in language and culture from the indigenous inhabitants.

Occasionally, migrations are forced upon people when, for example, a valley is flooded to form a reservoir. Haweswater in the Lake District is a small scale example - the ruins of the old village are still visible when the water is low. Several thousand people had to move when the Aswan High Dam in Egypt was completed in the 1960s and, in the late 1990s, over a million Chinese had to move as the Three Gorges Dam was being built.

Environmental accidents In 1986, the explosion at the nuclear reactor near Chernobyl caused an area of 50,000 square kilometres to be permanently evacuated. Whole towns and villages had to be abandoned. The area around the plant is too radioactive for people to live safely. The accident occurred in the old Soviet Union but today the area affected lies in northern Ukraine and southern Belarus (see unit 2.5 for a more detailed account of this incident).

Figure 1.38 A refugee camp in Rwanda

Africa has been the location of many forced migrations There are also refugees from war in both Asia and Europe. For example, civil war in Bosnia during the mid-1990s led to ethnic cleansing in which the three main factions, the Serbs, Croats and Muslims, drove minority ethnic groups out of 'their' areas by systematically destroying houses and killing people who resisted. Throughout former Yugoslavia, and in neighbouring countries, there are tens of thousands of displaced persons and refugees caused by ethnic conflict.

Figure 1.39 Volcanic eruption on Montserrat

During 1997, ash and volcanic debris made the southern end of Montserrat uninhabitable. The capital, Plymouth, was evacuated.

Natural hazards Hurricanes, floods and volcanic eruptions sometimes drive people from their homes but are rarely the cause of permanent migrations. However, there are exceptions. In 1997, a volcanic eruption on Montserrat (see unit 7.3) forced over half of the islanders to flee. Out of an original population of 11,000, only 3,200 residents were left by 1998. The capital, Plymouth, was evacuated and an exclusion zone was enforced around the volcano. Today, only the northern part of the island is inhabitable. Some people have migrated abroad, to neighbouring Caribbean islands or to the UK. Others have tried to set up new homes in the north. The depth of volcanic ash and danger of new eruptions mean that the towns, villages and homes in the south have been abandoned.

Famine is sometimes classed as a natural hazard although, in most cases, the cause is partly human. For example, the 1980s famines in Ethiopia and the 1990s famines in Sudan were partly due to drought but were also the result of civil war. Lack of rainfall caused crops to fail but people died when international food aid was blocked by warring factions. Refugees were forced to walk great distances to reach the safety of feeding stations.

During the mid-nineteenth century, the Irish famine was again due, in part, to human factors. The potato crop - on which the poorest people completely relied - was destroyed by blight (a fungus disease). However, there was still food in Ireland that could have been used to feed at least some of the population. Even at the height of the famine, grain was being exported. But,

there was no system in place to provide the people with the food that was available in Ireland and elsewhere. The poorest people did not have any money to buy food and the government was unwilling to arrange sufficient food aid. The result was that approximately one million died, one million emigrated to the United States and one million moved to Britain. (The issue of famine is discussed in unit 1.4.)

Economic factors Many voluntary migrations are for economic reasons, for example to obtain a job or to earn higher wages. These people move to improve their standard of living. They hope to live in a good house with consumer comforts and take advantage of social provisions such as health care and schools.

It is the 'pull' factor that is likely to determine their destination. For example, the opportunity to improve living standards by working in West Germany (as it was then) attracted many Turks and southern Europeans in the 1950s and 60s. The 'German economic miracle' created many jobs in manufacturing and the building industry. There was a labour shortage and migrants were recruited in their hundreds of thousands.

Figure 1.40 Retirement in the sunshine

In Europe and North America an increasing number of elderly people have moved south to enjoy winter sunshine. Many live in purpose built retirement homes. For example, an estimated 50,000 French Canadians from Quebec have moved permanently to Florida where they are joined each winter by another 350,000 'snowbirds' from the same province.

Social and cultural factors Some people migrate because they are attracted to the 'bright lights' of cities and major urban areas. Theatres, cinemas, concert halls, fashionable shops and night clubs are amongst the attractions of cities like London, Paris, New York and Los Angeles. Such migrants tend to be young adults.

At the other end of the age scale, in Western countries, more and more retired people migrate to warmer and sunnier places. In the UK, the south coast and the South West are popular retirement locations. The Mediterranean coasts of France and Spain have purpose built settlements for elderly people, as do Florida and Arizona in the United States. In addition to warm, dry weather, many elderly people are attracted by the prospect of relatively crime-free, clean environments.

Activity ▸ Lifeblood of rural Mexico drains north

Farmers are treading a well-worn path in search of a better life. Santa Ines, like many other towns and villages in north-western Michoacan state, about six hours by car from Mexico City, is dying. Its population is being drained away by a seemingly irreversible process of emigration to the United States. The unskilled go north to work as seasonal farm workers in California or as domestic servants in affluent suburbs. There are better job opportunities for those who have skills or an education.

Enrique and Consuelo Meza are among the few migrants who have returned to the once-thriving farming community. 'When we came back 10 years ago, there wasn't a house in the village for sale or rent - now there are hardly any that aren't, but no one's buying,' says Consuelo.

In a decade, the population of Santa Ines has fallen by around two thirds, to about 500. Teenagers grow up fast in rural Mexico: it is not uncommon for a girl to start a family at 14. But husbands are in short supply, and the young women who gather in the plaza in the evening have little hope of finding one. 'As they grow up, they start leaving, and then they only come back for holidays,' says Mirna, aged 12.

Michoacan's second city, Zamora, is about 40 minutes away. Exchange bureaux on many street corners hint at the importance of remittances (ie, money sent home) from relatives in the north. Every day, a queue forms at the Elektra store, where people can pick up money wired to them from Western Union in cities such as Chicago, Atlanta or Los Angeles. Eladio Romero, the credit manager, says 20 or 30 people a day pick up an average of about $250 each. Alicia Martinez, an unemployed agricultural worker with four children and three grandchildren to support, is desperate for the money. Her husband and one of her sons live in California. For the country as a whole, remittances from migrant labour represent an annual inflow of between $3 billion and $6 billion - more than Mexico's agricultural exports. Exporting people not only improves the balance of payments, it also relieves the pressure for jobs - and for political and social reform - back home.

A combination of Mexico's economic crisis and increasing anti-immigrant sentiment in the US is beginning to change the pattern of migration. It is tougher to cross the border, so people pay fewer visits home. Lack of employment opportunities in Michoacan means migrants are willing to undergo greater hardship in making the journey north. The guides, or polleros, accept a 'cross now, pay later' scheme for those whose relatives will guarantee their $400-800 fee. Meanwhile, the future looks bleak for Santa Ines. 'Every time an old person dies, another house is boarded up,' says Consuelo Meza. 'The way things are going, it's only future is to disappear.'

Adapted from the Guardian, 20th May 1997

Questions

1 In your view, are the Mexicans who move to the USA economic migrants or refugees? Explain your answer.

2 Classify the reasons that cause these migrants to move into 'push' and 'pull' factors.

3. What is the impact of migration?

The impact of migration can be considered in three ways: the impact on the migrant; the impact on the receiving country; and the impact on the country left behind.

Migrants

If they are fortunate, economic migrants can enjoy all the benefits that come from paid employment and a regular income. In addition to the material advantages of a comfortable home, a car and other consumer goods, better health care and educational opportunities might be available. Migrants may also improve their job skills, knowledge and experience.

However, migrants often face hardship, poor living conditions and discrimination when they move. This is particularly true if they have an African, Hispanic (ie, Latin American) or Asian ethnic background.

The United States has been described as a 'melting pot' where large numbers of white immigrants have been assimilated and have made good. But, many African Americans and Hispanics have been less successful. They tend to have the highest rates of unemployment, the lowest average incomes and they live in the poorest housing. In Western Europe, where a large proportion of recent immigrants are from minority ethnic and racial groups, assimilation has been slow. In many cases, the migrants still form the most disadvantaged and lowest income groups, often still living in separate communities in poor urban areas.

Social tensions sometimes arise within immigrant communities when second and third generation children start to grow up and become independent. They might not learn the 'old' language and customs and they might become alienated from their parents' culture.

In the case of refugees who are fleeing danger or persecution, migration brings relative safety and relief. However, the breakdown of community links and the possible separation of family members, combined with a lack of money or any other resources, can have a serious impact. Children are particularly vulnerable. Many become orphans or simply lose track of their parents - the fighting in Rwanda created thousands of such cases. Schooling is often abandoned. Living in refugee camps carries the hazards of diseases such as typhoid and cholera. There is also the uncertainty of having to rely on aid and charity, and not knowing if it will be possible to return home. All these factors contribute to a lack of self esteem and low social status.

Receiving or 'host' country

Immigration can bring costs and benefits for the receiving country. One benefit is that the inflow of people might fill labour shortages. Some of the jobs might be low paid and menial, such as domestic cleaners and manual factory workers. In other cases, the jobs might be skilled such as nurses and doctors. By increasing the labour supply at a time of economic growth, migration can reduce the rate of wage inflation and therefore enable further expansion to occur.

Migration adds to the cultural diversity of a country and can stimulate developments in the arts, literature and entertainment. For instance, much of the early success of Hollywood was due to the influx of foreign talent.

However, immigration can sometimes create social tension in host countries. This is especially the case if unemployment is high. Migrants are sometimes accused of 'taking our jobs' by certain people. Prejudice, discrimination and ethnic conflict can follow, particularly if the immigrants have distinctive racial or cultural backgrounds.

In the case of refugees, receiving countries might find it very difficult to cope with a large inflow. Sometimes the task of housing and feeding refugees has to be undertaken by governments which are unable to meet even the basic needs of their own populations. In the case of Rwandan refugees, Zaire and Tanzania were overwhelmed by the influx. The economic cost was very high and international agencies like the United Nations intervened to prevent a humanitarian disaster. The Rwandan crisis was made worse by continued fighting which spilled across the national boundaries. The remoteness of the region from ports and reliable transport, combined with the sheer volume of refugees, made the supply of food aid extremely difficult.

Like economic migrants, refugees who settle in their host country can make a positive contribution, particularly if they are skilled. In 1972, the government of Uganda, led by Idi Amin, expelled people of an Asian origin. Most of the refugees moved to Britain. They included many business people and professionals, such as lawyers and doctors, who have since prospered. Indeed, their energy and business skills have been so admired that, in the mid 1990s, the government of Uganda invited them to return and help that economy revive.

Source country

For the 'home' or source country, there can be some positive effects when people emigrate. Overcrowding might be reduced and there might be less pressure on social services such as health care. Remittances (ie, money sent home by the migrants) benefits the individual recipients and also the national balance of payments. The money can be used to pay for imports that the country would otherwise not be able to afford.

However, emigration can have a number of negative effects on the source country. The loss of economically active, energetic people is damaging. With fewer people left, local businesses face a falling demand for their goods and services. This can set up a spiral of decline if the businesses fail and more people leave. Many of the people who are left behind are either very young or old.

This creates an additional burden for the economy and on the working population who pay taxes. In some cases, remittances from abroad are used by people to escape from rural poverty and move into villages and towns. But the result is that farms are abandoned and food production falls.

When there is a mass exodus of refugees, whole regions are sometimes abandoned. Parts of rural Rwanda are deserted following the civil war because people are too fearful to return. It could take years for output to rise to its previous level. The situation might, however, take even longer to resolve. The history of the Rwandan, and other conflicts, is that refugees flee, then regroup and arm themselves. They then return and drive out their rivals - so continuing the cycle of violence.

 Activity **Economic migration – Germany**

By 1990, there were 5 million migrants living in Germany, including two million people of Turkish and Kurdish origin. These 'Gastarbeiter' (guest workers) helped rebuild the German economy following its destruction in World War Two. Most had migrated in the thirty years between 1960 and 1990. They took jobs that Germans could not fill or did not want, such as factory and building work, and they accepted low wages. This allowed the economy to grow at a fast pace without creating labour shortages or wage inflation that might have slowed the process. At first, many of the migrants lived in hostels and sent remittances home to their relatives. Often, later, they were joined by their families and set up home. A large number of the migrants were from small villages where unemployment was high and standards of living were low.

During the 1990s, after German reunification, economic growth slowed and unemployment rose. Large numbers of East Germans started to look for work in the former West Germany. At the same time, many ethnic Germans migrated to Germany following the collapse of the communist governments in Eastern Europe and the Soviet Union.

Figure 1.41 Frankfurt ▲

The skyscrapers of Germany's main financial centre symbolise the country's post-war reconstruction. The German 'economic miracle' attracted many foreign workers.

The German government encouraged ethnic minority migrants to return home by offering cash grants. The policy is known as 'voluntary repatriation'. However, many of the second and third generation children of the original migrants could only speak German and had lost contact with the customs and traditions of their 'homeland'. Social tensions rose as German nationals could not obtain jobs and there were incidents where migrants were attacked and killed. Some people blamed immigrants for the rising unemployment. Differences in skin colour and religion became more significant when the migrants were no longer wanted. Antagonism was often made worse because the minority population was generally concentrated in particular areas of cities and towns. These are usually where the cheapest housing is found and are often near the neighbourhoods where the poorest Germans are living.

The Schengen Agreement

In 1985, seven member states of the European Union signed the Schengen Agreement to remove all internal border controls, including the need to show passports. (Britain, Ireland and Denmark negotiated opt-outs from the Agreement which had, by 1997, been signed by a total of eleven EU member states.)

For two years, the Dutch and German governments blocked Italy's membership of the Schengen Agreement because they believed its external border controls were not strong enough. One problem is that Italy has an 8,000 kilometre coastline that is impossible to guard effectively. Another problem is that Italy is mid-way between Africa, the Eastern Mediterranean and northern Europe and so is a convenient staging post for refugees and illegal migrants.

Reports in 1997 suggested that tens of thousands of refugees from civil disorder in Albania and south east Turkey had been smuggled into Italy. In one week alone, 13,000 of the 16,000 Albanians who had entered Italy simply 'vanished' and became illegal immigrants.

Questions

1 Describe the advantages and disadvantages for (a) Germany, (b) the source countries and (c) the migrants of the large scale migration to Germany before 1990.

2 Discuss the advantages and disadvantages of a policy of voluntary repatriation (for both the ethnic minority population and for the ethnic Germans).

3 Outline the possible consequences of the Schengen Agreement.

4. What is the pattern of UK migration?

For centuries, the UK has been both a source and recipient of migrants. During the nineteenth century, large numbers of Britons migrated to the USA, Canada, Australia and New Zealand. Most were economic migrants. At the same time, there was a large influx of people from Ireland. Irish people moved to Britain following the 1845 famine when the potato crop was hit by blight. In just one decade, from 1841 to 1851, the number of Irish born dwellers in Britain rose from 49,000 to 734,000.

At the end of the nineteenth century, and again in the 1920s and 1930s, there were several waves of immigrants from Russia, Poland, Romania and Germany. They were mainly refugees from persecution and many were Jewish.

The next large scale migrations started in the mid-1950s. Reconstruction after the Second World War, and job opportunities in many countries, encouraged economic migration. People from Britain moved to Canada, New Zealand and Australia. Skilled migrants were offered £10 assisted passages to Australia as an encouragement. At the same time, immigrants arrived in the UK from Ireland, the West Indies (peaking in the 1960s), India and Pakistan (peaking in the 1970s), East Africa (particularly the Ugandan Asians expelled in 1972), Africa and Bangladesh (both peaking in the 1980s).

Since 1962, legislation has been passed that has gradually ended the influx of migrants. Immigration controls have changed the nature of migration from being one of mainly young males to one of 'family reunion' involving wives and dependents.

Since the late 1980s, there has been a large increase in the number of asylum seekers - from low income countries, particularly in Africa, and also from eastern Europe and the Balkans. It is proving extremely difficult for the immigration service to determine whether these people are genuine refugees or economic migrants.

Figure 1.42 Immigrant and ethnic minority population, UK 1901-96

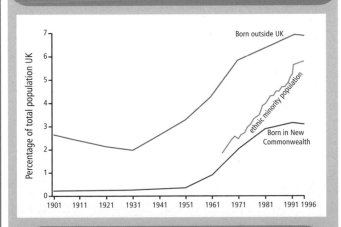

The 'New Commonwealth' includes the former colonies in Africa, Asia and the Caribbean (as opposed to the 'old' Commonwealth of Australia, New Zealand and Canada). Most migrants from the New Commonwealth are non-white, ie they are classed as being in the ethnic minority.

The majority of immigrants into the UK in the post-war period have been from the 'New Commonwealth', ie the former colonies in the Caribbean, Africa and the Indian sub-continent. At first, entry was unrestricted. Most of the migrants moved for economic reasons - to escape poverty and unemployment. They were attracted by the prospect of a higher living standard. Many were recruited to fill the labour shortages that occurred between the 1950s and 1970s. For example, large numbers of West Indians were recruited to work in London Transport and the health service. Many Asians were recruited to work in textile and clothing factories in Lancashire, Yorkshire and the East Midlands. Often the migrants did jobs that were dirty and menial. They were generally low paid and often worked unsocial hours.

Like earlier Irish and European migrants, the new immigrants to the UK tended to settle in areas of lowest priced housing - near the inner cities. By 1996, an estimated 3.3 million people from ethnic minorities were resident in the UK. Most of these were from the New Commonwealth or were children of migrants. The 1991 Census showed that the majority of immigrants and their descendants lived in Greater London, Greater Manchester, the West Midlands, West Yorkshire and Merseyside. Within these conurbations, the distribution of ethnic minority groups is very uneven. Certain districts have higher concentrations than others because particular ethnic groups have tended to cluster together. For instance, only 20 percent of people with a Pakistani origin live in London compared with over 50 percent of people with a Bangladeshi origin (who live mainly in the East End; eg, Tower Hamlets). A large proportion of the migrants from Pakistan and their families live in the towns and cities of the North of England. This is partly because many early migrants from Pakistan were offered employment in Northern textile mills. Once people settled in particular areas, families and friends were able provide support for newcomers. Migrants feel more comfortable if shared linguistic, cultural and religious traditions exist in the places they settle. Discrimination, and the fear of discrimination in 'new' areas, are reasons why the concentrations of ethnic minorities persist.

Migration within the UK

Since 1981, the pattern of migration within the UK has mainly been:
- from north to south,
- from urban to rural,
- and from inner to outer city areas.

During the 1980s and 1990s, a total of 1.25 million people left the major metropolitan areas of Britain (Greater London, West Midlands, Greater Manchester, Merseyside, West Yorkshire, South Yorkshire, Tyne and Wear and Glasgow). Greater London lost the largest number of people - over 600,000 - ie, almost half the overall total. (The causes of population movements out of urban areas are described in more detail in unit 3.3).

Between 1981 and 1996, there was a net inflow into the south of England (defined as the South East, the South West, the East Midlands and East Anglia) of 400,000 people. The flow slowed down when unemployment rose in the early 1990s but then resumed. The main reasons for this movement are the higher wages and lower unemployment in the south compared with the north. For several decades, the economy in southern England has been relatively prosperous while that of the north has relatively declined. (The reasons for this are described in more detail in unit 2.1.)

Almost half the changes of address in the year before the 1991 Census involved moves of under 5 km. Only one in eight moved 200 km or more (see figure 1.43). People tend to move short distances rather than long distances because they do not wish to break ties with family, friends and the local community. Also, it is easier to obtain information about new job opportunities in a local area, often by word of mouth, than it is over longer distances.

The most mobile people at the time of the 1991 Census were in their twenties with men being slightly more likely to move than women. The most mobile social group were professionals (eg, highly educated people with qualifications) and the least mobile were the unskilled. There are several reasons for this. People who go into higher education often move away from home because their university is in a different town or city. Then, when they start employment, they find it easier to move again because their ties to home and family are already partly broken. Another reason why professional people are more mobile is that they tend to be well paid and can therefore better afford the cost of looking for a new job and home compared with low paid workers.

Figure 1.43 Internal migration by distance, UK 1991 Census

Distance moved (km)	Internal migrants (%)
0-4	47.1
5-9	13.2
10-49	14.4
50-199	12.4
200+	12.9

Activity) Migration within the UK

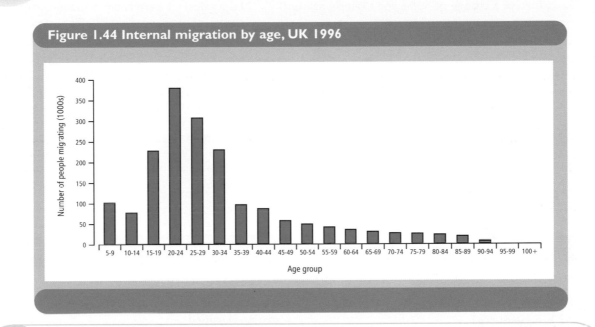

Figure 1.44 Internal migration by age, UK 1996

Question

1 Describe and give possible reasons for the pattern of migration shown in figure 1.44.

unit summary

1 In recent decades, large scale migrations for economic reasons have taken place into Western Europe and North America.
2 Large numbers of refugees have fled from civil wars in sub-Sahara Africa, the former Yugoslavia and Afghanistan.
3 In forced migrations, all age groups move. In voluntary migrations, young adults are the most likely to move.
4 The main 'push' factors are poverty, unemployment, war, persecution and natural hazards. The main 'pull' factors tend to be economic and social, for example the opportunity to have a higher standard of living.
5 Migrations have a three-fold impact: on the migrants themselves, on the source country and on the receiving country.
6 Post-war immigration to the UK has been in waves, from Ireland, the West Indies, India, Pakistan, East Africa and Bangladesh. Immigration controls have drastically cut the flow of migrants but there has been an increase in asylum seekers.
7 Within the UK, recent internal migration has mainly been from north to south, from urban to rural, and from inner to outer city.

key terms

Asylum - sanctuary or shelter for refugees.
Circulation - population movements that do not involve a change of home, for example seasonal work, commuting and tourism.
Economic migrants - people who migrate to improve their standard of living.
Emigrants - people who migrate abroad.
Ethnic cleansing - when one ethnic group deliberately forces another ethnic group to leave an area.
Forced migration - when people flee from war, persecution or other hazard; these people are classed as refugees when they cross a national boundary.
Immigrants - people who have migrated from abroad.

Internal displaced persons (IDPs) - people who are refugees within their own country.
Migration - a permanent or semi-permanent change of residence (in UK official statistics, a change of residence for a year or more).
Pull factors - the reasons why people are attracted to somewhere new.
Push factors - the reasons why people wish to leave somewhere.
Remittances - money sent back to the 'home' country by migrants.
Voluntary migration - occurs because people wish to move, for example to obtain a new job.

Unit 1.4 Population and resources

key questions

1 What is a resource?
2 Are there too many people?
3 Which theories help to explain the relationship between population and resources?
4 How might competition for resources be resolved?

1. What is a resource?

A **resource** is anything that is useful in producing the goods and services that people consume. **Natural resources** include plants, animals, minerals, the soil and, most importantly, the Sun's energy. Sometimes, a resource will not be useful unless the technology to exploit it is available. For example, wind was not useful to people as a source of electricity until the necessary technology was developed.

In its widest sense, the term resource also includes people themselves, their energy, skills and enterprise. Some writers suggest that this is the most important resource of all.

Certain resources are not natural but are manufactured. For example, factories and some manufactured goods are used to produce other goods. A textile mill, a weaving loom and a reel of cotton are all resources used in the production of textiles.

Classifying resources

There are a number of different ways in which resources can be classified.

Whether **renewable** or **non-renewable**:
• renewable: those resources that are in infinite supply; they can be used again and again, for example the power of the Sun or the tides
• non-renewable: resources that are in finite supply; they can only be used once, for example fossil fuels such as coal, oil and natural gas.

The distinction between renewable and non-renewable resources is, in practice, blurred. For example, metallic minerals are in finite supply but they can be recycled. Soils also are in finite supply but they can be used indefinitely if managed properly.

By **origin**:
• natural resources are from the environment; for example, timber, minerals, the soil and solar radiation
• agricultural resources are produced on farms or plantations; for example, cotton, wool and rubber
• manufactured resources are made by people: for example, the capital equipment (eg, machinery and factories) used to produce other goods

Whether **estimated** or **proven**:
• proven; ie, those resources which are known to exist and the quantities are certain
• estimated; ie, those resources where the amount is only an estimate.

It is generally the case, for natural resources such as minerals, that total reserves are unknown. For example, in the Atlantic Frontier off the west of Shetland, it is certain there is oil, but the total recoverable quantities are, as yet, only estimates. Even in established North Sea oil fields, new drilling technology can raise the quantity of recoverable oil, thus increasing the proven reserves.

2. Are there too many people?

Whether there are too many people in the world for the available resources is a matter of opinion and debate. The existence of widespread poverty and hunger would tend to support the view that there are too many people. According to the World Bank, in 1995 over 40 percent of young children were malnourished in seven countries: Ecuador, Nigeria, Ethiopia, Pakistan, India, Bangladesh, Nepal, Laos and Vietnam. In 1997, the United Nations reported that 6 million children die of malnutrition every year - more than the total killed by disease, war or natural disaster. Half the under-5s in South Asia and almost a third in sub-Sahara Africa are malnourished (see figure 1.45). The main cause, it is

argued by some, is a shortage of food and other resources leading to dietary deficiency. A better diet, including a simple, low-cost nutritional supplement, could improve children's health and raise resistance to malaria, pneumonia, diarrhoea and measles. In India and Bangladesh it has been estimated that vitamin and mineral deficiencies cost the equivalent of at least five percent of national output by causing premature deaths, disability and low productivity.

Although malnutrition is widespread throughout low income countries, some people do not accept the idea that there are too many people for the available resources. They believe that the issue is more complex than this. The problem is not a shortage of resources, but rather a problem of distribution. In other words, the difficulty is not that there is insufficient food, rather it is a matter of how to get the food to the people who need it most.

Evidence to support this view is that over the past 30 years the two most populous countries, India and China, have managed to increase food production in pace with their populations. The same is true on a world scale. Thirty years ago, according to the United Nations, the global food supply was 2,360 calories per person per day. By the mid-1990s, this had risen to 2,740 calories per person per day. At the same time, in Europe and North America, governments have even paid farmers to cut food output. Many people in low income countries are still suffering from famine and malnutrition but this, it is argued, is not due to a lack of food or resources. Several studies, from 1940s Bengal to modern sub-Sahara Africa, have shown that famines can occur when food output is rising. The usual problem is that poor people do not have enough money to buy the food that is available. This has been called a failure of 'entitlement'. In other words, the affected people do not have access to, or control over, the food resources that are available.

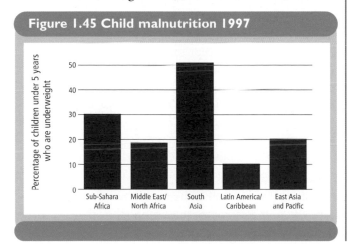

Figure 1.45 Child malnutrition 1997

Percentage of children under 5 years who are underweight

- Sub-Sahara Africa
- Middle East/North Africa
- South Asia
- Latin America/Caribbean
- East Asia and Pacific

Activity **Famine in Ethiopia**

During 1984, after a succession of dry years, there was a widespread crop failure in northern Ethiopia. Grass and other plants withered, causing sheep, oxen and cattle to die. Drought is a persistent problem in Ethiopia and it occurs on a regular basis. However, most inhabitants of that region had, in the past, developed farming systems that were adapted to the unreliable rainfall. The main cause of the famine in the early 1980s was not drought but civil war.

At the time, television news showed thousands of starving people who had walked to towns and refugee camps in the hope of relief. These pictures were the stimulus to Bob Geldof and others who organised the Band Aid concerts and recordings. Over £70 million was raised and large numbers of people were saved from starvation by emergency food supplies. But, almost a million died.

People fled from their land because they were afraid of being killed in the civil war. In many areas, farm animals and crops were left untended and seeds were not sown even in the areas least affected by drought. Fighting made it impossible to organise relief convoys to the worst affected areas. Some food that did get through was stolen by soldiers. Most of the refugees had to leave all their possessions behind. They were too poor to pay for food or to organise transport to safer areas.

Simply giving food surpluses to the poorest people can solve a short term famine but, in the long run, is not a good solution. If food is given away, local farmers have no incentive to produce food for sale, and a population becomes reliant upon aid. Although it is easier said than done, economic development that raises the buying power of the lowest income groups appears to be the best long-term solution. And, of course, this process cannot even start until fighting and civil conflict is ended.

Questions

1 Can the 1984 Ethiopian famine be classed as a 'natural' disaster? Explain your answer.
2 Outline the difficulties that aid agencies face in a war zone.

3. Which theories help explain the relationship between population and resources?

Over two hundred years ago Thomas Malthus expressed the view that population was rising too fast for the available resources. The result, he predicted, would be famine and misery. This issue still creates intense debate today. The ideas and theories that lie behind the debate are outlined below.

Optimum population

This theory is illustrated in figure 1.46. An optimum population is the population total at which the income per person is at a maximum. If the population and labour force are too small to fully utilise a country's resources, the country is described as **underpopulated**. At this population level, a rise in population would enable income per person to rise. This is because there would be a bigger workforce to use the resources more efficiently. However, if a country's population goes beyond the optimum level, it is said to be **overpopulated**. As the population rises, the per capita income then falls. This is because the increase in output cannot keep pace with the rise in numbers of people. Those who believe that the world as a whole has too many people say that it is overpopulated - in other words, it has gone beyond the optimum population size.

There are several difficulties with the idea of an optimum population. Often, the terms 'underpopulated' and 'overpopulated' are used imprecisely without defining what they mean. A more important criticism is that it is a 'static' concept that does not take technological or economic change into account. Nor does it take into account the fact that human ingenuity can make more efficient use of the resources that are available. The experience of Hong Kong illustrates these points.

Hong Kong is sometimes described as being overpopulated. Most of its food and even drinking water have to be supplied from mainland China. Its

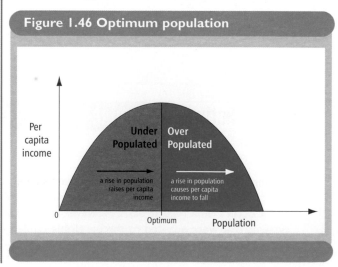

Figure 1.46 Optimum population

population density is 6,100 people per square kilometre (compared with 240 per sq. km. in the UK). It is dominated by high rise housing that is often of poor quality. The urban areas are overcrowded and several new towns have been built to try and relieve population pressure. During 1998, one million chickens were culled following a health scare when chicken flu spread to humans. This type of cross species contamination occurs most often in very densely populated conditions.

Yet, as the former colony's population has risen, so has its level of average income. According to figure 1.46, this implies that its population is smaller than the optimum size - in other words, it is underpopulated! This is surely not the case. The problem is that the concept of optimum population does not take into account changes in production and income that are caused by anything other than a change in the population size. The six million inhabitants of Hong Kong have innovated and used new technology to such an extent that their incomes have risen despite having almost no natural resources.

Some people take the view that what has happened in Hong Kong can also happen on a global scale. They believe that, although the world will be a more crowded place, economic and technological change will increase food and other output to match population growth.

Carrying capacity

Carrying capacity is the maximum number of people that can be supported by a given area of land. It is a concept that relates the size of population to the available resources in a given area. Unlike optimum

Figure 1.47 Hong Kong

population, it is not a static concept. It takes account of changes in, say, technology that might increase the output of an area over time. Figure 1.48 illustrates three different views on the relationship between population and resources on a world scale.

Broadly speaking, views on population growth and resources can be divided into pessimistic and optimistic. Pessimists believe that overpopulation will lead to famine and catastrophe. They suggest that the world will run out of vital resources and there will be irreversible environmental damage. These views are based on the ideas of Malthus and were further developed by the so called Club of Rome. Optimists believe that population growth will stabilise and that technology will overcome problems of poverty and hunger. These views are expressed in the work of Boserup.

Figure 1.48 Population and resources

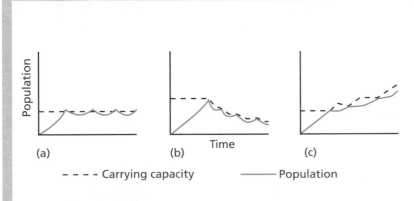

(a)   (b)   Time   (c)

- - - - Carrying capacity   ——— Population

(a) *Constant carrying capacity This view implies that there is an upper limit of resources and output against which population presses. It is a Malthusian view.*
(b) *Falling carrying capacity This implies that resource depletion and degradation (eg, soil erosion, air pollution) will cause the population to decline. It illustrates the gloomy predictions of the Club of Rome.*
(c) *Rising carrying capacity This implies that technical innovation and the discovery of new resources will match population growth. It is essentially an optimistic view, based on the ideas of Boserup.*

Thomas Malthus

Malthus wrote his *Essay on the Principles of Population* in 1798. His views led to much debate at the time and they are still very influential. Malthus believed that population increases exponentially, at a geometric rate. An example of such a rate is: 1 - 2 - 4 - 8 - 16 - 32 etc. At the same time, he believed that the limited amount of land available means that food supply can only increase at an arithmetic rate, for example: 1 - 2 - 3 - 4 - 5 - 6 etc. So, the inevitable outcome is that population growth will always tend to outstrip food supply. The result of this, Malthus suggested, is that the rise in population will be checked by famine, war and disease. However, he also accepted that 'moral restraint', ie later marriage and abstinence from sex, might also limit population growth.

Malthus' ideas were used by people opposed to poor relief. In their view, helping the poor only encouraged them to marry and have children - at a time when the population of the UK was already rising very rapidly. Malthus and his followers believed the outcome could only be misery and disaster.

Malthus wrote his book two hundred years ago. At first sight, his predictions appear to be incorrect. Today, the UK has a population seven times the size it was when he wrote, and living standards are much higher. During the nineteenth century, food was imported from abroad to support the growing population. But, by the late twentieth century, farming techniques had improved so much that the UK was largely self sufficient in food. At the same time, birth control has greatly reduced the average family size so that the population is almost stable. In several European countries, the number of births has even fallen below the number of deaths. In China, where almost a quarter of the world's population live, government policies to reduce birth rates have been very successful and per capita food supply has risen. (See unit 1.1.)

Neo-Malthusians (modern supporters of Malthus' views) believe that, for parts of the world, his gloomy predictions were not wrong - just mistimed. Famine, disease and civil war in sub-Sahara Africa, from Sierra Leone to the Sudan and from Ethiopia to Angola are said to demonstrate evidence of Malthusian 'checks'. Many of these areas are environmentally fragile and liable to great damage if population pressure increases. Persistent and recurrent droughts have made the problem worse. This view is illustrated in figure 1.48 (a). It shows that population growth is limited by the 'carrying capacity', ie there is an upper limit of resources and output against which population presses.

Some writers believe that the Sahel region, south of the Sahara Desert, is an example of how population pressure leads to land 'degradation' (ie, the soil is eroded and loses fertility). The growing population needs fuel and food. Trees are cut down to provide fuelwood and to clear land for farming. Once roots die or are removed from the soil, there is nothing to bind it together. Exposure to the wind and rain then causes soil erosion and the spread of desert like conditions. (The topic of 'desertification' is described in more detail in unit 14.4).

Shortage of productive land in the Sahel means that some marginal, semi-desert areas have to be used every year to grow crops. Previously, a system of 'shifting' agriculture was used in which land could be left fallow for several years. During this time it was not farmed so it regained its fertility. But now, over-use causes the soil to lose its nutrients and become friable (ie, crumbly), and even more liable to erosion. A related problem is that, in areas where water is available, herders tend to congregate. As population grows, the herds increase in size. The land is then over-grazed by sheep, goats and cattle and, once the soil loses its protective covering of grasses, it is quickly eroded.

Figure 1.49 Sahel landscape, Niger

Population pressure may be causing irreversible environmental damage in parts of the Sahel region of sub-Sahara Africa. Overgrazing and cutting down trees for fuelwood are causing land degradation. The predictions of Malthus - hunger, disease and war all appear to be occurring in the region.

The Club of Rome

A gloomy viewpoint on the relationship between population growth and resources was expressed in 1972 by the Club of Rome, a group of scientists, politicians and academics from 10 countries. They came together in Rome to establish a research project on the future of the human race. Their findings were summarised in a report called *The Limits to Growth* (see also unit 2.5.) Their conclusion was:

'If present day trends in world population growth, industrialisation, pollution, food production and resource depletion continue unchanged, the limits to growth on this planet will be reached sometime within the next one hundred years. The most probable result will be a rather sudden and uncontrollable decline in both population and industrial capacity.'

Other influential writers had a similar message. In *The Population Bomb*, written in 1968, Erlich wrote: 'Our world is on the verge of famines of unbelievable proportions. Feeding six billion people is totally impossible in practice'.

Such 'doomsday' predictions have not proved accurate - largely because food output has risen. As a result, attention has turned away from a shortage of resources to the environmental damage being caused by population growth and economic development. This viewpoint was outlined in *Beyond the Limits* (1992). It predicts a collapsing world population caused by a decline in 'carrying capacity' resulting from pollution, land degradation and environmental damage. This pessimistic view is illustrated in figure 1.48 (b).

The optimistic viewpoint

Opponents of the Club of Rome and neo-Malthusian views suggest that resources are not fixed in quantity but are discovered, invented and created by human ingenuity. One such writer is the Danish economist, Ester Boserup. In her publication *The Conditions of Agricultural Growth* she states that population pressure is a stimulus to technological change in agriculture, not a cause of disaster. In her view, people will alter the way they farm in order to support a larger population.

A number of 1990s studies in parts of the Sahel and East Africa support Boserup's ideas and contradict the mainstream view of increasing land degradation. Research has shown that increased agricultural productivity can follow a rise in population. Instead of the land becoming desert, it is farmed better and more intensively than before (see unit 4.1). Although it cannot be denied that famine and environmental damage have occurred in the Sahel, it might be the case that political instability and civil conflict in places such as southern Sudan have been the main causes. For instance, if large numbers of people are forced into particular areas by fighting, environmental damage is likely to follow.

The optimistic ideas of Boserup and others have sometimes been summarised as 'necessity is the mother of invention'. This view is illustrated in figure 1.48 (c). It shows a rise in 'carrying capacity' when population growth pushes upwards.

The **Green Revolution** is sometimes used as evidence to support Boserup's views. Researchers in Mexico and the Philippines produced improved varieties of wheat and rice in the 1950s. These new varieties called HYVs (High Yielding Varieties) were transplanted with great success to Asian countries, including India and Pakistan. The governments promoted the use of the HYVs and a range of new technology to go with them, including the

Figure 1.50 Average annual growth rates for population and agricultural output for selected countries

| | Population growth (%) | | Change in agricultural output (%) | |
	1980-90	1990-94	1980-90	1990-94
India	2.1	1.8	3.1	2.9
China	1.5	1.2	5.9	4.1
Bangladesh	2.4	1.7	2.7	1.9
Kenya	3.4	2.7	3.3	-1.5
Ghana	3.3	2.8	1.0	1.8
Zimbabwe	3.3	2.5	2.4	1.6
Brazil	2.0	1.7	2.8	3.2
Ecuador	2.5	2.2	4.4	2.0
Venezuela	2.6	2.3	3.0	2.3

Adapted from the World Development Report, 1996

use of fertilisers, insecticides, irrigation and farm machinery. Great increases in yields of rice and wheat were obtained in areas where farmers adopted the new measures. The HYVs produced a heavier crop and, in some areas, more than one annual harvest was made possible by using irrigation and fertilisers.

The Green Revolution in India has enabled food production to rise at a faster rate than population during the 1980s and 1990s (see figure 1.50). This has also been the case in China and many other Asian and South American countries. But, there has been a cost in terms of social change. For instance, rural depopulation

has occurred because of the increased use of machinery and decrease in demand for manual labour. There has also been environmental damage caused by the use of fertilisers and irrigation (see unit 2.5 on the negative impact of development). Whether the rise in output can be maintained, and whether the benefits continue to outweigh the costs, remain to be seen. A key question is whether the undoubted progress in South America and Asia can be matched in Africa. The data in figure 1.50 show that, in the three African countries selected, food output did not keep pace with population growth.

Activity — Food inadequacy (1970 – 1995)

The regions listed in figure 1.51 include those countries classified by the World Bank as being 'middle' or 'low' income. They do not include 'high' income countries. So, for example, East and South East Asia does not include Japan although that country is geographically part of the region.

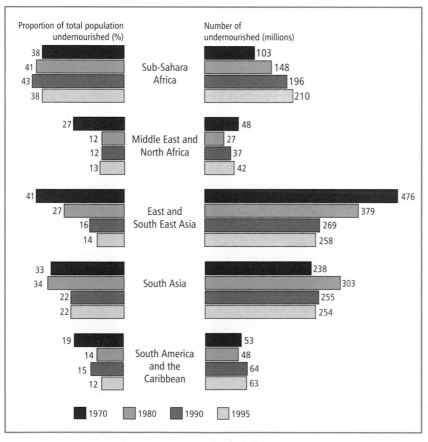

The population of East and South East Asia rose from 1,166 million to 1,753 million between 1970 and 1995. Yet, at the same time, the proportion of undernourished people fell from 41 to 14 percent.

Questions

1 Describe the main trends shown in the data.
2 To what extent does the data support the view of neo-Malthusians or of Boserup?

Figure 1.51 Food inadequacy
Source: FAO World Food Survey (1996)

4. How might competition for resources be resolved?

Most resources are limited in supply so there is often competition for their use. The developed, Western world is often accused of using far more than its 'fair share' of these resources. For example, according to the 1998 Human Development Report of the United Nations, the richest 20 percent of the world's population consumes 85 percent of all goods and services produced.

It seems likely that there will always be clashes of interest between countries and groups of people over how resources are used. The issue of how scarce resources are allocated (ie, shared out) is closely related to the issue of population size and growth. Disagreement and conflict over, say, fishing rights, energy resources and irrigation water are bound to be more serious in a world of 10 billion people (in the 21st century) compared with the 6 billion of the late 1990s.

Although the relationship between population and resources is generally considered at a global or national level, it is often also a matter of debate at the local level. For instance, urban sprawl and the movement of people out of UK cities raises issues on how scarce rural land should be used. Similarly, the rise in traffic volumes increases the demand for new roads and motorways to be built on land that could be used for farming or residential use.

If two or more groups of people want to use the same resource, then competition occurs. But, if one group or another refuses to accept the outcome, then conflict can arise. Examples of competition and conflict over the use of resources can be given at different scales: local, national and international (see figure 1.52).

In the competition for resources, the **market mechanism** usually determines who wins. This means that resources go to the highest bidder. So, in the case of a plot of land, the person or company who is willing and can afford to pay the highest price will become the owner. This type of arrangement works well when the ownership of the land is clear-cut and all parties agree to use the price mechanism.

A disadvantage of the market mechanism arises when people or countries have little income and therefore no market power. On a world scale, the market mechanism appears to reinforce the inequality between rich and poor. The 80 percent of the world's population who consume just 15 percent of all goods and services produced have little market power by which they can acquire a bigger share.

When no established ownership rights to resources exist, the market mechanism does not work because no one has the right to sell the resource. Unless some agreement is reached, the result can be a free for all in which resources are simply grabbed by the most powerful. To prevent this happening, some form of agreement has to be reached. In the case of Antarctica, most territorial claims are disputed and several countries claim to own the same parcels of land. So, in this region, a method has had to be devised to settle issues such as who can exploit the mineral wealth. The outcome is that an International Treaty has been negotiated and agreed by all the countries involved. This ensures that any development is organised within a framework of agreed rules and regulations.

At the local level, in the UK, a disputed development is often settled through the **planning process**. The proposal is discussed by a local authority planning committee and any one who has an objection can make their case. The planning committee then makes a decision on whether or not the development should go ahead. If this does not settle the dispute, an appeal can be lodged with the Secretary of State for the

Figure 1.52

	Competition	Conflict
Local	A plot of land being bid for by rival supermarket chains.	The second runway at Manchester airport when protesters were forcibly evicted.
National	Cities bidding for the resources to build the Millennium exhibition (before Greenwich was chosen).	During the break up of the former Yugoslavia different ethnic groups claimed and fought for the same land.
International	Exploration of the Southern Ocean and its mineral resources.	The 1992 invasion of Kuwait by Iraq was partly motivated by Saddam Hussein's desire to gain control over Kuwait's oil wealth.

Environment (a government minister). A full public enquiry might then be held, after which a decision is made.

However, during the past decade, an increasing number of people have not accepted planning decisions or public enquiry outcomes. The result has been the tree top and underground protests by 'ecowarriors' at Twyford Down, the Newbury bypass and Manchester Airport. The protesters have taken the view that the planning process is 'rigged' in favour of new roads and other forms of so-called economic development. They believe that insufficient attention has been given to the interests of those who want to 'save' the countryside and preserve the natural environment.

International conflicts and civil wars are the hardest disputes to settle because there is no legal framework or system that can force one side or the other to abide by a peaceful means of settlement. The United Nations has no power to enforce agreement on countries which refuse to cooperate. In the former Yugoslavia, Bosnia and Kosovo became a patchwork of warring ethnic groups as Croats, Serbs and Muslims fought to control 'their' areas. All sides used policies of ethnic cleansing to force minority civilian populations out of their homes and villages. At least in part, the conflict was over land, and the ownership of land - the most basic of resources. Only the intervention of NATO and the use of military force ended the fighting and allowed a truce in which - it was hoped - a negotiated settlement could be reached.

Activity ▸ Newbury bypass

The bypass around Newbury was an important and significant source of conflict between the 'road lobby' and conservationists. At the heart of the dispute was a difference of opinion on how scarce natural resources - in this case the countryside - should be used. The scheme, started in 1996 at a cost of £85 million, was designed to reduce traffic congestion on the A34 that passes through Newbury. This bottleneck was the only section of single carriageway on the road that links the industrial Midlands with the ports of Southampton and Portsmouth.

Planning permission was originally granted in 1982 and two public enquiries in 1988 and 1992 supported the proposal. However, environmental campaigners saw the bypass as an act of destruction. It symbolised the ever growing threat of road traffic to the countryside. Their view was that new roads encourage even greater volumes of traffic and that alternative transport policies should be promoted. When all legal remedies were exhausted, the protesters took direct action and built tree houses and tunnels along the proposed route. It cost £1.5 million and took 85 days to clear the route - during which time there were 768 arrests.

Opponents of the bypass claimed that the route would damage :
* the Rack Marsh nature reserve and two other Sites of Special Scientific Interest
* valuable farmland
* a dozen sites of archeological value
* the river banks of the Avon and Kennet
* people's health and wellbeing because the overall effect would be to increase road traffic volume.

They also stated that projected traffic increases would soon overwhelm the new road and there would be no long term saving in travel time.

Supporters of the bypass claimed:
* 50,000 vehicles per day passed through Newbury on the A34 causing pollution, noise and danger
* daily traffic jams in the town were damaging local business and causing delays to emergency services
* traffic congestion was costing the national economy nearly £20 billion per year in delays to people and freight
* reduction in through traffic in the town would save an estimated 28 lives in a 30 year period
* the bypass would save an average 15 minutes on through-journey times
* projected increases in road traffic would make congestion in Newbury even worse in years to come.

A local petition collected 17,000 signatures in favour of the bypass.

Figure 1.53 Greenfield land near Newbury

The Newbury bypass involved damaging parts of a nature reserve and other woodland areas.

Questions

1 To what extent can the Newbury bypass protest be considered a conflict over resources? Which resources were involved?
2 Describe the 'normal' mechanisms for settling disputes over land use in the UK. Why did they not work in the case of the Newbury bypass?

unit summary

1 People use resources to provide food, shelter, clothing and consumer goods.
2 Widespread hunger and poverty in the Third World might suggest that there are too many people in the world given the available resources. Yet, farmers in Western countries are being paid to grow less food, and in both India and China, per capita food output is growing.
3 Food shortages can be caused by drought or other natural disasters but famines are generally caused when there is a breakdown in distribution and access to food. This is often caused by war and/or the inability of poor people to afford the food that is available.
4 There are two broad views on population and resources:
   • Neo-Malthusians believe that population growth will tend to outstrip resources. The related, Club of Rome view is that population pressure in low income countries and wasteful consumption in the Western world will lead to environmental damage and resource depletion. This may become so serious that population will eventually decline.
   • The optimistic view, expressed by Boserup, is that population growth acts as a stimulus to food output. Also, it is hoped, economic development will lead to lower population growth because fertility rates decline when people become better off.
5 Because most resources are in limited supply, there is always competition for their use. Mostly, this competition is resolved in a peaceful fashion, either by using the market mechanism or by using an agreed set of rules and procedures.
6 Conflict over resources can arise if one or more party refuses to accept an agreed framework of rules. When this happens on a large scale, wars or civil wars might occur. On a smaller scale, civil disobedience or unrest can arise.

key terms

Carrying capacity - a concept that relates population size to resource availability over time.
Market mechanism - the free market system by which resources go to those who are willing and able to pay. It is sometimes also called the price or profit mechanism. When there is competition for scarce resources, it is the highest bidder who usually wins.
Natural resource - any naturally occurring resource such as solar radiation, minerals, plants and animals.
Neo-Malthusian - a school of thought that believes population growth will inevitably outstrip resource availability.
Non-renewable resources - those resources which are in finite supply, such as fossil fuels and other minerals.
Optimum population - a concept that relates population size to per capita income. The optimum population is the population size at which the per capita income is maximised.
Overpopulation - a population that is above

the optimum size. The term is also often used in a less technical sense to describe any very densely populated region.
Planning process - a system of deciding how resources are used that does not involve the market mechanism. Instead, a government or planning authority decides what will happen according to a framework of rules and regulations. These rules are generally established by using criteria such as the greatest public good or the least damage to the environment rather than simply the greatest profitability.
Renewable resources - those resources which, in effect, are in infinite supply, such as solar energy, the wind, tidal power and plants and animals which can reproduce.
Resource - anything that is useful in producing goods and services.
Underpopulated - a population that is below the optimum size. It implies that a population is too small to exploit effectively a region's natural resources.

Unit 1.5 Ageing Population

key questions

1 Who are the elderly?
2 What are the causes of an ageing population?
3 What is the impact of an ageing population?
4 How does an ageing population affect particular markets ?

1. Who are the elderly?

The term elderly is used to describe older people. It is not a precise term and definitions vary between countries. In the UK, the traditional definition is related to the ages at which people are eligible for a state pension, ie 60 and over for women and 65 and over for men. The definition may change in the future because after 2010, the state pension age for women is set to rise so it matches that for men.

It is important to note that the characteristics of elderly people are not uniform across the age group. What a 65 year old requires in terms of health and

social care may be completely different from the needs of an 80 year old. It is the case that many older members of the age group are very active whereas some younger members are infirm and need a lot of support. However, in general, the older the person, the greater the health care required.

Many high income countries are at a point in their demographic transition where they have an increasing number of elderly people and fewer younger people (see unit 1.1). This has the effect of raising the average age of their populations. In the UK, it is projected that the number of over 65s will outnumber the under 16s by 2008 - for the first time ever.

2. What are the causes of an ageing population?

An ageing population is one in which the proportion of elderly people is rising. There are two main causes. The first is that the number of young people is stable or falling - due to a fall in the fertility rate. Reasons for this are explained in unit 1.1. They include the widespread

Figure 1.54 Life expectancies for selected countries (1997)

Country	Life expectancy at birth All (years)	Life expectancy Men (years)	Life expectancy Women (years)
Brazil	67	64	70
China	70	68	71
Indonesia	65	63	67
Sweden	79	76	82
Uganda	42	42	42
UK	77	74	80
Zambia	43	43	44

use of contraception combined with the greater role that women play in the paid workforce. The second cause is increased life expectancy. This is brought about by better nutrition, improved social care for the elderly and advances in public health (eg, the provision of clean drinking water). Developments in medical science such as the flu vaccination have also been important. Shorter working hours and safer working conditions have helped bring about high life expectancies in the richest countries.

Figure 1.54 shows life expectancies for selected countries. It can be seen that, on average, women live longer than men. There are a number of reasons for this. In general, women play a smaller part in the paid workforce and are therefore less subject to industrial injury and disease. Another important factor is that fewer women smoke than men. It may also be that there is a genetic basis for gender differences in life expectancy.

Between 1970 and 1996, average life expectancy for the world as a whole rose from 55 to 66 years. If this trend continues, it is likely that the world's population structure will become more like that of the UK, with a smaller proportion of young people and a larger proportion of elderly people.

Figure 1.54 shows the marked difference in life expectancy between low income countries such as Zambia and Uganda, and rich Western countries such as Sweden and the

UK. Such differences illustrate the tremendous gap in development between the two groups of countries. This issue is discussed in detail in unit 2.1.

Some countries have life expectancies that are higher than might be expected. In China, for example, despite low average incomes, there is a well developed system of social and medical care. This contributes to that country's relatively high life expectancy. Figure 1.54 shows that the life expectancy in China is higher than in Brazil - yet Brazil's per capita income is more than double China's.

Figure 1.55 Life expectancy

In the UK, life expectancy increased by almost 30 years during the 20th century.

Activity) Life expectancy in different countries

Figure 1.56 Life expectancy and national income (1996)

Life expectancy	Number of countries	GNP per capita $
Less than 55	36	250
55-64	28	420
65-69	34	2,040
70-74	50	1,730
75 and over	47	25,840

Note: *Gross National Product (GNP) per capita is a measure of average national income. This World Bank data groups the countries of the world according to the average life expectancies of their populations. The average per capita GNP is given for each group of countries.*

Questions

1 Describe the relationship between life expectancy and GNP per capita as shown in the data.
2 Suggest possible reasons for the relationship between life expectancy and GNP per capita.

3. What is the impact of an ageing population?

The impact of an ageing population is complex. It is too simple, and a disservice to the elderly, to talk simply of their economic burden on the active population. Their impact is both positive and negative.

Positive impact

People who are elderly make a significant contribution to society. It is said that statesmanship, tolerance and wisdom are all characteristics associated with age. The knowledge and experience of elderly people can be of benefit in politics, in local communities, in commerce and in family affairs. Some societies value age and experience more than others. In very general terms, it is true to say that Eastern cultures show a greater respect for the elderly than Western society.

Elderly people are less likely, on average, to commit crimes or be associated with violence than young people.

It might be the case that falling crime rates in some Western countries are caused, at least in part, by the ageing population and the smaller proportion of young people.

The elderly's consumption of goods and services helps sustain particular sectors of the economy, as will be seen later in this unit. They also contribute in running clubs, societies and charities and, as grandparents, often provide support for working couples.

Negative impact

An ageing population normally has the effect of raising the dependency ratio (see unit 1.1). This is the number of economically inactive people (ie, children and pensioners) as a proportion of the economically active (ie, people of working age) in a population. In the European Union as a whole, the rising number of elderly people is expected to cause the dependency ratio to rise even though the number of young people is falling (see figure 1.57).

Figure 1.57 Actual and projected population of the EU by age, 1960-2050

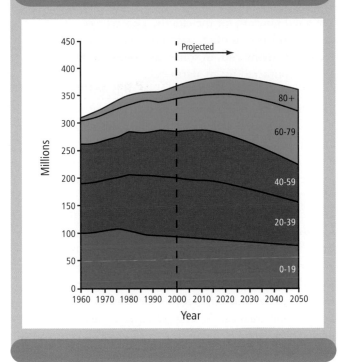

In 1960, the dependency ratio for the EU was 82 percent (elderly: 13% of the total population), in 1995 it was 85 percent (elderly: 20%) and in 2050 it is expected to be 111 percent (elderly 33%). When the dependency ratio rises above 100 percent it means that there are fewer people in the active or working age population than outside it.

The economic implications of there being more elderly dependents in relation to the working age population are very important. Not only will there be more pensioners, there will be more of the very elderly who cost a disproportionate amount in terms of health and social care. The cost of caring for people who are infirm and incapable of looking after themselves is very high.

The driving force of any economy is its active population who work and pay taxes and social security contributions to the government. From these payments, health care, social services and pensions are all funded. If the active population falls in proportion to the elderly, the economic burden on the working population increases. This means that taxes have to rise or, alternatively, pensions and other benefits have to fall.

If taxes rise in order to support an ageing population there is some evidence that this acts as a disincentive to the working population. In other words, they will be less inclined to work hard and create wealth if an increased proportion of their income is being taken in taxes.

Some economists have suggested that an ageing population might slow economic growth in other ways. Older people tend to be less flexible and mobile than younger people. People in their twenties generally have fewer family ties or financial commitments than those who are older. They are also readier to learn new skills and techniques. They are therefore more willing to move from job to job or region to region. A dynamic and growing economy requires this type of flexibility if it is to be successful.

Caring for the elderly

How to fund rising pension, medical and social care costs is an issue that faces most Western countries. In the UK, the government has encouraged people to take out a private pension to supplement their state pension. This is intended as a means of partially shifting the cost of looking after elderly people away from taxpayers. Between 2010 and 2020, the state retirement age of 65 for men and 60 for women will be changed to 65 for both sexes. The reason for this change is to equalise treatment between men and women. However, the decision to make the pensionable age 65 rather than 60 was also based on a desire to reduce the state pension bill. If the retirement age had been set at 60, or a figure between 60 and 65, the effect would have been to raise the bill.

In 1998, a UK Royal Commission recommended that the state should pay for the nursing care needed by elderly people. Most medical treatment in the UK is paid for by the state but most social care, including residential care and home help, has been treated differently. Elderly people must pay for their care until they can no longer afford it. This is determined by a means test in which a person's financial assets are taken into account. If the person has more than a certain level of wealth, the state does not make any contribution. In many cases, elderly people have to sell their homes in order to pay for care. A criticism of this system is that it reduces the incentive for people to make their own provision for old age. There is a widespread view that this system needs reform but there is no agreement on how it should be done. The Royal Commission estimated that state provision of nursing care to the elderly would cost £1.6 billion annually. Other estimates suggested that the cost would rise to £6 billion as the number of people who need care increases.

Nearly all countries are faced with the problem of paying for elderly care. Different solutions are being tried. Japan, for example, has the highest life expectancy in the world. In 1995, 14 percent of the population was over 65 years and this number is expected to increase to 25 percent in 2020. Everyone in employment has to pay into a state run insurance fund. In return, ninety percent of the costs of care and other services used by an individual will be met by the state fund.

4. How does an ageing population affect particular markets?

The elderly are consumers of a wide range of goods and services. Although many elderly are dependent on state pensions, there is a rising proportion who are wealthy and have surplus money to spend. Increasingly, companies cater just for this market. For example, holiday companies like SAGA specialise in destinations that are designed to appeal to the over-50s. Supermarkets stock more and more single portions of convenience foods designed, at least in part, for elderly people who live on their own. Clothes retailers, magazine publishers and insurance companies have likewise specifically targeted this market segment.

The care industry, providing residential and nursing homes, as well as home helps, is expanding rapidly throughout the UK. A wide range of job opportunities has become available in this sector. Specialist medical care, paid increasingly by private insurance schemes, is another growth area. So is the provision of private sheltered housing for the elderly. This type of accommodation is often specially designed with lifts, security systems and, in some case, with caretakers who can be contacted by an alarm bell.

Increasing numbers of retirement villages and apartments are being built in attractive locations. The number of people living in UK resort and retirement areas increased by 14 percent to 2.5 million between 1971 and 1995. In 1994, there were ten local authority districts in which the percentage of the population aged 60 or over exceeded 30 percent. All these were coastal areas in the South West or South East of England. Coastal districts such as Bournemouth and Eastbourne have high concentrations of elderly people because they are scenically attractive and have a milder climate than inland or further north. They are also perceived as being less dirty, safer and more crime free than major urban areas. Rural areas on the edge of cities are also popular with elderly people. Again, the quiet environment and lack of city stress are the attractions. Leisure and other facilities tend to follow because many elderly people have spare disposable income and the time to enjoy their retirement. Just like the 'snowbirds' from Canada and northeast USA who move to Florida in the winter, more and more elderly north Europeans are doing the same - to the Mediterranean coast of Spain, the Algarve in Portugal and Tenerife. Some are moving permanently, attracted by warm sunshine and purpose built retirement resorts. It is the more wealthy members of the elderly who migrate to coastal or rural areas. This leaves poor, elderly people within the city boundaries, particularly in inner city and public sector housing. There is a big difference between the lives of those trapped in urban council flats and those living in custom built retirement accommodation. The poverty in which large numbers of elderly people live is seen by many as a failure of social justice and highlights the difficulties experienced by one section of the ageing population.

Figure 1.58 SAGA brochures

SAGA specialises in the over-50s market.

Activity ▶ An ageing population

	Number of live births	Total fertility rate	Life expectancy	
			Males	*Females*
1971	901,600	2.4	69	75
1997	725,800	1.7	74	80

▲ **Figure 1.59 UK population statistics**

0-4	9
5-15	4
16-44	8
45-64	8
65-74	13
75+	20

▲ **Figure 1.60 Hospital in-patient care as % of age group 1995, UK**

65-69	4
70-74	6
75-79	12
80-84	18
85+	40

▲ **Figure 1.61 % of age group using a home help (local authority and private) 1995, UK**

	1971	1997
60-64	5.8	4.7
65-74	8.5	8.5
75-84	3.8	5.4
85+	0.8	1.8
	18.9	20.4

▲ **Figure 1.62 Elderly people as a percentage of the total UK population**

'Europe faces a grey future'

The European Commission has published a report that reveals a striking picture of what Europe will be like in 2025. A rising number of elderly people are expected to migrate southwards towards the Sun. There will be an extra 37 million in the number of people aged over 60 - an increase of nearly 50 percent. In the UK, there is expected to be a 44 percent increase in the population aged over 60 and a 3 percent drop in the population of working age. In Ireland, the changes will be more dramatic with a projected 67 percent increase in the retired population and a 25 percent drop in the working population.

The report states that the labour market will have to adapt to a different kind of demand, mainly in the fields of housing, health, transport and leisure. This will have to be done precisely at a time when those producing the goods and services needed by the economy are decreasing in number. Changing social patterns, including the decline of the family unit, may make it more difficult to accommodate the generational shift. In other words, there will be fewer 'conventional' family units to look after their elderly relatives. More and more, the state will have to provide care, or schemes will have to be put in place to encourage private provision. Although the increasing numbers of the very old may need more care, it should not be forgotten that the vast majority of people aged between 60 and 70 are active, fit and healthy. These people are often willing and able to make a valuable contribution in voluntary and charity work. They are also less likely to commit crimes or drive at high speeds than younger people. The ageing population should therefore not always be labelled a 'problem' - there are also positive effects.

Adapted from the Guardian, May 15th 1996

Fig 1.62 Grey power

Increasing numbers of elderly people are able to enjoy their retirement. They have the spending power and political influence to affect decisions made by companies and governments.

Questions

1 Briefly outline the factors that are causing an ageing UK population.
2 Describe the likely impact of an increase in numbers of the very elderly ie, people over 85.
3 To what extent are the consequences of an ageing population likely to be positive or negative?

unit summary

1 The population of the UK and many other developed countries is ageing. This is because the fertility rate is falling and life expectancy is rising.
2 The rising proportion of elderly people bring social and economic costs and benefits.
3 The cost of health and social care rises steeply in the later stages of old age. Governments in the UK and other countries are trying to develop a mix of private and public provision to pay for this care.
4 An ageing population has an impact on the market for many goods and services including leisure, housing and health.

key terms

Ageing population - a population in which the proportion of elderly people is rising.

Elderly people - generally defined as people older than the state retirement age (in the UK, 60 for women, 65 for men).

Unit 1.6 Social and political change

key questions

1 What is devolution and separatism?
2 How does nationalism cause political change?
3 Why do some countries join together?
4 Why has the European Union formed and how is it organised?

1. What is devolution and separatism?

The issue of whether countries join together or break up is important within the UK, within Europe and also on a world scale. The social and political consequences of such changes have an impact on most of the topics in human geography. For instance, migration, trade flows and industrial development are all affected. In the UK, there are seemingly contradictory processes at work. At one level, there is joining together as power is transferred to the European Union. Yet, at the same time, there is devolution to the Scottish Parliament and the Welsh Assembly.

Devolution can be defined as the transfer of power to a regional or local assembly. It is not the same as separatism which involves the creation of independent, self-governing countries. For many years, people in Scotland and Wales have argued that policies are decided in London without taking their local interests into account. This was particularly true in the 1980s and early 90s when Conservative Governments made policies for Scotland and Wales yet did not have a majority of votes in either country. The dispute over the poll tax, a form of local taxation, was particularly fierce in Scotland when it was introduced - some say imposed - a year earlier than in England.

The 1997 Labour Government was elected with a mandate to devolve power, and **referendums** were carried out in both Scotland and Wales. An overwhelming majority in Scotland and a small majority in Wales voted to establish their own decision making bodies. Control over foreign affairs and most taxation will stay in Whitehall, although the Scottish Parliament will have the power to make small changes to income tax.

In both Scotland and Wales, separatist parties campaign for full national independence. They believe that their respective countries would be better off without England and, importantly, their national culture, tradition and language would be easier to protect. They favour membership of the EU and see a 'Europe of the Regions' as a means of gaining the benefits of free trade and regional policies without having to suffer domination by the English. The EU principle of **subsidiarity** - ie, of devolving power to the lowest appropriate level - suits them very well. The biggest decisions would be made at European level and then most others at the regional (ie, Scottish and Welsh) level.

In the 1997 referendum campaigns for devolution, people had very different and contrasting motives. Nationalists saw devolution as a half way house to independence. Their opponents saw it as a means of satisfying the Scots and Welsh by granting them power over their own affairs and, therefore, of reducing the impetus towards complete separation.

Activity ▷ Devolution and the English regions

'Home rule for English regions?'

In Scotland, devolution is seen by some people as a stepping stone to full independence. Others view it as a means of giving Scots a greater say in their own affairs while remaining part of the UK. If Scottish and Welsh devolution is successful, the campaign for English regional government will be strengthened. There are many people who believe that there is a strong economic case for English regional government. As in Scotland and Wales, the North of England and the South West have suffered from policies decided by, and in the interests of, people in the South East. Because the South East is the most prosperous region, and the first to recover from recession, its economy is the first to 'overheat'. Rising incomes, labour shortages and rising house prices all start in the South East and then 'trickle down' to the regions. Successive governments have had to put the brakes on the economy, ie raised interest rates and taxes, to prevent overheating and inflation in the South East before the signs of recovery have been showing in the North and West. The result, over the long term, has been to damage the regional economies and to prevent them catching up with the most prosperous areas. The case for regional assemblies is that they would be more likely, and better able, to protect the economic interests of the regions than the present system of small local authorities.

Questions

1 With reference to the UK, explain the difference between devolution and separatism.

2 To what extent is the case for English regional assemblies the same as that for the Welsh Assembly and the Scottish Parliament?

2. How does nationalism cause political change?

Nationalism is the desire by people who share a common tradition, culture and language to have their own country. In the nineteenth century, Italy and Germany formed from many small individual states. The process continued in the twentieth century as European and colonial empires collapsed. In Europe, countries such as Hungary and Czechoslovakia were formed and, in Africa, many former colonies such as Zambia and Zimbabwe became independent.

Since the collapse of communism in the late 1980s, a new wave of nationalist change has occurred in Europe. The first changes were when the communist dominated regimes of Eastern Europe were swept away by popular uprisings. East Germany, maintained as a separate state by the Soviet Union since 1945, was reunited with West Germany in 1990.

The biggest changes came about in 1991 when the former Soviet Union broke into 15 separate countries (see figure 1.64). The Baltic States of Latvia, Lithuania and Estonia were the most Western (both geographically and culturally) and were the first to break away. The changes in the Soviet Union started under the leadership of Mikhail Gorbachev. He had introduced policies to reform the country and improve its economic performance. However, the result was a breakdown in Communist Party control which allowed different ethnic groups to assert their independence and break free from Moscow. Within Russia itself there remain many ethnic groups who wish to set up their own nation states, but, so far, they have not been successful. The tremendous bloodshed and destruction caused by Russia's military response to an armed uprising in Chechnya shows how determined Moscow is to resist any more breakaways.

Figure 1.63 The new states in the former Soviet Union

Although most of the post-communist changes in Eastern Europe were peaceful, Yugoslavia has been an exception. The country, formed in 1918 out of the southern part of the old Hapsburg Empire, had always been an uneasy grouping of different ethnic groups. For many years the country was held together under a strong communist leadership led by Tito. When the nationalist and democratic movement spread across Eastern Europe in the late 80s, the attempts by different ethnic groups to govern themselves were resisted by the Serb dominated government in Belgrade. Civil war started and, by 1992, Slovenia and Croatia - the two most wealthy regions - had gained their independence.

The situation was more complex in Bosnia because three ethnic groupings, Croats, Serbs and Muslims lived together in a patchwork of communities. During fierce fighting between 1992 and 1995 the three groups used tactics such as ethnic cleansing to clear rival groups from 'their' areas. At first the United Nations, then NATO, intervened. Only after NATO launched airstrikes on the Serbian forces which were besieging the Muslim population of Sarajevo did the fighting cease. The result was the formation of an independent state of Bosnia which still includes the three rival ethnic groups. It remains to be seen whether the result will be a viable country.

Within the former Yugoslavia, several other potential nationalist disputes remained after the Bosnian settlement. A large number of ethnic Hungarians live in northern Serbia and have had their limited self-rule withdrawn by the Serbs. In the region of Kosovo, ninety percent of the population are Muslim. They are ethnic Albanians and their desire for self determination led to conflict in 1998. Large scale ethnic cleansing by the Serbs caused almost a million ethnic Albanians to flee their homes. During 1999, NATO airstrikes were again used to force the Serbian government to reverse its policy and allow the refugees to return.

The desire for self-determination

The desire by national groups for self-determination (ie, the wish to rule themselves) remains a difficult problem in many parts of Europe and the rest of the world. Some of these groups desire unification with their 'home' country. For example, ethnic Hungarians in Romania wish to reunite with Hungary, and Irish nationalists in Northern Ireland wish to form a united Ireland. Other groups simply want independence or greater self-rule. These include Basques and Catalans in

Spain, Bretons and Corsicans in France, Walloons in Belgium and, in the UK, Welsh and Scottish people. Long standing nationalist conflicts in other parts of the world involve Kurds (possibly the largest ethnic group in the world without their own state), Palestinians in the Middle East; French Canadians in Quebec; Tamils in Sri Lanka and Sikhs in India.

3. Why do some countries join together?

Although nationalism remains a strong force within Western Europe, the need to compete with Japan and the United States has been a motivating force for countries to join together. On their own, the countries of Europe do not have sufficiently big home markets to gain the economies of scale (ie, efficiencies arising from larger scale production) necessary for modern industries. However, with a single market of 370 million people, European companies can compete on equal terms with any global competitor. The growth and impact of the European Union are covered in more detail in the next section of this unit.

Other powerful economies such as the United States and Canada have joined together, with Mexico, to form the North American Free Trade Area (NAFTA) in order to gain the benefits of larger home markets. Similar organisations exist in South America (Mercosur: Argentina, Brazil, Paraguay and Uruguay), South East Asia (ASEAN: Brunei, Indonesia, Malaysia, the Philippines, Singapore and Thailand), the Caribbean Community and Common Market (Caricom: 17 Caribbean countries), the Economic Community of West Africa (Ecowas: 16 West African states) and the European Economic Area (EEA: comprising of all EU members plus members of the European Free Trade Area (EFTA): Iceland, Norway, Liechtenstein and Switzerland) (see figure 1.65).

The motive behind such groups of countries is generally economic, ie to promote trade and to increase efficiency in a larger and more competitive market. For some countries, an additional motive is to increase their strength in relation to transnational corporations (TNCs). Some of these powerful global corporations have a turnover that is bigger than the Gross National Product of individual countries. By grouping together, countries are better able to withstand the pressure that a company such as Ford or Sony can exert. (This topic is described in more detail in unit 2.4.)

When countries join an organisation such as the EU,

Figure 1.64 Free trade areas or 'trading blocks'

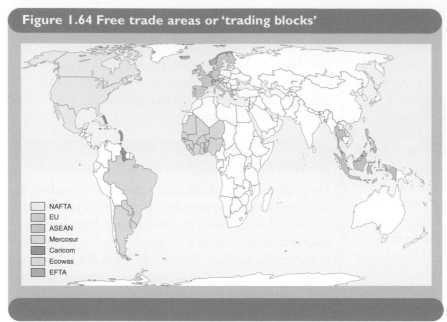

- NAFTA
- EU
- ASEAN
- Mercosur
- Caricom
- Ecowas
- EFTA

they agree to pool sovereignty. In other words, they give up some of their national independence in favour of collective decision making. This trend in world affairs is relatively new and runs counter to the strong nationalist movement that has dominated politics for so many years.

4. Why has the European Union formed and how is it organised?

The Second World War was the third time in less than 100 years that France and Germany had fought each other. At the end of the war there was a strong feeling that this must not happen again. Leaders from several West European countries agreed that closer economic and political cooperation would help prevent conflict. So, in 1952, the European Coal and Steel Community (ECSC) was formed with a membership of six: France, Germany, Italy, Belgium, Luxembourg and the Netherlands. The UK was invited to join but declined, mainly because of its close ties with the Empire and Dominions (later to become the Commonwealth) and to the USA.

Development of the EU

The Coal and Steel Community was so successful that the six members agreed, at the 1956 Treaty of Rome, to set up a Common Market - to be known as the European Economic Community (EEC). Again the UK decided not to join. The EEC stimulated development and trade between members which helped rebuild their

economies. Policies on agriculture (ie, the Common Agricultural Policy or CAP), regional development and external trade were all formed at this time. Later on, when Britain did join, it became clear that these policies had been framed in a way that suited the mainland European conditions but which sometimes worked against Britain's interests.

In the 1960s, UK governments, envying the greater economic success of the EEC, applied to join. Twice entry was blocked by France which distrusted the UK's close ties with the US. However, in 1973, the UK application was successful, along with that of Ireland and Denmark (see figure 1.66).

In 1981 Greece joined the EEC, followed by Spain and Portugal in 1986 and Austria, Finland and Sweden in 1995. Twice Norway has applied to join but then changed its mind after negative votes in national referendums.

In 1986, the Single Market came into force. Its aim was to ensure the completely free movement of goods, services and people across European boundaries. The EEC was renamed the European Community (EC).

Then, in 1993, the Maastricht Treaty set up a

Figure 1.65 The growth of the EU

- Original Members
- Joined in 1973
- Joined in 1981
- Joined in 1986
- Joined in 1990
- Joined in 1995
- Possible entry by 2003
- Possible entry in long term

N

IRELAND
UNITED KINGDOM
NETHERLANDS
BELGIUM
LUXEMBOURG
FRANCE
SWITZ
PORTUGAL
SPAIN
DENMARK
WEST GERMANY
EAST GERMANY
CZECH REPUBLIC
AUSTRIA
SLOVENIA
ITALY
SWEDEN
FINLAND
ESTONIA
LATVIA
LITHUANIA
POLAND
SLOVAKIA
HUNGARY
ROMANIA
BULGARIA
GREECE
TURKEY
CYPRUS

timetable for European Monetary Union (EMU). The same treaty changed the name again, this time to the European Union (EU). The aim was that, by 2002, a common currency - the Euro - would be in circulation throughout member states. At the same time, a European central bank setting common interest rates would be in operation. Only countries whose economies had 'converged', ie had low rates of inflation and sound public finances, were allowed to join. When, in 1998, the list of EMU members was announced, only Greece failed to meet the entry criteria. However, the UK, Denmark and Sweden had previously negotiated 'opt-outs' and they decided not to join in the first wave.

During 1998, membership applications to the EU were accepted from 11 countries. Six (Poland, Hungary, the Czech Republic, Slovenia, Estonia and Cyprus) were deemed ready for detailed negotiation with a target date for membership in 2003. The other five applicants (Bulgaria, Romania, Slovakia, Latvia and Lithuania) were told that economic reforms and stronger free market systems were required but that applications would be kept under annual review. Turkey, which applied for membership as long ago as 1963, was told that it must improve its human rights record and strengthen its democratic institutions before membership could be granted.

EU institutions

The supreme policy making body of the EU is the Council of Ministers. This is made up of the representatives of the member governments. When important decisions are to be made, the Prime Ministers or Presidents of member countries attend. On other matters, the relevant ministers meet - for example, the Ministers of Agriculture attend when the Common Agricultural Policy is discussed. The most important issues are decided by unanimous vote. This system means, in effect, that each country has a veto because a single 'no' vote is enough to stop a proposal. This has sometimes made decision making slow or even impossible so, for an increasing range of issues, a system known as 'qualified majority voting' exists. Votes are weighted according to population size (Germany, France, Italy and the UK each have 10 votes, Spain has 8, Belgium, Greece, Netherlands and Portugal each have 5, Austria and Sweden each have 4, Ireland, Denmark and Finland each have 3 and Luxembourg has 2). For a qualified majority, 61 out of the 87 votes are required.

The European Commission is the body that carries out

the policies of the Council of Ministers. It can also propose and suggest policies to the Council. The European Parliament has the job of scrutinising the work of the Commission and ensuring that Commissioners are democratically accountable. The European Court of Justice is the body that oversees the legality of EU actions and it is the place where disputes between members, particularly on policy implementation, are resolved.

EU policies

The policies of the EU have an impact on everyone who lives in the member states. Farming, fishing, trade, economic development, competition and transport are all areas which are controlled or regulated by EU policies and rules. In the future it is likely that monetary union will have an impact on inflation, interest rates and, therefore, mortgage payments - even in those countries which have opted out.

Before the EU expands to 21 or even 26 members, reform of the institutions and policies will be vital. Unless majority voting is introduced across even more areas, a single country's veto will be able to halt all decision making. But, of course, giving up the veto is a clear loss of sovereignty and might work against a country's vital national interests.

Reform of the Common Agricultural Policy and regional policy are equally urgent. The support given to farmers already costs every person in the EU an equivalent of £20 per week. To support the small scale and inefficient farmers of Eastern Europe on this same scale would be impossibly expensive. Just one example illustrates this. In Poland, in 1998, there were 1 million dairy farmers with an average of 4 cows each. In the UK there were just 30,000 dairy farmers with an average of 87 cows each. To provide the Polish and other East European farmers with the same level of support as UK farmers receive would bankrupt the CAP.

As for regional policy, the applicant countries' per capita incomes are all well below the lowest in Western Europe. If the present rules for regional support were maintained, the effect would be that all the aid would go to the new members and none to the present members no matter how badly off their poorest regions were.

The effect of EU policies on specific areas of economic and social life are dealt with in different units of this book. So, for instance, the impact of the Common Agricultural Policy is covered in unit 4.1, the impact on trade is covered in unit 6.2 and the impact on regional development is covered in unit 2.2.

Activity | Growth paves the way for entry into the club

Designer-clad young accountants and lawyers relax in open-air street cafes, their gleaming Jeeps and BMWs mounted on the kerb. Bejewelled and well-coiffed women chat into mobile phones as they browse in boutiques that sell expensive European fashions. Stroll through central Nicosia or Limassol and the prosperity of Greek Cyprus is on proud display. In just a generation, what was a colonial backwater dependent on agriculture has changed into a booming tourist destination, that is also fast becoming a regional financial hub. Cyprus already meets most of the Maastricht Treaty convergence criteria for monetary union with the European Union.

Per capita gross domestic product is nearly $13,000, which is far higher than any of the Eastern European countries also earmarked for EU membership talks. Inflation stands at just over 3 percent. The boom years that saw annual growth rates topping 5 percent may now be over, but a provisional 2.5 percent growth rate for this year is still in line with the EU average, and a 4.5 percent growth rate is forecast for 1998. Perhaps most crucially for a country clamouring to enter the EU, Cyprus is considered to have full employment. 'Cyprus certainly would not be a burden to the Community budget and could even be a net contributor,' says Constantinos Mavrantonis, an economic adviser with the European Commission delegation in Nicosia.

There are sound economic reasons why Greek Cypriots should want to join the EU, which absorbs about 50 per cent of their exports and accounts for 55 per cent of their imports. But their motivation is overwhelmingly political. They believe entry could help re-unify the island which has been divided between the Turkish north and Greek south since the 1974 invasion by Turkey.

Yet because Cyprus remains divided, they realise their application presents political problems for Brussels that those of the Eastern European applicants do not. For that reason the Greek Cypriot authorities are keen to ensure there are few reservations about the economy.

Less enthusiastic about the EU challenge are those involved in traditionally protected and labour-intensive industries such as clothing and footwear, where rising wages and small units have made their products less competitive. 'The way ahead for the manufacturing sector is to go for quality, innovation and enter partnerships with European companies,' says Mr Mavrantonis. Economists say there are good prospects for chemicals and food processing.

The once important agricultural sector, whose contribution to the GDP has shrunk to less than 10 per cent, is expected to do well from EU entry because domestic support to farmers in Europe is higher than in Cyprus. Farmers who grow citrus fruits, potatoes, table grapes and vegetables, the main agricultural exports, are expected to benefit most.

Adapted from The Times, 11th September 1997

Questions

1 Suggest reasons why Cyprus might wish to join the EU, and reasons why the EU might welcome Cyprus.
2 To what extent, in your view, does the EU represent a movement away from nationalism and self-determination?

unit summary

1 The desire for greater home rule has led to the formation of the Scottish Parliament and the Welsh Assembly. In both countries, some separatists want to go further and gain complete independence.
    Within Europe, there have been simultaneous, contradictory trends - the move to greater unity within the EU and, at the same time, the break up of the Soviet Union, Yugoslavia and Czechoslovakia, and the nationalist movements of Scottish and Welsh people, Basques and others.

2 The EU has grown from 6 to 15 members and has accepted applications in principle from 11 other countries.

3 The EU was established for political reasons yet has a social and economic dimension that affects all citizens within its member states.

key terms

Devolution - the decentralisation of power to local or regional governments. In the UK the term is generally used to describe a measure of Scottish and Welsh home rule short of complete independence.

Nationalism - a feeling shared by people of common culture and language who wish to establish or maintain their own nation state.

Referendum - a national vote on a single issue. Strictly speaking, the plural is referenda but 'referendums' has now gained common usage.

Separatism - the desire for complete independence as advocated by nationalists.

Subsidiarity - the EU policy of devolving power to the lowest appropriate level of government.

CHAPTER 2 Development

Introduction

Development is about economic growth and social progress. It is also concerned with the gap between rich and poor, both within countries and on a world scale. Why, for instance, do people in Sweden have average incomes of $20,000 per year while people in Sierra Leone have average incomes of $400 per year?

The study of development also raises other issues. Economic growth can create harmful side effects. Some of these effects are social, such as the breakdown of traditional values and ways of life. Other negative effects are environmental, such as pollution and the depletion of natural resources. For all societies, a judgment must be made - is development a good thing? So far, most people have taken the view that the benefits outweigh the costs.

Chapter summary

Unit 2.1 examines how development is defined and measured and describes the world pattern.
Unit 2.2 summarises the main theories on development and looks at policies which promote development.
Unit 2.3 looks at health and welfare.
Unit 2.4 considers the impact of globalisation on different countries' economic growth.
Unit 2.5 describes the negative effects of development.
Unit 2.6 investigates the issue of sustainable development - the maintenance of economic and social progress whilst minimising the environmental impact.

Unit 2.1 What is development?

key questions

1 How is development defined and measured?
2 What are the benefits and costs of development?
3 What is the pattern of development?
4 What factors cause inequalitites in development?

1. How is development defined and measured?

Development is a process that improves living standards. According to the United Nations Development Programme (UNDP), 'the three essentials of development include the ability to lead a long and healthy life, to acquire knowledge, and to have a decent standard of living'.

In other words, development is more than simply an increase in income and an ability to buy more cars or televisions. As well as these economic goals, there are also social goals such as improvements in health and educational standards.

Although there is broad agreement on the social and economic factors which affect living standards, there are differences of opinion on their relative importance. For instance, does a rise in mobile phone ownership increase living standards as much as a rise in the number of children who attend nursery school? There is no clear answer to this question, it is a matter of judgment.

Some people believe that democratic government and freedom of speech are important factors that affect people's quality of life, and should therefore be included in any definition of development. The UNDP states that 'development involves political, economic and social freedom, and opportunities for being creative and productive'. This is a controversial viewpoint in a world where the majority of people live in countries that do not have Western style democratic governments. Because it is controversial, and also because it is very difficult to measure freedom and opportunity, this aspect of development is generally ignored when measures of development are drawn up.

Measuring development

Development is generally measured by using economic and social indicators. These are statistics that show, for example, the level of average income, the average life expectancy, and the level of literacy within a particular population.

A problem with these indicators is that they can be misleading. Most are averages and therefore they do not show how the benefits of development are shared within a

Figure 2.1 Shopping at the mall

Development is often associated with mass consumption. But there is more to development than shopping at malls and buying expensive goods.

population. This sometimes makes it difficult to measure progress. For example, between 1990 and 1997, the average income in China rose by 10 percent per year. This indicates that people were better off, but it does not tell us whether everyone benefited or just a minority. In fact, what happened was that some urban workers in fast growing industrial sectors became much better off, and some rural inhabitants in more remote regions saw little improvement in their living standards.

Another problem with most measures of development is that they do not show the harmful side effects that can occur. For instance, a rise in car ownership indicates a general rise in living standards, but a family living next to a main road that becomes busier will suffer from increased noise and air pollution. They might well take the view that their living standards have fallen.

As with all statistics, development indicators are sometimes incomplete or inaccurate. They rely on national statistics and, in some countries, the data is not reliable. For instance, in a country such as Angola, there has been civil conflict for many years. The government can only estimate the population size and the numbers, for instance, of children at school. This makes comparisons between countries difficult. Another problem is that most low income countries have a large subsistence sector that does not involve cash transactions. In other words, many people in these countries grow their own food so, because is not bought or sold, its value is not included in national income statistics.

Economic indicators Gross National Product (GNP) is sometimes used as an economic indicator of development. GNP is the sum total of a country's annual economic output, expressed in money terms. Economic output includes all the goods and services that are produced for sale. When the goods and services are sold, someone in the country receives an income, so GNP is also a measure of total income earned. Often, GNP is divided by the total population of a country to give GNP per capita - this is an average figure.

Another economic indicator, Gross Domestic Product (GDP) is also commonly used. Like GNP, it is a measure of national output and income. GDP is calculated in the same way as GNP but it takes 'net property income from abroad' into account. For instance, if an American company such as Ford transfers some of its UK profits to the US, this is an outflow of property income and is not counted in the UK's GDP. If Virgin, a UK company, transfers some of the profits it earns in the US back to this country, it is counted as part of the UK's GDP.

The World Bank classifies the countries of the world into income groups. The 1997 classification is summarised in figure 2.2.

Figure 2.2 Countries by GNP per capita, 1997

	GNP per capita (US$)	Number of countries	Total population (millions)
Low Income	(less than $785)	61 countries	2,036
Middle Income	($786 - $9635)	95 countries	2,857
High Income	(more than $9636)	54 countries	927

Figure 2.3 GNP per capita, 1997

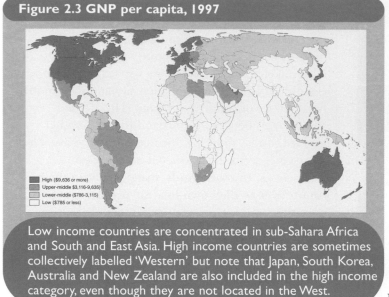

- High ($9,636 or more)
- Upper-middle $3,116-9,635)
- Lower-middle $786-3,115)
- Low ($785 or less)

Low income countries are concentrated in sub-Sahara Africa and South and East Asia. High income countries are sometimes collectively labelled 'Western' but note that Japan, South Korea, Australia and New Zealand are also included in the high income category, even though they are not located in the West.

Social indicators Social indicators give a broader measure of development than per capita GNP. Levels of adult literacy, life expectancy, nutrition and access to clean drinking water are all used as measures of social progress.

Sometimes, a number of indicators are combined. This gives a more complete indication of development than using a single variable. One method used by the UN is called the **Human Development Index** (HDI). This ranks countries on the basis of education, health and income. It has the advantage of combining social indicators with income per head which is an economic indicator. However, it carries a value judgment that income, life expectancy and educational attainment are of equal weight.

Geographers tend to concentrate on inequalities between spatial units such as countries and regions. But there are some inequalities which do not have a spatial dimension. These are based on factors such as gender, social class and ethnicity. Women for example, are much more likely to have incomes lower than the average, as are ethnic minorities, disabled people and elderly people.

In an attempt to assess the difference between male and female levels of development, the United Nations has calculated a Gender-related Development Index (GDI). Like the Human Development Index, it measures life expectancy, educational attainment and income per head. But it also takes into account the disparities between men and women. The greater the gender gap in terms of these factors, the lower a country's GDI compared with its HDI.

According to the UN Development Report (1997), 'Gender equality is essential for empowering women - and for eradicating poverty. Women are in the front line of household and community efforts to escape poverty - but too often they do not have a voice in decision making. As part of a strategy to eradicate poverty, countries should:

- focus on ending discrimination against women in all aspects of health and education
- ensure equal rights and access to land, credit and jobs
- take action to end violence against women.'

Activity) Comparing levels of development

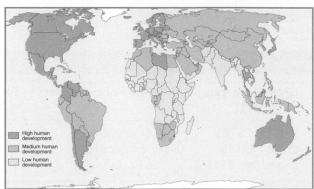

- High human development
- Medium human development
- Low human development

Figure 2.4 Human Development Index (HDI), 1997

The Human Development Index is calculated using:

- *income per capita*
- *life expectancy at birth*
- *educational attainment (measured by adult literacy and average number of years of schooling).*

Country	HDI rank	GDI rank	per capita GNP rank
Canada	1	1	10
Japan	7	12	6
UK	15	13	14
Ireland	17	29	20
Russia	67	46	59
Saudi Arabia	73	95	29
China	108	90	65
India	138	118	92

◀ **Figure 2.5 Selected HDI, GDI and per capita GNP rankings (1997)**

Note: *the per capita GNP figures are 'corrected' to purchasing power parity (PPP); ie, they are adjusted to take account of different costs of living in the different countries.*

Questions

1 Describe the pattern of development, on a world scale, as shown by the Human Development Index (figure 2.4)
2 With reference to specific examples in figure 2.5, explain why a country with a particular HDI rank might have a different rank on the GDI or per capita GNP scale.

2. What are the benefits and costs of development?

There are many benefits arising from development, especially in meeting people's basic needs of food and shelter. It is when the less definable social, cultural and environmental aspects are also considered that it becomes more difficult to identify what has been gained and lost in the development process.

Benefits

When comparing life in a high income country with life in a low income country, it is easy to see why people strive hard for economic development. So many aspects of life that people in Britain take for granted are simply not available in large areas of the poorest countries. For example, piped, clean drinking water, a sewerage system and electric power are available to virtually everyone in high income countries. Likewise, consumer goods such as TVs, cars, cookers and washing machines are owned by the great majority of families in Britain. They are owned by only a small minority in low income countries.

Social services such as health and education are available to everyone in Britain but in poor countries they might only be available in some urban areas. Another advantage of living in a high income country is that, in most cases, the state acts as a safety net. People in Britain who are disabled, unemployed or retired usually receive financial support from the state whereas, in low income countries, people often have to rely on their family or charities for help.

Because there are systems of social and medical care, the average person in high income countries enjoys better health and has a higher life expectancy than most people in low income countries.

Costs

There are many ways in which development can lead to pollution and environmental damage. Examples include air pollution that is caused by increasing traffic volumes, and water pollution that is caused by agricultural fertilisers which are washed out of the soil. There are also extreme events such as radioactive contamination of thousands of square kilometres of land after the Chernobyl nuclear reactor accident in 1986. (The issue of negative environmental impact is covered in detail in unit 2.5.) Development also brings social costs. For instance, economic growth appears to create a hectic lifestyle that can be stressful. Critics of the development process sometimes suggest that it leads to the 'Westernisation' of culture. They say that lives are dominated by large corporations which decide what people eat, what they wear, how they look and where they work. Local drinks are replaced by Coca-Cola and local restaurants are replaced by McDonald's.

People in high income economies often seem too busy to help each other and, it is said, they lose the spiritual values that tie communities together. Tradition, local culture and heritage become lost or submerged by modern, mass culture that is dominated by Hollywood films and Western television programmes.

Activity) **Development in a Javanese village**

Balearjo, an east Javanese village of almost 4,000 people, is an example of what development means for individuals. The village is about eight kilometres from the town of Gondanglegi and is connected to the outside world by bumpy but passable dirt roads. Research conducted in 1955 and 1995 shows how the lives of its inhabitants improved greatly in the intervening years.

Fertilisers and new seed varieties caused rice yields to increase dramatically, from 2 tonnes to 6 tonnes per hectare. A labourer's wage for a day's work increased from 2 kilograms of rice to nearly 4 kilograms. In 1955, clothes were worn until they were in tatters, and few people had shoes. A typical house was made of thatch and bamboo, with an earth floor. There were few furnishings. Almost nobody in the village could read and there was little contact with the outside world. Villagers had to ration their food carefully and, when the harvest was poor, people went hungry. Few people in the village lived until they were 50 and those who were older had to rely on their children for support.

By 1995 things had changed. Rice was in good supply throughout the year. Clothing was better and everyone wore shoes. Most villagers had radios and some had televisions. Nearly all the houses had been rebuilt in brick with concrete floors. Chairs and tables were now common and most homes had electricity. Literacy and education had improved with the opening of a local primary school. A mobile clinic brought basic health care to the villagers for the first time. People often travelled outside the village and knowledge of national events was commonplace. Physically demanding tasks such as carrying water from wells and pounding rice were no longer done manually - making life easier for women in particular.

But education and knowledge of the outside world caused dissatisfaction amongst many younger, enterprising people. Some left the village to find work in the nearby town or Jakarta, many hours away by road. Although they sent money back to their parents, this was the first generation in the history of the village that did not stay together and live as extended families.

Adapted from the World Development Report, World Bank, 1996

Questions

1 Outline the benefits that have arisen from development in Balearjo.
2 Suggest some possible problems that development has created.

▲ **Figure 2.6 Balearjo, Java**

3. What is the pattern of development?

No matter how it is defined, it is clear that there are great inequalities in development. In some parts of the world, such as in Ethiopia and Bangladesh, many households struggle to survive on incomes of a few hundred pounds per year. This is less than most British households spend on their annual holiday.

According to the Food and Agriculture Organisation (FAO), 20 percent of people in low income countries do not have an adequate diet. However, this is an improvement on the position in 1970 when 35 percent of their populations had an inadequate diet. Despite an additional 1.5 billion mouths to feed, the estimated numbers of malnourished people fell from 906 million in 1970 to 841 million in 1995. So there has been progress, but there is still a very long way to go before hunger is overcome.

Figure 2.7 shows that the countries with the highest calorie intake are in Europe, North America, Japan and Australasia. These 'Western' countries are sometimes labelled 'developed'. But, development is a relative concept and therefore the label 'More Economically Developed Country or **MEDC** is also used. Low and middle income countries are described as 'underdeveloped' or Less Economically Developed Countries or **LEDCS**. **First World** is often used instead of MEDC. **Second World** countries are the former communist or centrally planned economies, and the **Third World** covers other low and middle income countries. These terms came into fashion in the 1960s

and 1970s. The descriptions **North** (high income countries) and **South** (low income countries) became common in the 1980s. In the late 1990s, the term Third World once again became widely used as a means of classifying the LEDCs.

Most Third World countries are located in Latin America, Africa and Asia. Although diverse in language, culture and religion, they share many common features. They have low or middle incomes (as defined by the World Bank). They also have relatively low levels of nutrition, health care and literacy. Most are deeply in debt. Another common feature is a high level of vulnerability to natural or human hazards. Because they lack resources and financial reserves, disasters such as hurricanes or the collapse of export markets create great hardship. Similar events can, of course, occur in high income countries but here the governments and populations have more money to repair the damage and to help the worst affected people.

At the other end of the scale, the First World countries are mainly in the northern hemisphere - in Europe, North America and East Asia; (Australia and New Zealand are exceptions in that they are in the southern hemisphere). The highest income countries are members of the OECD (Organisation for Economic Cooperation and Development). The largest of these economies form the G7 (Group of Seven - USA, Japan, Germany, France, UK, Italy and Canada) - a group of rich countries which meets and discusses issues of mutual interest.

In the Second World of former communist countries, some within Eastern Europe are successfully changing to market based economies. Countries such as the Czech Republic and Hungary are classed as middle income by the World Bank. They are also known as 'transition economies'. Not all the countries of Eastern Europe and the former Soviet Union are managing the transition successfully. For example, in Russia, the Ukraine and Romania, economic output fell during the 1990s. These countries found it hard to adjust from centrally planned economies to free markets in which individuals and companies make the key decisions.

A complication in the global picture has been the success of several former Third World

Figure 2.7 Dietary Energy Supply (DES), per capita 1992

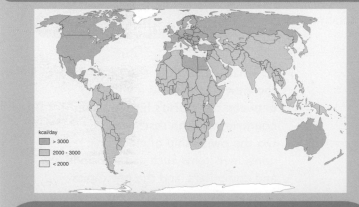

kcal/day
- > 3000
- 2000 - 3000
- < 2000

This data was published by the Food and Agriculture Organisation (FAO) in its Sixth World Food Survey. The FAO suggests that the minimum 'critical' diet is 2,500 calories per day so those countries with an average DES of less than 2,000 calories per day are well below this level.

countries in becoming **Newly Industrialising Countries** (NICs). (Sometimes they are called NIEs - Newly Industrialising Economies.) They are described more fully in unit 2.2.

In Asia, the NICs include the 'Four Tigers' of Hong Kong, Singapore, South Korea and Taiwan. These countries achieved such rapid economic growth in the 1980s and early 1990s that their per capita GNPs reached Western European levels. In Latin America, Brazil and Mexico are sometimes classed as NICs

although their economies have not grown as much as the four Asian economies. By the mid-1990s it appeared that some other Asian countries, such as Malaysia, Thailand and Indonesia, were close to achieving similar success. However, financial crises hit all these countries in the mid and late 1990s (Mexico in 1994; the Asian economies in 1997/98; Brazil in 1999). These setbacks reversed some of their earlier economic growth and showed that development is both complex and difficult to achieve

Activity The world's rich and poor

	Televisions per 1,000 people	Personal computers per 1,000 people	Electricity consumption per capita (kW hours)	
	1996	1996	1980	1996
Low and middle income countries				
Sub-Sahara Africa	43	Less than 1	444	437
Middle East and North Africa	145	17.1	485	1,122
South Asia	53	1.5	116	300
East Asia	41	4.5	243	575
South America and Caribbean	217	23.2	859	1,298
Eastern Europe and Central Asia	353	17.4	3,189	2,798
High income countries (all)	611	224.2	5,557	7,748

▲ **Figure 2.8 Development indicators**

Human Development Report, United Nations 1998

'It is estimated that the additional cost of achieving and maintaining universal access to basic education, reproductive health care for all women, adequate food for all and safe water and sanitation for all is roughly $40 billion per year.' It is also estimated that the people of North America and Western Europe spend $37 billion per year on pet food, perfumes and cosmetics.

Questions

1 To what extent does the data support the view that there is a wide gap between the world's high income countries and the rest?

2 Do the ownership of electronic consumer items such as televisions and computers, and the per capita consumption of electricity provide good indicators of development? Explain your answer.

Regional disparities

Differences in the level of economic development exist on a regional and local scale as well on an international scale. Although the European Union is relatively prosperous, some regions at the 'periphery' of Europe within Spain and Portugal, in Greece, and in Southern Italy, are much poorer than the central 'core' regions (see figure 2.9).

In the periphery, agricultural employment is generally higher than in the core; transport and communications are less developed; manufacturing is more likely to be labour-intensive and based on old technology. Wages are lower, education facilities (especially for further and higher education) are less developed, and health care is less advanced than in other parts of Europe. Such areas require help to enable them reach the levels of prosperity found in the core regions of the EU. The same is also true of the former communist East Germany and the prospective new EU members of Eastern Europe such as the Czech Republic.

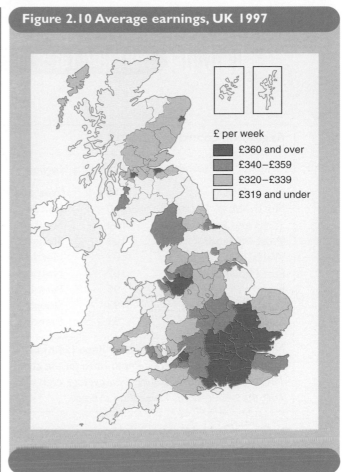

Figure 2.10 Average earnings, UK 1997

£ per week
- £360 and over
- £340–£359
- £320–£339
- £319 and under

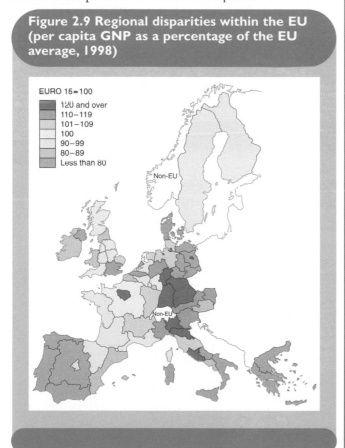

Figure 2.9 Regional disparities within the EU (per capita GNP as a percentage of the EU average, 1998)

EURO 15 = 100
- 120 and over
- 110–119
- 101–109
- 100
- 90–99
- 80–89
- Less than 80

In the UK, there is a broad 'North-South divide' in terms of income levels. However, as figure 2.10 shows, there are variations in this pattern. The South West and the Isle of Wight have relatively low average earnings and, for example, Aberdeen and Cheshire are relatively prosperous.

Throughout Britain, cities contain relatively prosperous suburbs and relatively deprived inner areas. Within Greater London, which has one of the EU's highest per capita incomes, an inner city borough such as Tower Hamlets is much poorer than the outer suburbs. Not only does its population have a lower average income and a higher unemployment rate, the residents also have a lower average educational attainment and a lower life expectancy. Some writers have suggested that rather than a 'North-South' divide, it is more accurate to think of an inner city-outer city divide. The same is true in the USA. For example, a man living in Washington DC has a life expectancy of only 62 years, barely higher than if he lived in the Third World. Yet twenty miles away, in Virginia's prosperous Fairfax County, male life expectancy is 15 years higher. As in the UK, the gap between rich and poor in the USA has widened, not narrowed, over the past 20 years.

Activity ▶ Mortality rates in England and Wales, 1998

Region or country	SMR	Local Authority area (Highest and lowest SMR in each region / country)			
		Highest	SMR	Lowest	SMR
North East	116	Tyne and Wear	117	Darlington	112
North West	110	Halton	129	Cheshire	100
Yorks and Humberside	104	South Yorkshire	109	North Yorkshire	95
West Midlands	103	Stoke-on-Trent	110	Herefordshire	94
Wales	102	Merthyr Tydfil	127	Ceredigion	84
East Midlands	102	Nottingham	108	Rutland	77
Eastern	95	Peterborough	108	Cambridgeshire	92
South East	93	Slough	109	East Sussex	86
South West	91	Swindon	102	Dorset	83

Note: *the Standardised Mortality Ratio (SMR) is the ratio of actual number of deaths in an area to the number expected if the age specific death rates for the country as a whole applied. In other words, if the SMR is above 100, the death rate is higher than average even after taking the age structure into account. If the SMR is below 100, the death rate is lower than average.*

▲ **Figure 2.11 Highest and lowest mortality rates**

Questions

1 Suggest how the Standardised Mortality Ratio might be an indicator of development.
2 To what extent does the data support the view that there is a 'North-South' divide in England Wales?

4. What factors cause inequalities in development?

There are a wide range of factors that cause some countries and regions to be more developed than others. These inequalities in development have both natural and human causes.

Natural resources

There are many regions in which development has been based on the exploitation of local natural resources. For instance, in Britain, the rest of Western Europe and in the northeast USA, much early industrialisation was based on the use of coal for energy. The mills and

factories were often built on coalfields. In the twentieth century, countries such as Brunei, Kuwait and Saudi Arabia have high average incomes due to their oil wealth.

However, there are some countries that have developed despite a lack of natural resources, for example Japan and Singapore. It is sometimes said that these countries based their development on human resources - ie, the hard work, ingenuity and innovation of their populations.

Also, there are examples of countries that are richly endowed with natural resources but have not developed. For instance, in the Democratic Republic of Congo (formerly Zaire) the wealth from copper mines was channelled into the pockets of President Mobutu and his followers, rather than being spread to the mass of the people. Sometimes, as in this example, corruption may be a severe hindrance to development.

Environmental factors

Some parts of the world are too dry, too cold or too mountainous for agriculture or industry to develop - at least without expensive investment to overcome the difficult physical conditions. Such investment might be economically worthwhile if valuable minerals are exploited, as in Alaska - but this is exceptional. So, most of the world's tundra regions, deserts and high mountain regions remain undeveloped.

In geography texts written in the early part of the twentieth century, it was sometimes stated that the temperate lands of the northern hemisphere offered the best environment for human activity. It was said that the relatively cool climate of north western Europe and northeast USA encouraged hard work and enterprise. This was the reason for their early economic development. Such texts, however, were written before the rise of sunbelt industries (ie, new, often high-tech, industries) in the southern states of the USA and in Mediterranean areas, and the decline of rustbelt industries (ie, old, often heavy engineering industries such as iron and steel) in the formerly prosperous, cool temperate regions. There are now few people who believe that climate, apart from the extreme cases, has any great effect on development.

Geographical location

Places that are near the central core of an economy are more likely to be prosperous than places at the periphery or edge. For example, within the UK economy, the London region is in the core and has an average income that is 25 percent higher than Cornwall which is at the periphery. Within the European Union, Southern Italy, on the periphery, has an average income that is 50 percent less than southern Germany which is in the core. New investment (eg, spending on new factories, roads and offices), inward migration and rising prosperity often occur at the centre of a region whereas there is decline and emigration from the periphery. (This point is developed in unit 2.2.)

Political and economic change can sometimes affect whether a region is at the core or at the periphery. For example, North West England was at one time at the heart of the Industrial Revolution. Liverpool was a gateway for trade between Lancashire and the rest of the world. Now, however, mainland Europe is Britain's main trading partner and Liverpool is facing the 'wrong way'. This partly explains the city's declining population and relative loss of prosperity. At the same time, ports such as Dover and Felixstowe are gaining employment by their location in the South East, closer to the EU core.

However, this factor can be overstated. For example, throughout the 1990s, the Republic of Ireland enjoyed the fastest rate of economic growth in the EU. Yet the country is on the western edge of the Europe. Other considerations such as Irish government tax policy, EU subsidies and the skills of the workforce outweighed any disadvantage arising from location.

Social and political factors

The different ways in which countries are organised (ie, their social and political systems) also contribute to differences in their level of development. In the West, most people believe that democracy

Figure 2.12 Northern Canada

Extreme climatic and physical conditions make it very expensive to develop some regions.

is a key element in development. It might be that political freedom creates the conditions for sustained development by allowing free expression and the exchange of ideas. The fact that the former Soviet Union never matched the economic growth of Western countries is sometimes given as evidence to support this view.

It would also seem that a country which is inward-looking is at a disadvantage in development, compared to one which is open to influences from the outside world. For example, there is a huge contrast between the closed system of North Korea, and the outward looking South Korea - even though both countries started at roughly the same level of economic development fifty years ago. In North Korea, the economy is extremely weak, and famine occurred during the late 1990s. In South Korea, the per capita GNP in 1997 was the 24th highest in the world, similar to that in Greece and Portugal.

In another example, the military rulers of Burma (Myanmar) have cut contacts with the outside world for many years. Previous government hostility to Western companies has made them wary of investing in the country. This is one of the reasons why Burma lags far behind its neighbours Thailand and Malaysia in economic output.

Countries that are destabilised by civil war or conflict have the greatest difficulty in becoming developed. People within these countries, and foreign companies, are reluctant to invest in long term projects if there is a danger that employees will be killed or property destroyed. This partly explains why countries such as Somalia, Angola and Sierra Leone are amongst the world's poorest.

The role of government can be positive in promoting development if the 'correct' policies are applied. Investment in free, compulsory education has been an important factor in the growth of the East Asian economies. A well educated workforce is more likely to be enterprising and innovative than one that is illiterate.

The Irish Republic's low tax policies, designed to encourage inward investment by foreign companies, is another example of a positive government policy. Initiatives at the local level can also help. For instance, Corby in the East Midlands has promoted and advertised itself very successfully. As a result, the town has managed to attract sufficient new companies to overcome the high unemployment that followed the closing of a major steel works.

Activity ▸ Barriers to development

The graph is based on research by the World Bank. It shows, for selected countries, the under-5 mortality rates for children whose mothers received no formal education, whose mothers attended primary school, and whose mothers attended secondary school.

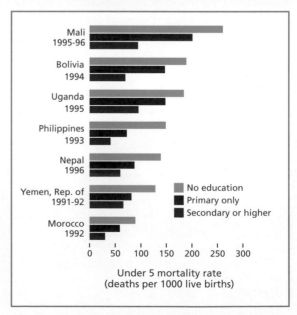

▲ Figure 2.13 Child mortality and educational attainment of the mother

According to the World Bank, formal education helps mothers raise healthier children in four main ways:

- basic information about nutrition and child care might be part of the school curriculum
- women are less likely to rely on traditional remedies for children's ailments and are more open to new ideas
- women gain the self-confidence to use public health services such as clinics
- increased literacy allows women to read written instructions on medicines, to follow advice given in health leaflets and to be aware of information in newspapers and magazines.

Questions

1 Briefly describe and explain the relationship between child mortality and the educational attainment of mothers.
2 What factors might influence the proportion of women who attend formal education.
3 Apart from its effect on child mortality, suggest other ways in which education might raise the level of development.

Colonisation

Some inequalities in development are rooted in history. For example, if a country was colonised, its economy might have been weakened as a result. Some former colonies in Africa overspecialised in cash crops (eg, tea and rubber, grown for sale overseas) or mineral production, because this was in the interests of the colonial powers. As a result they were made vulnerable to downturns in world markets. Zambia's reliance on copper exports is an example. When the world price of copper falls, Zambia has few other exports to fall back on. Another example is in Central America where some countries became dominated by American transnational companies. The 'banana republics' such as Guatemala and Honduras might have developed more quickly if they had not become over-reliant on the export of fruit.

Sometimes, local industries were damaged in the colonial era if free trade was imposed by the more efficient imperial power. Mahatma Gandhi, the leader of Indian independence, campaigned to protect village cotton producers from the output of Lancashire cotton mills, but to little avail. The Lancashire cotton was cheaper and the Indian producers were forced out of business. In unit 2.4 on globalisation, links to the global economy are shown to be crucial in determining which areas shall prosper or decline.

Cultural and religious factors

A traditional explanation of why some countries have developed faster than others is based on religion and the cultural values associated with particular religious

beliefs. Because it is said to encourage a strong work ethic, Protestant Christianity has been identified by some as a factor in encouraging development. Catholicism and Islam, by contrast, are said to be less concerned with money or economic growth so countries dominated by those religions have been slower to develop. Today, the role of Confucianism is sometimes regarded as a key element in the success of Japan and the 'Four Tigers'. The Confucian faith emphasises obedience to authority and the importance of working towards the collective good. These beliefs are, it is said, reasons why workforces in East Asia have been prepared to work so hard and to accept the changes that occur during rapid economic development.

There may be some truth in these views, but they cannot be a complete explanation of why development occurs faster in some countries than others. Confucianism has existed for 2,500 years and yet it is only recently that the East Asian economies have prospered. Mexico and Brazil have been relatively successful in development, as have France and Italy before them, and yet all have large Catholic populations. In the UK the established religion is Protestantism, yet the country contains some of the poorer parts of the European Union.

A cultural factor not normally associated with religious beliefs is the savings ratio. This is the proportion of income that people are prepared to save and invest in wealth creating activities. There is a strong positive correlation between investment and economic development. Those countries that invest the most are those in which growth is fastest. Part of the success of Japan, Singapore and South Korea has been the willingness of their populations to sacrifice present consumption and use their savings to finance future growth. Investment is not only in factories, machinery and communications. Social investment in education and health care are important factors in creating the conditions for economic growth. A skilled, literate and healthy workforce is essential for development to occur.

Activity | **Development in Mali**

▲ **Figure 2.14 Mali**

Profile of Mali:

- located in West Africa on the southern margin of the Sahara Desert
- population: 10 million, growth rate 3.1% per year (1996); urban population 19%; religion: 70% Moslem
- area: 1,220,000 sq km (UK: 241,000 sq km)
- the northern part of the country is arid and semi-arid, the southern part is grassland savanna; there is a short wet season in summer but this rainfall is variable and unreliable
- the Senegal and Niger Rivers flow through the southern part of the country and are used for irrigation
- Mali was a French colony, ruled in the interests of France. Since independence in 1960, political instability and economic mismanagement have hindered development. In the early 1990s, civil conflict disrupted much of the country
- GNP per capita (1996): $710 (ranking 151st out of 157 countries); growth rate -0.2% per year (1990-96)
- total GNP: $2,422 m (1996); total external debt: $3,020 m
- life expectancy: 50; child malnutrition: 31%; access to safe drinking water: 41% (all 1996)
- adult literacy: males 39%, females 23% (1995); daily newspapers per 1,000 people: 4 (UK: 351); telephone lines per 1,000 people: 2 (UK: 528) (both 1996)
- paved roads as a percentage of all roads: 12% (1996)
- main exports: cotton 47%, live animals 29%; food import dependency: 10% (all 1992)
- agricultural output as a percentage of GNP: 48%; proportion of the workforce in the agricultural sector: 88% (1996)

Questions

1 Summarise the key indicators that illustrate Mali's relatively low level of development.
2 With reference to the data, suggest reasons for Mali's lack of development.

unit summary

1 There is no general agreement on how development should be defined. A range of economic and social indicators are generally used.

2 Development can bring many benefits to people, especially in meeting their basic needs of shelter, food, clothing and social care.

3 Development also has its costs, such as deterioration in environmental quality and the breakdown of tradition and local cultures.

4 Development indicators at the national scale may hide differences in development at the regional or local scale within a country.

5 There are large inequalities in development between countries and regions. These inequalities are the result of a wide range of factors, including geographical and environmental variations, different levels of natural resources, contrasts in investment patterns, past history and differences in how countries are organised.

key terms

Core - regions which are at the centre of the development process.

Development - a process of improvement in the income and welfare of people.

First World - the high income economies of the world. (They are also known as More Economically Developed Countries, MEDCs.)

Human Development Index - a measure developed by the UN which ranks countries according to a range of development indicators - income, life expectancy and educational attainment.

Newly Industrialising Countries (NICs) - those countries which have achieved rapid industrialisation in recent decades.

North / South - the wealthy countries of the North (Europe, North America, Japan and also

Australasia) and the generally poorer countries of the South (Africa, Asia, Latin America).

Periphery - regions at the margins of the development process.

Rustbelt - those areas of early industrialisation in Europe or North America which are in decline.

Second World - the former communist countries.

Sunbelt - areas previously in the periphery, such as parts of the South of the United States, in which economic development is taking place.

Third World - the low and middle income, less developed countries of the world. (They are also known as Less Economically Developed Countries, LEDCs.)

Unit 2.2 Development theories and policies

key questions

1 What are the main theories on development?

2 How have the Newly Industrialising Countries developed?

3 What part does aid play in the development process?

4 How have UK governments promoted regional development?

1. What are the main theories on development?

A number of different ideas have been put forward to explain how development occurs and why certain places are more developed than others. Some of these ideas are outlined in the section that follows.

Rostow

An influential theory on how development occurs was

proposed by Rostow in 1960. The theory is essentially optimistic. It suggests that, once the process starts, it builds up momentum and becomes self sustaining.

The basis of Rostow's theory is that a country goes through a number of stages as it develops. To begin with, the economy is mainly based on agriculture. Then, as development occurs, there is a relative decline in the primary sector of the economy (ie, farming, fishing, forestry, mining) and a relative increase in output from the secondary sector (ie, manufacturing). Eventually, the tertiary sector (ie, services) becomes the most important sector. Figure 2.15 shows the stages that countries pass through.

Rostow stated that traditional societies are mainly rural, with a subsistence economy. In other words, most people grow their own food and produce little for sale. When development starts, wealthy landowners, business people and the government start to make productive investment. This involves spending on workshops, small businesses and 'social capital'. The latter can include roads, railways, power stations, schools and hospitals. This investment creates the preconditions for **take-off**. This stage can last for 20-30 years and is the start of industrialisation in which manufacturing industry develops. A steady, sustainable increase in output must be achieved for take-off. This occurs when investment rises to 10 percent of national income and one or more manufacturing sector (or **leading sector**; eg, textiles or engineering) achieves a high growth rate. The country then develops a framework of banks and other service institutions to help businesses grow. The drive to maturity involves growth in all parts of the economy. Eventually the age of mass consumption is reached in which the population is able to buy a wide range of consumer goods and services.

Rostow's theory was influential because it seemed to provide a good explanation of how development occurs.

It gave to the world the terminology of 'take-off' and 'leading sector' and people used it as a model in the UN 'Development Decade' of the 1960s. But, since then, the theory has been criticised because:

- it is based on the historical experience of just a few Western countries; other countries have not developed along the same lines; there have been a variety of pathways to development
- the theory describes but does not explain why the changes occur; ie, it emphasises the 'stages' through which countries pass but neglects the processes involved in development
- 'leading sectors' might not be required for development to occur, instead growth might be broad based across all sectors
- 'take-off' can take much longer than 30 years; and experience has shown that it is not inevitable.

Hirschman

Writing in the 1950s, Hirschman emphasised the spatial dimension of development. He suggested that development can spread from region to region. The process starts in successful industrial regions (or **growth poles**), into which private and public investment is channelled. Rising output in these regions can then cause **multiplier** effects in surrounding areas. For example, investment in the motor vehicle industry in one region might stimulate growth in the component industry in other regions. Hirschman believed that development would **trickle-down** or 'spread' from the growth pole to other parts of the country which were previously lagging behind.

Myrdal

Myrdal, also writing in the 1950s, accepted that economic development could spread to less prosperous regions. However, he also suggested that economic forces might widen rather than reduce regional differences in income. He described a 'cycle of cumulative causation', in which new industrial development in one region attracts capital, resources and high quality labour to it from other regions. Instead of 'trickle down', **backwash** occurs as wealth and population migrate to the more prosperous region (see figure 2.16). The effect becomes cumulative as the growth region

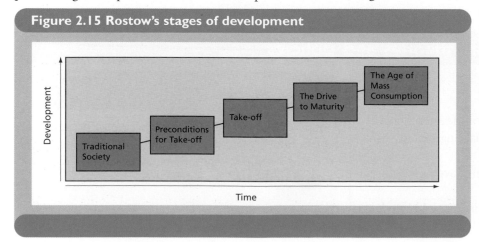

Figure 2.15 Rostow's stages of development

Figure 2.16 Trickle down and backwash

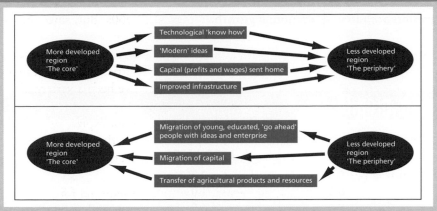

The top diagram shows trickle down; development spreads outwards to the periphery. The bottom diagram shows backwash; development flows inwards to the core.

sucks in resources, and the less prosperous regions go into a cycle of decline.

A later writer, Friedmann, in the 1960s, developed Myrdal's ideas and used the terms 'core' and 'periphery' to describe the regions at the centre and at the margins of economic development.

Frank

In the late 1960s, Frank developed a theory to explain the wide gap in development between different countries. He suggested that there was an unequal relationship between the centres of power in North America and Europe and their 'satellites' in Latin America, Africa and Asia. The term **dependency** is used to describe this relationship in which the rich are said to exploit the poor. Exploitation, Frank argued, occurs because the high income regions are able to use their economic and political power to their own advantage. By controlling trade and industry they can set the prices of goods on world markets. As a result, Third World producers are forced by economic circumstances to provide low cost food and raw materials to satisfy the demands of the high income countries. The result is that the rich became richer and the poor remain poor. It follows from this idea that development is by no means an inevitable process. As long as they remain in a state of dependency, low income countries will not achieve the take-off to industrial and economic development.

The ideas of Frank were particularly influential in the 1970s and 1980s. The dependency theory reflected the powerful economic position of rich countries and the weak position of poorer countries. Some felt, however, that dependency was overstated. A modified view suggests that there is interdependence between rich and poor countries. So, while the Third World depends on the First World, the First World also needs the raw materials and markets of the Third World. This idea of interdependence formed the basis of the Brandt Report which was published in 1980 by a group of academics and politicians. (Brandt had been the Chancellor of West Germany.)

The rise of the Newly Industrialising Countries (NICs) also appears to weaken the case for the 'dependency' school of thought. During the 1980s and 1990s, a number of economies broke through the barriers which dependency apparently put in their way. For instance, by 1996 Singapore and Hong Kong both had higher per capita Gross National Products than the UK. Their growth has become a model for other countries and many researchers have sought to analyse the 'secret' of their success. In recent years geographers have tended to move away from broad theories of development and have, instead, concentrated on how development has occurred in practice.

2. How have the Newly Industrialising Countries developed?

Beginning in the 1960s, a number of countries in East Asia and Latin America began to achieve rapid economic growth. They are called Newly Industrialising Countries (or, sometimes, Newly Industrialising Economies). During the 1990s, an alternative expression, **emerging markets** came into use. This term covers a wider range of countries including those former communist East European economies which are developing market based systems.

In Asia, Hong Kong, Singapore, South Korea and Taiwan (known as the 'Four Tigers') developed quickly in the decades after 1960. In Latin America, Mexico and Brazil were the leading countries. More recently, Thailand and Malaysia, Indonesia and China have also begun a rapid industrialisation.

In 1997/98, a series of financial crises affected countries in East Asia and Latin America. The value of their currencies fell and some foreign investors withdrew their money. But, after a period of slow down, it appears that most of the Asian NICs have resumed their economic growth.

Activity Economic growth

Figure 2.17 Average annual growth (%) in GDP for selected countries

	1965 - 1980	1980 - 1990	1990 - 1997
Brazil	8.8	2.7	3.1
Mexico	6.5	1.0	1.8
Hong Kong	8.6	6.9	5.3
Singapore	10.1	6.4	8.5
South Korea	9.6	9.4	7.2
Taiwan	8.6	8.2	6.5
Malaysia	7.3	5.2	8.7
Thailand	7.2	7.6	7.5
Indonesia	8.0	6.1	7.5
China	6.4	10.2	11.9
UK	2.4	3.2	1.9

Note: *Gross Domestic Product (GDP) is sometimes used as an alternative to Gross National Product. Both are measures of national output. The UK's GDP growth is given for comparison.*

Question

1 Compare the growth in GDP between the Asian countries, the Latin American countries and the UK.

There are a wide variety of explanations of why the NICs have been so successful in developing their economies. Some economists have suggested that the NICs' industrialisation is due to policies of 'laissez-faire'. This means 'let do'. The idea is that if business people are left to get on with their activities with minimal government interference and taxation, then economic prosperity will follow. The alternative term 'free market' is also used to describe economies in which there is little government intervention in the production and sale of goods and services.

As noted in unit 2.1, in East Asia, Confucianism has also been suggested as a key factor in the development of the NICs. Confucian ideas play down the role of the individual in favour of the broader society. Hierarchy and deference to authority are also emphasised. So, it is said, workforces in East Asia have been willing to make sacrifices - to work hard for low wages - for the common good. They have accepted change because their leaders have told them that the country as a whole will benefit. In Singapore, for example, the government has maintained a tight social and political control but, in return, has delivered spectacular economic growth.

Although laissez faire and Confucianism may be important factors in East Asia, most researchers believe that other factors are at work. In particular, the strategy of export led growth is said to be crucial. The example of Hong Kong shows that this and many other factors have also played a part.

Hong Kong

Hong Kong, which means 'Fragrant Harbour', has become one of the world's most dynamic economies. Hong Kong island was ceded to Britain in the First Opium War with China, in 1841 (at this time, Britain was trying to force China to open up its trade to foreigners, and to buy opium produced in India). The population was then 5,000. A small area of the mainland called Kowloon, with 3,000 inhabitants, was transferred to Britain following a Second Opium War in 1860. Then, in 1898, Britain leased the 'New Territories' from China for 99 years. This land had a population of 100,000 and made up the bulk of the area of Hong Kong. With the lease on the New Territories due to expire in 1997, the small area left would not have been viable. Therefore, Hong Kong was returned to China on July 1st, 1997. The Chinese Government agreed to keep Hong Kong administratively separate and to respect the former economic and political system.

Situated in the Pearl River delta, only 120 kilometres downstream from Canton (Guangzhou) and next to the prosperous Chinese province of Guangdong, the location of Hong Kong as a trading base was excellent. Another advantage is that the harbour is sheltered from the 'great winds' ('tai-fun' or typhoons) of the South China Seas.

Hong Kong soon developed into a major 'entrepot', a port in which goods are processed and trans-shipped in and out of China. Shipbuilding, ship-repair and related port activities followed, and banking and related services also grew to finance the local 'Hongs' or companies.

A setback came, in 1949, when the People's Republic of China (PRC) was founded as an independent communist country. For a time, Hong Kong lost its entrepot status and was flooded with hundreds of thousands of refugees from China. In the early 1950s, Hong Kong's situation seemed desperate. The border was closed to refugees in 1950 when the population had reached 2,400,000. Nevertheless, illegal immigrants continued to reach the colony. The indented coastline made it difficult to patrol and the refugees were often helped by relatives already in Hong Kong.

The refugees put great pressure on housing, sanitation and health care, but they also provided a new labour force. They were willing to work very hard, often in small family businesses which were to become the cornerstone of Hong Kong's prosperity. They were non-unionised, unskilled, and would tolerate very low wages and sweatshop conditions.

Figure 2.18 Dynamic Hong Kong

Some of the richer refugees brought financial capital, and even factory equipment such as textile machinery from Shanghai. The Hong Kong government improved the urban infrastructure, particularly by building new housing. It also provided protection from the mainland regime, and led trade negotiations on behalf of Hong Kong's businesses. These policies cannot be described as laissez faire because they were a form of economic intervention. However, the colonial government did keep taxation to a minimum and, for the most part, simply provided a stable framework within which businesses could operate.

At first, Hong Kong's manufactures of textiles, plastics and electrical goods (such as T-shirts, toys and radios) were viewed as being 'cheap and nasty' by the world outside. The economy was dominated by small businesses (family owned, often operating from domestic premises). By 1971, these formed 91 percent of industrial enterprises. Often short of capital, and producing inferior goods in inferior conditions, these establishments nevertheless found a market at the global level. Links with overseas Chinese in North America, Australia, Singapore and Britain helped this trade.

When new competitors, such as Taiwan and South Korea, and later the People's Republic of China itself, entered the market and began to undercut Hong Kong's wage rates and prices, Hong Kong companies started to move up-market, producing higher quality goods. These included electronic consumer goods, fashion garments and high technology equipment.

The most recent stage in its development has seen Hong Kong businesses invest heavily in China itself, as China opens up its economy to foreign investment. Now it is Hong Kong people who provide the trade links and management expertise, with the mainland Chinese providing cheap labour, land (in very short supply in Hong Kong) and other resources. Places such as Shunde City and Panyu in the Pearl River delta are themselves becoming large cities, thanks in part to the stimulus of Hong Kong investment. This is a good example of how development can spread or trickle down. Hong Kong has acted as a core and the neighbouring mainland province has been the periphery. Now, the Chinese government has set up Special Economic Zones across the border from Hong Kong. These, in turn, are acting as growth poles for the rest of China.

It is worth noting that Hong Kong's success would not have been possible without the approval of the communist government in China. The Chinese developed a policy which was, if not fully supportive, at least willing to ignore the fact that Hong Kong had become a capitalist showpiece. At any time, China could have disrupted the colony, by cutting off its water or food supplies, by allowing wholesale migration from Guangdong province, or by using its agents in the colony to encourage civil unrest. Only in 1967 was such unrest encouraged, and this only briefly, during the 'Red Guard' era in China.

In summary, Hong Kong's rise as a NIC was due to a wide range of factors, including its:
- location near Canton and the Pearl River Delta
- sheltered site and harbour
- wealthy inheritance from past trade
- stable, relatively uncorrupt government
- high government investment in infrastructure such as housing, transport and power, and education
- low taxation
- political security under British protection, with a 'blind eye' from China
- plentiful supply of (initially) cheap labour
- small family businesses which displayed enterprise and initiative
- larger companies, Hongs, which built up global trade links
- concentration on a range of manufactured goods for export
- decision to move up-market by producing high quality and high value goods, and, eventually, investing in China.

According to the World Bank, by 1996, Hong Kong's per capita GNP (corrected for cost of living differences) was the fifth highest in the world - higher than Japan, Germany or the UK. The experience of Hong Kong suggests that Third World countries can break free of dependency. By investing in certain key sectors, the Hong Kong economy has been able to modernise and develop from a traditional society to one of mass consumption. Virtually the only natural advantage that Hong Kong enjoys is its harbour and position near the Chinese mainland. Its success has been almost entirely due to human factors such as having a stable, supportive government and a culture of enterprise.

Activity Big emerging markets

According to the US Department of Commerce, the biggest commercial opportunities for US exporters are to be found in the 'big emerging markets'. These include the Newly Industrialising Countries and a 'second tier' of countries that are close to achieving similar economic growth.

	Value of imports US$ millions
Hong Kong	277,500
China	164,031
Singapore	153,220
South Korea	145,000
Taiwan	132,000
Malaysia	101,230
Mexico	89,700
Thailand	80,100
Brazil	54,665
Turkey	49,500
Indonesia	47,100
Philippines	40,900
Poland	37,030
India	35,000
South Africa	29,700
Czech Republic	27,709
Argentina	21,700
Vietnam	13,910

Note: *Hong Kong's trade statistics are reported separately from China's even though it is now politically controlled by China.*

▲ **Figure 2.19 The 'big emerging markets' and their 1997 imports**

The US Department of Commerce has reported:

- the GDP of the big emerging markets is 25 percent of that of the industrialised, 'Western' world (ie, USA, Canada, Western Europe, Japan, Australasia) and is rising rapidly
- US exports to these emerging markets exceeds exports to Europe and Japan combined
- with a combined GDP of over $2,000 billion, these economies already account for a bigger share of world output than Germany and the UK combined
- these countries are making 'significant progress' towards market economies (ie, they are reducing state controls and are opening their economies to Western style systems of free enterprise; in particular they are allowing transnational corporations to operate freely)
- there are increasing opportunities for US companies in these markets to export industrial and farm machinery, electrical power generating equipment, transportation equipment and a range of high technology manufactures.

Questions

1 Describe the distribution of the big emerging markets as defined by the US Department of Commerce.
2 Outline the possible advantages and disadvantages to Western economies arising from the industrialisation of the big emerging markets.
3 What lessons might be learned by other countries from the success of Hong Kong?

3. What part does aid play in the development process?

Many people believe that low income countries should be helped to develop. This view is sometimes based on moral concern - because helping others is the right thing to do. Others base their view on self interest because, as incomes rise in poor countries, the market for Western goods and services will expand.

There is no consensus on how help should be provided. Some believe that aid should be given directly, others believe that a fairer trading system would have the same result.

What is aid?
Aid is defined as a transfer of resources, from richer to

poorer countries, on terms which are 'concessional'. In other words, the aid is in the form of a gift or a loan at a lower rate of interest than charged by banks. Resources might be in the form of money, food, training or materials.

Aid is classified as **official aid** (sometimes termed **Official Development Assistance** or **ODA**) which comes directly or indirectly via governments, or as **voluntary aid**. This comes from charities and other bodies such as Oxfam or ActionAid. These bodies are called **Non-Governmental Organisations**, or **NGOs**.

Aid is **bilateral** when it is given directly from one country to another, and **multilateral** when it is given indirectly via organisations like the World Bank or agencies of the United Nations such as the Food and Agricultural Organisation (FAO).

A distinction is sometimes made between

development aid and emergency relief. Although both forms of help are included in official figures, there is a difference. Development aid is generally provided to finance medium and long term projects such an irrigation scheme or a water treatment plant. Emergency relief is used to alleviate short term famine or to help in the aftermath of a natural disaster.

During the 1990s, many donor countries reduced their official aid. In 1996, the proportion of GNP given by high income countries was just 0.27 percent. This was the lowest figure since data collection began in 1950 - and far below the UN recommended level of 0.7 percent. Total voluntary aid is only about one-eighth the total of official aid.

Figure 2.20 Food aid in Uganda

Emergency food aid prevents famine so solves a short term problem but it does not promote long term development. When free or low cost food is provided over a long period, local farmers might cease production because they lose their market.

Benefits of aid

Researchers for the World Bank have studied Official Development Assistance between 1970-1993. They found that 'foreign aid accelerates economic growth and reduces poverty in those developing countries that pursue sound policies'. But, in countries with 'poor' policies, aid 'has had no measurable effect'. The researchers' definition of 'sound policies' includes free trade without import or export controls, fiscal discipline (ie, governments should not spend more than they raise in taxes) and the avoidance of high inflation.

The study notes that in a well run economy, aid can help reduce infant mortality, increase the confidence of foreign investors in a country's economy and encourage economic growth. Countries such as Bolivia, El Salvador, Ghana and Honduras have benefited, while those with 'poor' policies, including Tanzania and Zambia have not.

Aid can help countries avoid getting into debt. During the 1970s and 1980s, many banks persuaded low income countries to borrow money at commercial rates of interest without properly assessing whether the money could be repaid. Often, these countries cannot afford to repay the loans and, in some cases, cannot even afford to pay the interest on the debt. Tanzania, for example, currently pays more in debt interest each year than it spends on education and public health combined. For such a country, aid in the form of gifts or interest free loans would have been a far better form of help than commercial bank loans.

Criticisms of aid

There is a view that much aid is wasted. The poorest countries remain poor, despite the aid that is provided. It is said that some countries are unwilling to help themselves, and that aid is being squandered or stolen by governments or ruling elites. The example of Zaire (now the Democratic Republic of Congo) is often quoted. The corrupt Mobutu regime simply stole millions of pounds of aid which should have benefited the local population.

Aid has also been criticised on political grounds. During the 1970s and 1980s, the World Bank was accused of giving aid almost exclusively to countries which supported capitalism rather than socialism. In other words, aid was given to gain political allies rather than for its own sake. It was used as a weapon in the Cold War between the West and the Soviet Union. Also, often, it was used to buy weapons rather than to help social and economic development.

The World Bank has also been criticised for its poor record on environmental concerns, providing funds for projects which have had a damaging impact on the environment and on local people. A report on 39 dam projects financed by the World Bank in the 1980s showed that the overall, positive impact had to be balanced by the displacement of 750,000 people.

Bilateral aid is sometimes criticised because the donor might have objectives that are not necessarily in the best interests of the recipient population. In a well known example, during the 1980s, Britain supplied £200 million of aid to help build the Pergau Dam in Malaysia. The motive, it is said, was partly to enable British companies to win contracts for work on the dam, and also as a 'sweetener' or bribe for the Malaysian government's purchase of warplanes from the UK.

Critics of aid suggest that, at its worst, it:
- creates dependency (ie, it encourages reliance on aid rather than self-help) and props up bad governments
- promotes a culture of corruption and over-consumption by uncaring Third World elites
- distorts local markets in the Third World; for example, food aid undercuts the prices that local farmers can get for their produce
- is skewed towards countries and regimes that are political allies rather than towards those most in need
- introduces technology which is often expensive and inappropriate, difficult to maintain and is 'tied' (ie, the equipment must be bought from the donor country)
- is used for military equipment rather than for economic development

Activity | World Bank aid in Bangladesh

In the early 1990s, the World Bank reviewed the effectiveness of its aid programme in rural Bangladesh. In a study of 16 villages, a comparison was made between the development of villages that had benefited from new public infrastructure and those that had not. Public infrastructure included new roads, electric power, schools, health centres and banks.

The study found that, in the villages where there was investment in infrastructure, there was a one-third increase in average household incomes. Crop income rose by 24 percent and income from livestock and fisheries by 78 percent. These changes were found to benefit the poorest households more than richer people.

Better roads and transport encouraged the production of agricultural output for sale at nearby markets rather than simply for family subsistence. New farm products included perishable commodities such as vegetables and eggs. Small scale industries also developed, helped by the provision of electric power. In some cases, this involved the processing of farm produce, for example the milling of grain. As a cash based economy grew, more use was made of banking facilities. This allowed people to borrow capital to buy new seed varieties and fertiliser.

As local incomes increased, there was more work for landless labourers in a range of occupations including construction, food processing and services. The study showed that households in the developed villages worked no more days in the year than in the undeveloped villages. However, the work they did was more productive and, more often, for wages rather than as unpaid family work.

Questions

1 Briefly outline the benefits arising from the World Bank aid in rural Bangladesh.
2 To what extent would aid in the form of: (a) free food (eg, sacks of rice), or (b) a Western designed and built automatic flour milling plant be appropriate and in the best interests of the Bangladeshi villagers?

Fair trade

There are some agencies, mainly Non-Governmental Organisations, which believe that 'fair trade' is the best form of aid. Oxfam and Traidcraft, for example, try to help Third World producers gain markets and sell goods at fair prices in the UK and elsewhere. This type of assistance promotes a system of self help and encourages self esteem. Instead of relying on aid hand outs, people in the Third World can produce and sell agricultural products, such as tea and coffee, clothing and other textile goods, and craft items.

Since the mid-90s, Oxfam and other NGOs have focussed their fair trade campaigns on particular industries such as textiles and footwear. By lobbying governments and high street retailers, and by information campaigns, NGOs have publicised the poor working conditions of many people in the Third World. In particular, the NGOs have highlighted the role of transnational corporations which produce and buy clothes in countries where wages are lowest - for example, in the Dominican Republic, Indonesia, the Philippines or Bangladesh. The NGOs have shown that, for instance, a worker in Indonesia might only receive a few pence in wages for producing a pair of Nike or Reebok trainers that costs £50 in UK shops. If workers were paid a 'fair' wage, it is said, there would be less need to give aid. The same would be true if there was a fairer trading system that passed the benefits more directly to the Third World producers rather than to the Western owned transnational corporations.

The fair trade campaign raises several questions. For instance, are the low wages and poor working conditions a necessary part of development? Are the sweatshop conditions in Third World countries part of a process that countries must go through in the early stage of industrialisation? Does trade and investment by transnational corporations help or hinder the process of development? These issues are covered in more detail in unit 2.4 on globalisation.

Activity › Clothes production in Bangladesh

During 1998, Oxfam highlighted the plight of workers in the Bangladeshi textile industry. Bangladesh is one of the world's poorest countries. Oxfam produced testimony from some clothing workers:

> **Bokul**: *'I sew collars on shirts. I am paid £4.64 a month. I often have to work unpaid overtime but my normal hours are from 7.00 am to 10.00 pm. We have 30 minutes for meal breaks but are not allowed to leave our machines.'*

> **Shadjena**: *'Even when I am sick, I am not allowed time off. If I miss a day, I shall be sacked.'*

> **Rani**: *'I'm always afraid that if I make a mistake, they'll hit me.'*

Working conditions in most Bangladeshi factories are hot, noisy and dusty, with poor lighting. Child labour is common. In 1995, nine child workers died in a factory fire after 500 workers panicked - there were no emergency exits.

But, some benefits arise from the clothing industry. Fifteen years ago the industry was virtually non-existent - now it earns 63 percent of Bangladesh's export earnings, worth more than $1.4 billion per year. By 1995 there were almost 3,000 factories in Bangladesh making shirts, blouses, trousers and skirts for Europe and the USA. 1.2 million people are directly employed in garment factories and a further 5 million indirectly - supplying thread, cloth and buttons, processing documentation and transporting the goods.

Women make up the bulk of the workforce and there have been benefits for them. Helen Rahman of Shoishab, an organisation that helps disadvantaged children in Dhaka (the capital of Bangladesh), says: 'The garment industry has caused a silent revolution of social change. Before, it was not acceptable for a woman to work outside her neighbourhood. Now, the income a woman earns gives her social status and bargaining power. One very positive result is that the average age of marriage has risen - and the birth rate has fallen.'

For the future, some uncertainties exist. Social unrest and strikes for better conditions might cause transnational corporations to shift production elsewhere. At the same time, countries like China, Cambodia, Nepal and Vietnam are ready to develop their export industries by undercutting Bangladeshi wages.

Questions

1 Outline how the textile industry has contributed to Bangladeshi development.
2 What negative effects have arisen from the growth of the textile industry in Bangladesh?
3 In your view, to what extent might fair wages and fair trade help Bangladeshi textile workers?

4. How have UK governments promoted regional development?

Within the UK, some regions are more prosperous than others. Regional development policies are used to help those parts of the country that have the highest unemployment and the lowest incomes. Since 1934, a policy of regional assistance has been adopted by all UK governments.

There are a number of reasons why help is provided to less well off regions. One is that investment in 'social capital' such as roads, schools and hospitals is wasted if a regional economy collapses and the population leaves. Also, if this happens, problems of congestion and a shortage of social capital arise in the successful regions to which people move. There are also the potential social consequences of regional decline to consider - for example, unemployment and poverty. If the government does not intervene, there is a financial cost in the form of social security payments and, possibly, a political cost to the government at election time.

One method of measuring the difference in regional development is by looking at the unemployment rates in different parts of the UK (see figure 2.21). Disparities in unemployment are

less in the 1990s than in previous decades . Nevertheless, in 1999, the region with the highest unemployment (the North East) had a rate almost three times as high as the region with the lowest rate (the South East).

A wide range of policies to promote regional development has been tried by successive UK governments. These policies include:
• Assisted Areas; grants and other forms of assistance are provided to companies which set up in these areas

Figure 2.21 UK unemployment rates

Country or region	Unemployment rate (%)		
	1979	1989	1999
North	8.3	10.7	
(North East)			7.3
Yorkshire and Humberside	5.4	8.0	5.5
North West	6.5	8.8	4.1
East Midlands	4.4	6.0	4.0
West Midlands	5.2	6.9	4.6
East Anglia	4.2	3.8	
(Eastern)			3.2
South East	3.4	3.1	2.6
South West	5.4	4.8	3.4
Wales	7.3	7.9	5.4
Scotland	7.4	9.8	5.4
Northern Ireland	10.7	15.4	7.0

Note: The boundaries of the Standard Regions changed between 1989 and 1999. The North was split; part became the North East and the rest went into the North West. East Anglia was extended to include part of the South East.

- Regional Development Agencies; these bodies have the task of attracting investment to the regions
- European Regional Policy; although this is a European Union initiative, the UK government provides matching funding for any assistance provided by the EU
- New Towns; the construction of New Towns throughout the UK has played a part in regional development
- Urban Development Corporations; these bodies have directed assistance to particular urban areas.

Assisted Areas

The first regions in Britain to be designated as Assisted Areas were located in the north and west of the country. (In 1934 they were called Special Areas, see figure 2.22.) They included the North East of England, Central Scotland, South Wales and Merseyside. The economies of these regions relied on coal, steel, heavy engineering and port industries which were all hit by falling demand and foreign competition.

The government provided the Assisted Areas with funds to help in retraining the workforce and for new infrastructure (eg, road building). Grants were offered to companies which set up in the Areas. At the same time, in the more prosperous South East and West Midlands, planning controls restricted the growth of new industries.

In the 1980s, the Conservative Government took the view that these policies had been economically wasteful and inefficient. Regional policy was seen as merely shifting jobs around, mainly from non-assisted to assisted areas. As a result, the national economy as a whole had not benefited. Also, firms were being persuaded to locate in unsuitable locations where production was inefficient. Examples such as the Linwood car plant near Glasgow were used to support this view. Government money partly financed this plant but it eventually closed because it was not profitable. It was too far from its major markets and from the main component

manufacturers in England. An additional argument against regional policy was that the planning controls in the South and Midlands had put a straitjacket on their economies. These regions, it was said, were prevented from diversifying and expanding because new industries were forced to locate elsewhere.

As a result of these criticisms, regional policy in the 1990s was made more flexible so that companies in Assisted Areas did not automatically receive financial aid. Instead, they had to bid for funds and show that new jobs would be created. Following a review in 1999, some further changes were made. The areas in Britain that are eligible for assistance are shown in figure 2.22. 'Tier 1' areas are those in which the GDP per capita was less than 75 percent of the EU average (in the years 1994-96). They receive the most help. These areas are also defined as having 'Objective 1' status in terms of eligibility for EU funding (see later in this unit). 'Tier 2' Assisted Areas are those in which the problems are not as severe as in Tier 1 but there is a combination of high unemployment, declining industry or evidence of rural decline. There is also a 'Tier 3' of Assisted Areas. They are areas of relatively high unemployment in which assistance is only available to small and medium size companies.

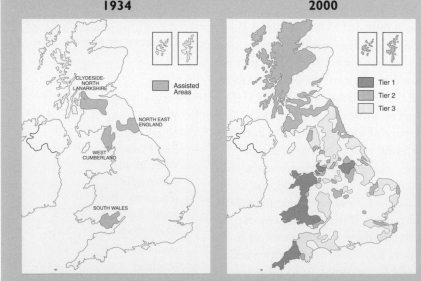

Figure 2.22 1934 Special Areas and Assisted Areas in Britain after 2000

After more than 60 years of regional policy, the areas that needed assistance in the 1930s are still in need of help today. Note that Northern Ireland has special arrangements and is not included in the categories shown. The 'Tier 1' areas which receive most assistance are Cornwall, West Wales, Merseyside and South Yorkshire.

Regional Development Agencies

Local partnerships between private companies and local government grew in the 1990s. By working together it was found that private and public sectors could be effective in attracting investment from major companies and also from the EU. After 1997, the Labour government developed these partnerships into Regional Development Agencies (RDAs) for the English regions. They are the equivalent of Scottish Enterprise and the Welsh Development Agency, the bodies which promote Scottish and Welsh development. The tasks of the RDAs are to:

- promote the region and represent its interests in Whitehall and Brussels
- monitor and report on trends in the regional economy
- develop local and regional economic development strategies
- help in the attraction of inward investment to the region and the UK.

The Welsh Development Agency (WDA) has been particularly successful in attracting foreign investment. By 1998, there were 75,000 employees of foreign owned companies working in South Wales. Traditional Welsh employment in coal and steel has been in decline for many years. However, improved communications with South East England, via the M4 and Severn Bridges, have helped persuade new companies to set up. The additional advantages of a pool of skilled labour - and relatively low wages - have been strong selling points for the Development Agency. A wide range of consumer and electronic goods, ranging from televisions to microchips, are now manufactured in South Wales. Companies such as Sony, Panasonic, Hitachi and Bosch have established large factories along the M4.

In some cases, pre-built factories have been offered to the new companies. In other cases, access roads, power lines and rail links have been provided. Critics of the WDA suggest that it has, on some occasions, 'bribed' companies to set up in South Wales at the expense of other UK regions. The 1997 announcement by LG (a Korean company) that it was to set up a microchip factory in Newport, eventually employing 6,000 workers, followed fierce campaigning by other development corporations. A figure of £200 million was put on the package that the WDA offered LG - equivalent to £30,000 per job created!

Figure 2.23 A new factory site in South Wales

Development Agencies sometimes pre-build factories to encourage new companies to set up in their region.

European Regional Policy

UK regional policy is affected by European Union regional policies. The European Union's Structural Funds are allocated to regions categorised as Objective 1 or Objective 2. Objective 1 status means that a region's average income is less than 75 percent of the EU average. Objective 2 status means that a region is seriously affected by industrial or agricultural decline.

Within the UK, up to the year 2000, Merseyside, the Highlands and Islands of Scotland, and Northern Ireland had Objective One status. Following a review of all EU regional policy, after 2000, Merseyside retained its status and was joined by South Yorkshire, Cornwall, West Wales and the Welsh Valleys. Northern Ireland and the Scottish Highlands lost their status because their per capita GNP had risen (though they were given funding during a 7 year 'phase-out' programme).

Merseyside is one of the poorest UK regions. Between 1981-1995, there was a net loss of 115,000 jobs in Liverpool. This was proportionately more than any other major UK town or city. The Liverpool region has suffered from the loss of traditional port industries such as refining and milling. It is also on the wrong side of Britain for trading links with the EU. The result has been above average unemployment, social deprivation and out-migration. Over a fifty year period (1945-1995), Liverpool's total population declined by 50 percent as people left to find jobs elsewhere.

Applications for European Regional Development Funds or European Social Funds (subdivisions of the EU's Structural Funds), are made in a competitive bidding process. Between 1989 and 1999, the UK received £14 billion of assistance from these funds. On Merseyside, the first funding programme started in 1994 and was planned to last for 6 years. Approximately £640 million was provided by the EU, with a matching sum from the UK government. The overall aim was to create 50,000 new jobs.

Five priority areas were identified for Structural Fund action:
- promoting inward investment
- provision of premises and training for small and medium size local enterprises (SMEs)
- research and development, particularly into new and clean technology
- developing the cultural, media and leisure facilities of Merseyside
- training and career development for local people.

Activity **Merseyside regional assistance**

The following articles appeared in Liverpool newspapers during the late 1990s:

Better communications give jobs boost

Objective 1 cash is helping to fund an exciting new regeneration programme in south Sefton. Eurogateway is an £11 million package of measures designed to upgrade road links between the A5036 and Liverpool Freeport and the docks.

The four year programme will create or safeguard up to 3,000 jobs by developing sites and premises, attracting new businesses, supporting existing companies and by the creation of projects to boost the jobs prospects of local people. Residents will also benefit from measures to cut down levels of pollution and congestion in the area. There will be improvements in public transport and extensive landscaping around the new road.

Exciting plans for Bold Street

A £70 million regeneration package funded by regional development grants will enhance the area's reputation as the city centre's creative quarter. Up to 50 separate schemes will provide commercial and office space, craft and media workshops, private student and low cost housing, and specialist retail outlets.

There will be support and training packages to help local small businesses. The multi-cultural nature of the area will be reflected in particular training schemes to develop the economic prospects of the local Chinese and black communities.

Investment success for Knowsley with Objective 1 support

Knowsley, an 'overspill' town just outside Liverpool, is setting the pace as a popular location for inward investment. In less than 12 months the borough has seen over 25 investments from new and existing companies. These investments have created or safeguarded 1,800 jobs.

European money is being used to improve infrastructure and the environment in local industrial and business parks. Landscaping, new roads and better access have attracted the new investors. Direct Line is to create its first purpose built Accident Management Centre on Knowsley Industrial Park at a cost of £2 million. Over 200 new jobs will be created. A training company, Telematics Centre - a joint venture with John Moores University - will help companies keep pace with technological changes in employee training.

▲ **Figure 2.24 Liverpool Pierhead**
Regional assistance is providing new jobs and an improved environment in Liverpool.

Questions

1 Describe the regional development policies that are being funded on Merseyside.
2 Explain why the UK government and the EU spend money on regional development.

New Towns

During the twentieth century, New Towns have played an important part in UK regional policy. The New Town concept was heavily influenced by the idea of the 'garden city' put forward at the end of the nineteenth century by Ebenezer Howard. Appalled by urban congestion and squalor in Victorian Britain, Howard proposed that new garden cities should be built. These would give people a good quality environment as well as employment, leisure and recreational opportunities. The new settlements would balance the attractions of town and country. Letchworth (1903) and Welwyn Garden City (1920) were early examples.

The New Towns Act was passed in 1946 as part of a programme of social reconstruction following the Second World War. Fourteen New Towns were designated by 1950, one more (Cumbernauld) in the 1950s, and then a further fifteen in the 1960s. Now there are 32 New Towns in the UK. Each was set up with its own Development Corporation which had the power to cut through red tape and 'fast track' the planning process.

The UK New Towns were intended to have a regional, as well as an urban role. They were part of a regional plan, designed to promote new industries, linked eventually by the motorway network. Their aims included:

- the provision of good quality residential, educational and recreational facilities in a planned, clean environment
- the relief of congestion and squalor in inner city areas (from which the New Towns received population)

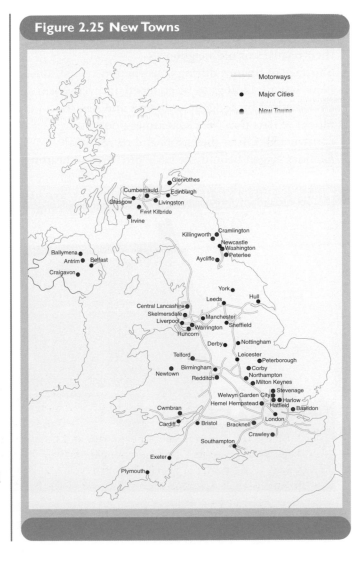

Figure 2.25 New Towns

- the creation of new employment by encouraging investment in new industries
- better access for motor vehicles with wide carriageways linking neighbourhoods and industrial estates.

Towns like Basingstoke in the South East, Washington in the North East, Skelmersdale in the North West and Cumbernauld in Central Scotland became the centres of new populations and employment. They drew residents mainly, in these cases, from their local cities of London, Newcastle, Liverpool and Glasgow.

Despite the good intentions of planners and politicians, there have been many criticisms of New Towns:

- They are often said to have a soulless quality, lacking in character. 'New Town Blues' (in France, 'Sarcellitis', after Sarcelles just outside Paris) is a term used to describe the sense of isolation felt by some residents. In many of the old urban areas there had been a sense of community in which families and neighbours helped each other. This was often lacking in the new surroundings because people no longer lived near their relatives or old neighbours.
- Shortage of finance during construction caused some New Town buildings to be cramped and very basic - characterised by concrete walkways and low rise blocks of flats that were sometimes poorly constructed. Often the leisure and recreational facilities lagged behind the basic provision of housing.

- There was insufficient consideration given to the social aspects of moving mainly low income urban dwellers to new surroundings. Many of these people could not afford cars yet the New Towns were planned for the benefit of private road users. There is now a need for improved public transport provision within them.
- In employment terms, the New Towns were generally a success, but some people continued to work in the old city, adding time and costs of commuting to their budget.
- The expansion of New Towns contributed to the decline of the old urban areas. They drew employment from the inner cities to the new locations and, arguably, worsened the plight of those urban areas that they were originally designed to help.

On the positive side, New Towns did help to reduce urban sprawl by providing discrete urban centres away from the old cities. Also, in general, the new housing is of better quality than that left behind. Now that there is a second and third generation of New Town dwellers, social cohesion and community spirit has improved. New social relationships have developed that do not rely on returning to the old urban neighbourhoods.

Urban Development Corporations

For much of the twentieth century, the regional problem in Britain was seen as a North-South divide. Average incomes, economic growth, life expectancy and educational attainment were all higher, on average, in the South compared with the North. However, from the 1980s onwards, it became clear that the situation was not so clear cut. Pockets of poverty and unemployment in inner London were as high as anywhere in the North. Likewise, parts of the North, in Cheshire, Cumbria and North Yorkshire, had lower unemployment and higher living standards than many places in the South. It was realised that, to some extent, the 'regional problem' had become an 'urban' problem. Deprivation, poverty and low living standards were concentrated in the inner cities of London, Bristol and Southampton just as much as in Newcastle, Glasgow and Liverpool.

In an attempt to tackle the urban problem, Development Corporations were

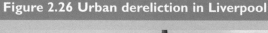

Figure 2.26 Urban dereliction in Liverpool

Many inner city areas in Britain are run down, with derelict land and empty housing.

established in inner cities after 1979. They were based on the model of the New Town Development Corporations and had wide powers to raise finance and oversee development. An early example was the London Docklands Development Corporation which transformed parts of London's East End and encouraged the building of Canary Wharf. Similarly, the Merseyside Development Corporation redeveloped Liverpool's previously derelict south docks, especially the Albert Dock area which is now a major tourist attraction.

Sometimes there was opposition to the new bodies. In London, for example, the Joint Dockland Action Group opposed the 'gentrification' and 'yuppificiation' of the East End. They claimed that when housing was improved, it became too expensive for locals to buy and 'yuppies' (young, urban professionals) moved in. Development Corporations

were also seen as undemocratic, steamrollering their projects through - against the wishes of long established residents. Locals in Toxteth in Liverpool, or the Isle of Dogs in London argued that money was being put into prestige projects which provided employment for outsiders rather than local people. They argued that resources were being diverted away from their essential housing, health and education needs towards these projects.

However, the Development Corporations did achieve improvements in the environment and infrastructure of urban areas. They also changed the image of areas such as Merseyside for the better. But their job creation record was less good, and they had little lasting impact for the worst-off people in the cities. As a result, in the late 1990s the Urban Development Corporations were closed down.

Activity Merseyside Development Corporation

▲ **Figure 2.27 Liverpool redevelopment**
Some of the old dockside warehouses have been converted to high quality apartments.

The Merseyside Development Corporation (MDC) was established in 1981 as one of 12 Urban Development Corporations (UDCs). Its task was to regenerate the largely run-down, southern dockside area in Liverpool. Along with all the other UDCs, it was abolished in 1998.

Although the MDC was criticised in its early years as being outside the control of the democratically elected local councillors, it had some notable achievements. The 1984 International Garden Festival in Liverpool involved one of Europe's biggest ever land reclamation schemes. Previously the land had been derelict. Wharves, warehouses and processing plants had been largely abandoned when the old port industries declined. The Albert Dock tourist development, where the northern Tate Gallery is housed, involved the renovation of Britain's largest single group of Grade I listed buildings (ie, buildings of the highest architectural merit).

During its existence the MDC was responsible for:

• 365 hectares of derelict land reclamation
• 3,600 new housing units
• 555,000 square metres of new commercial floor space
• 84 km new roads
• 17,000 new jobs
• £461m of new private investment
• £385m of government investment.

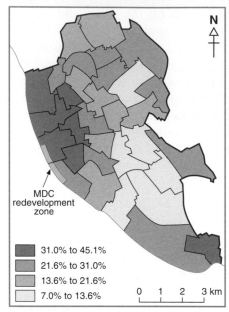

MDC
redevelopment
zone

31.0% to 45.1%
21.6% to 31.0%
13.6% to 21.6%
7.0% to 13.6%

0   1   2   3 km

**Figure 2.28 Liverpool
unemployment by ward, 1991**

However, critics of the MDC point out that many of the new jobs
are in the service sector, mainly in tourism, and many are part-time.
Compared to the number of unemployed in the Liverpool travel-
to-work area (41,000 in June 1998), not enough jobs were created.
Also the ratio of private capital to public investment on Merseyside
was low compared with other UDCs (for example, the London
Docklands Development Corporation attracted £6,300m of private
finance with a public outlay of £1,900m).

Questions

1 To what extent can the MDC be judged a success or a
   failure?
2 With reference to Liverpool, outline the case for and
   against regional development policies that focus on
   inner city areas.

unit summary

1 Some theories are optimistic about development, believing that the process follows a natural
   progression. Benefits can 'spread' or 'trickle down' from development 'growth poles' or 'leading
   sectors' of industry.
2 Other theories are more pessimistic, believing that richer areas prosper by drawing in people and
   resources from poorer areas, and by exploiting the less well off.
3 The Newly Industrialising Countries have successfully developed, mainly by concentrating on
   manufacturing exports.
4 There are different types of aid, ranging from famine relief to long term investment in
   infrastructure.
5 At the regional level in the UK, a range of policies have been used by different governments to
   assist regions and urban areas. It is generally accepted that some form of regional policy is
   necessary to reduce inequalities in development.

key terms

Aid - a transfer of resources, from richer to
poorer countries, on terms which are
'concessional' (ie, as a gift or a loan below
commercial interest rates).
Assisted Areas - areas within the UK which are
eligible for regional funding.

Backwash - the opposite of 'trickle down',
resources flow from the periphery to the core -
so widening the gap between regions.
Bilateral aid - aid provided directly from one
country to another country.

Dependency - the idea that some countries are dependent on others due to unequal relations between them - the state of dependency prevents development from taking place.

Development Corporations - organisations established in the UK to build and run New Towns from 1946, and were used in inner cities from the 1980s.

Emerging markets - countries which are successfully industrialising and developing; the term is increasingly used instead of 'newly industrialising countries'.

EU Structural Policy - policies which direct funds to less well off regions in the European Union.

Growth Poles - areas to which resources are channelled, in the belief that development will take place there, with benefits spreading to surrounding areas.

Industrialisation - the growth and development of manufacturing industry.

Leading sector - a manufacturing industry such as textiles or electronics that leads the development of the rest of the economy.

Multilateral aid - aid that is channelled via organisations such as the World Bank or United Nations.

Multiplier - the degree to which an investment leads to a rise in regional or national income; the term is often used in a more general sense to describe the 'knock-on' effect of new business enterprise on the surrounding economy.

Official aid (or Official Development Assistance, ODA) - aid that is provided directly or indirectly from governments.

Regional Development Agencies (RDA) - organisations which co-ordinate regional development in England.

Regional Policy - government action to assist and promote declining regions.

Take-off - this is when a steady, sustainable rate of economic growth is achieved.

Trickle down / spread effects - the positive impact of growth that 'trickles down' from the core to the periphery.

Voluntary aid - aid from charities and other bodies (eg, Non-Governmental Organisations, NGOs).

Unit 2.3 Health and welfare

key questions

1 What is the world pattern of health and welfare?
2 What is the impact of disease and ill-health?
3 How can health and welfare be improved?

1. What is the world pattern of health and welfare?

Health and welfare are fundamental human concerns. The charter of the United Nations states that people 'have a right to lead long and fulfilling lives'. However, the reality for many people in low income countries is that their lives are overshadowed by the threat of early death. Poor diet, disease and unhealthy living conditions prevent them from having good quality lives.

Despite the undoubted progress of medical science in preventing and curing disease, in many countries infant mortality rates are high and life expectancy is low. Often health and welfare systems are either non-existent or inadequate. Some diseases such as tuberculosis (TB), which were once thought to be under control, are making a comeback. The poor and the homeless are especially vulnerable, even in high income countries.

There is a close relationship between income and health. The populations of high income countries are generally healthier than those in Third World countries. Ill-health causes high death rates and, in particular, high infant mortality rates. The highest rates of infant mortality are found in the countries of sub-Sahara Africa (see figure 2.29). (The infant mortality rate is defined as the number of deaths of children under one year old per 1,000 live births.) In 1995, the infant mortality rate was 5.8 for Australia and 6.4 for the UK. It was slightly higher in the US, at 8.5, but still low in comparison with the figures for Eastern Europe where, for instance in Romania the rate was 23.4. This figure may seem high but, in the Third World, rates are much higher. For instance, India had a rate of 68 deaths per 1,000 live births, Uganda's rate was 98 and Sierra Leone's was 179.

Countries with high infant mortality rates also have low life expectancies. For example, the average life expectancy in Sierra Leone in 1995 was 40, in Uganda it was 42 and in India it was 67. In Eastern Europe, the figure was 70 for Romania. By comparison, in a high income country such as Australia, the life expectancy was 77.

Since the collapse of communism and the break-up of the former Soviet Union, the public health system in some of the newly formed countries has suffered from disorganisation and a lack of resources. As a result, life expectancy has fallen. In Russia, for example, average life expectancy fell from 69 to 65 between 1992 and 1996.

The world pattern of health and welfare has been influenced by the spread of disease. AIDS, for example, probably originated in the tropical rain forest of Africa. Its rapid spread is, at least in part, due to sexual transmission and the movement of infected people. Migration, business travel and tourism by long distant jet have caused the disease to make a global impact. (See unit 1.1 for more details on AIDS and its effect on death rates.)

However, the spread of disease between countries is not new. When Europeans started to colonise other parts of the world, they carried with them diseases to which they were largely immune. These diseases spread among the indigenous peoples and wiped out hundreds of thousands who had not built up natural immunity. The Spanish carried smallpox and influenza, for example, to South America. Smallpox alone is estimated to have killed one-third of the native people between 1518-1531. Measles is estimated to have killed more than 20 percent of the population after it was introduced to Fiji and Samoa in the 1870s. The sexually transmitted disease syphilis was introduced by Captain Cook's crew into Hawaii in 1778. Along with smallpox and influenza, it killed 90 percent of the local population.

Occasionally, **pandemics** (ie, world-wide epidemics) occur. These are usually caused by new strains of a disease to which there is no widespread immunity. In the years following World War One, an estimated 20 million people died of Spanish flu. Its impact was most severe on young people who sometimes died only a short time after the first symptoms appeared. The large scale movement of troops around the world was one of the factors that caused the rapid spread of the disease.

The diseases of poverty

The diseases of poverty are mainly infectious diseases. These spread by transmission between infected people or other living organisms. Their impact is greatest in low income countries. Some diseases, such as cholera, are spread by drinking contaminated water whilst others, such as malaria, are spread by parasites.

There are a number of factors that explain why low income countries are most affected. Poor people are often vulnerable to disease because they are more likely to be malnourished and living in overcrowded, unhealthy conditions. The Food and Agricultural Organisation (FAO) of the United Nations has estimated that up to 40 percent of people in sub-Sahara Africa are undernourished. At the global level, there are 850 million people whose food needs are not fully met (see unit 2.1). These people find it much harder to resist disease than people who are well fed.

In low income countries, there is the additional problem of governments having fewer resources than high income countries to spend on public health and medical provision. Because there are fewer doctors and medical facilities, there is less chance that ill people will be cured. In Australia in 1995, there was 1 doctor per 445 inhabitants, in the UK there

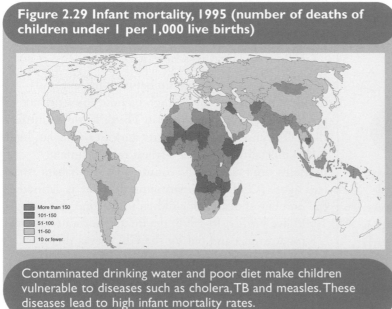

Figure 2.29 Infant mortality, 1995 (number of deaths of children under 1 per 1,000 live births)

More than 150
101-150
51-100
11-50
10 or fewer

Contaminated drinking water and poor diet make children vulnerable to diseases such as cholera, TB and measles. These diseases lead to high infant mortality rates.

was 1 per 667 but, in India, there was just 1 per 2,140 and in Sierra Leone the figure was 1 per 10,830. Similarly, for hospital beds, in the UK there were 5.4 beds per 1,000 people but in India there were only 0.8 beds per 1,000 people.

In the past, the population of Western Europe suffered from the health problems that exist in low income countries at the present time. For instance, in France before 1750, infant mortality was 200 deaths per 1,000 births, a higher rate than in Third World countries today. Diseases such as scarlet fever, influenza, smallpox and pneumonia were often fatal. Typhoid and cholera were especially dangerous in the cities where polluted drinking water, overcrowding and lack of sanitation were largely to blame. Government action to build sewers, provide clean water, and reduce overcrowding all helped to reduce the spread of infectious diseases. In the 1860s local authorities in Britain started to treat all sewage before it was discharged into rivers. As a result, death rates fell. The last major outbreak of cholera in London was in 1866.

In many Third World countries, however, only limited progress has been made in these areas of public health. A shortage of money and resources means that the diseases common in Europe over a hundred years ago are still major causes of death in poor countries. In order to improve health care, the World Health Organisation (WHO) was established in 1948. It has had some notable successes - particularly with mass vaccination campaigns. Smallpox (which killed 2 million per year as recently as 1966) was completely eradicated by the 1970s. But, in many Third World countries, particularly in large cities and in remote rural areas, health programmes still miss many people. For example, programmes to vaccinate against polio, diphtheria and measles have proved difficult and expensive to organise and the benefits are sometimes not made clear to all people - especially where literacy rates are low.

Diseases such as sleeping sickness, yellow fever, dengue fever and malaria are common in the tropics. Regions with hot, humid climates appear to provide the most favourable conditions for the growth and spread of deadly parasites and viruses, and many of the countries with the lowest average incomes are located in the tropics. So, although there is no direct causal link between low incomes and tropical diseases, it is people

Figure 2.30 Tropical rain forest in central Africa

Hot and humid conditions encourage the growth and spread of parasites and disease.

who live in tropical, low income countries that are the most vulnerable.

The diseases of affluence

The diseases of affluence are most common in high income countries. They include cancer, strokes and heart attacks (cardiovascular diseases), asthma and diabetes. These are non-infectious diseases and are caused, to some extent, by unhealthy diet, an inactive lifestyle and by atmospheric pollution.

Cancer kills up to one-third of people in wealthier countries. This is a much higher rate than in low income countries. Some environments and lifestyles encourage the development of particular cancers. Cigarette smoking is dangerous, for example. So are vehicle emissions from diesel engines. Eating too much red meat is also thought to increase risk.

However, the link between cancer and income is not straightforward. There might be other explanations for the higher rate in affluent societies. For instance, people in Western countries live longer and are less likely to die of infectious diseases, so they die of different things, and cancer is one of these. Also, because diagnosis is better, a death recorded as 'cancer' in the UK might be recorded as 'natural causes' in a Third World country.

Some medical conditions are on the increase in Western countries. Asthma, for example, used to affect a relatively small number of people, and appeared to run in families. But, by the mid-1990s, 3.5 million people in the UK had the condition. One causal factor might be poor air quality caused by vehicle and power station emissions. The droppings of microscopic dust mites are

Figure 2.31 Part of a typical diet for many people in Western countries

Obesity, poor diet and lack of exercise all help contribute to the diseases of affluence

which means there is more time for the condition to develop.

Studies show that psychological disorders such as depression are more common in high income than in low income countries. This might be stress related. However, there is little agreement on whether this is the case. Also, there is a school of thought that questions the validity of the data. For instance, is depression really more common in the West or is it simply diagnosed more? Do people in some Third World countries just 'get on with it' - possibly because there is more social stigma attached to mental illness?

The pattern of psychological disorder, like other forms of ill-health, can be analysed at a regional or local scale as well as at a national level. For example, geographical studies have shown that there are high rates of schizophrenia in inner cities. Schizophrenia has many symptoms - the most common being delusions (ie, persistent ideas which are clearly untrue but are experienced as true). It is not certain whether inner city conditions cause schizophrenia, or whether schizophrenics choose to live in inner cities. The latter might be the case because people with schizophrenia find it hard to hold a regular job and therefore live in places where there is low cost housing. On the other hand, low incomes, low status, and poor housing might be conditions that make the development of schizophrenia more likely. This problem of interpretation raises an issue that is known as the 'ecological fallacy'. Simply because something happens or occurs in a particular place does not mean that the location is the cause. Other, unrelated factors might be the actual reason.

also thought to be a cause of asthma. It seems that modern comforts such as fitted carpets, heavy curtains and central heating are responsible for an increase in the number of dust mites.

Diabetes is also increasing. In the UK, a 1997 report by the British Diabetic Association estimated that the number of cases would increase by 1.5 million within ten years. Globally, the number of people with diabetes was estimated as 123 million in 1995, and this will be 220 million by 2010, according to the report. The rise is attributed to such factors as unhealthy diets, less physical exercise, obesity, and a longer life expectancy

Activity) Lung cancer in the UK

The pattern of ill-health varies between countries, regions and localities. By mapping the incidence of ill-health, it is sometimes possible to analyse the causes. In the UK, lung cancer is the most common cancer for males and the second most common for females.

▼ Figure 2.32 Smoking and cancer

	Death rates from lung cancer (per 10,000 population) 1996		Heavy cigarette smoking (percentage of total population) 1996	
	Males	Females	Males	Females
England	7.7	4.2	11	7
Wales	7.4	3.9	11	8
Scotland	10.3	6.4	16	12
Northern Ireland	8.1	4.0	15	10

Note: *Heavy smoking is defined as smoking 20 cigarettes or more per day.*

Questions

1 Describe the relationship between heavy cigarette smoking and deaths from lung cancer in different parts of the UK.
2 What additional information would be useful in analysing the pattern of lung cancer within the UK?

Models of disease

It has been suggested that an epidemiological transition occurs when countries become more developed. (Epidemiology is the study of disease.) The idea is that, as countries increase in prosperity, there is a change in the types of disease suffered by their populations.

As already outlined in this unit, in low income countries, many infectious diseases such as cholera and typhoid are transmitted through dirty drinking water. Poor diet weakens people and makes them more vulnerable to illness. But, if development occurs, governments have more money to spend on sewerage systems and the provision of clean water. They can also afford to build hospitals and clinics, and employ more health care workers. When personal incomes rise, people can afford better diets and better living conditions. As a result, the diseases of poverty gradually decline. They are replaced by the

diseases of affluence such as strokes and cancer. These are known as 'chronic' (ie, long lasting) diseases. With an increase in life expectancy, the problems of old age also become more important. For example, forms of senile dementia such as Alzheimer's Disease impair mental and physical abilities, and rheumatism and arthritis impair mobility.

Figure 2.33 Health models

THIRD WORLD: INFECTIOUS DISEASE MODEL

Mainly agrarian society, desire for large families

High fertility

Society predominantly young

Unsanitary water supplies and malnutrition of preschool children contribute to:
1. Infestations (parasites)
2. Infections

High mortality of preschool children

FIRST WORLD: CHRONIC DISEASE MODEL

Mainly industrial society, desire for small families

low fertility

Society increasingly elderly

Life styles
1. Leisure time
2. Affluence
3. Lack of exercise
4. Diet high in animal fats and protein

Chronic diseases
1. Coronary heart disease
2. Cancer
3. Stroke
4. Senile dementia
5. Diabetes

Two models of First World and Third World health are shown in figure 2.33. Although simplifications, they are an attempt to describe and explain health differences. The Third World model focuses on infectious disease, whereas the First World model is concerned with chronic disease. Note that the age structure of the populations is different and this contributes to the contrasting patterns.

The health models are useful in highlighting the different causes and effects of disease in high and low income countries. However, they do not show that diseases sometimes spread between countries - an increasing problem in a world with global linkages. Another disadvantage of the models is that they ignore differences within countries. It is the case, in First and Third World countries, that the two models might exist side by side. For example, there might be an urban/rural divide or an inner city/outer city divide in the types of illness that occur.

Activity — **UK trails Mexico in world health study**

The UK is one of the unhealthiest places to live in Western Europe and has also fallen behind Mexico and Israel, according to a new analysis.

Bad diet and a high number of deaths from cancer and circulatory diseases helped to put the UK 15th in a survey of 25 countries, despite having respectable figures for average life expectancy. People born in the UK today are expected to live about eight years longer than those born in 1950.

The new study uses 12 indicators of public health to judge each nation's physical wellbeing (ie, the quality of health that people enjoy during their lives), whereas other surveys in the past have relied solely upon estimates of life expectancy. The Economist Intelligence Unit examined figures published by international organisations to compare how nations performed in crucial health factors. These included immunisation rates, maternal mortality, HIV, infant mortality, and rates of cancer, heart disease and respiratory disease per head of population, as well as life expectancy.

The poor showing for the UK was partly blamed on diet because of the amount of fatty, processed foods eaten by so many people. Health care specialists welcomed the report. One commented: 'The idea was to get away from the life expectancy figure in order to give a truer picture. Under the old system of comparision, the figure really only showed the state of health which existed in the past. This gives a true snapshot of the state of health at present because it includes the current state of peoples health'.

An important conclusion from the study must be that a nation's health is only partly determined by the amount spent on health care. Clearly, some systems of health care give better value for money than others. Diet, lifestyle and living conditions are also crucially important. The figures show that the United States is 13th in the league table, even though its per capita spending on health care is almost the highest in the world. The study blames this on the increasing numbers in America who do not have any medical insurance and who cannot afford to pay for private medical care. The number of uninsured is estimated to be 45 million, roughly 16 per cent of the population.

Adapted from The Times, 14th April 1997

Rank	Country	Life expectancy (1995)	Public spending on health care (1995, % GDP)	Rank	Country	Life expectancy (1995)	Public spending on health care (1995, % GDP)
1	Sweden	79	6.0	14	United Kingdom	77	5.8
2	Israel	77	2.1	15	Poland	70	4.8
3	Netherlands	78	6.7	16	South Korea	72	1.8
4	Canada	78	6.8	17	Singapore	76	1.3
5	Japan	80	5.7	18	Malaysia	71	1.4
6	Switzerland	78	7.2	19	China	69	2.1
7	Australia	77	6.0	20	Hungary	70	6.8
8	Spain	77	6.0	21	Argentina	73	4.3
9	France	78	8.0	22	Turkey	67	2.7
10	Italy	78	5.4	23	Russia	65	4.1
11	Germany	76	8.2	24	Brazil	67	2.7
12	Mexico	72	2.8	25	India	62	0.7
13	United States	77	6.6				

▲ **Figure 2.34 Rank order of countries surveyed, in order of healthiest to unhealthiest**

Questions

1 Describe the distribution of the most and least healthy countries surveyed. Which parts of the world appear to have been neglected in the survey?
2 Why does life expectancy on its own not give a complete picture of a nation's health?
3 Outline the main factors that affect the global pattern of health.

2. What is the impact of disease and ill-health?

Disease and ill-health sap the energy of the people who are affected. It weakens both families and the wider community. At a personal level, it can cause distress and poverty, especially if the affected person can no longer work. At a national level it can slow economic growth by causing lost output and by reducing the energy and enterprise of the working population. The examples of malaria and sleeping sickness, outlined below, show the impact of two major diseases on Third World countries. The example of drug and alcohol abuse illustrates how unhealthy lifestyles can have an impact in high income countries.

Malaria

Malaria was relatively common in England in Elizabethan times, particularly in low lying, marshy areas. For a long time it was thought to be caused by 'bad air' - hence its name. The traditional treatment for malaria in South America, and later Europe, was to make a medicine from the bark of the cinchona tree, found in Peru. The drug quinine was eventually developed from this bark.

In the 1880s, thousands of workers building the Panama Canal died of malaria. This gave an impetus to research on the causes of the disease. It was found that malaria is caused by a parasite that lives in the stomach of the female Anophelese species of mosquito. When the mosquito bites, the parasite spreads into the victim's blood stream.

Early solutions involved disease prevention. Public health officials began to drain swamps and marshes where the mosquitoes bred. Then a powerful pesticide which killed mosquitoes, DDT, was discovered in the 1930s. Once sprayed, it remained active on the land for

Figure 2.35 The world distribution of malaria

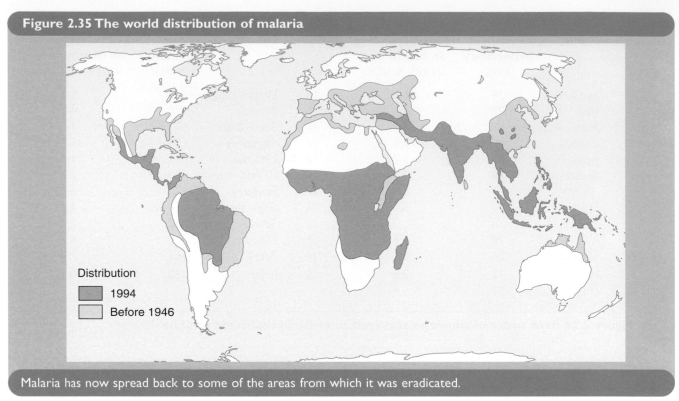

Distribution
- 1994
- Before 1946

Malaria has now spread back to some of the areas from which it was eradicated.

weeks which meant that frequent re-spraying was unnecessary. In 1945 there were 300 million cases of malaria globally, but with DDT, it was hoped by the World Health Organisation that malaria could be completely eradicated by 1963.

Unfortunately, insects adapt and reproduce quickly and some mosquitoes became resistant to DDT. Also, it was found, the pesticide had entered the food chain. High concentrations were found in birds and other creatures which eat insects. The effect was to cause a decline in their populations. As a result, DDT was banned and replaced by other pesticides that damaged the environment less - but were not as effective. The parasite itself became resistant to drugs such as quinine or chloroquine.

Malaria cases dipped in the late 1950s but then rose again. In Sri Lanka, for example, cases (not deaths) were 1 million in 1955, 80,000 in 1964 and 500,000 in 1969. Likewise, in India, cases were reduced to only 100,000 in 1961, but rose again to 2.5 million by 1974. There were three times as many cases of malaria in the early 1990s as in the early 1960s. By 1997, world wide, it was estimated that four children were dying of the disease every minute. Now, as many as 500 million people become ill with malaria each year, and up to 2 million die. Ninety percent of all deaths are in sub-Sahara Africa. For those who are infected but do not die, they become

weak and find activity difficult. They also lose resistance to other diseases. In the worst affected regions, economic development has either slowed or stopped altogether.

Malaria not only poses a risk to local populations. Each year, an estimated 20 million Western tourists visit affected areas. This number is likely to rise as the disease spreads back to areas such as the Mediterranean basin from where it was once eradicated.

Sleeping sickness

Sleeping sickness is a disease that is also widespread in sub-Sahara Africa. It is caused by a parasite which is carried by tsetse flies. There are two types of sleeping sickness. There is the less severe Gambian or West African type and the more severe East and Southern African type. The latter is especially lethal, and infects horses, cattle and dogs, as well as humans. It causes a wide range of symptoms and, if it reaches the brain, it brings on an overwhelming urge to sleep, usually leading to death. Between 1896 and 1906 it killed over 250,000 people around Lake Victoria, and many more in the Congo basin. Today, outbreaks are less dramatic. But along with malaria, bilharzia and tuberculosis it is still one of Central Africa's main causes of death and a major factor in that region's low level of economic development.

Drug and alcohol abuse

In Western societies, drug and alcohol abuse create major health and social problems. Alcohol abuse is the cause of many road accidents in the UK. Approximately 1 in 20 drivers involved in a traffic accident in which there is a personal injury fail the breath test. Excessive drinking of alcohol is also blamed for many acts of public and domestic violence. It is also a factor in causing liver damage.

Tobacco contains nicotine, an extremely addictive drug. Although smoking is not generally classified as a form of drug abuse, it causes emphysema, lung cancer and heart conditions such as angina. In 1995, the Health Education Authority estimated that 90 percent of lung cancer deaths among men, in the UK, and 78 percent among women were attributable to smoking.

It is not always obvious why some drugs are legal and some are illegal. In the nineteenth century, opium and cannabis, both now illegal, were sold over the counter as health cures. Cocaine was originally one of the ingredients of Coca-Cola but was withdrawn when the drug became illegal, even though the name was retained. The main reason for criminalisation (ie, drugs becoming illegal) is that authorities believe that users are a danger to themselves. There is a belief that illegal drug use leads to addiction. This damages a person's health, and creates wider social costs, for example in higher NHS bills.

Illegal drug use has a geographical dimension. Certain drugs are closely linked with particular groups of people in particular locations. For instance, some UK council housing estates have high rates of heroin use. The use of ecstasy and amphetamines has been associated with inner city night clubs. Also, the production and transport of drugs is associated with certain locations. It is one of the ironies of economic development that many illegal drugs come from the Third World, for example Colombia, Afghanistan and Burma, but are sold in the First World. If the trade was legal, and all the proceeds were returned to the producers, there would be a massive shift in resources and income from rich to poor countries - possibly greater than the current total sum given in official aid.

3. How can health and welfare be improved?

Health and welfare are complex issues. There is no single method by which they can be improved. In Third World countries, public health spending on clean drinking water and sewerage systems is clearly important. Improving people's diet is also vital, both in terms of quantity and quality. Vaccination campaigns against infectious diseases can work - as the eradication of smallpox shows. For these policies to be effective, governments and individuals need money and resources. This requires either that funds are transferred from other areas (such as military spending) or that new wealth is created through economic growth.

In high income countries, disease prevention takes different forms. For example, public awareness campaigns on diet and lifestyle, the reduction of air pollution, higher taxes on cigarettes and alcohol, and anti-drug programmes all play a part.

Once people become ill, the level of medical care becomes the key factor. The number and quality of nurses, doctors and hospitals are important. So is the availability of effective medical drugs to treat people. The funding of medical care is a major issue in all countries. There is a catch-22 situation in that better care leads to longer life expectancy which, in turn, leads to higher demand for medical services. Since 1970, spending on health care (as a percentage of GDP) has almost doubled in countries such as the USA, France and the UK. Nevertheless, in these countries there are still many people who are ill or who have medical conditions that are not being treated. Advances in medicine, new treatments and new drugs are often very expensive and they create an ever rising demand for treatment. For example, when a new drug such as Viagra is developed, there is often a strong demand. Publicly funded health care systems then have to choose whether to raise their overall spending or ration the use of the new drug - or limit the use of other treatments to finance the new treatment.

The National Health Service in the UK is a state controlled system of medical care that is funded out of taxation. Other countries, such as the USA, have largely private systems that are funded by insurance. The advantage of the NHS is that it is free at the point of treatment and therefore available to all. But, because it is funded by taxes, there is always a political incentive to limit spending. A system of private insurance generally provides a high level of health spending but is limited to those who can afford to pay the insurance premiums. This excludes those people who are on low pay, or who are unemployed, chronically sick or elderly.

Activity | Healthy Cities - Liverpool and Delhi compared

The World Health Organisation (WHO) started promoting the Healthy Cities Movement in 1987. A 'healthy city' is defined as one that is designed, built and managed to contribute to the health and well-being of all its inhabitants. By the late 1990s, a network of cities around the world had joined the Healthy Cities Movement. These include Liverpool, and Delhi in northern India. The two cities share some common problems but also have major differences.

Both cities suffer from the 'normal' urban problems of traffic congestion and air pollution. Liverpool has a relatively low average income and high unemployment compared with the rest of the UK, and its population is in decline. Nevertheless, its population has a far higher material standard of living than most people living in Delhi. For instance, most households in Liverpool own consumer goods such as video recorders and freezers. The majority of households in Delhi do not own these items.

Figure 2.36 Delhi ▲

Large numbers of people in Delhi are homeless. They live on the pavement or, as in this case, in cement pipes.

Delhi is expanding rapidly with an estimated 1.5 million slum dwellers. This is three times bigger than the total number of people who live in Liverpool. In Delhi's slums, literacy rates are low and malnutrition is common. There is very high unemployment, poor shanty housing and, in most areas, there is no sewerage system. In 1988 there was an outbreak of cholera. However, the city has a wealthy elite and a growing middle income group who enjoy a Western standard of living.

Liverpool

Liverpool was one of the first cities to participate in the Healthy Cities Movement. The local government and other agencies set up a task force to develop a City Health Plan which was launched for consultation in 1995.

CITY HEALTH PLAN FOR LIVERPOOL

Strategy 1 - Housing for Health
To provide dry, warm, appropriate and secure accommodation within a well-equipped, safe and attractive environment.

Strategy 2 - Poverty and Unemployment
To get people into employment and ensure that individuals and families receive the benefits to which they are entitled.

Strategy 3 - Improving the Environment
To create a better environment with clean and pleasant surroundings.

Strategy 4 - The Heart of Liverpool
To develop and implement plans which will help ensure 'heart health' for all people; to prevent and treat coronary heart disease; to tackle differences caused by social class, geographical area, race, culture and gender.

Strategy 5 - Cancer
To develop public awareness of cancer risks and to plan policies of prevention, treatment, care and rehabilitation.

Strategy 6 - Accidents
To reduce ill-health, disability and death caused by accidents by creating safer environments where risk of accidents is reduced and the effects are minimised.

Strategy 7 - Sexual Health
To work towards sexual health for all people in Liverpool from prevention of ill-health through to treatment and care.

Strategy 8 - Mental Health
To reduce the level of mental distress which is a leading cause of illness and disability; to improve the health and 'social functioning' of mentally ill people.

Strategy 9 - Substance Misuse (including Alcohol)
To provide information and support in the field of drug and alcohol misuse.

Strategy 10 - Action for Children and Young People
To improve the 'life chances' of our children and adolescents, particularly by raising educational standards.

Questions

1 Suggest which of Liverpool's Health Plan strategies are specifically targeted at the diseases of poverty and which are targeted at the diseases of affluence.
2 How might a City Health Plan in a Third World city, for example Delhi, differ from that in Liverpool?

unit summary

1 Infectious diseases (eg, cholera), are associated with poverty, and are most common in Third World countries.
2 Chronic diseases (eg, cancer), are associated with affluence, and are most common in First World countries.
3 An effect of globalisation is that diseases can be rapidly transmitted.
4 Disease affects all countries, both rich and poor; the effect is felt at the personal level and also at the wider community level in terms of low productivity and lost production.
5 The improvement of health and welfare requires a wide range of policies; in the Third World, countries need to improve public health and nutrition; in the First World, the need is to alter people's diet and lifestyle.

key terms

Diseases of affluence - diseases that are mostly associated with high income countries, for example cancer and heart disease.
Diseases of poverty - diseases that are mostly associated with low income countries, for example cholera and malaria.

Epidemiological transition - the idea that the types of disease change as countries develop from low to high income.

Unit 2.4 Globalisation

key questions

1 What is globalisation?
2 What are the roots of globalisation?
3 What are the effects of globalisation?

1. What is globalisation?

Globalisation can be defined as a process in which

national economies are becoming more and more integrated into a single **global economy**. Actions and decisions taken in one part of the world have knock-on effects in other parts. Increasingly, the largest companies design, produce and market goods on a global rather than on a national scale.

The motor vehicle industry is an example of how globalisation affects particular markets (see figure 2.37). People in the UK have a huge range of choice in terms of which car to purchase. A consumer might choose a

Figure 2.37 The 'UK' car industry

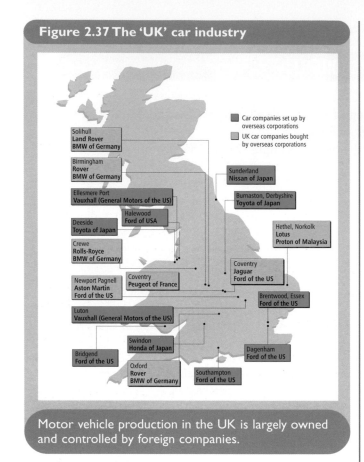

Car companies set up by overseas corporations

UK car companies bought by overseas corporations

Solihull
Land Rover
BMW of Germany

Birmingham
Rover
BMW of Germany

Ellesmere Port
Vauxhall (General Motors of the US)

Halewood
Ford of USA

Deeside
Toyota of Japan

Crewe
Rolls-Royce
BMW of Germany

Newport Pagnell
Aston Martin
Ford of the US

Coventry
Peugeot of France

Luton
Vauxhall (General Motors of the US)

Bridgend
Ford of the US

Swindon
Honda of Japan

Oxford
Rover
BMW of Germany

Sunderland
Nissan of Japan

Burnaston, Derbyshire
Toyota of Japan

Hethel, Norfolk
Lotus
Proton of Malaysia

Coventry
Jaguar
Ford of the US

Brentwood, Essex
Ford of the US

Dagenham
Ford of the US

Southampton
Ford of the US

Motor vehicle production in the UK is largely owned and controlled by foreign companies.

car that is assembled in Britain by an American company - Ford or General Motors. The car could have an engine which has been made in Germany, seats made in Spain and tyres in France. Alternatively, the consumer might buy a Rover, which is now owned by the German company, BMW, or a 'Japanese' car which is assembled in Derby (by Toyota) or in Sunderland (by Nissan).

Globalisation has increased the range of choice for consumers but, in the car industry, it has taken control away from the UK. Decisions about style, design, location and scale of production are largely made abroad. These decisions are not necessarily made in the best interests of the UK economy.

The role of transnational corporations (TNCs)

Over 40 percent of world trade is now carried out by the biggest 350 companies. These companies - IBM, Motorola, Philips, General Motors, Sony and many others - have extended their activities far beyond their original national base. They are known as **transnational corporations (TNCs)** or **multinational corporations (MNCs)**. The terms 'transnational' and 'multinational' are often used interchangeably. Note, however, that some writers define a transnational as a company that has its headquarters in a single country, employs people mainly from that country, and controls most of its activities from there. A multinational is defined as a company that is organised so that people in a number of countries are involved in directing its activities. This is a less common arrangement.

2. What are the roots of globalisation?

Globalisation, on its present scale, is very much a modern process. However, long-distance contact between peoples can be traced far back in time. During the Roman period, goods were traded between the Mediterranean region and eastern Asia, along the ancient route which became known as the Silk Road. Arab traders and travellers between the 9th and 15th centuries established trade links from North Africa and the Mediterranean to South and East Asia. They carried their religion, Islam, to these lands and traded in spices and other products.

In the 15th and 16th centuries, Spanish and Portuguese explorers hoped to find these same regions. By chance, they reached the 'New World' of the Americas. They established their dominance over **indigenous** (ie, local or native) peoples in relatively short and brutal wars of conquest, and began to exploit the natural resources. The Dutch, French and British soon began to compete with

Figure 2.38 BP's global operations, 1998

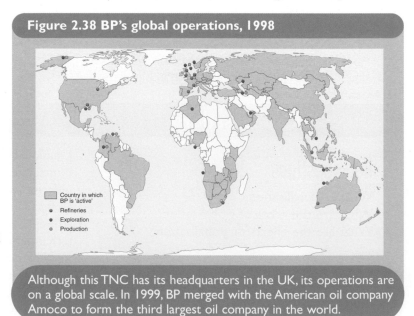

Country in which BP is 'active'
- Refineries
- Exploration
- Production

Although this TNC has its headquarters in the UK, its operations are on a global scale. In 1999, BP merged with the American oil company Amoco to form the third largest oil company in the world.

Figure 2.39 European Empires and spheres of influence

European colonies and spheres of influence 19th and early 20th centuries

- British
- Spanish
- French
- Portuguese
- Italian
- German
- Dutch
- Belgian
- Russian
- Independant countries

the Spanish and Portuguese, and with each other. Trading patterns were established in which routes were centred upon the colonial ports and capitals.

It was in the 19th century that European power reached its peak. Industrialisation spread from Britain to other European countries. The new factories required raw materials as inputs and also required markets for their output. This led the powers of Western Europe towards the era of colonisation. Regions of the world became locked into a global system of control which was centred on Britain, France and other European powers (see figure 2.39).

In many regions of the world, monoculture was established by the colonisers. (Monoculture is the production of a single agricultural crop or **commodity**). For example, Europeans set up rubber plantations in Malaya and Indochina, and tea plantations in India and East Africa. In Central and Latin America, the United Fruit Company, from the USA, set up many plantations in so called 'banana republics'.

Figure 2.40 shows the manufacturing output of selected countries during the 19th century. Note that Britain was still the leading European manufacturer at the end of the century. Germany's share had risen to 13.2 percent, while the United States had become the largest manufacturer worldwide, at 23.6 percent. The economies of China and India went into decline because of competition from the new industrial manufacturers. In many cases, the Europeans used military power to force their colonies or other countries to give free access to the factory produced goods. The local hand-produced manufactures simply could not compete.

During the first half of the 20th century, wars and economic slumps damaged the world economy. There was a determination that this should not happen again. So, at the end of the Second World War, a number of international organisations were set up to promote trade and development (see figure 2.41).

Figure 2.40 Percentage share of world manufacturing output, 1800-1900

	1800	1860	1900
Britain	4.3	19.9	18.5
France	4.2	7.9	6.8
Germany	3.5	4.9	13.2
Russia	5.6	7.0	8.8
USA	0.8	7.2	23.6
China	33.3	19.7	6.2
Indian sub-continent	19.7	8.6	1.7

Figure 2.41 Major post-war global organisations

Acronym	Full title	Date of foundation	Task
GATT	General Agreement on Tariffs and Trade	1948	To promote free trade and reduce barriers to trade.
IMF	International Monetary Fund	1945	To promote international monetary cooperation, currency stability and international trade.
UN	United Nations	1945	To increase international cooperation and reduce conflict.
IBRD	International Bank for Reconstruction and Development (World Bank)	1946	To provide funds and expertise to promote economic development.

Note: GATT has since been renamed the World Trade Organisation

Since 1945, advanced industrial nations have largely dominated the world economy. The low income countries of the Third World have relied primarily on commodity production and the exploitation of natural resources for their export earnings. Prices of these commodities are generally controlled by the Western economies. In an attempt to assert their power and influence, in 1973, the 13 members of the Organisation of Petroleum Exporting Countries (OPEC)(see figure 2.42), announced a 400 percent rise in the price of oil. This 'oil shock' had a marked effect on the world economy. Income to the OPEC countries rose from $14.5 billion in 1972 to $110 billion in 1974.

Some of the oil producers, such as Kuwait and Saudi Arabia, became rich. At first, the Western countries suffered, with high unemployment and high inflation occurring simultaneously. However, they soon recovered. New sources of oil were discovered, and energy saving measures reduced demand. By the late 1990s, the real price of crude oil had fallen back to its pre-1974 level.

It was the non-oil producers of the Third World that were hardest hit by the oil shock. With few financial reserves, many borrowed to keep their economies going. The large debts which they built up at that time are still a tremendous burden.

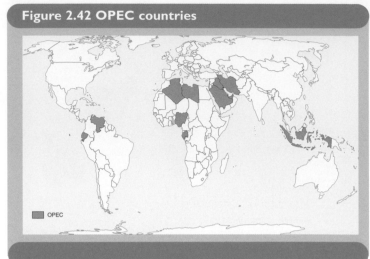

Figure 2.42 OPEC countries

OPEC

In the 1990s, the collapse of communism left the world even more dominated by the Western economies and Western based transnational corporations. However, some non-Western newly industrialising countries were able to take advantage of the new global opportunities. East Asian economies such as Taiwan and Hong Kong were able to share in the growth of trade and prosperity. But other regions, such as sub-Sahara Africa, found it much harder. They remain 'losers' in the process of globalisation.

Activity) Manufactured goods and commodities

Within the global economy, those countries that produce and export manufactured goods are in a state of interdependence. They buy and sell goods from each other at prices that tend, on average, to rise from year to year. Countries that rely on exports of commodities (ie, food, fuel and raw materials) are also part of the global economy but are in a relatively weak position. They rely on richer countries to buy their produce and the prices they receive can vary dramatically.

Beverages (tea, coffee and cocoa) are examples of commodities. Nine African countries rely on beverage exports for around a half of their export earnings. They are:

Cameroon (cocoa)	**Ethiopia (coffee)**	**Ghana (cocoa)**
Ivory Coast (coffee, cocoa)	**Kenya (coffee, tea)**	**Malawi (tea)**
Tanzania (tea)	**Uganda (coffee)**	**Zimbabwe (tea)**

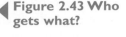

Figure 2.43 Who gets what?

The revenue from a £1.75 jar of coffee in a UK supermarket is distributed in the following way:
- grower 30p
- transport to Europe 8p
- transport and distribution in Europe 13p
- jar, label and boxing 21p
- UK manufacturer's costs and profit 50p
- supermarket costs and profit 53p.

The revenue from a £2.90 box of tea bags in a UK supermarket is distributed in the following way:
- plantation wages 20p
- other plantation costs and profit 27p
- transport to Europe 4p
- packaging 21p
- UK manufacturer's costs and profit 130p
- supermarket costs and profit 88p.

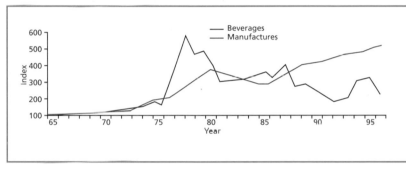

▲ **Figure 2.44 Price indices for beverages and manufactured exports (1965-96)**

The graph shows how the export prices of beverages and manufactured goods have varied. Each price is shown as an index (with the base year 1965 = 100).

Questions

1 Describe and compare the changes in export prices of beverages compared with manufactures over the period shown (in figure 2.44)
2 What does the data suggest about the power of beverage producers in the world economy?

3. What are the effects of globalisation?

Within the globalisation process, there are winners and losers. The winners are those countries, companies and populations that are able to control their destinies and ensure that are successful in the global economy. The losers are those who are excluded or who are most vulnerable to decisions made elsewhere. The gap between those who benefit from globalisation and those who do not is only partly shown by wage differences. A way of illustrating the true gap is by looking at the time it takes a worker to earn enough to buy a Big Mac (which is itself a symbol of globalisation). In a 1998 survey, an average worker in a North American city took just 11 minutes to earn enough. By contrast, an average worker in Nairobi, Kenya, took more than three hours

to earn enough to buy the same product. And, of course, the person in Nairobi was 'lucky' because a very large number of people in that city do not have any regular income at all.

The failure by Kenya and the other countries of sub-Sahara Africa to benefit from globalisation is shown by trade and investment figures. For instance, in the mid-1990s, the 570 million people of sub-Sahara Africa earned less export revenues than the small city-state of Singapore with a population of just 3 million people. The picture is very similar in terms of **foreign direct investment** (FDI). In 1995, the whole of sub-Sahara Africa received $1.8 billion in private investment. This compared with $11.9 billion that went to just one Asian country, Malaysia, with a population of 20 million.

Transnational corporations are reluctant to invest if

there is a threat of civil war or corruption on a scale that damages their interests. What they require is stable government and a friendly attitude towards foreign investment. Unfortunately for the people of sub-Sahara Africa, these conditions are met in very few countries.

Transnational corporations (TNCs) and globalisation

TNCs are symbols of globalisation. They create both positive and negative effects.

Positive effects of TNCs There are a number of reasons why most governments are eager to encourage foreign investment from these corporations:

- employment is created in the host country
- new technology might be introduced
- advanced management skills and practices might spread from the TNCs to other local producers
- the skills of local workers are upgraded
- exports are generated which help the balance-of-payments of the host country
- the local or regional economy can be regenerated by spin-offs, for example the growth of component suppliers
- links with the global economy are developed.

Sometimes, a cluster of TNCs is attracted to a particular location. They might supply each other with components or might wish to tap into a pool of skilled labour. Local colleges and training agencies might start courses specifically designed to upgrade the local workforce. As an example, Silicon Glen has grown across Central Scotland as a region of hi-tech manufacturing. It gets its name from the Silicon Valley area of California which was an early centre of the computer industry. The M4 corridor is another area where the spin-offs from foreign investment have led to rapid economic growth (see Figure 2.45).

Negative effects of TNCs Some potential disadvantages can arise when TNCs set up a new plant:

- a 'branch plant' is at the mercy of decisions made by corporate executives overseas
- the full range of advanced technology might be withheld and the new factory might be treated simply as an assembly plant; research and development (R&D) processes which form the basis of modern industry might be retained at the corporate headquarters - leaving the 'metal bashing' to the foreign branches
- grants and regional assistance given to attract TNCs might be very costly - and might be better used elsewhere in the economy
- environmental costs might be high if safeguards are relaxed in order to attract the TNCs
- profits might be repatriated overseas (ie, transferred back to headquarters).

The loss of local control is a major concern for countries which host TNCs. The company has the interest of its shareholders at heart rather than the interests of the local workforce. It might regard its overseas plants as 'branches' which will be closed first if the company has financial problems. Severe local unemployment can be the outcome.

An example of how TNCs sometimes operate in their own, narrow interests occurred in 1997. Renault, the French transnational car company, announced that it was making a financial loss and that it was shutting its plant in Vilvoorde, Belgium, at a cost of 6,000 jobs. This was an example of a TNC closing its foreign branches first when times were hard. However, there was more controversy when it was discovered that Renault was planning to build

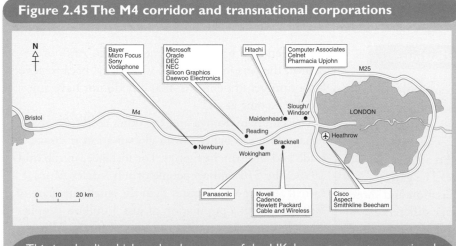

Figure 2.45 The M4 corridor and transnational corporations

This is a leading high technology area of the UK, home to top transnational corporations in electronics, telecoms, pharmaceuticals and information technology. The TNCs are attracted by the nearness to Heathrow airport, the M4 motorway, nearness to London and an educated workforce. (See also unit 5.1 on industrial location.)

a new plant in Valladolid, in Spain. The Spanish government had, it was said, offered millions of pesetas in grants to the company. There was widespread belief that Renault was playing the Belgian government and workforce off against the Spanish government and workforce. If the Belgian government would match the Spanish offer, and if the Belgian workers' wage bill could be cut, the company would perhaps not switch production. The beneficiaries of the situation were the French owners of Renault, the losers were, potentially, Belgian workers and Spanish taxpayers.

Figure 2.46 Advertising by American TNCs in Beijing, China

Coca-Cola is often seen as a symbol of Westernisation

The political and social impact of globalisation

Globalisation is not simply an economic process. It has an impact on politics, society and culture. At the political level, for example, globalisation is about the challenge to nation-states posed by the actions of TNCs, and by the inability of nation-states to control the activities of the global economy. It is estimated that the 100 largest transnationals now own $1,700 billion of assets in their foreign branches or affiliates. Therefore they have an enormous overseas impact, and the scale of these activities is way beyond the capacity of an individual country to control.

The 1997/98 economic crisis in South Korea was an example of how vulnerable countries are to disturbances in the global economy. Leading world banks lost confidence in South Korea's ability to repay its debts. They therefore demanded their money back at once, creating a financial crisis and almost causing the whole economy to collapse. The world's richest countries organised a rescue package of $55 billion for South Korea. They knew that the consequences of a collapse of the world's 12th largest economy would be damaging to them. Even so, the UK suffered as major Korean companies announced that investments in South Wales and the North East would be slowed or cancelled.

In social and cultural terms, globalisation is causing a movement towards a global society and a global culture. People across the globe share the same musical tastes, television programmes, films and also ideas. As with TNC investment, there are positive and negative aspects to this. The positive elements include the reduction in racism and nationalism as people with different nationalities work together in the TNCs. They become aware of social concerns at a global level and build what might be called a 'global consciousness'. A criticism of globalisation is that it is **Westernisation** in just another guise. It is Western values and culture that are becoming dominant with, some say, too great an emphasis on material goods and consumption, and too little emphasis on spiritual values and care of the natural environment.

As the global economy develops, the negative environmental effects of industrialisation are becoming apparent on a worldwide scale. For example, global warming and acid rain are having an impact across national boundaries. Solutions cannot come from individual countries acting alone, but from concerted action by countries acting together. The issue of environmental damage and possible solutions is described more fully in units 2.5 and 2.6.

Activity **TNCs and national governments**

Figure 2.47 The 12 largest TNCs, by turnover and the total GNP of selected countries ▶

TNC	Head Office	Annual turnover 1996 ($m)	Selected countries	Total GNP 1996 ($m)
General Motors	US	168,000	Denmark	169,000
Ford Motors	US	153,000	Norway	151,000
Shell	Neth/UK	131,000	South Africa	132,000
Exxon	US	120,000	Greece	120,000
Mitsubishi	Japan	117,000	Portugal	100,000
Toyota	Japan	90,000	Chile	70,000
BP	UK	73,000	Egypt	64,000
DaimlerBenz	Germany	72,000	New Zealand	57,000
Volkswagen	Germany	66,000	Czech Republic	49,000
Hitachi	Japan	63,000	Bangladesh	31,000
Siemens	Germany	62,000	Kenya	9,000
Mobil	US	59,000	Tanzania	5,000

Note: in 1996, just 24 countries had GNPs that were bigger than General Motors' turnover. GNP, or Gross National Product, is the total value of output of goods and services of one country in one year.

Questions

1 Outline what the data shows in terms of the relative power of TNCs compared with nation states.
2 What is the distribution of the head offices of the 12 largest TNCs? How might this distribution affect the world pattern of economic development?

unit summary

1 Globalisation is a process that is growing in importance. Transnational corporations are heavily involved in the process.
2 The roots of globalisation lie in the political and commercial dominance of the former colonial powers.
3 The winners in globalisation are the people and organisations which can benefit from the opportunities which globalisation provides. They are located in places such as Europe or North America, or in newly industrialising countries in South East and East Asia.
4 The losers in globalisation are those people and regions which are excluded from the global economy. They are found in all parts of the world, but especially in sub-Sahara Africa.
5 TNCs are key agents of globalisation, extending their reach into many countries, with both positive and negative effects.

key terms

Commodity - agricultural products such as coffee, sugar and tea; minerals, timber and fuel.
Foreign Direct Investment (FDI) - investment from overseas.
Global economy - a single, worldwide, economy in which production and marketing are organised on a global scale.
Globalisation - the development of a global economy; the term is also used to describe the wider social and political implications of the economic changes.
Indigenous people - local or native people, the original inhabitants of a region.

Monoculture - the production of a single crop such as rubber or tea.
Oil Shock - the impact of the oil price rise organised by OPEC (Organisation of Petroleum Exporting Countries) in 1974.
Transnational / multinational corporations (TNC/MNC) - companies which operate in more than country.
Westernisation - the spread of Western products, ideas, values and attitudes around the globe.

Unit 2.5 The negative impact of development on the environment

key questions

1 What are the negative effects of development?
2 What causes air pollution?
3 What causes water pollution?
4 What causes land pollution?
5 Is industrial development causing global warming?

1. What are the negative effects of development?

Development can bring many benefits, but it also has some drawbacks (see unit 2.1). The benefits include higher personal incomes and longer life expectancy. The drawbacks include social and environmental effects which are sometimes called **negative externalities**. The negative social effects include the loss of traditional cultures and lifestyles, and the more hectic pace of life that is required when competing in the global economy.

The environmental impact of development includes air, water and land pollution. This unit examines the causes of pollution, and unit 2.6 considers whether development can take place without causing irreversible environmental damage.

Figure 2.48 Industrial plant

Development brings many benefits but it has negative side effects. These include pollution and the destruction of the natural environment.

2. What causes air pollution?

Pollution is due to human activity. It can be defined as the introduction of harmful substances into the environment by people. Most air pollution arises from the burning of fossil fuels (eg, coal, oil and gas) by industry, by electricity power generators, by domestic users and by motor vehicle users. When the fuel is burnt, there are harmful **emissions** into the atmosphere including sulphur dioxide, carbon monoxide and carbon dioxide, nitrogen oxides and 'particulates' of lead. Other sources of air pollution are aerosols and cooling systems which contain CFCs (chlorofluorocarbons).

During the 19th century, industrial cities and the surrounding land became black with soot and smoke deposits. 'Where there's muck there's money' became a well-known saying in the north of England. Today, the effects of pollution are less visible but they are nevertheless a serious hazard. Air pollutants can have a local, national or even global effect. For example, lead particles from petrol can cause brain damage to children who live near major roads. Sulphur dioxide can cause acid rain which has a regional and even international impact. Carbon dioxide emissions are widely blamed for global warming, and CFCs damage the ozone layer which protects the Earth from dangerous radiation.

Acid rain

Acid rain is caused by sulphur dioxide and nitrogen oxides which are released when coal and oil are burnt. These gases mix with water vapour in the atmosphere and make the rain more acid. (Rain is already slightly acidic because naturally occurring carbon dioxide in the atmosphere combines with water vapour to form a weak carbonic acid.) Due to prevailing westerly winds, Scandinavians experience acid rain that is blown from Britain, East Europeans receive acid rain from Western Europe and Japanese suffer from acid rain caused by Chinese industry.

One effect of acid rain is to increase the rate at which nutrients and metals are leached (ie, washed out) of the soil (see unit 13.3). People are at risk because metals such as aluminium are released from soils into freshwater rivers and streams which are then used for drinking supplies. Studies have shown that Alzheimer's Disease is more likely to develop when people absorb concentrations of aluminium. There is also strong evidence that acid rain can kill trees if the loss of soil nutrients is severe. Leaching removes the nutrients

which trees need to remain healthy and survive. River and lake ecosystems are damaged because some organisms cannot survive in the more acid conditions and some cannot tolerate the higher concentrations of metals in the water.

An additional effect of acid rain is that it increases the rate of chemical weathering. This process occurs when rocks are broken down by chemical processes (see unit 8.1). The effect is noticeable on statues and old buildings such as cathedrals, particularly in large urban areas where acid rain is most severe.

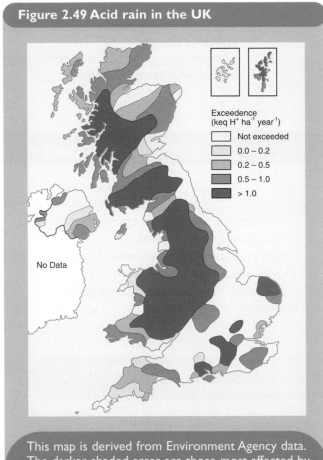

Figure 2.49 Acid rain in the UK

Exceedence
(keq H$^+$ ha^{-1} year^{-1})

- Not exceeded
- 0.0 – 0.2
- 0.2 – 0.5
- 0.5 – 1.0
- > 1.0

No Data

This map is derived from Environment Agency data. The darker shaded areas are those most affected by acid rain. The scale represents hydrogen ions per hectare per year. (The more hydrogen ions - the more acidic are the conditions.)

Figure 2.49 shows areas in the UK where acid rain has most effect. The map is constructed by calculating the amount of acidity that is deposited on soils, over and above what is known as the 'critical load' factor. This factor is an estimate of the natural acid neutralising capacity of soils - which, in turn, is dependent on the underlying rocks. If underlying rocks are alkaline, this tends to neutralise the effect of acid rain. However, if underlying rocks are acidic, this tends to reinforce the effect.

The map shows that acid rain has most impact on the upland regions of north and west Britain - areas where precipitation is heaviest and the underlying rocks are generally acid. However, parts of lowland Britain are also affected, most notably the West Midlands, parts of East Anglia and also the Hampshire basin. The least affected areas overlie chalk or limestone because the soils formed on these rocks tend to be alkaline.

The high income countries of Western Europe, North America and Japan have the resources to reduce acid rain and its side effects. In these countries, expensive 'scrubbers' are being fitted inside power station chimneys to filter out the sulphur dioxide. According to the European Environment Agency, sulphur dioxide emissions halved in EU countries between 1980 and 1995. In parts of Scandinavia, crushed limestone is dropped by air to counteract the acidity of some lakes and rivers. This has the effect of neutralising the acid. However, many forests are still at risk because the acid rain washes out soil nutrients faster than they are naturally replaced by the decomposition of organic matter in the soil.

It is in middle and lower income countries, particularly those relying on coal power, that the effect of acid rain is most severe. For example, many power stations in the Czech Republic and Poland rely on lignite and coal which has a high sulphur content. The result is that large areas of forest have died in both countries.

One of the worst affected locations for acid rain is the fast-growing city of Chongqing in central China. In the high summer temperatures, sulphur dioxide reacts with water vapour to form acid very quickly. China is dependent on coal-fired energy production, and the local coal has a high sulphur content. It has been estimated that 820,000 tonnes of sulphur are emitted into Chongqing's atmosphere each year. Because air flow is restricted by surrounding mountains, winds do not disperse the smoke and much of the sulphur comes back down as acid rain. Acidity is so high that steel is corroded. In 1990 it was reported that the city had spent US$250,000 on replacing lamp-posts and buses that had been damaged by this rainfall.

Smog

Some of the acid rain in Chongqing is due to residential coal fires. Before central heating was widely available, most homes in Britain also had coal fires. 'Smog' was a major health hazard, especially on cold overcast winter days when the air was still, typically in high pressure conditions. The name 'smog' comes from a combination of smoke and fog. It is caused by the condensation of water vapour on smoke particles and often appears yellow. It causes respiratory ailments such as bronchitis or asthma which can be fatal. Over 4,000 people died in the Great London Smog of 1952. The result was a public outcry and pressure to clean up the urban atmosphere. As a result, Britain introduced the Clean Air Acts of 1956 and 1968 to encourage the use of smokeless fuels and to reduce the sulphur dioxide emissions from homes and power stations. Today in Britain, there are relatively few coal fires and smogs are much reduced.

However, smogs continue elsewhere. For example in South Africa, until recently, black townships around Cape Town and Johannesburg lacked access to electricity. Most people used coal, paraffin or wood for fuel - so air quality was often poor. In China's capital, 'Beijing Throat' is a well-documented health hazard. The combination of dust from building work, fine sandy soil ('loess') blown in from the lands to the west, plus vehicle pollution and smoke pollution from coal fires, all combine to irritate people's noses and throats.

In cities where temperature inversions are common, smogs can be very persistent. (A temperature inversion occurs when cooler air is trapped below warmer air - see unit 12.2.) In Los Angeles, onshore surface winds blowing over the relatively cool Pacific Ocean are prevented from moving inland by the San Bernardino mountains. The cool air from the ocean collects in the Los Angeles basin and is trapped below relatively warm air from inland. The effect is that car exhaust emissions build up to form a petro-chemical smog that can be hazardous to asthmatics and young children in particular.

Vehicle emissions

Vehicle emissions are an increasing source of air pollution, especially in cities. In Britain, a 1997 report for the Department of Health estimated that up to 24,000 people per year die because of traffic fumes, and a similar number are admitted to hospital. Elderly people and those with respiratory conditions are especially at risk. Dust particles, mainly from diesel engines, cause 8,100 deaths and nitrogen oxides from vehicle exhausts

Figure 2.50 Los Angeles

The city has a geographical location that promotes the formation of temperature inversions, and the highest private car ownership in the world. These factors combine to cause some of the worst air quality anywhere in the USA.

cause 3,500 deaths per year. Ozone, which is vital in the upper atmosphere as a radiation filter, is a major source of pollution at street level. Ozone emissions from vehicles cause 12,500 premature deaths each year.

The UK government announced in 1998 that a new system of public warning about poor air quality would be introduced. By monitoring five different gases, pollution levels would be graded from 'low' to 'very high'. Once the 'very high' level was reached, the government would issue an alert, and ask motorists to cut unnecessary car journeys. Asthmatics would be advised to stay indoors. But, at this level, even healthy people could expect eye irritation, coughing and pain on breathing deeply. In Paris, the French government has taken more severe action. During 1997, when nitrogen dioxide levels reached 200 parts per billion, the French government made public transport free in Paris and banned half the cars from the capital's streets (by using the odd and even numbers on licence plates).

The effects of air pollution are found in cities around the world. Bangkok is a city that is badly affected by traffic congestion. A study in 1994 showed that lead from vehicle exhausts is causing irreversible brain damage and loss of IQ in large numbers of children. In Mexico City, it has been estimated that 2.4 working days per person are lost due to air pollution, and 6,400 deaths are caused by this each year. Annual health costs from air pollution in Mexico City are estimated by the World Bank to exceed US$1.5 billion.

In an attempt to improve air quality, California has introduced ever-tighter legislation to reduce vehicle emissions. The state was one of the first places to insist on catalytic converters being fitted to exhausts. Strong financial incentives are now in force for employers to organise 'car pools' where people can share lifts. On the freeways, there are lanes restricted for use by cars with at least one passenger. Great efforts are also being made to develop and encourage the use of electric cars which will have zero emissions.

As a result of these measures, despite vehicle numbers in Los Angeles increasing from 6.4 million in 1970 to 10.6 million in 1995, ozone levels (at street level) declined from 0.58 parts per million in 1970 to 0.33 parts per million in 1995. This is significant because it shows that air quality can be improved, even if vehicle numbers increase.

CFCs

CFCs are a relatively modern form of air pollution. They are used in the making of refrigerators, in cooling systems, in aerosol sprays and in the production of plastics. Research has indicated that CFCs accumulate in the upper atmosphere and cause ozone to break down. Ozone protects the Earth from the Sun's ultra-violet (UV) rays. If the ozone layer weakens, more UV radiation reaches the Earth's surface, and causes eye cataracts and skin cancers,

Figure 2.51 Sunbather

If the ozone layer disappears, sunbathing will become even more dangerous than at present.

especially among those who are fair-skinned. In the 1980s it was discovered that a hole had appeared in the ozone layer above Antarctica. Severe ozone depletion has since been recorded over the Arctic, northern Eurasia and North America. The hole gets bigger during winter and early spring, then appears to shrink.

According to estimates by the US Environmental Protection Agency, if ozone loss in the upper atmosphere is 10 percent by the year 2050, an additional 2 million cases of non malignant skin cancer will occur in the US alone. Fortunately, this type of cancer can be treated successfully and deaths are few. But a more dangerous type of malignant skin cancer would cause 4,000 deaths per year in the US, and 18,000 if the ozone depletion reached 50 percent.

Following an international agreement in 1987, known as the Montreal Convention, CFCs are being phased out. The hope is that the ozone hole will start to mend itself by 2010. In most Western countries, industries have switched production techniques and no longer use CFCs. Aerosols are now sold as 'CFC-free', as are refrigerators. However, the problem remains of how to dispose safely of old refrigerators which contain CFCs. Also, CFC production continues, albeit at reduced levels than before. As with acid rain, higher income countries can more easily find the resources to change production techniques than lower income countries. In a relatively rare example of international cooperation, in 1997, the World Bank gave Russia $30 million to phase out CFC production in seven factories over an eighteen month period. This was equivalent to half the world's production. China and India are also being paid millions of dollars by Western countries to shut down CFC manufacturing plants. Even so, the CFCs that have already accumulated in the atmosphere will have a damaging effect for many years to come.

Activity | Air pollution and cement production

Cement kilns under a cloud

Burning hazardous waste in cement kilns is a controversial issue. Cement factories use this fuel as a way of keeping energy bills down, but environmental groups and people who live nearby believe it is a poorly regulated process and a danger to health.

A long running UK dispute over emissions from Castle Cement's Ribblesdale plant, near Clitheroe, Lancashire, looks set to escalate as the company has asked permission to burn high-chloride industrial waste and rubbish such as tyres, textiles and carpets. Ribblesdale already uses 'secondary fuel', a

▲ **Figure 2.52 Castle Cement**

mixture of solvents and industrial waste, in its kilns. The company burned 43,000 tonnes of the fuel in 1996. Instead of paying £28 per tonne for coke, it was paid £5 a tonne by waste disposal companies to take the secondary fuel.

Clitheroe is an old market town set in the relatively unspoilt Ribble Valley. For many years, local people have accepted the large limestone quarries and chimney smoke as the price they pay for jobs and a prosperous local economy. But now, residents have started to complain of smells and irritation from the factory smoke plume. They say that the smell of sulphur is unpleasant and they are worried that there are also emissions of heavy metals which can cause cancers and damage to the nervous system. The Pollution Inspectorate, forerunner to the Environment Agency, reported in 1995 that the concentrations of sulphur dioxide in the plume when it 'grounds' can cause eye, nose and throat irritation. In response, Castle

Cement - who say that the sulphur dioxide is a by-product of cement making and not the new fuel - are building a flue gas scrubber which will remove 90 percent of the sulphur dioxide from the kiln gases. It will cost £4 million.

The company, which faces competition from other UK and European producers, believes that it must use the low cost fuel to survive. The company's Development Manager has stated: 'We either run a cement plant or we don't! We could switch off the kilns, or use coke, but we would go out of business.' If the company closed the plant, many local people would lose their jobs.

The Environment Agency has been criticised for its lax attitude towards the plant. A House of Commons Environment Committee announced in 1997 that the Agency 'must act to restore confidence in its regulation of the cement industry'. A difficulty that the Agency faces is that if it sets standards that are too stringent, foreign competitors will be able to produce cement more cheaply. To overcome this problem, the European Union issued a draft directive to come into force in the year 2000. It sets the same emission standards for all EU producers.

Adapted from the Financial Times, 11th May 1997

Pollutant	Limits set in draft EU directive (2000)	Environment Agency limits (1997)
Particulate matter	10	100
Nitrogen oxides	No limit	1,200
Sulphur dioxide	50	2,300
Carbon monoxide	50	No limit
Hydrogen chloride	10	No limit
Total organic compounds	10	No limit
Dioxins	0.1ng	1ng
Cadmium/thalium	0.05	0.1
Mercury	0.05	0.1
Other heavy metals	0.5	1

Note: *Figures are mg/cubic metre except where otherwise stated*

▲ **Figure 2.53 Emission limits for cement kilns burning hazardous wastes as fuel**

Questions

1 Assess the costs and benefits that arise from cement production at Castle Cement's Ribblesdale plant.
2 Explain why it might be preferable for the European Union rather than the Environment Agency to set new, lower emission limits.

3. What causes water pollution?

The main sources of water pollution are human waste, industrial waste and agricultural waste. In the UK, it is the responsibility of water companies to provide clean drinking water and to ensure that river and coastal waters are not polluted. The Environment Agency is the government body which monitors water quality and, where appropriate, prosecutes the polluters. Increasingly, in the UK, the USA and other countries, the policy of 'make the polluter pay' is used to reduce water pollution. The cost falls on industrial plants to clean up their own production processes and so avoid the discharge of liquid pollutants. If they do not, they are fined.

Human and domestic waste

Liquid domestic waste comes mainly from washing and from flushing the toilet. The invention of the flush toilet and the development of sewage systems have brought great benefits to public health. As is shown in unit 2.3 on health and welfare, typhoid and cholera epidemics in the UK were largely brought under control by the improvement in sanitation and waste disposal in Victorian cities. However, sewage systems are costly to install and maintain. As a result, in most low income countries, sewage is often simply discharged untreated into rivers.

In the UK, most sewage is treated at sewage treatment plants, with various filters diluting and eliminating toxic and dangerous material. One objective is to reduce the volume by drying out the sewage into sludge. The filtered water is recycled to the river system. Reuse then takes place downstream. There are some concerns that this water is not sufficiently clean. It may still contains nitrates for example, and small quantities of other materials including hormone affecting chemicals. The UK's Environment Agency has reported that sex changes in fish are more common in water that is recycled from sewage treatment plants than elsewhere. This is possibly because of pollutants remaining in the water. Only expensive upgrading of the treatment works will eliminate this danger.

There is much debate within the UK over the issue of sewage discharge into the sea. In some places, for example near Scarborough on the east coast, and Blackpool on the Irish Sea coast, partly treated sewage which has been filtered for 'solids' is discharged through long pipes into the sea. Environmental and other pressure groups, such as Surfers Against Sewage, argue that the waste should be fully treated. This treatment, they say, should include the use of ultra-violet light to kill bacteria which is a hazard to bathers. The water companies, in response, point out that this treatment will cost large amounts of money and that people will have to pay more in their water bills.

Sewage is not the only source of water pollution from households. Domestic waste water, from sinks, dishwashers and washing machines, is a source of pollution because it contains detergents. These are a cocktail of chemicals which are harmful to both plants and aquatic organisms. Expensive treatment by water companies is required to remove the detergent and bring the water quality to an acceptable level.

Industrial waste

Industrial liquid wastes come from activities such as mining, power stations, iron and steel works and chemical plants. Dangerous metals such as arsenic, cadmium, lead and mercury are released into water courses. Mercury poisoning causes brain damage and is especially toxic. The metal is still used by miners in processing gold ore and is contaminating rivers in, for example, the Amazon basin.

Coal-burning power stations release arsenic and mercury, and iron and steel plants release metals such as chromium and molybdenum. Some industrial processes produce chemicals known as synthetic organic compounds. They are considered to be especially dangerous when they enter the food chain - causing

Figure 2.54 Oil pollution and wildlife

Transport of crude oil in supertankers has increased as more and more people around the world drive cars. Inevitably there are accidents where wildlife is killed and, in the case of the Sea Empress, holiday beaches are polluted. The beaches can be cleaned - at a cost - but it takes much longer for the natural environment to recover.

birth defects and cancer in some cases. One type of toxic chemical, known as PCB (polychlorinated biphenyl) has been discovered in remote regions such as the north coast of Canada. This is many thousands of kilometres from the nearest industrial centre.

In some places, old mine workings are a major cause of water pollution. When the mines are operating, water is pumped out and dispersed. But, when the mine closes and the pumping stops, the mine's shafts and tunnels fill with water. This can become contaminated with minerals that are sometimes toxic. When the water eventually overflows into surface streams, the effect can be to kill plants and fish. Examples of this type of pollution have occurred in old tin mines, in Cornwall, and in old coal mines in Yorkshire. On the River Don, near Sheffield, a 10 km stretch of the river has been poisoned by high concentrations of iron. The river, for many years, was made orange in colour by drain water from the Bullhouse Colliery (which closed in 1918). No plants, fish or even insects could survive in the toxic water. In 1998, plans were announced to spend £1.2 m on a treatment plant. Settling ponds will hold the mine water which will pass through filters to remove the iron.

Thermal pollution of water is caused by discharges of hot water. In most cases, the water has not been used as part of an industrial process but as a coolant, particularly in power stations. It harms some fish species, including salmon and trout. Oxygen levels are reduced in the hot water and toxic 'blooms' of algae become more common.

Oil spills are a specific type of water pollution. They mostly occur when a tanker runs aground. Because oil floats on water, it tends to spread over a wide area. It can take many years for the marine environment to recover from the effect of oil and, in some cases, from the effect of detergent used in the clean-up. In the UK, the Torrey Canyon (1967), the Braer (1993) and the Sea Empress (1996) were all notable examples of large spills. Often, sea birds and mammals become covered with oil. Despite the efforts of volunteers who clean oil off rescued seabirds, research has shown that most of these birds die of stress or poisoning.

Some of the 85,000 tonnes of oil from the Sea Empress was washed up in tourist areas. Although most of the beaches were quickly cleaned, the adverse publicity damaged the South Wales tourist industry for a whole holiday season.

The sea is often used as a dumping ground - particularly by governments. The UK has, in the past, dumped old munitions in the Irish Sea, and the former Soviet Union has sunk unwanted old nuclear submarines in the Arctic Ocean. Because waste disposal on land is a costly process, the cheapest option is simply to dump the material in the sea. It is always tempting to take this low cost approach. The power and scale of the Earth's natural processes are so great, some believe, that wind and water will dilute and break down harmful pollutants over time. The opposite point of view is that the long term consequences of sea pollution are unknown, and therefore the sea should not be used as a dumping ground.

These contrasting views were highlighted in 1991. Shell proposed that the decommissioned Brent Spar oil storage platform should be sunk in the deep waters of the Atlantic Ocean, 250 km off the west coast of Scotland. Perhaps, on its own, this would not have caused long term damage to the environment. However, protesters - including Greenpeace - campaigned against Shell. They argued that large numbers of North Sea oil platforms would eventually need to be scrapped, and dumping was not an environmentally friendly option. Eventually Shell bowed

to public pressure and the platform was taken to be dismantled, at a cost of £40 million, in a Norwegian fjord.

Agricultural waste

Nitrates and phosphates are used as fertilisers on farmland. They help to increase food yields. When they enter the water system, however, they pose many problems. **Eutrophication** is the process by which surface water is over-enriched by these fertilisers. The fertilisers encourage the growth of algae which, in the case of blue-green algae, are highly toxic. The algae use up oxygen in the water, so reducing the amount available for fish. Sometimes 'red tides' are found along the coastline or in estuaries when the water is coloured by algae and other pollutants. These tides are hazardous to aquatic life, and seafood from these infected areas can cause illness or even death.

Run-off containing fertiliser from agricultural land has caused the pollution of aquifers, particularly in Eastern England. (An aquifer is a layer of rock that absorbs and holds water.) Before the underground water can be used for drinking supplies, expensive treatment is increasingly required to remove the nitrates. Nevertheless, in some areas, the concentration of nitrates in drinking water remains above EU guidelines. A scheme to pay farmers to use less fertiliser in 'nitrate vulnerable zones' is one remedy that is being tried.

During the 1990s, organo-phosphates (OPs) were used in UK farming to kill parasites in cattle and sheep. These OPs have been linked with cases of nervous disease in humans and, in some reports, to BSE in cattle. Similar chemicals were used to control human parasites in the Gulf War and have been blamed, by some, for the range of disorders known as Gulf War Syndrome. There is evidence that OPs have leaked into the soil and water courses, particularly from sheep dips. In 1998, the Environment Agency reported that over a quarter of sheep dipping facilities which they inspected carried a high risk of pollution due to their proximity to watercourses. In 5 percent of the sheep dips, the drains ran directly into streams. The Environment Agency stated that in intensive sheep rearing areas such as Wales and the North West of England, dipping was having an adverse impact on the environment on 'a significant and widespread scale'.

Pollution from slurry and silage pits has also been identified as being a cause of water contamination throughout the UK. (Slurry is liquid manure from farm animals that is spread on the land as a fertiliser. Silage is grass that has been cut and stored while still green.)

Activity Aral Sea

The fate of the Aral Sea has been described as 'the greatest ecological tragedy of the former Soviet Union'. It is an example of large scale water pollution and environmental damage. In the former Soviet Union, large scale water transfer schemes in the Aral Basin had ambitious aims to provide water for irrigation, for drinking and for new industry. Unfortunately people did not know enough about the environment to fully predict the consequences. In the 1920s, the Soviet government began to divert water from the two main rivers feeding the Aral Sea (which is in a completely enclosed basin). The aim was to irrigate land in Central Asia and so make the country self sufficient in cotton. Much bigger schemes were started in 1956 and the flow of the two rivers, the Amu Darya and the Syr Darya became a trickle. The result has been devastation for the Aral Sea which has:

- lost 60 percent of its water volume and 40 percent of its area since large scale transfers began in the 1960s; the water has tripled in salinity
- become polluted by concentrations of pesticides and nitrates
- had its ecosystem devastated, and its rich fauna and flora destroyed
- become a site for dust storms which have deposited millions of tonnes of salt over surrounding areas.

At one time, the fishing industry in the Aral Sea supported 60,000 jobs. Today, salinity and pollution have killed all the fish and the old fishing boats are rusting many kilometres inland from the present shoreline. The people of Uzbekistan have one of the lowest per capita incomes of any of the former Soviet Republics. They need the income that cotton and other crops provide but, in towns near the Sea, the cost is high. Salt and pesticides are blown from the evaporated lake bed, causing a five-fold increase in throat cancers. The infant mortality rate is 60 per 1,000 (it is 6 per 1,000 in the UK).

▲ **Figure 2.56** *This was once the coastline of the Aral Sea. The prosperous fishing industry has collapsed.*

▲ **Figure 2.55** *The shrinking coastline of the aral Sea*

Questions

1 Briefly outline how and why, in the case of the Aral Sea, development has not brought its intended benefits.
2 What lessons might the Aral Sea provide other countries which wish to develop their water resources?

4. What causes land pollution?

A major cause of land pollution is the dumping of waste. This might be in the form of household waste, industrial waste or radioactive waste. In most industrialised countries, toxic wastes from old industrial processes have been dumped in the past. Some of these sites are threatening groundwater and surface water supplies because chemicals are leaking into the environment. Much stricter controls are now generally in force in Western countries. But, in some cases, this has had the effect of increasing toxic dumping in Third World Countries where controls are weaker or are not enforced. In 1998, for example, television news reports showed drums of toxic chemicals from the West being stored at unregulated dumps in Cambodia. Acids and mercury were leaking into the ground - close to people's houses and drinking water supplies.

Radioactive waste

Radioactive waste is a by-product of the nuclear industry. The Sellafield Plant in Cumbria reprocesses spent fuel from the UK's nuclear power stations. It also takes material from other countries including Germany and Japan. By 1998, the site held 45 tonnes of high level radioactive waste and this is projected to rise to 100 tonnes by 2010. The problem of nuclear waste is potentially much more dangerous than other forms of waste.

Radioactivity is a serious concern because of the very long time it takes for radioactive materials to become safe. It will take thousands of years for some types of the stored plutonium to break down. Radioactivity is known to cause cancers such as leukemia, and birth defects and genetic mutations. The most dangerous waste is from reprocessing. How to dispose of this safely is a continuing problem.

Sellafield has been allowed to discharge small amounts of low level radioactive materials into the Irish Sea, as well as into the atmosphere, for many years. Now, parts of the sea bed are dangerously radioactive. In 1998 a cull of pigeons nesting on the plant was ordered after they too were found to be radioactive. The owners of the plant, British Nuclear Fuels, have been prosecuted on a number of occasions for exceeding the discharge regulations.

From 1949 to the early 1980s, the UK dumped most of its low level nuclear waste in the sea. This was stopped after international protests. Now it is dumped on land at Drigg, a site near Sellafield. The nuclear industry wishes to store intermediate level waste underground. In the 1980s a number of sites were examined, such as north Lincolnshire and Billingham near Middlesbrough. These sites were rejected following vigorous **NIMBY** ('not in my backyard') campaigns. A later proposal was to build a half mile deep storage chamber under Sellafield itself. The local council and environmentalists objected to the proposal because the west Cumbrian geology is complex, with many faults and fissures. The fear was that contaminated groundwater might eventually find its way to the surface. Opponents of the scheme prefer the material to be stored at ground level where it can be monitored.

The biggest problem is high level waste. This will be dangerous for 250,000 years. Waste from the 1950s is now cool enough to be mixed with glass and turned into 'vitrified' blocks. This material has to be kept cool and stored for a very long time and, as yet, no long term solution has been agreed. The waste is in sealed containment buildings, above ground. It is under armed guard because it is potentially vulnerable to terrorist attack and, if some was stolen, it could be used to make nuclear bombs.

An additional hazard arising from the nuclear industry is that accidents such as those at Three Mile Island in the USA in 1979, or Chernobyl in the former USSR in 1986, have the potential to contaminate huge areas of land. The Three Mile Island accident, in Pennsylvania, was due to human error, made worse by a lack of accurate monitoring data within the plant. A near meltdown of the nuclear reactor took place and radioactivity was released. The operating company, General Public Utilities was nearly bankrupted by the $1 billion clean-up costs. As a result of public concern, no new nuclear power station has since been commissioned in the United States.

Chernobyl in the Ukraine, was a much worse accident than Three Mile Island and many deaths occurred. Again, human error was involved, but the basic design was also faulty. An explosion and meltdown took place, sending nuclear fallout into the atmosphere. This spread across large areas of the Soviet Union and across Europe.

In some parts of Western Europe, heavy rain caused particularly high deposits of radioactive material. In upland areas such as the Lake District in northern England, 2,000 km distant from Chernobyl, some grazing land was heavily contaminated. Ten years after the accident, sheep from those areas were still not allowed to be slaughtered for human consumption.

As details from Chernobyl became clear, Western European governments looked on in concern, but were able to do little. On the Soviet side, the government organised an inept and inefficient response to the disaster. Official Soviet reports state that 250-350 of the clean-up team died of radiation poisoning. More reliable Ukrainian estimates are that 7,000-10,000 people died in the clean-up and immediate aftermath. A 30 km exclusion zone is now placed around Chernobyl and the impact on local people continues (see figure 2.56). The World Health Organisation estimates that a total of 4.9 million people received dangerous doses of radiation in the Ukraine, Belarus and Russia. There are many cases of child cancers, particularly thyroid and leukemia, and birth defects from radiation are being passed down through generations. The economic cost is also huge. Clean-up costs plus the costs of guarding the site, rehousing the evacuees and compensating the victims are estimated to take 15 percent of Ukraine's national income each year.

Industrial waste

Dumping of waste from industry as spoil heaps or 'tips' is the most visible form of land pollution. Many of these tips are located in mining and steel-making areas. The Aberfan disaster in South Wales, in 1966, occurred when a tip of coal waste became unstable and slid onto the local school. Over 140 people died, mainly children, and the public outcry led to efforts in Britain to level or stabilise such spoil heaps (see unit 8.2). However, spoil

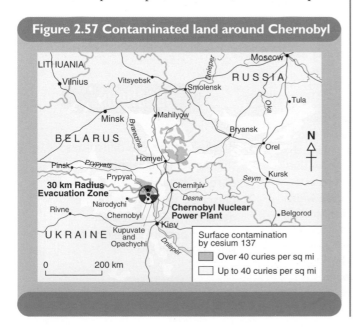

Figure 2.57 Contaminated land around Chernobyl

heaps are still deposited in mining and other industrial areas around the world.

Derelict industrial land is sometimes contaminated with poisonous metals and other chemicals which are dangerous if inhaled as dust. Asbestos is a health hazard that can cause cancer and lung disease. In the past, it was often used in buildings as insulation and as a fire barrier. When the buildings become derelict or are cleared, asbestos can remain on the ground unless an expensive clean-up takes place.

Municipal waste

Landfill sites (ie, 'holes in the ground') are the traditional means of municipal waste disposal. This is the waste that comes from people's dustbins. In some Third World countries it is common to see people picking through these sites for reusable materials such as metal and plastic. In the UK and Australia, landfill takes most municipal waste, whereas in Japan, two-thirds is incinerated.

Landfill sites can pose long term health threats, due to leakage of toxic waste, or the combustion of methane gas. The methane comes from decomposing organic matter. Unless it is safely vented, it can build up and cause explosions if ignited. Landfill sites have to be carefully managed, and sealed when full, because they can become a health hazard if rats and gulls spread the waste. Whenever new sites are proposed, local people often campaign against them because of the smell, the possible health hazard from leakage, and because of the increase in road transport by lorries which carry the waste. As a result, there is a growing shortage of suitable sites.

In the UK, a 'landfill tax' has been introduced. This is a tax on land fill waste and is designed to slow down the process of dumping, and encourage alternative arrangements. Incineration is a possibility. However, this can itself cause air pollution and also produces ash and other solid waste which still have to be disposed of.

In an ideal system, people would sort their waste at source. This would include full separation into glass bottles, plastics, clothing, waste paper and cans, for example. Recycling and reuse would be on a much bigger scale than at present. Supermarket companies would insist on suppliers using less packaging, and all packaging would be biodegradable. Some countries, such as the Netherlands are well advanced in such policies. They have legislation and tax systems that encourage recycling and the minimisation of waste.

Activity | **Derelict land**

	Urban	Rural
North	2,333	2,740
North West	6,285	2,368
Yorks and Humberside	3,569	1,897
West Midlands	3,019	1,922
East Midlands	1,835	2,550
East Anglia	293	729
South West	798	4,744
South East	2,347	2,173

▲ **Figure 2.58 Derelict land in English regions, hectares 1993**

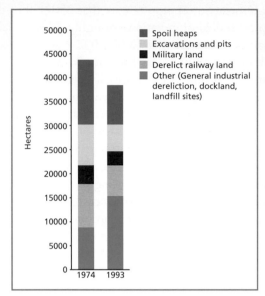

▲ **Figure 2.59 Derelict land in England, by type of dereliction, 1974 and 1993**

Derelict land reclamation

The reclamation of derelict land poses particular difficulties. Asbestos, metal and chemical waste has to be cleared from contaminated land before it can be reused. In some areas, toxic residues are so high that trees and other plants will not grow. Nevertheless, many derelict sites are in potentially valuable locations. These include railway sidings, dock areas and industrial land close to urban centres. Some of the new regional shopping centres such as Bluewater in Kent, Meadowhall in Sheffield and the Trafford Centre in Manchester have been built on land that was once derelict.

An early scheme to reclaim derelict land was in South Wales. In the lower Swansea Valley, nineteenth century mining and metal smelting had left an area of slag heaps, old mine shafts and derelict industrial buildings. Poisonous fumes from the spoil heaps had killed vegetation, leading to localised soil erosion.

Starting in 1961, the Lower Swansea Valley Project gradually transformed the area which was almost 500 hectares in size. Financial help for the scheme came from local government, the Welsh Office (ie, national government) and the EEC (now the European Union). The first task was to clear the old tips and make the land safe. Several trials were conducted to see which grasses, shrubs and trees could survive on the site. Eventually areas were successfully planted with pines, birch and alder - trees that are relatively shallow rooting. A forest park, nature trail and riverside walk were all constructed. Some housing, a new school and a large industrial estate were also built.

Questions

1 Briefly outline the difficulties that arise in reclaiming derelict land.

2 Describe the distribution of derelict land in England. Suggest possible reasons for this distribution.

5. Is industrial development causing global warming?

In recent years it has become widely accepted that **global warming** is taking place. At the 1997 Kyoto Climate Conference, most delegates accepted that increased emissions of carbon dioxide (CO_2) from burning fossil fuels are the main cause of rising temperatures. The Earth, however, has always had cycles of cooling and warming, and was warmer 1,000 years ago than it is now. So, whether today's global warming is fundamentally different from that in the past is a matter of debate. Warming is certainly taking place, and does seem to be at a rapid speed. The key issues are not whether it is occurring, but why - and what are the consequences?

Evidence to support the view that present day global warming is due to human activity comes from rising carbon dioxide levels in the atmosphere. Carbon dioxide increases the **greenhouse effect** which insulates the Earth and retains heat. Other gases produced by industrial activity, including CFCs, are also thought to have the same effect. The more greenhouse gases that are produced, the more heat will be retained within the Earth's atmosphere.

Figure 2.61 shows that, in the UK, the two main sources of CO_2 are power stations and road transport. On a world scale, the biggest CO_2 producer is the USA. Figure 2.60 shows that if other countries created the same per capita level of

Figure 2.61 Source of UK Carbon Dioxide (percentages, 1995)

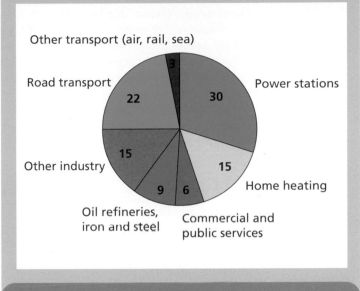

emissions as the USA, the overall increase would be massive.

The consequences of global warming are uncertain. Nevertheless, a consensus of scientific opinion suggests that sea levels will rise, and droughts and extreme weather events will become more frequent. In addition, climate zones might shift - causing changes in agriculture and also in the breeding grounds of insects such as mosquitoes.

(The causes and consequences of global warming are covered in more detail in unit 12.6.)

Figure 2.60 CO$_2$ Emissions

Selected countries	Population (millions) 1995	Energy use (kg oil equivalent) per capita 1994	Total energy use (million tonnes oil equivalent) 1994	CO2 emissions (tonnes) per capita 1992
China	1,200	650	780	2.3
India	929	250	232	0.9
Kenya	27	100	3	0.2
UK	58	3,750	217	9.8
USA	263	7,800	2,051	19.1

unit summary

1 Development creates negative effects including environmental pollution and social changes such as the breakdown of traditional cultures and ways of life.
2 People pollute the air, water and land with waste products from homes, industry and agriculture.
3 Pollution can pose dangers to human, plant and animal life. It is often difficult and expensive to dispose of waste. Radioactive waste is especially difficult to deal with.
4 Pollution affects the environment from the local scale to the world scale. Global warming and ozone depletion are two examples of world-wide effects.
5 Governments and other agencies have begun to tackle pollution issues. The Climate Conference held at Kyoto in December 1997 agreed new targets for reduction in greenhouse gas emissions.

key terms

Acid rain - rain which reacts with sulphur dioxide and nitrogen oxides to become more acidic. It is corrosive and helps speed chemical weathering.
Emissions - release of harmful substances from industry, vehicles or other sources.
Eutrophication - the process in which water is over-enriched by fertilisers; so depleting the water's oxygen supply.
Global warming - the rise in the Earth's average temperature, possibly due to increased emissions of greenhouse gases.
Greenhouse effect - the insulation of the Earth's surface by atmospheric gases.

Greenhouse gases - gases such as carbon dioxide which contribute to the greenhouse effect and global warming.
NIMBY - Not In My Back Yard; the name given to campaigns which object to waste disposal (or development projects in general) in a particular local area.
Negative externalities - the negative side effects arising from development.
Ozone layer - a layer in the atmosphere which protects the Earth from harmful ultra-violet radiation from the Sun.
Pollution - the introduction of harmful substances into the environment by humans.

Unit 2.6 Sustainable development

key questions

1 What is sustainable development?
2 Are current levels of consumption sustainable?
3 How can sustainable development be measured?
4 How can sustainable development be achieved?

1. What is sustainable development?

Sustainable development can be defined as economic growth and social progress that does not damage the prospects of future generations. It requires that resources (eg, raw materials and energy) are used and managed in ways that do not store up problems for the future. According to a former UK government minister, it means 'maintaining or improving our standard of living without cheating on our children's inheritance'.

Two examples from forestry help explain the idea of sustainability. If timber is cut faster than new growth occurs, then this is unsustainable in the long run. Similarly, if pollution is allowed to kill trees faster than new ones can grow, this is not sustainable. In both cases, timber output will eventually fall because there will be fewer trees. However, if new trees are planted and they grow healthily, and timber is then cut at a rate equal to the growth of new trees, the output can be sustained in the long run.

Long term sustainability also requires that the natural environment is not destroyed or permanently damaged. This relates to the concept of biodiversity. It is increasingly accepted that biodiversity is as much a resource as a coal deposit or a region of fertile soil. Biodiversity can be defined as the variety of flora and fauna (ie, plants and animals) in an area. The effect of development has been to reduce biodiversity. For example, in the UK, many species of plants and animals have disappeared as their habitats have been destroyed. Large scale intensive agriculture, involving high applications of fertiliser, harms bird and insect species. For example, in Britain, 17 bird species have declined by over 50 percent in the past 25 years. These include the lapwing, tawny owl and skylark - all of which were once common.

Tropical rain forests are especially rich in biodiversity but these are under great threat from farmers, loggers and plantation owners. Some species of plants and animals, for example mountain gorillas, are close to extinction as a result.

Biodiversity is important because it is part of our natural inheritance and should, it is said, be protected as a matter of duty. There is also a more selfish reason for maintaining diversity. The natural gene pool of the plant and animal world might contain cures for diseases such as cancer, AIDS and typhoid. If the environment continues to be damaged by human action, then the possibility of using the natural environment for medical purposes will be lost forever.

(Note: unit 4.3 includes case study material on the sustainable exploitation of natural resources such as minerals, timber and fish stocks. Unit 14.3 considers the issue of sustainable agriculture.)

The idea of sustainable development arose during the 1970s and 1980s. It was the main issue discussed at the **Earth Summit** held at Rio De Janeiro in 1992, officially known as the United Nations Conference on Environment and Development. The conference produced three main policy documents:

- the **Biodiversity Convention**, relating to the protection of flora and fauna
- the **Climate Change Convention**, relating to global warming (see units 2.5 and 12.6)
- **Agenda 21**, relating to Sustainable Development in the 21st century; the document proposed that countries should adopt policies to conserve the environment and resources.

The environment was defined as the air and water; natural vegetation and wildlife; and the social and human environment; ie, buildings, historic sites, and ways of life. Resources were defined as minerals (ores and fuels); fish and other marine life; and forests. To some extent these definitions of environment and resources overlap. Together, though, they constitute the renewable and non-renewable raw materials that people need to survive.

The UK government has published objectives for sustainable development. The aim is to 'ensure a better life for everyone, now and for generations to come' through:

- social progress which meets the needs of everyone

Figure 2.62 Brazilian rain forest

Many modern medicines have been developed from plant extracts. If the number of species declines, there is less potential for new discoveries and cures.

- effective protection of the environment
- prudent use of natural resources
- maintenance of high and stable levels of economic growth and employment.

The government's view is that protecting the environment does not necessarily involve cutting present consumption. Whether this view is true or not is an important theme that runs through this unit.

2. Are current levels of consumption sustainable?

The amount of land needed to produce the goods and services for one person's consumption is sometimes known as an ecological footprint. For the average Westerner, the **ecological footprint** is an estimated 5 hectares of land. This is the area of land required to produce the food, fuel and other raw materials that each person consumes. Yet, in 1995, the total available productive land in the world was only 1.7 hectares per person.

This means that people in Western countries consume far more of the world's resources than people in the Third World. It also means that the world as a whole could not sustain even its present population at Western levels of consumption. The total population of the world is projected to almost double within 100 years. As a result, the average area of productive land will fall to less than 0.9 hectares per person (assuming that the area of productive land does not alter). Under these circumstances, will the majority of people in less developed countries ever achieve higher living standards? And will the living standards enjoyed by most people in rich countries be sustainable in the long run?

The issue of **equity** or fairness is an important aspect of sustainable development. Will the world's 1.3 billion people who live in absolute poverty, on incomes of less than $1 a day, continue to consume less than their 'fair share' (see figure 2.63)?

The consequences of everybody in the world using resources at the rate, for example, of the average American is incalculable. To illustrate the point, David Bellamy has pointed out that our children will live in a world of almost 10 billion people. If they all consume like us, they will require 3 billion trees per year just to produce enough toilet paper to wipe their bottoms! This is approximately twenty times the number of trees growing in the whole of the UK today.

A similar point can be made about energy. If every inhabitant of China switched on one extra light bulb it would require the energy equivalent to 30 of Britain's largest coal fired power stations. Already China burns a quarter of the world's coal output in its power stations and this consumption is forecast to rise by 85 percent over the next 25 years. Even then, China's per capita electricity consumption will be less than the levels of North America or Western Europe today.

The issue of sustainability is not solely one of resources. There is no immediate shortage of many basic non-renewable raw materials. Even at current rates of consumption there is enough copper, iron and fossil fuel to last for many decades. More urgent is the concern relating to the 'life support' systems that we take for granted. These include the climate, soil fertility and the availability of fresh, clean water.

So, although it might be possible for China and other low income countries to find sufficient fossil fuel to burn in their power stations, the environmental impact might be severe. For instance, many believe that the process of global warming caused by increased carbon dioxide emissions will bring about unpredictable climatic changes.

Political leaders at the 1992 Earth Summit agreed that a world of 10 billion people cannot sustain present Western style levels of production and consumption. Given the projected population growth and the 'catching up' of less developed countries in levels of consumption, the increase in output is likely to create serious and irreversible damage to the environment.

Several possibilities exist. Pollution and environmental damage might cause the world's population to collapse in a 'Malthusian' disaster of famine, war and disease (see unit 1.4). Or the distribution of income and resources might remain as unequal as at present - though this

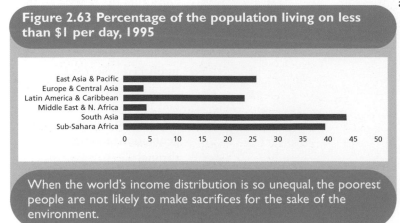

Figure 2.63 Percentage of the population living on less than $1 per day, 1995

When the world's income distribution is so unequal, the poorest people are not likely to make sacrifices for the sake of the environment.

will run the danger of tension and conflict between the Third World and high income countries. More optimistically, sustainable growth policies might be adopted that create new wealth while, at the same time, minimising the negative consequences of growth. These harmful side effects include:
- pollution of air, sea, rivers and groundwater
- global warming / climate change / rise in sea level
- ozone depletion
- acid rain
- soil erosion
- reduction in biodiversity.
    (These topics are described in more detail in units 2.5 (pollution and waste disposal), 12.6 (climate change) and 13.3 (soils).)

Because the negative effects of development are unpredictable in terms of scale, time and location, there is always the temptation to avoid making policy changes now. This is particularly true if the policies are politically unpopular. For example, raising the tax on petrol to discourage the use of private motor cars might help 'save the planet' but it risks losing the next election. The degree to which the negative effects of development come about will depend upon whether sustainable policies are implemented. These policies are discussed later in this unit.

Activity Private cars

Figure 2.64 London traffic ►

Questions

1 In 1997, 2 million new cars were registered in the UK (with a population of 59 million). In the same year, 0.5 million new cars were registered in China (with a population of 1,227 million). For the world as a whole, in 1997, there were 37 million new car registrations.
    Calculate the number of cars that would have been registered in China if new car ownership had been the same as in the UK. Comment on this number in terms of its impact on the use of resources and on the environment.
2 In your view, is the current upward trend in private car ownership sustainable? Explain the reasons for your answer.

According to environmental campaigners, the present use of minerals and fossil fuels is both wasteful and damaging to the environment. Oil is a hydrocarbon that is finite and precious. Each year, people in the UK burn oil that took an estimated two million years to form. Although there might still be sufficient oil reserves for decades of production, the oil could be used to produce recyclable plastics, pharmaceuticals and, as yet uninvented, new materials. Instead it goes up in smoke - producing carbon dioxide and other pollutants.

In Europe, only 10 percent of the potential energy in fossil fuel is used. The USA is even more wasteful. Internal combustion engines are inefficient and are a major cause of respiratory disease.

Cars and lorries in the UK are consuming twice the fuel they did 25 years ago because of congested roads. Any technological advances in fuel efficiency are being overwhelmed by the sheer volume of traffic according to Department of the Environment statistics. In 1995, road transport used a quarter of the total energy consumed in the UK.

Government agencies in the UK are starting to recognise that present trends in private car usage are unsustainable. More cars are burning fuel, but going nowhere! They are caught in longer and longer traffic jams. Over 60 percent of urban air pollution is caused by vehicles. Bypasses, new roads and motorways are being built which destroy our environment, yet average traffic speeds are slowing down.

3. How can sustainable development be measured?

At the Rio Earth Conference, it was agreed that a set of **sustainable development indicators** should be established. These indicators would measure economic growth, social progress and environmental impact. Unless there are systems of measurement, it is difficult for governments and other agencies to set targets and monitor progress.

At present, most countries measure economic growth by calculating changes to their per capita Gross National Product (GNP). This is the value of total output of goods and services, in a given year, divided by the total population.

Because GNP only measures the output of goods and services, it does not give a complete picture of standards of living. The United Nations Human Development Index (HDI) is an attempt to combine economic and social indicators and so give a truer indication of living standards (see unit 2.1). As well as per capita GNP, the index also measures two other basic components of human development - life expectancy and educational attainment (ie, adult literacy together with combined primary, secondary and tertiary enrolment). However, the HDI does not give an indication of environmental impact.

In the UK, an attempt to measure sustainable development was made by the Office of National Statistics (ONS) when it produced its first set of 'green' national accounts in 1996. These green accounts included factors that have an impact on the environment:
* the rate at which North Sea oil and gas reserves are being depleted

Figure 2.65 Polluted waterway

A green GNP is a measure of national output less the cost of environmental damage.

* the sources of air pollution
* the amounts spent by various industrial sectors on cleaner technology.

Some environmentalists have urged the government to go further and put a monetary value on the negative consequences of economic growth. This figure could then be subtracted from GNP to produce a **green GNP**. However, the statisticians in ONS argue that it is impossible to put a true or accurate monetary cost on, for instance, air pollution. For example, if poor air quality causes someone to have an asthma attack, how can the cost to the individual be assessed?

Development Watch is a United Nations agency which is monitoring progress on sustainable development. It has proposed a draft list of environmental indicators. These measures relate to the key factors which, in the agency's view, are important when assessing the environmental impact of development. The indicators include:

Water
* annual withdrawals of ground and surface water as percentage of available water
* industrial / municipal discharges into freshwater lakes and rivers
* household consumption of water per capita
* catches of fish and other marine species.

Land
* land use change
* area affected by soil erosion
* area affected by desertification
* deforestation rate / annual timber production
* arable land per capita / use of fertilisers and pesticides per km^2
* rate of extinction of protected species.

Atmosphere
* emissions of carbon dioxide, sulphur dioxide, nitrogen oxides
* production of ozone destroying substances.

Waste
* quantity of waste recycled as a proportion of total municipal and industrial waste
* generation of toxic wastes / area of land contaminated by toxic waste.

Development Watch also monitors whether:
* international agreements on environmental issues have been ratified (ie, incorporated into national law)

- programmes for setting up environmental indicators and statistics are in place
- sustainable development strategies are established
- representatives of indigenous peoples are included in national decision making.

(This latter point covers, for example, whether rain forest dwellers in Amazonia and Indonesia have had some say in how 'their' land is developed.)

Although the Development Watch indicators are comprehensive, there are practical difficulties in using them to produce a single environmental index that could be used to compare progress. Different countries use a variety of means to collect statistics and some measures might not allow easy comparisons. For example, 'land use change' could mean completely different things in different countries. And, in any case, is a change in land use always a 'bad thing'? If trees are planted on derelict industrial land, this could be an improvement. Another problem arises in defining terms. For instance, the definition of 'forest' varies between countries and this makes any comparison of deforestation rates unreliable. There is also the problem of inaccurate and incomplete data collection, particularly in those Third World countries with few resources or where there is civil conflict.

Even if reliable statistics could be collected, there is the difficulty of converting them into a simple numerical scale or index so that comparisons can be made. It is doubtful if any consensus could be reached on the weighting that should be given to any single indicator. For instance, should the size of fish catches be given an equal weight to the emission of carbon dioxide? These issues make it unlikely that a single environmental index will ever be generally agreed.

Activity environmental indicators

Figure 2.66 ▶ Selected environmental indicators for ten countries

Country	Per capita water use (average 1980-96, cubic metres)	Annual deforestation (average % 1990-95)	Carbon dioxide emissions (tonnes per person 1995)
Brazil	246	0.5	1.6
Canada	1,602	-0.1	14.7
Egypt	921	0.0	1.6
India	612	0.0	1.0
Malawi	98	1.6	0.1
New Zealand	589	-0.6	7.6
Philippines	686	3.5	0.9
UK	204	-0.5	9.3
USA	1,839	-0.3	20.8
Zambia	216	0.8	0.3

Note: a negative figure for deforestation indicates an increase in forest cover.

Questions

1 To what extent do these indicators provide a useful guide to the state of the environment in the selected countries?
2 For each of the indicators, place the countries in rank order according to impact on the environment (ie, make the 'worst' country number 1 and the 'best' country number 10.) Add up the ranks and use these totals to construct an overall index.
3 Outline the strengths and weaknesses of the index that you have constructed.

4. How can sustainable development be achieved?

Sustainable development requires less wasteful use of energy and raw materials; more recycling of waste; greater energy conservation; more use of renewable energy sources such as solar and wind power; and more use of clean, ie non-polluting, production methods. However, the methods of achieving sustainable development are much easier said than done. Most of the commitments made at the 1992 Earth Summit have not been honoured - the environment is being damaged at an increasing pace. Nevertheless, progress has been made in certain areas. Some of the policy issues are outlined below.

Urban dwelling

The traditional view of urbanisation and, in particular, the rapid growth of some Third World cities, is that the process is harmful. Big urban centres are seen as exploding out of control, unable to support their populations and causing great damage to the environment. However, there is some evidence that, contrary to the mainstream view, urban living can provide solutions to environmental problems. Cities can accommodate large numbers of people on relatively small areas of land. In the Third World, fertility rates are significantly lower in cities than in rural areas and statistics show that the urban poor are three to five times better off than the rural poor.

At the United Nations Habitat II Conference, held at Istanbul in 1997, some optimistic views on cities were expressed in contrast to earlier 'doomsday' scenarios of cities collapsing in chaos. At the Conference, speakers pointed out that many Third World cities produce much of the food necessary to feed their populations. For example, in China, city gardens provide 90 percent of the vegetables that their inhabitants consume. In Kenya, researchers have found that two thirds of urban households grow some of their own food, and half of them keep livestock. Around the world, rooftop and balcony gardening, and animals in the backyard, produce a much bigger

output than previously realised. So, it might be the case that urban living is not the ecologically unfriendly and unsustainable process that many writers in the past have suggested. Rather, the opposite might be true and the trend towards urban living that is occurring in most parts of the world should perhaps be welcomed and encouraged.

In places such as Britain, where people are leaving cities, the government should possibly develop policies to encourage urban living and discourage 'counter-urbanisation' (see unit 3.4). Urban living has a number of advantages. Terraced inner-city homes can be more energy efficient than detached rural homes because they have fewer exterior walls. And, if new housing is built on 'brownfield' sites within urban areas, rather than on 'greenfield' sites in the countryside, less environmental damage is caused. City dwellers travel shorter distances in commuting, and their waste processing installations can be more efficient than those for rural populations.

Energy

At the 1992 Rio summit, high income countries agreed to peg fossil fuel emissions at 1990 levels by the year 2000. The aim was to cut carbon dioxide levels in the atmosphere. Only the UK and Germany managed to achieve this target. In Germany, it was achieved by closing down the dirty and inefficient coal power

Figure 2.67 New housing on a brownfield site

Over the next 20 years, an estimated 4.5 million houses are needed in the UK. If most of these can be built on brownfield sites, rather than greenfield sites, the environmental impact will be less severe. The problem is that, for developers, it is cheaper to build in the countryside rather than on land that has already been used for building and then cleared.

stations of the former East Germany. In the UK it was achieved by running down the coal industry and switching from coal fired power stations to gas powered. Burning gas emits much less pollution than coal. Whether this 'dash for gas' is sustainable in the long run is very much open to doubt because North Sea gas reserves will, one day, be exhausted.

In the future, the UK and the rest of the world need sources of energy that are environmentally friendly and sustainable. These will include solar power and energy from wind and waves. The issue of renewable energy is covered in more detail in unit 4.2.

Government policies

Many governments have started to promote sustainable development by a range of policy measures. These involve taxation, legislation, setting up protected areas and also direct action.

'Green' taxation This is the name given to taxes that are 'environmentally friendly'. For example, in its 1996 Budget, the UK government introduced a landfill tax. This tax, levied at a fixed rate per tonne, is paid by businesses and local authorities which dump waste in landfill sites. At present, most UK household waste is dumped as landfill.

The tax aims to encourage councils to recycle a greater proportion of waste and so reduce landfill. For every tonne of paper, metal, glass and plastic recycled, less tax has to be paid. However, the rate set in 1996 was considered by many environmentalists to be too low - even though it added an average £5 per year to every council tax bill. A 1995 estimate stated that a tax of £20 per tonne would be required to get 12 percent of domestic waste recycled. In the 1999 Budget, it was announced that the tax, then set at £10 per tonne, would rise by £1 per tonne each year in the future.

In Norway a 'carbon tax' was introduced in 1991. This raises the price of fossil fuels according to the amount of CO_2 they emit when burnt. The result has been to reduce carbon emissions from power plants by over 20 percent per year. Similar taxes have been introduced in the UK. The government's target of cutting carbon dioxide emissions by 12.5 percent, by 2010, is one reason for annual rises in petrol duty (ie, tax) and the reduction in car tax for small engined cars.

In 1997, the EU proposed a worldwide tax on aviation fuel. Although air travel only contributes 3 percent of greenhouse gases, it is the fastest growing form of transport. The pollution is delivered high in the atmosphere where it takes immediate effect. Another point in the tax's favour is that it would be paid mainly by people from the rich, industrialised world who take holidays abroad and travel by air, ie those most able to pay. To be effective, the tax would have to be levied on a worldwide scale. A single country or group of countries could not levy the tax effectively because the airlines would simply refuel elsewhere.

Legislation Governments sometimes use the law to promote sustainable development. For instance, throughout the EU, the law now requires that an Environmental Impact Assessment is carried out for all large scale civil engineering projects, eg motorways, tunnels and oil field development. Whenever a company or developer wish to carry out a project, they must first complete an environmental impact assessment before planning permission can be considered. In a 1998 landmark ruling in the UK, the courts prevented the extension of a limestone quarry in the Pennines because a full Environmental Impact Assessment had not been carried out.

Many countries have established Environmental Protection Agencies (in the UK- the Environment Agency) which have a legal responsibility to monitor and control pollution and other forms of environmental damage. There is always tension between those who wish to promote new developments, perhaps creating jobs and increasing incomes, and those who wish to conserve the environment. This tension is greatest in Third World countries where many people live in poverty.

However, there are examples of environmental protection in low income countries. For example, in 1997, the Supreme Court of India supported conservationists and ordered all large commercial shrimp and prawn farms to close in five coastal states. The Court ruled that the industry was acting illegally by polluting the coastline.

Protected zones Often countries try to control development in their most valuable and sensitive environments by setting up specially protected zones. In the UK, there are agencies with the responsibility for looking after wild plants and animals (ie, the country's biodiversity) and the natural features. In England, the body is called English Nature (there is also Scottish Natural Heritage, the Countryside Council for Wales and the Environmental and Heritage Service in Northern Ireland).

Activity | Environmental protection in coastal India

◀ **Figure 2.68 Traditional fishing in south Asia**

Traditional fishing methods are under pressure in parts of south and east Asia. Widespread environmental damage is caused by large scale commercial shrimp and prawn farms. In most Third World countries, the pressure to earn more money from exports outweighs local environmental protection legislation.

The value of Indian shrimp and prawn exports to Japan, the USA and Europe is $500 million each year. India, with Indonesia, Thailand and Ecuador produce 70 percent of the world's farmed prawns. However, the large scale prawn and shrimp farms do great damage to the environment. They require massive quantities of water. To raise one tonne of shrimps, 20 to 30 million litres of fresh water are needed - a serious burden in regions where clean drinking water is scarce. Each kilogram of produce generates about 15,000 litres of effluent, including toxic residues. These chemicals are often released untreated into the sea. After only four or five years, the coastal lands become so contaminated that they are abandoned. It can take up to twenty years for them to recover.

Shrimp production is also very wasteful in energy terms. During their lives, shrimps eat three times their harvested weight but convert only 17 percent of this feed into edible flesh. Since the creatures are mainly fed on fish meal, it encourages local fishermen to trawl all fish stocks, including under-size fish, to supply the industry's needs. Scientific studies in India suggest that the environmental damage is actually costing India more than it is earning through shrimp exports.

It is possible to farm prawns and shrimps in an environmentally friendly way. Using a 'closed' system which recycles and cleans waste water, farmers would not have to abandon polluted stretches of coast after just five years of use. However, the filters and other equipment are so expensive that costs would be raised. Other unregulated producers, in India and other countries, would undercut prices and drive the 'green' farmers out of business.

Questions

1 Briefly outline why unregulated shrimp farming is unsustainable in the long run.
2 What policies or strategies could be used to promote environmentally friendly systems of shrimp farming?

These agencies have responsibility for a large number of protected areas. For example, in England there are approximately 200 National Nature Reserves (NNR), 4,000 Sites of Special Scientific Interest (SSSI), 150 Special Protection Areas as well as over 500 Local Nature Reserves. These are in addition to the National Parks and Areas of Outstanding Natural Beauty (AONB) which have their own special planning rules (see unit 6.3).

The protected sites are places where particular wild

flowers, animals, insects or bird life, or sites of landscape or geological interest are found. The NNRs tend to be publicly owned and generally bigger than the SSSIs which are mostly privately owned.

Direct government action Both local and national governments sometimes take direct action to promote environmentally friendly activity. Instead of passing laws or regulations, the government directly intervenes in the process. Examples of direct action include government departments making their own buildings more energy efficient, and spending money on public transport subsidies.

Cheshire County Council has produced a Sustainable Transport Strategy. It has set targets for reducing the growth in private car usage and for increasing the use of public transport, walking and cycling. The Council recognises that road transport is the largest source of air pollution in the county and accounts for one third of Cheshire's energy consumption. Road vehicles are the biggest single source of accidents and injuries, and the biggest generator of noise.
The County's targets include:
- a reduction in the proportion of journeys to work by car from 70 percent in 1991 to 60 percent by 2011
- an increase in the proportion of journeys to work by public transport from 7 percent in 1991 to 14 percent by 2011
- an increase in the proportion of journeys to work by cycle from 4 percent in 1991 to 10 percent in 2011
- a limit to road traffic growth in Cheshire of 16 percent above the 1991 level by 2011 (compared with the national traffic forecast growth of 32 percent).

The Council's actions to achieve these targets include:
- a publicity campaign, 'Travel Wise', to raise awareness of the consequences of car use and to promote alternatives like walking, cycling and public transport
- using the planning procedure to ensure that new developments maximise and encourage the use of public transport, walking and cycling
- using the available transport funds to provide footpaths, cycleways and bus lanes
- scaling down new roadbuilding, recognising that increased congestion will persuade more people to use alternatives to cars
- urging national government to set tighter controls on vehicle emissions.

Figure 2.69 Cycleway in Cheshire

One means of reducing CO_2 emissions and conserving resources is by encouraging the use of bicycles.

Non-governmental organisations (NGOs)

In addition to action by governments, there are a range of other organisations which are promoting sustainable development policies. These bodies include charities and environmental campaigners.

Intermediate Technology Development Group This NGO is a development agency and charity established in 1966 by E.F. Schumacher, author of *Small is Beautiful*. This influential book set out a development strategy that emphasised helping people by improving their access to appropriate technology. This is small scale, low cost technology that local people can use and maintain themselves. It does not rely on foreign experts or high cost technology that is too expensive for most Third World countries. Examples of the agency's work include:
- Sri Lanka - design and production of lightweight bicycle trailers by local workers. The trailers enable food and other produce to be marketed more quickly and efficiently by small scale farmers and traders.
- Zimbabwe - production of low cost, low technology tools for small scale mining.
- Peru - disaster protection; improving building design by incorporating flexible structures to make houses less vulnerable to earthquakes and landslides.

World Wide Fund for Nature (WWF) This pressure group campaigns to protect the natural environment. For example, in 1997, the WWF called on all governments to grant complete protection for at least 10 percent of their forests by the year 2000. The WWF also takes a lead role in development work, maintaining a balance between conservation and human development. For example, in Madagascar, the WWF helps run a project in the Zombitse rain forest where new settlers are threatening the unique ecological system. Local people have been encouraged to set aside particularly sensitive areas of forest from any logging or farming activity. People who ignore the rules are arrested and fined by the village authorities, and any income is confiscated. In return, the project provides schools and health care clinics. With other NGOs, the WWF is working to protect 29,000 hectares of forest. At the same time, eco-tourism is being developed to provide local people with income. Spectacular forest scenery, rare birds, and animals such as lemurs provide the attraction. The aim is to attract tourists, yet maintain local culture and traditions. Unlike many other Third World tourist destinations, the income generated is ploughed back into the local area.

In another project, the WWF has turned unsustainable snowdrop bulb collection in the Toros region of Turkey into a lucrative business. Until the 1990s, villagers in this mountain region uprooted millions of wild snowdrop and aconite bulbs for sale in Western European garden centres. Now, with the help of WWF project staff, the villagers have learned how to propagate the plants and are growing them commercially. During 1996, over 500kg of bulbs were harvested in this way - providing a secure and sustainable income for local people.

Greenpeace This is a pressure group that campaigns on environmental issues. It specialises in raising public awareness. For instance, in 1997 it displayed solar panels at exhibitions around the UK. Greenpeace claimed that 24 panels installed on a private house would meet 50 percent of a family's electricity needs. This would reduce the emission of CO_2 by 40 tonnes over the 30 year lifetime of the system.

Also in 1997, Greenpeace urged the UK government to refuse oil exploration licences to companies searching for oil in the Atlantic Frontier. This is the basin on the edge of the continental shelf west of the Shetland Islands. Greenpeace argued that granting licences, at a time when greenhouse gases are increasing, would contravene the commitments of the Climate Convention agreed at the Rio summit. This called upon countries to 'take precautionary measures to anticipate, prevent or minimise the causes of climate change'.

Forest Stewardship Council (FSC) This is an international pressure group which has set up a scheme to promote sustainable forestry. The aim is to monitor and certify forestry producers and forest products - checking that they comply with sustainable policy guidelines. So, for example, forests should not be 'clear cut' and trees should be replanted in an ecologically sensitive fashion. In this way, forests will not be destroyed but will be maintained as long term sources of income for local people. This policy contrasts with that of other pressure groups such as Greenpeace which urge a total boycott of tropical forest products.

Sustainable forestry means that habitats are preserved - so maintaining biodiversity and the way of life of indigenous peoples. Because trees convert CO_2 into oxygen, replanting forests also reduces the buildup of CO_2 in the atmosphere.

The FSC system works through publicity and commercial pressure on retailers. For instance, in the UK, B&Q pledged that by 1999 it would only buy timber products with FSC certification. In 1997, the company announced that it already stocked over 600 individual items from certified forests in Malaysia, Poland, South Africa, Zimbabwe, Sri Lanka and the UK. B&Q hopes that customers will be attracted by its 'green' policy and will not buy lower priced products from clear cut forests.

 Activity **Ecological footprints**

London has an 'ecological footprint' 125 times the size of its surface area. So, with 12 per cent of the UK's population, it requires the equivalent of the country's entire productive land to support its level of consumption. Much of the land supplying London is, of course, in the fields of East Anglia, the prairies of Kansas, the forests of Malaysia, the coalfields of Yorkshire and the tea plantations of

Kenya. These are some of the places that supply the food, fuel and raw materials that Londoners use. Its high income population is able to buy resources from around the world in order to maintain its standard of living.

Questions

1 Explain in your own words, with reference to London, what is meant by an 'ecological footprint'.

2 In your view, is the level of consumption enjoyed by people in London sustainable in the long term? Give reasons for your answer?

3 How might it be possible for Londoners to reduce the size of their 'ecological footprint'?

▲ Figure 2.70 The 'ecological footprint' of London is 125 times the size of its surface area.

unit summary

1 Sustainable development is a process of economic growth and social progress that conserves resources and the environment for people in the future.

2 All major countries have accepted that sustainable development is one of the most important challenges facing humanity. However, progress has been very limited through the 1990s. High income economies use most of the world's resources and do most damage to the environment. Low income countries see this as unfair.

3 For targets to be set, and progress measured, a set of sustainable development indicators is required. During the 1990s, CO_2 emissions have been the most widely used indicator.

4 Sustainable development requires less wasteful use of energy and raw materials; more recycling of waste; greater energy conservation; more use of renewable energy sources such as solar and wind power; more use of 'clean', ie non-polluting, production methods.

key terms

Biodiversity - the variety of flora and fauna (ie, plants, animals and other organisms) in an area.

Equity - fairness.

Earth Summit - the 1992 United Nations Conference on Environment and Development, held at Rio de Janeiro.

Ecological footprint - the area of land required to maintain the consumption of an individual or community.

Green GNP - the total value of goods and

services produced in a country in one year, less the cost of the negative side effects arising from economic activity.

Sustainable development - economic growth and social progress that does not damage the ability of future generations to meet their needs.

Sustainable development indicator - a statistic or set of statistics that can be used to measure economic, social and environmental progress.

CHAPTER 3 Settlement

Introduction

Settlements are places where people live. They can vary in size from an individual dwelling to a sprawling 'megalopolis' where several cities have joined together. Small settlements such as villages are usually described as rural, and large settlements such as towns and cities are described as urban, although in practice the distinction between these is blurred.

Economic and social development has been closely connected with the growth of settlements. Mayan and Inca civilisations in the Americas, Greek civilisations in Europe and Chinese civilisations in Asia were all based on urban communities. Today, cities such as Tokyo, Los Angeles, Shanghai and London provide the focus for new economic and social activity.

This chapter looks at the development of cities and the processes that operate within them. It also examines the reasons why some rural settlements in the UK are in decline while others are growing rapidly.

Chapter summary

Unit 3.1 examines settlement patterns.
Unit 3.2 considers the issues facing rural settlements.
Unit 3.3 looks at the urbanisation process and the world pattern of urban development.
Unit 3.4 examines counterurbanisation - the movement of population away from cities.
Unit 3.5 investigates the structure and pattern of land use within urban areas.
Unit 3.6 summarises the ways in which urban problems are managed, and contrasts the problems of cities in high income countries with those in low income countries.

Unit 3.1 Settlement patterns

key questions

1 What factors influence the site and situation of settlements?
2 What factors influence the pattern of settlements?

1. What factors influence the site and situation of settlements?

Site

The site of a settlement is the actual land on which it is built. When describing a particular site, it is conventional to note certain features:
- the angle of slope (eg, whether the land is flat or is steeply sloping)
- the aspect (ie, the direction in which a slope faces)
- the height above sea level
- the dimensions (ie, size) of the settlement
- the morphology of the settlement (ie, the shape; for instance whether the settlement is compact or whether it is linear)

- any physical features that mark the boundaries of the site, for example a river or coastline.

The site of Starbotton, in the Yorkshire Dales, is described in figure 3.2

Figure 3.1 Starbotton from the west

Figure 3.2 Starbotton in Upper Wharfedale (scale 1:25 000)

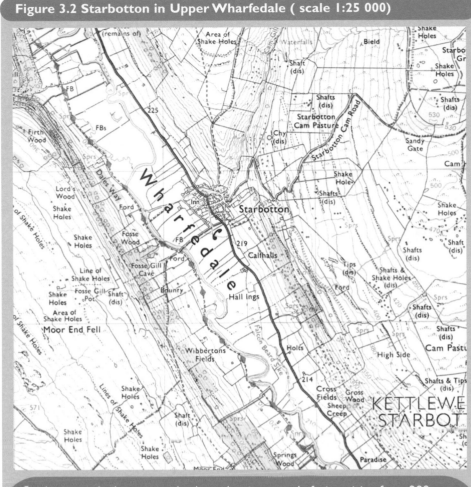

Starbotton is built on a gentle slope that is westerly facing, rising from 200 metres above sea level on its western side to 240 metres above sea level on its eastern side. It lies just above the flood plain of the River Wharfe, 300 metres east of the river. The village is small and relatively compact, with a diameter of approximately 200 - 250 metres. Starbotton is on the eastern side of Wharfedale, sheltered from the coldest winds and facing the afternoon sunshine. A small stream flows through the village from a narrow valley to the north east.

- is well drained, away from marshy areas where 'biological hazards' such as malarial mosquitoes are present
- has an aspect that maximises sunshine hours and provides shelter from cold winds
- has good transport links; eg, natural routeways such as rivers valleys; bridging or fording points on rivers; or inlets that make sheltered natural harbours
- has a supply of building materials such as timber or stone
- is close to valuable mineral deposits (eg, near a gold deposit)
- is near to farmland for its food supply
- is easily defended.

For any particular site, only some of these factors will normally be present. People usually have to make compromises in their choices so, for instance, the desire to build on flat land might be outweighed if the land is marshy and a breeding ground for mosquitoes.

When people choose the site for a new settlement, they normally try and ensure that it is safe, ie free from natural hazards such as flooding or volcanic eruption. Of course, people sometimes make mistakes in siting a village or town but these settlements often do not survive. The example of Pompeii near Mount Vesuvius, which was covered by volcanic ash in 79 AD shows that people can miscalculate the risks. So does the much more recent 1998 destruction by mudslide of Sarno, a village on the slopes of the same mountain. Another example, on a much larger scale, occurred in 1985. The town of Nevado del Ruiz in Colombia was destroyed and 25,000 people died when a nearby volcano erupted. The snowcap on the mountain melted and mudflows surged down the slopes (see unit 7.3). The town had been built on the solidified remains of an old mudflow. This should have been a warning that a similar event might occur.

A number of factors influence people's decisions on where to site a new settlement. The relative importance of these factors varies from place to place. The factors also vary depending on when the settlement was built. For instance, the reasons why a particular site was chosen in, say, Roman times might be very different from the reasons why a site is chosen today.

The factors that have influenced decisions on where to build a new settlement include whether the site:
- is free of danger from natural hazards (eg, flooding, volcanic eruption, landslide)
- has a nearby supply of drinking water
- is relatively flat (this is because slopes are sometimes unstable, especially if they bear the weight of buildings)

Figure 3.3 A small hill settlement in Greece

At one time, defensive locations were important considerations when choosing the site for a new settlement.

Sometimes generations of people are lucky and live their lives on unsafe sites. It is estimated that four million people live in the Naples area - one of the most densely populated and volcanically active regions in Europe. Over half a million live on the slopes of Vesuvius between the mountain and the sea. Many of the houses were built with complete disregard for local planning and zoning laws which try to steer people away from potentially dangerous sites. Vulcanologists know that it is only a matter of time before an eruption destroys some of these buildings.

Some factors that were once important influences on siting decisions are now less crucial. For example, in arid regions of Arizona and southern California, many new settlements have been built despite there being no local supply of drinking water. Aqueducts bring water from the Colorado River, in some cases to settlements 400km away. In general, it is only in high income countries such as the USA that people have the resources to finance such schemes.

A local food supply is not always necessary for a settlement as long as the population generates enough income to buy the food it needs. For instance, Singapore is a city state of 3 million people, built on a sand bar at the southern end of the Malay Peninsula. The site was chosen because it provided a safe anchorage on a trading route between the Indian and Pacific Oceans. The city has become an important port and manufacturing centre despite having to import most of its food.

A good defensive location was often a vital consideration when choosing a site. For example, in Spain, southern France and Italy, many towns and villages are built on hilltops. Such sites enabled inhabitants to keep a look out across a wide area and also gave defenders an advantage over enemies who had to attack uphill. The inside of meander loops, and islands in rivers were also good defensive sites because attackers would be slowed down when crossing the river channel. Paris is an example of a city that has grown from a site originally on an island - in its case, in the River Seine. Now, however, defensive locations have become irrelevant. Modern weapons mean that hill top and river island locations are no safer than anywhere else.

Situation

The situation of a settlement is its position in relation to other physical and human features. For example, its distance from a coastline, river or mountain range, or its location in relation to other settlements, or to political and administrative boundaries. Situation refers to a wider geographical area than site.

Figure 3.4 London

London is situated in South East England. The city is built on both the north and south banks of the River Thames, approximately 50km inland from the North Sea. It lies in a basin with the South Downs to the south and the Chiltern Hills to the north west.

In general, people do not choose the situation of a new settlement, they choose a site and this determines the situation. In other words, the situation of a settlement is a consequence of a siting decision. For example, the original site of London was chosen because it was an area of relatively dry land near a fording point (and later a bridging point) across the Thames. The settlement's later importance as a regional and then national administrative centre partly came about because of its situation - centrally located in southern England with good communication links in all directions.

In some cases, people do choose a situation for a settlement, and then look for a suitable site. Canberra, the capital of Australia is an example. Its location was the result of a political decision to locate away from the large cities (Sydney and Melbourne) that were rivals to become the capital. Another example, Brasilia, was chosen as a symbol of Brazil's new 'frontier' - away from Rio de Janeiro and Sao Paulo - in the sparsely inhabited and unexploited interior of that country.

2. What factors influence the pattern of settlements?

The way that settlements are spaced (ie, distributed) across a landscape gives rise to settlement patterns. In the case of individual houses, the pattern can be nucleated or dispersed.

A **nucleated** pattern exists when houses are clustered together in villages or larger settlements. There are a number of reasons why this occurs:

* The houses might have been built close together for defensive reasons. In violent and lawless times, there was safety in numbers and people living in large settlements were better able to defend themselves than those living in isolated farmhouses. Settlements on the borders of England and Scotland exhibit this pattern, as do hill towns in southern France and Italy.
* If shops and services are located together in towns or villages rather than spread across the landscape, the amount of travelling that people have to undertake is minimised. Rather than having to travel to different centres for their needs, people only have to travel to one. It follows that travelling time and costs are also minimised if people live in the settlements where the shops and services are located.
* In old coal mining areas such as Durham and South Yorkshire, pit villages were sited next to the mines which were spaced across the coalfields. It was

convenient for the miners if their houses were as close as possible to their place of work.
* In places where water is scarce, settlements might be clustered near a spring or well.
* Sometimes the system of land tenure (ie, land ownership) favours the growth of villages. In southern Europe, the traditional pattern of tenure is one of large estates that are worked by hired farm workers. This system spread to Latin America with the Spaniards and Portuguese. The farmworkers and their families generally live in villages that have been built and are owned by the estate.

A **dispersed** pattern occurs when individual houses, farms or hamlets are spread out across a landscape. The reasons for this pattern include:

* The pattern of land use and tenure. By the end of the eighteenth century in parts of England, the rural settlement pattern had changed as land became 'enclosed'. Previously, many people had lived in dwellings clustered near a manor house, and farmed strips in large open fields. During the 'enclosure movement', the land was subdivided into individual farms. People moved to farmhouses, built on the farms. This saved time and energy because people were nearer the land they farmed and they did not have to travel to separate strips of land that might be some distance apart. As a result, dwellings became increasingly dispersed.
* In some places, the move from a nucleated to a dispersed pattern in the English countryside coincided with a greater degree of law and order. It became safer to live in isolated farmhouses and there was less need of the protection provided by village life. A pattern of dispersed, even isolated, dwellings is typical of many areas settled during the past two hundred years. So, for instance, the spread of farming into upland areas such as the Pennines and Cumbria created a pattern of dispersed farmhouses in the nineteenth century.
* In northern Europe, there is a tradition of farmers owning or renting the land on which they farm. This system spread to the USA and Canada. It was encouraged by government land grants to settlers who were willing to set up their own farms. This gave rise to a dispersed settlement pattern of individual farmsteads. Now, it should be noted, in some places there is a reverse trend. A combination of rural isolation, loneliness and the availability of modern transport has caused a growing number of American 'suitcase' farmers to live in larger settlements and only travel to their farms when need be.

Although it is convenient in theory to divide settlement patterns into nucleated or dispersed, there is no clear cut dividing line between the two. One pattern can, in places, gradually merge into the other or, even, can overlie the other. Often this is a matter of scale. For example, a small local area might have a dispersed pattern of farm houses. But, when the surrounding region is examined, the same area might also have a pattern of nucleated villages between which the individual farm houses are scattered.

In some places, the distribution of settlements such as villages and towns gives rise to particular patterns. **Linear pattern** In England, along the foot of the Cotswolds and Chilterns, villages have formed on 'spring lines'. These are lines of springs where a supply of water emerges, usually along the foot of a chalk or limestone ridge. In South Wales, villages that were built next to coal mines also form a linear pattern. This is a result of the physical landscape of parallel valleys. The mines were built in these valleys, close to the coal seams, and the pit villages followed this pattern.

In the American Midwest and prairies, settlements form a linear pattern for a different reason. Towns and cities developed along the railway lines which brought settlers in the nineteenth century. The railways were the only practical way that bulky farm produce could be transported large distances overland. The settlements became centres for warehousing, processing and transporting grain and livestock.

Regular pattern Sometimes nucleated settlements form a regular, grid like pattern. This is typical of planned settlements such as those found on reclaimed land (or 'polders') in the Netherlands. The planners designed a pattern of small towns and villages, evenly spaced across the flat landscape. This arrangement is efficient in that it minimises the number of schools and other services that have to be provided, and also minimises the distances that people need to travel to reach these services.

Activity — **Nucleated and dispersed settlement patterns**

The two map extracts are both from the 1:50,000 scale OS Landranger map of the Lincoln area.

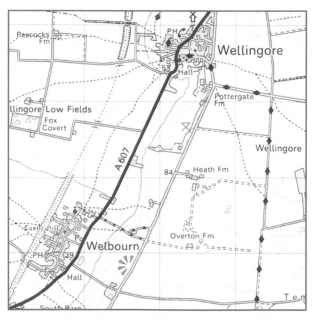

▲ **Figure 3.5 Welbourn and Wellingore**

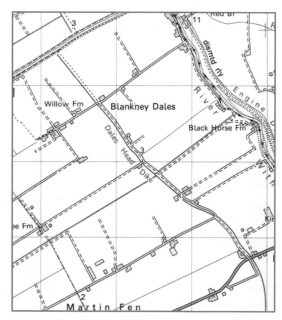

▲ **Figure 3.6 Blankney**

Questions

1 Compare and contrast the site of Welbourn with that of Wellingore.
2 Describe the settlement pattern in each of the map extracts.
3 What additional information would be useful in comparing and explaining the settlement patterns in the two areas?

Central place theory

Central place theory is an attempt to explain the size and distribution of settlements by looking at general principles rather than particular examples. First developed in the 1930s by Christaller, the theory was based on his research in southern Germany. Christaller proposed that distinct patterns of central places would arise, assuming that there was a uniform (ie, flat) landscape. A central place might be a village, town or city. People who live in the area surrounding a central place, within its 'sphere of influence', are assumed to travel to their nearest central place for goods and services.

A number of terms and ideas are used in central place theory:

Settlement hierarchy: this is a rank order of settlements, ranging in size from isolated farmhouses and hamlets, to villages, towns and cities.

Settlement functions: these are the services that are provided by settlements. In Britain, the functions for different sized settlements typically include:

- farmhouse or hamlet - accommodation for inhabitants, possibly a post box and a bus stop
- village - public house, post office, general store, primary school, church
- town - many shops, banks, secondary school, town hall, police station, hospital, bus and railway station, cinema, professional football team, library
- city - cathedral, university, many financial and administrative services, multiplex cinema, shopping centre.

Each settlement in the hierarchy fulfils not only its own functions but also fulfils those of the smaller settlements. In general, the bigger the population, the more functions there are.

Threshold: this is the minimum population required to make a function viable. Below this level there are not enough customers to provide sufficient revenue or, in the case of public services, there are not enough people (eg, school pupils, hospital patients) to make provision worthwhile. So, for example, the threshold population for a GP (a family doctor) is between two and three thousand people. For a Woolworth store it is approximately 20,000 people and for a Marks and Spencer store it is approximately 50,000.

Range: this is the distance that people are prepared to travel to take advantage of a particular function. In general, the more expensive the item, the greater the range. People are not normally prepared to travel far to buy low cost, **convenience** (or 'low order') goods such as bread, newspapers or groceries. Central places selling these goods will be relatively closely spaced and will have a small sphere of influence. For more expensive **comparison** (or 'high order') goods, such as furniture, clothing and electronic goods, people are prepared to travel further and shop around to get the best deal. These goods are sold in central places that are relatively widely spaced and have a large sphere of influence.

Figure 3.7 shows the pattern of central places and spheres of influence that Christaller predicted would arise, given certain assumptions. In particular, he assumed that different goods and services will have different ranges and thresholds. Within settlement hierarchies, the 'low order' functions found in the smallest settlements such as villages will have a low range and threshold. The 'high order' functions in large towns and cities will have a high threshold and range. He also assumed that people will travel to the nearest central place that provides the service they desire. These ideas on retail behaviour form the basis of what Christaller called the 'marketing principle'.

(Christaller also presented two variations on his central place theory, based on a 'transport principle' and an 'administrative principle'. These ideas have had less influence than his work based on retailing.)

Christaller's theory was influential in the 1960s and 1970s. At that time, geographers sought to identify hierarchical patterns in central places, and also to predict the flow of shoppers between lower and higher order settlements. Today, however, central place theory is seen as being of mainly historical interest. Since Christaller's work was first published, there have been many social and economic changes - especially for consumers in high income countries. These changes mean that most of the assumptions behind Christaller's theory are no longer valid. The idea that different sized settlements have distinct functions and spheres of influence is no longer realistic. Nor is the assumption that people will shop at the nearest outlet.

Mass car ownership, one-stop shopping and the increasing proportion of women in paid employment have significantly altered the way that people shop (see unit 6.1 on retail services). The rising number of

supermarkets, edge-of-city shopping centres and improved motorway networks have contributed to these changes.

Out-of-town shopping now accounts for nearly 30 percent of all retail sales in the UK. Meadowhall, to the east of Sheffield and next to the M1, has nearly 300 shops, a cinema and many restaurants - yet it is situated in between 'central places' rather than inside them. It attracts more than 25 million visits per year and many people are prepared to drive over 50 miles to go shopping there. In the USA, changes in shopping patterns have been faster than in the UK. The heart of many American cities has become dead in terms of retailing and entertainment. People travel in their cars to the suburban malls where, increasingly, other functions such as financial services are also located.

In the UK and elsewhere, a rising number of rural villages provide no services at all. Their only function is to serve as dormitory settlements for commuters or to provide weekend homes for city dwellers (see unit 3.2). People stock up on food weekly or monthly by driving to a supermarket, and buy other goods and services by 'direct line' or mail order. In many homes, central heating, satellite TV and video recorders mean that people do not even need to go out for their entertainment.

To illustrate the changes that have occurred in retailing, consider where a 'typical' UK family might buy a loaf of bread. According to Christaller's theory, the family will buy the loaf at the nearest shop, possibly in a village store or a suburban bakery. Today, however, it is just as likely that the family will drive past these outlets on their way to a supermarket. They might buy enough bread for a whole week and store it in their freezer. At the same time, they will do the rest of their weekly shopping, buying meat, fruit and vegetables, and ready made meals. Depending on where they shop, the family might also buy some clothes items, some household goods such as cups and saucers, and possibly some leisure goods such as a CD or video tape - all from the same supermarket where they buy their food. The purchases will then be transported home in the family car. Speed and convenience are the key factors that influence this family's behaviour.

The outcome is that shopping patterns are far more complex than in Christaller's time. As a result, it is not surprising that the hierarchy of regularly spaced settlements and spheres of influence predicted by central place theory do not exist.

Figure 3.7 Christaller's central place theory

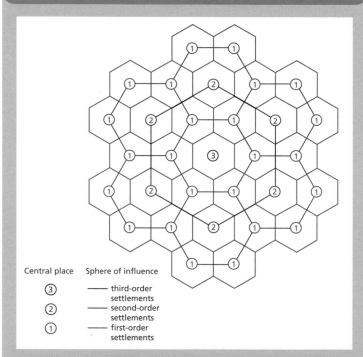

Central place   Sphere of influence

③ ——— third-order
        settlements
② ——— second-order
        settlements
① ——— first-order
        settlements

This diagram shows three 'orders' of central place (for example, first order: villages; second order: towns; and third order: cities). Around each central place, there is a 'sphere of influence'. People who live within the sphere of influence of a central place are assumed to travel to that central place to buy goods and services. For low order goods such as bread, they travel to their nearest low order settlement. For higher order goods such as clothes and electrical items, they travel to the nearest settlement that provides those goods. Christaller suggested that a hierarchy of regularly spaced settlements would result from these patterns of behaviour. The spheres of influence are hexagonal in shape because this is the most efficient geometrical pattern that covers the region without any overlap.

Activity ▷ **The range and threshold of Premier League football clubs**

Football is part of the leisure industry and clubs are providing a service in much the same way as a department store or a theme park. From a commercial point of view, the clubs need to attract as many customers as possible. Although soccer clubs generate income from television and other activities (eg, selling replica kits), they still rely on gate receipts for much of their income. The number of people who watch matches depends, to some extent, upon the size of the local population and the distance that people are prepared to travel. Clubs which have the biggest gates are often the most successful because they can afford to buy the top players and pay the highest wages.

Figure 3.8 Urban areas in England and Wales and ▼ Premier League teams (1997/98 season)

Rank	Urban areas in England and Wales	Popn (000s)	Number of Premier League teams	Average gate size (000s)
1	Greater London	7,652	6	27
2	West Midlands	2,296	1	36
3	Greater Manchester	2,277	2	40
4	West Yorkshire	1,446	1	35
5	Newcastle	886	1	37
6	Liverpool	838	2	38
7	Sheffield	633	1	29
8	Nottingham	613	-	
9	Bristol	522	-	
10	Brighton/Worthing	437	-	
11	Leicester	416	1	21
12	Portsmouth	409	-	
13	Middlesbrough	369	-	
14	Stoke on Trent	368	-	
15	Bournemouth	358	-	
16	Reading/Wokingham	335	-	
17	Coventry	331	1	20
18	Hull	310	-	
19	Cardiff	308	-	
20	Southampton	278	1	15
30	Derby	223	1	29
33	Barnsley	211	1	18
46	Blackburn	135	1	25

Note: *population figures are from the 1991 Census. Urban areas are as defined by the Office for National Statistics. This creates certain anomalies; for example Bolton is included in Greater Manchester but Coventry is not included in the West Midlands. The West Yorkshire urban area includes Leeds and Bradford.*

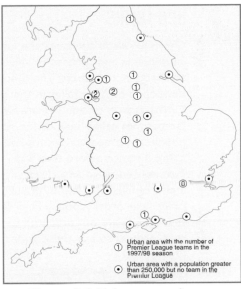

① Urban area with the number of Premier League teams in the 1997/98 season

⊙ Urban area with a population greater than 250,000 but no team in the Premier League

▲ **Figure 3.9 Urban areas in England and Wales with Premier League teams (97/98 season) and/or populations greater than 250,000**

 Questions

1 To what extent were Premier League clubs (in the 97/98 season) located in the urban areas with the biggest populations?

2 Outline the factors that might influence the threshold and range of a Premier League club.

unit summary

1 The location of settlements can be described both in terms of site and situation.
2 Settlement patterns can be described as being nucleated or dispersed although there is no firm dividing line between the two patterns.
3 Settlement patterns depend on several factors including the physical characteristics of the land, the ownership of land, and historical factors such as the need for defence.
4 Central place theory predicts that there will be a hierarchy of settlements. Each 'order' of settlement provides different functions and has a different sized sphere of influence. As a result of modern consumer patterns and lifestyles, combined with the development of motorway systems and edge-of-city shopping centres, the assumptions behind central place theory are no longer valid.

key terms

Central place theory - the idea that settlements and spheres of influence are arranged in a hierarchy. The theory was developed by Christaller in the 1930s.
Comparison goods - relatively expensive items (sometimes called 'high order' goods) for which people are prepared to shop around and travel some distance before they buy.
Convenience goods - 'everyday' goods such as a pint of milk or a loaf of bread (sometimes called 'low order' goods). Their low cost means that people are not prepared to travel far nor shop around to buy these goods.
Dispersed (settlement pattern) - individual dwellings are spaced apart.
Function - the services that a settlement provides, for example shops or public services.
Nucleated (settlement pattern) - individual

dwellings are clustered together in compact settlements.
Range - the maximum distance that people are prepared to travel in order to buy or obtain goods or services.
Settlement hierarchy - a rank order of settlements (eg, individual farmhouse - hamlet - village - town - city).
Site - the land on which a settlement is built, for example its aspect, angle of slope, height above sea level and its physical boundaries; also its shape (ie, morphology) and dimensions.
Situation - the location of a settlement in relation to other settlements and to physical and other human features.
Threshold - the minimum number of potential customers needed to make a business or public service viable.

Unit 3.2 Managing rural settlements

key questions

1 Why are some rural settlements in decline?
2 Why are some rural settlements growing?
3 How can changes in rural settlements be managed?

1. Why are some rural settlements in decline?

In the UK, a rural settlement is usually defined as a village or smaller settlement. (The issue of what is 'rural' and what is 'urban' is complex. It is discussed in detail in

unit 3.3.) In 1997, the Rural Development Commission (RDC) carried out a survey in rural parishes throughout England. Its findings are summarised in figure 3.10. Most rural parishes now lack basic services that were once available just a few decades ago.

The English rural areas in most decline are those which are remote from urban areas, for example north Norfolk, west Cumbria and the north Pennines. The same process is occurring in mid-Wales and in parts of the Scottish Highlands and Islands. The decline in these areas is cumulative. People leave, and this causes some services to close down because they become uneconomic. As a result, more people leave - and so on.

Figure 3.10 The percentage of rural parishes with basic services, 1997, England

Police station	8
Bank or building society	9
GP (family doctor)	17
Daily bus service	25
General store	27
School	51
Post Office	58
Library (permanent or mobile)	88

Note: *a rural parish is a local government district. It normally comprises at least one village and the surrounding area.*
Source: *adapted from the Rural Development Commission. (The Rural Development Commission was replaced by the Countryside Agency in 1999.)*

An estimated 11 million people live in rural Britain and almost a quarter of these are in poverty according to the Rural Development Commission. They live mainly in small and scattered communities. The physical isolation of remote villages in places like Norfolk or Northumberland is made worse for young people by the lack of local leisure or recreational facilities. According to the RDC, only 32 percent of rural parishes have a youth club. Two-thirds of young people move away from their homes in rural areas after they have finished their education. They are, in effect, forced to move in order to obtain jobs. There is often no local employment and public transport services are unavailable to take them to work.

Loss of jobs

In some cases, changes in employment patterns have had a major impact on the rural population. For example, since 1984, 60,000 jobs have been lost in rural collieries in Britain. This has been due to the overall decline in coal mining and the switch to gas fuelled power stations.

There has also been a fall in the number of farm workers. During the 1990s, 65,000 jobs were lost in the agricultural sector. This was partly due to increased mechanisation. Larger tractors can now complete tasks faster and more efficiently than previously. Also, caring for animal stock is increasingly mechanised. For example, fully automated feeding systems are used in many large cattle sheds. There are even automatic scrapers that clear bedding straw and dung from cow stalls onto a conveyor belt and then outside. These changes in technology mean that fewer farm workers are needed. At the same time, there has been a general fall in farm incomes so that, for example, beef and sheep farmers have either had to cut farm workers' hours or lay them off altogether.

Decline in public transport

People on low incomes in rural areas have great transport difficulties. There are very few railway stations in villages and bus services have declined. Deregulation since the 1980s has enabled bus companies to compete more freely but the effect has been to cut services on unprofitable routes. Higher car ownership for the majority of the population has eroded the profitability of most rural bus routes so the net effect has been for these services to be cut. This has left the rural poor with very restricted access to shops, jobs and services, including health and social care. The young, the old and the infirm are particularly affected because they, in general, do not drive.

Figure 3.11 North Yorkshire countryside

Living in the countryside can be pleasant and peaceful. However, poor public transport makes it difficult for young, old and low income people to live in remote rural areas.

Housing

A lack of affordable housing has forced young people to leave some rural areas. This is particularly true in places which are scenically attractive. For example, in parts of Cornwall and the Lake District, second homeowners and retired newcomers have pushed up the cost of housing beyond the reach of local people. The problem has been made worse by the 'right to buy' legislation of the 1980s. Under this law, council house tenants are allowed to buy the property in which they live. The result is that, now, there is much less housing for rent. So, in many rural areas, as young people leave home and become independent, they find that they have nowhere local to live and they must move away. Although the net effect on the population total might be neutral if older people move in, the loss of skills and enterprise causes long term damage to the rural economy.

Activity Village shops

There is no longer a village shop in 73 percent of England's parishes, revealed the Rural Development Commission (RDC) in a 1997 report. The Commission is funding a pilot scheme to reverse this decline. It is providing grants of between £1,500 and £5,000 to help rural shopkeepers upgrade their businesses. A spokesperson for the Commission has written: 'The village shop is not just a business; it also fulfils a social function, particularly for disadvantaged groups more tied to the village than commuter families. It is the last bastion of services.' RDC consultants also help shopkeepers with advice, training and business plans. 'We will only help with grants if the shop has a chance,' the RDC says. 'If we feel it is going to go down anyway, we would not offer to help. In the end, market forces will prevail.'

At Wilbarston, near Market Harborough in the East Midlands, new shop owners in the village hope the Commission can help them. They say: 'We have been thinking about imitating supermarkets, putting scanning in. We could serve customers quicker, make fewer mistakes, and could automatically monitor stock. For instance, you can easily miss sell by dates in a little shop.' The store's Post Office section is also going to offer banking services. It already offers travel insurance and foreign currency. The owners bring in fresh bread from the nearby town, make up bacon rolls, and order toys for customers. The Lottery has been a great draw. Now, on a Saturday afternoon, people come out of the pub and buy their ticket at the shop.

In Upper Boddington, Northamptonshire, the village shopkeeper has received a £5,000 RDC grant, and has matched this with his own funds. He plans to widen services, the latest being photocopying and faxing facilities. That's on top of the dry cleaning, film processing, delicatessen, Post Office, off-licence, pet food and general food and provisions. He also organises wine-tastings, and loans glasses free to customers.

▲ **Figure 3.12 Rural post office**

The owner concentrates on finding gaps in the market and on providing a convenient service. It has meant changing his stock. So, for most items, he carries just one or two brands - meeting the needs of people who run out of something, rather than trying to compete with the wide range that supermarkets offer. Nevertheless, there is an impressive row of sweet jars. 'I have discontinued a lot of things,' the owner states, 'but those are still very popular. There is an older generation who come here to shop on a Thursday morning with £20, but they are few and far between,' he says. 'You can't expect people to come and do all their shopping here when they can go to Tesco's.'

Adapted from the Independent, 4th November 1997

Questions

1 Suggest reasons why there has been a decline in the number of village shops.
2 Outline strategies which might help village shops to survive.
3 To what extent does it matter that some rural communities are in decline?

2. Why are some rural settlements growing?

Not all rural settlements are in decline. Each week during the 1990s, in the UK, an average 1,700 people left urban areas to live in nearby villages and rural locations. (In units 1.3 (migration) and 3.4 (counterurbanisation) this movement of people from urban to rural areas is described in more detail.) People moved to escape the problems of urban living and were attracted by the image of a green and pleasant countryside. In many cases, the migrants still work in towns and cities but live in commuter villages. This process has been made possible by the rise in average incomes. Higher wages allow more and more people to afford cars and pay the associated motoring costs. These commuters make a powerful political lobby and, in the past, successive governments have been willing to build new roads and motorways to meet their needs. As the new roads have been built, the effect has been to enable even more people to move out of the urban areas.

Although the population of many commuter villages is rising, some symptoms of decline are nevertheless present. The newcomers tend to be affluent, often owning two cars. They still use urban areas for shopping, leisure and entertainment. Edge-of-city shopping malls and supermarkets have been built to cater for their needs. Because they do not make use of the village shops, rural buses and other local services, these decline. Sometimes the villages simply become dormitory settlements. The commuters sleep there but do not have the time or inclination to maintain the village traditions and sense of community.

Conflict sometimes arises between newcomers and the original residents. Often the new people are wealthier than the locals and have different tastes and attitudes. During the 1990s, there have been reports of disputes over farmyard smells and churchbells which the ex-urban dwellers have found objectionable but which the locals accept as a normal part of rural life.

3. How can changes in rural settlements be managed?

It is clear that rural settlements in different parts of the country face very different problems. On the one hand there are the isolated regions which are facing rural decline. On the other hand there are the settlements within commuting reach of urban centres which are facing pressures of growth and expansion. Managing these changes is a difficult task. A range of government departments and agencies are involved in the UK. In the EU, the problems of rural areas receive special attention.

Central and local government

The Department of the Environment, Transport and the Regions is the central government agency with responsibility for most rural affairs (excluding agriculture). In 1998, the government announced five 'themes' for the countryside:

- a living countryside: improving education, health care, social services and the environment
- a working countryside: creating jobs in rural areas using the Regional Development Agencies
- one nation: narrowing the divide between town and country
- enhancing the environment: promoting sustainable development
- a countryside for all: increasing access to the countryside for everyone.

One practical example of government policy has been to grant a 50 percent rate reduction to post offices or general stores in small rural settlements - defined as less than 3,000 people. (The rates are a local property tax on businesses.) Local authorities have the discretion to increase the rate relief to 100 percent if they choose. The effect of this measure is to reduce the tax burden on small rural shops and post offices which, it is recognised, supply essential services and provide a focal point for village life.

Another form of government help is the provision of

subsidies to rural bus services. In 1998, for instance, the government announced an extra £40 million subsidy to bus companies in the 'most rural' counties. They include Cornwall, Kent, Lincolnshire, Somerset, Suffolk and North Yorkshire. It was hoped that the money would reverse the trend in declining bus services.

Planning controls Local authorities and central government can use planning regulations to prevent urban sprawl and to manage the increase in housing in rural settlements. As part of this policy, Green Belts have been designated around most urban areas. (A Green Belt is a zone in which, under most circumstances, no development is allowed.)

The growth of commuting has placed tremendous pressure on the Green Belts because it has caused a shortage of housing in the very areas where the new commuters wish to live. The effect has been to drive up

Figure 3.13 New rural housing

There is great pressure on some rural areas from people who want to move out from urban areas.

property prices and, in some villages, to force local young people on low incomes to move elsewhere.

Population estimates in 1998 suggested that 4.4 million new homes would be needed in the UK by 2016. The government announced that 60 percent of the new houses should be built on 'brownfield' sites (ie, on infill or reclaimed land within urban areas), but that still leaves over 1.5 million to be built in rural areas. Opponents of this decision point out that, since 1945, an area greater than the combined total of Greater London, Berkshire, Hertfordshire and Oxfordshire has already been urbanised. They say that no new major housing developments should be allowed in rural areas.

The difficulty for the government is that more and more people do want to live in rural areas or, at least, not in the old urban areas. In the past, New Towns were planned around London to accommodate the 'overspill' population (see unit 2.2). For example Stevenage was built, despite a fierce local protest, and by the 1990s housed 70,000 people. To meet the needs of the new generation, the government accepted in 1998 that 10,000 new houses must be built on Green Belt land next to Stevenage.

The government's dilemma is that it wishes to protect the countryside yet also satisfy the demand for new homes. The irony is, of course, that the people living in the 10,000 new houses near Stevenage will not be living in any 'greener' countryside than the people left living in London. However, from a conservationist point of view, it might be better to concentrate the new housing in large new centres rather than allowing bit by bit expansion of small villages.

Rural Development Commission (RDC) During the 1990s, the Rural Development Commission provided funds for rural development projects. One example of its work was the financing of an IT network in the rural Durham coalfield. Since the coal mines closed, this region of pit villages had become an area of high unemployment. People have moved to Newcastle and Sunderland to find work. In an effort to revitalise the economy, the RDC helped set up a communications network of voice, video and data information services. Local people, services and businesses can now use the network to communicate with each other and with the outside world. One such link is a 'telemedicine' service through a video channel to doctors' surgeries. Another important part of the scheme is the provision of training to residents and small businesses in the area.

One function of the RDC has been to lobby

government on rural issues. In 1998 it campaigned to ensure that telecommunication companies would maintain and extend their networks in rural areas and that their pricing policies were fair and did not discriminate in favour of towns and cities. Noting that most of the economic growth in rural areas in the past 15 years has been in businesses using new technology, the RDC urged that internet and cable links should be expanded. It is clear that advances in IT can make rural life less isolated and also provide employment opportunities such as 'teleworking'. This is where people set up their home as an office and use a fax and/or modem to carry on their business or work.

European Union

The EU has a number of regional policies designed to help rural areas in decline. These areas are given **Objective 5b** status. In the UK, most of rural Wales, Northern England, much of Scotland, the South West and parts of Eastern England are covered. The primary aim is to help people diversify from agriculture and set up alternative activities. Individuals, businesses and local authorities can apply for investment grants to create jobs in, for example, tourism, renewable power or recycling schemes, and in environmental protection. Help is also provided for businesses in training and research and development. Between 1994 and 1999, over £600 million assistance was given to the Objective 5b regions in the UK.

The Common Agricultural Policy (CAP) of the EU is another important means by which assistance is given to rural areas (see unit 4.1). One aim of the CAP is to ensure a satisfactory standard of living for farmers and to sustain the rural economy. This involves a system of subsidies and the purchase of surplus farm production. However, the policy has resulted in over-production and the creation of 'food mountains'.

During the 1990s, changes were made to the CAP to discourage surplus production. Some of these policies had the effect of limiting or reducing farm incomes. At the same time, the high value of the pound against other European currencies had the effect of cutting the value of CAP subsidies and of making imported food cheaper.

Unfortunately for farmers, there is little room for manoeuvre within the CAP. To reduce farm surpluses, the prices paid to farmers must fall. It is possible to compensate farmers by paying them not to produce food, but this tends to be unpopular with consumers and taxpayers. An alternative system, using quotas that set numerical limits on output, is used in milk production. This protects the incomes of the farmers who own the quotas but forces others out of production altogether. In 1998, the EU Commission recognised that the quota system was damaging rural communities and so allowed an extra quota to young farmers. The aim was to ensure that a new generation of dairy farmers would be able to make a living and thus stay in the countryside.

Activity   Housing development

Concrete proposal

The Government is running into trouble by supporting plans for thousands more homes on greenfield sites. When John Prescott stood up at the Kyoto Climate Summit this month and lectured the world about saving the planet for our children's children, some people in his own backyard were not impressed. For the Environment Secretary had just decreed that yet more of Britain's battered countryside should be concreted over. He has insisted, for example, that West Sussex needs 50,000 more houses.

Half the county is in designated Areas of Outstanding Natural Beauty such as the South Downs and the Weald. Because of a shortage of land, many houses would have to go on greenfield sites. Councillors of all parties agree that West Sussex neither needs nor wants so many houses- they would be bought by incomers who would, in their thousands, drive to London to work. However, a Department of the Environment spokesman said: 'These figures are not imposed from above, they are based on trends which exist in society. We have to meet the needs of all and cannot always pander to NIMBY (not in my backyard) viewpoints'.

Adapted from the Guardian, 24th September 1997

Super-village development arouses Green Belt fears

One of the largest schemes for new homes in Britain ever given planning permission is to be built in East Anglia. The settlement of 3,300 homes will house 8,000 people and is to be one 'super-village' constructed seven miles west of Cambridge, in a region under severe pressure from strong economic growth.

Alfred McAlpine announced on Monday that it had found two other house builders - Bryant Homes and Bovis Homes - to join the £450 million development, nominally called Cambourne, which covers 1,000 acres and will take at least 10 years to complete.

The consortium's announcement has been made against the background of pressure on planning authorities to encourage house building following the Government's call for 4.4 million new homes by 2016. The Green Belt is under pressure and counties such as Cambridgeshire, which is one of the country's fastest growing areas, are having to examine where the houses might be fitted in.

A spokesperson for South Cambridgeshire District Council, which has given outline planning permission for the development, said yesterday: 'We decided in principle 10 years ago that, in an area where there was a need to meet the demand for new houses, we would do it as a new settlement. We didn't want to fill the villages with new housing and therefore ruin all the reasons people had for wanting to come here in the first place'.

Adapted from The Times, 4th December 1997

▼ **Figure 3.14 New housing**

Questions

1 Outline the case for and against new house building in rural areas.
2 What strategies might the government adopt to conserve the countryside?
3 Explain why some rural settlements are growing while others are in decline.

unit summary

1 Some settlements in remote rural areas are in decline due to factors which include: low incomes, high unemployment, lack of public transport, loss of services and lack of affordable housing.
2 Some rural settlements near towns and cities are growing as more people escape from urban problems and seek a greener environment. Unfortunately, when people move to the countryside, the new development can destroy the rural tranquillity that is attractive in the first place.
3 Governments and other agencies use a range of policies to promote rural development and to control urban sprawl.

key terms

Objective 5b - a policy objective of the EU designed to promote development in rural areas; to qualify for assistance, a region must meet two of the following three criteria: a high proportion of employment in agriculture; a low level of agricultural incomes; a low population density or a high degree of out-migration.

Green Belt - a zone of land around an urban area that receives special protection from development.
Common Agricultural Policy - the EU policy that aims to ensure an adequate food supply for consumers and also maintain farmers' livelihoods.

Unit 3.3   Urbanisation

key questions

1 What is an urban area?
2 What is the world pattern of urbanisation?
3 Which factors cause urbanisation?
4 What is the impact of urbanisation?

1. What is an urban area?

On the face of it this is a simple question. An urban area is a city or town. Most people have an image of what a city looks like, and can contrast this with their image of the countryside. A city contains crowds of people, traffic, high-rise buildings, hotels, offices and shops. The countryside, in contrast, contains fields and woodland, low-rise buildings, minor roads and few people.

However, in reality, the issue is more complex. Some rural areas in south and east Asia, for example, have a higher population density than some urban areas in Europe. In Britain, a rural area might contain a busy motorway interchange, quarries or mines, or large buildings in which food is factory farmed. On the other hand, some 'garden' cities have mainly low-rise buildings, and contain fields and other large open spaces within their boundaries.

A particular problem in defining what is urban and what is rural arises when the official boundary of a city does not coincide with the edge of the built up area (ie, the land that is covered with buildings). Sometimes, within a city boundary, there are areas of fields and farms that are clearly rural. Also, often, the urban area extends beyond the city boundary. For example, in the UK, the local authority district that forms the City of Manchester had a population of 431,000 in 1996. But the city extends beyond the district boundary and

includes Salford, Trafford, Bolton and several other local authority districts. These form a continuous urban area and the whole 'conurbation' of Greater Manchester had a population of 2,576,000 in 1996. However, within this area, there are extensive stretches of open moorland that are definitely rural.

Figure 3.15 Central London

It is much easier to identify what is an urban area than it is to define one.

153

So, what constitutes an urban area is not a straightforward issue. Governments in different countries use a variety of criteria to judge whether an area is 'urban'. The criteria include:
• population size and density
• land use
• occupation of residents
• functions
• way of life.

Population size and density

The population totals of settlements, or the population densities of particular areas, are two ways of defining what is 'urban'. For example, if a given area has a high population density, or a settlement has a population over a certain size, they might be classed as urban. However, there are problems with using these criteria. In parts of Bangladesh, for instance, population densities along some river valleys and deltas are very high, sometimes rising to over a thousand people per square kilometre. Most of these families are engaged in farming which is a rural occupation. Although their population density is higher than in parts of UK towns and cities, these areas are not normally classed as urban.

At the other extreme, in a country like Sweden, population densities are low. Therefore a relatively small settlement, with as few as two hundred inhabitants, is considered by the Swedish government to be urban. There is no consistency between governments on this issue. By contrast with Sweden, Japan, with its high population density has a much bigger (30,000) threshold for defining an urban area.

Land use

In the 1991 UK Census, urban areas were defined on the basis of land use. So, for example, areas which were classed as urban comprised:
• built-up sites; ie, land that was covered by permanent buildings
• any area completely surrounded by built-up sites
• transportation corridors (such as roads, railways or canals) which had built-up sites on one or both sides, or which linked built-up sites less than 50 metres apart
• transportation features such as airports, railway yards and motorway service areas
• mine buildings.

In addition, to be classed as urban the area had to extend at least 20 hectares and also have a minimum population of 1,000 residents. Using this definition, the Census found that 90 percent of people in Great Britain lived in urban areas and 53 percent lived in urban areas with populations of 100,000 or more. There were five urban 'agglomerations' with a population over 1 million (Greater London, 7.6m; West Midlands, 2.3m; Greater Manchester, 2.3m; West Yorkshire, 1.4m; and Glasgow 1.3m). Together these contained 27 percent of Great Britain's population.

Occupation of residents

'Urban' is sometimes defined in terms of what people do. Farmers are clearly rural; office workers are clearly urban. But, what if the office workers work from a home in the countryside, via a modem? Likewise, a farmer might run a large agro-industrial business that involves factory farming and a processing plant. Is this a rural or urban activity?

In Israel, two thirds of a settlement's workforce must be engaged in non-agricultural activities for it to be defined as urban. In India the figure is three-quarters. However, these definitions are not entirely straightforward because it is not always clear what constitutes a non-agricultural activity.

Functions

Another way of defining urban is by considering the functions which a settlement performs. If the settlement provides only a few services, such as a grocery store, a pub and a garage then it is probably a village and therefore rural. A town which has a wider range of functions including, for example, banks, a police-station, a hospital, shops and supermarkets is more likely to be considered urban. A city usually has a full range of services, catering for a regional, national or even international markets and is certainly urban.

However, again, such divisions are not clear-cut. Regional shopping centres such as Lakeside in Essex have hundreds of shops and other services - but no permanent population. The function of such centres is clearly urban even though some have semi-rural locations.

Way of life

An urban area might be defined in terms of the way of life and the culture which it contains. Theatres, cinemas, cultural activities and 'sophisticated' life styles are associated with cities but not with the countryside. Urban living also tends to be more anonymous and lacking in community spirit. However, squatter settlements or shanty towns found inside some Third World cities are not sophisticated in any way. They are more like 'urban villages' in that relationships tend to be close-knit, with people retaining many ties to the rural

Figure 3.16 Farming under glass

Is the production of agricultural produce in a heated glasshouse a rural or urban activity?

2. What is the world pattern of urbanisation?

The process of **urbanisation** is more than simply the growth of the urban population. It is the growth of the urban population as a proportion of the overall population - and may be caused by internal growth or by inward migration, or by a combination of both. It generally involves the spatial growth of urban areas, ie the cities become geographically bigger.

Urbanisation is closely linked with industrialisation - ie, the growth of manufacturing industry, and is often regarded as a key element in the development process. In general, the more developed the country, then the more urbanised it is, and vice-versa. Today, countries such as China and Malaysia are investing heavily in urbanisation by building new urban settlements. Their governments believe that urbanisation speeds development. Urban centres are seen to provide employment opportunities and are key links between local, regional, national and global economies.

Global variations

Most First World countries have highly urbanised populations. According to the World Bank, the urban percentage (all figures are for 1995 unless stated) in the USA was 76.2 percent, in France it was 72.8 percent and in Sweden it was 83.1 percent. Singapore and Hong Kong, were 100 percent urban but these are more properly city-states rather than countries.

In the former communist 'Second World', Russia's population was 73.0 percent urban (1996) and Hungary was 62.6 percent (1996). In Asian Third World countries, India was only 26.8 percent urban, China was 28.6 percent (1994) and Vietnam was 20.8 percent. In Africa, Tanzania was only 24.4 percent urban, Nigeria was 39.3 percent and Mali 26.1 percent.

In Latin America, the pattern is different. Brazil has a high percentage of urban dwellers - in 1995 it was 78.2 percent urban. Argentina was even more urbanised, at 86.9 percent (1991), and Chile 85.8 percent. These high percentages are possibly the result of Spanish and Portuguese colonial policies in which power was very centralised in regional capitals.

area from which they have come. The 'high culture' of the city is unlikely to have any impact on these areas. Often, this culture, does not reach the mass of suburban dwellers in Western cities either.

Not all cultural events, however defined, are urban. Woodstock - a turning point in 1960s youth culture, the Glastonbury Festival and the Glyndebourne Opera are all examples of cultural events held in the countryside. So, again, the distinction between what is urban and what is rural is not clear.

The outcome of looking at different criteria on what constitutes an urban area is that there is no clear definition. It is better, perhaps, to think of a 'continuum', with rural at one end of the scale and urban at the other, rather than having a strict dividing line with urban on one side and rural on the other. Some places are clearly rural, some clearly urban. Many, however, are difficult to place in one or the other category.

In the next section of this unit, the world pattern of urbanisation is considered and data is drawn from different countries. Although not fully satisfactory, the simplest approach is to accept that there is inconsistency between the definitions used. So, for example, when countries provide the United Nations with data on their urban populations, they will have used different definitions of what constitutes urban.

Activity   World urbanisation

▼ **Figure 3.17 1950**

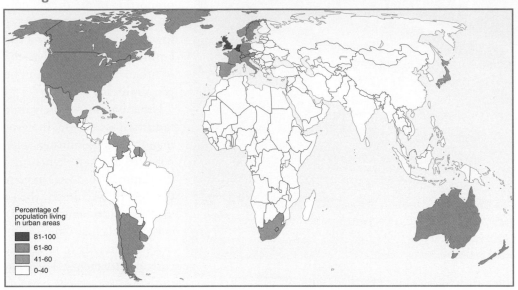

Percentage of
population living
in urban areas

■ 81-100
■ 61-80
■ 41-60
□ 0-40

▼ **Figure 3.18 1995**

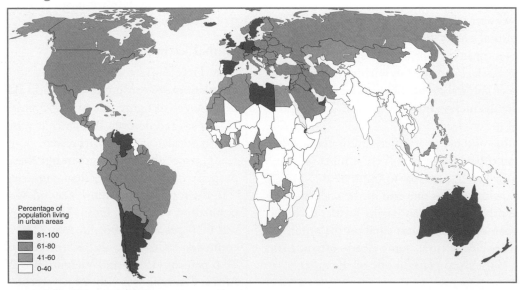

Percentage of
population living
in urban areas

■ 81-100
■ 61-80
■ 41-60
□ 0-40

Source: World Urbanisation Prospects, United Nations, 1996

 Question

1 Compare world urbanisation in 1950 with that in 1995.

Rate of urbanisation

From 1800 to 1900, the proportion of the world's population living in urban centres of 5,000 and over increased from 3 percent to 13 percent. This represented a numerical increase from 27 million to 219 million. The urban population reached 717 million by 1950. The momentum increased after World War II and, in the 1950s, the total urban population increased by over 1,000 million, to 1,800 million. It was estimated to have reached 3,100 million by the year 2000. The United Nations predicts that half the world's population will be urban by 2005 and that this will rise to three fifths in 2025.

In the Third World countries of Africa and Asia, the urban percentage is currently low, although the rate of urbanisation is high. In other words, urban populations are growing fast, but from a low base. The opposite is true in the First World. In the West, cities are expanding slowly, if at all, but from a high base. In some Western countries, urban populations are on the decline due to the process of counterurbanisation (see unit 3.4). Evidence from these countries suggests that urbanisation might have a threshold or maximum level beyond which a decline will take place. Figure 3.19 shows the rate of urbanisation for Europe, Africa and the world as a whole. The projections are based on United Nations estimates.

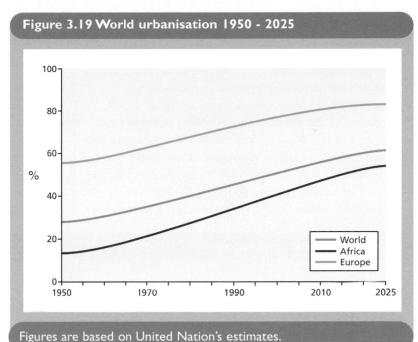

Figure 3.19 World urbanisation 1950 - 2025

Figures are based on United Nation's estimates.

Primary and secondary cities

Western cities, including those of Japan, have a key role within globalisation and the global economy (see unit 2.4). They are communication centres, often containing the headquarters of transnational companies and the stock exchanges, banks and finance companies which drive the global economy. London, New York and Tokyo remain in the first rank of these global cities. Figure 3.20 shows some linkages between cities. It

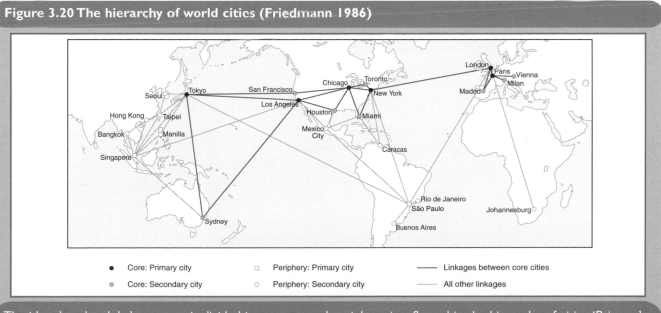

Figure 3.20 The hierarchy of world cities (Friedmann 1986)

- ● Core: Primary city
- ○ (grey) Core: Secondary city
- □ Periphery: Primary city
- ○ Periphery: Secondary city
- —— Linkages between core cities
- —— All other linkages

The idea that the global economy is divided into a core and periphery is reflected in the hierarchy of cities. 'Primary' cities have the biggest influence on the world economy and are linked to 'secondary' cities which are less influential.

illustrates the core-periphery model that is described in unit 2.2. The model suggests that economic growth and development are centred in core regions or cities, and that these exercise control over the periphery. The idea is that there is an urban hierarchy of 'primary' and 'secondary' world cities - classified in terms of their importance in the world economy. Most of these cities are located in the Western, capitalist core economies and only two primary cities, it is suggested, are in the periphery. Although the city authorities of cities like Mexico City and Singapore, aided by their national governments, are working hard to develop a major role within the global economy, there is still a long way to go before these new cities can be as successful as the old.

Primacy

Studies of urban patterns show that, in some countries, there is a relationship between the population of a specific city and its position in the urban hierarchy. This is called the **rank-size rule**. For example, the second ranking city in a country will (according to the rank-size rule) have a population half the size of the biggest city. The third ranked city will have a population one third the size of the largest city, and so on. There is no clear theoretical reason for the 'rule', it is based on empirical evidence of what sometimes occurs.

However, in many countries the rank-size rule does not operate and the urban hierarchy is dominated by a single, large primate, city (see figure 3.21). This is many times bigger than the second ranked city. Bangkok in Thailand, Kuala Lumpur in Malaysia, Teheran in Iran, Cairo in Egypt, Lima in Peru, and Lagos in Nigeria dominate other urban centres in their respective countries. London and Paris similarly dominate in Britain and France. (In a country such as Brazil where two cities, Sao Paulo and Rio de Janeiro, are dominant, it is known as a binary pattern.)

Primacy has important implications for a country. It can lead to an over-concentration of resources and wealth in the primate city. It can also lead to an unwillingness to spread the benefits of economic growth evenly around the country. Doctors, teachers and other professionals will prefer to work in the primate city rather than in the regions. This can contribute to the 'backwash effect' noted by Myrdal (see unit 2.2). Rather than economic development spreading to peripheral regions, the primate cities suck in resources and make the periphery poorer.

Figure 3.21 Rank sizes for selected countries

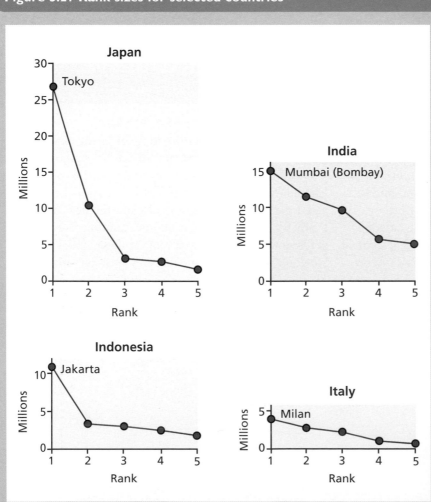

Indonesia is dominated by Jakarta and Japan by Tokyo. Both are larger than the rank-size rule would suggest - Jakarta very much so, possibly the result of it being the former Dutch colonial capital and centre of imperial control. By contrast, India and Italy do not have dominant primate cities. This pattern may be due to these countries being made up of previously independent (or semi-independent) smaller states, each having their own capitals before unification.

Activity ⟩ Mega-cities

▼ **Figure 3.22 Mega-cities**

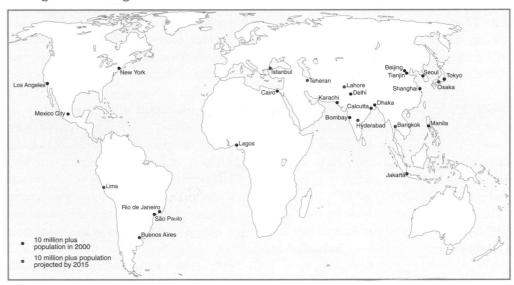

▼ **Figure 3.23 The 10 largest urban centres ranked by population size, 1950, 1990 and 2015 (estimate)**

Rank	1950	million	1990	million	2015	million
1	New York	12.3	Tokyo	25.0	Tokyo	28.7
2	London	8.7	New York	16.1	Bombay/Mumbai	27.4
3	Tokyo	6.9	Mexico City	15.1	Lagos	24.4
4	Paris	5.4	São Paulo	14.8	Shanghai	23.4
5	Moscow	5.4	Shanghai	13.5	Jakarta	21.2
6	Shanghai	5.3	Bombay/Mumbai	12.2	São Paulo	20.8
7	Essen	5.3	Los Angeles	11.5	Karachi	20.6
8	Buenos Aires	5.0	Beijing	10.9	Beijing	19.4
9	Chicago	4.9	Calcutta	10.7	Dhaka	19.0
10	Calcutta	4.4	Buenos Aires	10.6	Mexico City	18.8

Source: World Urbanisation Prospects, United Nations, 1996

Questions

1 List and classify by continent those cities with populations over 10 million in 2000 and those with projected populations over 10 million in 2015. Comment on the expected changes.
2 Describe the changes that occurred (and are predicted to occur) in the size and distribution of the ten largest urban centres between 1950 and 2015.

3. Which factors cause urbanisation?

One explanation of urbanisation relates to the push and pull factors that cause migration. Push occurs from rural areas, due to factors such as overpopulation, rural poverty, indebtedness, inequalities in land ownership and increasing farm mechanisation. Pull is exerted by the bright lights of the city and the image of the city streets being paved with gold. The rural poor know from radio and, increasingly, from television that the incomes, employment opportunities, health care and educational provision are often better in the cities than in the countryside. The opportunities, or perceived opportunities, of the city act like a magnet to the rural dweller who moves first himself (usually) and then his family to the urban area. (See unit 1.3 for a more detailed account of why people migrate.)

But, push and pull factors on their own do not explain urbanisation. They show why people migrate to cities but they do not fully explain the growth in importance of cities. Factors such as agricultural change, industrialisation and globalisation have all had an impact.

Historical factors

Ancient cities developed in many parts of the world, for example the Middle East, Central America and East Asia. These cities often developed as centres of specialisation in which people produced goods such as pottery, cooking utensils, weapons and works of art. The city became a centre of command and control over the surrounding countryside.

These ancient cities required the production of a food surplus in the rural economy. Some writers have suggested that it was developments in agriculture that led to an increase in food output, and so enabled urbanisation. The surplus gave people the opportunity to specialise in manufacturing and also allowed people time for religious contemplation, education and planning. In this interpretation, it was agricultural change which caused urban growth.

However, other writers believe that the reverse is true. The drive to urbanisation might have come first, as people decided to move away from a rural society. Perhaps they wished to avoid the seasonal toil of farming.

They produced goods such as textiles and metals, and developed trade to provide themselves with the goods they needed. The urban dwellers drew in an agricultural surplus by extending their power and control over the surrounding area. The farmers might be organised in a more productive way by encouraging irrigation projects, for example. New or improved implements, such as hoes and ploughs would be made for agriculture, and loans provided to support farmers through lean years. In this interpretation, urbanisation was caused by the specialisation of production in cities and the greater efficiency that this brought. The production of an agricultural surplus was stimulated by the growth of cities, not the other way around.

From about 1500, the nature of cities began to change. In Western Europe, places such as Bruges, Genoa and Amsterdam became 'merchant cities'. They traded not just with their immediate neighbours, but increasingly at a European and even global scale. As the European empires expanded, so did the power and influence of the merchants and traders in the home cities.

Cities must generally trade with cities. Because rural populations are generally spread out, there have to be 'hubs' and channels to focus activities. Where towns and cities already existed along trade routes, their expansion was encouraged by Europeans. Where centres were non-existent or small, new towns and cities were founded in the colonies. Lima, Manila, Singapore, Hong Kong,

Figure 3.24 Cambodia

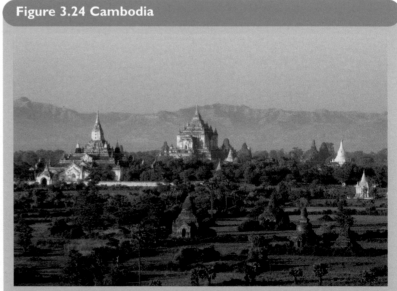

Did the production of surplus food in the countryside allow urbanisation to start or did urban settlements stimulate increased food production?

Cape Town and many other cities owe their origins to this period. From then onwards, urbanisation became closely linked to the wider development process.

Industrialisation

Beginning in the nineteenth century, cities such as Glasgow, Manchester, Birmingham, Chicago and Paris showed a dramatic increase in population as the factories, steel works and other features of the Industrial Revolution were established. Cities became centres of mass production, and people moved to them from far afield. Urbanisation and industrialisation became, for a time, interwoven. Increases in production caused the cities to grow and, at the same time, the growth of cities stimulated new production.

Globalisation

Modern urbanisation, and the increased attraction of cities, can be viewed as part of the globalisation process (see unit 2.4). The development of global-scale activities, in consumption, service provision and production has led to urbanisation being even more important than before. Businesses, whether corporate headquarters, banks or stock exchanges, prefer to locate in urban areas. There they have access to the range of accountancy firms, software companies, advertising agencies and media services which modern business enterprises require. Despite the spread of the internet and satellite technology, the urban location remains crucial. The spread of the market economy and the increase in trade at the global level is channelled more and more through cities. As the prosperity of cities increases, the effect is to attract ever more of the rural poor.

4. What is the impact of urbanisation?

At the present time, it is in low income countries that urbanisation is having the most obvious impact. Large scale migration from rural areas, and high urban birth rates, are causing cities to grow. In many Third World countries, farm mechanisation is reducing the need for hired manual labour. At the same time, some researchers have suggested that the feminisation of agriculture is taking place, leaving males free to look for alternative employment in towns and cities. Often, this employment is not in the formal sector in the sense of a full-time, regularly paid job. Rather it is in the informal sector with part-time or casual work, or insecure forms of self-employment such as scavenging or street vending.

The relative lack of industrial employment in cities has led to the term 'over-urbanisation' being used to describe the urban growth in parts of the Third World. It is becoming clear that, in many African and south Asian countries, urbanisation is not following earlier Western patterns. Unlike in nineteenth century European cities, industrialisation is not the same driving force behind urban growth. Cities are expanding at a faster rate than their industrial and manufacturing base.

The typical Third World city has become a city of contrasts. Masses of people eke out a living in squatter settlements, slum conditions, or even on the streets. In contrast, a small elite live in protected luxury conditions, either in the heart of the city or, increasingly, on the outskirts. Urbanisation creates tremendous contrasts in wealth and opportunity. Nor is this confined to the Third World. In cities such as Los Angeles, New York and London, polarisation between rich and poor is also found. For the rich, globalisation is providing worldwide opportunities, and access to enormous resources. Technological change and information flows are used by the 'information rich' to accumulate knowledge, power and influence. Modern urbanisation is at the heart of this process.

At the other end of the scale, however, the 'information poor' have little access to the wealth created by the global economy. A major process of exclusion seems to be at work. So, for example in New York between the mid-1980s and mid-1990s, 340,000 jobs were created in advanced services of the economy, in professional and skilled technical posts. During the same period, 140,000 manufacturing jobs were lost. Unemployment and underemployment therefore increasingly exist side by side with high-level, high-salaried employment. As technology changes, the global economy needs fewer unskilled manual workers but needs more people skilled in using the new information systems. Lima, in Peru, for instance, has become a major financial centre in Latin America with investment in telephone lines, a fibre-optic network, and expansion of the stock exchange, banking and insurance sectors. Yet, a 1995 study by the International Labour Office (ILO) showed that the percentage of the city's population living below the poverty line increased from 26 percent in 1980 to 78 percent in 1993. The result of the changes therefore appears to be a low standard of living for the many, paralleled with high wages for the few. (The management of urban problems in both high and low income countries is discussed in more detail in unit 3.6.)

Activity Mumbai (Bombay)

During the mid-1990s, the municipal government renamed Bombay, reverting to its pre-colonial name of Mumbai. The city is located on the west coast of India and has a large natural harbour. Its site is on seven islands that have been joined by causeways. Much of the land between the islands has been infilled. Because of restricted space, there is a very high population density - rising to 17,000 people per square kilometre in places.

The city's population is increasing at such a rate that, according to United Nations figures, it is already the second largest in the world (after Tokyo). Tens of thousands of migrants arrive in the city each year from all over India. Many are homeless and either sleep on the pavements or in new shanty settlements. Some of these are on patches of reclaimed land and some are on the outskirts of the city. The biggest slum, Dharavi, is approximately 8km north of the city centre. It is sometimes described as the worst slum in Asia with 700,000 people living in overcrowded conditions.

Between 1954 and 1970, the city government ran slum clearance programmes to rehouse the growing population. They cleared shanty housing and built concrete apartments. By the late 1960s, only 10 percent of the population lived in slums. However, since then, the rate of migration into the city has overwhelmed the government. In the mid-1990s, 55 percent of Mumbai's population lived in slums or shanties. Most of these people have no private water supply or sewerage. People go to the lavatory in public latrines which either discharge into septic tanks or directly into the Arabian Sea. Drinking water is in such short supply that some of the public taps are turned on for just a few hours during the night. It is not surprising, given these unsanitary conditions, that many people die from stomach and respiratory disorders. Cholera, TB, malaria and leprosy are all present. In one typical shanty settlement, Appapada, at the northern edge of the city, 200,000 people have the services of just one doctor, three mornings per week. Because people cook on open hearths, fires are a major hazard in the shanties made from cardboard, wood and plastic sheets. Fires are sometimes deliberately started, it is believed, by developers who wish to build on the land.

Although Mumbai has enormous social problems, it is India's richest city. An estimated one third of the Indian government's total tax revenue comes from Mumbai. It is a financial and a textile manufacturing centre and there are also many port based, processing industries. Jewellery and diamond cutting are based in the city, and it is home of the large Indian film industry - giving rise to the name 'Bollywood'. There is, in consequence, a rich elite and a growing middle income group who live close by the street people and shanty dwellers. The security guarded villas and apartments of the wealthy residents, for example in Colaba near the ocean front, are only a walking distance away from some of the worst slums. Because the city's site is so restricted, traffic is often chaotic. Up to 4 million people commute by train each day and 3 million by bus.

Despite its problems, Mumbai attracts migrants from as far away as the Himalayan foothills, Bengal and the southern tip of India. Many are driven by a land shortage. Their family plots are too small to support them. Some couples move because of 'love marriages' - they wish to marry the person of their choice rather than have a traditional arranged marriage. In some cases, it is skilled people, builders, electricians and craftsmen who move because they know that wages are higher in the city and there are more opportunities. Those who are unskilled often work as domestic cleaners or street vendors of food and drink to the city office workers. A large number of children are beggars.

◄ **Figure 3.25 Mumbai**

The very poor and the very rich live close to each other in Mumbai.

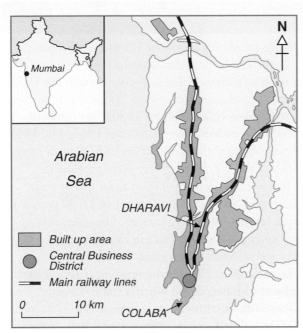

	millions
1900	0.8
1950	2.9
1960	4.1
1970	5.8
1980	8.1
1990	12.2
2000	18.1
2010 (est)	24.3

Figure 3.27 Population growth in Mumbai

Figure 3.26 Mumbai

Key (from map):
- Built up area
- Central Business District
- Main railway lines

0   10 km

Questions

1 Describe and give some of the reasons for Mumbai's growth in population.
2 Outline the consequences of rapid urbanisation in Mumbai.

unit summary

1 There is no clear cut or generally agreed definition of what constitutes an urban area.
2 Urbanisation has increased markedly in recent years; almost half the world's population is estimated to be urban. The Third World is where urbanisation is now occurring at the fastest rate, although it is proceeding from a low base.
3 Large cities, known as primate cities sometimes dominate the societies in which they are found.
4 Urbanisation is caused by a wide range of factors which, over the centuries, have included agricultural change, industrialisation and globalisation.
5 Urbanisation can create tremendous contrasts in wealth and opportunity, with a polarisation between those who are part of the global economy and those who are largely excluded from its benefits.

key terms

Primate city - a city which excessively dominates the country in which it is located; it is far bigger than would be expected from the rank-size rule.

Push/pull factors - these are explanations of why people move (in this case from rural areas to urban area); they explain why people migrate but do not explain the growing importance of cities.

Rank-size rule - an observed pattern in some countries in which the population of any specific city is related to its ranking in the urban

hierarchy; for example, the second ranked city has half the population of the largest city, the third ranked city has one third of the largest city's population, and so on.

Urban area - a town or city, it can be differentiated from a rural area by a range of criteria, including population size and/or density, land use, employment patterns of local people, functions or culture.

Urbanisation - the process in which a rising proportion of the population lives in urban areas.

Unit 3.4 Counterurbanisation

key questions

1 What is counterurbanisation?
2 What causes counterurbanisation?
3 What are the consequences of counterurbanisation?

1. What is counterurbanisation?

The term counterurbanisation came into use in the USA during the 1970s to describe the movement of people out of urban areas. Between 1970 and 1973, the Department of Agriculture noted that the population in non-metropolitan (ie, rural) counties was growing faster than in metropolitan (ie, urban) counties. This was unexpected because, until then, the country had been rapidly urbanising.

Today, in the US, evidence suggests that population is being filtered down the urban hierarchy (ie, moving from bigger cities to smaller ones) and also out into rural areas - but at a slow rate. In 1995, the percentage living in urban areas was estimated to be 76.2 percent compared to 76.7 percent in 1987. This 0.5 percent change represents a total of 1.3 million people.

In the UK, census data suggest that counterurbanisation began earlier than in the United States. Population movements into and out of urban areas were in balance in the 1950s, but outward movement became dominant after 1961. The 1991 census, showed that population had fallen in most large cities in the UK in the thirty years previously.

In the 1990s, out-migration from urban areas continued, with a net movement of 1,700 people per week leaving for rural locations. However, this movement was slower than in the 1980s and was reversed in some urban areas.

In most West European countries, urban growth appears to have peaked but the trend towards counterurbanisation has not been as strong as in the UK. In countries such as France and Italy, there is still a movement of population into urban areas. However, the proportion of people living in large cities (defined as having a population greater than one million) has fallen slightly. For instance, in France, the percentage of urban dwellers living in large cities fell from 30 percent to 29 percent between 1970 and 1996, and in Italy the fall was from 43 percent to 36 percent.

 Activity ▶ Urban population

▼ Figure 3.28 Population change 1961-97 in selected English cities (figures in thousands)

Year	Greater London	Inner London	Birmingham	Liverpool	Manchester	Newcastle
1961	7,977	3,481	1,179	741	657	336
1971	7,529	3,060	1,107	610	554	312
1981	6,806	2,550	1,021	517	463	284
1991	6,890	2,627	1,007	481	439	278
1997	7,122	2,727	1,014	464	428	280

Note: 1961-91 figures are census data. The 1997 figure is a mid-year estimate based on survey data from the Office of Population Censuses and Surveys (OPCS).

Questions

1 Calculate the percentage change in population for Greater London, Inner London and the selected cities between 1961 and 1997.
2 Describe the main trends that have occurred.

Figure 3.29 Urban traffic

Counterurbanisation has occurred in most urban areas in Britain since the 1960s. Large numbers of people have left cities to live in quieter rural areas.

Figure 3.30 is a general model that illustrates the process of urban population movement. In phase 1, the city 'core' (ie, the centre of the urban area) is dominant, providing jobs and services, and drawing in people from rural areas. This is typical of the urbanisation process. Cities have gone through this phase in Western Europe and North America, and are at this stage today within most of the Third World.

Phase 2 begins when increased affluence and better transport systems allow people to move to the suburbs ('suburbanisation') and leave the central city area. People might also move down the urban hierarchy towards smaller towns, or move directly out to rural villages. At the same time, however, even in this phase other people are still attracted to the city from rural areas or small towns.

Phase 3 shows the present position in the UK and USA. Suburbanisation and counterurbanisation are the dominant trends but there is also movement of some households back from the suburbs to city centres.

2. What causes counterurbanisation?

The urbanisation / counterurbanisation model in figure 3.30 is descriptive. To understand the process it requires an explanation of why the trends occur. There seem to be key 'tipping points' between the various phases. At first, in phase 1 during urbanisation, the city acts as a magnet. But eventually, in phase 2, pressures grow in the urban core from which people seek to escape. These pressures include traffic congestion, pollution and fears of crime - particularly street crime

(eg, mugging), burglary and car theft. Generally, it is the more affluent and more mobile who can escape. Such people are most likely to be in the child-rearing family phase and to be keen for their children to avoid the perceived disadvantages of the city location. Housing developers, estate agents and car manufacturers all encourage the outward movement, and profit by them.

During phase 3, some people decide that rural or suburban locations do not meet their needs. These people are mainly young adults and are generally childless. However, some older people also desire a move back to the city. They might have grown up families, or are perhaps divorced or separated. They prefer the convenience of city living. The advantages include shorter commuting times, the nearness of shops, and a nightlife that includes restaurants, clubs and theatres. Such people are most likely to move to city centres if developers provide suitable apartments and town-houses with security systems and maintenance services.

At the same time, other people continue to leave the city. It should be remembered that these various movements are not simply a question of what individuals desire or want to do. It is also a matter of having the income, wealth and opportunity to carry out these wishes.

Figure 3.30 A model of population movement

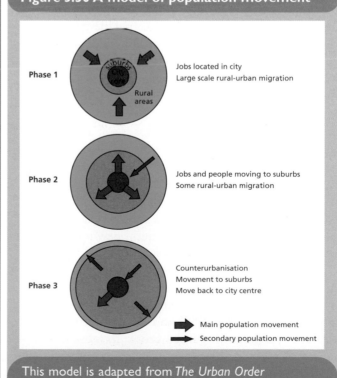

This model is adapted from *The Urban Order* by J. Short

Figure 3.31 New flats along the redeveloped canal area in Leeds city centre

Although counterurbanisation remains the dominant trend in British cities, there is some movement back into city centres. These flats in Leeds are easy to maintain and are within walking distance of the city centre. They have no gardens, but this suits the mainly young adults who live there. Security systems safeguard the residents' cars and property - so removing one of the perceived disadvantages of urban living.

Technological change is an important contributor to counterurbanisation. People find it much easier to live in a rural location if they have, for example, a fax, a computer with a modem, a freezer, a telephone, a television and a car. These allow a rural lifestyle without the disadvantage of isolation. The growth of 'teleworking' or 'electronic commuting' in which people work from home is another factor that encourages rural living.

For people who have to commute into cities by car, improvements in road and motorway networks have made the task easier. However, this is not a straightforward issue. When a new motorway or bypass is built, commuters find that their journey time falls. But, eventually, the improved roads encourage more people to move out of cities and become commuters. Congestion eventually increases and there is then often pressure on the government to build new roads or widen existing roads. The cycle then starts again.

A factor that has contributed to counterurbanisation in the UK is the process of urban renewal undertaken by some local government authorities. In many towns and cities during the 1950s and 1960s large slum clearance programmes caused people to move from inner city areas. Although some people were rehoused in the same neighbourhoods, the new housing densities were much lower than the terraced properties that were

demolished. This meant that most people had to be rehoused elsewhere - either on council estates that were usually built on the urban outskirts or in New Towns or overspill settlements beyond the urban area.

3. What are the consequences of counterurbanisation?

The consequences of counterurbanisation are felt both in rural areas and in the cities that people have left.

Rural areas and the rural-urban fringe

When large numbers of people move to the countryside, the increased demand for rural property can cause house prices to rise. As a result, in some places, local young people cannot afford to buy homes in their own villages. This causes resentment. Another problem that occurs is that newcomers might not appreciate the traditional customs of village life. The original inhabitants sometimes feel swamped by new residents and then conflict arises. If rural villages become dormitory settlements for commuters, they tend to lose vitality and community spirit. (The issue of urban dwellers moving into rural villages is discussed in more detail in unit 3.2.)

Counterurbanisation affects not only rural areas but also the rural-urban fringe - the zone where the city meets the countryside. In Britain, edge-of-city council estates and private housing estates have been built in the rural-urban fringe. As a result, urban sprawl has become a major problem. Edge-of-city shopping centres and road networks have increased the pressure in these areas.

To rural residents who live near the fringe, the spread of the city towards them can be a threat and an opportunity. Some do not want to live near urban dwellers, nor do they wish to lose the rural character of their surroundings. Some, though, make money from the process. Farmers can make large sums by selling land to urban authorities or to developers. Speculators sometimes buy land on the edge of cities in the hope that the city will move in that direction, and they can then make a large profit. If this land is left untended, it soon becomes a derelict wasteland.

To deal with urban sprawl in Britain, special planning controls have been introduced. Green Belts have been designated around most cities. In these areas, it is extremely difficult to gain planning permission for new housing or other development. In England, 12 percent of all land is designated as Green Belt and, in the South

East, this rises to 24 percent. However, developers are continually seeking to build on Green Belt land, arguing that suitable sites are unavailable within the cities.

Inner cities

Although the problems of inner cities are not all due to counterurbanisation, the process has been a contributory factor. The people who leave cities to live in rural areas tend to be in skilled or professional occupations. They are often well educated and earn regular salaries. Most are home-owners rather than tenants. They are also likely to be white.

People who are left behind in the urban areas tend to be in lower income groups, less skilled and less educated, and more likely to be unemployed. They also comprise a higher than average proportion of the elderly, of tenants, of ethnic minorities, of people dependent on welfare and in ill health.

Figure 3.32 Most and least deprived wards at the 1991 census

Rank	Ward name	Local authority
1	Spitalfields	Tower Hamlets, London
2	St. Dunstan's	Tower Hamlets, London
3	Liddle	Southwark, London
4	Everton	Liverpool
5	Vauxhall	Liverpool
6	Sparkbrook	Birmingham
7	University	Bradford
8	Princess	Knowsley
9	Granby	Liverpool
10	Hulme	Manchester
1582	Cranham West	Havering
1583	Biggin Hill	Bromley
1584	Cheam South	Sutton
1585	Norden and Bamford	Rochdale
1586	Packwood	Solihull
1587	Selsdon	Croydon
1588	Woodcote	Sutton
1589	Streetly	Walsall
1590	East Bramhall	Stockport
1591	St. Alphege	Solihull

Source: 1991 Census, OPCS

The lowest ranked wards were the most deprived, the highest ranked wards were the least deprived. The most deprived wards had the highest rates of unemployment, the lowest average incomes and the worst housing conditions.

Because of population decline, the cities have lost local taxation revenue (eg, council tax) and central government grants. This has led to a vicious circle in which funds for transport, housing, education, leisure and other services have diminished, so causing a further deterioration in the quality of urban life. Employers have left the city for greenfield sites, and more people have left to escape the impoverished situation left behind. The proportion of poorer people remaining in the cities has then increased.

In Glasgow, for instance, the city's population fell from over 1 million in 1960 to 623,000 in 1996. Of the families left, 50 percent did not have anyone in full-time employment. Only 180,000 households had an income that was high enough to pay council tax.

Analysis of the 1991 census in Britain shows that 9 out of 10 of the most deprived urban wards were in inner cities (see figure 3.32). The exception was a ward in Knowsley, an overspill settlement near Liverpool with a high proportion of council housing. The least deprived urban wards were in the suburbs or in the rural/urban fringe. Deprivation was measured by using a number of variables including unemployment and overcrowding.

The outer city

In Britain, as noted previously, large council estates were built at the edge of urban areas in the 1950s and 1960s. Most people now agree that building these estates was a mistake. Today, parts of the Easterhouse estate in Glasgow, Wester Hailes in Edinburgh, Speke in Liverpool, Kirkby in Knowsley and many others have been labelled as 'sink estates' by some writers. They have a reputation for petty crime, vandalism and drug abuse. The presence of a Knowsley ward in the top 10 most deprived wards is evidence that there is an 'outer city' problem, not just an inner city one.

The council estates were built with the best of intentions. Planners and politicians saw the inner city areas as being congested and overcrowded. There were few open spaces, and many houses were damp and lacking in basic facilities such as a bathroom or indoor toilet. It was thought that a move to greenfield suburban locations would improve people's lifestyles, as well as enable new developments to be constructed in the vacated central areas. However, many factors worked against these good intentions:

- people were uprooted from family and friends, so often felt isolated
- the developments were followed by a decline in job opportunities due to rising unemployment in the 1970s and 1980s
- housing was often badly designed and poorly built; there were often problems such as dampness and condensation, lack of security, lack of noise insulation and lack of privacy; planners created public open spaces that were vandalised and felt threatening to residents
- spending on facilities such as shops, entertainment, community centres and schools often lagged behind the house building
- because average incomes were low, not many families owned cars - this increased the sense of isolation and distance from friends and relatives, and also made people reliant on expensive public transport for shopping and travel to work.

To some extent, the problems of edge-of-city estates are similar to those in New Towns (see unit 2.2). However, New Towns were better financed and often had better management structures. Therefore their problems were not on the same scale as in the worst of the outer city locations. Despite the best intentions of the planners, councillors and developers who created such estates, they are sometimes unpleasant and threatening for the people who live in them.

Figure 3.33 Knowsley, Merseyside

The edge-of-city council estates were built to give inner city dwellers a new start in modern homes away from urban problems. The reality was that one set of problems were simply replaced by a different set.

Activity   Population change in Leeds

▼ **Figure 3.34 Leeds Metropolitan District - ward boundaries**

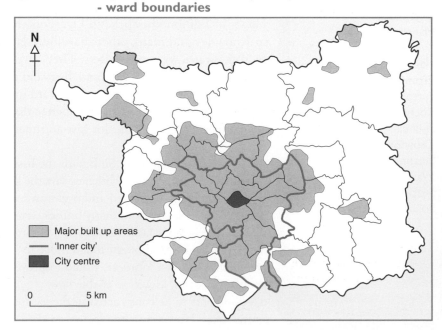

N

Major built up areas
'Inner city'
City centre

0   5 km

Leeds City Council defines its 'inner city' as those 12 wards that are most socially deprived. However, two of these wards (Seacroft in the east and Middleton in the south) are near the edge of the built up area. They both contain large estates of council housing. Most of the non built-up land in Leeds Metropolitan District is designated as Green Belt.

▼ **Figure 3.35 Population totals in Leeds Metropolitan District**

	1971	1991
Inner City	298,740	227,747
Other wards	440,191	452,918
Total	738,931	680,665

Questions

1 Describe the changes in population totals in Leeds between 1971 and 1991.
2 Suggest reasons for these changes in population.

Leeds profile, selected statistics:
Textile and clothing companies within the city lost 45 percent of their jobs in the 1980s.
Engineering companies within the city lost 33 percent of their jobs in the 1980s.
Service industries including retailing, finance and public administration all gained jobs in the 1980s.

In 1991, 33 percent of the total population lived in the inner city, yet:
• 60 percent of all unemployed people lived in the inner city
• 68 percent of the ethnic minority population lived in the inner city.

In 1991, in the inner city:
• 58 percent of all adults had no vocational qualifications (compared with the Leeds average of 37 percent)
• 44 percent of all households had no access to a car (compared with the Leeds average of 22 percent).

unit summary

1 Counterurbanisation is a process in which certain groups of people, often the better off, leave the urban areas for rural ones.
2 Counterurbanisation generally occurs when urbanisation reaches a high level. It is a complex process because some people will still be moving into urban areas as others are leaving.
3 The movement out from city centres is selective in terms of age, income and lifestyle. It has contributed to what is seen as the inner city problem. Inner cities have become the location for many disadvantaged groups in society. The loss of revenue from those who have moved out makes it difficult for local authorities to tackle the problems which face the people left behind.
4 The building of edge-of-city housing estates has created a set of social problems for those who live there.
5 The expansion of the city gives rise to pressures on the rural-urban fringe. To some extent these can be tackled by setting up specially protected zones called Green Belts.

key terms

Counterurbanisation - the movement of population out of urban areas.
Inner city - the urban centre and nearby zone in which population decline has contributed to a range of social problems.
Outer city - suburbs of private or council housing; the creation of poor quality council estates has contributed to social problems on the edge of some cities.
Rural-urban fringe - the zone where the city meets the countryside, often under pressure from urban sprawl.

Unit 3.5 The structure of urban areas

1 What are urban land use models?
2 What are the main land uses within urban areas?
3 Which processes are at work in urban areas?

1. What are urban land use models?

Urban land use models are attempts to describe and explain the patterns of land use in cities. Three influential models of urban land use were developed in the first half of the twentieth century. The models were presented by Burgess, Hoyt and the third jointly by Harris and Ullman. Generalised versions are shown in figure 3.36.

These models have formed the basis of many studies. Geographers have examined present day and historical cities in order to discover whether the urban patterns fit one or other of the models.

Burgess

The Burgess model was developed in the 'Chicago

School' during the 1920s. The Chicago School were sociologists who focused on the study of urban ecology. (Ecology is the study of living organisms, and the relationship between each another and their surroundings.) The researchers sought to show the interconnections between land use patterns and processes in the city. Burgess identified a number of concentric zones of land use from the city centre outwards. He called them the:

• Central Business District (CBD)
• Zone in transition (and factory zone)
• Zone of workingmen's homes
• Zone of better residences
• Commuters' zone.

Burgess described the zones as they applied to Chicago. The CBD is at the centre and contains a full range of retail, cultural, office and other activities. It is the heart of the city - the most accessible location, drawing people towards it. The CBD is surrounded by a rather seedy and run-down 'zone in transition'. This contains factories, warehouses and decrepit dwellings with shared occupancy. Slums, criminal activities and vice are sometimes associated with this area. It is the zone which receives the immigrants to the city - people who do not have the money to live away from their employment in the factories or the CBD.

Next comes a zone of factory-workers' homes. People here are often second generation migrants. They have reached a level of prosperity which enables them to live away from their work in higher quality housing. Further out from the centre, wealthier residents live in even better property. Beyond the city boundary is the zone of commuters. These people have escaped the urban area for greater space and tranquillity.

The Burgess model borrows from ecology the ideas of 'invasion' and 'succession' that occur within plant communities. Just as a species of plant might take over an area of ground, a change in urban land use might be caused by a wave of migrants taking over an inner city area. Alternatively, the change might be caused by CBD functions such as retailing invading the zone in transition. This zone in turn invades the zone of workingmen's homes, and so on through to the commuter zone.

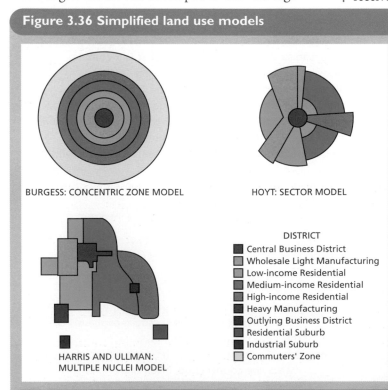

Figure 3.36 Simplified land use models

BURGESS: CONCENTRIC ZONE MODEL

HOYT: SECTOR MODEL

HARRIS AND ULLMAN: MULTIPLE NUCLEI MODEL

DISTRICT
- Central Business District
- Wholesale Light Manufacturing
- Low-income Residential
- Medium-income Residential
- High-income Residential
- Heavy Manufacturing
- Outlying Business District
- Residential Suburb
- Industrial Suburb
- Commuters' Zone

Competition for land is the key factor that determines land use in this model.

The model has provoked much debate. In the 1960s, geographers used computers to analyse land use data within cities and compare the results with the model. But, by the 1970s this was increasingly seen as a misguided activity. Although the Burgess model fitted Chicago in the 1920s quite well and also fitted other American cities of the inter-war years, there was little reason to expect that it should fit other societies at different time periods.

Present-day criticisms of the model include:
- it applies to a specific, historic period of transport and commercial development
- it only fits industrial cities in a period of industrialisation
- it does not fit well when there is a government which uses a planning system to control development
- it only fits a free market system which emphasises competition rather than cooperation
- in reality, gradients of change occur rather than sharply defined zones
- it encourages stereotyping of those living in the zone in transition as being undesirable elements
- terms such as 'invasion' and 'succession' are inappropriate when sensitive issues such as housing and ethnic groups are being discussed.

Hoyt

Hoyt developed his model of urban land use in the 1930s. He mapped 8 variables for 142 cities in the US, and focused on housing characteristics and rent patterns. Hoyt suggested that those who can afford the highest rent will occupy the land along the 'best' sectors outwards from the CBD. These sectors might be along the fastest transport routes, or on high ground free from floods, or along rivers or lakes where such land has not been occupied by industry. The demand for this land will exclude those who cannot afford high rents or land prices. Hoyt suggested that, as zones expand over time, they are more likely to do so outwards in the sectoral pattern shown in figure 3.36. Given that this model was derived from work in many cities it had a wider applicability than that of Burgess, derived from Chicago alone. But similar criticisms can be made to those of the Burgess model. It was based on US cities in the inter-war years and is therefore unlikely to apply to cities in other societies and at other times. In addition, the analysis mainly involved housing characteristics and largely ignored other land uses.

Harris and Ullman

Harris and Ullman published their model in 1945. They suggested that the land use pattern in many cities is based around not one single centre, as described by Burgess and Hoyt, but rather around many centres. They also suggested that heavy industry migrated out from the heart of the city to new suburban centres. Harris and Ullman said that four main factors were at work in the urban area:
- some land uses (such as retail or industrial activities) tend to locate near good transport routes
- some, similar, activities cluster together (such as wholesaling, and financial services)
- other, dissimilar, activities repel each other (such as industrial development and high-income residential accommodation)
- some land uses (such as bulk wholesaling or low income housing) are unable to afford the high rents of the most desirable sites

The Harris and Ullman model was largely based on North American experience and therefore shares the limitations of the Burgess and Hoyt models. Harris himself noted that it is most applicable to American cities of the early 20th century. He has stated that there is a need for a 'peripheral model' to take note of the outward movement in modern US cities. Others have noted that the European situation is quite different from that in the US. In the US, for example, some city centres are run down, whereas in European cities the central areas are often lively and prosperous, albeit surrounded by rings of deprivation.

In summary, the three land use models described here have been useful in stimulating debate. However, it should not be expected that models developed in one particular country at a certain time should fit cities from other countries at different times. Even if the patterns do fit, the processes at work to produce these patterns might be quite different. Most geographers now prefer to focus on the processes themselves rather than the patterns. These processes are described later in this unit.

2. What are the main land uses within urban areas?

The main urban land uses are retailing, commerce (ie, offices), industry and housing. Other land uses include transport (eg, roads and railway lines), and open space for recreation such as parks and sports grounds.

Central Business District (CBD)

The CBD is an important feature of most cities. It is the commercial centre, often dominated by high rise buildings, providing employment in a wide range of financial, office and retail activities. Generally it is the most accessible location within the urban area. It is the hub of the transport system so can attract the largest number of potential consumers and employees to the businesses located there. Because the demand for land is high in the CBD, it is the place where rents and land values are the most expensive.

Internally within the CBD, different land uses cluster together. For example, in London, the West End is dominated by retailing and the City is dominated by financial services. Within the City, insurance services cluster around Lloyds and banks cluster around the Bank of England in Threadneedle Street. Businesses group together because they use each other's services. For instance, banks might need accountancy and insurance expertise from nearby companies. Despite the use of computers and video-conferencing, face-to-face communication is still preferred in many transactions. There is also an advantage to be gained through informal contacts, in the pub for instance, where trade gossip can be exchanged.

National newspapers were at one time based in Fleet Street in the centre of London but many have now relocated to Wapping and other parts of Dockland.

These moves have given them more space for modern printing presses and so have increased their efficiency. The new sites have also made road transport for newsprint and newspapers quicker and cheaper than in the old, cramped locations.

Within the CBD, particular retail activities often cluster together. It is common, for example, that one part of the CBD is associated with exclusive shops for the wealthy, such as Bond Street in London or Fifth Avenue in New York. Another area might have many department stores, such as Oxford Street. Shoe shops are likely to be located near each other, as are clothes shops and travel agents. This clustering allows comparison shopping, and actually increases turnover, rather than decreases it.

Some activities can afford high rents and can therefore dominate the central area, others can only afford to locate on the periphery of the CBD. Marks and Spencer, for example, is a useful indicator of centrality in a British city centre. Because it has been very profitable in the past, it has been able to afford the best and busiest sites.

The growth of hypermarkets and shopping malls, accessible by motorway on the edge of cities, threatens the viability of city centre retailing. (See unit 6.1 for a more detailed account of changes in retailing). This has led local authorities to compete in 'place-marketing' to attract high-level retail and other activities. For instance, Leeds has sought to revitalise its central shopping area and has been successful in attracting a branch of the exclusive Harvey Nichols shop to its city centre. This was the first branch to open in the North of England. The publicity given to the event was used to promote the image of Leeds and illustrates the competitive nature of retailing between cities, not just within them. Pedestrianisation has been another means by which the city centre is made more attractive to shoppers. Enclosed shopping centres and pavement cafes are being developed in many towns and cities to provide pleasant and attractive environments and lure shoppers back to the retail part of the CBD.

Retailing outside the CBD

Retail areas are found throughout cities, not just within the CBD. These often lie along main roads in suburban areas. They mainly sell convenience goods such as food, drink

Figure 3.37 Canary Wharf from central London

London's CBD is spreading eastwards to Docklands as newspaper publishing and some financial services have moved from the cramped conditions within the City. The Canary Wharf tower seen in the distance is 5 km east of London Bridge.

Figure 3.38 McArthur Glen shopping centre, York

New shopping centres pose a threat to the traditional retail functions of the CBD. This mall on the outskirts of York has 80 shops selling clothes, footwear and household goods.

and household items. Local residents and passers-by use these shops for their everyday needs.

In recent years, new shopping centres have developed in the UK, closely following the North American pattern. Sometimes they are within the urban area, in retail parks but in other cases they are on the outskirts. Typically they contain supermarkets and also large stores selling household and electrical goods. The advantage of these locations to the retailer is that floor space is much cheaper than in the CBD. Also, the road network enables access not just to a large customer base, but ensures that that the products themselves can easily be transported around the country. When linked to computerised systems (via bar codes, for example), the information about sales is transmitted direct to warehouses, and even manufacturers. Goods can be moved overnight in large lorries, and the system is fast and efficient. There is much less danger that delivery will be slowed by city centre congestion.

The customer also benefits from reduced costs and speed of access. One-stop shopping is made easier which is an important consideration for families where both parents are in paid employment. The new shopping centres are also, increasingly, the focus of family leisure time with a trip to the mall seen as 'a day out'.

Industry

In Britain, few traditional industries remain in central urban locations. Newspaper publishing was one of the last to leave. Like engineering firms and clothing companies, these businesses found the centre of cities too crowded and congested to be profitable. Large scale modern machinery, warehousing and container transport all require larger floor spaces than most companies had available. Given the high price of city centre land, it made sense to sell the old site for redevelopment and move to the suburbs where land is cheaper. In many urban areas purpose built industrial estates have been built on the outskirts. These locations are closer to the road and motorway network and are less likely to be congested. The suburban road networks also create a large catchment area for the potential workforce. Local authorities and private developers who have built the new industrial estates have usually 'zoned' them away from residential areas - so minimising noise and traffic nuisance.

Some run-down industrial sites, including dockside locations, have been redeveloped by Urban Development Corporations (see unit 2.2). Initiatives such as Enterprise Zones were used in the 1980s to try and regenerate old industrial areas. Lower taxes and freedom from planning controls were incentives used to attract new firms. In most cases, redevelopment has taken the form of retailing, commercial and residential expansion. In areas such as London's Docklands, few manufacturing jobs have been generated. Industrial companies have preferred to locate on greenfield sites, away from the central urban areas.

Housing

Residential areas take up much of the space in urban areas. In some cities there are broadly concentric zones of housing types as in the Burgess model. For example, near the centre of British industrial cities, housing is most likely to be nineteenth century terraced property. This is high density accommodation with small houses and few, if any, gardens. Often the roads are laid out in a grid pattern (see figure 3.39). Because the land is central, it is relatively expensive. This means that any replacement housing is also likely to be high density - either high rise or small town houses.

With distance from the city centre, housing tends to be newer and lower density. Typically, in British cities, there are zones of 1920s and 1930s semi-detached properties and then, on the rural fringe, estates of modern detached houses. These are built at a much lower density than the inner city terraces. The street pattern is also different, with crescents and cul-de-sacs designed to slow the speed of motor traffic.

Although the housing pattern in some British cities has concentric features, when studied in more detail, the picture is more complex. Sometimes, this is because high income groups live in expensive inner city property, in otherwise poor districts. In London, Notting Hill is an example of such an area. Elsewhere, in prosperous suburban areas, local authority housing estates might be located as a result of decisions taken in the 1950s and 1960s. These council houses tend to be smaller and more closely spaced than private housing estates nearby.

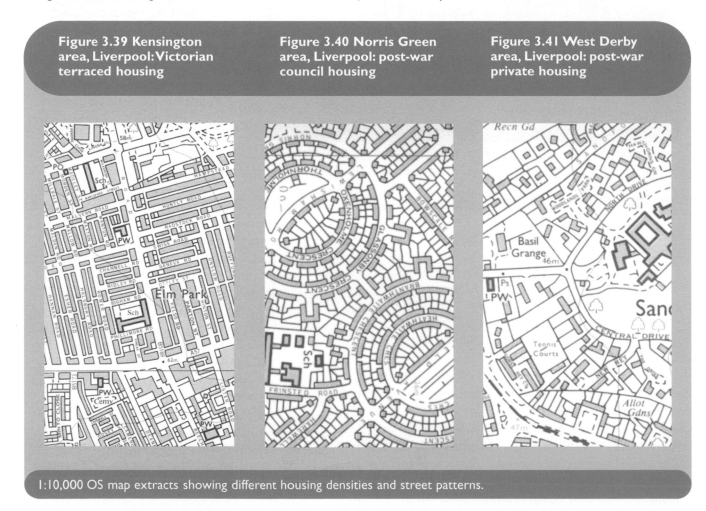

Figure 3.39 Kensington area, Liverpool: Victorian terraced housing

Figure 3.40 Norris Green area, Liverpool: post-war council housing

Figure 3.41 West Derby area, Liverpool: post-war private housing

1:10,000 OS map extracts showing different housing densities and street patterns.

An increasing feature of many inner cities are waterside developments, in which canalside or riverside warehouses are refurbished as apartments for residence. In the Isle of Dogs in the East End of London, in Liverpool's docklands, at Salford Quays in Manchester, in Amsterdam, in Baltimore and many other cities and towns around the world, new residences are being created from old urban structures. These residences are often part of wider-scale regeneration. The areas are upgraded by such means as improved landscaping (eg, tree planting), reclamation of derelict land and transport improvements. The residents of the new apartments are likely to be young, urban, professional people ('yuppies'), often in couples with dual incomes and no children ('dinkies'). The process of 'gentrification' in which run down residential areas are transformed is dealt with in the next section of this unit.

Activity **Urban land use**

▼ **Figure 3.42 Urban scenes**

Questions

1 Describe the different land uses typically found in any large city.
2 Suggest reasons why particular land uses are found in city centres.
3 Give examples of business and commercial activities that have moved to edge-of-city locations. Suggest reasons why they have moved.

3. Which processes are at work in urban areas?

The processes at work in urban areas can be viewed from different perspectives. It is possible, for example, to see the city as the product of many individual decisions. In this view, people choose to locate their businesses or homes in particular areas. There might be competition and conflict between these individuals, and the urban area can be regarded as an arena of struggle between them. Or the city might be viewed in terms of social groups, rather than individuals, with different groups congregating in specific areas for different reasons. Conflict or cooperation is group-based, rather than individual-based.

Urban processes can also be considered as part of the wider social and economic process. Businesses, governments and even global financial institutions can all have an influence.

These different perspectives are considered in the section that follows.

Individual decision making

Residential land use can be seen as the result of many choices by individuals. A focus on how individuals make decisions can help in understanding urban processes. Newcomers to a city are likely to seek a place to live where there are people of similar status and income. If the newcomer is single and relatively poor, this is likely to be in a run-down area near a railway or bus station. If the person is homeless, she or he might have to sleep rough or in a hostel. If the person can afford bed-and-breakfast accommodation, this is probably in an area at the edge of the CBD, in the zone in transition between the CBD and the wealthier suburbs. Perhaps, however, the individual has sufficient income to buy a house. The price of property, the image of different areas and the

Figure 3.43 Estate agent sign

Processes of change within a city's residential area can be viewed as the sum total of many individual decisions to buy or to sell.

quality of local facilities such as shops or schools will influence where the person will buy.

Individuals might also choose locations on the basis of their stage in the life cycle, whether they have children and what age these are. Location might be related to schools, and the suitability of an area for the children to grow up in. People might choose to live near friends, relatives or workmates, in an area where they feel comfortable.

Social processes

Urban processes are sometimes described in terms of an interaction between social groups. These groupings might be based on a number of criteria, such as income, job, or home ownership for example. Often, when analysing census or survey data, people are classified into social classes or socio-economic groups. At one end of the scale there are highly qualified, professional people such as lawyers or doctors. At the other end are unskilled and economically inactive people. Many geographical studies in the 1960s and 1970s focused on social classes and 'social areas' of cities, occupied by different groups in society. As might be expected, the highest income groups tend to live in the best housing - ie, in the biggest detached houses with large gardens, located in 'leafy' suburbs. The lowest income groups tend to live in smaller houses, more closely packed together - in the worst locations, often near to the city centre, perhaps near main roads or industrial premises.

Ethnicity has also been identified as an important factor influencing residence in urban areas. In the US, the description 'racial apartheid' has been applied to the situation in some cities. (The term comes from South Africa where, until 1994, racism was the basis of the official 'apartheid' policy and laws prevented different ethnic groups from living near each other.) Although in the USA no laws enforce racial separation, different ethnic groups tend to live in different neighbourhoods. This segregation has a number of causes. To some extent, different ethnic groups cluster together because they can maintain their traditions, culture and language more easily if they live in the same neighbourhood. However, in the case of some minority groups such as African Americans, discrimination also plays a part. These groups fear, correctly in some cases, that they will face hostility and abuse if they move to white neighbourhoods. Because they tend to have low average incomes, such groups are often clustered in areas of poor housing.

Figure 3.44 Chinatown, San Francisco

The original ghetto was the area within Venice where Jewish people were forced to live. Ghetto areas inhabited by one ethnic group might be the result of individual choices but might also be the result of social processes such as discrimination.

Political and economic processes

The processes at work in urban areas can be considered as being part of the wider economic and political system. So, in countries where market forces operate freely, land use in cities is the result of the way in which the market system operates. In other words, land is sold to the highest bidder and the owner decides on how it will be used. In the UK, market forces often determine urban land use but these forces are modified by the planning system operated by local government.

Bid-rent theory is the name given to one particular explanation of how the market system works. It explains how some land uses become concentrated in certain areas. The theory is based on the idea that businesses will wish to locate in the most accessible part of the city - where there will be most customers. All things being equal, this is the city centre which is the hub of the transport system. Firms try to outbid each other for the best sites and this drives up the price of the most accessible locations.

Retail activities earn relatively high profits so can generally bid more for land than can other users such as industry. Within retailing, department stores can usually outbid shoe shops which, in turn, can outbid furniture stores. Grocery stores cannot compete with these because they tend to be less profitable, and must locate in less accessible places. The outcome is, according to the

theory, concentric rings of different users changing with distance from the city centre. This is shown in figure 3.45. At first sight the pattern appears similar to the Burgess model. The basic bid-rent diagram does indeed suggest that there will be concentric zones of land use. However, if all lines of access and transport are included in the model, a modified pattern is a more likely outcome. This has places where rents are high outside the CBD, for example at accessible locations where a ring road meets an arterial road. (An arterial road leads in and out of the 'heart' of an urban area.)

The bid-rent theory helps explain some aspects of urban land use but has been criticised for a number of reasons:

* The relationship between centrality and accessibility is less strong than it once was. In other words, the CBD may no longer be the easiest place for all the urban dwellers to reach. Traffic congestion is an important reason why CBDs are becoming less accessible. Some businesses are therefore no longer prepared to pay the highest rents for city centre locations.

Figure 3.45 Bid-rent theory

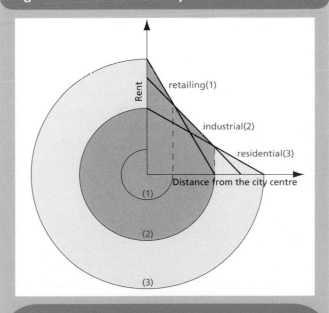

The bid-rent theory was developed by Alonso in 1964. It plots the amount of money ('rent') that land users are prepared to pay on one axis, and the distance from the city centre on the other axis. The land users who are prepared to pay the most rent gain the use of the land.

- Bid-rent theory assumes that users of land know precisely where accessibility is greatest and what rents are charged, and that they will always wish to make as much profit as possible. But, in reality, their information will not be perfect (ie, not complete). Nor will they always desire the most profitable location. For instance, they might be willing to sacrifice some profit to locate in a pleasant area, away from the city centre.
- Particular plots of urban land might only rarely come up for sale or rent - so many land users have to settle for second-best locations. Some landowners might keep their land for many years, not seeking to develop it because they hope its value will rise in the future. A study in Liverpool in the 1990s, for example, showed that vacant sites owned by private landlords were much less likely to be developed than vacant sites owned by Liverpool City Council.
- In UK towns and cities, planning controls and the need for planning permission mean that land use is influenced by political controls and not purely by market forces. This point is illustrated by the example from Birmingham described below. Although the changes to land use were mainly financed by private companies, it was the city council that took the initiative for the redevelopment scheme.

Figure 3.46 shows some of Birmingham's recent redevelopment. Private developers, financial institutions and local government have worked together in planning and financing the scheme. The local council hopes to create a positive image for the city and so attract further development. The two main projects are:

- Broad Street Redevelopment, with more than £380 million invested by the city council on a 16 hectare site. The EU has also provided 'regeneration' funds. Much of this money has been spent on the new International Convention Centre. Other new buildings include the privately financed 5-star Hyatt Regency Hotel and the National Indoor Arena.
- The Heartlands Initiative, an area of public-private partnership in a zone of formerly derelict and contaminated land. The area is large (900 hectares) and contains a wide mix of land uses. These include industrial and office developments, business parks (eg, along the Waterlinks area), and the Aston Science Park, linked with Aston University. High quality landscaping and building design are features of this development.

Figure 3.46 City centre redevelopment in Birmingham

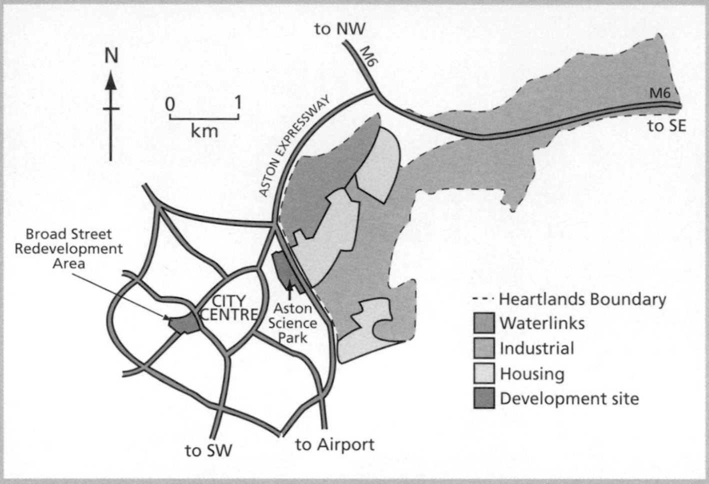

In derelict and run down urban areas within the UK it is generally local government that takes the initiative in determining how land is used. Private developers are often reluctant to spend money on new buildings or renovating property if the area has a bad reputation or is considered unfashionable. It is generally only when government 'pump primes' a project that private development will start. For instance, a local authority might spend money on landscaping - planting trees and creating attractive

Figure 3.47 A gentrified neighbourhood

Improving the housing stock might have the result of driving out the current inhabitants. This inner city area in Liverpool became run down in the 1950s and 1960s. Many of the houses were subdivided into flats and bedsits. Now the area is becoming gentrified and the houses are being reconverted into single residences for high income groups.

open areas. Money might be spent on narrowing roads (to slow traffic and improve parking) and on features such as attractive street lights and traffic bollards. Improvement grants might be offered to residents so that the houses can be rewired or replumbed. The hope is that the investment by the local authority will persuade private redevelopment companies also to invest.

When urban renewal takes place, it is sometimes followed by **gentrification**. This is when relatively affluent newcomers displace lower income groups. It is a process which improves the quality of the housing stock and takes the area upmarket. In other words, the houses are renovated and, as a result, their value increases. Some local people might be hostile to the process and resent the change in character to 'their' neighbourhood. As houses within the area come up for sale, newcomers from higher income groups with different tastes and attitudes might eventually replace the original inhabitants.

Activity   Regeneration in city centres

During the 1960s and 1970s a large number of glass and concrete office blocks were built in UK towns and cities. Many of these buildings are coming to the end of their useful life. For instance, over 1 million square feet of office space is vacant in old blocks in Birmingham. Modern office technology requires cabling and electricity supplies that are simply uneconomic to install in the old office buildings.

Many of the blocks will be demolished and replaced by new buildings. However, an extra lease of life might be given to others if they are converted into residential property. Millennium Apartments is a development company that has started to convert a 1970s Telecom building in Birmingham into 63 apartments. The 14 storey block will also house sports facilities and a restaurant as a means of attracting the young professional tenants that the company hopes will move in. The new residents, it is believed, will be tempted by the prospect of not having to commute to work and by living within walking distance of the city's attractions.

The government is expected to give backing to similar schemes as a means of providing some of the 4 million new homes it estimates are needed by 2016. By converting redundant offices and industrial premises, there will be less pressure on the out-of-town greenfield sites that most wish to see protected from development. Local authority leaders are calling on government to give them more powers to encourage office conversions. For example, if local councils could increase the business rates (the local property tax) on empty offices, and lower them on new developments, this would give a big incentive to such schemes.

Analysts suggest that additional benefits can flow from such office redevelopments. If there is good quality residential accommodation within walking distance of the main financial centre, the city becomes a more attractive location for business. The upwardly mobile, go-getting young professionals that local companies need to recruit are more likely to want to work in places with desirable housing. In turn, their spending power attracts other businesses, so giving another boost to inner city regeneration.

Adapted from the Financial Times, 18th February 1998

▲ **Figure 3.48 A 1960s office block**

Questions

1 If significant numbers of young professional people move into converted office blocks, how will this affect the land use pattern in UK cities?
2 Describe the processes at work in the scheme to convert old offices into residential accommodation.

unit summary

1 Early models of urban land use were developed in the United States. They are now generally regarded as being obsolete because they refer to specific US locations and time periods, and are therefore not generally applicable to most modern cities.
2 Retail, commercial (ie, offices), industrial and residential land use are the main urban land uses. Renewal areas are becoming important elements in most UK cities
3 A wide range of processes are at work in urban areas. These processes are influenced by the actions of individuals, social groups, and also by political and economic forces.

key terms

CBD (Central Business District) - the heart of the retailing and business activity of the city, usually the most accessible location.
Gentrification - the process in which residential urban areas are improved or renewed; low income

groups are displaced by higher income groups.
Segregation - the separation of different population groups into different areas. This often occurs along ethnic lines and, in some cases, the most disadvantaged groups live in ghettos.

Unit 3.6 Managing urban settlements

key questions

1 How do cities compare in different parts of the world?
2 What solutions are used to overcome urban problems?
3 What causes traffic congestion and how can it be resolved?

1. How do cities compare in different parts of the world?

Most large cities have some, or all, of the following characteristics:
- high rise office blocks and hotels in a Central Business District
- new buildings, often showing similar architectural features
- an international airport
- high rise or mid-rise housing estates, often on the edge of the city
- historic buildings of character which are under threat from new developments
- problems of waste disposal, of different types
- conspicuous consumption side by side with poverty

(ie, there are some very wealthy individuals who spend money on luxuries, and some very poor people who struggle to survive)
- lack of permanent shelter for the poorest people or new migrants
- a range of ethnic groups, some living in specific parts of the city
- traffic congestion (because this is such a widespread and serious problem it is treated separately in the last section of this unit).

Despite the similarities between First World and Third World cities, the processes operating within them are often different. Sometimes these differences are due to specific local conditions. In other cases, however, they are due to the different timescale in which urban development has taken place.

Cities in the First World, for example, often expanded rapidly in the 19th century, rather than the 20th. Their expansion was closely linked to industrialisation and the growth of employment in manufacturing. To tackle the health, environmental and other problems which they faced, the cities developed systems of municipal administration. These local governments financed and organised the provision of clean water supplies and sewerage disposal. By the early 20th century, planning controls were being used to direct and limit urban

Figure 3.49 Manila, Philippines

Many common features are found in First World and Third World cities. However, the processes at work are often very different.

expansion. In recent years, urban regeneration has become necessary due to the decline in the urban fabric - particularly in inner city areas. Despite such problems, Western cities, including those of Japan, are generally rich and powerful, with a 'global reach' based on connections built up over a long time period. They are located within wealthy societies, and so the overall level of prosperity in the urban population is relatively high. In particular, the cities have a large middle income group which generally forms the majority of the population.

In the Third World, the cities are located in societies which are generally poor. Industrial manufacturing is often important but, due to mechanisation, cannot provide the employment which it did in 19th century Britain, for example. Many people only have casual work rather than jobs with regular wages or salaries. Often, these are migrants from rural areas - where tap water, flush toilets, and electricity might not be available. Such people face a massive challenge of adaptation, probably greater than the equivalent challenge to 19th century migrants. Due to the scale and speed of urban expansion in the Third World, the severity of urban problems is often very great. City governments are sometimes simply overwhelmed. Arguably, the difficulties are greater today in Third World cities than in Victorian Britain because they lack the resources to cope with such problems.

In Eastern Europe, the former USSR and the People's Republic of China, cities grew under the communist system. In these societies, planning and state intervention was dominant. In the former East Berlin, in Moscow, in Beijing, and in other socialist cities, the CBD was practically non-existent. There was no free market in land to draw finance and retailing towards a central point. Instead, huge squares such as Red Square in Moscow or Tiananmen in Beijing became the focal point. They were symbols of the power of the socialist state.

Today, the former communist countries of Eastern Europe are being transformed. In China, 'market socialism' or 'socialism with Chinese characteristics' is now dominant. The cities in these societies, therefore, are also being transformed. State controls are being relaxed, and property markets, housing markets and other markets are being allowed or encouraged to grow.

Housing

The difference between cities in high income and low income countries is illustrated by the contrasts in housing. In most high income countries, the overwhelming majority of urban residents live in good quality housing. Houses are generally warm and dry, they have clean piped water and flush toilets. In low income countries, some urban residents also live in good houses. However, poor quality **shanty housing** is a feature of many Third World cities. The shanties are a consequence of a housing shortage, due to the rapid rate of population expansion, coupled with the lack of resources or political desire to provide housing in sufficient numbers and of sufficient quality for new migrants. Often, newcomers join previous migrants from their home village or town, and build their homes on land unused by the authorities or developers. They become squatters on this land. Packaging, scrap metal and other waste products are scavenged to build

Figure 3.50 A Rio de Janeiro shanty town

In 1998, an estimated 2 million people lived in the shanty towns or 'favelas' of Rio de Janeiro.

properties which are, at first, ramshackle. Electricity might be tapped from overhead power lines, and water carried from a well or tap some distance away.

Figure 3.50 shows a shanty town in Rio de Janeiro. Some of these settlements are built next to high income housing. Large numbers of Brazil's rural population are moving to cities because of the greater opportunities on offer and also because mechanisation is reducing the demand for farm labour.

The makeshift shanties are made from corrugated iron, plastic and wood. Large numbers of people have to share communal taps and there is no sewage system. Increasingly, drug dealing has become an important part of the informal economy in some Rio shanties. Drug gangs maintain control by a mixture of fear and community involvement. It is not unusual for the gangs to organise a creche, local health post and cut price food outlet. Tension between the gangs sometimes erupts into violence - 120 bodies were found by police in different incidents in just one month in 1998. Some of the wealthier residents are fleeing the city and moving to purpose built, bullet proof apartments, surrounded by electric fencing, that have sprung up at the city outskirts.

In the 'socialist cities' of the former communist countries, shanty towns were absent. This was due partly to the commitment of the state to provide housing for the working classes. It also reflected controls on the movement of population from rural areas. In China, for example, for most of the Maoist era which lasted from 1949 to 1976, to be housed, work and even eat in the city required registration and a ration card. It was virtually impossible to live in a city without approval from the authorities. Urban growth was tightly controlled for most of this period. Large-scale housing estates were built to house urban dwellers. These mainly mid-rise developments seem bleak and poorly maintained today, but were often an improvement on previous conditions. In the 1990s, controls on internal migration were relaxed and an estimated 130 million have moved to China's cities. Many of these people live in overcrowded conditions, but not as bad as in the shanty towns of other Third World countries. Housing still has a high priority in China, and by the mid-1990s, over 4,000 large housing developments had been built in the previous fifteen years. However, concerns over safety and quality have been expressed about some of the rapidly constructed dwellings, and there have been reported instances where blocks of flats have collapsed.

Employment

In First World cities, most employees work full time, in jobs that have regular hours and set wages. In Third World cities, the nature of employment is often different from that in the West. A high proportion of the urban population is engaged in what is called the **informal sector**.

Work in the informal sector is irregular and casual, generally unregulated by the government or urban authority. Mostly it is labour-intensive (ie, there is no expensive equipment or machinery involved), small-scale, cash-based, and often unskilled. People might sell fruit or vegetables at stalls, or just by the roadside. Some might shine shoes, or sell matches or cheap lighters. Others sell cooked food to office and shop workers, especially at lunchtime. The informal sector workers are sometimes exploited by having to work long hours for little return. They are in a weak position in the labour market because so many others are waiting to

Figure 3.51 A street trader in Bangkok

Many people in Third World cities work in the 'informal' sector. This is low paid, casual and insecure employment.

Figure 3.52 Female Third World factory workers in Dhaka, Bangladesh

Concern is often expressed that Third World female labour is exploited in textile, footwear and electronics factories. Others point out that the women are receiving a wage that gives them a greater degree of independence than they could otherwise obtain.

take their place. Also, there are few, if any, laws to protect their interests and no trade unions to defend their rights. Every so often, the local government might act to rid the streets of the informal activities. The authorities do this because they want to have a cleaner, neater environment in the hope that an improved image will make the city more attractive to business investors - particularly from abroad.

However, many workers in the formal sector (ie, people in regular employment) need the relatively cheap goods and services that the informal sector provides. The incomes of people in the formal sector might even be used to finance the activities of those in the informal sector. The two sectors therefore interact in a process of mutual benefit, although the benefit is unevenly distributed.

A controversial aspect of employment in many Third World cities relates to female labour in factories. Often, employers prefer female labour because women are perceived to be more docile, hard-working and dexterous than men. In countries such as Malaysia, Taiwan and China, female labour has been employed in large numbers, especially in the clothing, footwear and electronics industries. Many have argued that this labour is being exploited, with low wages and poor working conditions.

There are others, however, who claim that factory employment can be liberating for women, especially in patriarchal (ie, male dominated) societies. This may be the only opportunity for women to escape domestic drudgery, and to have some money of their own. This is a complex debate and the judgment probably depends on specific factors at work in each location.

Of course, unpleasant working conditions are found in Western cities, and there is also an informal economy. However, it is the degree of both that is the main difference in Third World cities. In the West, there are regulations that govern, for example, unsafe factories, exploitation of workers, food handling and hygiene. These combine to minimise the conditions which are common in the Third World.

Environmental conditions

Contrasts in environmental conditions are also a matter of degree between cities in different parts of the world. The level of regulation and control tends to be less in Third World countries. This is because economic growth is often sought at any cost.

The lack of adequate sewers and drains is often a severe problem. The UN estimated that by the year 2000, 446 million of the urban population in low income countries were without a clean water supply. The number without sanitation facilities (ie, a sewage system) was 632 million (see figure 3.53).

Overwhelmingly it is the urban poor who are without such basic facilities. For example, in Jakarta, Indonesia, 30 percent of wealthy households do not have regular waste collection facilities, but this rises to 81 percent of the poorest households. Often, the city authorities lack the financial resources to deal with such issues, and are restricted in the local taxation that they can raise. The combination of untreated sewage, domestic waste and contaminated water, in hot, humid conditions, makes the health hazards lethal.

Figure 3.54 Clean water and sewage systems

	Urban dwellers without a clean water supply 2000 (millions)	Urban dwellers without a sewage system 2000 (millions)
Africa	79	90
Latin America	47	89
Asia	314	453

Activity | Smokey Mountain

Smokey Mountain is the name that was given to the world's largest rubbish dump - in Manila, Philippines. It was closed down and removed in 1993 to make way for new housing. It is hoped that 25,000 'scavengers' who once made their living on the tip will be rehoused in apartments.

Most of the people who worked on the dump were shanty dwellers living on, or next to, the four hectare site. It contained an estimated 2.2 billion tons of rotting rubbish, piled as high as a 20-story building. The scavengers scoured the dump to find bottles, metal and plastic for recycling. It was a dangerous occupation. Methane gas leaked from the decomposing refuse, causing smoke and, occasionally, explosions. Accidents were common on the dump as people followed the bulldozers around. Other people became ill with lung and respiratory ailments. The shacks in which people lived gave little shelter and had no access to clean water or any form of sewage system. Flooding was a common problem.

One former resident, Tessie Cayago, is a 59 year old mother of nine children. Four had died on the dump. She objected to the rehousing scheme; 'In spite of all the problems, it was our home and the only way we can make a living'. Several forcible evictions had been tried in the 1980s but, in every case, the local shanty dwellers had resisted successfully. This time, the government was more determined and the promise of apartments made opposition weaker.

The scheme will cost the Philippines government £175m. It was determined to clear the site because it was a health hazard and, also, because of embarrassment at the negative image of Manila that the dump created.

▲ Figure 3.54 Tip scavengers on Smokey Mountain, Manila

The government and private charities set up temporary shelters for the displaced people and provided health clinics and teachers. For most of the children it was their first experience of education. Before, they had helped contribute to the family income by scavenging. Now, it is hoped, training in basic literacy, business studies and IT will help the residents get jobs in the formal economy. The new apartment complex is planned to have its own school, hospital and landscaped grounds. Running water and lavatories will be provided for all residents. However, the doubt remains whether the scheme will work. For the older Smokey Mountain residents, scavenging is all that they know and the monthly apartment rent of £13 might be too much for them to afford.

Adapted from the Guardian, 11th September 1997

Questions

1 Outline the advantages and disadvantages, from both the government's and the scavengers' point of view, of bulldozing Smokey Mountain and the shanty settlement.
2 Explain why features such as shanty settlements and scavenging on rubbish tips are more common in Third World rather than Western countries.

Crime

Crime and the fear of crime are common features of most urban areas - in low and high income countries. There are several reasons why this is the case. Firstly, the opportunity for theft is high because cities contain many wealthy people and large amounts of valuable property. Secondly, the size of cities allows some people to live anonymous lifestyles and so more easily escape detection than in a small settlement. Thirdly, there is less of a sense of community than, say, in villages where most people know each other. Fourthly, the great contrasts in wealth and income in most cities might cause some less well off people to feel tempted to gain a share for themselves.

The fear of crime is one reason why some people leave inner urban areas and move to the suburban / rural fringes (see unit 3.4 on counterurbanisation). According to the British Crime Survey (a biennial report by the government), the types of crime that people fear most are violence (eg, mugging), burglary, car theft and vandalism. Crime statistics support the view that these offences are more common in urban areas than in rural areas. For instance, in 1997, the mainly urban West Yorkshire police area had the highest rate of burglary in England and Wales, at 18 offences per thousand population. Dyfed-Powys in rural Wales had the lowest rate, just 2 per thousand. All the major urban areas in England and Wales had burglary rates of over 12 per thousand compared with under 6 per thousand in rural areas such as East Anglia, Cornwall and Shropshire.

Activity **Burglary and vehicle crime**

'I don't know anyone who hasn't been burgled'

The Hyde Park area of Leeds is typical of many inner city residential areas. The nineteenth century housing contains a mix of mainly low income families and students who live in flats. All the shops and many of the houses have metal doors and window grilles, often with more than one padlock. One street in the Hyde Park area, Chestnut Avenue, became infamous three years ago as 'the most burgled street in Britain'. The residents complain that the police seem powerless to stop the burglaries. One claimed that; 'I don't know anyone who hasn't been burgled'. In many cases it is believed that local children are to blame. Often they are too young to prosecute. The pattern, repeated elsewhere, seems to be that it is people on low incomes who are most at risk from burglary and other property crime.

On Chestnut Avenue, cars are regularly broken into and stereos are stolen. Sometimes cars are driven away by thieves and joyriders but there is also a risk that the cars will be vandalised or set on fire. In one major incident recently, more than 20 cars were burnt after police were accused of harassment during a drugs raid.
Adapted from the Guardian, 12th May 1997

	Residents of council estates and low income inner urban areas	Residents of high income suburban and rural areas
Vehicle crime (thefts and vandalism)	33	20
Burglary	9	4

Adapted from the British Crime Survey

▲ **Figure 3.55 Risk of being a victim of crime (1995-97), percentages, England and Wales**

Questions

1 To what extent can certain types of crime be considered an urban problem?
2 Suggest reasons why crimes such as burglary and car theft are more common in some areas than in others.

2. What solutions are used to overcome urban problems

A variety of policies are used to try and solve urban problems. In high income countries, such as the US and UK, cities are trying to overcome the difficulties arising from counterurbanisation and the loss of manufacturing industry. In low income countries, cities are trying to cope with rapid urbanisation.

Promoting an image

If a city can gain a positive, modern image, it will find it easier to attract investment and employment from transnational corporations and local companies. Slogans, advertising campaigns, sporting and cultural events are used to promote cities in all parts of the world. An example was the 'Glasgow's Miles Better' campaign of the early 1990s. The city's image of a run-down, working-class environment was partially transformed by the success of this campaign (and the real improvements which were being made in the city). As part of the process, Glasgow become European City of Culture in 1990. This upstaged its rival in Scotland - Edinburgh, and enabled Glasgow to join the front rank of Europe's culture capitals. Theatres, art galleries, festivals, museums and other aspects of culture were promoted. This encouraged national and international tourism during the year itself, and also left an improved stock of facilities from which further progress could be made.

Cities need a niche or even gimmick with which to promote themselves in the highly competitive global market for investment. Birmingham's regeneration projects, for example (see unit 3.5) were promoted by **place-marketing**, using slogans such as 'Birmingham - the Big Heart of England' and 'Birmingham - the European Business Venue'. It now seems that cities can no longer rely on businesses coming to them by chance; instead businesses must be attracted and persuaded to come.

Staging the Olympic Games is a very high profile means of gaining the world's attention. This prestige event, held every four years, is often regarded by urban authorities as a way of kick-starting large scale urban renewal, and providing a wide range of leisure facilities for the city's inhabitants. Cities such as Manchester, London, Athens, Los Angeles, Seoul, Sydney, Tokyo, Atlanta and Beijing have all bid in recent years for the right to host the event. The bidding process is costly, however, and a large investment must be made in facilities to stage the event. For cities such as Barcelona, which hosted the 1992 Olympics, the effect was worthwhile. Commerce, tourism and trade all prospered as a result of the Games.

The '24-hour city' or 'night-city' is another idea being used to promote a positive image in UK and US cities. The aim is to revitalise the urban core and solve the problem of the 'empty heart' of cities when office workers and shop assistants leave the CBD in the early evening. Cinemas, restaurants, bars and night clubs are being licensed to later and later hours in an attempt to attract and retain customers around the clock. By such means generally more use of urban facilities can be made, as peaks and troughs of use are smoothed out. Manchester, for instance, has heavily promoted its image as a centre for night life, and previously decaying urban areas have been revitalised by the opening of clubs, bars and restaurants.

Figure 3.56 Sydney, Australia

2000 Olympic Games. High profile sporting events can boost a city's image and have a long term beneficial spin-off in terms of investment, transport links and tourism.

Some council estates in Britain have a severe image problem. Like other urban areas that face difficulties, the very real problems that exist are reinforced by a negative image. The government's Social Exclusion Unit has identified 17 'worst' estates in which 'people's lives are wasted' and for which 'we all have to pay the cost of dependency and social division'. A 1998 survey of council tenant's attitudes on one such estate, the Blackbird Leys estate in Oxford, highlighted the issues.

Percentage of people who mentioned the issues as being important:	
Lack of shops / poor shops	24
Crime / feeling unsafe	22
Vandalism / threatening behaviour	21
Unsupervised youngsters	12
Traffic / speeding cars	8
Poor public transport	8
Lack of community spirit	7
Litter / general appearance	5

▲ **Figure 3.57 Residents' dislikes about their estates**

Studies have shown that pockets of poverty exist in some council estates that are in otherwise relatively prosperous areas. In the estates surveyed, unemployment is over double the regional average, teenage pregnancy is 50 percent higher and mortality rates are 33 percent higher. Council estates are often at the edge of urban areas and, because public transport is generally poor and car ownership is low, people are trapped. Local shops, if they exist at all, charge up to 60 percent more than supermarkets.

Announcing a £800 million New Deal for Communities programme, the government said that it would not repeat the mistakes of the past. Too often, short term fixes had been imposed on local areas and had failed. This time, the programme would be long term. It would only take place in communities where a partnership between the local authority, residents and businesses had prepared action plans. Targeted areas would be relatively small scale, ranging from 1,000 to 4,000 houses. The aim would be to renovate buildings, clean up the environment, improve services and tackle the problem of anti-social behaviour of a minority. A crucial part of the process would be to improve the image of such areas.

Adapted from the Independent, 8th September 1998

Questions

1 Explain why some council estates have an image problem.
2 Discuss the New Deal For Communities as a possible solution to the problems that council estates face.

Diversifying out of manufacturing

Cities in North America and Western Europe are having to cope with the loss of manufacturing jobs. (The issue of 'deindustrialisation' is described in unit 5.2.) Many cities are trying to overcome this problem by diversifying out of manufacturing and generating jobs in the service sector. An example of a successful attempt to diversify

has occurred in Lowell, 20 miles to the north of Boston, USA. This city was established as a textile centre in the 1820s. By 1848, Lowell was the biggest industrial community in the United States. But then competition developed and, by the 1920s, the textile industry had moved to the 'sunbelt' of the southern States or overseas, leaving derelict industrial buildings and a city in decay.

Figure 3.58 An old textile mill

Lowell has replaced its once important textile manufacturing base by promoting links between education and high-tech industries, and by developing a tourist industry around its heritage sites.

In 1975, local bankers founded the Lowell Development and Financial Corporation to raise funds and stimulate business expansion. Partnership between the public and private sectors was a key element. Success was achieved in the 1980s by the attraction of investment from the computing industry (especially via the Wang Corporation), plastics, a new National Historical Park (an industrial heritage park which attracts one million visitors per year), and the founding of the University of Massachusetts at Lowell by the merger of two higher education institutions. The city thrived in the 1980s on this diverse, upmarket, range of activities.

Old mill structures were converted into good quality housing for new residents. Businesses were attracted to the heritage industry, medicine, the defence industry, biotechnological/ environmental industries and a wide range of recreational/ cultural activities. 'Lowell Means Business' and 'City of Innovation' were two of the slogans used by the city government in promoting its image.

The 'brown agenda' in Third World cities

The previous examples are mainly from the UK and USA where cities are trying to cope with deindustrialisation and population loss. In the Third World many cities are also trying to promote a positive image in the hope of attracting employment, but they are also having to cope with population gain and consequent environmental and housing pressures. The so called 'brown agenda' in low income countries is largely concerned with the unequal access of the poor to decent facilities - particularly in terms of public health care and clean water. These services are sometimes provided at high cost, mainly for the benefit of the middle and upper income groups in society. For example, the World Bank estimates that in Third World countries, 80 percent of water supply and sanitation expenditure is on high cost water treatment technology that is used by only 20-30 percent of the population - mainly higher income groups. Poor people have to use communal taps that provide dirty water and public latrines that empty into septic tanks. In many cities water is sold by vendors rather than being provided from piped supplies. It is an expensive system in which the poor pay a higher proportion of their income for water, often up to 30 percent, compared to the better-off who pay only 1 or 2 percent.

The problem in most low income countries is that the provision of piped, clean water requires large amounts of public spending. This money is simply not available in many cases, and even when investment is made, the rise in population often outstrips the provision.

Housing

Large numbers of people in Third World cities live in squatter or shanty settlements. Some city authorities have a very negative view of these slums and try to solve the problem by clearing them. Bulldozing the shanty houses has the advantage of being a 'quick fix', especially if the settlement is highly visible, near an airport or

Figure 3.59 Slums near the Yamuna River, Delhi, India

The provision of housing, public health care and clean water are massive problems in most Third World countries.

road. Another advantage of clearing is that it might discourage migrants from moving to the city. However, this 'solution' does not provide a long term answer to the housing shortage. Also, it has been challenged by some researchers who have studied the processes at work in shanty towns. They suggest that it is better to allow residents to improve their homes. By providing low cost materials, social infrastructure such as power and piped water, and, most importantly, security of tenure, the local authorities can help people to help themselves. Security of tenure is crucial because the shanty residents will not improve their homes if they fear that the site is going to be cleared, or that the original landowner can seize the improved housing in the future.

Figure 3.60 shows the processes that have been identified in some Third World shanty towns. 'Bridgeheaders' are the new migrants who seek, primarily, to live near casual work and who endure the minimum of facilities. At first, they might even sleep in shop doorways, on the streets, or on someone's floor when they reach the urban area. Then they might locate in a shanty town, perhaps a recently established one. The 'consolidators' have been in the city for several years and are more concerned to ensure legal tenure for their residence. This might involve joining a local activist or community group to lobby the authorities to grant secure rights of tenure to their shanty-town area. The authorities in some countries are now willing to provide

this. For residents who have successfully negotiated this phase, they might become 'status-seekers' who wish to improve their family situation by moving into modern housing stock.

Conservation

How to conserve the best of the old is an issue that arises in most cities. New, high-rise buildings are being constructed at a rapid pace and demolition and reconstruction is common. The old is being rapidly swept away in favour of the new. In some Third World cities there is often little concern for conservation, sometimes because the old, and beautiful, buildings of the past are associated with the colonial era. For example, the impressive waterfront buildings of the Bund (an area of Shanghai that was built by foreign powers) were left to decay for many years. Investment was channelled instead to new developments such as those across the Yangtze River in Pudong. There is a now a growing awareness in China that some of these old buildings are worth preserving.

Similar concerns have emerged in Quito, Ecuador. Recognised as a World Heritage site by the United Nations in 1978, the city has the largest historic centre in South America. Conservation has become a priority - to attract tourism and to preserve the city's heritage. Streets have been pedestrianised, pavements widened and more light introduced to squares by the removal of trees. In all, the central area has become more pleasant a place to visit and live in. However, a negative aspect to this is that some local inhabitants have been priced out of the central area as it has become 'gentrified'. Also, in an effort to 'tidy' the area, street vendors have been cleared - hitting the incomes of some of the poorest people.

In low income countries, it is especially difficult to resolve the tension between developers and local residents. City governments sometimes prioritise issues of heritage, prestige and image - at the expense of the inhabitant's short-term needs of food, shelter and employment. The best solutions often arise when local people and communities are involved in the decision making process. However, this is easier said than done - particularly in countries where democracy is fragile or nonexistent.

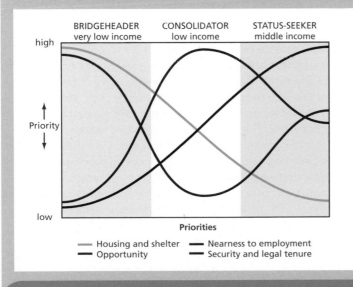

Figure 3.60 A model of changing priorities by shanty town residents

The model is based on research in Lima and other Latin American cities by John Turner.

Activity | **UN Habitat II Summit: growing good news in cities**

Expert reports made for Habitat II, a United Nations conference held in Istanbul during 1996, suggested that there was some good news for cities as well as bad.

- Although more of the world's population live in cities, urbanisation is reducing population growth. There has been a dramatic drop in fertility rates and family sizes as people have left the countryside.
- Although there is tremendous poverty in Third World cities, the urban poor are between three and ten times better off than the rural poor.
- Predictions that cities in the Third World would explode out of control have turned out to be wrong. Mexico City was predicted to have a population of 31 million by the turn of the century, according to forecasts in the 1980s. The latest estimate puts the figure at little more than half that (16.4m).
- Urban farming is lifting hundreds of millions of people out of extreme poverty and improving nutrition and health standards around the world. An estimated 800 million - just under a third of the world's city-dwellers - grow food or keep livestock in cities for consumption or as a source of income. In China, cities produce 90 per cent of the vegetables their inhabitants consume. Twenty per cent of the nutritional requirement in Africa is produced in towns and cities. The revelation that rooftop and balcony gardening and animals in the backyard combine to form a bigger 'industry' than anyone realised comes in a report from the Urban Agriculture Network, a Washington-based research group.

The Habitat findings show that some Third World cities are making progress to overcome their problems. But this does not mean that today's cities are not growing or that their problems of pollution, poverty and homelessness are not severe. Each year, 60 million people move into cities and 10 million city dwellers die of disease caused by poor sanitation. Waterborne diseases kill 4 million city children annually. Air quality is worsening through a rise in car ownership in many large cities. Airborne lead concentrations from petrol are often above World Health Organisation guidelines, causing high risks for children's health and mental development.

Homelessness has gone up as investment in public housing is cut in countries that have large debt burdens. However, evictions of squatters and shanty dwellers appear to have declined thanks to greater tolerance by national and city governments and tougher resistance by the squatters.

One new worry is 'gentrification', as cities upgrade low income areas or 'clear' or 'beautify' them, often in advance of major events such as the Seoul Olympics or the meeting of the World Bank in Bangkok. In Seoul between 1983 and 1988, 720,000 people lost their homes and 90 per cent of those evicted did not get flats on the redeveloped site.

Slow progress at solving urban problems since the first Habitat conference twenty years ago has led to a radically new approach for Habitat II. Instead of calling on governments to act, the Conference addressed itself to local authorities, urging them to go into partnership with the private sector, citizens' groups and community organisations. It focused on 'good governance' rather than 'big government'. The message is that low-cost finance has to be mobilised to allow communities and individuals to build their own homes, and that local authorities must do more to provide or organise decent services. There should not be an automatic assumption that shanty settlements should be cleared. High density is not the same as overcrowding if sanitation, drainage and clean piped water and health and education services are available. Most squatter settlements have densities no higher than expensive city centre blocks of flats in Europe.

Adapted from the Observer, 4th May 1996

▲ **Figure 3.61 India**

Varanasi on the River Ganges is typical of many Third World cities. It is overcrowded and does not have sufficient clean drinking water.

Questions

1 Outline the main urban problems faced by Third World countries. How do these problems differ from those in British cities?

2 With reference to examples, suggest ways in which the urban problems in Third World cities might be overcome.

3. What causes traffic congestion and how can it be resolved?

The issue of traffic circulation - ie, the daily movement of commuters - creates serious problems for most cities in the world. Traffic congestion causes not only wasted time for commuters and delays in freight transport, but also a worsening of air quality from vehicle exhaust fumes. In Third World cities such as Jakarta and Bangkok, rising car ownership and inadequate road systems cause daily traffic jams that can last for hours. But the experience of First World cities shows that building more roads does not solve the problem.

A city such as Los Angeles with its network of urban motorways suffers frequent traffic jams as commuters travel to and from work. The pollution from car exhausts causes smog, not only in Los Angeles, but in most major cities, from London to Tokyo. Nitrogen oxides and hydrocarbon vapours from exhausts combine with sunlight to create ozone and petrochemical smog. With increasing frequency, cities around the world are having to issue public health alerts - warning people that the air quality is so poor that they should stay indoors. High risk groups such as young children and asthmatics are particularly vulnerable.

Traffic congestion has increased as rising incomes have led to higher car ownership. Combined with improved road networks for commuters, this has allowed more and more people to move out of First World cities and travel into work by car. Living in the suburbs or in dormitory villages is what many people prefer. Where possible they also wish to travel by car, from door to door in climate controlled transport. The result, shown in figure 3.62, is that average commuting distances have increased and, at the same time, average journey times have also risen. Studies show that, for instance, in London the average speed of traffic is no higher now than it was one hundred years ago. During the morning peak rush hour, speeds have actually fallen, from an average 18.1 mph in 1968 to 15.8 mph in 1994.

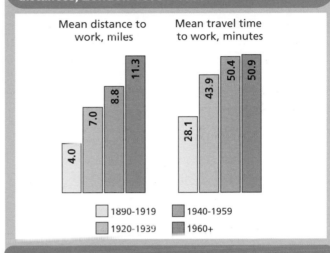

Figure 3.62 Average travel times and journey distances, London 1895 - 1995

In London, the proportion of commuters travelling by different modes has been remarkably stable over the past 30 years (see figure 3.63). It might have been expected that more people would switch to public transport instead of suffering long and frustrating drives to work. However, the privatisation of public transport, combined with government tax policies meant that the cost of rail travel rose in real terms by 70 percent since 1972, and bus travel by 58 percent, yet the price of petrol fell by nearly 10 percent.

Figure 3.64 The proportion of London commuters by mode of transport

Mode of commuter traffic (%)		
	1972	*1996*
Surface rail	38	39
Underground	33	35
Car	15	15
Bus	12	7
Coach	1	2
Bicycle / motorbike	1	2
	100	100

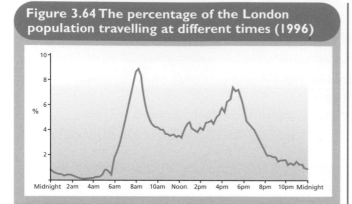

Figure 3.64 The percentage of the London population travelling at different times (1996)

In Britain as a whole, over the whole of the twentieth century, the pattern of commuting has changed markedly. One hundred years ago, more than 50 percent of commuters walked to work. By 1950 this had fallen to 20 percent, with approximately the same proportion cycling and almost as many travelling by train, bus or tram. But, by the 1990s, cars were used for over 70 percent of all commuter journeys, with walking and cycling together only making up 7 percent of journeys to work. In all British towns and cities except London, car travel is overwhelmingly the main form of commuter transport.

Solutions to traffic congestion

It is widely recognised that building more roads is not a viable means of solving traffic jams. New roads simply persuade ever more people to use cars - and cause worse air pollution. Solutions to the problem are relatively straightforward. More people have to use public transport, or cycle or walk. Urban areas, including new shopping centres and business parks must be planned in such a way that private car transport is not essential. However, stating the solutions is far easier than achieving them. Using the price mechanism to discourage driving, ie by making car usage more expensive, is unpopular and unfair to lower income groups. Politicians are therefore often reluctant to press for such measures.

Nevertheless, 'road pricing' solutions are being used in Singapore and are under study in many other cities including Edinburgh and Oslo. The problem in Singapore is particularly severe because it is a very densely populated island with little room for new roads. The government of Singapore has placed taxes on new cars that make them three times more expensive than in Europe. Before a new car is bought a 'certificate of entitlement' costing £30,000 must also be purchased.

An electronic toll system is used to charge for road usage. As a car passes under an overhead gantry, the toll is electronically transferred from a plastic card in the car windscreen. If the card does not have sufficient funds in credit, a photo is taken of the car and the driver is fined.

Less draconian schemes are being used elsewhere. In Los Angeles, for example, the city government uses the local tax system to encourage companies to set up car sharing schemes for employees. In the same city, the authorities have set aside motorway lanes for use by cars which are carrying passengers, and have set targets for the increased use of electric cars to reduce emissions.

In Canterbury, Kent, the council has set up park and ride schemes, cutting road traffic by 10 percent. A similar scheme in York has cut road traffic by 16 percent. Other measures adopted in York include pedestrianising over 30 city centre streets, doubling the charges for long stay car parks in the centre, and building a network of cycle ways. In 1998, over 20 percent of local commuters travelled by bicycle compared with the national average of just 1 percent. The scheme has not only cut road traffic and pollution from vehicle emissions, it has cut road casualties and has increased the number of passers by on the shopping streets that are now closed to traffic. However, critics of park and ride schemes complain that the edge-of-city car parks are ugly and intrusive, and that they encourage urban sprawl. The Council for the Protection of Rural England (CPRE) has suggested that the schemes might actually encourage fewer people to use public transport. This is because some people will choose to park and ride rather than use a bus or train for the whole journey. They predict that, if such schemes become widespread, the result will be a 'sea of car parks' around towns and cities.

In cities such as Manchester and Sheffield, new tram systems have been built to provide frequent and reliable commuter services. However, progress in developing the networks has been slow. They are expensive to build and rely on taxpayers' money for funding. Politicians are always very wary of raising taxes for such schemes.

For Third World cities, the issues of traffic congestion are the same as in UK cities. Rising prosperity has enabled an increasing number of people to achieve Western standards of living. For governments to tell these people that they cannot use their new cars for commuting is politically unpopular. It remains to be seen how many governments will follow Singapore's example in restricting car use and how many allow their urban traffic to grind to a halt before action is taken.

Activity — Traffic congestion

Questions

1 Outline the reasons why traffic congestion is a problem in cities.
2 Discuss the policies that could be adopted to relieve urban traffic congestion.

unit summary

1 Cities across the world often share similar features - such as new high rise buildings in their centre; but many of the processes at work in the Third World are different from those in First World cities.
2 Shanty towns and the informal sector are key elements of Third World cities. They provide homes and jobs for many people. Housing, employment and public health care (ie, drinking water and sewage provision) are important issues facing most Third World cities. In the First World, the main issues are a loss of manufacturing employment and, in some cases, a loss of population.
3 Solutions to urban problems include redevelopment via prestige events like the Olympics, concepts such as the '24 hour city', place marketing to promote cities at the global level, and cultural activities.
4 In the Third World, the urban problems require low-cost provision of basic services such as clean water and housing.
5 Traffic congestion is a severe problem in most major cities. New road building is not a viable long-term solution. Remedies include reducing the number of cars on roads, by road pricing and other means. Better public transport is also required.

key terms

Brown agenda - a focus on the environmental and health hazards of Third World cities.
Informal sector - where a large proportion of people in Third World cities earn a living, in an unregulated, cash economy based on labour-intensive and small-scale activities.
Place marketing - where cities try to market themselves by means of slogans and other publicity to attract outside investment and tourists.
Shanty town - an area, usually in a Third World city, taken over by people to build their own homes. It is now recognised that it might be better to encourage the shanty town dwellers to improve the area rather than to demolish it.

CHAPTER Primary Production

Introduction

Economic activity can be classified into primary, secondary and tertiary sectors. The primary sector is concerned with the exploitation of natural resources. It includes activities such as farming, fishing, forestry and mining. The raw materials produced by the primary sector are processed or manufactured in the secondary sector. For example, iron ore is turned into steel, crude oil is refined into petrol and wheat is milled into flour. The tertiary sector provides services, for example banking, transport and retailing.

This chapter describes the primary sector, chapter 5 looks at the secondary sector and chapter 6 examines the tertiary sector.

In the UK, the primary sector has declined in relative importance as, first, the secondary and, later, the tertiary sectors have grown. Today, the share of UK GDP (ie, national output) produced by the primary sector is approximately 4 percent, compared with manufacturing's share of 20 percent and the tertiary sector's share of 76 percent. A similar pattern has occurred in most high income countries.

Countries with the lowest per capita GDPs generally have the biggest primary sectors. So, for example, in the mid-1990s, the agricultural sector's output in one of the poorest countries in the world, Tanzania, was approximately 55 percent of GDP. Middle income countries, for example the Newly Industrialising Countries of south and east Asia, have experienced a relative decline in their primary sectors and growth in their secondary sectors. In Malaysia, for instance, between 1980 and 1995, the share of GDP contributed by agriculture fell from 22 to 14 percent and the share contributed by manufacturing rose from 21 to 32 percent.

Chapter summary

Unit 4.1 examines agriculture and food production.
Unit 4.2 considers energy resources, including renewable sources.
Unit 4.3 looks at non-energy resources, including minerals, forests and marine resources.

Unit 4.1 Agriculture and food production

key questions

1 How can agricultural systems be classified?
2 What factors influence agricultural land use?
3 What trends are occurring in food production?
4 How do conflicts arise in rural land use?

1. How can agricultural systems be classified?

Agricultural systems can be classified into broad categories. These categories often overlap and are sometimes inconsistent, but they make it easier to understand what farmers do and how land is used.

Commercial / subsistence agriculture

Commercial farmers produce crops and livestock for sale. The system is sometimes called 'cash cropping'. Those farm products that are sold on international markets are called **commodities**. Examples include wheat, soya beans, tea, coffee, sugar, cotton and orange juice.

In subsistence agriculture, farmers produce food purely for their own family's consumption. It is a system more common in the Third World than in First World countries. This is because, as economies develop and become more urban, a market for food develops. In a low income country such as Kenya, where 70 percent of the labour force work on the land, most farmers produce a mix of subsistence and commercial produce. For instance, they might grow maize and beans to eat themselves and cotton, tea or bananas to sell.

Figure 4.1 Papaya plantation in Honduras

Plantation agriculture is an example of commercial farming in which a 'commodity' is produced.

Intensive / extensive agriculture

The intensity of an agricultural system is related to the quantity of labour or capital that is used per hectare of land. Where there are high inputs of labour and capital, the agriculture is said to be intensive and where inputs are low per hectare the agriculture is extensive.

Capital refers to the amount of money spent on items such as machinery, buildings (eg, greenhouses) and fertiliser. An example of capital intensive agriculture is horticulture in the Netherlands where fruit, vegetables and flowers are grown in heated greenhouses. An example of labour intensive agriculture is rice growing in the Ganges Delta where most of the field preparation, planting and harvesting is done by hand.

Note that intensity relates to the ratio of capital and labour inputs to an area of land. So, for instance, in the American Midwest, very expensive tractors and combine harvesters are used to produce wheat and maize, but the area of land is so large per unit of capital that the farming is described as extensive.

Arable / pastoral / mixed agriculture

Arable agriculture is the growing of crops such as cereals. It also includes plantations, which produce crops such as coffee and rubber, orchards which produce fruit, and horticulture. When a single crop is grown over many years, as is typical in plantations, the system is known as 'monoculture'.

Pastoral agriculture is livestock farming. It includes milk and beef production together with pig, sheep, goat and poultry farming. When both arable crops are grown and animals are reared, the agriculture is said to be mixed.

The classification of agriculture into arable, pastoral or mixed is not straightforward. One source of confusion arises because arable land, in official UK statistics, includes land that has been ploughed, and sown with grass. It is not permanent grassland but it is used for pasture or silage. (Silage is cut grass that is fed to animals.) Another difficulty occurs because it is not always clear whether the terms arable and pastoral refer to land use or farm output. For example, an increasing number of dairy farmers in the UK use a technique known as **zero grazing**. Cattle are kept indoors all year round and are fed on fodder, such as grass silage and maize that is grown on the farm. The land use is clearly arable yet the farm's output, milk, is clearly pastoral. To avoid this problem, the terms 'crop production' and 'livestock production' are often used rather than arable and pastoral. They refer to farm output rather than land use.

'Nomadic pastoralism' is a form of pastoralism that is distinct from other types. It involves the herding of cattle, sheep or goats over wide areas, generally in a seasonal pattern. Examples are found in East Africa where Masai herders move their cattle from pasture to pasture, and in Central Asia where sheep and goats are moved from summer to winter grazing. Typically this is a subsistence system of agriculture and, although wide areas of land are used, only relatively small numbers of people are involved. In most areas, nomadic pastoralism is dying out as a way of life because population pressures are causing more 'sedentary' farming systems to develop. These permanent farms eventually make it impossible to wander freely across the once open ranges.

Figure 4.2 Modern livestock farming

When animals are kept indoors, as in this intensive pig unit, it is not easy to classify the farming in terms of arable or pastoral. Much of this farmer's land is used to grow crops which are fed to the pigs. Although the land use is arable, the main source of farm income is from livestock.

'Shifting agriculture' is a type of arable farming that, like nomadic pastoralism, does not involve permanent land use. The main areas where it is found are in the rain forests of Amazonia, central Africa and South East Asia. Plots of land are cleared and burnt, then planted with seeds. (The system is also known as 'slash and burn'.) At first the ground is made more fertile with the ash from burning but, after a few years, the land is abandoned and allowed to lie fallow and recover fertility. Shifting agriculture is a system that works well when relatively low numbers of people use large areas of land. The seeds are planted with 'digging sticks', rather than ploughs, and natural vegetation is allowed to grow between the crops. In this way, the ground is protected from soil erosion. Pressure from new settlers, logging companies and plantation owners means that this type of agriculture is in decline.

Both nomadic pastoralism and shifting agriculture are 'low-input, low-output' systems of farming. This means that inputs of labour and capital are low and that yields, per hectare of land, are also low. The systems tend to be ecologically friendly in that their impact on the environment is short lived and causes no permanent degradation. However, if population rises, environmental damage can occur when the same systems are used more intensively. Leaving the land fallow for shorter and shorter periods, or overstocking with grazing animals, may not allow vegetation long enough time to regenerate. This can cause the soil to lose fertility and become exposed to wind and water erosion.

Tropical / temperate agriculture

Different crops require different climatic conditions in which to thrive. For example, bananas grow best in tropical conditions, and apples grow best in temperate conditions. In some cases it is not the amount of precipitation or average temperature that is critical, rather it is the vulnerability of crops to particular pests or diseases that is crucial in determining suitability to a particular climatic zone. For instance, wheat is rarely grown in humid tropical areas beacause it is not resistant to the fungal diseases that flourish in the hot, wet conditions.

When considering the UK's self sufficiency in food production, the distinction is sometimes made between those crops that are grown in temperate latitudes and those crops, such as tea, rice or pineapples that are grown in the tropics. So, although the UK only produces 50 percent of its agricultural needs, this figure rises to 70 percent when temperate produce alone is considered.

Although classification by climate can be useful, it is important to note that there is not a rigid divide between temperate and tropical crops. Greenhouse production and, increasingly, genetically modified crops mean that it is possible to grow most crops anywhere. It is usually a matter of cost that determines whether, for example, strawberries are grown in heated greenhouses in Britain during winter, or are air freighted from Kenya after being grown outdoors. In such circumstances the distinction between tropical and temperate becomes blurred.

Agroecosystems

Sometimes agricultural systems are classified in terms of efficiency based on inputs and outputs. This ecosystem approach considers the food chain as an energy flow. The inputs include solar energy, human labour, artificial fertiliser and fuel for farm machinery. The key output is food production.

Plant biomass can be consumed directly by humans or indirectly through livestock. Figure 4.3 shows that cereal production for direct human consumption is eight times more efficient than feeding the cereals to beef cattle for meat. This issue is, of course, extremely important when considering population growth and world food supply. There is less likely to be a food shortage if more efficient, ie mainly vegetarian, systems of food production are promoted. The problem is that, as people aspire to First World standards of living, meat eating becomes the norm.

Figure 4.3 Pounds of grain that are needed to produce one pound of bread or one pound of live weight gain in each animal.

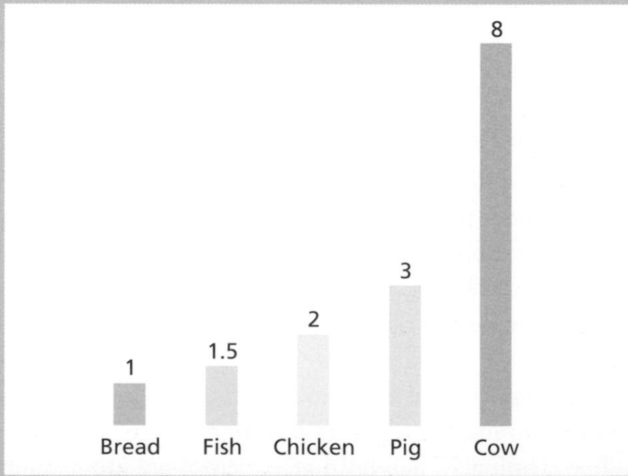

In the world as a whole, livestock are fed 40 percent of all grain that is harvested.

2. What factors influence agricultural land use?

The factors that influence agricultural land use can be divided into environmental and human. The environmental factors are the physical conditions, such as climate and soil type, that influence farmers' decisions. Human factors include the social, political and economic forces that affect what is produced.

At one time, agricultural geography was heavily influenced by 'environmental determinism'. This approach explained land use purely in terms of the physical environment. For example, it might have been stated that 'rice is grown in the Ganges Delta because there is a plentiful supply of water and there are at least three months per year with average temperature above 20°C'. This type of explanation was criticised, particularly in the 1960s and 1970s, because it did not take human factors sufficiently into account. So, the emphasis changed from environmental explanations to economic models of land use. These were widely used in explaining both land use and intensity of production.

In the 1990s, most agricultural geographers continued to regard farming as primarily an economic activity, with land use being heavily influenced by political decision makers. At the same time there has been an increased awareness of the industrialisation of agriculture and the influence of 'agribusinesses'. These are food producing and food processing companies that are, in some cases, developing global markets for their products.

Environmental factors

Environmental factors that influence agricultural land use include not only physical factors, such as climate, soil type and altitude, but also biological factors such as pests and diseases. Although these factors are not generally regarded as being the most important in determining land use, it is still recognised that they do have an influence.

Climate Although it is possible to create artificial climatic conditions in greenhouses, the cost is high. Therefore, under most circumstances, it is the natural climatic conditions that determine what can be grown. Precipitation and temperature are the key factors although the number of sunshine hours, the number of frost free days and, in some places, wind strength are also important.

Precipitation is a significant factor not only in terms of the annual total but also in terms of seasonal distribution,

reliability and duration. Clearly, heavy rain in summer thunderstorms has a very different effect from, for example, the same amount of precipitation falling as light steady rain. In the former case, fields might be flooded or crops flattened. In the latter case crops might thrive, but fail to ripen if the rain is continuous.

In Britain prolonged droughts are rare and even during the exceptionally dry period of 1996 and 1997 most crop yields were not significantly reduced. However, rainfall in the Sahel region of Africa, for instance, is much more variable than in Britain and many people there rely on subsistence farming. Droughts in the region during the 1980s had a severe effect as crops failed and animals starved.

Temperature affects crop growth in several ways. There is a minimum temperature below which crops will not grow. For example, grass requires a minimum temperature of 6°C. The length of the growing season is also critical because, for instance, wheat requires approximately three months to grow and ripen. The number of frost free days is also sometimes important. Some fruit, such as limes, cannot tolerate frost at all whereas other crops, such as apples, cherries and pears, are only vulnerable to frosts at blossom time.

Temperature has an effect on evaporation and therefore the moisture available to plants. To provide a given amount of moisture, regions with high average temperatures require a higher rainfall than cooler regions.

Relief This refers to the physical landscape of an area and includes altitude, aspect and angle of slope. Altitude mainly affects agriculture indirectly through its effect on temperature. On average, temperature falls by 0.6°C per 100 metres. This is the reason why, for instance, cereals cannot be grown in upland areas of Britain despite being grown over large areas of the south and east. The higher altitude lowers temperatures and makes the growing season too short.

In tropical regions, the effect of altitude is to moderate the very high temperatures that would otherwise occur. For example, in Kenya the highlands are a prosperous agricultural region with an altitude that averages 1,500 metres above sea level. Although the area is close to the equator, temperate crops such as maize and tobacco are grown.

Altitude also affects land use because of the way that cold air sinks into hollows. Such frost pockets are the reason why fruit trees and vines are grown on the slopes rather than the valley bottoms in places such as the Rhone Valley in Switzerland.

The angle or gradient of a slope is an influence on agriculture for two main reasons. Firstly, machinery such as tractors cannot be safely driven on slopes above approximately 10 degrees. Such slopes are therefore difficult to plough. Secondly, steep, bare slopes are vulnerable to soil erosion from running water. In some parts of the world, such as south and east Asia, steep slopes have been terraced to protect them from erosion and they can then be used to grow crops.

The aspect of a slope is the direction it faces. In the northern hemisphere, south facing slopes are warmer and sunnier than north facing slopes. The name given to the south facing valley side in the French speaking part of the Alps is 'adret' and the north facing slope is the 'ubac'. The adret is generally the valley side where there are settlements and hay meadows. The ubac is more likely to be uncultivated and tree covered.

Soil Soil type can influence agricultural land use but is not normally a crucial factor. This is because most soils can be improved or modified by draining, liming, fertilising or deep ploughing. However, because it is expensive to completely alter the character of a soil in a given area, soil characteristics do sometimes play a part in affecting land use. For example, in West Lancashire, there is a mixture of peat soils, formed from drained mosses, and clay soils formed from glacial deposits. The peat soils are relatively fertile, quick to warm in spring and well drained. The clay soils tend to be heavy in texture, poorly drained and slow to warm. Most of the peat areas are used to grow cereals and horticultural produce whereas the clay soils are mainly kept as pasture for dairy cattle. However, this pattern was not always the case. Before the mosses were drained, many of the clay soils were used for arable farming and today, due to changes within the dairy industry, an

Activity Arable land and permanent grass in the UK

The map shows the proportion of arable land and permanent grassland on farms in different parts of the UK in the mid-1990s. The definition of arable used here is based on land use rather than farm output. It includes land that has been under grass for less than five years and is part of a rotation (ie, it will be ploughed and used for a different crop in the future.). Some of the farms, therefore, are specialising in livestock production even though their land is classed as arable. The permanent grassland includes rough grazing, ie upland areas that are used for pasture. The figures exclude woodland and land that is 'set-aside' (ie, not presently used for crops).

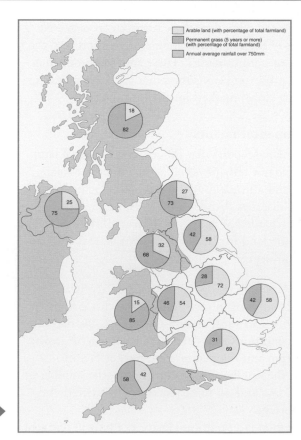

Figure 4.4 Arable land and permanent grassland in the UK ▶

Questions

1 To what extent do the proportions of arable land and permanent pasture reflect the rainfall pattern within the UK?
2 What physical factors, other than rainfall total, might affect the proportion of farmland that is arable or permanent pasture?

increasing area of clay is again being ploughed for crops such as oilseed rape and maize.

Pests and diseases Diseases such as phylloxera which killed large areas of vines in southern Europe during the late nineteenth century, or pests such as the Mediterranean fruit fly, are major influences on land use in certain areas. In some cases, resistant varieties of crops have been introduced and the farming system has continued but, in other areas, production has ceased completely.

The impact of pests and diseases is greatest where monoculture is practised or where significant numbers of people rely on just one crop. One of the most notable instances occurred during the 1840s in Ireland when potato blight, a fungal disease, caused successive crops to fail. This resulted in starvation and emigration for the poorest section of the population who relied on potatoes for their staple diet.

A modern example of how agriculture is affected by pests and diseases comes from sub-Sahara Africa. The tsetse fly carries parasites called trypanosomes which it transfers to humans and animals when it bites. This causes sleeping sickness in people, and a disease called nagana in animals. In both cases, these diseases can be fatal. This is one reason why cattle and other farm livestock are rarely kept in the low lying tropical regions where tsetse fly are most common.

Human factors

Human factors that affect agricultural land use include economic, social and political influences. It is important to note that these influences, together with environmental factors, are 'filtered' through a decision making process. In other words it is the way that the various influences are perceived by farmers that is critical in determining land use.

This behavioural aspect of agricultural geography has been recognised as playing a key part in explaining what farmers do. An example comes from agriculture in the Third World. The Food and Agriculture Organisation (FAO) of the United Nations estimates that it is women farmers in sub-Sahara Africa who produce most of the food in that region. Despite this, most farm assistance programmes are traditionally organised by men, for men. A World Bank study in the mid-1990s showed that investing in primary education for girls produced a 24 percent rise in food output. This was because the increased literacy and awareness brought about by schooling made the women farmers much more likely to adopt new seed and crop varieties, and to use more efficient farming methods. This illustrates the point that the way farmers learn, understand and process information can be just as important as the external factors that traditionally explain land use.

Fig 4.6 African woman farmers in Zimbabwe

Throughout sub-Sahara Africa it is women who carry out most of the food production. Land use is therefore heavily influenced by the decisions that these women make.

Economic factors These relate to the costs of farm production and the revenue earned by selling produce. If the cost of producing crops or livestock is greater than the price at which they can be sold, the farmer makes a loss and eventually switches production or stops farming completely. An important exception to this occurs when governments intervene and subsidise farmers. So, for example, within the European Union, most hill farmers would go out of business without the financial support provided by the Common Agricultural Policy. This political influence on agriculture is covered later in the unit.

In many cases, the cost of transport of produce to market is an important consideration when transporting perishable items such as soft fruit and vegetables. For instance, the production of horticultural produce in southern Spain for the northern European market only became worthwhile when fast container road transport was developed. Similarly, fruit, flower and vegetable production in East Africa for European consumers only became viable when relatively low cost air freight systems were introduced.

In general, the cost of farm inputs such as labour, land, machinery, fertiliser or seed are relatively stable. The costs change over time but they are not so volatile as the revenue earned from selling produce.

This revenue varies for two main reasons. Firstly, farm output can be affected by drought, floods, frosts, pests or diseases. Whole crops might be ruined by, for instance, a late frost. Whole herds might have to be slaughtered if there is an outbreak of foot and mouth disease or swine fever. Secondly, farm incomes are affected by fluctuating market prices. As with other commodities, farm prices tend to rise and fall cyclically. This is often because of the fluctuations in supply and the time lag involved in producing new output. For example, if a potato crop fails, the price will rise as merchants bid against each other for available supplies (see figure 4.7). Then, the following year, some farmers might be attracted by the higher price and plant more potatoes - so raising supply. This will tend to cause lower market prices and may persuade farmers to plant fewer potatoes the next year. Similar cycles occur for very many food commodities although, in some cases the length of the cycle is longer than a year because output cannot be so quickly adjusted. This is the case for livestock, such as pigs, and for plantation crops such as coffee.

Food prices also fluctuate because of short term changes in demand. These are often caused by health scares in which the public becomes alarmed by the risks associated with certain foods. Two examples from the UK are the salmonella scare of the 1980s when sales of chickens and eggs suddenly fell, and the BSE scare of the 1990s when the sale of beef fell by more than a third.

One other economic factor that has an important influence on land use is the availability of capital. This is money that is used to pay for items such as machinery, buildings, drainage, irrigation, fertiliser and seeds. In general it is in the high income, First World countries that there are financial and banking systems which can supply finance to farmers. It is in the same countries that the financial returns to farmers are high enough, at least most of the time, to enable them to pay interest on the capital loans.

One means by which some Third World countries raise capital is by allowing transnational companies to

Figure 4.7 Fluctuating farm prices for potatoes

Year One	Year Two	Year Three
Dry weather causes a fall in potato yields	Farmers plant more potatoes because of the higher price	Farmers plant fewer potatoes because of the lower price
Potato output falls - prices rise	Potato output rises - prices fall	Potato output falls - prices rise

Figure 4.8 Farm capital

The availability of capital to build glasshouses or buy machinery is an important influence on land use.

set up and organise agricultural production. Often this is in a plantation system. Examples include Brooke Bond tea in Uganda, Firestone rubber in Liberia and United Fruits in Costa Rica. Although these companies provide capital, employment and export earnings, they are sometimes criticised for using land in a monoculture system. The local population's ability to grow its own food is also diminished if the best land is used by the transnational corporations.

Capital is required to develop and finance technology in farming. For example, corporations such as Monsanto invest many millions of dollars in developing fertilisers, pesticides and genetically modified strains. Farmers have to pay large sums to buy the new seeds and therefore their use is to some extent dependent on the availability of capital. (The issue of genetically modified crops is covered later in this unit.)

Von Thunen An economic model that has been used to explain and predict land use was developed by Von Thunen in the 1820s. He was a landowner in Prussia. His model became influential in the 1960s and 1970s when an English translation was written. The ideas appealed to geographers who were interested in models against which actual patterns could be tested.

The basis of the model is that, given a set of simplifying assumptions, land use is determined by distance from the market and the profit (ie, revenue less costs) derived from any particular produce. So, for example, near the market, horticultural products might be grown if they earn the highest profit. Further away from the market, the cost of transporting the produce causes profit to fall and something else, for example milk, might become more

profitable. The pattern repeats itself resulting in a series of concentric land use rings around a market.

As with other land use models, Von Thunen's ideas have lost favour. The assumptions of a uniform physical landscape (ie, soils, climate and relief), together with the idea of a single, central market are considered over-simplifications. Changes in food processing, such as fast freezing, together with developments in transport also make it less likely that the pattern will be replicated. Another criticism is that the model ignores the wider social and political influences that affect the decisions of farmers.

However, although concentric circles of land use are rarely found around urban centres, the basis of the Von Thunen model still has some validity. In particular, its emphasis on financial returns and profitability for farmers does provide a better explanation of land use than purely environmental factors.

Social factors These influences on land use include land tenure and farm size. Cultural influences such as religion are sometimes also important.

Land tenure is how the land is owned. In Britain, most farm land is either owned directly by farmers or is rented by tenant farmers from landowners. The tenant farmers are legally protected from eviction - as long as they act reasonably - and they can pass their farms on to their children. This security of tenure is important because it gives farmers an incentive to improve their land and conserve its fertility. In countries where tenants have no security, or where farms are organised into large estates, there is less incentive for individuals to improve the long term productivity of the land. For this reason, land reform (ie, the breaking up of large estates into smaller farm units) has been promoted in many parts of the world where 'latifundia' or 'hacienda' estates exist. This has been the case in southern Europe, for example in Italy and Spain, and in parts of South America. The process is rarely easy or straightforward because the estate owners are generally rich and powerful and they resist the change.

Since the collapse of communism in the former Soviet Union, and the introduction of market economics in China, many of the large scale collective farms of these two countries have been privatised and broken up. In both countries, the peasants had resisted the earlier forced 'collectivisation' of land and had resented the virtually forced labour they had to perform. Central organisation of farming and bureaucratic control had greatly added to the inefficiencies of the system.

Activity Land reform

Zimbabwe, in southern Africa, has a population of 11.3 million. This is growing at a rate of 2.4 percent per year. Most of the population are black although there is a white minority that numbers approximately 80,000. Before independence, in 1980, the country (then called Rhodesia) was ruled largely for the benefit of the white colonialists. They had acquired the productive farmland, ie the most fertile and the best watered, for themselves. The white farmers owned over 50 percent of all farmland, produced 90 percent of all marketed farm output and contributed 40 percent of all exports by value.

Since independence, political and social pressure from landless black people has grown. In some cases squatters have simply occupied land and started farming. As a means of avoiding further social discontent the Zimbabwe government under President Mugabe announced in 1996 that it would start a programme of land reform. A list of 1,500 white owned farms was drawn up with the intention of confiscating them and resettling 150,000 black families. However, Zimbabwe owes a very large debt to global financial institutions and is therefore vulnerable to foreign pressure. Britain and other Western governments objected the scheme. So, in 1998, instead of confiscating the land, the first white owned farm was bought by the government and then given to 40 landless families.

To an extent, Zimbabwe relies upon the output of the white farmers for its export earnings. Large amounts of capital have been spent on the farms. Because most are so big, they generate sufficient wealth either to invest directly or to use as security for loans from banks. Mechanisation and irrigation systems have made the farms efficient and the exports of tobacco and cotton provide much needed foreign revenue.

Difficulties with land reform in Zimbabwe have not been helped by other policy initiatives. Government programmes to help the urban poor, particularly in setting controls over the price of maize, have backfired. The low prices have been a disincentive to farmers and, when prices have been raised, food riots have followed.

In the future, any large scale attempts to bring about land reform might have the effect of reducing farm output. Subdividing the white owned farms into family sized plots will lower food supply if the farmers only produce enough for themselves. Without finance to invest in fertiliser, irrigation and new seed varieties, and without the large farm sizes to gain economies of scale, the land reform programme will fail. Social and political justice might be achieved - but at the cost of slower economic development.

Questions

1 Describe the problems that Zimbabwe faces in its programme of land reform.
2 Suggest how farming might change if white owned farms are split into small family owned plots.

Farm size is a factor that affects how well land is used. Because owner occupation or secured tenancies of farms are generally regarded as the most productive system of land tenure, there is an 'optimum' size for most farms. If the farm is too big, it is unmanageable by one farmer - so becomes less efficient. If it is too small, it is uneconomic because economies of scale cannot be gained. These are the savings that come from increased size - such as buying seeds or fertiliser in bulk, or in negotiating bank loans at favourable rates of interest.

Inheritance laws are an important influence on farm size in different countries. The tradition in France, for example, has been for farms to be split between a farmer's sons, whereas in Britain the tradition is to hand the farm on to the eldest son. In one case, farm sizes fall over time while in the other the farm sizes do not fall. A related issue is one of 'fragmentation' where land holdings are scattered. This makes for inefficient farming because farmers have to spend time travelling between their plots and it might not be worthwhile to invest in machinery under such circumstances. The consolidation of such plots (the process is called 'remembrement' in France) is often promoted by governments as a means of increasing productivity.

Activity The Green Revolution in India

During the 1960s, developments in plant breeding led to the introduction of new high yield varieties (HYV) of wheat and rice. The wheat was first developed in Mexico, and the rice was developed in the Philippines, but both spread quickly to other countries. The impact was rapid. In Punjab, in north west India, wheat yields rose from 1.5 tonnes to 4 tonnes per hectare. On the Ganges flood plain, rice yields rose from an average of 1.2 tonnes to almost 4 tonnes per hectare.

The resulting surge in food output in India and in other Third World countries was called the Green Revolution. One consequence of the change was the need to use inorganic (ie, artificial) fertilisers, pesticides and irrigation to sustain the high yields. This has had a negative impact on some regions. For example, in parts of the western Punjab, the fertiliser and pesticides have polluted waterways and drinking water, and poorly managed irrigation has caused waterlogging and salinisation of the soil. This is a build up of salt on the ground after water evaporates.

The most dramatic effects of the Green Revolution in India have been restricted to two states, Punjab and neighbouring Haryana. The reasons for this are social and economic. It has become clear that the rise in yields was the result of more than simply a 'miracle of science'. According to an Indian government agricultural expert, 'the Punjab revolution was a revolution of inputs. The farmers needed more fertiliser, and they needed more water, and for both they needed more credit (ie, borrowed money)'. This was easier to obtain in Punjab and Haryana than other states because the state governments had pushed through a programme of land consolidation. The large number of farm small-holdings had been concentrated into 5 hectare plots. This contrasts with the rest of India where 60 percent of farmers still have plots smaller than 1 hectare. Many states even have laws which limit the size of farm holdings as a means of redistributing land to poorer people. The farms are too small to provide the income and security necessary to borrow money. Without credit, the farmers cannot afford to buy fertiliser or seeds. The fragmented holdings also make it difficult to organise efficient irrigation schemes. So, for instance, in states such as Bihar and West Bengal in the Ganges Valley, many rice farmers subsist on small plots that are barely sufficient to support a family let alone create a surplus to invest in more efficient farming systems. The plots are too small to gain the economies of scale that could be obtained by, for instance, investing in farm machinery.

Nevertheless, despite such difficulties, by the late 1970s India no longer relied on regular food imports. Even though the population has risen in thirty years by more than 300 million, to a figure that has now reached one billion, the country has not faced mass starvation. This is not to say that there are no food shortages - almost a third of the population does not get enough calories per day for an adequate diet. The problem, however, is not so much that the food is not available, as that the people do not have the money to buy it. The government has the dilemma of whether to keep food prices low, so that poor people can afford it, or to allow prices to rise and give farmers the incentive to grow more. What is clear is that something needs to be done. The effect of the Green Revolution is wearing off and food output in the 1990s only rose by one percent per year. With the population growing at over 2 percent per year some new breakthrough needs to be made.

▲ **Figure 4.9 Traditional farming in India**

Farm productivity rises when larger plots of land are created. Farmers can then raise loans to buy modern equipment.

Questions

1 Briefly outline what the Green Revolution was and what it achieved.
2 What factors made the Green Revolution more successful in some Indian states than others?
3 Suggest how a Third World government might resolve the dilemma of either controlling prices to enable poor people to afford to buy food, or allowing prices to rise in order to provide incentives for farmers to produce more.

Farming systems can be affected if certain diets are prohibited by religious beliefs. For example, most Muslim and Jewish people do not eat pork and most Hindus do not eat beef. It is therefore unlikely that farmers will produce these foodstuffs in countries where the majority of the population will not buy them.

Cultural attitudes can also affect the demand for various foods. Traditionally, as countries have developed economically, their populations have consumed a larger proportion of animal protein. This pattern has repeated itself in the newly industrialising economies of East Asia. However, a counter trend has developed in some Western countries as vegetarianism has increased. Caused by a combination of moral objection to meat eating and health fears associated with food safety, this trend appears to be causing a long term reduction in the demand for meat products.

A related trend, also mainly associated with high income countries, is caused by the rising demand for organic produce. This is food produced without using artificial fertilisers or pesticides on crops, and without using hormone growth promoters on livestock, or feeds that are not organically produced. People who buy organic food desire a healthier diet and may also wish to promote more environmentally friendly farming methods. Because organic yields tend to be lower than conventional farm yields, the selling price is higher.

If sufficient numbers of people signal their demand by buying organic foods it might reinforce the trend in UK farming away from a concentration on quantity to a greater emphasis on quality. Concern over animal welfare is also having an effect on how farmers operate. Battery production of eggs, chickens and pigs is seen by many as being cruel. A market for 'free range' produce has grown and legislation is forcing farmers to make stall and cage sizes bigger and, in some cases, to phase out battery farming altogether.

Common Agricultural Policy (CAP)

The CAP is a major political influence on UK and European Union agriculture. It was developed in the 1960s by the six original members of the Common Market (now the European Union). The policy had five main aims:
- to increase farm productivity
- to ensure a fair standard of living for farmers
- to stabilise markets
- to assure food supplies
- to provide consumers with food at reasonable prices.

It is clear from these aims that the policy was far wider than simply one of ensuring food supplies. The issues of farm incomes and rural standards of living were central to the policy. When the UK joined the Common Market in 1973, the policy was already fixed and UK farming had to adapt to the new regime.

The CAP operates by setting guaranteed minimum prices for most farm products. If the market price falls below this level, the surplus is bought and put into storage. To prevent foreign produce from undercutting CAP prices, import tariffs are placed on imported foodstuffs.

This 'dear food policy' has been, in many ways, too successful. The incentive of guaranteed high prices has caused food production to increase massively. Even the UK, traditionally a food importer, has become virtually self sufficient in many sectors such as cereals and dairy produce. The overall result has been a build up of surpluses and the creation of food 'mountains' and wine and milk 'lakes'. Storing these surpluses, together with the price support for farmers has created a huge financial burden. In the mid-1990s it was estimated that the CAP was costing the average British family £20 per week.

Environmental impact The EU incentives to increase farm production have had an adverse effect on the UK environment. By digging up hedgerows to create ever bigger fields for cereal production, natural habitats have been lost. Between 1980 and 1995 an estimated 40,000 miles of hedges were removed by farmers - mainly in the south and east of England. Huge areas of East Anglia now resemble North American prairies with a monoculture of cereals year after year.

Increasing amounts of inorganic fertiliser have been used to raise yields but this causes nitrates and phosphorus to leach into streams and ground water. The effect is to promote poisonous algae 'blooms' in waterways and to pollute drinking water.

In upland areas, EU subsidies are given to farmers per head of sheep. This has encouraged overstocking. The resulting overgrazing has killed large areas of heather and, in some places, has caused soil erosion.

The effect of the CAP on dairy farming has been to intensify production. Hay meadows that were once rich in wild flowers have been ploughed and reseeded with more nutritious Italian rye grass. This gives higher milk yields per cow but has the effect of reducing biodiversity. Techniques of zero-grazing have contributed to serious pollution in some water courses

Figure 4.10 Arable farmland from which hedgerows have been removed

In many parts of England, hedgerows have been removed by farmers to make larger fields. This increases efficiency because machinery is easier to use and also the area of land on which crops are grown is extended. However, the bushes and field margins which provided a natural habitat for wildlife are lost.

because of leakage from silage stores and slurry tanks. (Silage is cut grass, compacted in 'clamps' and slurry is liquid animal excrement.)

Fluctuating exchange rates Each year, the level of subsidies and minimum prices for agricultural produce are set by EU farm ministers. These prices are fixed for all member states and are converted into national currencies - using the so called 'Green Pound' in the UK. If exchange rates fluctuate, this causes difficulties. For example, if the pound rises against other currencies, as it did in 1997 and 1998, the effect is to make UK produce dearer (ie, less competitive) and imported goods cheaper. The value of EU subsidies also falls. A mechanism exists to compensate farmers for this fall in income but, as it requires a contribution from UK taxpayers, the government chose not to make these payments.

The result, during 1997 and 1998 was that farm incomes fell steeply. Pig farmers, for example, could not compete with cheaper imports from Denmark, and hill sheep farmers found that the value of their subsidies went down. If the UK joins the Euro (the common EU currency), exchange rates will become fixed and the problem of the fluctuating pound (against other EU currencies) will disappear.

Reforms to the CAP To reduce both the cost and

surplus production, reforms to the CAP began in the late 1980s. The basis of the reforms was that production had to be reduced. Dairy output was cut by introducing 'quotas'. These are maximum production totals that are shared out between the member countries and then allocated to individual farmers. Cereal production was cut by, in effect, paying farmers to produce less. This was achieved by a system of 'set-aside' in which payments are made for land that is taken out of production.

The Farm Diversification Scheme was setup to help farmers maintain their income by branching out into new activities. For instance, grants were made available to convert farm buildings into tourist accommodation.

The CAP reforms were accompanied by a new policy initiative. It was realised that the adverse environmental impact of previous policies could be reversed by setting up new **agri-environment schemes**. These would promote less damaging farming methods and, as a useful side effect, cut production. By the late 1990s several such schemes were operating in the UK:

- Arable Stewardship
- Countryside Access Scheme
- Countryside Stewardship
- Environmentally Sensitive Areas (ESAs)
- Farm Woodland Premium Scheme
- Habitat Scheme
- Moorland Scheme
- Nitrate Sensitive Areas
- Organic Aid Scheme.

Fig 4.11 Oilseed rape

By subsidising non-cereal crops such as oilseed rape, the CAP has influenced how land is used.

Figure 4.12 Environmentally Sensitive Areas (ESAs) in Britain, 1998

The agri-environment schemes vary in detail and scope. The ESA scheme, for example, only operates in designated areas such as the Somerset Levels and the Pennine Dales. There were 38 of these areas in 1998 covering approximately 10 percent of agricultural land in Britain (see figure 4.12). The ESAs are chosen for their special landscape or wildlife value. In Upper Swaledale in Yorkshire, for example, farmers receive payments for delaying hay making until flower seeds have set, and for not using artificial fertiliser. The reason for this is that fertilised grass grows vigorously and 'crowds out' wild flowers.

The Countryside Stewardship scheme operates in non-ESA areas. Farmers can enter a 10 year agreement, for example, to restore hedgerows or leave an uncultivated margin around field boundaries. As with ESAs, additional payments are made for allowing public access.

In 1998 there were 32 Nitrate Sensitive Areas, mainly in the arable farmland areas of eastern England. They were chosen because ground water pollution caused by leaching and runoff from high concentrations of artificial fertilisers had reached potentially dangerous levels. Fears about certain cancers and other medical ailments had prompted the scheme. Paying farmers money to reduce their use of fertilisers was a cheaper option than reducing nitrate levels in water treatment plants.

The agri-environment schemes are designed to encourage environmentally friendly farming. They are voluntary and they offer payments to farmers who agree to manage their land for the benefit of wildlife, the landscape, resource protection or public access. In some cases such as marginal hill farms, they provide farmers with a source of income that keeps their businesses going. Without this money, some farmers would not make a living.

Some payments are based on the agricultural income which farmers lose by participating in the schemes. This has caused criticism and controversy. A well publicised case in the mid-1990s occurred when a farmer on the South Downs ESA ploughed up 100 hectares of land in order to obtain a £590 per hectare CAP subsidy for planting flax. The previous landowner had only recently been paid £125,000 to plant and manage a wildflower meadow on the same land.

Agenda 2000 This is a plan to reform the CAP and was first proposed by the EU Commission in 1997. It was prompted by three main factors. Firstly, the possible enlargement of the EU (see unit 1.6) will make the present CAP too expensive to operate. For example, compared with the present EU in which only 5 percent of the workforce are farmers or farm workers, Poland has approximately 25 percent of its workforce in agriculture. Unless the system is changed, the new members will be entitled to massive farm subsidies.

Secondly, it is widely accepted that too much money goes to farmers in relatively prosperous regions. Money will have to be diverted to 'Structural Funds' which are used to finance regional aid policies - particularly in the new East European member states.

Thirdly, there are increasing objections to EU food import controls. Countries such as the USA, Australia, New Zealand and Argentina are major food exporters. They claim, with some justification, that it is unfair of the EU to restrict imports of food while insisting on free trade in manufactured goods. The World Trade Organisation is likely to condemn the present system of EU tariffs when its next round of negotiations takes place.

Although there is a strong desire to reduce the cost of

the CAP, the EU Commission wishes to protect farm incomes. The Agenda 2000 proposal states that, 'landscapes of scenic beauty and rich in biodiversity have been shaped by agricultural production over centuries. In many places, abandonment of land use would endanger the maintenance of the cultural and environmental inheritance.' In other words the Commission does not wish to see mass bankruptcies of farmers or widespread abandonment of farms and farmland. The use of agri-environmental schemes is proposed as the means by which farmers can be persuaded to maintain the landscape in an environmentally sound condition.

During inter-EU government negotiations in 1999 it was agreed that the guaranteed minimum prices for farm produce would gradually be reduced. By allowing EU prices to fall to world price levels, farmers will be encouraged to increase efficiency. At the same time, there will be less need for import controls because EU prices will become competitive. Market intervention, ie the purchase of surplus farm produce by EU agencies, will only take place as a safety net when world prices fall to very low levels.

On its own, such a proposal would cause many, and possibly most, EU farmers to go out of business. The Commission therefore will implement a system of direct payments to farmers to supplement their incomes. These subsidies might be in the form of payments per head of livestock or per hectare of crops grown. Like most aspects of EU policy, the final shape of CAP reform will depend upon political negotiations between the member states. The issue serves as a clear example of how political decisions affect what farmers do and how land is used.

Activity › Farming in the UK

Within the UK there exists a very wide range of farming enterprises. Some are small, for example specialising in capital intensive horticulture. Others are large, for example hill farms specialising in sheep production. It is virtually impossible to pick out a typical farm in terms of size, scale or type of production. However, the factors that influence farmers' land use have many common features. It is always the case, for example, that the environmental and economic factors are filtered through a decision making process. In other words, the factors have to be weighed by a decision maker and then a judgment is made.

Rocks Farm

At Rocks Farm, in Northumberland, the farm manager has chosen to spread risks by developing a wide range of enterprises. The farm estate is large with 560 hectares of cropped land, and it lies between 60 and 100 metres above sea level. It is only 6 kilometres inland and therefore both winter and summer temperatures are moderated by the sea influence. The annual average precipitation, 600mm, is relatively low because the region is in the rain shadow of the northern Pennines. The soil is generally well drained and ranges from light sandy soils to heavier sandy clay loams.

Partly by good fortune, but also partly because of the rotation of land use, pests and diseases pose no major problem for the farm.

A variety of crops are grown. In a typical year, land use on the farm includes:

- winter wheat (ie, planted in autumn) - 225 hectares
- winter barley - 60 hectares
- oilseed rape - 100 hectares
- peas - 10 hectares
- winter oats - 15 hectares
- organic oats (aimed for the muesli market) - 12 hectares
- set-aside - 20 hectares
- permanent pasture and other grassland (1,000 ewes) - 120 hectares.

Changes in land use are influenced by a number of factors. For example, approximately 30 hectares are now registered with the Soil Association. This body certifies that the land is farmed organically (ie, without pesticides or artificial fertiliser) and is therefore able to grow produce for the expanding organic market. Another change came in 1997 when beef production was ended. The fall in consumer confidence during the BSE crisis had reduced the price of beef and it had become more economic to concentrate on lamb production.

The pea crop is an an attempt at diversification out of oilseed rape. Up to now, rape has received support from the CAP but the farm manager believes that this will change and crops such as peas and beans will come into favour. Rape is a difficult crop to replace because it ripens in mid-summer. This gives it a double advantage because the crop provides early cash flow and also makes use of expensive farm machinery which would otherwise be waiting for the wheat and barley to ripen.

When beef production stopped, new uses were investigated for some of the vacated buildings. In one attempt at diversification, an indoor riding arena was established. Another idea being investigated is whether to join the Countryside Stewardship Scheme. This would increase income and would also be more environmentally friendly. Wider field margins would be planted with grass and left uncultivated to provide wildlife habitats. Under the Farm Woodland Scheme, 20 hectares of new woodland was planted three years ago with the same motive of improving wildlife habitats. Eventually, the woodland will be used for timber production.

Adapted from the Farmers Guardian, 21st August 1998

▲ **Figure 4.13 Rocks Farm**

Questions

1 Classify the type of farming that takes place at Rocks Farm.
2 Outline the factors that have influenced land use on Rocks Farm.
3 Explain how changes in the CAP might influence future decisions about land use on the farm.

3. What trends are occurring in food production?

Food production and population growth

The rapid rise of world population has not caused mass starvation on the scale that some writers predicted in the 1970s. The Green Revolution has saved India, China, Indonesia and Bangladesh from the terrible fate that would have occurred if food production had not kept pace with population growth. This is not to say that famines have not occurred. In 1997, according to the FAO, 29 countries were facing acute food shortages requiring emergency aid. More than half were in sub-Sahara Africa where civil wars or disorder had disrupted normal farm activities.

New sources of food must be found. In Asia, for example, the population is rising by over 50 million per year. By 2025 the current rice crop of 520 million tonnes must rise to 770 million tonnes in order to feed the population. With gains from the Green Revolution slowing down there are concerns about how this is to be achieved. Industrialisation and urban development are reducing available farmland. Salinisation, waterlogging and erosion caused by intensive farm production are also causing a net reduction in irrigated lands throughout Asia. For example in China, between 1976 and 1996, the area under rice cultivation fell from 37 to 31 million hectares.

However, a lesson from the 1970s might be that predictions of food shortages and famines made on the basis of conventional wisdom are not always accurate. The ideas of Ester Boserup, first published in 1965, might be relevant here (also see unit 1.4). She suggested that a rising population stimulates food production by providing more labour and by providing a market for more food. Two case studies from Africa (see opposite) suggest that conventional ideas of overpopulation leading to land degradation and inadequate food supplies might be mistaken.

Kenya When overgrazing kills grasses, allowing rain and wind to erode the soil, the result is **desertification**. In the drought prone Machakos district, east of Nairobi, outside 'experts' have been predicting disaster in most decades since the 1940s. During British colonial rule in 1952, a soil inspector said that the area was 'an appalling example of environmental degradation' in which 'inhabitants are drifting to a state of poverty and their land to a parched desert of rocks, stones and sand'. Yet the land has not turned to desert. Instead it is greener, more planted with trees, more productive and less eroded than in the 1950s. Since that time, the region has recorded one of the fastest population growth rates anywhere in the world and there are now five times as many people living there.

Population pressure forced the farmers to switch from cattle herding to settled farming. Many of the farmers are women who organise much of the communal effort. The extra labour provided by the rising population enabled people to dig dams, plant trees and construct terraces to trap rainfall and prevent soil erosion. The farmers combine subsistence agriculture - they grow maize to eat - with commercial farming of mangoes, oranges, French beans, tomatoes and coffee. Some of the produce is sold in Nairobi and exported to Europe and the Middle East. Cattle are kept to supply milk to a local dairy and they also provide manure for the soil. Techniques that are sometimes labelled 'appropriate technology' are used by the farmers. For example, horticultural plots are trickle irrigated simply by using a perforated hosepipe fed from a bucket. This is a cheap and easily repaired system.

UN researchers who have studied the Machakos district have commented that 'although there are more mouths to feed, there are more brains to think and more hands to work'.

West Africa A broad region of mixed savanna grassland and forest extends across West Africa from Guinea in the west to Nigeria in the east. Further north is the semi arid grassland known as the Sahel and, to the south, the natural vegetation is rainforest. The conventional view of the region is that population pressure is leading to deforestation and a degraded landscape. During the 1990s, however, researchers in Guinea discovered aerial photographs of the mixed forest and savanna region taken in the 1950s that show there is more forest cover today than in the past.

Local people cultivate forest plots around their villages in order to give shade and shelter from hot, drying winds. The trees also provide fruits, nuts and medicines. Within the sheltered area, the people cultivate plots of vegetables, cassava, yams and peanuts. The soil becomes richer and moister as it is manured and intensively hand cultivated. Seedlings of trees and bushes grow up and thrive in between the growing crops. They are protected from the sunshine, bush fires and the wind that would scorch them in the open grassland. Typically, the plots of arable land are used for about ten years and then allowed to lie fallow. During this time the bushes and trees can grow tall. As population has increased, the number of farmed plots has increased - so causing a rise in the forested area.

The examples from West and East Africa illustrate the difficulty in analysing trends in land use and agriculture in Third World countries. Pressure groups such as the World Wide Fund for Nature (WWF) assert that West African forests are being lost at a faster rate than anywhere else. While it is true that rain forests are being cleared, the overall rate of deforestation might be exaggerated. The new research has shown that local people often know best how to look after their land and that it should not be automatically assumed that population pressure leads to land and soil degradation.

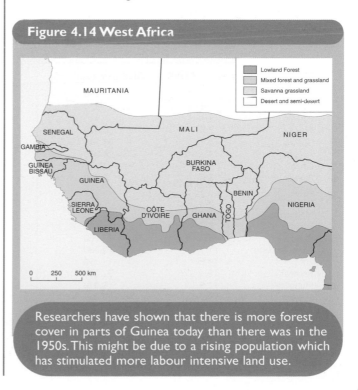

Figure 4.14 West Africa

Lowland Forest
Mixed forest and grassland
Savanna grassland
Desert and semi-desert

Researchers have shown that there is more forest cover in parts of Guinea today than there was in the 1950s. This might be due to a rising population which has stimulated more labour intensive land use.

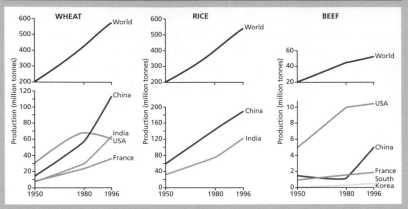

Figure 4.15 Food output in selected countries 1950 - 1996

World output trends

Figure 4.15 shows the rise in output for selected food products in certain countries between 1950 and 1996. The most striking point is the massive increase in production. Rice and wheat output has risen by over 3 times and beef output has risen by two and a half times. Food supply has therefore more than kept pace with world population which has approximately doubled over the same period.

Figure 4.15 also shows the impact of the Green Revolution in India and China. Both countries now produce more wheat than the USA which, in 1950, was the leading producer. The wheat and beef output for France is included to illustrate the rise in production typical of EU countries. Protected from cheaper imports, and with the incentive of high guaranteed prices, French farmers have produced food surpluses that in some cases have simply been put into storage.

The beef production figures illustrate two trends. Output in South Korea has risen as its average income level has increased. This is typical of countries that experience rapid economic growth.

The second notable trend in beef production is the relatively slow increase in high income countries. Concerns about the health effect of eating too much red meat, and animal welfare issues, have persuaded many people to reduce their beef consumption.

Activity ▸ Meat consumption

Figure 4.16 Meat consumption and level of income (selected countries) ▶

	Meat as % of DES	GDP per capita ($)
Tanzania	2.7	110
Malawi	1.4	210
Ghana	2.1	450
Mexico	7.7	3,470
USA	14.9	23,240
Argentina	19.2	6,050
Chile	9.1	2,730
Brazil	8.0	2,770
India	0.9	310
China	9.2	450
Malaysia	8.1	2,790
Japan	6.3	28,190
Australia	19.3	17,260
New Zealand	17.1	12,300
UK	14.8	17,790
France	18.4	22,260
Hungary	12.9	2,970
Sweden	10.2	27,010

Notes: DES is dietary energy supply. It is a measure of how much food people eat. Note also that the horizontal axis on the scatter graph is a log scale.

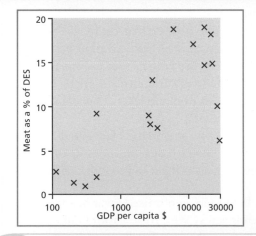

Questions

1 Describe what the data in Figure 4.16 shows.
2 Suggest possible reasons for the general pattern in the data and any exceptions.

Agribusiness

A trend that is occurring throughout agriculture is the industrialisation of farming. Food processing and food production is increasingly dominated by large companies. Although most land is still farmed by individual farmers, what they grow and how they grow it is influenced by outside business interests.

Contract farming This is a system in which farmers agree to sell their produce to food companies. Before crops are grown, the quantity, quality and price are fixed. An example from the English Midlands illustrates how the system works. At Holmebrook Farm, near Tamworth, the farmer has a contract with McCains to supply 800 tonnes per year of Maris Piper potatoes. McCains is a food processing company which supplies frozen chips to the domestic market and catering trade. The company specifies Maris Piper because of its suitability for freezing. Even though the region receives an average of 27 inches precipitation per year, this variety of potato does best with irrigation in the light gravelly soils on the farm. To supply the water, the farmer has built an 8.5 million gallon reservoir covering almost one hectare. This example shows the degree of influence that food companies sometimes have over how land is used.

It is not only in high income countries that contract farming is expanding. In northern India, near the Himalayan foothills, farmers are being contracted by McDonalds to grow potatoes for their outlets in that country. In another example, Pepsi, which owns Kentucky Fried Chicken, contracts hundreds of small farmers in the Punjab to grow tomatoes for processing into ketchup. The company supplies the high-yielding 'designer seeds' and the chemical pesticides to maximise production.

For poor farmers the system offers a stable income and provides the raw materials necessary to start production. The seeds and fertiliser ensure high yields and consistent quality. Some concerns are expressed, however, that the result is a uniformity of crop species that reduces biodiversity. Nevertheless, Indian state governments see the system as providing jobs and higher incomes for their populations. Uttar Pradesh, for example, gives interest free loans to the transnational companies that set up food processing plants in the state. By freezing peas, canning mushrooms or producing ketchup locally, the process of 'adding value' takes place at the production end of the distribution chain rather than at the consumer end.

Air freighting farm produce This is a relatively new trend in agriculture. In the 1990s the increased capacity of freight planes, and their lower running costs, allowed a new trade to develop in high value, perishable items. Flowers, vegetables and soft fruit are the main commodities traded.

In Kenya, an export trade has developed in cut flowers. It is the fastest growing sector of that economy and the fourth largest earner of foreign exchange. Over 35,000 tonnes of flowers are air freighted annually to Europe. Daily flights take most of the flowers to the Netherlands for sale at auction and then distribution throughout Europe. Approximately 15 percent of sales are made direct to supermarkets within the UK.

The two main flowers produced are roses and carnations. Local growing conditions are favourable with fertile volcanic soils and high average temperatures. Drip irrigation and, in some areas, growing under polythene tunnels, allow year round production. Pests such as caterpillars, and diseases such as mildew and rust, are a constant hazard to the growers and have to be chemically controlled. The two main production areas are at Thika, to the north of Nairobi, and Lake Naivasha to the west. A vital element in the trade is nearness to an international airport and an infrastructure to handle and transport the fragile flowers. Local growers have formed the Kenya Flower Council to promote the business, to oversee quality control and to ensure environmentally friendly production methods. They know that a positive public image in the consumer countries is an important element in keeping ahead of their main competitors in Colombia, Israel and Zimbabwe.

Factory farming This is the name sometimes given to capital intensive livestock production. It usually involves zero-grazing and includes methods such as battery cages for hens and chickens, veal crates for young cattle and pig stalls for sows and piglets. Farmers claim that these systems are the outcome of consumer pressure for increased production and lower prices.

Keeping animals indoors and in closely confined spaces causes a high risk of disease and infection. For this reason, some animals are routinely given antibiotics. The practice has been criticised because it promotes the development of antibiotic resistant diseases which might be hazardous to humans as well as to animals.

Some farmers use 'growth promoters' which are hormones that encourage the growth of muscle tissue in cattle. Again the justification is that food can be produced more cheaply this way but the practice is controversial because of fears regarding the affect on humans who eat the meat.

Where large numbers of animals are kept indoors, the local farmland often cannot produce sufficient fodder to support them. This means that supplementary foodstuffs have to be bought in. The use of infected meal, derived from the ground up carcasses of cattle and other animals, is thought the most likely cause of BSE. This disease was first identified in cattle in 1986. In 1996, the government announced that cases of 'new variant' CJD (a human form of BSE) might have been caused by people eating infected beef. Shortly afterwards the EU Commission banned all beef exports from the UK and beef consumption within Britain fell sharply.

Since then a cull of all cattle over 30 months old, combined with a ban on using ground up animal remains as animal feed, has greatly reduced the number of BSE cases. In 1998, the EU Commission partially lifted the UK ban on exports by allowing sales from Northern Ireland. A computerised tracking system for cattle, developed in Northern Ireland, was then extended to the rest of the country. It is hoped that this will reassure buyers that cattle sold for beef do not come from infected herds.

Because it is not known how long it takes for CJD to develop in humans, it will be many years before the full impact of BSE is clear. By 1999, there had been 40 human deaths from BSE related CJD. The worst case predictions are of a major epidemic, while optimists hope that numbers will not rise steeply. It is not certain how many BSE cases there have been in cattle because the over 30-month cull has in effect removed the evidence. It is known, however, that between 1986 and 1993 there had been 100,000 cases.

To some people, BSE is a classic example of the dangers in industrialised farming. It has reinforced the growing lobby of people who campaign for animal welfare and 'natural' farming methods. Even those who feel that the dangers have been exaggerated cannot deny the impact that BSE has had on land use, farmers and food consumption.

Genetically modified (GM) crops These are varieties that have been changed by manipulating the gene structure within seeds. This is done to increase yields, shorten the growing time or improve resistance to pests and diseases. In the future it might be possible to make foods more nutritious or better tasting. Research is also taking place to produce crops that have medicinal effects. The transnational food and chemical companies that have developed this biotechnology say that the process is simply a speeded up version of what has taken place over generations of farming.

Genetically modified types of soya, cotton, maize, sugar beet and tomatoes were developed in the mid-1990s and intense research into other crops has continued since then. Monsanto, one of the main companies involved, has created a variety of cotton with the 'Bollguard' gene. This protects the plant from attack by the bollworm and therefore allows farmers to use less pesticide. Another product developed by the same company is a soya bean with the 'Roundup Ready' gene. This allows the plant to tolerate 'Roundup', a herbicide also manufactured by Monsanto. By using this weedkiller, it is said that fewer applications are needed and it also removes the need to hoe or till the soil to get rid of weeds. This conserves moisture and reduces the danger of soil erosion.

Genetic modification of crops is a controversial topic. Supporters say that the new seeds are needed to feed the world over the next century. During that time, population numbers are predicted to almost double. GM will enable food production to increase because yields will be higher and farming will be possible in areas that are too dry or too cold at present. But opponents fear that unknown side effects might result and that more time is needed to assess the possible risks. Emotive descriptions such as 'Frankenstein food' are used by people opposed to the introduction of GM food. The worry, for some people, is that genetically

Figure 4.17 Factory farming

Pigs, poultry and cattle are kept indoors on many farms. The livestock are housed in climate controlled conditions and their feed is precisely regulated.

modified organisms might migrate to other species, mutate and multiply. Any mistakes could be irreversible.

What is clear is that most people in the UK have eaten genetically modified food whether they wished to or not. During the late 1990s, many United States farmers grew genetically modified soya. This was mixed with conventional soya and used by food companies around the world. Sixty percent of processed foods, including baby foods, chocolate, cake and bread contain soya products and most do not carry labels to say that they contain GM material. (Unit 14.3 includes a section on the environmental impact of agriculture and discusses how agriculture could be made more sustainable.)

Activity   Organic farming

Figure 4.18 Organic farming: pigs ▲
These pigs are kept in more natural conditions than factory farmed animals. They are fed grain that has been organically grown.

▼ **Figure 4.19: leeks**
These leeks are grown without the use of artificial fertiliser or pesticides.

The views of an organic farmer:
'Industrialised agriculture has stretched animal welfare to the limits, and transformed the once patchwork quilt landscape into prairie. Cornflowers have disappeared, along with several dozen species of insect and 100,000 miles of hedgerow. The survival of once-common birds such as thrushes and skylarks is in doubt. And the Ministry of Agriculture, Fisheries and Food advises us to peel carrots to get rid of organophosphates.
BSE has cost £4.5 billion to clean up and water companies spend £150 million per year removing pesticides from drinking water. It is time the CAP stopped promoting the high input - high output form of agriculture that it has favoured so far.'

Questions

1 Briefly outline the adverse consequences that are said to result from industrialised agriculture.
2 Suggest why the EU has promoted a 'high input - high output' form of agriculture.
3 What factors might affect the rate of organic food production in the future?

4. How do conflicts arise in rural land use?

There are many competing uses for rural land. Apart from farmers, other groups who might wish to use land in the UK include:

- developers wishing to build houses, factories, roads or golf courses
- recreational users such as walkers or cyclists
- conservationists who might wish to maintain the land in a natural state or manage it for the benefit of wildlife
- mineral companies hoping to extract sands, gravel, coal or limestone (also see unit 10.4)
- power companies who might wish to build power lines or wind farms.

In countries where population growth is rapid, conflicts can arise due to pressure of numbers. Demands for land reform might result in large estates being broken up. In Brazil and Indonesia, settlers are sometimes encouraged to start farming in virgin forest areas which are the traditional hunting grounds of indigenous peoples.

Competition for land is often resolved by the market mechanism. Whoever can afford to buy the land can choose how it is used. However, in the UK, this freedom is limited by the planning process. For most developments a change in land use has to be approved by the local authority planning committee. In National Parks, it is a separate planning board that oversees such applications. By these means it is hoped that an element of democratic control can be exercised over land use.

How the system operates on a small scale is illustrated by a farmer's proposal in 1998 to build an animal incinerator on his land near Ormskirk in West Lancashire. The development could not take place until planning permission was granted. The plan had to be published so that local people and other interested parties could make their comments and, if they wished, campaign against the proposal (see figure 4.20). Local authority officials checked the proposal to see that it conformed to health and safety regulations and that it fitted in with any local development plan. Then the local council planning committee met to decide whether to approve or reject the application. This was not the final stage because either side could object to the decision and request a review by central government. The minister might decide to overrule the decision on the advice of a planning inspector (who is a civil servant). For controversial applications, a public inquiry might be held where people can make their case to a planning inspector. Again the final decision is made by a government minister acting on the recommendation of the inspector.

Right to roam

Sometimes the planning process cannot resolve land use disputes. Although the legal position might be clear, one side or another still pursues its case. During the late-1990s one such conflict centred on the so called 'right to roam'.

For many decades, some people in England and Wales (the law in Scotland is different) have campaigned for free access to open countryside. Although most land is privately owned, the campaigners claim that there

Figure 4.20 Public campaign against an incinerator

Posters urging local people to oppose planning permission for an animal incinerator. In the UK, landowners do not have complete freedom over how they use their land. In this case, the protesters won and the farmer was not allowed planning permission

should be a right to roam freely across such land.

In the 1930s, ramblers groups, particularly from the industrial cities of northern England, started to use 'direct action' to gain free access. In 1932, six people were sent to jail for leading a mass trespass on Kinder Scout in the Peak District.

Over the years since then there have been many attempts to establish a right to roam. Some local authorities have set up voluntary access agreements with landowners who are paid a 'rent' to allow the public onto their land. On parts of the Forest of Bowland, in Lancashire, one such agreement exists between landowners and the County Council. The land is used in three main ways. The owners maintain grouse shooting rights, tenant farmers graze their sheep and walkers are allowed access (except in the shooting season). In order to protect the landowners' and farmers' interests, the County Council has organised a Countryside Ranger Service. These Rangers maintain footpath signs and try to ensure that walkers observe the local bye-laws. For example, dogs have to be kept on a lead and people are not allowed to fly kites - because they might disturb nesting grouse.

Over a long period, there have been many attempts to establish a legal right to roam. The first parliamentary bill for freedom to roam was introduced as long ago as 1884. All such attempts failed. Then, in the 1997 General Election campaign, the Labour Party pledged to 'give greater freedom for people to explore our open countryside'. Once in government, Labour announced a period of consultation on how best to achieve this aim. Interested parties were invited to submit their cases and two opposing views quickly emerged. The Ramblers' Association urged a statutory right to roam (ie, backed by law), while the Country Landowners Association campaigned for a voluntary scheme.

In 1999, the Government announced that it would legislate to allow the right to roam over open countryside including moors, heathland and hills.

Activity Two opposing views on the right to roam

These views are summaries of the representations made by the Ramblers Association and the Country Landowners Association during the Government's consultation exercise in 1998/99.

Ramblers' Association (RA)

This organisation represents the interests of walkers. It believes that there should be a legally enforced right to roam on 'open countryside', defined as mountain, moor, heath, down and registered common land. The RA conducted an opinion poll in 1998 in which 85 percent of people said they favoured a legal freedom to roam. The Association's view is that access should be free and unrestricted on uncultivated land. Fresh air, open spaces and access to the most scenically attractive uplands are a citizen's right and should not be the preserve of a few wealthy landowners. Voluntary access has largely been a failure, according to the RA, because local authorities have rarely had the funds to set up such schemes. In addition, it is said, many of the voluntary access areas are simply not publicised and therefore receive few visitors.

▲ **Figure 4.21 Yorkshire Dales**

The Ramblers Association believe that people should have the right to roam on open countryside but not on cultivated land.

It is not proposed by the Ramblers' Association that free access should be allowed on cropland, or into people's gardens or in sensitive wildlife areas. A Code of Practice would, for example, make clear that walkers were entering land at their own risk, that they should not damage property nor allow their dogs to worry farm animals.

The RA believes that there is no justification for compensating landowners for free public access because there would be no extra costs involved. Others point out that landowners and farmers already receive massive subsidies from taxpayers, both from the Common Agricultural Policy and from Inheritance Tax exemptions, and that the public has therefore already paid for access many times over.

Country Landowners Association (CLA)

This organisation represents the interests of landowners and farmers. It is strongly opposed to any legal right to roam and urges instead a scheme for encouraging voluntary access. The CLA has carried out its own opinion polls and declares that most people do not want access to distant open countryside but would prefer new access on waymarked paths within 5 miles of their homes.

The CLA estimates that there are 210,000 miles of footpaths and 3 million hectares to which the public has access before any new rights are granted. Voluntary arrangements already cover, according to the CLA, a quarter of the whole farmland area of England and Wales.

A point that the CLA strongly makes is that the cost of a statutory scheme would be very high - possibly £60 million. This comes from the costs to Local Authorities of mapping, signposting and wardening the access areas, together with the cost of compensating landowners. Such compensation could be as high as £20 per hectare for land with grouse shooting rights.

Supporters of the CLA have declared that the right to roam is 'effectively the nationalisation of land'. People from towns and cities would be able to walk across farmers' back gardens and have picnics wherever they liked. Litter and damage would be caused and vandals and criminals would be given access to property that is the 'sole source of farmers' livelihoods'.

Questions

1 Suggest why the right to roam issue is a source of conflict.
2 Summarise the advantages and disadvantages (to the parties involved) of legislation that allows the right to roam on open countryside.

unit summary

1 Agricultural systems can be classified in a number of different ways. The classifications can be useful when analysing how land is used and what food is produced.

2 Agricultural land use is influenced by a large number of environmental and human factors. The environmental factors include physical influences, such as climate, relief and soil type, and biological factors such as pests and diseases. Human factors include economic, social and political influences. Within the UK, one of the most important factors is the Common Agricultural Policy of the EU.

3 All the factors affecting land use are 'filtered' through the perceptions of the farmers who make the final decisions. Their perceptions are influenced in many ways, not least by their level of education and training.

4 Population growth and pressure are affecting the way that land is used in most Third World countries. Pessimists believe that land degradation is an inevitable outcome while optimists believe that population growth can stimulate more productive farming methods.

5 Overall food output has kept pace with population growth over the past 30 years. The introduction of high yielding varieties of wheat and rice (the 'Green Revolution') have contributed to this increase in output.

6 The intensification and industrialisation of agriculture is having a profound effect on the way that food is produced. The adverse side effects of 'factory farming' are a concern to many people.

7 Conflicts arise because there are many competing groups who have a stake in how land is used. The 'right to roam' issue is an example of a conflict between people who farm the land and people who wish to use the land for recreation.

Key terms

Agribusiness - a term used to describe the industrialisation of agriculture. It refers to the increased domination of big business in food production and food processing, and to the intensification of food production in 'factory farming' systems.

Agri-environment scheme - policies designed to promote more environmentally friendly farming methods.

Agroecosystem - the name given to an agricultural system when it is analysed in terms of inputs, outputs and energy flows.

Arable agriculture - the growing of crops.

CAP - the Common Agricultural Policy of the European Union.

Commercial agriculture - farming in which crops and livestock are produced for sale.

Commodity - a primary product that is traded in markets. Agricultural commodities include wheat, cotton and coffee.

Desertification - the spread of desert. It has been blamed on overgrazing leading to the destruction of grassland and the subsequent erosion of topsoil.

Extensive agriculture - farming in which relatively low amounts of capital or labour are used per hectare of land.

Green Revolution - the introduction and use of high yield varieties of rice and wheat in the 1960s.

Intensive agriculture - farming in which relatively high amounts of capital or labour are used per hectare of land.

Land tenure - the system of land ownership, for example owner-occupied or tenant farmed.

Mixed agriculture - farming where crops and livestock are both produced.

Pastoral agriculture - strictly defined this is livestock farming where animals are grazed on grass pasture. The term is commonly applied to all livestock farming.

Zero grazing - livestock farming in which the animals are kept and fed indoors or in stockyards rather than in fields.

Unit 4.2 Energy resources

Key questions

1 What is the world pattern of energy consumption?
2 What is the case for and against nuclear energy?
3 What are renewable energy sources?
4 What is energy conservation?

1. What is the world pattern of energy consumption?

Coal, crude oil and natural gas are known as **fossil fuels** because they derive from plant and animal remains. Together they provide 90 percent of the world's commercially traded energy. (This excludes fuelwood, peat and animal waste that is gathered and used mainly by people in Third World countries and for which reliable energy statistics do not exist.)

Crude oil is the single most important source of world energy. It provides approximately 40 percent of total commercially traded energy requirements (see figure 4.22). Nuclear power supplies approximately 7 percent of world energy and 3 percent comes from renewable resources. This is energy that is produced from sources

Figure 4.22 World energy consumption, 1972-1997

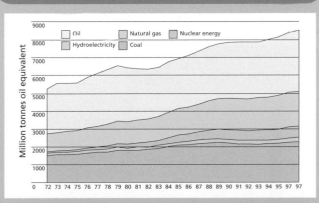

The world consumption of energy has risen since 1972. The rise has been in a series of steps with the most rapid increases occurring at times of rapid economic growth in the Western world. Throughout the period, oil has remained the main source of energy.

that are not burnt or used up in the process. The biggest source of renewable energy is hydro-electric power (HEP) but also included are tidal, wind and solar power.

All these sources of power, including coal, oil, gas, nuclear and HEP, are known as **primary energy**. This is because, in most cases, they form the 'raw material' for other forms of energy. For example, coal is burnt to generate electricity, and crude oil is refined to produce petrol.

Consumption of energy has increased as the world's population has grown and as average incomes have risen. High income countries consume most of the world's energy production (see figure 4.23). The per capita energy consumption in the USA, for example, is more than one hundred times greater than in Bangladesh. Not only does the USA have more industries which require fuel, its domestic consumers have more household appliances, its buildings are centrally heated in winter and air conditioned in summer, and its population drives more cars.

The least developed regions of the world consume relatively little energy. For example, the whole of Africa consumes less fuel than the United Kingdom. However, once economic development begins in a country, energy consumption rises rapidly. The fastest growth in energy use in the 1990s came from the Newly Industrialising Countries of south and east Asia.

Crude oil

Crude oil has many uses. It is refined into petrol and diesel fuel, fuel oil for heating systems and lubricants. It is also used as a raw material in the petrochemical industry to produce a large range of goods such as plastics, synthetic rubber, paints, cosmetics, detergents and fertilisers.

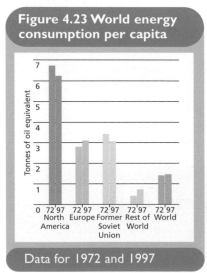

Figure 4.23 World energy consumption per capita

Tonnes of oil equivalent

72'97 North America   72'97 Europe   72'97 Former Soviet Union   72'97 Rest of World   72'97 World

Data for 1972 and 1997

Production The Middle East is the biggest producer of crude oil and Saudi Arabia is the main producing country (see figure 4.24).

The collapse of communism and subsequent economic difficulties caused oil production in the former Soviet Union to almost halve in the 1990s. Production in the USA has also fallen, primarily because oil fields are being depleted faster than new fields are being developed. Another country to experience a fall in production has been Iraq which, since the 1992 Gulf War, has been subject to United Nations' controls on its exports.

Overall, however, production of crude oil rose during the 1990s. The biggest rise was in Saudi Arabia but significant increases also occurred in Kuwait, Iran, the United Arab Emirates and in Europe (particularly Norway).

Consumption The consumption of crude oil is very closely correlated with national income and standards of living. The United States consumes approximately 25 percent of world output, followed by Europe (excluding the former Soviet Union) which consumes just over 20 percent, and Japan which consumes 8 percent.

By contrast, China and India with a total population of over 2 billion, together consume only 7 percent of world output. This is equivalent to the amount consumed by France and Germany, with a combined population of just 140 million. The whole of Africa consumes less crude oil than Germany on its own.

Like other commodities that are traded on world markets, the price of crude oil fluctuates a great deal. During the 1970s, the major oil exporting countries (OPEC) restricted output and increased the price. For a time OPEC was successful, raising the price from $3 per barrel in 1973 to over $20 per barrel in 1979.

The effect of the price rise was twofold. It stimulated new exploration for oil in regions that previously had appeared uneconomic. For example, North Sea oil fields with their expensive offshore oil platforms and pipelines would never have been developed if the price had stayed at $3 per barrel. Secondly, the price rise stimulated research into more fuel efficient vehicles and heating systems. Even in the United States where petrol is cheap by European standards, the average miles per gallon of motor vehicles has doubled since the 1970s.

New exploration and development The biggest technological development in the oil industry since the 1970s has been the rise in offshore production. For example, the output in the Norwegian sector of the North Sea rose from 815,000 barrels per day (bpd) in 1985 to 3,360,000 in 1997. Offshore production has also risen sharply in the South China Sea and the Gulf of Mexico. New developments are taking place in the 'Atlantic Frontier' to the west of the Shetland Islands and the Caspian Sea. Offshore production has stimulated new technology in the building of oil

Figure 4.24 Crude oil production by area 1997

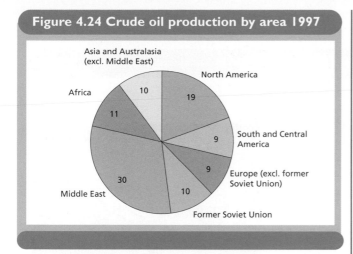

Asia and Australasia (excl. Middle East)

North America

Africa

South and Central America

Europe (excl. former Soviet Union)

Middle East

Former Soviet Union

10 / 19 / 9 / 9 / 10 / 30 / 11

production platforms and in drilling techniques. Oil wells no longer have to be sunk vertically but can now be angled to tap a wider area or even different small fields from the same rig.

The largest oil discovery of the 1980s and 1990s was at Tengiz in Kakakhstan, near the northern Caspian Sea. However, a combination of low world prices and political instability has slowed the development of the oilfield. In particular, conflict in southern Russia and the former Soviet republics in the Caucasus have made it difficult to find a safe route for a pipeline to the Black Sea from where it can be shipped to world markets.

During the 1970s it was feared that the world would run out of oil during the 21st century. North Sea production was expected to have ended by 2010. However, the discovery of new reserves, and the development of techniques to extract more oil from any given field, has made these predictions incorrect. UK North Sea production was higher in 1997 than in 1985, and the world total of 'proved reserves' rose from 666 billion barrels in 1975 to 1,037 billion barrels in 1995.

Natural Gas

Natural gas has the advantage of being a very clean fuel. When burnt in power stations and domestic heating systems it produces virtually no sulphur dioxide and between 60 and 80 percent less carbon dioxide that either oil or coal. Unlike coal, it does not produce ash or dust. However, it has an important disadvantage compared with these two other fuels. Because of its flammable nature and volume, it has to be transported by pipeline or as 'liquefied natural gas' (LNG). LNG is relatively expensive because it requires special plants to convert the gas into liquid, and special bulk carriers to transport it.

These factors mean that most internationally traded gas is by overland pipeline. The biggest movements are from Canada to the USA and from the former Soviet Union to Western Europe. Japan, because of its lack of domestic fossil fuels, and because it is an island, relies heavily on LNG from South East Asia, particularly Indonesia and Malaysia, and from gas fields off the north west coast of Australia.

Consumption As with crude oil, the consumption of natural gas is very closely correlated with national income and standard of living. High income countries use far more gas per person than low income countries. The main use is for domestic heating and cooking, and increasingly for electricity generation. As with oil, the United States' share of total world consumption is over 25 percent. By comparison, the whole of Africa's share of world consumption is just 2 percent.

Production Because of the particular difficulty of transporting natural gas, the main areas of production tend to be near their markets - for example, in the North Sea. The biggest producer is Russia, followed by the USA. Although the Middle East has 45 percent of the world's known gas reserves, it produces only 6 percent of the world output. This is because of its remoteness from major markets that can be served by pipeline, and because Japan can meets its needs from the nearer gas fields of South East Asia.

Large new discoveries in the Caspian Sea in Azerbaijan might be piped to Turkey if a route can be agreed. As with the Caspian oil fields, development has been slowed by the political uncertainties in the Caucasus region. Until border disputes are settled and a general peace treaty agreed, it is not likely that the investment in a pipeline will take place. When it does, the Shah Deniz gas field has been estimated to hold sufficient reserves to supply the whole of Turkey for at least 25 years.

Figure 4.25 North Sea oil platform

Offshore production has become important since the 1970s.

Activity **The 'dash for gas' in the UK**

Following the privatisation of the UK electricity industry in 1989, there has been a rapid rise in the number of gas fired power stations. Between 1989 and 1998, over 20 new gas power stations were built. Official figures suggest that by 2020 more than half of UK electricity will be generated from gas. The so called 'dash for gas' has been an important reason for the swift decline of the UK coal industry.

Many of the new power stations have been built at locations close to pipeline terminals from offshore fields. In some cases, their location has also been influenced by the position of older coal fired power stations. They have been built on the same site as the old power stations so that the existing electricity grid can be used.

There is a concentration of five plants in north Lincolnshire using North Sea gas. Two more are located in Cumbria and two on Deeside, these using gas from the Liverpool and Morecambe Bay fields.

▲ **Figure 4.26 The 340MW King's Lynn gas power station**

The arguments in favour of gas fuelled power stations include:

- they are quicker and cheaper to build than coal power stations
- they employ fewer staff and are therefore cheaper to run; for its employees, the gas industry is less dirty and dangerous than the coal industry
- they produce electricity more cheaply than nuclear power stations
- they are cleaner for the environment, they produce almost no sulphur dioxide (which contributes to acid rain) and little carbon dioxide (a greenhouse gas). They therefore help the government meet its internationally agreed targets in these areas.

In Britain, an important reason why new gas fired power stations have been built has less to do with environmental protection and more to do with the structure of the electricity industry. After privatisation, the generating companies who produced the electricity were split from the distributing companies (or Regional Electricity Companies, RECs) who sold the electricity to consumers. Because the RECs did not want to be totally reliant on the generators, they decided to produce some of the electricity themselves. Gas was the cheapest option available to them.

The case against the dash for gas includes:

- it is seen as a wasteful use of a natural resource. Assuming no new discoveries, at the end of 1995 the UK had only 10 years of gas reserves left at the current rate of consumption. These reserves will soon be used and, then, the UK will become dependent on imports - making the cost of electricity and domestic gas possibly more expensive.
- the rapid run down of the coal mining industry and coal power stations has had a high human and social cost. Many people have become unemployed as pits and power stations have closed. The speed of the change has made it very difficult for the individuals and communities to adjust.
- although it is accepted that building a new gas fired plant is cheaper than building a new coal burning plant, new power stations were not needed because the older coal burning stations had many years of service left.

Questions

1 Outline the advantages of gas powered electricity generation compared with coal powered generation.
2 What are the possible disadvantages of the 'dash for gas' in the UK?

Coal

Coal is the second most widely used form of primary energy (after crude oil). Its use is rising steeply in the Third World where there is an increasing demand for electrical power. However, in most First World countries, its use is in decline. In the UK, in 1947, the mining industry employed 700,000 men in 960 pits. Fifty years later there were fewer than 10,000 men in less than 20 pits. By 1997, coal provided only 18 percent of the UK's energy needs and that proportion is still falling.

Consumption and production In the UK, the demand for coal has fallen for a number of reasons. Since the 1950s, pollution controls and Clean Air Acts have largely ended coal's use in domestic heating. The decline of heavy engineering and manufacturing, combined with greater fuel efficiency have reduced the demand for coal from industry. More recently, environmental concerns over acid rain and greenhouse gases have encouraged governments to look for cleaner alternatives in electricity generation.

During the 1980s, the political decision was made to diversify the UK's energy sources away from coal. To a large extent this was to weaken the position of the

Figure 4.28 Coal consumption 1985 - 1995 (Million tonnes oil equivalent) - selected countries

	1985	1997
UK	62.9	40.4
Germany	147.6	86.8
France	23.0	13.2
China	436.5	681.8
India	76.4	146.4

National Union of Miners who, in both the 70s and 80s, had organised strikes against Conservative Governments. The prime minister, Margaret Thatcher, was determined to ensure that any future miners' strike could only have a minimal effect on power generation. It is now clear, however, that there has been a similar decline of coal mining in other First World countries and the political decisions in Britain probably only speeded an inevitable process (see figure 4.28).

At one time, coal mining was a labour intensive industry employing large numbers of underground miners. Now, coal is increasingly extracted using large scale machinery in open cast sites. By 1998, almost a quarter of UK coal was mined in this way. As the trend continues, environmental campaigners have started to raise more and more objections to this form of mining. Not only are large holes made in the ground, the 'overburden' of overlying rock and waste have to be tipped until restoration takes place. Open cast mining increases the productivity of mineworkers but decreases the work force required. This, combined with the closure of so many pits, has caused high levels of unemployment and the associated social problems in areas once heavily dependent on mining.

Despite concerns over the environmental effects of coal

Figure 4.27 West Burton Power Station

This is one of Britain's remaining large, coal powered electricity generators. Situated in Nottinghamshire, near the River Trent, the power station burns up to 19,000 tonnes of local coal per day. It also uses 200 million litres of river water per day for cooling. West Burton produces 2,000 MW of electricity per year - enough for 2 million people. The plant is investing heavily in equipment that will cut its sulphur dioxide and carbon dioxide output.

burning, it is still likely to constitute a major proportion of world energy consumption into the future. As developing countries increase their industrial output so the demand for energy will increase. In countries such as China, India and South Africa, coal is widely available and relatively cheap to mine. It is the main source of energy in these countries.

2. What is the case for and against nuclear energy?

Nuclear power contributed approximately 7 percent of the world's energy in 1997. The proportion in individual nations varies a great deal, for example 8 percent in the USA, 11 percent in the UK and 42 percent in France.

Because of the high development costs and the need for specialised scientific and technological expertise, most nuclear energy is generated in First World and Second World (former communist) countries. Of the Newly Industrialising Countries, only South Korea and Taiwan have invested significantly in nuclear power. The only nuclear power stations in Africa are in South Africa.

The case for nuclear power

In the 1950s, nuclear power was seen as the energy of the future. Virtually limitless in supply, it would solve the world's energy needs when fossil fuels ran out. It was claimed to be cheap to produce and clean compared with coal or oil. Only relatively small amounts of raw uranium were required to generate the same power that many tons of coal or oil could produce.

Massive amounts of money were invested in the new power stations in the UK, Western Europe, Japan, the USSR and North America. Supporters of nuclear power point out its good safety record, particularly, for example, when the number of nuclear related accidents and deaths is compared with the far worse record of coal mining. Some lingering doubts about safety were met by siting most of the power stations in relatively remote locations.

The case against nuclear power

Compared with the 1950s, optimism about nuclear energy has largely evaporated. Accidents at Windscale, now renamed Sellafield (Cumbria), Three Mile Island (USA) and Chernobyl (former USSR) (see unit 2.5) have shown that the technology is not completely safe. In addition, the proliferation of nuclear weapons is now seen as a deadly threat. Nuclear power stations produce plutonium - the vital ingredient for atomic bombs - as a by product. So,

the more nuclear power stations there are, the more chance that plutonium will fall into the wrong hands.

People have also become more aware of the difficulty in storing and reprocessing nuclear waste. 'Low level' liquid waste has been pumped out to sea over many years, for example on the Normandy and Cumbrian coasts. Large quantities of radioactive sediment now lie on the sea bed and currents have spread the radioactivity from Cumbria around the coast of Scotland as far as Scandinavia. 'High level' waste poses a particularly severe problem. It will remain radioactive and dangerous for thousands of years. Where and how to dispose of it is an unresolved problem. In Britain most of the waste is transported to Sellafield in Cumbria. It is stored and kept cool, under guard, in purpose built buildings. Proposals to bury the waste deep underground in special sites are opposed by people who fear that it will leak and contaminate ground water. It is safer, they say, to keep it above ground and monitor its condition.

A similar, and related problem lies in the uncertainty over how to deal with decommissioned nuclear power stations. These are stations which have come to the end of their life. They will remain dangerously radioactive for centuries. Is it safer to dismantle them and move the radioactive parts to a storage location or should they be maintained and guarded on site? No clear cut answer has been given to these questions.

Although the cost of running nuclear power stations is relatively low, it is now recognised that when all the safety, reprocessing, waste storage and decommissioning costs are included, nuclear power is not a cheap option.

Figure 4.29 Sellafield, Cumbria

Radioactive waste from this plant is a major environmental concern.

Activity | Electricity generation in the UK

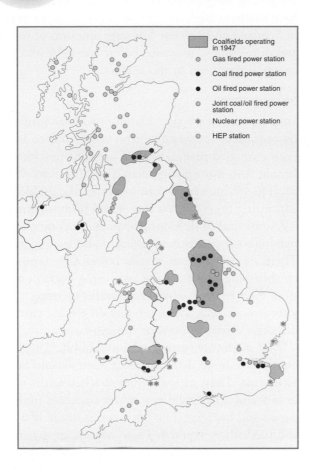

Coalfields operating in 1947

○ Gas fired power station

● Coal fired power station

● Oil fired power station

○ Joint coal/oil fired power station

✳ Nuclear power station

○ HEP station

Figure 4.30 Electricity generation in the UK, 1999

Questions

1 Describe the location of the coal and oil power stations.
2 Outline the factors that might be important in locating a new gas power station.
3 Describe and suggest reasons for the location of the nuclear power stations.

3. What are renewable energy sources?

Many people believe that an increase in the use of **renewable energy** is a vital component of sustainable development policies (see unit 2.6). At the Climate Summit in Kyoto in 1997, the UK government called for a reduction in CO_2 emissions of 20 percent (from 1990 levels) and a target of 10 percent of electricity needs to be generated from renewable sources by the year 2010.

There are five main sources of renewable energy - water power, solar power, wind power, geothermal energy and **biofuel** (ie, organic matter such as wood, agricultural produce and human or animal waste). (Note that, strictly speaking, only biofuel is renewable because it is the only one that can be regrown. The others are, more accurately, 'inexhaustible resources' in that they

can never be used up. However, in practice, this distinction is rarely made.)

Although renewables are generally more environmentally friendly than fossil fuels, they only provide approximately 3 percent of the world's energy needs. The unit costs of producing 'renewable' electricity are still generally higher than conventional methods of coal, gas or oil burning. Therefore it has generally been necessary for governments to subsidise the cost to keep the electricity at a competitive price.

Hydroelectric power (HEP)

HEP generates electricity in three main ways. In each case, the flow of water is used to turn turbines.

Conventional dam and reservoir This is the most widely adopted type of HEP scheme. Examples include the dams along the Colorado River in the USA and the Aswan Dam in Egypt (see unit 9.4 for details). Some of these schemes are multi-purpose in that they also provide water for drinking and irrigation, or they help in flood control.

The requirement for such schemes is that the river is large enough to provide sufficient water to keep the reservoir full, and the valley is narrow enough to build a dam. In addition, the bedrock must be sufficiently strong to support the dam wall and weight of water, and impermeable enough to retain the water.

Once HEP schemes are in operation, the electricity is relatively cheap to generate. However, the cost of construction is often very high. Another major disadvantage is the disruption and dislocation caused to people living in the area, and the loss of farmland. In one of the largest ever HEP schemes, the Three Gorges Project on the River Yangtze in China will eventually require the resettlement of 1.3 million people.

Pumped storage scheme This type of scheme involves using two reservoirs that are at different heights. During the day, water flows down from the top reservoir and turns the turbines. During the night, surplus electricity from conventional power stations is used to pump the water back up from the bottom reservoir.

Dinorwig, near Llanberis in North Wales, is an example of such a scheme (see unit 10.3 for details). The Dinorwig power station is built inside a mountain to preserve the landscape of the Snowdonia National Park. As well as being very expensive to construct, such schemes require two reservoirs that are relatively close together, yet are at different heights above sea level. The advantage of such a power station is that it can respond to peak demands for electricity and can supply energy to the national grid within seconds.

Energy from the sea Both the tide and waves can be used to generate electricity. Tidal power is harnessed at La Rance in Brittany. However, despite being a reliable and regular form of energy, no similar tidal schemes have been built. Proposals to build tidal barrages across the Severn estuary and Morecambe Bay have faced technical, economic and environmental objections. The technical difficulties include the need to protect turbines from the corrosive effect of sea water. In addition, the timing of electricity generation depends upon the state of the tide rather than consumer demand. The cost of building such a scheme is very expensive and there is also an adverse impact on the coastal ecosystem. Tidal

mudflats are flooded, wading birds are affected and fishing might be disrupted.

Harnessing energy from waves is even less developed than tidal HEP. Potentially, waves could supply large amounts of energy but the technical problems of converting wave power into electricity, on a large scale, have not been overcome. Small schemes are in operation in Scotland and Norway but large amounts of research and development is needed before competitively priced energy is produced by this method.

Solar power

Solar power has the potential to provide a significant proportion of the world's energy requirements. It has been estimated that an hour of sunshine provides Britain with more energy than it obtains from all the fossil fuel it burns in a year. However, the problem is converting the Sun's rays into useful forms of energy.

A great deal of development work is taking place on making solar panels more efficient and less expensive. There are several types of solar power. One type works by absorbing heat from the Sun, using water or oil to store the energy. A second type works by using photovoltaic cells. These produce an electric current and can drive electric motors or run appliances.

Solar panels are increasingly used in places such as Southern Europe, Israel, parts of Australia and Southern California. They are sometimes attached to the roofs of houses and other buildings. Water circulates through the panels and heats up. The hot water is stored in a tank and used when required. These systems are generally intended to supplement conventional heating systems.

Solar power stations which generate electricity have been built in Southern California. For example, 'Solar

Figure 4.31 Solar panels in southern California

One' produces 10 MW of electricity using a system of mirrors that track the Sun's rays. The mirrors focus heat to a boiler from which steam is used to turn turbines.

Solar panels and solar power stations are relatively expensive to build and install. For this reason they are generally only found in high income countries. As well as their high cost, they also have the disadvantage that they can only produce power during the daytime.

Most solar energy installations are built in sunny locations in order to obtain the best return from the capital investment. However, even in mainly cloudy locations such as northern Britain, solar energy has been successfully used in domestic heating systems. UK government policy at present is to encourage the building of energy efficient houses that make the best use of 'passive' solar energy. In other words, to design buildings using their fabric, structure and positioning to maximise the contribution that the Sun can make to direct heating and lighting.

Wind power

Windmills have been used for centuries to provide power - to pump water or to ground corn. However, it is only in the past three decades that wind has been used to produce electricity on a commercial scale. Wind turbines are now the fastest growing form of renewable energy. Developments in design and technology have increased the efficiency of wind power to the point that it is competitive with coal and nuclear energy. It also enjoys the advantage, like other renewables, of creating no emissions of carbon or sulphur dioxide, and no hazardous waste products. In Europe, there is the additional benefit that it is windiest in winter - just when demand for energy is highest.

A major disadvantage of wind power is the intrusive visual effect of the turbines and the noise they make when turning. Because hill top or coastal locations are the windiest sites, the turbines can often be seen from many miles away. In Britain, some of the best locations are in areas of high landscape value, in National Parks such as Snowdonia, or in Areas of Outstanding Natural Beauty such as the Forest of Bowland in Lancashire. For this reason there are often objections to proposed new wind farms. Another disadvantage is the unreliability of wind power. Some days it is not windy enough to turn the blades and, occasionally, the wind can be too strong

Figure 4.32 Coal Clough wind farm near Burnley in Lancashire

This area is approximately 350 metres above sea level on the western side of the Pennines. The 24 turbines produce enough electricity for 7,500 homes. Although the turbines are visually intrusive, the surrounding land can still be used as sheep pasture.

- risking damage to the mechanism. Critics of wind power also point out that most of the suitable locations for generating power are distant from the major centres of population where the electricity is needed.

The UK has over half of Europe's total 'wind resource', ie suitable locations where consistently high wind speeds have been recorded. All along the western coastline and on the hills of north and west Britain there are potential sites. The first commercial wind farm in Britain was built in 1991 and since then over 40, with 200MW of capacity, have been built. Sites are located in Cornwall, West Wales, Anglesey, North West England and West Scotland. It is estimated that wind power is already reducing CO_2 emissions by 700,000 tonnes per year. However, this form of energy remains relatively small in the UK and it supplied only a quarter of a percent of the country's energy needs in 1998 compared with, for example, Denmark's 3.7 percent.

A proposal to overcome the environmental objections to wind farms is by building them offshore, either as solid structures or on floating platforms. Some offshore sites have been developed in Denmark and two are proposed off the east coast of England, one off the Northumberland coast and one off East Anglia. The problem with this solution is that it raises the capital costs and involves building transmission lines back to the shore.

On a world scale, Europe has overtaken the United States in terms of wind generated energy with an installed capacity of over 2,500MW. The relative cheapness of wind turbines has made them a viable alternative to fossil fuels in the Third World. For example, by 1998, India had a wind energy capacity of 500MW.

Geothermal power

In geologically active areas, near tectonic plate boundaries, or where the Earth's crust is thin, underground heat can be used to turn water into steam. This then powers turbines. In Iceland and New Zealand, where hot steam escapes naturally from the ground, it is also piped directly to heat homes and other buildings.

Geothermal schemes are only economically feasible where the underground rocks are sufficiently hot at relatively shallow depths. The countries of the 'Pacific Ring of Fire', the active volcanic region around the Pacific Ocean, have the biggest potential for geothermal energy. In Indonesia, 60 kilometres south of Jakarta, holes have been drilled 2,000 metres underground near the dormant Salak volcano. Hot water under pressure comes out of the ground and turns into steam when the pressure is released. This is used to drive turbines. By 1997, Indonesia produced 330MW of geothermal electricity. This scheme has the advantage that the water is relatively free of corrosive minerals. A similar scheme in the Philippines had to be abandoned because the hot water contains dissolved minerals and acids which corrode pipes and machinery.

Biofuels

These are forms of energy that are produced from organic matter. In some cases the raw material is an agricultural product, in others it is a waste product or is the result of organic decay.

Biogas Fermenting domestic and industrial waste in landfill sites produces methane gas. It can be used in just the same way as natural gas, to heat water in a boiler and generate electricity in a steam turbine. The North of England, with its long industrial history and high population density, contains many land fill sites that produce gas. An increasing number are being used for small scale power schemes. For example, near Wigan in Lancashire, two 1MW generators supply electricity to the national grid and heat a local factory. Similarly at Withnell, near Blackburn, a gas extraction system is used to supply electricity for 1,300 homes.

In many Third World countries, the use of biogas is seen as an example of 'appropriate technology'. In other words, it is low cost and small scale. It uses locally produced raw material (human and animal excrement) and the generating plant can be built and maintained by local people. The material is mixed with water and allowed to decompose. The end products are a nutrient rich liquid that can be used for fertilising crops, and methane gas that can be piped off and used for heating or cooking. Such schemes are increasingly used in rural India and Nepal. They are particularly important in preserving local forests which might otherwise be used for fuelwood.

Biomass In this context biomass is defined as vegetation. The use of wood as a source of domestic fuel is common in Third World countries. Although it is a renewable resource, in many areas wood is being used at a faster rate than it is growing, and deforestation is occurring (see unit 4.3). Nepal is a well documented example of a country where population pressure is rapidly depleting forest resources. The country is mountainous and experiences very heavy rain in the annual monsoon. Without the forest cover there is severe soil erosion, landslides, disruption of communications and loss of farmland.

In some places, biomass is a by-product of agricultural production. For example, in Brazil, sugar cane has been successfully refined to produce fuel for motor vehicles. Although useful as a means of disposing of surplus crops, the scheme became uneconomic following the fall in the price of crude oil in the 1990s.

Burning the waste by-products of agriculture is another means of using biomass. Because the raw material is virtually cost free, such schemes are economically efficient. In Hawaii, the burning of sugar cane waste supplies approximately one third of the state's electricity needs. In a similar scheme, announced in 1998, the biggest power company in Spain outlined plans to build an olive fuelled electricity generating plant. The 14MW power station will burn the waste after the olive oil has been extracted.

In the UK, a small scale wood fuelled power station was opened in 1999 near Selby, Yorkshire. In this case, the fuel is grown specifically for use in the scheme. The fuel is short rotation coppice (SRC) willow. Local farmers are being encouraged to grow the willow which is harvested every three to five years. Willow is tolerant to a wide range of soil conditions and can be grown on reclaimed coal waste tips and old gravel pits. Advantages of this scheme are that the willow trees provide habitat for wildlife and also a diversified source of income for farmers. The electricity produced is sufficient to meet the daily demands of 18,000 people.

Wood fuel is 'carbon neutral' in that the amount of carbon dioxide emissions from burning are the same as that taken up by the growing trees. Another advantage is that, because wood has a negligible sulphur content, the power plant releases virtually no sulphur dioxide. If the Selby plant is successful, supporters of the scheme suggest that a 1,000MW plant could be built, using wood from 150,000-200,000 hectares of coppice woodland.

Activity ▸ UK electricity

▼ **Figure 4.33 UK electricity generation 1970 to 1997 (% share)**

	1970	1980	1990	1997
Coal	67	73	65	38
Oil	21	11	11	2
Gas	*	*	*	27
Nuclear	11	14	21	30
Hydro	*	*	*	*
Other fuels	-	*	*	2

Note: * is less than one percent but more than zero

Questions

1 Describe the changes that have taken place in UK electricity generation between 1970 and 1997.
2 Suggest reasons for the changing pattern of fuel use.
3 What effect will the changes have on levels of air pollution?

4. What is energy conservation?

Energy conservation involves the more efficient use of energy - in homes, in businesses and in transport. It reduces the demand for energy and, therefore, the emission of greenhouse gases. It also cuts people's fuel bills. In the UK, the 1995 Home Energy Conservation Act set a target of a 30 percent reduction in domestic energy consumption within 10 years. Local councils were given the task of using a mixture of guidance, advice and financial grants to achieve this aim.

The main domestic energy savings come from better insulation and also from draught exclusion. Double glazing, together with wall, loft, hot water tank and pipe insulation can cut the energy used by more than 60 percent. If all homes in Britain were as energy efficient as those being built under current regulations, the country would easily meet its target for a 20 percent reduction in CO_2 emissions by 2010.

The UK government increasingly uses the tax system as a means of cutting fuel consumption. In particular,

Figure 4.34 Conventional power station cooling towers

In conventional power stations, energy in the form of hot water is wasted. It is cooled in cooling towers rather than being used as part of a local heating scheme.

'carbon taxes' on motor vehicle fuel are designed to reduce the use of cars and lorries and to persuade people to buy more fuel efficient vehicles.

Activity — Combined Heat and Power [CHP]

Two policies by which the UK government aims to meet its target of reducing CO_2 emissions are by supporting renewable energy schemes (such as wind power and landfill gas) and by promoting energy efficiency. The latter involves better insulation for homes and other buildings, and installing more efficient heating systems. In particular, the government is in favour of Combined Heat and Power (CHP) stations. These are small scale, locally based systems for generating electricity. Unlike in conventional power stations where the steam used to drive turbines is cooled and discharged into rivers or the sea, CHP schemes use the steam for heating. It is fed through pipes to central heating systems in nearby buildings. The systems are normally small scale because there is rarely sufficient local demand for all the potential heating that a large power station could produce.

The government estimates that for every 1,000MW of new CHP capacity, annual energy costs will be cut by £100 million and CO_2 emissions by 1 million tonnes. Since 1989 there has been a 50 percent increase in CHP capacity providing heating for industry and local housing schemes.

New factory for Heinz

In 1996, H J Heinz, the food processing company announced that a new factory would be built at its Harlesden (London) site. BP Energy would install a CHP system using natural gas to produce both electricity and heating. Fuel costs would be cut by £0.5 million per year and CO_2 emissions by 26,000 tonnes per year.

Land Rover

In the mid-1990s, Land Rover replaced its conventional heating system, fuelled by electricity from the national grid, with 10 smaller CHP units using natural gas. The system, built at a cost of £6.5 million now saves £0.45 million per year in fuel bills. The hot water produced in the new boilers not only provides space heating but it is used for functions such as degreasing vehicle components and maintaining paint at high temperature for vehicle spraying.

ICI

The company's annual energy bill of £400 million is equivalent to 5 percent of its UK turnover. Since installing new energy saving schemes in 1990, the company has reduced its fuel bill by 18 percent. At its Teesside plant, a CHP unit supplies heating and power to the site and sells surplus electricity to the national grid.

Questions

1 Explain the advantage of CHP schemes over conventional power stations.
2 What disadvantages might CHP schemes have when compared with electricity generation in large coal fired power stations?
3 Outline the factors that might persuade people to install energy conservation measures such as:
   • more insulation (for example thicker loft insulation)
   • renewable energy systems such as solar panels.

unit summary

1 Most of the world's energy is consumed by First World countries. As countries develop economically, their demand for energy increases - to operate new industries, to meet the needs of consumers who desire electrical appliances, for central heating and/or air conditioning, and to provide greater mobility in motor vehicles.
2 Oil, gas and coal provide most of the world's energy. These fossil fuels produce greenhouse gases and are widely blamed for global warming.
3 Nuclear power is in decline due to safety fears and the high cost of dealing with radioactive waste.
4 Renewable energy sources are generally more expensive than oil or gas but they are 'clean' and, by definition, will not run out.
5 Energy conservation is increasingly seen as an important component of policies designed to reduce the use of fossil fuels.

key terms

Biofuel - energy derived from organic matter including wood, agricultural products and human or animal waste.
Combined Heat and Power (CHP) - schemes that generate electricity in steam turbines and which use the steam in heating systems rather than let it go to waste
Fossil fuel - gas, oil and coal, formed from plant and animal remains in previous geological eras. They are non-renewable energy sources.
Fuelwood - wood that is used for domestic heating and cooking, usually in rural areas of Third World countries. It is a renewable biofuel.

Geothermal power - energy that derives from underground heat using either naturally produced steam, or water that has been pumped into the ground and heated.
Primary energy - energy sources such as oil, gas or uranium that are used to produce 'secondary' energy such as electricity or petrol.
Renewable energy - energy from sources (such as the wind or solar radiation) that are not used up in the process. (Note that some writers call these 'inexhaustible resources' and reserve the term 'renewable' for resources such as biofuel which can be regrown or replenished in a human time scale.)

Unit 4.3 Non-energy resources

key questions

1 Where and how are non-energy mineral resources exploited?
2 Where and how are forest resources exploited?
3 Where and how are fishery resources exploited?

During the 1970s there was great concern that the world would soon run out of vital raw materials. Described as a 'doom and gloom' view, it was most clearly expressed in *The Limits to Growth* report of 1972. This influential document was produced by a group of respected academics and politicians who suggested that the world's energy and other natural resources were being depleted (see unit 1.4 for a fuller account of this viewpoint). However, despite a rapidly rising population, the most pessimistic predictions have not come about. New discoveries and production methods, combined with more recycling and efficient use of resources, have averted a global crisis. Natural resources have not 'run out' and, in some cases, are cheaper now than in the 1970s.

This is not to say that severe problems have not occurred. There has been increased pollution resulting from mineral exploitation, fish stocks have collapsed in some areas, and there is rapid deforestation in many tropical countries. Because of these developments, the fear that non-renewable resources will run out has now been replaced by concerns that the environment and renewable resources such as forests and fish stocks are being irreversibly damaged. These issues are examined in this unit.

(The wider issue of whether current rates of economic development are sustainable in the long run is dealt with in unit 2.6.)

1. Where and how are non-energy mineral resources exploited?

Non-energy minerals can broadly be divided into metals and non-metals. Metals include 'industrial metals' such as iron, copper, aluminium and tin, and 'precious metals' such as gold, silver and platinum. A further classification, 'strategic metals' is sometimes made. These include cobalt, chromium and tungsten. They are produced in relatively small quantities but are vital raw materials in high quality steels and in other advanced technology production.

Non-metal minerals include diamonds, phosphates (used in fertilisers), limestone (used in cement making) and borax (used in glass fibre and ceramics).

Mineral production

Minerals are a vital raw material in the production of virtually all consumer goods, from cars, to televisions. Even the page on which this text is written is coated with titanium dioxide - a widely used white pigment.

In terms of volume, iron ore is by far the most important non-energy mineral. World production of this ore is twenty times greater than all the other metals combined. However, because it is relatively abundant (it forms approximately 5 percent of the Earth's crust), it is not an expensive mineral. The most expensive minerals, like gold, are those which are relatively rare but are in high demand.

Like many other aspects of production and trade, the mineral industry is increasingly dominated by transnational corporations (TNCs). Globalisation (see unit 2.4) has created a global market for minerals. The large TNCs have the resources to explore and develop new resources around the globe. For example, Rio Tinto Zinc (RTZ) is one of the world's biggest mining companies (see figure 4.35). It is a leading producer of iron ore, copper and bauxite (aluminium ore), together with a wide range of other minerals such as borax, salt, talc and diamonds. Its operations are on a global scale. RTZ has the resources and market power to negotiate on equal terms with, for example, large steel producing companies and all but the largest national governments.

An issue that affects the production of minerals (as well as other **commodities** such as agricultural produce), is price volatility. The demand for commodities rises and falls depending on the state of the world economy. For example, during the early 1990s when the economies of leading industrial nations slowed down, the demand for raw materials fell. Whenever this happens there is a time lag before supply adjusts. This is because producer countries and companies are reluctant to cut back their production immediately. So, a surplus develops and this causes prices to collapse. Eventually the production of raw materials does fall - as mines close or reduce their output. Then, when economies recover and demand rises, there is a shortage. It takes time to reopen mines so prices rise sharply.

The rise and fall of commodity prices has been an important reason for the slow economic development of

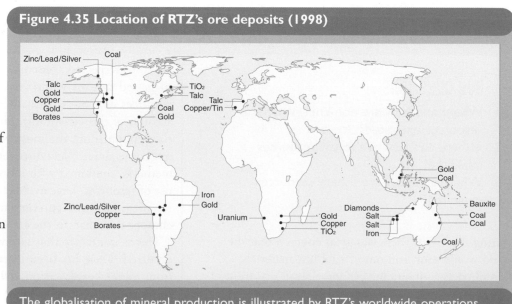

Figure 4.35 Location of RTZ's ore deposits (1998)

Zinc/Lead/Silver — Coal
Talc
Gold
Copper
Gold
Borates
Coal — Gold
TiO₂
Talc
Talc
Copper/Tin
Gold
Coal
Zinc/Lead/Silver
Copper
Borates
Iron
Gold
Uranium
Gold
Copper
TiO₂
Diamonds
Salt
Salt
Iron
Gold
Coal
Bauxite
Coal
Coal
Coal

The globalisation of mineral production is illustrated by RTZ's worldwide operations.

those Third World countries that are over-reliant on a single commodity export. Zambia (copper), the Democratic Republic of Congo (copper), and Bolivia (tin) are examples of countries that have suffered in this way. The lack of a steady and stable income has made management of these economies very difficult.

Costs of production

Deep mining is the most expensive form of mineral production. In deep mines, a shaft has to be dug and then passageways to the mineral deposit have to be tunnelled. Water must be pumped out and air circulated within the working area. The development costs are expensive, as is the employment of skilled miners who operate machinery at the mineral face. Because deep mining is so costly, it is used mainly for those minerals that are highest in value. This explains why the deepest mine in the world, Western Deep Levels in South Africa, is a gold mine.

One form of deep mining that is less expensive is where deposits can be exploited simply by pumping water underground and dissolving the minerals. This occurs both in Cheshire and North Lancashire, near Fleetwood, where salt deposits are extracted in this way. The brine solution that is extracted is piped to nearby chemical works.

For the majority of minerals it is much cheaper to use open cast mining techniques than deep mines. Large scale earth-moving equipment strips away the overburden above a mineral deposit and then giant mechanical shovels scoop the ore directly onto lorries. The development costs of such mines are much less than opening new shafts in deep mines. Some open cast pits are very large. The world's biggest is at Bingham Canyon, Utah, where the copper workings cover an area over 7 square kilometres and are 800 metres deep.

Where there is no overburden and the deposits are at the surface, quarrying can take place. In Britain this technique is used to obtain limestone, kaolin (for pottery), slate (for building) and granite (for road building).

Environmental issues

The exploitation of mineral resources inevitably has an environmental impact. In open cast mines, the removal and disposal of the overburden causes a visual impact, it reduces the amount of agricultural land, it destroys natural vegetation and it can disrupt local drainage. The noise and dust created can also be a problem for local people. As environmental concerns have increased, the

Figure 4.36 Bingham Canyon near Salt Lake City, Utah

The ore extracted at Bingham contains an average of 0.7% copper. About 6 kg of copper can be recovered from each tonne of ore. For such a low concentration it would be unprofitable to operate an underground mine.

requirement to restore old open cast workings by infill and re-vegetation has become normal, at least throughout Western Europe and most of the First World.

For deep mines, the need to store waste rock and **tailings** (finely ground rock waste) is a difficult environmental problem. Often the tailings contain toxic substances that are dangerous to human, animal and plant life. Another severe problem in some areas is subsidence, caused by the collapse of old underground workings. It can cause buildings to collapse and it can disrupt water channels causing localised flooding.

When disused deep mines are abandoned, they quickly fill with water. During their working life the water is pumped out and drained away, sometimes after storage and treatment. But, when pumping ceases, the water level rises. This water can become contaminated with toxic materials from within the old mine.

An additional environmental impact arising from mineral extraction comes from the transport of material away from the mining area. When purpose built railways are used, for example, to transport iron ore through remote areas in north western Australia, the human impact is minimal. However, when the minerals are transported by lorry, perhaps along narrow roads and through small villages, the impact is severe. It is the noise, danger and vibration from lorries that environmental campaigners most frequently cite in their objections to, for example, limestone quarries in the northern Pennines.

Toxic waste The environmental hazards arising from old mine workings have been highlighted in southern Spain, near Seville. The Los Frailes zinc and lead mine, owned by a Swedish-Canadian company, is on the same site as an older, abandoned mine (see figure 4.37). The trailings from the mine were held in a reservoir with an earth dam wall. In 1998, the dam wall collapsed releasing 5 million cubic metres of waste. This included toxic residues of zinc, lead, cadmium and other heavy metals.

The first effect was to cause a 500 metre wide flood over 2,000 hectares of nearby farmland. The crops of tomatoes, sunflowers and rice were either washed away or made unfit for consumption by the toxins. Local communities were warned not to drink water from wells that had become contaminated.

At risk, sixty kilometres downstream, was the Donana National Park, a nature reserve and wetland site of international importance. An estimated 1 million birds use the area as a stopover on their migration between northern Europe and Africa. In addition, 125 different

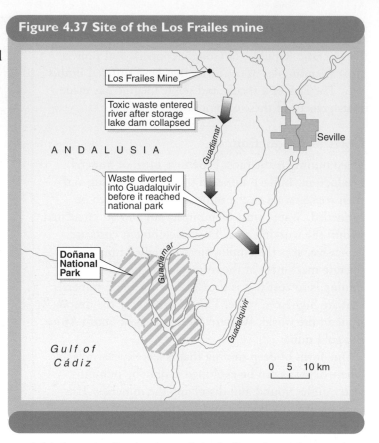

Figure 4.37 Site of the Los Frailes mine

- Los Frailes Mine
- Toxic waste entered river after storage lake dam collapsed
- Waste diverted into Guadalquivir before it reached national park
- Doñana National Park
- Seville
- ANDALUSIA
- Guadiamar
- Guadalquivir
- Gulf of Cádiz
- 0 5 10 km

bird species live in the park including the endangered imperial eagle, together with ibis, spoonbills and heron.

It is hoped that prompt action by the Spanish government in diverting the river into a different channel will have saved the wildlife site but it will be many years before the full impact is known.

Activity Tin production: Cornwall and Malaysia compared

Tin was one of the world's first metal ores to be exploited. With copper it was made into bronze and was the basis of early civilisations in the Middle East. Today, tin is used as a coating for steel on 'tin' cans and on other everyday objects such as pins and staples. Its value comes in preventing the steel from rusting and it stops weak acids in food from damaging the inside of cans. The only other major use for tin is in solder.

Since the 1970s, the use of tin has declined. World production peaked in 1973 at 214,000 tonnes but this has since fallen to 175,000 tonnes in 1998. The main reason has been the switch to aluminium by can producers. Aluminium cans are lighter and cheaper than tin/steel cans and are now widely used for most drinks and canned foods.

China, Malaysia and Indonesia are the world's leading tin producers. As recently as 1950 the UK was the world's second largest producer (after Malaysia) but, in 1997, the last Cornish tin mine closed.

During the 1970s, producer countries successfully joined together in a cartel. Known as the Association of Tin Producing Countries, they were able to raise the world price of tin by limiting production and stockpiling ore. For a time the strategy worked. But, when consuming companies started to switch to aluminium, the cartel collapsed and the stockpiles were sold - depressing the price further.

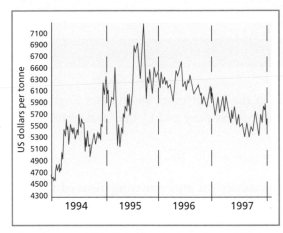

▲ **Figure 4.38 Graph of tin prices 1994 - 1998**

Like most commodities, the price of tin is very volatile.

▲ **Figure 4.39 A former tin mine in north Cornwall**

There is no longer any tin mining in Cornwall.

Cornwall

For 2,500 years Cornwall was a major producer of tin and copper. In the mid-nineteenth century there were 400 mines and 50,000 miners. They obtained the ore (tin ore is called cassiterite) from mineral veins found in the igneous granite rock that underlies much of the county.

Copper mining collapsed in the late nineteenth century following the discovery of large deposits in the USA and Chile. The tin mining industry followed and, by 1918, was in severe decline. In 1997 the last mine, South Crofty near Redruth, closed. Efforts to save the mine in 1995 when the world price briefly rose above $7,000 per tonne had to be abandoned when the price later fell below $5,500 per tonne.

The deep mine was simply too expensive to operate compared with lower cost producers in China, Malaysia, Indonesia and Thailand who were mining large scale surface deposits. By contrast, the Cornish miners had to operate 700 metres underground in hot, humid conditions, working narrow veins. Rio Tinto Zinc owned the mine until 1988 but had found it unprofitable to continue at that time. New owners took over but, despite a pay cut for the miners, contributions from local people and a government loan, the effort to save the mine failed.

A factor which has contributed to the decline of mining in Cornwall and indeed the rest of Western Europe, has been a reduction in long distance transport costs. Before large scale transport by sea was introduced in the late nineteenth century, there was an advantage for mineral producers to be near their main industrial markets. Today, this is no longer the case. Transport by sea in bulk carriers is now so inexpensive, per tonne, that mineral resources can be shipped around the world at virtually no cost disadvantage to the producers or end users.

For Cornwall, one legacy of the mining industry is a high unemployment rate. The South Crofty mine closure gave yet another impetus to the generations old tradition of emigration. It is an irony that, around the world, Cornish engineers have provided skills and enterprise to the very competitors that have driven their own industry to collapse.

Another legacy is one of abandoned mines and spoil heaps. Contaminated water from the old workings is a major hazard to some drinking water supplies. Because the mining industry was largely bankrupt before it closed, there are no industry funds to finance a clean-up. The financial burden has therefore fallen on local residents and water consumers.

Malaysia

In Malaysia tin ore is found in surface, alluvial gravels. The deposits are located along the western side of the Malay Peninsula. Relatively low cost dredgers are used to scoop the gravel from the beds of rivers or shallow lakes. The deposits are then dumped from the dredger buckets onto sieves and into settling tanks from where it can be recovered.

On solid ground, where it is not possible to use dredgers, the alluvial deposits are 'gravel pumped'. Jets of water are used to dislodge the ore which is collected in ponds. The material is allowed to settle and is then pumped out.

Despite being an efficient, low cost producer, Malaysia suffers from the general difficulties that all tin producers face. There are three main problems. Firstly, the demand for tin is in long term decline. Secondly there is increased competition from neighbouring producers such as Indonesia and Thailand. Thirdly, the world price remains volatile making investment and planning difficult.

Question

I If, in the future, alluvial deposits of tin were discovered in the estuaries of South West England, what factors would need to be considered by a) the mining company and b) the local planning authority, before mining could take place.

2. Where and how are forest resources exploited?

Trees are an important natural resource. Timber production is both a source of income and employment. Kielder Forest in Northumberland, for example, produces 25 percent of all trees harvested in Britain and is a major employer in that remote area. Countries such as Canada, Finland and Brazil export large amounts of timber and timber products. The value of this trade worldwide was estimated as being $114 billion in 1998. Further down the production chain, sawmills, pulp mills and furniture manufacturers also provide income and employment for large numbers of people.

Trees provide wood for building and construction, pulp for paper making and, in much of the Third World, fuel for domestic cooking and heating.

In addition to these economic benefits, woodland and forests are a source of biodiversity and they provide habitats for many other species of plants and animals. Trees are also a source of natural beauty, making urban areas more pleasant in which to live. In towns and cities they also reduce wind speeds and noise levels, and they trap dust and fumes in their leaves and branches.

An additional function of trees is that they 'store' carbon dioxide. Trees convert carbon dioxide and water from the atmosphere into oxygen and timber. Therefore, the more trees that are growing, the less carbon dioxide there is in the atmosphere. This is an important factor in the debate on global warming because carbon dioxide is a greenhouse gas (see unit 12.6).

World production and consumption of timber

Timber can be classified as softwood (mainly from coniferous trees) or hardwood (from non-coniferous trees). Coniferous trees, such as fir, pine and spruce mainly grow in cool temperate latitudes. They form the natural vegetation in much of Canada, Scandinavia and northern Russia, including Siberia. They tend to be quicker growing than non-conifers and their wood is softer. The forests are sometimes called 'boreal' (from the Latin borealis which means northern) or 'taiga' (which is the Russian name for the belt of coniferous forest in that country).

Hardwoods can be classified as temperate, such as oak and beech, or tropical, such as mahogany and teak. Temperate hardwoods form the natural vegetation in Britain and Western Europe, and in similar latitudes where the climate is moist. Tropical hardwoods form the natural vegetation is the world's rain forests including Amazonia, the Congo Basin and South East Asia.

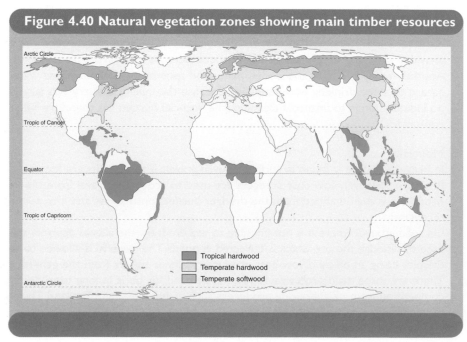

Figure 4.40 Natural vegetation zones showing main timber resources

Figure 4.41 World production of forest products

	(million cubic metres)		
	1970	1994	% increase
Fuelwood and charcoal	1,185	1,891	60
Industrial roundwood	1,278	1,467	15
Paper and paperboard	126	269	113

Roundwood is wood in its natural state - before sawing or pulping.

Most temperate hardwood trees are deciduous (ie, they lose their leaves at the same time) and are sometimes called 'broad leaved'. Tropical hardwoods in rainforests are mainly evergreen (ie, they do not lose all their leaves at the same time) but in some tropical areas which experience a dry season (for example where there is a monsoon climate) the trees are deciduous.

Figure 4.41 shows the total world production, in 1970 and 1994, of the main forest products. According to the United Nations Food and Agriculture Organisation (FAO), fuelwood is the most important forest product in Third World countries. The need for fuel has risen in line with the growth of population in these countries. The FAO estimates that fuelwood is the main source of domestic energy for forty percent of the world's population.

The main industrial uses for timber are in building, construction and paper making. As well as supplying sawnwood for joists and planks, timber is used for wood chip and particles to make board, and thin veneers to make panels. Wood pulp is used to make paper and cardboard. This is mainly produced from softwood.

From figure 4.41 it is clear that the biggest growth in the use of timber products has been for paper and paperboard making. Demand for newsprint (the paper used for printing newspapers) and tissue has been growing fastest in Third World countries though their average consumption of these products still lags a long way behind First World countries.

A significant trend in wood production during the 1980s and 1990s was the increasing involvement of transnational corporations (TNCs). For example, Shell owns plantations in Chile, South Africa, Congo (Democratic Republic), Thailand and New Zealand. The world's biggest forest product company, the US based International Paper, has sales in over 120 countries. The TNCs not only control timber production, they are also involved in transporting and processing the wood and wood products.

Some of the TNCs are based in Third World countries such as Indonesia, Malaysia and China. Their involvement reflects a shift in the global production of industrial timber towards tropical plantations and away from the temperate softwoods. The traditionally dominant wood producers, Canada, the USA and the former USSR are facing increased competition from, in particular, Indonesia and Brazil. An advantage for most tropical producers at the present time is that they are less restricted by environmental considerations than the First World producers. In other words, they are less closely regulated by governments in terms of the environmental damage that they cause. This has the effect of lowering their production costs.

Sustainable forestry

Sustainable forestry has been defined as 'the use of forests and lands in a way, and at a rate, that maintains their biodiversity, productivity and regenerative capacity'. This definition, at a 1993 Helsinki conference on European forestry, clearly suggests that sustainable forestry is more than simply replanting a greater number of trees than are cut down. So, for instance, clear cutting a 'virgin' forest and then replanting the same number of trees cannot be described as sustainable. Only by selective and limited logging, preferably in forests already replanted, can the wider environmental considerations be addressed.

According to the FAO, the world's total forest cover was 3,454 million hectares in 1995. Slightly more than half of this total is in Third World countries. The FAO estimates that the net rate of deforestation between 1980 and 1990 was 15.5 million hectares per year, and that between 1990 and 1995 the rate was slightly lower at 13.7 million hectares per year. For the forestry industry to be sustainable in the long run, the net rate of deforestation must fall to zero. In other words, the number of trees planted must equal the number of trees that are felled.

Most of the deforestation is occurring in Third World countries. In North America and Europe there was a small net increase in forest cover because new planting occurred at a faster rate than clearing. In Africa, Asia and South America, the rate of new planting is slower than the rate of clearing. However, the replanting rate has risen and there are now an estimated 80 million hectares of forest plantations in the Third World.

In the rain forests of West and Central Africa, it is logging companies which are responsible for most of the deforestation. Countries such as Ghana, Nigeria and Senegal have already been cleared of their prime timber. The logging companies have moved on to countries such as the Congo (Democratic Republic), Gabon, and Cameroon where an estimated 200,000 hectares of forest are being cleared each year.

Most of the deforestation in South and Central America occurs because the land is being cleared for agriculture. In some cases it is peasant farmers who clear the forest, in others it is cattle ranchers or plantation owners. The same is true in much of South East Asia where large areas of rain forest were burnt in 1997 and 1998 as a cheap way of clearing land for farming (including new plantations). This is not to say that logging companies are not involved. They often clear tracks into the forest, enabling them to extract the most valuable timber such as teak. This then allows access to

Figure 4.42 Loading logs for shipping

Although most of the world's industrial timber is obtained from coniferous forests in temperate latitudes, the fastest increase in output is from tropical plantations.

farmers and settlers who complete the destruction of the natural forest.

During 1997 and early 1998, large areas of forest in Indonesia were cleared simply by burning. Exceptionally dry conditions caused by the El Nino weather pattern (see unit 12.6) meant that small fires quickly burnt out of control. They were started by settlers wishing to extend their cultivated area or by companies wishing to establish new oil palm plantations. The resulting smog from the fires created a health hazard across much of South East Asia.

Deforestation can cause severe soil erosion in humid, tropical areas because the tree roots no longer hold the soil together and the tree canopy no longer protects the soil from heavy rain drops. The result is bare, rocky hill slopes and silted up streams and water channels. Where it is not washed away, the soil quickly loses its fertility and a hard baked 'laterite' layer (see unit 13.3) is sometimes exposed. Then the land can become virtually useless for agriculture and is not therefore able to support the local population.

As described previously, forests 'store' carbon dioxide from the atmosphere. The reduction of this greenhouse gas is one means by which global warming can be reduced. But, because more trees are being cut down than replanted, the present net effect is to increase the amount of carbon dioxide in the atmosphere.

Forests are an important source of biodiversity and they provide habitats for over 70 percent of land-living plants and animals. So, when they are cleared, the environmental damage can be serious. **Clear cutting** (ie, where all the trees are cut down) completely destroys local ecosystems and risks losing whole species. When a species of plant is lost there is a potential loss of pest or disease resistant genes that might prove useful in the future. Any medicinal drugs that might be developed from the plant are also lost.

When forests are cleared, the indigenous people lose their homes and way of life. The history of development in, for example, Amazonia and Irian Jaya (Indonesia) has been accompanied by the persecution of native tribes. Sometimes they are physically attacked by settlers and, in nearly all cases, they are decimated by contact with diseases such as measles or chicken pox. This is because they have not previously been exposed to these diseases and therefore they have not built up any immunity.

Forest Stewardship Council (FSC) In an effort to promote sustainable forestry, environmental groups have campaigned to stop clear cutting and to insist on the replanting of trees. The FSC is an international organisation, based in Mexico, which aims to persuade logging companies to adopt sustainable policies. It was founded in 1993 by environmental and human right campaigners, timber users and representatives of indigenous peoples. It 'certificates' woodland and forests that are managed in a sustainable fashion and it allows the timber extracted to carry the FSC logo.

In consuming countries people are urged only to buy FSC certificated timber. In the UK, B&Q were the first major retailer to commit themselves to stock only those timber products approved by the FSC. By 1998, four million hectares of forests had been certificated in countries such as Poland, the UK, the USA, South Africa and Papua New Guinea.

In 1998, the FSC approved the national standard for forest management in Sweden. In that country, concern about the depletion of forest resources had been raised as far back as the late nineteenth century. As a result of legislation to promote new planting, that country's forest stock has almost doubled in a hundred years.

In Europe and North America, growing public awareness of the issue has persuaded many logging companies to change their policies. Some have realised that there is a marketing advantage to be gained by claiming their products are 'environmentally friendly'. The independent certification provided by the FSC scheme is now widely regarded as the best means by which consumers can ensure that their purchases are truly 'green'.

Figure 4.43 A clear cut forest in Washington State, USA

Most environmental damage is caused when forests are clear cut. Soil erosion occurs and natural habitats disappear.

Activity   Clear cutting in British Columbia [BC]

British Columbia, in western Canada, has been the scene of a major dispute between environmental campaigners and logging companies. In the early 1990s the transnational company MacMillan Bloedel started clear cutting the original forest at Clayoquot Sound on Vancouver Island. Already, since 1950, two thirds of the island's forests had been cleared. Some of the trees were 1,000 years old, 100 metres in height and with a circumference of 20 metres. The trees form part of what is known as a 'temperate rainforest'. This rare ecosystem consists of giant conifers, such as red cedar, and now only exists in small areas of western Canada and the USA.

The forest forms the habitat for animals such as the cougar, black bear, wolf, elk and wolverine. After the trees are cleared, resulting soil erosion causes the salmon rivers to become silted and the discharge into the sea damages the feeding grounds of otters and whales.

In 1993, a combination of environmental groups and native Kyuoquot people started to protest against the logging. Greenpeace became involved and organised international pressure against the company and the British Columbia government. Campaigners hoped that the BC Government would protect the rain forest by legislation. Consumer boycotts were organised in many countries. Scott, the makers of Andrex tissues and Kimberley-Clark, the makers of Kleenex, both announced that they would no longer buy pulp from MacMillan Bloedel. Some retailers and local councils in Britain declared a boycott of products from clear cut Canadian forests. In a different form of protest, mass acts of civil disobedience at the logging site resulted in over 1,000 arrests as campaigners blocked access roads.

For a time, MacMillan Bloedel resisted the pressure. Because clear cutting is cheaper than selective logging, the rise in the costs of production would make the company less competitive. The logging company was supported by the provincial government which was concerned that jobs and tax revenues would be lost. Nevertheless, the consumer boycott eventually became too widespread to ignore and the company suspended operations at Clayoquot. In 1998, MacMillan Bloedel announced the formation of 'Ancient Forest Zones' in which there would be no more clear cutting of 'primary' forest. In the future it would concentrate its logging on 'secondary', replanted forests.

However, other logging companies continue to clear original rain forest in British Columbia. Protest activity has now shifted to the Great Bear Rainforest on the mainland. This contains most of the remaining pristine (ie, untouched) rainforest on Canada's west coast.

▲ Figure 4.44 'Primary' forest in British Columbia

Questions

1 What are the consequences, both positive and negative, that can arise from consumer boycotts of the forest products of particular companies?

2 What is sustainable forestry? Why is it seen as an important objective?

3 Outline the factors that will determine the rate of deforestation of the world's remaining original forest cover in the future.

3. Where and how are fishery resources exploited?

The total world harvest of fish and shellfish was 113 million tonnes in 1995. Of this, almost a fifth was produced by **aquaculture** (ie, in fish farms). Most of the output of the fishing industry, approximately 80 million tonnes, is used for direct human consumption. This provides around 15 percent of all animal protein consumed by the world's population. The remainder of the output is used for fish oil (used in processed foods) and for fishmeal (used as animal feed).

The FAO estimates that the number of people who make a living by fishing and fish farming has more than doubled in recent decades. From a total of 13 million in 1970, the figure rose to 30 million in 1995. Over 90 percent of these people live in south and east Asia.

'Capture' fishery production (ie, fish caught at sea as opposed to farmed) has been relatively static for more than a decade. The peak catches in the North Atlantic, for example, occurred in the 1970s. Since then there has been a decline. Because fish stocks have become depleted in most of the seas near populated regions, distant water fishing fleets have grown in importance.

Figure 4.45 shows that Asian countries catch or harvest more than a third of total production. The Pacific coast of South America is also an important fishing ground. Although fishing is locally important along European coasts, the combined EU catch only makes up approximately 7 percent of the world total.

Fishing methods

Although much small scale fishing is carried on by traditional means, using methods that have changed little over hundreds of years, modern systems are more efficient. For instance, sonar (an underwater tracking

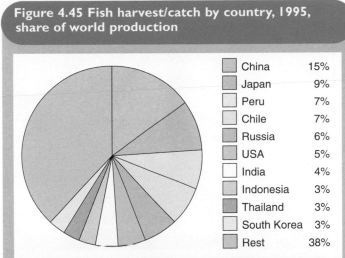

Figure 4.45 Fish harvest/catch by country, 1995, share of world production

China	15%	
Japan	9%	
Peru	7%	
Chile	7%	
Russia	6%	
USA	5%	
India	4%	
Indonesia	3%	
Thailand	3%	
South Korea	3%	
Rest	38%	

system) is so sophisticated that it can distinguish both the size and species of fish shoals. Fishing boats can now use satellites to pinpoint their position and to monitor weather patterns.

Large, modern boats can stay at sea for months at a time. These boats have a bigger range and storage capacity than older boats. They also have more efficient nets such as the 'purse seine' which can catch whole shoals of surface feeding fish such as mackerel. The boat drops one end of the net and then circles round a shoal, dropping more net. Once the circle is complete, the bottom of the net is drawn together, trapping the fish. Another form of net is the driftnet which can be several kilometres long. It traps everything in its path, including dolphins, whales and seals. Opponents of these nets have labelled them 'walls of death'. Under pressure from environmental campaigners, and some fishing communities concerned at overfishing, the EU has set a 2.5 kilometre limit on driftnets and has agreed to phase out their use completely in the Mediterranean and North East Atlantic by 2002.

Trawling is the method by which bottom feeding species, such as cod, are caught. The funnel shaped net is pulled along behind the boat. Weights are attached to the bottom of the net and floats are used to keep the 'mouth' open.

Resource management

It is widely accepted that fish resources have been over exploited in most seas and oceans of the world. Some fish species have virtually disappeared from what were once prosperous fishing grounds. The herring fisheries of the North Sea and the cod fishing grounds of the

Grand Banks, off Newfoundland, are now only folk memories. At the same time, fishing has become uneconomic for many fishing boat owners and fishing communities. The depletion of stocks, combined with the greater efficiency of modern fishing boats, has led to intense competition and rivalry between fishing communities and countries.

The United Nations, the FAO and the EU have all have recognised that there is a crisis in the fishing industry. The FAO has issued a Code of Conduct for sustainable fishing and has called for better fishery management. However, in most countries there is little effective control over fishing catches and, at the same time, some governments give subsidies to fishing fleets in an attempt to win votes in coastal areas.

In an effort to protect fish stocks, many countries have claimed 200 mile exclusion zones around their coastlines and they prohibit foreign fishing boats from entering the area. Iceland adopted such a policy in the 1960s. This started a 'cod war' with Britain whose long distance trawlers had traditionally fished in the Icelandic waters. Eventually the Icelanders won and the trawlers of Hull and Fleetwood withdrew. Now there are virtually no long distance fishing boats based in either of these ports.

European Union Common Fishery Policy For Britain, a 'go it alone' policy similar to that adopted by Iceland is not possible. On joining the EEC (now EU) in 1973, Britain agreed to abide by a Common Fishery Policy that included free access to fishing grounds for all member states. For this reason, fishery management has become an EU responsibility rather than a national responsibility, although it is left to individual countries to enforce the policy.

The basis of the EU policy is the establishment of fish quotas (for the main fish species) in the various fishing grounds. Based on expert evidence, the quotas are supposedly the maximum catches compatible with sustaining fish stocks. The quotas are then shared out between the EU members after a great deal of haggling and argument.

Within Britain, the quotas are allocated to the fishing fleets and each boat must have a licence to fish. Controversy has arisen because some British fishing boat owners have gone out of business and have sold their licences to Spanish boat owners. The catches by the Spanish owned boats are then counted as part of the British quota.

A further difficulty with the quota system is that it is relatively easy to 'cheat'. It appears to be common practice for some fishing boats to catch more than the quota allows and then quietly off load the fish at small, unregulated ports. Such catches are known as 'black fish'.

The Common Fishery Policy aims to decrease the number of fishing boats by paying compensation to boat owners who stop fishing. This policy has had some effect in terms of reducing the number of boats, but it has had little overall impact. The problem is that it is the smallest, oldest and least efficient boats that are generally taken out of service. If these are replaced by just a few modern boats, using high technology methods, the amount of fish caught rises rather than falls.

A third aspect of EU fishing policy is in regulating mesh and net sizes. Small mesh nets are banned because young and immature fish are caught. This obviously reduces the future potential catch. Only fish of a certain minimum size may be legally sold. However, this regulation has an unfortunate side effect. Small fish, and fish of the 'wrong' species that are caught, are simply thrown back into the sea. The FAO estimates, world-wide, that 20 million tonnes of fish are discarded in this way by commercial fishing boats each year.

Regulating and eventually banning driftnets is, as described previously, an EU policy. These nets have been mainly used for tuna fishing in the Bay of Biscay and the Mediterranean. Fishing boat owners in Cornwall, Ireland and France lobbied against the ban. They argued that their investment in new gear would be wasted and the

Figure 4.46 A Spanish fishing boat in the Mediterranean

The EU policy of compensating fishing boat owners for scrapping their boats has not cut the overall catch. Some of the older boats are simply replaced by bigger, more efficient boats.

already high unemployment in the depressed fishing ports would rise. Supporters of the ban claimed that up to 15,000 dolphins were being drowned each year in driftnets, as well as whales and sharks. Spain and most Spanish fishing boat owners also supported the ban. They mainly catch tuna by the old fashioned 'rod and line' technique and were concerned that the drift netters would soon destroy the fish stocks.

Activity | North Sea industrial fishing

It is estimated that over half the weight of fish caught in the North Sea is used for industrial processing. It is made into oil for margarine, biscuits and cakes, and the residue is used as fish meal to feed pigs, chickens and other livestock. Two thirds of the catch is sandeels. This is a small fish that forms a staple part of the diet of other species including cod, haddock, seals, dolphins, whales, and birds such as puffins. Despite being such an important part of the marine food chain there are no quotas or restrictions on the size of catch.

Over a quarter of the North Sea sandeel catch is processed at a single site, the '999 Plant' in Denmark. This modern plant is one of the largest industrial fish processors in the world.

'Wee Bankie'

This area of shallow sea off the Firth of Forth in eastern Scotland is an important fishing ground for sandeels. The fish shoal in great numbers in early summer attracting large numbers of sea birds (guillemots, kittiwakes, puffins, razorbills and gannets) and marine mammals (minke whales, porpoises and dolphins). The fish also attract industrial fishing trawlers from Denmark, Scotland, England and Norway.

Since 1996, environmental groups have lobbied the Government to ban industrial fishing in the North Sea. They claim that the trawlers 'hoover' the sea, and sea bed, of virtually all living creatures. The marine ecology is irreversibly damaged and other species, including marine mammals, are deprived of their food. In addition, it is claimed, the fishing is unsustainable and soon the sandeel stocks will disappear. This will not only stop the industrial fishing but it will harm the livelihood of other fishing communities. They catch fish such as cod and haddock that feed on the sandeels. Without the sandeels, these 'table' fish will also be lost.

As part of their campaign, the environmentalists have targeted the food companies that use processed fish products. By appealing to the companies and, possibly, because of the implicit threat of adverse publicity and a consumer boycott, the campaigners have persuaded Unilever, Sainsbury's and McVitie's to phase out their use of fish oil products.

**Figure 4.47 ▶
Puffins**

Sandeels form a vital part of the marine food chain. These seabirds rely on sandeels for their diet as do cod and haddock.

Questions

1 Outline the policy options for the EU in managing industrial fishing in the North Sea?
2 Discuss the advantages and disadvantages of each of these policy options.

unit summary

1 Non-energy minerals are subject to severe price fluctuations. Transnational corporations increasingly dominate world output and trade.
2 Open cast mining is much cheaper than deep mine production. The environmental costs associated with all types of mining can be high.
3 Forests are an important store of carbon dioxide, they are also a source of biodiversity and they provide habitats for humans and many animal species.
4 Most industrial wood and pulp is produced in the northern temperate coniferous forests but the fastest growth in output is from tropical plantations created from cleared rainforests.
5 The promotion of sustainable forestry in which trees are replanted and ecosystems are not irreversibly damaged is the aim of organisations such as the Forest Stewardship Council (FSC).
6 Fish are caught both for human and animal consumption. Overfishing and the depletion of fish stocks has caused static or falling catches in many areas. Approximately one fifth of world fishery output comes from fish farming or aquaculture.
7 Policies to conserve fish stocks in the EU include quotas on catches, controls on net and mesh sizes, and subsidies to fishing boat owners who leave the industry.

key terms

Aquaculture - fish farming, both inland and in coastal waters.
Commodities - agricultural products, timber and minerals that form the raw materials for other industries. Their prices are more volatile than manufactured goods.
Clear cutting - all the trees in an area are cut down and transported away. None are left to provide natural habitats or to bind the soil together.
Sustainable forestry - the use of forests in a way and at a rate that maintains their biodiversity, productivity and regenerative capacity.
Tailings - finely ground rock waste produced at mineral workings. Sometimes they contain toxic chemicals that can contaminate ground water or poison plants and animals.

CHAPTER 5 Manufacturing

Introduction

Britain was the first country in the world to industrialise and develop a large manufacturing sector. The rise in manufacturing output after 1750 was so great that the term Industrial Revolution was used to describe the change. During the nineteenth century, Britain was known as the 'workshop of the world' because it dominated large sectors of global manufacturing. However, since then, many other countries have industrialised and some have overtaken Britain in industrial production.

During this period of relative decline, the numbers working in British manufacturing have fallen while the numbers working in the service sector have grown. Today, approximately 17 million Britons are employed in services (eg, banking, retailing, tourism) compared with approximately 4 million in manufacturing. Nevertheless, the process of manufacturing remains a vital part of the British economy. The people who work in services rely on the manufacturing sector to provide them with goods such as processed food, clothing, vehicles and household articles.

Chapter summary

Unit 5.1 considers the main types of manufacturing and examines where they locate.
Unit 5.2 looks at deindustrialisation and investigates its causes and consequences.

Unit 5.1 Location of Manufacturing

key questions

1 What are the main types of manufacturing industry?
2 Which factors influence industrial location?
3 What factors have affected the global location of steelmaking?
4 How do models help explain where companies locate?

1. What are the main types of manufacturing industry?

Manufacturing literally means 'production by hand' but its modern usage includes production by machine. Before the Industrial Revolution most goods were produced manually in small workshops, or in people's homes. This type of manufacture is known as craft production or 'cottage industry'.

Then, in Britain during the 18th and 19th centuries, groups of workers were gathered together in factories. Output increased, with people specialising in different jobs within the factory system. The introduction of machinery by innovators such as Arkwright (water frame), Hargreaves (spinning jenny) and Watt (steam engine) enabled a further rapid rise in output. The use of machinery in production is known as **mechanisation**.

The resulting system was very profitable and enabled the **mass production** of textiles and other goods. Mass production can be defined as the large scale output of identical products. With the development of the moving assembly line, more goods could be mass produced. The process is today known as **Fordism**. It is named after the founder of the Ford Motor Company, Henry Ford, who set up the first large scale car assembly plant in Detroit in 1908. Large numbers of standardised products are now produced in this way.

Modern manufacturing industry is often highly **automated** (ie, the machines are electronically controlled). Robots and computer systems are used to mass produce consumer products such as motor cars, TVs, microwaves and dishwashers. However, older plants and outdated production systems still exist side-by-side with the new because of the high start-up cost of new manufacturing methods.

Assembly line production is now being transformed by new systems and methods of organisation. These modern techniques were first used in Japanese manufacturing plants. They require great flexibility, both from the workforce and the management. Team work, continuous improvement and quality control are essential aspects of the new production methods. The development of global production, marketing and competition is stimulating this

Figure 5.1 A car assembly line

Modern mass production has developed using assembly line techniques. The assembly lines are becoming increasingly automated. Japanese management ideas have changed the way that production line workers are organised.

rapid change and innovation. The new systems of manufacturing are sometimes described as **lean production** in order to emphasise their 'fitness' and efficiency. The term **post-Fordism** is also used to describe the new manufacturing methods.

Heavy and light industry

A distinction that is sometimes made by geographers is between 'heavy' and 'light' industry. Heavy industries are associated with bulky inputs of raw materials such as iron ore or petroleum, and bulky outputs, such as large machines, chemical fertiliser and ships. Heavy industries are traditionally based in large industrial plants. Their public image is one of noisy, dirty and relatively unpleasant working conditions.

Light industries, by contrast, have less bulky inputs and outputs. Examples of light industry include food processing, clothing manufacture and the production of electronic consumer goods. Light industry generally has a positive image because it offers a more pleasant working environment and produces less noise, smoke and dust than, say, a steel plant.

Vertical and horizontal integration in manufacturing

Throughout the twentieth century, the trend has been for manufacturing companies to increase in size. Sometimes they have become bigger by taking over or combining with other companies at the same stage of the production process. This is known as **horizontal integration**. Examples include the BMW takeover of Rover and the Nestle takeover of Rowntree.

When companies grow by merging with companies at different stages of production, the process is known as **vertical integration**. It might be 'forward' to the market or 'backward' to the raw materials. For example, if BP buys an oilfield, it is an example of backward integration. If BP buys a chain of petrol stations, it is an example of forward integration.

There are two main motives for companies growing in size and merging with others. The first is to increase market share and reduce competition. The second reason is to gain **economies of scale**. These are cost savings that can be made by increasing production levels. Examples include the savings that can be made by buying raw materials in bulk, or by using machinery to full capacity. Also, advertising and research costs can be spread across a higher volume of output, so reducing the unit cost. Another advantage that comes from larger size arises when companies need to raise funds for expansion. Banks and other financial institutions are more willing to lend money, at cheaper rates, to large companies than to small companies.

Activity) Motor vehicle production

Because of its mass sales and the large number of components which are required in a modern car, the motor vehicle industry has a key role in nearly all developed economies.

The first cars were made by skilled craft workers. They used hand tools to make a high quality product that could be modified to suit customer requirements. But, because skilled workers' wages are high and manual production is slow, this is a very expensive process. The system is now only used for luxury cars like Rolls Royce and for racing cars such as Ferrari.

Most motor vehicles are assembled on a moving production line. For 60 years after Henry Ford's first factory, the system was for unskilled and semi-skilled employees to perform a single task on the assembly line. For example, one worker might fasten the wheel nuts, another might fit the windscreen. In recent decades, robots have been used to perform the most repetitive and easily automated tasks such as welding. Robots are more accurate and reliable than people and they do not get tired or make mistakes.

Since the 1970s, lean production techniques have been adopted. These attempt to combine the best elements of craft production and mass production. Workers are organised in teams and they take responsibility for their own quality control. They are often 'multiskilled' and are expected to carry out simple maintenance and repair jobs as well as vehicle assembly. Just-in-time (JIT) procedures (where components are ordered and delivered when needed rather than kept in stock) are used to cut the cost of stockpiling components. This encourages a close working relationship between the car company and suppliers.

Toyota was one of the first companies to develop the lean production techniques but these are now spreading to most other producers. Success or failure in the car industry is closely related to the speed at which manufacturers can adopt the newest ideas. New plants tend to have an advantage over old plants because they can incorporate modern techniques. Just as importantly they can train a new workforce that has not become accustomed to older inefficient working practices.

An advantage of lean production is that cars can be 'mass customised'. This means that different models are constructed around the same basic frame while high volume output is maintained. Overall, the system is more efficient than traditional vehicle assembly and greatly improves quality. Generally there are improved relations with employees because they are encouraged to develop a team spirit and they have more varied tasks to perform.

	Plant	Country	Vehicles produced	
			Total	Per employee
Nissan	Sunderland	UK	289,000	105
VW	Navarra	Spain	311,000	76
Opel (General Motors)	Eisenach	Germany	174,000	76
Fiat	Melfi	Italy	383,000	73
Toyota	Burnaston	UK	172,000	72
SEAT	Martoreli	Spain	498,000	69
Renault	Douai	France	385,000	68
General Motors	Zaragoza	Spain	445,000	67
Renault	Valladolid	Spain	213,000	64
Honda	Swindon	UK	112,000	64
Ford	Dagenham	UK	250,000	61
Fiat	Mirafiori	Italy	416,000	61
Ford	Saarlouis	Germany	290,000	59
Ford	Valencia	Spain	296,000	58
Peugeot Citroen	Mulhouse	France	349,000	53
Vauxhall (General Motors)	Luton	UK	154,000	43
Skoda	Mlada Boleslav	Czech Rep.	287,000	35
VW	Wolfsburg	Germany	650,000	32
Rover	Longbridge	UK	281,000	30

▲ **Figure 5.2 Productivity of selected European car plants, 1998**

Opel in Eisenach

Eisenach, in former East Germany, is the site of Opel's newest car plant. It started full production in 1993 and, in the words of its management, 'it has used every Japanese trick in the book' to achieve high productivity levels. It takes just 18 hours to complete a car compared with over 30 hours at rival plants. Cars produced at Eisenach average 6 defects per vehicle compared with more than 20 at Vauxhall's Luton plant.

Everyone who works at the plant wears the same uniform. All are expected to perform a range of tasks and are organised in teams of six to eight. Virtually all routine maintenance is carried out by the production workers. Absenteeism averages 3 percent compared with 10 percent in most other German plants. All the assembly processes that can be automated are carried out by robots. The body work (ie, welding the car panels together) is 96 percent automated. By using just-in-time techniques the storage and workspace is half that in older plants. Two to three hour's worth of stocks are placed in boxes next to the production line and there are three day's worth in the warehouse. This compares with three week's worth at other Opel

Questions

1 Summarise the main points from figure 5.2.
2 Briefly outline the advantages of lean production to: a) manufacturers, b) employees and c) consumers.

2. Which factors influence industrial location?

There are many different factors that influence industrial location. In some cases, a single factor is dominant but, often, there is a combination of factors at work. The main factors are outlined in the section that follows.

Transport costs

The cost of transporting raw materials and finished products is an important consideration for some companies in deciding where to locate. In some cases, transports costs are minimised if production is near the source of raw materials. In other cases, transport costs are minimised if production is close to the market.

Nearness to raw materials Many heavy industries are located near their raw materials in order to minimise transport costs. The early iron and steel industry is an example. Large scale iron manufacture in Coalbrookdale, Shropshire, for instance, was heavily dependent on local supplies of iron ore, charcoal and then coal. Production had to be close to the raw materials because it was uneconomic to transport the ore and coal long distances until canals and railways were developed.

During the nineteenth century, iron and steel production in Britain mainly centred on coalfield locations in areas such as Central Scotland, South Wales, and the 'Black Country' of the West Midlands. However, as the century progressed, locational changes took place. In South Wales, for example, after 1870 the depletion of local iron ores caused a relocation down-valley from the coalfield to the coast. The coal was transported by rail to the coast, but the ore was brought in by ship.

This shift in location to the coast is now typical for large steel plants around the globe, with both coal and ore being brought in by bulk carriers. Transport costs now form a small proportion of the overall cost of finished steel. Relatively low shipping costs mean that raw materials can be purchased from anywhere in the world and sources can easily be switched if cheaper supplies become available.

In general, those industries that 'lose weight' in manufacturing are located near their raw materials in order to reduce transport costs. Paper and pulp mills are an example. The finished product, paper, weighs less

Figure 5.3 A coastal paper mill, Sweden

Many paper and pulp mills in Scandinavia have a coastal location near the source of their timber.

and is cheaper to transport than the raw material, timber. So, in Europe, for instance, there are large numbers of paper and pulp mills in Sweden and Finland, near the coniferous forests which supply their raw material.

A factor favouring coastal sites is that they are **break of bulk** locations. These are points at which bulky goods are unloaded from ships and reloaded onto smaller scale transport such as trains, lorries or barges. It is cheaper to process bulky materials at the point where they are unloaded from ships rather than reload them onto trains for processing at an inland location. It cuts down the number of times that the material has to be handled. This explains why flour mills and vegetable oil refineries are found at port locations such as Southampton.

Nearness to markets In general, light industries that produce consumer goods such as kitchen appliances or processed foods are located near their markets. This minimises their transport costs. For example, in Britain, a third of the population lives in the South East and any company selling to that market will reduce its transport costs by locating within that region.

One reason for the growth of high technology companies along the M4 corridor (see unit 2.4) is their nearness to Heathrow airport. These companies have world wide markets. They produce high value, low bulk products that are relatively inexpensive to send by air freight to customers. By locating near the airport, they minimise their transport costs.

Some products 'gain weight' in manufacturing. For example, in the brewing industry water is added to malted barley and hops. The volume and weight of the finished product, beer, is far greater than the volume and weight of the barley and hops. So, it costs less to brew the beer, at the market, and transport the hops and barley to the brewery rather than brew near the hop or cereal farms and transport the beer. In the nineteenth and early part of the twentieth centuries, there were large numbers of small breweries serving their local markets. The distance the beer could be transported was limited by the time it took for the beer to 'go off'.

Since the 1960s, changes in the brewing process have affected the location of breweries. The development of keg beers, which have a much longer shelf life than traditional beers, means that beer can be transported further. As a result, breweries have amalgamated and concentrated production in bigger, more efficient plants that are regionally or nationally based. In this way, they have gained economies of scale. Most small breweries which cannot achieve these savings have closed down.

Fuel supply

Certain processes require large amounts of energy and this influences their location. Aluminium smelting is an example. A big smelter needs as much electricity as a city of 500,000 people. Most aluminium companies site

Figure 5.4 The Rank Hovis flour mill at Southampton

Heavy industries such as refining and bulk processing are often found at dockside locations. These sites cut transport and handling costs and also make it easy for producers to purchase materials from different sources.

their plants near power stations from which they can buy relatively low cost electricity. So, for example, the biggest aluminium smelters in the world are located near hydro-electric plants (HEP) in Kitimat (British Columbia) and Alma (Quebec). In the UK there are smelters at Kinlochleven and Lochaber near Fort William with their own hydro-electric plants (see unit 10.3). When HEP is not used, aluminium smelters are still generally located near their power supplies. For instance, a smelter at Lynemouth in Northumberland uses local coal for its electricity generation.

Modern energy supplies for industry come mainly from electricity, gas or oil. These are widely available within most high income countries from a grid of pipelines or power lines. As a result, fuel supply has become an irrelevant locational factor for most industries unless they have particularly high energy needs. This is one reason why much of modern industry is **footloose**. In other words, it is not tied to one particular location but it can locate anywhere that is convenient for the owners and decision makers.

Labour supply

The availability and cost of labour can be a key factor in determining industrial location, though its importance varies from industry to industry. Some companies need to locate where there is a highly skilled or educated workforce. Others might prefer to locate where unskilled, low wage employees are available.

In clothing manufacture, it is extremely difficult to automate the sewing and garment assembly processes. These tasks are therefore mainly done by hand or with manually controlled machines. A large amount of labour is required relative to the amount of machinery or capital equipment that is used. In such 'labour intensive' industries, the cost of labour forms a high proportion of total costs. For this reason, basic and medium cost clothing is increasingly manufactured in low wage countries such as China, Vietnam, India or the Dominican Republic. More expensive designer garments are still made in First World countries with the higher labour costs being absorbed in the higher selling price.

Agglomeration economies

These are also sometimes known as 'external economies of scale'. They are the efficiency savings that can be made when companies locate near to each other. For example, transport costs were minimised in the early West Midlands car industry when component

manufacturers located in the same area. Windscreens, tyres and electrical components were all produced by companies within a short distance of the Coventry and Birmingham car plants.

Today, in the car industry, the situation is more complex because new Japanese plants have been built in non-traditional areas - North East England, Derbyshire and Swindon. To some extent these locations were deliberately chosen away from traditional car making areas because the managements wanted to train their work forces in new working methods. Nevertheless, in these areas, component manufacturers are becoming established and are developing close working relationships with the main manufacturing plants.

Some agglomeration economies arise because an area develops a pool of skilled labour that can be recruited by both new and existing companies. Silicon Valley, near San Francisco in California, the M4 corridor in England, and 'Silicon Glen' in Central Scotland are examples of where high technology companies have set up near each other. Not only can they share the same pool of labour, they can exchange ideas more easily when there is close physical proximity.

Decision makers

For many industries the decision where to locate is not clear cut. There might be a wide range of alternatives that are equally satisfactory and, as is stated earlier, many industries are footloose. They are not tied to a power source, raw material or particular market location. In these circumstances, the influence of the decision maker(s) in a company is crucial. Often it is the owner who makes the choice, and the decision might simply be made on the basis of personal preference of where to live. Henry Ford chose Detroit and for a time it became 'Motor City - USA'. Of course, he might have chosen a location in Hawaii, but it is unlikely that we would have ever heard of him in that case. Detroit was a good choice because it was close to iron and steel making plants and there was an experienced engineering workforce available. However, he might have chosen Cleveland or Chicago and either would probably have been as suitable as Detroit.

Efforts by local and national governments to attract businesses are often partly based on an appeal to the decision maker's personal preferences. For example, a pleasant rural environment, good golf courses, or successful schools are sometimes seen as factors which might sway the decision maker's choice.

Activity | High technology companies in the Cambridge area

Cambridge, in East Anglia, claims to be Europe's leading centre for high technology industry. Employment in this sector in 1998 was over 30,000 with more than 1,000 companies established in or near the city. The local council set up a Science Park as long ago as 1970 and, today, 'Silicon Fen' to the north of the city has attracted many of the world's leading information technology and biotechnology companies.

Sun Microsystems, Muscat and the European Research Lab of Microsoft are examples of IT companies that have been established there. Chiroscience, Peptide Therapeutics and Ethical Pharmaceuticals are amongst the biotechnology companies that are locally based.

The main reason for Cambridge's success in attracting the high-tech firms is the availability of a highly skilled and educated workforce, combined with links to university research departments. Many of the new ventures are 'spin-offs' from this academic work. Graduates and post-graduates provide a pool of labour that the companies can employ. Once the region became well known as a centre for high technology, a self-perpetuating momentum built up. Agglomeration economies arose as companies found it in their interests to locate near similar, related businesses. Not only can they share the same pool of labour, they can more easily share ideas and use each others' services as component manufacturers or sub-contractors.

The city of Cambridge has a number of secondary advantages that have helped its success. Its mediaeval core consists of beautiful buildings and its atmosphere is semi-rural and 'green'. These are significant factors for many of the new entrepreneurs, ie business venturers, who consider quality of life to be important issues in locational decision making.

The local council has supported the new industry, as has the University, and this has made it easier to obtain land and planning permission for development. Because the new industries require few raw materials, and the products are generally small and light, but of high value, existing transport links have proved adequate. London is less than two hours away by train and the M11 motorway provides a fast link to the South East.

▲ **Figure 5.5 Modern premises on a science park**

Questions

1 Outline the factors that might persuade a new high technology company to locate in a Cambridge science park.

2 Suggest which type of industries might not wish to locate in Cambridge.

Technological change

Changes in the way that products are made can be an important factor in determining location. In the nineteenth century, the most profitable location for steel production changed after innovations such as the Bessemer process and the Siemens-Martin (open-hearth) furnace became widespread. These reduced the coal input needed for steel making, so lessening the advantage of coalfield locations.

Technological innovation has also affected transport costs. Iron ore, from places such as Western Australia and Labrador in Canada, is often 'pelletised' before transport. This reduces bulk, and therefore transport costs, making it more economic to produce steel in consumer countries such as Japan, rather than in the ore producing countries.

Container transport and 'roll on - roll off' ferries have reduced transport costs to the extent that companies can treat the whole of Western Europe, including Britain and Ireland, as a single market. The Channel Tunnel has reinforced this trend. Before the roll on - roll off ferries were introduced, goods had to be unloaded by cranes from lorries or trains and placed in the holds of cargo ships. The process was time consuming, costly, and risked damage and pilferage.

Government policy

Government policy is an increasingly important influence in the location of industry (see unit 2.2 for details of these policies). Governments might choose to offer incentives for businesses to locate in regions with high rates of unemployment or low average incomes. Assisted Areas, designated by the UK government, and the EU's Objective One regions are locations where financial assistance is available. Individual cities and regions also attempt to attract inward investment by 'place marketing'. In other words they organise advertising and use slogans to convey a favourable image to industrialists who might wish to set up a new plant.

Capital

An important consideration for the owners and management of companies who are choosing a business location is the availability of capital, ie the money needed to finance the venture. Many financial institutions operate on a world-wide scale and there is rarely a problem in raising finance for a large transnational company with a proven track record. For smaller, less well known companies, raising capital can be difficult. It is in these circumstances that the decision makers might be especially swayed by offers of low interest loans, grants or low tax rates by particular national governments or regional development agencies.

Inertia

Sometimes the factors determining a location have changed but the plant remains because it is too costly to move. In such circumstances, the location is said to be caused by inertia. An example is the furniture industry in High Wycombe. This industry once relied primarily on local wood supplies as its raw material but now mainly uses wood that is bought in from elsewhere.

Globalisation

The growth of transnational corporations (TNCs) has had a marked effect on industrial location. The turnover of the biggest TNCs is greater than the national incomes of most countries. TNCs have the resources to switch production from country to country and they are often criticised for acting in their own interests rather than any particular national or regional interest. Clothing and footwear manufacturers such as Nike and Reebok operate on a world-wide scale rather than a national scale. They produce and buy from low cost producers in the Third World and market their goods mainly in the First World.

In the motor vehicle industry, a global market and production system have also developed. Ford and General Motors (from the USA), Toyota, Honda and Nissan (from Japan), Peugeot Citroen (from France) and BMW (from Germany) control the UK car industry. They decide where manufacturing plants are to be located and where to produce their models - in Britain or abroad. Their decisions are based on factors such as relative labour costs, financial incentives from national and local governments and on exchange rates (ie, the strength of the pound). One reason why Japanese car companies have located within the EU is to get round import restrictions that European countries have set up against them.

(The issue of globalisation is described in more detail in unit 2.4.)

Activity) Nike production

Manufacturing footwear is a labour intensive process so wage costs are a crucial factor in determining location. Although Nike, the world's biggest sports shoe company has its headquarters in the US, most of its products are made by sub-contractors in Asia.

It started production in Japan in early 1972, then switched to South Korea and Taiwan in 1975 and from 1987 began to expand rapidly in Thailand, China and Indonesia. Nike's choice of production location was based not just on labour costs but also on criteria such as political stability, staff quality and freedom from import and export duties.

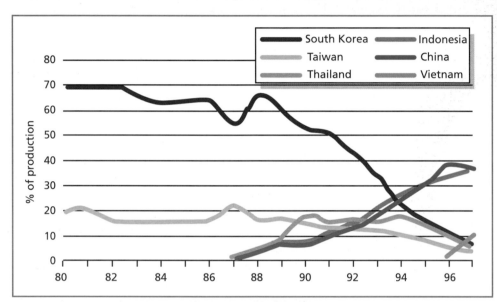

Figure 5.6 Nike trainer production in Asia, 1980 - 1997

Questions

1 Describe the changes in Nike production shown in Figure 5.6.
2 Suggest why production might have increased then decreased in Thailand.
3 What are the features of the footwear industry that enable it to move from country to country?
4 Which other industries might 'migrate' in the same way as footwear?

Site factors

Once a decision is made to set up a plant in a particular city or region, the precise location and plot of land must be chosen. At this point, local site factors become important.

Land Modern manufacturing plants often need a large flat site. This is to allow ease of access and turning space for lorries, and warehousing for components and finished goods. Large scale machinery and assembly lines also require a large floor space. For example, the Toyota plant in Derbyshire is on an old airfield that is over 200 hectares in size.

The cost and availability of land can also be an important factor. Generally speaking, land close to the centre of an urban area is more expensive than suburban and rural land.

Figure 5.7 New industrial units in Southampton

Local authorities often zone new industrial units in purpose built industrial parks. These premises are located near good communication links and away from residential areas.

In Britain, the need to obtain planning permission from a local authority also affects which land can be used. In most areas land is zoned for particular purposes. Industrial premises are increasingly located in business parks or on industrial estates that have been designated by local councils for industrial use. This is often suburban land, away from large residential areas and close to a good road network.

Planning regulations are used to ensure minimum environmental impact. Councils are very much aware of the 'NIMBY' factor (not in my back yard), and know that local residents will object to industrial premises that are noisy or generate traffic or fumes. This is another reason for the growing number of purpose built business parks.

Safety Sometimes safety considerations are important in siting decisions. A plant that produces toxic or hazardous substances is likely to be located away from a residential area. In First World countries, planning and zoning laws are generally strictly enforced to ensure that this is the case. In Third World countries, there might be no controls or they are less well enforced. As a result, plants are sometimes sited in unsafe locations. For instance, the Union Carbide factory disaster at Bhopal, India, in 1984, killed 2,000 and injured 200,000. The effect of the pesticide leak was made worse because the plant was located near high density housing.

In the UK, nuclear power stations and reprocessing plants are located in relatively isolated, mainly coastal locations because of safety fears. Nuclear industry supporters would say that the location is simply because the public perception of danger is high and there is no real hazard. Opponents of the industry might point to accidents at Windscale in Cumbria (now Sellafield), Three Mile Island in the USA and Chernobyl in the former USSR, and suggest that the public perception of risk is warranted.

Cooling and waste water disposal An additional factor that explains why industries such as nuclear power have coastal locations is the need to dispose of large quantities of hot water. The water comes from steam turbines which drive the generators. Similarly, for coal burning power stations, a river or coastal location meets the same need. For example, along the River Trent between Lincolnshire and Nottinghamshire, a series of large coal fuelled power stations discharge hot water into the river.

Transport links Most manufacturing plants need to transport raw materials and finished products. Nearness to motorway junctions, railway lines, airports or ports are therefore important factors.

Traffic congestion is sometimes a factor that influences a locational decision. In most urban areas in Britain, manufacturing industry has largely deserted inner city locations. This is partly because of the difficulty of access for large lorries, and the risk of being delayed by traffic jams. The printing of newspapers is an example. The traditional home of London newspapers was Fleet Street in the centre of the city. Most have now moved eastwards to larger and more accessible premises in Docklands. Throughout the country, the pattern has been the same with provincial newspapers moving from town centre sites to suburban locations on ring roads or beyond.

Activity | Perry Foods and Photronics

Food processing in Telford New Town

Telford is a New Town in the Midlands. It has been successful in attracting a wide range of companies which manufacture products ranging from automotive parts to plastic packaging. In 1998, Perry Foods, a company which processes foodstuffs, announced that it was locating its entire production at a new plant at Telford. There would be a workforce of 150 - 200.

The company chose Telford for a number of reasons. The town is linked by the M54 to the motorway network and has good rail connections to the rest of the West Midlands and London. There is a local workforce of 60,000 people and a potential 500,000 within 30 minutes drive.

Once the company had chosen Telford, it had to decide on a particular site. An important consideration for Perry Foods was the help it received from the Commission for New Towns (CNT) which had parcels of development land for sale. The company wanted to build a 1 hectare processing plant but also required extra land for future possible expansion. The CNT was able to offer a 4.9 hectare site, including 0.7 hectares of woodland, at a competitive price. The company liked the site because it was 'greenfield', ie there were no old buildings that

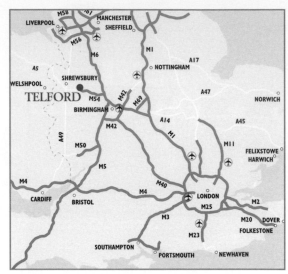

▲ **Figure 5.8 The location of Telford**

The Commission for New Towns promotes Telford by stressing its position on the motorway network.

would need to be demolished. This had the advantage of saving on building costs and also avoided the possible danger of contamination from old industrial premises. This was an important consideration for the food company. The site had good road transport links and was big enough to accommodate the plant, road turning space and parking. In addition, it had a 'green' and semi-rural atmosphere which made a pleasant working environment.

Adapted from the Commission for New Towns newsletter, summer 1998

Photronics' new factory in Manchester

Photronics is a US company that manufactures high value, precision components for the electronics industry. Many of its customers use just-in-time techniques and require deliveries at 24 hours' notice. The company is not able to supply the growing European market from its US base so needs a location in Europe.

The site that Photronics has chosen is in Manchester's Trafford Park Industrial Estate. It is two miles from the M60 motorway and 20 minute's drive from Manchester Airport. Local development agencies are providing £3 million in grant aid to the company and are clearing a pleasant two acre waterside site for the new factory.

Adapted from the Financial Times, July 16th 1998

Questions

1 Compare the needs of Photronics with the needs of Perry Foods in deciding a location for a new plant.
2 Suggest a rank order of factors that Perry Foods might have considered important when choosing its Telford site. Explain your reasons.

3. What factors have affected the global location of steelmaking?

World steel production spread from early industrialising countries to new producers as they became industrialised. First Britain, then the USA, Germany and the USSR became major producers as their economies developed. Today the biggest producers are in East Asia - China and Japan. China became the world's leading producer in 1996, with an output of 100 million tonnes.

As countries become richer and more developed, their industries' demand for steel rises. Because steel production is the basis of most engineering industry, including motor vehicle production, it provides a useful indicator of the manufacturing strength of different countries and regions. So, for instance, Japan produces over 13 percent of total world steel output compared with the whole of Africa and Latin America which together produce less than 10 percent.

When steel producers build new plants they tend to gain a cost advantage over older producers. This is because they are able to incorporate the latest and most efficient technologies. Often they integrate iron and steel production on one site. This saves energy that is otherwise wasted by allowing the iron to cool before transporting it to the steel mill. Most new production is at coastal or river locations to take advantage of imported ore and coal. These raw materials can be shipped by bulk carrier from wherever supplies are cheapest.

Unless old producers increase their efficiency they find that their steel cannot compete in price with the new plants and eventually they close down. Competition from new steel making areas has led to the closure of many small, inland plants in Europe and North America. Hundreds of thousands of steel jobs have been lost in Western Europe and in the USA. In 1980, British Steel employed 166,400 workers; by 1998 this had fallen to 39,000.

Steel production is sometimes regarded as a matter of national prestige and status. During the Communist period the governments of the USSR and Eastern Europe boosted steel output as a means of showing that their systems worked. But, since the collapse of communism, job losses have hit their steel making communities. The governments can no longer afford to subsidise the largely old and inefficient steel plants.

Within the steel industry, investment in research and development has led to the development of 'minimills'. These recycle scrap steel rather than make it directly from iron ore and coal. In the past two decades, US minimill capacity has increased seven times, to around 30 percent of total crude steel production. Minimills require much lower capital investment per tonne of capacity than conventional iron and steel plants. They are also more footloose than the big integrated plants in that they are less tied to supplies of raw materials. This is because the volume of scrap steel that a minimill uses as a raw material is much less than the volume of coal and iron ore that a conventional plant would use. In the USA, they have tended to locate closer to their markets, in new Southern 'sunbelt' (ie, new developing industrial areas) rather than North Eastern 'rustbelt' (ie, old, declining) locations. Over 40 percent of capacity is in 6 Southern states. Minimills only require an annual output of 1 - 2 million tonnes to gain maximum economies of scale compared to the 4 - 5 million tonnes required by traditional steel plants.

The development of minimills is an example of how the old established steel producers can compete with new producers. At one time, in the 1970s and 1980s it seemed that world steel production would switch completely to the Newly Industrialised Countries, particularly in Asia. But, during the 1990s, the steel companies of Western Europe and the USA have managed to maintain their market share (see figure 5.9).

Figure 5.9 World steel production by area

	1991	1997
	(% of total production)	
South and East Asia	33	39
Western Europe	23	22
North America	15	16
Former USSR and Eastern Europe	21	14
South America	4	5
Africa and Middle East	3	3
Australia and New Zealand	1	1
World total (million tonnes)	733	794

Activity | UK steel production

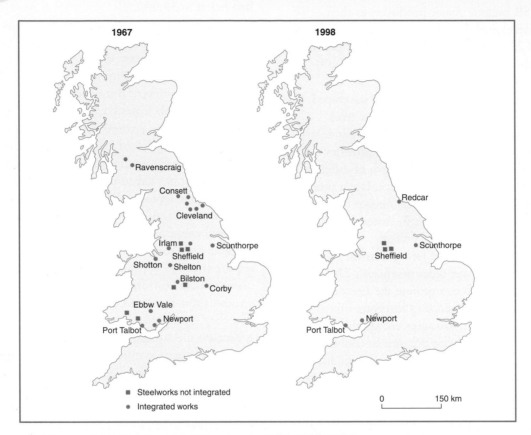

▲ **Figure 5.10 Steel production in the UK 1967/1998**

The example of British Steel in the 1980s and 1990s has been a model for many other countries. The company transformed itself from a loss-maker to a highly profitable and - according to some measures - the world's most efficient producer. In 1977 it produced 114 tonnes of steel per employee, by 1998 this had risen to 521 tonnes per employee. The company closed its older, less efficient plants and concentrated investment in just four locations.

Questions

1 Contrast the location of steelmaking in the UK in 1998 with that in 1967.
2 Suggest reasons for the changes between 1967 and 1998.
3 Make a list, in rank order, of the factors that you think would be most influential in choosing a location for a new steel minimill in Britain. Consider as wide a range of factors as possible in your answer and explain your choice of main factors.

4. How do models help explain where companies locate?

In an attempt to understand the complex nature of industrial location, a number of theoretical models have been developed. Two of the models are outlined below. These models were particularly influential in the 1960s and 1970s when geographers sought to analyse the location of particular industries in terms of the models' predictions.

Weber

An early model of industrial location was published by the economist Alfred Weber in 1909. He suggested that decision makers would take a 'least cost' approach to transport costs in their choice of location. Other factors, such as agglomeration economies or labour supply, would be less significant. His approach assumes that the cost of transporting raw materials and finished goods is the major influence in determining the location of a factory or industrial plant.

For an industry which 'loses weight' in the manufacturing process, such as steel production, the industry will be drawn to the raw material source. In other words, because the volume of raw materials (iron ore, coal and limestone) that are used in steelmaking is more than the volume of the finished steel, transport costs are minimised if production is located near the raw materials.

For an industry that 'gains weight' in production, such as brewing, the industry will be drawn towards the market. This is because the cost of transporting the bulky final product (beer) is higher than the cost of

Figure 5.11 Weber's locational triangle

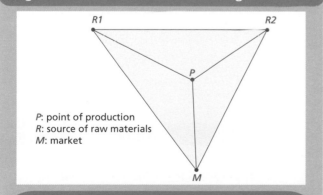

P: point of production
R: source of raw materials
M: market

The precise position of P depends on the relative costs of transporting the raw materials and finished product. If, for instance, the product 'gains weight' in processing, then P will be close to M. If, however, the product 'loses weight' in processing, then P will be closer to R1 or R2.

Figure 5.12 Spatial margins of profitability

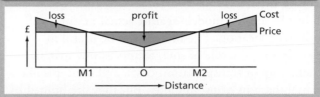

A company will maximise its profits at point O, and will make profits at any point between M1 and M2. In other versions of Smith's model, the price might vary over space (because demand is higher in some places than in others) and the costs remain constant, or both price and costs might vary.

transporting the raw materials (malted barley, hops and water). This is especially the case if one of the raw materials is ubiquitous (ie, found everywhere). Water is an example of a ubiquitous raw material. It costs very little to transport water to a brewery, especially if the water is piped from a well on site, but once the water is incorporated in the beer it is expensive to transport in barrels or tankers.

Weber's model can be illustrated by using a locational triangle, as shown in figure 5.11. It assumes that there is a single market location (M) and two raw material locations (R). The point of production (P) is the point in the triangle where the costs of transporting raw materials and the finished product are minimised.

Smith

The geographer David Smith reworked Weber's ideas in the 1960s using different assumptions. The main difference was that all the costs of production, and the revenue earned from selling the product, were now included in the calculations rather than just the transport costs. Smith's model is based on the the profit or loss that a company might make in different locations. When revenue from sales is greater than costs of production, a profit is made, and when revenue is less than costs, there is a loss. The model predicts that companies will choose an optimum (ie, best) location where profit (revenue less costs) is maximised.

One possible outcome is shown in figure 5.12 with an optimum location O and the **margins of profitability** M1 and M2. Profitable production can be at any location between these margins. In this example, the level of demand, and therefore price, is assumed to be the same everywhere. (It is said to be 'constant over space'.) However, costs of production vary because some locations have lower costs of transporting raw materials or perhaps, lower labour costs.

Criticisms of models

During the late 1960s and 1970s, attempts were made to test locational models against actual examples of industrial location. The models can be useful in highlighting the role of such factors as raw material availability or transportation costs, and concepts like spatial margins of profitability. But they are limited by their assumptions and they generally fail to explain actual location decisions.

Weber's approach has been criticised for treating the market as a single point whereas, in practice, markets are more likely to be whole regions or even bigger. Also, it is not likely that transport costs are the determining factor for many companies in choosing a location. Even if that was the case, it is not realistic to assume that these costs could be calculated accurately for every possible location. Although Smith takes more factors into account than Weber, his omission of issues such as planning permission and government regional policy limit the model's usefulness

One problem with the models is that they assume 'perfect knowledge' on the part of the decision makers. In other words, they assume that businesses have accurate and complete information on which to base a judgment. This is rarely the case. Often estimates have to be used in assessing, for example, the level of demand. Therefore, chance plays a part in whether the right location is selected.

Because it is clear that people's knowledge, perceptions and motivation are important in locational decision making, theories have been developed that take these factors into account. For example, one suggestion is that decision makers are not always optimisers seeking the best location. Instead, they might be **satisficers** willing to trade off some profitability to find a location that is satisfactory rather than perfect. And, in some cases, decisions might be based on personal preferences regarding where to live rather than on a profit and loss calculation.

Today, models are rarely used to explain the location of particular businesses. Instead, most geographers concerned with the study of business location prefer to examine the overall context in which industry operates. The role of government policies and global factors are seen to be crucial in understanding why plants locate in specific areas. In addition, the motivation of decision makers is recognised as being of key importance.

Activity — Location of sugar beet factories

The first British sugar beet factory was set up under Dutch management at Cantley, Norwich in 1912. At that time, sugar beet was not widely grown so local East Anglian farmers were asked to supply the crop. During the First World War (1914-1918) the UK price of sugar rose because of a shortage in continental and imported cane supplies. This led the newly formed British Sugar Beet Society to promote the establishment of a British owned industry. A plant was opened at Kelham, Nottinghamshire, operating as the Home Grown Sugar Company. Kelham was close to railways for transportation, and water supplies for use in processing. But the choice of Kelham seems a strange locational decision. It lies 170 km to the west of Norwich. Other locations were just as convenient for rail transport and water supply, and nearer to the main beet farming area in East Anglia. A key factor, however, was that the British Sugar Beet Society owned an agricultural estate in Kelham. Given favourable weather, the Society could guarantee supplies from its own land but, as it turned out, there were not sufficient other local growers to meet demand.

▲ **Figure 5.13 Land being prepared for sugar beet planting in East Anglia**

Location models suggest that processing plants for bulky agricultural raw materials such as sugar beet should be close to the farms where the crop is grown. They do not explain why two out of three of the first sugar beet refineries in England were built away from the main growing areas.

The Kelham factory was established in 1921. However, the plant was idle during the following year due to a sugar beet shortage! The plant had to be rescued by a takeover in 1923. In the meantime, another company, the Anglo-Scottish Group, was seeking a location for a new sugar processing plant. It also chose Nottinghamshire, mainly because the Home Grown Sugar Company was already there and therefore, Anglo-Scottish assumed, it must be a good location. Anglo-Scottish actually sited their plant 14 miles to the west of Kelham, even further away from the main areas of sugar beet farming.

Both the Nottinghamshire plants were unprofitable. Adding to their difficulties the world price of sugar had fallen sharply when French and German sugar beet output recovered after the First World War. In 1925, the UK government decided to subsidise production to safeguard domestic supplies and prevent bankruptcies. This state support encouraged new producers and, by 1928, there were 18 sugar beet factories. Most were located in East Anglia, near the areas of arable farmland where beet was grown. Because subsidies were clearly going to be needed in the long term, the whole industry was eventually reorganised into the partly government owned British Sugar Corporation in 1936.

Questions

1 With reference to sugar beet, explain why 'wrong' location decisions for manufacturing plants might sometimes be made.
2 To what extent do the Weber and Smith models help in explaining the location of sugar beet processing plants?

unit summary

1 Manufacturing processes have developed from craft production to mass production. Modern systems of lean production are changing the way that manufacturing is organised.
2 Location of manufacturing is influenced by a range of factors, including raw material availability, fuel supply, transportation costs, labour supply and technological change.
3 Factors such as state intervention, regional policy and globalisation are increasingly seen as important influences on business location.
4 Models of industrial location are based on either a 'least-cost' or a 'profit maximisation' approach. Behavioural factors affect the validity of such models. These factors are concerned with the motivation of decision makers and their less than perfect level of knowledge.

key terms

Agglomeration economies (or **external economies of scale**) - the savings that can be made by organising production near companies in the same industry. For example, costs can be reduced by sharing component suppliers or training facilities.
Automation - the use of computers or electronic systems to control mechanical

production.
Craft production - generally small scale, manual production by skilled workers.
Economies of scale - cost savings that can be made by expanding production, for example by bulk buying raw materials.
Footloose - a company that is not tied to a particular location.

Fordism - a term used to describe mass production based on a moving production or assembly line.

Heavy industry - manufacturing associated with bulk inputs of raw materials such as coal, iron ore and petroleum, and bulk outputs, such as steel plate or fertilisers.

Horizontal integration - the merger of companies at the same stage of production.

Light industry - manufacturing that does not use bulky inputs or produce bulky outputs.

Mass production - the large scale output of identical products.

Mechanisation - the use of machinery in the manufacturing process.

Post-Fordism - flexible manufacturing systems in which products can be 'mass customised', ie they are not all a standard design. Employees are set a greater range of tasks than on traditional

assembly lines, and there is often team working. The system emphasises continuous improvement of quality and productive efficiency. (It is also described as lean production.)

Satisficer - a decision maker who is prepared to accept a location that is satisfactory but not necessarily the best. It might simply take too long to work out the best location, or the information available might not be sufficient. A decision maker who tries to search out the best location is called an optimiser.

Spatial margins of profitability - geographical limits of profitability. Within the margins, a company can make a profit, outside the margins the company cannot.

Vertical integration - the merger of companies at different stages of production, eg forward to the market or backward to the raw materials.

Unit 5.2 Deindustrialisation

key questions

1 What is deindustrialisation?
2 What causes deindustrialisation?
3 What are the consequences of deindustrialisation?
4 Can reindustrialisation occur?

1. What is deindustrialisation?

Deindustrialisation is the decline in the manufacturing sector of an economy. It is defined in two slightly different ways. Some economists state that it involves an absolute decline in manufacturing output. Others suggest that it is a relative decline. In other words, manufacturing output is growing, but not as fast as the service sector. It is generally agreed that deindustrialisation is accompanied by a fall in manufacturing employment.

It is in First World countries that most job losses in manufacturing have occurred. Studies in these developed countries appear to show that there is a maximum level of manufacturing employment reached during industrialisation. This threshold varies but is generally between 25 and 35 percent of civilian employment. After that level is reached, the percentage begins to decline.

Figure 5.14 An old manufacturing plant being demolished in Manchester

Deindustrialisation is the decline in the manufacturing sector. It is accompanied by a fall in manufacturing employment.

Figure 5.15 Percentage of the workforce in sectors of employment for selected First World countries, 1910-1996

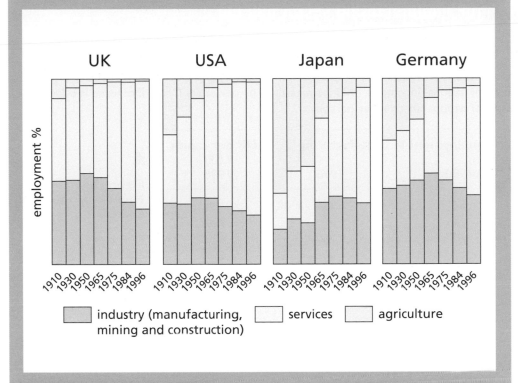

Source: World Bank. Note that the definition of 'industry' used here includes mining and construction as well as manufacturing. The data for 1950-1984 refers to West Germany only.

Economic maturity When deindustrialisation was first noted as a trend, it was suggested that the process was caused by economic maturity. In other words, it occurs when a country is fully developed and has reached a high income level.

Figure 5.15 shows how this process can operate. During the industrialisation phase of development, manufacturing employment rises at the expense of agricultural employment. Then a peak, or threshold, level of manufacturing employment is reached beyond which further growth does not occur. At this stage, the service sector begins to expand - at the expense of manufacturing. This is because, in a mature economy, average incomes are high. People have money to spare after they have bought the basics - food, shelter and clothing. So, they begin to spend a bigger proportion of their income on services. Services include leisure and tourism, financial services, health care, education, and personal services such as hairdressing and beauty care. As demand for these services grows, so does the employment in this sector.

The idea that an economy reaches a state of maturity helps to explain why Britain started to deindustrialise before other countries. Because it was the first country to industrialise, it was the first to deindustrialise. However, this explanation does not explain why countries which industrialised later, for example Canada and Australia, should have begun deindustrialising as early as the 1960s. The maturity explanation has also been criticised because it implies that nothing can be done to reverse the trend - that it is an inevitable process. This is by no means certain - as the regeneration of the UK car industry, albeit under foreign control, appears to show.

Figure 5.15 shows changes over the period from 1910 to 1996 in selected First World economies. In the UK and USA, the percentage working in manufacturing began to fall from the late 1950s. In (West) Germany and Japan the decline did not begin until the 1970s. During the 1990s, the loss of manufacturing employment continued in all four countries.

2. What causes deindustrialisation?

The causes of deindustrialisation are complex and there is no general agreement on why it occurs. Explanations can broadly be divided into traditional views and new explanations.

Traditional explanations

The traditional explanations of deindustrialisation involve ideas of economic maturity, economic failure and also of financial failure.

Activity | **The manufacturing sector and GDP**

The table shows the proportion of the labour force employed in manufacturing (including construction) in 1980 and 1990, and the level of national income in 1988 (as measured by per capita Gross Domestic Product). Per capita GDP is a measure of national income per person.

Country	Employment in manufacturing %		GDP per capita (US$)
	1980	1990	1988
India	13	16	340
Dominican Republic	24	29	720
Morocco	20	25	830
Honduras	15	20	860
Mexico	29	24	1,760
Poland	38	36	1,860
Greece	29	27	4,800
Spain	37	33	7,740
Singapore	42	36	9,070
France	35	29	16,090

Figure 5.16 Manufacturing and GDP

Questions

1 What is the relationship between the change in manufacturing employment and per capita GDP as shown in the data?

2 To what extent does the data support the view that economies begin to deindustrialise when they have reached a certain level of economic development? What other information would be useful in answering this question?

Economic failure A second explanation for deindustrialisation is centred on the notion of economic failure. In the 1980s, this became a popular idea. In Britain and in other countries, it was stated, manufacturing companies had became complacent. They took too much profit and did not invest sufficiently in new equipment. UK industry failed to continue exporting sufficiently, perhaps because of poor management and a lack of marketing expertise. Unlike companies in Japan, for example, which seemed to have the attitude 'export or die', UK companies seemed unable to remain competitive.

In the UK there was also what became known as 'the British disease' of poor labour relations. There were many strikes, not just over wages, but also over working conditions, and then over the redundancies which deindustrialisation brought. Some suggested that these conflicts were partly the result of the British class system. The company directors and management, largely educated in public schools, had no understanding of the working classes, and those educated in the state schools similarly had no understanding of the employers' attitudes.

Financial failure Another theory that aims to explain the severity of deindustrialisation in Britain relates to the financing of industry. In this view, British finance has operated for the benefit of the City of London and the financial sector rather than for the benefit of the manufacturing industry. British banks, it is said, have for over a hundred years failed to invest in industry, unlike their competitors in Germany or Japan. Evidence for this view comes from the contrasting fortunes of British and Japanese car companies at the time of the 1973 'oil shock'. This was a big oil price rise that caused an economic crisis in the world economy and, for a time, cut the demand for new cars. British banks refused to provide a loan of $1.2 billion requested by British Leyland. However, in Japan, the Sumitomo Bank which was already an investor in Mazda, actually increased its loans to the company by $1.5 billion. It also invested in a new range of cars. British Leyland became virtually bankrupt and was eventually rescued by the British Government, but job losses were high. Production fell, and in 1994, as Rover, it was sold to the German car maker, BMW. While British Leyland's production halved between 1973-83, Mazda's increased by two-thirds.

Like other explanations based on the failure of industry, the idea that financial institutions are to blame for deindustrialisation might be true for some manufacturing industries. However, it does not explain why manufacturing employment has also, more recently, fallen in Germany and Japan. Nor does it explain why motor vehicle output in Britain has increased in the 1990s.

New explanations

Because of weaknesses in the traditional explanations of deindustrialisation, other ideas have been developed. These focus on globalisation (ie, the development of a global economy - see unit 2.4) and the 'New International Division of Labour' (NIDL).

Globalisation In one view, it is the activities of transnational corporations (TNCs) that are at least partly responsible for deindustrialsation. In Western Europe and the USA, less successful manufacturing plants are being closed as production is moved abroad. This is especially the case for branch factories. These foreign owned subsidiaries of TNCs are particularly vulnerable if the company wishes to cut costs. Because so much of world manufacturing output is controlled by TNCs such as Sony, Ford and Siemens, they are in a powerful position to switch production from one country to another.

New International Division of Labour (NIDL) The concept of NIDL was developed in France during the late 1960s and gained acceptance within the English-speaking world during the 1980s. The idea is that the traditional international division of labour (manufacturing employment in the First World, agricultural employment in the Third World) is being replaced by a new pattern. In the new international division of labour, low skilled, manual work is being transferred from the First to the Third World in order to take advantage of plentiful labour and low wages. This explains why TNCs are investing overseas, particularly in low income countries, whilst simultaneously closing plants in high income countries. In this view, the success of the Newly Industrialising Countries (NICs) such as Hong Kong and Taiwan (see unit 2.2) is partly based on this process. A development of the NIDL idea is the so called 'Newer-IDL'. Companies that are based in the NICs are now investors in other countries of south and east Asia. They are losing their lower skilled, manual jobs to economies such as Bangladesh and China. An example of this is given in figure 5.6. It shows the decline in production of Nike trainers in South Korea, which is a successful NIC, and the increase in production in China where wages are much lower.

Activity   UK deindustrialisation

The decline in UK manufacturing employment gathered pace during the 1970s. Research into 30 UK manufacturing companies during the period 1975-83 showed that they cut their UK workforce by 422,000. At the same time, these same companies increased their overseas employment by 163,000. This migration of jobs overseas occurred at a time when the overall total of manufacturing jobs was also in decline. Between 1975 and 1983, overall manufacturing employment in the UK fell from 7.3 million to 5.4 million.

▼ Figure 5.17 Employment changes in 8 selected UK companies, 1975-83

Company	Sector of industry	% Employment Change		UK job losses
		Home	Overseas	
BIC Cables	Engineering	-19	+30	7,120
International Computers	Electrical engineering	-30	+53	7,007
Rank, Hovis, McDougall	Foodstuffs	-24	+11	3,567
Pilkington	Glass	-21	+29	6,501
Tootal	Textiles	-45	+28	8,818
Turner & Newall	Engineering	-21	+12	4,269
British Leyland	Motor vehicles	-51	+34	83,754
Imperial Group	Food and tobacco	-5	+463	4,728

Questions

1 With reference to the data in the table, explain what is meant by the term 'deindustrialisation'.
2 Suggest possible reasons for the UK job losses shown in the table.

3. What are the consequences of deindustrialisation?

Deindustrialisation can be a painful process for people who lose their jobs. Whole communities can be affected, especially if they are reliant on one major employer or if the region has specialised in manufacturing. Areas like Merseyside and South Yorkshire in Britain, the Ruhr in Germany and the industrial states of Illinois, Indiana, Ohio, Michigan, and Wisconsin in the United States have all suffered from deindustrialisation. Although some badly hit areas in the UK are beginning to revive, even reindustrialise, the new industries and the new jobs rarely require the skills and abilities of the old. Deindustrialisation therefore poses tremendous challenges, for families, communities and policy-makers alike.

Impact on individuals

An estimated 4 million people have lost their manufacturing jobs in the UK since 1970. In the USA, in just one decade between 1970 and 1980, more than 30 million jobs were lost in US manufacturing industry. Unskilled and semi-skilled 'blue collar' workers were especially vulnerable, although now white collar support staff are just as likely to lose their jobs.

People who lose their role of 'breadwinner' often suffer a severe loss of self-esteem. Redundancy payments might at first seem quite adequate, but are rarely enough to replace not just the work but the companionship which the factory or workshop offer.

In many cases, even the jobs that are left have shifted location. In the steel industry of the USA, studies show that few workers from the massive plants that have closed in Illinois, Ohio and Pennsylvania found jobs in the new minimills of Colorado, New Mexico or Utah. Workers who were once highly paid have found themselves 'skidding downwards' into piecemeal employment in machine repair shops or as attendants in petrol stations. For those who are middle-aged, the prospect of never working again is very real.

Figure 5.18 A blue collar worker in heavy engineering

Deindustrialisation is a painful process for workers who have spent all their lives in traditional heavy industries. They might have to retrain and move to a different place in order to get a new job. Many take early retirement because they cannot find new employment.

There is some evidence to suggest that manufacturing has been 'defeminised' during deindustrialisation, ie a bigger proportion of women have lost their jobs than men. The concern to protect male jobs, by male dominated management and trade unions, has often meant that female jobs have been cut first. From 1979-1997, for example, there was a bigger percentage fall in female employment in UK manufacturing than in male employment.

Given that divorce rates are on the increase, and that many one parent families have the mother as breadwinner, the impact of redundancy has had a severe impact on some of the poorest groups in society.

In some parts of Britain, job losses in manufacturing have been matched by a rise in the service sector (see unit 6.1). However, the service sector tends to offer more part-time and casual work than manufacturing. Job insecurity has risen because increasing numbers of

people are employed on short term contracts. Also, there has been a rise in 'flexible working' in the service sector which involves working shifts or at weekends. This is particularly true of retailing where shops are often open for 12 hours per day or more, and are also open on Sundays. The outcome is that the regular 40/40 pattern (40 hours of work per week for 40 years) that was typical for many workers in industry is now largely a thing of the past.

Impact on communities

Because manufacturing industry has tended to cluster in particular regions, deindustrialisation has had a wider impact than simply on individuals or companies. The effect on some communities has been severe.

The former steel centres of Gary, Indiana, and Magnitogorsk, Russia, provide typical examples. A 1997 study of Gary highlighted the problems of poverty and social breakdown which can come to a community which is over-reliant on a single industry. The report noted that the city had the highest murder rate of all US cities. Although the problems of Magnitogorsk have not reached that level of violence, the issues are similar. The city of 430,000 became famous in World War Two for its production of tanks which helped stop the German invasion. It was a 'city of heroes', known as 'Miraculous Magnitka'. But the collapse of communism in the Soviet system left the steel industry to compete with the modern plants of overseas competitors. The transition to the capitalist system has been painful, as it has been elsewhere in Eastern Europe. Now the city is seen as a 'city of social victims', with high unemployment and high inequalities of income.

Labour mobility

Another result of deindustrialisation is population movement. In the 1980s, a Conservative minister, Norman Tebbit, called on people to 'get on their bikes' and find work - as his father had done in the 1930s.

This was much criticised at the time because it seemed to blame the unemployed for their plight, rather than the process of factory closure. In reality, people who have a house to sell in a depressed area, and whose family are settled, find it very difficult to move - even if suitable jobs are available. Tenants who live in council houses find it even harder to move because they go to the bottom of the housing list in their new area. Nevertheless, many people have moved in an effort to find employment. Since 1981, there has been a net inflow into South East England of 400,000. Many of the people who moved were young, free of family ties, and relatively well educated.

The loss of population in regions hard-hit by deindustrialisation can lead to a further loss of wealth and social stability, contributing to the general air of gloom, dereliction and decay. The negative image in turn makes it more difficult to attract new employers. Demand for local goods and services falls, and there is a vicious circle of decline as those who can move do so.

The main destination for those who move, the South and East of England has become an expensive and more congested region in which to live. Places like Cambridge and the M4 corridor have attracted inward investment with their high-tech image. But fast economic development in the region has contributed to overheating of the British economy. Labour shortages and rising house prices have fuelled inflation - causing successive governments to put the brakes on the national economy. This has made it doubly difficult for peripheral regions to cope with the deindustrialisation process. These areas typically have only just started to recover from recession when the next economic downturn occurs.

Future trends

Despite efforts to slow the process, deindustrialisation continues in First World countries. Between 1970 and 1999, the numbers employed in UK manufacturing halved from approximately 8 million to 4 million. There is no reason to expect that this trend will not continue.

In labour intensive processes, where labour costs are high, production is likely to relocate to the Third World. In other industries, machines will be used to replace people wherever possible. A positive aspect is that this helps people avoid drudgery and dirty work. Also, the environment will be improved by ending the old 'smokestack' industries. It is even possible that manufacturing output will not fall. Production will be concentrated in automated plants that use modern management techniques and employ a relatively small number of highly skilled people.

The pain of deindustrialisation depends upon the the speed and scale of job losses and how well the process is managed by governments and industry. Deindustrialisation is set to spread further around the globe. Some analysts already refer to the NDCs rather than NICs - 'Newly Deindustrialising Countries' rather than 'Newly Industrialising Countries'. It seems only a matter of time before other places and other communities will have to come to terms with the end of the manufacturing phase of industrialisation.

Figure 5.19 A new housing development near the M4

House price inflation and labour shortages in the South East can create problems in less prosperous regions if the government is forced to raise taxes and interest rates.

4. Can reindustrialisation occur?

For the reasons already outlined, it seems likely that manufacturing employment in Britain and other high income countries will continue to fall. However, in some places, there are attempts to slow the trend and to maintain a manufacturing base. Often this involves 'leaner and fitter' companies. They employ fewer people yet retain high levels of output by using automated production systems. In many instances the type of manufacturing changes - away from 'metal bashing' and other low productivity activities to high-tech, 'knowledge based' activities. It is by concentrating on this type of production that some places are managing to reindustrialise.

Efforts to reverse deindustrialisation

It can take decades for a community to recover from the social and economic impact of factory closures. Sometimes assistance comes from foreign investment. In South Wales, for example, Japanese electronics investment helped ensure that manufacturing employment in 1991 was equal to that in 1981. By 1998, one third of Welsh manufacturing workers were employed by foreign owned companies. Over £11 billion of investment had taken place by Japanese, South Korean, Taiwanese, American and European companies. Their output ranges from televisions to pharmaceuticals and computer components. The impact of these companies has been to create a 'multiplier' effect in the local economy because new suppliers, sub-contractors and service providers were all needed and these, in turn, created new jobs. Similarly, Japanese investment in steel and automobile plants has been important in the American Midwest and northeastern 'rustbelt'.

In part, this investment is encouraged by government regional policy (see unit 2.2). Government incentives can mean the difference between attracting foreign investment or losing it to other areas, including those overseas. Provided that the incentives do not outweigh the benefits from the investment, this is accepted as a sensible policy.

Activity Reindustrialisation in Wales and the North East

Port Talbot
Port Talbot in South Wales lost 8,000 jobs from its steel plant by early 1996. The numbers employed fell from 12,000 to 4,000 Likewise, BP Chemicals closed part of its plant in 1994, with the loss of 600 jobs in total. In an attempt to regenerate its manufacturing base, Port Talbot launched a £230 million regeneration plan to become the 'green industrial town of Europe'. This was centred on a 650 acre 'energy park', on land owned by BP Chemicals and the council. The longer-term target was to attract 3,000 new jobs, and ensure that planned South Korean and Japanese investment would have a multiplier effect within the region. £71 million of the regeneration money is from the public sector, including £39 million on a new road to the docks. Environmental improvement is to be a key element, including brightening up the town centre, improving shopping facilities and reviving the old sea front area of Aberafon. The local council realise that a clean environment and new image are essential parts of the job creation process.

Consett
Consett in County Durham is an example of a place where revival has already occurred. It too, like Port Talbot, was dependent on steel and the British Steel plant employed 7,500 people in the 1970s. By 1980 this was down to 3,500, and the plant closed completely in 1982. The town of 30,000 people had an unemployment rate of 28 percent.

Regeneration funds came from such sources as British Steel itself, the UK government, the European Coal and Steel Community Fund and from the private sector Derwentside Industrial Development Agency. Instead of concentrating on attracting private foreign investment, a 'bottom-up' strategy was developed, with local people encouraged to start new businesses. Landscaping and environmental improvements were carried out, factory premises were built by the government-owned English Estates, and business parks were established by 1985. Ten years later, 180 companies had made investments. Of these, 98 were new local start-ups, 51 were expansions of previous companies and only 31 were inward investments. By 1995, over 5,000 people were employed in Consett, more than before the closures, although not as many as in the heyday of the 1970s. Successful start-ups included Derwent Valley Foods (Phineas Fogg snacks), Pure-Plas (packaging milk in plastic bottles), Penlea Plastics (thermo-formed food packaging) and Integrated Micro Products (high performance computer systems). Now Consett is developing 'Genesis', the renaissance of 750 acres on the old steel site with 400 acres for leisure activities and 350 acres for business parks.

Figure 5.20 The old steelworks in Consett

This plant closed in 1982. When traditional industries such as steelmaking close it requires a big investment in infrastructure to create a modern image that will attract new companies.

Questions

1 Outline the consequences for a community when its major industrial employers close down or 'downsize' (ie, cut the numbers employed).
2 Suggest ways in which manufacturing industry can be regenerated.
3 Describe the difficulties faced by towns such as Consett in regenerating its manufacturing base.

unit summary

1 Deindustrialisation is the decline of the industrial sector of an economy. It began in the 1950s in some countries but has speeded up in recent decades.

2 Different ideas are put forward to explain deindustrialisation. Many believe that it reflects the shift in manufacturing employment from older industrial centres in high income economies such as Britain or the USA to new locations such as South East Asia. A 'New International Division of Labour' is thus created. Investment by TNCs is a key element in this process. It now seems that even those Newly Industrialising Countries which received this investment are beginning to be affected by deindustrialisation.

3 Deindustrialisation has a dramatic and severe impact on those communities which suffer factory closures. It can take decades for the affected localities to recover. The new jobs usually do not require the same skills and labour force as the old.

4 Reindustrialisation is possible in some cases, but must be supported by government, by industry and by local people to ensure success.

key terms

Branch factories - foreign subsidiaries of TNCs which are especially vulnerable to closures and job losses when the TNC wishes to cut costs.
Deindustrialisation - a decline in the industrial sector of an economy, generally involving a decline in manufacturing employment.

New International Division of Labour (NIDL) - the shift of manufacturing jobs from traditional First World centres to overseas locations where labour costs are lower.
Reindustrialisation - the revival of industrial growth in an economy.

Introduction

Tertiary production is the fastest growing and largest sector of the UK economy. Unlike the primary and secondary sectors which produce goods, the tertiary sector produces services. In most high income countries the tertiary sector has overtaken the secondary (ie, manufacturing) sector in importance - both in terms of value of output and of numbers employed.

Chapter summary

Unit 6.1 considers changes in the service sector and examines the reasons for these changes.
Unit 6.2 looks at the pattern of UK and world trade.
Unit 6.3 describes the growth and impact of the leisure and tourism industry.

Unit 6.1 Changes in the service sector

key questions

1 What is the service sector?
2 What has caused the growth of the service sector?
3 What are the changing patterns of retailing?
4 What is the impact of new technology - the 'quaternary' sector?
5 What are the recent trends in transport services?

1. What is the service sector?

The service sector includes finance (eg, banking and insurance); retailing; leisure and tourism; personal services (eg, hairdressing); transport; and public services (eg, police, health care and education). Services are provided both by private companies and the **public sector**. The latter consists of local and national government, and corporations owned by the government (such as the Post Office and the BBC).

Solicitors, accountants and similar professions are sometimes known as **producer services**. This is because they provide, in part, specialist services for other firms and institutions. Many of their employees are highly skilled and have well paid jobs. Services such as retailing, education, health and transport are called **consumer services** because they deal more directly with the public. In general, they employ lower paid workers than the producer services.

Most of the jobs in the service sector are **white collar** as opposed to **blue collar**. The terms white and blue collar come from people's traditional work clothes. Manual labourers often need to wear overalls whereas most non-manual workers do not need to wear protective clothing.

2. What has caused the growth of the service sector?

Within the UK, the service sector employed just over 75 percent of the working population in 1998. This had grown from 55 percent in 1974. Similar trends have occurred in other countries. For example, in France, the proportion working in the service sector rose from 50 to 70 percent over the same period. The trend appears to be a normal aspect of industrial and economic development.

The size of the service sector in the UK is slightly bigger than in most comparable countries. For example, in 1998 the proportion of the workforce in services in the USA was 73 percent, in Sweden 71 percent, in Japan 61 percent and in Germany 60 percent.

The growth of the service sector in the UK has occurred for three main reasons. Firstly there has been a rise in the demand for services; secondly, there has been a decrease in employment in the agricultural and manufacturing sectors; thirdly there have been social, political and economic changes which have had an effect. These reasons are outlined in more detail on the next page.

Figure 6.1 The service sector: catering

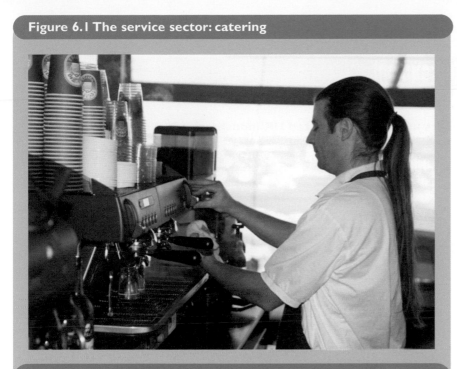

Approximately 75 percent of UK employees work in the service sector.

controlled by computers. Although this reduces the demand for manual workers, it increases the demand for IT specialists. Many of these people are employed in service sector companies that do work for manufacturing companies.

The rise in tertiary employment has also been caused by a change in the way that some companies are organised. In an effort to concentrate on their main activity, many manufacturing firms have subcontracted work such as cleaning and catering to outside companies. These tasks would have previously been done by the company itself. This has meant that the numbers employed by manufacturing firms have gone down, whilst the numbers employed by service sector companies have risen (even though the total number of employees may not have changed).

Rising demand

Higher disposable incomes (ie, incomes after tax and national insurance) have increased the demand for services - particularly since the 1950s. Most people now have money to spare after they have paid for their basic needs. According to official UK statistics, the average family spends just 40 percent of its total spending on food, housing, fuel and clothes. This means that they have 60 percent to spend on non-basic items. Rising affluence has increased people's expectations, for example in their demand for services such as meals out, for entertainment, or for higher education. Longer paid holidays and shorter working hours have raised the demand for leisure and tourist services (see unit 6.3), and for retailing which is now often seen as a leisure activity.

Decline in primary and secondary sectors

In the primary sector, many jobs have been lost in farming and mining. In the secondary sector, deindustrialisation (ie, the decline of manufacturing - see unit 5.2) has also led to the loss of many jobs. These changes have released people to work in the service sector, particularly in the more prosperous regions of Britain where the demand for services has increased most strongly.

One reason why employment in manufacturing has fallen is that machines are becoming automated and

Political, social and demographic change

Changing demographic patterns have had an impact on the demand for services. Partly, this has been due to an ageing population (see unit 1.5). Rising numbers of pensioners have created a demand for social services and health care. As a result, there is an increased need for home helps and staff in nursing and rest homes. This trend has been reinforced by changes within the family. Higher divorce rates and the rising proportion of women in paid employment have made it less easy for families to look after ageing people in the family home. At the same time, greater mobility within families means that fewer adults live near to their parents. This has caused a rise in demand for paid child care and nursery provision.

The financial services industry has grown, to some extent, because of political and social changes. For example, the political decision to privatise public sector businesses such as British Gas and British Telecom in the 1980s and 1990s led to an increase in the number of private individuals who own shares. There has also been a big rise in the number of people who have started private pension plans rather than relying on the state pension. Both these factors have increased the demand for financial advisers and companies who can handle transactions in shares and other forms of saving.

Activity) UK employment

▼ **Figure 6.2 Numbers employed in selected UK industries (000s)**

	1985	1998	Percentage change
Selected services			
Health and social work	2,021	2,585	27.9
Education	1,629	1,870	14.8
Financial services	870	1,059	21.7
Computing, research and other business activities	1,736	2,697	55.3
Hotels and restaurants	1,004	1,334	32.9
Wholesale and retail trade	3,355	4,033	20.2
All services	14,428	17,602	22.0
Primary sector			
Agriculture, forestry, fishing	366	289	-21.0
Mining, quarrying, gas, electricity, water	560	222	-60.4
Secondary sector			
All manufacturing	5,002	4,074	-18.6

Note: figures exclude the self-employed and HM forces

Questions

1 Briefly outline the main trends shown in the data.
2 Suggest reasons why some service industries have grown more than others.

3. What are the changing patterns of retailing?

Prior to the mid-1960s, most shopping in the UK was done at local shops for everyday items such as groceries ('low order goods') or in urban centres for clothes and furniture ('high order goods') (see unit 3.1). The shops selling high order goods could afford the more expensive rents for property in the urban centre. Their location made them easily accessible for people living in the areas around. Most shoppers used public transport into the urban centre or walked to their local shops.

This pattern still exists, but it is in decline as new patterns emerge. The nature of shopping has changed for many people. So called 'everyday' goods are now bought weekly or even less frequently in supermarkets.

Shopping for high order goods, for an increasing number of people, has become a leisure activity involving a drive to an out-of-town shopping centre.

Supermarkets

In the UK, the development of supermarkets started on a large scale after 1964. In that year, Resale Price Maintenance (RSM) ended. Before then, food manufacturers had been able to set the selling price of their products and they insisted that all shops kept to the same price. After 1964, the new supermarkets were able to advertise cut price 'loss-leaders' to tempt customers into their stores. Because local grocers could not compete with the lower supermarket prices, many went out of business and closed down.

Since then, the increase in car ownership has allowed

Figure 6.3 A new supermarket in Ullapool, Scotland

The five biggest supermarket chains account for over 75 percent of all grocery sales in the UK. Even in the most remote parts of Scotland, supermarket chains have set up outlets.

more and more people to shop for groceries in bulk at supermarkets. The number of households with deep-freezers has risen from almost zero in the 1960s to over 90 percent in 1998, and food companies have reinforced the trend by producing ready prepared, pre-packaged meals. The increasing proportion of women in paid employment means that families have less time to spend on their daily chores. Customers are therefore looking for convenience and one-stop shopping.

In order to keep ahead of their rivals, the supermarket chains have diversified into many non-food lines. Clothing, household and electrical goods are now commonly sold and some supermarkets also contain florists, hairdressers, travel agents, dry cleaners and pharmacists. In their car parks, they sell cut price petrol as an additional means of attracting customers. In the late 1990s, supermarkets started to offer banking facilities with competitive rates for loans and credit cards. Loyalty cards, where shoppers get money back or other incentives, have also become widespread. They not only aim to boost 'repeat custom' but they also allow the supermarkets to build up knowledge of the tastes and preferences of their customer base.

Following the 1990s reforms to trading laws, supermarkets now open on Sundays and for longer hours during the rest of the week. This trend is intended to meet the needs of customers who, increasingly, are in occupations where 'flexible working' has become the norm. These people work shifts or irregular patterns and

therefore need to shop outside the traditional '9 to 5' opening hours.

Town and city centres

During the 1970s and 1980s, many town and city centres developed new retailing areas. Covered shopping malls like the Arndale Centre in Manchester and Eldon Square in Newcastle were built. Multi-storey parking was provided to make access easy. The new shopping centres offered 'weather free' browsing and revitalised many urban centres. But, in the 1990s, they faced new competition from out-of-town (or 'edge-of-city') shopping centres. The main problem that town and city centres face is traffic congestion. Not only are the urban roads increasingly jammed, parking fees have also risen.

Out-of-town shopping centres

Large retail parks containing furniture and electrical stores are now a common feature of suburbs in UK towns and cities. Free parking and good road access make them attractive to customers. The shop owners favour these sites for the additional reason that rents and property prices are lower than in the urban centres. They can therefore afford more floor space to display their goods.

Regional out-of-town shopping centres (or malls) are on a much bigger scale than the suburban retail parks. They are found on the edge of large conurbations, often near motorway junctions. Most are within easy travelling distance of several million potential customers. There are now 9 in Britain including the MetroCentre near Newcastle, Lakeside in Essex and Merry Hill in the West Midlands. They contain as many as 350 shops, including all the high street shops that would be found in a city centre. There are also other attractions such as food courts (containing different style cafes and restaurants), entertainment areas with cinemas and amusements, and plenty of free parking. They are aimed at car owners but they also make provision for consumers who rely on public transport.

As well as protecting people from the weather, the shopping centres offer a safe, relatively crime free environment. Security staff patrol the public areas. Beggars and homeless people are discouraged. These features are designed to appeal to people who might feel insecure in the large urban centres. Shop owners also like the extra security. Because the malls are closed during the night there is reduced risk of vandalism and robbery.

Out-of-town shopping now accounts for over a quarter of all retail sales in Britain. The busiest centres attract over 25 million shopping visits per year and are by far the most profitable retail locations in the country. It was reported in 1998 that MetroCentre had an annual turnover bigger than the combined total of all the retail outlets in Oxford - a medium sized city.

Critics of the regional shopping centres say that they damage the traditional urban centres. Retail sales in Dudley, in the West Midlands, fell by 70 percent when the nearby Merry Hill Centre opened. Evidence from the USA, where the trend is more advanced than in the UK, confirms this effect. Many central shopping areas in US cities have suffered a complete decline. They are now dominated by run down discount stores, second hand shops and boarded up buildings.

The regional shopping centres are also criticised for reinforcing the upward trend of car ownership. The difficulty in reaching most of the centres by public transport is one factor that encourages the increased use of private cars. This runs counter to government policy which is to slow the growth of motor traffic.

For these reasons, in the mid-1990s, the government made it harder for developers to gain planning permission for new centres. However, the schemes already being built, such as the Trafford Centre in Manchester and the Bluewater development in Kent, were allowed to continue.

Figure 6.4 Out-of-town shopping malls in the UK

Name of mall and nearest urban centre	Number of shops	Shopping area and leisure space (millions of square feet)	Opening date
MetroCentre, Gateshead	350	1.8	1986
Bluewater, Dartford, Kent	300	1.6	1999
Merry Hill, Dudley, West Midlands	250	1.4	1989
Lakeside, Thurrock, Essex	350	1.2	1990
Meadowhall, Sheffield	270	1.1	1990
Trafford Centre, Manchester	280	1.0	1998
Cribbs Causeway, Bristol	130	0.7	1998
Braehead, Glasgow	100	0.6	1999
White Rose Centre, Leeds	100	0.6	1997

Activity Trafford Centre

Figure 6.5 Trafford Centre guide

Located directly on an exit of the M60 ring motorway to the west of Manchester, the Trafford Centre is within 60 minutes driving time of 9 million people. The centre is built on land that was derelict, near the Trafford Park Industrial Estate. It contains 280 shops, including leading stores such as Selfridges and Debenhams, a multi-screen cinema, a leisure centre and 25 restaurants and cafes. 10,000 parking places are provided together with a 'traffic management scheme' that controls entry and exit onto the motorway network.

Before the Trafford Centre was built, opponents suggested that local shopping centres such as Stockport and Warrington, as well as the city centre of Manchester, would suffer. Nine out of ten local authorities in Greater Manchester opposed the scheme when it was in the planning stage. It was only given the go-ahead after central government over ruled local opposition.

Critics also predicted traffic problems for the motorways and roads around the centre. The M60 already suffered daily congestion before the centre was opened and this was expected to worsen as traffic increased.

1 Outline the positive and negative social, economic and environmental impact of the Trafford Centre.
2 In your view, will regional shopping centres eventually 'take over' the traditional patterns of shopping? Explain your answer.

Mail order shopping

In the UK, mail order shopping is growing rapidly and is expected to form 6 percent of all retail sales by 2002. The growth is caused by a number of factors. For customers, it is a convenient method of shopping. Families in which all the adults are working, and perhaps working on flexible shift patterns, find it difficult to spare the time for weekday shopping. They find it much quicker to look at goods in a catalogue and then phone or write for their order. About half of total mail order sales are for clothing, the rest are mainly for household and electronic goods.

A second important reason for the expansion of mail order has been a change in the type and range of goods sold by catalogue. Traditionally, catalogues were used by low income groups who could buy their goods - mainly clothes - on extended credit. Today, specialist catalogues target higher socio-economic groups and focus on niche markets such as designer clothing. Also aiming for the same higher income groups are retailers such as Next and Marks and Spencer who have launched their own catalogues.

New trends in home shopping are likely to enlarge the sector further. Satellite and cable TV have introduced home shopping channels to the UK, and internet shopping (e-commerce) is expanding rapidly. These forms of retailing are sometimes called 'direct sales'. In the USA, during the late 1990s, the volume of internet sales doubled each year. Traditional markets, such as books, have been transformed by internet shopping. For example, Amazon Books recorded sales of $150 million in its first full year of operation. Customers are able to browse through the electronic catalogue of over 1 million books. They then order online using a credit card. As well as being convenient, the internet stores are able to offer discounted prices because they do not have the overhead costs of high street shops and a distribution network. However, as

with all mail order shopping, postage and packing have to be paid.

Some supermarkets have started, in limited areas, to offer internet shopping and home deliveries. Their customers save the time spent in travelling and in 'picking' the goods but, of course, they generally pay extra for the service. For some people, this new style of shopping is ideal. But those who value the social interaction in shops, and those who enjoy shopping as a leisure activity, are likely to resist the trend towards home shopping.

4. What is the impact of new technology - the 'quaternary' sector?

The development of computer and information technology systems has led to new types of industry. They are sometimes classed together as the **quaternary sector** to distinguish them from older 'tertiary' services. Examples include the telesales and call centres that banks and other commercial institutions have set up. They rely on new technology to access customer records, and new communication systems, such as cable or satellite to transfer data. The growth of this sector is transforming the location pattern of offices.

Reinforcing the trend is the need for offices to have wiring and cabling systems that can, for example, handle the increased volume of telecommunications data. Fax machines, computer networks and video-conferencing require amounts of wiring that cannot easily be installed in old buildings. The result is that offices built as recently as the 1970s are becoming redundant.

The location of quaternary industry

The CBD is the traditional location for offices because, until recently, it was the most accessible location. Road, rail and bus networks converge on urban centres and this enables companies to attract the widest possible

Figure 6.6 New offices on the outskirts of Greater Manchester, near the M61 motorway.

Many new office developments are taking place outside the traditional CBD.

number of potential customers and employees. The clustering of offices allows close physical contact between companies who might rely on each other for services. Examples include the head offices of companies, solicitors, accountants and insurance brokers. The high demand for such locations causes rents to be highest in city centres.

In the 1990s, the traditional CBD location for offices started to lose favour and many new developments were located outside the CBD, at the edge of urban centres or even beyond. For example Canary Wharf in London's Docklands attracted many companies that previously were in the City of London. In Manchester, the Refuge Assurance Company moved from the city centre to Wilmslow, south of the city in Cheshire. Outside Bristol, Aztec West is a new business park next to a motorway junction. The regional shopping centres such as Lakeside and Bluewater are expected to become business centres with large office developments.

As outlined previously, the new offices often need to be in purpose built premises that can handle the latest communications systems. This requirement has provided an opportunity for many companies to relocate. High city rents are sometimes an important factor in encouraging firms to locate out of the CBD. Also, congestion in urban centres often makes suburban locations more accessible, particularly if they are near the motorway network. Research in the USA, where the trend is more marked, suggests that out-of-town office employment is particularly attractive for highly skilled suburban based female workforces. Women in

particular, it is said, prefer to work in offices that are a short drive from home, are in pleasant surroundings, and not too far from supermarkets and shopping malls where they can pick up groceries. The American studies calculate that employers would have to spend 15 to 20 percent more in wages to attract the same calibre of staff in the CBD.

A factor that is allowing offices to move out of cities is the increased use of communications technology. This makes it less important for offices to be near their customers. For example, Hewlett Packard's European customer service centre is in the Netherlands and all calls are routed to that location. If a UK customer wants Hewlett Packard to collect or deliver some equipment, the caller is transferred from the Netherlands to the Federal Express service centre which is based in Dublin.

Because call centres can be based in virtually any location, at least anywhere that proficient staff are available, some companies have used the opportunity to reduce their wage bills. So, for example, banking direct line centres are rarely located in the South East where wages are highest, instead they are located in places such as Skelmersdale and Sunderland where average wages are much lower. The process has been criticised by some union leaders in Britain and other countries because it is said to take advantage of 'cheap labour'. Typically, labour costs make up to 70 percent of total costs in running a call centre so there is a big incentive for companies to locate where wages are relatively low. This has been one reason why some transnational companies have located, for example, in Ireland. The availability of a well educated, English speaking workforce is another factor. One such company is American Airlines which uses a call centre in Dublin to handle its European reservations. Three hundred staff now do the work that was once handled by eight separate centres across Europe.

The new quaternary sector is not completely based in offices and the service sector. It also includes the high technology manufacturing industries that produce IT hardware and software. In Britain these are concentrated along the M4 corridor west of London, in the Cambridge area and in 'Silicon Glen' in Central Scotland. (See unit 5.1 for details.) An important reason that motivates the owners and employees to work in these suburban or semi-rural locations is the desire for a high quality lifestyle. City centres are seen as noisy, dirty, crowded and, sometimes, dangerous. Unlike the traditional office based service industries, the new quaternary industries can choose from a wide range of locations. It is not surprising, therefore, that they prefer to be sited somewhere that is 'green and pleasant'.

Teleworking

New technology has allowed the development of 'teleworking'. This is where people work from home using computers and modems to communicate with an office or with other teleworkers. In the UK, in 1998, it was estimated that 1.9 million workers operated outside a formal office environment. In the USA, there are over 11 million teleworkers and teleworking increased by 30 percent between 1996 and 1998.

The growth of this sector has allowed even more flexibility in the location of quaternary businesses. Employees are able to combine their working life with their family commitments more easily and they save on commuting time. For society as a whole, reduced motor traffic means less congestion and pollution. For companies, the advantages are that office overheads are reduced and staff retention is higher. The disadvantages are that managers have less control over their staff and, in some cases, the lack of social contact gives the employees a sense of isolation.

Activity) The growth of call centres

▼ **Figure 6.7 The largest UK call centres, with numbers of employees, 1999**

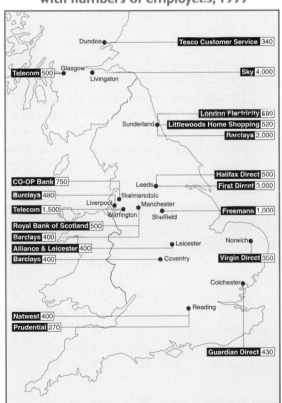

In 1998 it was estimated that 200,000 people in Britain worked in 7,000 call centres. The number was expected to double by the year 2000 making it the fastest growing occupation in the country. Businesses that operate call centres include banks, insurance companies, airlines, railway companies, mail order companies, and gas, water and electricity utilities.

The tasks performed by call centres range from telesales to help lines. Some, such as Virgin Trains, are selling a product or service, others such as Railtrack provide information, while others such as computer companies operate helplines.

The staff who answer the phones ('computer telephonists'), usually work in large open plan offices with rows of desks and screens. Their performance is monitored to check that they are giving correct information and are not taking too long between calls. The work is high pressure and there is a big labour turnover in some centres. About a quarter of the staff are graduates - reflecting the need for articulate and adaptable operators. Some call centres require specialist language staff. For example, the IBM helpline based at Greenock near Glasgow handles calls from 15 European countries in 11 languages.

Most of the call centres are in purpose built buildings designed to accommodate modern IT equipment. Many are on greenfield sites in industrial estates, attracted by incentives from local development agencies who value the employment they provide. The lower average wages typical of Northern England and Scotland are an important locational factor. Some companies also cite the availability of suitable workers, and their regional accents, as additional factors. It is widely believed that customers find soft regional (and Scottish) accents more 'trustworthy' than standard southern accents. This is an important consideration for those companies selling financial services.

▶ **Figure 6.8 A call centre employee**

Questions

1 Outline the reasons why call centres have grown in importance.
2 Suppose that you are given the task of deciding a location for a new call centre (operating a banking service for supermarket customers). List the factors (in rank order) that would influence your choice. Briefly justify your answer.

5. What are the recent trends in transport services?

The transport industry is an important part of the service sector. Not only does it provide jobs, it is an essential part of a modern economy. Without an efficient transport system, people and goods cannot easily move around. This wastes time and reduces economic output.

Trends in passenger traffic

For the past fifty years the most significant trends in passenger transport have been the rise in air travel and the increase in road traffic. This has been the case not only in the UK and other high income countries but also in newly industrialising countries. Both air travel and road traffic are closely related to the level of national income and standard of living of a country. As people's incomes rise, they make more journeys by plane and car.

Figure 6.9 shows the distances travelled within the UK using different modes of transport in the years 1961-1997. The biggest increase in percentage terms was by

air travel, followed by car travel. In absolute terms, however, car travel is overwhelmingly the most important mode accounting for over 86 percent of the total distance travelled.

Since the 1960s, annual car travel has almost doubled to an average of 6,500 miles per person while travel by bus and coach has dropped by almost a quarter to 600 miles a year. Rail travel declined and then rose slightly over the same period, and travel by bicycle has more than halved.

Figure 6.9 Distance travelled by mode within the UK (1961 - 1997), billion passenger kilometres

Mode		1961	1971	1981	1991	1997
Road		255	381	458	638	670
	Car	157	313	394	582	619
	Bus and coach	76	60	49	44	43
	Bicycle	11	4	5	5	4
	Motorbike	11	4	10	6	4
Rail		39	36	34	38	41
Domestic air		1	2	3	5	7
All modes		295	419	495	681	725

Note: a passenger kilometre is one person travelling one kilometre.

During the late 1990s, the number of rail passengers increased - possibly due to increased road congestion. But overall, this form of transport is still losing market share. In 1961, rail travel accounted for 13 percent of passenger distance travelled. By 1998, this percentage had fallen to less than 6 percent.

Trends in freight traffic

The trends in passenger transport are mirrored by the trends in freight transport. Road haulage has grown in importance while rail has declined. Between 1986 and 1996, the volume of UK freight moved by road (measured in tonne kilometres) increased by 46 percent whereas the volume moved by rail fell by 21 percent.

Air freight, both domestic and international, almost doubled in the period 1986 - 1996. In 1986, the total was 360,000 tonnes and in 1996 it was 655,000 tonnes. Other notable trends include the large increases in tonnage carried by pipeline (from 79 million tonnes in 1986 to 181 million tonnes in 1996), and the increase in seaborne freight carried in roll-on roll-off containers (from 53.1 million tonnes in 1986 to 93.1 million tonnes in 1996).

Reasons for the transport trends

Passenger road traffic For most of the twentieth century, official transport policy in the UK gave priority to roads and to private transport. As more people bought cars, new roads were built to accommodate the traffic. These roads in turn reinforced the trend towards car ownership because they made it quicker and more convenient to travel by car. Even as recently as 1989, the UK government announced a £23 billion programme of new roads, bypasses and motorway extensions. It was based on the assumption that private car ownership and usage would continue to grow at the same rate as previously.

Figure 6.10 shows that approximately 30 percent of families owned a car in 1961 but that this had risen to 70 percent in 1997. By that date, over 20 percent of families had two or more cars. These figures are reflected in the number of people with full driving licenses, rising from nearly 11 million in 1975 to 30 million in 1997.

The rise in car ownership and car usage has been caused by a number of factors. More people are able to afford a car now than in the 1950s. Average incomes have risen and the price of cars in real terms (ie, as a proportion of people's incomes) has

fallen. The cost of running cars has also fallen in real terms whereas bus and train fares have risen in real terms.

Generally, when people can afford to buy a car they choose to do so. Cars offer door-to-door, comfortable transport. Drivers and passengers are protected from the weather and they can travel at a time they desire. Official government policy, as described previously, has favoured motorists at the expense of other transport users so, where congestion and bottlenecks have occurred, the response from governments has been to build a new bypass or motorway. This has then encouraged more people to drive along those routes. The resulting increase in the number of motorists has had a negative effect on public transport provision. Falling numbers of passengers have made bus and train services less profitable so, in some cases, they have been closed down or made less frequent. This, of course, has then persuaded even more people to travel by car.

A factor that is sometimes blamed for adding to the decline in UK public transport is the deregulation and privatisation of bus and train companies that occurred between the mid-1980s and mid-1990s. The change caused competition between the new operators, but little overall improvement in services. Passengers are often confused over which companies are running particular routes. The operators themselves tend to concentrate on the most profitable routes while neglecting their loss making rural and off-peak services. The lack of investment in new buses and trains during the privatisation period contributed to break downs and delays that worsened services. At the same time, competition and lack of coordination between transport

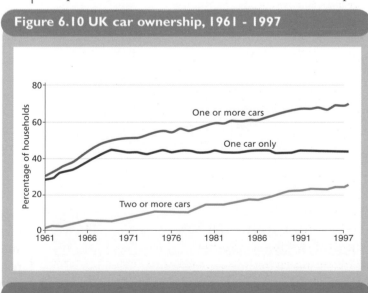

Figure 6.10 UK car ownership, 1961 - 1997

operators made it difficult for passengers to plan journeys. Combined with unreliable and persistently late services, the overall effect has been to discourage travel by public transport.

Passenger air traffic The number of people travelling by air has more than doubled since 1981. This is true of international air traffic as well as domestic travel. In 1981, there were 43.7 million international air passengers either entering or leaving UK airports, and by 1997 this had risen to 105.4 million. As with car travel, the increase in air traffic is due to the rise in people's incomes and the fall, in real terms, of the cost of air travel.

Holidays abroad, particularly to sunny locations such as the Mediterranean and, increasingly, to long haul destinations such as Florida and the Caribbean, have become affordable to millions of people on average

Figure 6.11 Air travel

Passenger air traffic is the fastest growing mode of travel in the UK.

incomes. Families which might have taken a week's holiday in Brighton or Blackpool in the 1950s now have much higher expectations. They want to travel somewhere with warmer weather and exotic surroundings. Holiday companies are able to offer package flights and accommodation much cheaper than individuals can arrange themselves. As a result, there has been rapid growth in the numbers taking foreign holidays by air. For example, in 1970, 51,000 Britons travelled to the USA for a holiday. By 1997 this number had risen to 2.1 million.

An additional reason for the growth in air travel has been a rise in the number of business travellers. This is due to the increasing dominance of transnational companies that have operations in many countries. The managers of these companies spend a great deal of time travelling between their subsidiaries. Globalisation of trade has created world wide markets for many products. So, companies that are based in just one country need to send sales staff abroad in order to compete with their rivals.

Freight traffic As with private cars, the rise in the number of goods lorries has persuaded governments to build more bypasses and motorways. This, in turn, has stimulated yet more road traffic. Hauliers find road transport quicker, cheaper and more flexible than rail transport. In particular, time and expense are saved in trans-shipping goods to and from railway wagons. It is also easier to keep track of goods when they are in lorries rather than in goods marshalling yards or railway sidings.

The use of containers has reinforced the trend towards road traffic, especially for goods that are being transported abroad. Roll-on roll-off ferries between the UK and mainland Europe allow containers to be moved on lorries from factory to foreign destination with no need for extra handling. Train operators hope that, in time the Channel Tunnel might reverse the trend away from railways. High speed trains will be able to transport containers and lorries from destinations anywhere in Britain to mainland Europe but it is not expected that the rail links will be complete until at least 2005.

Although road transport has increased in importance over recent decades, it is not the cheapest option for all types of good. Oil, gas and some chemicals cost less to move by pipeline. Bulky materials such as coal, iron ore and crushed limestone are generally cheaper to move by rail. However, in the case of coal, the decline of the UK mining industry in the 1980s and 1990s has reduced the overall volume that is transported.

Consequences of road traffic growth

An important consequence of rising road traffic is the increase in congestion. In 1996, the Confederation of British Industry (CBI) estimated that road congestion was costing the economy £20 billion per year. This was the value of wasted fuel, late deliveries and people's time spent queuing in traffic jams. Surveys by the AA suggest that congestion not only wastes people's time, it is a major cause of stress. For instance, over 90 percent of motorists state that they sometimes experience 'road rage'.

The worst jams occur in urban areas during rush hours though, increasingly, sections of the motorway network such as the M25 and the M6 near Birmingham are congested for much of the working day. (The issue of managing commuter traffic in urban areas is covered in detail in unit 3.6.)

Vibrations from heavy vehicles cause damage to road surfaces, to underground utilities such as sewers and to the foundations of buildings. Studies by the Association of State Highway officials in the USA suggest that the damage a vehicle does to the road is proportionate to its axle load to the power of four. This means, for example, that a 44 tonne lorry causes a million times more damage than an average sized family car. The UK government announced in 1998

that it was going to raise the weight limit for lorries from 38 to 41 tonnes. This was less than the EU average but it still required a £2 billion programme to strengthen bridges.

Road traffic also has other side effects including air pollution and noise. Exhaust emissions produce 30 percent of airborne particulates, 50 percent of nitrogen oxide and virtually all the carbon monoxide present in urban air. When the pollutants become concentrated, a petro-chemical smog forms. The pollutants are particularly harmful to people such as young children and asthmatics. The smogs are worse in summer when high pressure systems trap air over a city. Public health alerts warning people of poor air quality may then have to be issued. These have become more frequent during the 1990s, not only in London but in other major cities such as Paris, Athens and Tokyo.

In addition to the pollutants listed above, vehicle exhausts emit about 20 percent of the total UK carbon dioxide output. This 'greenhouse gas' is held responsible for global warming (see unit 12.6). At the 1997 Kyoto Climate Summit the UK and other EU governments agreed to cut carbon dioxide emissions by 15 percent. An important aspect of this policy will be to reduce the growth of road traffic.

Activity UK transport policies

▲ **Figure 6.12 Twyford Down**

The case against new road building has become more vociferous since the early 1990s. Big public campaigns against the M3 extension through Twyford Down near Winchester, the M65 extension in Lancashire and the Newbury bypass highlighted the issues involved. By the time of the 1998 Transport White Paper (a government policy statement), it was clear that public opinion had turned against large scale road schemes. Official policy now recognises that spending money on new roads does not solve the problem of traffic congestion. In the short term there might be alleviation but soon, traffic volumes increase and the situation becomes worse than ever. Experience from the M25 and its partial widening in the mid-1990s helped people realise that no matter how much countryside was covered with tarmac, the jams would continue.

The pressure group Transport 2000 campaigns to reduce road traffic and to encourage the use of public transport. Its suggestions include:

* the introduction of taxes on workplace parking
* higher taxes for company car users
* road tolls for commuters (with higher charges on days when air quality is poor)
* the introduction of a lorry-weight tax (that rises with vehicle weight)
* reducing roadspace for cars by introducing more bus and cycle lanes and having wider pavements
* a 20 mph speed limit in urban areas
* traffic calming measures (eg, speed bumps and lane narrowing)
* lorry routing restrictions
* improvements in the number and quality of train and bus services
* providing households with accurate information on bus and train timetables (including up to the minute 'real time' information at bus stops and stations)
* the introduction of travel cards that can be used on all modes of public transport
* building new style, low-floor buses to help passengers with young children or those who are carrying shopping.

Questions

1 Summarise the case against building more roads and motorways.
2 Identify the different groups who might be affected if the Transport 2000 policies are implemented. Assess the possible advantages and disadvantages of the policies to each of these groups.

unit summary

1 The service sector is the largest sector in the UK economy and in most other high income countries.
2 Service sector growth has been caused by increased demand for services (due to rising incomes and changing demographic patterns). The decline in the numbers employed in agriculture, mining and manufacturing has released people to work in the service sector.
3 Increased car ownership and changing lifestyles have stimulated new retail developments. Supermarkets have overtaken local shops for 'everyday goods' retailing. Out-of-town centres are now challenging urban centres for their traditional trade. A growing consumer desire for convenience has led to the increase in home shopping by mail order, cable TV and internet.
4 Computer and information based industries are sometimes labelled the 'quaternary sector'. They are growing quickly, particularly on sites away from the traditional office locations in the CBD.
5 The growth of air and road traffic, and the relative decline of rail, bus, cycle and pedestrian traffic have been major trends in UK transport over the past 50 years.
6 There is a growing acceptance that the current rate of growth in road traffic is not sustainable and that alternatives must be found.

key terms

Blue collar - manual occupations or employees.
Consumer services - services that are provided directly to the public, eg hairdressing, health care.
Producer services- services that are provided for companies or institutions, eg accounting.
Public sector - that part of the economy that is owned by the government. It includes national and local government and public corporations

(such as the Post Office and the BBC).
Tertiary sector- that part of the economy that produces **services** and not goods.
Quaternary sector- the name given to new industries based on information technology and computer systems.
White collar - non-manual occupations or employees.

Unit 6.2 Trade

key questions

1 What is the pattern of world trade?
2 What is the pattern of UK trade?

1. What is the pattern of world trade?

Trade between different peoples is an ancient activity. For example, the Silk Road was an important route between China and the Mediterranean nearly 2,000 years ago. Pack horses and camels were used over land. Ships were small, and bulky goods and perishable items (in preservatives) could be moved only in small quantities. This pattern remained virtually unchanged until the nineteenth century when the invention of steam power and refrigeration enabled a massive increase in the movement of goods. Later came the bulk carriers and huge oil tankers of today. Aeroplanes have also become important in modern freight transport, typically carrying expensive or fragile items. On a more local scale, articulated lorries have become the major form of land transport.

Trade underpins the globalisation process in which a global market for goods is developing (see unit 2.4). For First World consumers especially, the range of goods in supermarkets is immense. Food, drink, flowers and household goods are imported from hundreds or thousands of miles away. Similarly, in shops selling clothing and electronic goods, there is a huge range of goods on offer from different countries. For those who can afford to buy, trade brings an increase in choice and quality of goods on offer.

Figure 6.13 Modern container transport

Low cost transport by sea has enabled international trade to increase.

Activity Trade patterns

Area/Country	1970	1997
Africa	**4.4**	**2.3**
Americas	**22.6**	**24.2**
USA	13.0	14.7
Canada	4.4	3.8
Mexico	0.5	0.2
South America and Caribbean	4.7	5.5
Asia	**16.7**	**26.6**
Japan	5.7	7.1
Hong Kong	0.8	3.7
China	0.7	3.1
South Korea	0.4	2.6
Other Asia (excl. Middle East)	6.5	7.2
Middle East	2.6	2.9
Europe	**54.2**	**45.4**
EU (1997 members)	35.9	38.6
Other Western Europe	6.5	3.4
Eastern Europe	11.8	3.5
Oceania	**2.1**	**1.5**

Note: 'Merchandise' includes food, fuel, raw materials and manufactured goods. It does not include services.

◀ **Figure 6.14 Percentage shares in total world merchandise trade, 1970-1997, by continent and with selected countries**

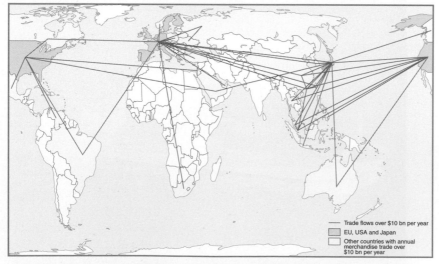

Trade flows over $10 bn per year

EU, USA and Japan

Other countries with annual merchandise trade over $10 bn per year

▲ **Figure 6.15 Ten billion dollar merchandise trade flows, 1997**

Questions

1 Describe the main features of world merchandise trade in 1997.

2 Compare the pattern of world trade in 1997 with that in 1970.

Comparative advantage

In the early nineteenth century, the economist David Ricardo developed the theory of comparative advantage. This theory helps explain the world pattern of trade. Ricardo showed that all countries can benefit from trade if they produce and then export those goods in which they have an advantage. In modern terms, he demonstrated that trade is not a 'zero sum' game in which the number of winners must equal the number of losers. Rather, by specialising in the production of those goods in which a country is most efficient, and exchanging these with different goods produced by other countries, all can be winners. Ricardo used the example of textiles and wine to illustrate the point. If Britain is most efficient at producing textiles, and Portugal is most efficient at producing wine, both countries can gain if they specialise and trade goods. So, in this case, Britain should produce and export textiles, Portugal should produce and export wine.

Ricardo also demonstrated that both countries can benefit from trade even if one country is more efficient at producing everything. If that country specialises in producing the goods at which it is 'most best' (ie, where its advantage is greatest), and leaves the other country to produce the goods at which it is 'least worse', then overall output will rise and both can gain. For example, suppose that Portugal is more efficient than Britain at producing both textiles and wine, but its advantage is greatest in wine production. The two countries can still gain from trade if Portugal specialises in producing the good at which it is 'most best', ie wine, and Britain specialises in producing the good at which it is 'least worst', ie textiles.

Because Ricardo's theory of trade is widely accepted, there is general agreement that long term benefits can be gained by all countries if specialisation and trade are encouraged. The advantages are greatest if there is free trade. (Free trade means trade without import restrictions. Examples of import restrictions include quotas, ie numerical limits on imports, and tariffs, ie import taxes or duties.)

For agricultural commodities, whose production is linked closely to physical conditions such as climate, the idea of specialisation and trade is fairly straightforward. For example, Caribbean countries can produce bananas more cheaply than, say, in Britain where greenhouses are needed to grow them. It therefore makes sense for Britain to import bananas from the Caribbean.

For manufactured goods, Ricardo recognised that

Figure 6.16 Caribbean fruit

It makes economic sense for countries to buy goods from wherever they can be produced most efficiently and cheaply. This principle helps explain the pattern of world trade.

'labour productivity' was the main factor in determining comparative advantage. This not only means how hard people work but also includes how much machinery (ie, capital equipment) they have available and how well they use it. The success of Japan as a trading nation is often explained in terms of its comparative advantage in producing manufactured goods.

In the twentieth century, the idea of 'factor endowments' has been used to explain why some countries are more efficient than others. For those countries with rich natural resources, such as Australia or Brazil, it makes sense to specialise in producing those goods (eg, iron ore, agricultural products) which reflect these endowments. A country such as Singapore, which has almost no natural resources, is richly endowed with 'human capital' and has been able to specialise in the production of manufactured goods. Human capital is a country's workforce and, in Singapore's case, it is extremely efficient because it is healthy, well motivated and well educated.

The theory of comparative advantage explains imports and exports in terms of relative costs of production and shows why some producers specialise in producing particular goods for export. According to this view, world trade flows are the result of differences in efficiency between producers. However, some trade cannot be explained by the theory of comparative advantage. Also, the theory does not explain why the production of particular goods might switch from country to country within a relatively short period of time. The following section of this unit provides explanations for these trade patterns. The explanations involve the product life-cycle, protectionism and intra-industry trade.

Product life-cycle

Much industrial production has moved from First World to Third World locations. This shift can be explained in part by the product life-cycle idea, first outlined in the 1960s (see figure 6.17). In this explanation of trading patterns, it is changes in the methods of production during a product's 'life' that are responsible for the shift.

During the twentieth century, high incomes in the USA led to rising demand for new products, especially labour-saving appliances such as washing machines, vacuum cleaners and dishwashers. In the early stages of production (Phase I), the products were non-standardised and required skilled labour to make them. As the products caught on and standardisation occurred, competitors eventually established themselves in Europe (Phase II). The higher cost US producers were then displaced from the European market, and they switched exports to the lower income countries of the Third World, eg Latin America and East Asia. They were then displaced from Third World outlets, again largely on cost grounds. Finally, near the end of the product life-cycle, standardisation was such that production could be moved to the even cheaper and less-skilled labour locations of the Third World, exporting back to the United States itself (Phase V).

When the product life-cycle idea was first proposed in the 1960s, the final stage had not yet occurred. It has since become an important feature of global production and trade flows. China provides an example of the current pattern - it exports an increasing volume of consumer goods to the USA.

Protectionism

The pattern of trade is sometimes affected by import restrictions which are designed to protect domestic producers from competition. Although free trade can create long term benefits for all, at times of high unemployment governments are sometimes tempted to control imports in an effort to save jobs. The same policy is also used to help new or 'infant' industries, or

to protect 'strategic' industries such as defence manufacturers. This policy can work for a short time but backfires when other countries retaliate and set up their own trade barriers. The economic problems of slow growth and high unemployment which the world faced between the World Wars were partly due to the lack of trade between countries. Figure 6.18 shows the contrast between that era (1913 - 1950) and the periods before and since. The fast economic growth of the 1950s and 1960s was heavily dependent on the rising world trade of that time. Growth began to slow following the 'oil shock' of 1973 (the sudden rise in oil prices - see unit 2.4) and was especially slow in the 1980s. The economic slowdown and rising unemployment in the 1980s increased the pressure on governments to restrict imports. However, such protectionist measures run counter to the rules of the **World Trade Organisation** (WTO) whose task it is to promote free trade.

To get round the rules of the WTO, 'Voluntary Export Restraints' (VERs) have become common. Trading partners are asked to 'voluntarily' limit their exports of sensitive goods. Motor vehicles and semi-conductors (used in computers) are common examples. For instance, Japan has for many years 'voluntarily' agreed to restrict its car exports to the European Union. This is one reason why Japanese car companies have set up production within the EU. Such agreements are normally made bilaterally between countries or between trading blocs. (See figure 1.65 for a map of world trading blocs.)

Trading blocs or free trade areas, such as the EU or NAFTA (North American Free Trade Area) have become an important feature of international trade. Their objective is usually to have completely free trade within their borders, but trade is often restricted beyond

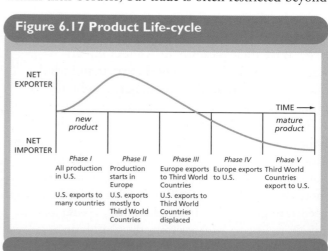

Figure 6.17 Product Life-cycle

Figure 6.18 World Output and Trade Growth, 1820-1995 (annual average % change)

	Output growth	Trade growth
1820-1870	2.2	4.0
1870-1913	2.5	3.9
1913-1950	1.9	1.0
1950-1973	4.9	8.6
1973-1980	4.0	5.0
1981-1987	2.0	2.5
1988-1995	2.5	10.6

their borders. The European Union, for instance, has created the Single European Market which aims to provide the free movement of goods, services and people between the member states. The effect of trading blocs is often to increase trade within the bloc, but at the expense of trade with countries outside the bloc. For example, the EU has set up import controls on grain and other foodstuffs from the USA and other low cost producers, and so the imports from these regions are relatively low. However, within the EU, trade in grain between members is relatively high, despite the fact that grain grown in France or Spain is more expensive than that from North America.

During the nineteenth and early twentieth centuries, the traditional pattern of trade for Western European countries was to export manufactured goods to their colonies and the 'New World', and buy food and raw materials in return. Some remnants of this pattern remain and are reinforced by protectionist measures. For example, the EU gives preferential treatment to certain former colonies although such links are increasingly under challenge.

During the 1990s, the EU's policy of allowing the Caribbean producers of bananas free access to the European market, while placing tariffs on other Latin American producers, caused a trade dispute. The Windward Islands, for instance, were allowed to export their bananas duty free to the EU because they were former UK colonies. The US fruit companies that control Latin American production - on large scale, lower cost plantations - claimed that the arrangement was unfair. This led, in 1999, to a threat from the US government to retaliate by setting up tariffs against selected EU exports - including cashmere knitwear from Scotland.

After a decision by the WTO in favour of the US, the EU had to alter its trading arrangements. The Windward Islanders and other Caribbean producers feared that a change in the agreement would cause them to lose their market and force them to stop production.

The dispute illustrates both the advantages and disadvantages of protectionism and free trade. The eventual outcome might be that all the parties involved could be 'winners' - US companies, Latin American producers (eg, Ecuador and Costa Rica) and European consumers who will be able to buy cheaper bananas. The less efficient Caribbean Island producers might also benefit if they can cut their production costs or switch to producing another crop for which there is a demand. This, at least, is the theory. In practice, the Windward Islanders and others might take decades to recover or might never find an alternative way of making a living. There is also a possibility that some might be tempted to switch production to illegal drugs - for which there is a ready market.

Intra-industry trade

A feature of world trade that is difficult to explain using the theory of comparative advantage is intra-industry trade. Almost half of all international trade is intra-industry. This is trade between countries in the same products. For example, the UK exports cars to Spain and Spain exports cars to the UK. France sells steel to Germany, but also buys steel from Germany.

One explanation comes from the activities of transnational companies (TNCs). These set up production in different countries and then transfer parts and finished goods between subsidiaries. So, for instance, Ford

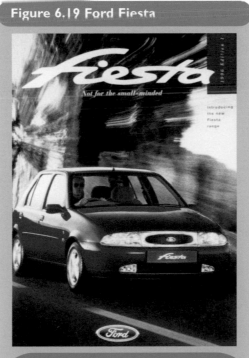

Figure 6.19 Ford Fiesta

It is convenient and profitable for Ford and other motor companies to produce cars in different countries and then transfer them between subsidiaries.

Spain supplies the Fiesta to the UK and Ford UK supplies the Focus to Spain. By locating in different countries, TNCs can gain tax advantages. They can also 'play-off' work forces and governments against each other, threatening to switch production to somewhere that wages are lower or the government is more helpful.

Another explanation for intra-industry trade is the growing demand for consumer choice. This might explain why some people buy foreign goods even though similar goods are made by domestic producers. For example, the USA sells Bourbon whisky to Scotland, and Scotland sells Scotch whisky to the USA. Similarly, English people buy French cheese and French people buy Stilton - an English cheese. Europeans buy American jeans and Americans buy European jeans. A wide range of goods, it appears, are desired by consumers simply because these items have a foreign label or image.

 **Activity** **Trade flows**

▼ **Figure 6.20 main merchandise trade patterns for 6 selected countries, 1995.**

Country and per capita GNP (US$)	Main Exports	Main Destinations	Main Imports	Main Origins
Bolivia $830	Zinc 13.8% Gold 12.1% Soya beans 10.9%	USA 23.3% UK 15.1% Peru 14.2% Argentina 12.0%	Machinery 43.3% Raw materials 36.9% Consumer goods 19.4%	USA 18.2% Brazil 14.5% Japan 13.8% Argentina 10.4%
Germany $28,870	Machinery and transport equipment 49.6% Chemicals and chemical products 13.5%	France 11.6%	Machinery and transport equipment 34.4%	France 10.7%
Hong Kong $24,290	Clothing and textiles 31.9% Electrical machinery 13.8%	China 33.3% United States 21.7%	Machinery and transport equipment 37.1%	China 36.2% Japan 14.8%
New Zealand $15,720	Food and live animals 43.7% Basic manufactures 26.0% Minerals, chemicals and plastics 11.1%	Australia 20.8% Japan 16.3% USA 10.4%	Machinery 24.5% Minerals, chemicals and plastics 20.7% Transport equipment 17.2%	Australia 19.5% USA 18.9% Japan 13.7%
Niger $200	Uranium 70% Agricultural products 22%	France 55.3%	Consumer goods 71.2% Machinery 28.9%	France 21.8%
USA $28,020	Machinery and transport equipment 48.2%	Canada 21.6% Japan 11.0%	Machinery and transport equipment 47.1%	Canada 19.2% Japan 16.5%

Note: only categories 10% and over are shown.

Questions

1 To what extent do high income countries have a different pattern of trade from low income countries?
2 Suggest possible reasons why countries like Germany and the USA import and export the same category of goods (ie, 'machinery and transport equipment').
3 Why might reliance on a single export commodity create problems for a country such as Niger?

2. What is the pattern of UK trade?

Up until the late eighteenth century, trade to and from the British Isles was of only minor international importance. The main exports were tin, wool and cloth, and the main imports were spices, wine and sugar. The Industrial Revolution caused a huge shift in this pattern. The export of British manufactured goods came to dominate world trade. Food, fuel and raw materials became the main imports. The main export markets for British goods were the colonies and the 'New World', and these locations were the source of most imports.

Manufacturing exports were greater than manufacturing imports from the time of the Industrial Revolution until the early 1980s. Britain's main exporters became famous all over the world, for example Vickers, Rolls Royce, Jaguar, Leyland Motors and Cammell Laird. Ships, armaments, railway engines, motor vehicles, textiles and machinery were the main exports.

However, during the late nineteenth and early twentieth centuries, other manufacturing countries such as the USA, Germany and later Japan caught up and overtook British industrial output. As a result, the UK's share of world trade fell and manufactured imports started to rise. In 1983, manufactures went into deficit (imports of manufactures exceeded exports) for the first time in two centuries. This was partly caused by deindustrialisation (see unit 5.2). The change in the pattern of trade was accompanied by a change in trading partners. Because manufactured imports increased in volume, the countries that supplied these goods became major trading partners. Today, overwhelmingly, the UK's trade is with other high income, industrialised countries such as Germany and France, and not with the former colonies.

During the 1980s, the UK became self-sufficient in oil from the North Sea and this helped cushion the impact of the decline in manufacturing. Likewise, changes in the agricultural sector have caused a major change in the UK's trade. Improvements in farm productivity, together with EU subsidies, have made the UK largely self-sufficient in temperate foodstuffs such as dairy produce and grain. Only tropical produce such as tea, coffee and fruit are imported on a large scale.

Trade in services

International trade takes place not just in merchandise (ie, manufactures, raw materials and food) but also in services. This includes financial services such as banking and insurance, the profits from overseas investments,

Figure 6.21 A dealing room in the City of London

The City earns billions of pounds for the UK in sales of financial services to other countries.

spending by foreign tourists, earnings from UK ships and planes, and sales of music, films and TV programmes. Until recently they were collectively known in official statistics as 'invisibles'. Now they are called 'trade in services'.

For over two hundred years, the UK trade in services has been in surplus (ie, earnings are greater than payments). On a world scale, during the late 1990s, the UK was the second biggest exporter of services - after the United States. A large proportion of these earnings come from the activities of the City of London. The strength of the City comes from a number of factors including:

- the advantage of English being the international language of business
- the historical links with former colonies and trade partners
- the convenience of time zones (London, Tokyo and New York allow 24 hour trading)
- the deregulation of the financial markets in 1986 ('Big Bang') which made the City more competitive and efficient
- the large number of foreign financial institutions located in the City
- the size and strength of the EU economy and the Eurocurrency markets.

Activity UK trade

Figure 6.22 UK merchandise trade (1997)

	Exports (£m)	%	Imports (£m)	%
Food, drink and tobacco	11,389	6.9	17,540	9.6
Raw materials (eg, timber, metal ores)	2,621	1.6	6,306	3.5
Fuel	11,030	6.6	7,060	3.9
Manufactured goods	140,865	84.9	151,080	83.0

	Exports (%)	Imports (%)
European Union	57.0	54.2
of which: Germany	12.3	14.8
France	10.2	9.6
USA	11.8	12.3
Japan	2.5	4.9
Canada, Australia, New Zealand, South Africa	4.0	3.1
South Korea, Hong Kong, Singapore, Taiwan	4.4	5.8
Rest of world	21.9	19.3

Figure 6.23 UK Trade in services (1997)

	(£m)
Exports (ie, sale of services)	52,900
Imports (ie, purchase of services)	44,003

Share of total imports and exports	%
European Union	34.1
USA	10.7
Japan	4.1
Canada, Australia, New Zealand, South Africa	5.2
South Korea, Hong Kong, Singapore, Taiwan	4.3
Rest of world	41.6

Questions

1 Describe the main features of UK trade in 1997.
2 The traditional pattern of UK merchandise trade a hundred years ago was: import of food, fuel and raw materials, and export of manufactured goods; the main trading partners were colonies in Africa, south Asia, Australasia and Canada. To what extent has this pattern changed?

unit summary

1   Trade is an important feature of modern life, underpinning the globalisation process. It is explained by theories such as 'comparative advantage' and the 'product life-cycle'. The activities of transnational companies are increasingly important in determining trade flows.

2. The benefits of free trade are generally accepted. However, some nations or trading blocs use protectionism to gain short term advantages, protecting infant or strategic industries by a range of measures against imports.

3   For over 200 years, the UK relied on manufacturing exports to pay for food and raw materials. The main trading partners were the former colonies. Today the UK's merchandise trade is mainly involved with buying and selling manufactured goods, and the EU is the major trading partner.

4   The UK is a major exporter of services and has a large surplus in this sector.

key terms

Comparative advantage - a theory that explains how overall output can rise if countries specialise in making those goods at which they are relatively most efficient.

Free trade - trade that is not restricted by import barriers such as tariffs, duties or quotas; these are examples of protectionism.

Human capital - the productive value of the workforce, including their education and skills.

Intra-industry trade - trade where one country imports and exports the same or similar products.

Invisible earnings - overseas earnings from banking, insurance, tourism and other service activities. Now called 'trade in services' in official statistics.

Product life-cycle - the production process for a good as it moves through several stages. This has an important geographical dimension because the product is more likely to be designed in the First World and then manufactured in the Third World later in the product life-cycle.

World Trade Organisation - an international agency that promotes free trade and monitors compliance with free trade regulations. It was formerly known as GATT (General Agreement on Tariffs and Trade.)

Unit 6.3   Leisure and Tourism

key questions

1   What are the main trends in leisure and tourism?
2   What impact does increased leisure and tourism have on the economy and the environment?

1. What are the main trends in leisure and tourism?

Leisure can be defined as free time. In other words it is the time that is not spent in paid work, performing household chores or doing other necessary tasks such as sleeping or travelling to work. Leisure activities are what people do in their free time. In the UK, in the 1990s, the main home-based leisure activities, in rank order, were TV viewing, entertaining visitors and listening to the radio.

According to the 1996 General Household Survey, over 80 percent of the UK adult population participate in some form of sport or physical activity (including walking). However, the single most popular leisure activity away from home is visiting a public house. In the 1996 Survey, 65 percent of people aged 16 or over said they had visited a pub in the three month period prior to being interviewed. The next most common activity was eating a meal out (62 percent). Other examples of leisure activities were going to the cinema (36 percent), visiting a sports event (22 percent) and visiting a theme park (12 percent).

Tourism is an activity that involves a visit away from home. The World Tourism Organisation (WTO) defines a tourist as someone who spends at least one night away from their normal place of residence. The visit might take the form of a leisure activity (ie, a holiday) although the WTO also includes journeys made for business, or other reasons such as visits to relatives, religious pilgrimages or trips to obtain health treatment. In the UK, the Office for National Statistics uses a wider definition of tourism that includes a 'leisure day visit' - for example, a day trip to a theme park or to the seaside.

UK trends

In 1970, the main leisure activities, as today, were watching television, going to the pub and going for meals out. However, although this pattern of leisure activity might seem unchanged, there are differences between then and now. People watched, on average, 19 hours of TV per week in 1970 compared with 25 hours per week in 1996. In 1970, virtually all televisions were black and white and there were only three channels. By the late 1990s, over 80 percent of households owned a video recorder and many people also had satellite and cable TV, often with large screens and stereo sound. Combined with the improved quality and comfort of people's homes, these developments made watching TV a completely different experience from the 1970s.

During the 1950s when most families bought a television for the first time, the impact on cinema attendance was very marked. From annual admissions of 1.4 billion in 1951, the number fell to 53 million in 1983. It seemed that soon there would be no cinemas left as more and more closed. This has not happened, mainly because of the development of out-of-town multi-screens. People were attracted to the new multi screens which offered more choice, ample parking and, in many cases, fast food outlets. By 1997, cinema attendance had recovered to 139 million. The relocation

Figure 6.24 Meals out

The proportion of people in the UK who regularly eat meals out has doubled in thirty years.

of cinemas from urban centres to out-of-town sites mirrors the changing retail pattern that also occurred in the 1990s (see unit 6.1).

Eating meals out was a regular activity for just 30 percent of people in 1970. By 1996 this had risen to over 60 percent. Predictions that improved in-home comfort and entertainment would reduce the number of people going out have not come about. The rise in cinema attendances and the increase in the number of people who eat out are evidence that away-from-home leisure activities remain popular.

Activity **Sports participation**

▼ Figure 6.25 Participation in the most popular sports, by gender, Britain 1996

	Percentage of adults taking part in sporting activity		
	Women	Men	Total
Walking	64	73	68
Swimming	41	37	40
Keep fit / yoga	29	10	21
Cycling	16	27	21
Snooker / pool	8	33	19
Ten pin bowls	13	18	15
Golf	4	19	11
Weight training	6	14	10
Running / jogging	5	12	8
Soccer	1	18	8
At least one sport	77	87	81

▼ Figure 6.26 Participation in sport by age and social class, Britain 1996

Percentage of people participating in at least one sport

By age:	20-24	30-34	60-69
Men	90	80	61
Women	73	66	51

By social class:	Professional	Skilled manual	Unskilled manual
Men	78	66	54
Women	85	53	42

Source: adapted from the General Household Survey; data is based on respondents' activities in the 4 weeks prior to interview.

Questions

1 Briefly outline the main features shown in the data.
2 With reference to particular sporting activities, suggest what factors might influence the participation rates shown in figures 6.25 and 6.26.

Figure 6.27 Foreign holiday destinations, UK residents

	1970		1997	
	(000s)	(% of total)	(000s)	(% of total)
Spain	1,499	26.3	7,663	26.3
France	205	3.6	6,731	23.1
USA	51	0.9	2,156	6.7
Greece	257	4.5	1,369	4.7
Italy	496	8.7	1,224	4.2
Portugal	143	2.5	1,165	4.0
Irish Republic	912	16.0	1,049	3.6
Turkey	-	-	903	3.1
Netherlands	177	3.1	816	2.8
Belgium	171	3.0	641	2.2
Total holidays	5,703		29,138	

Note: the 1970 figure for Turkey was below 10,000

The proportion of the UK population taking at least one holiday per year has remained almost static at 60 percent since 1970. There have, though, been major changes. The total number of holidays has risen from 35 million a year to 57 million in 1997. This is because over 20 percent of the population now take two or more holidays per year. Many of these are 'short breaks' in the UK although an increasing number are winter holidays, either skiing or to sunny destinations. During the same period, the number of foreign holidays rose from 5.7 million per year to 29.1 million in 1997 (see figure 6.27). This is perhaps the biggest single change in UK leisure and tourism in the late twentieth century.

In 1997 there were 1.3 billion 'tourist leisure day visits'. These are defined as being for entertainment purposes as opposed to trips for business, shopping or visiting relatives. This was a 20 percent increase over the 1991 figure.

Theme parks have attracted a growing number of visitors. The first theme park in Britain, Thorpe Park in Surrey, opened in 1979. By 1997 a further 14 had been built including Legoland, near Windsor, and Alton Towers in the Midlands. This type of leisure activity is expected to grow. Owners of theme parks hope that UK trends will follow the US experience where, on average, people make five times more visits annually than in Britain.

Figure 6.29 shows the rise in visitor numbers for selected tourist destinations. They include the main theme parks and cultural attractions. Not only has attendance at the established locations risen, there are an ever increasing number of new attractions. These include not only new theme parks but 'indoor family entertainment centres' which contain facilities such as bowling alleys, sports centres and swimming pools.

Figure 6.28 New York

The number of UK tourists visiting the USA has grown by nearly 4,000 percent in just thirty years.

Figure 6.29 Selected tourist attractions - numbers of visitors (millions)

	1991	1997
Blackpool Pleasure Beach	6.5	7.8
British Museum	5.1	6.1
National Gallery, London	4.3	4.8
Alton Towers	2.0	2.7
Madame Tussaud's	2.2	2.7
Tate Gallery, London	1.8	1.8
Chessington World of Adventures	1.4	1.8
Legoland	-	1.4

Reasons for the leisure and tourism trends in the UK

There are a number of reasons why there is an upward trend in the number of people participating in leisure and tourist activities. Rising living standards and increased opportunities have raised demand, and changes in the leisure and tourism industry have raised the supply of potential activities.

Rising real incomes Overwhelmingly the biggest reason for the changing pattern in leisure and tourism is the rise in the average standard of living. As people's incomes have risen, so have their expectations. Whereas a week in Margate or Blackpool was the ambition of most working people in the 1950s, now a package holiday to Ibiza or Tenerife is the norm. By travelling abroad people can enjoy warmer and more predictable weather. They also can experience 'exotic' surroundings that allow them to forget their everyday circumstances back home.

The rise in average incomes means that people have more money left over after buying their basics needs. Official UK data on household spending shows that in 1970 the average family's expenditure on food (eaten in the home) was 25 percent of total spending. By 1998 this had fallen to just 13 percent. Over the same period, the 'real' price of furniture and electrical goods (ie, their price as a proportion of income) also fell - again leaving people with more disposable income. Much of this 'spare' income is used for leisure and entertainment. So, in 1998, the average family spent 15.5 percent of its total spending on meals out, accommodation, leisure goods and leisure services. This compares with just 8.9 percent in 1970.

Holiday entitlement A second explanation for changing trends in tourism has been the increase in holiday entitlement. Most people in work now receive at least four weeks paid holiday per year and 25 percent of full time employees receive five or more weeks annual holiday. This contrasts with the position in the 1960s when 97 percent of full time manual employees had an entitlement of two weeks or less. It was not until the mid-1980s that the four week annual holiday entitlement became established. Combined with the rise in average incomes, the extra holiday entitlement made it easier for people not only to take an annual holiday but also enabled them to have more short breaks and day visits.

Hours of work Although the number of paid holidays has increased, the average number of hours worked in a week has not fallen. In 1970, the average number of hours worked by men in the UK was 45.7 per week. In 1996 this had actually risen to 45.8 hours. Over the same period the number of women in paid employment doubled from 5.5 million to 11.9 million. Together, these factors put pressure on families in terms of how much time they have available. This is a possible reason for the increase in the number of meals out that people consume. Rather than find the time to buy and prepare a meal, families increasingly eat pre-packaged convenience foods, or buy a take-away, or go out to eat.

Lifestyle A number of factors have caused a rise in the number of people who participate in some form of sporting activity (including walking). Advice from doctors and health officials has persuaded large numbers of people to take some form of regular exercise. The decline in manual work and the rise in the use of cars has meant that most people are less naturally fit than previous generations - and sport helps them compensate for this. There is also a fashion motive in some of the activities. Keep fit and weight training are popular because they help keep people's bodies in the 'right' shape.

Package holidays An important reason for the growth in foreign tourism has been the availability of relatively low price packages. The introduction of wide-bodied jets and charter flights, combined with purpose built apartment and hotel complexes, has reduced the price of foreign holidays. By buying transport and accommodation in bulk, the holiday tour operators are able to sell holidays more cheaply than independent travellers can arrange for themselves. Fierce competition within the holiday industry has meant that a week in, for example, Majorca costs little more than a week in a British seaside resort.

Resort life-cycle An idea developed in the 1980s is that tourist resorts go through a life cycle. To start with, there is an 'exploration' stage in which tourists first discover an area. There follow a 'development' stage in which the resort grows, a 'consolidation' stage in which the resort caters for a mass market and then 'stagnation' followed by 'decline'. To some extent, British seaside resorts fit this model. Places such as Blackpool, Scarborough and Brighton were discovered by holiday makers in the eighteenth and nineteenth centuries. Railway transport opened up a mass market and many hotels were built. The peak of their popularity was between the 1920s and 1960s when very large numbers of families visited the resorts. With the advent of package holidays and foreign travel, the British seaside resorts have suffered a relative decline. Some have developed 'extension strategies' to prolong their tourist trade. Blackpool, for example, has its illuminations and Brighton has developed a marina in order to attract visitors.

Trends in world tourism

There are two broadly contrasting views on the growth in world tourism. On the one hand, the World Travel and Tourism Council (WTTC), speaking for the tourist industry, stresses the positive aspects. It claims that travel and tourism is the world's biggest industry contributing 11 percent of global GDP. According to the WTTC, the industry is a 'catalyst for the construction, food and retail sectors' of low income countries.

The alternative, negative view is expressed by Tourism Concern, an environmental pressure group. It accepts that tourism can bring benefits but suggests that these are seldom spread evenly or fairly. The result of tourism,

Figure 6.30 Tourist arrivals (000s) by region 1996

Europe	347,437
Americas	115,511
East Asia/Pacific	90,091
Africa	19,454
Middle East	15,144
South Asia	4,485

Figure 6.31 Top ten tourist destinations (000s) 1996

	International arrivals
France	61,500
USA	44,791
Spain	41,425
Italy	35,500
China	26,055
United Kingdom	25,800
Mexico	21,732
Hungary	20,670
Poland	19,420
Canada	17,345

it says, is that 'religious and cultural traditions are debased, and environments are degraded'.

Trying to reconcile these two opposing viewpoints is the World Tourism Organisation (WTO), an agency of the United Nations. It has stated that 'tourism is a driving force both to create job opportunities and to preserve natural and cultural resources through sustainable development'. The issue of sustainable tourism is dealt with in more detail later in this unit.

According to the WTO, the number of international tourist arrivals worldwide was 457 million in 1991. This grew to 594 million in 1996 and is projected to reach 1.6 billion in 2020. Receipts from tourism increased from $282 billion in 1991 to $423 billion in 1996 and could reach $2,000 billion by 2020.

Figures 6.30 and 6.31 show the main tourist destinations in the mid-1990s. Europe had by far the highest number of international arrivals with six out of the top ten destinations. The pattern of tourism very closely reflects the average level of incomes of the various regions. European and North American countries generate more tourists because their populations have, on average, far higher incomes than people in other regions. Most of these tourists visit countries within their 'home' regions.

China is exceptional in that it is the only low income country in the top ten destinations. Its rise has been rapid, moving up from 25th place in 1990. Since the relaxation of travel and visa controls by the communist regime in the 1980s China has become a popular destination. Its cultural wealth and exotic image have attracted visitors from Europe, North America and other East Asian countries such as Japan.

Figure 6.32 Paris

France is the most popular destination for international tourists. It offers seaside resorts, historic sites, spectacular mountain scenery and cultural events.

Reasons for the trends in world tourism

Trends in world tourism are closely influenced by three main factors - incomes, security and the cost of travel. The level of disposable income earned by a population is the key factor in determining how many people can afford to travel abroad. The East Asian 'tiger economies' (South Korea, Taiwan, Hong Kong, Singapore) and Japan were the fastest growing economies of the early and mid-1990s and they generated the fastest growth in tourist numbers. However, following the financial crises that hit these countries in 1997, their currencies lost value and their average real incomes fell. Unemployment rose and people in work feared that they might lose their jobs. The result was a marked slowdown in tourism and total receipts fell in the East Asia/Pacific region in 1998. This contrasted with the continuing growth in, for example, Europe where both France and Spain's tourist receipts rose by 7 percent.

An important factor in determining tourist destinations is the level of security and safety in particular locations. Not surprisingly, civil disorder, military conflicts and terrorist attacks have the effect of reducing tourist visits. For example, the massacre of 58 European tourists in Luxor, Egypt, in 1997 had the effect of cutting 1998 tourism to that country by 80 percent. Similarly, conflicts in the Balkans, Algeria, Sri Lanka and the Middle East have all reduced the number of tourists to those destinations during the 1990s.

A third factor influencing world tourism has been a fall in travel costs. The larger, more efficient jets that are used by charter companies have cut air fares. Also, tour companies have introduced package techniques to **long haul** holidays (ie, destinations in a different world region or continent). This has allowed, for example, North Americans and Europeans to take holidays in Caribbean destinations that previously were enjoyed only by the very rich. So, for instance, the most popular long haul destinations for UK holidaymakers in the mid-1990s included the Dominican Republic, Barbados, Antigua and Jamaica. In 1995, 24 percent of all international tourism was long haul. The WTO predicts that this will rise to over 30 percent by 2020.

Activity — World Tourism Organisation predictions of future trends

In a 1998 report, the WTO predicted that tourist growth would be fastest in the areas of cultural tourism, ecotourism, thematic tourism, adventure tourism and cruises.

Cultural tourism

A significant number of potential tourists are the 'baby boomers' of Europe and North America. These are the large numbers of children born in the years following World War Two and who are reaching late middle age. They are less likely to look for 'sun and sand' compared with younger people but they are increasingly interested in holidays to historic sites and cultural centres. They have the spending power and the time, when they retire, to become a major influence in the tourist market. Cities such as Venice, ancient monuments in places like Egypt and relics of former civilisations throughout the world are all expected to have an increase in tourist visitors.

Ecotourism

A growing awareness of the environment and a concern to see wildlife in its natural state is fuelling this type of holiday. Visits to rain forests in Central America, whale watching off California or New Zealand, and safaris to African nature reserves are all examples of ecotourism.

Thematic tourism

This is the name given to holidays where a special interest is the main motivator. It includes visits to theme parks in locations such as Orlando, Florida, but also other types of holiday such as night clubbing in Ibiza, shopping trips to Paris or New York, or gambling in Las Vegas.

Adventure tourism

Treks to remote mountain regions, visits to the 'ends of the earth' and even underwater voyages are a fast growing form of tourism. For example, by the mid-1990s there were over 40 passenger submarines in service and they carried more than two million passengers in 1996. Antarctica had over 10,000 visitors in 1997 and this was set to increase as scientific bases were adapted to meet tourist needs. Treks to the Himalayas, Andes and other mountain chains have become so popular that litter and rubbish disposal has become a problem at places such as Everest base camp.

Cruises

Cruising holidays are growing at a very fast rate. According to the WTO, in 1997 there were 7 million cruise passengers and this was forecast to grow to 9 million by 2000. In 1998, there were over 40 cruise ships under construction in shipyards around the world and there were plans to build a 250,000 tonne ship which would carry 6,200 passengers.

▲ **Figure 6.33 Cruise ships in the Virgin Islands, Caribbean**

Questions

1 Explain why all types of tourism (and in particular those listed) are expected to become more popular.
2 Suggest the possible factors that affect the UK's position (6th) in the world 'league table' of tourist destinations.

2. What impact does increased leisure and tourism have on the economy and the environment?

The impact of tourism can be both positive and negative. For example, positive effects include job creation and the regeneration of historic and cultural centres. The negative effect includes damage to the environment, traffic congestion and the loss of traditional cultures if mass tourism develops.

Positive effects

According to the Office for National Statistics, tourism related industries in Britain employed 1.5 million people in 1998. This was a rise of over 300,000 since 1986. The British Tourist Authority (BTA) claims that 20 percent of all new jobs are in leisure and tourism. In 1998, the tourist industry as a whole earned over £40 billion, equivalent to 5 percent of GDP. Almost £13 billion of these earnings came from the 26 million foreign visitors to Britain.

There are three main areas of employment within the leisure and tourism industry - accommodation and catering, travel and passenger transport, and tourism related leisure services (eg, theme park or leisure centre employees). Many leisure activities have a **multiplier effect** (ie, their impact has a knock-on effect on other industries within the economy). For example, a hotel buys supplies of food, drink and items such as furniture, bed linen, stationery, floral decorations and cleaning materials from other businesses. Similarly, the incomes of hotel employees are spent on goods and services from other sectors of the economy.

Approximately 60 percent of employees in leisure and tourism in the UK are female although only half of these work full time. The jobs are widely spread throughout the country but there are higher concentrations of workers in seaside resorts such as Brighton, Bournemouth and Blackpool. In these locations there is a problem of seasonal unemployment because most visitors take their holidays in the summer. Resorts such as Blackpool have tried to extend their season by special attractions such as the Illuminations or by hosting conferences in the spring or autumn.

The growth of tourism has been recognised as an important driving force in economic development. As stated previously, tourism is claimed to be the world's biggest industry. The World Tourism Organisation and the World Bank in a joint 1998 report expressed the view that 'tourism is a labour intensive sector that can alleviate poverty through its capacity to create jobs'. In addition, they stated that tourism can stimulate the construction industry and can provide a market for agricultural produce. The same report predicted that travel and tourism would generate globally, directly and indirectly, 100 million new jobs by 2010.

For an individual country, tourism brings in foreign currency that can be used to finance imports or pay off debts. Money spent by First World visitors in Third World countries is a direct transfer of resources from high to low income economies. It is not only the tourist industry that benefits. Tourist spending and earnings from tourism are taxed by governments. This raises money that can pay for health care, education or public infrastructure such as roads, water supplies or power plants. In some countries, tourist development has led to 'growth poles' in which regional economies have been stimulated by the investment which tourism generates (see unit 2.2). Early examples of this occurred in the 1960s in Spain when the 'Costas' were first developed as package tour destinations for northern Europeans. The effect was to transform the local economy. Modern examples include resorts in Mexico (eg, Cancun) and in the Dominican Republic.

Negative effects

An unfortunate side effect of tourism is that it can destroy the very features that originally attract visitors. Purpose built ski resorts in the Alps (see unit 10.3), Mediterranean beaches lined with apartment blocks and overflowing car parks in National Parks are all features that spoil the natural environment. Social and cultural traditions of local people are often swamped by visitors, or are repackaged as tourist attractions. It is the eating and drinking habits, and cultural values, of incoming tourists who increasingly dominate holiday destinations from Benidorm to Bali.

However, many believe that these negative outcomes are not inevitable. At the 1992 Rio de Janeiro Earth Summit, delegates supported an 'Agenda 21' commitment to sustainable development (see unit 2.6) . Part of that Agenda was a policy statement on **sustainable tourism**. It was based on the view that well managed tourism could be a powerful instrument for good. Sustainable tourism can be defined as tourist development that meets current needs without damaging the ability of future generations to meet their needs.

Ulixes 21 is a EU funded project to promote sustainable tourism within the Mediterranean Basin. The project promotes tourist development that respects natural, social and cultural resources. It defines sustainable tourism as being:

- environmentally friendly, adapted to the carrying capacity of the 'natural and cultural spaces' (ie, it does not intrude on the landscape in an ugly fashion, nor does it swamp local communities)
- year round, avoiding marked seasonal effects
- well planned and economically viable over the long term
- diversified in terms of integrating the hinterland and avoiding total dedication to tourism
- participatory, ie local people, towns and villages have a say in the development.

The Mediterranean region is the world's main tourist destination, receiving 176 million visitors in 1996. Over 5 million jobs rely on the industry which earns more than $100 billion per year. The Ulixes 21 project starts with an acceptance that tourist development since the 1950s, particularly in France and Spain, has not been sustainable. In particular, mass tourism has:

- been predatory, ie it has not conserved natural systems or natural resources
- emphasised growth in tourist numbers rather than quality of environment
- not distributed the benefits evenly
- not included the surrounding areas.

A Ulixes report states that tourism has caused 'a devastating effect on the coastal environment. Water pollution, soil erosion, degradation of underwater flora and fauna and, especially, landscape degradation have been the results'. It goes on to say that development is concentrated in time and space - on a narrow coastal strip during the summer months.

Figure 6.34 Near Gerona on the Mediterranean coast of Spain

Apartment blocks have been built all along this coastline.

In the mid-1990s, the Mediterranean Basin's share of world tourism fell by 3 percent. One motive behind the Ulixes project is concern that environmental degradation might be responsible for the region's failure to maintain its share of the tourist market.

Activity Malham - the Yorkshire Dales National Park

The village of Malham in the Yorkshire Dales is an example of a **honey pot** (ie, a focus of tourist activity). It has a resident population of just over 200 but it receives approximately 500,000 visitors a year who come to look at the spectacular limestone scenery.

The Yorkshire Dales is one of the most popular National Parks in England and Wales. In 1998, a total of 8.3 million days were spent by visitors in the Park, mainly from the large urban centres just to the south. The Park is within an hour's drive of Leeds and Bradford and within two hour's drive of over 9 million people in Yorkshire and Lancashire. The visitors spend approximately £50 million per year and provide employment in hotels, cafes and restaurants. Just over 18,000 people are permanent residents in the Park area.

The main attractions of the Park are the scenery, for example the limestone cliff at Malham Cove, the stone built villages, and tourist attractions such as underground caverns, historic monuments and craft centres. Many visitors spend time walking or cycling, and some people use the Park for more strenuous activities such as climbing, caving and riding.

The Yorkshire Dales National Park is one of eleven in England and Wales. In some countries, such as the USA, a **National Park** is a wilderness area owned and managed by the government. This is not the case in Britain where the land within the Parks is privately owned and is mostly farmed. Each Park has a planning authority whose duty is to 'conserve and enhance the natural beauty, wildlife and cultural heritage'. But, at the same time, there is an obligation to 'foster the economic and social well-being of local communities'. In practice, managing the Parks involves compromises between the sometimes conflicting demands of recreation, conservation and the local economy. An example of such conflicts is the desire by walkers in the Dales for free access to upland areas and the needs of farmers to use the land for their sheep or cattle. Similarly, some local people work and earn their living in limestone quarries but these are an eyesore for visitors.

(The National Parks in England and Wales were originally chosen for special protection because of their scenic qualities and also because they contained open spaces for recreation. Other areas which merit protection but which do not contain as much open space have been designated Areas of Outstanding Natural Beauty (AONB). The local authorities in these areas are given special planning powers to control development).

Pressures on the Park

Over 90 percent of visitors to the Yorkshire Dales National Park travel by car. This traffic causes noise, it makes the narrow valley roads dangerous for walkers and cyclists, and it causes air pollution. During the summer of 1997, for a total of 500 hours, air quality in some of the Dales was so poor that it was a hazard to young children and people with asthma. In a mid-1990s survey, 60 percent of people rated 'peace and quiet' and 70 percent rated 'fresh, clean air' as 'very important' to their visit. The effect of traffic is therefore to destroy the very qualities that attract visitors

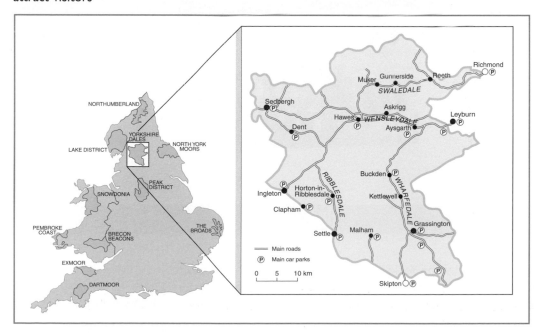

Figure 6.35 The Yorkshire Dales National Park and other National Parks.

An additional problem caused by cars is the need to provide car parks. Rather than let people leave their cars on verges or in narrow lanes, the National Park Authority has built car parks in most large villages and at most tourist attractions. The parking fees provide useful revenue to the National Park but the car parks themselves are often visually intrusive. People visit the Dales to see beautiful scenery, picturesque villages and green fields, but their first experience when they arrive is to see rows of parked cars.

The large number of tourists cause additional problems once they leave their cars. Footpath erosion is so serious that the National Park Authority has created new paved paths in popular locations. These prevent gullies from forming when grass cover is destroyed. However, they can change the character of the area from being open countryside to something more like an urban park. Farmers suffer when walkers trample wide paths across their hay meadows or leave gates open so that sheep and cattle escape. Tourists with dogs sometimes allow them to wander off the lead, worrying sheep and causing stock losses.

The character of Dales villages has been completely altered by the tourist influx. In Malham, for example, the village is dominated by tourist shops, cafes and accommodation. Facilities for local residents have closed or been converted to meet the more profitable tourist needs. An additional problem is that, because Malham and many other villages are beautiful, an increasing number of houses have been bought as second homes by weekend visitors. The effect has been to price out local people from homebuying and also to make the villages 'dead' during the week.

▼ **Figure 6.36 Malham**

Car park in Malham

Souvenir and gift shop

Shop selling drinks and ice cream

Questions

1. List the reasons why the Yorkshire Dales receive so many visitors.
2. Briefly summarise the main issues facing Malham and the Yorkshire Dales.
3. Discuss means by which sustainable tourism could be promoted in the Yorkshire Dales.

Activity ▷ Tourism in Kenya

Kenya was one of the first African countries to embrace mass tourism. Its natural features - beautiful coasts with white sandy beaches and coral reefs, and wildlife reserves - are the main attractions. Tourism is the country's second biggest source of foreign revenue after agriculture. In 1997, Kenya earned over $450 million from tourism. This income is particularly valuable because the two main agricultural exports, tea and coffee, suffer severe fluctuations in price on the world commodity markets.

More than half the tourists come from Europe, mainly from Germany, Britain and other EU countries. Over two thirds stay at coastal resorts and many also spend some time on safari to an inland wildlife reserve. The best known of these is the Masai Mara National Reserve which borders the Serengeti National Park in Tanzania. In the dry season, between July and October, the reserve is the scene of one of the world's most spectacular natural events. Seven hundred thousand animals, including over half a million wildebeest, migrate northwards into the reserve in search of pasture. Then, once the grass has been eaten and fresh rains to the south have fallen, the animals move back. The reserve also has a permanent population of many other species including lions, elephants, rhinoceros and giraffes.

Tourists to the reserve generally stay for a few nights in lodges or special camp sites. They are driven to see the animals in minibuses and there are also balloon excursions.

The Kenyan government set a target of 1 million tourists by 2000 but this was more a hope than an expectation. Publicity regarding muggings and harassment, particularly in coastal areas, has had a negative effect. For example, following violence in 1997 that was widely reported in Spanish and Italian newspapers, over 80 percent of bookings from those two countries were cancelled. A second factor likely to reduce tourist numbers is the economic crisis in East Asian economies that started in 1997. Lower incomes and fears about job losses have had a drastic effect on the number of travellers from that region.

Tourist development in Kenya is also likely be affected by problems related to the issue of sustainability. In particular the concentration of tourists in sensitive areas has a potentially negative effect on both wildlife and on the local population. For example, the minibus drivers in the Masai Mara, hoping for tips from tourists, sometimes drive too close to the animals. This has caused a change in natural behaviour patterns. Minibuses also churn up large areas of the bush by not staying on roads. This creates dust storms and soil erosion. When several minibuses gather in one place, for instance surrounding a pride of lions, the effect for the tourists is not a 'wilderness experience' at all. Balloon safaris have been criticised for frightening animals. The burners used to keep the balloons in the air can be very noisy and the shadows cast by the balloons can startle wildlife.

▲ Figure 6.37 An elephant in the Masai Mara National Reserve

The indigenous people of the Masai Mara are the Masai. Their pattern of life is one of nomadic pastoralism. They move their cattle and goats in search of pasture and water. Although the reserve is within their traditional homeland, the Masai have been moved out. However, wild animals such as wildebeest can still move freely onto Masai grazing land in surrounding areas. This sometimes causes conflict. The Kenyan government is now fostering a more cooperative approach to local people whose lives have been disrupted by the wildlife reserves. In some cases, compensation is paid to the Masai for being moved off their traditional lands. Local villagers are being persuaded to take advantage of tourism, for example by supplying camp sites and lodges with fire wood. It is felt that if they have a stake in wildlife conservation they are less likely to hunt or poach the animals in the reserves. Several Masai settlements are now used as tourist attractions. However this is controversial because it is said that the people on display lose their dignity and their traditional way of life.

▲ **Figure 6.38 Kenya wildlife reserves**

Tourism also sometimes causes social and cultural conflict on the coast where many Kenyans are Muslims. The presence of westerners, especially women, wearing only beach attire can be offensive to locals. Community leaders are worried about the influence on younger Kenyans who see western women less fully clothed than religious custom dictates. An additional source of tension is the sale of alcohol. Its consumption is contrary to Islamic beliefs but hoteliers know that it is expected by western visitors.

Also worrying for local residents is the possibility that a sex industry will develop in the tourist areas. Prostitutes are attracted by the prospect of wealthy visitors and there is evidence from other Third World countries, notably in South East Asia, that some westerners are willing to exploit the poor and disadvantaged.

Various environmental problems have arisen along the coast as a result of tourism. People walking on the coral, and boats running aground or dragging anchors on the reefs have damaged parts of the fragile ecosystem. The shoreline itself has also been degraded. The first hotels were built with little regard for the surrounding environment and do not blend in with the landscape, although later developments have been more sensitive. The provision of swimming pools, clean water and electricity in hotels can cause resentment amongst local people who may have no running water or other basic utilities.

Despite these negative effects, the Kenyan government and people cannot afford to lose their tourism revenue. The government is trying to strike a balance between encouraging tourism and not letting it destroy the very features that attract visitors. So, for example, game wardens are employed to check that safari minibuses are not too close to wild animals, and marine wardens patrol the coral reefs. Tourists are encouraged to be sensitive to local culture and to dress appropriately.

A dilemma facing Kenya, like most low income countries, is how to finance tourist development. Foreign companies, which own 80 percent of the hotels and organise the package tours, supply much needed investment. In return, they take most of the profits back home. One solution, which the government is adopting, is to set up joint ventures with foreign operators. In this way, development can be steered to less crowded areas and more of the benefits can be retained within the country.

Questions

1 Outline the benefits and negative effects of tourism in Kenya.
2 To what extent in your view, is current tourism sustainable in Kenya?
3 Suggest policies that the Kenyan government might adopt to promote more sustainable tourist development.

unit summary

1 As incomes and holiday entitlements grow, people spend an increasing proportion of their incomes on leisure and tourist activities.
2 The number of foreign holidays taken by UK residents has risen five fold in 30 years.
3 Holiday trends are influenced by levels of disposable income, rising expectations and the cost of travel (and also, on a world scale, concerns over security).
4 Leisure and tourism provide jobs and incomes to large numbers of people. Tourism is said to be the world's biggest industry.
5 Tourism brings negative effects of landscape degradation and the erosion of social and cultural traditions.
6 Sustainable tourism is a policy that attempts to reconcile the conflict between tourist development and the damaging side effects that can destroy the very features that attract people.

key terms

Honey pot - a focus of tourist activity.
Leisure - 'free time'; what people do in their free time includes watching TV, going to the cinema or participating in a sporting event.
Long haul - travel to destinations in a different continent or world region.
Multiplier effect - the knock-on effect that spending in one sector of the economy has on other sectors.
National Park - in the UK this is an area of countryside with a high landscape value that is subject to special planning controls. It is generally privately owned farmland. In other countries, for example the USA, National Parks are owned and managed by the government.
Sustainable tourism - tourist development that meets current needs without damaging the ability of future generations to meet their needs.
Tourism - an activity that involves a visit away from home. It might be for leisure or business.

Introduction

The Earth is formed from gases and dust orbiting around the Sun. Inside the Earth, temperatures are high enough to melt rock but on the surface the crust has cooled sufficiently for life to evolve. The Earth's crust is relatively thin and it floats on the material below. It is broken into plates which slowly move, causing earthquakes and volcanic eruptions. The movement of these plates also causes mountains and rift valleys to form.

Studying the structure of the Earth helps explain the distribution of continents and oceans, mountains and plains. It also helps our understanding of earthquakes and volcanic eruptions, and might in the future enable people to be safer from these hazards.

Chapter summary

Unit 7.1 looks at the Earth's crust and explains the theory of plate tectonics.
Unit 7.2 considers the distribution, causes and effects of earthquakes.
Unit 7.3 looks at the distribution, causes and effects of volcanoes.
Unit 7.4 examines people's perception of and response to tectonic hazards.

Unit 7.1 The Earth's crust and plate tectonics

key questions

1 What is the structure of the Earth?
2 What is the structure of the Earth's crust?
3 What is plate tectonics?
4 What happens at plate boundaries?

1. What is the structure of the Earth?

The Earth was formed at the same time as the Sun and other planets in our solar system. About 4.5 billion years ago, a rotating cloud of dust and gas (a nebula) was compacted by gravity. This raised the temperature and pressure at its centre and caused a nuclear reaction. Some hydrogen in the cloud fused into helium, releasing vast amounts of energy and this formed our Sun. Further out, orbiting material cooled and crashed together producing larger and larger lumps that would eventually become the planets - of which the Earth is one. The spinning of the planet Earth caused the densest particles to go to the centre, forming the core where temperatures are still hottest. The least dense material moved to the surface where, eventually, it cooled and formed a crust.

By studying patterns of shock waves (caused by

earthquakes), scientists have been able to analyse the Earth's structure. They have identified a number of layers. These have different densities, chemical compositions and physical properties.

When analysed in terms of density and chemical composition, the Earth can be divided into three layers, the crust, the mantle and the core (see figure 7.1). The core is at the centre and is formed of the densest material, mainly iron and nickel. The temperature in the core is approximately 5,500°C. Next comes the thickest layer, the mantle. It is formed of less dense silicate rocks, rich in iron and magnesium. The surface layer of the Earth, or crust, is formed of the least dense material. It is described in more detail in the next section of this unit. The boundary between the crust and the mantle is called the **Mohorovicic (Moho) Discontinuity** (after the Croatian scientist who discovered it).

When the Earth's structure is analysed in terms of its physical properties, the layers are slightly different from those based on chemical properties. ('Physical properties' means whether the material is solid and rigid, or plastic and fluid.) The outer layer is known as the **lithosphere**. It comprises the crust and the top layer of the mantle. This layer is formed from material that is solid and rigid. Below the lithosphere, is a zone known as the **asthenosphere** in which the material is relatively fluid. The rock is soft and plastic and it flows in slow convection currents. Below the asthenosphere is the mesosphere which is less fluid, and then the core which is subdivided into a liquid outer layer and a solid inner layer.

Above the surface of the solid rock which forms the Earth's crust is the **hydrosphere** which is the name given to the total mass of water on the surface of the planet. About 98 percent is in the oceans. Without this water, life would not exist. As water moves over the Earth's surface it erodes, transports and deposits material, and so creates and changes landforms. The term **biosphere** is sometimes used to describe that part of Earth where life exists - the land, sea and air.

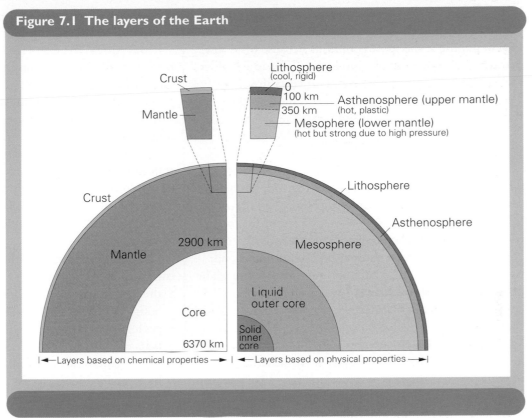

Figure 7.1 The layers of the Earth

Crust
Mantle

Lithosphere (cool, rigid)
0
100 km — Asthenosphere (upper mantle) (hot, plastic)
350 km — Mesophere (lower mantle) (hot but strong due to high pressure)

Crust
Mantle
2900 km

Lithosphere
Asthenosphere
Mesosphere

Liquid outer core

Core
6370 km

Solid inner core

|← Layers based on chemical properties →| |← Layers based on physical properties →|

2. What is the structure of the Earth's crust?

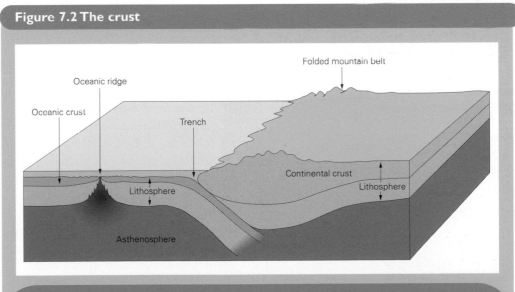

Figure 7.2 The crust

Folded mountain belt
Oceanic ridge
Oceanic crust
Trench
Continental crust
Lithosphere
Lithosphere
Asthenosphere

Oceanic crust is only about 8-10 km thick, made of dark, dense rocks such as basalt. Continental crust is 35-60 km thick. It is less dense and lighter than Oceanic crust. Mountains formed from continental crust are counterbalanced by thicker crust pushing down into the mantle. This diagram shows new oceanic crust being formed from material rising from the mantle at an oceanic ridge, and oceanic crust being destroyed as it sinks into the mantle at an ocean trench.

The Earth's crust can be subdivided into two types, oceanic and continental (see figure 7.2).

Oceanic crust is less than 200 million years old. This is very recent in terms of the Earth's entire existence. Oceanic crust is mainly formed from basalt, a dark, heavy rock rich in silica and magnesium (**sima**). It is about 8-10 km thick. Oceanic crust is far denser than continental crust and it can sink down into the mantle.

Continental crust is thicker than oceanic crust, varying between 35 km and 60 km in depth. It is also lighter (ie, less dense) than oceanic crust, consisting mainly of rocks rich in silica and aluminium (**sial**) - granite is the most common. Because of its low density, it cannot sink into the mantle. It is much older than oceanic crust - up to 3.8 billion years in age. Slowly it is being worn away by rivers and by other forms of weathering and erosion.

3. What is plate tectonics?

The theory of **plate tectonics** states that the Earth's surface is made up of rigid **plates**. These plates form the lithosphere. They consist of crustal rock and the top layer of the mantle. Some plates contain only continental crust, some contain both continental and oceanic crust and others contain only oceanic crust. The plates 'float' on the asthenosphere, powered by convection currents that derive their heat from the Earth's interior.

By taking measurements from satellites and lasers, it has been shown that Europe and North America are moving apart at the rate of approximately 3 cm per year. This has been happening for over one hundred million years and explains how the Atlantic Ocean was formed.

When geologists first developed the idea of continents moving on the Earth's surface, the idea was called 'continental drift'. Now the term 'plate tectonics' is used. The older term implied that it was just the continents that moved whereas, in fact, it has become clear that plates containing oceanic crust also move.

The word tectonics comes from the Greek word 'tekton' meaning builder. The term is used because the movement of plates has been shown to cause periods of mountain building. The process is described later in this unit.

It was Alfred Wegener (1880-1930) who first proposed the theory of continental drift in 1912. A German meteorologist and geophysicist, he built on other scientists' works to show that land masses and magnetic poles move. He suggested that there was originally one supercontinent, which he called 'Pangea', that evolved 280 million years ago (see figure 7.3). This split into two - a northern continent called 'Laurasia' (now North America and Eurasia), and a southern continent called 'Gondwanaland' which later split into South America, Africa, Antarctica, India, New Zealand and Australia.

The evidence to support the idea of plate tectonics / continental drift includes:

- the jig-saw fit of continents, particularly Africa and South America
- geological evidence; matching rocks and mountain belts extend through, for example, South America, Africa, Antarctica and India
- biological evidence; fossils of the same species are found in matching sediments on the continents that once formed Gondwanaland - for example, the fossils of a freshwater reptile called Mesosaurus are only found in South Africa and South America
- climatological evidence; climate variations in certain parts of the Earth have been too great to be the result of global climatic change - for example, coal seams in Antarctica are now covered by ice that is more than one kilometre thick. However, these deposits must have formed in tropical or sub-tropical forests and the only logical conclusion is that the continent of Antarctica was at one time much closer to the equator and that it has drifted southwards. Similarly, evidence of glaciation in Brazil and southern Africa suggests that these areas must, at one time, have been in a polar region.

Modern support for the theory of plate tectonics comes from the study of 'paleomagnetism' which helps show the age when rocks were formed. ('Paleo' means ancient.) The evidence came in the 1950s and 1960s when new techniques for dating rocks were developed. The research was conducted on the mid-Atlantic Ridge where plates are

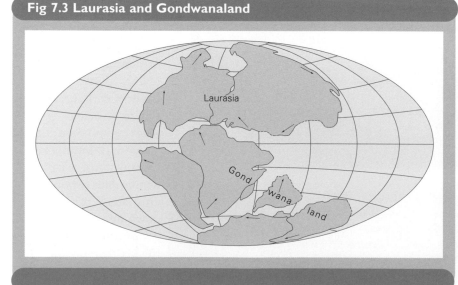

Fig 7.3 Laurasia and Gondwanaland

Laurásia

Gond wana land

Figure 7.4 Convection currents

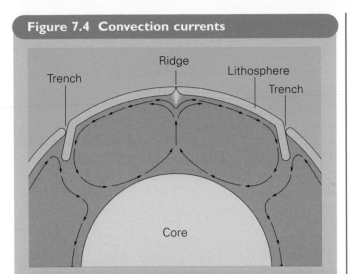

Hot currents in the asthenosphere rise, cool and sink. These are convection currents. This process slowly moves the 'floating' plates of the lithosphere. Scientists are not certain how deep the convection currents extend nor where the heat source that powers them exists.

moving apart and magma is rising to form the Ridge and volcanic islands such as Iceland.

When magma (ie, molten rock from within the Earth) comes to the surface and cools, the particles within the rock are 'polarised'. In other words, they line up like mini-magnets towards the poles. Because the Earth's magnetic field has reversed at known times in the Earth's history, it is possible to use this information and date the geological time period when rocks were formed.

On either side of the mid-Atlantic Ridge, the rocks have been dated and they show that the ocean bed is composed of parallel bands of successively older basalt rocks. This is strong evidence that the ocean floor is 'spreading' along a line

of upwelling magma. This discovery led researchers to believe that the rocky plates of the Earth's lithosphere were moving on the semi-molten asthenosphere below, powered by convection currents (see figure 7.4).

Plate boundaries

The Earth's lithosphere is made up of seven large plates and several smaller ones (see figure 7.5). At the edges of the plates, there are ridges or trenches where crust is being created or destroyed. It is at plate boundaries that most of the world's earthquakes and volcanoes occur. Where the plates move apart, molten rock wells up from below. The mid-Atlantic Ridge is one such place where new crust is being constantly created, moving North America and Eurasia apart.

Where plates collide, mountains can be formed. For example, India is pushing northwards into Asia, creating the Himalayas in a process that is still continuing. In other cases, crust is being destroyed as one plate sinks below another.

Because the Earth is not getting larger or smaller, the rate at which new crust is being created must be equal to the rate of crustal destruction. This is a state of 'dynamic equilibrium' - ie, change is occurring but the overall balance remains the same.

Figure 7.5 The main tectonic plates and their direction of movement.

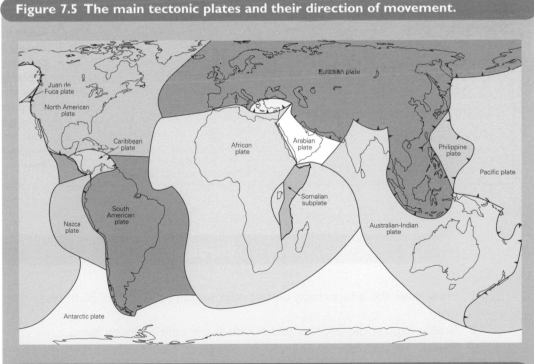

Note that there are plate boundaries around most of the Pacific Ocean. The Pacific 'Ring of Fire' is the name given to this zone of volcanic activity.

In 1997, research undertaken by the British Antarctic Survey suggested that the slow movement of plates caused by convection currents cannot adequately explain the break-up of the southern supercontinent of Gondwanaland. The process had to be aided by some type of eruption from the depths of the mantle known as a mantle plume.

Research into the rocks of the area reveal that a mantle plume under Brimstone Mountain in Antarctica 'domed up' Gondwanaland 2 to 3 km high, making it crack open and spread apart. The vast amount of molten rock that flowed out broke off rafts of the supercontinent. Because the mantle plume caused the crust to rise upwards in a dome, once the split occurred the rafts moved apart by gravity down each side of the bulge. These huge rafts of older rock are embedded in dolerite (a rock formed when magma cools underground) and can be found today.

It appears that Mount Erebus, in Antarctica, is located at the top of another mantle plume from 100 million years ago. This caused Australia and New Zealand to drift off northwards. Antarctica itself is still being split in two, divided by a rift near the Ellsworth Mountains.

Activity ▸ Plate tectonics

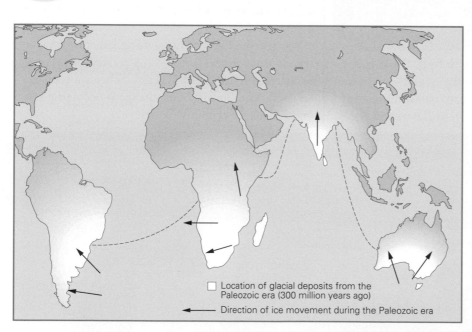

Figure 7.6 The location of glacial deposits and direction of ice movement in southern continents.

During the Paleozoic era (about 300 million years ago), ice sheets covered large parts of the landmass in the Southern Hemisphere. The deposits left by these ice sheets and the direction of ice movement have been identified by striations (deep scratches) and grooves along exposed rocks. Evidence from other glaciations makes it very unlikely that the ice moved from the sea onto land.

□ Location of glacial deposits from the Paleozoic era (300 million years ago)

← Direction of ice movement during the Paleozoic era

Questions

1 How does the information on this map support the idea of plate tectonics / continental drift?
2 Briefly explain the process which causes the continents to move.
3 Sketch the possible positions of the Southern Continents at the time of the Paleozoic glaciation.

4. What happens at plate boundaries?

At plate boundaries, the plates might:
• converge (move together);
• diverge (move apart); or
• move sideways alongside each other.

Convergent Plates

Where two plates move together and collide, the outcome depends on whether the plates contain mainly continental or oceanic crust. If one continental and one oceanic plate, or two oceanic plates converge, it is known as a **destructive margin**. If two continental plates converge it is known as a **collision margin**. Examples of each type are described below.

Destructive margin When a continental and an oceanic plate converge, the lighter, less dense continental plate rides up over the heavier, denser oceanic plate which is forced down into the heat of the mantle. As it sinks, it cracks and partially melts. This creates gases and molten rock which move upwards through weaknesses in the continental crust above, and forms volcanoes. Where the oceanic plate sinks down, a deep sea trench is formed. Such a plate boundary is sometimes called a **subduction zone** (see figure 7.7). An example is on the west coast of South America. The Andes have been formed as the Nazca oceanic plate has pushed into and under the South American plate.

The same process occurs where plates made of oceanic crust converge. This happens near Japan where the Pacific plate pushes into and moves under the edge of the Eurasian plate (which at this location is formed of oceanic crust). The resulting volcanoes form an **island arc**. This, and other arcs, form an almost continuous string of islands from the Aleutians in Alaska to New Zealand. Another example of a subduction zone where two plates formed of oceanic crust converge is the Caribbean arc of islands.

Collision margin Where two plates formed of continental crust collide, **fold mountains** are formed as neither crust is dense enough to sink beneath the other. **Sediments** (ie, layers of rock deposited in seas and oceans) are squeezed into folds and slowly pushed up by the steady advance of the two plates, eventually forming thick layers. Two mountain ranges formed in this way, the Alps and Himalayas are still rising faster than they are being worn away. This process of mountain building is known as an **orogeny**.

The formation of the Himalayas illustrates what happens at a collision zone (see figure 7.8). The single supercontinent Pangea broke up around 200 million years ago. The Indo-Australian plate split from present-day South Africa, spun around and moved northwards towards the Eurasian plate. Sediments from the plates were washed into the 'Tethys Sea' which lay between them. The sea became ever smaller as the Indo-Australian plate headed north. About 45 million years ago, the sea closed up completely and the Indo-Australian plate pushed into the larger Eurasian plate. The sedimentary rocks, such as sandstone and limestone, were forced into giant folds, crumpling and also cracking along faults that slipped or buckled. This is the reason why fossils from sea beds can be found at the top of Himalayan mountains. The weight of the sediment also forced the underlying crust down, forming a 'root' that is well below the Earth's surface.

Figure 7.7 The subduction zone at a destructive margin where two plates converge.

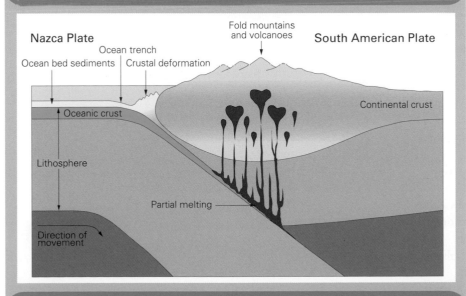

This example shows the plate boundary that runs down the western edge of South America. The Andes were formed at this destructive plate margin.

Figure 7.8 A collision margin between two continental plates

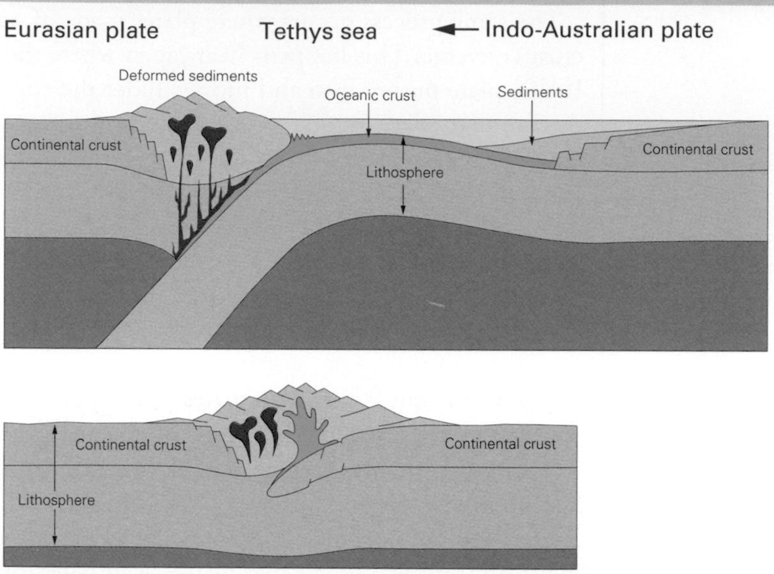

Eurasian plate   Tethys sea   ← Indo-Australian plate

Deformed sediments
Oceanic crust   Sediments
Continental crust   Continental crust
Lithosphere

Continental crust   Continental crust
Lithosphere

The Himalayas are formed from sedimentary rocks that were formed below sea level. The lower diagram shows the position of the plates after the sea has closed.

Although converging plates have enormous energy and have formed the world's highest mountains, it should be remembered that the process is imperceptibly slow. It takes millions of years to happen and, of course, it is happening at the present time.

Divergent Plates

Where two plates move apart, they leave a gap through which magma (molten rock) oozes up. The magma is called lava when it reaches the surface. The rock formed from the lava is mainly basalt - it is an example of an **igneous rock**. These plate boundaries are sometimes called **constructive margins** because new crust is being created.

When two oceanic plates move apart, the magma rises up onto the sea bed and forms a **mid-ocean ridge**. The process is known as **sea floor spreading**. On contact with the water, the magma cools and forms spectacular rock formations. It also warms the water and enriches it with sulphur, producing a rich diversity of marine life. The largest mid-ocean ridge is the mid-Atlantic Ridge, running from

inside the Arctic Circle to the Antarctic Circle.

Iceland lies on the mid-Atlantic Ridge and is widening by around 3 cm a year. The submarine volcanoes along the ridge sometimes rise above sea level and form new islands - for example, Surtsey, south of Iceland.

The mid-Atlantic Ridge is along a line where two plates are moving apart. Figure 7.9 shows the process by which it formed. At first, there was an upwelling of magma that caused a split in a plate that consisted of continental crust. Then a 'rift valley' formed between parallel lines of faults. The block of crust between the faults sank and eventually flooded - forming, at first, a narrow sea. As convection currents moved the plates further apart, magma continued to flow out. This formed a ridge in mid-ocean and, as the sea floor 'spread', also formed new oceanic crust.

Figure 7.9 The mid-Atlantic Ridge: a constructive margin

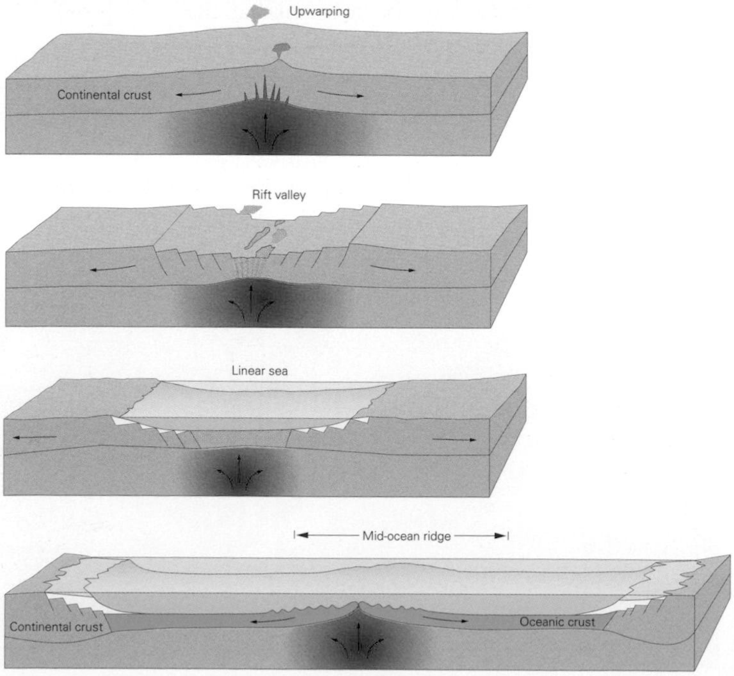

Upwarping
Continental crust

Rift valley

Linear sea

Mid-ocean ridge
Continental crust   Oceanic crust

Activity | Iceland

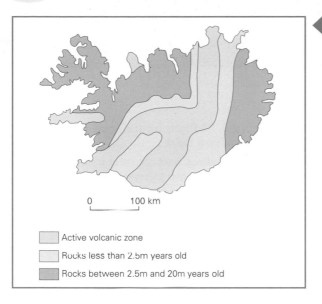

0   100 km

Active volcanic zone

Rocks less than 2.5m years old

Rocks between 2.5m and 20m years old

Figure 7.10 Iceland showing the age of its volcanic rocks

Questions

1 Describe the pattern of rocks shown on the map of Iceland.
2 Explain how the pattern of rocks provide evidence for Iceland lying on a divergent plate boundary.
3 Outline the process that causes plates to diverge.

Divergent plates in continental crust Divergent plate boundaries sometimes occur on land. The East African Rift Valley is an example (see figure 7.11). It is part of a rift valley system that stretches 5,000 km from Israel in the north to Mozambique in the south. At the northern end of the system, the Arabian Plate (north east of the Red Sea) is moving north eastwards whilst the African Plate is moving south westwards, widening the Red Sea. To the south, the African Plate is being cracked apart and the rift valley system is split into a western and eastern section. Tension in the crust has caused parallel faults to form and the blocks of crust between the faults to sink downwards. In places, the rift valley's sides are over 500 metres high and its width varies between 10 and 50 km. Lakes such as Lake Malawi and Lake Tanganyika have formed inside the rift valley and volcanoes such as Mount Kenya and Mount Kilimanjaro have formed on the edges of the valley.

Transform (or conservative) margins

Where plates slide past each other in a transform margin, crust is neither created nor destroyed. The friction caused as the plates grind past each other causes cracks or faults in the crust.

Earthquakes can be caused by friction and the build-up of pressure between the moving plates - the plates

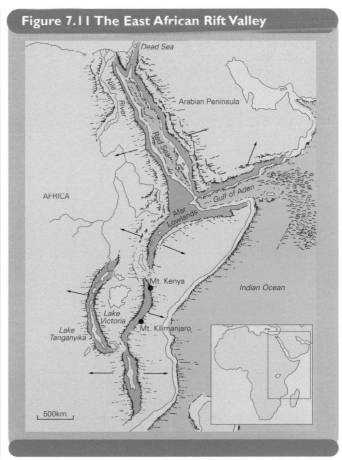

Figure 7.11 The East African Rift Valley

Dead Sea

Nile River

Arabian Peninsula

Red Sea

AFRICA

Afar Lowlands

Gulf of Aden

Mt. Kenya

Indian Ocean

Lake Victoria

Mt. Kilimanjaro

Lake Tanganyika

500km

'stick', then suddenly jerk. The best known and most studied transform margin is in California where it forms the San Andreas Fault. This is the boundary between the North American Plate (moving northwest at a rate of 1 cm a year) and the Pacific Plate (also moving northwest but faster, at 6 cm a year). Faults radiating from the San Andreas Fault run under Los Angeles and were the cause of a major earthquake in 1994 (see unit 7.2). A much bigger earthquake in 1906 caused great damage to San Francisco.

Activity   The San Andreas Fault

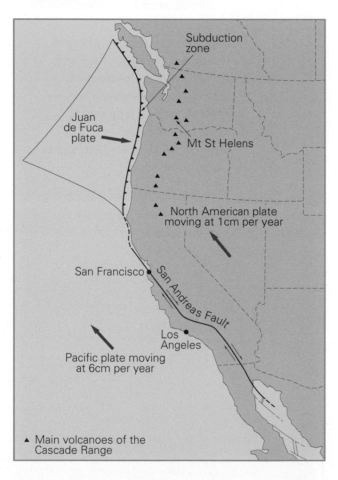

▶ **Figure 7.12 Plate boundaries on the west coast of the USA**

The San Andreas Fault occurs at a transform plate boundary where two plates are sliding past each other. Further to the north, the small Juan de Fuca plate moves under the North American plate forming a destructive margin. Fifteen major volcanoes - one of which is Mt St Helens - are found along the Cascade Range mountain chain which has built up along this plate boundary.

Questions

1 With reference to the west coast of the USA, explain the difference between a transform plate margin and a destructive plate margin.
2 Briefly outline how the Cascade Range of volcanoes formed.

Unit Summary

1 Scientists have identified three main zones or layers in the Earth in terms of chemical composition and density: the core, mantle and crust.
2 The crust is the thinnest layer and can be subdivided into lighter, thicker Continental crust (sial) which forms mainly land, and the denser, thinner and younger Oceanic crust (sima) which forms oceans basins.

3   The top layer of the mantle is cool and rigid. Together with the crust it is called the lithosphere and this is broken into plates. Underneath is a zone of hotter, 'plastic' rock that is capable of flow. This is known as the asthenosphere.

4   Heat in the Earth's interior generates convection currents within the mantle.

5   Plate tectonics is a theory that explains continental drift and the movement of the plates.

6   The plates are in continuous motion so the relative positions of the continents are constantly changing.

7   The destruction and creation of crust is in a state of dynamic equilibrium. In other words, the destruction is balanced by the creation of new crust.

8   When two plates diverge (move apart), new crust is created.

9   When two plates converge (move together), crust is destroyed and recycled as it sinks into the mantle, or is forced up into fold mountains.

10 At transform plate boundaries, the plates move past each other.

11 Most volcanoes and earthquakes occur near plate boundaries.

key terms

Asthenosphere - the plastic layer of mantle below the lithosphere.

Biosphere - the land, sea and air where life exists.

Collision margin - where two plates formed from continental crust converge and create fold mountains.

Constructive margin - where two plates move apart, creating new crust by sea floor spreading or in rift valleys.

Core - the densest, hottest, innermost layer of the Earth.

Crust - the least dense, thin outer shell of the Earth divided into **oceanic crust** and **continental crust**.

Destructive margin - where two plates (one or both being oceanic plates) converge; one is destroyed as it is forced under the other in a **subduction zone**.

Hydrosphere - the water on the Earth's surface.

Igneous rock - rock formed from **magma**. This is the molten material that comes from inside the Earth's mantle.

Island arc - a chain of islands formed by volcanic activity at a subduction zone.

Lithosphere - the upper, solid layer of Earth that includes the crust and top layer of mantle.

Mantle - the layer between the crust and the core where convection currents are generated.

Mohorovicic (Moho) Discontinuity - the dividing line between mantle and crust marked by a change in density and therefore speed at which shock waves can move through it.

Orogeny - the process of mountain building when continental plates collide.

Plates - sections or pieces of the Earth's lithosphere (the crust and rigid upper layer of the mantle).

Plate margin - the boundary or edge of a plate.

Plate tectonics - the theory that explains continental drift. The theory states that the Earth's surface is broken into a number of separate plates. These move in relation to each other in response to convection currents in the mantle.

Sedimentary rock - rock laid down in layers, mainly on the sea bed. It is formed mostly from eroded debris transported by rivers. Examples include sandstone and clay. During orogenies, it is folded and faulted.

Subduction zone - the line along a plate margin where oceanic crust is forced down into the mantle below another plate.

Transform margin (or conservative margin) - where two plates pass each other and the friction generated causes faults and earthquakes.

Unit 7.2 The distribution, causes and effects of earthquakes

key questions

1 What causes earthquakes and can they be predicted?
2 What are the effects of earthquakes?

1. What causes earthquakes and can they be predicted?

An earthquake is a sudden movement or shaking of the Earth's surface. Another name for earthquakes is **seismic activity** (seismos is Greek for earthquake).

Each year there are more than one million earthquakes. Only about 1,000 per year are strong enough to be felt by humans and, on average, 150 cause serious damage. Ninety percent of earthquake activity is concentrated near plate boundaries. It should be noted,

though, that some powerful 'intraplate' earthquakes have been recorded away from plate boundaries.
Earthquakes are caused in two main ways:
• tectonic quakes - these are the most frequent form of earthquake. They are the result of movements or fractures in the Earth's crust. Stresses build up and are released - causing vibrations and tremors.
• volcanic quakes - lava rising in a volcano can set off an earthquake. These are rarer and usually less serious than tectonic quakes. (Volcanic activity is covered in unit 7.3.)
People can also cause earthquakes, for example by filling large reservoirs with water. The weight of water can put stress on underlying rocks and can set off minor quakes. These become dangerous if the retaining dam is damaged. Underground nuclear testing and large-scale dumping of liquid chemicals in bore holes can also trigger earthquakes.

Activity Where do earthquakes occur?

▼ **Figure 7.13 The location of major earthquakes 1900-1999**

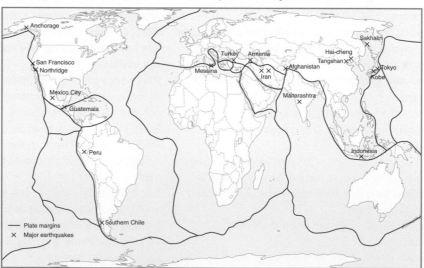

Questions

1 Describe the location of the major earthquakes between 1900-1999.
2 To what extent were the earthquakes near plate margins?

Figure 7.14 The focus and epicentre of an earthquake

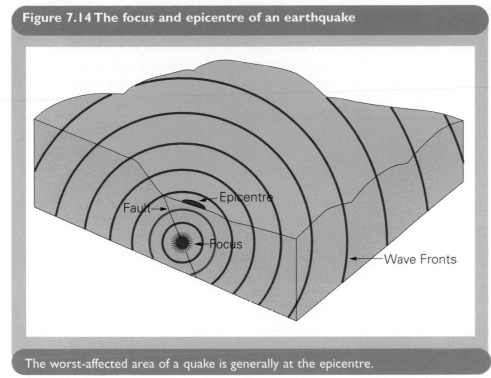

Fault → Epicentre

Focus

Wave Fronts

The worst-affected area of a quake is generally at the epicentre.

When the plates that form the Earth's crust converge or move past each other, the zone between them is under great stress. It becomes deformed by pressure. The ground first bends, then, upon reaching a certain limit, breaks and 'snaps' to a new position. In the process of breaking or 'faulting', vibrations are set up that are the earthquakes. Some of the vibrations are of very low frequency, whereas other vibrations are of such a high frequency that they are audible to humans.

Faults are simply cracks or fractures in the Earth's crust. Large numbers are found near plate boundaries. When stress builds up on opposite sides of a fault, at first slippage might not occur due to friction within the rock. But, if the pressure becomes too great, movement will occur at the weakest point along the fault. This point is known as the **focus** of the earthquake (see figure 7.14). The focus can be up to 700 km deep, well below the lithosphere. However, most earthquakes that are felt on the surface are less than 70 km deep. The point on the surface immediately above the focus is known as the **epicentre**.

Earthquake predictions

There are three variables to be considered in earthquake prediction:
• where will it occur;
• when will it occur; and
• how big will it be ?

Because most earthquakes occur near plate margins, on fault lines, their general location is well known. Also of course, there are historical records which show where past quakes have occurred. However, the precise location of the next quake in a particular region, its timing and size are impossible to predict at the present time.

In high income countries such as Japan and the USA, scientists continually monitor quakes and plot the sites that are most at risk. Seismometers (or seismographs) detect earth tremors, and laser beams are set up across known faults to detect earth movements on the surface. By building up this knowledge, and by analysing 'return intervals' (the usual time gap between quakes in a particular area), it is hoped to improve predictions in the future.

Observing unusual animal and fish behaviour is a less scientific method of predicting earthquakes than using seismometers. However this method is claimed to have saved thousands of lives in the 1975 Hai-cheng quake in China. The population was evacuated from buildings when people were alerted by rearing horses, mice fleeing houses, dogs barking and fish jumping - all the result of their sensitivity to the preliminary tremors. Unfortunately, this method of prediction has rarely worked. The more serious Tangshan quake a year later was not predicted and an estimated 240,000 people died. This was the most destructive earthquake of the twentieth century. Eighty percent of the buildings in this million strong industrial city in north east China were damaged or destroyed. There had been no foreshocks or seismic activity in the area in the previous two months.

Using return interval data, the regularity of earthquakes in an area can be plotted (see figure 7.15). For example, in the Tokai area of Japan, major quakes have occurred, on average, every 72.5 years since 1623. The last one was in 1923 so the next one is now due. Although this information is useful in predicting where an earthquake will occur, it does not tell people precisely whether it will be this week, next week, or next year! Nor does it give an indication of how big it will be.

Figure 7.15 Return interval data for Tokai

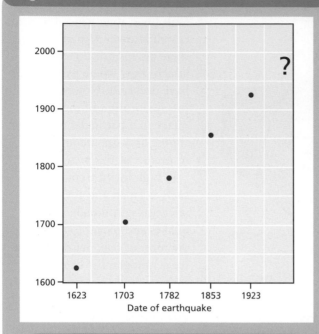

Tokai is a densely populated region to the south of Tokyo in Japan. The Pacific plate is moving towards Japan at the rate of 8 cm per year. It appears that the build up of pressure causes a major earthquake at regular intervals.

Many scientists believe that there is no prospect, for the foreseeable future, of making accurate predictions of the precise time, location and size of earthquakes. Indeed some suggest that there are so many variables involved that attempts to predict quakes are futile and a waste of money. In this view, it is simply not possible to monitor the build up of stress along every section of all known faults. Nor is it possible to predict whether movement along a fault will be slow and gradual, or sudden and 'jerky'.

Some geologists have suggested that it might be possible to prevent earthquakes along sections of known faults. Studies have shown that injecting fluid into faults might slowly release the strain rather than allow it to build up. This could be particularly valuable along the San Andreas Fault because it lies so close to heavily populated areas. However, fears of unforeseen and adverse side effects have so far stalled this idea.

At present, it seems that the best policy is to learn how to live with the consequences of earthquakes. Buildings should be designed and built to withstand earth tremors. High risk areas should be avoided for high density building, and emergency plans should be prepared for coping with the aftermath. (These issues are discussed in unit 7.4.)

Activity   Californian earthquakes

▼ Figure 7.16 The San Andreas Fault

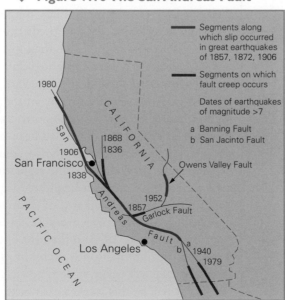

The San Andreas is the main fault in an intricate fault network that cuts through rocks in the California coastal region. The entire San Andreas fault system is over 1,200 km in length and extends to a depth of at least 15 km. In detail, the fault is a complex zone of crushed and broken rock from tens of metres to two kilometres across. Many smaller faults branch from the San Andreas fault zone. The whole region is subject to faulting and stress as the Pacific Plate moves north at a faster rate than the North American Plate. The boundary between these two plates is the San Andreas Fault. Places built on the Pacific Plate, including most of Los Angeles, are moving faster than places on the North American Plate, including San Francisco. At the present rate, Los Angeles will lie next to San Francisco in six million years time!

Blocks of land on opposite sides of the San Andreas fault line move horizontally. During the 1906 earthquake in the San Francisco region, roads, fences, and rows of trees that crossed the fault were moved several metres, and the road across the head of Tomales Bay ended up with a seven metre gap between the two sections on either side of the fault. In each case, the ground west of the fault moved relatively northward. The sudden movements that cause large earthquakes occur on only one section of the fault at a time. Total movement accumulates through time in an uneven fashion, primarily by movement on first one, and then another section of the fault. The sections that produce big earthquakes remain 'locked' and quiet over a hundred or more years while strain builds up; then, in great lurches, the strain is released, producing a large earthquake. Other stretches of the fault, however, bear the strain by a process of slow 'fault creep' rather than by sudden movements. In historical times, these creeping sections have not generated earthquakes of the magnitude seen on the 'locked' sections.

Geologists believe that the total accumulated relative movement from earthquakes and creep has been at least 550 km along the San Andreas fault since it came into being about 15-20 million years ago. Although this amount of movement in the Earth's crust is large, the overall rate is similar to the rate measured in historical times. Present day surveys show a relative movement of the plates at the rate of as much as 5 cm per year.

Questions

1 Why does California experience large earthquakes?
2 Explain why it is more dangerous to live near a section of the San Andreas Fault that is 'locked' rather than near a section that experiences 'fault creep'.
3 Outline the difficulties in predicting earthquakes along the San Andreas fault.

2. What are the effects of earthquakes?

The effects of earthquakes can be divided into the physical effects and the impact on people.

Physical effects

Earthquakes are caused by the passage of shock (or seismic) waves through the Earth. There are three sorts of waves that radiate out from the focus of an earthquake (see figure 7.17). First, the pressure or primary waves (known as **P waves**) cause back and forward movement compressing and expanding the rock as the wave moves through. It is rather like a crowd of people standing on a bus when it stops suddenly - they all get pushed together, then spread out again. These are the fastest waves and reach the surface first. They start at the focus and travel through both solids and liquids at 6-13 km a second.

Next come the sheer or secondary waves (known as **S waves**) which cause a sideways shaking and can tear the rocks. These secondary waves only travel through solid material and are slower than P waves, moving at 3-7 km a second.

Thirdly, there are the **surface waves** causing a 'rolling sea' effect on the surface. These waves cause the most damage to buildings and other structures.

To demonstrate the sequence of events, imagine a stone being thrown into a pond. The point it hits on the surface is the focus and the point on the bed directly below is the epicentre. The water is compressed in front of the stone as it drops through the pond (the P waves). Ripples then radiate outwards from the focus (the S waves) and finally, the surface is disturbed and 'wobbles' before it returns to normal. In an earthquake, the same sequence occurs (except that the focus is underground and the epicentre is at the surface).

Figure 7.17 Motion caused by the different types of seismic waves

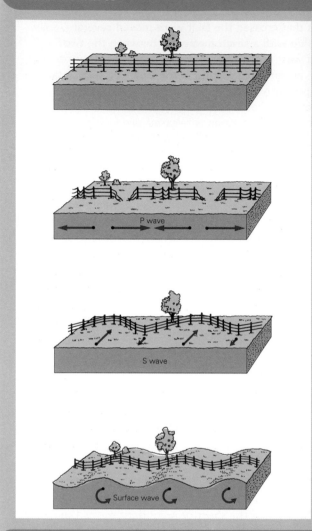

motion ten times greater than the next lowest number. So, for example, a magnitude 7 earthquake causes ten times more motion than a magnitude 6 earthquake. An earthquake's destructive power (its intensity) is measured by observing the damage caused. An intensity scale from 1 to 12 was first drawn up by an Italian, G Mercalli, after whom the scale gets its name.

Liquefaction is an important and damaging physical effect of earthquakes on soft or sandy ground. The surface, for a time, turns into a liquid. The effect is similar to being on a beach at the edge of the sea where the sand is wet. If you dabble your feet up and down, water rises to the surface and very soon you are standing in a puddle with sloppy sand around your feet. The same happens in an earthquake; the surface waves cause vibrations that make the ground water rise and the whole surface briefly acts like a liquid, resulting in the collapse of buildings and bridges as their foundations give way and they slide down.

Tsunamis are ocean waves caused by earthquakes under the sea bed. They are hardly noticeable in the open ocean but, as they move into shallower coastal waters, the resulting wave can rise up to 30 metres high. They can cause widespread damage. Sometimes, confusingly, they are called tidal waves, but they are more accurately referred to by their Japanese name of tsunami.

The speed of tsunami can be as high as 1,000 km/hr. In 1960, an earthquake in Chile triggered a tsunami that caused 11 metre waves in Hawaii and, 22 hours after the quake, caused $70 million damage on the Japanese coast. The most destructive tsunami in historic times was not associated with an earthquake but with the 1883

The physical effect of an earthquake depends upon its **magnitude** (energy) and its **intensity** (destructive power) (see figure 7.18). The amount of energy is measured by a seismometer and the tremors are recorded with a trace pen. By timing the arrival of the different types of wave, it is possible to calculate the distance of the focus from the observer and thus the magnitude of the earthquake. This is given as a number on the Richter Scale (named after the American geophysicist CF Richter who devised it). The Scale is logarithmic so each whole number represents ground

Fig 7.18 Earthquake scales

Mercalli Scale		Richter Scale
Only felt by instruments	1	Under 3
Felt by a few people	2	3 - 3.4
Like the rumble of traffic	3	3.5 - 4.0
Windows rattle	4	4.1 - 4.4
Light bulbs swing	5	4.5 - 4.8
Plaster cracks, furniture moves	6	4.9 - 5.4
Walls crack, chimneys fall	7	5.5 - 6.0
Severe structural damage	8	6.1 - 6.5
Underground pipes crack, houses collapse	9	6.6 - 7.0
Landslides, cracks in ground	10	7.1 - 7.3
Big gaps in ground, bridges destroyed	11	7.4 - 8.1
Total destruction	12	Over 8.1

volcanic eruption of Krakatoa. An estimated 36,000 people lost their lives when the wave hit the shoreline.

The effects of earthquakes on people

The effect of an earthquake depends on the rock type on which an urban area is built. Solid rock withstands earthquakes far better than silt or clay where liquefaction is a serious threat.

In a built-up area, the effect of an earthquake can be devastating if it is above 6 on the Richter Scale. The impact is most severe in low income countries where buildings are often poorly constructed. This is because there are fewer resources to design and build reinforced buildings. Also, in low income countries, there are often fewer regulations to ensure that buildings are safe, and even when there are regulations, they are less likely to be enforced than in high income countries.

The **primary effects** of a major earthquake are the immediate consequences. For instance, inside a house, ornaments, book cases and fitments might shake and fall, perhaps trapping occupants. An open fire in the grate, or flames on the cooker, might set the house alight. If people rush outside in panic they risk being hit by falling slates, gutters and chimneys. On the street, cracks form in the roads, and bridges collapse causing traffic pile-ups to occur and blocking the road to emergency services. Communication links, power sources and utilities are also cut as high tension cables, gas mains, water pipes and sewers fracture. Buildings might collapse and, in the case of high-rise blocks, might 'concertina' downwards. People are trapped, injured and frightened - all in the first few minutes following a big earthquake.

The **secondary effects** of an earthquake are the consequences that follow in the days and weeks after the event. Sometimes these effects kill more people than the initial earthquake damage. In the immediate aftermath of a major quake, shocked, stunned and injured people try to cope with the devastation and loss of homes, security and family. Fires at petrol stations and leaking gas mains might continue to burn and their smoke pollutes the air. Contamination from sewage is a serious danger, bringing the risk of disease, and there is little fresh water for washing or drinking. Buildings are often unstable and some people might still be trapped inside. Rail, road and telephone links are often cut, and airports damaged - so aid from outside is difficult and slow.

How people cope, and how quickly they can get back to some normality, largely depends on where the earthquake occurs. In high income countries, there will be contingency plans and financial support. In low income countries, there will be fewer resources to help the disaster area.

The secondary effects will have both social and economic consequences. Many factories, offices and homes might be so damaged that work cannot resume straight away - costing money in wages, lost production and future orders. The community might also be threatened by disease, hunger and, possibly, social disorder.

In an urban area, the effect of an earthquake on the environment can be severe. Air pollution from fires can cause a build-up of ozone or smog, and ruptured pipes might release toxic gases from chemical plants. Water courses become polluted if they are contaminated by sewage and other wastes. If there are large areas of derelict land where buildings have been destroyed, uncollected refuse and decomposing organic material will attract flies and rats.

In rural areas, farmland and crops will be seriously affected if drainage or irrigation systems are disrupted. In addition, the soil structure might be damaged if it liquefies. In places where landslides have blocked roads and railways, farmers will have difficulty in getting their produce to market.

 Activity) The effect of earthquakes in urban areas

The islands that form Japan are part of an island arc created by the convergence of major plates. Throughout history the country has experienced both earthquakes and volcanic eruptions. However, in the Kobe area there had been little seismic activity for several decades before 1995. Early on the morning of January 16th, the converging plates caused a sudden movement on a fault 20 km underground. The result was an earthquake that measured 6.9 on the Richter Scale. First, a P wave rose vertically, not in itself causing much damage. Then an S wave caused violent sideways shaking. Although it lasted barely a second, it liquefied soft and unconsolidated ground - particularly near the harbour. Finally came the surface wave, which lasted for 20 seconds and literally shook the ground.

▲ Figure 7.19 Kobe port area

During the earthquake large cracks appeared. The ground shifted three metres in some places.

Many buildings and roads were destroyed. Afterwards, questions were asked about the construction methods which were supposed to be 'quake proof'. This was particularly the case for the elevated Hanshin highway on which 5 sections collapsed, killing 12 drivers. If the quake had hit later, in the rush hour, many more would have died. Housing in lower income areas, mainly built of wood and tar paper, caught fire as gas lines ruptured. Large areas burnt as firefighters were hampered by blocked roads and broken water mains. More than 100 hectares of the city were completely burnt and approximately 4,500 people died. Over 12,000 buildings were damaged and destroyed, and, a week after the quake, 100,000 households had no electricity and 850,000 had no gas. The economic life of the city with 1.4 million people completely came to a halt.

After the initial shock and confusion, a well coordinated relief operation quickly began. Emergency services were able to provide first aid, shelter and food to the people made homeless. In particular, drinking water and portable toilets were supplied to prevent the outbreak of water borne disease. Nevertheless the quake, which was the biggest in mainland Japan for nearly 50 years, badly shook the faith of many Japanese. They had believed that modern, reinforced buildings and contingency planning would prevent the scale of loss of life and damage that occurred. In historic terms, the earthquake was not very powerful. The 1923 earthquake which hit Tokyo was over 25 times more powerful - causing fears that a much bigger disaster could happen in the future.

Los Angeles - Northridge 1994

On January 17th, a magnitude 6.6 earthquake struck Northridge, just north of Los Angeles. The quake was small compared with the magnitude 8.2 earthquake that hit San Francisco in 1906. Nevertheless it caused the death of over 50 people and caused $30 billion in property damage.

The earthquake occurred on a previously unknown fault that lies under the prosperous and heavily populated San Fernando Valley. The epicentre lay several kilometres away from the much bigger San Andreas fault - responsible for California's biggest earthquakes.

Most people died when apartment blocks collapsed. Several freeway overpasses also collapsed - raising doubts about the design and building regulations which were meant to protect people from much bigger quakes. There was extensive secondary damage as landslips blocked the Pacific Coast Highway and other roads. Overall, the Earth's surface was ruptured along a 15 km stretch with the ground, in places, lifted by a metre. Electrical power was cut for 3 million people and one unlucky man died when his hospital respirator shut down. Over 250 gas mains broke and several buildings burnt down in the resulting fires. Other buildings were flooded when water lines were broken.

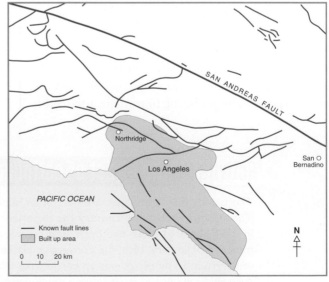

▲ Figure 7.20 Faults in the Los Angeles area

The wavelength of the surface waves was an estimated 300 metres. Little, single story buildings bobbed up and down as the peaks and troughs passed - like corks caught in a sea swell. But bigger buildings were rising at one end and sinking at the other in the same second. This stress caused some to collapse.

Mexico City 1985

This earthquake was unusual because the epicentre was 400 km distant from the most severe damage. The quake, which measured 8.1 on the Richter Scale, was centred on Mexico's Pacific Coast where only mild tremors were felt. However, when the shock waves reached the centre of Mexico City, they were intensified to five times that experienced elsewhere. The reason was that much of the city centre is built on an ancient lake bed that has been infilled. Lax building regulations meant that most buildings did not have sufficiently deep foundations. The soft sediments liquefied in places and, in others, created surface waves that caused the ground to rise and fall 40 cm every two seconds for nearly two minutes. Such shaking was too intense for many poorly designed buildings. Approximately 7,000 people died - mainly in collapsed apartment blocks. The situation was made worse because of previous subsidence in the soft material of the lake bed.

The wave motion caused multistorey buildings to sway back and forth by as much as one metre. This caused many, particularly in the 5 to 15 storey height range, to collapse completely or to 'concertina' on one or two floors. Many people were trapped inside buildings. In some cases there were miraculous survivals - in one case, 58 new born babies survived after being trapped up to seven days in a collapsed maternity hospital.

▲ **Figure 7.21 Northridge, Los Angeles**
A section of the Interstate Highway 14 collapsed during the earthquake.

Questions

1 Summarise (a) the physical effects and (b) the effects on people of the three earthquakes.
2 Suggest reasons why some powerful earthquakes cause more damage than others.

unit summary

1 Earthquakes occur most often near plate boundaries when pressure builds up along faults.
2 Seismic movement is monitored and recorded by seismometers (or seismographs). The magnitude of earthquakes is graded on the Richter Scale.
3 Previous locations and return intervals help to calculate the probability of future earthquakes. However, accurate prediction of the timing, scale and location of earthquakes may be impossible.
4 In a quake there are three types of wave: first, the Pressure wave compressing the rocks, then the Shear wave at 90 degrees to the first that tear the rocks and lastly, the surface waves that cause most damage.
5 Earthquakes can have immediate (primary) and longer term (secondary) social, economic and environmental consequences.

key terms

Epicentre - the point on the surface immediately above the focus of an earthquake and usually the location of maximum destruction.
Focus - the starting point, deep underground, of an earthquake.
Intensity - the destructive power of an earthquake, measured on the Mercalli Scale.
Liquefaction - a process in which the ground's surface acts like a liquid.
Magnitude - the size or energy of an earthquake.
P Waves, **primary** or **pressure waves** - these waves compress the crust.
Richter Scale - a logarithmic scale, scaled from 1 to 9, that measures earthquake magnitude.
S Waves, **secondary** or **shear waves** - these

occur at 90 degrees to the P waves in an earthquake.
Seismic activity - an alternative term for earthquakes.
Seismometer and **Seismograph** - instruments used to record and measure earth tremors.
Surface waves - these waves occur on the ground making the surface 'roll'.
Tectonic earthquakes - caused by plate movements.
Tsunami - an ocean wave sometimes caused by undersea earthquakes. The wave can rise up to 30 metres in shallow coastal waters.
Volcanic earthquakes - caused by volcanic eruptions or movements of magma underground.

Unit 7.3   Volcanic activity

key questions

1 Where do volcanic eruptions occur?
2 What landscape features are the result of vulcanicity?
3 Can volcanic eruptions be predicted?
4 What are the effects of volcanic activity?

1. Where do volcanic eruptions occur?

Where the Earth's crust is fractured or weakened, molten rock called **magma** can find its way through to the surface, either gently oozing out or violently erupting. Where this happens, the feature is called a **volcano**. Although the popular image of a volcano is a steep sided mountain pouring out smoke, ash and lava, this is not always typical. Many volcanoes are no more than vents or cracks in the Earth's surface through which lava flows. Also, there is far more volcanic activity under the sea than on land.

Volcanoes get their name from Vulcan, the Roman God of Fire. The Mediterranean island of Vulcano was named after the God because of the smoke and fire it emitted. It was supposed to be his workshop.

For over four billion years, volcanoes have moulded the face of our planet. It is likely that they created the conditions for life to begin. Eruptions released gases from the mantle to form the primitive atmosphere. Water vapour from deep in the Earth condensed onto the surface to produce the oceans. Without volcanoes, the Earth would probably be a lifeless desert with no oceans, rain, clouds or people. But volcanoes also have the potential to destroy life. A huge eruption could blot out the Sun for decades and, without light, the food supply would dwindle. The Earth would cool and a new Ice Age might begin. Even small eruptions have the capacity to kill many people and destroy property.

Distribution of volcanoes

There are approximately 500 active volcanoes around the world. Many more are dormant (at present inactive) or extinct (dead, unlikely ever to erupt). Most volcanoes are located near plate boundaries, either at destructive plate margins (eg, around the Pacific Ocean) or at constructive plate margins (eg, the mid-Atlantic Ridge). However, some volcanoes do occur away from plate margins at locations known as 'hot spots'. Hawaii is an example. See figure 7.22 for a map showing the distribution of major volcanoes.

Figure 7.22 World distribution of major volcanoes

If this map is compared with figure 7.5, it is clear that most volcanoes are located on or near plate boundaries.

Destructive plate margins At destructive margins, oceanic plate is forced down into the mantle (see figure 7.7). This occurs round the Pacific Ocean and causes the 'Ring of Fire' where tectonic plate boundaries give rise to earthquakes and volcanic eruptions. Where the Pacific Plate and the smaller Juan de Fuca, Nazca and Cocos Plates meet the North and South American Plates, there is a line of volcanoes running from Alaska to Chile. Where the Pacific Plate meets the Eurasia Plate, the ring continues through the Aleutian Islands, Kamchatka Peninsula and Kuril Islands. The Ring of Fire then runs southwards through Japan and the Philippines, along the subduction zone between the Eurasia and Philippine Plates and then it curves through the Solomon Islands and onto New Zealand.

Where oceanic crust is forced down into the mantle, it is called a subduction zone, and there is partial melting of the subducted plate. The melted rock is less dense than the surrounding rock so it rises upwards and forms a volcano if it reaches the surface. It melts the continental crustal rocks as it passes through, mixing to form an acidic magma. The viscous (ie, sticky) nature of this magma makes it difficult for gases to escape - so creating bubbles and pockets of hot gas under great pressure. A rock commonly formed from this type of lava is andesite - named after the South American Andes where it is abundant.

Because there is a build-up of gases under high pressure within this type of magma, these volcanoes often explode when they erupt. They tend to cause much more violent eruptions than those elsewhere. Ash clouds can reach 80 kilometres high and, not surprisingly, these are the most dangerous type of volcano for humans. They can produce **pyroclastic flows** (pyroclastic means fiery, shattered rock). These are avalanches of hot rock, gas and ash at over 1,000°C and moving at 300 km per hour, destroying everything in their path. Pyroclastic fragments can vary in size from fine ash to large volcanic bombs. Large pieces of froth like lava, called pumice, may also be formed. Two examples of this type of eruption from recent decades were at Mount Soufriere on Montserrat in 1996 and Mount St Helens in the USA in 1980. In both cases the top of the volcano bulged before the violent explosion, then collapsed, causing pyroclastic flows down the steep valleys.

The intense heat during a volcanic eruption causes air to rise, frequently resulting in heavy rain. The rain mixes with the ash and forms mud flows capable of carrying cars, houses, bridges, trees, and boulders. The term **lahar** is sometimes used to describe such a mud flow.

Some volcanoes release both pyroclastic material and lava. They are called **composite volcanoes** because they are formed of layers of both ash and lava (see figure 7.23). One such, Mount Etna in Sicily, has erupted over

Figure 7.23 The features of composite volcanoes

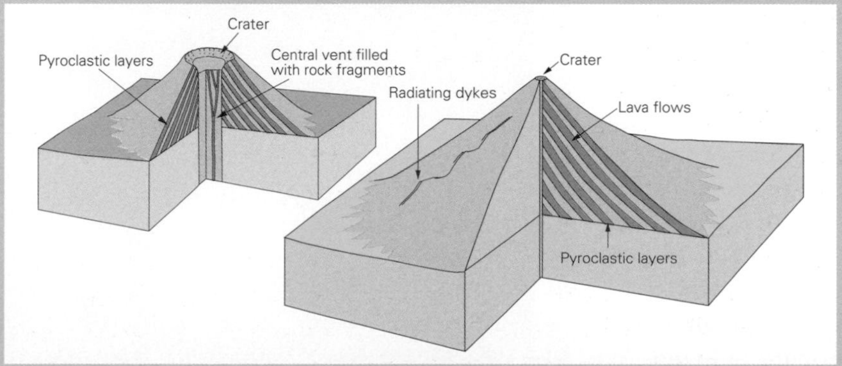

Crater
Pyroclastic layers
Central vent filled with rock fragments
Radiating dykes
Crater
Lava flows
Pyroclastic layers

In explosive eruptions a crater might be formed.

Figure 7.24 Mount Shasta, California

This volcanic peak in the Cascade Range of northeastern USA has the classic shape of a composite volcano.

100 times in the last 4,000 years, with several major eruptions in the last 50 years. On a small island, 100 km to the north, is Stromboli. This volcano erupts 'gently' and regularly, so there is no major build-up of pressure. It is typical of many composite volcanoes. However, 220 km further north, another composite volcano, Mount Vesuvius, is an exception. This poses a constant threat to the city of Naples which lies within 10 km of the crater. It was the location of a major eruption almost 2,000 years ago.

The settlements of Herculaneum and Pompeii had grown up at the foot of the volcano, along the Bay of Naples. The towns were home to 15,000 inhabitants who enjoyed a high standard of living. They were totally unprepared for the

eruption that occurred on August 24th, 79 AD. Eye witness accounts from across the Bay reported seeing an ash cloud rising high above the mountain. Then, pyroclastic flows swept down the slopes. In recent times, archaeologists have found the skeletons of a few Herculaneans who had sheltered in caves, only to be killed by the overpowering heat and gases. Falling ash had sealed the cave entrances, setting into pumice as it landed. In nearby Pompeii many people were enveloped by a dense cloud of super-heated ash that set around their bodies, incinerating them and leaving empty moulds. Upon their discovery by archaeologists, these were filled with plaster to reveal each person's last seconds. The ash preserved the houses, murals and mosaics so that today, tourists are able to observe the scene.

Constructive plate margins Where tectonic plates move

Figure 7.25 Iceland

Lava flowing from a fissure at a constructive plate margin.

Figure 7.26 Fissure eruption in Iceland at night

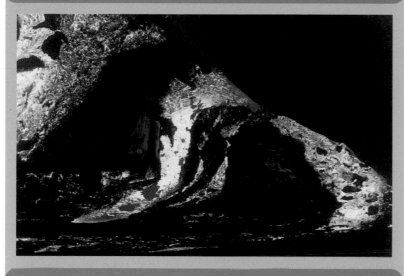

When the lava solidifies it forms basalt.

apart, the boundary is called a constructive margin. Mid-ocean ridges and rift valleys are examples of constructive plate margins. Under the oceans, magma rises to the surface at mid-ocean ridges and oozes out to create new sea floor. When the magma reaches the Earth's surface it is called lava; the rock it forms is mainly basalt. Underwater eruptions, especially along mid-ocean ridges, result in 'pillow lava'. The water cools the liquid rock but the pressure of lava behind is so great that it bursts through causing distinctive patterns that look like a jumbled mass of pillows. Basaltic lava is also found along the edges of rift valleys where it forms volcanoes or lava flows.

Volcanoes at constructive margins tend to erupt as gentle lava flows, often from fissures - long narrow cracks in the crust (see figure 7.25). An example is at Heimay in Iceland where, in 1973, a 3 km long fissure opened up near to the port. At first, black ash buried hundreds of houses. This was followed by lava flows which threatened to block the fishing port. Millions of gallons of seawater were sprayed onto the flow. It set and acted as a natural barrier to further flows which then bypassed the port and flowed into the sea, extending the sea wall and thus enlarging the harbour.

Hot spots Hot spots are areas of volcanic activity not associated with the edges of crustal plates. They are caused by **mantle plumes**, thought to

be isolated, long, slender columns of hot magma that rise from within the mantle. When oceanic plates move over the hot spot, the magma breaks through and a volcano forms. If the hot spot lies beneath continental crust, there may be hot springs as underground water is heated by the magma below. Yellowstone in the western USA is an example.

Over a hot spot in the ocean, the volcano might form an island. Volcanic activity on the island diminishes as the plate moves from the hot spot but, behind it, the hot spot remains and creates a new volcanic island. In this way, an island chain may be formed. The lava in these cases is 'basic' (ie, not acidic) and fluid. It produces low, gently sloping **shield volcanoes**. The islands of Hawaii in the Pacific Ocean were formed in this way (see figure 7.27).

Figure 7.27 Volcanic islands formed over a hot spot

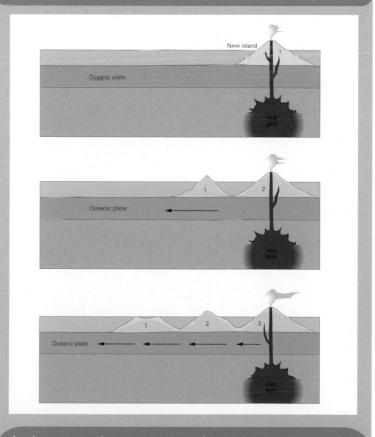

As the oceanic plate moves over a hot spot, a succession of volcanoes are formed. Sometimes they form islands and, in time, they are eroded away.

Figure 7.28 Mauna Loa: a shield volcano

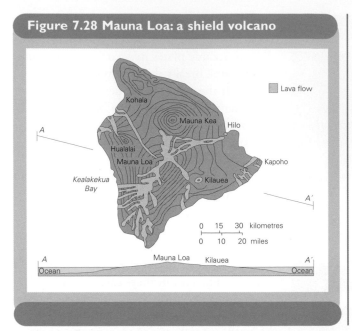

Mauna Loa is the largest volcano on Hawaii (see figure 7.28). It rises 9,000 metres above the ocean bed (5,000 metres are below sea level). To the southeast of Mauna Loa, Mount Kilauea has erupted almost continuously since 1966. In 1991, new lava flows slowly moved through tropical forest towards the town of Kalapana. After seven years, the lava eventually engulfed the whole town. Many people were able to load their houses onto trailers and move, leaving the area a blackened wasteland.

All of the Hawaiian islands are made of basaltic lava which forms long rivers of molten fluid. In places, the surface cools and solidifies, making a roof, whilst lava continues to run underneath in a tunnel or tube. Sometimes parts of the roof collapse and it is possible to observe the flowing lava. Research has shown that the lava can flow at 300,000 litres per minute and has a temperature of almost 1,000°C.

Figure 7.29 Volcanic cones in Hawaii

Eruptions over hot spots tend to be gentle rather than explosive.

Activity | Classification of volcanoes

▼ Figure 7.30 Classification based on the shape and composition of the volcano

Type	Description	Example	Composition
Fissure	Cooled lava may form a plateau or gently-sloped area along a long crack.	Heimay, Iceland	Basic basalt lava
Shield	Gently sloping, concave-sided cone formed by successive flows of runny lava.	Mauna Loa, Hawaii	Basic basalt lava
Acid Dome	Sticky, acidic lava forms steep convex-sided volcanic dome.	Mount Pelee, Martinique	Acidic andesite lava
Ash Cinder	A concave-sided cone made of successive layers of ash and cinders; easily eroded.	Paracutin, Mexico	Pumice
Composite	The 'classic' volcano shape; a cone shaped by alternate layers of ash and acidic lava.	Mount Etna, Sicily	Ash and andesite
Caldera	A collapsed or exploded dome; leaving a wide crater.	Krakatoa, Indonesia	

*Note: A **caldera** is a basin shaped depression. It is formed when an explosive eruption occurs - either blasting the summit of the volcano away or causing the summit to collapse into the magma chamber.*

▼ Figure 7.31 Classification based on the violence of the eruption

Type	Description
Icelandic or Hawaiian	Gently flowing lava from a vent or fissure
Strombolian	Small but frequent eruptions.
Krakatoan	Exceptionally violent

▼ Figure 7.32 Classification according to location

Location	Description
Constructive Margin	Basaltic, gentle fissure eruptions of basic lava.
Destructive Margin	Acidic and composite, violent eruptions.
Hot Spots	Basaltic, shield island chains.

Questions

1 Explain why different types of volcano occur in different parts of the world.
2 What factors affect the violence of volcanic eruptions?

2. What landscape features are the result of vulcanicity?

Volcanic activity can produce many different features depending on the type of volcanic activity which produced them. When magma cools it produces what is known as an **igneous** rock. This might be **extrusive** (from lava and ash on the Earth's surface) or **intrusive** (from magma that cools and solidifies below the Earth's surface).

Extrusive landforms

These landforms are produced when magma and other volcanic material reach the Earth's surface.

- Volcanoes form hills or mountains. These differ greatly in size and shape from steep sided composite cones to gentle sloped shield volcanoes. However, they share some common features. There is a pipe or vent through which material erupts. It is fed from an underground **magma chamber** containing molten rock and dissolved gases. Gas from the chamber might keep the pipe or vent open; if not, the magma sets and subsequent eruptions have to blast this blockage out of the way forming a crater, or break

Figure 7.33 Devil's Postpile, California

Hexagonal columns of basalt have been smoothed by ice.

through the sides forming a secondary or 'parasitic' cone.

- lava plateaux or **flood basalts**. These are horizontal layers of basalt that are formed when lava flows from fissures and then solidifies. Examples occur in India (the Deccan Plateau) and in the north west USA where the Columbia Plateau extends over 5 million square kilometres and is up to 2,000 metres thick. When lava cools on the Earth's surface, it does so relatively quickly - causing the crystals within it to be very small. This is typical of basalt. In some places, where flood basalts occur, jointing in the cooling lava has formed distinctive columnar, hexagonal shapes. Examples occur in Antrim at the Giant's Causeway, at Fingal's Cave off the island of Mull and in California at the Devil's Postpile near Mammoth.

In most volcanic regions, including many where volcanoes are extinct, heat and gases are trapped in the rocks. This underground heat creates a variety of surface features:

- Fumaroles These are ponds of hot mud, often with clouds of steam rising above them. Below the ground surface, the water is above 100°C but the intense pressure prevents it from turning into steam - so it becomes 'superheated'. As it emerges from the ground, the drop in pressure enables it to vaporise and become steam. Examples are found in active volcanic regions such as Iceland and North Island, New Zealand.
- Solfatara These features are named after a volcanic area near Naples, Italy; they are emissions of smelly, sulphurous gas.
- Geysers These are intermittent fountains of hot water. Water trickles into the ground from the Earth's surface and is heated by the hot rocks below. It turns to steam and, as pressure builds up, the water and steam explode to the surface. The word 'geyser' is Icelandic and there are several examples in that country (see figure 7.34). Another well known geyser is 'Old Faithful' in Yellowstone National Park, USA.
- Hot Springs These remnants of volcanic activity occur where water trickles through warm rocks and becomes heated. It re-emerges, often having absorbed sulphur or other minerals to form hot springs or mineral spas. The springs sometimes become tourist attractions or health resorts where people sit in the water, or drink it, hoping to become more healthy. Dax, in south west France, is one such location - far from any present day volcanic activity. Since Roman times, people have gone to Dax to bathe in the hot natural springs and to 'take the cure'.

Figure 7.34 Geyser at Krisuvik, Iceland

The intense heat and pressure can alter these to form a new rock. These altered rocks in the 'contact zone' are called **metamorphic**. For example, limestone turns into marble, sandstone becomes schist and mudstones and clays become shale and slate.

Volcanic plugs These features are the remnants of eroded volcanoes and are formed from the more resistant rock of the vent or pipe. They generally form small, steep sided hills. Edinburgh Castle is built on such a volcanic plug and the Puy area of France has many examples.

Dykes These features are formed when magma intrudes (ie, pushes) vertically through the crustal rocks, perhaps along a fault. A dyke is a vertical intrusion that cuts across bedding planes. Sometimes dykes radiate from a batholith to make a 'dyke swarm'. When exposed, dykes can look like dry stone walls cutting across the landscape. They are very prominent when they cross beaches - there are many examples in north west Scotland and the Scottish islands. Not all dykes produce ridges. In places where a dyke is formed of rocks less resistant to erosion than the surrounding rock, it can form a long, narrow ditch like depression.

Intrusive landforms

Intrusive landforms result from volcanic activity where magma does not reach the surface. When magma is forced up through the crust it might push along bedding planes (ie, surfaces separating layers of sedimentary rocks) and faults, or form huge underground domes. After millions of years, weathering and erosion might uncover the solidified magma. Because these intrusive rocks might be more, or less, resistant to erosion than the surrounding rocks, a variety of landforms can be created.

Batholiths These features are formed when large domes of magma cool underground. They are recognisable in the landscape only when the overlying rocks are eroded to reveal the dome-shaped hills. Dartmoor and Bodmin Moor, in south west England, are examples. In north east Scotland, large intrusions have been exposed by weathering to form the Cairngorm Mountains. Batholiths typically contain granite which, because it has cooled relatively slowly underground, is formed from quite large crystals. When magma moves through the crust, it comes into contract with the surrounding rocks.

Figure 7.35 A ridge dyke at Largybeg, Arran

The igneous rock that forms this dyke is more resistant to weathering than the surrounding rock.

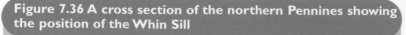

Figure 7.36 A cross section of the northern Pennines showing the position of the Whin Sill

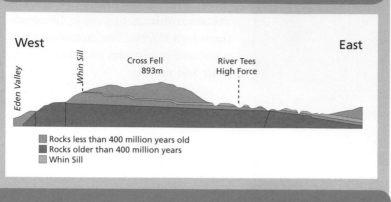

West   East

Eden Valley

Whin Sill

Cross Fell
893m

River Tees
High Force

■ Rocks less than 400 million years old
■ Rocks older than 400 million years
■ Whin Sill

3. Can volcanic eruptions be predicted?

Because volcanoes can be inactive or dormant for centuries, it is difficult to predict when, and with what ferocity, they will erupt. However, there has been some progress in research. For example, the US Geological Survey has devised methods of remote sampling of volcanic gases. Using a vehicle-mounted device which measures sulphur dioxide levels in the smoke plume, scientists in the mid-1990s had some success. Instruments were set up on Popocatapetl, an active volcano in Mexico. Twenty million people live within the danger zone. By monitoring the wavelengths of light coming through the plume, it was possible to record the sulphur dioxide concentrations. Using this technique, a normal rate of sulphur dioxide emission from Popocatapetl was established (17,000 tonnes per day). When, six months later, emissions reached 700,000 tonnes per day, the Geological Survey accurately predicted an eruption. Changes in the gas mix had indicated that new magma was moving into the magma chamber, making an eruption likely.

In Japan, similar research has been undertaken. For example, near the active volcano Sakurajima, a 200 metre tunnel has been bored into the side of the cone. Instruments monitor the fluctuating gas pressure in the magma chamber. However, this effort has only achieved limited success. It is now possible to predict an eruption 20 seconds before it occurs - not long enough to give people sufficient warning.

More recent research has turned to remote-sensing and monitoring of volcanic activity by satellite. Using satellite images, scientists can observe volcanoes and monitor the thermal (heat) patterns and changes in the shape of the ground. Again, there is much reliance on the change in the wavelength of light passing through gases and other airborne particles (aerosols) emitted by the volcano. Thermal monitoring can also detect temperature changes, and thermal images of a volcano can establish its normal or dormant pattern from which changes can be detected.

Sills These features are formed when igneous rock intrudes horizontally along bedding planes. Sills can produce striking features in the landscape when exposed by weathering. An example is the Whin Sill, in north Cumbria and Northumberland (see figure 7.36). Part of the exposed sill was used by the Roman Army as a foundation for Hadrian's Wall - it forms an imposing frontier when viewed from the north. The sill is exposed for over 60 km before dipping underground to re-emerge on the coast at Bamburgh. Here it creates a defensive site for a castle and, further out to sea, it forms the Farne Islands. In some places, the sill is 80 metres thick but, in other places, it is only 1 metre thick. Where rivers flow over the resistant edge of the sill, waterfalls occur. An example is High Force on the River Tees.

Figure 7.37 Drumadoon sill, Arran

This sill has been exposed by weathering of overlying rock.

Sometimes predictions are inaccurate. For example, in 1976, La Soufriere on the Caribbean island of Guadaloupe, began to emit smoke and ash. Fearing a major eruption, officials organised the evacuation of over 75,000 people. However, nothing more happened. The cost of disruption and evacuation was estimated to have been several million dollars.

On the other hand, there have been successes. In April 1991, Mount Pinatubo in the Philippines started to show danger signs. Increased sulphur dioxide emissions, dozens of shallow earthquakes and the rapid growth of a lava dome suggested new activity in the magma chamber. Monitoring instruments were installed and scientists called for nearby villages to be evacuated. Minor explosions began on June 12th and, on June

15th, a huge blast blew out the side of the mountain. Fortunately, 60,000 people had been evacuated. The warnings saved many lives in villages and at the nearby Clark Air Force Base. Nevertheless, nearly 900 people died - mostly when the weight of ash caused roofs to collapse or when lahars swept downstream.

Whether completely accurate predictions on the timing and intensity of eruptions will ever be possible is a matter of debate. Sometimes volcanoes start to smoke and have small eruptions, then become inactive again. But in other cases, the warning signs are followed by a major eruption. At the present time, there is no certain way of knowing what will happen. The issue of how people cope with volcanic hazards is covered more fully in unit 7.4.

Activity Mount Pinatubo, 1991

▼ **Figure 7.38 The volcanic eruption of Mount Pinatubo, Philippines**

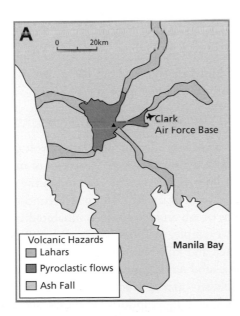

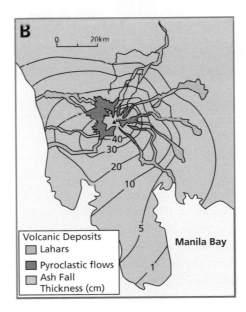

Map A is a volcanic hazard map drawn prior to 1991. The map was constructed by plotting where material from previous eruptions had been deposited. There were no detailed historical accounts of eruptions because Pinatubo had been dormant for at least 400 years.

Map B shows the distribution of material deposited in the 1991 eruption.

Figure 7.39 Clark Airbase
A cloud of ash from Mount Pinatubo threatens the airbase.

Questions

1 Describe the main hazards forecast by geologists before the Pinatubo eruption.
2 To what extent was the hazard map accurate?
3 Outline the difficulties that arise in making successful predictions of volcanic eruptions.

4. What are the effects of volcanic activity?

The effect of volcanic activity can be considered at both a global and at a local level.

Global effect

On a global scale, volcanic eruptions can cause climate change. For example, when Mount Pinatubo (in the Philippines) erupted in 1991, global temperatures dropped by an average of 0.5°C. The explosion carried aerosols (ie, particles of ash and droplets of sulphur dioxide) high into the atmosphere and filtered out some of the Sun's radiation. The eruption of the Indonesian volcano Tambora, in 1815, caused poor harvests and food shortages around the globe in what was called the 'year without a summer'.

It seems certain that much bigger eruptions in prehistoric times must have had a severe impact on global climate and, therefore, on all life forms. For example, in India 65 million years ago, massive lava flows formed the Deccan Plateau. The resulting loss of sunlight, reduction in photosynthesis and lower temperatures may have caused mass extinctions of plant and animal species. It seems likely that this has occurred several times during the Earth's history.

Local effect

In general, it is only the very largest volcanic eruptions that have a global impact. The effect of most eruptions is felt only on a local scale - although the impact can be severe. Sometimes the effect of an eruption is to send clouds of ash and gas towards inhabited areas.

For example, in 1902, Mount Pelee on Martinique erupted and killed nearly 30,000 people. The volcano is near a subduction zone on an island arc in the Caribbean - at a destructive plate margin. The magma is viscous, causing eruptions to be explosive because trapped gases cannot easily escape. After a month of emitting steam and fine ash, a massive eruption occurred. Dense, hot ash swept down the slopes in an avalanche. It took less than two minutes to engulf the town of St Pierre, 10 km away. Every flammable object was set on fire and almost no one survived - a condemned prisoner being held in a deep cell was one of the few lucky people.

A pyroclastic flow of this type is sometimes called a 'nuée ardente' (ie, glowing cloud). The Mount Pelee example shows that escape is impossible once a major eruption has occurred; the only safe option is to evacuate when volcanic activity begins.

Although eruptions at constructive plate margins tend to be less explosive that at destructive margins, they can still be lethal. For example, in Iceland in 1783, upwelling magma opened a system of fissures over 25 km long. It was known as the Laki Eruption. Over 550 square kilometres of land was covered by lava - the largest flow in recorded history. A blue haze of toxic gases also flowed from the fissures, killing 75 percent of Iceland's sheep and horses, and causing a famine that killed 20 percent of the country's population.

Why do people live near volcanoes?

Nearly 500 million people live near active volcanoes - and the number is rising as the world's population increases. Some people will always take a chance, even when they know the risk. As long as they can make a living in the area, they will ignore the danger or become adjusted to it.

There are some benefits to living in volcanically active areas. The most important attraction is that of fertile soil. Lava and ash weather rapidly into deep, rich soils that are ideal for farming. For example, Java, in Indonesia, has a very high population density, partly explained by the productive agriculture that takes place on the island's volcanic soils.

Volcanic activity sometimes produces valuable minerals such as gold, copper, lead and silver. Although most mining occurs in areas where volcanoes are extinct or where igneous rock has been exposed by erosion, sulphur is extracted from volcanoes in Indonesia that are still active.

The presence of volcanoes, geysers, or deep-seated 'hot rocks' in decaying volcanic areas provide the opportunity to develop geothermal power. Hot water and steam from underground are used to drive turbines or to supply central heating directly. In New Zealand, 7 percent of all electricity is generated from geothermal power and most Icelandic homes are centrally heated using hot water from underground. Some geologists believe that up to 10 percent of the United States' energy needs could be met by geothermal power (see unit 4.2).

Volcanoes, geysers and hot springs are tourist attractions in places such as Hawaii, Yellowstone and Iceland. This is another reason why people live close to volcanoes or volcanic regions.

The way that people perceive the risk and adapt to volcanic hazards is covered in more detail in unit 7.4

Activity   Volcanic eruptions

Krakatoa, 1883

This is a volcanic island to the west of Java in Indonesia. It is part of an island arc along the subduction zone where the Australian-Indian plate sinks under the Eurasian plate. The volcano had been dormant for two hundred years when it erupted in four great explosions in 1883. One was heard nearly 5,000 km away in Australia. The whole northern part of the island, standing 600 metres above sea level was blown away leaving a massive caldera or crater. Some of the ash circled the globe for two years causing a dip in world wide temperatures. However, the most serious effect was a tsunami that killed 36,000 people in Java and Sumatra.

Since 1927, the volcano has been active again, building a new island called Anak Krakatoa (Child of Krakatoa).

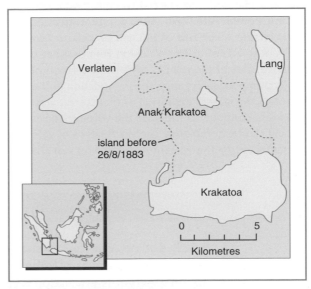

▲ Figure 7.40 Krakatoa

Mount Saint Helens, 1980

Mainly because it occurred in the United States and therefore was convenient for well funded scientists to monitor, this was one of the best documented eruptions of recent times. The mountain lies in the Cascade Range which contains 15 large, composite volcanoes. It lies above a zone of subduction where the Juan de Fuca plate pushes below the North American plate.

After being dormant for 123 years, a series of small earthquakes during 1980 suggested that there was renewed activity in the magma chamber. Small eruptions of steam and ash occurred for six weeks, during which time a zone around the mountain was evacuated.

Then a bulge was observed on the north side of the mountain, growing at the rate of 1.5 metres per day. At the same time, emissions of sulphur dioxide were increasing. Two months after the first activity, a massive eruption occurred. An earthquake, magnitude 5 on the Richter Scale, shook the mountain and caused the whole of the north flank to collapse. The release of pressure caused a blast that levelled the forest in a zone 35 km wide and 23 km outward from the mountain.

The eruption had three main effects. Firstly, pyroclastic flow, moving at 120 km/hr, extended for 9 km. Secondly, ash clouds rose 18 km. Some ash quickly fell to earth downwind. Some remained in the atmosphere and, in two weeks, had encircled the Earth. Thirdly, lahars - mixtures of steam, mud, ash and melted snow - raced down nearby valleys. The Toutle River became a 1.5 km wide torrent of mud, heated to 90°C, flowing 20 metres higher than normal.

Despite the evacuation, 54 people died, mainly because the eruption was so large. Only 3 people had ignored warnings and were in the exclusion zone, the rest thought they were safe.

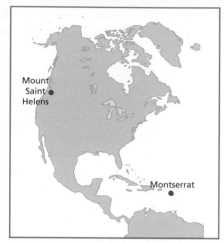

▲ **Figure 7.41 Mount St Helens and Montserrat**

▲ **Figure 7.42 Mount St Helens**
In the 1980 eruption the north flank of the mountain collapsed.

Montserrat, 1996

This Caribbean island lies on the same island arc as Martinique (the location of Mount Pelee). In 1995, the Soufriere Hills volcano started to emit steam, ash and small volcanic bombs. After two years of intermittent activity, most of the southern part of the island had become uninhabitable. Thick falls of ash and pyroclastic flows caused the evacuation of the former capital, Plymouth - just 6 km from the volcano. An exclusion zone was set up into which entry was punishable with a $250 fine or jail sentence. Out of the island's original population of 11,000, more than 7,500 people have been moved. Many now live in cramped, emergency accommodation in the north of the island.

Although the largest explosion in Montserrat was only one tenth as powerful as the Mount St Helens explosion, geologists continue to monitor the volcanic activity and full evacuation plans are ready. As with most volcanoes, nothing can be completely certain. Analysis of volcanic deposits shows that the northern part of the island has not been affected by the volcano for 2 million years, but that gives no guarantee for the future.

Questions

1 Briefly outline what causes explosive volcanic eruptions.
2 Summarise the effects of volcanic eruptions.
3 To what extent is evacuation a sensible option for people living near active volcanoes?

unit summary

1. Volcanoes have created the conditions for life but they also have the capacity for destroying life.
2. Eruptions at constructive margins and at hot spots tend to be gentle lava flows; at destructive margins they tend to be explosive.
3. Basic (basalt) lava is runny and flows quickly whereas acidic (andesite) lava is viscous and slow.
4. Explosive eruptions are the most dangerous and can cause pyroclastic flows.
5. Volcanoes can be classified according to location, shape and composition, and violence of eruption.
6. Volcanic features can be extrusive or intrusive.
7. Predicting eruptions is difficult, but recent developments measuring light wavelengths travelling through volcanic plumes can identify changes in gases in the magma chamber.
8. Volcanic eruptions can cause global climatic change.
9. People live near volcanoes for economic reasons, sometimes out of necessity because of pressure for living space and also because of the desire to farm rich volcanic soils.

key terms

Batholith - a large body of intrusive igneous rock sometimes exposed by the erosion of overlying rock

Caldera - a large depression or crater formed by a volcanic eruption. The summit may have been blasted away in the explosion, or it may have collapsed into the volcano's magma chamber.

Composite volcano - a volcanic cone created by layers of both ash and lava. The resulting shape is the classic shape of a volcano.

Dyke - an intrusive rock formed when magma pushes through vertical cracks or faults, across the bedding planes of the surrounding 'country rock'.

Extrusive rock - igneous rock formed above the Earth's surface.

Flood basalt - an extrusive feature formed by a lava flow from a fissure (or fissures); sometimes creating a large plateaux.

Hot spots - areas of volcanic activity not associated with plate margins.

Igneous rock - rock formed when magma cools.

Intrusive rock - igneous rock that solidifies beneath the Earth's surface - sometimes exposed by erosion of overlying rock.

Lahar - a destructive mud flow formed from water and volcanic ash.

Lava - the name given to magma when it reaches the Earth's surface.

Magma - molten rock material beneath the Earth's crust.

Magma chamber - the source of magma beneath a volcano.

Mantle plumes - columns of hot magma that rise below the crust to form hot spots.

Metamorphic rock - a rock formed when pre-existing rocks are subject to intense heat and/or pressure.

Pyroclastic flow - an avalanche of hot ash, gas and rock.

Shield volcano - a volcano shaped like a flattened dome (or shield), formed from basic lava flows. The slopes are rarely more than 10 degrees, ie they are very gentle slopes.

Sill - a horizontal sheet of rock formed when magma pushes along a bedding plane.

Volcanic plug (or **neck**) - the solidified magma that originally filled a volcanic vent, now exposed by erosion.

Volcano - a place where magma flows or erupts onto the Earth's surface.

Unit 7.4 Tectonic hazards

key questions

1 How do people perceive tectonic hazards?
2 How do people respond to tectonic hazards?

1. How do people perceive tectonic hazards?

A hazard is an event which can threaten both life and property. Tectonic hazards arise from earthquakes and

Figure 7.43 The Transamerica Pyramid, San Francisco

People living in San Francisco are threatened, everyday, by an earthquake hazard. Although they know that one day the 'big one' will come, they can be fairly confident that it will not be today! So, in the meantime, they get on with their lives, they make their homes as safe as possible and plan what to do in an emergency. The 853 feet high Transamerica Pyramid is constructed to withstand an earthquake as powerful as the one in 1906 which measured 8.2 on the Richter Scale.

volcanic activity. They include earth tremors, explosive emissions of ash and debris, mud flows (lahars), lava and pyroclastic flows, and tsunamis. As the world's population grows, the danger posed by tectonic hazards becomes relatively greater. This is because more and more people live in the danger zones.

Given the uncertainty of predicting tectonic events, the only way to ensure complete safety is to assume the worst and evacuate the area at risk. This option saved thousands of lives when Mt Pinatubo in the Philippines erupted in 1991 (see unit 7.3). When the threat is clear and imminent, and the population is small, evacuation is a viable option. The experience of Montserrat is evidence for this. But, when the threat is less clear cut, and the population is large, evacuation is not a viable option. This is particularly the case for earthquake hazards which occur with much less warning than volcanic eruptions. For example, in both Tokyo and San Francisco, a major earthquake is expected within the next few decades but nobody seriously proposes that everyone should leave these cities now. In zones of tectonic activity, the normal human response is to assess, adapt and accept. Most people know the risks they are living with, and are willing to accept them having made whatever preparations they feel appropriate to their circumstances.

Perceptions

People's perceptions are influenced by past experiences, present attitudes and future expectations. Not surprisingly, perceptions of particular hazards alter as time elapses since the last occurrence. For example, before the 1994 Northridge earthquake in Los Angeles, state authorities sometimes failed to persuade residents to take the potential dangers seriously. A primary school was built on a known fault line in the city's northern suburbs and people were unwilling to accept the additional taxes needed for emergency planning. However, immediately after the quake, it was a different story. Residents' associations demanded more safety measures. But now, several years after the event, the feeling of security, well-being and 'lightning doesn't strike twice in the same place' has once again emerged.

There are many reasons why people live in hazardous areas. Some people close their minds to the danger and hope that it will never happen. Others who have been born and brought up in a hazardous area often have little choice due to social and economic factors. For instance, families cannot easily uproot and move. Also, there is the fear of change and the unknown which leads to inertia. Some people might assess the risk and think it is worth taking. They might be farmers working the rich volcanic soils, or tourist workers in a resort in a volcanic region.

This combination of resignation, calculation and acceptance is most people's response to a hazard; those in constant fear will move away to re-establish peace of mind. Only those accepting the hazard will remain.

The factors that affect people's perception and acceptance of risk include:

- time scale: if the risk is of a sudden, catastrophic event (eg, a pyroclastic flow), it will be perceived as more dangerous than a delayed action event (eg, a slow eruption of lava from a fissure).
- frequency: if the hazard often occurs, people can become immune. On the other hand, if it is occasional or unlikely then - when it happens - it can be more shocking. For example, frequent, low scale earth tremors can become an acceptable feature of people's lives.
- media coverage: the more attention that is paid by the media to a hazard, the more aware people will be of the risks involved.
- randomness: a random event (such as a tsunami along a coastline) will be perceived as posing a lesser threat than an earthquake on a major fault line. This is simply because there is less chance of it occurring.
- number of potential fatalities: a hazard in a wilderness area (such as around Mount St Helens) will be perceived as posing less risk than a hazard in a densely populated area.
- voluntary acceptance of risk: people who voluntarily put themselves in danger (such as vulcanologists observing an active volcano) might accept a higher level of risk than other people.

2. How do people respond to tectonic hazards?

Volcanic hazards

Over the past decades, experience has shown that the main volcanic hazards have been:

- ash falls that cause buildings to collapse
- volcanic debris flows or lahars

- pyroclastic flows
- volcanic gases
- tsunamis
- lava flows.

This list is ranked in decreasing order of importance - in terms of the number of fatalities. Ways in which people cope with these hazards are described below.

It seems unlikely that volcanoes can ever be controlled. Nor, as we have seen in earlier units, is completely accurate prediction of these hazards a realistic goal. However, improvements have been made in monitoring volcanic eruptions (see unit 7.3) and it is now sometimes possible to give advance warning. This gives time for people to evacuate. So, those responsible for managing hazards are turning their attention to planning evacuation procedures and improving community awareness. Effective response by public services is now seen as a key element in saving lives. However, the administration of aid and relief programmes in the vital days after a disaster is an issue still sometimes neglected, especially in low income countries.

In many areas at risk from tectonic activity, **hazard mapping** is seen as a key part of the management policy. This technique maps the hazards and the areas likely to be affected. Once 'at risk' areas are identified, land use can be zoned. Vulnerable areas are then given

Figure 7.44 Mount Fuji, Japan

Japan is situated in one of the most active volcanic and earthquake prone zones in the world. In high risk areas Japanese children are taught to dive under their school desks at the first sign of an earth tremor.

over to land uses where damage to people and property would be minimal, for example parks and nature reserves. This also makes allocation of resources more effective by targeting help to those areas most at risk.

Hazard mapping has been effective in both earthquake and volcanic areas. Analysis of the morphology (ie, shape and structure) of a volcano can show where lava and pyroclastic flows, and lahars are likely. People can then avoid building in the vicinity. Near Sakurajima, in Japan, a popular tourist island and home to 10,000 people, massive concrete bunkers provide a refuge from the volcanic bombs - up to 50 kg in weight - that are sometimes hurled up to 8 km from the crater. Knowing the potential danger from lahars, concrete-lined drainage channels have been built around the island to intercept and direct the lahars out to sea. Each channel has a remote sensing camera to monitor the flow.

Hazard mapping has also shown itself useful in other volcanic areas. Basaltic lava can move fast but it can sometimes be redirected by excavating channels and by cooling the flow using water pumped through hoses. This technique has been used with mixed success in Iceland at Heimay and in Sicily on the slopes of Mt Etna.

People on Sakurajima accept and have learned how to live with the presence of the nearby volcano. Children attending the local schools wear hard hats as a compulsory item of uniform and even cemeteries have pitched roofs to protect the graves from falling ash. Once a year the whole island is evacuated - a practice run in case of a massive eruption. This coordinated management plan, based on hazard mapping, has proved very successful so far. In the event of a disaster it is hoped that it will help the local community stay calm and safe.

Figure 7.45 Reinforced girders in a new San Francisco building

In both California and Japan, high building standards are enforced in order to minimise earthquake damage.

Earthquake hazards

The ways in which people cope with earthquake hazards have some features in common with coping strategies for volcanic eruptions. But, with earthquakes, it seems even less likely that accurate predictions will ever be possible. Despite years of research, and some successes, Chinese scientists were not able to predict the major Tangshan earthquake in 1976 (see unit 7.2). One problem is that large and small earthquakes start in the same way. Even if it was possible to predict that, for example, a fault was about to slip, it would still be impossible to predict the magnitude of the resulting quake. So, because accurate prediction seems unlikely, the strategy that is adopted in many high risk earthquake zones is to minimise the effects.

Building design in earthquake zones includes features that ensure structures have a reasonable chance of surviving an earthquake. In California there is a saying that 'buildings kill people not earthquakes'. Yet, despite the designers' and builders' best efforts, the Los Angeles quake of 1994 caused $30 billion worth of damage. Kobe in 1995 suffered damage costing $80 billion. Both disasters forced engineers in the US and Japan to reexamine the design of buildings, roads and bridges.

New buildings in, for example, San Francisco and Tokyo, must have steel frames and be able to sway. Bricks are not used because of the danger when they fall. Fire resistant materials are compulsory. In Tokyo one new long block of flats, the Shirahige-Higashi complex, is specially designed and located to act as a fire break across a residential area. Behind it is a huge area of open space with room for 60,000 evacuees.

Hazard mapping of earthquake zones can help to identify potentially high risk areas. This assists in planning emergency services. It also allows **land use zoning** in which planning authorities control where building can take place. This is important because good designs alone are not sufficient to ensure that buildings can withstand an earthquake. The ground material is also a key factor. Solid rock offers the best foundation and clay should be avoided because it is prone to liquefaction. In Mexico City, in 1985, some modern buildings conformed to current earthquake proof designs, but still many collapsed. This was mainly due to liquefaction - the city being built on an old lake bed. Similar lessons were learned in the 1989 San Francisco quake when the only buildings to collapse were in the Marina district, built on reclaimed land. In Tokyo, large areas of the city are built on river delta mud or reclaimed land. To avoid the problem of liquefaction, foundations of modern buildings have to reach down 40 metres to the underlying rock.

In high risk areas, public bodies, private companies and individuals have to be prepared for the dangers they face. For example, public information leaflets and advice are provided in California by both state and federal governments. Residents in Japan's danger zones observe

'Disaster Day' every September 1st. It is a public holiday to prepare for the next earthquake. Public information posters and the media remind people what to do in a quake. They show how to make furniture secure, put out fires, switch off gas supplies and remain calm!

Figure 7.46 Landslide caused by earthquake

In Southern California and other regions affected by earthquakes the disruption of communications is a major hazard.

Activity **Preparing for an earthquake**

Official advice from the US Federal Management Agency for private householders includes:

Before the event:
- fasten shelves securely to walls
- place large, heavy objects such as televisions on lower shelves
- store bottles and other breakable items in low, closed cabinets with latches
- hang heavy items like mirrors away from beds, chairs or couches
- keep potential fire hazards such as gas and electrical fittings well maintained
- secure a water heater with straps and wall studs, and bolt it to the floor
- identify safe places   - under sturdy furniture
                              - away from windows, near an inside wall
                              - outside, away from buildings, bridges, power lines or trees.

Teach all members of the family how to turn off water, gas and electricity.
Have disaster supplies ready (first aid kit, portable radio, torch, batteries, water, food).
Prepare an emergency communication plan - where to meet after a disaster.

During the event:
- take cover
- stay inside (if already inside) - the most dangerous thing is to go outside and risk falling objects
- if outside, move away from buildings and other hazards
- in a car, park away from buildings, power lines and, especially, bridges and overpasses
- watch pets closely, dogs and cats can become aggressive in an earthquake - prepare emergency shelter, food and water for pets

After the event:
- beware of aftershocks that can destroy weakened buildings
- help trapped and injured, but do not move seriously injured
- call for help but be aware that communications might be broken and emergency services will be at full stretch
- listen to a radio for emergency information
- check water, sewage, gas and electricity lines for damage.

Questions

1 Briefly summarise how individuals can prepare for an earthquake.
2 Outline what public authorities can do to help people cope with an earthquake hazard.
3 For people living in a high risk area, such as San Francisco, summarise the factors that will affect their perception of danger.

Middle and low income countries

So far, this unit has focussed on the situation in high income countries. In middle and low income countries, the position is often very different. Constructing strong buildings to earthquake proof designs is very expensive, so most poor people in earthquake zones around the world live in buildings that are far more likely to collapse than the average Californian's. Likewise, emergency planning and co-ordination of rescue services is expensive and requires a degree of organisation impossible in most Third World countries.

Even in a middle income country such as Turkey, the August 1999 earthquake killed far more people than would have been expected in a high income country such as Japan. The quake hit a rapidly growing urban area where many new apartment blocks had been quickly built. There was strong evidence that some builders had bribed officials to overlook breaches of building regulations. In particular, many had not reinforced the structures with steel frames. In the aftermath of the disaster in which up to 20,000 people died, a Turkish journalist was quoted as saying that 'corruption kills people, not earthquakes'. In the first few days after the earthquake, it was clear that government officials were overwhelmed by the scale of the disaster. They did not have an emergency plan that could cope with the numbers of trapped people, nor did they have adequate arrangements to house and feed the homeless.

Figure 7.47 Golcuk, Turkey, 1999

Many thousands of people died when apartment blocks collapsed. The old mosque and minaret in the foreground survived the earthquake. Most of the buildings that collapsed had been built during the previous 15 years. It seems that, in many cases, building regulations had been ignored.

Activity | Responding to earthquake hazards in low income countries

It has been suggested that there is no such thing as a 'natural disaster' - only disasters made more or less serious by the economic conditions which people experience. Professor Dobson of Keele University has written, 'It was not a 'miracle' that prevented a higher death toll in the Los Angeles earthquake in 1994, but money. A much weaker earthquake killed two hundred times more people in India in September 1993, because they were poor and could not afford to build sturdy houses. Nor was it a case of Californians knowing what was coming. All the advance knowledge in the world will not help if you cannot afford to prepare properly.'

▼ **Figure 7.48 Notable earthquakes, 1900 - 1999**

Date	Location	Magnitude	Number of deaths	Comments
1906	San Francisco	8.2	700	Fires caused most damage
1908	Messina, Sicily	7.5	100,000	Tsunami
1923	Tokyo	8.2	150,000	Fires caused most damage
1960	Southern Chile	9.5	5,000	Tsunami, most powerful quake in recent times
1964	Anchorage, Alaska	8.6	130	Most powerful in recent US history
1970	Peru	7.8	66,000	Rock slide and floods
1975	Hai-cheng, China	7.5	Few	First major quake to be predicted
1976	Tangshan, China	7.6	240,000	Not predicted
1976	Guatemala	7.9	22,000	Most deaths in poorly built shanty settlements
1985	Mexico City	8.1	7,000	Epicentre was 400 km distant
1985	Armenia	7.0	25,000	Many poorly built apartment blocks collapsed
1989	San Francisco	7.1	63	Reclaimed coastal land liquefied
1990	Iran	7.7	50,000	Landslides blocked relief
1992	Indonesia	6.8	2,200	Many buildings collapsed
1993	Maharashtra, India	6.3	10,000	Not close to any plate boundary
1994	Northridge, Los Angeles	6.7	51	Damage to freeways believed to be 'quake proof'
1995	Sakhalin, Russia	7.5	2,000	Major quake in remote area
1995	Kobe, Japan	6.9	4,500	Most damage in fires
1997	Iran	7.1	2,400	Over 100,000 homeless as weak buildings collapsed
1998	Afghanistan	6.1	4,000	Landslides, many poorly built houses collapsed
1998	New Guinea	7.0	2,000	Undersea quake triggered 8 metre high tsunami
1999	Colombia	6.0	1,000	Many buildings collapsed in the city of Armenia
1999	Turkey	6.7	20,000	Large numbers of new, high rise blocks collapsed
1999	Taiwan	7.6	2,500	A relatively small number of new buildings collapsed

Iran pleads with West for help in quake zone

An international relief operation was gathering momentum last night to help Iran cope with the aftermath of an earthquake that devastated a remote mountainous area in the east of the country. An estimated 2,400 people are dead and an unknown number are missing or injured.

The United Nations has been asked for emergency supplies of food, tents, blankets, clothing, four wheel drive vehicles, ambulances, water tankers and infra-red life detectors.

Iranian television has shown mass destruction in the stricken zone. Dazed children and weeping adults wander almost aimlessly, shocked by the sudden disaster. Some villagers are tearing the rubble with spades and bare hands to release people trapped inside the collapsed houses. Most were built of mud bricks without any reinforcement.

A government spokesman reported, 'The area is completely cut off. The communications are down, most roads are blocked by landslides. The nearest airport is Mashad but that is seven hours away even when the roads are clear'.

Adapted from The Times, 12th May 1997

Questions

1 Briefly outline why earthquake hazards pose a greater danger to people in low income countries compared with high income countries.

2 To what extent does the data in figure 7.48 support the view that there is 'no such thing as a natural disaster'.

unit summary

1 A natural hazard is a danger or threat arising from a natural event, for instance from a volcanic eruption or earthquake.

2 Peoples' perceptions of tectonic hazards vary for a wide variety of reasons. One of the main factors is the length of time since the last event.

3 The prevention of tectonic hazards is not possible, nor, at the present time, is it possible to make precise and accurate predictions of when earthquakes and volcanic eruptions will occur.

4 Management of a hazard's consequences is the key to reducing the impact and cost.

5 Hazard mapping and land use zoning are the first important steps in managing the risk.

6 Public information and community awareness is vital in reducing tectonic hazards.

7 Good building design and solid foundations, together with the enforcement of building codes, are important elements in reducing risks.

key terms

Hazard mapping - mapping the source and likely extent of a hazard and the damage it might cause.

Land use zoning - deciding on appropriate land use depending on the level of risk. For example,

avoiding building high rise accommodation close to a known fault line.

Perception - how people view something.

Tectonic hazard - the danger, threat or risk arising from volcanoes and earthquakes.

Introduction

Weathering transforms solid rock into smaller fragments. It is an important process because these fragments eventually form the soil on which we depend for agriculture and food supply. Other products of weathering provide valuable minerals such as bauxite (for aluminium) and kaolinite (or 'china clay' for pottery).

Rocks disintegrate and decompose when they are exposed to the atmosphere. The rate of weathering depends upon both the climatic conditions and the nature of the rock. The process is slow, although in some places it occurs at a faster rate than in others. For example, in an English churchyard, 200 year old gravestones made from sandstone might be so weathered that the lettering is impossible to read. Yet, in Egypt, granite columns have lettering that has remained virtually unchanged for 2,000 years or more. Chemical pollutants in the air, from vehicle exhausts and from industry, speed up the process of weathering. Industrialised regions suffer from air pollution far more than less developed regions. This is one of the reasons why the rate of weathering is faster in England than in Egypt.

This chapter looks at different types of weathering and how weathered material is transported or removed. The resulting landforms on various rock types, and in humid and dry conditions, are also examined.

Chapter summary

Unit 8.1 looks at weathering processes
Unit 8.2 examines mass movement and slope development
Unit 8.3 considers how geology affects landforms
Unit 8.4 looks at the particular processes and landforms found in arid regions.

Unit 8.1 Weathering

key questions

1 What is weathering?
2 What is mechanical weathering?
3 What is chemical weathering?
4 What is biotic weathering?
5 What is urban weathering?

1. What is weathering?

Weathering is the disintegration and decay of rocks at the Earth's surface. It is caused by a range of mainly **sub-aerial** processes (ie, at the Earth's surface as opposed to underground or underwater). These processes break down and alter rocks by mechanical, chemical and biotic means.

- Mechanical weathering: the physical break down of rocks without any change in their chemical composition
- Chemical weathering: the break down of rocks caused by changes to the chemical structure of minerals in the rocks

- Biotic weathering: the break down of rocks by plants and animals.

When rock is exposed to the air, it is open to attack by weathering. The process is mainly controlled by climate and is more effective under wet conditions than dry conditions. The reasons for this are explained later in the unit.

The rate of weathering is also influenced by the factors that make a rock more or less resistant. A rock's resistance to weathering is influenced by its chemical and physical composition. For example, a rock that is deeply jointed is more vulnerable than a massive, unjointed block. This is because the joints create a bigger surface area on which the weathering processes can operate.

There is a tendency in weathering for rounded (or 'spheroidal') shapes to evolve. Exposed corners of rock are weathered from all sides so are rounded off. Further weathering reduces the size but there is no change in the shape.

The result of weathering is to produce a layer of rock fragments overlying the solid bedrock. This layer, including soil, is called the **regolith**.

The processes of mechanical, chemical and biotic weathering break down rocks into smaller pieces in a number of ways:

- **shattering**: this is when a rock breaks into irregular, angular fragments, for example as might be found on a scree slope
- **granular disintegration**: this is when a rock breaks down into individual grain particles, for instance, sandstone sometimes disintegrates into the individual quartz crystals from which it is formed
- **exfoliation**: this is when surface layers of rocks become loose and 'peel off'. The result can be a rounded dome of rock that can look like a partly peeled onion.

Shattering is mainly caused by mechanical weathering. Granular disintegration and exfoliation can be caused by either mechanical or chemical weathering. Often it is a combination of processes that is at work. Mechanical weathering increases the surface area on which chemical action takes place. Chemical weathering in turn promotes further mechanical disintegration. The balance between the processes depends to a large extent on the nature of the rock and the climatic conditions.

A broad distinction is made between **weathering**, **mass movement** and **erosion**. Weathering refers to the decomposition of rocks 'in situ' (ie, in place). The term mass movement is used to describe the process when gravity causes the downslope movement of the weathered material. Erosion is the removal and transport of weathered material by 'agents of erosion' (eg, the wind, rivers, glaciers or waves).

To illustrate these processes, consider what happens on a cliff face. Firstly, weathering might loosen a rock fragment. When gravity causes it to fall, this is an example of mass movement. If the rock fragment is washed away and transported by a stream, this is an example of erosion.

Some geographers consider mass movement to be a type of erosion while others treat it as a process distinct from both weathering and erosion. In this chapter, it is treated as a separate process.

The overall process of wearing down the land is known as **denudation**.

2. What is mechanical weathering?

Mechanical weathering (also called physical weathering) is the disintegration of rocks by forces which do not involve a chemical change in the rock. There are three main causes of mechanical weathering: freeze thaw, sheeting, and salt crystal growth.

Freeze thaw

This process is also known as 'frost shattering', 'cryofracture' or 'frost wedging'. When water freezes, it expands by approximately 9 percent in volume. A force of over 20MN m^{-2} (20 million newtons per square metre) is generated. If water collects in cracks and pore spaces in rocks, and then freezes and thaws many times over, the effect is to cause 'fatigue failure'. In other words, the rock eventually cracks and shatters. The same process causes pipes in domestic heating systems to burst in winter if they freeze, and causes drink cans to burst if they are left in a freezer.

Freeze thaw action is most effective when there are frequent changes of temperature above and below freezing. Where there is a diurnal (ie, daily) cycle of freezing at night and melting in the day, the weathering process is more active than if there are only seasonal temperature changes. Those tropical regions which never experience freezing temperatures are not affected at all. In polar regions (and places at high altitude) that remain well below freezing throughout the year, there is only limited freeze thaw action. Similarly in continental interiors, where the winter conditions are dry and intensely cold, there are few freeze thaw cycles. It is in maritime, cool temperate regions that the process is most active, for example in the mountains of Western Europe or Western Canada.

The composition, structure and strength of rock affects how it resists frost shattering. A rock such as granite has a tensile strength (ie, resistance to being pulled apart) of approximately 21MN m^{-2} whereas sandstone has a tensile strength of only 13 MN m^{-2}. For this reason, sandstone is more prone to freeze thaw weathering than granite. The permeability of rock is also an important factor. Water must penetrate into the rock and be trapped by initial surface freezing for maximum pressure to be exerted. It is therefore in well jointed, sedimentary rocks such as limestone that the process is generally most effective.

Figure 8.1 shows how freeze thaw action can create a large scree (or talus) slope. Gravity causes the shattered rock fragments to fall down the slope. The momentum of larger blocks causes them to fall to the bottom while smaller particles rest higher up. The scree eventually builds up until the whole of the cliff face or mountain slope above becomes covered. The angle of slope depends upon the type of rock and the size of fragments but, in general, averages 25 to 35 degrees.

Figure 8.1 Freeze thaw action

Freeze thaw action occurs when water seeps into cracks and expands when it freezes. The expanding ice forces the rock apart and produces loose, angular fragments that move downslope by gravity. They accumulate at the foot of the slope as scree.

Sheeting

Rocks deep within the Earth's crust are under massive pressure from the weight of overlying layers. If this overlying material is removed by erosion there is 'pressure release' and the buried rocks expand in volume. This can cause cracks to form parallel with the surface in a process called sheeting. It can occur in quarries. When blocks of rock are removed, the quarry floor sometimes expands and a sheet of rock several centimetres thick can burst up. Pressure release also occurs if the weight of a glacier or ice sheet is removed by melting.

Granite is formed deep underground, under great pressure, and is therefore particularly prone to sheeting. Once the layers of rock and cracks are exposed to the atmosphere, other weathering processes, for example freeze thaw and chemical weathering, start to work. The result can be spectacular, creating 'exfoliation domes' such as Half Dome in Yosemite, California or the Sugar Loaf at Rio de Janeiro, Brazil.

Salt crystal growth

This form of weathering occurs where salt accumulates. Most ground water (ie, underground water) contains dissolved mineral salts. In hot, dry climatic conditions, evaporation and capillary action can draw the water upwards and deposit a layer of salt on the rock surface. Salt can also accumulate in places where the wind carries and deposits salt spray inland from coastal areas.

When salt crystals form in surface rock pores they exert pressure as they grow. In laboratory experiments it has been shown that they can expand by up to three times their original size. The pressure this exerts can weaken, and eventually shatter rock. Evidence suggests that salt crystal growth may be the most important mechanical weathering process in tropical arid and semi-arid zones such as the Sahara Desert.

Figure 8.2 Half Dome, Yosemite, California

The granite forms an 'exfoliation dome'. A combination of mechanical and chemical processes have created this feature.

Insolation weathering

In hot desert regions, there can be a daily temperature range of more than 40°C. Because skies are generally cloudless, the daytime insolation (ie, the Sun's radiation) is intense, and at night the heat escapes into the atmosphere. This causes the surface layer of rocks to heat and expand in daytime and contract at night when it is cooler. Within the rock, there is also differential expansion and contraction because some crystals which have different colours and chemical compositions heat up and expand faster than others.

At one time thermal expansion and contraction caused by insolation was thought to be a significant cause of mechanical weathering. However, research in laboratories has cast doubt on whether the force exerted is sufficient, on its own, to disintegrate rocks. It is now believed that water must also be present, and this promotes other mechanical and weathering processes.

Activity   Shattered rocks

Figure 8.3 Glyder Fawr, North Wales
This area is almost 1,000 metres above sea level. At this height the temperature falls below freezing on many nights of the year. The rocks are volcanic in origin.

Questions

1 Describe the landscape feature shown in the photograph.
2 How might freeze thaw action have caused the rock to shatter?
3 Suggest why some types of rock are more prone to weathering than others.

3. What is chemical weathering?

During chemical weathering, rocks are decomposed. Their internal mineral structure is altered and new minerals are formed. Water is important in the process. It plays a direct part in some chemical reactions and in others it transports the elements that do the work.

The process occurs in most parts of the world, but is least effective in deserts and polar regions where there is little rainfall or where the water is frozen. However, even in deserts, it sometimes rains and chemical weathering then occurs. In general, chemical reactions are faster in high rather than in low temperatures. For these reasons, chemical weathering is most active in equatorial zones that have hot, humid climates.

Rocks consist of minerals held together in various structures and forms. They vary in vulnerability to chemical weathering because some are relatively stable while others decompose quickly. For most rocks the potential for chemical weathering increases with acidity. This acidity arises in three main ways:
- rainwater combines with carbon dioxide in the atmosphere to form dilute carbonic acid
- where air pollutants such as sulphur dioxide or nitrogen oxides are present the effect can be to create dilute sulphuric or nitric acid
- when rainwater washes into the soil, it combines with organic acids that are formed by decomposing vegetation.

The main types of chemical weathering are hydrolysis, hydration, carbonation, oxidation and chelation.

Hydrolysis

This is a chemical reaction between water and a mineral. Wetting the mineral causes a chemical exchange to occur in which hydrogen ions from the water displace ions in the mineral. The way that hydrolysis works can be illustrated by looking at how it affects granite. This rock consists of quartz, mica and feldspar. Quartz and mica remain relatively unchanged when exposed to weakly acidic rainwater but feldspar decomposes. Hydrogen ions from the dilute carbonic acid displace potassium ions in the feldspar which then breaks down into a clay mineral. This is known as kaolinite or 'china clay' and is used in the pottery industry. Deposits of this mineral are found in South West England where granite outcrops are exposed at the surface. In places, the material is so decomposed that it can be extracted using high pressure hoses.

Hydration

This process occurs when minerals absorb water (or 'hydrate'). It causes a chemical change and also a physical change in that the mineral swells. This weakens the rock. An example of hydration is when water comes into contact with anhydrite to form gypsum. The gypsum is relatively soluble in water and is washed away.

Carbonation

This process is a chemical reaction that occurs when rainwater (dilute carbonic acid) reacts with calcium carbonate to form calcium bicarbonate. This is soluble and is carried away by water. Because chalk and limestone largely consist of calcium carbonate, carbonation is an effective form of weathering where these rocks outcrop.

Carbonation and its effects on limestone produce a distinctive type of scenery called karst (karst landscapes are described in detail in unit 8.3). The term comes from the Slovenian region where it is particularly well developed. Karst landscape is typified by depressions, dry valleys and extensive underground drainage. It is likely that the weathering process occurs not only where the rock is exposed to the atmosphere but under the soil as well. Where ice sheets have scoured the landscape and have removed the soil, as in the limestone areas of northern England, the bedrock is deeply weathered.

Oxidation

This process occurs when a mineral combines with oxygen. The oxygen might come from the air or it might be dissolved in water. Iron is particularly prone to this type of weathering. It readily oxidises and it occurs in many rocks. Oxidation changes blue-grey ferrous iron compounds to ferric compounds that are a rusty red. The process weakens the mineral structure and also makes the rock more vulnerable to other forms of weathering.

Chelation

This process occurs when rocks and soil weather through the action of organic acids. These acids are produced by bacterial action when vegetation decomposes. One such acid is 'humic acid'. In the chelation process, rainwater mixes with the organic acids and then combines with aluminium and iron. These metals are washed out of the soil as rainwater percolates through.

Activity — **The relative importance of chemical and mechanical weathering**

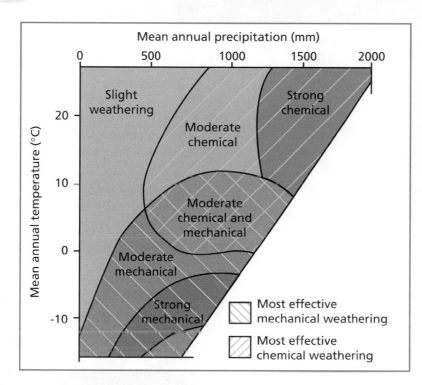

Figure 8.4 Weathering and climate

Figure 8.4 is based on the work of Peltier (1950) who studied the relative importance of chemical and mechanical weathering under different climate conditions.

Questions

1 What are the mean temperatures and precipitation levels under which the most effective: a) mechanical and b) chemical weathering takes place?
2 In which parts of the world would you expect: a) mechanical and b) chemical weathering to be most effective? Explain your reasons.

4. What is biotic weathering?

Biotic weathering is caused by the action of plants and animals (ie, by biota). It can be a mechanical process, for example where rocks are forced apart by plant roots, or a chemical process where organic acids from decomposing vegetation are released. Often it is a combination of both types of factors.

Micro-organisms

Micro-organisms such as lichens, algae, fungi and bacteria grow directly on bare rock and can cause weathering to occur. They attach to the rock and extract nutrients in dissolved form. This produces holes in which the organisms can live, gaining protection from the elements and from predators. For example, blue-green algae can bore holes into limestone 1mm deep. This 'pitting' of the rock surface increases the surface area exposed to attack from other forms of weathering.

In places, rocks are covered with grey, yellow and green coloured communities of algae and lichens (see figure 8.5). These micro-organisms are eaten by slugs

Figure 8.5 Algae and lichens

Micro-organisms growing on a rock in North West Scotland

example, burrowing animals open up cracks and joints in soil and in weathered rock fragments. This exposes the rock to weathering and allows increased percolation of rain water. Animals also mix rotting plant material into the soil and aerate it. As this material decomposes, organic acids are formed which can seep through the soil and chemically weather the bedrock.

Another type of biotic weathering is found on coasts. Some animals, such as limpets and barnacles, secrete an acid as they hold onto rocks. This increases the rate of chemical weathering.

and snails. Research has shown that snails erode the rocks as they feed on lichens and can collectively remove a tonne of rock per hectare per year. Also, excreta from these and other animals acts as fertiliser encouraging more plant growth as well as causing further chemical weathering.

Micro-organisms can mechanically weather rocks by absorbing water. When this happens the organism's volume increases and exerts pressure in pores on the rock surface. Lichens are one of the most common early colonisers of bare rock and are very efficient water absorbers.

Plants

Some plants send roots deep below the ground surface. They start as fine hairs penetrating pore spaces and joints, and enlarge as the plant grows. This widens cracks and forces rocks apart. Trees can exert massive force in this way, as can be seen in suburban streets when pavements and walls are sometimes buckled by roots. Sometimes when trees fall or blow down, huge amounts of rock are levered out or loosened.

Weathering by root systems is relatively important in those areas where most plant biomass is below the ground surface. For instance, in some desert plants, 80 percent of their mass is below ground and in tundra plants this can be as high as 90 percent.

Animals

Animals can weather rocks directly or indirectly. For

Figure 8.6 Tree roots

Tree roots can widen cracks in rocks

Activity The type and extent of weathering from equator to pole

▼ **Figure 8.7 Weathering in different climatic conditions**

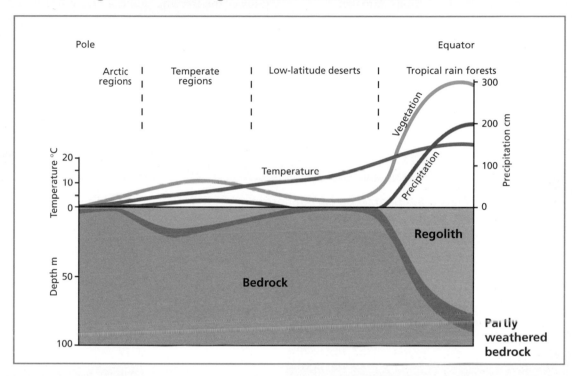

Questions

1 Describe how the average depth of regolith varies from equatorial to polar regions.
2 Suggest why the regolith varies in depth.
3 Apart from the factors indicated on the diagram, what other factors affect the rate of weathering?

5. What is urban weathering?

Weathering tends to occur at a higher rate in urban areas than in rural areas. This is because the process is fastest where there is the most severe air pollution. It is directly related to the amount of fossil fuels that are used. Sulphur dioxide is produced when coal and oil are burnt. When it combines in the atmosphere with water it forms a dilute sulphuric acid. Nitrogen oxides, from vehicle exhausts, combine with water to form dilute nitric acid. Together these increase the level of acidity in the atmosphere over urban and industrialised areas. The **acid rain** (see unit 2.5) that is produced contributes to weathering both directly and indirectly. The acids themselves decompose rocks chemically. Once cracks or holes are formed, mechanical weathering then plays a part in the process. The effect is most severe on old buildings in industrial cities. For example, on cathedrals, statues and carvings lose their detailed features and even on newer buildings there are often signs of crumbling brick and stonework.

Another weathering process occurs when sulphur

dioxide in the air reacts with calcium carbonate to form gypsum. This causes a soft crust to develop on limestone buildings. The crust is often blackened by soot from burning coal and oil emissions (especially diesel fumes). Eventually the surface begins to exfoliate (ie, peel off). Once cracks or gaps appear in the stonework, freeze thaw action can cause further serious damage.

Smokeless zones (ie, legally enforced curbs on coal burning) have led to a drop in sulphur dioxide levels in most UK cities and this has reduced one type of air pollution. However, levels of nitrogen oxides, especially from vehicle exhausts, have increased. Nitric acid

dissolves calcium carbonate and is a direct cause of chemical weathering. Higher nitrogen levels act as a fertiliser, so encouraging lichen and algae growth on buildings. This increases the rate of biotic weathering.

Some weathering occurs in urban areas in the UK because salt is applied to roads in winter. This is to lower the freezing point of water and so reduce the risk of ice. The salt splashes onto pavements and roadside buildings, crystallising and hydrating in pores within the stone. This can cause granular disintegration and also honeycomb weathering in which the surface becomes deeply pitted.

Activity   Weathering

▼ **Figure 8.8 Shattered carboniferous limestone, north Pennines**

▶ **Figure 8.9 Sandstone gravestone in a Leeds graveyard**

◀ **Figure 8.10 Honeycomb weathering on coastal sandstone, Arran**

▲ **Figure 8.11 Quartzite outcrop, Stiperstones, Shropshire**

Question

1 For each of the photographs, suggest which weathering processes might be at work. In each case, explain your answer.

unit summary

1. The main types of weathering are mechanical disintegration and chemical decomposition. Biotic factors also plays a part in the weathering process. Because air pollution is highest in urban areas, the rate of weathering tends to be fastest in towns and cities.
2. Freeze thaw, sheeting and salt crystal growth are the main forms of mechanical weathering.
3. The main types of chemical weathering are hydrolysis, carbonation, oxidation and hydration. Chelation is a form of chemical weathering in which acids are mainly formed from the decomposition of organic matter.
4. The effectiveness and rate of weathering depend upon the resistance of a particular rock. This is controlled by its chemical and physical composition.
5. Climate greatly influences the type and rate of weathering. The major controlling climatic factors are precipitation and temperature.

key terms

Biotic weathering - the disintegration and decomposition of rocks by plants and animals.
Carbonation - this process occurs when rainwater combines with carbon dioxide to form dilute carbonic acid which then reacts with calcium carbonate (in chalk and limestone). The resulting calcium bicarbonate is soluble in water and washes away in solution.
Chemical weathering - the decomposition of rocks in which their internal mineral structure is altered and new minerals are formed.
Crystal growth - salt deposits from groundwater, or that are wind borne, accumulate in rock pores and expand causing disintegration.
Denudation - the overall process of wearing down the land involving weathering, mass movement and erosion.
Erosion - the removal and transport of weathered material by 'agents of erosion' (eg, the wind, rivers, glaciers or waves).
Exfoliation - the surface layer of a rock 'peels off'. It can be caused by both chemical and mechanical processes.
Freeze thaw (or **frost shattering, ice wedging** or **cryofracture**) - water in rock spaces freezes, expands and shatters rocks. The process is most effective where there are frequent freeze thaw cycles.

Granular disintegration - the break up of rock into individual grain size fragments. It can be caused by both chemical and mechanical processes.
Hydration - this process occurs when minerals absorb water and expand.
Hydrolysis - this is a chemical reaction between water and a mineral.
Mass movement - the downslope movement of weathered material caused by gravity.
Mechanical (or **physical**) **weathering** - the physical disintegration of rock with no change to its chemical composition.
Oxidation - oxygen in water or air combines with a mineral to form a new mineral.
Regolith - the layer of weathered material, including soil that overlies solid bedrock.
Scree (or **talus**) - angular fragments resulting from freeze thaw action. Loosened and shattered rock falls downslope under the force of gravity. An accumulation of scree at the foot of a cliff face is called a scree slope.
Sheeting (or **pressure release**) - when weight is removed from the Earth's surface, underlying rocks expand and crack parallel to the surface.
Sub-aerial - at the Earth's surface as opposed to underground or underwater.
Weathering - the disintegration and decay of rocks at the Earth's surface.

Unit 8.2 Mass movement

1. What causes mass movement?

Mass movement is the downhill movement of regolith (ie, weathered material) caused by gravity. The movement might be a slow creep or a fast landslide. The material which moves might be rock, soil or mud - or a combination of all three. (Sometimes snow avalanches are also included in classifications of mass movement even though no weathered material might be involved. This topic is covered in unit 10.3.)

Mass movement takes place on slopes and is an important process in the development of slopes. New material is added to a slope by the weathering of bedrock and by the downhill movement of material from further upslope. The material eventually accumulates at the foot of the slope or, more often, it is removed by agents of erosion - waves, rivers or glaciers.

Downslope movement depends upon the balance between two forces. These are **shear stress** and **shear strength**. Shear stress is the downhill pull exerted by gravity and the weight of material. Counterbalancing this is shear strength which is the resistance to downhill movement. Sometimes the terms 'stick' and 'slide' are used to help understand the process. Imagine a rock particle resting on a slope. Whether the particle 'sticks' in place or 'slides' down the slope depends upon the balance between shear strength and shear stress (see figure 8.12).

Shear strength depends upon friction and cohesion. Most rock and soil particles have rough surfaces that increase the friction between them. In addition, their shapes might help them interlock like jig-saw pieces. Also, particles of clay within slope material carry an electric charge that increases cohesion. In other words, the clay 'glues' material together and therefore increases shear strength.

If shear strength exceeds shear stress, mass movement does not take place. But, if shear stress is greater than shear strength, slope failure occurs and material starts to move downhill. The movement might be slow - or more rapid if stress suddenly increases. There are several factors that affect the likelihood of slope failure. They include the angle of slope, the amount of water that is present, the vegetation cover and the possibility of earthquakes.

- Mass movement is more likely on steep slopes than on gentle slopes. The steeper the angle, the greater is shear stress relative to shear strength.

- If material on a slope becomes wet, due to either precipitation or snow melt, mass movement also becomes more likely. Water adds to shear stress because the weight of material is increased when it is wet. At the same time, water acts as a lubricant - reducing shear strength because friction and cohesion are lower. In saturated conditions, water fills the spaces (pores) between the soil and rock particles. This creates what is known as 'pore-water pressure'. It forces the particles apart and increases the possibility of slope failure. Mass movement can occur on slopes with angles as low as 3 degrees if the material is sufficiently wet.

- For all slopes, vegetation with a strong root system reduces the likelihood or speed of movement.

Figure 8.12 Forces acting on a rock particle

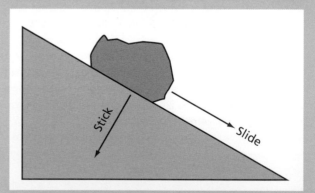

Shear stress ('slide') depends upon the weight of the particle and the angle of slope. The particle remains stable as long as shear strength ('stick') is greater than the downslope force. If the weight is increased, or if the angle is steeper, or if friction and cohesion are decreased, movement is more likely. The steepest angle at which a particle remains at rest is called the **angle of repose** or 'equilibrium angle'.

- Earthquakes increase the likelihood of mass movement because their shockwaves loosen the regolith. This creates a major hazard in earthquake zones that are hilly or mountainous.

2. What are the main types of mass movement and what features do they produce?

There are several different ways of classifying types of mass movement. The following criteria are all used:
- speed of movement - eg, from slow creep to rapid rockfall
- type of material - eg, rock, or soil, or a mixture of rock and soil debris
- type of slope failure - eg, fall, slide, slump or flow
- water content - eg, wet or dry.

To some extent, these classifications overlap and any particular mass movement will combine elements from the different criteria. So, for example, a 'flow' might be fast or slow, it might have a high or low water content, and it might consist of rock or mud.

Another difficulty in classifying mass movement is that it might occur, for instance, very slowly or very quickly, or at any speed in between. Similarly, the material might be saturated or very dry, or somewhere in between. In other words, the processes operate on a continuum rather than at fixed points along a scale

In this unit, a simplified classification is used. It divides mass movement into four main types: slide, flow, creep and fall. A fifth type of movement, subsidence, is also described although it does not play a part in slope development.

Slide

Sometimes the term 'landslide' is used to describe any form of rapid mass movement. However, strictly speaking, a slide is a movement along a 'slip plane'. This is a line of weakness in the rock or soil structure. The moving material slides downslope along the slip plane, more or less intact, until it reaches the bottom of the slope where impact usually breaks it up. A slide of mixed rock and soil is called a **debris slide**. When a slab of solid rock breaks loose along a bedding plane or line of weakness it is known as a **rock slide**.

A slide might be on a large scale such as the one that caused the Vaiont Dam disaster in Northern Italy in 1963 (see figure 8.13). The dam was completed in 1961 and, from the start, slow movement occurred on the mountain side above. During October 1963, the movement became quicker and then, suddenly on

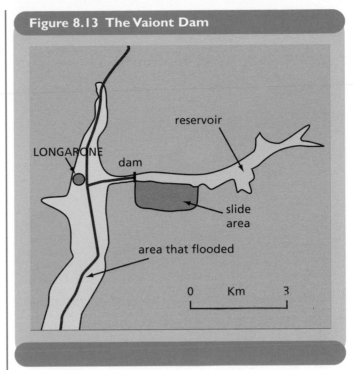

Figure 8.13 The Vaiont Dam

October 9th, a large section of mountain side slid down. The debris caused a wave of water over 100 metres high to wash over the dam wall. More than 2,500 people died in the resulting flood and much of the small town of Longarone was destroyed. The mountain side above the dam consisted of limestone interbedded with layers of clay, dipping downwards parallel with the slope. This geological structure provided ideal conditions for a line of weakness to form along a slip plane. Heavy rain that fell during the two weeks prior to the event are thought to have saturated the rock, contributing to the slide. It is estimated that 240 million cubic metres of material slid down into the reservoir.

Slides on a much smaller scale than Vaiont are fairly common. Thin turf and soil might absorb water until they become so heavy that the whole mass slides down a few metres. This sometimes occurs on older motorway embankments and in railway cuttings. The design of embankments has now been modified to improve drainage and reduce infiltration from rain water.

A **slump** is a type of slide that involves a rotational movement along a curved plane. (It is also sometimes called a rotational slip or slide.) Examples often occur on clay. It cracks in dry weather and then, during rain, water trickles down the cracks and is absorbed in the rock. When the clay is saturated, its cohesion is so weakened that it slides down on a slip plane. The result can be dramatic. For example, the Holbeck Hall Hotel in Scarborough collapsed in 1993 after clay at the top of

Figure 8.14 Quiraing, Skye

Horizontal beds of basalt overlie relatively weak beds of shale at this location. Large blocks of basalt have slid down from the cliff face.

Flows can occur on gentle slopes of 3-6 degrees but are more usual on angles of over 10 degrees. They cause a 'scar' where the flow starts and a 'lobe' of material that spreads out at the base of the slope.

Mudflows consist of a high percentage of fine silt and clay sized particles. They tend to occur when the ground is saturated after sudden thaws or heavy rain. The high water content (up to 30 percent) causes clay and other soil materials to reach their 'liquid limit' (ie, the point at which they act like a liquid). Mudflows often follow stream beds. They can be rapid but they can also flow slowly on quite low angled slopes.

Because of their density, mudflows have exceptional erosional and transporting power. Large boulders can be carried over slopes as gentle as 5 degrees and even barns and houses can be moved. In desert wadis (ie, normally dry river beds), mudflows 2 metres deep have been observed moving so fast there are waves on the surface. If they reach open country at a mountain foot they spread out into large lobes or fans. Mudflows are most common in areas with sparse vegetation cover and where torrential rainstorms occur.

Mud and debris flows sometimes occur on mineral waste dumps where mining has taken place. In South Wales a disaster occurred in 1966 when coal waste on a tip above the village of Aberfan became unstable. Over 100 children died when the waste flowed down onto the local school.

Lahars are a type of mudflow that occur when water

sea cliffs slumped (see figure 8.15). It happened when a period of wet weather followed a dry spell. A contributory factor at Scarborough was that sea erosion had steepened the angle of slope below the hotel.

Flow

A flow consists of mixtures of rock fragments, mud and water that move down slope as a viscous (ie, thick) fluid. The distinction between slumps and flows is not always clear cut because the movement at the bottom of slumps often becomes a flow. This is particularly the case if there is a high water content and the moving mass breaks up as it moves. Speed of flow can range from very slow, for example 1 cm per day to very fast, for example 100 metres per second. The greater the water content, the greater is the velocity. This is because water decreases friction between particles and increases the weight of the material.

Figure 8.15 Scarborough

In 1993 an estimated one million tonnes of clay slumped 100 metres. The Holbeck Hall Hotel collapsed when this happened.

washes away the unconsolidated ash and dust on volcanic slopes. They create torrents of mud capable of washing bridges, vehicles and buildings away. In 1985, a lahar engulfed the town of Armero, Colombia when the ice capped Andean volcano Nevado del Ruiz erupted. More details of this event and the Aberfan disaster are given later in this unit.

Solifluction is the name given to a flow of a saturated soil in periglacial conditions (see unit 10.4). These are the conditions found in tundra regions. In summer, the surface soil layer thaws but the meltwater cannot soak away because the subsoil remains permanently frozen (ie, it is 'permafrost'). The saturated surface layer (sometimes called the 'active layer') can flow down even gentle slopes. Its movement is helped by reduced friction with the frozen subsoil. The rate of flow varies from place to place but is generally slow - often less than 1 cm per day.

This type of flow creates solifluction lobes which are up to 50 metres wide and 2 metres high. Such features are found in periglacial regions of the arctic and sub-arctic. They also occur in many mountainous areas, for example in Scotland's Cairngorms above 1,000 metres. There are also 'fossil' solifluction lobes on the chalk Downs of Southern England. These lobes were formed at the time of the last glacial advance when the region experienced periglacial conditions.

Creep

This is a very slow, almost imperceptible downslope movement of soil and rock particles. Most slopes with an angle over 6 degrees show signs of creep. One result is a build up of soil behind walls. Telegraph poles and fence posts on a slope start to tilt downwards as soil builds up behind them and is removed from in front. Soil creep is caused by expansion and contraction (or 'heaving') in the surface layer of regolith. This is due to two main processes - wetting and drying, and freezing and thawing.

When soil particles become wet, they expand in volume. They push up from the slope at a perpendicular angle. Then, when they dry, they contract in volume and sink down vertically. The result is a zig-zag downhill motion for the soil particles (see figure 8.16). The same process occurs when soil moisture freezes and expands. Material is lifted and then moved downslope when the ice thaws. Sometimes, when wet soil freezes, needle ice (or 'pipkrake') grows perpendicular to the surface. It can lift thin loose layers of material over 10 cm above their

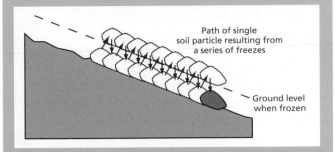

Figure 8.16 Soil creep

Path of single soil particle resulting from a series of freezes

Ground level when frozen

Every time that the ground freezes, water in the soil expands and raises the particle. When the ground thaws, the particle moves vertically downwards.

original position. When the ice needles melt, the material sinks downslope.

Creep is affected by climatic conditions. In regions that experience cycles of wet and dry weather, or where the temperature frequently rises above and below freezing, the movement is quickest. Also, if soil contains a high proportion of clay, the wet - dry process of creep causes relatively fast movement. This is because clay minerals have the ability to absorb large volumes of water and therefore expand considerably in size.

On grass covered slopes, small terraces (called 'terracettes') sometimes form (see figure 8.17). They are usually less than a metre wide. It is not certain whether terracettes are natural features caused by creep, or are caused by trampling cattle and sheep. Their common name, 'sheep tracks', suggests an animal origin but it may be that sheep are simply taking advantage of a natural feature and making it more pronounced.

Figure 8.17 Terracettes in Smardale, Cumbria

Fall

Falls only occur on the steepest of slopes, generally with angles greater than 45 degrees. Although gravity causes a fragment of rock to fall, it has to be loosened in the first place. Freeze thaw (see unit 8.1) is the main agent that is responsible, so falls are more common in areas which experience cold conditions at least some of the time. In hotter areas, chemical weathering can play a part in loosening material. Once detached, a particle of rock falls, rolls and bounces down the slope until it reaches a point where the slope angle is low enough for it to come to rest.

Scree (or 'talus') is a classic feature produced by falls. Rock fragments are detached from a cliff face (or 'free face') and then fall. This creates scree slopes of unconsolidated rock fragments at angles generally between 34 and 40 degrees. 'Active' scree slopes on which new rock is falling are normally over 36 degrees while 'inactive' or 'fossil' screes are less steep. The rate of activity on a scree slope depends on the rock type, structure, and climate. Weaknesses in the rock determine the size of the fragments and the rate of weathering.

The rate of supply of scree material is related to the height of the free face on a cliff. The higher the cliff, the faster the scree builds up. The free face weathers and

Figure 8.18 A scree slope in the Bernese Oberland, Switzerland

This active scree slope is over 300 metres high. The rock fragments have fallen from the cliff face above.

retreats at a steady rate but, as the scree accumulates, it covers the base of the cliff and protects it from weathering. Eventually this process creates a curved profile.

Material in screes is sorted as it falls. The largest boulders travel the furthest because of their momentum, so are found at the bottom of the scree slope. The result is a 'boulder apron' at the base of the scree. Smaller fragments 'stick' further up the slope, filling gaps and acting like ball bearings for larger pieces to roll over.

 Activity   Classifying mass movement

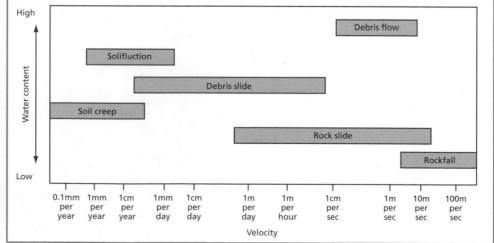

Figure 8.19 Mass movement

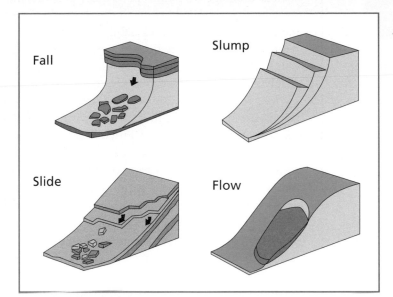

Figure 8.20 Types of slope failure

Questions

1 Summarise the information in figure 8.19.
2 Describe the difference between a fall, a slide, a slump and a flow.

Rain splash and surface wash

These processes cannot be classed as mass movement because they are not primarily caused by gravity. However, their effect is to increase the rate of downslope movement and so are included here.

Rain splash occurs when raindrops fall. A 2 mm drop has a terminal velocity of 6.9 m/sec and, in a heavy storm, one spot of ground can be hit over 20 times per hour. When a raindrop hits, soil particles can be splashed several centimetres high. The particles tend to bounce downslope when they land. Studies have shown that raindrop impact can move 180 tonnes of soil per hectare in just one hour of heavy rain. The largest particles are left on the slope while the finer material moves towards the base of the slope.

Surface wash occurs on slopes when the soil is saturated or cannot absorb heavy rain. The result is 'overland flow' of water. If it occurs as a thin continuous layer of flowing water, it is called 'surface wash' or 'sheet flow'. Silt and clay sized particles are washed downslope when the flow of water reaches a velocity powerful enough to overcome the resistance and cohesion of the soil particles.

Both rain splash and sheet wash are very effective on bare slopes. These conditions occur, for example, on farmland under cultivation when the surface has been loosened prior to planting, up to the time the crop is big enough to protect the soil. The processes are also effective in arid and semi-arid areas when rain falls in rare torrential downpours and vegetation cover is low.

Where plants and roots protect and bind the soil, the effect is much reduced.

Subsidence

Subsidence is a vertical downward movement of material at ground level. Generally there is little or no horizontal movement. The main force producing subsidence is gravity but other factors also play a part in first creating an underground hole. For instance, in some places, it occurs when overlying material collapses into caves or underground caverns. In central Florida where there is underground limestone, and in the Vale of York where underground potash occurs, the soluble rock is being dissolved by water.

Underground mining can lead to subsidence when the ground surface collapses into disused workings. In many coalfields this has caused depressions that fill with water and form small lakes. Damage to roads and buildings is common in these areas as the ground underneath them sinks.

Pumping of underground water and oil can also cause subsidence. Buildings in Mexico City have subsided due to excessive pumping of water from the underground aquifers. Similarly in Long Beach, California, subsidence of 10 metres in 30 years is due to the extraction of oil. These problems can be solved by injecting water back underground and raising the fluid pressure. Unfortunately this does not work for disused coal mines and a 'controlled drop' is often the only solution.

3. How do people cope with hazards caused by mass movement?

Mass movement is a continuous, natural and normal process. However, it is worth noting that human activity can sometimes speed the process or even cause it to happen. People sometimes increase the rate of mass movement by:

- increasing the water content of slope material; eg, by poorly planned drainage
- removing vegetation cover that stabilises the slope, especially by deforestation
- increasing the slope angle; eg, by constructing roads in cuttings
- adding weight to a slope; eg, by building on it
- shaking the slope; eg, by using machinery or making a noise (particularly on snow slopes).

Landslides (defined here in general terms as any form of rapid mass movement) are ranked high on a scale of natural hazards that affect people. Worldwide, from 1945 to 1995, there were 33 landslides that each killed over 50 people and they cause around 600 deaths a year. Large scale landslides are, fortunately, relatively rare in Britain. Countries that experience torrential rain and/or earthquakes are most at risk. For example, in the Central American countries of Honduras and Nicaragua, the combination of heavy rain, house building on unstable volcanic slopes and deforestation caused many landslides in 1998 at the time of Hurricane Mitch.

Hazard management

There are several ways in which the hazards arising from mass movement can be managed. Methods include:

- Increasing slope stability - by engineering techniques such as drainage (to reduce pore-water pressure and so increase shear strength), terracing or 'regrading' (to reduce the slope angle) and stabilising (by using retaining walls, rock anchors or steel mesh) (see figure 8.21). The drawbacks to this approach are the cost involved and the responsibility for enforcement. Official regulations can set the required building standards, but ensuring they are observed is often not easy - even in countries with efficient government systems. (This form of hazard management is sometimes called 'modification of the event'.)
- Avoiding the danger - this requires that hazards are assessed and then mapped to show areas most at risk. Planning and building controls can be used to avoid development in the most hazardous zones. If development has already taken place, systems for forecasting, warning and evacuation are needed. (This form of hazard management is sometimes called 'modification of vulnerability'.)

Figure 8.21 Stabilising slopes at Scarborough

In this example, the slope has been stabilised by a retaining wall. (In other places, steel mesh is used. Sometimes, rock anchors are drilled down to the bedrock to 'tie' the surface in place.) An undersoil drainage system has been constructed to reduce the pore-water pressure and so increase the shear strength of the slope. Above the wall, terracing has been used to reduce the overall slope angle. Such measures are expensive and are only generally used to protect valuable property - in this case, the sea front chalets.

- Insurance - private insurance companies rarely provide cover in the most hazardous locations and charge above normal premiums for areas at risk. This acts as a disincentive to development. Sometimes insurance companies charge lower premiums if they are satisfied, for example, that all safety procedures have been followed on a hill slope development. Systems of insurance do not reduce the likelihood of mass movement but they do reduce the financial risk involved.

- Managing landslides - this solution is only undertaken where people are at risk and sufficient resources are available. Near Mt Sakurajima, Japan, for instance, concrete and metal barriers and deflectors are built in stream beds and on volcanic slopes where lahars might occur. These techniques slow and divert the flow. Television monitors and instruments on the mountain are in place to give people warning and time to evacuate. Similar techniques are used to reduce the risk from snow avalanches in alpine resorts.

 Activity ⟩ **Mass movement**

Aberfan, South Wales, 1966

Aberfan is a colliery village built on the slopes of the River Taff valley. Above the houses, tips of colliery waste from the Merthyr Vale mine had been dumped for many years prior to 1966. In some cases, the waste was tipped on slopes as steep as 25 degrees. Tip 7, begun in 1958, consisted of fine rock fragments. When it rained (the annual rainfall here is 1,500 mm) the surface turned into a mud-like fluid. In 1963, a small debris flow occurred on Tip 7 but, afterwards, the scar was filled in by more dumping. By 1966, the tip was 180 metres high.

When workmen arrived at Tip 7 on the 21st October, 1966, they found that the top surface had sunk, leaving a 3 metre depression. As they watched, material broke loose from the side of the heap and flowed downhill engulfing the village school where lessons had just begun. The final death toll was 116 children and 28 adults.

Later investigations revealed that the site lay over a previously unknown spring line which had saturated the lower layers of the tip. On the morning of the disaster, the weight of material above had liquefied the lower layers and a dense mix of debris and water had flowed out from the base - carrying the upper layers with it.

Nevado del Ruiz, Colombia, 1985

Nevado del Ruiz is the most northerly active volcano in South America. It is over 5,300 metres high and has an ice and snow cap that extends over 25 square kilometres. A series of small eruptions started in November 1984 and geologists began to monitor the volcanic activity. Then, a large explosive eruption occurred on November 13th 1985. Pyroclastic flows of gas, hot ash and pumice melted approximately 10 percent of the snowcap. Lahars began pouring down from the summit area and became concentrated in five main stream channels. The flow became faster and increased in volume with water and debris from the stream beds. It was estimated that the average speed of flow was 60 km/h and rose to 150 km/h in places.

In the narrow, upper Langunilla River valley, the lahar grew to 50 metres deep, destroying everything in its path. At a point approximately 50 km from the volcano, the valley widens. Here, the town of Armero was situated, built on solidified mud from previous lahars in 1595 and 1845.

Just over two hours after the volcano erupted, the first lahar 'pulse' or wave hit Armero - at 11.25 pm when most people were in bed. A second, bigger pulse arrived ten minutes later, covering the town with mud between two and five metres deep. The lahar's flow was described as having the consistency of liquid concrete. Over 5,000 houses were destroyed and 23,000 people died. When the mud 'set', it covered most of the town and surrounding area, leaving fragments of buildings sticking out above.

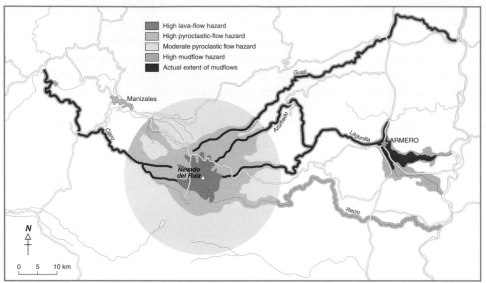

Fig 8.22 Hazard map for Nevado del Ruiz produced one month before the Armero lahar

High lava-flow hazard
High pyroclastic-flow hazard
Moderate pyroclastic flow hazard
High mudflow hazard
Actual extent of mudflows

Questions

1 Identify any features that the Armero and Aberfan disasters had in common.
2 Suggest how people might have been protected from the hazards at Armero and Aberfan.

4. What factors affect slope development?

Landscapes are made up of combinations of slopes. Studies of slope development therefore form the basis of people's understanding of landscape features.

A slope is a system in which material moves downslope, generally towards a drainage channel (see figure 8.23). Material on the slope is weathered into smaller and smaller particles which move downslope by gravity or are transported downhill. Eventually, a stream, river or glacier removes the material from the system. In the case of coastal slopes, wave action, sea currents and longshore drift remove the weathered material at the bottom of the slope.

The main processes at work on slopes are weathering and the downslope

Figure 8.23 Slope processes

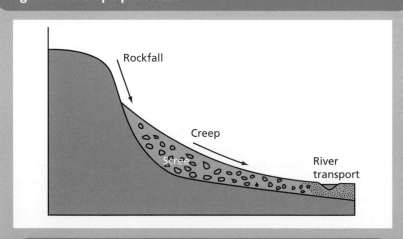

A slope is an 'open dynamic system'. This simply means that there is an input, an output and constant movement of material. New material comes from upslope, in this case from rockfall. Material is weathered on the slope by mechanical and chemical processes. It moves downslope by mass movement (such as creep) or is carried by running water in gullies or as surface wash. At the foot of the slope, the material is removed by a river.

Figure 8.24 Convex, straight and concave sections of a slope

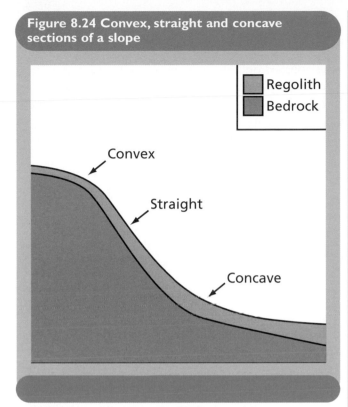

Regolith
Bedrock

Convex

Straight

Concave

movement of weathered material. Movement is either by mass movement (ie, by gravity) or by the action of running water. It is often difficult in practice to distinguish between mass movement and water transport because there is no clear cut dividing line between the two processes. For instance, an example of mass movement is a watery mudflow, whereas an example of water transport is a muddy, water flow.

Slope development is complex because there is interaction and feedback between many variables. For instance, the rate of weathering and the rate of removal of material determine the angle of slope. But, at the same time, the angle of slope influences the rate of weathering and removal of material. This is illustrated by looking at what happens on different parts of a slope.

At the top of a slope, weathered material is likely to move downhill, either due to gravity or due to transport by running water. The result is a loss of soil upslope, and a build up of soil downslope. Near the top of the slope, the rate of weathering of bedrock is likely to be higher than lower down because the thinner soil provides less protection to the underlying material. This will cause the upper slope to become less steep as the weathered material is removed - so producing a convex shape (see figure 8.24).

In mid-slope, there may be a straight section with a constant gradient (sometimes called a 'rectilinear slope').

However, this is not always the case and some slopes have a profile that moves from convex to concave without a straight section. It is the resistance of the rock and the amount of precipitation that are the controlling factors. For example, in upland Britain, there are many examples of upper, convex slopes that give way to slopes with a constant gradient. It is likely that straight mid-sections of slopes exist in these areas because the rocks are relatively resistant to weathering and there is very active downslope transport of material. This rapid removal of weathered material is caused by mass movement and by the relatively heavy rainfall which brings about overland flow and surface wash. In areas where rocks are less resistant, or where precipitation is lighter, there may not be a straight mid-slope section.

The bottom of slopes is often concave. This is because weathered material moves downslope and accumulates until it is removed by agents of erosion (eg, rivers, glaciers or waves). The material builds up as long as the rate of downslope movement is greater than the rate of removal.

Figure 8.25 Chalk cliff, Sussex

The cliff remains almost vertical because weathered material is removed from the base.

In general, the more dominant that the process of transport is over the process of weathering, the steeper the slope. On very resistant rock, the rate of weathering is slow compared with the rate at which material is transported away - so cliffs or 'free faces' are formed. On a sea cliff, rock fall and wave action completely remove the weathered material. Combined with the undercutting effect of the waves, this can keep the face almost vertical (see figure 8.25).

Factors influencing slope processes

A number of factors influence the rate at which slope processes operate. They include the climate, the aspect of the slope, the geology, the vegetation and the human activity.

- Climate Both temperature and precipitation affect the rate of weathering and downslope movement. For instance, in humid regions, downslope movement of material by water is more effective than in arid regions where there is little rain. In periglaciated regions, solifluction (ie, the downslope movement of saturated soil) is more rapid on slopes that undergo a surface thaw than on slopes that remain mainly frozen. Another factor is the rate of freeze thaw action which is affected by the temperature. The more freeze thaw cycles there are, the more weathering of material occurs.

- Aspect The direction a slope faces can be a factor in those regions where freeze thaw processes are active. Slopes that face the Sun at midday are likely to go through more freeze thaw cycles than slopes that are mainly in shadow and are therefore colder.

- Geology Both the structure and composition of rocks affects slope development. Different rocks have different resistances to weathering and this affects the angle of slope. In general, the more resistant the rock, the steeper the slope. Where there are alternating layers of soft and hard rock, slopes are generally less steep than in places where the rock is uniform. For example, if a layer of clay underlies a more resistant sandstone or limestone, the slope is liable to be unstable.

- Vegetation The angle of slope both affects and is affected by the plants that grow on slopes. For instance, deep rooted vegetation only grows on slopes that are sufficiently gentle for soils to develop. Once the vegetation is established, the root systems bind the soil together and reduce downward slope movement.

- Human activity Arable farming only occurs on slopes of approximately 10 degrees or less. Steeper than this, slopes are difficult to plough. Once farming is established on a slope, increased soil erosion can eventually modify slope angle by washing material downslope. In some cases, farmers have completely regraded slopes by building terraces and retaining walls. This allows the farmers to grow crops on land that otherwise would be too steep for agriculture. Deforestation and urban development can also influence slope processes. By removing vegetation that holds the soil and slows surface runoff, the rate of slope movement is increased. Also, construction of roads and buildings can affect slopes by increasing the load or by steepening the angle if cuttings are made.

Theories of slope development

Three models of slope development are shown in figure 8.26. They are attempts to explain, in a generalised fashion, how slopes develop under particular climatic and geological conditions. The models are now considered invalid, mainly because it is accepted that

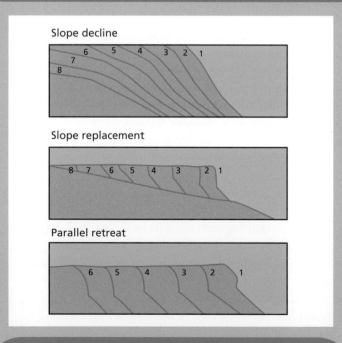

Fig 8.26 Models of slope development

Slope decline

Slope replacement

Parallel retreat

Slope decline: this theory was developed by Davis in the 1890s. The angle of slope declines over time.
Slope replacement: this theory was developed by Penck in the 1920s. The free face becomes smaller as scree builds up.
Parallel retreat: this theory was developed by King in the 1950s. The angle of slope remains constant.

slopes develop in many different ways and no single model can provide a full explanation. Modern research into slope development tends to focus on detailed studies of particular slopes.

Although the theories of slope development are now mainly of historic interest, some of the terminology survives. In particular, the ideas of Davis have had a long standing influence on how landscapes are described. He suggested that there is a 'cycle of erosion' which starts with the uplift of a land surface. In this 'youthful' stage, the land is deeply incised with steep slopes. Then the landscape goes through a stage of 'maturity' and finally reaches 'old age' in which the mountains are eroded and the landscape is a virtually flat 'peneplain'. A new cycle starts when the land is again uplifted.

Since the publication of Davis's ideas, it has become clear that tectonic movements and climate changes occur relatively frequently - in geological terms. These changes prevent the completion of any cycle of erosion. Nevertheless, terms such as 'youthful', 'mature' or 'old' landscapes are still sometimes used.

Activity | Slope features

Slopes are sometimes classified according to the balance between weathering and transport that is taking place:
- A **denudation** slope is a slope on which there is a net loss of material because transport processes remove the weathered material so quickly that it does not accumulate.
- A **transportation** slope is a slope on which the rate of accumulation of material (from upslope and from weathering) is equal to the rate of transportation downslope. There is no net gain or loss of material.
- An **accumulation** slope is a slope on which there is a net gain of material. Weathered material accumulates at a faster rate than it can be removed by transport processes.

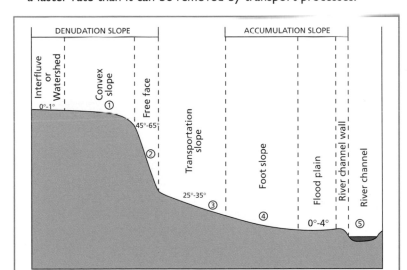

Figure 8.27 Slope features

At the points numbered 1 to 5 on the slope in figure 8.27, the main transport processes at work are:
1. Soil creep; formation of terracettes
2. Rock fall and slide
3. Mass movement by flow, slide, slump and creep; surface wash of material by overland flow of water
4. Redeposition of material; creep
5. River transport of eroded material.

Questions

1. Where on the slope profile would you expect scree to accumulate? Explain your answer.
2. Where on the slope profile would you expect the soil depth to be greatest? Explain your answer.
3. Outline the factors that will affect the future angle of slopes on the slope profile.

unit summary

1 Mass movement is the transfer of material downslope through the force of gravity. It occurs when shear stress is greater than the shear strength of slope material.

2 Two major factors that influence mass movement are the water content of the slope material and the slope angle.

3 There are different ways of classifying mass movement. In this unit, four main types are identified: creep, flow, slide and fall.

4 Hazards created by mass movement can be managed in different ways. These include prevention, avoidance of risk areas and emergency planning.

5 Slopes are open, dynamic systems in which there is an input of material from weathering and an output or removal of material by mass movement and water transport.

6   The angle of slopes is determined by the relative rates of weathering and transport of material. These are largely influenced by geology and climate. Other factors that affect slope development are aspect, vegetation and human influence.

key terms

Accumulation slope - a slope on which there is a net gain of material.

Angle of repose - the steepest slope on which loose material will remain in place and not move downwards. (Sometimes also called the 'angle of friction' and the 'equilibrium angle'.)

Creep - the slow movement of individual soil and rock particles downslope.

Denudation slope - a slope on which there is a net loss of material.

Fall - the airborne movement of material down a steep slope or cliff face.

Flow - the downslope movement of loose debris, soil or mud that behaves as a fluid.

Lahar - a mudflow formed from unconsolidated ash and volcanic material.

Mass movement - the movement of material downslope due to gravity; it is also sometimes known as 'mass wasting'.

Mudflow - a flow that consists of water mixed with a high proportion of fine silt or clay particles.

Scree (or **talus**) - rock fragments lying at the foot of a cliff face.

Shear strength - the resistance to downhill movement in slope material.

Shear stress - the downhill pull exerted by gravity and the weight of slope material.

Slide - the movement of a section of slope down a plane of weakness. It can be a debris slide of mixed soil and rock, or a rock slide.

Slope failure - the downhill movement of slope material following a loss of cohesion.

Slump - a slide along a curved plane (sometimes also called a rotational slide or slip).

Solifluction - literally 'soil flow', the term is used to describe the generally slow movement of saturated soil in periglacial conditions.

Subsidence - the vertically downward movement of surface material into an underground cavern.

Transportation slope - a slope on which there is no net gain or loss of material; the rate of weathering equals the rate at which material is removed.

Unit 8.3 Geology and landforms

1 How does geology affect the landscape?
2 What distinctive features are formed by chalk and limestone?

1. How does geology affect the landscape?

Features on the Earth's surface are the result of two sets of opposing natural forces. On the one hand, volcanic activity and tectonic movements create new landforms. On the other hand, the process of denudation wears these landforms down. (Denudation is the combined effect of weathering, erosion and transport of material.)

Geology (ie, what rocks are made of and how they are arranged) is an important influence on the rate and outcome of denudation. The degree to which a particular rock resists the processes of weathering and erosion depends upon its composition and structure.

Composition (or 'lithology') relates to a rock's characteristics - ie, its chemical and physical properties. These properties will determine the rock's physical strength and also its 'porosity' (ie, the volume of water that can be held within the rock). If a rock has a high porosity, it is said to be **porous**. In addition, a rock's composition will affect its resistance to chemical weathering. This is because some mineral components of rocks are more stable than others. For example, quartz (in sandstone) is very stable and is therefore resistant to chemical attack.

Structure relates to a rock's shape and form. It might be 'banded', with thin layers, or 'massive' with no obvious layering. If there are distinct beds, these might be horizontal, vertical or folded.

The rock might be well jointed or have no joints at all. (A joint is a vertical crack formed by pressure, or by cooling in the case of igneous rocks.) Rocks that have many joints and bedding planes tend to be **permeable** (ie, they allow water through).

In general, rocks that are strongest, least porous and most massive in structure are the most resistant to erosion. The fewer pores, joints and bedding planes there are, the less surface area is exposed to weathering. The degree of porosity and permeability are also important because this factor determines how much water can penetrate into a rock. Water not only increases the rate of chemical weathering, it also affects the rate of mechanical weathering in those regions where freeze thaw action occurs.

The composition and structure of rocks depends, to a large extent, on how they are formed. There are three broad categories: igneous, metamorphic and sedimentary.

Igneous rocks These rocks are formed when molten magma (from within the Earth's interior) cools and solidifies. When magma spills out onto the Earth's surface, it is known as lava. Because lava cools relatively

Figure 8.28 Sedimentary rocks at the Grand Canyon, Arizona

The layers of limestone, sandstone and shale are clearly seen. These rocks were laid down in a variety of conditions. The top strata are mainly sea deposits - formed from shells, corals and sponges. Lower down, some strata were formed on land from sand dunes, or in shallow freshwater. There are also beach deposits and flood plain deposits. The oldest sedimentary rocks in the Canyon are over 3 billion years old.

quickly, the rocks it forms tend to have a fine crystalline texture. Basalt and andesite are examples. Sometimes, in explosive volcanic eruptions, ash and larger 'pyroclastic' fragments are ejected and deposited on the ground. Tuff is an example of a volcanic rock formed from compacted ash. The rocks formed from lava and pyroclastic material are called 'volcanic' or 'extrusive'.

If magma cools before it reaches the surface, the rocks formed are called 'plutonic' or 'intrusive'. A slower rate of cooling tends to give these rocks a coarse crystalline texture. Examples include granite and gabbro.

The structure of igneous rocks varies a great deal depending on how and where they cool. Some are in the form of thin sheets while others form massive blocks. The landforms they create are described in detail in unit 7.3.

Sedimentary rocks These rocks are formed by the accumulation and consolidation of sediment. The origin of the sediment might be from the weathering of pre-existing rocks. Examples include sandstone, mudstone and clay. In other cases, there is an organic origin to the sediment. Examples include coal (from vegetation) and limestone and chalk (from marine organisms).

Sedimentary rocks are laid down in horizontal beds (or 'strata') which can vary in thickness from a few millimetres to several hundred metres. The surface on which a layer of sediment forms is known as a 'bedding plane'. Sedimentary rocks are often faulted or folded by tectonic movements. 'Synclines' (ie, downfolds) and 'anticlines' (ie, upfolds) are relatively common structures.

Metamorphic rocks These are rocks that have been modified by heat and pressure. The process occurs mainly in mountain building periods (or 'orogenies') where tectonic plates collide. Examples include marble (formed from limestone), quartzite (formed from sandstone), slate (formed from clay) and gneiss (formed from granite). These rocks tend to be resistant to both chemical and mechanical weathering.

The structure of metamorphic rocks is very variable depending on the type and location of the original rocks. In some places, the rocks form massive blocks but, in others, relatively thin structures are formed if the metamorphism is due to contact with intrusive magma.

Activity — The strength and porosity of selected rocks

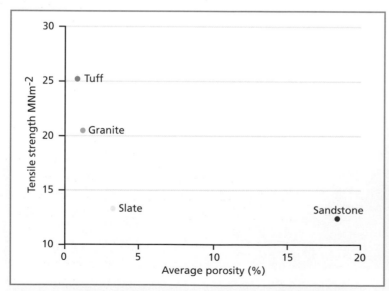

Figure 8.29 The tensile strength and average porosity of granite, tuff, slate and sandstone

Tensile strength is resistance to being 'pulled apart'. It is measured in million newtons per square metre. Porosity is the volume of pores in a rock expressed as a percentage of total volume. The figures on the graph are average values.

Questions

1 Which of the rocks in the diagram are igneous, metamorphic or sedimentary?
2 Which of the rocks is likely to be most resistant to weathering. Explain your answer.

Geology and landscape in Britain

In Britain, the most resistant rocks are the igneous, metamorphic and older sedimentary rocks that outcrop in the north and west. The least resistant rocks are the younger sedimentary rocks that outcrop in the south and east. This divide between more and less resistant rocks corresponds to the divide between upland and lowland Britain.

The cross section in figure 8.30 shows that the highest mountains in Snowdonia are formed from igneous rocks. It also shows the effect of differential erosion in South East England. The relatively resistant chalk, sandstone and limestone form ridges and less resistant clays form vales.

However, it should not be generalised from this that the most resistant rock always forms the highest ground. Tectonic movements create fold mountains that, in many cases, are formed from relatively weak sedimentary rocks. For example, in the Alps, some peaks consist of sandstones and limestones that are no more resistant to erosion than similar rocks in South East England. On the other hand, in Sutherland (north west Scotland), some of the oldest and most resistant metamorphic rocks such as gneiss form relatively low land.

The reason why relatively soft rocks sometimes form high ground and relatively hard rocks form low ground is related to the age of the rocks and landscape features.

The Alps are, on a geological time scale, much younger than the mountains of the far north west of Scotland. There has been less time for denudation to occur and therefore the Alps are higher.

When considering the resistance of particular rocks to denudation on a world scale, the issue of climate becomes important. Limestone, for example, is relatively resistant to weathering in warm, dry climates. In cool, humid climates it is less resistant. This is because it is vulnerable to both freeze thaw and chemical weathering by solution.

These points illustrate the fact that the same rock can produce different landforms under different climatic conditions and at different time scales. Landscape features therefore depend as much on the length of time that weathering occurs, and on the dominant type of weathering, as on the composition and structure of rock.

2. What distinctive features are formed by chalk and limestone?

Limestone and chalk are sedimentary rocks that are relatively resistant to erosion when compared, for example, with clay. They are formed when certain marine plants and creatures extract calcium carbonate from sea water and use it to construct their shells, skeletons and hard parts. When these organisms die, their skeletal remains accumulate on the sea floor. Over a long period of time, the deposits form limestone and chalk. These 'calcareous' rocks take many forms. Some contain impurities, such as mud and sand, while others are very pure. Some are massive while others are composed of well jointed, thinly bedded layers.

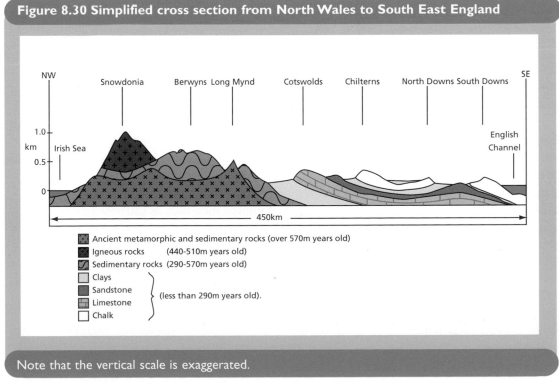

Figure 8.30 Simplified cross section from North Wales to South East England

Note that the vertical scale is exaggerated.

Figure 8.31 Chalk and limestone areas of Britain

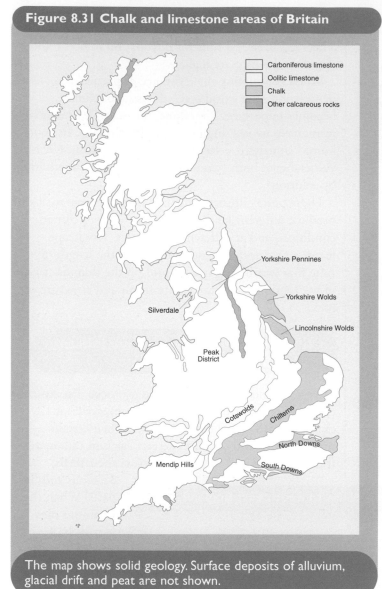

Carboniferous limestone
Oolitic limestone
Chalk
Other calcareous rocks

Yorkshire Pennines
Yorkshire Wolds
Silverdale
Lincolnshire Wolds
Peak District
Cotswolds
Chilterns
North Downs
Mendip Hills
South Downs

The map shows solid geology. Surface deposits of alluvium, glacial drift and peat are not shown.

Carboniferous limestones (see figure 8.31) were deposited approximately 320 million years ago. They were formed from shells and skeletons of sea plants such as crinoids (sea lilies) and corals. The Jurassic limestones were deposited approximately 200 million years ago. They include Oolitic limestone which has a different origin from most other calcareous rocks because it is not organic in origin. 'Oolites' are small, spherical grains of limestone formed when calcium carbonate 'precipitates' in water (ie, the mineral is deposited in solid form from a solution). This happens in warm sea water where there is a high concentration of calcium carbonate.

Both Carboniferous and Jurassic limestones contain impurities and are rather grey in colour, often with fossils

clearly visible. Limestone is not porous but it is permeable, ie water can drain through its joints.

Chalk is a very pure limestone formed from the skeletal fragments of microscopic organisms. Deposits in Britain are from the Cretaceous period, approximately 100 million years ago. The rock is porous and very white in colour though not well jointed.

Chalk and limestone are weathered mainly by the chemical process of carbonation. Rainwater is weakly acid because it absorbs carbon dioxide from the atmosphere. It reacts with calcium carbonate in chalk and limestone to form calcium bicarbonate - which is soluble and is washed away in solution. Precise monitoring equipment has been developed that can measure the rate of weathering. On average, it is estimated that limestone is lowered by 10 cm per 1,000 years but this rises to 30 cm per 1,000 years in areas of high rainfall.

Because weathering by solution removes dissolved material, there tends to be little weathered debris. Soils are generally thin - unless the rock contains a large amount of impurities, in which case the impurities accumulate and form the basis of soil.

Landscape features

Limestone and chalk scenery is distinctive because there is little surface drainage. In chalk, water slowly percolates through pore spaces. In limestone, water drains down joints and along bedding planes. Because streams and rivers do not generally run across the chalk and limestone surface, there is less erosion by running water than on rocks where there is surface drainage. Another reason why chalk and limestone scenery is distinctive is because most of the weathering and erosion is by carbonation and solution.

In a well jointed rock such as Carboniferous limestone, underground streams and caves are common. Running water dissolves the rock, so widening joints and bedding planes. Both the Malham area of Yorkshire, and central Kentucky in the USA, contain notable cave systems that extend for many kilometres.

'Classic' limestone scenery is called **karst** after the region in Slovenia (part of the former Yugoslavia) where it is found. It is a landscape of depressions and dry valleys. Some karst features occur in the Yorkshire

Figure 8.32 Limestone pavement, Hutton Roof, Cumbria

cases, solution runnels caused by rainwater or melt water. However it is believed that, in many cases, the grooves first developed when the rock was covered by soil or peat. Under these conditions, decomposing organic matter made percolating water more acidic - so increasing the rate of chemical weathering. This had the effect of widening joints in the limestone.

In parts of south east China, limestone has been subject to a long period of weathering under warm, humid climatic conditions. The result is a very spectacular landscape known as 'tower karst' (see figure 8.33). Most of the limestone has eroded away - leaving steep sided blocks as remnants of the former land surface. These towers are honeycombed with caves, arches and solution channels. During times of flood, water rises to the foot of the towers and this causes undercutting to occur.

Springs

A feature of both chalk and limestone is the existence of springs. Generally they emerge at a point where the permeable rock overlies an impermeable rock or where the water table is at ground level. Where a line of springs occur, this is known as a 'spring line'. (The **water table** is the upper level of groundwater in permeable or porous rocks).

Pennines and Derbyshire Peak District. In both these places, however, the landscape has been modified by glaciation. In Yorkshire, in particular, ice sheets have deepened valleys and scoured the upland. The result has been to form cliffs (or 'scars') and areas of bare rock known as **limestone pavement** (see figure 8.32).

In Northern England the grooves in limestone pavement are called 'grikes' and the paving blocks are called 'clints'. Similar features occur in parts of the Alps where there are limestone outcrops. The German term for the grooves is 'karren'. Some are shallow but others can be several metres deep. The formation of limestone pavement is probably due to ice sheets stripping away overlying soil and weathered material. The grooves are, in some

Figure 8.33 Tower karst, south east China

Figure 8.34 Cavedale, Derbyshire

A dry valley in an area of Carboniferous limestone.

In some locations, where an underground river emerges, the term 'resurgence' is used rather than spring. This feature is also known as a 'Vauclusian spring' - named after the Fontaine de Vaucluse in the Rhone Valley of southern France. An example in England is where the River Aire emerges at the foot of Malham Cove (see figure 8.35).

Dry valleys and gorges

Dry valleys are features common to most chalk and limestone areas. They are simply valley shaped hollows - but with no running stream. In some cases they were formed under periglacial conditions when the frozen ground was impermeable. Running water eroded the valleys but now, in a warmer climate, the water percolates underground. Some dry valleys - such as the one above Malham Cove in Yorkshire - may have been deepened by glacial meltwater. A large waterfall would have eroded the deep valley at the foot of the Cove.

In Carboniferous limestone, valleys are sometimes gorge-like in shape. Examples include the Cheddar Gorge in the Mendips, Winnats Pass in Derbyshire and Gordale Scar near Malham. At one time, such features were thought to be the remnants of collapsed underground caverns. Now it is believed they are the result of rapid erosion caused by periglacial run-off. However, in the case of Gordale, the existence of

a natural arch suggests that some collapse has also taken place.

In wet periods, the water table in chalk and limestone can sometimes rise and streams might reappear in formerly dry valleys. In the chalklands of southern England such intermittent streams are called 'bournes' or 'winterbournes'.

Solution depressions

In both chalk and limestone regions, enclosed depressions are formed by solution, or by the collapse of cave systems. Larger basins are called 'poljes'. They are relatively common in parts of Slovenia and Croatia. Examples in England occur near Silverdale, in north Lancashire.

Smaller depressions, from a few metres to over a kilometre in diameter, are called 'dolines'. Examples occur in both chalk, for instance Culpepper's Dish in Dorset, and in limestone areas. Sometimes such depressions also develop in locations where the permeable rock does not outcrop at the surface but is covered by a thin layer of other rock or glacial deposits. Here, the overlying material collapses into a widened joint and forms a 'subsidence doline' or 'shake-hole'.

Where a surface stream flows into a depression, the terms 'sink-hole', 'swallow-hole' and 'pot-hole' are sometimes used. Many examples occur in the Ingleborough area of Yorkshire where surface streams

Figure 8.35 Malham Cove, North Yorkshire

The River Aire emerges at the foot of the Cove. During periglacial times at the end of the last glacial period there was a large waterfall here.

Figure 8.36 Gaping Gill, Ingleborough

At this point a stream flows into a swallow-hole and then flows through underground caverns.

develop on impermeable rock and then flow onto limestone. An example is Gaping Gill. Here a stream flows into a depression and then drops over 110 metres into a large underground cavern (see figure 8.36). In such caverns, the calcium bicarbonate dissolved in dripping water sometimes precipitates into calcium carbonate and forms stalactites and stalagmites. The material which forms these features is called 'tufa' and it sometimes builds up into thick deposits near waterfalls or in cave systems.

Escarpments

(The term 'cuesta' is sometimes used instead of escarpment.) These features are elongated ridges on which there is generally a steeper 'scarp' slope and a gentler 'dip' slope. Where the scarp and dip slopes are of similar, steep angle, the feature is known as a 'hogsback'.

Escarpments are formed by the differential erosion of tilted strata. Relatively weak rocks, such as clay, form valleys and relatively resistant rocks, such as chalk, form ridges (see figure 8.37). In southern England, examples include the Chilterns, the North Downs and the South Downs (all chalk) and the Cotswolds (limestone). Spring lines occur along these escarpments and there are, for example, a number of 'spring line villages' along the scarp foot of the Cotswolds. These settlements are sited at the point where a reliable supply of fresh water emerges at the junction of the limestone and clay.

Where chalk outcrops occur in England, there is a distinctive rolling landscape of low hills. In the south of England, these are called Downs; in Lincolnshire and Yorkshire they are called Wolds. As in limestone areas, there are few surface streams. The landscape has been formed under both present and past climatic conditions. Because chalk is porous and has few joints, weathering by solution creates a relatively uniform surface. The landscape is worn down gradually and evenly. However, under periglacial conditions during past glacial advances, the ground was frozen so there was more surface drainage than there is now. It is likely that some valleys were eroded at that time. During the same period, the subsoil was permanently frozen and solifluction caused lobes of material to flow downslope. These deposits, called 'head' or 'coombe rock', have been identified on the South Downs and in other chalk areas of southern England.

Figure 8.37 A simplified cross-section across the Cotswold and Chiltern escarpments

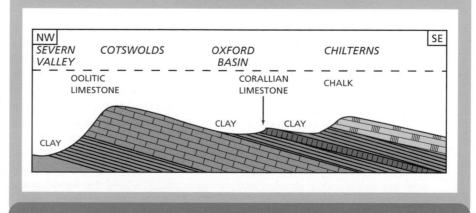

Activity Ingleborough

▼ **Figure 8.38 1:25,000 map of the Ingleborough area**

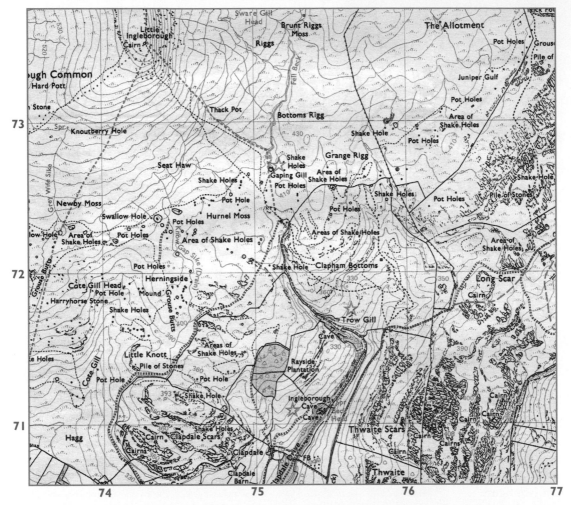

In the Ingleborough area of North Yorkshire, the Great Scar Carboniferous limestone is between 150-200 metres thick. It is sandwiched between two layers of impermeable rock. Above the Great Scar limestone are the Yoredale Series of shales, sandstones and thin beds of limestone. The south west edge of the Great Scar limestone outcrops along a fault line where it is exposed as a series of cliffs or scars (not shown on the map extract). Ingleborough itself is capped by a layer of resistant sandstone called Millstone Grit.

The area has been uplifted several times. Streams that drained the Yoredale Series cut deep valleys down to a former water table and exposed areas of limestone. When the land was raised, the water table fell - leaving a number of dry valleys. Today, the streams cross the Yoredale Series until they reach the limestone where they flow down joints. Solution is enlarging these joints to form swallow holes and underground caverns.

The water drains down to the present water table and seeps laterally along enlarged bedding planes. It emerges as resurgent streams and springs at places where the water table comes to the surface.

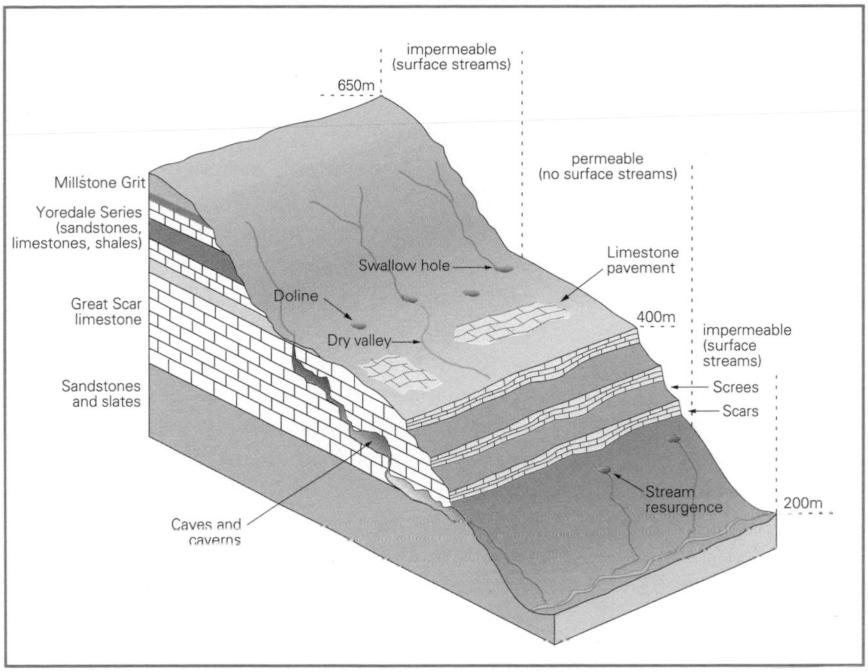
impermeable
(surface streams)
650m
permeable
(no surface streams)
Millstone Grit
Yoredale Series
(sandstones,
limestones, shales)
Great Scar
limestone
Sandstones
and slates
Swallow hole
Doline
Dry valley
Limestone
pavement
400m
impermeable
(surface
streams)
Screes
Scars
Stream
resurgence
200m
Caves and
caverns

Figure 8.39 Block diagram showing limestone features

Questions

1 Identify on the map and give the grid reference of: a) a dry valley; b) a resurgent stream; c) a swallow hole; d) an area of limestone pavement.

2 Draw a sketch map of the area shown on the map extract. Mark on your map the summit of Little Ingleborough, Gaping Gill and Ingleborough Cave. Mark and shade on the map the area where limestone outcrops at the surface.

3 Describe the map evidence that indicates where limestone outcrops at the surface.

unit summary

1 The composition and structure of rocks is largely determined by whether they are igneous, sedimentary or metamorphic.

2 Rocks that are most resistant to weathering tend to be those that are strongest and least permeable. These are generally igneous and metamorphic rocks.

3 Geology (ie, the composition and structure of rocks) is an important factor in landscape formation. However, timescale and climatic conditions are also important factors.

4 Igneous and metamorphic rocks often form distinctive landscape features because they are resistant to erosion.

5 Chalk and limestone form distinctive landscape features because they have little surface drainage and they weather by solution.

key terms

Composition (or **lithology**) - the chemical and physical characteristics of a rock and the particles that form the rock.
Dry valley - a valley in which there is no river or stream.
Escarpment (or **cuesta**) - an elongated ridge, generally with a steeper scarp slope and a gentler dip slope.
Igneous rocks - formed when magma cools and solidifies; volcanic or extrusive rocks are formed when magma reaches the Earth's surface; plutonic or intrusive rocks are formed if the magma cools underground.
Karst - 'classic' or typical limestone scenery.
Limestone pavement - a bare limestone outcrop in which blocks of rock (clints) are dissected by grooves (grikes).

Metamorphic rocks - formed when intense heat or pressure modify existing rocks.
Permeable - a rock that allows water to pass through, either along joints, cracks and bedding planes or through pores in the rock itself (in which case it is called porous). The opposite of permeable is impermeable.
Sedimentary rocks - formed by the accumulation and consolidation of sediment; the sediment might come from the weathering of existing rocks or from the organic remains of plants and animals.
Structure (of a rock) - the shape and form of a rock, how it is laid down and arranged.
Water table - the upper level of groundwater in permeable rocks.

Unit 8.4 Processes and landforms in desert regions

key questions

1 Where are the desert regions?
2 What are the main weathering processes in deserts?
3 How does wind affect the desert landscape?
4 How does water affect the desert landscape?

1. Where are the desert regions?

A desert is an arid region with little vegetation cover. Using this broad definition, more than one third of the world's land surface can be classed as desert. Although deserts are commonly associated with images of sand dunes, only a quarter of their surface area is sandy, the rest is rocky or stony.

There is no generally agreed, precise definition of what constitutes a desert. Sometimes it is defined as an area with an annual average precipitation of under 250 mm. This method has the advantage of simplicity. However, it is not completely satisfactory because it ignores evapotranspiration (ie, evaporation from the ground and transpiration from plants). In hot regions, where evapotranspiration is high, there is less moisture

available for plants than in cool locations where evapotranspiration is low. For instance, in some polar and tundra regions, the annual precipitation averages less than 250 mm but, because of low temperatures, there is generally little evapotranspiration. As a result, there is more water available for plants than in hotter regions which have much higher precipitation.

To get round this difficulty, deserts are sometimes defined on the basis of the balance between precipitation and evapotranspiration. For instance, a desert can be defined as a region with an annual 'moisture deficit'. This occurs if annual precipitation is less than potential evapotranspiration (ie, the actual precipitation is less than the estimated amount of evapotranspiration that would take place if there was more water).

Using this approach, in 1948, Thornthwaite devised a 'moisture index' which could be used to classify arid and semi arid regions. It is expressed by the formula:

$$MI = \frac{100(P-PE)}{PE}$$

MI is the moisture index, P is the precipitation and PE is the potential evapotranspiration.

Thornthwaite defined a semi arid region as having a moisture index of between -40 and -20, and an arid

Fig 8.40 Desert regions

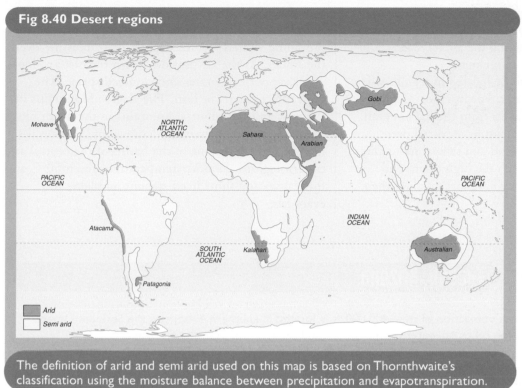

Arid

Semi arid

The definition of arid and semi arid used on this map is based on Thornthwaite's classification using the moisture balance between precipitation and evapotranspiration.

region as having a moisture index of below -40. Different measures have since been developed but most are still based on the **moisture balance** between precipitation and evapotranspiration.

Desert regions are sometimes classified by temperature. Parts of Central Asia, including the Gobi Desert, and Patagonia in Argentina are known as 'temperate deserts'. They are also, confusingly, called 'cold deserts' which is the same term used to describe polar and tundra areas with low precipitation. In temperate deserts, the average temperature is near to, or below, freezing for several months of the year.

The deserts located in the tropics or sub-tropics are known as 'hot deserts'. Their average temperatures are always well above freezing. They include the Sahara, Arabian and Australian Deserts. Because the skies over deserts are generally clear, radiation cooling is rapid at night time. This causes very large diurnal (ie, daily) temperature ranges. Day time temperatures in the Sahara can rise above 50°C, yet at night the temperature can fall below freezing. In the Negev Desert, in Israel, the air cools enough for dew to form on almost half the nights in the year and in the Mojave Desert, California, there are sub-zero temperatures on a third of all nights.

A feature common to most desert regions is the extreme variability of precipitation. This means that annual figures can be very misleading. For instance, at

Al Wejd in Saudi Arabia, there is an annual average of 25 mm but during some years there is no rain at all, and the average is only exceeded one year in three. At Biskara, in Algeria, the annual average is 150 mm, yet 200 mm was recorded there in just two days of storms in 1969.

Radar imagery from satellite photographs shows that some deserts previously had much wetter climates than now. For example, beneath Saharan sand dunes there are 'relic' landforms of well developed river and drainage networks. Historical and archaeological findings also provide evidence of climate change. Cave drawings in the central Sahara show flora and fauna that must have lived under wetter conditions than now. Even in Roman times, parts of North Africa were regarded as the bread basket of the empire.

Climate change, population pressure and overgrazing are blamed for causing the Sahara and other deserts to spread in present times. The process is known as **desertification**. The precise causes, and the degree to which it is occurring, are a matter of debate and controversy (see unit 4.1 and unit 14.4).

Location of deserts

The hot deserts are mainly located between 15 and 30 degrees north and south of the equator. They are in the zone of sub-tropical high pressure associated with Hadley Cells (see unit 12.1). At these locations, the subsiding air brings very stable climatic conditions.

Two additional factors add to the dryness of these deserts. Firstly, prevailing winds in the sub-tropics blow mainly from the east. This helps to explain why the hot deserts tend to be in the centre or on the western side of land masses. By the time winds reach these regions, they have lost most of their moisture and are very dry. Secondly, off the west coasts of the Atacama, Kalahari and Sahara Deserts there are cold ocean currents. The contrast in temperature between the land and sea causes local sea breezes to blow onshore (see unit 12.4). These surface winds are cool - making the air very stable and preventing the build up of rain clouds.

Temperate deserts tend to be located in regions where there is little marine influence. For instance, Central Asia is dry because it is very far from the sea or ocean. Winds that blow into the region have passed over thousands of kilometres of land and several mountain ranges. By the time they reach the high basins and plateaux of Central Asia, they have lost much of their water vapour.

In other regions, arid conditions are caused by a 'rain shadow' effect. Patagonia is dry because the prevailing westerly winds deposit their moisture over the Andes. As the air subsides down the eastern slopes, water vapour evaporates and clouds disperse. The same effect occurs in Iran. The Zagros Mountains in the west and the Elburz Mountains in the north block the path of easterly moving depressions. This results in very arid conditions in the basins of the central and eastern regions. Summer temperatures reach 50°C and this causes any short lived streams and lakes to evaporate.

 Activity **Tucson, Arizona**

Tucson has a population of over 400,000. It is located in southern Arizona, in the Sonoran Desert. Its population relies on water from underground aquifers and from the Colorado River.
As with most arid regions, annual precipitation is extremely variable. The long term annual average is approximately 300 mm but there are many years when it is less than this. Most precipitation falls in summer in the form of heavy convectional storms.

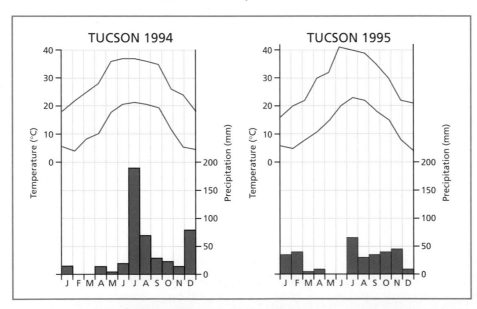

Figure 8.41 Mean monthly maximum and minimum temperatures and precipitation in Tucson, 1994 and 1995

Questions

1 Describe the pattern of weather in Tucson during 1994 and 1995.
2 What features of Tucson's weather in 1994 and 1995 indicate that the city is located in a desert?

2. What are the main weathering processes in deserts?

Desert landscapes take many different forms. Examples include areas of sand dunes (known as **erg** in Arabic), areas of bare stone and gravel (known as **reg** or **desert pavement**) and areas of bare rock (called **hamada**). These desert features are formed by a variety of weathering processes - some of which may have operated in former, wetter, climates. Under present conditions, the main weathering processes are 'exfoliation' and 'granular disintegration' (see unit 8.1).

Exfoliation occurs after overlying material is removed by weathering and erosion. 'Pressure release' causes horizontal cracks to form in rock and these cracks make the rock more vulnerable to chemical weathering. Layers then 'peel off', resulting in landforms such as Ayers Rock, Australia (see figure 8.42).

Granular disintegration is caused by a combination of chemical and mechanical weathering. At one time it was thought that expansion and contraction due to intense daily heating and night time cooling of rocks was sufficient to cause mechanical weathering. However, experiments have shown that heating and cooling - on their own - are not sufficient to cause rocks to disintegrate. It is now clear that moisture must also be present. This allows chemical weathering processes such as hydrolysis and oxidation to occur. The moisture comes from several sources. These include occasional rain, moisture from night time dews and, in some coastal areas, from fog drifting inland. In places, where an underground aquifer exists, and the water table is not too deep, moisture can rise to the surface by capillary action.

Most underground water contains dissolved salts. If the water reaches the surface and evaporates, crystals form. When these salt crystals develop in rock pores or cracks, the force they exert as they expand can cause disintegration. The salt can also chemically react with, and weaken, the minerals that form the rocks. When large amounts of salt accumulate on the ground surface, a crust (or 'duricrust') might develop. Depending on its composition, this crust has a variety of names such as 'calcrete' and 'silcrete'. In some places, capillary action and evaporation leave a stain or hard glazed coating of iron oxide or manganese oxide on exposed rocks. The feature is known as 'desert varnish'.

3. How does wind affect the desert landscape?

Because desert vegetation is sparse, plants provide only a limited ground cover and there are few root systems to bind weathered material together. This means that there is little to stop particles of sand and rock being blown by the wind. For this reason, deserts are particularly prone to wind (or **aeolian**) action.

Wind action can be divided into three main groups of processes; erosion, transport and deposition.

Erosion

The wind erodes in two main ways, by deflation and by abrasion. **Deflation** is the blowing away of fine material to leave larger, coarser fragments of 'lag gravel' behind. Desert pavements are formed in this way. Such features are common in most desert regions (see figure 8.43).

Figure 8.42 Ayers Rock, central Australia

This feature has been formed by a combination of chemical and mechanical weathering processes. Ayers Rock is also known by its Aboriginal name Uluru.

Figure 8.43 Desert pavement, southern Egypt

The wind has removed fine material leaving larger fragments in this stony desert.

Sometimes the wind removes so much material that hollows or depressions are formed in the desert. In Egypt, the Qattara Depression is 130 metres deep and over 100 km in length. The process of deflation is accelerated at this location because groundwater is close to the surface. Calcium carbonate, which 'cements' the sandstone formations on the surface, is dissolved by the moisture - leaving grains of sand that are removed by the wind.

Abrasion is the 'sandblasting' effect of wind as it transports grains of sand. Because large grains of sand are rarely lifted more than a metre above ground, abrasion is only of limited importance as a form of erosion. Nevertheless, a number of small, localised features are formed. They include **ventifacts** which are polished stones with one or more smooth faces, **yardangs** which are parallel ridges and troughs, and **zeugens** which are rock pedestals. In south east Iran, there are very large examples of yardangs sculpted out of soft silt, clay and gypsum

sediments. The largest of these ridges is 150 metres high and 300 metres long.

Transport

The wind can move grains of material in three ways, depending on the size and weight of the particles (see figure 8.44). Fine material, up to 0.15 mm in diameter, can be picked up and carried in **suspension**. Larger particles of sand are moved by **saltation** (bouncing or jumping) and by **surface creep** in which grains roll or slide along, striking against each other. Particles bigger than 1 cm in diameter are rarely moved by the wind.

Occasionally, large sand storms are formed by a strong downdraft of air from a cumulonimbus cloud. Relatively cool air sinks quickly to the ground and is then deflected upwards, carrying dust and sand. The Arabic name for such a storm is a 'haboob'. The leading edge of sand storms can move at 200 m/sec and the particles can rise over 2,500 metres into the atmosphere. Very rarely, strong southerly winds high in the atmosphere carry the sand northwards from the Sahara to Britain - depositing a fine red dust if it rains.

Figure 8.44 Movement of sand by the wind

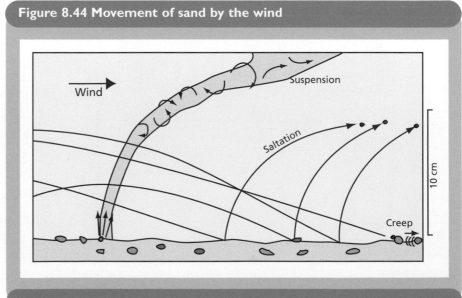

Figure 8.45 Sand dunes

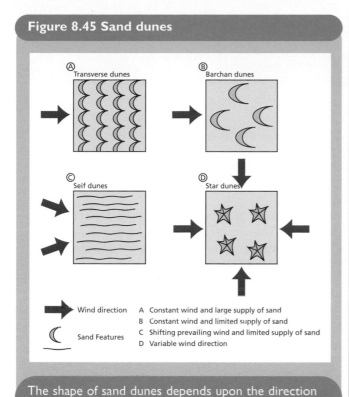

Wind direction
Sand Features

A Constant wind and large supply of sand
B Constant wind and limited supply of sand
C Shifting prevailing wind and limited supply of sand
D Variable wind direction

The shape of sand dunes depends upon the direction and variability of the wind and the amount of sand.

Deposition

The main depositional features formed by the wind are sand dunes. Where large numbers of dunes occur, the area is called a **sand sea**. Approximately a tenth of the Sahara Desert is covered by dunes and almost a third of

Figure 8.46 Sand dunes in the Sahara Desert, Morocco

This feature is called a sand sea. There are a number of relatively small barchan dunes in the middle distance.

Fig 8.47 Sand dune migration

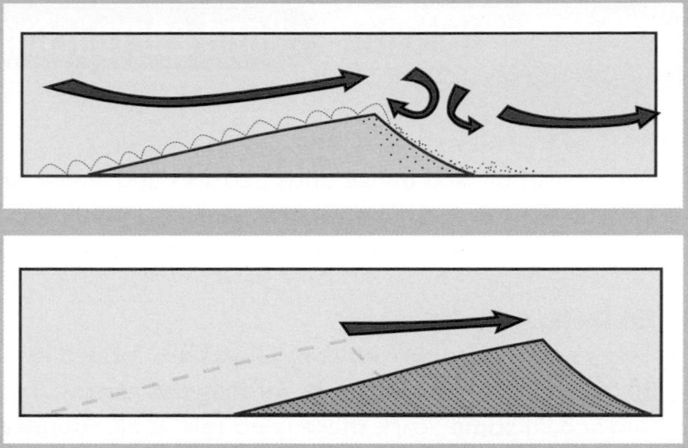

Sand dunes migrate down wind.

the Arabian Desert. In the 'Empty Quarter' of south east Saudi Arabia, some of the dunes are over 200 metres high.

Dunes can take many forms depending on the wind velocity, the variability of wind direction and the amount of sand (see figure 8.45). **Star dunes** have a central peak and a number of radiating ridges. They are formed in locations where wind direction is variable. **Transverse dunes** are wave-like in form, lying across the path of the prevailing wind. **Barchans** are crescent shaped dunes formed under similar conditions to transverse dunes except that there is only a limited supply of sand. Longitudinal or **seif** (Arabic for sword) dunes are long, parallel ridges. They form along the line of a strong prevailing wind that shifts slightly from time to time.

Sand dunes form in the lee or wind shadow of an obstacle such as a bush, rock or fence post. The obstacle reduces wind velocity and causes particles to accumulate. The dune then acts as a barrier, creating its own wind shadow and causing more sand to be deposited.

Once formed, sand dunes migrate down wind (see figure 8.47). The individual particles are blown along, up the slope of the dune, and then they roll down the sheltered slope. The result is a series of layers or 'cross-beds' that can be seen in some sedimentary rocks.

Activity **Sand encroachment**

The spread of sand dunes onto pastures and arable land is a form of desertification. The United Nations Environment Programme (UNEP) collects information from around the world on 'success stories' that show how desertification can be reversed. One such success has occurred at Ed Debba in northern Sudan.

Ed Debba, Sudan

This town and its surrounding villages are located on the banks of the River Nile, deep in the Sahara Desert. The 30,000 population survives by farming the narrow, irrigated flood plain. The average annual precipitation is just 20 mm and, in some years, there is no rain at all. Potential annual evapotranspiration is over 6,000 mm. Average temperatures range from 15°C in January to 35°C in July. Between April and October, the average daily maximum is over 40°C.

For decades the region has been threatened by advancing sand dunes. The wind which causes the greatest sand movement is the north easterly which blows strongly between October and May. Sand dunes in the area vary in size from just a few centimetres in depth to barchans which are over 40 metres high. According to local villagers, sand dune encroachment has become more severe since the 1950s. This, it is believed, has been due to over grazing and tree cutting on the marginal land at the edge of the flood plain.

By the 1980s, the wind blown dunes were moving at a rate of 25 metres per year, covering hectares of pasture, arable land and some houses. The people and livestock were forced into smaller and smaller areas, overusing the land that was left. Some attempts were made to halt the sand by using fences of date palm leaves. These proved ineffective, partly because the locals had little knowledge of how to construct such barriers and also because the barriers require a great deal of labour to maintain. At one time it was feared that the area would have to be evacuated - creating thousands of 'environmental refugees'.

However, help has come from SOS Sahel International - a British NGO (non-government organisation). Combining with the Sudanese Government, and with the active participation of local people, the dunes have been stabilised and some land restored. The method used has been to plant bushes and trees. People have been provided with seeds and shown how to tend the seedlings in nurseries. The plants include mesquite bushes (native to America) and eucalyptus trees (native to Australia). These drought resistant species have deep roots and thick leaf and branch systems. They act both as a windbreak and a barrier to prevent sand being blown onto fields. Planting has taken place at the edge of the cultivated area and on the windward side of dunes. Water to irrigate the new bushes and trees is obtained from boreholes to an aquifer where the water table varies between 9 and 15 metres underground. Shelter belts now protect the community and have saved 600 hectares of land. Proposals to plant date palms on 150 hectares of reclaimed land will provide a new source of income as well as additional shelter.

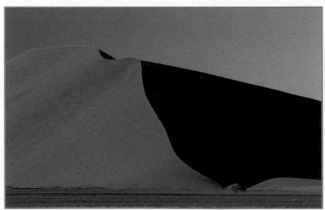

▲ **Figure 8.48 Large sand dunes such as this are encroaching on the Nile Valley**

Questions

1 Suggest why wind blown sand is a particular problem in very arid regions.

2 Summarise how the people of Ed Debba have prevented sand encroachment, and suggest why outside help was necessary.

4. How does water affect the desert landscape?

Although it might occur only once or twice a year, or even less frequently, rain does sometimes fall in deserts. When it rains, it is often in the form of short, intense storms. The resulting streams and rivers are generally intermittent (ie, not permanent) but they do play an important part in forming the desert landscape. As noted earlier, many desert regions had wetter climates in the past. Their landforms are therefore also partly a 'relic' of former conditions in which water was more plentiful.

When heavy rain occurs in deserts, surface wash quickly removes loose material. There is little vegetation to protect the ground. As the water gathers in rills and gullies, the rapid flow gains in erosive power as it picks up more material. Downward erosion creates steep sided gorges. These are called **wadis** in North Africa and Arabia, and **canyons** in the southwest USA. Note, however, that large scale features such as the Grand Canyon are the result of tectonic uplift as well as downcutting by permanent rivers. (Permanent rivers that flow through deserts, such as the Colorado, are known as 'exotic' or 'allogenic'.)

A sudden rise in water level following a desert storm is called a 'flash flood'. The leading edge or wave of flood water carries large amounts of debris down the stream channel. Then, once the force of water starts to weaken, infiltration into the stream bed is rapid. The rate of evaporation is fast and the debris carried by the water is deposited.

Sometimes water from desert streams flows into a temporary lake or **playa**. This type of inland drainage is called 'endorheic' (as opposed to 'arheic' areas which are so dry that no drainage channels develop).

Large amounts of sediment are transported into playas and these often form very flat, bare surfaces if the water evaporates. When this happens, salts are left covering the surface. The Great Salt Lake and the Bonneville Salt Flats in Utah are examples. In the Atacama Desert, nitrates in the salt are collected and commercially used as raw materials in chemical plants.

In the western states of the USA, from Utah to Arizona, there is a distinctive landscape known as 'basin and range'. It results from the uplift and faulting of blocks which form, alternately, mountain ranges and basins. Drainage into many of these basins is endorheic. Because the region is arid, and drainage is intermittent, the basins often contain a playa. Sloping down to the playa is a gentle, alluvial slope called a **bahada** (see figure 8.49). Upslope from this, typically, is a similarly angled slope eroded from from solid bedrock - known as a **pediment**. Such features are found in many other arid regions, including central Australia and central Iran.

The origin and formation of pediments is the subject of some debate. There is generally a marked break of slope at the top of the pediment where the angle becomes much steeper. It is possible that pediments are formed in a number of different ways - depending on the local geology and climatic conditions. Exactly why there should be a distinct break of slope in the bedrock at the top of the pediment is not clear. It might be due to the process of slope retreat. An alternative view is that it might be due to intense surface wash removing weathered

Fig 8.49 Landscape features in Death Valley, southwest USA

The flat ground in the foreground becomes a temporary lake or playa after exceptionally heavy storms. Rising above the flat ground is an alluvial slope or bahada, and there is an alluvial fan emerging from a side canyon in the mountains behind.

fragments at the foot of the steeper upper slope.

Where canyons emerge from upland onto a pediment, the sudden fall in velocity causes streams to deposit their loads - causing alluvial fans to form.

In parts of the southwest USA, horizontal strata, capped by resistant rocks, has led to the formation of **mesas** and **buttes** in the desert landscape. These are flat topped, steep sided plateaux and hills. Buttes are formed in the same way as mesas but are at a more advanced stage of erosion and are therefore smaller. In other areas of the world, similar features occur but their detailed appearance depends upon their geology. In parts of southern Africa, for instance, 'inselbergs' are formed from granite which tends to weather into more rounded shapes.

Activity Desert landforms

Figure 8.50 Monument Valley, southwest USA

Questions

1 Describe the landforms in the photograph.
2 Suggest how these features were formed.

unit summary

1 Deserts are arid regions with sparse vegetation. There is no generally agreed definition of what constitutes a desert. An annual precipitation less than 250 mm is sometimes used as a definition but, because this ignores evapotranspiration, alternative definitions based on the balance between precipitation and evapotranspiration are also used.

2 Deserts occur in the centre and western sides of land masses in sub-tropical regions. They also occur in rain shadows of major mountain ranges and in the interior of Asia.

3 The main ground features in deserts are desert pavements, sand dunes and bare rock surfaces.

4 Both mechanical and chemical weathering occurs in deserts. Moisture which is required for chemical processes comes from occasional rain, from dew, from fog in some coastal areas and from groundwater.

5 The wind erodes, transports and deposits material. Wind erosion tends to be of limited importance in creating landforms but it is effective in transporting material in desert environments.

6 Most desert features have been modified by running water. In places, 'relic' landforms are the result of former, wetter climatic conditions. Sudden, intense storms in deserts cause streams and rivers to erode and transport large amounts of unconsolidated debris.

7 Distinctive landforms of pediments, bahadas and playas are created in many arid regions, particularly where there is inland drainage.

key terms

Abrasion - erosion caused by the sandblasting effect of blown sand. Features formed in this way include **ventifacts** (polished and faceted stones), **yardangs** (linear rock ridges) and **zeugens** (rock pillars or pedestals).

Aeolian processes - wind processes.

Deflation - the removal of loose sand and dust by the wind. The particles move in **suspension** (blown in the air), or by **saltation** (bouncing) or by **surface creep** (rolling and sliding).

Desertification - the spread of deserts into areas where they did not exist in the recent past. The United Nations Environment Programme (UNEP) defines the process as 'the degradation of drylands, involving the loss of biological or economic productivity'.

Desert pavement (or **reg**) - an area of bare pebbles or rocks.

Hamada - an area of bare rock, sometimes a plateau surface.

Moisture (or **water**) **balance** - the balance between precipitation and potential evapotranspiration.

Playa - a temporary lake that forms in a desert basin. Salt deposits occur when the lake evaporates. The gentle alluvial slope that typically encloses a playa is called a **bahada**. Above this, in turn, is sometimes a gentle slope of solid bedrock called a **pediment**.

Sand dune - a ridge or mound of wind blown sand. It can take many forms including **transverse** (a ridge at right angles to the prevailing wind), **barchan** (crescent shaped across the wind), **star** (with a central peak and radiating ridges) and **longitudinal** or **seif** (parallel with the prevailing wind).

Sand sea (or **erg**) - a large area of sand dunes.

Wadi (or **canyon**) - a steep sided valley or gorge, sometimes with no permanent flowing water.

CHAPTER 9 Drainage Basins

Introduction

Flowing water erodes, transports and deposits weathered material. This process creates landforms such as river valleys, deltas and flood plains which have an important influence on people's lives. Streams and rivers supply water for drinking, for industry and for farming. In some cases they also provide navigable routeways and supply energy in the form of hydroelectric power. However, rivers can have a negative impact on people when they flood. Managing rivers to obtain their benefits and prevent their harmful effects is an important issue in many countries around the world.

Chapter summary

Unit 9.1 looks at the hydrological cycle and drainage patterns.
Unit 9.2 explains the processes of river erosion, transportation and deposition.
Unit 9.3 focuses on the landforms formed by rivers.
Unit 9.4 evaluates methods of river management - considering how best to use rivers and deal with the problem of flooding.

Unit 9.1 The hydrological cycle

key questions

1 What is the hydrological cycle?
2 Why and how does river discharge vary?
3 How do drainage patterns and densities vary?

1. What is the hydrological cycle?

Water is the most important agent shaping the landscape. Its movement over and through the ground is one part of the hydrological cycle. In this cycle water evaporates, mainly from the oceans, and enters the atmosphere as water vapour. Then precipitation occurs and water returns to the oceans, either directly, or indirectly via runoff from the land surface (see figure 9.1).

Geographers and hydrologists (people who study water flows) are particularly interested in the route taken by water through a **drainage basin** as it returns to the sea from land. A drainage basin (or **catchment**) is an area of land within which water collects and is then drained by a river system. The perimeter of a basin, separating it from its neighbour, is called a **watershed.**

A drainage basin is a system with inputs and outputs. The input is precipitation, either rainfall or snowfall. The main output is river discharge, ie the flow of river water out of the basin and into the sea. However, water vapour is also lost by evaporation from land or water surfaces, or by transpiration through the leaves of plants.

Figure 9.1 Transfers and stores of water in the hydrological cycle

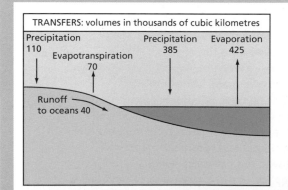
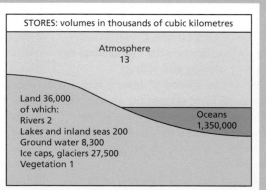

Within the hydrological cycle, there are transfers and stores of water. The runoff of water from the land to oceans is only a very small part of the total flow within the hydrological cycle. However, it is extremely important in terms of its effect on the landscape and on human activity.

Figure 9.2 Stores and transfers in a drainage basin

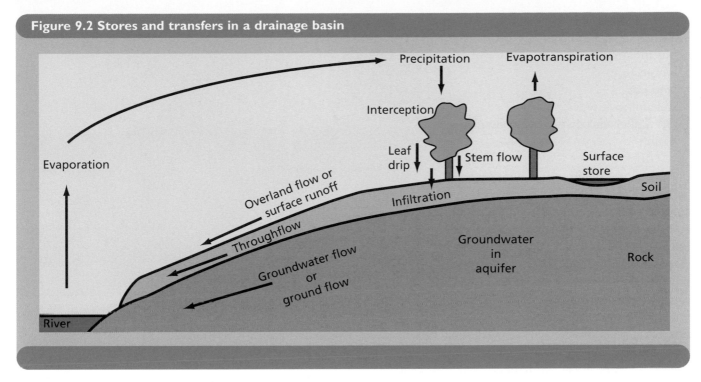

These last two outputs are collectively known as **evapotranspiration**.

Water is stored or transferred within a drainage basin in a variety of ways (see figure 9.2). When there is a large amount of vegetation cover such as in deciduous woodland, rainfall might be prevented from reaching the ground. Some rain will rest briefly as water droplets on leaves or bark This is called **interception**. On other types of plants, such as moorland grasses, the water runs to the ground more easily. A proportion of rain water that has been intercepted and held on the vegetation eventually reaches the ground by leaf drip or by 'stem flow' (ie, down the stems of plants and trees).

On reaching the ground, water enters the soil through pore spaces, and through holes created by growing vegetation or by fauna. This process is called **infiltration**. The maximum rate at which infiltration occurs in a soil (ie, the **infiltration capacity**) depends upon a number of factors. These include:

• the texture of the soil; eg, a clay soil has fewer and finer pore spaces than a sandy soil and so has a lower infiltration capacity
• the structure of the soil; eg, a crumb structure has larger pore spaces than a platy structure (see unit 13.1 for a detailed account of soil texture and structure)
• the temperature; eg, if the ground is frozen, infiltration cannot occur
• the current level of moisture in the soil; eg, if there

has been continuous rain for a period of time, the pore spaces may already be full of water. When the soil is 'saturated' (ie, the pore spaces are full), no more water can enter the soil. On a slope, water will flow downhill as overland flow (or surface runoff), and on flat land it will form surface puddles ('surface storage') until it can enter the soil or it until it evaporates. If rain continues under these conditions, flooding can occur.

Once in the soil, the downward **percolation** of water continues through the pore spaces. Lateral (ie, sideways) movement of water through the soil will also occur downslope, towards a stream. This lateral movement of water in the soil is called **throughflow**.

Some water will percolate through the soil to reach the bedrock. If this rock is permeable (ie, it can hold water) it is called an **aquifer**. The main examples are chalk and limestone. Water that is contained in the rock is called **groundwater**.

Factors influencing the stores and transfers within a drainage basin

Water is stored within a drainage basin in plants, in lakes, in the soil and in groundwater. It is transferred by streams and rivers, by overland flow, by throughflow (through soil) and by groundwater flow. The amount of water stored or transferred can vary greatly from one drainage basin to another. The five main variables that influence storage and transfers are:

- precipitation
- temperature
- land use
- soil and rock type
- physical characteristics of the drainage basin.

Precipitation The intensity, duration and variability of precipitation affect both the amount of water input in a drainage basin and the amount of infiltration that occurs. For example, heavy rain in thunderstorms sometimes falls so quickly that the amount of water greatly exceeds the infiltration capacity of the soil. Most of the water remains on the surface as standing water, or flows overland into rivers. In arid regions, 'flash floods' occur in this way. As stated before, the same effect can happen even with light rainfall if it continues over a long period of time. Eventually the ground becomes saturated and can hold no more water - so overland flow occurs. The amount of water already in the soil affects how quickly it becomes saturated. This amount is known as the 'antecedent moisture'.

When precipitation falls as snow, water is stored above ground and is released overland to rivers only when the temperature rises and the snow melts. The amount of infiltration depends upon the speed of the melt and also whether or not the ground is frozen.

Temperature When the temperature falls near to, or below, freezing, there are a number of effects. For instance, if the ground is frozen, water remains on the surface and cannot infiltrate. Also, cold temperatures

Figure 9.4 Los Angeles

Urban surfaces such as glass, concrete and tarmac are impermeable. Rainwater quickly flows into drains and culverts.

turn water into ice, and water 'flows' become water 'stores'. If plants are dormant, for example during the UK's winter, there is less interception and transpiration of water because most bushes and trees have lost their leaves. Cold temperatures also have the effect of slowing or preventing evaporation.

In warmer weather, when plants have regrown their leaves, more interception occurs. Transpiration and evaporation become important outputs in the drainage system. The hotter the weather, the more water is lost in this way. Because less water reaches the ground, infiltration and percolation are reduced. This causes UK groundwater and river levels to be lower in summer than in winter - even though precipitation is fairly evenly distributed throughout the year.

Land use There are three main land use factors which affect water flow. The first is natural vegetation cover. For example, tropical rain forest intercepts most of the rainfall it receives, whereas on bare, open ground there is no interception. This is why deforestation (the cutting down of trees on a large scale) can lead to increased overland flow, severe erosion and flooding in river basins.

The second factor is agricultural land use. This has a direct affect on vegetation cover. For example, permanent crops such as grassland slow down the water flow compared with annual crops such as cereals. Annual crops generally need a period of bare soil prior to planting and there is only limited ground cover while the plants are starting to grow. Figure 9.3 shows typical rates

Figure 9.3 Approximate percentage of rainfall intercepted by different vegetation

Vegetation	% intercept
Deciduous woodland (winter)	15
Deciduous woodland (summer)	30
Coniferous forest	40
Grassland	25
Wheat (ready to harvest)	20

of interception by different types of vegetation.

A third land use factor influencing water flow is whether the area is urban or rural. Increased urban development has created more impermeable surfaces such as roofs and roads, and rainwater quickly flows into drains and culverts. The effect of this artificial drainage is to prevent rain infiltrating into the ground, and to speed up the transfer of water into streams and rivers. This increases the risk of flooding in urban areas.

Soils and rock types Impermeable rocks and soils prevent infiltration because they have few pores or cracks in them for water to pass through. For example, clay soils and granite keep water on the surface whereas sandy soils and permeable rocks let water infiltrate. Chalk allows slow percolation through its pores but, in limestone, with its cracks and joints, water infiltrates and percolates more rapidly.

Physical characteristics of the drainage basin The drainage basin itself affects water flow. If it is in a mountainous region, water runs off the slopes more quickly than in a lowland region with gentle slopes. Also, if there are many surface streams (ie, there is a 'high drainage density'), water travels relatively quickly through a basin. The same is true for basins that are compact or small in area.

The water balance

Hydrologists and water engineers sometimes need to know how much water is available in a drainage basin. This is to calculate how much there is for people to use, or so that they can assess the risk of flooding. To do this they use an equation that gives the water balance (ie, the relationship between input, output and storage of water in a drainage basin):

$$S = P - Q - E$$

(Or, expressed in a different form: $P = Q + E + S$)
where:

    S = stores and transfers
    P = precipitation
    Q = river discharge
    E = evapotranspiration

This equation gives the volume of water that is in the system (S). It is equal to the input (precipitation) less the output (evapotranspiration and river discharge). Generally it is calculated for a particular time period. If S is positive it means that the amount of groundwater

Figure 9.5 Glacier National Park, Montana, USA

The headwaters of the Missouri River rise in this area. Water runs off the steep, bare slopes faster than on the more gentle grass and forest covered slopes.

will rise. If it is negative, the opposite is true and the amount of groundwater will fall. In turn this will lead the **water table** (ie, the level below which rocks are saturated) to fall.

The **soil moisture budget** is an alternative method of considering stores and transfers in a drainage system. It focuses on how much moisture is present in the soil over a period of time. Generally, in an average UK winter, there is a soil moisture surplus. This means that there is an excess of precipitation over evapotranspiration and the soil is saturated. Because the ground cannot absorb any more moisture, the surplus water runs off into rivers. In spring and early summer, temperatures become warmer, evaporation is higher, and there is renewed plant growth. More water in the soil is now taken up into plant roots. This continues until autumn when average temperatures fall and rainfall begins to recharge (top up) the soil moisture. By the end of autumn there is once again a soil moisture surplus.

In 1995 (an exceptionally dry year in the UK) the surplus of water during early spring was so low that a soil moisture deficit developed in the summer months. In other words, all the available moisture in the soil was lost through evapotranspiration. In different climates, the pattern will vary. In a hot, dry climate, for example, the potential evapotranspiration might normally be higher than the actual evapotranspiration that occurs. Under these conditions there is regularly a soil moisture deficit.

Activity Soil moisture budgets

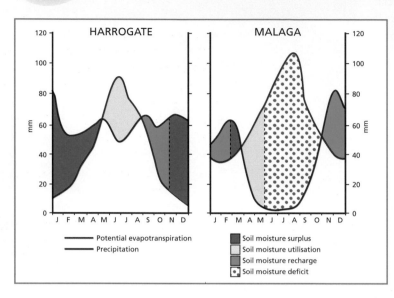

Figure 9.6 Soil moisture budgets for Harrogate and Malaga

On both graphs the average precipitation and potential evapotranspiration are shown for each month. Potential evapotranspiration mainly depends on the temperature and shows how much moisture would be lost by evaporation and transpiration if the moisture was available.

	Harrogate	Malaga
Annual average precipitation (mm)	770	450
Annual average potential evapotranspiration (mm)	485	760

Questions

1 Compare and contrast the two graphs.
2 Suggest possible reasons for the differences between the two graphs.

2. Why and how does river discharge vary?

The rate and volume of flow of water in a river is known as river discharge. Understanding why and how rivers respond to precipitation is an important aspect of hydrology. A storm hydrograph (see figure 9.7) shows how river discharge changes after a storm or period of heavy rainfall.

Storm hydrographs

The discharge of a river is defined as the volume of water passing a particular point in a given time period.

It is usually measured in m³/sec (cumecs) or, sometimes, in litres per day.

In figure 9.7, the small bar graph in the top left of the diagram indicates the start, intensity and duration of precipitation. The line graph shows the river's discharge over time. There is always a delay between the precipitation and rise in discharge because it takes time for the rainfall to flow into the river. The rise in the discharge marks the time when, first, overland flow and then throughflow (water moving laterally through the soil) have arrived. The discharge rises to a peak as more water flows into the river, before falling to a more normal level later. Throughflow takes longer to arrive at the river than

Figure 9.7 A storm hydrograph

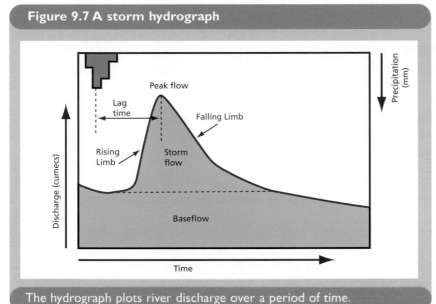

The hydrograph plots river discharge over a period of time.

overland flow, and causes the graph to fall less steeply than it rises. The delay between peak rainfall and peak discharge is called the 'lag time' and the rise in discharge above normal is called the 'storm flow'. The underlying flow, mainly coming from from groundwater (groundflow) and some from soil (throughflow) is called the **baseflow**.

The discharge pattern in figure 9.7 is an 'idealised' version. In reality, the response of a river to a storm varies from place to place and from time to time. The factors that influence the shape of a storm hydrograph are the same as those that influence stores and transfers within a drainage basin. For example:

- precipitation: heavy and prolonged rainfall will cause a high peak; however, snowfall might have little immediate effect because the water remains stored on the ground
- temperature: frozen ground will reduce infiltration and cause rapid overland flow with a short lag time
- land use: interception by trees will lower the peak discharge by reducing overland flow
- soil and rock type: impermeable surfaces (including tarmac and concrete in urban areas) will increase overland flow and produce steep curves on the hydrograph
- physical characteristics of the drainage basin: gentle valley sides will cause the hydrograph to be flatter because it will take longer for peak discharge to be reached.

River regimes

The regime of a river is the pattern of its annual discharge (see figure 9.8). It is, in effect, an annual hydrograph. The annual pattern of discharge for a river is mainly affected by climate. Rivers in monsoon regions, for example, have a peak discharge in the wet season and a lower flow in the dry season. In some large drainage basins, the main tributary rivers might have different discharge patterns and this will affect the regime of the main river. For example, the River Rhone in France is fed by Alpine glaciers which have a maximum flow after spring snow melt. Its tributary the Saone is fed mainly by rain and has a winter maximum. The result is a river regime with two peaks.

Figure 9.8 River Ouse - average discharge and precipitation during 1995

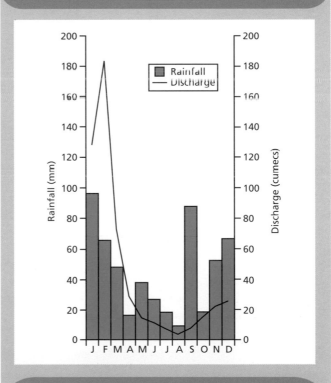

The precipitation was recorded at a weather station near York, on the Ouse. During 1995, Yorkshire suffered a severe summer drought. The river's discharge broadly followed the pattern of precipitation. However, the relatively high September rainfall was not followed by a rapid rise in discharge. This was because most of the rain percolated into the very dry ground and did not flow overland.

Activity | **The River Nile**

In 1970, the building of the Aswan High Dam in Egypt was completed. It fundamentally altered the flow of the lower Nile which had previously flooded annually. Since 1970, the river flow has been regulated downstream of the Dam so there is now a steady all year round discharge.

At the source of the White Nile (near Entebbe, on Lake Victoria), there is an equatorial climate that is wet all the year round. By contrast, the source region of the Blue Nile has a climate with distinct wet and dry seasons (Addis Ababa is in this region).

For most of its lower section, the River Nile flows through desert and, along the whole of its length, the river loses large amounts of water from evaporation. This is particularly true of the Sudd region in southern Sudan. The Sudd is a large area of shallow lakes, floating vegetation and wetlands through which the White Nile flows. It is estimated that 21 cubic kilometres of water flows annually from the White Nile into the Sudd, but only 14 cubic kilometres flows out. The rest is lost through evaporation.

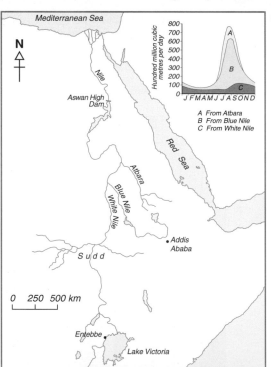

Figure 9.9 The Nile Basin and hydrograph (at the confluence of the Atbara and Nile)

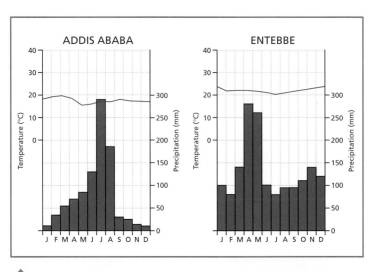

Figure 9.10 Climate graphs for Entebbe and Addis Ababa

Questions

1 Using information from figure 9.9, compare the river regimes of the White Nile and the Blue Nile.
2 Outline the reasons why the river regimes are different.

(**Note:** a follow up activity question on how the Nile is managed is included in unit 9.4.)

3 How do drainage patterns and densities vary?

A **drainage pattern** is the arrangement of rivers and tributaries within a drainage basin. The number of surface streams is an important factor in determining how quickly water flows through the system.

There are three main features of drainage patterns:
- the drainage network - the pattern of streams when seen from above
- the drainage density - the number of streams in relation to the area of the basin
- the stream order - the hierarchy of different sizes of streams in the basin.

Drainage network

When streams flow across a surface which has uniform geology, there are no controls over the pattern other than gravity. As a result, the pattern develops into a dendritic or tree-like form (see figure 9.11). The River Shannon in Ireland shows this pattern. Some very large river systems such as the Mississippi - Missouri also look like this.

Where there is a marked slope, the larger streams might flow in the same direction and have a parallel pattern. This is seen in northern Sweden, and in the Yorkshire Dales, where rivers flow eastwards from the Pennines into the Ouse.

Where there is a central high point such a volcanic peak or mountain area, the streams might flow outwards in all directions. This pattern is radial. The English Lake District has such a pattern.

In areas where there are different types of rocks, the drainage patterns are more complex. For example, when there are alternating ridges of more resistant and less resistant rock, a trellis pattern is typical. An example occurs in Surrey where outcrops of chalk, sandstone and clay have shaped the drainage pattern of the Thames tributaries, such as the River Mole (see figure 9.12). An additional factor at work in this region is that the original drainage pattern developed before the clay vales and chalk and sandstone ridges were formed by differential erosion (ie, the clay was eroded at a faster rate than the chalk and sandstone). Some rivers have kept their original courses and now cut across these ridges and vales. This is called superimposed drainage and, in the case of the North Downs, it has formed a gap where the river flows through the chalk ridge.

Figure 9.12 The River Mole drainage pattern

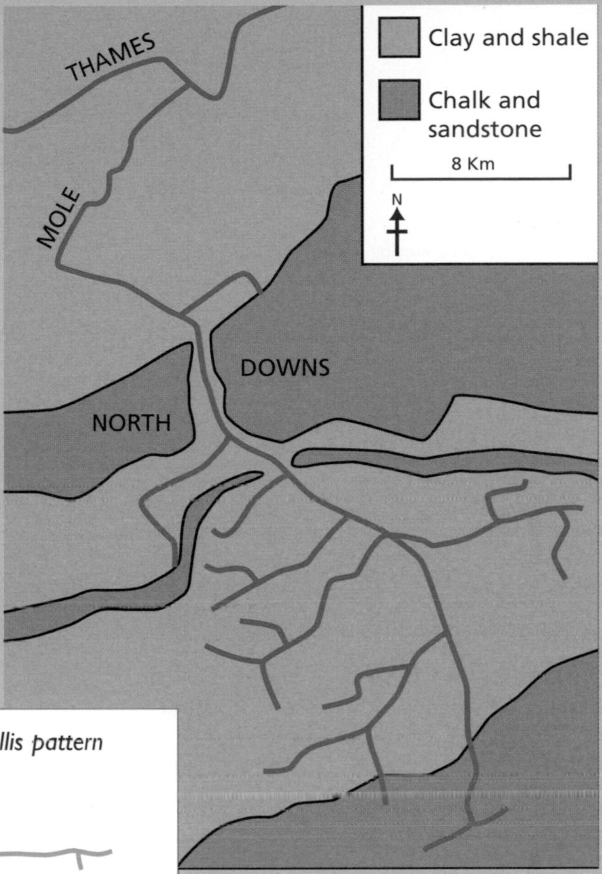

An idealised trellis pattern

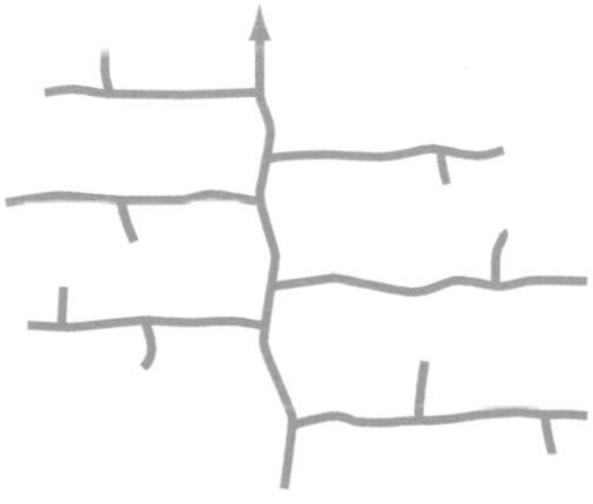

Figure 9.11 Three drainage patterns - dendritic, parallel, radial

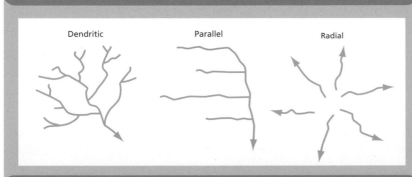

Figure 9.13 The capture of the Aire by the Ribble

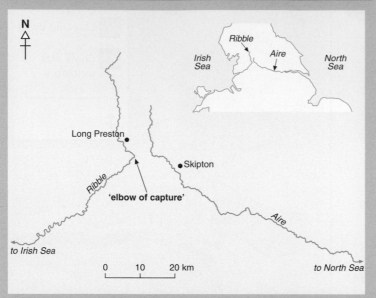

The steeper gradient of the Ribble makes it more erosive than the Aire

Factors such as glaciation (see unit 10.2) and earth movements might also affect the drainage patterns in river basins. For example, rivers might be diverted by ice sheets that block their flow, or along a fault line that causes the land to rise or fall in height.

Rivers which are more erosive than their neighbours sometimes increase their catchment areas by cutting headwards through their watersheds. For example, the River Ribble which drains part of the western Pennines is slowly increasing its drainage basin in this way (see figure 9.13). The River Aire, which flows eastwards, is the 'losing' competitor. Because the course of the Ribble to the Irish Sea is steeper than that of the Aire to the North Sea, the Ribble has been able to capture the upper drainage basin of the river Aire. Once this capture took place, the river system was 'rejuvenated' (see unit 9.3) and created rapids and a gorge. There is a marked change in direction of the River Ribble which marks the 'elbow of capture'.

Drainage density

Where there are impermeable rocks in areas of high rainfall, there are usually a large number of streams flowing across the land surface. This creates a high drainage density. Drainage densities are sometimes described in numerical terms by dividing the total length of streams by the basin area. This is a numerical way of describing a drainage pattern rather than using the subjective classification of 'radial', 'trellis' or so on.

Rivers on impermeable clay, sandstone or granite generally have higher drainage densities than those on permeable rocks such as limestone. A drainage density can differ from season to season, particularly on rocks such as chalk and limestone. In winter, when precipitation is higher and the ground may be frozen, there are more surface streams. In summer, when water percolates into the ground, these streams dry up and the valleys become dry.

Stream order

Another method of describing and analysing drainage basins is by considering stream order. Streams, or rivers, within a drainage basin can be ranked in a hierarchy, from small to large. The smallest, those without tributaries, are called first order streams (see figure 9.14). Second order streams are larger, and are created when two first order streams join, and so on. This type of analysis was developed in the 1940s by Horton and then modified by Strahler and others. It

Figure 9.14 Simple stream order diagram (using Strahler's system)

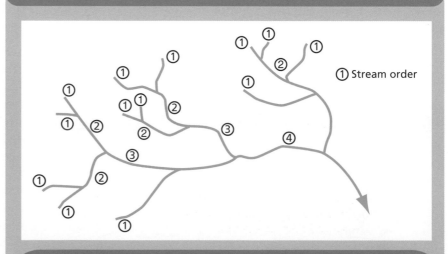

Note that where two first order streams meet, a second order stream is formed; where two second order streams meet, a third order stream is formed - and so on. Where a first order stream meets a second order stream, there is no increase in order at this junction.

provides an objective comparison between drainage basins. Also it allows a means of analysing the relationships between different variables, such as drainage basin area, stream length and number of streams.

Although drainage basins differ in size, and occur in very different landscapes and climatic zones, they share many common characteristics. These include:

- there are more low order (ie, first and second order) streams than high order streams
- the length of high order streams is greater than low order streams
- the gradient of high order streams is less than lower order streams
- the higher the maximum stream order in a drainage basin, the bigger the area
- the size of a valley increases downstream and is related to the stream order
- the stream channel becomes wider and deeper as the stream order increases.

Of course, these are generalisations and exceptions do occur. Nevertheless, these features and relationships have been shown to exist in many drainage basins, on different scales and in different parts of the world.

Activity   The River Ouse

The River Ouse in North Yorkshire is fed by a number of tributary rivers including the Swale, Ure and Nidd. In the early part of January 1982, a series of depressions passed over northern England bringing rain and mild temperatures. The period leading up to this had been cold with frosty conditions and heavy snowfall. The combined effect of heavy rain and a sudden increase in temperature produced dramatic changes in the discharge of the Ouse and its main tributaries.

The River Ure flows steeply down into the Vale of York, crossing mainly impermeable rocks along its lower course. However, in the Ure's upper basin there are extensive areas of limestone. The River Swale has a gentler gradient than the Ure and has a very flat lower course. The River Nidd has a number of small reservoirs in its upper tributaries.

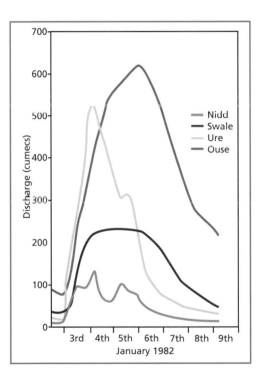

▲ **Figure 9.15 Storm hydrographs of the Swale, Ure, Nidd and Ouse.**

The discharges for the Swale, Ure and Nidd were measured upstream from York and the discharge for the Ouse was measured at a point below York.

▶ **Figure 9.16 The Ouse, Swale, Nidd and Ure**
Land over 200 metres is shaded.

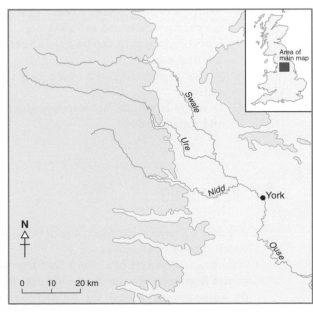

Figure 9.17 The Foss flood defence scheme in York

York is vulnerable to flooding. It is relatively low lying and the River Ouse, which flows through the city, is subject to large variations in flow. The tributary rivers of the Ouse that rise in the Pennines sometimes rise rapidly. To prevent the Ouse floodwater backing up into the River Foss, a steel barrier has been built. (The Foss is a small tributary that rises to the east of York and which flows through the heart of the city.) The barrier can be lowered when the level of the Ouse rises to danger levels.

Questions

1 Describe the drainage pattern of the rivers in figure 9.16.
2 Compare the storm hydrographs of the four rivers shown in figure 9.15.
3 Suggest reasons why the storm hydrographs are different in shape.
4 Outline the various climatic conditions that might cause the Ouse to flood and therefore require that the Foss floodgate be closed.

unit summary

1 A drainage basin forms one part of the hydrological cycle.
2 The input into a drainage basin is precipitation, the main output is river discharge.
3 Within a drainage basin, stores and transfers of water are affected by several factors including temperature, land use and soil type.
4 Storm hydrographs can be used to describe and analyse the response of a river to a particular weather event.
5 A river regime describes how a river's discharge varies over a year. It is mainly influenced by the climate.
6 Drainage basins can be described and analysed by looking at drainage networks, drainage densities and stream order.

key terms

Aquifer - a permeable layer of rock through which groundwater moves.
Baseflow - that part of a river's discharge which comes from groundwater flow and throughflow (ie, water flowing through the soil and rocks).

Catchment - a drainage basin.
Drainage basin - an area of land within which water collects and is then drained by a river system.
Drainage density - the number of streams in relation to the area of a drainage basin.

Drainage network - the shape or pattern that streams and rivers form when seen from above.

Evapotranspiration - evaporation of water from land and sea, combined with transpiration from plants.

Groundwater - this is normally defined as water that is below the Earth's surface in rocks. Some books also include soil moisture - the water that is contained in soil.

Hydrograph - a graph which plots river discharge over time.

Hydrological cycle - the system of evaporation and condensation by which water circulates on and above the Earth's surface.

Infiltration - water soaking into the soil.

Infiltration capacity - the maximum rate at which moisture can pass into the soil.

Interception - this occurs when precipitation does not reach the ground but rests on plants and trees.

Overland flow (or **surface runoff**) - water flowing over the ground surface.

Percolation - the movement of water down through the soil into underlying rock.

River discharge - the rate of river flow; expressed as a volume of water that passes a given point in a given time period.

River regime - the pattern of river discharge over one year, drawn graphically as an annual hydrograph.

Soil moisture budget (or **water budget**) - the balance between precipitation and evapotranspiration.

Stream order - a rank order of streams in a drainage basin from low to high order. The ranking depends on the number of tributaries.

Throughflow - water that flows laterally through soil.

Water balance - the balance between the input and output of water in a drainage basin.

Watershed - the boundary of a drainage basin.

Water table - the level below which rocks are saturated in an aquifer.

Unit 9.2 River processes

key questions

1 How do rivers erode?
2 How do rivers transport material?
3 What factors affect the deposition of material by rivers?

1. How do rivers erode?

Erosion is the process by which water and sediment carried by a river deepens and widens the channel. Four main processes of erosion are at work:

- **Corrasion** occurs when transported materials such as sand and gravel rub against a river channel's bed and sides. This sandpaper action is also called abrasion. It is the most important method of river erosion. Rapid erosion occurs in mountainous streams at times of flood when large boulders are moved by the water, scraping the channel as they pass by. Small cavities or potholes can be made in the stream bed by these impacts.
- **Hydraulic action** is the force exerted by water alone. It puts pressure on the banks of a river and removes loose material. Below waterfalls, and in rapids, air becomes trapped in the turbulent water and can be forced into cracks, so weakening the solid rock. Also, in turbulent water, a suction effect can dislodge material on the channel bed.
- **Attrition** occurs when the particles being moved by a river become smaller in size, and more rounded, as they collide with each other. Angular boulders in the upper course of a river are eventually transformed into small rounded particles found downstream.
- **Solution** occurs where minerals in rocks are dissolved in river water. This process is also known as corrosion. Minerals that are most vulnerable to solution include calcium (from chalk and limestone), magnesium and potassium.

The erosive power of a river depends on how much **energy** the river has, and how much of this energy is used for erosion. A river's energy comes from the force of gravity that causes water to flow downhill. It is calculated by using the formula: $E = 0.5M \times V^2$ (where E is energy, M is the mass of flowing water and V is the velocity of flow). Energy is directly related to discharge (which is generally measured in cubic metres of water per second). So, the greater the discharge, the greater is the river's energy. Most erosion occurs when there are **bankfull** conditions (ie, when the stream channel is full and there are high levels of discharge).

Up to ninety five percent of a river's energy is used up by by friction against the channel sides and river bed, and by eddies and swirls in the current known as turbulence. The rest of the river's energy is used to transport the water and its load (ie, the sediment it carries along), and to erode the river channel.

The amount of friction that occurs within a river channel depends upon its efficiency. The more efficient the channel is, the more energy is available to move sediment, to erode and to create new landforms. The most important factor affecting the efficiency of a channel relates to its shape (ie, its cross-section). Where the shape of the channel is semi-circular, there is least friction. Such a channel is highly efficient. To measure the efficiency of a river channel, its hydraulic radius is calculated (see figure 9.18). The larger its value, the more efficient the channel. The formula used is:

$$\text{hydraulic radius} = \frac{\text{cross-sectional area}}{\text{wetted perimeter}}$$

The wetted perimeter is the cross-sectional width of a river channel (ie, the distance across a channel bed and the height of the channel sides).

Studies have shown that maximum velocity in a straight section of river channel occurs in midstream,

Figure 9.19 Cross section through a river channel

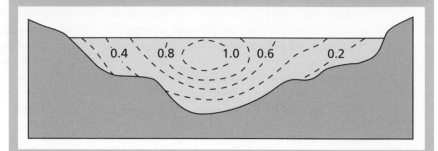

The pattern of velocity within the channel is shown by 'isovels' (lines of equal velocity). Friction and turbulence slow the flow near the channel bed. The numbers on the isovels are a proportion of the maximum velocity within the channel.

a little below the surface (see figure 9.19). This is where the effect of friction and turbulence is minimised.

It might be expected that a river would flow faster in its upper course than in its lower course because, in general, the gradient is steeper. However, this is not the case. In fact, the upper, steep sections of rivers typically flow at the same or lower velocity than the downstream sections. This is because shallow, upriver channels generally have a small hydraulic radius and low efficiency (therefore slowing velocity). Downstream, although the gradient is less, the hydraulic radius and efficiency are greater (therefore raising velocity). The roughness, or smoothness, of a river channel is another factor which affects a river's efficiency. Turbulence increases with channel roughness and slows a river down. Channels are most rough, or irregular, in the upper parts of rivers. This is an additional reason why rivers do not necessarily flow fastest in their steepest sections.

The relationship between a river's velocity and the shape of its channel is given by the Manning equation. This states that velocity is determined by the hydraulic radius, the channel slope or gradient and the degree of roughness of the channel. It is expressed as:

$$v = \frac{1.49 \, (0.67R \times 0.5S)}{n}$$

where: v is the river velocity
R is the hydraulic radius
S is the channel slope
n is the degree (or coefficient) of roughness.

Figure 9.18 Two stream channels

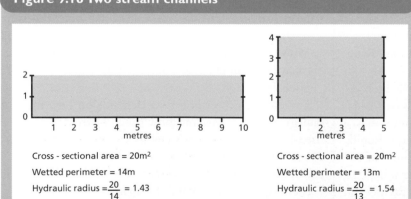

Cross - sectional area = 20m²

Wetted perimeter = 14m

Hydraulic radius = $\frac{20}{14}$ = 1.43

Cross - sectional area = 20m²

Wetted perimeter = 13m

Hydraulic radius = $\frac{20}{13}$ = 1.54

The deeper, narrower channel has the bigger hydraulic radius so is the more efficient. It therefore has more energy available to transport material and to erode.

Other things being equal, the Manning equation shows that velocity decreases as channel roughness increases, and vice versa.

The proportion of a river's energy available to erode material on the bed and on the sides of the river channel not only depends upon the overall amount of energy generated by the flowing water, but also on the proportion that is used to transport material. For instance, if a river transports a big sediment load, it has less energy available to erode. The opposite is also true so, if there is only a small quantity of sediment transported, there is more energy available for erosion. This explains why, below dams behind which sediment is trapped, so called 'clearwater erosion' is often very great.

Activity ▸ River channels

Figure 9.20 River Wyre, Bowland Fells, Lancashire ▸

This point is 3 km downstream from the source of the river.

▼ **Figure 9.21 River Wyre near Fleetwood, Lancashire**

At this point the river is 5 km from the sea.

Question

I Outline the factors that will determine how much energy there is available for erosion at the points on the River Wyre shown in figures 9.20 and 9.21.

2. How do rivers transport material?

A river's load, ie the material carried, includes materials derived from the surrounding slopes as well as from the channel bed and sides. The load can be transported in three ways:

- in **solution** - minerals such as calcium carbonate or sodium chloride are dissolved in the water
- in **suspension** - fine particles of material are carried along by rivers in the flowing water. The Hwang-He (Yellow River) in China, the Rio Negro in Amazonia and the White Nile all owe their names to the large amount of distinctively coloured sediment which they carry
- in **traction** - this process occurs when larger particles are moved along the bed of a river. The bed load slides, rolls and bounces along. The bouncing movement is sometimes called saltation.

As an example of how great a load a large river carries, the Mississippi River is estimated to deliver (annually) into the Gulf of Mexico:

- 340 million tonnes in suspension (64% of total)
- 150 million tonnes in solution (28% of total)
- 40 million tonnes by traction and saltation (8% of total)

The proportion of a river's load that is transported by the three methods depends upon several factors. They include the nature of the soil and rock within the drainage basin. For example, in a limestone region, more material will be transported in solution than, say, in a region of unconsolidated sandy material. Human activity can also be an important factor. Where forests are cleared, particularly in hilly regions, soil erosion can be rapid and this supplies a large amount of material which will be carried by rivers in suspension.

When dams are built, the transport of sediment in suspension and by traction is greatly affected. This is

Figure 9.22   Hjulstrom Curves

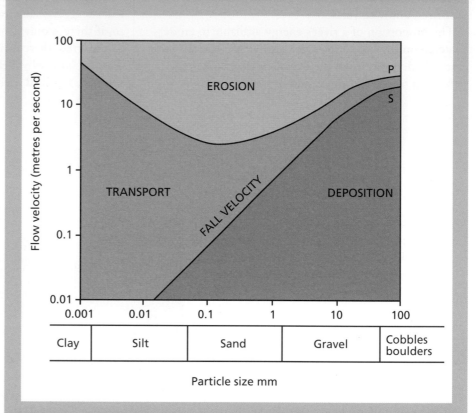

This diagram is named after the person who first published the data in 1935. It shows the threshold velocities at which different sizes of particles are picked up, transported or deposited.

because the velocity of flow, and therefore energy, is suddenly reduced as the river enters the reservoir. The suspended load and bedload are deposited in the reservoir behind a dam leaving only the dissolved load to flow downstream. As noted earlier in this unit, the river without this load then erodes more rapidly that it would do otherwise. It is estimated that the Aswan High Dam on the Nile has cut the annual supply of suspended sediment downstream from 120 million tonnes to less than 50 million tonnes.

Threshold velocity for sediment transport

The ability of a river to transport sediment is called its **capacity**, and the size of the largest particle that a river can move is called its **competence**. The relationship between river velocity and sediment transport is shown in figure 9.22. The size of particles that a river can pick up and move depends mainly on the velocity of the river. Line P in figure 9.22 represents the threshold velocities above which particles are picked up (or entrained) and start to move. Smaller particles of sand require relatively low velocities to pick them up, whereas larger gravels and boulders only start to move when velocities are high. The very smallest clay and silt particles tend to stick together (this is called 'cohesion') and resist being moved. This explains why these particles require a higher velocity to pick them up than slightly larger particles (shown on the graph where line P falls before it rises). Above line P, the zone on the graph is labelled 'erosion'. This indicates the velocities at which material is actively being removed by the river's flow.

The graph also shows the threshold velocity below which different sized particles are deposited (shown on the graph as line S). As velocity decreases, smaller and smaller particles are deposited on the channel bed. This point is covered in more detail in the next section of this unit.

Note that the zone on the graph between lines P and S is labelled 'transport'. This indicates that particles continue to move (either in suspension or by traction) at velocities that are lower than those required to start them moving.

3. .What factors affect the deposition of material by rivers?

Once material such as silt and gravel is picked up by the flowing water, it continues to move until the velocity falls to a level where it can no longer be carried along. Line S in figure 9.22 shows the critical 'settling' boundary between transport and deposition. This is the threshold velocity below which the river can no longer transport a particular particle. The bigger the particle, for example a cobble or boulder, the higher the velocity required to keep it moving. At lower velocities the smallest particles held in suspension start to settle on the channel bed.

The reason why deposition occurs when the velocity falls is that a river loses some of the energy it requires to transport material. Settling can be triggered by water leaving the channel and flooding over on to a floodplain, thus reducing river discharge and velocity. This sometimes has the effect of building up the bed and banks of the river - so creating the 'levees' (embankments) typically found in the lower Mississippi Valley (see unit 9.3).

Where rivers emerge from mountain areas onto flatter land, they experience a decrease in velocity relative to their load. The result is rapid deposition of material in the channel bed. The river may divide into a number of channels in a process known as 'braiding'. Where rivers flow into lakes or into the sea, the sudden reduction in velocity causes rapid deposition of load, so forming deltas in some places (see unit 9.3).

Along river channels, the slower velocities that occur below waterfalls, or on the inside of bends, also cause sediment to settle. It is often the case that this settling process sorts sediments by size. The result is a grading of particles from small to large along a zone of deposition. (In figure 9.20, some braiding is seen where the river splits and flows on either side of the material that has been deposited on the inside of the river bend.)

River sediment budgets

The amount of sediment eroded, transported and deposited within a drainage basin depends upon a number of factors. These include:

- the size of the basin, the drainage density and the main rock types
- the amount and intensity of precipitation, and the temperature within the basin area - temperature is important because it affects evaporation rates and also the amount of time that rivers are frozen
- vegetation cover; in general, dense vegetation slows the erosion of sediment compared with, for instance, bare ground in arid or semi-arid regions
- human activity; particularly deforestation which increases soil erosion and therefore sediment transfer, and dams which trap sediment within the system.

Modern research into drainage basins has focussed on the idea of treating the erosion, transport and deposition of sediment as a system. This is useful, for example, when calculating how quickly a reservoir will fill with sediment.

Difficulties have been found, however, in obtaining accurate measurements of the river sediment budget. This is the balance between inputs and outputs (ie, sediment 'in' and sediment 'out') of the system. Debate has also arisen concerning how much sediment is stored along a river's route in mid-basin. For example, within a drainage basin, some sediment might be deposited in a lake bed, or on a flood plain, and remain there for thousands of years. Then, perhaps when a river changes course, the sediment is once again transported to the river's mouth. Under these circumstances it has proved impossible to obtain anything other than approximations for the inputs and outputs of such a system.

Activity World drainage basins

▼ Figure 9.23: Annual discharge of suspended sediment for the world's 20 largest drainage basins

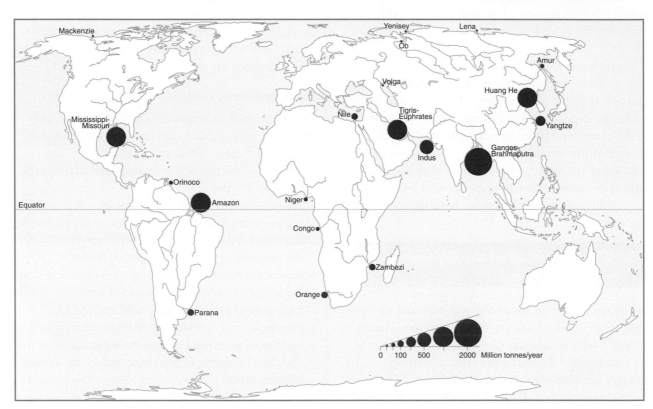

Questions

1 Describe the world distribution of rivers that discharge most suspended sediment.
2 Suggest possible reasons why the suspended sediment discharges are relatively small in northern Canada and in northern Russia.
3 What factors (other than those you have suggested in question 2) might explain why the biggest drainage basins do not necessarily have the biggest discharge of suspended sediment?

unit summary

1 The energy of rivers is derived from the force of gravity which causes water to flow downslope.
2 The energy that is available to erode and transport material down river depends upon a river's discharge and the efficiency of the channel along which the water flows.
3 Rivers erode material by the processes of corrasion, hydraulic action, attrition and solution.
4 Material is transported in solution, in suspension and in traction.
5 The velocity of flow is the main factor in determining whether a river will pick up and start to move or deposit material.
6 Deposition of load occurs when a river's velocity slows, for example when it reaches a lake or a break in gradient.
7 The total load transferred within a drainage basin is difficult to calculate. It depends upon many factors including climate and vegetation cover.

key terms

Attrition - erosion of material such as sand or larger rocks that occurs when they rub against each other.

Bankfull - the state of flow of a river when it completely fills its channel.

Capacity - the ability of a river to transport sediment.

Competence - the ability of a river to transport particles of a particular size. The size of the largest particle that can be transported is closely related to the river's velocity.

Corrasion (or **abrasion**) - erosion that occurs when particles such as sand or gravel rub against a river bed and channel sides.

Energy (of a river) - the power of a river to erode and move the water within it and its load from source to mouth.

Hydraulic action - erosion that is caused purely by the force of moving water.

Hydraulic radius - the cross-sectional area of a channel divided by the wetted perimeter. It provides a measure of how efficient a channel is in terms of the friction caused by the channel bed and sides.

Load - the material that is transported by a river.

River sediment budget - the balance between the inputs and outputs of sediment within a drainage basin.

Solution - the process in which soluble material such as salts dissolve in water.

Suspension - solid material that is held floating in water.

Traction - the process in which bedload is rolled or bounced (saltation) along a river bed.

Turbulence - the chaotic swirls and eddies in a current.

Wetted perimeter - the width of a river channel bed and the height of the channel sides up to the water level.

Unit 9.3 River landforms

key questions

1 What features are associated with river channels?
2 What features are associated with the long profile of rivers?
3 What occurs during rejuvenation?

1. What features are associated with river channels?

Water does not flow in a straight line, even if the slope is relatively steep. This is because the flow is turbulent - with swirls and eddies naturally occurring. Sideways movements are reinforced in rivers when the flowing water is deflected by bends or irregularities in the channel. The effect is to cause bends or meanders to form (see figures 9.24 and 9.25).

Many rivers form a **floodplain** (see figure 9.26). This is a flat area of sediment that is deposited by a river during times of flood. The alluvial soil formed from this sediment tends to be fertile and productive. It is along the floodplains of rivers such as the Nile, Ganges and Yangtze that some of the highest rural population densities are found.

Most large rivers deposit fine silt on their beds in their lower sections. This has the effect of slowly raising the level of their beds. If the river floods, water flows onto the surrounding lowland, depositing suspended load as a fine layer of sediment on the floodplain. At the point where the river water leaves the channel and spreads onto the floodplain, its velocity is slowed. It is at this point that the most coarse, heaviest sediment is deposited. Over time, this can have the effect of building

Figure 9.24 The formation of meanders

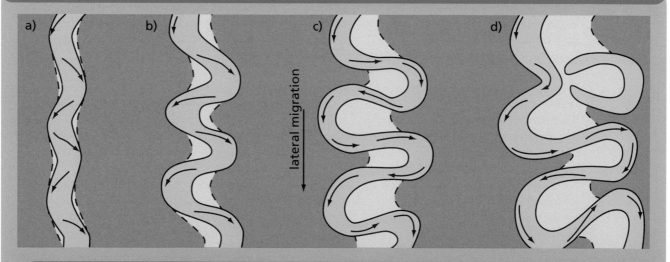

a) The line of maximum flow within a river channel is sinuous, ie it moves from side to side.

b) Meanders begin to form in the river channel. On the outside of a bend there is erosion and a **river cliff** might be formed. On the inside of a bend (or **slip-off slope**) the water velocity is relatively low and deposition occurs. This deposited sand and gravel forms a **point bar** which might be attached to the river bank or might run parallel, separated by a shallow trough. Alternating stretches of deeper and shallower water (called **pools and riffles**) often develop. Pools become deepest on the outside of bends and the riffles are formed where material is deposited between bends.

c) The meanders become bigger and migrate laterally. (The wavelength of a meander is the distance between meander loops. The radius is half the diameter inside a meander loop.)

d) The meanders migrate downstream and may form an **oxbow lake** or **cut-off**. This is a lake in an abandoned river meander - formed when the river erodes through the 'neck' of a meander.

embankments on either side of the channel. These are called **levees**. Eventually, the river might flow above the height of the floodplain, between the levees.

When this happens, drainage into the river is impeded and swamps form alongside the levees. Tributary rivers are sometimes diverted for many miles and flow parallel to the main river. These tributaries are called 'yazoos' along the lower Mississippi where the features are common.

Figure 9.25 A cross-section of a river channel at a meander

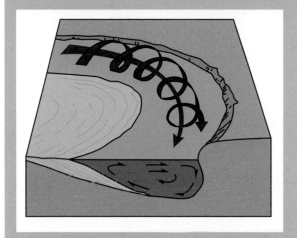

Water flows in a corkscrew fashion with higher velocities in the deeper outside of the bend and lower velocities in the shallower inside of the bend. The river's channel is asymmetric. The corkscrew pattern of water flow is sometimes called 'helical' or 'helicoidal'.

Figure 9.26 Features of a floodplain

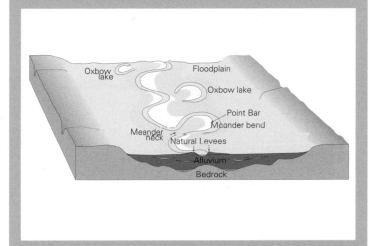

On both sides of the floodplain there is a line of bluffs. These are relatively steep slopes which form the edge of the floodplain.

Activity   Meanders on the River Ribble

▲ Figure 9.27 The floodplain of the River Ribble near Preston, Lancashire

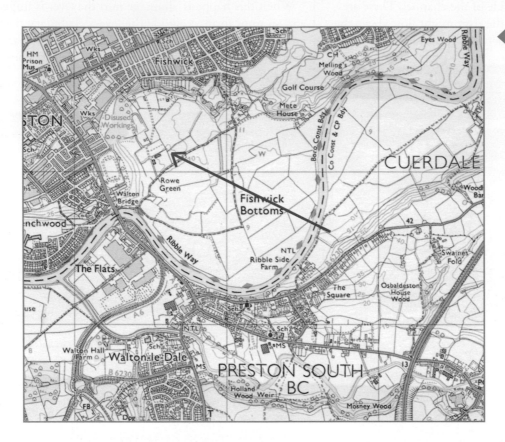

Figure 9.28
The River Ribble, 1: 25000 scale

The arrow marks the direction in which the photograph in figure 9.27 was taken.

Questions

1 Describe the natural features shown on the photograph in figure 9.27.
2 Explain how the floodplain was formed.
3 Suggest reasons for the land use in the area shown on the photograph.

2. What features are associated with the long profile of rivers?

The processes of erosion, transport and deposition of sediment are an important influence on landforms along a river's long profile (ie, from source to mouth). In general, there is a net erosion of material in the upper parts of drainage basins and a net deposition of material in the lower parts of drainage basins. However, it should be noted that some deposition does occur in upper river valleys and small flood plains might be formed. Likewise, erosion does occur in lower valleys - for example, on the outside of meander bends.

Upper drainage basin

Processes of river erosion in the upper parts of a drainage basin - where river gradients are steepest - take three main forms:

- removal of weathered material: soil and rock debris from the valley slopes is washed downstream and the general land surface is lowered
- downcutting of the river channel: corrasion and the other processes of erosion lower the river bed. In arid regions the result can be the formation of deep, almost vertical canyons. This is because other weathering processes in arid regions are generally not active enough to make the valley sides less steep.

Figure 9.29 Interlocking spurs, Swiss Jura

This steep sided valley is typical of upland areas that have not been heavily glaciated. The river winds along the valley at the foot of these interlocking spurs.

west Italy where rivers from the Alps drain into the flat valley of the River Po, and also along the eastern side of the Rocky Mountains in North America.

When a river flows into a lake or the sea, there is an abrupt decrease in water velocity. This causes the river to deposit its load and form a **delta**. Typically, when the water velocity slows, material is deposited along the side of the channel and also in the middle of the channel. This eventually causes separate **distributary** channels to form (see figure 9.30).

The eventual shape of a delta depends on the balance between two forces. On the one hand there is the river current that brings the sediment load. On the other hand there is wave and tidal action along the shoreline. Where river processes dominate, a 'bird's foot' delta is formed - for example the Mississippi delta in the Gulf of Mexico (see figure 9.31). Where shoreline processes dominate, an 'arcuate' delta is formed - for example the Nile delta in the eastern Mediterranean. Here, wave action redistributes the river sediment along the coast.

- headward erosion: at the point where water becomes concentrated into a stream channel, its velocity and energy increase; this causes a river to erode headwards (or upslope).

These processes of erosion create the landforms that are characteristic of upland areas - deep, steep-sided valleys or canyons, and dissected surfaces. Because of the tendency to meander, river valleys are rarely straight but typically form a series of **interlocking spurs** (see figure 9.29). These are ridges that slope down to a river along a winding valley.

Lower drainage basin

Most of the characteristic features of lower drainage basins are formed by deposition. As noted earlier in this unit, floodplains are commonly found along the lower sections of rivers. Where streams and rivers flow from an upland area onto lowland, and there is an abrupt change in gradient, deposition occurs and **alluvial fans** are found. Along a mountain front where several streams emerge from upland, the alluvial fans might merge together into a 'piedmont fan'. Such features occur in north

Figure 9.30 The formation of distributaries

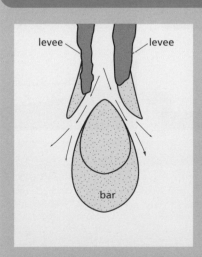
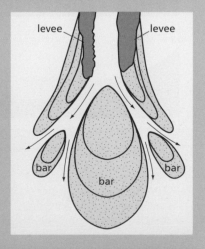

The deposited material builds up underwater and causes the channel to divide. Eventually the bars of sand and sediment become solid land and the process is repeated.

Figure 9.31 Bird's foot and arcuate deltas

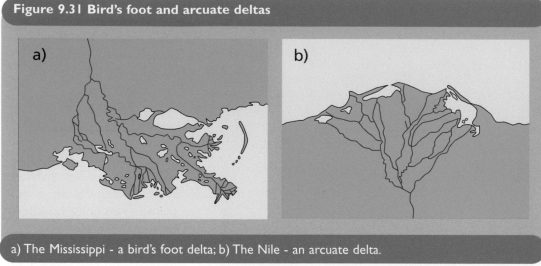

a) The Mississippi - a bird's foot delta; b) The Nile - an arcuate delta.

Like all other features of drainage basins, deltas are dynamic systems. In other words they are constantly changing. During times of flood, there are often shifts in the course of distributary channels. Breaks sometimes occur in the levees that line the channels and new deltas start to form. At least seven major changes in the course of the main channel have been identified at the mouth of the Mississippi. Old deltas have formed and then been abandoned as the main river channel has altered course. This has great significance for settlements such as New Orleans because the city lies partly below sea level on Mississippi delta land. The issue of managing a river's flow and protecting the land from flooding is covered in unit 9.4.

3. What occurs during rejuvenation?

Rivers erode down to a **base level** which is determined by the sea or lake level into which the river flows. Clearly, once a river has eroded the land down to sea level, it cannot go any lower. However, before a drainage basin is completely eroded to this level, rivers might be **rejuvenated** by a fall in base level (caused by a fall in sea level), or an uplift in the land level. Such changes in level are caused by:

* climatic changes during glacial periods when ice sheets form - so locking large volumes of water in the ice and causing the sea level to fall
* the melting of ice sheets after a glaciation - this removes weight from the Earth's surface and causes it to rebound (ie, rise) in the affected areas
* movements of tectonic plates - this can cause the land to rise, particularly during periods of mountain building (or 'orogenies').

Figure 9.32 Adjustment of a river profile after faulting

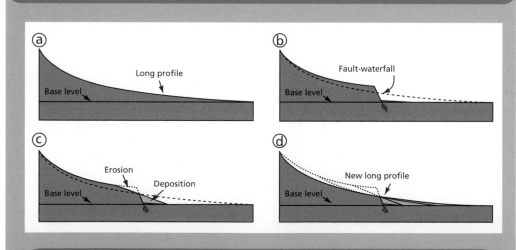

a) Original long profile of a river.

b) Movement along a fault line decreases the gradient downstream and increases the gradient upstream. A waterfall is formed at the fault line. The point at which the change in slope occurs is known as a 'knickpoint'.

c) Erosion occurs upstream of the fault, deposition occurs down stream. The waterfall erodes headwards, ie upstream - gradually becoming less high and eventually turning into rapids.

d) A new, smooth, 'graded' river profile is formed.

Figure 9.33 River terraces, Sutherland, Scotland

The Strathmore River is creating terraces as it erodes downwards. When it reaches a new base level, the river erodes laterally to form a new floodplain. This becomes a terrace when downward erosion reoccurs.

If either the sea level falls or the land rises, river gradient increases and there is renewed energy available for erosion. The same happens if a fault line shifts - so making one section of a river steeper (see figure 9.32).

Rejuvenation causes downward erosion of a river bed. When this occurs on a flood plain, the river starts to erode down to a new lower level - so creating a terrace. If several falls in base level occur, a series of terraces might be formed (see figure 9.33).

Where meanders occur, these might become deeply incised if the downward erosion is rapid. Examples occur in Britain on the River Dee near Llangollen, where the meanders are over 200 metres deep, and also on the River Wear in Durham where the castle and cathedral are built in the incised meander core.

Where rapid and prolonged uplift of land occurs, very deep gorges and canyons are formed. Examples include the upper Brahmaputra River in the Himalayas and the Colorado River in the southwest USA.

Activity ▷ Rejuvenation

Tectonic uplift of the land in the Grand Canyon region of southwest USA has caused the Colorado River to erode down through 1,600 metres of rocks. The Canyon is 16 km wide from rim to rim. Rock formations that are most resistant to weathering, such as Kaibab Limestone, form cliffs. Rocks that are less resistant, such as Hermit Shale, form gentler slopes. It has taken the river approximately 30 million years to erode the Canyon.

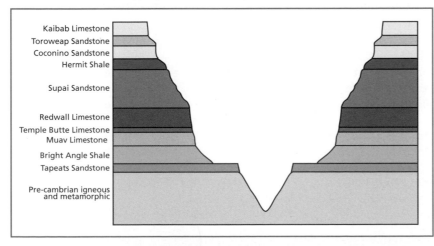

The photograph overleaf shows the San Juan River, Utah. It is a tributary of the Colorado River and the area through which it flows has been subject to the same process of tectonic uplift.

◀ **Figure 9.34 Cross section of the Grand Canyon**

The cross section is not to scale. The Canyon is 1.6 km deep and 16 km wide at the rim.

◄ **Figure 9.35 Incised meander, San Juan River, Utah**

Questions

1 Describe the features shown on the photograph in figure 9.35.
2 With reference to the Grand Canyon and San Juan River, explain what is meant by rejuvenation.
3 Suggest what natural features might be formed if the rapid downcutting of the San Juan River ended.

unit summary

1 Turbulence in a river's flow causes it to meander. This creates features such as river cliffs, slip-off slopes and floodplains.
2 Along the long profile of a river, in general there is net erosion of material on the upper part and net deposition on the lower part. Therefore, the features associated with a long profile of a river tend to be mainly erosional along the upper sections and mainly depositional along the lower sections.
3 Renewed erosion occurs when a river is rejuvenated - either by a fall in base level or by an uplift in land.

key terms

Alluvial fan - a fan shaped deposit of sediment formed at a point where a river emerges from a steep valley onto a wider and flatter plain.
Base level - the lowest level to which a river can erode (determined by the sea or lake level into which the river flows).
Delta - a deposit of sediment formed at the point where a river enters the sea or a lake.
Distributary - a river channel created where a river splits in a delta.
Floodplain - the flat land on each side of a river channel over which the river might sometimes flood.
Interlocking spurs - a series of ridges that slope down to the river along a winding valley.
Levee - a naturally formed embankment on either side of a river channel.
Meander - a loop in a river.

Oxbow lake (or **cut-off**) - a lake formed in an abandoned loop of a meander.
Point bar - a deposit of sand and gravel on the inside bend of a meander; it might be attached to the river bank or be separated from the bank by a trough.
Pools and riffles - alternating deeper and shallower sections along the course of a river.
River cliff - a steep slope or face on the outside bend of a meander.
Rejuvenation - an increase in a river's energy caused by either a fall in base level or an uplift in land.
Slip-off slope - the gentle slope on the inside bend of a meander.
Terrace - a relatively flat area of land bounded on one side by a relatively steep up-slope and on the other side by a relatively steep down-slope.

Unit 9.4 — Managing rivers and drainage basins

key questions

1 How do people use rivers?
2 What are the causes and effects of floods?
3 How is the River Nile managed?

1. How do people use rivers?

The earliest human civilisations depended, to a very large extent, on the use of river water for irrigation. In the valleys of the Nile, the Tigris and Euphrates, the Indus and the Yangtze, people built dams and channels to divert water onto their crops. By allowing the river water to flood onto the land and deposit sediment, the early farmers maintained the soil's fertility.

Today, worldwide, an estimated 18 percent of all arable farmland is irrigated. In some countries the proportion is much higher - over 50 percent in China and almost 100 percent in Egypt. As the world's population grows, more land is likely to be irrigated because food yields are higher when crops are regularly watered.

In the first civilisations, rivers were also used to provide water for drinking, for bathing and for washing. These needs are still met by rivers. In some cases there is direct extraction of river water and, in others, the river is dammed and water comes from reservoirs.

Since the start of the Industrial Revolution in eighteenth century Britain, river water has been increasingly used as a raw material or coolant in manufacturing processes. This is still the case in industries such as iron and steel and in coal powered electricity generation.

Rivers have many other uses in addition to providing water. Water wheels and, now, hydroelectric plants provide energy. Approximately 3 percent of the world's energy comes from HEP. Rivers also provide routeways. For many centuries, water transport was the cheapest and most convenient method of carrying freight. Although road and rail have become more important in modern times, rivers such as the Trent in England, the Rhine and Rhone in Western Europe, the Mississippi in the USA and the Ganges in Bangladesh provide locally important transport for bulky goods.

Rivers are sometimes used for dumping human and industrial waste. In most high income countries of the world, the waste is treated and is made safe. However, in many low and middle income countries, untreated waste is simply allowed to drain into rivers and then the sea.

In addition to their important domestic and industrial uses, rivers also provide an outlet for leisure and recreation. They also help create and preserve natural ecosystems of flora and fauna. So, for instance, people might spend their time bird watching on a river estuary, sailing or rowing in a river channel, or fishing. In some parts of Britain, salmon fishing, fish farming and fishing rights bring financial benefits. In low income countries, particularly in south and east Asia, river fishing is an important source of high protein food.

With so many demands on their use, it is not surprising that there are conflicts of interest between people who use rivers and river water. For example, in regions where water is scarce, there are often disputes between farmers who need water for irrigation and cities which need water for drinking. There are also international conflicts when, for example, the headwaters of a river are in one country but the river's water is used for irrigation downstream in other countries. One such dispute involves the River Tigris

Figure 9.36 River Nile, Cairo

Rivers bring many benefits such as water for drinking and for irrigation. They also provide a means of transport. However, they also create a hazard when there is a danger of flooding.

which rises in Turkey and then flows through Iraq. Turkish proposals to build a dam on their section of the river have been opposed by the Iraqi government.

So far, only the potential benefits provided by rivers have been outlined. Adverse or negative impacts of rivers have also to be considered by government agencies which manage drainage basins. By far the most serious negative impact arises when rivers flood. Urban development along floodplains, deforestation in upper catchments and channel straightening increase the rate of runoff and river discharge. This makes flooding more likely.

Developing flood prevention schemes and, at the same time, balancing the needs of river users are extremely difficult and complex issues. Examples of how these issues are tackled are described in the next sections of this unit.

Activity — Colorado River Basin

The Colorado River in the southwest USA is one of the most managed and controlled rivers in the world. It has been described as 'the world's greatest plumbing system' in which 'water flows uphill towards money'. Over 2,000 km in length, it rises in the Rocky Mountains and flows through an arid region of semi-desert until it reaches the Gulf of California. Before the first big dam was built (the Hoover Dam in 1935), the river's flow was very irregular. There was flooding after the spring snow melt, and low volumes of water later in the year. In 1922, the Colorado River Compact divided the region into the upper and lower basin (see figure 9.39: Wyoming, Utah, Colorado are in the upper basin; Nevada, Arizona and California are in the lower basin; New Mexico straddles the two basins). The upper and lower basins were each allocated 7.5 million acre-feet of water from the river per year and, in 1944, Mexico was guaranteed 1.5 million acre-feet per year. (An acre-foot of water is sufficient to flood an acre of land to the depth of one foot.)

Since 1930, the average annual river flow has been 14 million acre-feet and a further 2 million acre-feet are lost by evaporation from reservoirs. This compares with the 16.5 million acre-feet that have been allocated. The shortfall has been made up, so far, by some states not taking their full share. Under the Compact, in a drought year, the upper basin is obliged to deliver the lower basin's allocation before meeting its own needs. Rapidly rising populations in San Diego, Los Angeles, Las Vegas, Phoenix, Salt Lake City and Denver are putting more and more pressure on available supplies. People demand water not only for drinking and washing but for garden sprinklers and swimming pools.

▲ Figure 9.37 Lake Powell

▲ Figure 9.38 Hoover Dam

▼ **Figure 9.39 Colorado Basin**

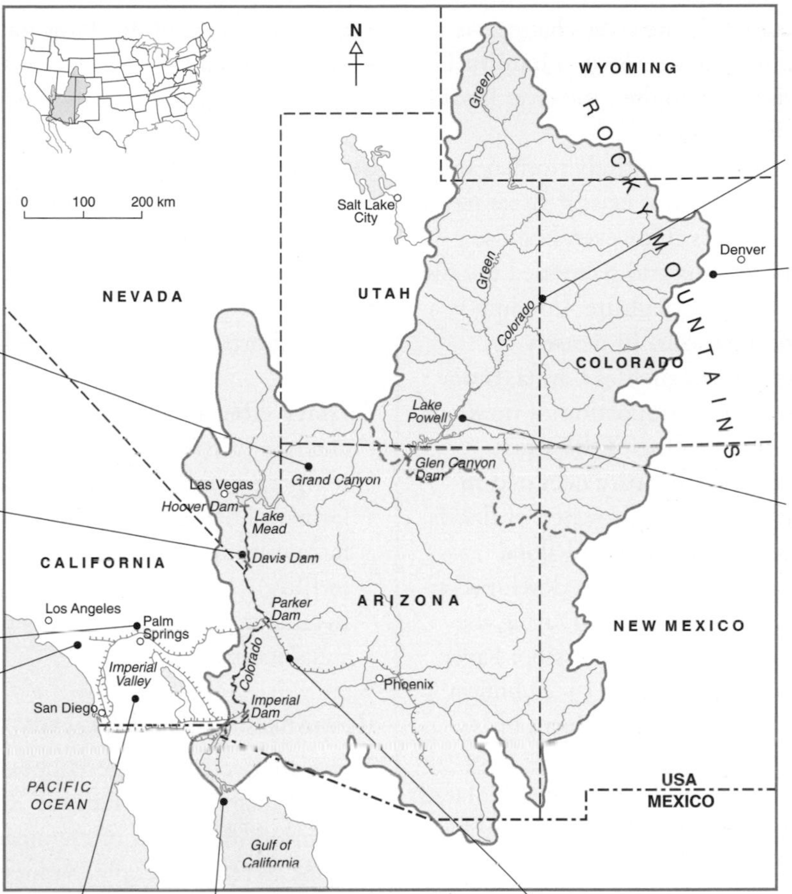

The Sierra Club (a pressure group of conservationists, walkers and climbers) proposes that the Colorado Dams (starting with Glen Canyon Dam) should be demolished - allowing the river and ecosystem to return to its natural state.

Dams along the Colorado generate 11,400 MW hydro-electricity (4% of US total). The river provides water for over 25 million people in the drainage basin and surrounding states.

Over 1.5 million gallons of water per day are used to keep Palm Spring's golf courses green in summer.

Over 30 percent of Southern California's domestic and industrial water supply comes from the Colorado River Aqueduct.

The Colorado carried an average 380,000 tonnes of sediment per day before the dams were built. Most of this is now trapped behind dams. Within a few centuries the reservoirs will fill with silt.

Tunnels, pipelines and canals divert water to Denver and 300,000 hectares of farmland on the eastern side of the Rockies.

Over 3 million people per year make holiday visits to Lake Powell. More than 20,000 people per year raft through the Grand Canyon.

Farmers use over 80 percent of the Colorado's water for irrigation. Imperial Valley's farms use 2.9 million acre-feet of water per year to grow over $1 billion worth of cotton, vegetables and grain.

At the mouth of the Colorado River, only a trickle of water reaches the sea. The river's intermittent flow and high salinity have altered the coastal ecosystem and destroyed the fishing and hunting way of life of local, native Americans.

Water from the river, reservoirs and irrigation canals seeps into underground aquifers. Communities in the lower drainage basin use this water pumped from wells.

Map labels: WYOMING, NEVADA, UTAH, COLORADO, CALIFORNIA, ARIZONA, NEW MEXICO, USA, MEXICO, ROCKY MOUNTAINS, Salt Lake City, Denver, Green, Colorado, Lake Powell, Glen Canyon Dam, Grand Canyon, Las Vegas, Hoover Dam, Lake Mead, Davis Dam, Los Angeles, Palm Springs, Parker Dam, Phoenix, Imperial Valley, San Diego, Imperial Dam, PACIFIC OCEAN, Gulf of California, N, 0 100 200 km

Questions

1 Make a list of all the different interest groups who have a stake in how the Colorado River is managed.

2 In your view, what are the main issues that will arise in managing the Colorado in the future?

3 Suggest what priorities you would have in allocating water from the Colorado River. Explain your answer.

2. What are the causes and effects of floods?

After heavy rain or a sudden snow melt, river discharge rises. If the water completely fills the river channel to the top of the river bank, it is said to be in a **bankfull stage**. If the water level rises any higher, the river is said to be in an **overbank** or **flood stage**.

Along most rivers, flooding is an entirely normal and natural event. Floodplains would not exist if rivers never rose above the top of their banks. However, because people have settled on floodplains and have used the flat land for housing, industry and agriculture, flooding is a serious hazard for these populations. In densely populated Third World countries such as China, India and Bangladesh, there are a high proportion of rural farmers who live on floodplains. One of the worst natural disasters of the twentieth century occurred in 1931 when nearly 4 million Chinese drowned in floods. In high income countries, such as the USA, flood prevention and warning systems have been developed to ensure that similar disasters do not occur. During the 1993 'flood of the century' along the Mississippi River, an estimated economic loss of between $15-20 billion was suffered (according to the US Army Corps of Engineers), but only 47 people died.

The chance of a flood occurring is generally calculated by analysing historic peak flows. From this data, a **recurrence interval** (or 'return period') can be calculated. This is the average period of time within which a particular scale of flood can be expected to occur. So, for instance, a '100 year flood' is a flood that might occur once in a hundred years. However, this is not to say that such floods will be regularly spaced or that they can be predicted. Expressed another way, a recurrence interval of 100 years means that there is a one percent chance that a flood will occur in any one year. Statistically speaking, it would be entirely possible for a flood of this scale to occur two years running - even though the probability is very low.

Hazards associated with flooding

Flood hazards are sometimes subdivided into primary, secondary and tertiary effects. Primary effects are due to the direct impact of floodwater, secondary effects are less immediate and tertiary effects are long term.

Primary effects include:
- loss of life by drowning - both people and livestock

- rapid erosion and undercutting of bridges, causeways and embankments
- water damage to homes, furniture, carpets, vehicles and commercial property
- contamination of drinking water by sewage
- crops washed away by floodwater
- sediment deposited in the flooded locations.

Secondary effects include:
- ill-health and disease from water borne sewage and toxins
- disruption of services such as gas and electricity
- disruption of communications (possibly leading to food shortages and famine in low income countries).

Tertiary effects include:
- changes to river and drainage channels
- temporary unemployment until services are restored
- farmland being covered by new sediment (reducing farm output at first but possibly raising long term soil fertility)
- insurance rates being increased for floodplain inhabitants.

Responses to flood hazards

There are two broad approaches which can be adopted when managing flood hazards. These involve flood prevention (by means of engineering) and setting up systems to reduce people's vulnerability to flooding.

Flood prevention

As noted previously in this unit, floods are natural and inevitable events. However it is possible, by using engineering solutions, to minimise flood damage in the most valuable locations. These are generally built up areas. Examples of 'hard' engineering include the building of embankments and the straightening and deepening of river channels ('channelisation'). These solutions work - but at a cost. As well as being very expensive, such methods can make flooding worse upstream. For example, in the 1993 Mississippi floods, the embankments near St Louis protected the city but they also slowed water flow and caused flooding to be worse upriver.

Dams and river barriers can be effective in reducing floodwaters but they are expensive to build. They also require accurate forecasting and flood prediction because preventative measures have to be taken before the event. In the case of dams in the upper drainage basin, the

Figure 9.40 Thames region at risk from flooding

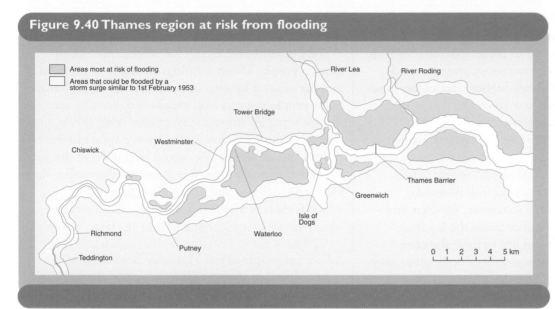

Areas most at risk of flooding

Areas that could be flooded by a storm surge similar to 1st February 1953

River Lea

River Roding

Tower Bridge

Westminster

Chiswick

Thames Barrier

Greenwich

Isle of Dogs

Richmond

Waterloo

Putney

Teddington

0 1 2 3 4 5 km

These are areas of floodplain that are designated as an outlet for floodwaters. By allowing water to flow onto land which is normally used for agriculture or recreation, the risk of flooding downstream is reduced. Such schemes are in operation on the River Witham near Lincoln and also along the Mississippi River near New Orleans.

reservoirs have to be part emptied before the floodwaters arrive - otherwise there is no extra storage capacity. In the case of flood barriers, they have to be closed before the water level rises.

The Thames Barrier in London is designed to prevent floods, not from swollen rivers, but from a surge in sea level. The damaging floods of 1953 were caused by such a surge. Very low atmospheric pressure, combined with a northerly wind and high tide, caused a funnelling effect in the Thames estuary and the southern part of the North Sea. Over 60,000 hectares of land were flooded and 300 people were drowned along the east coast.

To prevent a similar event from flooding central London, the Thames Barrier was built at a cost of over £1 billion (see figure 9.41). It was opened in 1982; it is 520 metres long and consists of four main gates. These normally rest on the river bed but, when raised, are as high as a five storey building.

A 'soft' engineering approach to flood prevention is the preparation of 'floodways' or 'washlands'.

Reduction of vulnerability to floods

This approach to managing flood hazards accepts that floods will occur but aims to reduce the risks involved. The first stage is to collect flood data and produce **hazard maps** for floods of different magnitude - for example, a 10-year flood, a 25-year flood and a 100-year

Figure 9.41 The Thames Barrier

The Barrier is designed to provide flood protection until at least 2030. By then, rising sea levels caused by global warming and the slow sinking of South East England might require the barrier to be raised in height.

flood. This information can then be passed on to residents and potential residents. Planning regulations and zoning laws can be used to prevent development in the most vulnerable areas. Insurance companies and mortgage lenders might charge higher rates in the zones at risk - and so discourage new residents.

It is important for flood prevention agencies to minimise urban development on floodplains for two reasons. The first is the obvious reason - to reduce the number of people at risk. The second is that urban development actually increases the risk of floods. Impermeable materials, such as tarmac, concrete and brick, reduce infiltration and decrease the lag time before peak discharge. Storm drains have the same effect. They might reduce local street flooding but they increase the rate of runoff and therefore peak flow.

By looking at the drainage basin as a whole (a 'holistic' approach), flood prevention agencies can devise integrated policies which lessen the flood hazard. Such policies include controls on floodplain development, and the creation of washlands by dismantling some of the artificial embankments which channelise the river.

The second stage in risk reduction is the accurate forecasting of rainfall, snow melt and ground saturation. River gauges are needed to monitor stream flow throughout the drainage basin. Data from these sources has to be collected and analysed, quickly and accurately. In places where flash floods occur, for example in the arid south west of the USA or in Mediterranean countries during the summer, it might be too late to wait for river levels to rise. Potential flood alerts have to be issued at any time there is sudden and heavy rainfall.

The third stage in risk reduction is the communication of flood warnings to people at risk and to the emergency services. The Environment Agency has the responsibility in England and Wales for flood defence and flood warning. It has a three level colour code of danger:
- yellow warning - flooding is likely on low-lying farmland and roads near rivers
- amber warning - flooding is likely in isolated properties, roads and large areas of farmland
- red warning - serious flooding of property, roads and farmland is likely.

When these warnings are issued, there needs to be an efficient system of communication to give people time to evacuate or prepare for flooding. Following the floods in the Midlands during Easter 1998, the Environment Agency was criticised for its failure to warn sufficient people. One of the problems was that the most severe flooding occurred overnight on the Bank Holiday weekend.

The Environment Agency has several methods of alerting people. Direct warnings are made in a limited number of areas by siren or by nominated flood wardens. Some people, most at risk, are phoned direct by the Agency using an automatic voice messaging system. Following the 1998 floods, the Agency agreed to increase the number of people who would be warned in this way.

The Agency also issues flood alerts to the media, via local radio, teletext and TV weather forecasts. In addition there is a 'dial and listen' Floodcall service which people can telephone to hear the latest warnings.

Advice for people at risk Households who live in the most vulnerable areas are given advice by the Environment Agency on how to cope with flooding. In the United States, the Federal Emergency Management Agency (FEMA) provides similar advice.

Before the event, people are advised to be prepared. This involves:
- knowing the risk, ie finding out whether the particular area is prone to flooding
- learning how flood warnings are given
- making sure that the property and contents are fully insured
- keeping valuable items upstairs or in a handy position to move
- for people who live in single storey buildings, asking neighbours who have upper floors to provide accommodation in an emergency
- keeping an emergency supply of food and drinking water together with a battery operated radio, a torch, first aid kit and warm clothes.
- finding out if the local council distributes sandbags, or keeping a supply in the property.

If a flood warning is issued, people are advised to take action to protect themselves and their property. These actions include:
- listening to local radio or telephoning Floodcall for the latest news
- alerting neighbours
- moving family, pets, livestock and most valuable belongings to a safe place
- switching off gas and electricity
- dressing in warm, waterproof clothing and getting emergency supplies ready
- blocking doorways and air vents with sandbags
- avoiding contact, if possible, with floodwater (it might be contaminated) and boiling tap water if it has to be used.

Activity | 1998 floods in England and China

Easter floods in the Midlands

Over the 1998 Easter weekend, the worst floods in 150 years were experienced in the English Midlands. Towns and cities such as Bedford, Northampton, Milton Keynes, Leamington Spa, Peterborough and Banbury were badly affected. Over 4,200 properties were flooded, five people died and many thousands of hectares of land were covered by the floodwater. An estimated £1.5 billion damage was caused to property. The main north-south railways and motorways were disrupted with the M40 being closed for several hours by floodwater.

The flooding was caused by exceptionally heavy rain. The ground was already saturated by above average rainfall when, on Wednesday 8th April and Thursday 9th, a frontal system became 'blocked' across the Midlands. The Met Office forecast was for the front to move steadily northwards but, instead, its progress was stopped by an area of high pressure. The result was that the front became almost stationary for 36 hours - during which time 75 mm of rain fell. This is equivalent to 6 weeks normal rainfall in the region.

Much of the Great Ouse, Nene and Avon catchment lies on limestone and sandstone covered by a layer of clay. Once the clay was saturated, the runoff quickly filled streams and rivers. Urbanisation in parts of the region, for example at Milton Keynes, increased the rate of runoff because the water quickly drained into storm drains. Readings from automatic river gauges in the upper catchment showed sudden increases in water levels. The extremely rapid rise in discharge was much faster than hydrologists had predicted.

One reason for the severity of the Midlands floods was that the flood defences in the region are not designed for the magnitude of flooding which occurred. This scale of floods might be expected once in 100 or 150 years but planners had designed defences to cope with what they classed as a 'severe event' - a 50 year flood.

After the floods, an independent review judged that the flood defences were in good order and had not suffered structural failure. The embankments were simply overtopped by the high water levels. The review did, however, criticise the Environment Agency for its failure to give adequate warning of the rising floodwaters. A quarter of the people whose properties were flooded did not receive any official warning. In one example, 500 properties in Leamington Spa were flooded at 6.00 am. The householders were completely unaware that the Environment Agency had issued a red alert for the River Leam at 11.15 pm the evening before.

In its defence, the Environment Agency said that the flooding was unprecedented and could not have been predicted from the Met Office weather forecast. It also suggested that tighter controls should be placed on floodplain development. In particular, planning permission for mobile homes and caravan parks sited next to rivers should be reconsidered. The Agency agreed that, in future, more emphasis should be placed on explaining the risks to people in the most vulnerable locations and also that investment should be made in better warning systems.

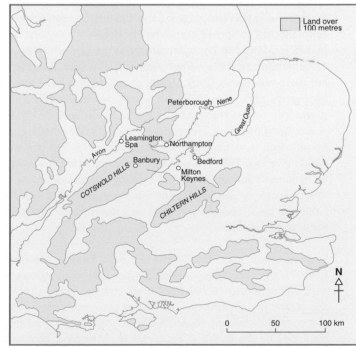

▲ Figure 9.42 Locations affected by the Easter 1998 floods

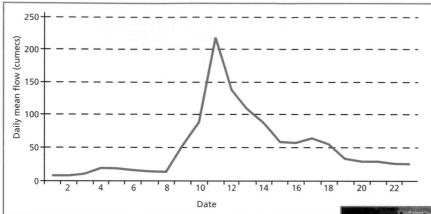

Figure 9.43 Hydrograph for the Great Ouse at Bedford, April 1998

The flow recorded for the 10th, 11th and 12th is based on an estimate by the Environment Agency. This is because, on each of those days, the upper limit of their recording device was exceeded.

▼ **Figure 9.44 Flooding in the English Midlands**

Summer floods in China

Between June and September 1998, the most damaging floods in 50 years hit China. The middle section of the 6,400 km long Yangtze River was the worst affected region. An estimated 2,000 people died. Most casualties were either caught in mudslides or were trapped in collapsed houses. Over 21 million hectares of farmland was flooded, 6 million homes were damaged and 14 million people evacuated. Many businesses and industrial units were forced to close because their premises were flooded or because communications were disrupted.

Prolonged and heavy rains over several weeks in the middle and upper catchment were blamed for the floods. Deforestation added to the speed of runoff and, in some places, river embankments made the flooding worse. By narrowing and straightening the channel, the banking caused the river to rise more quickly than if it had been allowed to spread across its floodplain.

In one incident, 150 km upstream from the city of Wuhan, soldiers were ordered to break down the embankment on the southern side of the Yangtze. Local farmers, armed with shovels and hoes, tried to resist but were overcome. Over 50,000 people had to be evacuated by the deliberate flooding of almost 200 square kilometres of farmland. Officials hoped that this would prevent flooding in Wuhan, with its 7 million inhabitants. It was also hoped that pressure would be reduced on the massive 6 metre high Jing Jiang embankment on the river's northern bank. This protects the valuable cotton growing plain of Hubei. At one time thousands of farmers and their families were camping out on top of the embankment - fearing that the flood defences would give way. Before water levels eventually fell, the river rose to within one metre of the top of the embankment and pools started forming on the north side - indicating that moisture was seeping through. When analysing the flood, after the event, officials decided that the deliberate flooding of the southern river bank had been necessary. Wuhan was saved from flooding and the more valuable farmland on the northern bank was also saved.

In an attempt to control floods along the Yangtze, the Chinese government is building the Three Gorges Dam. This is one of the world's biggest ever civil engineering projects. Scheduled for completion in 2010, the dam will generate 18,200 MW of electricity, create a reservoir 600 km long and enable safe navigation along the river's middle section - as well as preventing life threatening floods. Critics of the scheme suggest that the cost ($75 billion) could be better spent on smaller projects. Nearly two million people are being displaced by the dam and reservoir. Many historic sites will be covered by water and unforeseen changes will be caused to the river ecosystem.

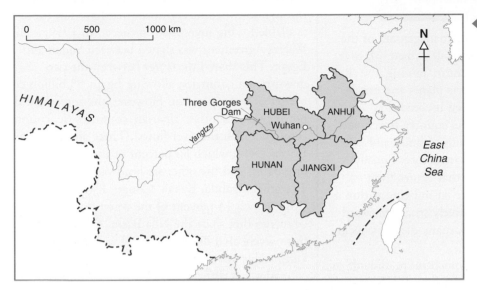

Figure 9.45 Provinces most affected by the 1998 summer floods in China

Figure 9.46 Site of the Three Gorges Dam, Yangtze River

The dam will prevent floods downstream and will generate large amounts of electricity. However, nearly 2 million people will be displaced by the reservoir.

Questions

1 Briefly describe the main causes and effects of the 1998 floods in (a) the Midlands; (b) the Yangtze valley.
2 Suggest why the 1998 flooding in China had a bigger impact on life and property than the Easter floods in the Midlands.
3 Summarise the ways in which flood defence agencies can protect the public.
4 Outline the case for and against building embankments along river channels.

3. How is the River Nile managed?

In the first activity of this unit the management of the Colorado River basin in the USA is described. Massive amounts of money have been spent in 'taming' the river and in building dams, hydroelectric plants and canals. The US has many advantages when it comes to managing the Colorado's flow. The country is rich and there are sufficient investment funds to build and maintain the dams and other infrastructure. Equally important is the political control that comes from virtually the whole of the drainage basin being within a single country. This makes it relatively straightforward to manage the river flow. Even so, many disputes occur over the use of the river water.

The River Nile, by contrast, is much more difficult to manage. It is over 6,000 km in length and flows through low income countries that have few funds available for big investment projects. In 1959, a Nile Waters Agreement was signed between Sudan and Egypt. This shared the water between the two downstream countries, allowing Egypt 55 billion cubic metres of water per year. However, the agreement did not include the other 'riparian' countries (ie, countries through which the river flows). These are Ethiopia and Eritrea (from which 86 percent of the river's flow originates) and the other six headwater countries - Tanzania, Uganda, Kenya, Congo, Rwanda and Burundi (from which 14 percent of the water flows). Of the ten countries that share the Nile Basin, six have suffered from severe civil disorder or civil wars in recent decades. Until stable governments are formed in all these countries it is difficult to see how a basin agreement can be reached. Even then, Ethiopia is in a position to veto any deal because it controls such a large proportion of the flow.

International development agencies and water engineers have outlined the advantages of a Nile basin 'action plan'. If political agreement, and peace, could be achieved, the Nile could be harnessed for the benefit of millions of low income people. The Blue Nile, as it falls from the Ethiopian Highlands, has sufficient hydro-electric potential to provide electricity in every home in the region. If the Sudd swamplands of the White Nile, in southern Sudan, were drained and then used for irrigated farming, the periodic famines which the region suffers could be overcome. Careful water management in the Sudd could reduce annual evaporation by 10 billion cubic metres. The benefits from such schemes, it is believed, would be so overwhelming that the World Bank and other agencies would supply the investment funds. However, they will not do so until there is political stability in the region.

Lake Victoria

Near the headwaters of the White Nile is Lake Victoria. This is divided between Kenya, Tanzania and Uganda. It is the second biggest freshwater lake in the world with a surface area of 68,800 square kilometres and a shoreline 3,500 km in length. The main river that feeds the lake is the Kagera which rises in Burundi and Rwanda. Approximately 85 percent of the water entering the lake evaporates and the remaining 15 percent forms the Victoria Nile. This flows, via Lake Albert and the Owen Falls, to form the White Nile.

Figure 9.47 The River Nile basin

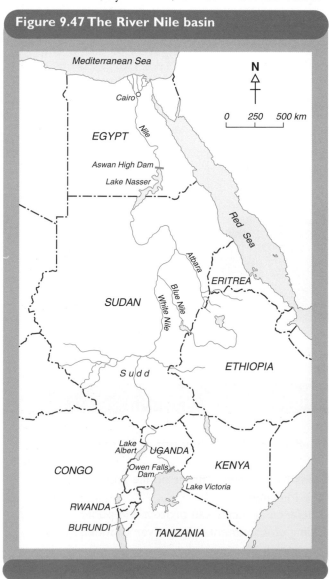

Lake Victoria's catchment supports approximately 25 million people. Most are engaged in farming and fishing. Some commercial fishing for export, and commercial farming of tea and coffee take place but most people subsist on their own produce. The annual growth rate of the local population is over 3 percent - one of the highest in the world. As a result, Lake Victoria is suffering from increased pollution by human and industrial waste. Nutrient inputs from fertilisers washing into the lake are also having an adverse effect. The result has been massive blooms of blue-green algae which are not only poisonous but deplete the oxygen on which fish rely. An additional problem is the spread of water hyacinth. This is a flowering plant, originally from Brazil, that is now spreading at a fast rate due to the high nutrient levels. The plant forms dense mats on the water surface, choking waterways, preventing fishing and threatening the intakes at the Owen Falls hydroelectric plant. It is also thought to act as a breeding ground for malarial mosquitoes and and other pests and diseases.

In an attempt to tackle their shared problems, Kenya, Tanzania and Uganda have agreed to the Lake Victoria Environment Management Programme. This was signed in 1994 as a recognition that individual governments working alone could not provide solutions to the catchment area's difficulties. However, it has proved difficult for these low income countries to overcome the environmental problems that pollution in the Lake is causing.

Egypt

Before the building of the Aswan High Dam in 1970 (also see unit 9.1), the flow of the Nile through Egypt was very irregular (see figure 9.48).

Egypt has a desert climate, with an annual average rainfall less than 200mm - even on the coast. Farming before 1970 was entirely dependent upon the annual Nile flood. Crops are irrigated and, for most of the year before the Aswan High Dam was built, water had to be lifted from the river onto nearby fields. For thousands of years, the height of the Nile flood indicated prosperity or famine. Too low and it would be impossible to water the fields, too high and it would wash the crops away. Floods of between approximately 14 and 18 metres in height provided just the right amount of water. The annual flood also brought the benefit of a fresh deposit of silt which maintained the soil's fertility.

So reliant is Egypt upon the Nile that, even today, 95 percent of the population live within 16 km of the river or on its delta. The country's rapidly rising population is putting pressure on the government to create more agricultural land. At present there are approximately 60 million people living in Egypt and this is forecast to rise to 85 million by 2015.

The government has responded to this pressure by announcing a scheme to settle 3 million people in the New Valley - a large oasis in the Western Desert. A canal, almost 250 km long, would be needed to carry water from the Nile at Aswan. Ten percent of the Nile's flow would be diverted to the new settlement. Critics of the proposal say that a 10 percent reduction in discharge would make navigation dangerous along parts of the lower Nile. Others suggest that it is unwise to plan more irrigation when both the Ethiopian and Sudanese populations are rising rapidly. These countries are likely to demand more of the Nile's water in the future, not less.

Figure 9.48 Nile discharge before and after the Aswan High Dam

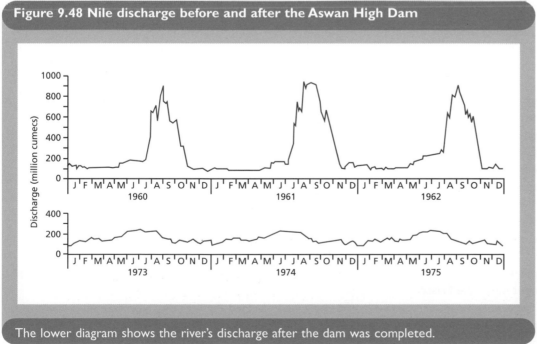

The lower diagram shows the river's discharge after the dam was completed.

Activity — The Aswan High Dam

Completed in 1970, the Aswan High Dam, is a symbol of Egypt's determination to achieve economic growth and national prestige. Almost 1,000 km upriver from Cairo, the dam has created the world's third largest reservoir, Lake Nasser. This stretches into Sudan which has a joint agreement to share the water.

Like most large dams, the scheme has been controversial because it has created both benefits and drawbacks. Groups who benefit do not necessarily share their good fortune with the 'losers'. The strongest opponents of such schemes suggest that it is the multinational construction companies who have most to gain, and that local people are often left with debts which they cannot repay.

Benefits:

- the Nile's flow has been stabilised - higher year round water levels allow double cropping (ie, two crops per year), an increase in irrigated land area (800,000 hectares) and higher food output; Egypt manages to feed its population (which has doubled since the dam was built) and also exports cotton and early vegetables to the European market
- 10,000 MW of electricity are generated by the dam's turbines - approximately 20 percent of Egypt's consumption; the power has increased living standards and has made industrial development possible (steel, textile and chemical fertiliser plants have been set up at Aswan)
- the controlled water level has made navigation along the Nile safer; in turn this has been beneficial to trade, transport and tourism (allowing year round cruises to Nile temples along the river)
- sediment and nutrients flowing into Lake Nasser have caused an increase in fish stocks in the lake.

Drawbacks:

- almost 100,000 people had to be relocated from land that was flooded by the dam; some were moved 600 km from their original homes
- over 95 percent of the river's sediment load (120 million tonnes per year) is deposited in Lake Nasser; sediment is no longer deposited by the annual flood on irrigated lands on the river banks or in the delta - so artificial fertiliser has now to be used instead
- without the annual flood, salt deposits that are created by salinisation on irrigated land are not washed away; this salinity reduces crop yields
- former seasonal wetlands and swamps along the Nile have dried, killing vegetation and reducing the habitat of animals such as the Nile crocodile
- the Nile delta is eroding at a rate of over 30 metres per year because no new sediment is being deposited at the coast; saline water from the Mediterranean is contaminating parts of the delta and has seeped 30 km inland
- the 'clear' water discharged from the dam erodes the river bank more vigorously than before; three old dams downstream and several hundred bridges have been undermined by the river's flow
- sediment and nutrients carried by the river used to support a flourishing sardine and shrimp fishery in the eastern Mediterranean; overall fish catches have fallen by over 20 percent and sardine catches by 95 percent
- before the Aswan High Dam was built, the lower water level between December and June allowed the ground next to the river to dry for part of the year; this limited the spread of the waterborne bilharzia parasite - carried by snails and causing schistosomiasis in humans (a damaging liver disease which now affects almost half the population)
- high evaporation rates and seepage into porous sandstone cause an annual water loss approximately equivalent to 14 percent of the input into Lake Nasser
- rich archaeological remains were either covered by the rising water behind the dam or, in the case of Abu Simbel, had to be expensively relocated above the new waterline.

▼ **Figure 9.49 Lake Nasser**

▲ **Figure 9.50 Irrigation fields**

Irrigation water from the Nile is pumped onto the narrow flood plain. In places, the river's banks have been reinforced to protect them from erosion.

Clear skies and high temperatures cause high rates of evaporation from Lake Nasser.

Questions

1 In your view, do the benefits arising from the Aswan High Dam outweigh the drawbacks? Explain your answer.
2 When sediment is trapped behind a dam, what effect does this have on the river and its features?
3 What lessons might other countries learn from the Aswan High Dam?

unit summary

1 People use rivers and river water for many purposes including power generation, navigation, water for drinking and irrigation. Conflicts often arise between the different users.
2 Floods are natural and inevitable events. Their impact can be reduced by flood defences and by reducing the vulnerability of people most at risk.
3 The flow of the River Nile has been controlled in its lower section but massive untapped potential remains in the upper basin. This requires political stability that does not exist at present.
4 Dams are controversial because they create many drawbacks in addition to benefits. Groups who benefit from dams do not always share the gains with the 'losers'.

key terms

Bankfull stage - the flow or discharge of a river when the channel is completely full and the water is almost to the top of the river banks.
Flood stage (or **overbank stage**) - the flow or discharge of a river when the river overtops its banks and starts to flood.
Hazard map - a map that shows locations at risk from a particular event (for example, the land that would be covered by a 10-year flood).
Recurrence interval (or **return period**) - the average length of time between floods of a particular scale. For instance, a 10-year recurrence interval implies that, on average, such a flood can be expected to occur within ten years. Expressed differently, there is a 10 percent chance that such a flood might occur in any one year.

CHAPTER 10 Glaciation

Introduction

During the Earth's geological history, there have been several cold periods in which ice sheets have expanded. These periods of glaciation are known as **ice ages**. At their maximum, ice sheets extended over almost a third of the planet's surface. Just 20,000 years ago, much of Britain north of the Thames was covered by ice that was over a kilometre thick. Today, approximately 10 percent of the Earth's land surface is covered by ice. Ice sheets scour and erode the landscape. Landscape features are changed again when ice melts and deposits the material it has transported. It is not only the physical landforms that are changed. During ice ages, the climate of the whole planet is altered, the sea level is lowered and parts of the Earth's crust are depressed by the weight of ice. There are also biological effects - on both plants and animals.

Ice ages are not single continuous events. The most recent began over 2 million years ago but, during that period, there have been many warm 'interglacial' phases when average temperatures were higher than today. This chapter concentrates on the effect of the most recent ice age in terms of its impact on the physical landscape and also on human activity.

Chapter summary

Unit 10.1 investigates glacial processes.
Unit 10.2 looks at glacial landforms.
Unit 10.3 examines the human impact and considers how people use glaciated areas.
Unit 10.4 investigates periglacial environments, and looks at how people cope with living in such conditions.

Unit 10.1 Glacial processes

key questions

1 What happens during ice ages?
2 How do glaciers form?
3 What processes are at work in glaciers?

1. What happens during ice ages?

Evidence for what happens during an ice age comes mainly from the most recent, 'Pleistocene', glaciation. Analysis of fossils and mud in deep ocean sediments suggests that, during this period, there have been many advances and retreats of ice sheets. Until fairly recently, it was believed that there had been only four major advances and retreats but this now appears to be an underestimate.

Most of the land affected by the Pleistocene glaciation is in the northern hemisphere because, apart from Antarctica, there are no large land masses near the southern polar region where ice could accumulate (see figure 10.1). During the Pleistocene glaciation, ice sheets (at their maximum) covered North America, approximately as far south as the Great Lakes, and Eurasia, approximately as far south as southern England. It appears that parts of Alaska and Siberia were not completely glaciated, probably because there was too little snowfall to generate ice sheets.

For an ice age to occur, average temperatures in temperate latitudes must be approximately 5°C below the present level. Different theories have been put forward to explain this cooling. They include:

- variations in the solar energy output, possibly associated with sun spot activity
- cyclical changes in the Earth's orbit and angle of tilt towards the Sun, causing changes in the amount of solar radiation received at different places on the Earth's surface (so called 'Milankovitch cycles')
- changes in atmospheric circulation and ocean currents, possibly caused by movements of land masses in the process known as continental drift
- changes to the composition of atmospheric gases. For example, a decrease in greenhouse gases such as carbon dioxide leads to cooling. So does an increase in sulphur dioxide (from volcanic eruptions) which blocks out solar radiation.

Unfortunately, no one theory precisely fits the complex pattern of global warming and cooling that has occurred. (See unit 12.6 for a more detailed account of climate change.) Throughout the Earth's existence, ice ages have

Fig 10.1 The extent of the most recent, Pleistocene glaciation

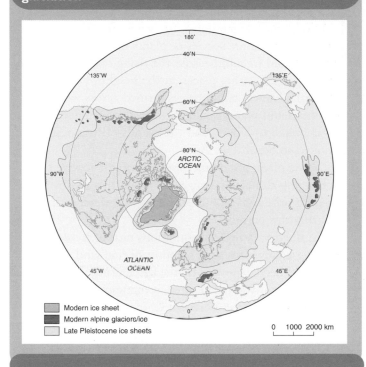

Modern ice sheet
Modern alpine glaciers/ice
Late Pleistocene ice sheets

0 1000 2000 km

The start of a glacial period

At the start of a glacial period, snow begins to accumulate. Relatively small changes in temperature are required for the process to start. For instance, it would only take a 1°C fall in average temperature for snow to remain all year in the Scottish Cairngorms and build into a snowfield. If the temperature continued to fall, the snow depth would increase, ice would accumulate and glaciers would form.

Once the ground is covered by snow, more of the Sun's energy is reflected back from the Earth's surface. This 'albedo effect' results in further cooling. The result is a change in the climate pattern and atmospheric circulation. This is because, over ice sheets, the air is cooled and tends to sink and blow outwards. The air is relatively dry and there is little precipitation. Eventually, it is believed, the low precipitation causes the ice sheets to thin and retreat. This process may partly explain the cyclical pattern of advance and retreat during ice ages.

During an ice age, the sea level changes. This occurs for two main reasons. Firstly, during a glacial advance, a large amount of water freezes and becomes trapped in ice sheets. This causes the sea level to fall. Approximately 20,000 years ago, when ice sheets were at their maximum, the sea level was 100 metres below that at present. Then, as the ice melted, the sea level rose. These are called **eustatic** changes. Secondly, the weight of ice in an ice sheet is so great

not occurred at regular intervals and, within ice ages, there have been many warm interglacial periods. Currently the mainstream view is that the variations in orbit and tilt of the Earth are the trigger for cyclical changes during the ice ages but other factors must also be at work to start the process.

Towards the end of the last glacial period, approximately 15,000 - 20,000 years ago, the ice sheets melted across most of North America and Eurasia. Evidence for this comes from air samples trapped in polar ice cores These samples also suggest that many abrupt changes in climate have occurred in the past. Yet, for 10,000 years, the Earth's climate has been very stable (see figure 10.2). During this period, agriculture and human civilisation have developed. It remains to be seen whether the present period of global warming marks the complete end of the ice age or, more likely, is simply another interglacial phase.

Figure 10.2 Climate change during the past 160,000 years

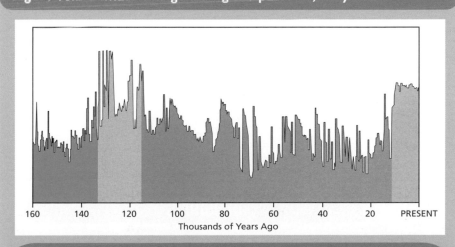

Thousands of Years Ago

Relatively warm interglacial periods are marked in red. The data comes from the analysis of ice cores from the Greenland ice sheet. It shows that there have been many climate changes in the past. For most of the past 160,000 years, the Earth has been colder than now. However, there have also been warmer periods - for example, between 115,000 and 135,000 years ago.

that the Earth's crust is depressed. The land surface then rebounds when the ice has melted. These are called **isostatic** changes. In parts of Scotland, the effect has been to cause a 300 metre rise in the land surface and the land is still rising at 3 mm per year. The result is a fall in the relative sea level, causing features such as 'raised beaches'. In southern Britain, the isostatic rebound to the north has caused the land surface to tilt downwards. The effect has been to drown river valleys - forming estuaries and 'rias' (see unit 11.2 for a more detailed account of sea level changes).

At the margins of continental ice sheets there are zones of tundra and permafrost, ie permanently frozen ground (see unit 10.4). During glacial periods, these 'periglacial' conditions extended into what today are temperate zones. So, for instance, 20,000 years ago, England south of the Thames had a climate and natural vegetation similar to that found today in northern Scandinavia. Other zones of natural vegetation migrated southwards (in the northern hemisphere) as the ice sheets advanced, and then moved northwards as the ice melted. Combined with the changes in sea level

that first linked the British Isles to mainland Europe and then broke the link, this has had a marked effect on natural vegetation. At the end of the last glacial period, when vegetation zones were migrating northwards, some species of plants never recolonised Britain and Ireland because the rising sea level blocked their path. In other places, at the height of the last glacial advance, land bridges formed across which animals and plants could migrate. For instance, Alaska was linked to Siberia and the islands of Indonesia were linked to South East Asia.

Some plant and animal species did not survive the changing climate and vegetation pattern - for instance, mammoths and sabre-toothed tigers became extinct during this period.

In the dry, periglacial conditions near to ice sheets, strong winds blow large amounts of fine sand and silt that has been deposited by the ice. During the last glacial advance, this was redeposited, sometimes hundreds of metres thick, across northern China, Western Europe and the American Midwest. It is called **loess** ('limon' in France) and now forms a fine, fertile, soil.

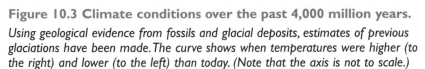

Activity ▸ Previous ice ages

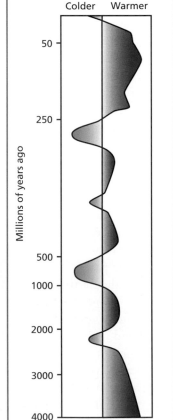

Figure 10.3 Climate conditions over the past 4,000 million years.

Using geological evidence from fossils and glacial deposits, estimates of previous glaciations have been made. The curve shows when temperatures were higher (to the right) and lower (to the left) than today. (Note that the axis is not to scale.)

Questions

1 Describe the climate pattern shown on the graph.
2 Based on the evidence in figure 10.3 (and in figure 10.2), how certain is it that the Pleistocene ice age has ended?

2. How do glaciers form?

In high latitudes, and at high altitudes, snow accumulates in snowfields above the permanent snowline. This happens where more snow falls in the winter than melts or evaporates in summer. Figure 10.4 shows the present snowline across the Earth's surface.

Snowflakes are ice crystals, usually hexagonal in shape. When snow builds up, the weight of overlying layers causes the ice crystals gradually to change into more compact granules. These form **névé** (or 'firn') which is opaque in appearance. When the depth of snow is more than about 30 metres, the névé is further compressed and recrystallised into glacier ice (see figure 10.5). This has a bluish colour and is formed of solid, interlocking grains. By this stage, most of the air trapped within the ice crystals has been squeezed out. If the ice thickness is greater than 60 metres, its lower layers become 'plastic'. The ice then flows downslope under the force of gravity.

In mountain regions, flowing ice might be compressed in a valley and is then known as a **glacier**. On a plateau, the ice might cover all the land and form an ice cap or, on a much bigger scale it is called an **ice sheet** or **continental glacier**.

On a glacier or an ice sheet, there is a **zone of accumulation** (where the supply of snow exceeds that lost by melting and evaporation) and a **zone of ablation**

Figure 10.5 The relative volumes of an equal weight of snow, névé and ice

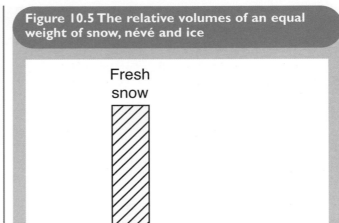

When snow is compressed into neve and ice, the volume decreases as the air is squeezed out.

(where melting and evaporation cause a net loss of ice) (see figure 10.6). The rate of accumulation and ablation depend mainly upon precipitation and temperature which, in turn, partly depend upon altitude and aspect. So, for instance, in the northern hemisphere, most valley glaciers flow from mountain snowfields on the north and east side of the highest peaks. This is where precipitation is greatest and where melting is least.

At the present time, in most parts of the world, glaciers and ice sheets are retreating because ablation is greater than accumulation. (Note, of course, that the ice is still moving forwards even though the front of the glacier is retreating.)

Within a glacier system, the balance between accumulation (input) and ablation (output) is called the **mass balance** (or 'glacial budget'). If the input equals the output, the mass of the ice

Figure 10.4 Snowline

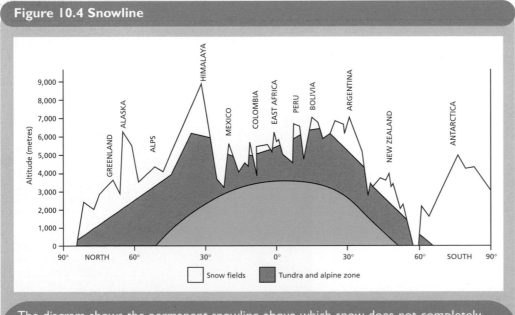

The diagram shows the permanent snowline above which snow does not completely melt in summer. The altitude of the line varies with latitude but it is also affected by local factors such as aspect and amount of precipitation.

Figure 10.6 Glacier

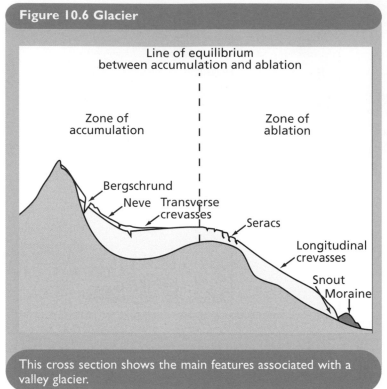

Line of equilibrium
between accumulation and ablation

Zone of
accumulation

Zone of
ablation

Bergschrund

Neve Transverse
crevasses

Seracs

Longitudinal
crevasses

Snout
Moraine

This cross section shows the main features associated with a valley glacier.

remains constant and the front of the glacier remains stationary. If the input exceeds the output, the glacier advances and, if the input is less than output, the glacier retreats.

During summer, ice melts and forms 'supraglacial' streams on top of the glacier. These sometimes flow down through cracks and holes ('mills' or 'moulins') to join the 'subglacial' streams flowing beneath the ice. The point at which the meltwater emerges from a glacier is called the **snout**.

Near the backwall of the glacier, there is often a deep, narrow crevasse in the ice. It is called a bergschrund (or rimaye in French). Water seeps down this crack and can cause freeze thaw to occur on the rock. At one time it was thought that this process was a major factor in causing erosion of the backwall. However, modern research suggests that this is not the case because the water generally just freezes once and then does not remelt. For the process to be more effective, there have to be many freeze thaw cycles.

How do glaciers and ice sheets move?

The ice within glaciers moves downhill through the force of gravity. The movement can be divided into 'internal flow' and 'basal sliding'.

Internal flow (This is sometimes also known as internal deformation.) It occurs in two main ways. Individual ice

crystals melt under pressure caused by the weight of overlying ice. The water then moves and refreezes downslope in a process known as 'regelation creep'. Also, within the glacier, pressure from the weight of ice causes stresses to build up. This causes 'shear planes' to form along which layers of ice slide past each other, like a pack of cards.

Basal sliding (Also known as basal slip.) This is the sliding movement of a glacier over the underlying rock surface. As the ice partially melts under pressure, pockets of water form that reduce friction and lubricate the process (see figure 10.8).

When an ice sheet moves, there is friction with the ground underneath. In valley glaciers, there is also friction with the side walls. This causes the ice to move slower near the base and sides than at the surface and in the middle. The stresses that build up cause cracks or **crevasses**. The speed of movement is too slow to see at any given moment but experiments confirm the differential movement (see figure 10.9). Most crevasses form

Figure 10.7 Mer de Glace, Chamonix, France

This photograph was taken in summer. The ice appears grey in colour because of the large amount of rock debris (or 'moraine') that it is transporting.

Fig 10.8 Internal flow and basal sliding

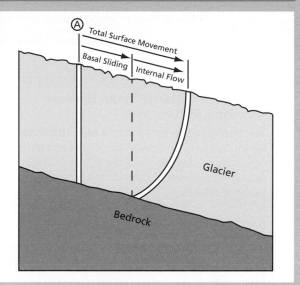

In an experiment, a flexible steel tube was pushed through a glacier at point A. After a few years, the tube had moved downslope and bent, showing both the basal sliding and the internal flow.

Figure 10.9 Glacier Blanc

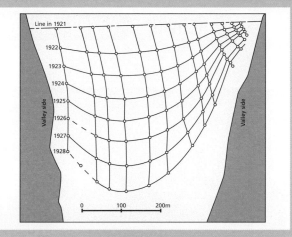

The diagram shows the results of an experiment that was carried out in the French Alps during the 1920s. Painted stones were placed in a straight line across Glacier Blanc in 1921. Their position was recorded annually - confirming that movement is fastest in the centre.

where the glacier moves over uneven ground or where the underlying slope is steepest.

Gravity causes glaciers to flow fastest down steep slopes. Here, the ice becomes stretched and thinned. On very steep sections, an 'ice fall' may form with many crevasses and blocks of ice called 'seracs' (see figure 10.10). Where this happens, there is said to be 'extending flow' as opposed to 'compressing flow' which occurs when the gradient is less steep.

The overall speed of flow in a glacier depends upon the gradient, the volume of ice, the amount of snowfall in the zone of accumulation, and the temperature. Large valley glaciers in Switzerland can move up to 180 metres per year, smaller ones at 90-150 m/year. The fastest movements in the world at the present time - over 8 km/year - occur in west Greenland. Here, 'outlet glaciers' extend westwards from the main ice cap. They are pushed through mountain passes by the great mass of ice that has built up in central Greenland.

Most of the time, glaciers flow at relatively stable rates but, occasionally, a surge occurs. In one example, the Bering glacier in Alaska advanced 225 metres in one day in 1993. This may have been due to rapid basal sliding following a build up of subglacial water under pressure. On other occasions, surges might follow an avalanche

or landslip that suddenly add weight to the glacier.

A distinction is sometimes made between cold glaciers (in polar regions) and warm glaciers (in temperate regions). On average, cold glaciers in places such as Antarctica tend to move more slowly than warm glaciers in temperate areas such as the Alps. This is because there is more meltwater in the temperate zones during summer and this acts to lubricate the ice flow. Under these conditions, basal sliding is the dominant process.

Fig 10.10 Seracs on the Argentiere Glacier, Chamonix

This is a steep section of the glacier.

Activity ▶ Valley glaciers

◀ **Figure 10.11 Glacier in the Bernese Oberland, Switzerland**

Two hundred years ago, during a cool climatic period known as the 'Little Ice Age', this region was more snow covered than now and the glacier extended much further down its valley. At the present time, the glacier is retreating.

Questions

1 Briefly describe how glaciers form and how they move.
2 Explain what happens when a glacier retreats.
3 Summarise the factors that cause glaciers to advance and retreat.

3. What processes are at work in glaciers?

A glacier can be described as a river of ice. The processes at work are the same as those that occur in rivers - erosion, transport and deposition.

Glacial erosion

In some mountain areas, glaciers have eroded troughs that are two kilometres deep. Clearly glaciers are very powerful agents of erosion. However, the ice they contain is not as strong as solid bedrock because, when it is under great pressure, ice tends to melt or 'deform'. This property of ice means that other factors must cause the erosion. These factors include: freeze thaw action; glacial processes of abrasion, attrition and plucking; glaciofluvial processes (ie, erosion by meltwater); and pressure release.

- **Freeze thaw** is a weathering process that can occur whenever and wherever the temperature falls below freezing. It is a major factor in creating glaciated landforms. When water freezes, it expands by approximately 9 percent. If this happens in cracks within rocks, fragments are loosened or fractured. (The process is also known by several other terms including 'frost shattering' and 'ice wedging'.) In a glacial landscape, freeze thaw is active in two broad zones. Firstly, it occurs on the valley slopes above a glacier. From these slopes, large amounts of shattered rock fragments fall onto the sides of the glacier. Secondly, it occurs underneath the glacier when meltwater seeps into cracks, then freezes, expands and shatters rocks.

- **Abrasion** (also called 'corrasion') occurs when rocks are embedded in the underside of a glacier. These rocks gouge and scrape the bedrock and soil as the glacier moves along. Sand and silt particles in the ice have the effect of polishing the underlying rock, and larger fragments cause scratches or 'striations'. Experimental work in Iceland has shown that abrasion can be a very effective form of erosion. Over a twelve month period, blocks of marble were worn down by 3 mm and blocks of basalt by 1 mm.

- **Attrition** occurs when solid rock fragments, embedded on the underside of a glacier, are ground against the bedrock. The rock fragments themselves become smoother and smaller. When the rock is ground into very fine material, it is called 'rock flour'.

- **Plucking** occurs underneath a glacier. Fragments of bedrock may be loosened by freeze thaw and become frozen to the ice. As the glacier moves, the rocks are pulled or plucked away - leaving a jagged surface. This occurs on the sides and on the backwall of a glacier, and also underneath the ice.

- **Glaciofluvial** erosion occurs when meltwater streams run beneath the ice. The flowing water can be at very high pressure if it is confined in narrow channels under a glacier. These subglacial streams, loaded with eroded rocks and debris, are very powerful forces of erosion.

- **Pressure release** is the name given to a process that occurs when ice sheets or glaciers melt and the weight is removed from the Earth's surface. The result can be an expansion of the rock that causes a series of cracks parallel to the surface to form - so exposing the rock to weathering. There is some dispute over the exact nature of this process and it is believed by some researchers that the removal of ice alone is not sufficient. Overlying layers of rock may have previously been removed by erosion and this has caused the pressure release. (The process is also known as 'unloading' and 'dilatation'.)

Glacial transportation

A glacier is very effective in transporting eroded material. Partly this is because it is made of solid ice and can therefore carry much heavier material than rivers. Massive blocks of rock, known as erratics can be moved hundreds of kilometres by ice sheets. In Alberta, Canada, one erratic field contains over 100,000 blocks, the biggest weighing several thousand tonnes. However, most erratics are much smaller. Some found along the North Sea coast of England are just pebble sized. Well known examples of erratics in England are at Norber, to the south of Ingleton in the Pennines. Here, dark coloured rocks of sandstone are perched on top of the much lighter coloured local limestone.

Transported material is carried along within the ice (englacial), on the ice (supraglacial) and beneath the ice (subglacial). Eroded material is also transported in the streams that flow on and under the ice in summer. Such glaciofluvial streams are often milky in colour,

Fig 10.12 Norber erratic

The block of sandstone is perched on limestone. It was transported by ice during the last glacial period.

containing large amounts of finely ground rock flour in suspension.

Glacial deposition

When ice sheets or glaciers melt, the material they deposit is called **drift**. It is often classified as stratified (in layers) or unstratified (with no layers). The stratified deposits have been sorted by meltwater streams, either under the ice or beyond the ice margin. They are generally formed of gravels, sand and silt and are called glaciofluvial deposits.

The unstratified deposits, called **till** (or 'boulder clay'), have simply been dumped by the melting ice. The material consists of angular rock fragments in a mixture of fine clay particles and rock flour. The landforms created by these deposits is known as **moraine**. In some places, the moraine is in the form of a ridge but, in others, it is a sheet deposit that masks the original landscape. This 'ground moraine' is 100 metres thick in parts of East Anglia.

The term moraine is, confusingly, used in two slightly different ways. Landscape features formed from till are called moraine but the term is also used to describe the eroded rock fragments carried along on the surface of a glacier. The line of debris at the side of a glacier is called a 'lateral moraine' and, where two glaciers meet causing the lateral moraines to be more central, the feature is called a 'medial moraine'.

(See unit 10.2 for a detailed account of glacial landforms.)

Activity | Glacial processes

Figure 10.13 The Mer de Glace showing moraine and crevasses

Questions

1 Briefly describe the glacial processes of erosion, transport and deposition.
2 Describe the photographic evidence (in figure 10.13) that indicates particular glacial processes are at work.

unit summary

1 The cause of climate change that triggers an ice age is not well understood, although several theories have been proposed.
2 The most recent ice age began over 2 million years ago, during which time there have been many warmer interglacial periods. Throughout the Earth's history, ice ages have been relatively infrequent.
3 The effects of an ice age include changes to landscape features, to drainage systems and to plant and animal life.
4 Ice ages also cause changes to the relative sea level because of the amount of water trapped in the ice and because the Earth's crust is depressed under the weight of ice.
5 At the margins of glaciated regions, there are periglacial conditions. The landform features, climate and vegetation typical of such areas extended over wide areas during the last glacial advance.
6 Glaciers are systems of flowing ice that form in areas where more snow accumulates than melts.
7 A glacier erodes the land surface, it then transports and deposits the eroded material.
8 Glaciers can be classified as valley glaciers - in mountainous regions, or as continental glaciers (or ice sheets) covering much bigger areas.

key terms

Basal sliding (or **basal slip**) - the process by which a glacier moves over the underlying ground surface. The partial melting of the ice under pressure lubricates the process.
Continental glacier - a large scale ice sheet.
Corrasion (or **abrasion**) - the erosion caused

when rocks and other fragments frozen in glacier ice grind against the underlying land surface.
Crevasse - a crack in a glacier, most common where the ice is moving over uneven ground or down a steep slope.
Drift - a general term for all material deposited

by glaciers and ice sheets, including till and glaciofluvial deposits. The UK Geological Survey defines the term more broadly and includes non-glacial deposits such as peat and blown sand.

Eustatic change - the rise and fall in sea level caused when water is 'locked' into ice sheets during an ice age, or is released when the ice melts.

Freeze thaw - a mechanical form of weathering that occurs when water seeps into cracks and joints of rock. When the water freezes it expands and shatters or loosens the rock. (The process is also called 'frost shattering' and 'cryofracture' and, in American books, 'ice or frost wedging').

Glacier (or **valley glacier**) - a river of ice, confined within a valley. It is formed from a mass of ice that is thick enough to become 'plastic' and flow downhill.

Glaciofluvial - the processes and landforms related to the action of glacial meltwater (sometimes also called fluvioglacial or fluvio-glacial processes).

Ice age - a period in the Earth's history when average temperatures fall and ice sheets expand to cover present day temperate latitudes. During an ice age there are periods of cold conditions interspersed by warmer interglacial periods.

Isostatic change - the depression of the Earth's crust caused by the weight of ice, and the rise or 'rebounding' when the ice melts.

Mass balance (or **glacial budget**) - the balance between input (accumulation of snow) and output (ablation - melting and evaporation) in a glacier system. If the input equals the output, the mass of the ice remains constant and the glacier front (or **snout**) remains stationary. If the input exceeds the output, the glacier advances; if input is less than output, the glacier retreats.

Moraine - landforms made from till. The term is also used to describe the accumulations of till carried on a glacier surface (lateral and medial moraine).

Névé (or **firn**) - compacted, granular snow - an intermediate stage between snow flakes and glacial ice. (Névé is the French word, firn is German.)

Periglacial - the climate and landscape features typically found at the margin of ice sheets.

Pleistocene - a period within the Quaternary geological era. It started over 2 million years ago and ended approximately 10,000 years ago.

Till - unsorted material that is deposited by melting ice. It consists of rock fragments in a mixture of finer materials. The term boulder clay is also used but is now generally considered outdated.

Zone of ablation - the lower part of a glacier system where ice melts (and evaporates) faster than it is replaced.

Zone of accumulation - the upper part of a glacier system where snow collects faster than it melts (or evaporates).

Unit 10.2 Glacial landforms

key questions

1 What landscape features are formed by glacial erosion?
2 What landscape features are formed by glacial deposition?
3 How has the most recent ice age affected Britain and North America?

1. What landscape features are formed by glacial erosion?

The features formed by glacial erosion are most clearly seen in upland regions. In Britain, glacial erosion has had a major impact on the mountain landscapes of North Wales, the Lake District and the Scottish Highlands. The effect of ice in these areas has been to deepen and straighten valleys, and to transform rounded mountain tops into sharp ridges.

Although most of lowland Britain north of the Thames has also been eroded by moving ice, the features formed are now largely masked by glacial deposits.

Figure 10.14 Glaciated features in an upland region

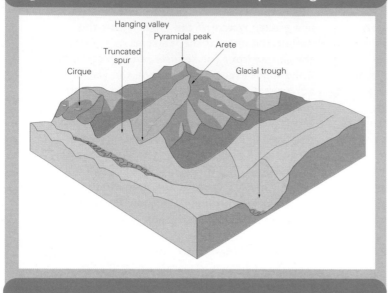

Labels: Hanging valley, Pyramidal peak, Truncated spur, Arete, Cirque, Glacial trough

Cirque

A cirque is called a 'cwm' in Wales and a 'corrie' in Scotland. It is a deep, armchair shaped basin with a steep backwall (see figure 10.15). It might contain a small glacier, or a lake - called a 'tarn' in the Lake District. Cirques are found most often on the north and east side of mountains (in the northern hemisphere). They are thought to originate as hollows where snow accumulates. Freeze thaw action deepens the hollow and allows more snow to accumulate. The process is called 'nivation'. As the volume of snow increases, it turns into névé and, when it reaches a critical weight, it slides in a rotational movement. This causes more deepening and, when the ice melts, the lip of the cirque can create a natural dam, so causing a small lake to form.

Above the permanent snowline, large cirques become zones of accumulation for glaciers. Typically a large crevasse (or bergschrund) forms where the moving ice shears away from the backwall of the cirque.

Aretes and pyramidal peaks

When two or more cirques form on either side of a ridge, the result can be a sharp edge - or arete. Striding Edge in the Lake District is a well known

example in England. If large cirques form on all sides of a mountain, the result can be a pyramidal peak or 'horn' in German. The Matterhorn is a famous example.

Glacial troughs

These are the U-shaped valleys typical of glaciated uplands. They are formed by valley glaciers which deepen and straighten the pre-existing river valleys. Typically they have very steep sides and flat bottoms. The Yosemite Valley in California is a spectacular example (see figure 10.16).

Sometimes, after a valley glacier melts, moraine that has been deposited blocks the valley and creates a **ribbon lake**. Buttermere in the Lake District was formed in this way. In coastal regions, glacial troughs might flood and form a **fiord**. These are found in western Norway, and also in South Island New Zealand, southern Chile, British Columbia and North West Scotland. Because glaciers can erode below sea level, some fiords are up to 1,000 metres deep.

Valley glaciers cut off the ends of the interlocking spurs found in river valleys and form **truncated spurs**. Side valleys are often not eroded as deeply as the main trough and are left as **hanging valleys**. Sometimes these create waterfalls where tributary rivers drop down to the lower valley floor.

Figure 10.15 Cirque de Gavarnie, Pyrenees, France

The backwall of this large cirque is over 1,200 metres high.

Roche moutonnée and crag and tail

A roche moutonnée is a polished outcrop of bedrock, smooth on one side and jagged on the other. The jagged downslope side is believed to be the result of freeze thaw action under the glacier. The feature is formed when a glacier scrapes over resistant rock, often causing striations. Partial melting occurs due to the increased pressure caused when the ice is forced over an outcrop, and the water then refreezes in cracks. The loosened rock fragments are removed by 'plucking' as the glacier ice freezes onto them. Roche moutonnée means rock sheep in French, possibly because the feature resembles a sheep - though there is some dispute over the precise origin of the term.

Although many roche moutonnée are small, there are some large examples. Lambert Dome in Yosemite, for example, is 200 metres high. In the north west of the Scottish Highlands, large groups of roche moutonnee occur, interspersed with small water filled basins. The landscape of bare rock hillocks and small lakes is called 'cnoc (or knock) and lochan'.

When a glacier's flow is blocked by an outcrop of very resistant rock, the ice is forced round or over the obstruction. The outcrop protects the downslope from erosion, leaving a 'tail' of original rock or deposited moraine. In the British Isles the best known example of a crag and tail is in Edinburgh. The castle is built on a crag formed from a volcanic plug and the Royal Mile is the street running down the tail.

Figure 10.16 Yosemite Valley, California

This is a spectacular example of a glacial trough. The valley has been deepened and straightened by a large glacier. On the right hand wall of the main valley there is a waterfall flowing from a hanging valley.

Figure 10.17 Roche moutonnée, Duddon Valley, Cumbria

The ice was moving from right to left in this photograph.

Figure 10.18 Glacially smoothed and striated rock, Glen Brittle, Skye

The ice was moving from left to right in this photograph.

2. What landscape features are formed by glacial deposition?

Depositional features are widespread in lowland regions of Britain north of the Thames. They are also found in upland glaciated valleys.

As described in unit 10.1, the term drift refers to till and **glaciofluvial** material that has been deposited by glaciers and ice sheets. Till is material dumped by the ice. Glaciofluvial deposits are sorted and stratified by meltwater, either on or under the glacier, or beyond the ice margin. The particles are generally smoother and rounder than the particles in till. This is because they have been subject to the action of fast running water and attrition within the glacial streams.

Figure 10.19 Glaciated features in a lowland region

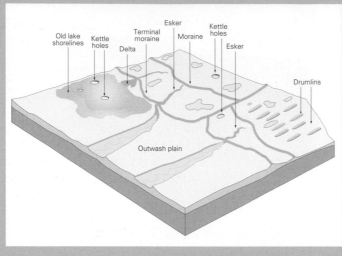

Till is generally unsorted and unstratified and the particles vary in size from finely ground rock flour to large boulders. Often, the long axes of the particles are orientated in the direction of glacier flow. Till can be classified by origin as 'lodgement till', ie subglacial material deposited underneath the moving ice, or 'ablation till', ie material deposited as the ice melts.

Moraine

This is a deposit of till. It might be in the form of a ground layer ('ground moraine') or in the form of a ridge. Lateral and medial moraines are ridges parallel to the flow of ice. (The terms lateral and medial moraine are also used to describe lines of glacial debris being carried on the surface of a glacier.) Terminal moraines are ridges roughly at a right angle to the ice flow (see figure 10.19). They are formed at the point of maximum advance when the ice front is stationary for some time, allowing a build up of material. Recessional moraines are similar to terminal moraines except that they form during a pause in a period of glacial retreat.

Typically, terminal and recessional moraines are steeper on their up-slope, ice contact side because that is the side into which the glacier has been pushing. The best known example in England is the

Cromer Ridge in Norfolk, 90 metres high and 8 kilometres long. Continental moraines can be much larger, the Bloomington Moraine in Illinois is more than 300 km long.

Drumlins are egg shaped mounds formed under the moving ice, orientated in the direction of ice flow. They have a streamlined shape with the upstream end generally being blunter than the downslope end. Sometimes they are 100 metres high and often they are found in 'swarms' or 'drumlin fields'. There are many examples in the north eastern United States, in central Ireland and in northern England. Swarms occur to the east of the Lake District in the Eden Valley, and further south in the Ribble Valley. The landscape in these areas is sometimes described as 'basket of eggs' topography.

The way that drumlins are formed is not clear. It is possible that they are produced when lodgement till is deposited from the underside or base of glaciers in the zone of ablation. These deposits are then shaped as the glacier, containing embedded till, moves over them. A slightly different view is that drumlins form when glaciers or ice sheets re-advance over ground moraine that has previously been deposited. The material is reshaped when the re-advancing ice passes over.

Outwash plain

Large amounts of water flow out from glaciers and ice

Figure 10.20 Jokulsarlon, Iceland

The dark line of eroded debris on the glacier (from the centre distance to the front left is a medial moraine. As the ice moves forwards, the debris is deposited at the front of the glacier. If the glacier melted completely, the material would form a ridge.

sheets in summer. Gravel, sand and silt are carried by the water and are redeposited at the margins of the ice. This glaciofluvial material is stratified and sorted, the coarsest material is deposited first, the finest material is transported furthest. Sometimes the material is laid down on top of existing ground moraine.

Outwash plains are characterised by 'braided' stream channels in a landscape of alluvial deposits. The term braiding is used because the streams contain an interconnected network of channels just like the strands of a braid. In between the channels there are shifting ridges of sediment. Braided channels develop in streams which have an irregular annual regime. In late spring and summer the meltwater transports large amounts of debris. But, during colder months, the stream flow might stop completely or become a trickle and only small amounts of sediment are moved. When streams are supplied with more sediment than they can carry, they deposit the excess material on the channel floor as sand or gravel bars. This deposition is what causes the stream to split into separate channels when discharge falls.

Where lakes form at the edge of the ice, sediment is deposited in layers or 'varves'. These typically are a mix of coarser fragments deposited in summer when the volume of meltwater is greatest, and finer layers of silt or clay deposited during winter when material in suspension settles on the lake bed.

On outwash plains there are often **erratics**, boulders or rocks brought from elsewhere by the ice. There might also be **kettle holes**, small depressions created when large blocks of ice break off the glacier and are partly submerged in outwash material. When the ice melts, the hollow often fills with water to form a pond or small lake.

Kames are irregular mounds of sand and gravel formed from the alluvial fans created by glacial streams. They might be on the edge of a valley glacier or at the snout. The fan collapses when the ice melts, leaving the mound behind. A 'kame terrace' is a flat topped ridge that is formed of alluvial material deposited along the edge of a valley glacier, between the ice and the valley slope. It is formed by meltwater streams that flow along the side of the ice.

Eskers are narrow, sinuous ridges of coarse sands and gravels deposited by glacial streams. Some debate exists over the formation of eskers. They might be formed in subglacial channels, or they might be formed by material dumped where streams emerge from ice sheets at times of rapid glacial retreat (ie, like an elongated alluvial fan).

Outwash features such as eskers, kames and kettle holes are found in many locations including the Fylde, Lancashire; the Tay Valley, eastern Scotland; County Meath, Ireland; and in both Sweden and Finland.

Activity — Glacial deposition

Figure 10.21
Esker, Tayside

Figure 10.22
Drumlin field,
Ribble Valley,
Lancashire

Figure 10.23
Hummocky
moraine,
Langdale,
Cumbria

Questions

1 Describe the features shown in figures 10.21, 10.22 and 10.23.
2 Briefly explain how the features were formed.

3. How has the most recent ice age affected Britain and North America?

British Isles

Since the start of the most recent, Pleistocene ice age over two million years ago, there have been many ice advances and retreats. The traditional view, based on evidence from glacial deposits, was that there were four such advances. However, new studies show that there have been a far higher number of 'glacials' (ie, ice advances) and 'interglacials' (ie, ice retreats) than previously thought. This research is based on fossil evidence from ocean floors. By looking at the relative proportions of two oxygen isotopes contained in the fossils, it is now possible to calculate the proportion of oceanic water that was frozen in ice caps at different times in the past. This evidence shows that possibly as many as thirty interglacials have occurred during the Pleistocene period.

At its greatest extent, ice covered most of the British Isles as far south as the Thames Valley. The most recent advance, known as the Loch Lomond, was 11,000 years ago (see figure 10.24).

Figure 10.24 Glaciation in the British Isles

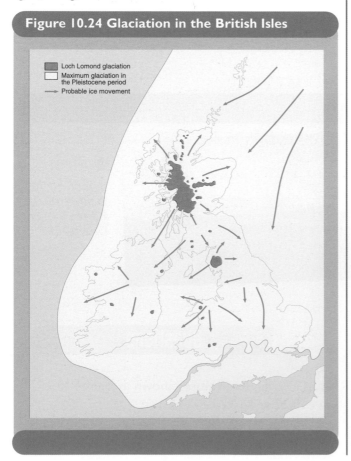

Loch Lomond glaciation
Maximum glaciation in the Pleistocene period
Probable ice movement

During the last glacial period, ice caps formed over the highland regions of the UK, and the Scandinavian ice sheet extended westward across the North Sea. As described in unit 10.1, the weight of ice depressed land in northern Britain. Since the ice melted, the crust has rebounded. This isostatic readjustment is causing parts of Scotland to rise by 3 mm per year. The result has been a succession of raised beaches and fossil cliff lines. In southern Britain, the rebound has caused the crust to tilt the opposite way. This has created the drowned estuaries (rias) of south west England. The Thames estuary is still sinking.

Most of the mountains of Britain exhibit some features associated with glacial erosion. Pyramidal peaks, aretes and glacial troughs are found in North Wales, the Lake District and the Highlands of Scotland. However, not all upland areas exhibit the 'classic' glaciated features, mainly because of local geological factors. For example, the horizontally bedded limestone areas of the northern Pennines do not contain sharp ridges or pointed peaks, although the valleys are clearly glaciated.

Depositional features are found throughout Britain but are most common in lowland areas. Drift covers much of East Anglia and Eastern England with many examples of moraine and outwash material. South of a line from the Thames to the Severn estuary, periglacial conditions existed during the last major ice advance. The frozen ground allowed surface drainage patterns to develop on the otherwise permeable limestone and chalk of the Cotswolds and Downs. Solifluction occurred on the slopes and changed their profiles. When warmer conditions returned, much of the drainage went underground, leaving behind dry valleys and gorges (see unit 10.4).

Retreating ice sheets have had an important influence on drainage patterns. When ice sheets melt, massive volumes of water are released. The streams and rivers that flow out carry big loads of sediment - so making them very efficient agents of erosion. They sometimes create **meltwater channels**. These might be marginal channels formed along the front of an ice sheet ('urstromtaler' in Germany) or subglacial channels which are cut by meltwater underneath an ice sheet.

Spillways (or overspill channels) are formed when water in 'pro-glacial' lakes (ie, water that is dammed by the ice) drains over watersheds. In the Midlands, it is believed that a large lake ('Lake Lapworth') was formed as the last ice sheets retreated. Rivers flowing eastwards from Wales were blocked by ice from draining northwards. A spillway formed to the south, cutting the

Figure 10.25 Glaciation in North America

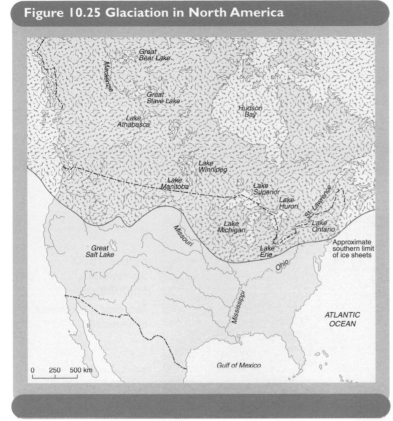

melted, these rivers continued to drain southwards.

The Great Lakes formed along the ice margin around 16,000 years ago. At first they drained southwards but, as the ice retreated, they formed new outlets. The Hudson-Mohawk Gap in New York State was eroded. Then, as the ice receded, the present drainage pattern towards the St Lawrence became established. As water flowed from Lake Erie to Lake Ontario, it flowed over the Niagara escarpment. The resistant limestone of the escarpment overlies weak shales which are quickly eroded. The Niagara Falls are retreating at a rate of 1.3 metres per year and have eroded a gorge 11 kilometres long (see figure 10.26).

To the west of the Great Lakes, an even bigger lake was formed against the ice margin. Its remnants include the present Lakes Winnipeg and Manitoba. Deposits on the old lake bed now form the fertile, stone free, soils of the wheat belt in North Dakota, Minnesota and Manitoba.

In the north western states of the USA, other large lakes formed in the basins between mountain ranges. New drainage channels were scoured and the present, flat, dried up lake beds were created. 'Lake

Ironbridge Gorge through which the River Severn now flows. Previously, this river had flowed northwards towards what is now the Dee estuary.

North America

Much of North America, as far south as the Ohio and Missouri Rivers, was covered by ice sheets 20,000 years ago. In parts of central Canada, soil and weathered rock to a depth of 15 - 25 metres were eroded and removed by ice. Today a patchwork of lakes and irregular drainage exists across the scoured landscape. The eroded material was redeposited as till or outwash material across the Midwest from Ohio to Montana.

Isostatic rebound around Hudson Bay has already been 300 metres and it is estimated that the land will rise another 80 metres before it reaches its preglacial level. The general rise in sea level caused by ice sheet melting has caused parts of the Atlantic shoreline to retreat by between 100 and 200 km.

Before the glaciation, much of the Midwest had drained northwards towards Hudson Bay or north eastwards towards the St Lawrence estuary. The ice sheets diverted drainage and caused a series of lakes to form along their southern margin. The present courses of the Ohio and Missouri Rivers developed as meltwater channels at this time. When the ice

Figure 10.26 Niagara Falls, US/Canada border

The Niagara Falls and gorge have formed since the last ice sheets melted and allowed drainage to revert northeastwards towards the St Lawrence.

Bonneville' was, at one time 300 metres deep and 50,000 sq km in extent. Its old shoreline, terraces and deltas are now high and dry. The remnants of the lake now form the Great Salt Lake in Utah.

In the periglacial conditions to the south of the ice sheets, wind blown deposits of fine glacial material called loess were created. These now form rich soils across much of the Midwest. Coarser sand deposits formed large dunes in western Nebraska. These are now largely stabilised by a covering of grass.

 Activity | **Glaciated uplands**

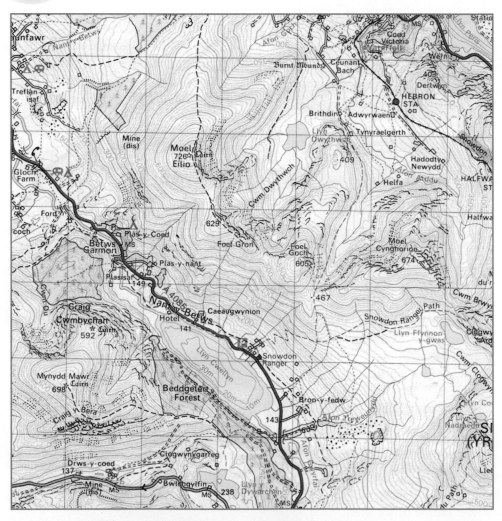

**Figure 10.27
Snowdonia
1:50000 scale**

This area is northwest of Snowdon.

 Questions

1 Describe the landscape shown in the map extract
2 Outline the glacial processes that have helped form this landscape.

unit summary

1 Landscape features formed by glacial erosion (eg, cirques, aretes, pyramidal peaks, glacial troughs, hanging valleys) are most commonly found in mountainous regions.
2 The features formed by glacial deposition (eg, moraines, drumlins, outwash plains, kames, eskers) are most commonly found in lowland regions.
3 The landscapes of many present day temperate regions, including much of Britain and North America, have been greatly modified by glacial processes.

key terms

Arete - narrow ridge between cirques.

Bergschrund - a crevasse between the moving ice of a glacier and the ice attached to the solid rock backwall.

Cirque (or **corrie** in Scotland or **cwm** in Wales) - an upland hollow with steep back and side walls.

Crag and tail - a resistant outcrop that has protected downslope material from glacial erosion.

Drumlin - a smooth, streamlined hillock. Collectively drumlins are called a 'swarm' or 'field'. The term 'basket of eggs' is sometimes used to describe such a landscape.

Esker - a narrow ridge formed from glaciofluvial deposits.

Fiord - a flooded glacial valley, normally on a coastline.

Glacial trough - a U-shaped valley formed by a glacier.

Hanging valley - a tributary valley left high above a main glacial trough.

Kame - a glaciofluvial deposit formed from an alluvial fan.

Kettle hole - a depression, often flooded, caused when a large block of ice detaches from a retreating glacier.

Meltwater channel - a valley created by water from melting glaciers or ice sheets. They include 'marginal channels' formed along the front of ice sheets. These are called 'urstromtaler' in Germany and are broad and fairly shallow. Subglacial channels are cut by meltwater underneath a glacier or ice sheet.

Moraine - a landform made from till. This might be a ridge formed at the end of a glacier (terminal or recessional moraine) or parallel with the glacier (lateral and medial moraine), or the moraine might be in the form of a sheet (ground moraine). The terms lateral and medial moraine are also used to describe the ridge like accumulations of till carried on top of a glacier's surface.

Outwash plain - the area beyond an ice sheet where glaciofluvial material is deposited.

Pyramidal peak (or **horn**) - a sharply pointed peak with cirques on all its sides.

Roche moutonnée - a solid rock mound polished on one side and jagged on the other.

Spillway (or **overflow channel**) - a valley that is often deep and steep sided that has been carved by the overflow of an ice-dammed lake.

Truncated spur - previously interlocking spurs cut off by a valley glacier.

Varve - a layer of deposits that build up annually on glacial lake beds.

Unit 10.3 Glaciation and human activity

key questions

1 Why is hydroelectric power generated in glaciated uplands?
2 Why are summer and winter tourists attracted to glaciated uplands?
3 Why are snow avalanches hazardous?

1. Why is hydroelectric power generated in glaciated uplands?

Hydroelectric power (HEP) is the most widely used renewable form of energy (see unit 4.2). Although globally it accounts for only 6 percent of all electricity generated, in some countries it provides much more. Norway, for example, produces 96 percent of its electricity from HEP.

The scale of HEP schemes varies enormously. In some Alpine villages, small HEP generators supply the power for a single house or hotel. At the other extreme, large HEP stations feed directly into the UK national grid.

The advantage of HEP is that running costs are very low and power is instantly available. The main disadvantages are that initial building costs are high, the visual impact might damage the scenic value of a landscape, and the demand for energy is often some distance away. Some ecological damage is also caused if the migratory routes of fish, such as salmon, are blocked. Fish ladders are sometimes built to avoid this problem. Also, when water passes through HEP schemes, the effect of the vertical drop can be to increase the amount of dissolved oxygen and nitrogen in the water. This can be harmful to fish, causing gas bubble disease.

HEP comes from the conversion of potential energy, in water stored behind a dam, into kinetic energy from water moving down a slope. The moving water drives turbines which generate electricity. The kinetic energy depends on the volume of water and speed of flow (together known as the **head** of water). HEP can be generated with either a small volume and high velocity, or large volume and low velocity of water. Clearly, most power can be obtained if the volume and velocity are both high.

HEP in Britain is mostly generated in the glaciated uplands of North Wales, Cumbria and the Scottish Highlands. This is for two main reasons. Firstly, mountain areas receive the highest rainfall in Britain. For a successful scheme to operate there must be a reliable supply of running water - otherwise the turbines will not turn. Secondly, the physical relief is favourable. Glacial troughs, steep stream gradients, hanging valleys and lakes provide the ideal conditions. If natural lakes do not occur, glaciated valleys are relatively cheap to dam because they tend to be narrow and steep sided.

Although technology is being developed to transmit electricity longer distances, the transmission costs are high. An important disadvantage of HEP in Britain, as in most other countries, is that few cities and industrial centres are located in or near mountainous regions.

Scotland: Kinlochleven

Near Fort William, in the Western Highlands, the small settlement of Kinlochleven provides an example of how HEP is used for industrial production. The local climate and the glaciated mountain features were the key factors in choosing this location.

In the late nineteenth century, a new process of refining aluminium was discovered that required large amounts of electricity. The British Aluminium Company was set up in 1894 and it started looking for sites where HEP could be generated relatively cheaply. Kinlochleven was chosen for several reasons. The local annual average precipitation of 2,000 mm per year ensures that sufficient water is nearly always available. Above the settlement, to the east, the Blackwater Valley provided a good site for a dam. It is a long valley with a large catchment area.

By 1909 the dam had been completed and a reservoir 12 km long was ready to supply water to the turbines. At the time, it was the biggest hydroelectric scheme in Europe. Every minute, 675,000 litres of water is fed through the system. The water passes through pipes (called 'penstocks') to the HEP plant which is 6 km away. The vertical drop of 300 metres into the glacial trough of Loch Leven gives sufficient head to generate 24 MW of electricity.

Today the plant is owned by Alcan, a Canadian transnational company. Raw bauxite, mainly from Ghana, is first converted into alumina and then transported to Lynemouth in Northumberland. From there it is carried by train to the Kinlochleven smelter. The refined aluminium ingots are taken away by road transport. Unfortunately for Kinlochleven, the plant is old and relatively small - with an annual capacity of just 8,000 tonnes. This compares with the 130,000 tonne capacity at Lynemouth (in a coal powered plant) and the 38,000 tonne output at the more modern (HEP) Alcan plant in nearby Lochaber (Fort William). Even these are small compared with the 272,000 tonne annual output at the world's biggest HEP powered plant at Kitimat, British Columbia. In Canada, Alcan's total capacity is 1.1 million tonnes - all hydroelectric power driven. The company is currently building a new 375,000 tonne smelter at Alma in Quebec. By comparison, the old Kinlochleven smelter is inefficient and nearing the end of its economic life. But in the future, even when the smelter closes, it is likely that the HEP plant will continue to operate, feeding electricity into the national grid.

Cumbria: Glenridding

The village of Glenridding is near Lake Ullswater in the Lake District. A small HEP scheme supplies enough power for the village and also feeds into the national grid. High above the village, water from a stream is extracted at a weir beside an old lead mine. The water runs underground in plastic piping to turbines housed in the old mine's power house. Unobtrusive and clean, the scheme was partly financed by a 1992 government initiative to subsidise alternatives to fossil fuels.

Figure 10.28 The turbines at Kinlochleven

In the early 1900s, the Kinlochleven hydroelectric plant was the biggest in Europe.

Figure 10.29 The intake at the Glenridding HEP scheme

Water is piped from this point to a turbine lower down the valley.

Similar small scale power generation is found throughout Norway and Sweden, and in the Alps. Their relatively low initial costs, and almost zero running costs, make such schemes very attractive to communities wherever the physical conditions are suitable and there is reliable rainfall.

The disadvantage of schemes like Glenridding which do not operate with a storage reservoir are that, in exceptionally dry periods, there might be no power. This is not a problem for Glenridding because of the link to the national grid but, in other locations, it could be more serious. Another problem arises if there is too much water. Summer thunderstorms are normal events in many mountain regions. They cause large amounts of sediment to be carried down in the streams. In the Alps, rock flour (finely ground glacial material) in suspension can make the water milky after heavy rain. This can quickly destroy the turbine blades if the scheme's filters become clogged with debris. A reservoir or lake is therefore an advantage because it acts as a settling tank for sediment before the water is taken into the HEP pipes.

Activity | **HEP in a glaciated upland area, Dinorwig, North Wales**

The Dinorwig pumped storage power station near Llanberis in North Wales is the largest in Europe. It can provide 1320 MW of electricity to the national grid within 12 seconds. This is extremely useful because its turbines can be switched on to meet sudden surges in demand, or if another power station breaks down. It was opened in 1984 at a cost of £450 million.

A pumped storage HEP station requires two reservoirs, one that is high above the turbines and one that is below. At Dinorwig the six turbines are housed underground in an excavated cavern that is 180 metres long and 60 metres high. The scheme is designed so that, during the daytime, the turbines can supply electricity to the national grid, but at night (when demand for electricity is low) power from the national grid is used to pump water back to the top reservoir. In this way there is always sufficient water to meet demand.

The glaciated landscape of Snowdonia is ideal for HEP generation. At Dinorwig, two existing lakes, with a big vertical distance between them, are used. In addition, there is sufficient rainfall (annual average: 2,200 mm) in the area to keep the reservoirs topped up. The lower reservoir, Llyn Peris, is a ribbon lake in a glacial trough. The upper reservoir is an enlarged natural lake, Marchlyn Mawr. It is approximately 3 km from the turbines with a vertical drop of 557 metres. This provides the head of water to generate the electricity. At maximum output, the water flows down the hydraulic tunnels at a rate of 92,400 gallons per second.

Because the area is part of the Snowdonia National Park, great care was taken to reduce the scheme's visual impact. The enlarged upper reservoir and a short access road to the power station cavern are the only visible features. The electricity transmission cables are carried underground for nearly 10 km to a point where they join the national grid.

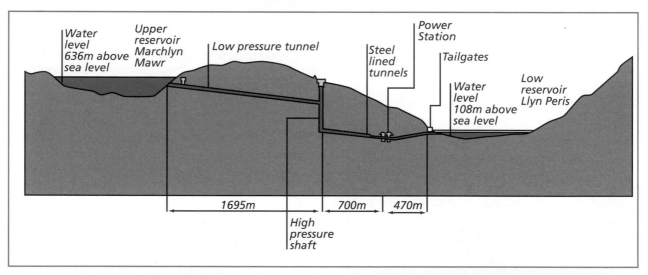

▲ **Figure 10.30 Dinorwig HEP scheme**

Questions

1 Explain why two reservoirs are used at Dinorwig rather than one.
2 What natural features make the Dinorwig site suitable for HEP generation?
3 Suggest reasons why more HEP stations are not built in Britain.

2. Why are summer and winter tourists attracted to glaciated uplands?

Throughout Europe and North America, glaciated mountain regions have become popular destinations for tourists in both summer and winter. The high scenic value of the Lake District and Snowdonia has been recognised by giving them protected status as National Parks. In the United States, Yosemite was one of the first areas to be similarly protected.

Rising average incomes and longer holidays mean that people have more leisure time and this has boosted the tourist industry. But, in some places, the attraction of the mountain areas has created problems of overcrowding and congestion. The peace and solitude that many seek has disappeared. For instance, in the USA, limits to the numbers allowed to enter Yosemite mean that traffic queues sometimes develop on the roads leading in. In the Lake District, small towns such as Ambleside become busy and noisy on summer weekends and, increasingly, at other times during the year.

In mainland Europe, some Alpine resorts developed in the nineteenth century as centres for convalescence. It was believed that the clean, cold air was healthy, and particularly good for TB sufferers. Large hotels and clinics were built to accommodate people fleeing from the polluted air of the cities. Today, summer tourists are attracted by the mountain views, the fresh air and the feeling of being close to nature. The more active visitors climb mountains, ride mountain bikes, sail, canoe or simply go walking. Mountain areas are often rich in flora and fauna which many people enjoy. In winter, the scenic attractions are just as strong, with snow adding the extra possibility of skiing or snowboarding.

Many resorts have deliberately promoted summer activities as a means of filling the hotels and apartment blocks built for the short, 3 or 4 month, ski season. In Scotland, the changeable maritime climate means that snow cannot be guaranteed. This has made it even more important for centres such as Aviemore to diversify out of purely winter based tourism.

Alpine resorts

In the French Alps, government regional policy has promoted tourism as a replacement for the declining farming and forestry industries. Since the 1960s, a number of purpose built ski resorts have been built. In order to ensure good snow conditions, most have been located above 1,600 metres on north facing slopes. Examples such as La Plagne, Les Deux Alpes and Tignes are self contained resorts with their own shops, restaurants and hotel complexes. Ski lifts operate from the resorts and people are able to ski back to their hotels and apartments.

By the 1990s, there were 500,000 bed spaces in the new French resorts. Such purpose built 'ski stations' have been much criticised. They are often ugly and obtrusive with concrete apartment blocks rising above the tree line, clearly visible from great distances. Likewise, ski lifts have completely changed the character of peaceful Alpine meadows. The older villages on the lower slopes and in the valleys have largely been bypassed by the tourist boom. The main beneficiaries have been the tour companies and property developers who financed the resorts.

In the eastern Alps, particularly in Austria, a different model of winter tourism has been developed. It is based in the villages, on a smaller scale, and providing facilities that locals can also use. Visitors stay in family run hotels or guest houses rather than in apartment blocks. The main drawback of this type of development is that the lower altitude, typically 1,000 to 1,500 metres, means that snow is less reliable and the season is shorter than in the higher French resorts.

As the numbers of winter tourists rise in the Alps, there are concerns over their environmental impact. In France alone, there are 50 million ski trips made by visitors each year. Trees have to be cleared to build resorts and make new ski runs. This deforestation increases both soil erosion and avalanche risk. The fragile ecosystems high on mountains often do not recover from intensive skiing, especially at the end of the season when the snow is thin.

The large number of people who drive to the resorts has increased the level of air pollution and acid rain. Some estimates suggest that 60 percent of the trees in Alpine areas are suffering from this rising acidity.

Whether tourism has had an overall positive or negative impact on Alpine areas is a matter of judgment. To some extent it depends on the perspective of the person making that judgment. For instance, in the French Alps, the sons and daughters of local farmers who now work as ski instructors or as restaurant staff might feel that tourism has given them employment and allowed them to stay in their home region. However, for many older local people the changes have not been welcome. The character of their mountains has been completely changed. Noise, weekend traffic jams and ugly buildings have spoilt the quiet mountain pastures and traditional way of life.

Activity Alpine skiing

Figure 10.31 Courcheval, French Alps

Questions

1 What features in Alpine areas attract tourists?
2 How does tourism affect mountain areas?

3. Why are snow avalanches hazardous?

Increased winter tourism has made the hazard posed by snow avalanches more severe. Ski resorts are faced with the dilemma of wishing to attract more people to snowy, mountain areas yet, at the same time, needing to reduce avalanche danger.

An avalanche is a rapid movement of snow, ice and sometimes rock down a slope. It occurs when the 'snowpack', ie the lying snow, becomes unstable. The causes can be subdivided into long term (background) and short term (trigger) factors.

The background factors include:
• the angle of slope (at angles less than 20-25 degrees the snow is generally stable; between 25 and 60 degrees the snow is unstable; above 60 degrees the slope is too steep for large depths of snow to accumulate)

• the type of slope - convex slopes are more prone to avalanche than concave slopes
• aspect - north facing slopes (in the northern hemisphere) are most prone to avalanches because the snow accumulates to a greater depth, and it tends to remain frozen rather than melting and refreezing on to the underlying layer. Lee slopes receive a bigger build up of snow than windward slopes - so are more likely to avalanche.
• the depth of snow (the deeper the snow, the less stable it is)
• the number of layers of older compacted snow that lie on each other
• the amount of forest cover (trees trap the snow and slow any downslope movement)
• the time of day, and month of year (most fatal accidents occur between noon and 2pm - when

temperatures are highest, and in January, February and March - when there is most snow).

The trigger factors include:

- a heavy fall of wet snow, particularly on a compacted or icy surface
- wind - this causes the top layers to form slabs which become unstable
- a sudden rise in temperature that causes snow to melt and percolate between layers, acting as a lubricant
- vibration from a sudden noise, a falling rock or passing skier. According to official Canadian statistics collected between 1984 and 1996, nearly 90 percent of fatal avalanches were triggered by human activity (walking, skiing or snowmobiling).

Loose or **powder avalanches** start at a single point. They are sometimes partly airborne and tend to be very fast - up to 70 metres per second. They can be dangerous because they are preceded by a blast of air. In very extreme cases this blast can be strong enough to shatter wooden buildings.

Slab avalanches tend to be bigger and they cause most avalanche fatalities in ski areas. They occur when a top layer of snow becomes detached and slides downwards.

Both types of avalanche can be either wet or dry depending on the amount of water absorbed in the snow. Although wet avalanches are more destructive (because of their greater mass), dry avalanches cause more fatal accidents because skiers are more likely to venture out in dry rather than wet snow conditions.

Avalanche hazards

Snow avalanches are hazardous to people, buildings and communications. Clearly they pose the greatest danger in high risk areas - on snowy mountain slopes in winter. During February 1999, the worst avalanches for several decades affected the Alps. In just one incident, at Galtur in Austria, 32 people died when an avalanche hit hotels and apartments in the village. Over two metres of wet snow had fallen in the previous 48 hours, making the upper slopes completely unstable.

Avalanches are natural events that have always occurred, but it is the growth of winter tourism that has increased the hazard. Not only are there more people in the danger zones, the clearing of trees to form vertical ski runs down the slopes has made avalanches more likely.

Avalanche protection comes from better warning systems and improved preparation. Throughout the Alps in winter, snow conditions are monitored and weather forecasts reported. At times of very high risk, for example during a sudden thaw, warnings are issued and ski runs are closed.

Hazard mapping is used to plan new installations and to warn where better protection might be needed. Communication links such as road and rail are put in tunnels or avalanche shelters. Measures to control avalanches include mounds of earth and concrete embankments to deflect the force from buildings or ski lift gantries (see figure 10.32). At the top of vulnerable slopes, metal and wooden fences are built to hold back the snow, and trees are planted for the same reason. In many resorts, after heavy snowfalls, explosions are set off to trigger controlled avalanches before the slopes are open to tourists.

The greatest danger for individuals is when they ski off-piste, ie off the prepared ski runs. In most years, the majority of avalanche casualties occur under these circumstances. The issue of how people perceive risk is an important factor in managing avalanche hazards. Most skiers buy rescue and medical insurance and therefore, to some degree, they recognise that they are taking a risk. The degree to which individuals should be allowed to participate in challenging and hazardous activities is, however, a matter of judgment.

Figure 10.32 Avalanche protection

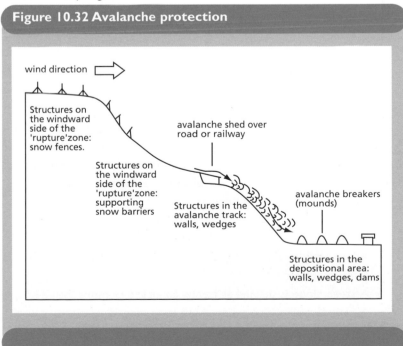

wind direction

Structures on the windward side of the 'rupture' zone: snow fences.

Structures on the windward side of the 'rupture' zone: supporting snow barriers

avalanche shed over road or railway

Structures in the avalanche track: walls, wedges

avalanche breakers (mounds)

Structures in the depositional area: walls, wedges, dams

 **Activity** **Snow avalanches**

▼ **Figure 10.33 Five point hazard scale now used in most Alpine ski and winter mountaineering areas:**

Degree of hazard	Avalanche probability
1 (low)	The snowpack is generally well bonded and stable. Only a few small natural avalanches possible. Virtually no restrictions on off-piste and back-country skiing and travel.
2 (moderate)	The snowpack is moderately well bonded. Triggering is possible with high additional loads. Virtually no hazard from natural avalanches. Generally favourable conditions. Routes should still be selected with care, especially on steep slopes.
3 (considerable)	The snowpack is moderately to weakly bonded on many steep slopes. Triggering is possible, sometimes even with low additional loads. In certain conditions, medium and occasionally large natural avalanches may occur. Traffic and individual buildings in hazardous areas are at risk in certain cases. Off-piste and back-country skiing and travel should only be carried out by experienced persons able to evaluate the avalanche hazard.
4 (high)	The snowpack is weakly bonded in most places. Triggering is probable even with low additional loads on many steep slopes. In some conditions, frequent medium or large natural avalanches are likely. Avalanches may be of large magnitude. In hazardous areas, closure of road and other transport is recommended in some circumstances. Off-piste and back-country skiing and travel should be restricted to low-angled slopes; areas at the bottom of slopes may also be hazardous.
5 (very high)	The snowpack is generally weakly bonded and largely unstable. Numerous large natural avalanches are likely, even on moderately steep terrain. Extensive safety measures (closures and evacuation) are necessary. No off-piste or back country skiing or travel should be undertaken.

Notes:

A high additional load might be a group of skiers or a piste machine A low additional load might be a lone skier or walker.

A steep slope is defined as having an incline of more than 30 degrees.

A natural avalanche is when there is no immediate human cause.

Report from Scottish Avalanche Information Service (SAIS):

AVALANCHE HAZARD 1500 HRS THU 01/01/98
Heavy snow showers overnight on a storm force S wind have deposited large amounts of deep, unstable, hard windslab. Sheltered gullies, hollows and slopes facing W through N to E, above 950 metres are particularly affected. The avalanche hazard for today is High (Category 4).

AVALANCHE HAZARD OUTLOOK FRI 02/01/98
A very brief thaw followed by more snow on a storm force SW wind will lead to further accumulations of windslab on top of the already weakly bonded snowpack. In sheltered gullies, hollows, and slopes facing N to E above 950 metres, avalanches will occur. The avalanche hazard will be High (Category 4).

Questions

1 Outline the factors that prompted the SAIS to issue a level 4 (High) avalanche warning on the 1st and 2nd January 1998.
2 What are the factors that have caused the growth in winter tourism to upland glaciated areas?
3 Discuss the means by which ski resorts can reduce the avalanche hazard.

unit summary

1 The physical features of glaciated upland areas provide ideal conditions for generating HEP. The main requirements are for a head of water and reliable precipitation. The disadvantages of generating HEP in these areas include remoteness from large cities and possible damage to the scenic beauty of the landscape.
2 In countries where people have high average incomes, increasing numbers of winter and summer tourists visit glaciated uplands. In addition to the spectacular views, fresh air and relatively unspoilt natural environment, more and more people participate in activity holidays such as skiing and mountain biking.
3 An important hazard facing people in glaciated upland areas is the danger of snow avalanches. Ski resorts are faced with the contradiction of wishing to attract more winter tourists and yet, at the same time, reduce the avalanche hazard.

key terms

Avalanche - a rapid downward movement of snow and ice; avalanches can be classified as **slab** or **loose/powder**.

Hydroelectric power - electricity that is generated when water drives a turbine.

Unit 10.4 Periglaciation

key questions

1 What processes are at work in periglacial areas?
2 What landforms are typical of periglacial areas?
3 How do people cope with periglacial conditions?

1. What processes are at work in periglacial areas?

Periglacial is a term used to describe the environment and processes at the margins of glaciers and ice sheets. It is also sometimes used in a wider sense to include any region where freeze thaw processes are dominant. Periglacial zones overlap, but do not completely coincide with, regions of **permafrost**. These are regions where the ground is frozen. They are sometimes subdivided into continuous and discontinuous zones. The definition of continuous permafrost is that the ground has been frozen for at least two years. Discontinuous permafrost is where zones of frozen ground occur within an area of unfrozen ground. In most permafrost areas, an active surface layer thaws in summer. This often becomes waterlogged because the frozen ground underneath is impermeable.

A mean annual temperature of -2°C marks the approximate southern limit of discontinuous permafrost in the northern hemisphere. In central Canada, this extends southwards to latitudes similar to those of England and Wales (see figure 10.34). In the discontinuous zone of permafrost, it is the south facing slopes and ground under lakes and streams that thaw completely in summer.

Periglacial conditions occur over approximately 10 percent of the world's land surface, mainly in northern North America and Eurasia (see figure 10.35). In addition, wherever mountains have a permanent or lengthy snow cover, periglacial conditions occur in a zone just below the snow line. Most of Antarctica is permanently covered by ice so it does not contain extensive periglacial areas. In the past, at the height of the last major ice advance, periglacial conditions existed in southern England and as far south as the Mediterranean.

Processes

Within periglacial areas, the distinctive processes of weathering and erosion include freeze thaw, solifluction and frost heave.

- **Freeze thaw** action is the dominant weathering process in periglacial environments. When water trickles into cracks and pores of rocks, and then freezes, it expands. This exerts so much pressure that rocks weaken and eventually shatter. Sandstone and granite typically break into grains and crystals, limestone into larger rock fragments. The greater the number of freeze thaw cycles, the greater the weathering. On steep rock faces, the weathered fragments fall and form **scree**. In Britain, large scree slopes occur in most glaciated upland areas, such as North Wales and the Lake District. Typically the angle of scree is approximately 30 degrees. There is some evidence that screes are largest and most common on south facing slopes (in the northern hemisphere). This is because the Sun's warmth causes some ice to melt during the daytime. If the water refreezes at night, and this occurs on a regular basis, the freeze thaw process becomes more frequent. On a north facing slope, there is less heat from the Sun, less melting and, therefore, less freeze thaw.
- **Solifluction** occurs on gentle slopes in periglacial regions. This process occurs when the active surface layer of soil thaws and moves slowly downslope. If the ground is saturated with meltwater, the process can take place on the gentlest of slopes (as little as 2 degrees).

Figure 10.34 Permafrost in Canada

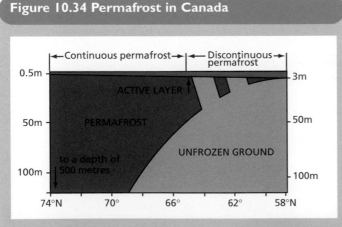

This diagram shows the approximate latitudes of continuous and discontinuous permafrost in Canada.

- **Frost heave** is a process caused by water freezing and expanding in the ground. Because different sized particles conduct and retain heat at varying rates, water in the ground does not freeze and expand uniformly. The effect is to move and sort the particles. Stones are pushed upwards until they reach the ground surface. Gravity then causes them to move slowly down the slope of low mounds that are formed in the frost-heaved ground. The effect is to form stone patterns. Under some circumstances, for example where the ground surface is dry and cracked, a more random mixing of the active top layer can take place. This is known as 'cryoturbation'. If a large crack forms in the ground, water and fine sediment might be washed down. During each freezing cycle, the crack becomes bigger and more material is deposited. This is known as 'ice wedging' and the resulting ice wedge can grow up to 30 metres deep. Frost heave and ice wedging have the effect of creating **patterned ground**. This can be in the form of 'stone polygons' on relatively flat ground, or 'stone stripes' on slopes. They are relatively common features in periglacial areas (see figure 10.37).

Because the margins of ice sheets tend to have little vegetation cover, and much of the ground is made up of unconsolidated material, wind and water erosion can be important processes. For instance, during the last glacial period, large areas of wind blown material, called loess, were deposited across Eurasia and North America (see unit 10.1). Glaciofluvial processes also erode and deposit large amounts of material on the margins of ice sheets. During periods of glacial advance and retreat in the British Isles, large areas of sand and gravel were deposited. These shallow deposits of moraine were laid down on outwash plains and in river valleys. This material is now a valuable resource for the construction and road building industry.

Figure 10.35 Permafrost in the northern hemisphere

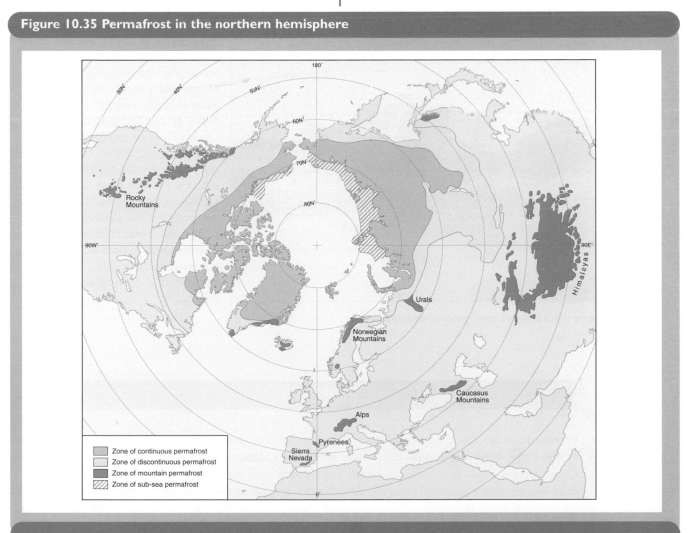

Zone of continuous permafrost
Zone of discontinuous permafrost
Zone of mountain permafrost
Zone of sub-sea permafrost

Activity | Sand and gravel extraction

During 1997, the Nene Barge and Lighter Company applied for planning permission to extract 780,000 tonnes of sand and gravel in north Cambridgeshire (in an area now administered by Peterborough City Council). Throughout the region there are deposits of outwash material that were laid down when periglacial conditions existed at the margin of ice sheets.

The location of the deposits is close to Burghley House. This is a famous Elizabethan building that is set in its own grounds. The government agency which protects sites of architectural importance, English Heritage, objected to the scheme. So did local residents and environmental groups. They feared the adverse visual impact of the scheme and the rise in road traffic that would be needed to transport the material from site. The issue of what would happen to the gravel pit was also raised. In some sites, the land is restored to agricultural use and in other locations it is left as a freshwater lake or even a nature reserve. However, in many cases, the pit is used for landfill, ie the dumping of household refuse. Although the government is trying to reduce the amount of landfill by taxing each tonne that is dumped, and also by encouraging more recycling, there is still a need for

waste disposal. Local residents often object to landfill because of the smell, the increased number of scavenging rats and gulls, and the danger that groundwater might become contaminated.

Although the Cambridgeshire County Council recognised that sand and gravel are vital ingredients for the building industry, and that local employment would be created, they rejected the planning application. It was felt that the environmental impact would be too great and that this consideration outweighed all others.

▲ **Figure 10.36 Sand and gravel extraction**

Questions

1 Briefly describe the climate and landscape that would have existed in Cambridgeshire at the time when the sands and gravels were being deposited.

2 Given that the building industry needs sand and gravel, suggest some policy guidelines that would help councillors decide whether to accept or reject a particular application to extract these deposits.

2. What landforms are typical of periglacial areas?

The periglacial processes of freeze thaw, frost heave and solifluction combine to create distinctive landforms. These are most clearly seen in places such as northern Canada and northern Scandinavia. However, some present landscape features in southern England, for example, are also the result of former periglacial conditions. Even today, at places in Britain such as the Cairngorm plateau, some periglacial processes are at work.

A number of periglacial landforms develop over ice lenses or cores which form when water collects in the otherwise frozen permafrost. The water might be from an underground aquifer or from water seeping into sediments beneath a small lake. As the water freezes, it expands and lifts the ground surface. The largest type of feature formed in this way, up to 80 metres high, is known as a **pingo**. If the ice core of the pingo melts, the dome collapses leaving a circular 'rampart' around a depression or lake. Pingoes are found in many periglacial areas, for example the Mackenzie Delta of northern Canada and also in eastern Greenland. So called 'fossil pingoes' have been identified in mid-Wales

and East Anglia. These are circular depressions surrounded by a low embankment and are evidence that periglacial conditions existed in Britain in the past.

Where smaller ice lenses form, they can cause 'tundra hummocks' which are no more than 0.5 metres high. They occur in many periglacial areas and 'fossil hummocks' are found in parts of Britain, for example on Dartmoor.

In some periglacial areas, the ground surface contains depressions caused by thawing of sub-surface ice. The depressions can be large, several kilometres across, and can form steep sided troughs. The name given to such a feature is an 'alas'. Examples occur across northern Siberia. Such a landscape is called 'thermokarst' because of its similarity to some limestone ('karst') areas where depressions also occur.

Dry valleys are landscape features that, in some cases, have periglacial origins. They are valleys that do not contain a river or stream at ground surface level. It is likely that at least some were formed during glacial periods when the ground was frozen. They occur throughout southern England in chalk and limestone areas, for example in the North and South Downs, the Chilterns and the Cotswolds. Because water could not percolate down through the frozen ground, 'normal' weathering and erosion occurred, and the valleys formed. Then, in warmer conditions, the drainage reverted to underground.

Evidence that at least some dry valleys are periglacial in origin comes from solifluction deposits found at the point where the valleys widen out. These deposits are called **head**, (or 'coombe rock') if they contain a high proportion of chalk. They are an unsorted mass of rock fragments and smaller particles. Where solifluction has occurred on a large scale, a series of lobes are sometimes formed.

Other evidence for a periglacial origin of dry valleys comes from their sometimes **asymmetrical** slopes. (This simply means that one valley side is steeper than the other.) South facing slopes formed under periglacial conditions (in the northern hemisphere) tend to be less steep than north facing slopes. The reason is

Figure 10.37 Patterned ground

At the end of the last glacial period much of Britain experienced periglacial conditions. Remnants of patterned ground still survive in the Stiperstones area of Shropshire. The quartzite rock weathers very slowly and it creates acidic conditions. As a result, soil and vegetation have been slow to develop and have not covered the stone patterns.

Figure 10.38 Haytor, Dartmoor

This tor is an outcrop of granite.

because the freeze thaw process of weathering is more active on slopes with a southerly aspect. Solifluction is effective at transporting the shattered rock downwards because of the greater amount of meltwater on these south facing slopes.

Freeze thaw action is also believed to be partly responsible for the formation of **tors** (see figure 10.38). These are outcrops of bare, resistant rock that stand above the surrounding landscape. Well known examples occur on Dartmoor, formed of granite. Others exist in Yorkshire, such as the Brimham Rocks formed of sandstone, and in Shropshire where the Stiperstones are formed from quartzite. Frost shattering of these well jointed rocks, and the removal of debris by solifluction, is the most widely accepted explanation. However, some researchers suggest that chemical weathering has also played a part in the formation of these landforms. It may be that chemical processes widened the rock joints during warmer climatic conditions prior to the last glacial period.

3. How do people cope with periglacial conditions?

High latitude areas that experience periglacial conditions are called tundra. Until the second half of the twentieth century the human impact on most periglacial areas was slight. A low density population of nomadic hunter gatherers was able to survive without threatening the ecological balance. This has now changed as a result of mineral extraction, tourism and the desire for a more settled lifestyle by many of the indigenous people. Periglacial areas are very fragile ecosystems. The low temperatures and short growing season mean that damaged vegetation takes a long time to recover. Also, pollutants remain in the environment longer in cold conditions because chemical processes of decomposition are much slower.

The spread of 'civilisation' to the native peoples of northern Canada, Alaska and Eurasia has been a mixed blessing. Health care, education and material comforts have improved. But damage to the environment and the loss of traditional culture have also occurred. In Canada, Inuit and native American languages have struggled to survive against the overwhelming influence of English language programmes on radio and TV. In addition, traditional ways of life based on crafts using marine ivory and seal products have been hit by trade bans and lobbying by wildlife groups who oppose seal and whale hunting. The result, for some people, is dependency on welfare and boredom leading to alcohol abuse.

Difficulties of living in periglacial areas

The most obvious difficulty facing people in periglacial areas is the extreme cold. Winter temperatures in tundra regions can average -50°C and, in summer, there might only be two or three months with an average daytime temperature above zero. So, keeping warm is a problem and modern settlements are reliant on large amounts of energy - normally oil that is flown in. Buildings have to be very well insulated with double or triple glazing in the windows.

Insulation is important, not only for keeping the inhabitants warm, but also in preventing heat escaping below the buildings. If the permafrost melts, there is a danger that foundations will sink, causing subsidence and collapse. On slopes, solifluction would cause structures to move laterally. For this reason, most structures are built on stilts above the ground. The same problem occurs with service pipelines for water, gas or sewerage. They have to be insulated and are generally built overground.

The trans-Alaska oil pipeline is an example of the extreme measures that have to be undertaken when building on permafrost. The pipeline runs for over 1,200 km from Prudhoe Bay on the north coast of Alaska to Valdez, an ice free port on the south coast. For much of its route, the pipeline crosses permafrost.

Figure 10.39 Trans-Alaska pipeline

The oilfield development on Alaska's North Slope has posed a great challenge. It has stimulated much research and development on living in periglacial conditions. The units on top of the vertical supports are automatic refrigeration systems which maintain the permafrost around each footing.

Because the temperature of the oil is 65°C when it is pumped from the ground, the pipeline must be insulated to prevent the ground melting and the pipeline rupturing. The daily flow is 1.4 million barrels of oil, supplying over 20 percent of the USA's domestic output. The economic and ecological consequences of a break in the pipeline would clearly be enormous. To prevent this happening, the pipeline is carried overground for much of its route, using 78,000 supports - many of which have their own refrigeration units to keep the permafrost frozen. (See unit 14.4 for an account of the environmental issues facing the oil industry on Alaska's North Slope.)

Transport and movement in periglacial conditions is easier in winter than summer because the ground surface is frozen. Ice roads and airstrips can support the weight of trucks and planes. Where all year round, permanent routeways are required, deep gravel pads are used. The effect is to insulate the permafrost and keep it frozen. The gravel also provides traction for wheels that would otherwise just sink into the top waterlogged layer in summer.

An additional problem in Arctic regions is the tremendous variation in river flow that occurs. For most of the year the water is frozen but in summer the flow can be torrential. Large amounts of sediment from unconsolidated glacial material is transported - and deposited when river discharge falls. The result can be braiding and constantly shifting river channels (see unit 9.2).

People living in Arctic and Antarctic regions must cope not only with extremely cold conditions but also with weeks of permanent darkness in winter. For some people, the long period without daylight causes psychological depression - the so called 'SAD' (seasonal affective disorder). The lack of sunshine can also cause a vitamin D deficiency that has to be treated with dietary supplements.

Ozone depletion (see unit 2.5) has caused an annual ozone hole to appear in the Earth's atmosphere - most noticeably in spring and early summer over polar regions. The effect of ozone is to block out harmful ultraviolet radiation. In places such as northern Canada, the result of the ozone hole is that people are exposed to the increased UV radiation. This is believed to raise the risk of skin cancer and eye cataracts.

Activity | Mountain permafrost in Europe

In 1998 it was announced that EU funding would be used to set up a research project into mountain permafrost. The project was called PACE - Permafrost and Climate in Europe.

Permafrost is found within Europe, from sea level in Svalbard to the mountains of the Sierra Nevada in southern Spain. Although most lowland regions have completely thawed since the last glacial period, some mountain regions still contain frozen ground. It is estimated, for example, that discontinuous permafrost underlies 5 percent of Switzerland.

Mountain permafrost in Europe is often only a few degrees Celsius below freezing. It is therefore highly sensitive to global warming. The combination of steep slopes and ice within the frozen ground leads to a potential geotechnical hazard. In other words, if the permafrost starts to melt there will be an increased risk from landslides and other forms of mass movement. This is particularly important for those places within, for example, the Alps and Pyrenees which rely upon winter tourism for much of their income.

One of the PACE Project's first tasks was to set up a network of instrumented boreholes in mountain permafrost zones across Europe. These were made in a transect from Svalbard in the north to the Sierra Nevada in the south. Data from the boreholes is monitored to assess the geothermal impact of global climate change. In addition, to assess the likely areas at risk, the mountain permafrost areas of Europe are being mapped. New theoretical models are also being developed to assess the effect of temperature change on slope stability in mountain areas.

Questions

1 Briefly describe the features and processes associated with permafrost.
2 Explain why a rise in average temperatures might create an increased hazard in mountain regions.
3 Suggest why a network of instrumented boreholes, in a transect from Svalbard to the Sierra Nevada, might be a useful means of monitoring changes in mountain permafrost.

unit summary

1 Periglacial conditions occur at the margins of ice sheets and also in other regions where freeze thaw processes are dominant. Permafrost is a characteristic feature of periglacial areas.
2 The main periglacial areas today are in northern North America and northern Eurasia. During the last major ice advance, periglacial conditions existed across southern England and as far south as the Mediterranean.
3 The main periglacial processes are freeze thaw, frost heave and solifluction. Meltwater or glaciofluvial action is also an important agent of erosion. Wind blown deposits are commonly found at the margin of ice sheets.

4   Periglacial landforms include tors, scree slopes, dry valleys, patterned ground, asymmetrical slopes, ice wedges, pingoes and solifluction deposits (head).

5   Periglacial conditions pose great difficulties for human inhabitants. Commercial exploitation, for minerals and tourism, has increased the human impact on the fragile periglacial environment. Traditional ways of life for hunter gatherers are in decline.

6   The difficulties that people must overcome in periglacial areas include the extreme cold, long winter darkness and the dangers arising from the ozone hole. In addition, all types of construction are very difficult on permafrost. If heat escapes downwards and melts the frozen ground, buildings, pipelines and other structures start to subside and collapse.

key terms

Asymmetrical slopes - one side of a valley is less steep than the other - caused by greater freeze thaw action and solifluction on south facing slopes (in the northern hemisphere).

Dry valley - a valley in chalk or limestone that contains no surface drainage; formed in a number of ways, including normal river drainage under periglacial conditions when the ground was frozen.

Freeze thaw - a weathering process caused by water seeping into cracks and joints in rock, and then freezing. The water expands when it freezes, causing rock to weaken, then shatter.

Frost heave - the upward movement of particles caused by the freezing and expansion of sub surface water.

Head - the mixture of sand, clay and stony material deposited at the bottom of a solifluction slope.

Patterned ground - stone shapes, lines or polygons, found on the surface of the ground; created by frost-heaving.

Periglacial - the processes and features found near ice sheets and in other zones where freeze thaw action is the dominant weathering process.

Permafrost - frozen ground; continuous permafrost has been frozen for at least two years; discontinuous permafrost is where unfrozen ground is interspersed in otherwise continuous permafrost. The active layer is the top layer of permafrost that thaws in summer.

Pingo - a dome shaped, generally low hill caused by successive freezing of underground water. When the ice core melts, the pingo collapses, leaving a round depression with low ramparts.

Scree - a relatively steep slope (30-35 degrees) of unconsolidated rock fragments that have fallen from a rock face; caused by freeze thaw action.

Solifluction - the flow of soil down a slope; an important process under periglacial conditions when the top, active layer can become waterlogged above a frozen impermeable layer. (The process is sometimes called 'gelifluction' under these conditions).

Tor - an isolated outcrop of solid rock; some tors are believed to have been formed under periglacial conditions.

CHAPTER 11 Coastlines

Introduction

Coastlines, though narrow in extent, are very significant landforms. They shape the world we see when we look at an atlas, a satellite image or a globe. The coastline is a frontier where marine (sea-based) and terrestrial (land-based) processes produce a variety of landforms. Some of these landforms are produced by erosion, others by deposition.

Living near coasts can be hazardous because of floods and coastal erosion. Nevertheless, coastlines provide an environment that attracts human settlement and economic activity. For example, 75 percent of the population of the USA live and work within 100 km of the coast and nearly 70 percent of the world's population live within 500 km of a coastline.

Coastlines are dynamic systems (ie, they are always changing). Yet, because coasts are also the place where so many people live, there is often a need to control or manage change. The costs and benefits involved in coastal management are important issues that concern people around the world, from Venice to Bangladesh, and from Fiji to London.

Chapter summary

Unit 11.1 shows how waves, tides and other factors combine to influence the processes of erosion, transportation and deposition.

Unit 11.2 focuses on two specific aspects of the physical geography of coasts - the impact of changes in sea level and the role of geology.

Unit 11.3 evaluates methods of coastal management - the options available and the decisions that people face.

Unit 11.1 Coastal processes and landforms

key questions

1 What factors influence coastal features?
2 What happens when waves reach the coastline?
3 What part do tides play in coastal processes?
4 How are coastal features shaped by erosion?
5 How are coastal features shaped by deposition?

1. What factors influence coastal features?

Coastal features are influenced by both marine and terrestrial processes. Cliffs for instance are affected not only by waves and tides, but by frost action, by rain and by running water. To distinguish between marine and terrestrial processes, the terms 'cliff-foot' and 'cliff-face' are sometimes used:

• cliff-foot refers to marine processes such as wave action (described in this unit)

• cliff-face refers to terrestrial processes such as freeze thaw or the action of running water (see chapters 8 and 9). Human activity has a big impact on coastlines. In some

cases, natural features might be completely altered by the development of a port or tourist resort. In other cases, natural processes of erosion or deposition might be disrupted by, for example, the building of a breakwater or sea wall. Weather and climate also have an important influence on coastlines, particularly through their effect on the sea. A summary of all the main factors that influence coastlines is given in figure 11.1.

Research has shown that marine processes tend to operate within relatively small coastal units or **sediment cells**. (The term 'littoral' cells - from the Latin word for 'shore' - is also used.) Erosion, transportation and deposition of sediment occurs within these cells. Eleven have been identified along the coastline of England and Wales (see figure 11.2). One such cell stretches from Flamborough Head to the Wash on England's eastern coastline. This cell can be further sub-divided into two parts, one north of the Humber estuary and one south. The part of the cell that is located between Flamborough Head and the Humber is known as Holderness. It is the focus of study later in this unit and also in units 11.2 and 11.3 where coastal management issues are discussed.

Figure 11.1 The factors at work on coasts

From people living at or near coasts
- disruption of natural processes
- use of land for development

From the land
- relief of the land
- shape of the shoreline
- presence (or lack of) a beach
- resistance to erosion of the rocks
- structure of the rocks
- processes of weathering and mass-movement
- nature of the coastal ecosystems

From the weather and climate
- wind strength and direction
- temperature and precipitation at the present time and in previous eras
- storms and severe weather

From the sea
- direction of the waves
- size and shape of the waves
- drift of local currents
- pattern of tides
- depth of water
- supply of sediment
- longer term changes in sea level

Figure 11.2 Sediment cells around England and Wales

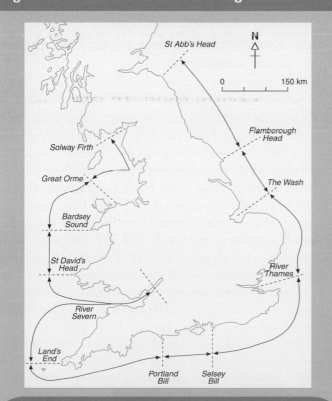

Within a sediment cell, the processes can be regarded as a system, with inputs of wave energy and outputs of sediment. There are also transfers of material between the sea and the land.

Figure 11.3 Processes within a sediment cell

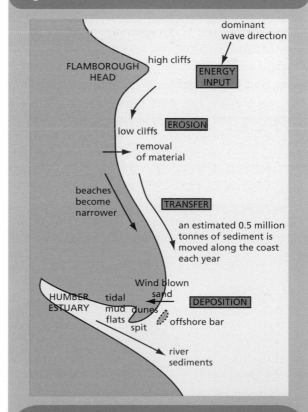

The diagram illustrates the processes at work along the Holderness coastline between Flamborough Head and the Humber estuary.

2. What happens when waves reach the coastline?

Waves are the main source of energy along a coastline and are created when wind blows over the surface of the sea. Waves which form in the open ocean are referred to as **swell**. Their size is related to the distance over which they have travelled across open water, called the **fetch**. The more exposed coastlines of the UK, such as those in South West England, sometimes experience waves which began several thousands of kilometres away in the Atlantic Ocean. **Storm waves** are created by more localised weather conditions offshore, and are the cause of rough seas. Both swell and storm waves can occur at the same time and superimpose upon each other. When both types of wave move away from their place of origin, they tend to become more regular and uniform.

Wave motion

When describing wave motion, a number of basic terms are used (see figure 11.4). These are **wave length**, which is the distance between two wave crests; **wave period**, which is the time between the passage of two successive waves; and **wave height**, the vertical distance between crest and trough. The **wave base** is the depth below which there is no orbital motion, it is approximately equal to half the wave length. The ratio of wave height to wave length is called the **steepness**. Research suggests that waves **break** if the ratio of wave height to wave length rises above 1:7.

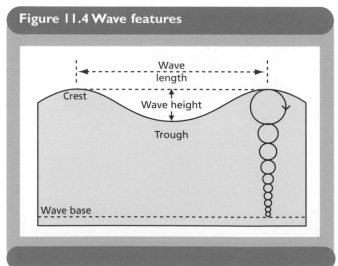

Figure 11.4 Wave features

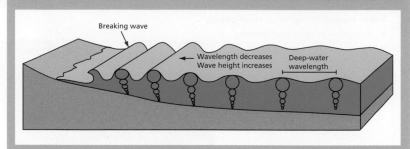

Figure 11.5 Waves breaking on a shore

When a wave breaks on a beach, the water ceases to move in an orbit - it moves forward towards the shore.

When a wave travels forward, the water in the wave moves in an orbital motion. This can be seen at sea when floating objects rise and fall as a wave passes. However, when a wave approaches a shoreline, the wave base touches the sea bed and the resulting friction slows it down (see figure 11.5). This causes the wave length to shorten and the steepness to increase. Eventually the wave breaks and water rushes forward up the beach. This shoreward movement of the 'breaker' is known as the **swash**, and the returning water is the **backwash**. If the coastal water is deep, as it might be at the foot of a cliff, a wave will keep its shape and not break. This is known as a **standing wave**.

Constructive and destructive waves

Waves can be divided into two types, based upon their effects. Constructive waves help build up beach material and destructive waves help remove material. The effect of these waves is to change the beach profile, ie the cross-sectional shape of the beach (see figure 11.6).

Constructive waves are relatively flat. Their swash, which is more powerful than their backwash, moves fine sandy material up the beach. Typically these waves occur where beaches are gently sloping. The effect of the gentle slope is to slow the wave's forward momentum. This is because the beach absorbs energy and also gives the sea water more time to percolate into the sand. Constructive waves are also known as 'surging' or 'spilling' waves. They have a long wavelength (their crests are generally over 20 metres apart), a long wave period (generally less than 10 waves per minute), and a relatively small wave height (generally less than 1 metre).

Destructive waves are sometimes called 'plunging' waves. They tend to be steeper than constructive waves, their crests are closer together, they break more rapidly and they are higher. In destructive waves, the backwash

Figure 11.6 Constructive and destructive waves

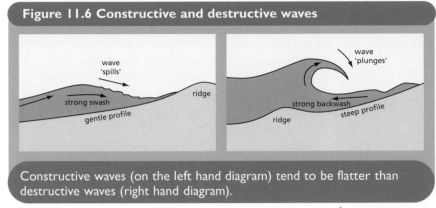

Constructive waves (on the left hand diagram) tend to be flatter than destructive waves (right hand diagram).

is dominant and the effect is to move coarser material down the beach, and often remove it altogether. Sometimes the material is redeposited as a 'longshore bar'. This is a sand bank or ridge that runs parallel with the coast and may be exposed at low tide.

Destructive waves are more common where beaches are steep and sea water runs off rapidly. Coastlines which are most affected by these damaging waves are

Figure 11.7 Wave rays off the Holderness coast

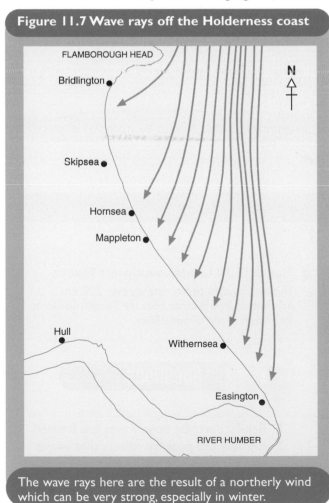

The wave rays here are the result of a northerly wind which can be very strong, especially in winter.

generally located where factors such as seasonal storms, strong winds or local tidal currents create a 'high-energy' environment.

The profile or shape of a beach constantly changes. This occurs slowly from season to season and, sometimes, rapidly during big storms. The effect of tides (dealt with in the next section of this unit) is to concentrate wave energy at different points up and down a beach at different times. Because, typically, a beach slopes more gently near the low tide line, the action of waves at this point is different from wave action near the high tide mark where beaches are generally steeper. As a result, waves are more likely to be constructive lower down a beach and destructive higher up.

Wave direction

So far, waves have only been considered in cross-section. Other characteristics of waves are best seen using a plan view of the coast. A technique sometimes used by coastal engineers is to plot the path of waves as they approach the shore in 'wave ray' diagrams. These are lines drawn at right angles to the moving waves. They generally follow the direction of either the prevailing (ie, most common) wind or the dominant (strongest) winds (see figure 11.7).

As waves move towards the shore, the depth of water can change wave direction. This is a key factor in coastal processes because it concentrates wave energy on headlands, such as Flamborough, and disperses it in bays, such as in Holderness. When a wave moves towards a headland, the frictional drag of the sea floor in the shallower water slows it down, but the wave continues to move at a faster speed towards a beach because the water is deeper. The effect is to bend or **refract** the wave as seen in figure 11.8. The same effect occurs when waves strike a coast at an angle, the drag effect of the shallower water on the landward side reduces their speed, and causes them to bend towards the shore.

Rip Currents

Rip currents are fast moving areas of backwash, channelled into beach runnels or depressions. They increase erosion locally by concentrating currents of water into narrow channels which are then scoured deeper. These channels are sometimes deep enough to

Figure 11.8 Wave refraction

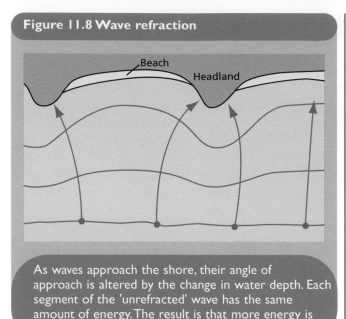

Beach
Headland

As waves approach the shore, their angle of approach is altered by the change in water depth. Each segment of the 'unrefracted' wave has the same amount of energy. The result is that more energy is concentrated on the headland than on the beach.

interrupt the line of incoming breakers. Rip currents can pose a danger to swimmers who risk being swept out to sea if caught unawares.

Longshore drift

Depending on wind direction and the shape of a coast, waves might strike the shoreline obliquely rather than head-on. The water will run up the beach at an angle and, when it has lost its momentum, it will return at

right angles to the shore, following the steepest path seawards. As each wave breaks, the swash moves material up the beach and backwash moves material down. With this process repeating itself every time a new wave arrives, the result is a zig-zag movement of material along the shore. This process is called **longshore drift** (see figure 11.9). Research suggests that a 30 degree angle of wave approach creates the most movement.

Longshore drift is a very important coastal process, particularly in locations where there is a strong prevailing wind - so causing the waves, and therefore movement of material, to be in the same direction for most of the time.

Figure 11.9 Longshore drift

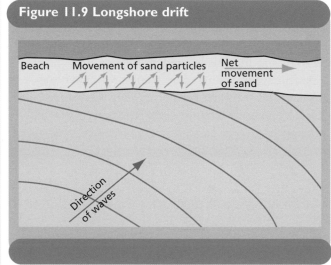

Beach   Movement of sand particles   Net movement of sand

Direction of waves

Activity   Waves and currents

◄ **Figure 11.10 Landes, southwest France**
This long straight beach extends over 200 km northwards from Biarritz near the Spanish border to the mouth of the Gironde River.

Questions

1 Briefly describe how waves are formed.
2 Outline the possible effects that waves and currents are having on this shoreline.

3. What part do tides play in coastal processes ?

Tides are the daily rise and fall of sea level. They are caused by the gravitational pull of the Moon and, less strongly, the Sun, together with the centrifugal force of the Earth's rotation. These factors cause two bulges in the oceans on opposite sides of the Earth. Because the Earth rotates every 24 hours, most coasts experience two high tides and two low tides per day. Each tide occurs a little later each day.

In enclosed seas such as the Mediterranean, there is only a very small tidal range. However, in bays and estuaries at the edge of large oceans there is a much bigger tidal range. For example, at Avonmouth in the Bristol Channel, the range is 12 metres and, at the Bay of Fundy in Nova Scotia, the tidal range is over 21 metres.

Approximately every 14 days, when the Sun, Moon and Earth are all in line, the difference between high and low tide is particularly large. This is called a 'spring tide'. Midway between spring tides, when the Sun and Moon are not in line, are the 'neap tides' which have a smaller range.

What effects do tides have?

Tides affect both the economic and the physical geography of coasts. They influence shipping patterns and port activities as well as creating distinctive landscapes along the shoreline. Tides are also a key factor in determining the nature of coastal ecosystems, particularly around estuaries (see unit 14.2).

Tides influence the level and variation of wave attack on all coasts. However, it is in the funnel shape of estuaries like the Severn (which opens into the Bristol Channel) that they have most impact. The mouth of the Bristol Channel, between Pembroke and Cornwall, is 150 km wide but this narrows to only 1.5 km near the Severn bridges. The effect is to concentrate the incoming tide so much that a wave known as the Severn bore occurs. This tidal wave moves many kilometres up river, at speeds reaching 30 km/h and over one metre in height.

In the Severn estuary, the 12 metre tidal range has led to feasibility studies into the building of a tidal barrage. The flow of water through the barrage could be used to drive turbines and generate clean (ie, non polluting) electricity. In the Rance estuary in Brittany, tides are already used to generate power in this way. However, as with all large engineering schemes, there is a significant environmental effect to be considered. The saltwater

ecosystem would be altered and the impact would range from disrupting local fisheries to removing the habitat of wading sea birds. The strong tides also have the effect of flushing pollutants and sediment from the lower reaches of estuaries like the Severn, Humber and the Mersey. A barrage would greatly reduce this effect.

Tidal surges (or storm surges) are exceptionally high tides caused by low atmospheric pressure associated with depressions or tropical storms. A fall of 100 millibars of air pressure can increase the sea level by 1 metre. If this happens at the same time as a high spring tide, there can be a much bigger effect. When combined with the large waves generated by storm force winds, and the funnel effect of a coastline, the overall result is a high risk of large scale coastal flooding.

This sometimes occurs along the North Sea coast when high tides, low pressure and northerly winds coincide. The effect is to concentrate the tidal surge southwards into the narrower and shallower waters at the southern end of the North Sea. On the west coast of Britain, tidal surges sometimes occur in the Bristol Channel and Irish Sea. They tend not to be as severe as in the North Sea.

Hurricanes and cyclones (the name given to hurricanes in the Indian Ocean) also cause tidal surges and, again, they cause most damage when funnelled into shallow inlets. In 1900, a surge occurred in the Gulf of Mexico. It caused massive damage and over 6,000 deaths in the city of Galveston, situated on a barrier island off the coast of Texas.

Most of the world's deadliest surges in the twentieth century have occurred during cyclones in the Ganges Delta. For example, in 1991, a six metre surge drowned an estimated 140,000 people in Bangladesh and West Bengal. Over 1.4 million homes were destroyed. The combination of very low atmospheric pressure and cyclone force winds caused the storm surge to be funnelled northwards into the narrowing Bay of Bengal where the low lying delta lands are extremely vulnerable to flooding.

The coastal areas of Bangladesh are densely populated with over 1,000 inhabitants per square kilometre. This means that there are very large numbers of people at risk. Because the country is so poor (with a per capita GNP of just $270 in 1997), the government cannot afford to build sufficient shelters to protect the population. It is estimated that 3,000 shelters are needed along the coastline but only 300 had been built by 1999.

Activity The 1953 tidal surge in the North Sea

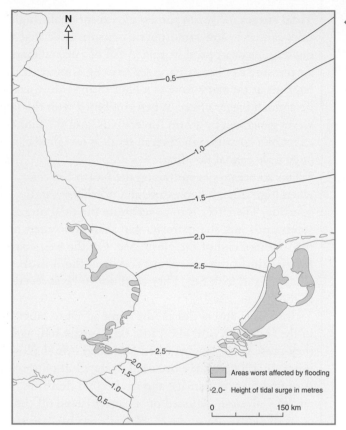

◄ **Figure 11.11 1953 floods**

In late January 1953, a 2.5 metre surge caused flooding in eastern England and the Netherlands. Almost 300 people drowned in England and 1,800 in the Netherlands. The surge was caused by a combination of events. A deep depression in the northern North Sea lowered atmospheric pressure by over 50 millibars. Gale force northerly winds created large waves which caused a build up of water in the southern North Sea.

Questions

1 Briefly describe what happens in a tidal surge.
2 Suggest why the southern coastline of the North Sea is more prone to damaging tidal surges than the northern coastline.

4. How are coastal features shaped by erosion?

There are four main processes of marine erosion:
• Abrasion (or corrasion)
• Attrition
• Hydraulic action (or wave quarrying)
• Solution (or corrosion)

Abrasion (or corrasion) occurs when rocks, pebbles and sand are thrown against cliffs by the waves. It is the most rapid of the erosion processes, and is most effective when there is high wave energy and large sized materials.

Attrition is the process by which rocks are progressively worn down in size, and made rounder in shape, as they are moved back and forth on the sea bed and against each other by wave action.

Hydraulic action (or wave quarrying) occurs when waves strike the shore. In storm conditions, the force of the waves can have a heavy impact - equivalent to 100 kg per square metre. Where there are joints or weaknesses in a cliff face, air might become trapped and compressed by the incoming waves. The resulting pressure expands and weakens the joints. This can cause large blocks as well as smaller fragments to be loosened and then removed by the waves.

Solution (or corrosion) is a chemical process. Rocks like chalk and limestone (formed of calcium carbonate) slowly dissolve in sea water which contains weak carbonic acid. Salt spray from the sea directly corrodes some rocks. It also causes disintegration in rocks because the salt expands when it crystallises in cracks and joints.

The Yorkshire coast

The Yorkshire coast illustrates many features and processes of coastline erosion including cliffs, headlands and bays (see figure 11.12). It extends over 100 kilometres in distance from north to south. In the north are the highest cliffs in England, at Boulby. The northern section, which forms part of the North York Moors, has a variety of rocks including limestone and shales that are exposed on the coast near Robin Hood's Bay. To the south are the chalk cliffs of Flamborough Head and then the less dramatic clay cliffs along the bay of Holderness.

The eastern edge of the Wolds, the chalk hills which arc round to the sea at Flamborough Head, once formed the coastline. But, during the last glacial period, ice sheets from what is now the North Sea deposited large amounts of till (or boulder clay) to the east. This clay, which in some places is rapidly eroding, lies on top of the underlying rocks.

Figure 11.13 Chalk cliffs at Flamborough Head

The joints and faults allow the sea to penetrate into the chalk producing caves and geos

Figure 11.12 The Yorkshire coastline

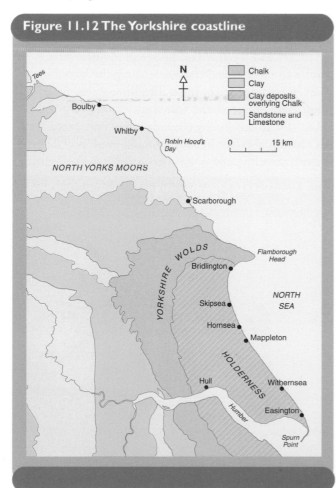

Flamborough Head rises almost 50 metres above the North Sea. The chalk, made of calcium carbonate, is a relatively resistant rock. Like other sedimentary rocks, it has potential weaknesses caused by its distinct layers or bedding planes, and by upright cracks known as joints. However, the fact that the chalk forms a high headland is evidence that it resists erosion. Indeed, studies show that the cliffs are only retreating at about 1 cm per year.

At Flamborough, waves have a maximum 700 km north easterly fetch and, in winter, the dominant northerly winds create high wave energy. The wave action is concentrated on weaknesses such as joints or fault lines. Hydraulic action and abrasion open up these weaknesses creating sea caves and narrow inlets in the cliffs called 'geos'. Most of this erosion takes place in storm conditions when waves cut a groove in the base of the cliffs. This groove or **wave-cut notch** gradually increases the overhang of the cliffs and causes rocks to fall into the sea. In this way, the cliffs retreat landwards yet retain their steepness. Fallen rocks remain at the cliff-foot until repeated attrition makes them small enough for removal by wave action and coastal currents. These rocks, of course, also act as ammunition in the abrasion process.

Tides set the upper and lower limits of this erosion and concentrate the waves' energy on just the lower part of the cliffs.

As the cliff retreats, the eroded remains are gradually planed off by the sea, making a gently sloping shelf or platform (normally less than 4 degrees in angle). This

Figure 11.14 Wave-cut platform, Flamborough

At low tides the wave-cut platform is exposed. At high tides the sea is eroding a notch at the foot of the cliffs.

wave-cut platform is generally visible at low tide, covered with rock pools and seaweed. It can be quite wide. The indentions on its surface show the effects of abrasion and solution. As the size of the platform grows, it can reduce the rate of cliff retreat by absorbing wave energy and protecting the foot of the cliff.

As described earlier in this unit, the process of wave refraction concentrates the waves' energy on a headland. The effect is to narrow the headland. Eventually, erosion on each side can cause sea caves to become linked, forming a **natural arch**. Continued wave action, and weathering, might lead to this arch collapsing, leaving an isolated rock known as a **sea stack**. The area between this and the new headland eventually becomes part of the wave-cut platform. The stack, now attacked from all sides, is also eventually worn down, though a stump of rock may well be visible at low tide on the platform.

This type of feature at Flamborough is found in other chalk coastlines. Examples include the Needles at the western tip of the Isle of Wight. Stacks also occur on other coastlines where there are cliffs and the rocks are resistant to erosion. The Scottish coastline provides examples such as the Old Man of Stoer in Sutherland and the Old Man of Hoy in the Orkneys which is the tallest stack in the UK.

Between Flamborough Head and the mouth of the Humber estuary is the Holderness coast. Formed of till (or boulder clay) which was deposited at the end of the last glacial period, it is the most rapidly eroding coastline in the UK. In recent years, the average rate of retreat of these cliffs has been over one metre per year (100 times greater than the rate at Flamborough). In some places, the erosion is even faster. At Great Cowden, south of the village of Mappleton, the rate is 10 metres per year.

The coastline has been inhabited and documented since Roman times, since when the coast has retreated by 5km. More than thirty villages have been lost to the North Sea. Some, like Dimlington, are still remembered by older residents, others are referred to in old documents and recorded on ancient maps (see figure 11.16).

The sea and weather conditions in Holderness are similar to those found elsewhere along the Yorkshire coast in terms of fetch, wind direction, wave energy and tides. Here, however, the soft clay cliffs are very vulnerable to erosion by running water and freeze thaw. An additional factor in causing rapid erosion is that the smooth coastline allows uninterrupted longshore drift.

Figure 11.15 Sea Stack, Flamborough

Figure 11.16 The erosion of the Holderness Coast

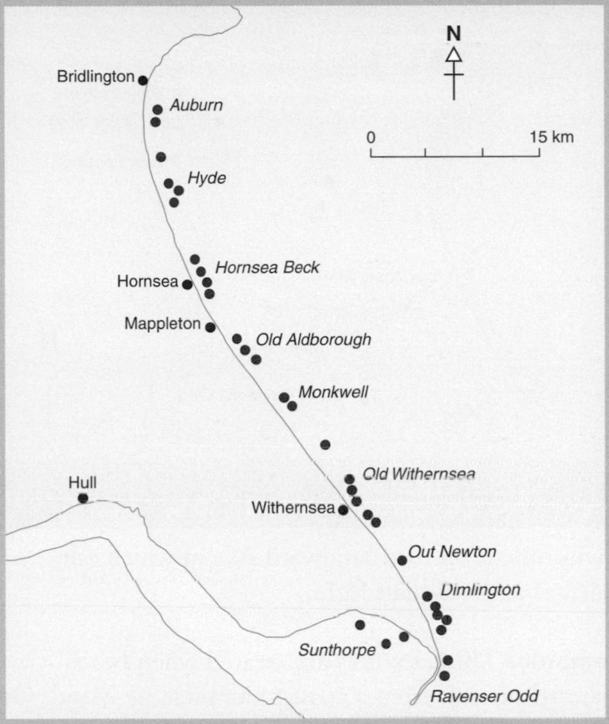

The 'lost villages' of the Holderness coast

South of Bridlington, there is only a narrow width of beach along the coastline. This is because most of the sediment in the area comes from the clay cliffs. When eroded, these produce very fine material which is easily suspended in water and so is quickly removed by the waves and longshore drift. Although the till does contain some larger fragments of rock, this does not provide enough sand or shingle to form large beaches.

The currents along the Holderness coast are important factors in the erosion of the cliffs. Rip currents remove material and so lower the level of a beach at particular points. Backwash is concentrated into channels which then form hollows. On the Holderness coast, these hollows are known as 'ords'. They allow neap as well as spring tides to reach the cliff base. Then, wave erosion soon undercuts the cliffs, causing landslips and slumping.

Studies into erosion at Easington, near to a BP owned North Sea gas terminal, have confirmed that ords accelerate the rate of erosion. In one example, a 15 metre retreat occurred in just six months immediately north of the BP site. The ords migrate southwards at a rate of about 0.5 kilometres a year - so causing erosion along the whole coastline.

Longshore drift carries away the eroded material southwards along the coast. It is estimated that over half a million tonnes of mud and clay are being moved each year. This is an average of almost 1 tonne per minute. Some of the material is re-deposited along the Holderness and Lincolnshire shorelines, but research suggests that some is transported to the coasts of Norfolk and even the Netherlands.

Activity Cliff erosion

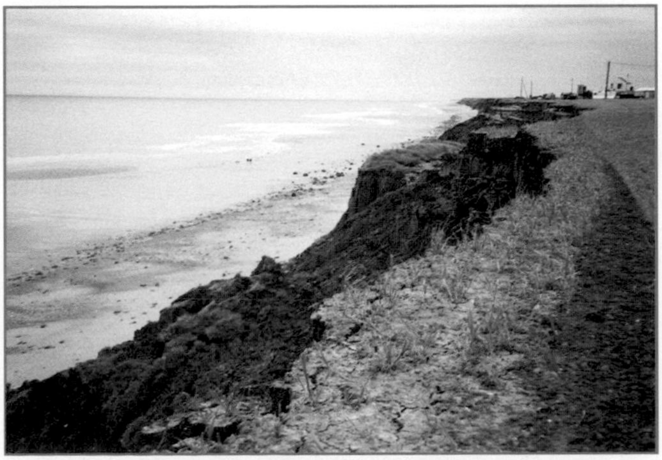

Figure 11.17 Collapsing cliffs at Mappleton

These cliffs on the Holderness coastline are formed from soft clay.

Questions

1 Outline the processes that have caused these cliffs to erode.

2 What factors make some coastlines more prone to erosion than others?

5. How are coastal features shaped by deposition ?

The process of marine deposition causes sediments to build up along shorelines in low energy environments. These are locations which are sheltered from the biggest waves and the strongest currents. Deposition also occurs when rivers, which transport sediment, reach the open sea. At this point, the river velocity slows, its energy is reduced and it is no longer able to carry its load.

Features caused by deposition along coastlines can be divided into four types:
- spits and related features
- beaches
- sand dunes
- mudflats and salt marshes.

Spits

A spit is a long narrow strip of sand or shingle which has one end attached to the coastline and the other end projecting out to sea, or into an estuary. The two factors necessary for a spit to form are, firstly, that sediment is carried along the coast by longshore drift and, secondly, the presence of some feature which interrupts this movement. This feature might be a change in the direction of the coastline, or a river mouth or estuary that forms a break in the coast.

If there is no human intervention, a spit will grow in length until there is a balance between deposition and erosion. In the case of Spurn, historical records suggest that the feature has a growth cycle of about 250 years. After this period of time the sea, driven by north easterly winds, breaks through at the narrow neck and causes the spit to become detached and quickly destroyed. Such events occurred in the 14th, 17th and 19th centuries. There have been a number of temporary breaches during the 1990s, perhaps indicating that the cycle is about to recur. At the same time, the spit is migrating westwards and growing in length by about 10 cm per year (see figure 11.18).

Spits are a common feature around the coastline of Britain. Examples include Orford Ness in Suffolk, Hurst Castle on the south coast, and Morfa Harlech in Wales. Larger examples fringe the Baltic coast of Poland and its eastern neighbours.

As spits develop, they are often turned inland by the effect of wave refraction and tidal currents, and they become recurved. This, together with their tendency to migrate landwards, sometimes provides a sheltered

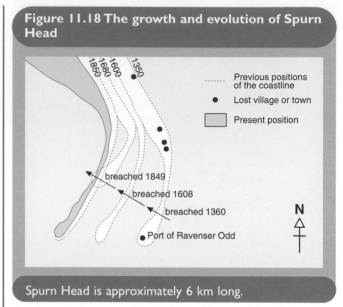

Figure 11.18 The growth and evolution of Spurn Head

Spurn Head is approximately 6 km long.

environment on their landward side in which salt marshes and mudflats form.

Tombolos These features are created when beach material extends from a coast to an offshore island. One example, Chesil Beach in Dorset, links the Isle of Portland to the mainland (see figure 11.19). This shingle ridge is 30 km in length and up to 13 m high, with a lagoon behind it. It is also notable because the shingle increases in size from the western to the eastern end. Another example of a tombolo is located near Llandudno in North Wales where the Great Ormes Head is connected to the mainland by a low lying neck of land.

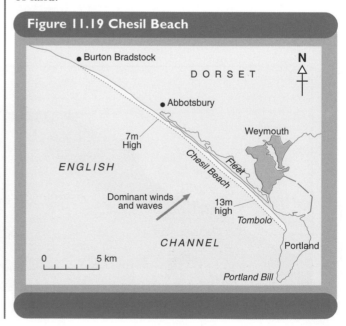

Figure 11.19 Chesil Beach

Figure 11.20 Dungeness

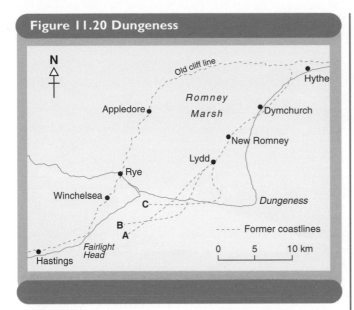

Tombolos are formed where an offshore island protects the mainland shoreline from wave action. This prevents longshore drift from moving material along the coast and, instead, it is deposited behind the island.

Bars Where a spit extends completely across a bay, it is called a bar. It forms in exactly the same way as a spit but, if there is no large river or estuary to limit its growth, it may reach the other shore. Loe Bar in Cornwall and Slapton Ley in Devon are UK examples and others are located on the Baltic coast of Poland.

Cuspate forelands These are triangular-shaped features which may have resulted from changes in the growth and direction of spits. In some cases, it appears that spits growing on either side of an estuary might have joined together across a bay.

Dungeness in Kent is the best known example in the UK (see figure 11.20). Much larger examples are located on the Atlantic coast of North and South Carolina in the south east USA.

Barrier islands These are long, offshore islands of sediment lying parallel to the coast. Most are cut by tidal inlets through which water flows to a sheltered lagoon. Although not common in Europe, except along the coast of the Netherlands, these chains of islands dominate the Gulf coast and eastern seaboard of the USA. They offer important protection to the hurricane-prone American coasts. Strong winds and storms sometimes force waves over these barrier islands,

and beach material is moved from the seaward side over into the lagoons and swamp land behind. The islands are therefore gradually moving landwards.

The precise origin of barrier islands, cuspate forelands, spits and bars is a matter of some debate. The traditional theory suggests that they are formed by longshore drift. More recent research, however, indicates that this may not always be the case. Alternative explanations involve the changing sea levels during ice ages. It is possible that material deposited offshore during a glacial period has been progressively brought landwards by normal wave action, assisted by rising sea levels. This might explain why so many features like bars, forelands, and even the tombolo at Chesil, do seem to run at right angles to wave direction. These 'swash-aligned' features (ie, facing dominant waves) appear to be as common as 'drift-aligned' features (ie, at an angle to dominant waves). In a swash-aligned feature, longshore drift cannot be the only process at work.

Beaches

A beach is a shoreline of unconsolidated sediment. It is a zone of deposition. Beaches lie between the low water mark and the highest point which storm tides reach. Sand is the most common beach material but some are composed of cobbles and pebbles, and some of fine silt and mud. In general, the larger the beach material, the steeper is the beach and vice versa. The characteristics of a beach such as its composition, shape and slope, depend mainly on wave energy. However, the supply of sediment material from either inland or along the coast is also important.

Beaches generally form in bays, where the sheltered conditions and shallower water protect them from the biggest waves and strongest currents.

Figure 11.21 Beach features

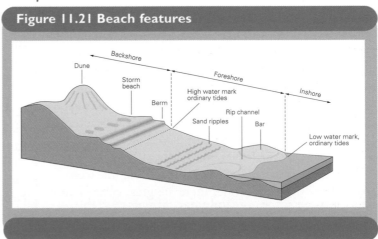

Figure 11.21 shows the main beach features. There are three shoreline zones on a beach - the backshore above the normal high water mark, the **foreshore** between the normal high and low water marks, and inshore which is where waves break in the sea.

On the lower foreshore and inshore zone it is common to find ridges of sand brought down the beach by destructive waves. These 'longshore bars' may be up to one metre high, running across the beach parallel to the waves. They are not continuous but are cut through at intervals by channels formed by rip currents or backwash from the waves. Inland of the bars, runnels form. These are hollows which often remain filled with sea water at low tide.

Higher up the foreshore, there are sometimes small ripple marks made by the waves as the tide moves over the beach. A network of drainage channels often forms at low tide returning water seawards.

Towards the top of the foreshore, where material is larger in size, the slope typically increases to produce a concave profile. Here a large unbroken ridge might be constructed by the waves. This 'berm' marks the normal high tide mark and often has crescent-shaped hollows on its seaward side, made by the swash of the waves.

On the backshore there might be a storm beach consisting of pebbles and even larger boulders. It is formed when there is a combination of storm waves and spring tide conditions.

Sand dunes

When onshore winds dry and then blow sand inland, sand dunes can form. They commonly occur behind large open beaches and can migrate many kilometres inland. Examples occur at Spurn Head, on the seaward side of the spit and at many other locations in the UK. The most extensive area of dunes in Europe is in the Landes region of southwest France. For over 200 km there is an almost continuous sandy beach backed by sand dunes. Some of these dunes are over 100 metres high.

Behind the beaches and sand dunes along the west coast of the Outer Hebrides there are grass covered areas of sand that are called 'machair'. Some of the sand is formed from broken sea shells which have a high

Figure 11.22 Beach on the west coast of Barra, Outer Hebrides

Behind the beach and the sand dunes is the fertile machair.

calcium content. This increases the fertility of the land and so provides good grazing for sheep and cattle (see figure 11.22).

Sand dunes have fragile ecosystems (see unit 14.2) and are vulnerable to damage by human activity. For example, people tramping on a footpath across dunes can damage the roots of grasses and plants which bind the sand. The result can be rapid erosion and a 'blow-out', creating a hollow in the dunes.

Although dunes are found on coasts, their formation is not strictly due to a coastal process. The material is deposited on beaches by waves and currents but is then transported inland by the wind.

Mudflats and salt marshes

In sheltered coastal locations, for example on the western side of Spurn Head, the waves are generally small and there is no strong tidal current. In this low energy environment, fine silt and sand is deposited to form mudflats. Other examples in the UK are located in estuaries, such as the Thames, and in inlets and bays, such as Morecambe Bay. Examples in mainland Europe include the mudflats in lagoons at the head of the Adriatic Sea - on which Venice has been built, and the lagoons behind the Dutch barrier islands. In the latter case, some of the mudflats have been made into farmland by building sea walls and pumping the sea water out.

The sediment that forms mudflats is brought by tides

and by streams and rivers flowing into the sheltered zone. Eventually, as more and more material is deposited, some of the mudflats become completely exposed apart from during the highest tides. Salt tolerant plants then might start to colonise the highest parts and a salt marsh forms. The plants have the effect

of trapping more silt and sand so the area eventually becomes land - and is only covered by sea water at exceptional times. Such a salt marsh is typically criss-crossed by creeks and channels which fill at each high tide. The ecology and plant succession of salt marshes is described in more detail in unit 14. 2.

Mudflats and salt marsh
These have formed from silt and mud on the sheltered Humber Estuary side of the spit. In this wet environment, the bare mud is colonised by a succession of salt-loving plants. Yorkshire Wildlife Trust has a reserve in this area. It is an important international site for wading birds and wildfowl.

Beach and sand dunes
These have formed from sand and shingle on the exposed North Sea side. Wind blows sand from the beach to form the dunes. The beach is small and getting smaller. Holiday resorts to the north protect their beaches by building groynes - sea defences designed to trap the drifting sand. This has meant that less sand is moving south to replenish the beach.

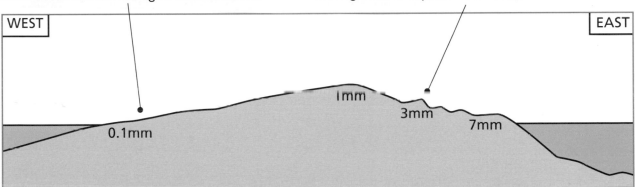

▲ **Figure 11.23 Spurn Head - cross section**
The average diameter of sand and silt particles at different points across the spit are marked.

▲ **Figure 11.24 Spurn Head from the south**

The Spurn Head community
If, in the future, storms do break through and turn Spurn into an island, then the lifeboat station might have to close. The men and their families would be moved across the estuary to Grimsby. Officials say that this will increase incident response times by vital minutes. For the small group of coastguards, lifeboatmen, pilots (who guide vessels up the Humber) and their families, Spurn Head is home. If they have to go Spurn would become uninhabited. There have been people living on Spurn Head since the 7th century, and in the 13th century there was even a port called Ravenser Odd. It is now long gone, washed away by the waves. During World War II, the spit had its own railway and, today, old fortifications are still visible.
Adapted from the Yorkshire Post, November 19th 1998

Spurn Head abandoned

In October 1995, Holderness Council decided to leave the spit to nature, acknowledging that it could no longer afford to maintain the access road that runs down to Spurn Point. Earlier efforts to save the road included the building of a 700,000 tonne, 3 kilometre long, 20 metre wide embankment in 1981. It was made of clay excavated from the site of the Easington Gas Terminal to the north. But, by 1995, much of the banking had been washed away; in one place only one metre remained.

Expert says 'let it go'

In a 1995 report, university professor John Pethick agreed that the spit should be left to the sea. The report concluded that £20 million is far too high a price to pay for its protection and, in any case, the spit has been breached many times over the centuries and has always regenerated itself.

Spurn Head cut off

In February 1996, gale force winds and high tides removed a further 200 metres of the concrete road that links Spurn to the rest of Yorkshire. Only four-wheel drive vehicles could now get through at low tide. Since then, the road has been repaired by the coastguard service but most agree that it is only a matter of time before it is swept away again.

Questions

1 Briefly outline the processes at work at Spurn Head.
2 Suggest reasons why the sediment size varies from the east to the west side of the spit.
3 Outline the case for and against spending money on protecting the spit from erosion.

unit summary

1 Coastlines are dynamic systems influenced by many factors: marine (eg, waves, currents and tides); terrestrial (eg, geology and weathering); atmospheric (eg, weather and climate change): and human (eg, building sea walls and reclaiming land).
2 Wind generated waves provide most of the energy in coastal processes.
3 Most coastal erosion is caused by the abrasive action of sand and gravel moved by waves and currents.
4 Coastal erosion creates cliffs, headlands, arches, stacks and wave-cut platforms.
5 Sediment is transported by waves and longshore drift. When deposited it forms beaches, spits, tombolos, bars, barrier islands and mudflats. Dunes are formed when dry sand is blown to the back of wide, sandy beaches.

key terms

Abrasion - the erosive process that occurs when sand and gravel is thrown by waves against a cliff face.
Attrition - the process by which rocks and pebbles are worn down in size.

Backwash - water flowing back down a beach after the forward momentum has ceased.
Bar - a strip of sand or shingle formed when a spit extends across a bay and is joined to the land at both ends.

Barrier island - a long offshore island formed from sediment.

Beach - a shore built of unconsolidated shingle or sand.

Beach profile - the cross-section shape of a beach.

Breaker (or **breaking wave**) - the point at which a wave steepens and causes the water to move forward.

Constructive wave - a relatively flat wave in which the swash is stronger than the backwash.

Cuspate foreland - a triangular shaped coastal feature formed of sand or shingle.

Destructive wave - a relatively steep wave in which the backwash is stronger than the swash.

Fetch - the distance that a wave travels across open water before it reaches land.

Foreshore - the zone on a beach between the normal high and low water marks.

Hydraulic action (or **wave quarrying**) - the erosive action of water when a wave hits a solid object.

Longshore drift - the action of waves when they strike a beach at an angle and move material along the beach.

Marine processes - the action of waves, currents and tides on the coastline.

Mudflat - an area of fine silt and sediment deposited in a sheltered location.

Natural arch - a feature formed when a narrow headland is undercut by erosion.

Rip currents - fast moving areas of backwash that scour channels down a beach.

Salt marsh - a feature that forms when salt tolerant plants colonise mudflats.

Sand dune - a mound of wind blown sand.

Sediment cell - a stretch of coastline within which marine processes of erosion, transportation and deposition operate.

Solution - a chemical process of weathering.

Spit - a long narrow strip of sand or shingle joined at one end to the coast.

Spring tides - the highest tides.

Stack - the feature formed when a natural arch collapses.

Standing wave - a wave that does not break before it hits a cliff face or sea wall.

Storm wave - waves generated by localised weather systems.

Swash - a breaking wave moving up a beach.

Swell - waves created by winds in mid-ocean.

Tidal surge - exceptionally high tides caused by a combination of low atmospheric pressure and strong winds.

Terrestrial processes - land based processes such as freeze thaw or erosion by running water.

Tombolo - a neck of land that attaches an offshore island to the shore.

Wave base - the water depth below which there is no orbital motion.

Wave-cut notch - a groove or hollow at the foot of a sea cliff caused by erosion.

Wave-cut platform - the flat area formed when cliffs retreat.

Wave height - the vertical distance between the crest and trough of a wave.

Wave length - the distance between two wave crests.

Wave period - the time it takes for two successive waves to pass by. Sometimes the term wave frequency (the number of waves per minute) is used instead.

Wave refraction - the bending of a wave as its base touches the sea bed. The effect is to concentrate wave energy on headlands and disperse it in bays.

Wave steepness - the ratio of wave height to wave length.

Unit 11.2   Coastal features

key questions

1 What is the effect of geology on coasts ?
2 How and why are sea levels changing ?
3 How are coastal features shaped by changing sea levels ?

1. What is the effect of geology on coasts ?

The geology of an area is very important in shaping the features of a coastline. There are two main aspects to consider:

- the **structure** of rocks - the way in which they are arranged (eg, massive beds or thin layers; faulted or folded layers)

- the **lithology** of rocks - what they are made of (ie, their physical and chemical composition).

These two characteristics influence the impact of erosion upon coasts. In unit 11.1 the effect of geology was illustrated on the Yorkshire coast. Resistant chalk forms the headland at Flamborough and less resistant clay forms the bay of Holderness. In this unit, the Purbeck and Swanage area of Dorset is used as a detailed case study.

The Purbeck coast

Exposed rocks in the Purbeck area generally run east to west. They are in alternating layers of more and less resistant material. These layers (or strata) have been folded and eroded to produce a pattern of ridges and valleys. On the coast, the more resistant rocks form cliffs and headlands, the less resistant rocks form bays. This variation is known as **differential erosion**.

Figure 11.25 shows that the southernmost line of rocks is limestone. It consists of Purbeck limestone and, on the seaward side, of Portland limestone. This is tough and well jointed. It forms cliffs which run west from Durlston

Figure 11.26 Durdle Promontory and Durdle Door

Resistant limestone has formed this headland. The main photograph looks west towards Durdle Promontory. The natural arch, Durdle Door, is on the western side of the Promontory.

Head and then intermittently to Durdle Promontory (see figure 11.26). Cracks and joints in the rock have been eroded to form a natural arch at Durdle Door.

Once the sea has broken through the outer protection of the harder Portland stone, the Purbeck limestone erodes more easily. This process is seen at Stair Hole

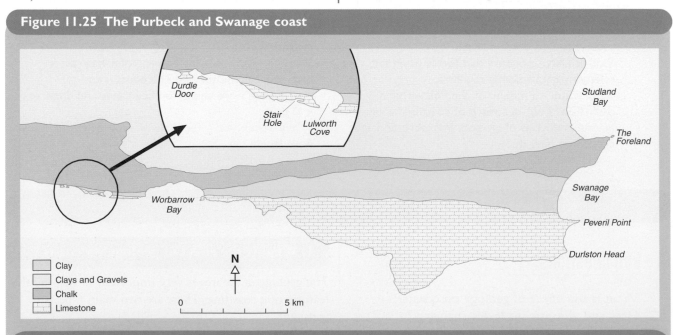

Figure 11.25 The Purbeck and Swanage coast

Durdle Door

Stair Hole

Lulworth Cove

Studland Bay

The Foreland

Worbarrow Bay

Swanage Bay

Peveril Point

Durlston Head

Clay
Clays and Gravels
Chalk
Limestone

N

0   5 km

The features along this coast show the effects of geology and differential erosion. A succession of resistant and less resistant rocks trends east to west in this area.

where the sea has cut caves and arches allowing the waves to scoop out weaker material from behind (see figure 11.28).

At Lulworth Cove, the process has gone further. North of the limestone rocks there is a vale of clay. This soft clay is more easily eroded than the limestone. Where the sea has broken through to the clay, it has widened the breach into a near circular cove. The further growth of this is limited by the shape of the inlet, and by the resistant chalk of the Purbeck Hills which forms the next rock type to the north.

At Worbarrow Bay, the sea has completely breached the line of limestone and is now eroding the chalk. Possibly a similar process occurred in the past to the east of Durlston Head - forming the bay that extends across to the Isle of Wight.

Swanage Bay

The coastline at Swanage Bay shows a different effect of geology from that on the Purbeck coast. This is because the coastline here cuts across the geological structure rather than being in parallel. Going from south to north, the resistant limestone forms the headlands of Durlston Head and Peveril Point. In between these headlands, the small Durlston Bay is the result of a fault

in the limestone which has allowed more rapid erosion.

Northwards is the broad sweep of Swanage Bay, where the clay lowland has been worn away by the waves. The bay is enclosed to the north by chalk hills. This resistant rock forms The Foreland and the stacks of Old Harry. At low tide, a wave-cut platform can be seen and there are also caves at the foot of the chalk cliffs (see figure 11.27).

To the north of the Foreland are more easily eroded clays and gravels. They form Studland Bay and Poole harbour. A shingle spit protects a zone of mudflats and saltmarsh inland. This section is a coast of deposition rather than erosion.

Concordant coasts

In areas such as the Purbeck coast where the structure of the rocks runs parallel to the coast, cliffs and coves are common features. Such a coastline is known as a concordant coast. Because similar features are found on the west coast of North and South America, from Alaska to southern Chile, the term 'Pacific coastline' is also used. In California, the San Francisco Bay is an example, on a much larger scale, of the same features and processes as at Lulworth Cove.

In Europe, an example of a concordant coast is found in Dalmatia - the Adriatic coastline of the former Yugoslavia. Here the coast has been 'drowned' and instead of a continuous shoreline there are a large number of long islands parallel to the mainland.

Discordant coasts

At Swanage, the structure of the rocks is at right angles to the coast. This is called a discordant coast or, alternatively, an 'Atlantic coastline' because similar features are found in Brittany, south west Ireland, Pembroke and the north and south coasts of Newfoundland in Canada. In all these cases, the more resistant rocks form headlands and the less resistant rocks form bays.

Figure 11.27 Old Harry Rocks, Swanage

The chalk has been eroded to form a narrow headland, arches and stacks.

Activity **Coastal features**

◀ **Figure 11.28 Lulworth Cove and Stair Hole**

This photograph looks east with Stair Hole in the foreground and Lulworth Cove behind.

Questions

1 Describe the features shown in figure 11.28.
2 With reference to the photograph and figure 11.25, explain how the coastal features have been formed.

2. How and why are sea levels changing?

Waves and tides produce short term effects upon coastlines, but changes in sea level have a much greater long term impact. These changes are classified into two main types:

- **eustatic** changes are largely caused by fluctuations in the Earth's climate; they are world-wide.
- **isostatic** changes occur when land moves up or down relative to the sea. These are regional or local events and have a number of different causes.

The combined effect of these changes has been, in some locations, to cause the emergence of land from the sea and, in other locations, to cause submergence of land into the sea.

Eustatic changes

It is estimated that the oceans hold 97 percent of all the water on Earth and the polar ice caps hold approximately 2 percent. If this balance shifts by even a small amount, the sea level will change significantly. So, for instance, if temperatures across the world fall as they did during the last glacial period, then there will be more ice and less ocean. Global warming has the

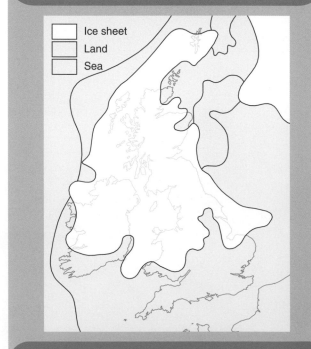

Figure 11.29 The approximate coastline and extent of ice around the British Isles 18,000 years ago

- Ice sheet
- Land
- Sea

As ice sheets melted, the continental shelf gradually flooded.

opposite effect. Higher temperatures cause the sea level to rise as the ice melts. Sea level also rises because the volume of water in the ocean expands as it gets warmer. This occurs at a rate of around 0.8 metres rise in sea level per 1°C rise in average temperature.

Approximately 18,000 years ago, average temperatures were about 5°C below those of today, and ice was at its maximum extent during the last glacial advance. Ice covered much more of the Earth's surface than today and there was less water in the oceans. As a result, the sea level was approximately 140 metres lower than at present. (See unit 10.1 and unit 12.6 for a more detailed account of glaciations and climate change.)

When the ice sheets started to melt at the end of the last glacial period, the sea level rose quite rapidly for 12,000 years and was within 6 metres of its present level by 6,000 years ago. Since then it has risen more slowly, creating the coastlines we recognise today. During the twentieth century, the sea level rose by about 15 cm.

Over the past few decades, there has been growing evidence of an increase in the rate of global warming. Many believe that this is due to the effects of greenhouse gases caused by human activity. Low-lying coastal locations are at risk. They face an increased likelihood of flooding and erosion, both from a rise in sea level and from the higher wave energy brought about by more violent storms (see unit 12.6).

Predictions about the future rate of sea level change vary, but a rise of a further 50 cm by the year 2100 is a widely accepted current estimate. It has been calculated that global sea levels would rise by 70 metres if all the ice in ice caps melted.

Present day shorelines are the result of rising sea levels since the last glacial period. Much of the continental shelf off north west Europe was above sea level 18,000 years ago. Approximately 11,000 years ago, the Irish Sea flooded and Ireland separated from Britain. Then, 9,000 years ago, Britain separated from mainland Europe. As the sea level rose and water flooded the lowlands and valleys, areas of higher land became isolated and formed islands. During the same period it is believed that the Black Sea became flooded by water from the Mediterranean. This might be the origin for the Noah's Ark story in the Bible.

Isostatic changes

Isostatic changes are caused by sections of the Earth's crust either sinking or rising. This happens because the lighter crust floats on the denser material in the mantle

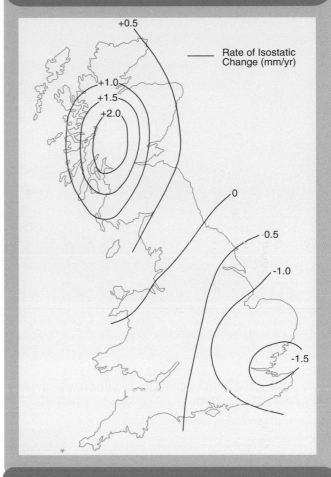

Figure 11.30 Current rates of isostatic change in Britain

Rate of Isostatic Change (mm/yr)

+0.5
+1.0
+1.5
+2.0
0
0.5
-1.0
-1.5

below (see unit 7.1). One cause of isostatic change is linked to the effects of glaciations. Ice sheets can be over 1 km thick. The massive weight causes the Earth's crust to depress down into the mantle. When the ice melts, the crust rebounds.

This process continues today in many parts of the world. Northwestern Scotland and the Hudson Bay area of Canada are both rising, and recent measurements in Scandinavia have recorded uplifts of over 1 cm per year. In the Great Lakes region of North America, the rebound since the last glacial period is thought to have been at least 300 metres. In the British Isles, there appears to be a tilting effect with the north and west rising and the southern and eastern areas, which were not covered by ice, subsiding (see figure 11.30).

In parts of the world along the edges of the Earth's crustal plates, there are isostatic changes caused by tectonic forces. Movements within the mantle are slowly lifting some areas and lowering others. Uplift is occurring

Figure 11.31 Kingsbridge ria, South Devon

This drowned lower part of a river valley provides sheltered anchorage for commercial and recreational shipping.

Many coasts show evidence of both types of movement. Currently, most of the world's coastlines are undergoing submergence - apart from those where isostatic 'rebound' is occurring at a relatively fast rate.

Submergent coastlines

When sea levels rose after the last glacial period, many lowland valleys were flooded. The estuaries of north west Europe formed at this time, creating extensive areas of mudflats and tidal creeks. The mouth of the River Thames and the Essex coastline are examples.

As the climate warmed, marshlands and forests grew, only to be submerged as the sea level rose. Tree stumps from these drowned forests have been found in many locations - particularly on the south and west coast of Britain. Examples occur near Southampton, in Cornwall, South Wales and along the Lancashire coastline.

In some parts of the world, the rise of sea level has

in the Andes, the North American Pacific coastal ranges and in the Himalayas. By contrast, some areas of the Mediterranean basin are being forced downwards.

Isostatic changes are also caused when the weight of sediment on the Earth's crust increases. Enormous quantities of sediment collect at the mouth of many of the world's major rivers, often in deltas. For example, where the Mississippi River enters the Gulf of Mexico, the weight of sediment presses down on the crust. This has depressed the region by an average of 2 mm per year for the past 10,000 years. The delta itself is also subsiding as the material within it settles.

3. How are coastal features shaped by changing sea levels ?

When the sea level changes, different types of coastlines are created:

- **Submergent** or drowned coastlines result from a rise in relative sea level.
- **Emergent** coastlines result from a fall in relative sea level.

Figure 11.32 Prince William Sound, Alaska

The glacier in the background at one time extended much further into the Sound. It eroded a deep trough that has now flooded to form a fiord.

divided coastal ridges into chains of islands. These sometimes run parallel to the coast as seen in the Frisian Islands off the coast of Germany and the Netherlands. When hilly upland areas are submerged, the resulting islands can form a very distinctive coastline such as the Dalmatian coast described previously.

Where the lower valleys of rivers have been drowned in hilly areas, funnel-shaped inlets called **rias** are the result (see figure 11.31). Examples occur in South Devon and Cornwall, Brittany, south west Ireland and north west Spain.

One of the most spectacular submergent features occurs on mountainous coasts when the sea has filled the lower portions of deeply glaciated valleys. Called **fiords** they occur on the west coasts of Norway, South Island New Zealand and Scotland, and on the south coast of Alaska. These steep-sided inlets are often very deep - some in Norway are over 1,000 metres in depth (see figure 11.32).

Unlike rias, which typically become deeper near the open sea, fiords become shallower. They have a lip of solid rock or glacial debris near the entrance. This is probably due to their formation by valley glaciers. At the seaward end of these valleys, the temperatures are slightly higher because of the lower altitude. The result is that the lower parts of the glaciers melt more quickly and the ice is not as thick. Erosion is therefore less effective here.

At the head of many fiords, the material eroded by streams is deposited when it reaches the sea. This forms deltas and fans of new sediment. Over a long period of time, it becomes valuable flat land for farming or settlements.

Emergent coastlines

During the Pleistocene ice age (ie, during the past 2 million years) there have been several warm phases when ice melted and sea levels rose. There is evidence that, 100,000 years ago, the sea level was perhaps 15 metres

Figure 11.33 Raised beaches, Islay, Scotland

At this location there is a 30 metre raised beach and, at a lower level, a former line of cliffs and caves that were eroded when the sea washed up to them. Since then, the land has risen.

higher than it is today. Old (or 'relict') cliff lines, such as one which runs from Flamborough Head to the Humber, and a similar example on the Gower Peninsular in South Wales, date from this time. Old beaches and other coastal features such as caves and shingle deposits are also found. These **raised beaches** remain as relics of former coastlines, now left high and dry.

Coastal areas that are rebounding from their depression during the glacial period also contain similar features. For example, there are many examples of raised beaches in western Scotland. They consist of shingle, sand or shell deposits on what is often an old wave-cut platform. The precise interpretation of these beaches is a matter of debate because they occur at several different heights, at 8, 15 and 30 metres. Nevertheless, they are clear evidence that land has emerged from the sea, and that this process has not been at a steady rate. In terms of their human use, raised beaches provide valuable sites for settlement, farming and coastal roads.

Relict cliffs are sometimes found on the landward side of raised beaches and some still have caves and notches cut by the sea (see figure 11.33)

Activity ▷ Coastal erosion

Coastline is on the edge of collapse

Experts fear that the Beachy Head collapse will be followed by others.

Yesterday, the Environment Agency warned sightseers to stay away from Beachy Head where an 80 metre section of the chalk cliff-face tumbled into the sea on Sunday night. Experts said that it was impossible to predict where the next collapse on Britain's coastline would occur. However, one said, 'You only need look at the geology of the British coast to see where it is at risk. The rate of loss is currently a metre a year on the south coast but, on the east coast, the rate is far higher'. Cliffs on much of the the east coast are formed from clay which was deposited by ice sheets between 15,000 and 30,000 years ago. The clays are softer than the much older chalk cliffs of the South. Both kinds of coastline are being undermined by wave action.

In the case of Beachy Head, it is believed by geologists that heavy winter rains, following the exceptional wetness of 1998, caused the sudden collapse. The chalk is riddled with fractures, fissures and cracks - often more than a metre wide. Some of these expand and become unstable because of rainwater seeping down through the chalk. Freezing temperatures can be a factor in causing cracks to expand, but in this recent case it is thought that temperatures have been too high. It is forecast that global warming might cause an average rise in sea levels of 25 cm in the next 50 years because of thermal expansion of the oceans and melting glaciers. Britain is also tilting because of movements associated with the last glaciation, with Scotland rising and the South of England sinking. When the tilt effect is included, sea levels in northern Scotland might rise by 15 cm and, in southern England, by 30 cm by 2050. Other features of global warming, including more violent storms, rainfall and waves, could hasten cliff collapse.

Adapted from The Times, 18th January 1999

▲ **Figure 11.34 Chalk cliffs near Beachy Head**

Questions

1 According to the article, why is the coastline of southern England expected to be increasingly vulnerable to erosion over the next 50 years?
2 How does geology affect the rate of coastal erosion?
3 If, instead of global warming, the Earth entered into a new glacial period, how might this affect the coastline at Beachy Head? Explain your answer.

unit summary

1 The geological structure and lithology of rocks can affect coastal features.
2 The general sea level is rising because a process of global warming is melting ice caps and also causing the water in the oceans to expand.
3 Localised changes in sea level are occurring due to rebounding following the last glacial advance (in areas which were once covered by great weights of ice). Tectonic movements of the crust, and depression by the weight of sediment at deltas are also causing localised changes.
4 Rising sea levels cause features associated with a submergent or drowned coastline.
5 Where the land is rising relative to sea level, features associated with an emergent coastline are found.

key terms

Concordant coast (or Pacific or Dalmatian coastline) - the geological structure runs parallel with the coastline.
Differential erosion - a process in which less resistant rocks are eroded at a faster rate than more resistant rocks.
Discordant coast (or Atlantic coastline) - the geological structure runs at a right angle to the coast.
Emergent coastline - a coastline resulting from a relative fall in sea level. Raised beaches are associated with this type of coast.
Eustatic change in sea level - a worldwide change in sea level.

Fiord - a flooded formerly glaciated valley.
Isostatic change in sea level - a localised change in sea level when parts of the Earth's crust either rise or fall.
Lithology - the composition and characteristics of a rock.
Ria - a flooded upland river valley.
Structure - the way that rocks are layered, faulted or folded, and the way in which different rocks occur adjacent to each other.
Submergent coastline - a drowned coastline. In lowland areas the resulting features include estuaries and island chains. In upland areas the features include rias and fiords.

Unit 11.3 Managing coastlines

key questions

1 What is the impact of people on coasts ?
2 How do people prevent coastal flooding and reclaim land ?
3 What methods are used to reduce coastal erosion ?

1. What is the impact of people on coasts ?

The human impact on coastlines depends on population density and the level of economic activity. The more people there are, and the more industrial development there is, the greater the effect. Examples of human impact range from urban development to tourism, and from port facilities to sewage disposal.

Some coastal land uses preserve and protect the natural environment, for example in nature reserves. However, in other cases such as harbour developments or hotel construction, the land use permanently damages the natural features. Sometimes conflicts arise in the way that coastlines are used. For example, the dumping of untreated sewage or nuclear waste is not compatible with tourism or inshore fishing.

There are three basic issues in coastal management:
• Coastlines form a naturally changing frontier between sea and land, but people want to fix them with sea walls and other defences to protect their homes and livelihoods.

Figure 11.35 Sand extraction at Southport

Coastlines change and evolve as part of a natural process. When people intervene, there can be unintended effects. For example, sand extraction (for use in the construction industry) is taking place in the Ribble estuary near Southport. This has been blamed for lowering beach levels in Blackpool, 10 km north along the coast.

- When coastal development takes place there is always an environmental and ecological impact. This may be small scale, for example when sand dune and wetland environments are used for recreation. On a bigger scale, the impact of pollution from rivers and from coastal cities affects areas as large as the North Sea and the Mediterranean.

- When trying to manage coastal processes and landforms in one location, people's actions often have unintentional effects elsewhere. Interrupting the process of longshore drift, for instance, might protect beaches in one resort but reduces the supply of sand further along the coast.

2. How do people prevent coastal flooding and reclaim land?

Flooding in coastal areas has a number of different causes. In valleys and deltas, heavy rains or rapid snow melt can cause water levels to spill on to river floodplains. Marine flooding occurs when the sea is driven by storms or high tides onto the land.

In most of the world's largest deltas and estuaries, river and sea flooding sometimes occur at the same time. The worst floods in, for example, the Ganges Delta or at the mouth of the River Rhine, have occurred when high river levels have coincided with storm surges in the sea. Management of these hazards is made more difficult by the rise in world sea levels and greater frequency of storms associated with global warming (see unit 11.2).

When low lying coastal regions, inlets, estuaries and mudflats are reclaimed from the sea, the land created is often very fertile. The sediments are rich in nutrients and therefore form valuable farmland. In the Netherlands, with its low lying coasts and high population density, land reclamation has been carried out for generations. Smaller scale schemes have been undertaken in England, for example, in the Wash, on the Essex coastline and on the west Lancashire coastline. However, the more land that is reclaimed, the greater is the danger of flooding.

Flood prevention

In unit 11.1, the 1953 floods of the Netherlands and Eastern England are described. These severe floods claimed many lives and prompted the building of large scale coastal defences in both countries.

In England, the Thames Flood Barrier was built to protect London from flooding. The Barrier is 620 metres long and consists of 4 main gates which are kept open, apart from testing and at times of flood alert, to allow shipping through. The Barrier cost over £1 billion and took 8 years to build. It was completed in 1984. The site at Woolwich was chosen because the river is comparatively straight there and the underlying chalk rock can bear the weight of the large scale construction (see unit 9.4).

The Netherlands is particularly vulnerable to flooding because 24 percent of the land area - in which 60 percent of the population live - is below sea level. In addition, the rivers Rhine, Scheldt and Meuse (Maas in the Netherlands) flow through the southern part of the country and form a large delta with low lying islands and many river channels. In 1995, there was flooding along the lower Rhine when the river reached record levels after heavy rain and rapid snow melt upriver. However, the main flood defences held and the major towns and cities were saved. After the 1953 floods, the Dutch government decided to strengthen the country's sea defences by spending the equivalent of £3 billion on a series of barrages known as the Delta Plan.

Activity ▷ Flood defence and land reclamation in the Netherlands

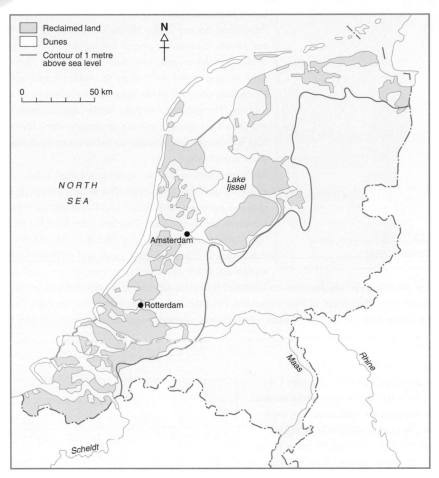

◀ **Figure 11.36**
The Netherlands

The Delta Plan

This scheme, completed in 1986 to protect the Rhine, Scheldt and Maas delta area, took 30 years to construct and has raised sea defences to one metre above the 1953 storm surge levels. In addition, it has improved road and shipping links, created new land for development, and conserved valuable water supplies and habitats. It is one of the world's biggest engineering projects involving dams, flood barriers and massive gates. The difficulties faced by the engineers included a three metre tidal range combined with strong river currents.

The last component of the scheme was the Eastern Scheldt surge barrier. It is a dam with gates which can be opened and closed. It was designed to meet the demands of oyster fishermen and environmentalists who wanted to keep the tidal flow of sea water.

At the start of the Eastern Scheldt stage of the project, a fleet of specially designed ships laid 65 'mattresses' made from reinforced wire, sand and gravel on the seabed. On top of each was placed a prefabricated 18,000 tonne pier which was then anchored with sand and 5 million tonnes of rock imported from Belgium, Sweden and Finland. Between each of these piers (each equal in height to a 12 storey building), were hung 62 steel gates, each weighing 400 tonnes.

The Delta Plan is seen by most Dutch people as a great success and is a source of national pride. Whilst some people regret the changes brought about by the barrier, most welcome the greater safety (and accessibility between islands) that it provides.

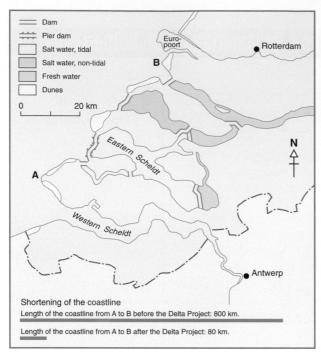

Dam
Pier dam
Salt water, tidal
Salt water, non-tidal
Fresh water
Dunes

0   20 km

Europoort
Rotterdam
B
Eastern Scheldt
A
Western Scheldt
Antwerp

N

Shortening of the coastline
Length of the coastline from A to B before the Delta Project: 800 km.

Length of the coastline from A to B after the Delta Project: 80 km.

Figure 11.37 The Delta Plan
The Eastern Scheldt barrier is the most recent component of the Delta Plan. The 3 km long tidal surge barrier must deal with both high tides and floodwaters

Land reclamation

Population density in the Netherlands in 1995 was 416 people per square kilometre - one of the highest in the world. Because of this population pressure, over the centuries Dutch people have developed the technology to reclaim land from the sea. More than one fifth of the total land area has been reclaimed in this way. The process has been made possible because much of the Dutch coastline is formed of estuaries and low lying mud flats. It is easier and cheaper to reclaim this land than, say, a rocky coastline of cliffs.

Reclaimed land in the Netherlands is called 'polder' and is generally used for agriculture. The older polders of South Holland, between Amsterdam and Rotterdam, are between 2 and 6 metres below sea level. They are now used for dairying, horticulture and bulb growing. This drained land is used intensively. In other words, a great deal of labour and capital equipment (such as heated greenhouses) are used to produce the agricultural output. In this way, maximum production can be obtained from the expensively reclaimed and protected land. Critics of land reclamation point out that large areas of freshwater and salt marsh have been lost in the process. These ecosystems provide habitats for a wide range of plants and birds - particularly migratory species such as ducks and geese.

The Zuider Zee Scheme

This scheme to reclaim land began in 1927 in North Holland. A barrier dam was built between the coastal dunes to separate Lake Ijssel from the North Sea. Having built the outer dam, embankments (or 'dikes') were built around the areas to be reclaimed. The next stage in reclamation was to drain the land. Traditionally, in older schemes, water was pumped from the land by windmill. Now, diesel and electric pumps are used to raise the water up into a network of drainage channels and then into the sea. In the early years, salt tolerant crops were grown and lime and fertiliser were added to the land. This has now created a deep, silty and fertile soil.

Not all the land is used for agriculture, some is used for urban expansion. The growing population of cities such as Amsterdam requires more homes, and industry is looking for new sites. There are demands too for improved roads and recreation facilities, such as lakes for sailing.

Further land reclamation is not likely in the near future. Because of increased farm productivity, the Netherlands now produces a food surplus. It therefore does not need to spend the large amounts necessary to reclaim more land. At the same time, there is ever increasing demand for water supplies from domestic users, industry and agriculture. The freshwater Lake Ijssel can provide this water, but cannot if it is drained. So, the emphasis has now changed away from creating new land to a policy of coastal protection and flood prevention.

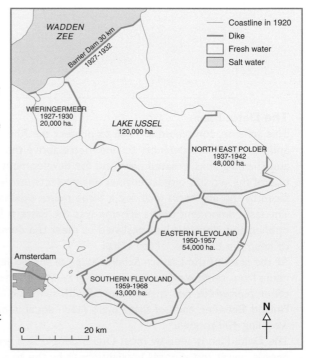

WADDEN ZEE

Coastline in 1920
Dike
Fresh water
Salt water

Barrier Dam 30 km 1927-1932

WIERINGERMEER
1927-1930
20,000 ha.

LAKE IJSSEL
120,000 ha.

NORTH EAST POLDER
1937-1942
48,000 ha.

EASTERN FLEVOLAND
1950-1957
54,000 ha.

Amsterdam

SOUTHERN FLEVOLAND
1959-1968
43,000 ha.

N

0   20 km

▲ **Figure 11.38 The Zuider Zee**

Figure 11.39 Reclaimed land
In the past windmills were used to drain reclaimed land. Today diesel and electric pumps are used.

Questions

1 Briefly outline the reasons why the Dutch have reclaimed land from the sea.
2 How is the Zuider Zee scheme different from the Delta Plan?
3 Explain why flooding is a particular hazard for the Netherlands.
4 Assess the costs and benefits of land reclamation.

3. What methods are used to reduce coastal erosion ?

Coastal erosion is a natural process. It becomes a hazard when it threatens people's lives and livelihoods. There are three different types of response to it:

* **Hard engineering** involves the building of structures, such as sea walls, to resist the power of waves and tides.
* **Soft engineering** adapts and exploits the natural processes at work, for example by replacing sand on beaches.
* **Strategic retreat** means abandoning land which is judged uneconomic to defend.

The first of these options has traditionally been the way that people have responded to coastal erosion. However because of the rising costs of building and maintaining these structures - and their environmental impact, the other two strategies are increasingly being seen as viable alternatives.

Since 1965, an estimated $3.5 billion has been spent on coastal defences in the USA. It is now increasingly recognised that much of this money has been wasted. In several states of the USA such as Maine, North and South Carolina, and Texas, laws have been passed that ban any new sea walls or other hard structures along the shoreline. Not only does the sea win in the end, but hard structures increase the scouring and erosion further along the coastline. An example of the new thinking occurred on North Carolina's Shell Island in 1998. Only 12 years previously, a nine storey apartment block was built on the coast of this barrier island. Erosion soon threatened the apartments and residents lobbied for a sea wall to be built. However, the decision was taken by the state to abandon the coastal defences and allow the apartment block to fall into the sea.

Hard engineering

In unit 11.1, two aspects of coastal erosion were described: cliff-foot (or sea) processes, and cliff-face (or land) processes. Coastal protection strategies can be subdivided in the same way:

* Cliff-foot strategies - these protect the coastline by absorbing or reflecting wave energy. The structures might be at a cliff foot, or on a beach, or in the zone of breaking waves. Examples include sea walls, revetments, rock armour, gabions, groynes and breakwaters (these are described overleaf).
* Cliff-face strategies - these try to reduce or prevent cliff damage resulting from subaerial processes of erosion (ie, those caused by gravity, frost and precipitation). Examples include stabilising cliffs, and cliff drainage.

Figure 11.40 Withernsea, Holderness

The old wall has been protected by rock armour. These boulders prevent waves scouring out the sand from beneath the wall's foundations. The new wall is sloped to absorb wave energy.

Sea walls These were built in many UK coastal resorts during the nineteenth century. Examples include Blackpool, Scarborough and Brighton. The sea walls are constructed of concrete, reinforced with steel. Relying on their massive strength, they withstand the waves in all but the worst storms. But, when they are built on beaches, backwash lowers the level of the sand, and the walls' foundations are gradually undermined. This can cause them to collapse if they are not regularly maintained. Sea walls are costly both to build and to preserve.

Modern designs often have curved and sloping features to reflect the waves and to absorb energy. However, with both the latest and the older designs, the effect of sea walls is often to protect a stretch of coastline but at the cost of increased erosion beyond the area of the wall. There is also some evidence that these rigid barriers increase current strength and therefore accelerate the erosion of beach material in front of the wall.

On the Holderness coast of Yorkshire, the older types of sea wall are found in resorts such as Bridlington and Hornsea. Withernsea has extended its old wall with a new section that has a more modern design. The old wall has been upgraded and further protected by placing large (5 tonne) boulders on the seaward side. The sea defences were strengthened after strong local pressure, particularly from the tourist trade. They cost £6 million (see figure 11.40).

Revetments These are structures designed to absorb wave energy while allowing the water to pass through. Concrete and steel versions are sometimes attached to a cliff foot by piles driven into the ground. Wooden revetments, called baffles, allow both sediment and water to pass through, so helping to build up the beach.

The cost of these structures is relatively cheap at around £1 million per kilometre, but they do not last long and need regular replacement. Older versions near Spurn Head have now failed completely.

Revetments can also be constructed from large boulders which are placed onto a beach. This effective form of rock armour is also called rip-rap. At Withernsea, the boulders used to protect the sea wall were brought by barge from Norway - sea transport being the most cost-effective means of moving such bulky material. A revetment made with large boulders at the BP North Sea gas terminal at Easington is a recent example of hard engineering along this coastline (see figure 11.41).

Figure 11.41 The BP terminal at Easington (looking north)

The BP terminal was a top priority for coastal protection because of its economic importance. The photograph was taken in 1998 before the coastal protection scheme had started.

Figure 11.42 Gabions at Skipsea near Bridlington

These are wire cages filled with rocks or concrete. They protect cliffs from erosion and provide a firm structure. Some local people have protested that this form of coastal defence is ugly and not suitable for a holiday resort.

Groynes These are, in effect, strong fences built on beaches at right angles to the sea (see figure 11.43). They work by capturing sediment as it is moved along the coast by longshore drift. The result is an increase in the amount of sand or shingle on the beach and this prevents waves reaching the cliff foot. Groynes are usually very successful at preventing the loss of sand in a holiday resort and they are also effective in reducing cliff erosion. In addition, they can be repaired relatively cheaply and easily.

At Mappleton, on the Holderness coast, new groynes constructed from boulders have been built in addition to rock revetments. This scheme has been successful at slowing beach and cliff erosion locally. However, it has been blamed for accelerated erosion down the coastline by reducing the transport of sediment and by causing an increased scouring action. Research suggests that groynes along the Holderness shoreline might have an impact in Lincolnshire, Norfolk and even in the Netherlands.

Breakwaters These are large walls built out into the sea, or offshore, parallel to the coast. They are designed to reduce the impact of destructive waves by absorbing some of the wave energy. They can be very expensive to build. Proposals to cut costs by using car tyres, colliery waste and oil drums, all suitably anchored, have been put forward for the Holderness coast in recent years.

Artificial reefs linking offshore bars in Florida do suggest that they can be effective, and the Environment Agency has an experimental scheme on the Norfolk coast. However, the ecological impact of such projects, and their effects on fishing and recreation, is largely unknown.

Stabilising cliffs One relatively simple way of making cliffs less liable to slipping or slumping is by reducing the angle of slope. Hard rock cliffs can be blasted to prevent rock falls, as on the coast of North Wales just west of Conwy. On the softer glacial clay cliffs of Holderness, at Mappleton, regrading (ie, reducing the angle using earth moving equipment) has greatly reduced the amount of slumping.

An alternative method is to secure cliffs which are likely to slip seawards by using steel piles driven vertically into the ground. Planting trees and shrubs has a similar

Figure 11.43 Groyne at Hornsea

Holderness Council has built a succession of wooden groynes at Hornsea which have successfully created a wide holiday beach. The work cost over £5 million. The beach is higher to the left of the groyne than to the right. This is because longshore drift and sea currents are moving beach material from left to right (ie, southwards) along the coast.

effect because the roots help bind the soil together. This strategy also reduces water runoff and prevents gully erosion. Where footpaths have made parts of the ground bare, such as at Flamborough and along the Cleveland Way (along the North Yorkshire coastline), the cliff tops are more vulnerable to erosion. This has become a severe problem in some areas.

Cliff drainage This is a relatively inexpensive method of reducing erosion, particularly on clay cliffs. It involves building drains and diverting running water from the cliff face and from potential lines of weakness behind the cliffs. In dry periods clay dries out and cracks can form. Then, when it rains, these cracks allow rain to seep down. The rain acts as a lubricant causing slumping to occur. However, this process is prevented if the water is drained away. A small scale cliff drainage scheme at Easington on the Yorkshire coast has been successful.

Soft engineering

Soft engineering involves adapting and working with natural processes. It includes, for example, the conservation of sand dunes by planting marram grass which binds the sand and prevents wind erosion. However the main focus of activity in tourist locations is beach nourishment.

Beach nourishment Where the store or supply of sediment is insufficient to protect a coast from erosion, or where longshore drift is eroding a beach, one solution is simply to bring sand from somewhere else. This approach is expensive and therefore only used where there are strong economic reasons.

Nevertheless, projects of this sort are becoming increasingly common. They range from the small scale mechanical movement of sand by local authorities in the UK, to massive schemes in the USA. One of the largest schemes in the UK is planned for Skegness on the Lincolnshire coast. On a far bigger scale, at Miami Beach, millions of tons of sand have been vacuum pumped off the seabed to form a new beach. The resort is built on a barrier island off the east Florida coast. It contains hotels and apartments valued at over $6 billion. By the 1980s, the beach of fine coral sand had almost eroded away - due mainly to scouring caused by the hard engineering structures built to protect the buildings along the coast. So, a $60 million beach nourishment programme was started and a 16

Figure 11.44 Miami Beach

Beach replenishment is an expensive option that only becomes economically worthwhile where there is a major tourist industry.

kilometre, 100 metre wide beach of coarse sand was created. Expensive projects like this can only be justified when the land is very valuable.

Such schemes are sometimes criticised as being environmentally unfriendly. By moving different types of sediment within an ecosystem, there is an impact on the flora and fauna. The removal of material from its source will also have an effect on currents and waves - and may cause an increased rate of erosion along the coast from where the sand is extracted.

Coastal zone management In recent years, it has become recognised that coastal protection in one area often has a knock-on effect in another. So, a strategy of integrated coastal zone management is sometimes used. The idea is to deal with sections of the coast in a coordinated way and draw up Shoreline Management Plans. One such plan has been proposed for the Dorset coastline. It involves planning coastal defences in such a way that unintended adverse effects do not occur further along the coastline.

Strategic retreat

Until relatively recently, coastal engineers generally assumed that they could successfully fortify all shorelines against erosion. However, many now realise that this is too costly and that some coastal areas should be left to natural processes. Although it is not sensible to abandon cities like Miami, some believe that undeveloped areas of farmland in, for example, Holderness should be left to the forces of nature and allowed to erode.

This approach is increasingly being adopted by planners in the USA. Under the National Flood Insurance Program, American property owners in high risk areas who are prepared to move and build inland, are offered 40 percent of the value of their property. Supporters of this approach in the UK suggest that local authorities could buy up threatened property and lease it back to residents until protection is no longer cost-effective.

In unit 11.1, the decision by the local council to abandon Spurn Head is described. A similar decision was taken in 1995 when the Ministry of Agriculture bulldozed a sea wall in south east Essex. The wall had been built a century earlier and protected over 30 hectares of farmland. The Ministry decided that it would cost millions of pounds to rebuild the sea wall high enough to withstand the combined effect of a rising sea level and tidal surge. The land was being used as rough grazing and was not so valuable as arable land. It was expected that, after the removal of the sea wall, the land would revert to salt marsh. This would then provide 'defence in depth' against the sea and protect the next sea wall inland. The Ministry calls this policy 'managed set back'.

How are decisions about coastal management made?

The decision making process on coastline protection involves identifying and answering a number of questions. These include:

- What is the problem or issue? This might be that coastal flooding or coastal erosion is becoming a hazard, or existing defences are failing.
- What are the physical processes at work? There is a need to understand the nature of any tidal surges, high energy waves, or unstable cliffs.
- Whose interests are involved? These could be tourists, farmers, fishermen, industrialists, local residents, or the military.
- What are the alternative solutions available? These include hard or soft engineering, strategic retreat, flood prevention, land reclamation, or simply doing nothing.
- How much will the options cost? These might involve both building and maintenance costs, in the short and longer term.

- What impact might there be? This could be economic, environmental or social. It might be positive or negative.
- Who needs to be consulted? Landowners, MAFF (Ministry of Agriculture, Food and Fisheries), the Environment Agency, other government departments, the National Trust, conservation groups, and civil engineers.
- How is the choice going to be made? Analysis is generally based on comparing costs with benefits, or by assessing the likely environmental impact.

Cost benefit analysis This decision making technique is used to compare the costs and benefits of a scheme. It involves putting a price on all the outcomes, whether direct or indirect. For example, it would include the direct costs of construction and maintenance of a sea wall. If the wall spoilt people's view of the sea, some value would also have to be put on this loss which is an indirect cost.

A value is also placed on the benefits. For example, there will be direct benefits such as reducing damage to property, and indirect benefits through saving jobs in tourist resorts. A major drawback of this approach is that it is often very difficult (or even impossible) to price the indirect effects such as environmental damage or loss of wildlife habitat.

When all the costs and benefits have been calculated or estimated, the net benefit can be shown. This might be used as a basis for a decision or as a means of comparing two different schemes.

Environmental impact analysis Increasingly this technique is used to assess civil engineering schemes. EU legislation makes it compulsory for all large projects. It weighs up the positive and negative effects of a scheme under environmental headings.

A list of relevant outcomes is drawn up that includes aspects of the physical, social and economic environment. For a sea wall, these might be the impact on the beach, on the coastline, on local wildlife and plants, on the tourist trade and on the local economy in general.

In some environmental impact assessments, scores are given (on a +5 to -5 scale) for the various impacts. Plus scores are beneficial effects, negative scores are damaging effects. The impacts might be weighted according to their perceived importance. In this way, the overall impact can be judged and compared with alternative schemes.

Activity | **Tackling erosion at Mappleton, Holderness**

Village sinking into the sea - newspaper extract from 1986
The tiny village of Mappleton sits on top of 15 metre cliffs of soft clay, on the road from Hull to Bridlington. Unless something is done quickly, it is doomed to follow other lost villages into the North Sea. Once the parish church was over 3 km from the sea, now it is less than 300 metres. Geoff Porter moved into his home in Cliff Lane 16 years ago when there were two houses between it and the cliff top. Now they've gone and he's in the front line. Villagers say that the village and coast road need protecting.

New defences - newspaper report from 1991
In 1991, Holderness District Council completed new sea defences to protect Mappleton. A groyne to preserve the beach and a sea wall, built with large boulders, were constructed. Villagers were happy that the Council was able to spend £2.1 on the new sea wall. The money came from an EU grant designed to promote tourist development. The grant was made on condition that facilities such as a car park and picnic area were also provided. Without the expenditure, the village would have been at risk in a few year's time. Officials from the Council accept that the new sea defences will only protect the village, not the farmland to the north and south.

Woman's crusade - newspaper report from 1996
A woman whose home had to be abandoned to the North Sea is trying to prove that Holderness Borough Council has made erosion worse by building the Mappleton defences. Sue Earle, whose farm is falling into the sea two kilometres south of the village, is taking the council to the Land Tribunal. She claims that the 10 metre per year rate of cliff retreat on her farm is due to the new sea defences. By protecting the coastline to the north, the effect is to increase scouring along unprotected stretches of coastline.

▲ **Figure 11.45 Mappleton**
Rock armour now protects the foot of the clay cliffs.

▲ **Figure 11.46 Sue Earle's farm, 2 km south of Mappleton**

Questions

1 Briefly describe the types of coastal defences that have been used at Mappleton.
2 What alternative forms of coastal defence could have been used at Mappleton.
3 Outline the advantages and disadvantages of building coastal defences such as those at Mappleton.

unit summary

1 People have an impact on coastlines when they try to fix what is a naturally changing frontier between sea and land.
2 In managing coastlines, people cause an environmental impact both locally and, often, at more distant locations.
3 Coastal flood prevention and land reclamation in the Netherlands has involved building massive barrages and sea walls.
4 Hard and soft engineering solutions can be used to prevent coastal erosion. There is a growing acceptance that, in some circumstances, it is not worth spending the money necessary to save the land from the sea.

key terms

Hard engineering - building structures such as sea walls and groynes (fences built down a beach to slow longshore drift) in order to prevent coastal erosion.

Revetments, rock armour (or rip-rap), gabions - are all hard engineering structures designed to prevent coastal erosion.

Soft engineering - adapting and using natural processes, such as beach nourishment (replenishing beach sand), to prevent or slow erosion.

Strategic retreat - abandoning coastal land that is judged uneconomic to protect.

CHAPTER 12 Weather and Climate

Introduction

The state of the atmosphere at any one time is described as the **weather**. This includes the temperature, precipitation, wind speed and cloud cover. **Climate** is the term that describes the average weather conditions in a particular place over a period of time. Weather and climate affect us in many ways, from the clothes that we wear to the food that is grown. Extremes of weather such as floods, drought or hurricanes can cause major upheavals in people's lives. These events tend to affect people in low income countries more than in high income countries. This is because they have fewer resources to cope with such hazards.

Weather changes all the time, sometimes several times in one day in Britain. Because climate is an average of weather conditions, it is more stable. However, it is not constant. There are short term fluctuations such as El Niño which occurs regularly and lasts for several months. It involves a reversal of normal weather patterns in the Pacific Ocean. Longer term fluctuations also take place. For example, global warming has now been occurring for at least one hundred years and, over a much longer time period, there have been a number of ice ages and warm interglacial periods.

This chapter describes weather and climate patterns and examines the factors that affect these patterns. It also considers how weather and climate affect people's lives.

Chapter summary

Unit 12.1 examines atmospheric processes and the factors that affect our climate.
Unit 12.2 looks at different types of precipitation and their causes.
Unit 12.3 describes large scale weather systems and their impact on people.
Unit 12.4 analyses local weather systems.
Unit 12.5 examines climatic zones on a world scale and in Britain.
Unit 12.6 reviews ideas on climatic change including El Niño and global warming.

Unit 12.1 Atmospheric processes

key questions

1 What is the structure of the atmosphere?
2 What causes the global pattern of circulation?
3 What factors influence Britain's climate?

1. What is the structure of the atmosphere?

Approximately 95 percent of the atmosphere consists of nitrogen and oxygen. The rest is made up of small quantities of water vapour, carbon dioxide, methane, ozone and other gases.

As distance from the Earth increases, the density of the atmosphere falls. It is in the lowest layer that weather systems operate. This zone, nearest the Earth, is called the **troposphere** and its upper boundary is the **tropopause**.

Figure 12.1 The structure of the atmosphere

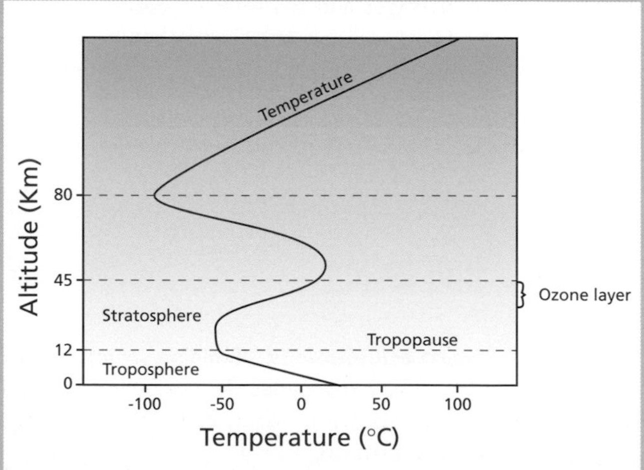

Note that there is an ozone layer in the stratosphere.

The height of the tropopause varies from approximately 8 km at the poles to 16 km at the equator. The troposphere is distinguished from the next layer above, the stratosphere, by its temperature lapse rate. This is the rate at which temperature changes with increased distance from the Earth's surface. Figure 12.1 shows how, in the troposphere, temperature falls with increased height. Then, above the tropopause, temperature remains constant with height and actually increases in the upper stratosphere.

Short wave radiation

The climate system is driven by short wave solar radiation which warms the planet's surface. Gases in the atmosphere such as carbon dioxide and water vapour act like a blanket to preserve this warmth. This is the so called **greenhouse effect** that is so important in maintaining life on Earth. Without these atmospheric gases it has been calculated that the average temperature on the surface would be -18°C rather than the actual 15°C.

When sunlight enters the atmosphere it is mainly in the form of short wave radiation. Approximately 47 percent is absorbed by the Earth's surface, and the rest is either reflected back into space or scattered in the atmosphere. The degree of reflection is called the **albedo**. Water droplets and ice crystals in clouds have a high albedo and, together, they reflect approximately 21 percent of incoming radiation (see figure 12.2).

In the upper atmosphere, a reaction takes place when short wave, ultra violet (UV) radiation strikes oxygen molecules. Ozone is formed. This gas, which consists of three oxygen atoms, helps shield the Earth from the dangerous effects of UV radiation. These dangers include skin cancer and eye cataracts in mammals.

In the 1980s it became clear that ozone holes were forming over polar regions during winter. Scientists have blamed these holes on the chlorine released from chlorofluorocarbons (CFCs) in aerosols and cooling systems. When chlorine atoms come into contact with ozone, it breaks down to oxygen. The polar regions are most affected because cold temperatures promote ozone destruction. In addition, the circulation pattern of polar winds means that there is little mixing with ozone rich, warmer air away from the poles. Attempts are being made to phase out the use of CFCs on a world-scale in order to prevent or slow down the development of ozone holes (see unit 2.5 for more details).

Long wave radiation

When incoming, short wave solar radiation reaches the Earth, it heats the surface. Some of this heat energy is emitted from the surface in the form of long wave radiation. A proportion of this is absorbed by carbon dioxide and water vapour, and helps warm the atmosphere. If the sky is cloudy, more of the radiation is absorbed by the water vapour and then re-emitted back to the ground. If the sky is clear, more of the radiation escapes. This is the reason why cloudy nights remain warmer than clear nights.

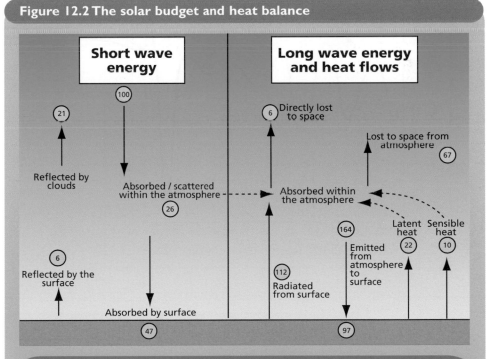

Figure 12.2 The solar budget and heat balance

The solar budget is the balance between incoming solar radiation and outgoing radiation (ie, **the net radiation balance**). Note: the figures are a percentage of total incoming solar radiation. This diagram shows average conditions for the Earth as a whole (and are therefore not typical of either polar or equatorial regions). Also, in any particular region, there is a positive radiation balance during the day time and a negative radiation balance at night when there is no incoming solar radiation.

It is important to emphasise that the atmosphere is warmed from below, not above. Although the source of the energy is solar radiation, it is only when this is reradiated at a longer wavelength from the Earth's surface that it heats the air.

Heat balance

The Earth's surface receives a net surplus of radiation. This is shown in figure 12.2 where incoming radiation that is absorbed at the surface (47 + 97 = 144) is greater than outgoing radiation from the surface (112). This would cause the surface temperature to rise indefinitely if there was not also an outflow of 'sensible' and 'latent' heat (10 + 22 = 32). (These figures are percentages of the total incoming solar radiation.) The transfer of sensible heat is by conduction and by convection. Conduction occurs when the ground warms the air immediately above it. Convection occurs when the warmed air starts to rise.

Latent heat is transferred when water changes from a solid state (ie, ice) to a liquid state, and again when it changes from a liquid state into a gas (ie, water vapour). So, for instance, when water evaporates, heat is extracted from the ground surface. This process occurs over both land and sea.

Activity Day and night time temperatures

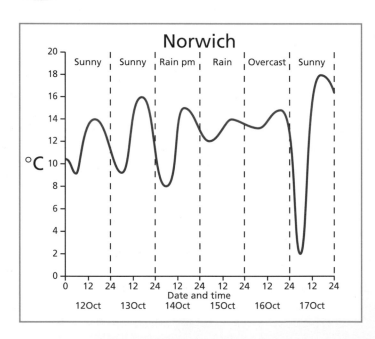

Figure 12.3 Temperatures in Norwich

The graph shows the diurnal (ie, daily) temperature variations in Norwich over a period of six days in October 1995. The daytime weather conditions are also shown.

Questions

1 Describe the temperature pattern over the six days and relate this to the weather conditions.
2 Explain why there is often a bigger diurnal temperature range when skies are clear compared with overcast conditions.

2. What causes the global pattern of circulation?

The global pattern of circulation within the atmosphere is complex. Air moves both vertically and horizontally, and in different directions at different altitudes. The basic force causing atmospheric motion is the variation in temperature between equatorial regions and the poles.

Solar radiation is most intense near the equator and least intense near the poles. This is because the Earth is a sphere. The Sun's rays shine almost vertically downwards at midday in the tropics and so concentrate energy on the surface. In polar regions, the Earth's curvature means that the Sun's rays hit the surface at an angle, even at midday (see figure 12.4). This reduces the intensity of radiation received. A second factor further decreases the energy received in higher latitudes. When solar radiation passes through the atmosphere, some is scattered and absorbed by water vapour, dust and gas molecules. Because the Sun's rays take a longer path through the atmosphere to reach the ground at polar regions, more energy is lost than at the equator.

When solar radiation reaches the surface, the level of absorption of energy varies from place to place. It depends upon the albedo. Over the sea, when the Sun is high, only 2 to 4 percent is reflected, so between 96 and 98 percent is absorbed. On fresh snow, between 75 and 90 percent of radiation is reflected, so 10 to 25 percent is absorbed. This variation reinforces the temperature difference between the snow covered poles and elsewhere.

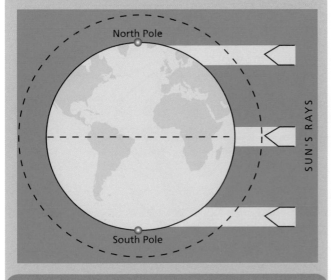

Figure 12.4 Solar radiation at the Earth's surface

North Pole

SUN'S RAYS

South Pole

This diagram shows the Sun overhead at the equator.

Regions which receive and absorb the most intense radiation would simply become hotter and hotter if energy was not transferred to cooler regions. This heat transfer takes place through the ocean and the atmosphere. It is the energy flows in the atmosphere that cause the variations in our weather.

Pressure

Differences in air temperature, arising from unequal heating of the atmosphere, cause differences in **air pressure**. This is the weight of the atmosphere on the Earth's surface. When air warms, it tends to rise and expand. This causes low pressure. Where cooling occurs, the air tends to sink and contract, causing high pressure. The difference between high and low pressure is known as the **pressure gradient**.

Air flows from areas of high to low pressure at the Earth's surface. In the upper troposphere, the flow is reversed. The horizontal flow of air is what we call wind. It blows most strongly where there is a steep pressure gradient, ie where there is a big pressure difference. Air pressure is mapped by plotting lines of equal pressure known as **isobars**. The closer the isobars are together, the greater the pressure gradient and the stronger the wind.

It might be expected that wind would blow directly from high to low pressure areas, at right angles across isobars on a weather map. This is not the case. The reason is due to the Earth's rotation, spinning on its axis once every 24 hours. The effect, known as the **Coriolis force** deflects the wind, to the right in the northern hemisphere and to the left in the southern hemisphere. Towards the equator the force is reduced, and at the equator there is no deflection at all.

One other important influence affects air flow. It is friction with the Earth's surface and the effect is to modify the Coriolis force. Over land, the wind is slowed more than over the sea because there is more friction.

The net result of the pressure gradient, Coriolis force and friction is that winds blow in a concentric, converging pattern towards an area of low pressure. Such an area is called a **depression** or **cyclone** (not to be confused with a tropical cyclone or hurricane). The wind blows in a concentric diverging pattern away from a high pressure area. This is known as an **anticyclone**.

Within a depression, the inflowing air at the Earth's surface escapes by rising upwards. The opposite occurs in an anticyclone, with outflowing air at the surface being replaced by sinking air. The typical surface airflow within a depression and anticyclone (in the northern hemisphere) is shown in figure 12.5.

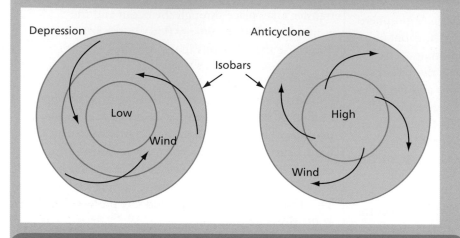

Figure 12.5 Surface air flow in a depression and anticyclone (in the northern hemisphere)

Depression

Anticyclone

Isobars

Low

Wind

High

Wind

Global circulation

The key to understanding the global pattern of pressure and wind is to remember that it is caused by unequal heating of the Earth's atmosphere at different latitudes. At the equator, intense solar radiation causes high temperatures. Air is heated, it expands and rises, then flows outwards towards the poles at high altitudes. Near the poles, the temperature is much colder. Air tends to sink and flow towards the equator at low altitudes.

A complicating factor is that the air moving away from the equator cools and sinks before it reaches polar regions. This occurs between 20 and 30 degrees latitude, causing sub-tropical high pressure belts. These are zones which experience a dry climate, and are typically desert regions over land, for example the Sahara Desert.

The subsiding air diverges, some returning towards the equator and some flowing polewards. The circular pattern of air flow, rising at the equator, flowing outwards, sinking and then returning to the equator is known as the Hadley Cell (see figure 12.6). There are two of these, north and south of the equator. Where the circulating air converges at the surface the area is called the Inter Tropical Convergence Zone (ITCZ). After it converges, the air rises causing clouds to form and creating a zone of high rainfall that is typical of equatorial regions. The ITCZ is an area of low pressure.

Polewards from the Hadley Cell, there are two more cells. These are the Ferrel cell and the Polar cell. Relatively warm, sub-tropical air flows at low altitudes towards the poles in the Ferrel cell until it meets cooler polar air, at which point it rises. This is an area of low pressure and is known as the Polar Front. It is along the Polar Front that depressions are formed.

The global circulation shown in figure 12.6 is sometimes called the 'three cell model'. It provides a starting point for understanding atmospheric motion. However, reality is far more complex. This is because air movement is also affected by the position of land masses and oceans. Temperature differences between land and sea influence winds on a local and continental scale. This effect is described in detail in units 12.3 and 12.4.

The Coriolis force deflects winds within the three atmospheric cells. Near the equator, at the ITCZ, winds tend to be light. This area is called the Doldrums.

Figure 12.6 Atmospheric circulation

Polar cell

Westerlies

Ferrel cell

NE Trade winds

Subtropical high-pressure belt

Hadley cell

ITCZ

SE Trade winds

Hadley cell

Subtropical high-pressure belt

Westerlies

Ferrel cell

Polar cell

Moving polewards, in the northern hemisphere, winds blow from the north east towards the equator. These are the trade winds that derive their name from an old expression meaning 'constant direction'. Over the ocean, these winds blow steadily and were useful at the time of sailing ships. The westerlies, in middle latitudes, blow on average from the south west but not as steadily as the trade winds. They are the winds within which depressions move. (These are described in more detail in unit 12.2.) Towards the North Pole, there is a zone of north easterly polar winds which tend to be irregular and variable.

In the southern hemisphere the pattern is similar except that the trade winds are from the south east, the westerlies from the north west and the polar winds from the south east.

In addition to the Coriolis force, the Earth's rotation causes swirls and eddies within the general circulation. The spiralling clouds and winds within depressions are one result. The effect is to create a complex, chaotic pattern that is difficult to predict. So, although Britain is located in a zone of south westerly air flow, the wind might blow from any direction at different times. This is one factor that makes the weather so variable.

Activity ▸ Atmospheric circulation

◀ **Figure 12.7 Southern Africa and the Indian Ocean**

Questions

1 Describe the distribution and pattern of cloud shown on the satellite photograph.
2 What does the cloud distribution imply about the pressure and wind systems at the time the photograph was taken?

Upper winds

Higher in the atmosphere there is less friction from the Earth's surface than at ground level. As a result, the winds are stronger and are deflected more by the Coriolis force. The outcome is that air circulation is more directly east-west than nearer ground level. In the tropics, the main movement is from east to west but, in higher latitudes, there are much stronger air flows from west to east.

Within these flows there are zones of exceptionally high winds called **jet streams**. The average speed of the high altitude westerly winds is 125 km/h although maximum speeds can approach 500 km/h. These high wind speeds are the reason why it takes less time to fly from North America to Europe than the opposite direction. Jet streams are formed where there is a rapid temperature gradient. A polar front jet stream exists at the tropopause above the Polar Front and a sub-tropical jet stream occurs at the boundary between the Hadley and Ferrel cells.

The winds in the upper troposphere do not flow in parallel lines directly around the globe. Those in higher latitudes have a wave-like pattern called **Rossby waves** (named after a Swedish scientist) (see figure 12.8). These waves change shape and wave length, creating a series of ridges and troughs.

The movement of Rossby waves and the polar front jet stream affects the weather in temperate latitudes. Alternating settled conditions (associated with high

pressure) and changeable conditions (associated with low pressure) are due to complex changes in the upper troposphere. The causes of Rossby wave patterns are not well understood although surface features such as mountain ranges and oceans are thought to play a part. Because the waves are unpredictable it is, as yet, impossible to provide accurate long range weather forecasts.

3. What factors influence Britain's climate?

In addition to the global circulation within the atmosphere there are several other factors that affect Britain's climate. These include the seasonal changes that occur, the moderating influence of the Atlantic Ocean, the prevailing wind direction and the height above sea level.

Seasonal changes

In Britain, there is an annual cycle of four seasons, spring, summer, autumn and winter. The main difference between these is the average temperature and its effect on natural vegetation. In other parts of the world, there are different patterns and there might only be two or three seasons. For example, in some equatorial regions there is a hot and wet season followed by a hot and dry season.

These seasonal variations are caused by the Earth's orbit around the Sun and the 23.5 degree tilt of the Earth's axis. Figure 12.9 shows why, in December, the North Pole is in permanent darkness. At this time of the year, the northern hemisphere is relatively cool because solar radiation has further to pass through the atmosphere, and strikes the ground at a lower angle than in the southern hemisphere. At midday on December 22nd (the winter solstice in the northern hemisphere), the Sun appears directly overhead at the Tropic of Capricorn. Then, six months later, the position is reversed as the Earth has half completed its orbit. The North Pole is in permanent daylight and the Sun appears directly overhead at the Tropic of Cancer at midday on June 21st (the summer solstice). On March 21st and September 22nd (the spring and autumn equinoxes), the Sun appears directly overhead at the equator.

The result of these movements is that the zone of maximum solar radiation moves north and south between the Tropics. This causes the Hadley and other cells to also move north and south, together with their associated wind and pressure systems.

Figure 12.8 Rossby waves in the northern hemisphere

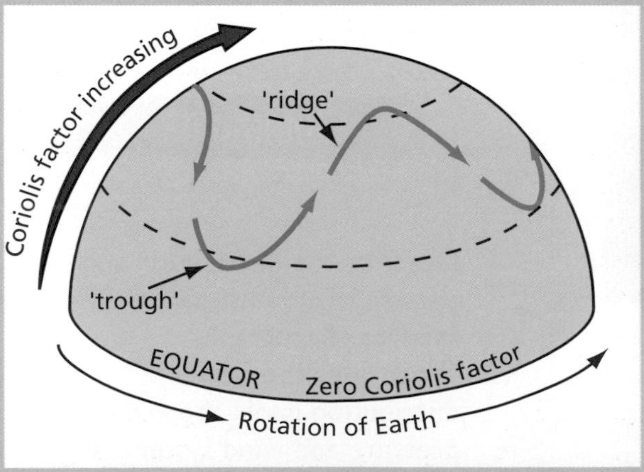

The wave pattern is divided into troughs and ridges. There are usually three to five waves around the hemisphere.

Figure 12.9 Earth's orbit

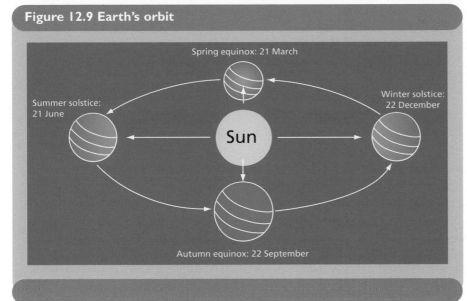

Spring equinox: 21 March

Summer solstice: 21 June

Sun

Winter solstice: 22 December

Autumn equinox: 22 September

In the Mediterranean region, the effect of seasonal changes is marked. In summer, the region is under the influence of subsiding air on the northern side of the Hadley cell. The result is clear skies and generally fine weather. In winter the belt of subsiding air moves south and is replaced by westerly winds that bring depressions and unsettled weather.

In Britain, the northward and southward movement of global wind systems has less effect because the country stays within the influence of the westerlies all year round. However, there are seasonal changes because of the different angle of the Sun's rays and the different length of day between summer and winter. For example, in December, the maximum elevation of the Sun at midday is approximately 16 degrees in London. Even on a clear day, the Sun shines for 8 hours at the most. These factors reduce the intensity of incoming radiation. In summer, the Sun appears much higher in the sky and there can be 16 hours of sunshine on a clear day. This results in a higher temperature than in winter.

Oceanic influence

Britain's maritime position on the eastern margin of the Atlantic Ocean has an important climatic effect. For comparison, consider the winter and summer temperatures of Winnipeg in central Canada, and London. Although they are approximately on the same latitude, the December average in London is 4°C compared with -18°C in Winnipeg. The July average is 17°C in London and 20°C in Winnipeg. The temperature range (ie, the difference between the summer and winter temperatures) is much less in London and this is because

of the moderating influence of the ocean. Two factors are at work. One is ocean currents, the other is the heat retaining properties of water compared with land.

Ocean currents There is a global pattern of circulation within the oceans just as there is within the atmosphere. Both are driven by the imbalance between solar radiation received at the equator compared with the poles. In the Atlantic, the Gulf Stream brings relatively warm water from the tropics northwards across from the Caribbean towards Western Europe. The northerly extension of the Gulf Stream is sometimes known as the North Atlantic Drift.

The effect is to make Britain significantly warmer that it would be otherwise. Compared with Labrador on the east coast of Canada, average January temperatures are at least 10°C higher. On the north west coast of Scotland at Inverewe Gardens, sub-tropical plants are grown in almost frost free conditions. At the same latitude in Labrador, the ground is frozen and snow covered for at least three months of the year.

Land and sea Water takes longer to heat than land and is slower to cool. As a result, in spring and early summer, the sea is relatively slow to warm and causes coastal temperatures to be lower than inland. Then, in autumn and winter, the sea retains its heat longer than the land and causes coastal areas to be relatively warm. The effect is to moderate the climate and reduce the temperature range of places near the sea or ocean. For example, Valentia on the south coast of Ireland has an average annual temperature range of just 8°C. Berlin, almost on the same latitude but 1,300 kilometres inland from the Atlantic, has an average annual temperature range of 20°C.

Prevailing wind

Britain and north west Europe lie in a zone of prevailing westerlies. (When the wind blows mainly from one direction, it is called a prevailing wind.) Earlier in this unit, the point is made that depressions and anticyclones pass over Britain. They cause the wind direction and weather to be variable. Nevertheless, the prevailing direction of the weather systems that cross north west Europe is from the Atlantic Ocean. The result is an air stream laden with moisture. This causes the climate to be wetter in the west than places further to the east. For example, at Penzance in west Cornwall, the average annual precipitation is 1,130 mm. At London, 400 km to the east, the annual average is 600 mm.

Altitude

In general, more rain falls over high ground than low ground. (The reasons for this are covered in unit 12.2.) For Britain, the result is to reinforce the effect of the prevailing wind that causes the west to be wetter than the east. The mountains of the north and west receive an annual average of over 2,000 mm precipitation compared with less than 600 mm on the lowland of East Anglia.

Altitude affects not only rainfall, it also affects temperature. On average, temperature falls by 6°C per 1,000 metres within the troposphere. This means that it is warmer at ground level than at higher levels. There are two reasons for this. Firstly, the atmosphere is heated from below, by radiation from the Earth's surface. Secondly, the density of the atmosphere decreases with altitude. The air is less able to absorb and retain heat as it gets thinner.

The effect of altitude can be illustrated by comparing the conditions on Ben Nevis with nearby Fort William which is at sea level. The summit of Ben Nevis is 1,343 metres above sea level. Its average temperature, over a whole year is just below freezing. The average temperature in Fort William is 9°C higher.

Activity **World temperatures**

▼ **Figure 12.10 January isotherms (°C)**
The map shows average temperatures in January that have been corrected to sea level. This means that they have been raised by 6°C for every 1,000 metres of actual altitude.

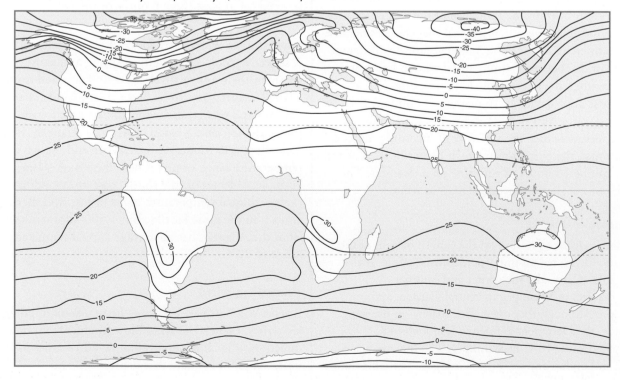

Questions

1 Describe the main features of the temperature pattern shown on the world map (ie, describe where it is hottest, where it is coldest, and what is the difference between land and ocean temperatures).
2 Compare the average January temperature in Britain with places at a similar latitude.
3 Suggest reasons for the world temperature pattern.

unit summary

1 The atmosphere mainly consists of nitrogen and oxygen. Greenhouse gases such as water vapour and carbon dioxide keep the Earth's average temperature above freezing.
2 The driving force of atmospheric motion is the heat imbalance between the equator and the poles, caused by the different intensity of solar radiation received at the Earth's surface.
3 Atmospheric motion creates wind and pressure systems that affect our climate and weather.
4 Air flows are affected by the Earth's rotation and by friction with the Earth's surface.
5 In the upper troposphere there are high speed air flows around the globe. The flows form waves in temperate latitudes and are concentrated in jet streams in some locations. Changes in these air flows have a marked effect on our weather.
6 Apart from atmospheric circulation, the main influences on climate are the seasonal changes brought about by the Earth's orbit around the Sun; the different capacity of water and land to retain heat; the prevailing wind; and altitude.

key terms

Air pressure - the weight of the air at the Earth's surface.

Albedo - the degree of reflection from an object or surface. Fresh snow reflects most incoming solar radiation and therefore has a high albedo.

Anticyclone - an area of high pressure in which air tends to sink and diverge (at low altitudes).

Climate - the average weather conditions at a particular place over a period of time.

Coriolis force - the effect, caused by the Earth's rotation on its axis, of deflecting air flows to the right in the northern hemisphere and to the left in the southern hemisphere.

Depression (or **cyclone**) - an area of low pressure in which air tends to converge (at low altitudes) and rise.

Greenhouse effect - the warming, blanket effect of atmospheric gases such as water vapour and carbon dioxide.

Isobar - a line on a weather chart joining points of equal air pressure.

Jet stream - a concentrated, fast flowing air flow in the upper troposphere.

Pressure gradient - the change in air pressure between two points. A steep gradient is shown on a weather chart by closely drawn isobars and indicates strong winds.

Prevailing wind - the wind direction that is most frequent.

Rossby wave - wave-like pattern of winds in the upper troposphere.

Tropopause - the upper boundary of the troposphere.

Troposphere - the lowest layer of the atmosphere within which most weather occurs.

Weather - the state of the atmosphere at any one time, for example temperature, precipitation, wind and cloud cover.

Unit 12.2 Precipitation

key questions

1 What is condensation?
2 What causes stable and unstable air?
3 What happens when condensation occurs?
4 What causes precipitation?
5 How do people observe and forecast the weather?

1. What is condensation?

In order to understand how precipitation occurs, it is first necessary to understand the atmospheric processes that cause condensation. Air contains water vapour which is a gas. When water turns into vapour, the process is known as evaporation. When the opposite occurs and water vapour changes to a liquid form, this is known as condensation. The main factors that determine whether condensation occurs are the amount of water vapour held in the air and the temperature.

For any particular air temperature, there is a maximum amount of water vapour that the air can hold. When this limit is reached the air is said to be **saturated**. At 10°C, a cubic metre of saturated air will hold approximately 9 gm of water vapour whereas, at 20°C, the same volume of saturated air will hold approximately 17 gm of water vapour. At 30°C, a cubic metre of saturated air will hold approximately 30 gm of water vapour. These figures show that the amount of water vapour that air can hold rises with temperature.

The ratio of water vapour that is actually present in air to the amount of moisture that the air can hold when saturated is known as the **relative humidity**. It is normally expressed as a percentage. As temperature falls, relative humidity rises (and vice versa). This is shown in figure 12.11. For example, if a cubic metre of air at 30°C actually holds 6 gm of water vapour, the relative humidity is 20 percent (because 6 gm is 20 percent of the 30 gm which could be held by saturated air at that temperature). If the temperature

falls to 20°C, the relative humidity of the same air rises to 35 percent, and at 10°C the relative humidity rises to 67 percent. If the temperature continues to fall, the relative humidity will rise to 100 percent at approximately 6°C. At this temperature, called the **dew point**, the air is saturated. If the temperature falls further, the water vapour in the air starts to condense in the form of water droplets. When condensation occurs near ground level, fog forms; when it occurs higher in the atmosphere, clouds form.

Lapse rates

Figure 12.11 shows that condensation becomes more likely when temperature falls. The rate at which temperature falls with increasing height from the Earth's surface is known as the **environmental lapse rate (ELR)** or vertical temperature gradient. (Unit 12.1 explains why temperature falls with increased altitude.) Lapse rates are important in determining whether condensation will occur within the atmosphere, and also at what height it will occur.

The environmental lapse rate averages 6°C per 1,000 metres although this varies under different conditions. Sometimes in still, calm conditions, the lapse rate is low and the temperature might even rise with height for a short distance, causing an inversion (see figure 12.12). However, under most circumstances, temperature falls as height increases.

The environmental lapse rate indicates the temperature of air at different heights above ground level. Rising air does not necessarily cool at this rate and figure 12.13 shows what might happen when a bubble of air rises from the ground. The bubble could be

Figure 12.11 Relative humidity

Air temperature (degrees C)	Quantity of water vapour held in I cubic metre of saturated air (gm)	Relative humidity (Actual water vapour held divided by maximum that could be held)
30	30	6/30 = 20%
20	17	6/17 = 35%
10	9	6/9 = 67%
6	6	6/6 = 100%

The table shows an example in which 6 gm of water vapour is actually contained in each cubic metre of air.

Figure 12.12 Environmental lapse rate and inversion

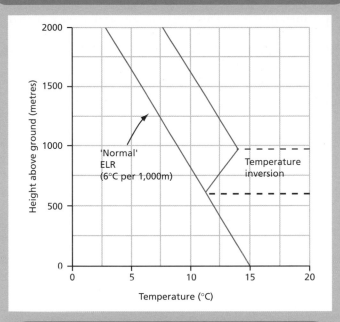

The normal lapse rate is indicated by the line which starts at 15°C at ground level and falls to 3°C at 2,000 metres. The temperature inversion is shown where temperature increases with altitude.

formed, for instance, over a small island that becomes warmer than the surrounding sea. As the bubble of air rises, it expands because atmospheric pressure is lower. This causes it to cool. The rate of cooling due to expansion is 9.8°C per 1,000 m and is called the **dry adiabatic lapse rate (DALR)**. The reason it is 'dry' is not because the air contains no moisture but because there is no condensation at this stage. 'Adiabatic' refers to a change in temperature caused purely by expansion (or contraction) of a gas.

If the rising air bubble falls in temperature below its dew point, condensation occurs and this reduces the lapse rate. This is because water vapour releases latent heat when it changes to a liquid. The heat has the effect of slowing the rate at which the rising air cools. The lower rate of cooling is called the **saturated adiabatic lapse rate (SALR)**. It is not a constant figure because it depends on how much moisture there is in the air. The more water vapour contained in the air, the more heat is released when it condenses - so lowering the SALR. The rate varies from

around 4°C per 1,000 metres to just below the DALR of 9.8°C per 1,000 metres.

Figure 12.13 shows an initial temperature of 20°C for the bubble of air at ground level, and the dew point is, in this example, 6°C. The **condensation level** at which clouds will start to form is approximately 1,430 metres. This is the height at which the bubble of air has cooled to its dew point. (It is calculated by dividing the fall in temperature to the dew point (ie, 20-6= 14) by the DALR (ie, 9.8) and multiplying by 1,000.) Above the condensation level, the air cools at the SALR.

2. What causes stable and unstable air?

The bubble of air shown in figure 12.13 starts to rise because it is warmer than the surrounding air. As long as it remains warmer than the air around it, the bubble will continue to rise. The air is said to be unstable. But, if the bubble of air falls in temperature at a faster rate than the surrounding air, eventually it will be cooler than its immediate environment. It will start to sink and, when this occurs, the air is said to be stable.

Figure 12.13 Lapse rates: DALR and SALR

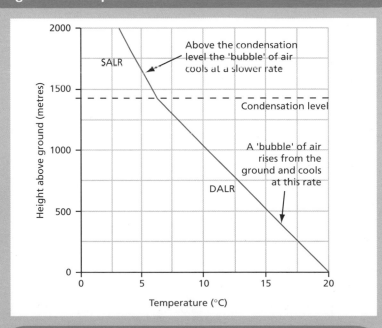

In this example, a bubble of air has an initial temperature of 20°C. It rises from the ground and falls in temperature at the DALR of 9.8°C/1000m. When its temperature falls to 6°C, condensation starts to occur. This releases latent heat and slows the cooling rate.

Stability and instability within the atmosphere depend upon the relative rate at which rising air cools and the environmental lapse rate (ie, the temperature of the surrounding air at different altitudes):

- **stable conditions**: if a bubble of rising air becomes cooler than the surrounding air, it will cease to rise and large clouds are unlikely to form. This occurs if the ELR is lower than the SALR.
- **unstable conditions**: if a bubble of rising air remains warmer than the surrounding air, it will continue to rise and large clouds are likely to form. This occurs if the ELR is higher than the DALR.
- **conditional instability**: this means that the bubble of air is stable as long as it does not fall in temperature to its dew point. Above the height where condensation occurs (ie, the condensation level), the air starts to

cool more slowly (at the SALR). It may reach a point where it becomes warmer than surrounding air and is then unstable. This situation can arise if air is forced upwards over high ground or over a cooler mass of air. It occurs if the environmental lapse rate is between the DALR and SALR.

Stability and instability in air are important because they affect the amount of cloud and therefore rain. When a flow of unstable air crosses Britain, there is likely to be wet weather. In a situation of conditional instability there might be fine weather over low lying areas because the air temperature remains above its dew point. But, over high ground, there might be rain if the air rises and cools sufficiently to become saturated and then unstable. This is one reason why it is wetter over mountains than over low land.

Activity ▶ Stability and instability

Figures 12.14, 12.15 and 12.16 show what might happen when a bubble of air rises. The ground air temperature is 20°C but localised heating warms the bubble to 21°C causing it to rise. The temperature of the rising air and the temperature of the surrounding air at different altitudes are given in the tables.

◀ **Figure 12.14 Stable conditions**

Altitude metres	Temperature (degrees Celsius)	
	Environment	Air bubble
2000	8.0	4.1
1500	11.0	8.1
1000	14.0	12.1
500	17.0	16.1
0	20.0	21.0

Note: In this example; the ELR is 6°C/1000m; the DALR is 9.8°C/1000m; the SALR is 8°C/1000m; the condensation level is 500m.

◀ **Figure 12.15 Unstable conditions**

Altitude metres	Temperature (degrees Celsius)	
	Environment	Air bubble
2000	0.0	4.1
1500	5.0	8.1
1000	10.0	12.1
500	15.0	16.1
0	20.0	21.0

Note: In this example; the ELR is 10°C/1000m; the DALR is 9.8°C/1000m; the SALR is 8°C/1000m; the condensation level is 500m.

| Altitude | Temperature (degrees Celsius) | |
metres	Environment	Air bubble
2000	8.0	8.6
1500	11.0	11.1
1000	14.0	13.6
500	17.0	16.1
0	20.0	21.0

Note: In this example; the air is forced to rise as it crosses a line of mountains; the ELR is 6°C/1000m; the DALR is 9.8°C/1000m; the SALR is 5°C/1000m; the condensation level is at 500 metres.

◄ Figure 12.16 Conditional instability

Questions

1 Sketch three graphs to show the data in figures 12.14, 12.15 and 12.16. (Use figure 12.13 as a guide, though note that you need to extend the temperature axis to 21°C.) Mark on the ELR and the lapse rate of the bubble of rising air. In each case, mark on the condensation level and, for figure 12.16, mark the altitude above which the air becomes unstable.

2 Describe what your graphs show.

3. What happens when condensation occurs?

When the air temperature falls below its dew point, condensation occurs. Under these conditions, dew, fog, mist or cloud might form.

Dew

Dew forms on cold surfaces at night when nearby air is cooled to the point where it is saturated. Under these conditions, the air cannot hold all its water vapour and moisture is deposited as tiny droplets. Most dew occurs on clear nights when there is no cloud cover to slow radiation cooling of the Earth's surface. Wind prevents dew from forming because it mixes the air and does not allow long enough contact between the air and the cold surface.

If the temperature falls below freezing, dew turns into frost and gives the ground a white appearance. If water droplets freeze on surfaces that are below freezing point, rime is formed. This is a deposit of white, opaque ice crystals. If there is a slight wind the crystals can build into feathery shapes on the windward side of objects.

Figure 12.17 Rime

When dew forms on freezing surfaces, ice crystals form.

Fog and mist

Within the atmosphere, condensation occurs around very small particles (or nuclei) of dust, smoke, sulphur dioxide or salt. When this happens at ground level, the result is that water droplets limit visibility. When visibility is less than one kilometre, this is generally defined as fog. Visibility between one and two kilometres is defined as mist.

There are two main types of fog - **advection** and **radiation**. Although they are both formed by condensation of water vapour, the causes are different. (The term hill fog is sometimes also used though, strictly speaking, it is simply low cloud over an upland area.)

Advection fog This is caused when relatively warm, moist air passes over a colder surface. The lower layers of air are cooled and, if they go below the dew point, condensation occurs. This can happen on coastlines where a cold ocean current cools the air above. Examples include the coast of central California, near San Francisco, and the coast of Newfoundland in eastern Canada. A similar process occurs off the east coast of England and Scotland in late spring and early summer. The North Sea cools during the winter and is slower to heat than the land in spring. Fog forms if relatively warm air blows offshore and is cooled. An onshore breeze can then blow the fog inland where it can persist for several kilometres. Eventually the warmer land heats the air and the water droplets evaporate.

Radiation fog This occurs when the Earth's surface cools at night, particularly in cloudless conditions. The cold ground causes the temperature of overlying air to fall below its dew point. The resulting condensation creates fog. It does not form in windy conditions because turbulent air does not stay in contact with the ground long enough for sufficient cooling to occur.

In hilly or mountainous regions, cold air tends to flow downhill at night so causing the temperature to be lower in valleys than on higher slopes. This explains why fog forms in hollows and valleys (see figure 12.18).

Fog can persist all day if cold air is trapped beneath warmer air in a temperature inversion. Under normal daytime conditions the ground warms causing air to

Figure 12.18 Valley fog

Cool air has sunk into the valley and the air temperature has fallen below its dew point causing condensation to occur. There is an inversion with warm air above.

rise. But, if it is foggy, the sunlight might not penetrate to the ground and there is no uplift of warm air to break the inversion. When this happens in urban areas, the combination of fog, smoke and vehicle exhausts can create smog. Only a wind that is strong enough to mix the air can clear the fog under these circumstances.

Cloud

When water vapour condenses within the atmosphere, clouds form. These consist of water droplets and, at high altitudes, also of ice crystals. Clouds are important to weather and climate because they affect the amount of precipitation and also the amount of solar radiation received at the Earth's surface.

There are many different forms of clouds (see figure 12.19). They can be classified by altitude and by shape. High clouds are typically above 6,000 metres, middle clouds are above 2,000 metres and low clouds are below 2,000 metres. Cloud shape can broadly be divided into layered (or stratiform) and vertically developed (or cumuliform).

Different clouds are associated with particular weather patterns and are therefore useful in forecasting. This is particularly true when a weather front is approaching. This topic is covered in the next section of the unit.

Some parts of the world are cloudier than others. Temperate regions, in the zone of westerly winds on the western margins of land masses, such as Britain and British Columbia, tend to be cloudy. So are equatorial regions at the Inter Tropical Convergence Zone - particularly later in the day when cumulus clouds have built up. Both types of region experience unstable air conditions.

The sub-tropical zones of subsiding air, for example in the Sahara Desert, are the least cloudy places on Earth. Even during the day, rising convection currents of warm air rarely cool below the dew point.

Figure 12.19 Cloud types

Cirrus	high, wispy cloud
Cirrostratus	high, layered cloud through which the Sun can shine - creating a halo effect
Cirrocumulus	high, bubbly cloud - its similarity to fish scales sometimes gives it the name mackerel sky
Altostratus	medium, layered cloud, thicker than cirrostratus, sometimes with a halo effect
Altocumulus	medium, bubbly cloud
Stratus	low, layered cloud causing overcast, grey conditions
Nimbostratus	low, stratus cloud from which precipitation is falling
Stratocumulus	low, generally unbroken cloud, grey or whitish in colour - in the shape of rolls or rounded masses
Cumulus	bubbly cloud that can vary in height from small fair weather cumulus to much larger storm clouds
Cumulonimbus	towering thunderclouds that can rise to the tropopause - the top may spread out in the form of an anvil

Figure 12.20 Cloud types

Cirrus

Stratus

Altostratus

Cumulus

Cumulonimbus

4. What causes precipitation?

Inside a cloud, there is a mass of water droplets. When they first condense they are very small and they float in the air. However, if there is a strong uplift of air, the droplets will collide and coalesce (ie, join together). Once they reach a certain size, gravity causes the water drops to fall as rain. The stronger the uplift, the higher that water droplets will rise in the cloud - so giving them a longer time to grow. If the temperature falls below 0°C, the droplets might not freeze immediately but remain as a liquid in a supercooled state. At temperatures below -10°C, ice crystals form and rapidly grow with the moisture from the supercooled droplets. When the crystals reach a big enough size, they fall as snowflakes. However, if the temperature is sufficiently warm at a lower altitude, the snowflakes melt and drop as rain - gaining size as they collide with more droplets.

In large cumulonimbus clouds, the droplets can sometimes fall and then be swept back up into the higher part of the cloud several times. If the droplet freezes, a new layer of ice is added each time that uplift occurs. This forms hail and, in some circumstances, hailstones can grow very large. Although most have a diameter less than 10 mm, some have been recorded weighing over 1 kg. When large hailstones fall there can be severe damage to property and crops.

Types of precipitation

Precipitation includes rain, snow and hail. Whether moisture falls in liquid or in frozen form depends upon the air temperature and the cloud conditions. Precipitation occurs due to a number of factors which cause air to rise and clouds to form. Different types of precipitation are classified according to the causes of upward air movement. There are three main types, convectional, cyclonic and relief.

Convectional precipitation This occurs when air is heated locally. The heat source might be an area of land or sea that has been heated by the Sun's rays. The air rises in a convection current. The stronger the uplift, the greater is the volume of condensed water vapour and therefore the chance of rain. It is in unstable air that most convectional rain occurs.

In equatorial regions where high temperatures and high humidity exists for most of the year, convectional rainfall is common. In temperate latitudes, convectional rainfall is most frequent in summer when the Sun's rays are at their strongest. It is the reason why continental interiors have a summer maximum of rainfall. Convectional rain can also occur in temperate coastal regions in winter when, for example, cold air is warmed by the relatively warm sea.

Thunderstorms occur most often in conditions of very rapid convectional uplift. They can cause heavy rain, hail and squalls (ie, sudden increases in wind speed) (see figure 12.21). The thunder and lightening that accompanies thunderstorms is due to a build up of a positive electrical charge high in the cloud and a negative charge at the base of the cloud.

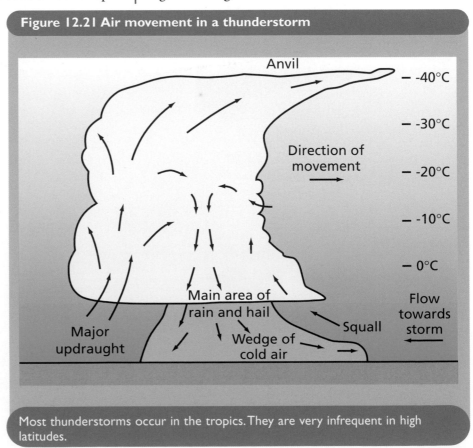

Figure 12.21 Air movement in a thunderstorm

Anvil

Direction of movement

Main area of rain and hail

Major updraught

Wedge of cold air

Squall

Flow towards storm

Most thunderstorms occur in the tropics. They are very infrequent in high latitudes.

Activity | **Thunderstorms and lightning**

▼ **Figure 12.22 Frequency of lightning strikes in the USA**

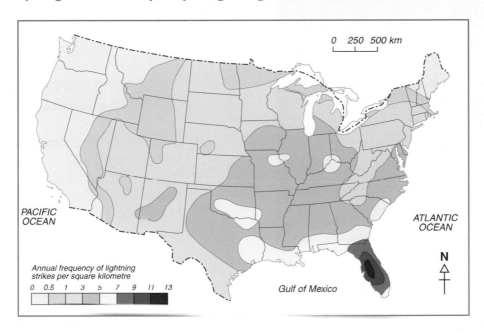

▼ **Figure 12.23 Climate graphs for Seattle and Miami**

Seattle is in the Pacific Northwest of the USA and Miami is in Florida.

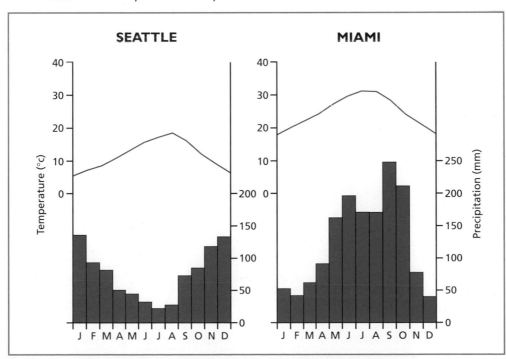

◀ **Figure 12.24 Lightning in Florida**

Questions

1 Describe the distribution of lightning strikes in the USA.
2 Suggest why lightning is more frequent in Florida than in the Pacific Northwest.

Cyclonic (or frontal) precipitation Cyclones are areas of converging and rising air, mainly occurring in temperate latitudes. They are also called depressions or 'lows' (because of the low atmospheric pressure associated with them). Note that a temperate latitude cyclone is not the same as a tropical cyclone or hurricane. To avoid confusion, the term depression is used in this chapter.

The cause of depressions is the air movement caused by the temperature difference between the equator and the poles (see unit 12.1). The Earth's rotation deflects the air flow and helps create a spiralling effect. Depressions form on or near the Polar Front. This is where the relatively warm air of the Ferrel Cell and the relatively cold air of the Polar Cell meet and is marked by a steep temperature gradient. The Polar Front Jet Stream flows in the upper troposphere at this point.

The formation of depressions (or cyclogenesis) is complex. For many years it was believed that they originated as waves in the

Polar Front and, as the wave developed, a warm sector of air became wedged between cold air. The leading edge of warm air is called a **warm front** and the leading edge of cold air is called a **cold front**. The process is shown in figure 12.25.

Although fronts are drawn as lines on a map, in reality they are narrow zones in which there is a steep temperature gradient. In other words, there is not a point at which temperature changes from warm to cold. Rather there is a zone in which relatively warmer and relatively colder air mix.

Figure 12.25 Traditional theory of depression formation

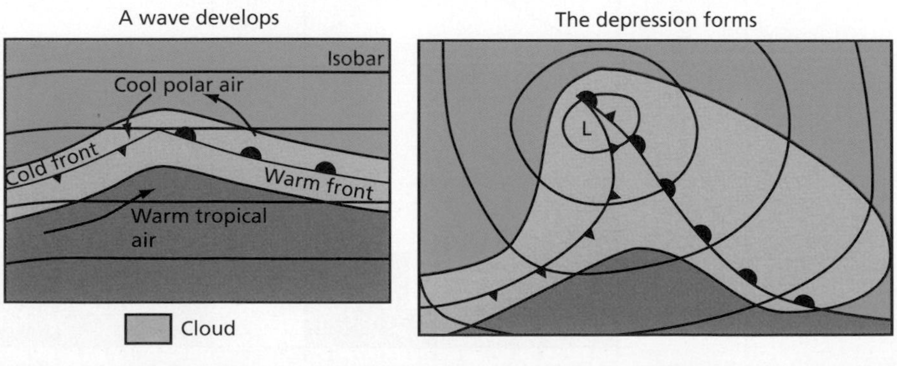

A wave develops

Isobar
Cool polar air
Cold front
Warm front
Warm tropical air

☐ Cloud

The depression forms

L

Figure 12.26 Upper air flow and depression formation

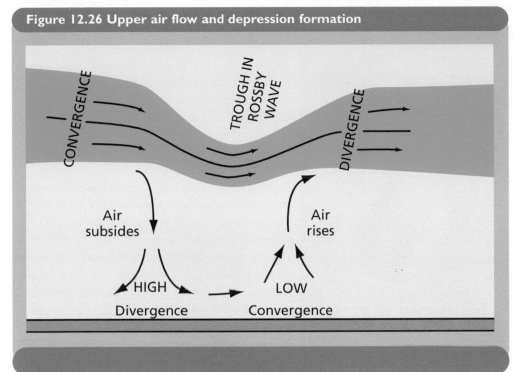

Research on the upper troposphere has shown that the traditional explanation of how depressions form may not be correct. It is now believed that fronts are caused by the rotation of air around a depression's centre and are a consequence of depressions rather than the cause. Waves in the upper troposphere's westerly winds (Rossby waves) and the position of the jet stream are thought to play an important part in depression formation. Where the upper winds converge before a trough in a Rossby wave, air tends to subside and then diverge at lower levels - causing relatively high pressure. Air moving away from the trough at upper levels tends to diverge and

causes air to rise from lower levels. This causes low pressure at the surface and is the point at which depressions form. Figure 12.26 shows the process.

In the normal pattern of Rossby waves (in the northern hemisphere) there is a trough above the east coast of North America. The diverging air in the upper tropopause to the east of this point causes air to rise from below. This helps to explain why most of the depressions that cross Britain form in the western Atlantic, between North America and Iceland.

Because depressions are zones of rising air, they tend to bring cloudy, wet conditions. Along the fronts, where relatively warmer and cooler air meets, the warmer air rises above the cooler air. A generalised cross-section is shown in figure 12.27. In reality there is great variation between depressions - in terms of temperature, stability, cloud pattern and precipitation.

The warm front is generally less steep than the cold front. Its approach is marked several hours ahead by high cirrus cloud. As the front approaches, the cloud thickens and rain begins to fall. Once the front has passed, temperature rises and the sky often becomes clearer. The passage of the cold front is often marked by

Figure 12.27 Cross section of a warm and cold front in a depression

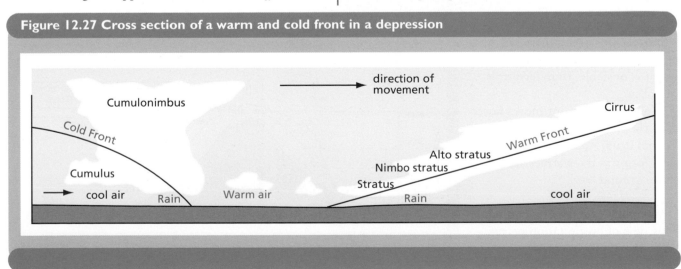

Figure 12.28 Satellite image of a depression approaching the British Isles

High cirrus clouds over the Irish Sea are a sign of an approaching front. At this point the front is occluded. To the south west of Ireland the cold front is bringing thick cloud. Behind the frontal system there is an area of cumulus cloud over the Atlantic.

rise. As the air rises, it expands and cools, clouds form and precipitation can follow. The rain is heaviest in conditions of cyclonic or convectional rainfall when the relief causes an extra uplift to air that is already rising.

An additional reason why precipitation is high over mountains is because the speed of air flow is reduced by friction. A belt of rain therefore takes longer to pass over high ground than, for instance, a region of low land.

Once an air flow has crossed high ground, it starts to descend and also warm. This is due to compression (the opposite of what occurs when air rises and expands). Clouds tend to thin as the moisture evaporates and this causes a **rain shadow** (ie, a relatively dry zone on the leeward or sheltered side of the high ground).

In some regions, the warming effect as air subsides on the leeward side of mountains can be very marked. Figure 12.29 shows how it occurs. On the windward side of the mountain range, the air rises. When the air temperature falls to its dew point, condensation occurs and it cools at the saturated adiabatic lapse rate (SALR). However, on the leeward side, the moisture evaporates and the air warms at the dry adiabatic lapse rate (which is higher than the SALR). In the Alps, the warm wind on the leeward side of the mountains is called the 'fohn' and in the Canadian Rockies it is called the 'chinook'. The result in winter can be a rapid thaw of lying snow and an increased avalanche danger.

a shorter but more intense period of rainfall. If the air in the warm sector is unstable, thunderstorms can occur.

Often the cold front moves faster than the warm front and sometimes catches it up. An occluded front then forms as the warmer air rises above ground level.

Orographic (or relief) precipitation
This type of precipitation occurs when an air flow meets a range of hills or mountains and is forced to

Figure 12.29 Fohn

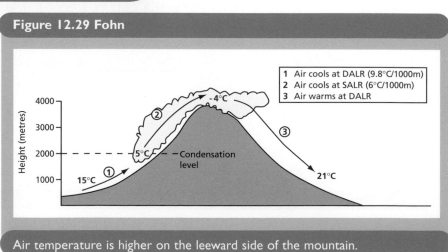

1 Air cools at DALR ($9.8°C/1000m$)
2 Air cools at SALR ($6°C/1000m$)
3 Air warms at DALR

Height (metres): 4000, 3000, 2000, 1000

-4°C
5°C — Condensation level
15°C ①
② ③
21°C

Air temperature is higher on the leeward side of the mountain.

Activity | North Wales and the Cheshire Plain

▼ **Figure 12.30 Relief**

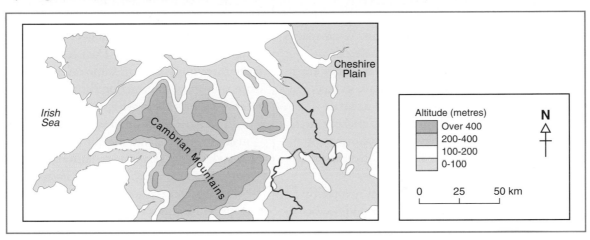

▼ **Figure 12.31 Precipitation**

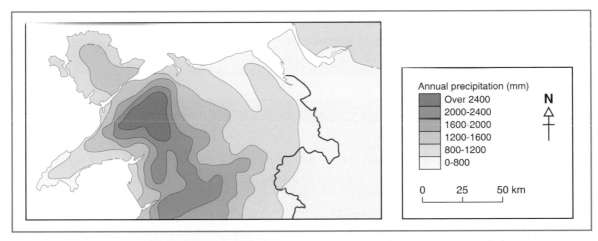

Questions

1 Describe the relationship between annual precipitation and relief as shown on the two maps.
2 Explain why the Cheshire Plain receives less precipitation than the Cambrian Mountains.

5. How do people observe and forecast the weather?

Weather forecasts are important for a number of reasons. For example, road conditions are affected by the weather. Fog warnings can reduce accidents and local authorities need to know if frosts are forecast so they can salt and grit roads. The Environment Agency, which is responsible for flood alerts, requires accurate predictions of the timing and intensity of precipitation. Wind speeds and direction affect shipping, oil rigs and aircraft.

Farmers need to know the likely weather if they are planting or harvesting crops, or if they have animals outside. Sporting organisations also need accurate forecasts if, for instance, an event such as cricket match is scheduled. On holiday, people often organise their time depending on the weather forecast - for example spending time on a beach or finding indoor entertainment. Even on a day-to-day basis, people find it useful to know the forecast so that they can decide what clothes to wear or whether to carry an umbrella.

In parts of the world which experience more extreme weather conditions than Britain, accurate forecasts can save lives. The National Hurricane Centre in Florida warns people in the USA and Caribbean region of likely hurricane and storm paths. There is then a chance that inhabitants can gain shelter or evacuate the danger area. In mountain regions with a winter sports industry, weather forecasts can also prevent loss of life. Heavy falls of snow, high winds and sudden thaws can all trigger avalanches. Accurate forecasting can reduce the risk from these hazards.

Making forecasts

In the UK, the Meteorological Office is the official agency which makes weather forecasts. It is also part of a world-wide network of weather forecasting organisations. These communicate via satellite links and contribute information to each other. There are three stages in making forecasts:

- making observations of current weather conditions
- collecting and analysing data
- producing the forecast.

Observations The Met Office gathers information in a wide variety of ways. Measurements are made of air pressure, from barometers; temperature, from thermometers; wind speed, from anemometers; and precipitation from rain gauges. Visual assessments of cloud cover are also made. Data is collected at least once every three hours and, in some cases, every hour. The main sources of information for the Met Office are:

- land stations: there are approximately 200 in the UK with weather recording instruments - observations are made by professional meteorologists and volunteers, though over 50 stations are automatic
- buoys: these are moored in the Eastern Atlantic collecting and transmitting data automatically
- ships and aircraft: there are over 500 ships and rigs of the UK Voluntary Observing Fleet
- balloons (or radiosondes): these are released every 12 hours and can reach heights of 20 km - they transmit data on temperature, humidity and wind speed
- satellites: these were first used in the 1960s - they

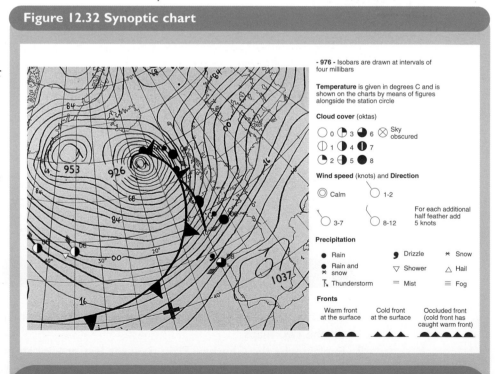

Figure 12.32 Synoptic chart

This chart was produced on the 9th January 1993. It shows a deep depression approaching Scotland, and high pressure over Spain. The chart was drawn by the Met Office in order to prepare a forecast.

provide information on cloud cover, wind speed and temperature
- radar: the British Isles are now covered by a network of weather radars that record rainfall intensity and duration.

Analysis The weather observations are collected together at the Bracknell Met Office centre. Meteorologists use the information to prepare a weather map (or synoptic chart) (see figure 12.32). Isobars, fronts, wind speed and direction are marked on the map. Data is also fed into the Met Office computer system.

Forecasting Using computer models of the atmosphere, forecasts are generated for up to ten days ahead. Human weather forecasters use their knowledge and experience to modify the computer predictions when they think it is necessary.

The Met Office claims over 80 percent accuracy with its 24 hour forecasts but this figure falls substantially for the 10 day forecasts. The problem is that the atmosphere is complex, dynamic and chaotic. Because it is constantly changing, small variations from the expected pattern can have a powerful and unpredictable effect.

Activity ▶ The Great Storm of October 15/16, 1987

On the evening of October 15, 1987, a BBC weather forecast presenter famously declared that 'a lady has phoned to say that a hurricane is on its way', and proceeded to tell her that she was wrong.

Later that night, winds of over 100 mph swept across southern England, killing 18 people and causing damage costing over £300 million. Most of the deaths were due to falling chimney pots, masonry and trees. In some cases, people in cars crashed into the fallen trees which lay across darkened roads. Railway lines were also blocked by fallen trees and over 100 flights were cancelled from Heathrow and Gatwick. Electricity lines and pylons were so damaged that much of South East England was without power for over six hours. In East Sussex, almost a quarter of all mature trees were blown down and Kew Gardens lost a third of its trees.

The cause of the storm was an explosive (ie, sudden and sizable) deepening of pressure in a depression over the Bay of Biscay. This means that there must have been a rapid increase in the rate of air convergence and uplift at the centre of the system. A big rise in air pressure took place just behind the depression and the steep pressure gradient caused the high winds. The mechanism that causes explosive storms is not clear although they do occur in other parts of the world. Such storms are rare in the UK. The Great Storm of 1703 was probably the last time that similar winds were experienced in the south of England.

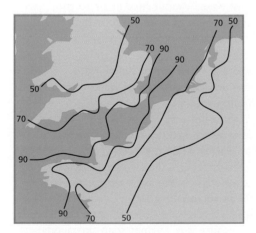

▲ **Figure 12.33 Highest recorded wind speeds during the Great Storm (in knots)**
Note: a knot is equivalent to 1.15 mph

Questions

1 Suggest possible reasons why an accurate forecast was not made on the mid-evening news of October 15th.
2 Using the map of wind speeds, describe the track of the storm.
3 To what extent could the deaths and damage have been avoided if a more accurate forecast had been issued?
4 Explain why the British Isles' weather is dominated by depressions.

unit summary

1 Condensation occurs when air cools and water vapour changes to a liquid form.
2 The stability and instability of air depends on the rate at which it cools when it rises, compared with the temperature of surrounding air.
3 When water vapour condenses in air it can cause fog, clouds, dew and frost.
4 There are three main types of precipitation, each related to the reason for the uplift of air that causes the condensation. They are called convectional, cyclonic and orographic precipitation.
5 Weather forecasting involves making observations, analysing data and making predictions. Short term forecasts are relatively accurate and are made possible by using computer models and data processing. Accurate long term predictions cannot at present be made because of the large number of variables involved and the chaotic behaviour of the atmosphere.

key terms

Cold front - the leading edge of relatively cold air in a depression or cyclone.
Condensation - the conversion of water vapour (a gas) to water (a liquid) - it occurs when there is a sufficient fall in temperature.
Condensation level - the altitude at which water vapour starts to condense.
Conditional instability - the condition in which air is stable at low altitudes but may become unstable if forced to rise above the condensation level.
Convectional precipitation - precipitation caused when relatively warm convection currents of air rise and cool - causing water vapour to condense.
Cyclone (or **depression** or **low**) - an area of converging, rising air with low atmospheric pressure at the Earth's surface.
Cyclonic (or **frontal**) **precipitation** - precipitation caused when air rises in a cyclone.
Dew point - the temperature at which water vapour condenses.
Dry adiabatic lapse rate (DALR) - the rate at which (unsaturated) air cools when it rises (or warms when it subsides).
Environmental lapse rate (ELR) - the rate at which temperature falls with increased height.
Fog - water droplets that have condensed at

ground level, reducing visibility to less than 1 km.
Inversion - a rise in temperature with increased altitude - the reverse of normal conditions.
Orographic (or **relief**) **precipitation** - precipitation caused when an air flow is forced to rise over high ground.
Rain shadow - an area of relatively low precipitation on the leeward (sheltered) side of high ground.
Relative humidity - the ratio of the actual amount of water vapour held in air to the maximum amount of water vapour that could be held if the air is saturated (expressed as a percentage).
Saturated air - air that is holding the maximum possible quantity of water vapour (at a given temperature).
Saturated adiabatic lapse rate (SALR) - the rate at which saturated air cools when it rises (or warms when it subsides).
Stable conditions - the air has no tendency to rise (because it it is the same temperature or cooler than surrounding air).
Unstable conditions - the air has a tendency to rise (because it is warmer than surrounding air).
Warm front - the leading edge of relatively warm air in a depression.

Large scale weather systems

key questions

1 How do depressions and anticyclones affect the weather?
2 What are tropical cyclones and what is their effect?
3 What is the monsoon and how does it affect people?

1. How do depressions and anticyclones affect the weather?

In the British Isles, the daily pattern of weather is largely determined by the passage of depressions and anticyclones. The formation of depressions (areas of low pressure) and anticyclones (areas of high pressure) is described in unit 12.2. They occur mainly in the mid-latitude westerly winds that circle the Earth.

Because air tends to rise in depressions, and also because fronts form in them, these low pressure systems generally bring precipitation. By contrast, anticyclones are associated with dry weather because the air is subsiding. As the air sinks, it warms and water droplets contained within it tend to evaporate.

At the Earth's surface, air moves from high to low pressure areas. However, the Earth's rotation deflects winds from a straight line path. It causes air to flow in a concentric pattern, converging anticlockwise towards the centre of depressions and diverging clockwise outwards from anticyclones (in the northern hemisphere).

As well as causing either wet or dry weather, depressions and anticyclones also influence the temperature. This is because the spiralling winds within these systems draw in **air masses** from different directions. An air mass is a

body of air with uniform temperature and humidity characteristics. It gains these characteristics from its source area. The British Isles are affected by air masses that are Tropical, Polar or Arctic in origin. (Air from a fourth source region - Equatorial - does not affect Britain.) The air masses are further subdivided according to whether they form over the ocean (maritime) or land (continental). The characteristics and source of air masses affecting Britain are shown in figure 12.34.

The character of air masses changes as they move away from their source areas. For instance, air moving towards the poles generally crosses cooler surfaces. In

Figure 12.34 Air masses and source regions

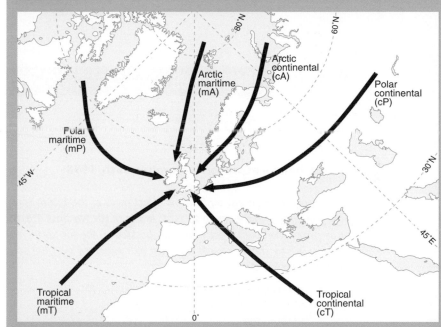

Air mass characteristics:

Air mass	Symbol	Characteristics
Arctic continental	cA	Very cold and dry.
Arctic maritime	mA	Very cold. Can become unstable when crossing warmer seas.
Polar continental	cP	Cold and generally dry in winter, dry and warm in summer.
Polar maritime	mP	Cool and moist. Can be unstable bringing showery weather.
Tropical continental	cT	Warm and dry. Can bring heatwave conditions in summer.
Tropical maritime	mT	Warm and moist. Brings mild, wet weather in winter, warm wet weather in summer.

winter, this might cause the lower layers of air to fall below their dew point and become saturated. This creates low clouds but the air remains generally stable.

When an air mass moves from its source towards the equator, its lower layers come into contact with warmer surfaces. This causes the air to become less stable and can result in convectional rain.

Because depressions and anticyclones draw in air from different sources, the weather in temperate latitudes can show marked variations over a short time period. The precise effect of an air mass depends upon its source region, its track and the speed of movement over intervening surfaces. For example, Polar continental air in winter is generally dry but, if it is relatively slow moving over the North Sea, it can pick up warmth and moisture. The east coast of Scotland and England can experience low cloud and snow under these less stable conditions (see figure 12.35).

Figure 12.35 Polar continental air flow

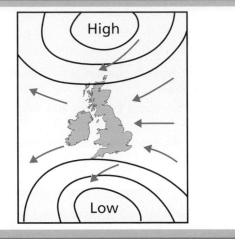

Note that the easterly air flow is caused by the relative positions of the high and low pressure systems.

 Activity) **Air masses**

A weather forecast for November 15th, 1998:

A relatively warm, moist air flow will affect most of the British Isles. Maximum temperatures will vary from 15°C in the south to 10°C in the north. No frost is expected. Winds will be moderate to strong from the south west with gales possible in the far north west.
The sky will be mainly cloudy with light rain expected over the south and heavier bursts over high ground in the north.

 ## Questions

1 Suggest, with reasons, which air mass was affecting the British Isles on the date of the weather forecast.
2 Draw a sketch map of the British Isles showing the relative position of high and low pressure areas (and wind directions) that could cause such weather conditions.
3 Explain why depressions and anticyclones are associated with particular weather patterns.

Sometimes an anticyclone becomes 'stuck' in a stationary position over the Eastern Atlantic or North West Europe. It is then called a **blocking high**. The effect is to divert the normal flow of depressions north and south of Britain and bring dry weather. Anticyclones are generally bigger than depressions. They might sometimes be over two thousand kilometres in diameter and can affect the weather for days or even weeks.

In Britain, the effect of such a blocking high depends on its exact position and the season in which it occurs. In summer, the result can be exceptionally warm, fine weather. The droughts of 1995 and 1996 were caused when depressions were diverted northwards and southwards of the British Isles by large blocking high pressure areas.

In winter, the effect can be to bring exceptionally cold weather such as that experienced in 1978/79 and 1987/88. If the anticyclone is centred on Scandinavia the clockwise winds bring very cold, dry air from Siberia. The conditions are not always sunny and clear in Britain because low cloud can sometimes form as the air passes over the relatively warm North Sea. If, during such a period, depressions and their fronts penetrate eastwards over the British Isles they can bring heavy snowfalls where the relatively moist air meets the colder continental air.

2. What are tropical cyclones and what is their effect?

In the zone of trade wind easterlies that circle the globe north and south of the equator, weather conditions tend to be less variable than in the mid-latitude westerlies. However, in summer and autumn, tropical cyclones sometimes occur. These are relatively small, intense, revolving storms that are called hurricanes in the Atlantic, cyclones in the Indian Ocean, willy-willies off Australia and typhoons in the western Pacific (see figure 12.36).

The precise cause of tropical cyclones is not well understood although the conditions in which they form is known. Cyclones generally form:
- over warm seas with a surface temperature of at least 27°C
- in the tropics, but not within 5 degrees of the equator

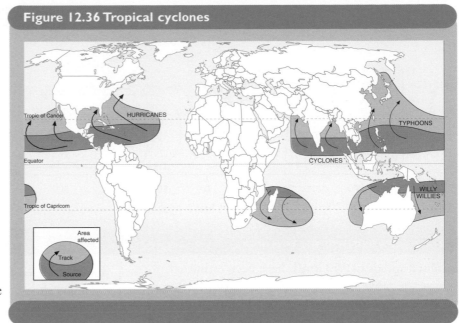

Figure 12.36 Tropical cyclones

(because the Coriolis force weakens towards the equator)
- between July and November in the northern hemisphere and between January and March in the southern hemisphere (ie, where the Earth's surface is hottest).

In the Atlantic, hurricanes form off the coast of West Africa. Rising convection currents within the atmosphere carry large amounts of water vapour upwards. The heat that is generated when the water vapour condenses is the main source of energy in the storm. As much as 200 million tonnes of seawater per day is recycled in a hurricane - first evaporated from the sea then deposited as rain. When hurricanes move over land, they lose their power because they no longer have a supply of moist rising air.

Once a rising column of air over the warm sea develops, more air converges and rotation starts. Large clouds form, heavy rain falls and winds strengthen. The vertical height of the clouds can be 10 - 12 km (see figure 12.37). As the storm moves westwards across the Atlantic it might gain strength and will be officially upgraded from a tropical storm to a hurricane when its winds reach 120 km/h. Then, depending on wind speed, it will be classed as a category one hurricane up to the most powerful, category five.

Hurricanes can be 800 km in diameter although the most powerful winds are in a much smaller area near the centre. At the very centre of the swirling winds and clouds there is a small 'eye' where calm and clear conditions occur. This is a zone of subsiding air. The strongest winds are experienced near the eye wall where

Figure 12.37 Cross section of a hurricane

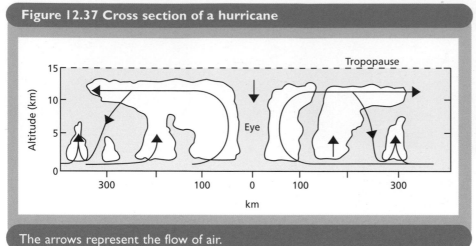

The arrows represent the flow of air.

localised speeds of 250 km/h have been estimated (above the range of most recording instruments).

The track of hurricanes is generally westwards, moving at a speed of 15-20 km/h. Their path is erratic and difficult to predict, eventually swinging polewards at the end of their life. The strong winds and very low pressure associated with hurricanes (pressure can drop by 50 millibars near the centre) cause the sea level to rise as the storm passes. This surge is a major hazard for people living in coastal areas.

Hurricane hazards

The damage and destruction caused by hurricanes has prompted the development of systems to warn and protect people. These efforts are well resourced in high income countries such as the United States and Japan. However, Third World countries often lack the warning facilities, organised evacuation plans and strongly constructed dwellings that reduce the hazard for US citizens. To give an idea of the difficulties facing low income countries, it is estimated that over 500,000 people have lost their lives as a direct consequence of tropical cyclones in Bangladesh in the past 25 years. The country has an extremely high population density and a very low per capita GNP (ranking 141st in the world). Many people live on low lying coastal and river margins, their houses are generally flimsy and there are only a relatively small number of concrete storm shelters.

The biggest hazard caused by tropical

cyclones in Bangladesh is flooding. On coasts and river banks, houses are swept away and people and livestock drown.

In parts of the world that are hilly or mountainous, tropical cyclones bring not only flooding but also mudslides and avalanches. During November 1998, the central American countries of Nicaragua and Honduras were very badly hit by Hurricane Mitch. These countries are amongst the poorest in the western hemisphere. The hurricane slowed as it crossed onto the land and, in some places, deposited almost a metre of rain in two days. The result was devastating mudslides, particularly where unconsolidated volcanic ash slopes were exposed. Deforestation and the removal of natural vegetation cover over previous decades increased the amount of soil and debris that was brought down into the swollen rivers.

An estimated 15,000 people died in Honduras alone and over a million people were made homeless. At the height of the floods, small streams were turned into torrents a hundred metres wide. The worst affected people were the poorest who lived in shanty settlements

Figure 12.38 Satellite photograph of a hurricane in the Gulf of Mexico

The eye is visible in the centre of the hurricane.

Figure 12.39 Hurricane damage in Honduras and Nicaragua

on river banks. The exact numbers who were drowned or buried in mud will probably never be known. Most bridges were destroyed, dirt roads were swept away and crops were flattened or washed away. Relief was very slow to reach remote areas because land communications were so disrupted. Helicopters were the only means to provide assistance but there were very few of these in either Honduras or Nicaragua. The first priority was to provide clean drinking water and prevent the outbreak of disease. Then shelter and food were required. In the longer term, substantial foreign aid will be needed to rebuild roads, bridges and other economic infrastructure. Some local politicians claimed that 40 years of economic development had been wiped out by the hurricane's impact.

➡ Activity ▶ Hurricane Georges

In September 1998, Hurricane Georges crossed the Dominican Republic, Haiti, the Florida Keys and then hit the southern US state of Mississippi east of New Orleans. The death toll in the Dominican Republic was estimated to be over 500, in Haiti it was over 100, yet in the US just 4 people died. The wind strengths were similar in all three countries - over 250 km/h as it crossed the US coastline - yet the consequences were much more severe in the two poorer countries. In the Dominican Republic, 100,000 people were made homeless, 70 percent of bridges collapsed or were swept away and 90 percent of banana plantations suffered destruction. This impact on the country's main food export caused long lasting damage to the economy which, even before the hurricane, had a per capita income level that was only 15 percent of the USA's.

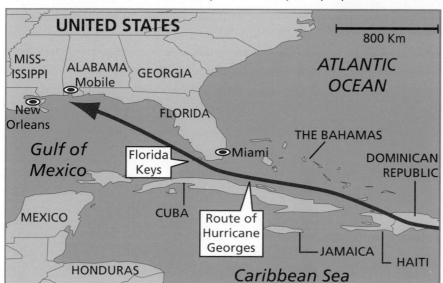

▲ **Figure 12.40 The track of hurricane Georges**

In the United States, as the hurricane approached, people tuned into TV and radio stations to hear the National Hurricane Centre's bulletins. The Centre tracks and monitors all Atlantic hurricanes and tropical storms using satellites and planes. During the hurricane season it names each one alphabetically. Since 1979, Atlantic hurricanes have been given male and female names in alternate years.

On the 24th September, the National Hurricane Centre warned southern Florida of an expected 5 metre storm surge, winds of over 200 km/h and 40 cm of rain. A similar warning was issued to New Orleans two days later. Both regions are vulnerable to flooding - the Florida Keys are a chain of low islands and much of New Orleans lies below sea level protected by levees (embankments). More than a million people evacuated the danger areas and drove northwards in their cars. Most of those who stayed behind gained protection from hurricane shelters that the State governments and local authorities prepared. In New Orleans, there was enough room to shelter 100,000 of the city's 450,000 population. One of the biggest shelters was the Louisiana Superdome - normally used as a sports venue. Curfews were imposed by local police departments to prevent looting of the evacuated areas.

At the height of the storm there were power failures as electricity lines were brought down but these only lasted a few hours in most cases. Trees were uprooted and many homes were damaged. In the aftermath of Hurricane Georges, the affected areas were declared Federal Disaster Areas so that they could claim government funds to repair the damage.

Questions

1 Why is the Caribbean and Gulf of Mexico region more at risk from hurricanes than West Africa?
2 Briefly outline the hazards that people face from hurricanes.
3 Explain why people in high income countries tend to cope with hurricane hazards better than people in low income countries.

3. What is the monsoon and how does it affect people?

The term monsoon comes from an Arabic word that means season. It is now used to describe the seasonal reversal of winds and rainfall that affect south and east Asia, northern Australia and east Africa.

A key feature of the monsoon is that winds blow outwards from central Asia in winter (in the northern hemisphere) and inwards in summer. When the air blows outwards from the continental interior it contains little moisture and so brings dry weather. When it blows inwards from the ocean it contains warm, moist air and so causes rain to fall.

Causes

There are two main causes of the monsoon. The first is the pressure change due to differential heating of land and water. In summer the land heats faster than the sea. Air above the central Asian land mass warms and rises,

Figure 12.41 Monsoonal wind pattern

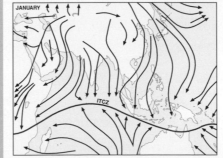

The wind pattern over south and east Asia reverses between January and July.

causing low pressure and drawing air in. In winter the land cools faster than the sea. This causes air to cool and subside over central Asia, and then flow outwards.

The second factor that causes the monsoon is the shift of wind and pressure belts northwards and southwards caused by the apparent movement of the Sun. The Inter Tropical Convergence Zone (ITCZ) moves far to the north in summer, almost to 40 degrees N in eastern China (see figure 12.41). By January it has moved south of the equator.

Figure 12.41 shows the reversal of winds in the Indian Ocean. Note that winds blowing across the equator bend as they are deflected by the Coriolis force. Rainfall occurs where the winds cross onto land after passing over the sea. So, for example, Northern Australia is wet in January, the mainland coasts of south and south east Asia are wet in July, and the islands of south east Asia are wet all year round even though the wind direction is reversed.

The highest rainfall is where moist monsoon winds are forced to rise over high ground, for example in the Himalayas. This mountain chain receives some of the highest rainfall totals in the world. Cherrapunji in north east India, at an altitude of 1,400 metres, recorded over 24 metres of rainfall in 1974 and holds the record for the wettest 24 hours ever recorded - 1.5 metres of rain in June 1995.

The impact of the monsoon in India and Bangladesh

The period before the monsoon 'bursts' in northern India can be very hot with average daytime temperatures over 40°C. The monsoon rains arrive at roughly the same week in the year. In northern India it is in late June. A period of mainly wet weather follows, accompanied by a dip in average temperatures due to increased cloud cover. Disturbances within the air flow, creating low pressure areas, sometimes bring wetter or drier periods during the rainy season.

By late October or November in northern India, the rains decrease and eventually the southerly winds are replaced by dry northerlies. The average temperature falls to

approximately 20°C and, on occasions, night time temperatures can go below freezing. Figure 12.42 shows the temperature and rainfall pattern for Delhi (in India) and Dhaka (in Bangladesh). The length of the rainy season and the amount of rain decreases with distance from the sea. Delhi is approximately 1,500 km from the Bay of Bengal whereas Dhaka is only 200 km away.

Monsoon reliability

With its population of one billion people, and large proportion of inhabitants relying on subsistence agriculture, the arrival of monsoon rains in India is vital. Rice is the main food crop. It requires minimum average temperatures of 20°C and a high rainfall over its three month growing period. Two crops per year can be grown in the south, where the monsoon rains last longest, and in the Ganges delta where irrigation is used. Wheat is the second most important food crop and is grown in north central and north west India. This is where monsoon rains are lightest and least reliable. For example, annual rainfall in Delhi varies from 400 mm in dry years to over 1,000 mm in wet years.

Drought In most years, the monsoon winds bring sufficient rainfall for agriculture. However, the monsoon rain sometimes 'fails' and causes drought. This occurred throughout the 1980s with particularly low rainfall totals in 1987 and 1989. The northern parts of India were more severely affected than the south. Because so many people grow their own food, drought and crop failure can cause food shortages and hunger.

During droughts it is generally the poorest farmers

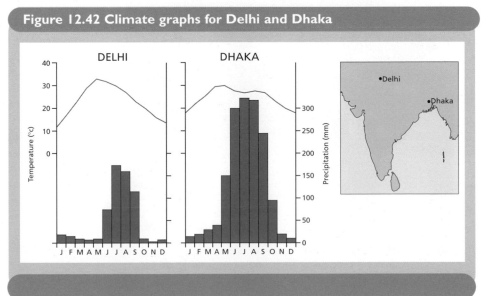

Figure 12.42 Climate graphs for Delhi and Dhaka

and farm labourers (and their families) who suffer most. They lack sufficient income to save money in 'good' years so cannot afford to buy food when crops fail. However, land reform schemes in the Punjab (north west India) have increased average farm sizes in that region and have raised incomes sufficiently for many farmers to afford irrigation schemes. They are therefore able to survive dry years.

Flood The variability of monsoon rains means that in some years the main hazard comes from flooding rather than drought. This particularly affects the low lying Ganges delta which is fed by rivers that rise in the Himalayas. High water levels and flooding are normal occurrences. It is estimated that over 2 billion tonnes of sediment are carried by the Ganges and Brahmaputra Rivers annually. Some of the fertile silt is deposited on flooded land and some is deposited at the coast or in river beds, creating new land. If the rivers do not flood, the land eventually loses fertility. But, during 1998, the rain was so prolonged and intense that the floods lasted more than twice as long as normal.

Activity — Bangladesh floods 1998

▲ **Figure 12.43 Dhaka**
Slum dwellers evacuating their homes as flood levels rise.

News report, September 8th:

The duration and magnitude of the 1998 flood has made it the worst this century. The flooding is also unprecedented in that the floodwaters are receding much more slowly than in the past. The result of more than 2 months of flooding, triggered by heavy monsoon rains, has been over 30 million homeless (out of a total 125 million people) and 700 deaths so far. During the last few weeks, continuous rainfall in Bangladesh and in the river catchment areas outside Bangladesh has led to the high water levels. Further monsoon rains and water from melting snow in the Himalayas are aggravating the situation. Unfortunately the flooding is expected to get worse before it gets better. The water level will not begin to recede until mid-September, weeks later than normal.

Aid agency report, mid-October:

Bangladesh has suffered catastrophic inundation over the past 12 weeks. At the height of the flooding almost two thirds of the country was covered by water. Over 11,000 km of roads and hundreds of small bridges have been swept away. Most of the autumn rice crop has been ruined and over 300,000 houses have been destroyed.

Aid agency report (continued):

Two million people have been driven out of the capital, Dhaka, by flood waters polluted by overflowing sewage pipes. Throughout the country, over 100 deaths have been caused by water borne diseases such as diarrhoea. Outbreaks of cholera, typhoid and hepatitis are feared. Other deaths have been caused by drowning, house collapse and mudslides.

Short term needs:

* *emergency food relief for the worst hit regions*
* *safe drinking water*
* *emergency health services and medical supplies to control water borne diseases and epidemics.*

Medium and longer term needs:

* *employment opportunities for landless labourers who have no work (and therefore no income) - so they have money to buy food*
* *construction programmes to rebuild roads and embankments*
* *provision of seeds and credit to farmers so they can plant winter crops of wheat, maize and potatoes.*

In the long term Bangladesh faces many severe problems. They include:

* *river flooding - strengthening and raising river embankments works in the short term but has the effect of raising river levels. This is because sediment is deposited on the river bed. Then, the next time there are floods, the consequences are more severe because the water level is well above the surrounding land. It is also feared that deforestation in the Himalayas will speed runoff and cause higher flood levels in the future.*
* *sea flooding - if global warming does raise the sea level by the predicted 50 cm in the next decades, the low lying coasts and river banks will be even more vulnerable to flooding and saltwater contamination of farmland.*
* *arsenic poisoning - for over 20 years the government and international agencies have helped people to sink wells so they can drink from clean groundwater. It has now been realised that many of the wells are in areas where the groundwater contains naturally occurring arsenic. Possibly as many as 18 million people are being slowly poisoned.*

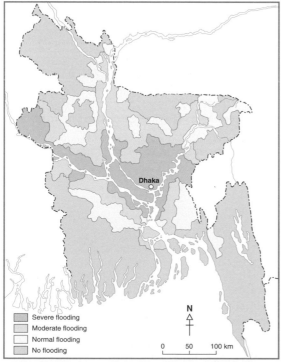

▲ **Figure 12.44 Bangladesh and its rivers**
The shaded areas show which parts of Bangladesh were most affected by the 1998 floods.

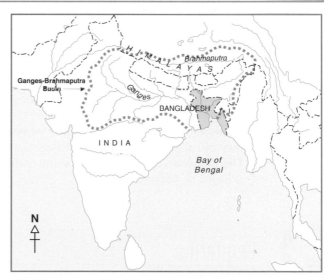

▲ **Figure 12.45 The Ganges-Brahmaputra Basin**

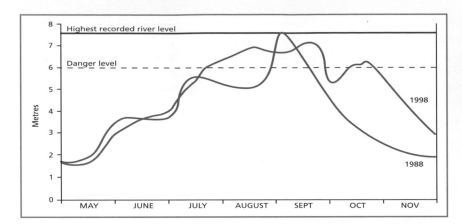

Figure 12.46 River level at Dhaka (May - October, 1988 and 1998)
The graph shows the water level of the River Buriganga at Dhaka. The danger level relates to flooding in the city. Rural areas experience flooding at river heights well below the city's danger level. The river's highest ever recorded level was in 1988.

Questions

1 Briefly outline the consequences for Bangladesh of variations in monsoon rainfall.
2 What made the 1998 floods worse than previous floods?
3 Suppose you have the role of an executive with an aid agency or the World Bank. In the aftermath of the 1998 floods, suggest strategies and priorities that you would recommend to the Bangladesh government. Explain your reasons.

unit summary

1 Anticyclones and depressions cause changes in precipitation and temperature. They draw in air masses from different directions.
2 Tropical cyclones or hurricanes are formed by disturbances in trade wind easterlies. The main hazard they cause is flooding and mudslides.
3 The monsoon brings rainfall to south and south east Asia. Variability in monsoon rains causes drought or floods.

key terms

Air mass - a large body of air that has similar temperature and humidity characteristics. Air masses are described according to their place of origin, eg Polar maritime.
Anticyclone - an area of high pressure in which air generally subsides - associated with dry weather.
Depression - an area of low pressure in

which air generally rises - associated with weather fronts and precipitation.
Monsoon - the seasonal reversal of winds and pressure systems in central Asia and the Indian Ocean.
Tropical cyclone (or hurricane or typhoon) - a destructive weather system with spiralling winds at speeds over 120 km/h, heavy rain and sometimes causing a storm surge.

Unit 12.4 Local weather systems

key questions

1 What causes local winds?
2 What are microclimates?

1. What causes local winds?

Local winds are caused by small scale temperature and pressure differences. They affect a much smaller geographical area than, for example, large scale systems such as monsoons, depressions or tropical cyclones. Three examples - sea breezes, valley winds and tornadoes - are described in this unit. A fourth example, the fohn, is a wind that blows over mountain ranges and warms as it descends. It is described in unit 12.2 in the section on orographic rainfall.

Sea breezes

This is a wind system that develops over coastal areas (see figure 12.47). It is caused by the different capacities of water and land to absorb and retain heat from the Sun. The same effect causes the monsoon. However, sea breezes involve a daily reversal of wind direction rather than the seasonal reversal that occurs in the monsoon.

During the day, if the weather is sunny, the land quickly absorbs solar radiation and starts to warm. Some of this heat is transferred to the air above, which starts to rise. By contrast, over the sea, the temperature does not rise so much because water warms relatively slowly. The temperature difference between sea and land sets up a pressure gradient - with relatively low pressure over the land and relatively high pressure over the sea. This causes air to blow inland as a sea breeze. Typically the breeze starts in the mid-morning and strengthens during the afternoon, subsiding in the evening when the Sun's rays are weaker.

Overnight, the land cools more quickly than the sea. This causes a reversal in the temperature and pressure gradient and a breeze develops from the land onto the sea. Because the temperature difference between land and sea is not so great at night time, the breeze is usually weaker than in the day time.

Regular afternoon sea breezes provide welcome relief from the heat in hot coastal regions. The strongest breezes occur when the temperature difference between land and sea is most marked. Calm, cloudless days in the tropics, and in temperate latitudes during summer, provide the most favourable conditions. Normally, sea breezes only extend inland a few kilometres although there are some instances in the tropics where the wind blows over one hundred kilometres inland.

Figure 12.47 Sea breeze

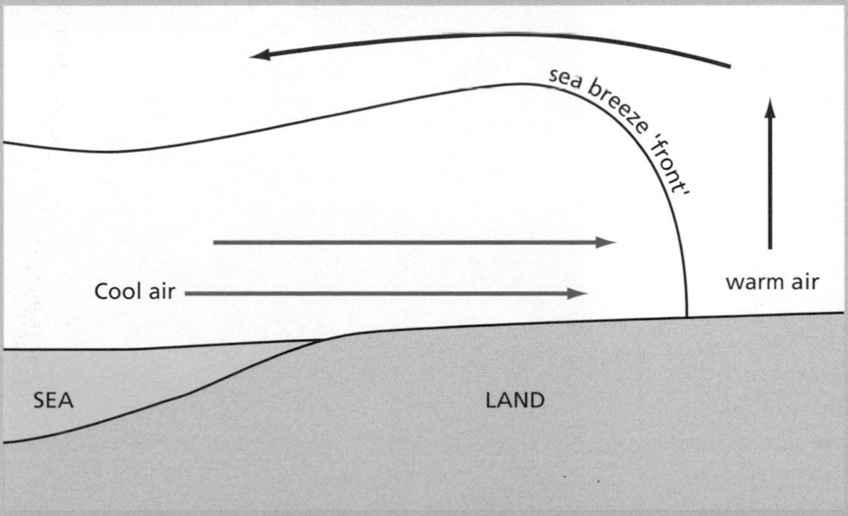

During the day, warm air over the land rises. It is replaced by relatively cool air from over the sea.

Valley winds

At night, the ground surface cools. This is particularly marked when the sky is clear because cloud cover acts as a 'blanket' and reduces the heat loss from radiation cooling. In mountain regions, the ground - and air - is coldest over snow and ice fields. The cold air is relatively dense and it starts to sink. If this flow continues, a cold wind develops down the valley - known as a **katabatic wind** (see figure 12.48). During the day, the wind flow is reversed. The Sun's rays heat the valley floor and slopes, causing relatively warm air to rise. If the flow develops up the valley it is known as an **anabatic wind**.

Figure 12.48 Valley winds

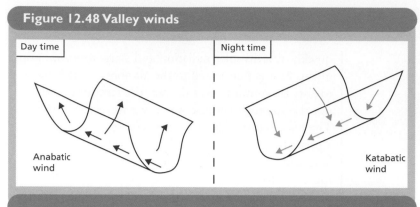

Day time | Night time

Anabatic wind

Katabatic wind

Firstly, the strength of the revolving wind can knock down most buildings that are not made from reinforced steel and concrete. Secondly, the flying debris creates great damage. Even large vehicles can be lifted from the ground and smashed into other objects. Thirdly, there is very low pressure at the centre of a tornado. As it passes over a building, the pressure difference can cause the building to explode outwards.

Tornadoes

A tornado is a relatively small and localised event in terms of its size but, because of its power, it can cause tremendous damage. Tornadoes are generally less than 500 metres wide and they rarely stay in contact with the ground for more than 20 km. In the most powerful tornadoes, wind speeds can be over 450 km/h (300 mph) (see figure 12.49).

The most frequent and dangerous tornadoes occur in spring in the American Midwest. However, they do occur in many other parts of the world and over 30 are recorded on average each year in the British Isles. The precise mechanism that causes a tornado is not certain although the conditions favourable to their development are known. If there is relatively cold, dry air moving over warmer, moist air, conditions become very unstable and large cumulonimbus clouds form. Funnels of rising air then sometimes develop and start to rotate - so creating the tornado. Often several tornadoes form beneath the same cloud. Occasionally, tornadoes occur during hurricanes but most develop during large thunderstorms that are called supercells. Because these storms tend to build in the afternoon and evening (when convection currents are strongest), this is when most tornadoes occur.

Almost 20,000 people have lost their lives in tornadoes in the USA during the twentieth century. On one day in March, 1925, 700 people died when seven large tornadoes touched down in Missouri, Illinois and Indiana. The National Weather Service of the United States issues warnings when tornadoes are likely but there is still no way of knowing exactly where one will form or how powerful it will be.

Tornado damage is caused by three main factors.

Figure 12.49 The Fujita Scale: a system used to classify tornadoes

F0: 40-72 mph, chimney damage, tree branches broken
F1: 73-112 mph, mobile homes pushed off foundations or overturned
F2: 113-157 mph, considerable damage, mobile homes demolished, trees uprooted
F3: 158-205 mph, roofs and walls torn down, trains overturned, cars thrown
F4: 206-260 mph, well-constructed walls levelled
F5: 261-318 mph, homes lifted off foundation and carried considerable distances, cars thrown as far as 100 metres

Figure 12.50 Tornado damage

In an F5 tornado most buildings will be severely damaged or destroyed.

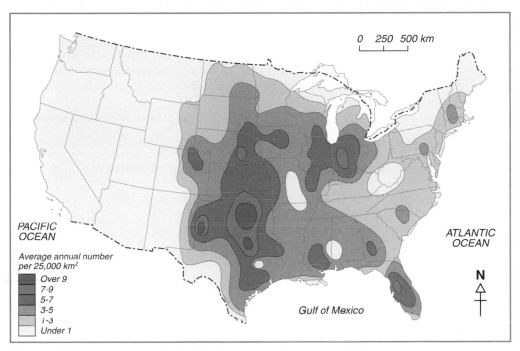

Activity | **Coping with tornadoes**

▲ Figure 12.51 **The distribution of tornadoes in the USA**

*The location where most tornadoes occur - in Texas, Oklahoma and Kansas - is sometimes
called 'Tornado Alley'. It is where warm, moist air from the Gulf of Mexico moves north and
meets cold, dry air from Canada, particularly in the March - June period. Earlier in the year,
in February, cold air sometimes penetrates further south and creates conditions favourable
for tornadoes to form in Florida.*

---

41 dead after storms batter Florida

At least 41 people were killed yesterday as 200 mph tornadoes carved an 11 mile path of destruction
across the Orlando region in central Florida, uprooting hundreds of homes and vehicles.

Twelve tornadoes struck in the early hours of the morning. Fields were littered with the remains of
roofs ripped from homes. Mobile homes, of which there are thousands in this holiday area, bore the
brunt. Thirty of the people who died were mobile home residents and another ten were in vehicles
when they were hit. Near one house, a pick-up truck was tossed into the branches of a tree.

'It is the greatest loss of life from tornadoes in Florida's history,' said Jim Luchine, a Miami
meteorologist. 'We've had so many tornado touchdowns we can't keep track of them,' said a
spokeswoman from the Seminole County sheriff's office. 'Most people were asleep and woke to find
their houses wrecked. The tornadoes were rated as F3 in strength - not as powerful as an F5 - but
caught people unawares because they were so late at night. '

Miami newspaper report, February 24th, 1998

At least 44 dead after tornadoes strike Oklahoma and Kansas
The most severe storms to hit the Oklahoma City area for 50 years struck on Monday. An estimated 70 tornadoes formed as thunderstorms passed the region. One tornado, classed as F5 in intensity, caused a half mile wide path of destruction through the city's suburbs. No houses were left standing along several blocks and a total of 2,000 buildings were demolished. The homes that were destroyed were substantial brick buildings. In some cases, there was literally nothing left standing apart from shattered tree stumps. A school bus, empty at the time, was lifted and carried two blocks by the 260 mph plus winds.

Officials praised the TV and radio stations which kept people informed of the tornadoes' tracks. Using weather radar, forecasters were able to monitor the storms and give people enough time to move into shelters. Many more people would have lost their lives without these warnings.
Oklahoma City newspaper report, May 4th, 1999

▼ **Figure 12.52 Tornado statistics, USA 1950 - 1997**

Month	Average number of tornadoes	Average number of deaths
January	48	2
February	20	6
March	52	13
April	104	26
May	171	18
June	161	11
July	94	1
August	58	2
September	38	2
October	27	2
November	29	3
December	17	3
Full year	819	89

Extracts from the Federal Emergency Management Agency's tornado safety tips brochure:
When a tornado is coming, you have only a short amount of time to make life or death decisions. Advance planning and quick response are the keys to survival.

Before
Decide which part of your home will make the best shelter - a basement cellar is best.
Prepare a stock of disaster supplies (eg, torch, radio, batteries, first aid kit, emergency food and water).
Prepare a plan for getting in contact if family members are separated.
Make sure that everyone knows the difference between a tornado watch (issued by the National Weather Service if there is a likelihood of tornadoes) and a tornado warning (issued when a tornado has been sighted or spotted by radar).
Mobile homes are particularly vulnerable because they can easily overturn. If a building with strong foundations is not available, shelter in a ditch or low-lying area away from the mobile home.
Learn the danger signs:
• an approaching cloud of debris (the tornado's funnel is not always visible)
• the wind might die away just before the tornado hits
• most tornadoes occur near the trailing edge of a thunderstorm.
Check local building codes to see if your home meets current specifications. Consider investing in structural changes - strengthening roof ties, reinforcing masonry and improving wind resistance.

During
Seek shelter in a basement, storm cellar or lowest level of the building.
Get away from windows, shelter under a heavy table or desk.
If outdoors: get inside a building with solid foundations or shelter in a ditch.
If in a car: tornadoes can change direction quickly; they are generally slow moving but can move fast (up to 70 mph) - never try and outdrive a tornado; get out of the car and take shelter.

After
Listen to the radio for emergency information.
Provide first aid if needed.
Stay out of damaged buildings; leave the building if you smell gas.
Check power and water utilities - do not drink tap water if you suspect the pipes are damaged.
Take photographs of damage for insurance claims.

Questions

1 Describe the distribution of tornadoes in the USA both in terms of their geographical location and the time of year.
2 Each year over a million holidaymakers from the UK visit Florida. Suppose someone you know is intending to take a holiday in Orlando next year but is worried because of a newspaper report on tornadoes. Write that person a letter setting out the risks and giving advice.

2. What are microclimates?

A microclimate is the climate in the lower few metres of the atmosphere, over a relatively small area. It might be, for instance, the climatic conditions on a valley slope, within a woodland or in an urban area. Local factors such as slope angle, vegetation cover and building material are all important influences. There is no set or agreed scale at which a microclimate operates. So, in a town or city, the whole urban area can be considered as having a microclimate and, at the same time, many smaller scale microclimates might exist between the individual buildings.

In places where relief has a marked climatic effect, the term 'topoclimate' is sometimes used to describe the conditions at a local scale. An example is the variation in temperature that can occur in valleys. This effect is described below.

Valley microclimates

A number of different microclimates might operate at various points within a valley - depending on aspect, slope angle and altitude. Earlier in this unit the diurnal

reversal of valley winds (katabatic and anabatic) is described. Because relatively cool air tends to sink downwards at night, valley bottoms are often cooler than higher slopes. This is particularly the case in clear, still conditions. Night time radiation from the Earth's surface escapes upwards and there are no turbulent

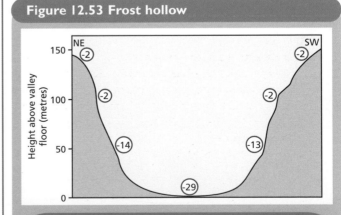

Figure 12.53 Frost hollow

The temperature (in degrees C) is shown at 50 metre intervals up the valley sides. The location is an Alpine Valley in Switzerland during January and the readings were taken at 6.00am.

winds to cause air at different levels to mix. Figure 12.53 shows the night time temperatures in an Alpine valley during winter. The readings were taken in January, at 50 metre intervals up the valley side. The extreme cold on the valley floor was exceptional but illustrates how **frost hollows** form. These are low lying areas in which frost is most likely.

The effect of frost hollows on farming is important. Plants that are sensitive to frost have to be grown on valley slopes rather than in the valley bottom. So, for example, in the Rhone Valley in Switzerland, vines and fruit trees are grown on the valley sides where frost is less likely to kill blossom and fruit. The cold air tends to sink down the slopes without accumulating near the fruit trees or vines.

Within hilly and mountainous regions the different angle and aspect of slopes creates different microclimates on opposite sides of valleys. This is especially true for valleys that trend east - west because there is a marked difference in the intensity of solar radiation that the north and south facing slopes receive. In the northern hemisphere it is south facing slopes that receive the strongest sunshine. On these slopes it is locations where the angle between the surface and the Sun's rays is 90 degrees that become warmest (see figure 12.54).

The different intensity of solar radiation on valley slopes affects not only the temperature but also the moisture content of soil. This is because evaporation rates are at a maximum where it is warmest. These

factors affect natural vegetation, settlement and land use.

In Alpine valleys that trend east - west, most farms and pastures are located on south facing slopes. In the French speaking parts of the Alps this slope is called the adret (Sonnenseite in German). The colder and damper north facing slope (ubac or Schattenseite) is often left as forest.

Farmers prefer to live on the sunnier and drier side of the valley because it is warmer and more pleasant. The higher temperatures on this side mean that grass has a longer growing season and therefore provides more feed for animals. Because many of the farm animals are dairy cattle, which need to be milked twice a day, it is convenient if farms are built close to pastures.

However, some modern tourist developments are on north facing slopes. These are purpose built ski resorts. They are located in positions where snow cover is deepest and longest lasting. By building ski runs on shady slopes, the skiing season can be extended longer than on the south facing slopes where the Sun melts the snow fastest.

Woodland microclimates

On hot days, it is often cooler in woodland or forests. This is because there is a distinct microclimate under the trees. Typically between 5 and 15 percent of incoming solar radiation is reflected by leaves, and much of the rest is absorbed by the tree canopy. It is not only the temperature that is affected. Trees provide shelter from the wind so air is often still in a woodland.

Because air movement is weak, moisture from transpiration is not quickly dispersed and humidity tends to be high. At night, the effect of a tree canopy is to retain heat, causing the range of temperature inside woodland to be less than elsewhere.

The precise microclimate within woodland depends upon the type of tree and season. Spruce trees, for instance, provide a very dense canopy that cuts out most of the light (see figure 12.55). By contrast, deciduous trees in winter provide very little cover and a high proportion of light reaches the ground.

The microclimate of woodlands affects the type of vegetation that grows at ground level. In general, the darker the conditions, the fewer plants will grow. So, there is little vegetation on the floor of a spruce plantation. Under deciduous trees there is often quite dense vegetation in spring with, for instance, bluebells and anenomes. This vegetation tends to die back in high summer when the tree canopy is most leafy.

Figure 12.54 Cross section of an Alpine Valley showing the Sun's rays

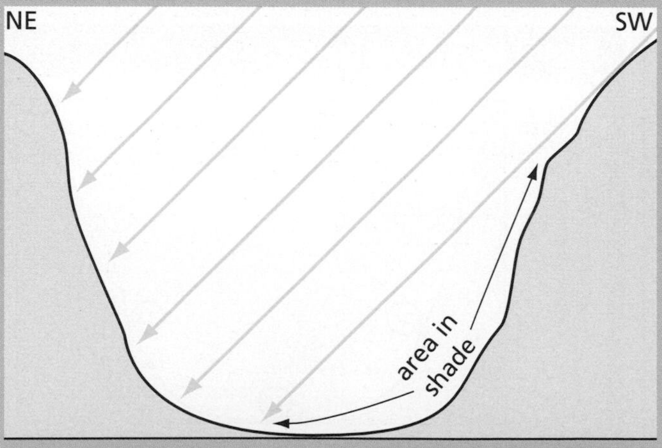

The diagram shows how (in mid-morning, in September) the Sun's rays shine on a valley that runs NE - SW. While some areas are in shade, others are receiving high intensity sunlight.

Figure 12.55 The average temperature difference at ground level in spruce woodland compared with outside the woodland

The dense canopy of spruce trees insulates the ground and retains heat during winter. In summer, the shade cuts most of the light and the ground is relatively cool.

Urban microclimates

Inside urban areas, much of the land is covered by concrete, tarmac, brick and glass. These surfaces have very different physical properties from soil and plants so it is not surprising that they create distinctive microclimates. The variable height of buildings and the street pattern affect not only air flow but also the intensity of solar radiation received at ground level. Some places might be in shade for much of the day whereas other places might receive extra light reflected from glass buildings.

Towns and cities are generally warmer than surrounding areas. The term **urban heat island** is sometimes used to describe this effect (see figure 12.56). In cities such as London and New York, the result is that there is less snow, and flowers bloom earlier than in nearby rural areas. However, it is much more than temperature that is affected. Urban areas also tend to be cloudier, rainier, less windy and less humid than rural areas. And, because urban air is more polluted than air elsewhere, less solar radiation reaches ground level. In general, the bigger the urban area, the more marked is the climatic contrast with the surrounding region.

Although incoming solar radiation is reduced by dust and smog particles, this cooling effect is more than counterbalanced by factors which cause urban areas to be relatively warm. Brick, concrete and tarmac are good absorbers of heat. In the day time, they become warm and then slowly release their heat at night - so preventing the temperature from falling as quickly as elsewhere. It is at night time that the difference between urban and rural temperatures is greatest. Research in both Australia and the United States suggests that, during hot weather, the cities' warmer nights can delay recovery from stress caused by heat. Aggressive behaviour and murder rates increase when night time temperatures are highest.

An additional factor that causes urban heat islands to form is the burning of fuel for energy. Central heating systems, vehicle engines and industrial processes all generate heat. It has been calculated that the centre of New York City, during an average January, receives over double the amount of energy from this human activity than it does from the Sun's rays.

Urban heat islands are most marked at times of light winds. When winds are strong the effect is to mix the air and reduce the urban - rural temperature difference.

The presence of tall buildings in urban areas creates

Figure 12.56 The Melbourne urban heat island

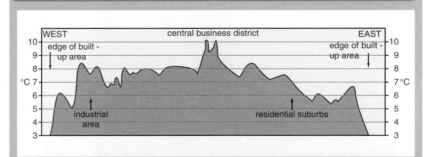

The temperatures in the diagram are the number of degrees above the surrounding area's average (for an east-west cross section of Melbourne, Australia).

friction and reduces the speed of air movement. This causes winds to be generally lighter than in rural areas. However, some exceptions occur when air is funnelled between tall buildings. The resulting gusts and eddies can be a localised nuisance if high rise buildings create such 'wind tunnels'. Litter and rubbish sometimes swirl around, and the draughty conditions are unpleasant. Often there is a significant difference in wind speeds between streets if some are built parallel with the prevailing wind direction and others are built at ninety degrees. In one case, the wind is strengthened as it is channelled down the street, whereas in streets at a right angle there might be very little wind.

Rainfall is higher in urban areas compared with surrounding regions, and thunderstorms are more frequent. American research suggests that in summer the likelihood of thunderstorms is increased by 30 percent in cities. A number of reasons contribute to the higher rainfall which, it has been found, is also experienced downwind of the urban areas. The higher ground temperature in cities makes convection currents more likely, and therefore increases the chance of rain. In addition, the frictional effect of high buildings sets up air turbulence and triggers upward air movements. The rising air cools, condensation occurs and cumulus clouds build.

Activity — Urban microclimate within Toronto, Canada

▲ **Figure 12.57 Toronto lakefront and CBD**

In the early 1990s, Toronto City Council commissioned a report into the likely effects of urban redevelopment on the city's microclimate. Four factors in particular were considered to be important for pedestrian comfort - solar radiation, wind speed, temperature and humidity. As a result of the report's findings, recommendations were made regarding building design and street layout.

The term **comfort zone** is sometimes used in bioclimatology to describe the range of temperature and humidity within which people feel comfortable. In general, the higher the temperature, the lower should be the humidity to obtain comfort. In Toronto, the associated factors of wind speed and wind chill are also important factors that affect people's comfort. Toronto is located on the north shore of Lake Ontario in eastern Canada. The city is at latitude 43 degrees N (approximately the same as Nice in Southern France). Its population is nearly four million. The local climate is one of cold winters and hot, humid summers. Winter is long, lasting from November to April with average temperatures below freezing in the coldest months. However, the city's 'heat island' protects the central areas from the most severe weather. In July and August, the average temperature rises to 25°C and relative humidity is generally over 55 percent. At this time of year the most pleasant conditions are often at the lakeside, under the shade of trees with a light breeze off the lake. Because the city retains the summer heat, night time temperatures can remain uncomfortably high.

Spring and Autumn tend to be short but, with average temperatures of around 18°C, they are the times of year that people find most comfortable.

In much of the downtown CBD, there are high rise buildings. Over the past three decades many of these have been linked by underground arcades and shopping malls, and they have direct access to the subway (ie, underground railway) system. Air conditioning in summer and central heating in winter allow many people to escape the weather almost completely. They can move from their offices to the shops and restaurants in the underground malls, and then commute by subway without going out of doors.

In 1990, the City Council began planning an extension of the CBD into an area of old railway tracks between the city centre and Lake Ontario. The aim was to create an urban environment that would not drive people underground but would serve as a pedestrian link between the business district and the lakefront.

Research findings

By making observations and using wind tunnel models, researchers found that wind speeds at street level are closely related to building height.

- Streets that are less than 20 metres wide and are lined by buildings no more than four storeys in height provide most shelter - they reduce wind strength by 25 to 50 percent.

- At street level, near some of the highest buildings, gusts can be 50 percent above the wind speed recorded just outside the city. During winter the wind sometimes blows at 30 - 50 km/h in the Toronto region so, in the vicinity of high rise blocks, gusts of 45 - 75 km/h are experienced. Gusts of this speed are difficult to walk in and, during the cold Toronto winter, they contribute to severe wind chill.

- When building heights rise gradually - creating a smooth profile - there is less gusting of surface wind than when there is an abrupt change of height.

- When the higher parts of tall (ie, over 100 metre high) buildings are set back from their bases there is a significant reduction in wind speed at street level (in other words, pyramid or tapered shapes are better than high vertical walls).

Computer modelling helped researchers calculate the relationship between building height, street width and hours of direct sunlight at ground level. This technique was used to work out the various combinations of width, height and aspect that would give three, five and seven hours of ground level sunshine around midday at a particular time of year (the 21st September was chosen). Figure 12.58 shows the results for two streets, one north-south and one east-west, that would provide three hours of direct sunlight at street level.

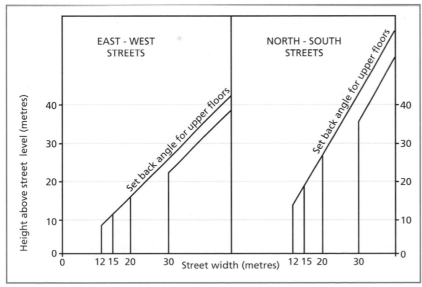

Report recommendations

A number of recommendations on how pedestrian comfort could be improved were made to the Toronto City Council. They included:

- tower blocks should be designed to provide a minimum of three hours direct sunshine at ground level in the commercial district, five hours on shopping and tourist streets, and seven hours in residential streets (at the time of the spring and autumn equinox)

- buildings should be set back from building lines and graded in height to minimise wind speeds

▲ **Figure 12.58 Building heights and street widths in Toronto that allow 3 hours of sunlight at street level in March and September**

- open arcades should be built at street level to give shelter from rain and snow, and from direct sunshine in summer
- open pavements should be built alongside the arcades so people can walk in the sunshine if they prefer - particularly in spring and autumn
- single or double rows of deciduous trees should be planted along streets - slowing wind speed and giving shade on hot, humid summer days, but not reducing sunlight in spring and autumn when there is no foliage.

Questions

1 With reference to figure 12.58, compare the maximum building heights that provide 3 hours of sunlight at ground level around midday (in September) on east-west streets compared with north-south streets. Explain why there is a difference.
2 What aspects of the urban climate in Toronto encourage people to seek shelter from the weather?
3 For a town or city centre that you know, write a brief report that outlines the main factors affecting pedestrian comfort. Suggest ways in which the microclimate could be modified to improve comfort levels.

unit summary

1 Local winds are relatively small scale systems that do not extend over wide geographical areas - generally no more than 100 km.
2 Examples of local winds include sea breezes, valley winds, the fohn and tornadoes.
3 Microclimates are the climatic conditions experienced near ground level over a relatively small area. Examples include the microclimates within woodland, in valleys and inside urban areas.
4 Urban areas as a whole have different climates from surrounding rural areas. In particular, urban areas tend to be warmer.

key terms

Anabatic wind - an upvalley wind caused by the convection of relatively warm air.
Comfort zone - the range of temperature, humidity (and in some places, wind speed) within which people feel comfortable.
Frost hollow - a valley or depression where frost is more likely than on higher slopes.
Katabatic wind - a downvalley wind caused by the sinking of relatively cold, dense air.

Microclimate - a distinct pattern of climatic conditions that occurs in a relatively small area.
Sea breeze - a wind that blows onshore during the day and offshore at night.
Tornado - a powerful rotating wind system that can be very destructive.
Urban heat island - an urban area where the temperature is higher than the surrounding region.

Unit 12.5 Climatic zones

1. Which are the main climate zones of the world?

Early attempts to classify climates were based on temperature. The system is still sometimes used today:

*   tropical climates have the highest average temperatures
*   temperate climates have medium average temperatures
*   polar climates have the coldest average temperatures.

These climates correspond to geographical zones of latitude. So, very broadly speaking, tropical climates are found within the tropics, ie between the Tropic of Cancer and the Tropic of Capricorn. Temperate climates are found between the tropics and the Arctic and Antarctic Circles. Polar climates are found between the Arctic and Antarctic Circles and the poles.

As with all climate classifications, this system is open to criticism. It implies that there is a clear dividing line between the different climate zones whereas, in reality, one zone merges into the next. It also oversimplifies because it does not take into account precipitation, seasonal changes or the effect of altitude. To overcome these difficulties many different classifications have been devised. All have been criticised as either being oversimplified or too complex to be useful.

In the 1930s and 1940s, an attempt was made (by CW Thornthwaite) to classify climates in terms of moisture availability for plants, ie taking evaporation and transpiration into account as well as precipitation. This approach recognises the close relationship between climate and natural vegetation. Indeed, some climate classifications are based on zones of natural vegetation (see chapter 14). So, for example, the terms 'equatorial rain forest' or 'savanna grassland' are used not only to describe ecosystems but also to describe the typical climate of these regions.

Figure 12.59 is a version of Koppen's climate classification that is widely used. Temperature is the main criteria used to classify the climate types although precipitation (in the case of dry climates) and the effect of altitude (in the case of highland climates) are also used. The system has the advantage of simplicity but can be criticised because it does not show seasonal variations either of precipitation or temperature.

Figure 12.59 Climate zones based on the Koppen classification

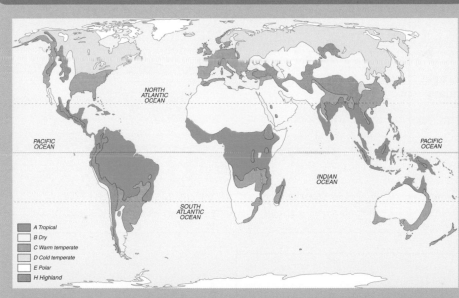

- A Tropical
- B Dry
- C Warm temperate
- D Cold temperate
- E Polar
- H Highland

In this system there are five basic types of climate (A - E), (plus highland climates (H) which share the characteristics of neighbouring regions except that temperature falls and precipitation generally rises with altitude).

A Tropical: mean monthly temperatures all above 18°C
B Dry: mean precipitation is less than 250 mm per year
C Warm temperate: mean temperature of warmest month above 10°C, coldest month above -3°C
D Cold temperate: mean temperature of warmest month above 10°C, coldest month below -3°C
E Polar: mean monthly temperatures all below 10°C
H Highland: climate significantly affected by altitude

For example, within Western Europe, Ireland and southern Spain are shown as being in the same climate classification - ie, 'warm temperate'. This hides the fact that, in Ireland, the rain is spread fairly evenly throughout the year whereas, in southern Spain, most rain falls in the winter months. Likewise, in tropical regions, the classification does not distinguish between areas which are wet for most of the year, eg Equatorial Africa, and regions which have distinct wet and dry seasons, eg those parts of India which experience a monsoon climate.

Climate patterns

The global pattern of pressure and winds is described in detail in unit 12.1. The intense solar heating at the equator compared with the poles is the driving force behind the climate system. Seasonal changes are caused by the orbit of the Earth around the Sun, and the Earth's tilt on its axis. In June, the Sun appears overhead at the Tropic of Cancer and this causes the northern hemisphere to be hotter than the southern hemisphere. Pressure and wind systems move north with the Sun, bringing rain to the northern tropics. The zone of sub-tropical high pressure also moves north, bringing dry weather to Mediterranean areas.

In December, the position is reversed and the Sun appears overhead at the Tropic of Capricorn. Wind and pressure belts move south bringing the highest temperatures and precipitation to the southern tropics. The sub-tropical high pressure belts also move south - leaving the Mediterranean basin under the influence of westerly winds and the depressions that these winds bring.

Activity | Precipitation in January and July

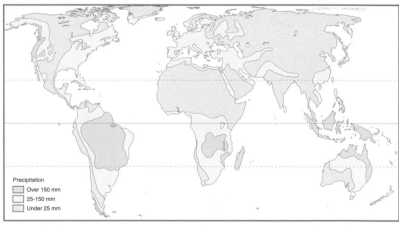

Figure 12.60 Average precipitation in January

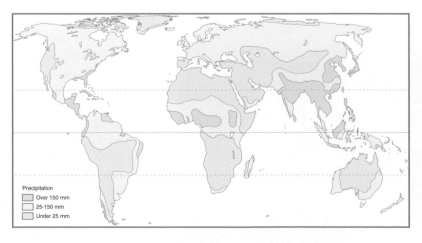

Figure 12.61 Average precipitation in July

Questions

1 Compare the zones of maximum precipitation in January with those in July.
2 For January, identify locations where a) cyclonic; b) convectional; and c) orographic (relief) precipitation might be expected. Explain your choice of locations. (You may need to refer to unit 12.2 to refresh your understanding of cyclonic, convectional and orographic precipitation.)
3 For each of the broad climatic types listed below, suggest a region of the world where such a climate might be found.
   a) hot and wet all year
   b) hot, wet season, warm, dry season
   c) hot and dry all year
   d) hot, dry season, mild, wet season
   e) wet all year, warm summer, cool winter

2. How does the climate vary within the British Isles?

The British climate is sometimes described as 'temperate marine' or 'temperate maritime'. It shares many features with other regions that lie on the eastern margin of an ocean in the zone of mid-latitude westerlies - for example, British Columbia, Southern Chile and South Island, New Zealand. All these locations receive precipitation throughout the year, their winter average temperatures are above freezing and their average summer temperatures are less than 20°C.

Precipitation

The main influence on the British climate is the westerly air flow that crosses the Atlantic, together with the depressions and anticyclones that develop in this air flow (see units 12.2 and 12.3). The British Isles receive frontal precipitation throughout the year. The fronts generally move from west to east causing the heaviest rainfall in western parts. By the time the fronts have reached eastern regions, they are often weaker and therefore rainfall is lighter.

This effect is reinforced by landscape features. Because orographic precipitation increases with altitude, it is the highest points of western Britain - in Cornwall, Snowdonia, Cumbria and North West Scotland that receive the most precipitation. To the east of high ground there is often a rain shadow effect that causes relatively low precipitation.

Convectional rainfall is most common in the summer months. Because southern and eastern England tend, on average, to be the warmest regions, they experience more convectional showers and thunderstorms than other parts of the country (see figure 12.62).

Figure 12.62 Average number of thunderstorms per year

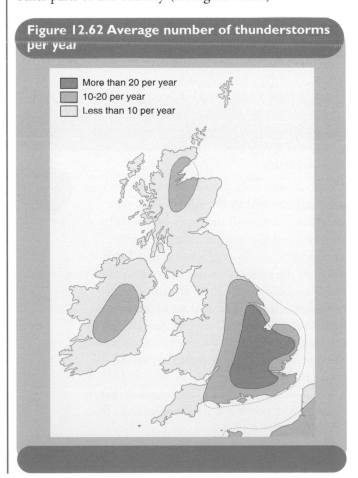

More than 20 per year
10-20 per year
Less than 10 per year

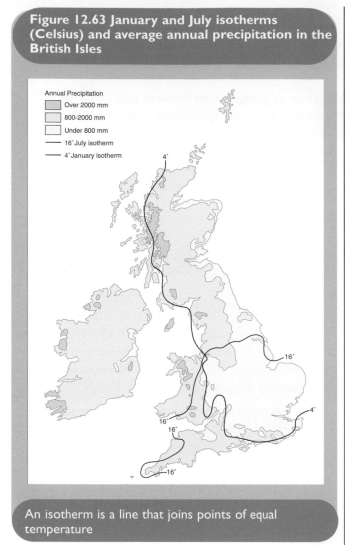

Annual Precipitation
- Over 2000 mm
- 800-2000 mm
- Under 800 mm
- 16° July isotherm
- 4° January isotherm

An isotherm is a line that joins points of equal temperature

Temperature

There are two main factors that affect average temperatures within the British Isles - the different intensity of the Sun's rays at different latitudes and the marine influence of the surrounding sea. It might be expected that the north of the country would be cooler than the south because the angle of incoming solar radiation is lower. The Sun never appears as high in the sky in the north of Scotland as in the south of England. So, even in June when the north of Scotland is light for over 16 hours per day, the intensity of solar radiation is less than further south. The result is that, in summer, the north is indeed cooler than the south (see figure 12.63).

However, in winter, this effect is counterbalanced by the warming influence of

the Atlantic Ocean. The west of the country tends to have higher average temperatures than the east because the ocean retains its heat more than land, and also because of the influence of the Atlantic Drift. This ocean current brings relatively warm water to the western coasts of Britain and Ireland.

The east of Britain, being closer to mainland Europe, is more influenced by the continental climate and less influenced by the Atlantic Drift. This is particularly marked when easterly winds bring dry air from the interior of the Eurasian landmass. These winds are relatively hot in summer and very cold in winter.

Climate variability

An important feature of the British climate is its variability. The average conditions of temperature and precipitation shown on figure 12.63 give a valid picture of the climate over a thirty year period but they hide short term variations. Changeable weather conditions are a result of the different air masses that depressions and anticyclones bring. In turn, these are influenced by the chaotic and unpredictable air flows in the upper troposphere associated with the polar front jet stream. The normal pattern is for changeable weather but this is sometimes interrupted by a 'blocking high' - an anticyclone that diverts depressions to the north or south of the British Isles (see unit 12.3). When this happens, there is a period of dry weather that can be prolonged if the anticyclone becomes fixed in position. It can cause a heatwave if it occurs in summer, and cold, frosty weather if it occurs in winter.

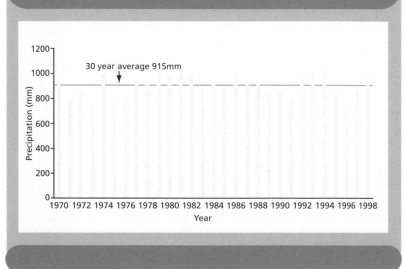

Figure 12.64 Average annual precipitation (England and Wales 1970 - 1998)

Figure 12.65 Average temperatures (England 1970 - 1998)

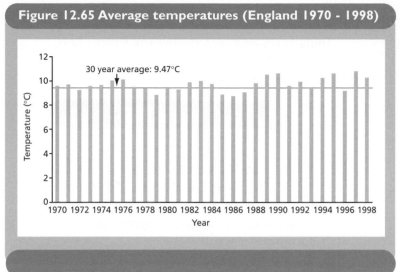

Figures 12.64 and 12.65 show the average annual temperature and precipitation for a period of nearly 30 years. The temperature figures come from an average of recordings made in England (roughly in a triangle, London - Bristol - Manchester) and the precipitation readings come from over 30 rain gauges throughout England and Wales. They show that both temperature and precipitation vary from year to year. Some years were exceptionally warm, such as 1990 and 1997, while others, such as 1986 and 1996, were relatively cool. Similarly for precipitation, there are marked variations between years. For example, in the 1990s, 1994 was a very wet year while 1991 and 1996 were exceptionally dry.

 Activity) Britain's variable weather

▼ Figure 12.66 Daily temperatures: selected days in February 1998

Date	Camborne (°C)			Norwich (°C)			Glasgow (°C)		
	Max.	Min.	Mean	Max.	Min.	Mean	Max.	Min.	Mean
1st	7.0	3.4	5.2	3.3	-2.2	0.5	8.6	2.4	5.5
2nd	8.0	0.5	4.3	6.2	-2.5	1.9	6.5	0.1	3.3
3rd	8.5	0.5	4.5	5.5	0.1	2.8	8.0	-3.0	2.5
4th	9.5	1.8	5.7	8.3	-0.2	4.1	8.7	2.9	5.8
5th	9.8	3.3	6.6	10.4	1.8	6.1	8.8	2.9	5.8
6th	9.9	6.3	8.1	10.4	3.9	7.2	9.4	6.9	8.2
7th	10.3	5.0	7.7	8.2	4.5	6.4	8.2	1.9	5.1
14th	13.6	5.7	9.7	17.4	6.7	12.1	13.0	10.4	11.7
15th	13.8	7.0	10.4	15.5	8.7	12.1	12.7	10.7	11.7
16th	11.0	8.7	9.9	12.3	9.4	10.9	11.3	7.8	9.6
February 1998 mean			8.4			7.8			7.8
Long term mean			6.5			3.0			3.2

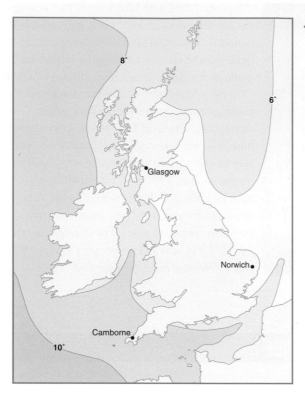

Questions

1 Describe the difference between the monthly mean temperatures for the three locations in February 1998. To what extent are these temperatures typical of the normal pattern?
2 Suggest reasons why the February mean monthly temperature in Camborne is normally higher than in Norwich.
3 With reference to the data, describe the variability of the temperature in the three locations. Suggest possible reasons for the changeable weather conditions.

Drought

In Britain, a drought is said to exist if there are at least 15 consecutive days during which there is no more than 0.25 mm of rain in any one day. A partial drought is defined as a period of at least 29 days during which the mean daily rainfall is less than 0.25 mm. However, there is no internationally agreed definition of a drought and the term is used loosely in newspapers and on TV. So, for example, the drought of 1995 and 1996 was featured in many headlines. During that time there were many days on which it rained so, technically, the whole period was not a drought. Nevertheless, as figure 12.68 shows, rainfall was exceptionally low.

No similar dry period has been experienced since records began. Manchester - normally one of Britain's wettest cities - had less rainfall than Madrid, Rome or Athens in 1996. At the start of 1997, January was the driest since 1779. It was feared that a major water crisis would arise later in the summer with domestic and industrial water supplies being at risk in many areas.

Then, in February 1997, the drought ended when rainfall was 50 percent above normal. A dry spell between July and September caused renewed fears but, by the end of the year, it was clear that most regions had received above average rainfall. The following year, 1998, was exceptionally wet in spring and early summer

Figure 12.68 Rainfall in Britain, April 1995 - September 1997

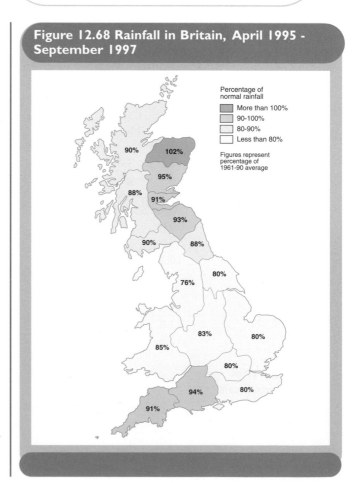

with, for example, April being the wettest in a hundred years and June the fourth wettest. By the end of 1998, reservoirs were full, groundwater levels were nearly back to normal and stream flows had returned to 1994 volumes.

Figure 12.68 shows that exceptionally dry weather was not experienced everywhere in Britain during 1995 - 1997. North east Scotland had above average rainfall and South West England was less than 10 percent below normal. It was in northern England that rainfall was lowest.

The climate pattern for Britain is that the north and west of the country receive the most precipitation, and the south and east receive the least. However, the biggest concentration of population (and therefore demand for water) is in South East England. This may cause long term difficulties if demand continues to rise in that region. Water supplies from rivers and underground aquifers are already inadequate in dry years and the long term solution may involve the construction of water pipes from reservoirs in the north and west. Alternatively, water metering which charges people for the actual amount used might be introduced on a wider scale than at present. This has the effect of reducing demand because people take more care to conserve water.

Activity ▶ Drought and water supplies

Figure 12.69 Rivington Reservoir, near Bolton
In August 1995 the reservoir was less than one third full.

Water companies impose hosepipe bans - *August 1995*

The drought has caused most water companies to impose bans on hosepipes and garden sprinklers. A total of 20 million people are covered by the bans which extend from Cornwall to south west Scotland. Yorkshire Water - which serves the worst hit region - has applied for permission to cut off household supplies by rota and supply people by standpipes on street corners.

Government orders water companies to stop leaks

- September 1995

An estimated 100 million gallons of water are lost each day through leaking pipes. Water companies have traditionally ignored this problem because supplies in reservoirs are much higher than demand in normal years. Now the government has told the companies to cut this waste and to start compensating customers for restricting supplies.

Drought relief operation

- November 1995

Reservoirs in West Yorkshire are at an all time low. Some have less than 12 percent of normal water volumes. As a means of avoiding cutting domestic water supplies, Yorkshire Water has started a shuttle service of 350 water tankers from Kielder Reservoir in Northumberland to drought stricken areas in the Huddersfield - Halifax region. Kielder is the biggest artificial reservoir in Europe and holds 44 billion gallons of water. This is more than enough to supply the people of the North East.

Environment Agency and conservationists object to drought orders *- April 1996*

Water companies in East Anglia and southern England are applying for permission to increase water extraction from rivers. The water is needed to maintain domestic supplies, for industrial processes and to allow farmers to irrigate their crops. Objectors say that river levels will fall too low - killing fish stocks and river plants.

Driest since records began

- November 1996

Water companies have drawn up contingency plans to cope with a severe water shortage next summer if the record breaking drought continues. Cuts in supply have not been ruled out and stockpiles of bottled drinking water have been made ready for vulnerable groups. The companies also want to push ahead as fast as possible with the introduction of water meters. These cut demand because people pay for the water they use rather than the present system of paying a flat rate depending on house value.

A spokesman for the water companies said: 'The drought has been longer and more severe than any experienced in this country since records began - at least 200 years. The water companies have to decide how much it is worth spending to ensure we can cope with a similar occurrence. We must remember that, in less fortunate countries, such a dry spell might have caused crop failure and famine. Here, the worst that most people have suffered is a hosepipe ban.'

Groundwater levels still not recovered *- September 1997*

Folkestone and Dover Water Company are desperately short of water. Most of their supplies come from underground chalk aquifers and water levels are still well below normal. There is a danger that further extraction will cause salt water from the Channel to seep into the chalk and contaminate drinking supplies.
The water company is hoping that the weather pattern will revert to normal this winter with plenty of depressions to replenish groundwater levels. Summer rain makes little difference to underground supplies because so much evaporates. It is only when the ground is saturated that water starts to seep downwards in significant quantities.

Questions

1 Briefly describe the causes and effects of the 1995/96 water shortage.
2 List possible measures by which future water shortages could be avoided.
3 Write a draft report that sets out the advantages and disadvantages of each of the measures you have listed.

Unit summary

1   There are many different ways of classifying climate zones. One simple method is by temperature - (ie, tropical, temperate and polar).
2   Climate zones move north and south with the apparent movement of the Sun.
3. Within the British Isles, climate differences between regions mainly occur because of the marine influence of the Atlantic Ocean and the lower intensity of solar radiation in northern areas.
4   The British climate is extremely variable - not only from day-to-day but also from year-to-year.

key terms

Drought - a continuous period of dry weather. There is no generally agreed precise definition.

Unit 12.6   Climate change

key questions

1   What are the causes and consequences of global warming?
2   What is El Niño and how does it affect people?

1. What are the causes and consequences of global warming?

Throughout the Earth's history, the temperature has fluctuated. There have been several ice ages and intervening periods that were sometimes warmer than today's climate. The most recent ice age began over 2 million years ago and, since then, there have been a series of glacial advances and retreats. On a geological time scale, it was only very recently - 18,000 years ago - that large ice sheets covered much of Britain. The ice then melted but, around 10,500 years ago, a dip in temperatures caused ice caps to reform over Scottish mountains. For the past 10,000 years, conditions have been warmer. It is possible that the ice age has ended though it seems more likely that we are living in an interglacial period.

Although conditions have been generally warm and stable for the past 10,000 years, there have been some variations. It is known, for instance, that temperatures

were high enough 1,000 years ago for wheat to grow in Iceland and for Viking colonisers to settle in Greenland. Then average temperatures started to fall, leading to a cold period. This lasted approximately 400 years from 1450 to 1850 and, in Europe, is known as the Little Ice Age. Although the fall in average temperatures was only 1.5 - 2.0°C, it was enough to cause Viking settlers to abandon Greenland and it forced a switch from cereal growing to sheep farming on Iceland. During this period, it was also sufficiently cold for the Thames in

Figure 12.70 Mont Blanc, western Alps

Since around 1850, most European glaciers have been retreating, indicating a general rise in temperatures.

545

London occasionally to freeze in winter. In the Alps, snow accumulated on the mountains because melting was reduced in the cooler summers. As a result, glaciers advanced down the valleys.

Since around 1850, global temperatures have risen by approximately 0.5°C. The rate of warming appears to be increasing with five of the hottest years ever recorded (1990, 1995, 1997, 1998, 1999) during the 1990s. There is a widespread scientific consensus that global warming will continue. The United Nation's best estimate is that average temperatures will rise by 1 - 3.5°C before 2100.

Causes of climate change

There are a number of different theories on why the Earth's climate has changed in the past and is changing now. It is widely accepted that present global warming is due to human activity - in particular the burning of fossil fuels and the increased emission of carbon dioxide into the atmosphere. This acts as a **greenhouse gas** which allows solar radiation to reach the Earth but cuts the radiation of heat from the surface back into space. The effect is to act like a blanket - making the Earth warmer than it would be otherwise. However, there are some scientists who suggest alternative causes of global warming and who also point to climate changes in the past that cannot be blamed on human activity.

Possible non-human causes for climate change:

*   Wobbles in the Earth's angle of tilt and orbit around the Sun create cyclical changes in the amount of solar radiation received at different places on the Earth's surface (known as Milankovitch cycles - after the person who developed the theory).
*   Variations in the amount of solar energy emitted by the Sun (possibly associated with sunspot activity) cause warmer and cooler periods.
*   Changes in atmospheric circulation and ocean currents (possibly caused by movements of land masses in the process known as continental drift or plate tectonics) cause the transfer of heat from the equator to the poles to be stronger at some times and weaker at others.
*   Natural changes to the composition of atmospheric greenhouse gases cause warmer or cooler conditions.
*   Volcanic eruptions create dust and sulphur dioxide droplets in the atmosphere - these reflect solar radiation and have a cooling effect.

One of the problems with research into climate change is that accurate records are not available for any great length of time. Global temperature records have

been collected only since 1860 although a complete series of recordings exists for England since 1659. Further back in time, historical data such as the Viking accounts of their voyages or records of wine vintages and harvests have to be relied upon.

Data from non-human sources is available but often does not give a very precise record. For example, growth rings on trees can be analysed to see in which years growing conditions were most favourable. This is useful but it does not provide actual temperatures. Similarly, pollen analysis in lake sediments shows which plant species were most common at the time the sediments formed. Because it is known, for example, that broad leaved deciduous trees are more likely to be found in warmer conditions than conifers, it is possible to estimate temperature changes in the past.

Pollen analysis, growth rings in trees and human evidence all point to the relatively stable climate conditions of the past 10,000 years. Fluctuations in temperature have occurred, as in the Little Ice Age, but these variations have been relatively small compared with changes over, say, the past 100,000 years (see unit 10.1).

Some historical evidence suggests that volcanic eruptions can cause short term climate change. For example, when the Indonesian volcano Tamboro erupted it was followed by 'the year with no summer' in 1816. In North America and Europe, average temperatures fell and harvests suffered. There seems little doubt that the dust and sulphur dioxide 'aerosols' thrown into the atmosphere caused a decrease in solar radiation reaching the Earth's surface. However, the effect was relatively brief and caused no long term climate changes.

Larger scale volcanic events such as the massive lava flows 65 million years ago in India certainly caused changes in the atmosphere and possibly caused the extinction of many species. However, the dates of major lava flows and ice ages in the Earth's history do not match. For example, 65 million years ago the climate did not cool sufficiently for an ice age to begin. Likewise, the onset of the most recent ice age over 2 million years ago does not appear to be connected with any particular volcanic event.

The analysis of ice cores from Greenland and Antarctica gives some clues as to climate change during the past 150,000 years. It is known that during relatively warm periods the atmosphere contained a higher proportion of carbon dioxide than during cool periods. This proportion is trapped within ice when it

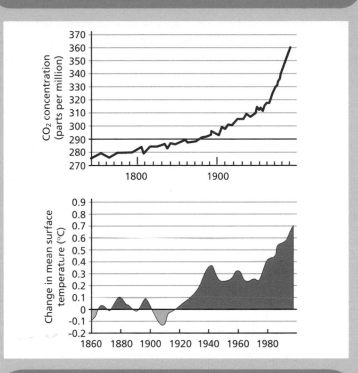

Figure 12.71 World temperatures (1860-2000) and carbon dioxide levels in the atmosphere (1750-1995)

The carbon dioxide levels in the top graph are estimates using Antarctic ice cores up to 1957, and direct measurements since then. The bottom graph shows the change in mean global surface temperatures relative to the temperature in 1900. There is a close correlation between carbon dioxide levels in the atmosphere and global temperature, but which is the cause and which is the effect is not certain.

isotope. Under normal conditions, the lighter isotope returns to the ocean via precipitation and river flow. But, during a glacial period, it becomes locked in ice sheets and the ratio of light to heavy isotopes in the oceans changes. By dating the fossils and analysing the oxygen isotopes contained within them, it is therefore possible to give a sequence of glacial periods. Researchers using this technique have identified almost 60 major climate fluctuations within the past two million years.

Two other techniques using marine evidence are also helping to provide details of climate change. One method involves the analysis of sea bed mud from the North Atlantic. Alternating layers of this sediment show that there have been quite rapid changes in climate. At times of maximum glaciation, large amounts of rock debris have been transported by ice from North America and then deposited on the sea bed. During interglacial periods this flow of material has stopped because the ice sheets have melted.

A similar picture of climate change emerges from studies of Caribbean coral reefs. These form in shallow coastal waters. They provide a useful record of sea levels in the past because the coral can be accurately dated. Tectonic activity is slowly raising islands such as Barbados and, as the land rises, the fringing coral reefs form terraces on the land. The resulting sequence of reefs shows that sea levels have risen and fallen many times in the past 250,000 years. This is evidence of climate change. At times of maximum glaciation, the sea level falls because so much water is locked in the ice caps and, during interglacial periods, the sea level rises.

These rises and falls in sea level show a close fit with the pattern predicted by Milankovitch cycles in the Earth's tilt and orbit. The variations in movement around the Sun combine to cause regular increases and decreases in the amount of solar radiation received at the Earth's surface. It is now widely accepted that the glacial and interglacial periods during the most recent ice age have been caused, at least in part, by this process.

However, during the Earth's history there have been lengthy periods of warm temperatures that do not fit this pattern. For instance, before the most recent ice age, there was a period of over 200 million years with average temperatures higher than today. This is not consistent with the idea that glaciation occurs in regular

freezes so, when samples of a known age are analysed, it is possible to estimate past temperatures. This evidence shows that marked variations have occurred. Unfortunately the techniques used to date the ice are not sufficiently precise to assess whether the increase in carbon dioxide came before or after the temperature changes. It might be that a rise in carbon dioxide increased the greenhouse effect - causing global warming. But, it might also be the case that a rise in temperature caused increased evaporation from the oceans and this released carbon dioxide which had been dissolved in the sea water.

Marine evidence Marine fossils are another method by which long term climate conditions can be assessed. Sea water contains two oxygen isotopes (different atomic forms of the same element) and these are retained in the fossils of dead marine organisms. The lighter of the oxygen isotopes evaporates more readily than the heavier

cycles. It seems that other factors must be at work to cause the onset of an ice age. One possible explanation involves the changes to global circulation caused by plate tectonics and continental drift. Air flow and ocean currents must be affected by the shifting positions of continents and the formation of new mountain chains. But, whether these changes are sufficient to trigger an ice age is not clear.

Studies of the marine evidence not only show **flip-flops** (ie, switches from warm to cold, and cold to warm) in the Earth's climate, but also that the changes can be very rapid. It appears, for instance, that average temperatures have sometimes risen or fallen by several degrees in just a few decades. Why this happens is not clear but it could possibly be related to ocean currents. One idea is that the Gulf Stream and its northern extension, the Atlantic Drift, at times become less powerful. If this happens, a huge source of heat energy is lost in the northern hemisphere and could cause the climate to flip. Then, at other times, the current becomes stronger - causing a rapid rise in temperatures. This idea, of course, does not explain why the ocean current switches on and off in the first place.

Solar radiation Some scientists do not accept that current global warming is primarily caused by greenhouse gases or human activity. Instead they blame variations in solar radiation. This is not a new idea. In the eighteenth century the astronomer William Herschel noticed that there was a relationship between sunspot activity and the price of wheat. It seemed that a high level of sunspot activity was followed by relatively warm weather and good wheat harvests - causing a fall in prices. It was also noted that the second half of the seventeenth century was relatively cold and that there was little sunspot activity.

Opponents of the greenhouse gas explanation for current warming also point to the more recent temperature record. The period from 1945 to 1970 experienced a slight cooling that cannot be explained if steadily rising carbon dioxide levels are to blame. However, during this period there was a slowing of the sunspot cycle and a reduction in the number of sunspots.

During the 1990s, two Danish meteorologists (Svensmark and Friis-Christensen) suggested an explanation for the link between sunspots and climate. They point out that the Earth is being constantly bombarded by sub-atomic particles from outer space

known as cosmic rays. These interact, they say, with gases and water vapour in the upper atmosphere to form clouds. In turn, these clouds reflect solar radiation and therefore cause lower temperatures on Earth. When sunspots occur there is a surge in sub-atomic particles escaping from the Sun. This 'solar wind' moves towards Earth and deflects cosmic rays - so causing less cloud cover and higher temperatures at the surface.

If this theory gains acceptance it will have an important affect on environmentalists and politicians. Government policies to reduce greenhouse gases (see later this unit) will have been pointless. However, at present, the solar radiation theory of global warming is not the mainstream view and further research is continuing.

Consequences of global warming

If the Earth's average temperature continues to warm, the effect is uncertain because so many variables are involved. It is likely that certain regions will become much warmer with some estimates suggesting that the temperature at the poles will rise by 4 - 7°C. If this happens, the sea level will rise and cause flooding on low lying coasts.

Climate change It is possible that higher temperatures will make the climate more extreme, more changeable and more prone to severe weather events. This will be due to increased instability caused by the higher temperatures. If the effect of global warming causes - as expected - the poles to warm relative to the equator, the temperature gradient between them will become less steep. Some meteorologists predict that this will weaken the jet stream causing it to become more 'wavy' and even less predictable than now.

Higher average temperatures are expected to cause the present climate zones to shift polewards by 200 - 300 km. So, for instance, the Sahara Desert might extend northwards - causing the Mediterranean coast of Africa and southern Spain to become even drier than at present. The Great Plains of the USA may also become drier. These changes will have a marked effect on agricultural output unless expensive irrigation schemes are installed.

The temperate climate zone will also shift polewards. It is possible that the higher temperatures might increase agricultural output in northern Europe and the Canadian Prairies. The growing season will be longer than now and the increased carbon dioxide in the atmosphere will also promote plant growth. However,

Figure 12.72 United Nations estimates of sea level rise

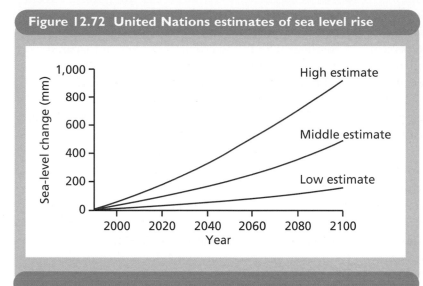

the ice displaces roughly its own volume in water. However, melting ice from the Greenland and Antarctica ice caps will add to the overall volume of water in the oceans. Only a relatively small amount of the ice is expected to melt - if the whole of the Antarctic ice cap melted, the oceans would rise by 70 metres.

Sea levels will rise not only due to melting but also because the higher global temperature will cause sea water to warm and expand in volume. Some researchers suggest that this effect will be equal to the rise caused by melting.

The United Nations' current middle estimate is that sea levels will rise by 50 cm, and the worst case prediction is 95 cm by 2100 (see figure 12.72).

The UN estimate of a rise in sea level by 50 cm may not seem much, but it is sufficient to flood many low lying deltas and coastlines. It also raises the base level for high tides and storm surges. Areas that are already protected by sea walls - such as the Netherlands - will need to strengthen their defences. The Nile delta in Egypt, the Ganges delta in India / Bangladesh and the deltas of eastern China and South East Asia are particularly vulnerable. They have very high population densities and it is very difficult to prevent flooding

further north there might be adverse effects if the permafrost melts. Many buildings, roads and railways in Alaska, northern Canada and northern Russia have foundations sunk into the permanently frozen subsoil. If this melts, there is a risk that many buildings and communication systems will collapse.

The effect on ski resorts is more difficult to predict. Higher temperatures might be expected to reduce the length of the winter season and reduce snow cover - for example in the Scottish Highlands. However, there is also the possibility that increased precipitation will occur in Alpine regions and this will cause more snow in winter.

There is already evidence that global warming is helping the spread of tropical insects and diseases. For instance, the malaria carrying mosquito has spread northwards into parts of the Mediterranean basin and the east coast of North America (see unit 2.3). It is likely that this trend will continue with other pests and diseases normally associated with the tropics becoming more common in temperate latitudes.

Sea level change Rising temperatures will cause more ice to melt in the polar regions. Where the ice is floating, for example at the North Pole, the overall effect on sea level will be slight because

Figure 12.73 A small island in New Caledonia, western Pacific Ocean

Low lying islands and river deltas will be flooded if sea levels rise.

when there are large numbers of river channels. In Egypt, the Nile Delta north of Cairo forms only 2.3 percent of the country's area but it contains 46 percent of total cultivated land, 50 percent of the population and 46 percent of industry. In Vietnam, 50 percent of the national rice harvest comes from the Mekong Delta. The United Nations estimates that, worldwide, there are 100 million people at risk from flooding caused by the predicted rise in sea level.

Forty two countries have formed the Alliance of Small Island States to form a pressure group in an attempt to protect their interests. Countries such as the Bahamas, the Maldives (Indian Ocean) and Tonga (Pacific Ocean) have low lying sandy or coral islands. Their populations are relatively poor and, in most cases, have nowhere to move when the water level rises. Their outlook is very bleak if the sea level rise is greater than currently predicted.

(See unit 9.4 for an account of the Thames Barrier and unit 11.3 for an account of flood defences in the Netherlands.)

Government responses to global warming

The United Nations and most governments in the world are working on the assumption that current global warming is being caused by increased carbon dioxide emissions. It is estimated that carbon dioxide in the atmosphere has risen from 280 parts per million (ppm) in the pre-industrial period to 360 ppm at the present time. If current trends continue, this will rise to 560 ppm during the twenty first century. Most carbon dioxide is produced by coal burning power stations and motor vehicles. In 1998, the USA accounted for 36 percent of total emissions, the EU contributed 24 percent and Russia 17 percent. In very broad terms, the industrialised world, with just 20 percent of the world's population, produces 80 percent of the total carbon dioxide output. (See unit 2.5 for details on the negative impact of industrial development and the sources of atmospheric pollution.)

It is clear that deforestation is also contributing to higher carbon dioxide levels. This is because trees absorb carbon dioxide and act as a store. The fewer trees there are, the more carbon dioxide is present in the atmosphere. It is also known that other greenhouse gases such as methane are increasing in the atmosphere. However, it is the burning of fossil fuels and the resulting carbon dioxide that is the focus of attention.

At the UN sponsored conference at Kyoto in December 1997, after much bargaining, industrialised countries agreed an overall cut in greenhouse gas emissions of 5.2 percent by 2012 (from a 1990 baseline). The EU agreed an 8 percent cut, Japan 6 percent and the US 7 percent. These are subject to ratification within each country. Russia agreed to stabilise its emissions, but Australia, Iceland and Norway were allowed to increase their global-warming pollution up to 2012, as special cases. Agreement between the countries was difficult for two main reasons. Firstly, businesses, especially US oil companies, argued that being forced to cut emissions will threaten economic growth and thus jobs. Secondly, countries in the Third World argued that they should be exempt because their economies are not developed and their emissions per person are much lower than in high income countries.

One proposal of the Kyoto Protocol (ie, agreement) is that emissions can be traded. In other words, the rich can buy the right to pollute. Under emission trading, the following situation might occur:
- an out-of-date power station in Eastern Europe emits a high level of greenhouse gases
- a US power company buys the plant, modernises it and reduces the emissions
- the US company buys the difference between the emissions levels before and after, and counts this saving as part of its overall reduction.

Optimists suggest that the result will be a fall in total emissions. But many environmental activists believe that Western energy companies will use the system to avoid reducing their own emissions.

Figure 12.74 US power station

The reduction of carbon dioxide emissions is being resisted by some energy companies.

Activity ▶ **Alliance of Small Island States [AOSIS]**

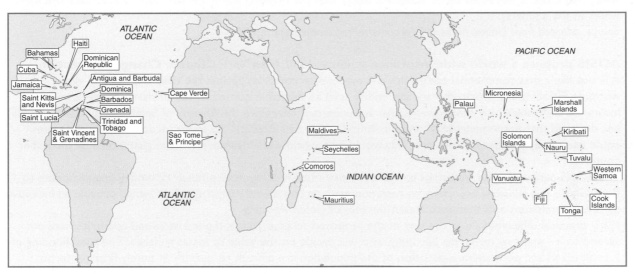

▲ **Figure 12.75 Members of AOSIS**

Country	Insularity Index	Vulnerability Index	Population (000) 1996	GNP per capita (1996 US$)	Protection cost as % of GNP
Bahamas	0.35	11	284	10,180	2.6
Cuba	0.03	3	11,019	1,300	0.1
Kiribati	1.59	180	82	920	18.8
Maldives	2.15	1833	256	1,080	34.3
Seychelles	1.08	183	77	6,850	5.5

Notes: Protection costs are the costs of building sea defences in urban and economically important districts. GNP is a measure of national income.

Insularity Index = length of coastline divided by the land area
Vulnerability index = insularity index multiplied by the population density

▲ **Figure 12.76 Indicators for selected members of the Alliance of Small Island States (AOSIS)**

The Maldives and climate change

Situated in the Indian Ocean, the Maldives consist of 1,200 coral islands - though only 190 are permanently inhabited. The highest point is just 3.5 metres above sea level. During 1988, most of the capital, Male, flooded when five metre high waves were generated by south west monsoon winds.

The difficulties faced by the Maldives are severe because the population is concentrated on just a few low lying islands. Rising sea levels and the expected greater frequency of storm generated waves will have a major impact. The physical nature and size of the islands mean that there is no inland or higher ground to which people can evacuate. Tourist developments which have been built on the beaches of a few resort islands are also very vulnerable.

The situation has been made worse by human activity. Coastal reclamation, the construction of sea walls and the mining of coral reefs for building material have reduced some of the islands' natural defences. This is because the developments have caused scouring by waves and currents - so removing beaches and corals that previously acted as breakwaters.

High population growth has increased demand for fresh water which comes from underground aquifers. As sea levels rise there is expected to be 'saline intrusion' into the drinking water (ie, salt water will replace the fresh water in the aquifers).

Source: adapted from United Nations Environment Programme Report, 1989

AOSIS propose a world wide insurance scheme: 1992 New York Climate Change Convention

It is not likely that commercial companies will ever insure countries against the risks arising from global warming. Flooding and storm damage are widely seen as inevitable consequences of rising sea levels and insurance companies only cover events that are uncertain. Therefore the Alliance of Small Island States (AOSIS) has declared that the industrialised nations should set up a fund which the lower income small island states could use to pay for loss and damage. This would be a world wide insurance scheme guaranteed by the richer countries.

The AOSIS proposal is for industrial countries to pay into the scheme an amount of money proportionate to their GNP - but adjusted according to each country's carbon dioxide emissions. This would provide an incentive to reduce emissions and therefore lessen the rate of global warming.

Many practical difficulties lie in the way of the proposed scheme. Firstly, the industrialised countries have not agreed to it - and may never do. Secondly, who will decide on the value of losses suffered? The total flooding of a small island and permanent evacuation of the population are difficult to quantify in purely financial terms. Thirdly, the proposal gives no incentive for coastal communities to prepare - either by organised retreat to higher ground or by building storm shelters and elevated buildings.

Source: adapted from AOSIS Insurance Annex, Climate Change Convention, 1992

Questions

1 Explain how the vulnerability index is constructed. What are the strengths and weaknesses of this index?
2 Outline the likely consequences of a general rise in sea level. Suggest possible means by which people might cope with these consequences.
3 To what extent do you consider it fair for industrialised countries to pay for losses caused by rising sea levels?

2. What is El Niño and how does it affect people?

The Earth's climate undergoes cyclical changes on different time scales. For example, there are long term variations that cause the glacial advances and retreats during ice ages. On a much shorter time scale are the changes associated with El Niño. This involves a reversal in the normal climate conditions across the width of the Pacific Ocean. El Niño refers to the baby Jesus (or Christ child) because Spanish settlers in Peru noticed

that the event often occurred at Christmas time. The effect on the Peruvian coast is that the sea water becomes much warmer than normal.

Sometimes, when an El Niño ends, the normal climate and sea temperature pattern strongly re-establishes itself. When this happens quickly, it is known as La Niña (or the girl).

El Niño Southern Oscillation (ENSO)

Scientists now generally use the term 'ENSO event' to describe El Niño although the latter name is still mainly used in the press and on TV. An oscillation is a term that simply means a switch in conditions - in other words, a reversal from normal and then back again. The use of the description 'southern' is misleading because ENSO events occur in equatorial waters, both north and south of the equator.

Normal conditions The normal pattern of atmospheric pressure and air movement in the tropical parts of the Pacific Ocean is known as the Walker Circulation (see figure 12.77). At surface level, easterly trade winds blow from a high pressure area off the coast of South America towards a low pressure area over Indonesia in the western Pacific. These winds blow almost directly from high to low pressure because, near the equator, there is very little deflection by the Coriolis force.

In the zone of high pressure, there is sinking air and generally fine weather. It is exceptionally dry in the coastal parts of Peru and northern Chile and the area is known as the Atacama Desert. Far to the west, in the zone of low pressure, rising convection currents cause condensation and heavy rainfall over Indonesia and South East Asia.

The easterly winds push warm equatorial waters westwards. This causes a build up of relatively warm water in the western Pacific. Here the sea level is approximately 50 cm higher than it would be otherwise. Off the South American coast a current of colder water from the south replaces the warm water. This is called the Humboldt Current and it is particularly rich in nutrients and plankton. Shoals of anchovy feed on the plankton and make the coastal waters of Peru one of the most productive fishing grounds in the world.

An ENSO event Every few years, the normal Walker Circulation reverses and there is an El Niño. This has happened many times in the past. The first El Niño recorded by the Spanish was in 1576 and, during the late twentieth century, one has occurred every 5 - 7 years. There were particularly strong El Niños in 1982/83 and 1997/98 with a weaker event in 1991/2. Some scientists suggest that global warming is causing more frequent El Niños. However, this is not certain

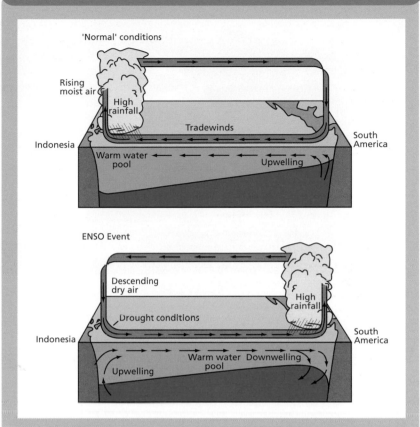

Figure 12.77 Walker circulation and ENSO event

The top diagram shows the normal Walker Circulation in the Pacific Ocean. The bottom diagram shows an ENSO event in which the normal circulation is reversed.

because the historical records are not always reliable. The cause of El Niños is unclear. The relationship between atmospheric and ocean circulation is very complex and there is no agreement as to whether the event starts in the atmosphere or in the water.

The onset of El Niño is marked by a fall in the pressure gradient across the Pacific. This means that the difference between the high and low pressure areas becomes less marked. The easterly trade winds then weaken and this reduces the westward flow of warm water. Eventually, in a strong El Niño, the Walker circulation completely reverses. High pressure forms over Indonesia and low pressure forms off South America.

The impact of El Niño

When the easterly winds blowing across the Pacific weaken and reverse, the warm water 'pool' near Indonesia starts to move eastwards. This water moves across the surface of the ocean at a rate of approximately 100 km per day. Eventually, in a strong El Niño, it

Figure 12.78 El Niño event

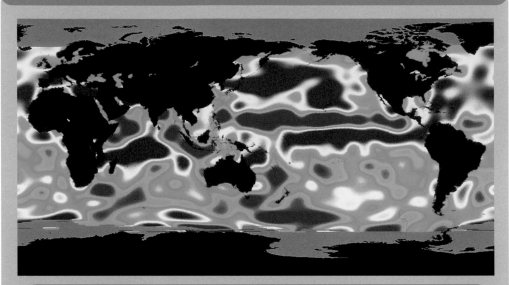

This NASA image shows the difference between average sea heights and those during an El Niño event. Colours run from purple (10 cm below normal), through blue, green (normal) and yellow to red (10 cm above normal). The patch of red in the Pacific Ocean along the equator to South America indicates a mass of warm water that moved eastwards in late 1997.

reaches the coast of South America where the water temperature rises by 6 - 8°C.

The warm water prevents the cooler, nutrient rich waters of the Humboldt Current from reaching Peru. The result is that the normally rich anchovy fisheries simply collapse. The shoals move far to the south and fish catches fall by 90 percent or more. Wildlife such as sea birds and seals also move south or die of starvation. The effect on the Peruvian economy is severe. In normal times, the country's fishing industry is one of the world's biggest. Most of the anchovies are processed into fish meal and exported as animal feed. It is therefore not only the fishermen who suffer but the economy as a whole. There is also a worldwide knock-on effect because a shortage of fish meal causes the price of other animal feeds, such as grain, to rise.

South East Asia During El Niño, the normally low pressure over South East Asia is replaced by high pressure. The result is drought that can extend far southwards into Australia. Crops fail, animals starve and, in the poorest countries, people go hungry. The dry weather also makes the region's forests more vulnerable to fire. During late 1997 / early 1998, large areas of rain on islands such as Sumatra and Borneo were burnt. Most of the fires were started by people who wished to clear a patch of forest for farming or oil palm plantations. In the

dry conditions, the fires got out of control and eventually thousands of square kilometres were burnt. Then, when the rains eventually did arrive, accelerated soil erosion silted up rivers and killed coastal corals by covering them with sediment.

North and South America On the eastern side of the Pacific, the warmer sea temperatures associated with El Niño cause increased evaporation and convectional rain. During the 1982/83 El Niño, parts of coastal Peru received over twenty times their normal rainfall. El Niño causes flower seeds in the Atacama Desert to germinate and bloom but the human impact is less pleasant. From northern Chile to California, storms batter the coasts and damage property. There are frequent mudslides. This is because vegetation cover is generally sparse in the normally arid areas and the rain simply washes down bare slopes. Houses are swept away, roads are blocked and bridges are destroyed. During the 1982/83 El Niño, almost 2,000 deaths and $8-10 billion damage was caused by storms and mudslides on the coastline of North and South America. In 1997/98, there were fewer deaths but damage was estimated at $33 billion and over 250,000 people were made homeless in Peru and Ecuador alone. On just one weekend, in March 1998, the Pan American Highway was blocked by 18 separate mudslides in Peru.

Because of the abnormally wet weather in Peru, there was an increase in the number of wet, marshy areas in which mosquitoes breed. As a result, during 1998, there were 30,000 cases of malaria - three times the average number.

Worldwide effect The Pacific Ocean is approximately 14,000 km wide at the equator. It is therefore not surprising that a reversal of normal climate conditions over such a big area has a worldwide ripple effect. Unfortunately there is no way of knowing for certain whether any particular effect is the result of coincidence or has a causal connection. To confuse matters there is a tendency for all unusual weather patterns to be blamed on El Niño.

However, there does appear to be a negative correlation between El Niño events and Atlantic hurricanes. It seems possible that westerly winds blowing across the Pacific in El Niño years continue across Central America and into the Atlantic. These winds shear off the top of Atlantic storms - so reducing the number of hurricanes that develop. However, at the end of the 1997/98 El Niño, atmospheric conditions reversed in a particularly strong La Niña. This coincided with the most damaging hurricane season in the Caribbean for 200 years.

Other correlations have been noted between, for example, droughts in Africa and El Niño events. During 1982/83, a particularly severe drought across southern Africa was widely blamed on the the strong El Niño at that time. However, during the 1997/98 El Niño, the conditions in southern Africa were wetter than normal. This does not necessarily disprove the connection but it serves to show that the global circulation is extremely complex and is subject to apparently random events.

Activity ▷ The impact of El Niño

Fires in South East Asia - April 1998
During the 1997/98 El Niño, exceptionally dry conditions allowed many fires to burn out of control in South East Asia when farmers and plantation owners cleared and burnt forests. In Sarawak (Malaysia), for instance, many people were affected by the resulting smoke. During one period, over 5,000 people per day were hospitalised due to smoke inhalation. Government authorities declared that an Air Pollutant Index (API) of between 100 and 200 was 'unhealthy' and anything between 300 and 500 was 'hazardous'. On the worst day, during mid-September 1997, the API reached 839 in the city of Kuching (the main city in Sarawak).
Officials were ill-prepared for the emergency. They had insufficient funds to supply everyone with effective smoke masks. Nor did they have the resources to stop the fires - many of which were burning across the national border in Kalimantan (Indonesia). Everyone hoped that rain would eventually put out the flames.

◀ **Figure 12.79 Schoolchildren in Kuching, Malaysia** *In early 1998 health authorities in Kuching reported a 50 percent increase in respiratory illnesses.*

California prepares for El Niño - October 1997

California state officials and experts from the Federal Emergency Management Agency (FEMA) are meeting to plan for possible severe weather over the winter. Satellite images and sea surface temperature readings from buoys anchored across the Pacific are showing the rapid eastward movement of warm water typical of El Niño. In 1982/83, floods and mudslides killed 160 people and caused $2 billion damage in the state when a similar event occurred. This time the government authorities want to be better prepared for the expected heavy rains. An expensive programme has been started. Already storm drains have been cleared and river beds stripped of foliage to speed water flow. Along vulnerable sections of the coast, 4 metre high sand banks are being built and embankments are also being strengthened along the Sacramento and San Joaquin Rivers.

Australia's farmers - November 1997

During the 1982/83 El Niño, Australia's agricultural economy shrivelled. Farm incomes fell by nearly half and farm related losses totalled $2.5 billion. In 1997, warned of the impending drought, many cattle ranchers sold off cattle and bought in extra animal feed, and arable farmers planted drought resistant crops.

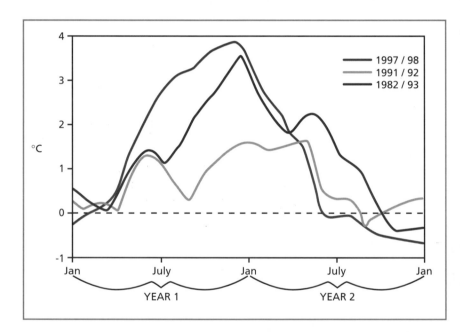

Figure 12.80 The sea surface temperature (SST) anomaly in the eastern Pacific during the strong El Niños of 1982/83 and 1997/98 and the weak El Niño of 1991/92.
The graph shows the temperature difference from normal of the Pacific Ocean's surface in the area between 5 degrees north - 5 degrees south, and 90 degrees west - 150 degrees east.

Questions

1 Describe the difference between the sea surface temperature anomalies during the strong and weak El Niños.
2 Outline ways in which people and governments might prepare for an El Niño event if they have sufficient warning.
3 Suggest reasons why disaster preparation might be more effective in high income countries compared with low income countries.

unit summary

1. There have been many variations in the Earth's climate. Several theories attempt to explain the climate changes but none is entirely satisfactory.
2. Global warming has been occurring for over 100 years. The mainstream view is that this is caused by an increase in greenhouse gases - particularly carbon dioxide from burning fossil fuels.
3. The consequence of global warming is that the sea level will rise and the climate will become more variable. It is also likely that climate zones will shift polewards.
4. El Niño is a cyclical climate change in the Pacific Ocean. A reversal of wind and pressure systems causes warm water to move from the western to the eastern Pacific.
5. El Niño causes drier than normal weather in South East Asia and wetter than normal weather on the western coasts of North and South America. World wide ripple effects also occur.
6. By monitoring atmospheric pressure and sea surface temperatures scientists were able to predict the 1997/98 El Niño so allowing some communities to prepare for the impact.

key terms

ENSO (El Niño Southern Oscillation) - the name given by scientists to the reversal of normal Pacific Ocean wind and pressure systems. Off the coast of Peru an ENSO event is marked by an increase in sea surface temperatures.

Flip-flop - the switch from one climate state to another, eg warm to cold, or cold to warm.

Greenhouse gas - an atmospheric gas, such as carbon dioxide or methane, which allows short wave solar radiation to reach the Earth's surface but then absorbs and retains long wave radiation (heat energy) emitted from the surface.

Introduction

There is a saying 'as common as dirt' which implies that dirt (ie, soil) is worthless. Yet people depend on the soil to survive. Without it, few plants could grow, the base of our food chain would disappear and life would no longer be sustainable. Nor would it be possible to produce natural products such as cotton and timber. So, although soil only forms a thin layer on the land surface, it is one of the most valuable of our resources.
But soil is a fragile resource that can easily be damaged or destroyed by human activity. It must be conserved and treated with care if future generations are to enjoy a sustainable food supply.
This chapter looks at how different soils are formed and considers the human impact on soils.

Chapter summary

Unit 13.1 looks at soil forming processes.
Unit 13.2 identifies the main soil types.
Unit 13.3 examines the human impact on soil.

Unit 13.1 Soil forming processes

key questions

1 What is soil?
2 What factors affect soil formation?
3 What are the main soil forming processes?

1. What is soil?

Soil is the thin, unconsolidated material that forms the top layer of the land surface. Together with the underlying weathered rocks of the Earth's crust it forms what is known as the **regolith**. Soil consists of minerals, from the weathering of underlying parent material, and organic matter which comes from decaying vegetation and animal matter on the surface. This is decomposed (ie, rotted and broken down) and mixed in the soil by fungi, bacteria, worms and other living **organisms**. The decomposed organic matter is called **humus**. Together the minerals and humus form soil particles. Between these particles are spaces (or pores) which might be filled either with air or water.

Soil profiles

Within most soils, there are layers or **horizons** that have developed over time. A cross section through the layers is called a **soil profile**. Soil can be divided into 'topsoil' (the

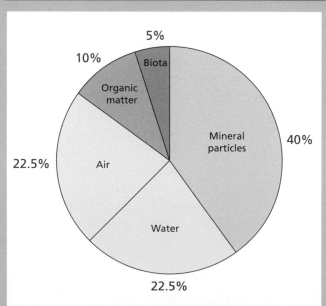

Figure 13.1 Soil constituents

5% Biota
10% Organic matter
40% Mineral particles
22.5% Air
22.5% Water

These percentages are typical values and vary from soil to soil. Biota are living organisms, eg plants, animals, insects, fungi and bacteria.

part containing most organic matter) and 'subsoil' (the part mainly consisting of the underlying weathered parent material). Figure 13.2 shows a typical soil profile for the UK.

Figure 13.2 Generalised soil profile

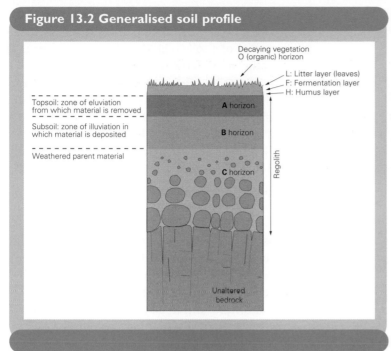

The O horizon is where leaves and other decaying vegetation lie on the surface. This mainly organic layer is sometimes subdivided into:

- L - litter; ie, leaves and other organic debris
- F - fermentation layer of partly decomposed organic matter
- H - humus; ie, fully decomposed organic matter.

Some of the material in the O horizon is carried downwards into the A horizon by insects and other small organisms. The A horizon is where most of the organic material accumulates and humus content is high. Soluble minerals and clay particles are washed down (or 'eluviated') from the A into the B horizon. This B horizon consists of weathered parent material and redeposited minerals and clay particles. It is sometimes called the 'zone of illuviation'. The C horizon is made up of weathered and disintegrated bed rock and other parent material.

The relative depths of each horizon vary from place to place. In tropical regions, with humid climates and undisturbed conditions, the bottom of the C horizon can be 60 metres deep. However, this is exceptional. In places where the soil has been ploughed or cultivated it might be difficult to identify separate horizons and, in some soils, there might be horizons missing altogether.

Soil texture

The mineral particles in soils are classified according to their size (see figure 13.3). Soil texture is the degree of coarseness or fineness of a soil and is determined by the proportions of sand, silt and clay (see figure 13.4).

It is possible to judge soil texture by feel. A sandy soil is light, it feels gritty and does not stick together when squeezed. It warms and cools quickly. It also allows water to soak through relatively quickly (ie, it is porous - because the sand particles form irregular shapes that leave gaps in between even when they are packed together).

A clay soil is heavy and sticky when wet, and can be rolled and moulded. It does not let water soak through as quickly as a sandy soil. This is because the fine texture allows the particles to pack close together. Although this makes the soil less porous, it allows more water to be retained in the soil. A silty soil feels smooth, almost soapy and will form a ball. Its qualities lie in between those of sand and clay. A soil that is a mix of clay, sand and/or silt is called a 'loam'.

Figure 13.3 Classification of mineral particles in soil by size

Diameter	Particle
Over 2 mm	Stones and gravel
2.0 - 0.2 mm	Coarse sand
0.2 - 0.02 mm	Fine sand
0.02 - 0.002 mm	Silt
Under 0.002 mm	Clay

Figure 13.4 Soil texture

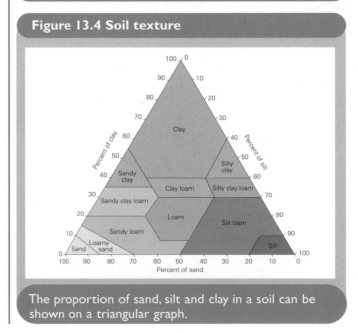

The proportion of sand, silt and clay in a soil can be shown on a triangular graph.

Figure 13.5 Soil structure

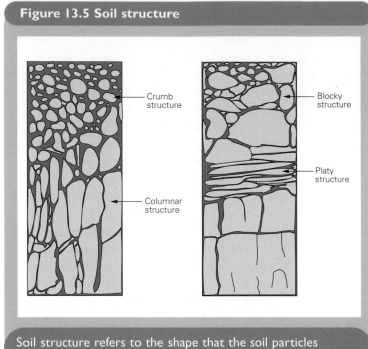

Crumb structure

Blocky structure

Platy structure

Columnar structure

Soil structure refers to the shape that the soil particles combine to form.

Soil structure

The individual particles in soil combine to form **peds**. Soil structure depends on the way that these peds are arranged, in other words - the shape they make (see figure 13.5). Fertile soils generally have a 'crumb' structure which means that the peds form irregular shapes approximately 2 to 4 mm in diameter. Air and water can pass through this type of soil, between the peds, and also through the peds themselves which are porous. A columnar (or prismatic) structure also tends to aid fertility because it allows good drainage and root development.

Some soils have a 'blocky' or 'platy' structure in which the arrangements of peds slows drainage and restricts root growth. Air and water cannot pass through easily and this reduces fertility.

Soil fertility

Fertility is the ability of a soil to provide sufficient water, air and nutrients for plants to grow. Both soil texture and soil structure influence fertility because they affect the water retaining properties of soil and the amount of air in it.

Soil moisture, ie the water content in soil, is vital because it supplies water for plants and organisms. It also contains dissolved nutrients. If there is not sufficient moisture in soil, plants begin to wilt and eventually die.

Air within the soil is also important because it contains oxygen which living organisms require. The ability of a soil to hold both water and air is a key factor in soil fertility. If water fills all pore spaces, the soil is said to be saturated. Under these waterlogged or 'anaerobic' conditions, the number of soil organisms is reduced.

Soil organisms - small animals, bacteria and fungi - are known as 'detrivores'. They break down 'detritus', ie dead and decaying organic matter from plants and animals. Without soil organisms, organic material would not be decomposed. The organic material is broken down to form the black coloured humus which gives soil its colour. Humus provides plants with many nutrients. It can also improve a soil's water holding capacity by its effect on soil structure. In sandy soils, it helps retain moisture, and in clay soils it creates larger particles that improve aeration, making the soil better drained and quicker to warm.

Decomposition is fastest in warm, airy soils because more organisms can live in these conditions than in cold, wet soils. It is mainly micro-organisms (bacteria and fungi) that decompose dead vegetation whilst bigger organisms, such as slugs, worms and ants, mix organic matter throughout the topsoil. As well as acting as decomposers, soil organisms make passageways or small tunnels that let air and warmth into the soil.

Nutrients are essential for plant growth. They come from five main sources: the air, rainwater, weathered bedrock, decomposing vegetation (humus) and fertiliser.

Three nutrients, carbon, hydrogen and oxygen, come mainly from rainwater and the air. Together they make up over 90 percent of plant tissue. The other nutrients come mainly from humus and minerals in rock particles, and also, sometimes, from artificial fertiliser or farm manure. They can be subdivided into six major nutrients (nitrogen, phosphorous, potassium, calcium, magnesium and sulphur) and nine minor nutrients, or 'trace elements' which are needed in smaller amounts (such as iron, manganese, copper and zinc).

The process by which plants take nutrients from the soil is very complex. There are several pathways. One group of nutrients, including calcium, potassium, sodium and magnesium, form positively charged **ions** (called cations). These attach to clay and humus particles in the soil known as **colloids**. Hydrogen ions, which are attached to plant roots, are replaced by the nutrient cations from the colloids. These nutrients are then absorbed by the roots in a process known as 'cation exchange'.

Another means by which plants take up nutrients is via soil solution. This is simply soil moisture that contains dissolved nutrients. The nutrients are absorbed into the roots when plants take in soil solution to replace water lost through their leaves (by transpiration).

Nitrogen is the plant nutrient needed in greatest quantities after carbon, oxygen and hydrogen. The process by which it is taken from the atmosphere into the soil is known as the 'nitrogen cycle'. It involves the decomposition of organic matter by bacteria which 'fix' nitrogen in the soil and make it available for plants. There are a number of different means by which this takes place. Some nitrogen is fixed within the bodies of micro-organisms and is released when they die and decay. More important are the bacteria which fix nitrogen onto root nodules of a group of plants called legumes (eg, peas, beans and clover). This is a major source of nitrogen within the soil.

Soil acidity

The acidity of soil is governed by a chemical exchange. When rainwater (which is slightly acid) passes through soil, it dissolves some of the nutrient ions attached to clay and humus colloids and washes them away. Their place is taken by hydrogen ions. The process is called **leaching**, and is described in more detail later in this unit.

The concentration of hydrogen ions in solution indicates how acidic the soil is. This is measured by using the pH scale (see figure 13.6). Like the Richter scale for earthquakes it is logarithmic - each point being ten times more (or less) acid than the next. On the pH scale, 7 is neutral. Below 7 is acid and above 7 is alkaline (or basic).

A pH of 7 means that, in one litre of pure water weighing 1,000 g, there is one ten millionth of a gram of hydrogen ions, ie 1/10,000,000 or, more simply, 10^{-7}. In a more acid soil, there is a higher concentration of hydrogen ions. For example, a pH of 3 means that in one litre of solution there is one thousandth of a gram of hydrogen ions, ie 1/1,000 or 10^{-3}.

Soil acidity is important because it affects fertility and plant growth. Increased acidity makes plant nutrients more soluble and so easier to leach out of the soil by rain. In addition, high acidity releases the iron, aluminium and other metals in soil which, in large amounts, are toxic to plants. Also, soil organisms generally avoid acid conditions, so fewer live in acid soils - making decomposition slower and reducing the humus content. These factors mean that, in general, acid soils are less fertile than those that are neutral.

The most acid soils have a pH of 3 to 4, whereas the most alkaline soils have a pH value of 8 to 11. In Britain, most soils have pH values in the range of 5 to 7. Generally, wetter upland soils tend to be acidic, and drier lowland soils tend to be more alkaline.

Soil system

Soil can be considered as a system with inputs, outputs and transfers (see figure 13.7). The main inputs are water from precipitation, the Sun's energy, mineral particles from the parent rock, and organic matter from decomposing vegetation. The main outputs are the nutrients that are consumed by plants, and moisture that is lost by 'evapotranspiration' (evaporation and transpiration from plants). Some moisture and nutrients are also lost in the downward flow of groundwater.

Nutrients are recycled within the system by plants which take them up through their roots, store them and then release them back to the soil when the plant dies or its leaves fall. Other transfers of material also occur within the system. For example, water moves downwards through soil, transporting nutrients, and also sometimes moves upwards in a process known as 'capillary action'. These processes are described later in this unit.

Figure 13.6 pH scale for soils

	pH	Hydrogen ion concentration	Liquids with similar acidity
acid	3	1:1,000	vinegar
	4	1:10,000	
	5	1:100,000	
	6	1,1,000,000	rainwater (contains dissolved carbon dioxide)
neutral	7	1:10,000,000	
	8	1:100,000,000	sea water (contains dissolved mineral salts)
	9	1:1,000,000,000	
	10	1:10,000,000,000	
alkaline	11	1:100,000,000,000	washing soda solution

Figure 13.7 Inputs and outputs in soil formation

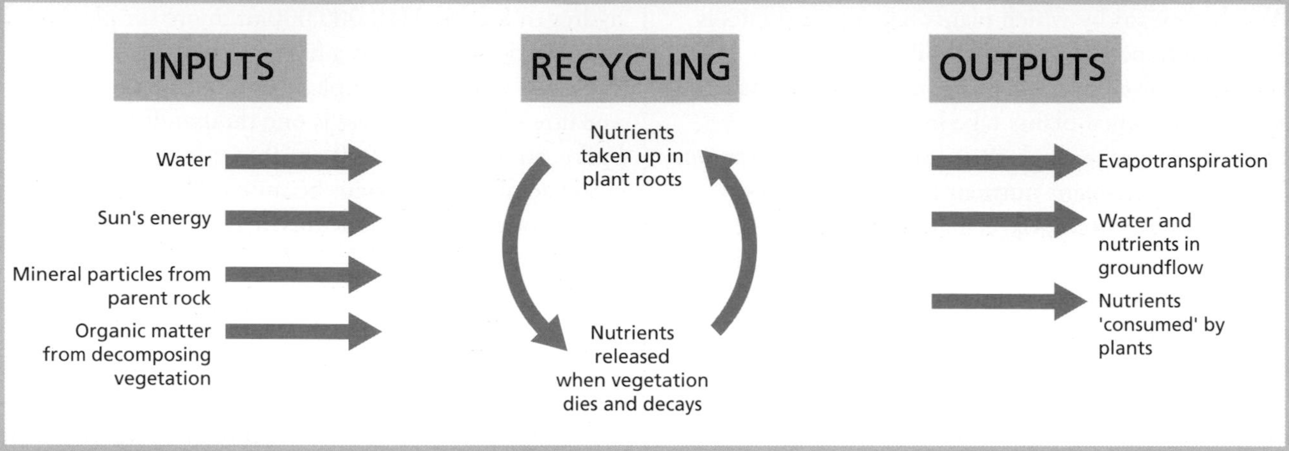

INPUTS	RECYCLING	OUTPUTS

INPUTS

Water →

Sun's energy →

Mineral particles from parent rock →

Organic matter from decomposing vegetation →

RECYCLING

Nutrients taken up in plant roots

Nutrients released when vegetation dies and decays

OUTPUTS

→ Evapotranspiration

→ Water and nutrients in groundflow

→ Nutrients 'consumed' by plants

Activity The composition of soil

◀ **Figure 13.8 Farmland being prepared for sowing, near Thetford, East Anglia**

This soil contains a mixture of particles: sand, 60%; silt, 30%; and clay, 10%.

Questions

1 Classify the soil in the photograph in terms of its texture (using the triangular graph, figure 13.4).
2 Explain the difference between soil structure and soil texture.
3 What factors will determine the fertility of this soil?

2. What factors affect soil formation?

The rate at which soil is formed depends upon a number of factors. These include:
- climate, particularly temperature and precipitation
- geological material from which the soil is formed (ie, the parent material)
- natural vegetation and soil organisms
- relief (ie, the variation in height and shape of the land)
- time.

Human activity can also be important - this is discussed in unit 13.3.

Climate

This factor controls the temperature and moisture content of a soil. Both temperature and precipitation have an important effect on the rate of weathering of the parent material (see unit 8.1). They also affect the number and type of organisms living within the soil, the type of natural vegetation growing on it, and, consequently, the soil acidity.

For example, in humid tropical regions, soils typically have a high humus content and a deep weathered layer. This is because the hot, wet climate favours the growth of lush vegetation and also favours a fast rate of chemical weathering of the parent material. By contrast, in arctic areas, the soil is generally thin. It is often waterlogged in summer and frozen in winter. Organic matter decomposes only very slowly under these conditions and the rate of weathering of parent material is also slow.

Parent material

Parent material not only includes bedrock but also unconsolidated gravels, sand or scree on which soil sometimes forms. The parent material has an important influence on a soil's texture and the mineral nutrients that it contains. Because different ratios of minerals are contained in different rock types, they weather and release minerals at different rates. Parent material also affects the depth, texture, drainage and colour of soil.

The parent material is broken down in two main ways. Mechanical weathering, such as freeze thaw action, tends to produce shattered rock fragments. Chemical weathering involves water, often in the form of carbonic acid (from rain) or organic acids from plants. The rock is decomposed into clay minerals, nutrients (for plants), and iron and aluminium oxides.

The outcome can be rock fragments or finer particles. In cases where the parent material is soluble, for example chalk, the material might be completely washed away in solution.

Vegetation and soil organisms

Growing plants use carbon and hydrogen from air and water, and nutrients from within the soil. When a plant dies, these are recycled and returned to the soil. Soft tissued plants such as grass, and deciduous leaves, decay rapidly. Woody material and coniferous needles decay much more slowly. In general, the slower the rate of decomposition, the more acid and less fertile is the resulting soil.

Research in English woodland illustrates this. Under deciduous woodland containing oak trees, the soil pH typically is in the 5.8 - 6.2 range. Under coniferous trees, the soil is typically much more acid at 4.7 - 5.1. The difference in pH is due to the rate and composition of decaying matter. The coniferous needles form an acid humus layer on the surface and are slow to decompose. On the other hand, leaves from broad leaved deciduous trees form a much less acid leaf litter. This attracts many soil organisms and therefore decomposes relatively quickly.

Organic material is decomposed by soil micro organisms. In neutral and alkaline soils, the majority of micro-organisms are aerobic (ie, oxygen using) bacteria, (up to 1 billion per gram of soil). In acidic soils, fungi are the main decomposers. In addition to these micro-organisms are the mites, worms, insects and mammals that eat and break down organic material and mix the soil up. Without their intervention, the bulk of plant residue would be left on the surface and not be of any use to plants.

Organic matter is decomposed in two stages:
- **mineralisation**: where it is changed into acids and plant nutrients
- **humification**: where some of the acids recombine to produce humus.

Under grasslands, with neutral or alkaline soil, there is generally a complete breakdown of the organic matter. Organisms mix up the material and produce a mull, or 'mild' humus. In slightly more acidic conditions - under deciduous woodland - decay is slower because there are fewer organisms. A thin layer of litter remains visible on the surface with a layer of partly decayed material below it. This is called **moder**. In very acidic conditions - under conifers or heathland - there are so few organisms that a thick layer of black, greasy, slowly decaying organic matter lies below the surface litter - this is **mor** or 'raw' humus. Where the soil is completely waterlogged, few soil organisms can survive because there is not enough air. Decomposition is very slow and plant material builds up on the surface to form **peat**.

Relief

Relief affects soil formation by causing different drainage conditions and by determining the aspect of soils (ie, the way they face, affecting how much sunlight or shade they receive). Soils formed on slopes are generally well drained, but are often thin because material is washed downslope. On flat land, soils can sometimes be waterlogged but they usually have a greater depth than on slopes. A sequence of soil types down a slope is known as a **catena** (which comes from the Latin for 'chain' - referring to the links between the soil types). Unit 13.2 includes an example of a catena in northern England.

Time

Soils develop only very slowly. Some in Britain have not had time to reach maturity (ie, a final, stable state) since the last ice sheets melted 10,000 years ago. By comparison, soils in tropical regions have had a much longer period of undisturbed development, and are therefore sometimes very deep.

Soils that are forming on recently deposited materials such as volcanic ash or lava, on sand dunes or glacial moraine, are so new that they show none of the characteristics of mature soils. They do not have recognisable horizons and there is little mixing of organic matter.

3. What are the main soil forming processes?

So far, this unit has shown that soil is a mixture of mineral particles and organic material (plus water and air) arranged in layers. The main processes involved in producing a soil are:
• the weathering of the parent material
• the decay and mixing of organic matter
• the arrangement of soil into horizons.

Figure 13.9 shows the main soil forming processes. These processes can be considered in more detail by looking at what happens under particular conditions. For instance, in some places, the downward movement of material through soil is dominant. In other places,

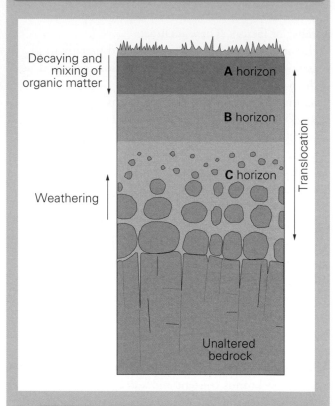

Figure 13.9 Soil forming processes

Decaying and mixing of organic matter — A horizon

B horizon

C horizon

Weathering

Translocation

Unaltered bedrock

Translocation is the movement of material either up or down through soil. Soil components move downwards by two main processes which are collectively known as eluviation. Chemical eluviation (or **leaching**) occurs when the material moves in solution, ie it is dissolved. **Mechanical eluviation** (or, confusingly, sometimes just eluviation) occurs where particles of material are washed down through the soil in suspension. Soil components move upwards through the soil by capillary action which is caused when high temperatures cause evaporation at the surface.

upward movement is dominant. Also, in different places, the conditions might be more or less acidic. The particular soil processes that occur under different conditions include:
• leaching
• podsolisation
• calcification
• gleying
• laterisation
• salinisation.

These processes, and the soils they produce, are described below. A description of where these soils occur and their relationship with the natural vegetation is given in units 13.2 and 14.4.

Leaching

In this process, a chemical exchange occurs on clay and humus colloids. Nutrient ions such as calcium, potassium, magnesium and sodium are exchanged for hydrogen ions. These hydrogen ions come from weakly acidic rainwater and organic acids as they move through the soil by gravity. When the proportion of hydrogen ions in the soil rises, the soil becomes more acidic and less fertile. The nutrient ions are removed from the topsoil as the rainwater percolates downwards (see figure 13.11).

The rate of leaching is related to the acidity of the percolating water. In more acid conditions, more soluble ions are washed down out of the A horizon.

Figure 13.10 The process of leaching

Precipitation is greater than evaporation

⬇

| Weakly acidic rainwater and organic acids | O horizon |

⬇

| Nutrient ions such as calcium and sodium are removed in suspension | A horizon |

⬇

| Redeposition of nutrients | B horizon |
| | C horizon |

For leaching to occur, precipitation must normally be greater than evapotranspiration. Acidic water percolates downwards, washing soluble soil nutrients such as calcium and potassium from the A horizon. The nutrients are redeposited in the B horizon or are removed by groundwater.

Podsolisation

This is an extreme form of leaching that leads to the formation of podsols (see figure 13.13). These soils are most common in cool climates where precipitation is in excess of evapotranspiration, and on well-drained parent material. The natural vegetation is usually coniferous forest, heathland or moor. This is vegetation that can survive in cold, wet conditions. The vegetation

Figure 13.11 A brown earth soil

This soil developed under deciduous woodland in England. It is typical of regions where leaching is the dominant soil forming process. The surface humus overlies the leached A horizon.

decomposes slowly and produces an acid humus. Rain passing through the organic material in the soil increases in acidity - the pH can be as low as 3.

Minerals such as calcium and potassium are leached out in solution. Iron and aluminium oxide are also washed out by **cheluviation**. This is a process that occurs under very acid conditions. The acid causes clay to break down into silica and soluble iron and aluminium oxides (known as sesquioxides). The result of these processes is that the A horizon is a pale, ash colour. (The name podsol means 'ash soil' in Russian.)

By contrast, the B horizon contains illuviated (ie, washed in) material that is darker in colour. Sometimes iron oxide is redeposited as a distinct layer that becomes very hard - known as an 'iron pan'. Where this happens, drainage can be much reduced - causing waterlogging above.

Figure 13.12 The process of podsolisation

Precipitation is greater than evaporation

Acidic rainwater and organic acids — O horizon

Removal of nutrients and oxides — A horizon

Redeposited nutrients and oxides — B horizon

— C horizon

There is an ash coloured A horizon from which minerals are lost by leaching and cheluviation. There is a dark layer in the B horizon where iron and aluminium oxides are redeposited.

Figure 13.13 A podsol

This soil developed under acidic heathland vegetation in south west Scotland. The ash coloured A horizon is clearly visible.

Calcification

In humid conditions (ie, relatively wet climates), leaching removes soluble calcium salts from the soil. However, in arid and semi-arid regions, these salts may not be entirely removed but are redeposited in the B horizon. The result can be light coloured patches of calcium carbonate and calcium sulphate (gypsum) in the lower soil levels. This process is most common in prairie grasslands of North America and the steppes of Ukraine and Russia. In these regions, black chernozem soils tend to form. The A horizon is dark coloured because it is so rich in humus (see figure 13.15).

Figure 13.14 Calcification

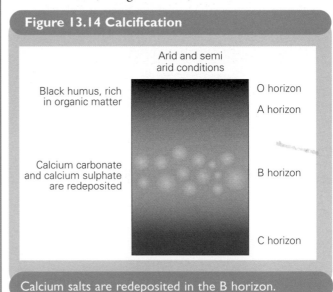

Arid and semi arid conditions

Black humus, rich in organic matter — O horizon / A horizon

Calcium carbonate and calcium sulphate are redeposited — B horizon

— C horizon

Calcium salts are redeposited in the B horizon.

Gleying

This process occurs in waterlogged soils, either in low lying river valleys or in areas where the underlying rock is impermeable. It also occurs in tundra regions where permafrost remains frozen underneath a thawed surface layer. The pore spaces in the soil fill with water and produce anaerobic conditions (ie, there is no oxygen). Iron oxide within the soil is 'reduced' (ie, chemically changed by the removal of oxygen). This causes the reddish coloured ferric oxide to turn into blue/grey ferrous oxide (see figure 13.17).

Where soil is waterlogged for only part of the year, it might contain reddish patches or 'mottles' in a grey/blue background.

Gley soils can have a wide range of pH values depending on where they occur. On acid moorlands they generally have a low pH, but in lowland areas which overly chalk or limestone, the pH might be relatively high.

Figure 13.15 Chernozem soil

This soil developed under prairie grassland in Alberta, Canada. It is an extremely fertile soil because leaching has not removed many nutrients. The humus rich surface horizon is almost black in colour.

Figure 13.16 Gleying

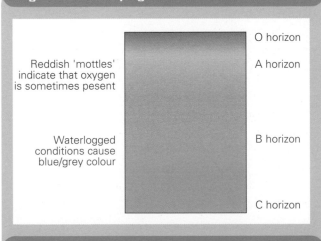

Reddish 'mottles' indicate that oxygen is sometimes pesent

Waterlogged conditions cause blue/grey colour

O horizon

A horizon

B horizon

C horizon

Gley soils form when pore spaces become waterlogged.

Figure 13.17 Gley soil

This soil has developed on the floodplain of the River Severn in the West Midlands.

Laterisation (or ferrallitisation)

In humid tropical areas, vegetation and leaf litter are quickly decomposed by micro-organisms. Chemical weathering of the parent material is also rapid. This produces clays that contain soluble compounds of potassium, calcium and magnesium, and iron and aluminium oxides. Under these conditions, leaching removes the soluble material but leaves the oxides in the A horizon. The resulting soils are called latosols (or ferrallitic soils) and are typically found in tropical rain forests where rainfall is heavy for most of the year. Iron oxide gives them a characteristic red colour - see unit 13.3.

In tropical areas where there is a wet and dry season, there is leaching followed by an upwards capillary action. In these conditions, the accumulation of iron and aluminium oxide can form a distinct layer. If this layer becomes hard and cemented, it is known as a **laterite**. (The term 'plinthite' is now also used).

Figure 13.18 Laterisation

Precipitation is greater than
evaporation for all or most
of the year

Humus decomposes
quickly   O horizon

Oxides remain   A horizon

Rapid removal of
nutrients by leaching   B horizon

Leaching removes nutrients and leaves a red coloured A horizon.

Figure 13.19 Latosol or ferrallitic soil

This soil has developed in Ghana, West Africa. It is intensely leached with a thin surface humus overlying a deep A horizon.

Salinisation

This process occurs when potential evapotranspiration is greater than precipitation. In other words, when the actual loss of moisture through evaporation and transpiration from plants (plus the amount of moisture that would be lost if it was available) is greater than rainfall.

Salinisation typically occurs in arid and semi arid regions with high daytime temperatures (see figure 13.20). The heat causes an upward movement of water through the soil. Dissolved salts in the water, such as sodium and potassium, are left as a crust of salt crystals when water evaporates from the ground surface. This can happen when the water table (ie, the upper level of saturated rocks) is near the surface, and also in irrigated areas, particularly when too much water is applied or when there is poor drainage.

Figure 13.20 A salt crust, Death Valley, southwest USA

Upward capillary movement of soil water has brought soluble salts to the surface.

Activity | Soil formation

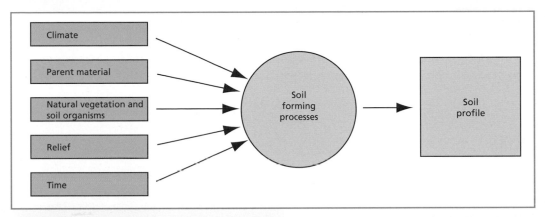

Figure 13.21
Soil formation

▲ Figure 13.22 Deciduous woodland, Oxfordshire

▲ Figure 13.23 Sparse vegetation in a semi arid landscape, Utah, USA

Questions

1 Outline the factors that will determine the type of soil that might develop in the locations shown in figures 13.22 and 13.23.

2 Suggest which soil forming processes might be dominant in each of the two locations.

unit summary

1 Soil contains air, water, organic matter and weathered parent material. These components combine to form plant nutrients.
2 The main natural factors that affect soil formation are climate; living organisms; relief; parent material and time.
3 Processes that create soils are the weathering of parent material, the decomposition of organic matter, and the rearrangement of soil components into horizons.
4 Under a variety of conditions, different processes can influence soil type. These processes include leaching, podsolisation, calcification, gleying, laterisation and salinisation.

key terms

Biota - living organisms including plants, animals, insects and bacteria.
Calcification - a soil forming process in which calcium salts are leached from the A horizon and redeposited in the B horizon.
Catena - a sequence of soil types down a slope.
Colloid - a very small particle that carries an electric charge. In soils, plant nutrients become fixed to clay and humus colloids.
Eluviation - see mechanical eluviation.
Gleying - a process that occurs in waterlogged soils. Red ferric oxide is changed to blue/grey ferrous oxide.
Humus - decomposed organic matter (plant and animal remains). It can range in acidity from mor (most acid) to mull (neutral). A layer of organic matter that is not decomposed is called peat.
Ion - a particle with either a positive charge (a 'cation') or a negative charge (an 'anion'). Ions of plant nutrients such as sodium, calcium, magnesium and potassium become attached to clay and humus colloids. The process by which these are absorbed by plants is known as cation exchange.
Laterisation - a process of soil formation typical of humid tropical areas. Nutrients are leached from the soil leaving behind aluminium and iron oxides (sesquioxides) which give the soil a reddish colour. The process is also known as ferrallitisation.
Leaching (or **chemical eluviation**) - the washing out of soluble material in soil.
Mechanical eluviation (or simply **eluviation**) - the washing out of material from soil in suspension.
Nutrients - chemical elements that are essential for plant growth.
Organisms - the micro-organisms (such as bacteria and fungi) and larger organisms (such as worms and ants) which decompose organic matter.
pH - a measure of alkalinity or acidity. (An alkaline substance is sometimes described as 'basic'.) Soils become more acidic when hydrogen ions replace nutrient ions on clay and humus colloids. When soils increase in acidity they lose plant nutrients and become less fertile.
Podsolisation - an extreme form of leaching in which some nutrient ions, and iron and aluminium oxides are washed out of the topsoil. The removal of the iron and aluminium oxides is called **cheluviation**. The resulting soils are called **podsols**.
Regolith - the layer of weathered material, including soil, that overlies solid bedrock.
Salinisation - a process that occurs mainly in hot, dry climates. Soil moisture rises through the soil by **capillary action** and evaporates at the surface leaving a deposit of salt.
Soil - a mixture of rock particles, minerals and decomposed organic (mainly plant) matter.
Soil moisture - the water content in soils. When all pore spaces are filled with water the soil is saturated.
Soil profile - a cross section through a soil from its surface to unaltered bedrock or parent material.
Soil structure - the shape of soil particles (or **peds**) determines the soil structure which can be, for example, crumbly or platy.
Soil texture - this refers to the size of the rock particles in soil, and is determined by the proportion of sand, silt and clay. A fine textured soil is formed from small clay particles. A coarse textured soil is formed from bigger sand particles.

Unit 13.2   Main soil types

key questions

1 How are soils classified?
2 What are the main zonal soils?
3 What are the main intrazonal soils?
4 What are azonal soils?

1. How are soils classified?

Although every soil is different, many share common features and so can be grouped together in broad categories. The first large scale attempt at classification was over one hundred years ago by Russian soil scientists. Soil names such as podsol and chernozem come from their work. Since then, many other classifications have been made, including the 1940s Soil Survey of England and Wales (similar surveys were carried out in Scotland and Ireland). Today, the two most commonly used soil classification schemes are the United States Department of Agriculture's 'Seventh Approximation', and the Food and Agriculture Organisation's 1985 Revision. (The FAO is a United Nations agency). The FAO scheme includes 27 soil groups and over 100 sub-groups. These more modern classifications give less emphasis to climate and natural vegetation zones than earlier systems, and depend more on soil forming processes and the soil horizon.

Because a variety of classification schemes are in use, different names are sometimes used to describe the same soil. For example, a 'eutric gleysol' (FAO scheme) is called a 'brown earth with gleying' by the Soil Survey of Scotland. In general, the soil names used in this unit are from the simpler, older classifications.

The traditional method of grouping soils was developed by a Russian scientist, Sibirtsev. He described soils as zonal, intrazonal and azonal. The most common world soils, broadly coinciding with major climatic zones, are called zonal. Where a particular local factor such as a limestone parent material is dominant, the soils are called intrazonal. Soils that are newly forming on unconsolidated material such as volcanic ash are called azonal.

It should be noted that, no matter which classification scheme is used, the boundaries between soil types are rarely clear cut. Just as climatic and vegetation zones merge into one another, so do soil zones.

2. What are the main zonal soils?

Zonal soils have had time to produce distinct horizons. They are mature and well developed. The distribution of these soils is closely related to the world's climatic zones. This is because temperature and precipitation have a great influence on natural vegetation. The vegetation provides the organic matter that decomposes into soil and, in turn, is recycled in plant nutrients. Not only does the climate affect the vegetation input into soil, it also affects the rate of weathering of the other main soil constituent, the underlying parent material. So, for example, in hot humid climates where chemical weathering is rapid, a deep soil layer is typical. The climate also influences processes within the soil. For instance, the rate of leaching and evaporation is controlled by temperature and precipitation.

The main zonal soils corresponding to the main climatic and vegetation zones from the equator to polar regions are shown in figure 13.24.

(A more detailed examination of natural vegetation zones and their associated soils is provided in unit 14.4.)

Figure 13.24 shows a very simplified sequence of soil types and processes from the equator to polar regions. In the humid tropics, latosols (or ferrallitic soils) tend to be deep and red coloured - a result of laterisation. Plant nutrients do not remain long in the ground but are rapidly recycled to the natural vegetation which is mainly rain forest.

Moving away from the equator there is a zone of savanna grassland where the climate typically has a wet and a dry season. Here the soils are leached during the wet part of the year but experience an upward movement of soil moisture in the dry period.

In hot desert regions where rainfall is low, salinisation occurs. Capillary action brings salts to the surface of the soil and, in some places, might cause a salt crust to form. Because vegetation is sparse there is little humus.

In the drier regions within temperate latitudes, grasslands form the main natural vegetation (eg, the prairies and the steppes). Deep, fertile, black soils (chernozems) develop in these conditions. In wetter temperate latitudes, forests are the main natural vegetation. In milder areas the trees are mostly deciduous, and brown earths that are rich in humus develop. In less mild areas, the natural vegetation is

Figure 13.24 Zonal soils from the equator to polar regions

	POLE					EQUATOR
Climate and natural vegetation zone	Tundra	Coniferous forest	Deciduous forest	Grassland	Desert	Humid tropics-savanna and rain forest
Main soil process	Gleying	Podsolisation	Leaching	Limited amount of leaching	Salinisation	Laterisation or ferrallitisation
Main soil type	Gley	Podsol	Brown earth	Chernozem	Desert soil	Latosol or Ferrallitic

mainly coniferous forest under which podsols form.

Finally, within arctic regions, there is tundra and ice cap. The tundra typically has a thin layer of soil that overlies the permafrost (ie, permanently frozen ground). In summer the soil is waterlogged, in winter it is frozen. The gley soils that form under these conditions are sometimes not classed as zonal soils because they occur in many other locations around the world - wherever the ground is waterlogged.

Climate, vegetation and soil are influenced not only by distance from the equator but also by altitude. For example, on high mountains in equatorial areas such as the Andes, there are vertical vegetation zones. These correspond to the equator-polar transect described above. So, for instance, there are zones of rain forest, grassland and coniferous forest at different altitudes. Underlying this vegetation are soils that are very different from those typically found near sea level.

3. What are the main intrazonal soils?

Intrazonal soils reflect the influence of one localised, soil forming factor other than climate and vegetation. They can be found in many parts of the world - wherever the particular conditions are suitable. There are three main types:
- calcimorphic - these develop on calcium rich chalk or limestone parent material
- hydromorphic - these develop in waterlogged conditions
- halomorphic - these develop in dry regions where salts accumulate at or near the surface.

Calcimorphic soils

These soils develop on limestone and chalk. The dominant soil forming factor is the parent material. There are two commonly identified types, **rendzinas** and **terra rossas**.

Figure 13.25 Rendzina

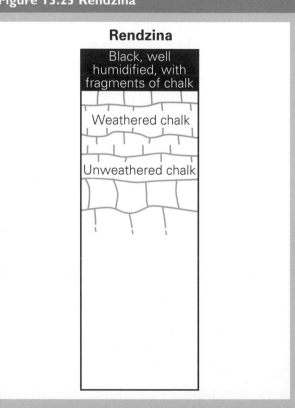

Rendzina

Black, well humidified, with fragments of chalk

Weathered chalk

Unweathered chalk

The humus rich A horizon overlies weathered bedrock. There is no B horizon.

Figure 13.26 Rendzina

This well developed rendzina has formed over chalk in the Lincolnshire Wolds.

Rendzina This soil is typically thin, with a rich A horizon of black or dark brown humus. It does not have a B horizon, mainly because the weathered chalk or limestone is removed downwards in solution - leaving little mineral material for soil development. Such soils are typical of the chalk and limestone uplands of southern England. The nutrients are quickly washed out into the underlying parent material and, when the land is used for arable farming, the natural soil fertility quickly declines (see figure 13.25).

Terra Rossa (or red earth) This soil is typically found in lowland Mediterranean areas where there is limestone parent material. The alternate dry summer and wet winter conditions promote the weathering of the parent material and its breakdown into silica and oxides of iron and aluminium. The build up of iron oxide in the B horizon gives the soil its characteristic red colour.

Hydromorphic soils

These soils can develop virtually anywhere in the world in waterlogged conditions. They include gley soils and **peat**.

Gley This soil forms as a result of the gleying process (see unit 13.1). Because the ground is waterlogged there is no air in the soil pores. The result is a chemical (and partly biological) process that changes red coloured ferric oxide to blue/grey coloured ferrous oxide. Such soils might develop where drainage is restricted by an impermeable layer (such as where an iron pan develops in a podsol) or where the groundwater level is high (such as on a river meadow).

Gley soils are generally infertile because the wet conditions slow the decomposition of organic matter and the release of nutrients. Also, few plant roots can survive these anaerobic conditions. However there is an important exception in the case of paddy field rice cultivation which takes place under water. Algae in the water fix nitrogen from the air and make it available as a plant nutrient (ie, the nitrogen is extracted from the atmosphere and converted to nitrates in the surface soil layer - see unit 14.1).

Peat This is defined by the Soil Survey of England and Wales as a layer of undecomposed organic matter, at least 40 cm thick. It sometimes forms as a surface horizon on another soil, such as a podsol or a gley.

Peat forms where ground conditions are saturated and there is insufficient oxygen for most micro-organisms to survive. An area of peat is called a bog and is often very acidic - particularly in upland regions. However, where it

Figure 13.27 Peat in South Uist, Outer Hebrides

This peat has developed in an area of acidic moorland vegetation. Local people cut the peat and use it as fuel when it is dried.

forms on lowland chalk or limestone (in places where the groundwater level is near the surface), the pH can be higher. This is because the groundwater dissolves some of the alkaline calcimorphic material and washes it into the peat. When such areas are drained, they can form very fertile soils, for example in the Fens of eastern England.

Figure 13.28 Rendzina, peat and podsol in England and Wales

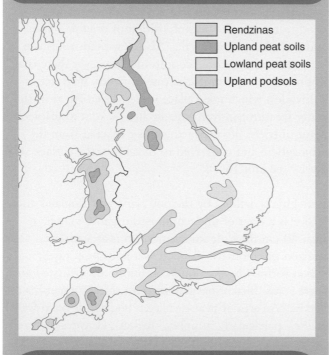

Rendzinas
Upland peat soils
Lowland peat soils
Upland podsols

The rendzinas are located on the chalk and limestone areas of southern and eastern England. The upland peats are mainly on the higher hills and mountains of the north and west, on impervious rocks such as sandstone and granite. The upland podsols are also found in the same areas, generally on better drained slopes which are not waterlogged. The lowland peat soils are found on drained marshlands such as the Fens, the Somerset Levels and the West Lancashire Plain.

Halomorphic soils

These soils develop where salinisation (see unit 13.1) causes high levels of salts in the upper soil or even on the soil surface. They occur where leaching is weak or non-existent, typically in hot arid regions. Evaporation of soil moisture at the surface causes a capillary action within the soil in which water containing soluble salts rises upwards. The most saline soils are sometimes called 'solonchaks' and, in some cases, have a surface crust of salt crystal. They tend to have a low humus content and are infertile because few plants can withstand such saline conditions.

When irrigation schemes in hot, arid regions are mismanaged, the process of salinisation can create halomorphic soils. A careful balance has to be achieved between allowing sufficient water to wash salts down through the soil, but not too much water to raise the groundwater level to the surface. (Salinisation caused by irrigation schemes is discussed in more detail in units 13.3 and 14.4.)

4. What are azonal soils?

These are immature soils which have no distinct horizons. They have not had enough time to develop because they are new or forming on unconsolidated parent material, for example on scree, river alluvium, sand dunes, mudflats or volcanic lava. In time, they might develop into recognisable zonal or intrazonal soils.

Most azonal soils are infertile. They contain little decomposed organic material and the parent material has not been sufficiently weathered to produce mineral nutrients. However, there is an exception in the case of fertile river alluvium which consists of fine silt and clay particles. For example, in south and east Asia, alluvial river deltas such as the Ganges and Mekong support high populations and very productive agricultural systems.

Figure 13.29 River alluvium

Although river alluvium is a zonal soil, it is often fertile because it contains nutrients deposited by the river.

Activity | Soils

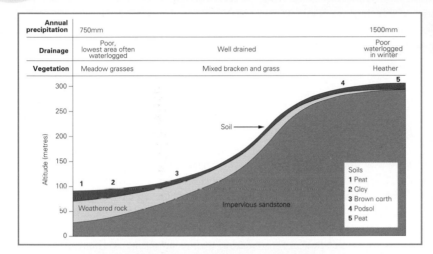

Figure 13.30 A soil catena in the northern Pennines

This catena is a sequence of soils found on a slope in an upland area of northern England. The underlying parent material is coarse, impermeable sandstone.

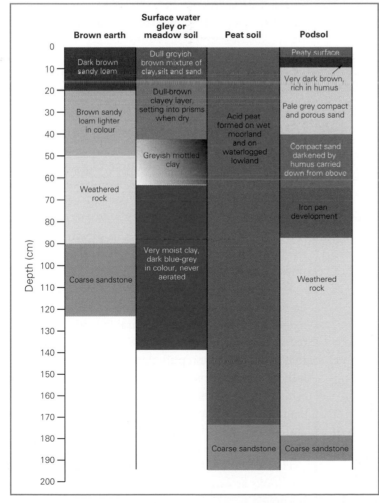

Figure 13.31 Soil profiles

These profiles represent the main soil types found in the soil catena.

Questions

1 Describe the soils that occur in the soil catena.
2 Outline the processes that have formed each of the soils.
3 Explain why each of the soils might have formed in the positions marked on the catena.

unit summary

1 There are a number of different ways in which soils can be classified.
2 A traditional method of classification is to group soils according to the main climate and natural vegetation zones in which they are found (zonal soils).
3 Other classifications are based on: a soil's parent material or on the dominant soil forming process (intrazonal soils); or on the degree of maturity of the soil (azonal soils).

key terms

Azonal soils - an immature soil on new material (equivalent to an 'entisol' (US Dept. of Agriculture) or a 'regosol' (FAO classification))
Calcimorphic soil - a soil formed on a calcium rich rock such as chalk or limestone.
Halomorphic soil - soils in which salt has accumulated at or near the surface.
Hydromorphic soil - a soil formed in waterlogged conditions.
Intrazonal soil - a mature soil influenced by a dominant local factor other than climate or vegetation, for example a calcimorphic, halomorphic or hydromorphic soil.
Zonal soils - a mature soil that is mainly influenced by climate and natural vegetation, for example a podsol, latosol or chernozem.

Unit 13.3 Human impact on soils

key questions

1 How does human activity affect soil?
2 What is soil erosion and how can it be prevented?
3 What is chemical and physical soil degradation?

1. How does human activity affect soil?

The human impact on soil can be positive or negative. People can increase the productive potential of soil by careful farming techniques. But, equally, careless techniques can cause damage or erosion to soils that have taken hundreds or even thousands of years to form.

A summary of human influences on the five main soil forming factors is given in figure 13.32. It shows ways in which human activity can improve or damage soil.

Soil degradation is the name given to soil damage. It includes:

• soil erosion (the removal of soil by water and wind)
• chemical and physical degradation; examples of chemical degradation are salinisation, pollution and soil exhaustion; examples of physical degradation are compaction by farm machinery and damage caused by ploughing.

The FAO (Food and Agriculture Organisation of the United Nations) estimates that, worldwide, between 5 and 7 million hectares of farm land are being lost each year. FAO statistics show that 55 percent of the damage is due to water erosion, 33 percent to wind erosion and the remaining 12 percent is due to chemical and physical degradation.

The FAO believes that the three main causes of soil degradation are overgrazing (causing 35% of the total damage), mismanagement of arable land (35%) and deforestation (30%). In a 1998 report, the FAO stated that soil degradation puts the livelihoods of nearly 1 billion people at risk. Prominent American and Russian ecologists have described the accelerating rate of soil degradation as 'the silent ecological crisis of the planet' and 'the greatest threat (short of nuclear war) to the prosperity of all humanity'.

This unit includes examples of soil degradation but also looks at ways in which soil has been conserved and improved.

Figure 13.32 Summary of human impact on the five main factors that control soil formation

Soil forming factor	Positive impact	Negative impact
Parent material	Adding fertiliser, shell and bone meal; burning vegetation to add nutrients	Harvesting crops removes nutrients; dumping toxic wastes
Relief	Terracing; reducing soil erosion	Increased erosion by deforestation and inappropriate farming methods
Climate	Adding water by irrigation; constructing drainage schemes; planting wind breaks	Removing ground cover; allowing soil to be exposed to the elements
Biota	Adding organic matter; leaving land fallow; introducing new plants and animals; controlling pests	Reducing plant and animal diversity; reducing organic content by overgrazing or overcropping
Time	Rejuvenating soil by adding new organic and parent material; reclaiming land	Accelerated removal of nutrients and vegetation cover; covering land with urban development, landfill or reservoirs

Figure 13.33 Soil erosion in northern Spain

This severe gullying and erosion has been caused by the removal of the natural woodland vegetation which, at one time, protected the soil.

2. What is soil erosion and how can it be prevented?

Soil erosion is a natural process that occurs when it rains or when the wind blows. However, it can be accelerated by human activity. Each year, according to the FAO, 25 billion tonnes of topsoil are washed or blown away. The United States has lost an estimated one third of its topsoil since settled agriculture began. Figure 13.34 shows the area of land in each continent that suffers from moderate to severe degradation by soil erosion.

It is clear that soil erosion is a global problem affecting all continents. It occurs not only in semi arid lands of Africa and on the western plains of the USA, but also in the UK. For example, in 1996, researchers found that 4 mm of topsoil was lost from a 16 hectare field in just one rainstorm in the English Midlands. In the 1970s, another study estimated that a relatively small thunderstorm in Cambridgeshire had caused the removal of 330 tonnes of topsoil per square kilometre. Both these incidents took place on arable land which was being prepared for seeding but which was lying bare at the time. Such events cause the loss of soil that has taken farmers hundreds of years to nurture and improve. Farming did continue after these two examples of soil erosion but, in the long run, such losses are not sustainable. Yields

Figure 13.34 Area affected by moderate to severe soil erosion (million hectares) (FAO estimates)

	Water erosion	Wind erosion	Total
Asia	440	222	662
Africa	227	187	414
South America	123	42	165
Europe	115	42	157
North and Central America	106	39	145
Australasia	83	17	100

begin to fall and, in extreme examples of total topsoil loss, farming cannot continue. The UK Soil Survey Research Centre believes that up to 20 percent of arable lowland is at risk from erosion. The 1996 Royal Commission on Environmental Pollution stated that the government should encourage farmers to draw up plans aimed at minimising the loss of soil from their land. Most erosion occurs on arable land where there are light soils or where the soil structure has been damaged by monoculture. One such example is on the South Downs where winter cereals are grown on the same land year after year. Because the seeds are planted in autumn, the soil is bare at a time (October - February) when heavy rain might be expected.

In Saskatchewan, in the Canadian prairies, arable farming only started one hundred years ago. It is estimated that over half the original organic content of the soil has been lost in that time, so reducing the amount of nutrients available to crops. Two periods of severe drought, in the 1930s and the 1980s, caused the most serious erosion when crops failed and the bare land was exposed to the wind. However, even under normal conditions, the soil structure is damaged every time the land is ploughed, leaving the soil more vulnerable to erosion.

Causes of soil erosion

Most soil erosion occurs when there is no vegetation to protect the soil from being washed or blown away (see figure 13.35). Clearing forests and removing wind breaks are major causes. So too is ploughing on steep slopes, or up and

down slopes rather than along contours. When hedgerows, walls or natural windbreaks are removed, the soil becomes more vulnerable to wind erosion. Overgrazing and trampling by animals can kill vegetation. This causes the roots which bind the soil together to die.

In areas of the world that are densely populated, more and more land is being used for intensive cultivation. To increase food supply, forests are being cut down. Then pressure is put on the soil by overgrazing, overcropping, lack of crop rotation and by reliance on artificial fertiliser. All of these weaken the soil structure and leave the topsoil open to erosion by wind or rain.

Figure 13.35 Vegetation cover and runoff

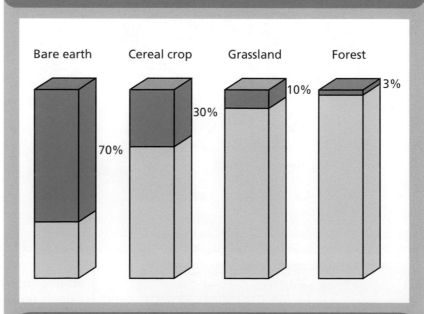

Bare earth — 70%
Cereal crop — 30%
Grassland — 10%
Forest — 3%

The diagram shows the typical proportion of rainfall that runs off the surface and that which is held by plants and the soil. The greater the vegetation cover, the lower the rate of runoff and soil erosion.

Consequences of soil erosion

Erosion removes the most productive part of soil - the topsoil - and causes farm yields to fall. When water carries eroded soil downstream, it can silt up rivers and fill reservoirs. Hydroelectric turbines can be damaged and river transport can be disrupted. Where large amounts of material are deposited on floodplains and deltas, drainage can be impeded. The result can be the formation of marshland and swamps - so creating breeding grounds for malarial mosquitoes. Because river beds are raised when sediment is deposited, floods become more frequent.

Soil conservation

The basic principle of soil conservation is to protect the bare soil from wind and rain - by covering it with vegetation. At the same time, the flow of water and the wind needs to be slowed down.

The most effective method of conservation is by afforestation, ie by planting trees. The leaves intercept rainfall and the tree roots bind the soil, increase infiltration and reduce surface runoff. At the same time, the ground is protected from the wind. However, in many places this is not an option because farmers need the land to supply food. In these areas, better farming techniques are required to reduce soil loss. These techniques include the terracing of slopes, contour ploughing, or the planting of grass strips along the contour. The effect is to slow the movement of water downhill, so reducing sheet erosion and the formation of gullies. An additional effect is to increase the infiltration of rain water, so increasing soil moisture content.

In arable farming, using organic fertiliser and leaving stubble in fields can improve soil structure, making it less likely to blow or be washed away. By planting trees as shelter belts, or strips of grass around field boundaries, both wind and water erosion can be reduced. 'Intercropping' alternate strips of taller and shorter plants can lift the wind off the land surface and cut the amount of soil blown away (see figure 13.36).

In pastoral farming, the most important method of reducing soil erosion is by limiting herds or flocks of animals to numbers that the countryside can sustain. Because overgrazing, and trampling of vegetation, are

Figure 13.36 Intercropping of wheat and vegetables in the Midwest, USA

This technique reduces both wind and water erosion.

the main factors that cause soil damage, reducing the number of animals is the solution. This, though, is easier said than done - particularly where population pressure is intense or where rainfall variability causes big fluctuations in the number of animals that the land can sustain. It is also difficult is to change cultural attitudes that equate wealth with the quantity, rather than the quality, of animals owned.

Although soil erosion is a growing global problem, there are examples of successful schemes that show it can be overcome. For instance, in 1979, the Chinese government, supported by UN agencies, began a scheme in the Mizhi region of north central China. This is an area of steep slopes and loess soils (formed from fine, sand blown deposits). Nearly two-thirds of the land lies at an angle greater than twenty degrees. It had one of the most severe soil erosion problems in the world. Solutions included planting trees on the steepest slopes and building more terraces. Annual crops such as wheat were replaced by perennials such as alfalfa, and farmers were encouraged to diversify into fruit growing and small animal production. By the mid-1990s, food production had risen by 70 percent despite the halving of cultivated land.

Another UN backed scheme, in southern Morocco, has been successful in reducing wind erosion. In the mid-1970s, villages, roads and palm plantations were being buried under wind blown sand. The problem was getting worse because overgrazing was killing vegetation, and trees and bushes were being cut down for fuel wood. Three methods of stabilising the sand dunes were used. In some places, palm branches were made into lattice wind breaks. In others, small concrete walls were built to stop the blowing sand. The third method was to sculpt sand banks along roads so encouraging sand to blow away rather than settle. Overgrazing and tree cutting have been stopped so that, now, the irrigation canals, roads and villages are safe from the blowing sand

Activity   **Dust Bowl USA – wind erosion**

▼   **Figure 13.37 The Dust Bowl**

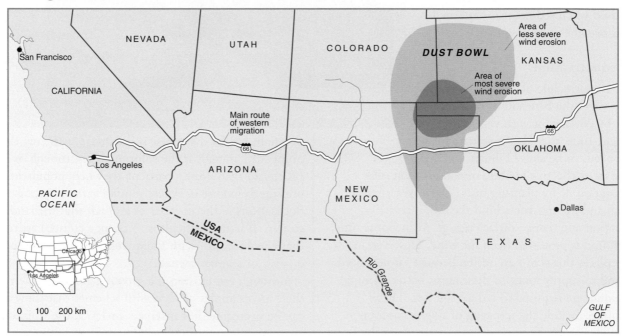

Western Europeans, used to farming in a temperate climate with reliable and regular rainfall, emigrated to the USA in the nineteenth and early twentieth century. They took their traditional farming methods with them. The Homestead Act of 1862 gave 160 acres of land to anyone would settle on it for five years. From Texas to Dakota there seemed an endless supply of rich, black chernozem soil. Its carpet of grass was quickly removed by new steel ploughs. Wheat and maize were grown by the farmers who enclosed the land to keep the ranched cattle out.

In 1889, the population of Oklahoma was 60,000, by 1900 it was 389,000 and between 1900 and 1910, nearly half a million new settlers arrived. The rising US population, and demand for food in Europe during and after World War One, gave farmers an incentive to increase their output. As a result, the soil became exhausted. The humus content was so reduced that the soil's ability to retain moisture was lost. The water table sank and the soil became a light dust during the 1920s.

Although drought years had been experienced in the region before, the period between 1930 and 1934 was exceptionally dry. Crops failed and the land was left bare. The problem was made worse by a world slump in grain prices that caused many farmers simply to abandon their land.

Strong winds sweeping across the plains created dust storms or 'black blizzards' that filled the air with grit and even choked cattle to death. In 1933 alone, an estimated 850 million tons of topsoil were blown away in the area that became known as the Dust Bowl. It had taken just 75 years since the first European settlers arrived to turn the region into a wasteland. Many of the farmers moved westwards to California. The poverty stricken migrants were called 'Okies' and became part of American folklore.

The United States government treated the Dust Bowl as a national disaster and set up the Soil Conservation Service. Its strategy was to:

- educate farmers in suitable techniques and to help them understand the causes of soil erosion
- encourage farmers to contour plough, to plant drought resistant grass strips, to leave the stubble in fields
- encourage annual crop rotation and the intercropping of strips of wheat and maize with crops such as alfalfa (which fixes nitrogen in the soil and so allows the soil to recover fertility)
- promote the planting of trees to act as windbreaks and to stop gully erosion
- show how 'dry farming' techniques such as leaving land fallow (ie, uncultivated) could build up and conserve soil moisture.

These strategies were successful and, within a few years, agricultural productivity was restored. By the 1960s, grain yields were higher than ever before.

Questions

1 Describe where the Dust Bowl was located.
2 Explain the cause of wind erosion in the Dust Bowl.
3 What lessons might present day farmers in the USA and other parts of the world learn from the Dust Bowl experience?

3. What is chemical and physical soil degradation?

This is the damage caused to soil by chemical and physical processes. Although these processes occur naturally, like soil erosion they are made worse by human activity. Chemical degradation includes laterisation, podsolisation, salinisation and the over use of artificial fertiliser. Physical degradation includes the compaction of soil by farm machinery and the changes brought about by artificial drainage.

Chemical processes

Laterisation This is a process that occurs in tropical areas (see unit 13.1). In regions which experience wet and dry seasons, the result can be to form a layer of aluminium and iron oxide within the soil. When this is exposed to the air, and dries, it can become so hard that it is virtually impossible to plough. The name laterite comes from the Latin word for 'brick' and the material is sometimes used for building purposes in India and elsewhere. Deforestation has greatly increased the

problem. If left bare, the topsoil is quickly removed by water erosion and the laterite layer is exposed. Without the forest cover, the micro-climate becomes less humid and this helps dry the crust.

Laterisation is an important reason why it is difficult to re-establish tropical forests once cleared. The only solution is to prevent the removal of vegetation in the first place.

The late 1940s Groundnut Scheme in Tanzania (then Tanganyika) illustrates the difficulties that arise with laterites. The British government urged landowners in Tanganyika to cultivate groundnuts on the tropical soils. The scheme failed, mainly because conventional tractor drawn machinery could not cope with the almost concrete like ground. It was reported that a set of discs, used for preparing the land, lasted less than a month under these conditions.

Podsolisation and acidification In Britain, over the past few thousand years, most upland forests have been cleared for arable and pastoral farming. The result has been to create acidic podsols with a moorland vegetation of heather and bracken. Burning the trees at first released nutrients useful for agriculture, but these have long since been washed away. Without the deciduous tree cover acting to replenish the soil, the conditions have gradually become more acid. Eventually, in some areas, waterlogged conditions with thick layers of peat have formed on top of the podsolic iron pan (see unit 13.1).

In an effort to bring the land into more productive use, deep ploughing is sometimes used to break the iron pan and improve drainage. Reafforestation by conifers (which can withstand the acid conditions) has occurred in areas such as Sutherland in the north and Galloway in south west Scotland. Opponents of conifer plantations claim that the trees are unsightly and that biodiversity is reduced. What is clear, however, is that the moorland they replace is no more natural than the conifers themselves.

In some regions, particularly the heavily polluted areas of central Europe such as the Czech Republic and southern Poland, sulphur emissions that cause acid rain have an important effect on soils (see unit 2.5). Where conditions are 'acidified', the effect is to release toxic metals such as lead and zinc from the soil. They then become more readily available to plants and grazing animals. Water draining from the acid soils can harm plant and animal life in rivers and lakes, and can also be hazardous to humans if drinking water is contaminated.

Salinisation This is the process by which calcium, sodium and magnesium salts are drawn upwards within the soil. In the most severe cases a salt crust forms on the surface (see unit 13.1). It occurs in arid and semi arid regions where temperatures are high and potential evapotranspiration is greater than precipitation. The salt is toxic to plants and greatly reduces farm yields. If the salt causes plants to die, the bare soil becomes more vulnerable to wind and water erosion. Irrigation schemes can increase salinisation by raising the water table near to the surface. The ground water dissolves salts in the rock and so becomes saline. If the water table rises to less than 3 metres below ground level, then capillary action will cause the soil moisture to rise to the surface in hot, dry regions.

Areas of southern Russia, the central Asian republics of the former Soviet Union, north west India, parts of the Middle East, south east Australia and southern California all experience moderate or severe salinisation.

Figure 13.38 Irrigated crops in southern California

Overwatering can raise the water table and make salinisation more likely.

In parts of Victoria, Australia, the water table is rising by 1 cm per year and is now only one metre below the surface. The FAO estimates that salinisation lowers the productivity of irrigated land in both China and Pakistan by 20 percent. (See unit 14.4 for a case study on salinisation and farming in Kazakhstan.)

The Euphrates Valley in Iraq is another region that experiences salinisation. An estimated 50 percent of irrigated land is either salt affected or waterlogged due to the use of irrigation schemes. It is not a new problem. There is evidence that the farmers of Ancient Mesopotamia (now Iraq) had to use salt tolerant plants more than 4,000 years ago. This was one of the first places in the world to develop irrigation. Salinisation caused crop yields to fall and, in some places, wheat growing had to be abandoned. It is possible that some of the first civilisations collapsed for this reason.

Managing the flow of water is the key to avoiding salinisation, but this is difficult to achieve. Enough water has to be supplied to allow crops to grow. But, if too much water is applied, the water table rises and increased salinisation occurs. There is then a vicious circle of adding ever more water to wash the salt downwards. The water table rises further and, in the worst cases, the land can become completely waterlogged.

Modern sprinkler systems that spray large amounts of water, and unlined canals that leak are blamed for some of the increase in salinisation. The solution is to use smaller scale, trickle irrigation schemes that use less water and apply it more slowly to the plants. Drainage schemes can also help because they remove the excess water and lower the water table. Salt accumulating plants, such as suaeda fruticosa can also be grown and harvested - so removing some of the salt.

Salinisation can sometimes occur in coastal areas that are neither arid nor irrigated. In the Netherlands, for example, the saline ground water near the coast is very close to the soil surface. This is particularly true of those areas under sea level. Concern has been expressed that the expected global rise in sea level will make the problem worse. During dry spells in summer there is a loss of soil moisture by evaporation and this brings salts close to the surface. A similar problem can occur near to coastal areas when fresh ground water is pumped for domestic use or for irrigation. Saline water is more dense than fresh water and it can seep into the aquifer (ie, the water bearing rock) and can contaminate the fresh water.

Salinisation is an important problem because irrigation is vital for food supply. On a world scale, 20 percent of harvested land is irrigated and it provides nearly 40 percent of food supplies. Yet, because of mismanaged irrigation schemes, the FAO estimates that there is now a balance between the amount of land that is newly irrigated and land that is becoming unproductive due to salinisation.

Artificial fertilisers Soil chemistry has been modified by human activity ever since farming began. The addition of organic manure from farm animals has been the traditional means of maintaining soil structure and fertility.

However, during the twentieth century, the invention of artificial, inorganic fertiliser, and the decline of mixed farming (ie, keeping animals as well as growing crops) has caused a change. The positive result has been a massive rise in agricultural production. The negative result has been a deterioration of soil structure and an increase in soil erosion. In addition, runoff from the fertilised soil contains a high proportion of nitrates and other plant nutrients. The consequence has been contamination of drinking water and 'eutrophication'. This is a process in which the nutrients stimulate a rapid growth in aquatic plant life which then depletes the water's oxygen supply. The result is that fish and other water life die. Official figures in the UK suggest that the water companies spend over £500 million per year in removing fertiliser and pesticide residues from the domestic water supply.

Physical degradation

Physical degradation of soil includes damage to the soil structure. This can occur due to compaction. However, soil structure is not inevitably damaged by farming. For instance, it can be improved by adding lime to clay soils. This makes the clay particles stick together in bigger peds (ie, they 'flocculate'). On sandy soils, adding clay improves structure, and adding organic waste improves all types of soil.

Compaction This occurs when tractor tyres and farm animals 'squash' the soil. It makes it harder for roots to penetrate the soil and for seedlings to grow. It also reduces soil oxygen and therefore the number of micro-organisms which decompose organic matter and produce plant nutrients. The rate of water infiltration is also reduced by the compacted surface - so increasing the rate of surface runoff and increasing the risk of gullying.

Ploughing can produce a compacted layer within the soil, at the base of the zone of ploughing. It is called a 'plough sole'. The plough leaves a loose surface layer over a dense subsoil where the soil peds have been compacted by the bottom of the plough. The effect is made worse if a field is always ploughed to the same depth or when heavy machinery is used to plough when the ground is wet.

Soil drainage By draining soils, farmers can increase agricultural productivity but there is also a danger that degradation will occur. The positive effects of digging field drains, surface ditches and dykes are that waterlogging is reduced and the water table is lowered. This gives plant roots a greater depth in which to grow and it increases the proportion of oxygen in the soil. Also, well drained soils warm up faster than wet soils so increase the length of the growing season. An additional advantage is that heavy machinery does less damage to dry soils than to wet soils.

However, improved drainage can reduce soil quality because soluble nutrients are washed out more quickly than otherwise. Also, when soils are drained, they shrink. In the lowland peat soils of Fenland and West Lancashire, the land has sunk in some places by over two metres. In parts of Florida, the soil is subsiding at a rate of over 3 cm per year. The result is that ever better drainage systems are required to prevent flooding. One other important problem associated with improved drainage is that wetland habitats are lost. Particular species of plants and birds decline and biodiversity is reduced.

Activity | Nepal - water erosion

This mountainous Himalayan country has a monsoon climate. There is a wet season from June to September during which heavy rains fall.

At one time, the country was largely tree covered. However, population growth during the twentieth century has caused much forest to be cleared. In some cases this has been to create land for cultivation, in other cases to provide fuel wood for heating and cooking.

Trees are vital in preventing erosion on steep slopes because their deep roots help bind the soil together. They also make it easier for rain water to penetrate the soil rather than flow across the ground as surface runoff. The tree leaves and branches intercept the rain and reduce its impact on the ground.

Nepalese people have traditionally used wood for fuel. Now, many face a shortage and use instead either stalks from harvested crops or animal dung. Previously, the crop stalks were used to feed animals whose dung is applied as a fertiliser - so recycling nutrients and maintaining humus and moisture content in the soil. The result is a loss of fertility and productivity, so creating the need to clear even more land for agriculture. At the same time, the degraded soil, with its reduced organic content, is more easily eroded.

The result is an estimated half a million tonnes of topsoil being washed off the Nepalese hillsides and into the Ganges each year. It is helping to form a huge sandbank in the Bay of Bengal covering 5 million hectares.

To try and reduce the soil erosion, the Nepalese government started a tree planting scheme as far back as the 1950s. New tree plantations were fenced off to keep animals and people out. Locals were rarely consulted or involved, and the scheme was not a success.

More recently, a new initiative based on village councils - called Panchayats - has been started. By involving villagers, and by providing them with trees to plant, people have been more positive in their approach. The fences around the trees are well maintained and locals are more willing to look after the new saplings. They feel that they have a vested interest in growing more trees and in reducing erosion. So far, the scheme has been judged a success but there is still a very long way to go before the erosion problem is overcome.

◀ **Figure 13.39 Soil erosion in Nepal**
Deforestation on the upper slopes has caused soil erosion and landslips. Only where the slopes are terraced and trees are planted is the problem overcome.

Questions

1 To what extent is soil erosion in Nepal a natural process?
2 With reference to the Nepalese experience, explain the difference between soil erosion and physical and chemical degradation.
3 Suggest why the involvement of local people might be important in reducing soil erosion.

unit summary

1 Soil degradation is one of the world's most serious problems because our food production depends upon the soil.
2 Soil erosion is accelerated by deforestation and by poor farming practices. Soil conservation techniques involve putting these processes into reverse.
3 Chemical and physical degradation of soil is largely caused by human activity. Mostly this is undertaken with good motives such as creating more farmland by irrigation or clearing forest to feed more people. It is when these schemes are mismanaged or are carried out in inappropriate locations that soil damage occurs.

key terms

Laterite - a hard layer formed of oxides of iron and aluminium in soils within humid tropical regions. (It also has the more modern name of 'plinthite'.)

Soil conservation - methods used to reduce or prevent soil erosion.

Soil degradation - the damage to soils caused by erosion and chemical processes (such as salinisation and podsolisation) and physical processes (such as compacting and draining).

Soil erosion - the loss of topsoil by wind or water action.

Introduction

The living part of the Earth is called the biosphere. It includes the water, the soil and the air of the surface zone where all life exists. It is where we live and so is of great importance and interest. The biosphere can be divided into units called ecosystems. These ecosystems vary in scale from biomes (ie, world zones of natural vegetation such as rain forests) to small scale places such as local wetlands or woodlands. Humans have a major impact on ecosystems. For instance, farming, forestry, mining and construction all have an effect on the natural environment. This chapter looks at how ecosystems work, their interacting components and the way that people alter and manage them on different scales. It includes the human impact on particular ecosystems such as coral reefs and on wilderness regions such as the Arctic tundra and Antarctica.

Chapter summary

Unit 14.1 considers what an ecosystem is and what processes operate within an ecosystem.
Unit 14.2 examines colonisation and succession within ecosystems.
Unit 14.3 looks at the impact that people have on ecosystems and how this impact can be managed.
Unit 14.4 describes the main global biomes and how people affect them.

Unit 14.1 Ecosystems

key questions

1   What are the components of an ecosystem?
2   What processes operate within an ecosystem?

1. What are the components of an ecosystem?

The term **ecosystem** is relatively recent. It was first used in 1935 by Arthur Tansley to describe the interaction between organisms (ie, plants and animals) and between organisms and their surroundings. He suggested that our understanding of the natural world is improved if the relationships between organisms and their environment are explored rather than simply studying living things in isolation.

There are many types of ecosystem even within a relatively small area such as Britain. Some are on land and some are on water but, within them, there are always the same basic components. These are:

• the **abiotic**, non-living component of the ecosystem; ie, the physical environment. This provides the living space, the raw materials and the energy, directly or indirectly, from the Sun. It includes the climate which affects the temperature, water availability, humidity and wind speed.

It also includes the rock type. Together, the rock type and the climate affect the rate of weathering and also the soil's acidity, fertility and texture.

• the **biotic** components of the ecosystem are the living organisms that exist there - the plants, animals, bacteria and fungi.

There is an interrelationship and interdependence between the abiotic and biotic components of an ecosystem. For instance, some micro-organisms affect the soil's fertility which, in turn, affects the plants that grow there. The plants then affect the micro-organisms by providing food and shelter so that, in this case, there is a loop or feedback effect.

The environment in which an individual animal or plant normally lives is called its **habitat**. The total number of a particular species living in a habitat is known as the **population**. Because organisms are selective about where they live, those that share the same kind of tolerances or requirements live in the same kind of habitat. For instance, in a shady woodland, there are populations of particular species of trees, shrubs, flowering plants, fungi, insects, birds and mammals. Organisms that share the same habitat might provide shelter for each other, compete with each other or, in some cases, they might eat each other. Collectively, these organisms make up the living **community** of that habitat.

Figure 14.1 A spider's web

Within a woodland habitat, plants and animals form a community. This spider has a niche within the habitat. In the food chain, it captures and eats smaller insects but is eaten by birds. In environmental terms, the conditions which are most favourable to the spider will be a sheltered location where its web will not be damaged by strong wind.

Habitats are rarely isolated from each other. A woodland habitat might have distinctive communities of organisms living on the woodland floor and also in the canopy of the trees. There might be a stream flowing through the woodland and animals in the stream habitat might feed on material falling from the trees. Such networks of habitats and communities generally have no visible boundaries. In reality, most ecosystems merge into each other.

Within a habitat, each species of plant and animal has a place in the order of things. This is called its ecological **niche**. The term is sometimes used to describe a species' place in the food chain - for example, whether it eats or is eaten by other species. The term is also used to describe the environmental factors (such as temperature and moisture) that are the most favourable for a particular species (see figure 14.1).

2. What processes operate within an ecosystem?

Within ecosystems, there are two main processes at work - energy flows and nutrient cycles.

Energy flows

All life ultimately depends upon the Sun. Within ecosystems, energy flows from the Sun via plants to other living organisms. Solar energy is captured by green 'chloroplasts' in plants in the process known as photosynthesis. The Sun's energy allows the plant to fix (ie, take in and use) carbon dioxide from the atmosphere and convert it to plant food in the form of carbohydrate. The process is described in the equation:

Carbon dioxide + water + light energy
$\longrightarrow$ carbohydrate + oxygen.

Energy is passed on to other organisms when they eat the plants. This movement of energy is called a flow because it occurs in just one direction (as opposed to being recycled through the system).

Photosynthesis occurs in plants that range in size from the largest trees to minute plankton in oceans. In total, billions of tonnes of carbohydrate are produced every year. However, less than one percent of the solar energy that reaches the Earth is converted into this stored energy. Much solar radiation falls not on green plants but on rock or ice or on buildings; some is reflected back and a large amount is the wrong wavelength for the plants to use.

The total amount of converted energy is called the **Gross Primary Production** (GPP). Some of this energy is used by the plants themselves for respiration (ie, the absorption of carbon dioxide and release of oxygen). The rest is stored in their tissues and is called the **Net Primary Production** (NPP). This is also the amount of energy that is available for anything that eats the plant. Since only net primary production is available for other animals, the NPP values are used to compare the productivity of different ecosystems.

During a plant's life, some of the NPP remains inside the plant and is used for growth, and some is lost when parts are eaten or fall off. The total mass of living organic matter in all plants in a given area is called the **biomass**. This is generally measured as 'dry weight' (ie, excluding water content) and is expressed in grams or in kilojoules if the energy content is known.

Activity | Productivity of ecosystems

Studies by the International Biological Programme have produced estimates on the productivity and the total biomass within different ecosystems.

▼ **Figure 14.2 Ecosystem productivity**

Ecosystem	Annual average NPP (kg per square metre)	Percentage of global biomass %
Tropical rain forest	2.2	44.0
Other tropical forest	1.8	22.0
Temperate deciduous forest	1.2	10.5
Temperate coniferous forest	0.8	14.0
Savanna grassland	0.9	4.5
Temperate grassland	0.6	1.0
Tundra	0.1	0.4
Desert and semi-desert	0.1	2.5
Open ocean	0.1	0.5
Coral reefs	2.5	0.6

Questions

1 What proportion of the global biomass is contained in forests? What does this tell you about the relative productivity of forests and other ecosystems?

2 Suggest why the percentage of total biomass contained in coral reefs is relatively low despite this being the most productive ecosystem.

3 The total area of the world's rain forests is roughly the same as that of the world's desert and semi-desert regions. Suggest possible reasons why the total biomass in rain forests is so much greater than that in deserts and semi-deserts.

Plants which convert solar energy and use it for their own needs are known as **autotrophs** (the term means 'self feeding'). They are the **primary producers** which produce food for the animals, fungi and bacteria that feed on them. Organisms that cannot feed themselves directly from the Sun but have to obtain energy from primary producers are called **heterotrophs** ('other feeders') or **consumers**. If they obtain their energy by eating plants they are called **herbivores**, if they obtain energy by eating other animals they are called **carnivores**. If they feed on the

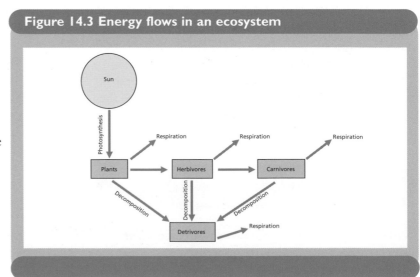

Figure 14.3 Energy flows in an ecosystem

decomposing remains of dead or waste material, they are known as **detrivores** or **decomposers** (see figure 14.3).

The transfer of energy through an ecosystem is called a **food chain** and the different stages in the chain are known as **trophic levels** (see figure 14.4). Food chains are a basic feature of all ecosystems. All chains start with 'producers' that make food using the Sun's energy. Other links in the chain are all 'consumers'. There might be four or even five trophic levels in a food chain if 'first' carnivores are eaten by 'higher' carnivores.

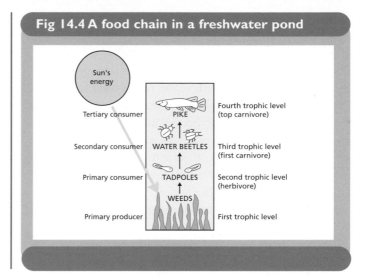

Fig 14.4 A food chain in a freshwater pond

Activity ▶ Biomagnification of toxic pollutants

PCBs are industrially produced chemicals that are toxic to animals and humans. In particular, they affect the physical and neurological development of babies and young animals. Studies during the 1970s in the Great Lakes region of the USA and Canada showed high concentrations of PCBs in human breast milk and in the tissue of various species such as eagles, herring gulls and otters.

However, the source of the PCBs was uncertain. The toxic chemicals were known to be released into the atmosphere and into waste water from industrial plants. But, within the water and sediments of the Lakes, the concentration of PCBs was below the level that could be measured by standard testing procedures.

Further research showed that a process known as 'biomagnification' was occurring. In Lake Ontario, it was found that the PCBs were working their way up the food chain - at each link in the chain, the concentration in animal tissue increased. Overall, between the level in the sediment and the tissue of the top predator carnivores such as herring gulls, the PCB concentration increased by a factor of 25 million.

▼ **Figure 14.5 Biomagnification of PCBs in freshwater organisms**

Filter feeding tiny animals called plankton absorb pollutants from sediments on the lake bottom. The diagram shows the increase in concentration of PCBs at each stage in the food chain compared with the concentration in plankton.

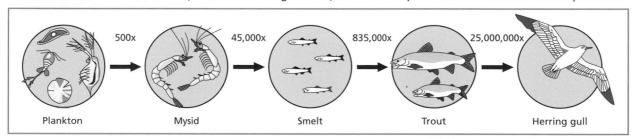

Questions

1 Describe the process of biomagnification as shown in the diagram.
2 Suggest how humans might receive toxic levels of PCBs.

In the food chain shown in figure 14.4, weeds use the Sun's energy to produce carbohydrate which is stored in their leaves. These food stores are eaten by tadpoles. Typically, only 10 percent of the plants' energy is used by the tadpoles for growth - the rest is used for respiration or to swim about. The same is true when the tadpoles are eaten by the beetles and, again, when the beetles are eaten by the pike. So, at each step up the chain, much energy is lost. As a result of this, higher up the chain, the total number of higher organisms that can be supported becomes fewer. A given number of tadpoles can support a smaller number of beetles and an even smaller number of pike. The result is what is known as the pyramid of numbers (see figure 14.6).

The food chain shown in figure 14.4 shows four trophic levels. The primary producer (ie the pond weed) is eaten by the herbivore which, in turn, is eaten by the carnivore, and so on. However, in reality, the situation is more complex. This is because some organisms are 'omnivores', ie they eat both plants and animals. For example, humans are omnivores and so operate at different trophic levels. This is true of different species. For instance, many birds eat both seeds and insects and, similarly, some species of mice do the same. Detrivores such as bacteria and fungi also

Figure 14.6 The pyramid of numbers

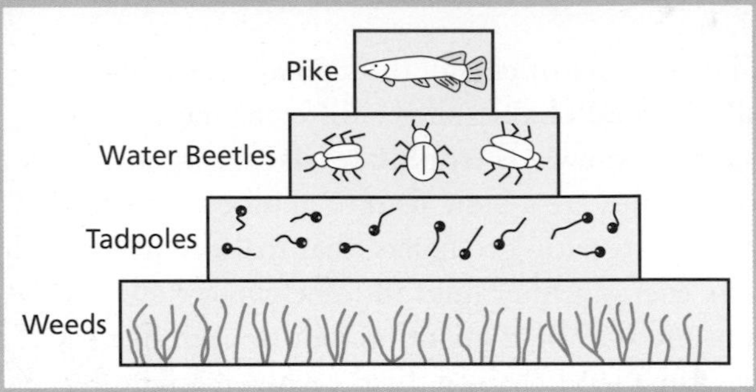

Pike

Water Beetles

Tadpoles

Weeds

The higher up the food chain, the smaller the number of organisms that are supported. This general rule also explains the pyramid of biomass in which the total mass of living organisms also falls at each higher trophic level.

sometimes operate at different trophic levels. In some cases they decompose dead vegetation but they also decompose animal matter.

Because these organisms have more than one food source, it is appropriate to think in terms of a **food web** rather than a food chain. A food web shows the linked food chains within an ecosystem. An example is provided in the Activity which follows.

Activity — Energy flows in woodland

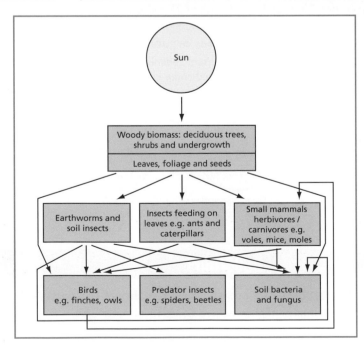

Figure 14.7 Typical energy flows in a deciduous woodland in England

Figure 14.8 A deciduous woodland

The study of energy flows in ecosystems requires long term investigation. Populations of plants and animals have to be studied over many years. This involves counting their numbers and measuring their weight - which is then converted to an energy equivalent. Seasonal and annual variations add to the difficulty. Even more difficult is to estimate the quantity and change in biomass underground - in root systems and soil organisms.

▼ **Figure 14.9 Estimated annual biomass production and consumption in a deciduous English woodland (kilojoules per square metre)**

	Production	Consumption
Deciduous trees and shrubs	45,000	
Insects feeding on plant material above ground eg, caterpillars		360
Predator insects eg, beetles, spiders		400
Small mammals: carnivores / herbivores eg, moles, weasels, voles, mice		125
Birds: carnivores / herbivores eg, owls, finches		25
Soil organisms including decomposers eg earthworms, soil insects, bacteria, fungus		not known

Questions

1 Summarise the main energy flows shown in figure 14.7.
2 Explain why it is more realistic to describe the diagram as a food web rather than a food chain.
3 With reference to figure 14.9 showing biomass production and consumption, what factors will determine the energy consumption of soil organisms?
4 Suggest why, in practice, it is difficult to provide precise figures for energy flows within a woodland ecosystem.

Nutrient cycles

In addition to a continuous supply of energy, living organisms require a supply of raw materials or **nutrients**. These are chemicals which are essential for plant and animal growth. They move from the Earth's atmosphere, water and soil into plants and animals, and back again. Because they are in finite supply, they have to be recycled - otherwise life could not continue.

Different nutrients have different cycles. Three main nutrients, carbon, oxygen and hydrogen form over 90 percent of all plant tissue. They come mainly from the atmosphere and water. Other nutrients, such as nitrogen, calcium, potassium and phosphorous, come mainly from the soil.

Each cycle consists, at its simplest, of plants taking up chemical nutrients which are then passed on to herbivores and carnivores. As organisms at each trophic level die, they decompose and the nutrients are returned to the system.

The carbon cycle and the nitrogen cycle are described below.

Figure 14.10 shows how carbon is recycled. Carbon is used by organisms to form proteins and carbohydrates. It comes from carbon dioxide in the atmosphere and is converted by photosynthesis into plant food. Animals obtain the carbon by eating plants. Carbon is recycled back into the atmosphere when it is excreted by organisms in respiration. It is also released by bacteria and fungi when they decompose dead tissue. These processes occur in the sea as well as on land.

When plants die, over a geological time scale, some organic material becomes trapped in rocks in the form, for example, of coal and oil. These fossil fuels represent a 'sink' (ie, a store) for carbon. The carbon is returned to

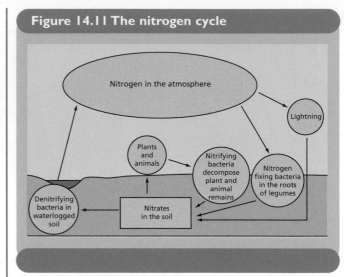

Figure 14.11 The nitrogen cycle

the atmosphere when the fuels are burnt. Carbon dioxide is a greenhouse gas that has the effect of blanketing the Earth and making it warmer. The more that is trapped underground or in living organisms such as trees, the smaller is the greenhouse effect. The opposite is also true - the more fossil fuels that are burnt, and the more trees that are cleared, the greater the greenhouse effect. This is believed to be an important factor in current global warming.

Figure 14.11 shows how nitrogen is recycled. Nitrogen is an essential part of the structure of plant proteins. It is the plant nutrient required in the greatest quantity after carbon, oxygen and hydrogen. Although nitrogen forms approximately 80 percent by volume of the atmosphere, it is a relatively inert gas - so cannot be used directly by plants. It is made available to living organisms by a process called nitrogen fixation in which nitrates are formed in the soil. Plants then obtain nitrogen by taking in the nitrates.

Nitrogen is fixed (ie, converted into a form which can be used by plants) in the soil in a number of ways. The biggest natural source of fixed nitrogen comes from a family of plants called legumes. These include clover, soya bean, alfalfa, lucerne and pea. Their roots have swellings, called nodules, which are caused by colonies of bacteria which fix nitrogen. It is a symbiotic (ie, mutually beneficial) relationship - the plant gets nitrogen in the form of ammonia from the bacteria and, in return, the bacteria get energy and nutrients from the plant.

Another source of nitrates in the soil are 'nitrifying' bacteria. These produce nitrates from the decomposing remains of animal droppings and from dead animal and plant tissue. Also, locally important in regions where thunderstorms occur, lightning can produce nitrogen

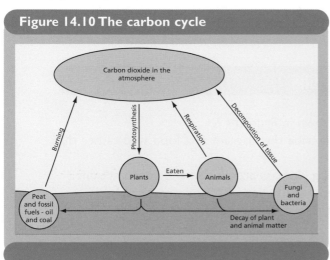

Figure 14.10 The carbon cycle

oxides in the atmosphere when it heats the air. This nitrogen is then washed into the soil by precipitation.

It is estimated, on a global scale, that a quarter of all nitrogen fixation is brought about by the use of artificial fertilisers in farming. These fertilisers are produced in chemical works and are used to increase soil fertility. Although it is not part of the natural nitrogen cycle, the process has important side effects. There are increasing concerns, for instance, over the leaching of nitrates into ground water and streams. Contaminated drinking water is a health risk to humans and there is also an adverse effect on marine organisms.

'Denitrifying bacteria' have the opposite effect to nitrifying bacteria. Particularly in anaerobic (ie, waterlogged) conditions, these bacteria convert nitrates back into nitrogen which is released into the atmosphere. On a global scale, their activity is beneficial because, without them, most of the atmospheric nitrogen would now be locked up in sediments.

Nutrient cycling within ecosystems

Within ecosystems, there are three stores (or compartments) of nutrients. These stores are the litter - the surface layer of vegetation which may be decomposed into humus; the biomass - the total mass of living organisms, mainly plant tissue; and the soil.

The stores are shown in figure 14.12. In this diagram, the nutrient stores and transfers between stores are shown as being of equal size. However, when particular ecosystems are described, it is conventional to show the

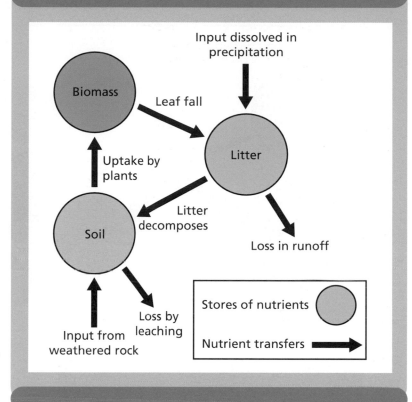

Figure 14.12 A diagrammatic model of a nutrient cycle

proportion of nutrients in each store by drawing different sized circles. Also, the thickness of the arrows between the stores is generally drawn in proportion to the amount of nutrient being transferred (see figure 14.13).

The main factors determining the size of nutrient stores and the rates of transfer are the density of vegetation and the climate, ie the availability of moisture, the temperature and the length of the growing season. Different ecosystems have different patterns. (These are described in detail in unit 14.4.).

 Activity   **Two nutrient cycles compared**

In a tropical rain forest, the biomass is the largest store of mineral nutrients. Relatively high rainfall and high average temperatures help promote rapid vegetation growth. The vegetation tends to be dense and multilayered. Litter is recycled quickly due to the climatic conditions and abundance of decomposing organisms. The soil holds only a relatively small proportion of the total nutrients because they are quickly taken up by fast growing trees and bushes.

▼ **Figure 14.13 Nutrient flows in a tropical rain forest and in a tropical plantation**

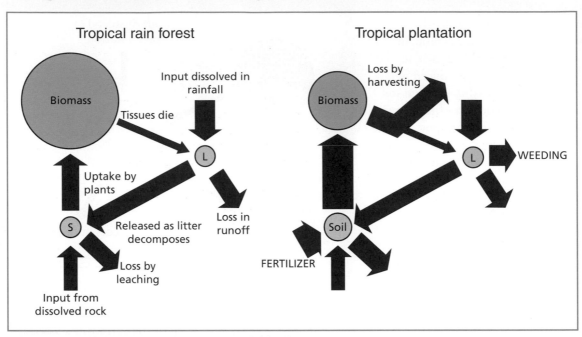

◄

Figure 14.14 A banana plantation, Guatemala

In central America, large areas of rain forest have been cleared for banana plantations. The effect has been to modify the nutrient cycle.

Questions

1 Compare the nutrient cycle in a rain forest with that in a plantation.
2 Suggest what might happen to the plantation's nutrient cycle if fertiliser is not added.

unit summary

1 An ecosystem is the interrelationship between organisms (ie, plants and animals) and between organisms and their environment. Ecosystems can be on very different scales but, within them, there will be a series of interconnected, self sustaining habitats and communities.
2 Ecosystems can be divided into their living (biotic) and non-living (abiotic) components. The abiotic elements include air, water, heat, nutrients and rock. The biotic elements are plants and animals.
3 Living organisms can be divided into autotrophs (or producers) - capable of converting sunlight into food energy by photosynthesis, and heterotrophs (or consumers) that feed on other organisms. These consumers are grouped according to diet into carnivores, herbivores, omnivores (that eat both plants and animals), and detritivores (or decomposers).
4 The level at which an organism feeds is called the trophic level. The flow of energy between trophic levels is called a food chain. Several may interlink to form food webs. At each trophic level, much energy is used by respiration, growth or mobility. This leaves less and less to be consumed by organisms higher up the food chain.
5 Nutrients are recycled within the ecosystem. The three main stores within a nutrient cycle are the biomass, the litter and the soil.

key terms

Abiotic - the non-living components in an ecosystem.

Biomass - the total mass of plant material in a given area (sometimes expressed as the energy equivalent of the plant mass).

Biotic - the living components in an ecosystem, ie plants and animals.

Community - the living plants and animals that depend on each other in a habitat.

Consumer (or heterotroph) - an organism that feeds on other organisms.

Ecosystem - the interrelationships between plants, animals and their environment.

Food chain - the transfer of energy through an ecosystem. It starts with a primary producer that is eaten by a consumer which is eaten, in turn, by higher consumers.

Food web - several connected food chains.

Gross Primary Productivity - the total amount of energy fixed by plants.

Habitat - the environment where a particular organism can live successfully.

Net Primary Productivity - the amount of energy made available by plants to animals.

Niche - the place within a habitat and point in the food chain that a species occupies.

Photosynthesis - the process that takes place in green plant cells in which sunlight provides the energy to convert carbon dioxide and water into oxygen and carbohydrates. Carbohydrates are a source of plant energy - for example sugar and starch.

Primary producer (or autotroph) - an organism that is capable of converting solar energy into food energy by photosynthesis.

Population - the number of a specific species in an ecosystem.

Trophic level - the level of the food chain which an organism occupies.

Unit 14.2 Colonisation and succession

key questions

1 What are the processes involved in colonisation and succession?
2 Which are the main types of plant succession?

1. What are the processes involved in colonisation and succession?

When new plants start to grow on bare rock or soil, the process is called **colonisation**. It is the start of a process of **succession** in which successive stages of plant communities develop. The final stage in the process is when a **climax community** becomes established.

The term **sere** is sometimes used as an alternative to succession as a way of describing the sequence of change in plant communities. Each stage in the process is known as a 'seral stage'.

The bare rock or soil at the start of the process of plant succession might result from a number of factors. For example, a volcanic eruption might create new lava flows or cover an area with ash. Blowing sand on coasts or at desert margins might cover land with dunes. In glaciated regions, retreating ice sheets or glaciers might leave bare rock and soil exposed. Human activity sometimes has the same effect, for instance if cultivated land is abandoned or if forests are cleared.

The succession from bare ground towards a 'seral climax' is called a **prisere** (or primary succession). A secondary succession occurs on previously vegetated ground that has been cleared, for example by burning or by deforestation. The pioneer plants will vary according to the area being colonised. Each type of area will have its own series of plants that can cope in the particular conditions. As one stage succeeds another, the species that colonise the area are influenced by:

- local climatic conditions, eg temperature and precipitation
- the physical and chemical properties of the rock and soil
- the types of plants that are locally available to colonise, and how tolerant they are to different conditions.

When, eventually, the vegetation reaches a balanced state or climax, no further changes will happen other than the death of old plants and animals and their replacement by the next generation. Of course, a climate change, a natural disaster or human interference can all disrupt the process at any stage in the succession.

The natural climax vegetation for lowland Britain is deciduous woodland. There are, however, a number of **arresting factors** that can prevent vegetation reaching this stage (see figure 14.15). For example, grazing by animals, burning or deforestation can stop the seral progression and keep it at a **sub-climax** stage. When the normal succession is stopped by human interference, the resulting sub-climax vegetation is called a **plagioclimax** community. An example is the moorland vegetation that is typical of upland areas in the north of England. Heather, grasses and bracken are dominant because trees and shrubs have been cleared. They are prevented from regrowing by sheep grazing and by deliberate burning (to provide new shoots for both sheep and grouse).

In a subclimax or plagioclimax community, if the arresting factor is removed, a secondary succession occurs. This might continue until the climax community develops. For example, on farms, if weeding, hoeing or ploughing stop, the process of succession starts again. Untended farmland is soon invaded by weeds which take

Figure 14.15 Colonisation and succession

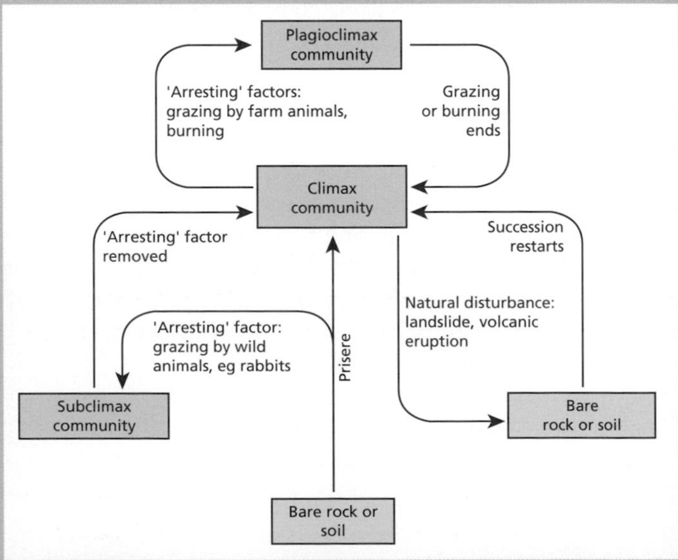

A climax community of natural vegetation might be prevented from developing by factors such as grazing by wild or farm animals, or by natural disturbances such as a landslide.

Figure 14.16 Heather moorland in the southern Pennines

Human activity sometimes prevents natural plant succession. By maintaining moors for sheep grazing and grouse shooting, a plagioclimax is created.

over from the cultivated plants. After a few years, shrubs and tree saplings will start to grow and, eventually, the area will revert to woodland.

2. Which are the main types of plant succession?

Priseres (ie, plant successions from bare ground) are often classified into four main types depending on the nature of the surface from which the succession starts. Two are on land environments and two are in wet environments:

- **lithosere** on bare rock
- **psammosere** on coastal sands
- **hydrosere** on fresh water margins
- **halosere** on salt marshes and sea estuaries.

Lithosere

This plant succession starts on bare rock. Initially a community of algae that can photosynthesise and so feed itself will colonise the rock. They are 'autotrophic primary producers'. Lichens also start to grow. They too are autotrophs - being part algae and part fungi. These colonisers can survive the extremes of temperature, lack of shade and water variations that occur on bare rock surfaces. They help to weather the rock surface and, as each generation dies, humus is added to the rock debris - so forming a thin soil that can support mosses. These add to the humus and organic content. Grasses and herbs then colonise and, because they are relatively tall, they shade out the lichens and mosses - so becoming the

dominant species. Taller meadow grasses, shrubs and fast growing trees, such as rowan, follow on. Finally, slow growing, broadleaved trees take over and form the climax vegetation. This succession is typical of wet, temperate climates such as in Britain but would be modified under different climatic conditions.

Each stage in the succession has a different dominant species. These will alter the microclimate by, for example, slowing air flow, reducing the rate of evaporation and increasing moisture retention. The new conditions will attract a different community of organisms. As each successive stage is reached, some of the earlier colonisers die out because they cannot compete, but others will continue to live alongside the new plants. This creates greater diversity at each stage.

Because the weathering of solid rock is very slow, a lithosere can take hundreds of years to reach a climax condition. The precise time scale depends upon the nature of the rock and the climate. If the rock is unbroken, it takes much longer than, for instance, on a stable scree slope where the rock is shattered into pieces.

Figure 14.17 Plant succession on bare rock, north west Scotland

The sandstone rock is being colonised by lichens and algae. Sufficient organic matter has accumulated in cracks for grass to become established.

Activity | **Plant succession after the Mount St Helens eruption**

When Mount St Helens erupted in 1980, it was the world's most powerful volcanic event for 60 years. The volcano is situated in Washington State, in the north west USA. Hundreds of square kilometres were covered with avalanche debris, ash and mud. Heat from the volcano melted snow on the mountain top. This mixed with ash and water from rivers to form lahars (mudflows) which swept down river channels and buried everything in their path. In places, deposits 5 metres deep were left in the channel beds and on the valley sides.

Since the eruption, the region has provided an ideal opportunity to observe plant succession. At one study location, the colonisation of plant species on the dried mudflow has been compared with the number of plants at the edge of the mudflow and with those in the relatively untouched, nearby coniferous forest. At the edge of the mudflow, the dense forest cover was swept away by the force of the lahar. Within the forest, apart from some airborne volcanic debris such as ash, conditions remained similar to those existing before the eruption. The forest floor is relatively dark, covered with pine needles, and the habitat is dominated by tall coniferous trees (in particular, the Pacific Silver Fir).

Plant species	Number of species		
	On the dried lahar	**At the edge of the lahar**	**In the forest**
Lichen	7	9	12
Moss	2	3	2
Grass	1	2	-
Fireweed	6	1	-
Lupin	1	1	-
Penstemon	6	-	-
Pearly everlasting	1	6	-
Huckleberry (S)	1	13	16
Douglas Fir (T)	3	1	-
Hemlock (T)	4	5	11
Willow (S)	1	1	-
Blackberry (S)	-	1	-
Vine maple (S)	-	1	1
Prince's Pine (S)	-	8	20
Pyrola	-	1	-
Rush	-	2	-
Salal (S)	-	1	-
Pacific Silver Fir (T)	-	-	26

Notes: T denotes large tree when fully grown; S denotes small tree, bush or shrub when fully grown. All the other plants listed are less than one metre in height when fully grown.

Figure 14.18 The number and variety of plant species within equal sized sample areas.

This research was completed 15 years after the Mount St Helens eruption.

Questions

1 Outline the possible factors that will have affected the colonisation of the lahar (mudflow) by new plants.
2 Compare the number and variety of species in the three locations.
3 Suggest possible reasons for the difference in vegetation between the three locations.

Psammosere

Figure 14.19 Marram grass

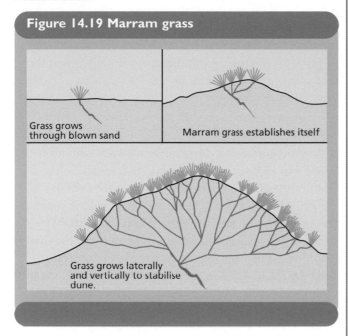

Grass grows through blown sand

Marram grass establishes itself

Grass grows laterally and vertically to stabilise dune.

This type of plant succession develops on coastal sands and on sand dunes where dried sand is blown inland. The first colonising plants might actually cause dunes to form if they trap blowing sand. The pioneer plants have to be able to withstand being buried in the sand. They also have to cope with a lack of humus, because there is little organic matter in the sand, and a lack of water, because moisture quickly drains through the sand. (The term 'xerosere' is sometimes used to describe a plant succession in very dry conditions.)

Lyme grass, sea buckthorn and marram grass are common pioneers. Marram in particular is drought resistant and salt tolerant. Its long roots help stabilise the sand dunes (see figure 14.19).

The early colonisers on sand dunes survive by reducing transpiration. Typically they have waxy or spiky leaves with only a relatively small surface area. This reduces moisture loss. Long roots tap sources of groundwater deep underground.

The pioneer species grow on the embryonic (ie, new and small) dunes and on the more established yellow dunes (see figure 14.20).

They are called yellow dunes because they are formed mainly of sand. Further inland, older dunes become stabilised by the surface cover of plants. A build up of humus changes their colour and they are sometimes called grey dunes. The humus can retain water and this allows a wider variety of plants to colonise and become established. In Britain, typical plants include gorse, heathers, red fescue grass, sea spurge, hawkbit and dandelion. With increasing distance from the sea, the height and variety of plants increases. Shrubs and trees such as maritime pine become dominant. Further inland, there are deciduous trees such as ash and oak. In between the sand dunes, low lying, marshy areas called 'slacks' are commonly found. Cotton grass, flag iris, rush and willow all grow here.

Around Britain, there are many examples of psammoseres. North of Liverpool on the Irish Sea coast, the Ainsdale and Formby areas contain protected sand dune areas. In the slacks between the dunes, the relatively rare natterjack toad survives. Further inland, the zone of Scots Pine is one of the remaining habitats for red squirrels in England.

Sand dune ecosystems tend to be fragile. If large numbers of people trample over dunes, the vegetation can easily be killed if the sand is disturbed (so exposing the roots) or if the leaves are crushed. When the plants die, there is nothing to hold the dunes in place and

Figure 14.20 The sequence of plants found in a typical psammosere

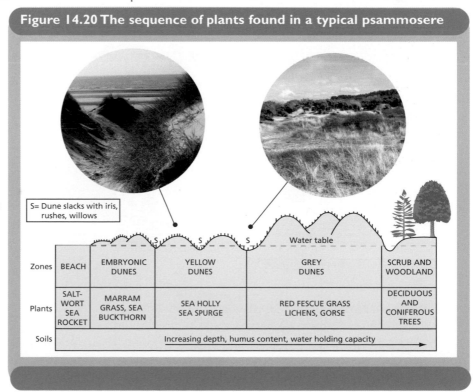

S= Dune slacks with iris, rushes, willows

Zones	BEACH	EMBRYONIC DUNES	YELLOW DUNES	GREY DUNES	SCRUB AND WOODLAND
Plants	SALT-WORT SEA ROCKET	MARRAM GRASS, SEA BUCKTHORN	SEA HOLLY SEA SPURGE	RED FESCUE GRASS LICHENS, GORSE	DECIDUOUS AND CONIFEROUS TREES
Soils	Increasing depth, humus content, water holding capacity →				

blow-outs (ie, wind hollows) can form. For this reason, many dune systems in populated regions are protected and the public are asked to keep to specific pathways that are often boarded.

Hydrosere

A hydrosere develops at the edge of fresh water ponds or lakes. Such features are continuously being filled in with sediment. Often this material is brought by rivers and deposited - so making the edges shallower and more fertile.

Furthest out from the edge of the pond or lake shore, floating plants such as pondweed or water lilies might form mats of vegetation. These provide habitats for organisms and also trap sediment. As the vegetation dies, the amount of organic matter builds up and the water margins become less deep. Marsh plants such as reeds and rushes can survive in these conditions and they encroach on the lakeshore. Plants which can survive waterlogged soil conditions are called 'hydrophytes'. They are able to absorb oxygen through their roots and stems more efficiently than most other plants.

Over time, as lakes or ponds infill, the zones away from the water's edge become drier and the soil depth increases. Trees start to grow. In Britain, willow and alder survive in the wetter areas (sometimes these

wooded, marshy areas are called 'carrs'). Alder in particular is important in the succession because it fixes atmospheric nitrogen in root nodules and therefore increases soil fertility. Birch, rowan and hawthorn start to grow on the drier ground and, eventually, when the lake is completely infilled, an oak - ash climax vegetation develops.

Halosere

This plant succession develops in the salty conditions found on sea coasts, typically in estuaries and inlets. In Britain, the zone is covered by water twice each day as the tide ebbs and flows. Sediment and sand are washed through the area with the tide. Where the water is deepest, green algae and eel grass are amongst the first colonisers. They are able to survive almost constant cover by sea water. As silt, sediment and organic matter build up, and the depth of water becomes shallower, other salt resistant plants start to colonise. These are called 'halophytes' and, typically, can survive being submerged in salt water for several hours per day. Spartina grass (Spartina anglica) is an example. This plant has spread widely over the past two hundred years. It developed as a hybrid between a European variety (S. maritima) and an American variety (S. alternifolia) that was introduced in 1820. It has long roots which trap mud and so helps raise the plant above water level.

Further towards the shore, where the tide covers the area for just a few hours per day, plants such as short turf grasses and sea lavender become dominant. There are few shrubs or taller plants, mainly due to high winds on the exposed salt marsh. Hollows in the marsh form creeks. Sometimes these dry out leaving a deposit of salt that is toxic to most plants.

Nearest the shore, the vegetation might be coved by sea water only during spring (ie, the highest) tides. Dwarf shrubs such as sea purslane, and plants such as sea lavender become established in this zone. The grass and other vegetation builds up a deeper organic layer in which, eventually, large shrubs and trees start to grow.

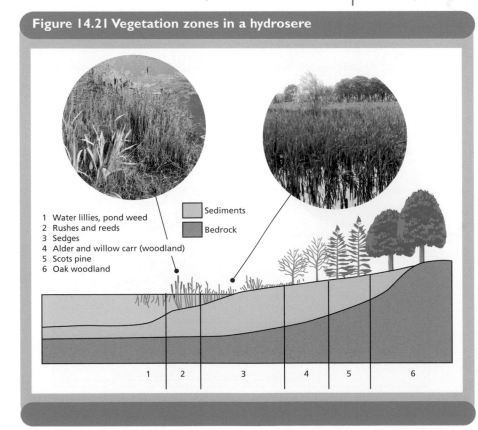

Figure 14.21 Vegetation zones in a hydrosere

1 Water lillies, pond weed
2 Rushes and reeds
3 Sedges
4 Alder and willow carr (woodland)
5 Scots pine
6 Oak woodland

Sediments

Bedrock

1 2 3 4 5 6

Activity | Plant succession on a salt marsh

The Kent estuary

The River Kent flows into Morecambe Bay in north west England. The Kent estuary is bordered by a number of salt marshes. The area contains an important bird reserve for migrating waders and is also used for sheep grazing on the drier margins.

▼ **Figure 14.22 Salt marsh in the Kent estuary**

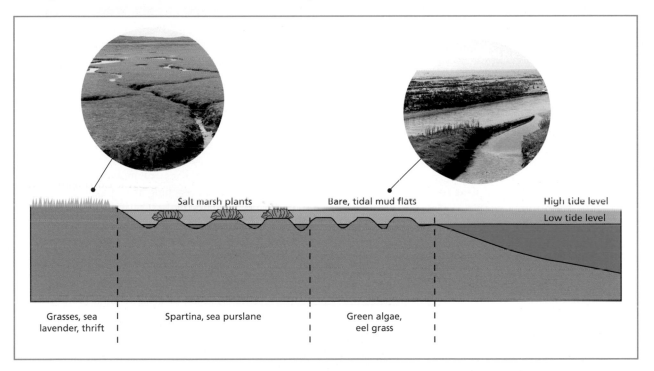

Questions

1 Describe the salt marsh and the succession of plants that occurs there.
2 Outline the factors that might influence plant succession on the salt marsh.
3 Some years ago, a scheme to build a barrage across Morecambe Bay was proposed. This barrage would have stopped the tidal flow of sea water into the Bay and would have changed the water in the Kent estuary from being salt to fresh water. Suggest how this scheme might have affected the local ecosystem if it had gone ahead.

unit summary

1 Bare ground will normally be colonised by a succession of plants, starting with pioneer species and ending with a climax vegetation. The stages in the process are, together, called a sere.

2 Different seres develop under different conditions, for example on bare rock, on sand, at freshwater margins and at saltwater margins.

3 If a plant succession is interrupted it will form a sub-climax community but, if then allowed to continue, it will eventually become a climax community.

key terms

Climax community - the final stage in a plant succession.
Colonisation - the process of plants becoming established in a new area.
Halosere - a plant succession starting at a salt water margin.
Hydrosere - a plant succession starting at a fresh water margin.
Lithosere - a plant succession starting on bare rock.
Plagioclimax - a plant community which has been prevented from reaching its climax by

human activity, for example by burning.
Psammosere - a plant succession starting on coastal sand.
Sere - a plant succession in which one community of plants succeeds another.
Sub-climax - a plant community that has been prevented from reaching its climax, either by natural events or by human action (in which case it is a plagioclimax).
Succession - the sequence of plant communities that replace one another in a particular environment.

Unit 14.3 The human impact on ecosystems

key questions

1 What is the human impact on ecosystems?
2 What is the difference between a natural and an agricultural ecosystem?
3 How can agriculture be made more sustainable?

1. What is the human impact on ecosystems?

For thousands of years, people have been altering the natural environment - by clearing forests, by farming and by building cities. Very few untouched wilderness areas remain. Even the remotest parts of the planet are affected by air-borne pollutants or by flotsam washed ashore on coastlines.

Some ecosystems are more at risk than others. Where valuable natural resources exist, for example in locations where there are minerals, timber or fertile soils, pressure from humans is intense. Certain ecosystems are particularly fragile because there are few species in each niche in the food chain. If one species is removed, or if a new species is introduced, the effect can be severe. When, for example, Europeans colonised Australia, New Zealand and tropical islands in the Pacific and Indian Oceans, their domestic animals (and escaped rats) quickly killed local species of flightless birds. Likewise, the introduction of the American grey squirrel into

Britain has brought about the virtual elimination of the European red squirrel in England and Wales.

This section considers how human activity has affected three natural ecosystems - the Scottish Highlands, raised peat bogs in England, and coral reefs in the tropics. Other examples of human impact are described in unit 2.5 (the Aral Sea); unit 4.3 (forestry in British Columbia); unit 9.4 (the Nile Basin and the Aswan High Dam); unit 13.3 (the American Dust Bowl of the 1930s) and unit 14.4 (rain forests, savanna grassland, arid regions, tundra and the Antarctic region including the Southern Ocean).

Forestry in Scotland

Under natural conditions, the climax vegetation of Scottish hills and mountains is pine forest with some birch. Scots pine, rowan, hazel, juniper and bilberry still cover some areas. The original 'Caledonian' forest supported a community of red squirrels, wild cats and pine martens as well as distinctive birds such as capercaillies, crossbills, crested tits and some ospreys. However, less than 2 percent of the original woodland now remains.

The land has been cleared for farming, for timber and for recreation. At first the pasture was used for cattle and then for sheep. During the nineteenth century, areas of the Highlands were cleared of people to provide open moorland for red deer and grouse. Large estates were established and shooting 'parties' became big business for the landowners. The natural forest has not regenerated because the red deer eat young tree saplings in winter and also because the moors are deliberately burnt to provide new shoots for grouse to eat.

During the twentieth century, large areas of Scottish uplands have been planted with conifers. After the First World War, it was decided that the UK should be less reliant on imported timber. So, in 1919, the Forestry Commission was set up with the aim of planting fast growing timber to replenish national supplies. Sitka spruce and lodgepole pine from North America were planted over huge areas. By the mid-1990s, commercial forest plantations covered 15 percent of the Scottish land area - both in the Highlands and in the Southern Uplands. Forestry brought much needed employment to remote regions. The industry now employs more than 10,000 people if those in paper mills and saw mills are included. Reliance on imports has fallen - so reducing the burden on the UK balance of payments.

Two other benefits arise from the forestry. Firstly, as more land is planted with trees, less is available as pasture - so easing the problem of over-production in the sheep meat sector of the farming industry. Secondly, because trees are a carbon store or 'sink', the more that are planted, the less carbon dioxide there is in the atmosphere. This has the effect of reducing greenhouse gases.

However, the planting of conifers in Scotland has been controversial and much criticised. Particularly in the early decades, the plantations were hurriedly created with little thought to aesthetic appeal. Dense and uniform rows of impenetrable trees were a blight on the landscape. Because the fast growing sitka spruce was generally planted, rather than the more open canopied native scots pine, biodiversity was reduced. Single species planting in geometric patterns became very unpopular with residents and visitors alike.

Figure 14.23 A coniferous plantation in Argyll, Scotland

Many of the early coniferous plantations in Britain were single species, planted in geometric patterns with little regard for the natural landscape.

Activity) The changing pattern of Scotland's forests

The Flow Country
In the 1980's, a huge afforestation programme took place in the Flow Country, an area of peat bog and moorland in Caithness and Sutherland. This region had been identified as a wetland habitat of global significance in which birds such as golden eagles and greenshanks survived. However, encouraged by the low price of land, by government grants and by tax relief, large areas were drained and planted. Some archaeological sites were ploughed up and the fragile blanket bog ecosystem was seriously affected. A severe, though temporary effect of planting was to damage water quality downstream of the new forest sites. Draining and ploughing the land released sediment and nutrients into the water - in some cases adversely affecting salmon fisheries.

Despite the negative effects arising from forestry, the government aims to double the forested area of Scotland by 2050. From an economic point of view, it is felt that the advantages outweigh the disadvantages. To promote the idea and to gain greater public acceptance, more sensitive planting schemes are already in use. Mixtures of species, non-geometric patterns that are in harmony with the landscape, and more open spacing have been introduced. Also, during the past decade, the Forestry Commission has encouraged the planting of native species. Over 70 percent of the trees now planted are native Caledonian pinewoods and broadleaved trees. The new plantations more closely resemble the original ecosystem and are visually attractive. It is hoped that increased tourism will be an additional benefit. Already, forest parks are popular destinations for tens of millions of people in the UK. An estimated 2 million Scots visit forests each year for recreation - walking, biking, fishing and orienteering. Creating mixed woodland and forest, with a wide variety of plant and animal species, will be good not just for the environment but also for the local economy.

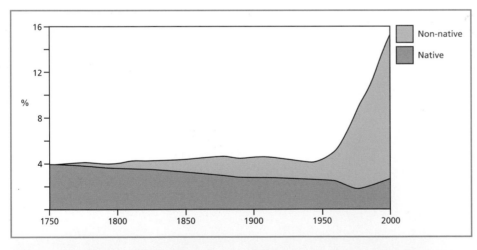

Figure 14.24 The changing percentage of woodland cover in Scotland - native and non-native species

A multi-benefit forest in the Scottish highlands
Within the Queen Elizabeth Forest Park, in the Trossachs, there are 20,000 hectares of forest. The Park is managed by Forest Enterprise, the Forestry Commission's management agency. The forest provides employment for about a 100 people, produces timber worth millions of pounds a year and provides a wide range of recreation facilities, enjoyed by hundreds of thousands of people annually. Within the Forest Park, there are important areas of native woodland, managed primarily for conservation. For many people living in the area, the Forest Park contributes to their livelihood and well-being.
Adapted from Forests for Scotland, Forestry Commission

Questions

1 How has the natural ecosystem of the Scottish highlands been affected by humans?
2 To what extent is it possible to reconcile the interests of local people and tourists with the desire to increase timber production?

Raised peat bogs

Peat is a layer of undecomposed organic matter, generally defined as being at least 40 cm deep. A peat bog is a thick layer of waterlogged peat. In Britain, peat bogs have formed in both upland and lowland areas. The upland bogs are found on flat or gently sloping hills and moors, from Dartmoor in the South West to the most northerly Highlands of Scotland. They are sometimes called **blanket bogs**.

The lowland bogs are found in valleys or basins. In some cases, the underlying rock is limestone or chalk and this causes the groundwater to be relatively alkaline. Examples include the Somerset Levels and the Fens of eastern England. When drained, these areas tend to be very fertile and so therefore are intensively farmed.

Where the underlying rock is sandstone or igneous, runoff from rain water tends to make the bog acid. In some cases, the ph can be as low as 3.8 - 4.2 (neutral pH is 7). As the bog develops and material accumulates, it often becomes dome shaped and is known as a **raised bog**. Raised bogs can form where there is underlying chalk or limestone if the depth of peat becomes so deep that the surface rises above the groundwater level. In these circumstances, the acidity of the decaying vegetation is no longer neutralised and the top layers become acidic.

Most raised peat bogs in Britain started as shallow lakes left at the end of the last glacial period (see figure 14.25). Over the past 10,000 years, the lakes have been gradually colonised by plants such as sedge and reed at the water's edge. Layers of partly decomposed organic matter have been deposited - forming peat beds. As the lakes became shallower, the vegetated fringe advanced towards the middle. Marsh plants colonised the drier margins, then trees such as willow and alder took over at the edge. Eventually the peat filled most of the lake. Relatively acidic rain water slowed decomposition and only species that could cope in the nutrient poor, waterlogged conditions were able to survive. The insectivorous sundew is one such plant. It derives most of its nutrients not through its roots but from the decomposing remains of insects trapped in its sticky leaves.

On top of the reed and sedge peat, bog mosses such as sphagnum grow in hummocks and form moss peat when they die. This creates a new layer over the old lake. Sphagnum moss absorbs and holds a large amount of water as it develops. In time, the moss peat forms a thick layer - up to 8 metres deep in some locations. It is thickest at the centre, so creating a dome. These features

Figure 14.25 The formation of a lowland raised bog

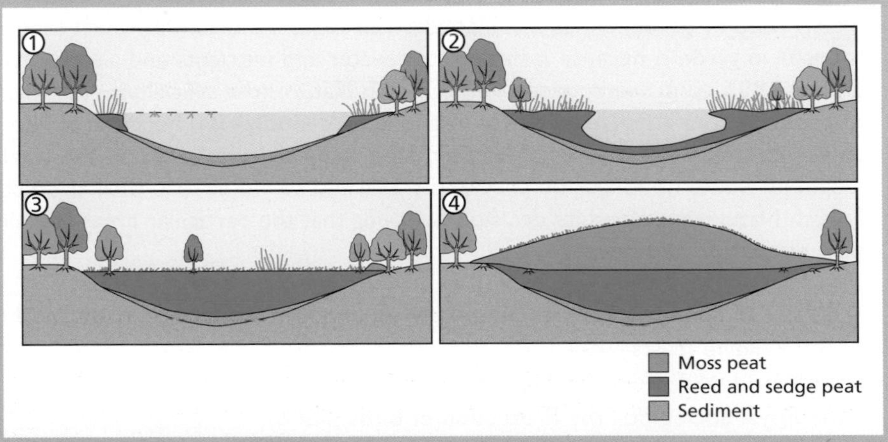

Moss peat
Reed and sedge peat
Sediment

1. Original lake with reeds and sedges around the margins.
2. The lake starts to infill with reed and sedge peat.
3. The lake becomes completely infilled but is still waterlogged and acidic.
4. Mosses growing on top of the reed and sedge peat form a raised bog.

are relatively stable as long as the input of rain water is balanced by an equivalent loss of groundwater. If something happens to disturb the equilibrium, for example if groundwater starts to drain at a faster rate, the bog might dry and a woodland vegetation would form. It has been estimated that a metre of peat takes 1,000 years to form in British climatic conditions. Examples of raised bogs are found at Thorne and Hatfield in south Yorkshire and also in Ireland, over much of the central region.

Raised bogs are becoming increasingly rare. At one time they formed approximately 5 percent of land area in Britain. Since 1840, an estimated 94 percent of lowland raised bogs have been drained or otherwise damaged. Many of those left have been listed as Sites of Special Scientific Interest in order to protect their diverse ecosystems. Orchids, over 5,000 species of insects and invertebrates, and birds such as the nightingale, nightjar and woodcock have all been recorded.

Figure 14.26 Shallow lake in north Lancashire

The lake is becoming filled by reeds and other vegetation. Willow trees are colonising the edge of the lake. If left undisturbed, a raised bog will form here.

Activity — Protecting Sites of Special Scientific Interest

Thorne and Hatfield Moors, located between Doncaster and Goole, are Britain's largest remaining examples of raised lowland bog. Although protected from new development by their SSSI status since the mid-80s, commercial peat extraction still takes place on both moors. This is because planning permission was given in the 1950s and Levingtons, the company working the peat, is able to continue its operations in certain areas.

Before the excavation takes place, the ground is drained by powerful water pumps. Large machinery is then used to strip the peat down to a thickness of just a few centimetres. Almost all the peat is bagged and sold as compost. It is mainly used by gardeners as a soil conditioner or as a medium in which seedlings or potted plants are grown. Peat is useful in gardens because it helps retain water and nutrients and also improves soil structure.

During 1997, controversy arose when English Nature (the official agency which advises the government on matters of conservation) announced that it intended to 'denotify' 100 hectares of Thorne Moor (approximately 6% of the total area) and 350 hectares of Hatfield Moor (approximately 25% of the total area). This meant that these locations would no longer be part of the SSSI and so would lose their protection from further development. English Nature explained its decision by saying that the particular areas had already been extensively damaged by peat extraction and drainage.

A variety of conservation groups and others opposed the change in status. They included:
• local Wildlife Trusts
• the World Wide Fund for Nature
• the Royal Society for the Protection of Birds (RSPB)
• the Council for British Archaeology (the waterlogged peat preserves ancient remains and some complete burial sites have, in the past, been found in similar locations)
• neighbouring local authorities
• the Environment Agency (the government's own body responsible for groundwater and river quality)
• Friends of the Earth.

The case against denotification was twofold. Firstly, the damaged sites were still valuable in terms of plant and animal biodiversity. Reducing the area of protection would put more pressure on the remaining undisturbed ecological system. Secondly, the change in status would be a reward to Levingtons for damaging the site. It would be a message that they, and other companies operating in or near SSSIs, would only need to do similar damage for the sites to lose protection. This would obviously be contrary to the intention behind SSSIs.

Following pressure from objectors, in 1998 English Nature reversed its decision to seek denotification of the sites.

Questions

1 Briefly describe how lowland raised peat bogs are formed.
2 Outline the case for and against protecting Britain's remaining lowland raised bogs from development.

Coral Reefs

Coral reefs are formed in tropical seas at depths of less than 90 metres. Most occur between 30°N and 30°S, in water temperatures over 20°C. Coral reefs are composed of colonies of polyps. These are marine organisms that secrete a hard skeleton around themselves - producing a wide variety of irregular shapes. Living in a symbiotic (ie, mutually beneficial) relationship with the coral polyps are zooxanthellae. It is these organisms that give coral its distinctive bright colours. When they die, the coral loses its colour and is said to be bleached.

Coral reefs support an abundance of marine life, providing food and shelter for a very diverse and rich ecosystem. An estimated 25 percent of all marine life is found on or near coral reefs, even though they form only a fraction of the total area of seas and oceans.

There are three main types of coral reef: fringing reefs along a coastline; barrier reefs that are offshore, parallel to the coast; and atolls which are rings of coral around a lagoon. They provide a natural breakwater - giving protection from strong waves and erosion by the sea. In some places, long sandy beaches are formed from eroded particles of coral. These beaches and the beautifully coloured reefs themselves attract many tourists. Worldwide, it was estimated in 1998 that visitors to coral reefs generated £500 million revenue.

In many places, coral reefs are under threat. Global warming and pollution are causing mass bleaching that is expected to increase. There are three major problems:

- rising average temperatures make the sea warmer; if the water heats by more than 1-2°C, the coral expels the zooxanthellae - causing bleaching; unless the sea temperature falls, the coral eventually dies
- rising carbon dioxide levels in the atmosphere are partially absorbed in the top layers of sea water; this makes the water too acidic for the corals to tolerate
- global warming is expected to raise average sea levels by 50 cm during the 21st century; although healthy corals might cope with this rate of rise, those under stress will not.

Figure 14.27 Bora Bora, French Polynesia, Pacific Ocean

This is an example of a fringing reef. Coral reefs have been described as the 'canary in the mine' for global warming. They will be amongst the first casualties of rising world temperatures. (Note: in the past, canaries were kept by miners in cages to warn them of a build up of methane gas.)

Activity ▸ Reef Check

During 1998, a network of conservation groups called Reef Check surveyed 300 coral reefs in 30 countries around the world. They found that 230 sites displayed some evidence of damage. The least affected reefs were in the Red Sea, relatively undisturbed by tourist or urban development, and with no rivers bringing sediment to the coastline.

In addition to the impact of global warming, some specific local problems were found to affect the health of coral reefs. They included:

- the 1998 El Niño (see unit 12.6); this raised sea temperatures in some areas - for example, in the Indian Ocean; coral reefs in the Seychelles, Maldives and Mauritius were badly affected by bleaching
- pollution and sewage contamination is killing coral near urbanised areas such as along the coast of Java near Jakarta; also in Java, runoff that is high in farm fertilisers provides nutrients to algae that smother the coral polyps
- deforestation is causing rising sediment levels in rivers throughout South East Asia; the sediment is deposited on the coast and prevents light reaching the coral
- fishing (using trawl nets or even dynamite blasting) is damaging coral reefs and reducing fish stocks in South East Asia and on the southern coast of China near Hong Kong
- mining of coral reefs for lime (used in the construction industry) is damaging reefs in many areas - for example, in southern Sri Lanka
- collection of coral fragments by and for tourists is having a damaging effect in many locations from the Caribbean to the South Pacific islands
- cyanide is used by divers in the Philippines and elsewhere to stun reef fish which are then sold to aquariums; this can kill coral
- tourist boats and divers damage reefs simply by knocking into the coral in busy tourist destinations such as the Florida Keys
- the Crown of Thorns starfish is a natural predator that has attacked coral in places such as the Great Barrier Reef off Queensland, Australia; its population can explode when plankton increases after an increase in nutrient rich agricultural run-off or sewage
- hurricane damage; for example, Hurricane Georges destroyed large areas of coral reef off southern Florida in 1998.

In response to these problems, some efforts are being made to conserve coral ecosystems. Southern Florida now protects certain reefs on the Florida Keys, and the Flower Garden Banks is a protected reef off the Texas-Louisiana coast. Visitor numbers are controlled and spearfishing by divers is banned because it tends to remove the top predators - so causing a cascade of effects down the food chain. Australia has created the Marine Park conservation area containing the largest system of coral reefs in the world - the Great Barrier Reef. The Park was established in 1975 to control mining and oil drilling that could have caused irreparable damage. The reefs support 1,500 species of fish, 400 species of coral and 400 species of shellfish, as well as being the breeding ground for 240 bird species. The number of visitors to various parts of the reef is regulated to limit disturbance.

Questions

1 Summarise the human impact on coral reefs.
2 Suggest what difficulties and problems might arise when marine conservation areas are set up and people are banned from visiting coral reefs.

2. What is the difference between a natural and an agricultural ecosystem?

Agricultural ecosystems (or **agroecosystems**) are modifications of natural ecosystems. They are plagioclimaxes in which the natural succession has been interrupted and altered. The difference between agroecosystems and natural ecosystems is that the former have fewer species and a less complex structure. Because, in most cases, a single species has been deliberately selected and planted, there is less genetic diversity. Farming deliberately reduces competition by weeding and pest control to ensure maximum productivity and yield for people. The food chain is reduced to 2 or at most 3 trophic levels:

plant $\longrightarrow$ people, or;

plant $\longrightarrow$ animal $\longrightarrow$ people.

Agricultural ecosystems are open systems with a greater number and volume of inputs and outputs than natural, closed systems. In other words, there is a far greater interaction with the outside compared with more self sustaining and self sufficient natural systems. Farmers are able to buffer production against environmental constraints that affect the natural systems of the area. For instance, by using pesticides, fertilisers, irrigation or glasshouses, farmers can overcome the constraints of climate, soil and relief.

Compared with natural ecosystems, agricultural ecosystems experience a continuous loss of nutrients because crops are harvested. The same is true in pastoral farming. When farm animals are taken for slaughter, they are removed from the system. Fewer nutrients are returned to the soil than would be the case if the animals died and decomposed on the land. So, farmers have to replace the lost nutrients by adding artificial fertilisers. The result is that most agricultural ecosystems are unstable and would collapse without constant inputs. In addition, monoculture (ie, single crop production) leaves the system more vulnerable to attack by pests and diseases than where rotations of crops are grown.

However, there are exceptions to these generalisations. One example is the traditional padi (ie, wet rice) ecosystem of South East Asia in which rice is grown in irrigated fields. The system is stable and self sustaining because the crop is grown in nutrient rich water. High inputs of manual labour are required to plant and harvest the rice, and to maintain the irrigated fields. Few outside inputs are required and the people who work on the land are largely fed by their own rice crop.

Activity ▸ Sustainable rice production

Rice typically requires a 3-4 month growing season in which the temperature must be over 20°C. In south and east Asia, rice has been grown for generations on flood plains, on river deltas and on terraced slopes. Large amounts of labour have been used to build and maintain the channels and embankments around padi fields.

▸ **Figure 14.28 Padi fields in Bali, Indonesia**

The key to the sustainability of traditional wet rice production is irrigation. The water is the primary means of supplying and maintaining nutrients in the system. Silt from the surrounding catchment is transported by the irrigation water to the padi fields, or is manually spread on the fields. The water contains dissolved nutrients. Organic fertiliser is often also added; typically several cartloads of manure, ashes and straw per hectare are ploughed in before flooding.

Working the waterlogged soil (ie, trampling by people and oxen) creates a puddling effect. This causes the pore spaces to become saturated and clay mineral particles to swell, making the soil impervious and so reducing the leaching of nutrients. The soil becomes an anaerobic sludge (ie, there is little oxygen). Various micro-organisms that can tolerate these conditions decompose organic material and slowly release nutrients. Most of the nitrogen in the system comes from this 'ammonification' of organic soil matter and also from atmospheric nitrogen fixed by blue green algae. Studies show that 16 tonnes of algae can accumulate per hectare, producing up to 100 kilograms of nitrogen. Semi-permanent flooding has the additional effect of releasing other plant nutrients from the soil and sediment, for example phosphorous, manganese and calcium.

Although this system of farming has the advantage of being largely self-sustaining, it is under pressure. The need to produce more food to feed growing populations has led to the development of high yielding varieties (HYVs) of rice (see unit 4.1 for details on the Green Revolution). These seed varieties provide more grain but they require more nutrients than are naturally available. Chemical fertilisers are therefore increasingly used. Unfortunately, artificial fertiliser inhibits the growth of blue-green algae and so the production of nutrients within the system decreases. Another side-effect of using the HYVs is that they tend to be more vulnerable to pests and diseases than older seed varieties. This means that farmers have to use pesticides.

The net effect of the changes is that the self-sustaining system is being replaced by less stable farming practices. In parts of the world where the process has been taken furthest, for example in the mechanised rice farms of central California, virtually all the inputs into the system are external. This modern agriculture has been described as 'energy intensive monoculture'. It is completely dependent upon chemical fertilisers, herbicides and pesticides.

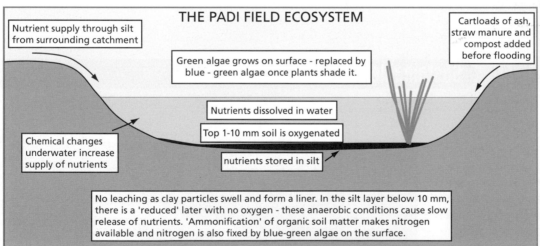

THE PADI FIELD ECOSYSTEM

Nutrient supply through silt from surrounding catchment

Green algae grows on surface - replaced by blue - green algae once plants shade it.

Cartloads of ash, straw manure and compost added before flooding

Chemical changes underwater increase supply of nutrients

Nutrients dissolved in water

Top 1-10 mm soil is oxygenated

nutrients stored in silt

No leaching as clay particles swell and form a liner. In the silt layer below 10 mm, there is a 'reduced' later with no oxygen - these anaerobic conditions cause slow release of nutrients. 'Ammonification' of organic soil matter makes nitrogen available and nitrogen is also fixed by blue-green algae on the surface.

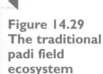

Figure 14.29 The traditional padi field ecosystem

Questions

1 Briefly explain how an agricultural ecosystem differs from a natural ecosystem.
2 Compare the traditional padi ecosystem with the more modern version which uses high yielding varieties of seeds.
3 Suggest what pressures might cause farmers to switch from traditional, largely self sustaining forms of agriculture to modern, high input, high output systems.

3. How can agriculture be made more sustainable?

Sustainable agriculture can be defined as producing the food needed by the present population without damaging the prospects of future generations to grow their food. (Unit 2.6 has a wider discussion of the whole topic of sustainable development.) The sustainable approach to agriculture requires farmers to avoid destroying the environment or undermining future productivity. To achieve this, farmers have to conserve the soil (ie, protect it from erosion and exhaustion) and to maintain biodiversity in the natural environment.

There are many obstacles to implementing sustainable agriculture on a wide scale. Agrochemical companies are naturally concerned to maintain the use of their products and they spend a large amount of money on promotion. Organisations which promote alternative methods are much less well funded by comparison. Another difficulty is the method of financial support given to farmers in the EU, the USA and elsewhere. At the present time, there is little financial incentive given to farmers to do anything other than maximise production by whatever means are available. A third obstacle is the relatively low funding given to researchers and scientists in this area of study. The interactions between crops, pests and pest predators are complex and not fully understood. For farmers, the easiest option at present is often simply to apply a technological fix, such as a pesticide spray, when faced with a problem.

Supporters of sustainable agriculture do not suggest that there should simply be a return to older, traditional types of farming. They recognise that yields have to be high, to feed the rising population, and farming must be profitable for farmers to maintain production. In order to achieve these goals, it is proposed that knowledge and science should be applied to the problems - but not in the same way as at present. So, for instance, rather than using large amounts of chemical fertiliser and pesticide, alternative methods should be used to maintain fertility and control pests. Farm profits can, it is suggested, actually be increased if there is less reliance on off-farm inputs such as energy and chemicals.

A number of ways in which farming can be made more sustainable have been identified. They include:
- crop rotation
- the use of cover crops
- soil enrichment
- the use of natural pest predators
- biointensive integrated pest management (IPM).

Crop rotation

This involves growing different crops in succession in the same field. It reduces the problem of pests because many have a preference for particular crops. Monoculture - the growing of the same crop year after year - guarantees pests a food supply and causes their population to increase. Growing different crops interrupts pest life cycles and so reduces their numbers. Tests in the United States, for example, have found that pests such as the 'corn borer' have significantly less impact on corn (ie, maize) if the crop is rotated annually.

In rotations, farmers can also plant crops such as legumes which fix nitrogen in the soil. Beans and peas are examples which add nutrients to the soil and so reduce the need for artificial fertilisers.

Cover crops

These plants are sown on otherwise bare ground between cropping periods. Examples include vetches, clover and oats. They are not harvested for sale but are used to prevent soil erosion and to suppress weeds. This can then reduce the need for herbicides.

Soil enrichment

Fertile, healthy soil improves yields and helps produce robust crops that can resist pests and diseases. Soil quality can be improved by incorporating animal manure and compost or by ploughing in the living plants that

Figure 14.30 A field of corn (maize), Iowa, USA

Monoculture gives pests a chance to gain a foothold. But if crops are rotated, the pests have less chance to become established.

were used as ground cover. Mixed farming (ie, raising of livestock as well as crops) makes this process easier because the animals provide manure on site.

Natural pest predators

Many birds and insects are natural predators of agricultural pests. Creating the conditions which encourage these predators can be an effective pest control method. Growing particular species of plants on which the predators feed in hedgerows and field verges is one technique that is used. The problem in most farms is that the indiscriminate use of chemical insecticides kills both predators and pests - so creating a vicious circle in which ever more pesticide is required.

Biointensive Integrated Pest Management (IPM)

This is a system of pest control that involves the prevention as well as the cure of pest problems. Crop rotation is part of this approach. So is the use of physical barriers such as agricultural fleece and polythene coverings that prevent pests from attacking plants.

Pest management is achieved more by biological than by chemical controls. Methods include the breeding of sterilised male pests. If released in sufficient numbers, they cause a collapse in the population of pests because the females are not fertilised. This technique has been used in California to combat the problem of fruit flies. Another method is the release of biocontrol agents which are simply predator insects that have been specially bred. Insects such as ladybirds are used in this way.

 Activity — **Farming in California's Central Valley**

Central Valley is approximately 600 km long and 80 km wide. Its rich alluvial soil and irrigation systems have helped it to become the most productive agricultural region in the USA, and probably the world. An annual farm revenue of over $12 billion comes from producing fruit, vegetables, rice, cotton and wheat. Most of the farms in the Valley use high input/high output systems based on subsidised water supplies, artificial fertilisers and pesticides. However, during the 1990s, increasing concerns were raised about the long term effects of this type of farming. Drinking wells were found to be contaminated with a cocktail of chemical fertilisers and pesticides. Some local people blamed clusters of cancer on the polluted water. In addition, consumer groups started to campaign against the indiscriminate use of pesticides. Fruit and vegetables were feared to be coated with toxic chemicals.

As a result, some farmers have started to reduce their use of agrochemicals. Instead, they are turning to biocontrol methods. Programmes of integrated pest management have been started along the whole of the Central Valley. Examples include the use of ladybird beetles to eat aphids. Some growers are planting plum trees to attract tiny wasps that will eat leafhoppers - a pest that attacks grape vines. Plants can also be part of biocontrol schemes. For example, strips of vetch planted between rows of crops repel nematodes (microscopic worms) that damage plants by attacking their roots. Marigolds have been found to have the same effect.

Although reducing the input of chemicals cuts farmers' costs, revenue is sometimes reduced as well. This is because the farmers' produce, particularly fruit, is sometimes marked and blemished because of minor pests and diseases - so some consumers are put off from buying. Consumers have become used to unblemished fruit and vegetables so, unless and until consumers can be 're-educated' in what to expect, many farmers will be reluctant to stop using artificial pesticides.
Adapted from the Los Angeles Times, 8th April 1999

▲ **Figure 14.31 Irrigation in the Central Valley**
Large scale irrigation combined with overuse of pesticides and herbicides has contaminated the groundwater.

Questions

1 Explain what is meant by the term biocontrol.
2 From a farmer's point of view, discuss the advantages and disadvantages of cutting the use of agrochemicals and adopting sustainable farming methods.

unit summary

1 People affect all natural ecosystems, often with destructive consequences. Increasing pressures on the environment increase the need to conserve species, habitats, resources and the biosphere.
2 Agricultural ecosystems are examples of plagioclimaxes and generally have only 2 or 3 trophic levels.
3 Agricultural ecosystems have less diversity of species, a simpler structure and less genetic diversity than natural ecosystems. Because they need inputs from outside the system, they are generally not self-sustaining or stable.
4 Sustainable agriculture requires systems that do not permanently damage the environment; the aim of sustainable agriculture is to maintain or even increase the productive potential.

key terms

Agroecosystem - an agricultural ecosystem; the ecosystem that exists in a farmed landscape.
Blanket bog - the acid, peat bog that covers much of upland Britain; in most cases it is a plagioclimax, ie formed as a result of human activity in clearing forests.
Integrated Pest Management - a system of pest control that emphasises the use of biological rather than chemical methods; it is an integrated approach that treats the agroecosystem as a whole rather than in its component parts.
Raised bog - a dome shaped area of moss peat formed over the site of a former lake or basin.

Unit 14.4 Biomes (and the human impact on them)

key questions

1 What factors affect the distribution of biomes?
2 What are the characteristics of tropical rain forest?
3 What are the characteristics of tropical grassland?
4 What are the characteristics of deserts?
5 What are the characteristics of temperate grassland?
6 What are the characteristics of Mediterranean regions?
7 What are the characteristics of broad leaf deciduous woodland?
8 What are the characteristics of coniferous forest?
9 What are the characteristics of tundra?
10 What are the characteristics of Antarctica and the Southern Ocean?

1. What factors affect the distribution of biomes?

A **biome** is a climax community of vegetation that extends over a wide area. Biomes generally correspond to world climatic regions. The length of the growing season (ie, the number of months with average temperatures above 6°C) and the availability of water are the key climatic factors that influence the distribution of biomes (see figure 14.32).

Apart from climate, the main natural factors that influence vegetation within biomes are relief (especially altitude), soils and biotic factors (ie, plants and animals). The effect of increased altitude is to cause lower average temperatures and therefore to create the climatic conditions found at higher latitudes. So, for example, the vegetation zones that exist in the Andes, near the equator between the coast of Ecuador and the summit of Mt Cotopaxi (5,896 metres high and 250

Figure 14.32 Generalised climate controls on natural vegetation

In regions where there is sufficient moisture for trees to grow:

Average temperature	Natural vegetation
All year above 6°C	Evergreen forest: consists mainly of broad leaved trees which shed their leaves at different times of the year.
About 8 months above 6°C	Deciduous forest: consists mainly of broad leaved trees which conserve moisture in the cold months by shedding their leaves.
About 4 months above 6°C	Coniferous forest: most trees have needle-like leaves which reduce moisture loss; most trees are evergreen so that photosynthesis can occur throughout the short growing season.
About 2 months above 2°C	Tundra: consists mainly of mosses, lichens and low vegetation of dwarf shrubs; the growing season is not long enough for large trees to grow.

In regions where the growing season is long enough for vegetation to grow:

Precipitation	Natural vegetation
Wet for at least six months of the year	Forests: trees form the natural vegetation.
A dry season of 3-6 months	Mediterranean: drought resistant shrubs and trees reduce moisture loss by having small, hard leaves, thick barks or deep roots.
	Tropical savanna and temperate grassland: there is generally insufficient precipitation for trees to grow.
Dry for most or all of the year	Deserts: scrub, cactus and succulent desert plants; most have deep roots and thick waxy leaves to retain moisture.

Figure 14.33 Vegetation zones related to latitude and altitude

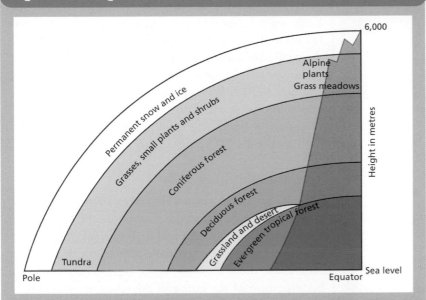

Note that this diagram is very generalised. In some mountain areas, certain ecosystems might not occur. For example, a vegetation zone equivalent to the desert biome might not always be found at higher altitudes. If such a zone occurs, it is most likely to be found on the leeward (ie, rain shadow) side of a mountain range where precipitation is relatively low. The tree line (ie, the highest altitude at which trees grow) varies from around 3,500-4,000 metres in equatorial regions to 2,000-2,200 metres in the Alps. In polar and tundra regions, the tree line is effectively at sea level.

km inland), equate to the biomes found at sea level between the equator and the north pole (see figure 14.33).

Biomes are zones of natural vegetation but all have been modified to some degree by human activity. For example, temperate deciduous woodlands have largely been cleared for agriculture. Tropical rain forests are currently being cleared at a rapid rate. Even the more undisturbed biomes such as deserts and tundra regions are increasingly being affected by mineral exploitation and pollution.

This unit looks at eight major biomes (and the Southern Ocean and Antarctic region). It also considers how people are affecting the regions. The biomes are described in sequence, starting at the equator and moving polewards.

2. What are the characteristics of tropical rain forest?

The Portuguese word selva is sometimes used to describe the tropical rain forest in Brazil. This term is also applied to similar types of vegetation elsewhere in the world.

Climate

In tropical rain forests there is no cool season. Average temperatures are high, typically 26-27°C throughout the year; the diurnal temperature range is much greater than the annual range, up to 10-15°C. In these hot conditions, plants can grow at all times of the year. The warm air holds large amounts of water vapour evaporated from vegetation - often giving humidity levels of 100 percent on the ground and resulting in frequent convectional thunderstorms in the afternoons. The annual average rainfall is high, over 1,800 mm, and it is wet throughout the year. In Manaus (Amazonia), July, August and September

Figure 14.34 Rain forests

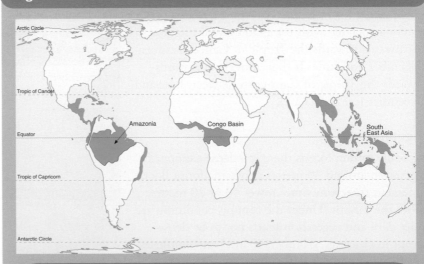

Rain forests are located in equatorial regions and in tropical areas where rainfall is high. This map shows where rain forest is the natural vegetation. Many areas have been cleared so that now only parts of Amazonia, the Congo Basin and South East Asia (particularly Sumatra, Borneo and Papua New Guinea) have extensive areas of virgin forest.

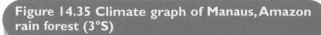

Figure 14.35 Climate graph of Manaus, Amazon rain forest (3°S)

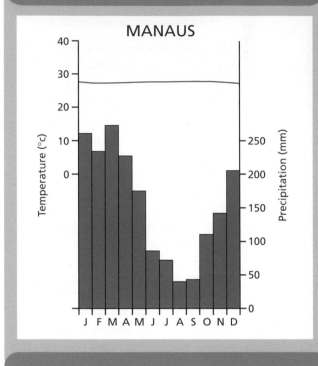

In rain forests, trees are mostly broadleaved and evergreen, allowing all year photosynthesis and growth. Large waxy leaves with pointed drip tips allow rain to fall off and aid rapid transpiration. Trees tend to have their own individual cycles so some are in flower while others are fruiting or leaf shedding. This maintains a constant leaf fall for recycling nutrients and provides a year round food source for birds, animals and insects. Productivity (ie, the net amount of biomass formed) is high - typically 2.2 kg per square metre per year.

Tropical rain forest soils

Soils are ferrallitic with a thin layer of humus and very active soil organisms which decompose the fallen leaves (see unit 13.1). The heat and high rainfall cause rapid leaching. Despite the luxuriant appearance of the vegetation, these are some of the world's least fertile soils because most of the nutrients are taken up into the vegetation or are lost through leaching. In places, a layer of iron and aluminium oxides remain in the A horizon. If this layer is exposed it can form a hard laterite crust that makes agriculture almost impossible.

The human impact on tropical rain forests

It is estimated that 15 percent of the world's land surface was, at one time, covered by rain forest. Approximately half has been destroyed and the rest is being cleared at a rate of 10 million hectares per year. This is equivalent to an area slightly bigger than the size of Belgium, Luxembourg and the Netherlands combined. In South

are less wet than other months but cannot be described as a dry season (see figure 14.35).

The climate of Manaus and other equatorial regions is influenced by surface trade winds which converge in the tropics and rise - causing a zone of low pressure. This is where rainfall is heaviest. The wind and low pressure system associated with the Hadley Cell migrates northwards towards the Tropic of Cancer between December and June. It then moves southwards towards the Tropic of Capricorn between June and December (see unit 12.1).

Vegetation

Typically in rain forests there is a dense canopy of vegetation around 30 metres above the forest floor. Emergent trees sometimes tower 10 or 20 metres above the canopy. Under the canopy, conditions are quite dark and vegetation tends not to be dense except in clearings. Climbers (lianes) and epiphytes (plants which grow on the leaves and branches of other plants) are common. Tree species such as teak or mahogany tend to be scattered throughout the forest. The trees are fast growing (to reach the light quickly) with long straight trunks and, in some cases, they have buttress roots to support their great weight.

Figure 14.36 Amazonia, Brazil

When viewed from above, the rain forest canopy is so dense that the forest floor is not visible.

Figure 14.37 The rain forest nutrient cycle

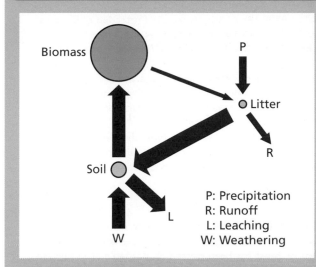

P: Precipitation
R: Runoff
L: Leaching
W: Weathering

The bulk of nutrients within the system are stored within the biomass. This is because litter is quickly decomposed and recycled through the soil into plant roots.

they are being covered in silt.
- Nutrients are lost from the system and cannot be replaced when the biomass is destroyed.
- Rainfall amounts are reduced - trees hold massive amounts of water which is lost when they are cut down. This reduces the amount of evapotranspiration and makes the regional climate drier.
- Global warming - trees are a store of carbon dioxide so, when forests are burned, more of this greenhouse gas is present in the atmosphere. Rising temperatures are expected to cause sea levels to rise and to create less predictable climate patterns (see unit 12.6).
- Indigenous peoples are under threat. In places such as Amazonia, New Guinea and central Africa, groups of people are losing their land and their lives as the rain forests are cleared. Cultures are lost and people are killed by settlers either deliberately or by diseases to which these people have no immunity.
- Biodiversity is reduced - half of all known living things come from rain forests; many medicinal drugs have been derived from rain forest plants and this potential is lost if species become extinct.

It is by no means certain whether remaining rain forests can be preserved. The pressure for commercial exploitation has, so far, been stronger than conservation efforts. For instance, widespread fires in South East Asia during 1997/98 were deliberately started to clear forests for farming and for palm oil plantations. However, some progress has been made. The Forest Stewardship Council (see unit 2.6) has tried to promote the idea of sustainable forestry. Consumers in western countries are urged to buy timber from sources which are properly managed and do not involve the destruction of virgin forest.

East Asia and Amazonia, most of the clearance is for agriculture or plantations. In Africa, most of the clearance is for timber (see unit 4.3 - forestry).

Deforestation on the present scale has important consequences. These include:
- Soil erosion - as the soil is no longer protected by the canopy, a single storm can remove over 150 tonnes of soil from one hectare of bare land; this silts up rivers and reservoirs. For instance, the Ambuklao reservoir in the Philippines will last 32 instead of 60 years due to rapid silting. On coastlines, corals are dying because

Activity ▶ Rain forest destruction

Amazonia

In the mid-1990s, an illegal logging operation was discovered on the 3,500 strong Kayapo (native Amerindian) reserve in Amazonia. Over 4,000 felled hardwood trees, including mahogany, were seized by the Brazilian Environment Institute en-route for the British furniture industry. The Kayapo's leaders were selling the trees despite having received financial help and support from environmental campaigners. In return for conserving their environment, the Kayapo had negotiated a health care programme with the Brazilian government, and trade in nuts and handicrafts had been organised by UK conservationists.

As a result of the incident, there were renewed calls for a total ban on the trade in mahogany by Greenpeace and Friends of the Earth. The ban would benefit the environment but would cost the Brazilian economy a valuable export trade. It is estimated that £800 million worth of illegally felled trees are sold each year. But, of course, because much of the trade is illegal, the profits do not figure in official Brazilian trade accounts.

West Africa

Approximately 60 percent of Sierra Leone was once rain forest. Today, only 4 percent of the original forest cover remains and this is threatened by loggers and farmers wanting to clear more land. The RSPB (Royal Society for the Protection of Birds - a UK organisation), with the Sierra Leone government, has established a 750 square kilometre nature reserve in the Gola Forest with the aim of managing the forest on a sustainable basis. The RSPB became involved because many Western European migratory birds pass through the area or spend the winter in Gola.

Gola is one of the least exploited areas of virgin forest left in the country and it is home to several rare and endangered species. Management plans have been prepared specifying where and how much logging can take place. Key areas have been identified as reserves and training programmes for forestry and wildlife management have started. A research station is planned with an education programme for local people explaining the need for management and conservation.

Unfortunately, since the mid-1990s, Sierra Leone has been destabilised by a series of civil conflicts. Most Europeans left when the fighting intensified and the government has relied on a Nigerian backed force to maintain power. Because central government authority broke down in many areas in the late 1990s, unauthorised logging, mining and farming increased. So has the hunting of the remaining chimpanzees which are regarded as 'bushmeat' by some local people.

South East Asia

Much of the original rain forest of South East Asia has been cleared for agriculture. Population pressure in the region is increasing and the remaining forests are under threat. The largest remaining areas of virgin forest are on the islands of Papua New Guinea, Sumatra and Borneo. Even there, an estimated 40 percent of forest has been cleared on Borneo and 35 percent on Sumatra.

During late 1997 and the start of 1998, large fires burnt in both Sumatra and Borneo. Most were started deliberately by people

▲ **Figure 14.38 Rain forest destruction, Borneo**

clearing areas for farming, for industrial pulpwood plantations and, especially, for palm oil plantations. Many of the fires spread, in some cases into virgin forest and protected areas. The problem was much more severe than in other years because the strong El Nino effect (see unit 12.6) had caused a drought throughout the region. The fires destroyed not only vegetation but threatened some of the world's most endangered species. Sun bears, which live in the forest, tigers, elephants, rhinoceros and orang-utans were all affected. Orang-utans are especially vulnerable. In 1998, it was estimated that the total population was less than 30,000 - a decline of 30-50 percent in a decade. The main reason for their decline is loss of habitat when forest areas are broken up into smaller and smaller pockets. They cannot swim so cannot easily move to safer areas.

Like the other animals listed, orang-utans are also hunted. In their case it is to be captured as pets or to be sold to zoos. Some of the other species, such as tigers and rhinoceros are hunted because parts of their bodies are used in traditional medicines. The elephants are sometimes shot or poisoned when they come into conflict with settlers who are trying to grow crops.

It is not only large mammals that are under threat. Freshwater species are also at risk from development. In places where new settlements are formed, crocodiles are generally quickly wiped out because of the danger they pose to settlers and also because of their valuable skins. Soil erosion that occurs when forests are cleared adds sediment to the rivers and this kills some types of fish. So does the rise in water temperature that occurs when tree shade is removed. Where agriculture and plantations have been developed, runoff containing pesticides and fertilisers also damages the freshwater ecosystems.

Questions

1 Summarise the reasons why rain forest ecosystems are under threat.
2 Suggest why conservationists and local governments find it difficult to protect rain forests.
3 To what extent does it matter that rain forests are being cleared?
4 Discuss the ways in which people in Western countries might help preserve remaining rain forests.

3. What are the characteristics of tropical grassland?

Tropical grasslands are called savannas in Africa, campos in Brazil and llanos in Venezuela.

Climate

In tropical grasslands there is a hot wet season and a very warm dry season. At Kano (northern Nigeria) the Sun appears overhead in the northern hemisphere's summer and this brings heavy convectional rain from May to September (see figure 14.40). Typically, between 500 mm and 1,000 mm rain falls each year. In the dry season, during winter in the northern hemisphere, winds blow from the high pressure zone over desert areas to the north east. The average temperature is high throughout the year with a January average of 20°C and a May average of nearly 30°C. During the rainy season, the temperature dips because of increased cloud cover. Although temperatures are high year-round, the growing season is limited by water availability.

Vegetation

The vegetation in tropical grasslands is a mixture of grassland and trees. The trees become more sparse in drier areas. There is a marked contrast between the wet

Figure 14.40 Climate graph of Kano, northern Nigeria (12°N)

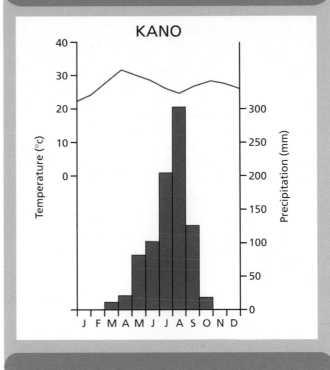

season with lush, green vegetation and the dry season when vegetation becomes parched and brown.

Tropical grassland vegetation is **xerophytic** (ie, adapted to drought) and **pyrophytic** (ie, adapted to fire). Many trees are deciduous, losing their leaves in the dry season to conserve moisture. Most have long roots and thick barks. Examples include acacia and, in Australia, eucalyptus trees. These have thick water retaining leaves. The baobab tree can store water in its large trunk. Grasses develop extensive root systems and grow rapidly when the rains start. They recover quickly after burning which can be caused by lightning or started deliberately by humans.

This type of ecosystem is relatively productive with a typical net primary productivity of 0.9 kg of biomass per square metre per year - slightly less than half that of the rain forest.

Figure 14.39 Tropical grasslands

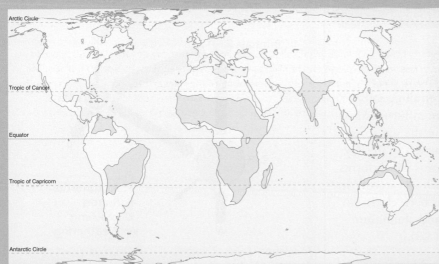

Tropical grasslands mostly lie within the tropics of Cancer and Capricorn in a zone between the equatorial rain forests and hot deserts. In East Africa, the savanna grassland extends across the equatorial zone because the climate is modified by the effect of altitude.

Figure 14.41 Tropical grassland vegetation, Kenya

Combat Desertification defines the term as: 'land degradation in arid, semi-arid and sub-humid areas resulting from various factors including climatic variations and human activities'.

Population pressure has led in some places to overgrazing and inappropriate farming methods. The result has been the destruction of natural vegetation leading to soil erosion in the affected areas. The gathering of fuelwood has reduced the number of trees and this has the effect of making erosion by wind and heavy rains more severe. The problem has been made worse, particularly in parts of the Sahel (along the southern margins of the Sahara Desert) by intermittent drought, and also by civil conflict preventing the normal migration patterns of nomads. Even in relatively peaceful places, such as in Kenya, the traditional nomadic lifestyle of cattle herders such as the Masai has been disrupted by increasing numbers of settled farmers.

However, the picture is not completely negative. Examples from Kenya, and Guinea in West Africa (see unit 4.1), show that desertification is not inevitable and may, in some cases, have been exaggerated. In both these instances, population pressure has led to more intensive agriculture but the net result has been for the land to become more productive. People have adopted techniques which conserve the soil rather than destroy it.

Figure 14.42 The nutrient cycle in tropical grassland

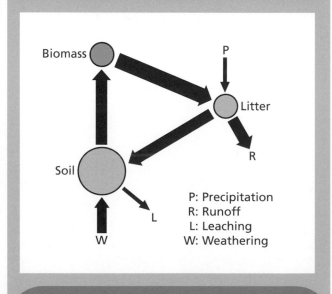

Much of the biomass is stored underground in root systems, and the litter store is reduced by fire. Compared with rain forests, a bigger proportion of nutrients are stored in the soil.

Tropical grassland soils

Soils formed under tropical grassland tend to have similar characteristics to the deep, red ferrallitic soils typical of rain forests, However, they are influenced by seasonal changes, being partly leached in the wet season and being subject to upward capillary action in the dry season. There is generally a store of humus which forms from decomposed vegetation during each wet season. In some cases where natural vegetation has been cleared or damaged, a hard lateritic layer of iron and aluminium oxide can develop (see units 13.1 and 13.3).

The human impact on tropical grasslands

There is a great deal of debate and research on the issue of desertification on the drier margins of tropical grasslands. This is a process which involves the spread of desert conditions. The United Nations Convention to

Activity **Desertification in the Sahel**

According to the United Nations Convention to Combat Desertification (UNCCD), 250 million people are directly affected by desertification. The problem is most severe in Africa. In the Sahel region which stretches from Senegal and Mauritania in the west to Somalia in the east, there has been a long term trend towards drier climate conditions. Average annual rainfall (generally in the 300 - 600 mm range) has decreased during the past two decades and has become more variable. At the same time, the wet season has become shorter.

Population totals in the region have more than doubled since 1960, according to the UNCCD. The result has been ever greater pressure on grazing land, fuelwood supplies and water resources. In Niger, over half the forest areas have been cleared in just 35 years; in Mauritania, increased wind erosion has caused sand dunes to migrate into populated areas; in Burkina, springs have dried and stream levels have fallen.

The governments of the region and the UNCCD have started programmes to reverse the trend. They share the view that the process of land degradation is not inevitable. Indeed, it has been noted by the UNCCD that much of the food aid that was supplied in the severe 1980s droughts came from parts of Australia and the USA that are not significantly wetter than many Sahel regions.

Policies to combat desertification include education, training and exchange visits so that local people can spread 'best practice' by word of mouth. In Niger, the UNCCD sponsored programme includes:
- population control policies - to slow the growth in numbers
- changes to land tenure laws - to give private ownership and a sense of responsibility to farmers rather than rely on communal ownership of land
- urban development - to increase overall income levels and to support the growing urban population (many of whom have migrated from rural areas)
- the creation of village woodlands - to provide shelter and fuelwood
- the setting up market gardens - to grow crops rather than rely on pastoral farming
- the adoption of soil and water conservation techniques - for example, stone lines are built along the contours of slopes to slow surface runoff and to prevent sheet wash of topsoil; hedges are planted, and woven brushwood windbreaks are built to slow wind erosion
- the development of domestic solar power systems to take the place of fuelwood for cooking.

Questions

1 Why is desertification a problem in the Sahel region?
2 Outline the obstacles that low income countries in the Sahel face in combating desertification.
3 Suggest how international agencies such as the UNCCD might help countries overcome the problem of desertification.

4. What are the characteristics of deserts?

Deserts are dry regions. They have an annual average precipitation generally less than 250 mm and high rates of evapotranspiration. (See unit 8.4 for a more detailed discussion of what constitutes a desert climate.).

Deserts are sometimes classified according to temperature. Hot deserts lie mainly between 15° and 30°N and S of the equator - generally on the western side or in the centre of continents. They include the Sahara, Kalahari, Atacama and Australian deserts. Temperate deserts lie in the interior of continents or in the rain shadow of mountain ranges. They include the Gobi and Patagonian deserts. Temperate deserts are sometimes called cold deserts which is also the name given to polar and tundra regions where precipitation is very low. This section looks at hot and temperate deserts.

Climate

The key feature of desert climates is their low rainfall. Average annual totals for such regions tend to be misleading because rainfall is extremely variable. In some years there might be very little rain or none at all, in other years there might be heavy convectional rainstorms for several days. Where deserts occur on the western margin of continents, such as the Atacama or Kalahari, advection fog can sometimes form. This happens when air passes over a cool ocean current and water vapour condenses.

Generally cloudless conditions in deserts allow intense solar radiation during the day but, at night, heat is

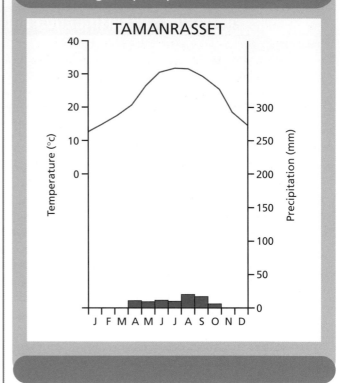

Figure 14.44 Climate graph of Tamanrasset, southern Algeria (23°N)

quickly lost. In hot deserts, day time temperatures in summer can reach over 50°C and night time temperatures in winter can fall below freezing. In temperate deserts, temperatures are not so high although the annual range can be just as great.

High day time temperatures in deserts often cause evapotranspiration rates to be greater than precipitation, leading to a moisture deficit. (Evapotranspiration is the combined loss of moisture due to evaporation from the ground and transpiration from plants.)

The climate of hot desert regions is dominated by high pressure systems. Subsiding air within the Hadley Cells (see unit 12.1) bring dry conditions in tropical deserts. The low rainfall in temperate deserts is caused by the long distance and/or mountain ranges over which winds must blow before these locations are reached. By the time air reaches these deserts, most of the moisture has already been deposited elsewhere.

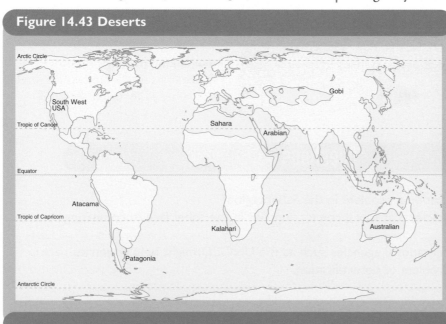

Figure 14.43 Deserts

Vegetation

Plants in deserts are xerophytic, having to withstand intense drought and high temperatures. Many varieties of cacti and succulents are found. Some have waxy leaves to reduce transpiration. Plants often have bulbous stems or thick leaves to store water, long roots to tap groundwater and sharp needles to discourage grazing animals and birds. Some plants are 'ephemerals' - only bursting into life after rain (such as the Rose of Jericho) whilst others are 'halophytes', able to grow in salty soils. Vegetation cover is generally sparse and well spaced to cut down competition for water. Animals that survive in deserts are well adapted. Some are nocturnal, to avoid the day time heat, and others such as camels are able to survive using stored food reserves and infrequent drinks of water.

Because desert vegetation is so thin, and because precipitation is low, decomposition of litter is slow and there is very little humus content in the soil. However, weathering breaks up the bedrock and, in places, a sandy soil rich in nutrients is formed. There is generally little leaching to wash out the nutrients so desert soils are potentially fertile if water is available.

Where groundwater is near the surface, capillary action in hot weather can bring salts to the surface of the soil. The process is called salinisation (see unit 13.3). Only a limited variety of plants can survive in these saline conditions.

Productivity is low in arid regions with a typical net primary productivity of 0.1 kg per square metre per year.

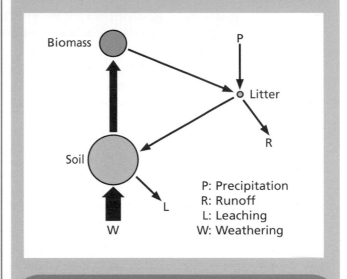

Figure 14.46 The nutrient cycle in hot deserts

P: Precipitation
R: Runoff
L: Leaching
W: Weathering

Because vegetation is sparse, nutrients are mainly stored in the soil. There is very little litter. Most recycling occurs through the decay of root material.

This is twenty times less than the biomass formed in rain forest conditions.

The human impact on deserts

Deserts are fragile ecosystems because water shortage means that it takes a very long time for plants to grow and regenerate if damaged. 'Desert varnish' is a thin layer of iron and manganese oxides that sometimes forms on the surface and stabilises the sand. It is easily destroyed by walking on it or driving over it. Once this crust is broken, the sand can more easily be blown - so causing sand dunes to spread.

Most desert regions remain relatively undisturbed. However, gas and oil exploitation, for example in North Africa and the Persian Gulf region, has had an impact. And, in some parts of western Egypt and Kuwait, the remnants of war time battles are still visible. In the deserts of southwest USA, recreational, off-road vehicles have damaged some areas by breaking the desert crust and crushing vegetation.

Figure 14.45 Cactus and scrub vegetation, Sonoran Desert, southwest USA

Activity Salinisation in Kazakhstan

Kazakhstan declared its independence from the Soviet Union in 1991. It is located in central Asia, bordered to the northwest and north by Russia, to the east by China, to the south by the Kyrgyz Republic and Uzbekistan, and to the southwest by Turkmenistan and the Caspian Sea.

Desert and steppe grasslands account for more than 80 percent of the total area. There was a dramatic increase in the cultivated area following the political decision in the 1950s to develop agriculture on semi-arid 'Virgin Lands'. From 7.8 million hectares in 1950, the cultivated area rose to 28.5 million hectares in 1960.

The climate is continental, with cold dry winters and hot dry summers. In the south, average temperatures range from -3°C in January to 30°C in July and the growing season varies from 8 months in the south to 6 months in the north. The average annual precipitation in central areas is 350 mm although this falls to less than 100 mm in the west. Evapotranspiration rates are very high throughout the summer.

In the mid-1990s, irrigation was used on 3.5 million hectares, or just over 10 percent of the cultivated area, and produced 20 percent of the country's crop production. Most of the water comes from rivers which rise in mountainous regions to the south and east. In some cases, such as the Syr Darya River, most of the water is extracted before it reaches the Aral Sea.

The main irrigated crops are fodder (mainly alfalfa), cereals, cotton, rice, fruit and vegetables. However, water efficiency is very low due to seepage in unlined canals and poorly controlled water supply on the land. This results in wastage of water and, in some places, a rise in the water table leading to salinisation. The problem can be made worse if more water is added to wash the salts down through the soil. If this happens, the soils can become waterlogged and unfit for agriculture. The effect of poor water management in Kazakhstan is that more than 10 percent of the irrigated land has been classed as saline or waterlogged. Some has become so salt encrusted that it cannot be used for any agriculture at all.

Because of economic difficulties following the break up of the Soviet Union, Kazakhstan does not have sufficient resources to slow down or reverse the salinisation process. One method that has been used successfully in parts of California, for instance, is to adopt micro-irrigation techniques such as drip-irrigation. This puts much less water on the land by using perforated pipes which limit water supply. However, the system requires sophisticated control methods that have broken down in those parts of Kazakhstan where it has been tried. Another solution is to use artificial drainage that takes excess water out of the ground in pipes. This prevents waterlogging and reduces capillary action. Unfortunately, in Kazakhstan, in the late 1990s, about 90 percent of the drainage systems that had been installed were not operating due to the high cost of pumping.

Other solutions, such as planting trees, have been successfully used in some countries - for example in parts of Australia. The effect is to lower the water table because the tree roots tap deeply into the soil, extract water, and then lose large amounts of moisture by transpiration. Also in Australia, salt absorbing plants have been grown in saline areas to reduce the salt content in soil. So far, these techniques have not been widely adopted in Kazakhstan - partly because of their cost and partly because of the slow rate of innovation on the farms. This is, to some extent, due to the legacy of the Soviet era when managers of state farms simply waited for government instructions rather than taking their own initiative. Even though most of the farms are now privatised, education and training on new techniques has been slow to develop.

▲ Figure 14.47 Kazakhstan

Questions

1 What are the physical and human factors that make salinisation a severe problem in Kazakhstan?
2 Discuss the possible methods by which salinisation can be reduced.

5. What are the characteristics of temperate grassland?

Figure 14.48 Temperate grassland

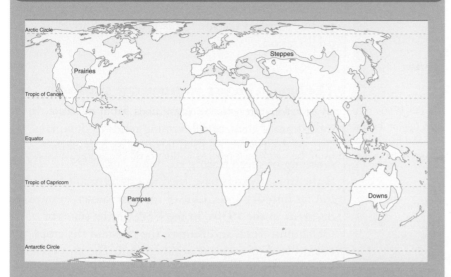

These grasslands are found within the temperate continental interiors of Europe, Asia (the steppes) and North America (the prairies); similar areas are found in New Zealand, Australia (the downs) and South America (the pampas).

Climate

The climate of temperate grasslands is continental with hot summers and cold winters. Summer average temperatures in the steppes and prairies are typically between 25-30°C and the coldest months can average -10°C (see figure 14.49). In winter, 3 or 4 months are below freezing and the growing season varies between 7 and 8 months. Precipitation is low, typically 500-750 mm per year. There is a marked summer maximum of precipitation - mainly convectional rain in the form of showers or thunderstorms. In winter, cold high pressure systems dominate - so only occasional depressions penetrate to bring snow. Evaporation rates are high in summer.

Temperate grassland soils

Soils are black earths (or chernozems) (see unit 13.1). They tend to be dark in colour from decomposing humus,

Figure 14.49 Climate graph of Omaha, USA (41°N)

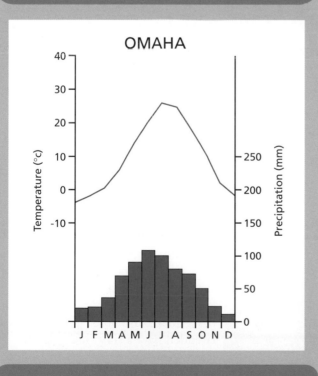

Figure 14.50 Temperate grassland, Wyoming, USA

There is insufficient moisture for trees to grow. Vegetation is dominated by short grasses and xerophytic plants. Typical values of net primary productivity are around 0.6 kg per square metre per year.

Figure 14.51 The nutrient cycle in temperate grassland

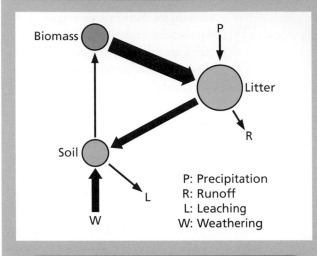

P: Precipitation
R: Runoff
L: Leaching
W: Weathering

Because the grass tends to become brown and die back in winter, most of the biomass is in the grass roots. Decomposition of the grass into humus is relatively fast, so the litter and fertile black soils hold most of the nutrients within the system.

and rich in calcium and other nutrients. Soil horizons tend to be indistinct because of mixing by burrowing animals, worms and other soil organisms. Leaching after the spring snow melt and capillary action in summer sometimes have the effect of creating calcium nodules within the soil. This process is known as calcification.

The human impact on temperate grasslands

Most temperate grasslands are used for agriculture. In more humid areas, cereal farming tends to dominate and, in drier parts, pastoral farming such as cattle ranching or sheep rearing are dominant.

Sometimes, farmers have tried to extend arable farming too far into dry areas. One of the best known examples occurred in the 1930s, in the USA. In the states of Oklahoma, Texas and Kansas, the rain and the crops failed - leading to severe wind erosion. The area became known as the Dust Bowl (see unit 13.3 for a more detailed account).

6. What are the characteristics of Mediterranean regions?

Figure 14.52 Mediterranean regions

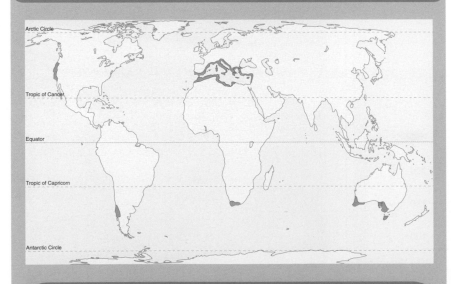

This biome is a distinctive ecosystem that gets its name from the Mediterranean basin. Other regions with similar climates have similar vegetation. They are mainly located on the western margins of continents, for example central California, central Chile, south west South Africa and south west Australia.

Climate

In summer, Mediterranean regions are dominated by sub-tropical high pressure systems that bring hot, sunny weather (see figure 14.53). Summer temperatures average between 25-30°C and evapotranspiration rates are high. In winter, depressions bring frontal rain. Frosts are rare and January average temperatures are typically around 10°C.

Vegetation

Mediterranean vegetation is adapted to the summer drought. Conifers such as the Corsican Pine have needle shaped leaves to reduce transpiration. Olive trees have deep roots and the cork oak has a thick bark. Some plants, such as lavender, have a short life cycle (ie, from flowering to seed production) to avoid the summer drought.

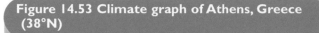

Figure 14.53 Climate graph of Athens, Greece (38°N)

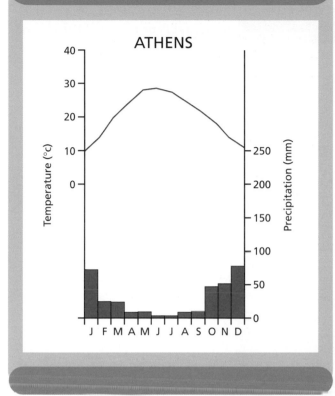

Mediterranean soils

Mediterranean soils vary a great deal depending on the annual precipitation, vegetation cover and bedrock. In woodland areas, the soils might be brown earths. In limestone areas, the soils might be terra rossas (or red earths). The alternating wet and dry seasons promotes weathering and the formation of iron oxides. These give the soil its typical red colour.

The human impact on Mediterranean regions

Many Mediterranean ecosystems have been severely affected by human activity. Forests have largely been cleared for timber or to create farmland. In Italy, for instance, much of the woodland was cleared by the end of the Roman period. Deforestation of hillsides made the soil vulnerable to erosion - particularly in summer storms. Without the tree roots to bind the soil together, large amounts of soil were swept into streams and rivers. This had the effect of silting valley bottoms and river mouths - so creating marshy breeding grounds for malaria carrying mosquitoes. It was only in the twentieth century that many of these areas were finally drained, so providing farmland at the same time as removing the mosquito's habitat.

In the Mediterranean region of southern Europe, the 'maquis' vegetation of small trees and bushes is a sub-climax - the result of fires and centuries of human activity in clearing trees and grazing animals. On limestone areas, water drains quickly and the summer drought is more severe. This results in the 'garrigue' vegetation of scattered herbs, grasses, juniper and gorse. In California, a similar scrub vegetation is called 'chaparral'.

Because of the variability in Mediterranean soil types and precipitation levels, there is no typical level of biomass productivity or nutrient cycle. In wetter areas, the ecosystem more closely resembles that of deciduous woodland. In drier areas, the ecosystem is more like that found in arid and semi-arid regions.

Figure 14.54 Olive groves in southern Spain

There are few parts of Mediterranean Europe where the natural vegetation remains. In many areas the land is used for agriculture. In other places, deforestation and soil erosion have permanently altered the natural vegetation.

7. What are the characteristics of broad leaf deciduous woodland?

Figure 14.55 Temperate deciduous woodlands

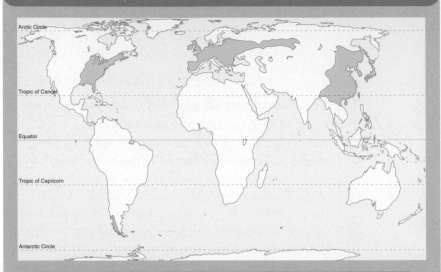

Most temperate deciduous woodland occurs in the northern hemisphere, in eastern Canada and the north eastern USA, in Western Europe and in eastern Asia. A small area occurs in southern Chile. Most other temperate woodland in the southern hemisphere is evergreen - in Tasmania, south east Australia and New Zealand. Only small areas of natural temperate woodland survive - most have been cleared for agriculture.

America) dominate. In summer, the woodland floor tends to be shady and dark, so ground vegetation is not dense. However, in spring, before the leaves fully develop, plants such as wood anenome and bluebell quickly grow and flower. Net primary productivity is high at 1.2 kg per square metre per year due to the long growing season and the relatively long summer days that occur in temperate latitudes.

Temperate woodland soils

Typical soils formed in deciduous woodlands are brown earths (see unit 13.1). Plentiful soil organisms decompose the fallen leaves, creating a fertile soil that is rich in nutrients. Because of mixing by burrowing animals and other fauna, the soil horizons tend to be indistinct.

Climate

North west Europe has warm, wet summers and cool, wet winters (see figure 14.56). Summer average temperatures are typically in the 15-20°C range and the coldest winter months generally average between 0-5°C. The growing season can extend all year round in the mildest, coastal locations but, in most places, it lasts 9-10 months per year. Precipitation occurs throughout the year although there is sometimes an autumn/winter maximum. Annual precipitation is normally well above transpiration rates. The weather tends to be extremely variable from day to day but, in general, there are no extremes.

In eastern Canada and north eastern China, the climate is more extreme than in north west Europe. The annual temperature range tends to be slightly bigger. So, for instance, two or three winter months average below freezing and summer temperatures average 20-25°C.

Vegetation

Deciduous trees shed their leaves in winter to retain moisture, conserve nutrients and prevent frost damage. Species such as oak, beech, ash and maple (in North

Figure 14.56 Climate graph of Antwerp, Belgium (51°N)

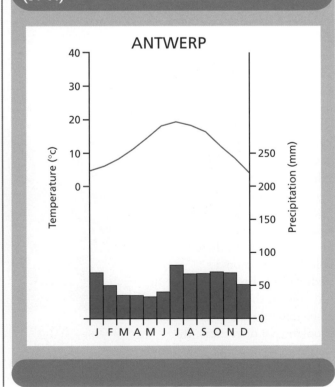

Figure 14.57 Broad leaf deciduous woodland, New England

Figure 14.58 The nutrient cycle in deciduous woodland

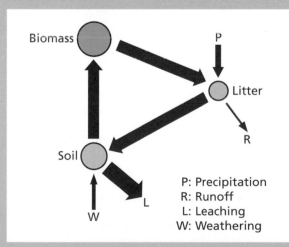

P: Precipitation
R: Runoff
L: Leaching
W: Weathering

Compared with tropical rain forests, there is a relatively large nutrient store in the soil. This is because the vegetation is less dense and also because the growing season normally does not extend all year. The result is that, for two or three months each year, the woodland is not producing new biomass whereas in the tropics this process does not stop.

The human impact on temperate woodland regions

Only small amounts of native woodland survive in regions where temperate deciduous trees form the natural vegetation. The trees have mainly been cleared for timber and for agriculture. In general, the brown earths found in deciduous woodland are fertile and productive for agriculture. With year round precipitation, these regions form ideal farmland - for pastures and for crops.

In Britain, where trees have been planted to replace the original woodland, these have often been conifers. The reason is that they grow more quickly than broadleaf trees and so bring a faster commercial return. However, starting during the 1990s, there has been a trend to plant native species such as oak, ash and beech. Partly this has been due to greater awareness of the ecological tradition. It has also been due to increased government and EU subsidies for native woodland planting schemes.

Activity **Maintaining biodiversity on arable farmland**

Seeds of destruction

The brown earth soils of lowland Britain provide rich farmland. Over a period of at least 2,000 years the land has been cleared of its natural woodland cover to allow food production. Traditionally, mixed farming techniques have been used in which animals and crops were raised on the same farms. To control pests and diseases, and to maintain soil fertility, farmers relied on a grass ley (ie, temporary crop) as a break after two or three years of growing cereals. The ley was grazed by sheep or cattle which returned fertility to the soil - ready for the next crop. Because the land was not ploughed for a year (or more), the number of earthworms and other soil organisms built up. These aerated the soil and helped decompose organic matter - so increasing the availability of nutrients and improving the soil structure.

The mixed farming system supported a diverse wildlife because it contained a variety of habitats. In addition, the traditional method of leaving cereal stubble (ie, the stalks and roots left after harvesting) in the fields over winter provided food to many species of seed eating birds.

However, since the 1970s, the influence of the Common Agricultural Policy of the European Union has led to a greater intensification of agriculture and the virtual ending of mixed farming. Because farmers get guaranteed prices for their cereals, there has been a big incentive to obtain higher and higher yields from the land. The south and east of Britain has come to specialise in cereal monoculture and the north and west have tended to concentrate on sheep and cattle farming. The arable farms rely heavily on agro-chemicals; pesticides to kill pests and prevent diseases, herbicides to kill weeds, and fertilisers to replace nutrients in the soil. In order to increase yields, hedgerows have been removed (at a rate of over 20,000 miles per year in the early 1990s) and fields have been made bigger.

The result has been a loss of biodiversity. For example, according to the British Trust for Ornithology, over a 25 year period, there has been an 89 percent fall in the population of tree sparrows, a 76 percent decline in bullfinches, a 73 percent decline in song thrushes and a 56 percent fall in the number of skylarks. In addition, the numbers of brown hares, pipistrelle bats and wildflowers have also declined dramatically.

Another side effect of farm intensification has been the overuse of fertilisers. Nitrates have contaminated drinking water after being dissolved in surface runoff and also being leached from soils into groundwater. Over application of phosphorus has led to eutrophication in which the surplus nutrients have washed into freshwater rivers and ponds. This leads to algal blooms and excessive growth of aquatic weeds. In turn, this has the effect of deoxygenating the water and killing the fish.

Adapted from the Sunday Times, 18th April 1998

Arable Stewardship Scheme

In response to the 1992 Rio Earth Summit's Biodiversity Convention, the UK government has drawn up a plan of action. Part of this plan involves the Arable Stewardship Scheme operated by the Ministry of Agriculture, Fisheries and Food (MAFF). The scheme aims to promote more ecofriendly land use and will, it is hoped, encourage sustainable farming techniques. An important aspect of sustainable agriculture is the maintenance of soil fertility for future generations. In addition, the aim is to prevent and even reverse the loss of biodiversity that has accompanied modern farming methods.

Farmers are paid to take part in the Arable Stewardship Scheme and must then agree to a range of measures. These include:

- the use of broader field margins and 'conservation headlands' in which wildlife (ie, insects, birds, mammals and wildflowers) can survive
- the planting of crops in spring (rather than in autumn) so that stubble can be left in the fields over winter - providing food for birds and also increasing the organic content of soil
- the undersowing of grass and/or clover in cereals so that, after the cereals are harvested, the land is left under grass or clover. This increases the organic content of soil and leaves soil organisms undisturbed - so promoting the decomposition of organic matter. Clover is a legume so it fixes nitrogen which can be used as a nutrient by the next crop. Another advantage of this technique is that weeds find it harder to become established - so reducing the need for herbicide.
- the planting of wild flowers in strips or in field margins to provide nectar, pollen, seeds and habitat for birds and insects. Plants are chosen to provide a succession of seeds through the year and also to attract useful insects such as hoverflies. These are a predator to aphids which are a pest because they eat young crops.

Questions

1 To what extent can it be said that the Arable Stewardship Scheme is an attempt to protect the natural ecosystem of lowland Britain?

2 Explain the impact of modern arable farming techniques on the brown earth soils of lowland Britain. Outline methods by which the quality of these soils and biodiversity can be maintained in the long run.

8. What are the characteristics of coniferous forest?

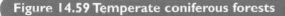

Figure 14.59 Temperate coniferous forests

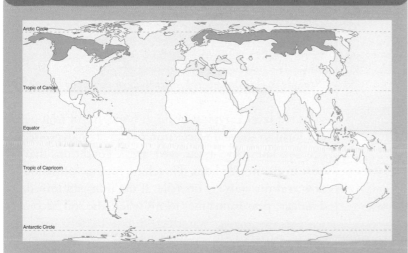

Most of the world's coniferous forests lie in a zone north of the northern hemisphere's temperate grassland and deciduous woodland, but south of the tundra. The term boreal is sometimes used to describe these forests which stretch across Canada and Eurasia ('borealis' is the Latin word for northern). The Russian word taiga is also used. There is no similar zone in the southern hemisphere because there are no land masses at the equivalent latitude.

Climate

The climate of the coniferous forest zone is sometimes called 'cold continental'. July temperatures average 15°C and winter temperatures average below freezing for 4-5 months (see figure 14.60). The growing season is short, generally 6 months or less. The days in summer are long although the Sun remains low in the sky. In winter, the days are very short and, during the long, often clear nights, extremely cold conditions are experienced. Precipitation is generally in the 500-750 mm range with a summer maximum of convectional rain. If depressions penetrate into the continental interiors in winter, the precipitation falls as snow.

Vegetation

Pine, fir and spruce are the most common trees in the coniferous forests of Canada and Europe. They tend to occur in stands (ie, particular species group together - generally depending on the soil conditions). Because these trees are evergreen, photosynthesis can start rapidly once daylight increases in spring and temperatures rise over 6°C. In much of Siberia, where conditions are colder and drier, the larch is more common. It is a deciduous conifer which reduces moisture loss by completely shedding its leaves. During the winter, when water in the ground is frozen, conifers have to conserve moisture. Transpiration is very slow through their tough, needle shaped leaves. Their conical shape and springy branches help them shed snow which might otherwise build up and break the branches. The dark, shaded floor in coniferous forests limits plant growth and the needles produce an acid litter that is slow to decompose. On the colder margins of the forests, either in higher latitudes or at higher altitudes, smaller, stunted trees allow light to reach the ground and bilberry, moss and lichens grow.

Productivity in coniferous forests is relatively low because the growing season is short and also because there is little undergrowth. The net primary productivity is typically 0.8 kg per square metre per year.

Figure 14.60 Climate graph of Moscow (56°N)

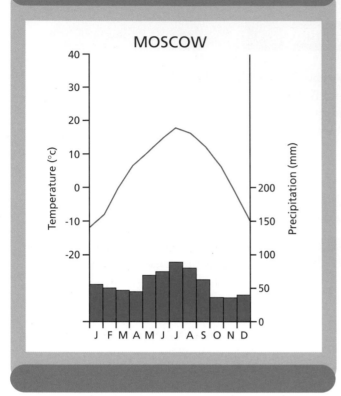

Figure 14.62 The nutrient cycle in coniferous forests

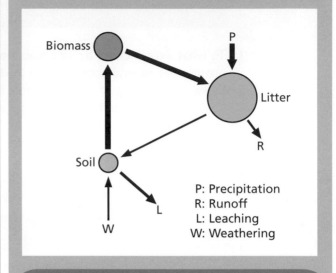

P: Precipitation
R: Runoff
L: Leaching
W: Weathering

Because vegetation is slow to decompose in the low temperatures and acid conditions, most of the system's nutrients are stored in the litter layer.

Soils

The typical soils of coniferous forests are podsols (see unit 13.1). They tend to be heavily leached - particularly during the spring snow melt. A pale, ash coloured layer is typical in the A horizon. An iron pan can form in the soil where iron oxides are redeposited. Few soil fauna live in the cold, acidic conditions that exist in the needle litter. Therefore, humus formation is slow and the soils are infertile. If the iron pan impedes drainage, peat sometimes forms where the soil becomes waterlogged. Few bacteria can survive to decompose the dead vegetation in these conditions.

The human impact on coniferous forests

Many of the accessible coniferous forests have been cleared for timber or pulp production. Eastern Siberia is the latest region to be exploited - mainly by East Asian producers from South Korea and Japan.

In Canada and Europe, conservationist pressure has ensured that replanting has kept pace with clearing. However, controversy has arisen over the clear cutting of remaining virgin forest - for example in British Columbia. (See unit 4.3 for a more detailed account of this issue.)

Figure 14.61 Coniferous forest, northern Russia

9. What are the characteristics of tundra?

Figure 14.63 Tundra

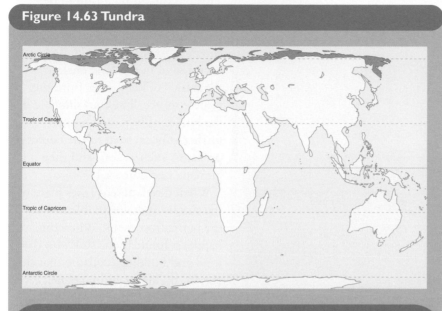

Tundra means 'treeless plain'. The tundra exists in high latitudes in northern Canada, Alaska, northern Siberia and northern Scandinavia. No equivalent zone exists in the southern hemisphere.

which reduce transpiration. There are extensive areas of bog or muskeg (a Canadian term) - dominated by cotton grass, mosses and sedge.

In summer, as soon as the temperature rises sufficiently, many tundra areas become covered with flowers. Large numbers of insects such as mosquitoes and blackflies breed in the marshy ground, taking advantage of the long daylight hours to complete their life cycle.

Tundra soils

Gley soils are common in tundra regions. The small amounts of dead vegetation decay only very slowly. The soil is frozen for most of the year and is underlain by permafrost. This restricts drainage, so causing waterlogging in summer. The conditions restrict bacterial action and cause peat to accumulate. Frost action within the soil heaves sharp angular

Climate

In tundra regions, high pressure and winds blowing from the Arctic create a dry climate with low temperatures all year round (see figure 14.64). The summer maximum typically averages 5-15°C and the coldest months in winter can be -40°C or even lower. It is below freezing for 8-9 months of the year and the growing season is very short, 6 to 7 weeks. The Sun remains low in the sky but there are 24 hours of daylight in mid-summer, contrasting with 24 hours darkness in mid-winter. There is little water vapour in the cold atmosphere so annual precipitation totals are usually under 250 mm. However, because of the low temperatures, there is also little evaporation.

Vegetation

During the short summers, thin, often waterlogged soils form above the permafrost (ie, permanently frozen ground). These conditions limit vegetation to shallow rooted plants with a very short life cycle. Bilberry, dwarf birch, saxifrages, anemones, buttercups, mosses and lichens survive. Strong winds blowing across the treeless plains also affect vegetation by stunting growth and increasing transpiration. Plants adapt by being low and ground covering, and by having thick or hairy leaves

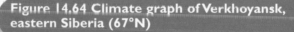

Figure 14.64 Climate graph of Verkhoyansk, eastern Siberia (67°N)

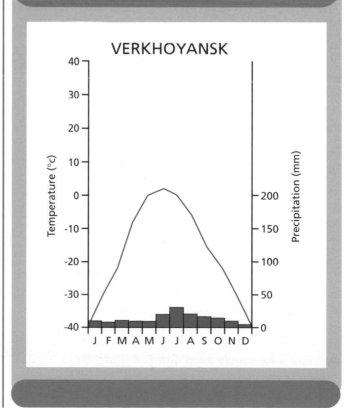

VERKHOYANSK

Figure 14.65 Tundra, northern Alaska

The landscape is treeless and often waterlogged in summer.

or pollution. Plants only grow slowly and decomposition is also very slow. This has caused pollution to be 'magnified' in certain areas. For instance, in northern Canada, chemical toxins such as PCBs have been found in the food chain, thousands of kilometres from the nearest source. These accumulate in the bodies of fish and are then further concentrated in the bodies of predators such as seals and then humans (see unit 14.1).

When development takes place on the tundra, a major problem arises if the permafrost melts. When this happens, foundations sink into the mud and buildings collapse. For this reason, buildings and pipelines have to be insulated from the ground. This is usually done by building them on stilts. Surface communication is easiest in winter when the ground is frozen but, in summer, can be difficult. Gravel roads are one solution - they insulate and protect the ground from melting.

fragments of rock upwards to form stone polygons and other features (see unit 10.4) .

Productivity is low in tundra regions. Typical values for net primary productivity are 0.1 kg of biomass per square metre per year.

The human impact on tundra

The very low population densities in tundra regions have, until recent decades, caused little human impact. Hunter gatherer people such as Inuits tended to live in ecological balance with their environment. However, during the past 50 years, this has changed. Discoveries of oil and gas in Alaska and Siberia have led to economic development (see unit 10.4). During the Cold War, the Arctic was the front line between the West and the Soviet Union and several defence installations were built by both sides in the tundra region. Since then, a related problem has arisen on the north coast of Russia where obsolete nuclear submarines and other radioactive materials have simply been dumped in the sea.

Because the conditions are so harsh, it takes a long time for tundra vegetation to recover from disturbance

Figure 14.66 The nutrient cycle in tundra regions

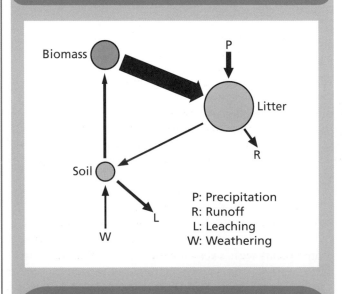

P: Precipitation
R: Runoff
L: Leaching
W: Weathering

The plants and their root systems store relatively large amounts of nutrients. When the vegetation dies, the nutrients are recycled very slowly so most remains in the litter.

Activity **The Arctic National Wildlife Refuge [ANWR]**

The ANWR was set up in 1960 (and extended in 1980) to 'preserve the unique wildlife of the wilderness area'. It is said to contain the greatest biodiversity of any conservation area in the Arctic. The Refuge lies in the north east corner of Alaska, with the Canadian border to the east, the Beaufort Sea to the north and the Brooks Range of mountains to the south. It is 200 km east of Alaska's large North Slope oil field at Prudhoe Bay.

Only 200 people live permanently in the ANWR. They are Inupiat who live on the coast at a village called Katovik. These Inuit people live mainly by fishing and hunting marine mammals. Inland, to the south, live the Gwich'in Athabascan people who are native Americans. They are semi-nomadic, spending much of their time hunting caribou.

The coastal plain in the north of the ANWR is featureless tundra that contains hundreds of small lakes in summer when the snow melts. It extends 160 km from east to west and 50 km from north to south. It is to here that a 160,000 strong herd of caribou migrates each year. They spend the winter in the forests to the south of the Brooks Range but, each spring, make the 1,000 km journey to the coast. The female caribou give birth to their calves in June when the vegetation is growing strongly. By gathering on the gravel beds of rivers and on the shoreline, the caribou gain some relief from mosquitoes in the height of summer.

Oil and gas exploration
For over 10 years, there has been fierce debate in the USA over whether to open the ANWR to oil and gas exploration. The Prudhoe Bay oil field currently produces 25 percent of US supplies, but production has peaked. A 1,250 km pipeline linking Prudhoe to Valdez, on Alaska's ice free southern coast, was opened in 1977. The US government has to decide on whether to allow development in the ANWR or to refuse permission, or to allow some compromise. For instance, limited development might be allowed with environmental safeguards.

The case for exploration:
• US oil production is not sufficient to meet present or future needs - so leading to greater reliance on foreign supplies
• an estimated 10 billion barrels of oil lie under the coastal plain of the ANWR
• up to 700,000 new jobs could be created in the US if the ANWR oil fields were opened; these jobs include construction, transport and equipment manufacturing
• Alaska's state revenues would be increased by oil taxes on the new production
• the majority of Alaskans are in favour of development, as are the Inupiat people who would receive royalty payments from the oil companies
• the Prudhoe Bay area has not experienced any major oil spillage or pollution incident in over 20 years of operation
• the 15-20,000 strong caribou herd which spends its summer near Prudhoe increased in number in the early years of development - mainly because predators became less common
• only 5,000 hectares out of a total 750,000 hectares of the coastal plain would be directly affected.

The case against exploration:
• the ANWR contains a unique, unspoiled ecosystem that would be damaged by new roads, pipelines and buildings
• the caribou calving grounds would be disturbed, endangering the future of the herd; the ANWR herd is much bigger than at Prudhoe and the impact of the exploration and development cannot be determined
• at Prudhoe, the caribou predators such as grizzly bears and arctic foxes became scavengers around the human settlements
• 170 bird species and 44 mammal species spend time in the ANWR; over 300,000 snow geese migrate there each year; developing the Reserve risks disrupting all these species
• oil and other pollution from development remains locked in the tundra ecosystem because decomposition is extremely slow
• the Gwich'in people oppose the development because they fear the impact on the caribou herd; without the caribou, their traditional way of life and culture would be destroyed
• the Exxon Valdez tanker spill in 1989 caused extensive damage to the Prince William Sound marine ecosystem on Alaska's south coast; a similar accident could happen on the North Slope or anywhere along the pipeline
• conservationists claim that if American cars increased their average efficiency to just 30 mpg by 2020, twice as much energy could be saved as it is projected that the ANWR could produce
• energy conservation (eg, insulating buildings, improving energy efficiency) creates jobs that are just as valuable as oil production jobs.

Questions

1 Explain why tundra regions such as the ANWR are fragile yet relatively unspoilt environments.
2 Discuss the options that face the US Government in deciding whether to open the ANWR to oil exploration.

10. What are the characteristics of Antarctica and the Southern Ocean?

The continent of Antarctica has a diameter of over 4,000 km. Most of the land surface (97%) is covered by ice, and the ice sheets are over 3,000 metres thick in places. The great weight of this ice has depressed the Earth's crust to below sea level in much of the central area. Some high mountains do stick out above the ice - mainly around the continental fringes (see figure 14.67).

Attached to the coast of Antarctica are ice shelves that float on the ocean. They are fed by glaciers that emerge from the continental interior. In winter, the sea around Antarctica freezes and pack ice can extend almost 2,000 km into the Southern Ocean. It has been estimated that the ice sheets in Antarctica contain 70 percent of the world's fresh water.

The Southern Ocean surrounds the continent of Antarctica. Its northern boundary is marked by a sharp divide between relatively cold surface water to the south and the slightly warmer, more saline water to the north. This boundary varies between latitudes 45°S and 60°S.

The Antarctic ecosystem

Because of the severe cold on Antarctica, there is virtually no plant life apart from algae and lichens. These organisms exist on bare rocks above the ice or in a small number of ice free, wind swept valleys. The mammals and birds that live in the region rely upon the ocean for their food supply so are mainly coastal. In places, there are large populations of penguins and seals and, in summer, of migratory birds such as terns.

The ecosystem within the Southern Ocean is relatively fragile and has a low productivity. This is because, for much of the year, there is no solar radiation which is needed for photosynthesis. Also, the water is relatively low in mineral nutrients because the land is not being actively eroded and therefore there are few sediments.

Primary production tends to peak sharply in December, January and February when there is 24 hours of daylight. Plankton, including a crustacean plankton called krill, multiply rapidly and are eaten by fish and whales. In turn, the fish are eaten by other predators such as seals and birds.

The ecosystem is fragile because the flow of energy is restricted through a small number of species. If, for some reason, the supply of plankton is restricted, this has a rapid knock-on effect up the food chain. This causes variations in the populations of birds and mammals.

Figure 14.67 Infrared satellite image of Antarctica

Ross Ice Shelf

The image is oriented with the Greenwich Meridian at the top.

Climate

The Antarctic climate is uniformly cold and dry. It is also windy because there are few landscape features to slow the wind. The coldest period is from May to September when there is almost no daylight. In 'summer' between December and March, the Sun can shine for 24 hours but, because it is low in the sky, the temperature remains cold. In most of Antarctica, even the summer months have a mean temperature below freezing.

In the cold conditions, the air pressure is generally high and there is little convection. Measuring the small amount of precipitation is difficult because the strong winds blow ice crystals into the air and it is impossible in practical terms to distinguish this from any actual snow fall.

Scientists at Antarctic weather stations monitor the local climate and they are also involved in researching wider climate changes. In particular, the impact of global warming and the depletion of the ozone layer are being studied. It is expected that a rise in global temperatures will cause some of the Antarctic ice cap to melt and, possibly, to cause the break up of the large ice shelves off the Antarctic coast. The speed at which this happens will have an important effect on sea levels (see unit 12.6 for a fuller discussion on global warming).

Ozone depletion in the upper atmosphere was first noted by researchers in the Antarctic. The layer of ozone provides a shield against ultra-violet radiation which can cause skin cancer and eye cataracts. It is believed that industrial pollutants, particularly CFCs used in refrigeration units, are causing the ozone to break down. (See unit 2.5 for an account of ozone depletion and the measures that are being undertaken to phase out the use of CFCs.)

The human impact

The human impact on Antarctica and the Southern Ocean is relatively small and the Antarctic continent is the largest wilderness area on Earth. There are no permanent inhabitants and there are only approximately 30 scientific stations scattered along the coastline (plus the Amundsen-Scott Station at the South Pole). So far, the limited number of ecotourists (mainly climbers and adventurers) and passengers on specialist cruises have not had a significant impact. The remoteness of the continent, the high travel costs and the severe climate are major obstacles that face any travellers to the region. Nevertheless, concern over the possible damage that development could bring has led to the region having a

special protected status. This is set out in the 1959 Antarctic Treaty (and subsequent treaties). Before then, there had been a risk that there would be a scramble for territory in the region. In the early part of the twentieth century there were a number of whaling stations established on the margins of Antarctica and, in more recent times, there have been moves to exploit the region's possible mineral wealth. Many different countries claim parts of Antarctica and some of these claims overlap.

To avoid potential conflicts that might arise, the Antarctic Treaty has demilitarised the continent. This means that no military bases can be set up there. There is also a set procedure of arbitration in which independent assessors are used to settle any disputes. The main provisions of the Antarctic Treaties (signed by all countries which claim an interest in the region) are:

- the continent is a Special Conservation Area
- no activities are allowed that will cause permanent damage to the environment
- there must be an environmental impact assessment before any new activity takes place
- native mammals, birds and plants (lichen and algae) are to be left undisturbed
- no non-native animal species or parasites are to be introduced
- no 'mineral resource activity' can take place
- waste disposal is to be organised in a way as to minimise the environmental impact; where possible, waste should be completely removed; open burning of waste is prohibited; the discharge of oil is prohibited.

These last points recognise that in the dry, cold environment, pollutants are very slow to decompose. Animal and human wastes can remain unchanged for tens of years or even longer. Archaeologists who examine the old whaling stations find that that they are exactly as people left them, decades ago.

The Southern Ocean The management of resources in the Southern Ocean has proved more difficult to organise than in Antarctica itself. Fish stocks, including krill, are relatively unexploited but are increasingly being caught for use as fish meal for farm animals. There is a danger that, in the future, unregulated fishing will lead to the depletion of stocks.

At the present time, the issue of whaling is the focus of much debate. In the first half of the twentieth century, a large number of countries had whaling fleets. Whales were caught for oil (by countries such as the UK and USA) and for meat (by countries such as Norway and Japan). By the 1950s, the market for whale oil declined as other oils (eg, vegetable oil and petroleum) became cheaper to use. Around the same time, fears started to grow about the extinction of certain whale species - such as the blue whale. So, as a result of world wide public pressure, the International Whaling Commission (IWC) announced a ban on whaling in 1982. This ban has always been resented by countries such as Norway and Japan who claim that their traditional industries are being discriminated against.

The IWC allows some limited exceptions to its ban. These include:
- 'aboriginal subsistence whaling' (ie, whaling by native people for their own use) in places such as Alaska, Greenland and northern Russia
- 'small species whaling' in some areas, eg pilot whales in the Faroe Islands and porpoises in Japanese coastal waters
- whaling for 'scientific research' - mainly by the Japanese who catch several hundred whales each year in the Southern Ocean.

Some countries (eg, Canada and Norway) are not members of the IWC and are therefore not covered by the ban. Whalers from Norway are estimated to have killed over 3,000 minke whales in the North Atlantic during the 1990s.

The issue of Japanese whaling in Antarctica for scientific research is extremely controversial. Opponents of whaling say that the Japanese are simply exploiting a loophole and that they do not need to kill the whales for research purposes. Partly, this opposition comes from Western groups who see whales as marine mammals - ie, kindred species to humans which have intelligence and should not be eaten.

The Japanese response is that the research is necessary to monitor the whale population. For instance, the IWC's own statistics suggest that there are over 750,000 minke whales in the Southern Ocean and that they are nowhere near extinction. The Japanese whalers claim that the research is expensive and that it is only fair that they should recoup some of the expense by selling the whale meat that they have collected. At a more fundamental level, many people in Japan feel that eating whale meat is a normal and natural part of their culture. There is nothing, apart from Western squeamishness, that prevents whaling from returning to being part of the mainstream world fishing industry. The issue is likely to remain unresolved because the resources of the Southern Ocean are common property. In other words, they are owned by no particular country or group of countries. There is therefore no means by which they can be protected from exploitation unless every country agrees.

Activity — Antarctic weather

A number of science stations in Antarctica monitor the weather. The readings in figure 14.68 were taken in 1995 at the McMurdo Base near the Ross Ice Shelf (78°S).

▼ **Figure 14.68 Temperature and wind**

Month	Mean °C	Maximum °C	Minimum °C	Mean wind speed km/h	Maximum wind speed km/h
January	-3.5	1.6	-8.1	11.5	49.0
February	-8.3	1.6	-15.9	16.5	63.0
March	-19.1	-5.9	-29.8	14.0	66.5
April	-25.0	-10.9	-37.4	12.6	56.0
May	-26.7	-10.9	-36.1	16.1	80.5
June	-24.0	-6.6	-36.9	12.9	63.0
July	-25.2	-16.8	-34.2	15.4	80.5
August	-24.6	-5.4	-36.1	14.0	66.5
September	-25.3	-9.9	-40.4	14.3	70.0
October	-17.8	-7.9	-26.6	14.7	80.5
November	-7.8	2.2	-19.8	13.6	105.0
December	-1.4	5.1	-6.9	10.5	49.0

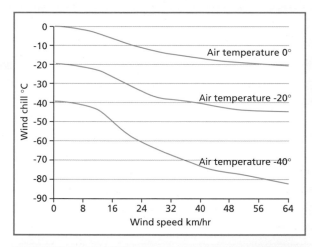

 Figure 14.69 Wind chill

The effect of cold wind on living creatures is to lower the body temperature. The stronger the wind, the greater the loss of heat. Hypothermia (ie, a lowering of the body temperature that can be fatal) becomes a serious risk for people if the wind chill falls below about minus 20°C, even if full winter clothing is worn. At temperatures lower than this, all parts of the body must be covered so as to avoid frostbite. If parts of the body become frozen, blood circulation ceases and gangrene can occur. In serious cases, the only remedy is to amputate. The graph shows the wind chill at different wind speeds for three actual air temperatures.

▲ **Figure 14.70 Pack ice, Antarctica**

Even in summer, floating pack ice can be a hazard for the supply ships which serve coastal scientific bases.

 Questions

1 Briefly explain why plants (other than algae and lichen) do not grow in Antarctica.
2 Using the data in figures 14.68 and 14.69, outline the risk of hypothermia and frostbite (in the form of a letter or memo) to someone newly arriving at the McMurdo Base science station.

 unit summary

1 The world can be divided into a number of biomes that range from tropical rain forest to arctic tundra.
2 Within each biome, there are characteristic features of vegetation, climate, soil and biomass productivity. Each has a typical nutrient cycle in which nutrients are stored, in different proportions, in the biomass, in the soil and in the litter.
3 There has been a human impact on all biomes. Some are more fragile than others but their survival has related more to their productive potential for agriculture than any other factor.

 key terms

Biome - a climax community of vegetation that extends over a wide area; biomes generally correspond to world climatic regions.
Desertification - the spread of desert conditions; the United Nations Convention to

Combat Desertification defines the process as: 'land degradation resulting from various factors including climatic variations and human activities'.
Pyrophytic - plants that are adapted to fire.
Xerophytic - plants that are adapted to drought.

Introduction

It is worth spending some time thinking about how you will learn rather than what you will learn. Being successful in your studies involves more than simply attending lessons and making notes. It is important to take responsibility for your own learning and be 'active' rather than 'passive'. In other words, you should think about and participate in the process rather than just let it happen to you.

As well as analysing your own learning, you must make sure that you know what is expected of you. How and when will you be assessed? What topics must you learn? What criteria will be used in marking your work? Reading through this study skills chapter will help you to learn more effectively. However, there are no 'short cuts'. You will have to work hard and practise your skills in order to obtain the grades that you deserve.

It might be useful if you return to this chapter at different times during your course - for example, when you have to write an essay or answer a data response question. Before any examination, you might find it useful to re-read the whole of the chapter and remind yourself of the main points of advice.

key questions

1 What is the best way to study?
2 How can assignment and examination techniques be improved?

1. What is the best way to study?

Instead of leaving all your revision to the end of your course, it is much better to learn the material as you go along. This does not mean that you should try and remember every detail, rather you should aim to build up a broad picture of each topic area. This will help you see the connections within the subject and will increase your understanding, as well as making final revision easier.

Analysing your own strengths and weaknesses

As a starting point, you should try and identify the style of learning that is best for you. There is an old saying: '*I forget what I hear, I remember what I see, but I understand what I do*'. Is this true for you? Different people have different ways of learning and you might find it easiest to remember things that you hear. Or, you might have a memory that works best when you see something. One way of thinking about this is to ask yourself the question: 'When I meet new people, am I best at remembering names or am I best at remembering faces?' If you are better at names, your aural memory is strongest, if you

are better at faces, your visual memory is strongest.

In either case, aural or visual signals can be reinforced if you actively 'do' something with the information. The more senses that you can use in processing information, the more likely it will be that you will remember and understand the material. So, for example, you could try reading your notes into a tape recorder and then listening to them. Alternatively, you could try drawing a flow chart, spider diagram or a 'mind map' to summarise each topic in your notes (see figure 15.1). Using colour, vivid images and a striking design in a diagram helps you remember the information, and the active process of drafting the drawing can help your understanding.

Figure 15.1 An example of a mind map / spider diagram

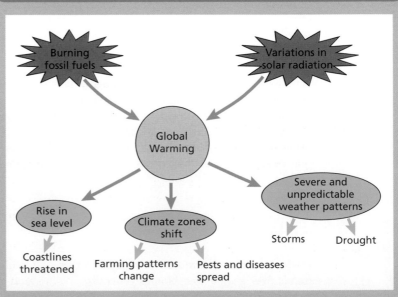

Creating your own design will help you remember the main points and also understand the connections.

When reading through notes or other written material, some people find it helpful to underline or highlight the important points. This again is an example of using more than one sense in processing information. It involves you thinking about which are the most important points and then actively 'doing' something with that knowledge. Of course, you should only do this in books that you own. Writing a brief summary in your own words is another way that you can use and make sense of information in an active way.

Asking and answering questions is also a good method of learning. Mature students in their twenties and upwards often have the confidence to ask questions in class or discuss their work with other students. Those students who do the same have a great advantage over those who stay quiet.

To summarise, the first stage of taking responsibility for your own learning is to work out how best you learn. Then, once you have decided on the strategy that suits you, you must continually 'process' the information that is in your notes. The ideas, theories and data contained in your file or text books is no use there - it must be understood and in your head!

Activity Mind maps

Use the following information to draw a diagram that summarises the key features. Try and give your diagram a strong visual impact.

Hazards that face human populations:

Human made hazards
- pollution
- radioactive contamination
- civil war/disturbance
- famine
- crime

Environmental hazards
- volcanic eruption
- earthquake
- tsunami
- mass movement
- hurricane
- tornado
- lightning
- flood
- drought
- plague/disease

Environmental hazards with a possible human causation
- global warming/sea level rise
- ozone depletion
- soil erosion
- salinisation
- desertification
- snow avalanche

Reading and making notes

Successful students spend a lot of time reading text books, magazines, newspapers and, for revision, their notes. As with most things, practice and effort can help you improve your level of skill. The point of reading is to gain knowledge and understanding. This is helped if you can quickly make sense of the information - where does it fit in with your other knowledge? One method which has been shown to work for some people is to follow a routine:
- scan the material to get an impression of what it is about
- read the material slowly
- put the book (or other written material) to one side and recite the key points to yourself or, better still, write them down
- if you cannot remember something, go back and review that bit again.

Make a written summary of what you have read. This has to be clear and legible. Use sub-headings, underlines and block capitals to break up the page and make it visually interesting. Draw a diagram if you can.

Then, file your summary in the proper place (ie, in a loose leaf file). Ensure that your notes are subdivided into subject and topic areas. Keep them in order and, at regular intervals, update a list of contents and number the pages. Also, as you go along, create a glossary of key terms that you will need to learn for the examination. One way of doing this is to create a card index or to use a word processing package that allows you to sort information into alphabetic order.

Action planning

There are two issues here. Each individual assignment needs a plan and, overall, you also need to plan how you will be an effective student. An action plan does not have to be formal or written out - but it is important to work out when, where and how you will study.

Planning for study As a first step, you should estimate how much time you need to study. This involves more than simply doing your set assignments. You should aim to spend some time in reading and reviewing your notes. These must be neat and complete. You should also find time to read text books.

Some people can work faster than others but you will need a minimum of several hours a week as study time. Once you have decided how long you need to study, you have to decide when you will do the work. Will it be fitted in during the day time, in the evening or at the weekend? It is important to be realistic about this. Part-time paid employment, outside interests and hobbies all take time that you might also have to take into account. Also, remember that short, intensive periods of work are often more productive than spending several hours at a stretch when concentration starts to fail.

Different people have different times of the day when they can work best. Try to do your work when you are most alert.

Finally, where will you work? Most people need somewhere that is quiet and comfortable. However, you might prefer to work with some music in the background. If your home does not provide you with ideal conditions, can you work in your school or college library? Consider the advantages and disadvantages of each place. The importance of a good working environment - somewhere that is convenient yet has the resources that you need - is often overlooked.

Remember, when you eventually sit your examination, the fact that you did not have enough time to study, or that you had nowhere quiet to work will not be counted as a valid excuse!

Figure 15.2 An outline Action Plan

Points to consider:
- Assignment title:
- Start date:
- Finish date:
- What do I need to find out: what information is needed to complete the task?
- What do I need to do: where will I find the information, how will I gather it?
- How long will it take and when will I do the work? Time will be needed for reading, researching, thinking, discussion, drafting and redrafting.
- In which order will I carry out the tasks?
- What is the final deadline and when must I complete the interim tasks to do the work on time?
- Review: how well did the plan work; was the outcome successful; could the work have been done in a better way?

Action planning for an assignment Every time that you are given an assignment to complete, you should prepare a plan. The key issues that you have to bear in mind are outlined in figure 15.2.

What is expected of you?

In general terms, you know that you are expected to work hard, attend lessons and hand assignments in on time! However, there are also specific 'assessment criteria' on which you will be judged. It is important that you are aware of these. Your final grade will depend to a large extent on how well you can display your ability in these areas. In particular, you need to show:
- knowledge and understanding;
- an ability to interpret and apply knowledge;
- an ability to evaluate (ie, to make judgments).

Early on in your course it can be off putting to look at the complete syllabus but, at some stage, you should make sure that you know what topics you are going to cover. For instance, you need to be aware of what geographical facts and ideas you are expected to know.

Skills development In addition to learning and understanding the syllabus content, you will be expected to develop a range of geographical skills. These will include:
- **cartographic skills**: drawing and interpreting a range of maps (including OS maps at different scales, land use

maps, weather maps, isopleth maps, choropleth maps)
- **graphical and diagrammatic skills**: drawing and interpreting graphs and diagrams (including line graphs, bar charts, histograms, scatter graphs, pie charts, triangular graphs, population pyramids)
- **statistical skills**: using and interpreting statistics (including mean, mode and media, correlation, sampling; note that some syllabuses require a wider range than this)
- **research skills**: gathering and interpreting data from primary and secondary sources.

It is possible that your school/college will take the opportunity to use your work in Geography to assess your performance in Key Skills. These include:
- **Information Technology**: using IT to present and analyse data; using IT to gather data (eg, CD Roms, Internet)
- **Application of Number**: performing calculations and presenting findings in mathematical form (note that much of this is covered by the statistical techniques that form part of most Geography courses)
- **Communications**: reading, writing, discussing and presenting information (again, this forms part of most Geography courses)

2. How can assignment and examination techniques be improved?

Students sometimes do not get the grades they deserve. Often this is NOT because they do not know the subject matter, but because they do not apply the knowledge that they have. To avoid this happening to you, it is important to learn how to answer questions that are set as assignments or as part of an examination. Different types of questions require different techniques, but there are some common features.

You will have heard many times that you should answer the question set. It is a frequently quoted instruction because it is ignored so often! Students are sometimes accused in examiners' reports of answering the question that suits them or writing everything they know about the topic, rather than answering the actual question. Under examination conditions, these are easy mistakes to make. You should concentrate very hard on making sure that they do not happen to you. Also, of course, you must check how many questions to answer and what mark allocations are given. This helps you to divide your time properly.

In assignments and examinations, the wording of the questions is crucial. Examiners use a range of key words that you must know and understand. These terms have a very specific meaning and they require a particular response. The words, and their meaning, include:

- **account for**: give reasons for something; explain why something happens
- **analyse**: break into parts, investigate and explain
- **annotate**: write explanations on a map, diagram or photograph
- **assess**: make a judgment; it is normally best to outline both sides of an issue before reaching a conclusion
- **compare**: point out the similarities between (also, if you think that there are marked differences, point these out as well)
- **contrast**: point out the differences between
- **describe**: give a detailed account of
- **define**: give the meaning of a word or phrase
- **discuss**: examine an issue by looking at more than one point of view; give reasons for and against
- **distinguish between**: show the differences between
- **evaluate**: make a judgment; outline the different possibilities and weigh the evidence before you give your conclusion
- **explain**: make clear; give reasons for
- **identify**: pick out the key features
- **outline**: give the main features of a topic, omit minor details
- **summarise**: give an account of the key points.

Other common key phrases are:
- **critically evaluate**: same as evaluate (see above), back your judgment by a discussion of the evidence
- **in your view**: you are being asked to make a judgment or express an opinion; marks will be awarded for the way that you discuss points for and against and for the way that you weigh the evidence; your actual conclusion will gain you few, if any, marks
- **to what extent**: discuss and make a judgment; make sure that you outline the case for and against before you make your conclusion
- **using specific examples**: you must give relevant examples, otherwise you will gain no marks
- **with reference to**: again you must refer to an example.

Essays

Often you will be asked to complete written answers. Some will be full essays and some will be parts of structured questions that may take only fifteen or twenty minutes to complete. The techniques that you need for these questions are broadly the same. Think of an essay (or any written answer) as an opportunity to 'show off' what you know and understand. In an examination, bear in mind the mark allocation and use this as a guide in terms of how much to write and how much time you should take. Spend some time thinking and planning what needs to be included. Quickly write the key words, issues and examples that you will need to include in your answer. Decide in which order you will make these points. Then draw a line through this rough work.

At the start of an essay you MUST define the geographical terms used in the question. Sometimes you will specifically be asked to do this but you should do it even if there is no formal instruction. This is the only form of introduction that your essay needs.

Next you should aim to answer the question by making relevant points. You should not make a list of these because you will gain no marks unless you explain each point. It is best to make the point, describe and explain what it means in detail, and give examples if appropriate. If you are unsure whether a point is relevant or not - you should include it. If you are correct, you will be given marks. If you are wrong, marks will NOT be subtracted. There is a penalty in that you have wasted some time and you should keep this in mind. Nevertheless, if in doubt - make the point. It is no use,

after the examination, realising that you should have included something that you had in mind. The examiner can only award marks for what is written down.

If possible, and where appropriate, illustrate an answer with an annotated sketch map or diagram. This demonstrates an important geographical skill and is often the best way of presenting a point.

Do not spend time writing a conclusion that repeats the points that you have already made. You will not be awarded marks twice for making the same point. If the question asks for a judgment, you must give one. Note that you will not be penalised if you give the 'wrong' answer - as long as you have backed it up with evidence in the body of your essay.

If you have time, read through what you have written. Check for spelling, punctuation and grammar. Do not be afraid of making changes or adding new material. If need be, mark the point in your text with an asterisk and then write your new text at the end.

Summary

- define the relevant geographical terms
- make clear, separate and relevant points that are explained and, where appropriate, are illustrated with an example
- conclude by providing a judgment, if required.

Sample essay question:

Explain what is meant by the 'net radiation balance' at the Earth's surface (9). To what extent, in your view, are human activities leading to long term climate change? (16)

Sample answer plan:

The first thing that you should note is the mark allocation. This gives a guide as to how much time you should take on each part of your answer and how many points you should make.

Start by defining the term *net radiation balance*. What does it mean? Show that you understand what *net* means in this context. You could draw a diagram to show the radiation flows towards and away from the Earth's surface, but note that you will gain few marks unless you explain and refer to the diagram in your text.

In the second part of your answer, you need to explain how human activities might be affecting the climate and, in particular, global warming. For each human activity in turn, describe and explain it, giving precise examples where appropriate. So, for instance, you might describe the burning of fossil fuels in cars. You could show how these cause emissions that contribute to the greenhouse effect and to global warming. Also give examples of which countries contribute most.

The question asks *to what extent......are human activities leading to long term climate change?* This requires that you discuss an alternative point (or points) of view and then assess the evidence for and against the ideas that you have outlined. For example, you could point out that climate variations have occurred in the historical past and these were not caused by human activity.

As a conclusion, you should express your own point of view. You could state that human activity is causing climate change, or that you believe the reverse to be true. It is also acceptable to write that there is insufficient evidence to confirm either view. You will not be penalised for giving the 'wrong' answer but you will be given credit for having made a persuasive case that is supported by evidence.

Data response questions

Data response questions come in many forms. Some provide you with a large amount of data that you have to describe and explain. Others provide a small amount of 'stimulus' material that gives you a starting point to show what you know. In either case, this type of question tests your knowledge and understanding of a particular topic and whether you can interpret and analyse data.

The information that is provided to you might be in numerical, graphical, pictorial or written form - or a combination of all four. There are some common features that you need to bear in mind. They are outlined below.

- When you answer a data response question, you will not be awarded marks for simply copying passages or numbers from the text. You have to express the data in your own words to be given credit.

- In your answer, refer to evidence that is provided in the data.
- Be sure to do the task that is set. For example, if you are asked to compare two items, this means more than simply describing them one after the other.
- As with other forms of question, if you are unsure whether a point is correct or relevant, include it anyway. You will not lose marks and you might gain some.
- Remember to use your answer as an opportunity to show what you know and understand about a particular geographical topic that you have studied.

When describing numerical or graphical data, get into the habit of using a set routine: what are the main trends, what/where is the biggest, what/where is the smallest, what are the anomalies (ie, the data that does not fit the general pattern). It is useful to go through this routine even if you have not been asked to write it out.

Sample data response question:
1. Define what is meant by the term 'urbanisation'. (3)
2. Outline the main trends in urbanisation as shown in figure a. (4)
3. Analyse the relationship between the level of urbanisation and per capita GNP. (8)
4. Discuss whether present trends in urbanisation are likely to continue. (10)

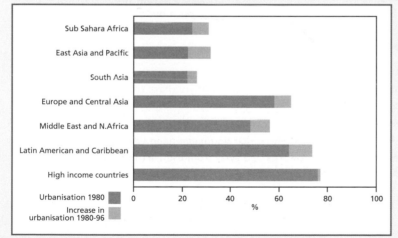

Figure (a) Urban population as a percentage of total population (High income countries are defined as those with a per capita GNP higher than $9,636. They are classified separately from low and middle income countries).

Figure (b) GNP per capita, 1996 US$ Region

Low and middle income countries:
Sub Sahara Africa	490
East Asia and Pacific	890
South Asia	380
Europe and Central Asia	2,200
Middle East and North Africa	2,070
Latin America and Caribbean	3,710
High income countries:	25,870

Sample answer plan:
Note the mark allocations for the different parts of the question. They give a guide to how much you are expected to write but also indicate different levels of difficulty. Descriptive answers are deemed to be easier than explanatory answers. Also note the key words in the questions: 'define', 'outline', 'analyse' and 'discuss'. It is most important that you do as you are asked in each case.
Before you start your answer, try and identify what part of your syllabus the question is testing you on. If you can focus on the key issues and ideas that you have covered in class, you will be in a better position to answer the question. Where data questions present you with a wide variety of data, skim through it all and work out what the links might be.

Question 1 requires a definition. You have to show that you understand the term urbanisation. The question does NOT ask for causes or consequences of urbanisation so do not be tempted to write everything you know about the topic at this point.

Question 2 asks for the *main trends* which means that you have to make a judgment. What are the most obvious features? In this case, it is that the level of urbanisation rose in all regions between 1980 and 1996. Note that it is always worthwhile to show that you have noticed the relevant dates and the units that are used in the data.
Pick out the region with the highest level of urbanisation and the region with the lowest. Refer to the data in the question. For example, you might write; 'The high income countries were the most urbanised in 1996 with 77 percent of their populations living in urban areas and South Asia was the least urbanised with just 26 percent of its population living in urban areas.'
Then pick out the regions with the fastest rate of increase and the regions with the lowest rate. Here you have to be clear whether you are describing an absolute rise or a percentage rise. The percentage rate of rise is the most appropriate measure but this requires you to calculate the change.

Question 3 asks you to analyse a relationship (although you should also be prepared to say, if appropriate, that there is no clear relationship). There are two main possibilities - the relationship might be negative or it might be positive. In this case, the rate of urbanisation rises as per capita GNP rises and there is a strong positive correlation. Look for any anomalies, ie anything unusual or something that does not quite fit the overall pattern. So, you might note that there is a very large difference between the per capita GNP of the highest income countries and Latin America but only a small difference between their rates of urbanisation. Analysis is more than pure description and you should make an attempt to explain and investigate the relationship. So, for example, you could give possible reasons why the highest income countries have the highest levels of urbanisation, and vice versa.

Question 4 asks you to *discuss* whether present trends will continue. This means that you have to briefly describe the present trends and then assess the likelihood of future changes. Whenever you are asked to discuss something, think of your answer as an opportunity to give different points of view. On the one hand, yes - the particular trend might continue because.....On the other hand, the trend might not continue because.....
This question expects you to bring in additional information from that provided. The data is the starting point of a discussion in which you are expected to display your understanding of the topic as a whole.

Pre-issued questions / decision making exercises (DMEs)

There are a number of alternative names for this type of question. What they generally have in common is that the data is issued to candidates some time before the written exam. Sometimes the material is in the form of a case study. Your teacher/lecturer will probably give you some specific guidance but it is your responsibility to prepare yourself as well as possible.

Your first task, after quickly reading the material, is to identify what topic area(s) are covered. Where is the subject matter covered in your notes and in your text books? Read through the relevant sections so that you are familiar with the topic area. This will help you make more sense of the material when you go through it again in detail. Identify and familiarise yourself with any geographical issues, theories or ideas that are relevant. On a second reading, make detailed notes of the facts and then write a summary of the key points. If you have been presented with maps, photos or statistical data, work through each of them and write a short summary of what each shows. In the case of DMEs, you will be given a variety of evidence that might include opinions. You should analyse these opinions - possibly in the form of a table that summarises the key points.

Your second task is to think what are the questions that the examiners are likely to set. It is highly unlikely that you will be set 'trick' questions. You might not be able to predict every 'angle' but you should work out in draft form what you would write in answer to straightforward questions.

When you eventually write your answers or complete the tasks set, remember that you should refer to evidence provided, but not copy out large sections of the data. Also remember that it is a Geography exam! In other words, your responses must display your knowledge and understanding of the subject. The examiners will be expecting you to relate the material to Geographical concepts and theories. Think of the examination as an opportunity to 'show off' your Geographical ability rather than simply an exercise in 'answering the question'.

Finally, remember that the examiners are looking for sound judgments that are based on solid evidence. Your explanation of why you choose a particular option - and why you reject another - will gain you more marks than the actual choice you make.

Coursework

It is likely that there will be a coursework component in your examination. In most cases, you will be given a choice of which topic to cover. This is the most critical aspect of coursework. If you make a mistake at this stage it is very difficult to recover.

The most common mistake that students make is to choose a topic that is impractical. At some stage, you have to collect data. You must be realistic in what you can gather - no marks are awarded for statements such as 'I could not obtain the necessary information'.

Unless you have a sure and certain personal contact, do not rely on local authorities, private firms or government agencies to supply you with any data - unless it is already published. Most of these bodies are simply too busy to provide individual students with detailed information. If your coursework requires detailed statistical information, again make sure that you know where the data is published before you commit yourself to a particular title.

The same advice stands for first hand research. You must be practical in terms of the time and effort that you can devote to primary information gathering. Footpath erosion in the Lake District or on the South Downs might be a topic that appeals to you - but is no good if you cannot visit these places several times in the time scale that is available to you. Similarly, a study on 'the decline of the engineering industry in the West Midlands' is far too big and impractical. However, a limited study on 'the impact of closure of "X engineering company" on its local community' might be possible.

A second common mistake that students make in their proposed coursework is to forget to relate it to a Geographical issue. Unless you can find the topic covered in a text book - avoid it! This is because you need to relate your study to an area of theory, preferably one that is covered on your syllabus.

Once you have chosen a topic, try and make the title into a question or hypothesis. This gives your coursework a focus and avoids the problem of open ended topics which simply go on and on. A hypothesis provides a start and a finish. The start is the explanation of why, in theory, your hypothesis is likely. The finish is your conclusion as to whether your research has provided evidence to support or reject the hypothesis. Note that it is very rare in Geography that you can ever say that a hypothesis is 'proved' or 'disproved'. This level of certainty is, in most cases, not possible.

As with the other forms of assessment already outlined, use your coursework report as an opportunity to display your Geographical knowledge, understanding and skills. This latter aspect is particularly relevant in coursework - for example, in presenting and analysing data.

When you are certain of your coursework topic and title, make a detailed plan of how you will collect your data. When, where and how will you gather information? Once you start your research, keep detailed notes of what you have found out and where the information came from. This is important because it is easy to become confused by a mass of data later on.

Confront any problems of data collection as soon as they occur. If you have difficulties, try alternative strategies or modify your plans. Discuss problems with your teacher as soon as possible - not after the coursework deadline has passed!

When it comes to the presentation of data, try to use a variety of techniques - maps, diagrams, photographs and different types of graphs. Spend plenty of time on thinking about your findings and then draft the points you will make in your analysis section.

Do not be afraid to discuss your work with people who can help you. Asking the right questions is a way of showing initiative and is not cheating. Also, do not be afraid of asking follow-up questions if you are unclear on issues relating to your coursework. Show your work in draft form to your teacher/lecturer or other knowledgeable person. Rather than ask open-ended questions, for example; 'Have I written enough?', ask specific questions such as; 'My intention is to present this information as a scatter graph, do you agree?'; or, 'Is the Spearman Rank Correlation coefficient the most suitable form of statistical analysis?'

Coursework report

Your coursework should be presented in an attractive and interesting manner. One possible format is outlined below:

Title: as noted above, try and make this in the form of a hypothesis or question.

Contents page: complete this at the very end of your coursework when you can number all the pages, diagrams, photographs and maps.

Introduction: a brief outline of the key issues and an explanation of how the topic relates to Geographical theory. If the title is in the form of a hypothesis, explain why it might be expected to be upheld.

Research methods: describe and explain in detail how you intend to gather the information that you need. Justify your methods of data collection in terms of how they relate to your coursework aims. Explain how you have ensured that your data is accurate and reliable (ie, not biased).

Findings: give a detailed account of your research findings. Present these results in appropriate forms - for example as numerical or graphical data and as maps. Try and use a variety of techniques. Include any photographs that you have taken. You must provide a written account that describes and explains in words any information that you present.
If any of your research methods have failed to give you satisfactory results, explain what went wrong and what difference this made.

Analysis: you have to interpret and evaluate your results. Where appropriate, use statistical analysis. Are your findings valid and reliable - in other words, are they accurate and do they provide solid evidence that supports your hypothesis?

Conclusion: does your research allow you to accept or reject the hypothesis, or is the answer inconclusive? Remember, if your results do not appear to support your hypothesis, or answer your title question, the coursework is not 'wrong'. Outline any weaknesses in your coursework, suggest improvements that might be made and briefly suggest what further research might be conducted on your chosen topic.

Appendix: include references, sources and bibliography. Also include rough work that shows evidence of your personal research. Be very careful to credit material that you have adapted from elsewhere.

Index

Acknowledgements

Cover and page design	Caroline Waring-Collins (Waring-Collins Partnership), Ormskirk, Lancashire
Page layout	Rob Gittins and Rebecca Leatherbarrow (Waring-Collins Partnership)
Graphics (maps)	Stephen Ramsay Cartography
Graphics (diagrams)	Andrew Allen, Susan Allen and Chris Collins
Advice and comments	Eve Calderbank
Reader	Mary Walton

Photograph credits

The publishers would also like to thank the following for use of photographs:

Associated Press: Japan quake / Koji Sasahara 320; Interstate collapse / Douglas C. Pizac 321; Philippinen Vulcan / Luis Garcia 332; Turkey quake / Hurriyet 341; Three Gorges / Xinhua 419; Bangladesh floods / Pavel Rahman 524; Malaysia pollution / Bernama 555.

BP Amoco: Easington terminal 486.

GeoScience Features Picture Library: Cirrus cloud 507; Altostratus cloud 507; Cumulonimbus cloud 507; Stratus cloud 507; Brown earth soil 565; Podsol 566; Chernozem soil 567; Gley soil 567; Latosol 568; Rendzina 573.

David Gray: Reservoir 543.

Mike Gosling: Geyser 329; Dyke 329; Sill 320; Glyder Fawr 347; Quiraing 356; Terracettes 357; Hutton Roof 371; Cavedale 372; Gaping Gill 373; Norber erratic 431; Roche moutonnee 435; Striated rock 435; Moraine 437; Tor 454.

Landform Slides: River Terraces, Sutherland 409; Drumlins 437; Esker 437; Durdle Door, Dorset 474; Old Harry stacks, Dorset 474; Stair Hole, Dorset 476; Kingsbridge ria 478; Raised beach, Islay 479.

Panos Pictures: Kosovo refugees 30; Imphos women's cooperative, Harare 200; Aid in Uganda 84; Kaohua camp, Rwanda 32; Homeless in Delhi 104; Mumbai, India 162; Beijing, China 111; Aral Sea, Uzbekistan 212; Slums, Rio de Janeiro 181; Smokey Mountain, Philippines 184; Slums, Delhi 188; Bangladesh garment factory 183; Erosion in Nepal 584.

Penny Ritson: Tree roots 350; Honeycombe weathering 352; Desert pavement 380; Lake Nasser 423; River Nile 423; Glenridding 443.

Rex Features: Holbeck Hall 356.

Science Photo Library: El Niño 554; Antarctica 636.

Additional photographs: Jim Nettleship; PhotoDisc, Inc.

Other data

Ordnance survey maps 139, 142, 174, 374, 406, 440: Reproduced from Ordnance Survey mapping on behalf of The Controller of Her Majesty's Stationery Office, © Crown Copyright. MC 014688

Meteorological Office: Crown Copyright. Reproduced by permission of The Controller of Her Majesty's Stationery Office. Office for National Statistics material is Crown Copyright, reproduced here with the permission of Her Majesty's Stationery Office.

Note: a more detailed list of sources, references and web sites is provided in Geography in Focus Teacher's Guide.

Every effort has been made to locate the copyright owners of material used in this book. Any omissions are regretted and will be credited in subsequent printings.

British Library Cataloguing in Publication Data
A catalogue record for this book is available from the British Library.
ISBN 1 873929 919
Causeway Press Ltd, PO Box 13, 129 New Court Way, Ormskirk, Lancashire, L39 5HP
First edition 2000
© Ian Cook, Bob Hordern, Helen McGahan, Penny Ritson

Typesetting by Waring-Collins Partnership
Printed and bound by Butler and Tanner Ltd, London and Frome

Geography in Focus

This book is due for return on or before the last date shown below.

**FOR
REFERENCE ONLY**

Don Gresswell Ltd., London, N.21   Cat. No. 1207

DG 02242/71